EDUCATIONAL PSYCHOLOGY

A DEVELOPMENTAL APPROACH

SEVENTH EDITION

Richard C. Sprinthall

American International College

Norman A. Sprinthall

North Carolina State University

Sharon Nodie Oja

University of New Hampshire

D0206665

Boston, Massachusetts   Burr Ridge, Illinois   Dubuque, Iowa
Madison, Wisconsin   New York, New York   San Francisco, California   St. Louis, Missouri

McGraw-Hill

*A Division of The **McGraw·Hill** Companies*

EDUCATIONAL PSYCHOLOGY:
A Developmental Approach

This book is printed on acid-free paper.

1 2 3 4 5 6 7 8 9 0   DOW/DOW   9 0 9 8 7

ISBN 0-07-060576-9

Editorial director: *Jane Vaicunas*
Sponsoring editor: *Beth Kaufman*
Editorial coordinator: *Adrienne D'Ambrosio*
Marketing manager: *Daniel M. Loch*
Project manager: *Paula M. Buschman*
Production supervisor: *Karen Thigpen*
Senior designer: *Laurie J. Entringer*
Photo research coordinator: *Keri Johnson*
Compositor: *ElectraGraphics, Inc.*
Typeface: *10/11 Palatino*
Printer: *R. R. Donnelley & Sons/Willard*

Library of Congress Cataloging-in-Publication Data

Sprinthall, Richard C. (date)
    Educational psychology : a developmental approach / Richard Sprinthall, Normal Sprinthall, Sharon Nodie Oja. — 7th ed.
      p.   cm.
    Norman A. Sprinthall's name appears first on 6th ed.
    Includes bibliographical references and index.
    ISBN 0-07-060576-9
    1. Educational psychology   I. Sprinthall, Norman A., 1931–
II. Oja, Sharon Nodie.   III. Title.
LB1051.S6459   1998
370.15—dc21   97-21840

http://www.mhcollege.com

ABOUT THE AUTHORS

Norman A. and Richard C. Sprinthall graduated from the same public high school and the same undergraduate college, Brown University. After completing his doctorate in psychology at the Graduate School of Boston University, Richard took an instructorship at American International College in Springfield, Massachusetts, and soon rose to department head in psychology and a full professorship. He currently serves as director of graduate studies in psychology. Norman completed his doctorate in counseling psychology at Harvard's Graduate School of Education and remained there to eventually become program head in counseling. He left Harvard to become chair of the counseling psychology program at the University of Minnesota, followed by a similar position at North Carolina State University. He recently entered a new stage of development as professor emeritus and continues to serve as author and educational adviser to universities, schools, and nonprofit foundations both here and in Europe. Both Norman and Richard have been prolific writers throughout their careers. In addition to being a regular contributor to professional journals, Richard has authored other texts in the field of statistics and research design, including the fifth edition of *Basic Sta-*

tistical Analysis. Norman has coauthored another successful McGraw-Hill text, *Adolescent Psychology: A Developmental View,* as well as other books and numerous journal articles. Both have received outstanding teacher awards for their classroom teaching.

Sharon Oja grew up in St. Paul, Minnesota, where she graduated from Central High School and Macalester College. While teaching high school mathematics, she completed a master's degree in mathematics education at the University of Minnesota. There she cofounded a school-university peer-teaching program in mathematics and science for disadvantaged junior and senior high school students (including African-Americans, Native Americans, Spanish Americans, and Euro-Americans). Her interest in teacher development grew, and she completed her doctorate in developmental education at the University of Minnesota. As a professor at the University of New Hampshire, she teaches courses in educational psychology and is director of field experiences in teacher education. She is coauthor of *Collaborative Action Research: A Developmental Approach.*

PREFACE

When we wrote the first edition of this book in the early 1970s, the world was different in many ways. The cold war, the Vietnam experience, the hippies and flower children, the early period of space explorations—all seem today to belong to a long-past era, to ancient history. On the other hand, from the standpoint of educational psychology, we continue to see many of the same issues, perhaps phrased in somewhat different language, yet highly parallel. The foundation of educational practice is still too often based on anecdote or even a transient fad without substance. Then, it was fashionable to speak of personal traits of openness, spontaneity, and "do your own thing." Now we hear of character virtues such as honesty, trust, and responsibility. Then, we heard of creativity; now it is test score achievement. Then, the trend was for more centralized curriculum efforts; now it seems to be for more decentralization and charter schools. The educational pendulum continues to swing. From our view, however, such swings do not always represent real progress. The difficulty often results from an inadequate basis for such changes in practice. In fact, given the increased complexity and diversity of our school populations, we need educational practices that are more than ever based on solid theory and research, and vice versa: practical theory and theoretical practice. Through successive revisions of our text, we have always worked toward this goal. This, our seventh edition continues this effort to provide educators-teachers, counselors, and administrators with the latest information base for the teaching-learning process. We decided to continue to build a developmental framework for education. It is our view that such an enterprise is too important to be left in the hands of overly theoretical, faddish, or anecdotal "educationist" practice.

For continuity, we've retained and expanded features from previous editions, namely the chapter summaries, the extensive glossary entries, many Spotlights on contemporary issues, extensive biographies, and end-of-the-chapter theory to practice assignments.

In the chapters focused on the domains of development, you'll find the latest information on the constructivist approach, including cognitive, moral, and personal identity. As one of the major theorists in this country, John Flavell, has noted, despite some shortcomings there is simply no adequate alternative to this approach. This means it is extremely important to understand the learning process with particular reference to Vygotsky's zone of proximal growth. Equally significant is the newest research on identity status development as an educative goal, even more so for students from culturally deprived backgrounds. It is clearly time to help such students get off, in Don Locke's phrase, "ethnic probation." These chapters present the latest research and practice supporting our approach to moral development. They thus form the building blocks, a basis for constructing effective teaching and learning methods.

In the sections on learning, we have devoted more coverage to the information processing framework of metacognition, episodic memory, schemata, and attention deficits. In the testing chapter we introduce new concepts, such as race norming and gender-equity testing. New spotlights have been added, including coverage of such issues as Ebonics, gender bias, single-sex schools, the gifted, self-esteem, conduct disorders, and sex education.

Given the increased diversity in the student population, we continue to ask how teachers can deal with the increased diversity in their classrooms and schools. In this edition we have added emphasis on teachers learning about the home communities of their students with examples from Shirley Brice Heath's research and that of K. Tsianina Lomawaima. New biographies of Linda Darling-Hammond and James Comer focus on the work being done nationwide on the issues of teaching quality and educational equity for all students. New sections on restructuring schools focus on reorganization of the school environment to meet the needs of all students as we move into the next century. We emphasize the new work in school-university partnerships and professional-development schools, where experienced teachers and administrators, beginning teachers, and university professors are teaming and learning side by side. We suggest how teachers can use networking and e-mail as well as collaborative action research to support their own reflective inquiry and professional development. In a new "Spotlight on Fairer Tales" we show how some students are very able to re-form old stereotypes from their own gender socializations when teachers give them the chance. From new studies on teaching effectiveness at elementary and secondary levels, we show the cross-validation of Herbert Walberg's prior studies. A new spotlight on scaffolding uses Lev Vygotsky's notion of the zone of proximal development and David Hunt's notion of accessibility channels to promote higher-order thinking and understanding. Research from the National Center for Organization and Restructuring of Schools adds to our knowledge of more authentic ways to assess student learning using performance measures, including portfolio assessment. But we also voice some cautions about mandating portfolio assessment, for example, without determining the necessary means of evaluation. This controversy continues as we go to press.

New sections on discipline focus on school-based conflict-management skills and peer mediation for resolving conflicts between students. We investigate the research in training elementary and secondary students on how to manage conflicts constructively by negotiation and mediation. Ruth Charney's examples for teachers to teach children to care are among those suggestions that focus on teaching activities and methods that are appropriate to developmental stages of students. A new Spotlight on Classroom Rules, within the developmental framework, lists some overall criteria for setting up classroom limits. We reinforce the teaching role as firm but fair. There is a new focus on parent-teacher communication, with examples showing how an authoritative teacher works with students to set up classroom rules and also starts early in the school year to build a working relationship with parents by informing parents of classroom expectations. The parent-teacher relationship continues to build throughout the year as the teacher shares positive information about the students and uses parental help to address recurring discipline problems. Suggestions are given for ways to avoid stereotyping of students and their family structures and to develop collaborative connections with parents.

For teaching pupils with special needs, we have outlined the 12 disability conditions listed in the Individuals with Disabilities Education Act (IDEA), the successor to Public Law 94-142. The widely developing new policy called "inclusion" suggests that schools are encouraging children with disabilities to enter the mainstream of the regular education classrooms. A substantial body of newly reported research supports the view that regardless of regular-education or special-education teacher roles, there is a common knowledge base for good teaching for all students. We describe these common teaching characteristics using the most recent research studies. This common knowledge base combines with current emphases in both special education and regular education on classroom contexts for learning, such as embedding instruction in meaningful activities with authentic performance-based assessments, promoting classroom dialogue for pupils' self-reflective learning, responding to individual learner needs and realities, and establishing learning communities in the classrooms. High school teachers of students with disabilities are participating in individual transition plans for the years from school to work. We have devoted new sections to the research on learning outcomes and social results for high school students with disabilities who have been included in regular-education classes. Throughout the chapter on inclusion, we stress the importance of collaborative problemsolving among special-education teachers and regular-education teachers. Collaboration of school staff and students with the community and parents is critical to the goals of inclusive education.

Many of our colleagues have been extremely helpful. Jim Rest, now retired, has continued important input on moral development, as have our international friends Bartolo Campos (Portugal), Fritz Oser (Germany), Monica Taylor (United Kingdom), and Renata Siemienska (Poland). Jerene Mortensen provided a very creative cross-cultural case study from her vantage point as a school principal. Our North Carolina colleagues Debra Stewart, Don Locke, Tracy Robinson, and Barbara and Tom Parramore have remained important resources. In addition, many thanks to Alan Reiman for colleagueship and creative artistry. We have also received helpful suggestions from many who have used earlier editions of the book. Most recently in this regard, M. J. Stockton from Jewell College has shared his course activities, a most valuable set of ideas for implementation. In Massachusetts, valuable contributions were made by Lee Sirois, Greg Schmutte, and Art Bertrand. We thank them for adding their expertise to the measurement chapter. We also thank Toni Spinelli-Nannen, Nancy Hayes, and Tom Nolan for their valuable suggestions for both the information processing and motivation chapters, and to Gerry Weaver for his excellent outline on grade-equivalent scores. We thank Gus Pesce for his important additions to the growth and development chapter, and both Barbara Dautrich and Carol Spafford for their outstanding work on attention deficits and dyslexia. Finally, we thank George Grosser for his comments on the chemistry of learning and Tom Fitzgerald for his statistical insights. Colleagues at the University of New Hampshire kept us abreast of some of the controversies in the field as we sought out the most recent research in teaching effectiveness, developmental discipline, and inclusion of students with disabilities. Special thanks go to colleagues Joe Onosko for suggestions in the sections on teaching objectives and teaching for higher-order understanding, Georgia Kerns for directions to the most recent laws for identifying children and adolescents with disabilities, and Ellen Corcoran for insight into the areas of discipline and classroom management. Tim Churchard and his educational psychology classes give constructive feedback on each new edition of the book. Middle-school teacher Trish Walton, a teacher-in-residence at UNH, and elementary school teacher Katharina Fachin Lucas, a current Ph.D. student, added their teaching experiences with the compelling notions of inclusion of students with special needs. Typing by Robin Hughes, Sandy Richards, and Micki Canfield is, as always, much appreciated. Closer to home, we do need to recognize both the professional and moral support from our spouses. Lois Thies-Sprinthall, an experienced teacher, is really responsible for the heavy emphasis on applying theory to practice. Her work in mentoring provides a rich arena in which to test out ideas in the real world of education. Dianne Sprinthall's background in art and art education continues to inform us of the importance of the visual mode in communicating ideas and feelings. And Ron McMillan has learned again what it is like for a spouse to work on a revision with tight deadlines and what seem like endless tasks. His support and understanding were important through the entire process.

Richard Sprinthall
Norman Sprinthall
Sharon Nodie Oja

CONTENTS
IN BRIEF

CONTENTS

1

INTRODUCTION AND HISTORY

At first sight it may seem that the process of teaching and learning is simple and straightforward, that all the educator has to do is arrange the material in a logical sequence, present it to the students, and then repeat the process across the curriculum. In fact William James, who originated psychology as a field of study on this continent, portrayed exactly such a circumstance by comparing teaching to warfare:

> In war, all you have to do is to work your enemy into a position in which the natural obstacles prevent him from escaping if he tries to; then to fall on him in numbers superior to his own . . . Just so in teaching, you must simply work your pupil into such a state of interest—with every other object of attention banished from his mind; then reveal it to him so impressively that he will remember it to his dying day; and finally fill him with devouring curiosity to know what the next steps are (James, 1958, p. 25).

From the teacher's perspective nothing could be plainer or simpler. The science of general pedagogics could not be clearer. Then James mentioned the other side of the classroom equation, schooling from the pupil's point of view, by reminding teachers that

> The mind of your own enemy, the pupil, is working away from you as keenly and eagerly as is the mind of the commander on the other side from the scientific general. Just what the respective enemies want and think and what they know and do not know are as hard things for the teacher as for the general to find out (James, 1958, p. 25).

Thus, teaching, like other forms of human interaction, only seems easy. In fact, as we shall point out, teaching is among the most complex of activities that humans can attempt. In this chapter we shall outline these issues, beginning with an inquiry into the nature of educational psychology: Is it mostly education or mostly psychology, or a hybrid, or some inadequate compromise? This inquiry will be followed by a discussion of the so-called two-culture problem of theory versus practice and the four-corner problem of teaching. To give you some historical perspective, we will then review the early beginnings of our discipline as a basis for the art and science of teaching.

The only prediction we can make with certainty is that teaching effectively will become an even more complex activity as the twentieth century draws to a close. The increasing complexity is due partly to a growing national awareness of the need for an educated and literate population that will include all segments of our society. Structural changes in our society, such as the dramatic increase in the number of families in which both parents work outside the home, the increase in single-parent families, the increase in the number of students from minority backgrounds, the recognition of the importance of early education, and the move toward more inclusive education, to name a few of the most obvious, confront all of us with the need to reach more pupils, more effectively (Goodlad, 1990). A postindustrial society such as ours needs workers with "thinking skills," but that's only part of the story. A democracy needs informed citizens to make intelligent decisions at both the local and national levels. We certainly cannot afford an educational system that loses one-third of our teenagers through dropouts and undereducates a second third (Heyns, 1988; Kozol, 1992). Our third president, Thomas Jefferson, said it best: "If a nation expects to be ignorant and free in a state of civilization, it expects what never was and never will be" (1816).

EDUCATIONAL PSYCHOLOGY: A BRIDGE STEPPED ON AT BOTH ENDS?

Educational psychology as a field of study has quite literally struggled throughout its history with an identity problem. Existing by definition somewhere between psychology and education, the discipline has experienced the crosscurrents and whirlpools often created when two great oceans meet. Psychology as the science of human behavior has as a major concern the discovery of laws. As such, it focuses on basic description and prediction to uncover the nature of human beings. In this mode psychology is a science, a body of knowledge about ourselves. In the tradition of rigorous science, the questions it raises are generic. The rate of progress is slow. Human beings have been and will be more complex than psychological theories. Indeed, psychology as a science is forever limited by the size of the cerebral cortex of the investigators. Ultimately, we study ourselves. Even at best, progress in basic theory proceeds more at the speed of a glacier than at that of great oceans on the incoming tide.

Psychology's theorists are committed to a careful and comprehensive analysis of what it means to be human. This is a long-term enterprise. The payoff lies in the future. As one professor of psychology and education puts it, "It's like investing in recreational land in Labrador. Don't expect an immediate return." At the same time theorists are quick to point out that without theory, practice has nothing to guide it. Thus, those who wish to act without an informed theoretical basis do so at their own hazard. The traditions of science require a conceptual framework for practice.

On the other side, we have the profession of edu-cation. A profession generally has exactly the opposite agenda to that of a science. Education—like law, medicine, and business—has practice as its foremost concern. The practical world is completely different from the scientific realm. To many in a profession, applied knowledge is the only kind that matters. Otherwise, they claim, "It's too theoretical" or "It will never work." "It's another case of excessive navel gazing," they might say, or, "Remember that according to theory the bumblebee can't fly." Such comments are understandable, given that educators, like other professionals, confront the realities of practice every day. A teacher, counselor, or school principal cannot withdraw in the middle of a class, counseling session, or budget proposal and say (perhaps wistfully?), "Well, we need more basic research on that point, so I'll stop now, close the school, and go back to the drawing board. Class dismissed for the next three years." Nor can a doctor in the middle of an operation stop suddenly, look up, and say, "We don't have an absolutely scientific basis for this surgery, so tell the patient (when he comes to) to take a number, and we'll get back to him as soon as we can." We cannot imagine a lawyer's leaving, halfway through a summation for the defense, with the words: "We don't have a completely clear framework of precedents, so (members of the jury) put everything on hold. More research is needed."

THEORY AND PRACTICE: TWO CULTURES?

C. P. Snow (1963) in a famous book denoted the problem of **theory versus practice** as a legitimate disparity between two cultures, the scientific and the humanistic. The same split can be seen in educational psychology. Neither tradition is better, although the status of the two cultures may be different. In fact, the status problem has only clouded the central difficulty. In this country, and certainly in nearly all modern technological societies, scientific achievement is more highly regarded than professional activity. Science is more glamorous. Breakthroughs are announced in media blitzes. Money flows to basic research. However, the status difference is not really central to the problem. In our terms the difficulty is that the two traditions have different histories, different pressures, different procedures—indeed, fundamentally different ways of understanding what the problem is in the first place.

As you experience both scientific and professional courses, you will gain firsthand knowledge of the distinctions between these two different cultures. When C. P. Snow uses the term *cultures,* he means two different societies, or what the Germans call

According to C. P. Snow, there is a disparity between scientific culture, which emphasizes objectivity, and humanistic culture, which is more subjective.

Weltanschauung—different world views. The behavioral scientist may interview literally hundreds of subjects to uncover possible systematic variations in cognitive processes. The teacher wants to know what to do at a given moment with a student. The movement here is from the general, the scientific, and the objective to the particular, the active, and the subjective. Both groups can become easily annoyed with each other. The scientist often answers the professional with a shrug followed by a long, complex, and seemingly evasive nonanswer. The professional may retort in frustration: "Well, why don't you emulate the philosopher Bishop Berkeley? He isolated himself in a cave for a very long time, trying to get his mind together. In the meantime, we will keep things going here as best we can."

As you enter the field of education, then, do not accept at face value any of the simpleminded statements that are made about educational psychology. The claim that we synthesize two diverse traditions with the wave of a hand does not hold up. Realize that comments such as "It's a connector science" or "It's an applied science" or "It's the science of education applied to the art of teaching" are oversimplifications. Educational psychology as a bridge between two different traditions is still being built. Indeed, the progress in the last decade has been substantial, but

the discipline as a bridge is still stepped on regularly at both ends. It isn't quite scientific enough for psychology, nor is it quite practical enough for the profession. However, the overall movement is positive. Just pick up some earlier reviews of teaching, for example. It was common to conclude in the past that educational psychologists didn't really know anything or have anything to contribute. Talk about a field in search of an accident about to happen! Researchers concluded after reviewing hundreds of studies on teacher effectiveness:

> Existing research has a long but disappointing history (Hyman, 1971).

> We do not know how to define, prepare for, or measure teacher competence . . . Reviewers have concluded, with remarkable regularity, that few relationships between teacher variables and effectiveness criteria can be established (Shulman, 1974).

> Research has not identified consistent replicable features of human teaching (Gage, 1978).

Notwithstanding these statements, later chapters in this volume will show clearly that the current state of the art indicates a solid basis for both theory and practice.

Why Theory? Why Practice?

Let's look at another aspect of the two-culture question. In most cases science reserves the most important place for theory, while the profession takes the opposite position—that practice is the overriding concern. The purpose of theory is to provide a set of abstract, logically coherent explanations. Theory provides reasons and principles and is therefore descriptive. Practice provides a series of concrete behaviors—activities to do—and is therefore prescriptive. The question, then, is whether we really need both. Well, let's imagine for a moment that we don't. Then the following scenario might unfold: A new theory has been proposed. Preliminary evidence shows that tall people and short people may have different learning styles. "So what?" you ask. "The new theory doesn't tell me anything about what I should do differently. I'm left with a general idea but no details. At best, all I can do is to speculate. Also, I just heard that another researcher claims that the only difference between tall and short people is in height, not learning style." So there you have it. The theory enables us perhaps to know something new about humans, yet the knowledge remains abstract.

Now, let's look at it the other way around. You are listening to some professionals. One says, "I decided to try something different in my class. I heard somewhere that another teacher had good luck in using the discovery method of teaching." That's it. By word of mouth, a promising practice is suggested. You have some specific details as to how to set up the room, ask open-ended questions, and use maps without cities designated. In fact, the suggestions for practice are very clear and very detailed. It is just the opposite of theory. As an educator you may instinctively feel that the second approach is clearly superior. You have the directions, but you don't have any explanation. You don't know why the method works. The danger is that all teachers will use the same method on all students. Without theory, you have no way of knowing when to use it and when not to use it. The practical advice doesn't allow systematic prediction of the outcome.

Another way to think about the issue is from the viewpoint of the performing artist, such as a violinist, a ballet dancer, or an opera singer. Such artists are clearly committed to practice, practice, practice. In fact they often avoid theory altogether. James Allen (1992) interviewed a gifted 13-year-old soloist with the question: "What goes through your mind when you play?" "Nothing," she replied (p. 8). The idea, of course, is that action and performance are the ultimate criteria. Anything else, such as reflection, discussion, or theory, seems to fail the test. "But what is

the use of that?" the performer asks rhetorically. Allen points out the mutual distrust and "reciprocal condescension" (p. 8) between the performer and the intellectual critic. The critic views the performer as an empty vessel, a robot, while the performer regards the critic as hopelessly removed from real life by a screen of abstractions and words, words, words.

The debate between theory and practice has a long history. Educational professionals and humanists often decry "cold" theory. The great German dramatist Goethe put the case clearly and emotionally: "Theory is all grey and the golden tree of life is green." The famous French philosopher Sartre criticized scientists in this way: They build "great theoretical cathedrals, but actually live in a small outhouse next door." On the one hand, then, theory without practice can be abstract speculation. On the other hand, practice without guiding theory may be random—or, even worse, frenzied—activity without point or consequence. One commentator remarked that practice by itself quickly becomes a fad wandering around somewhere between the cosmic and the trivial, without knowing which is which. We have scientific reasoning divorced from reality, or folklore separated from logic. Basic research can become sanctimonious aimlessness. Practice can become just aimlessness. Clearly, we need both, even though each tradition works against an overall integration. The Spotlight highlights this need.

One Theory or Many?

Still another related question, if you are convinced of the need for both theory and practice is: Which theory should be selected as a basis for informed practice? As any study of psychology quickly shows, there are many contending theories. How can you know which is best? Where is the supertheory for educational practice? Naturally, there is no easy answer. Many dedicated psychologists have given their entire adult lives to the search. Promising theories emerge but then do not stand up and so are replaced. The scientific community attempts to evaluate theory on the basis of two principles, parsimony and reductionism. Sometimes this is as difficult as serving two masters.

The first term means just what you think: *parsimony* equals stinginess. Like a person who spends money very carefully, theory should be succinct and compact. A parsimonious person doesn't throw money around needlessly. A theory should not be more elaborate or more abstract than it needs to be to explain the facts. For example, one of the current and largely justified criticisms of Freud's classic psycho-

SPOTLIGHT ON THEORY PROBLEMS

Goldilocks vs. Procrustes and the Ted Williams Solution

Two eminent educational theorists, Lillian Katz and James Raths (1985), have suggested one way to understand the theory problem. They point out that educational theory is often much too broad for educational practice, much as Papa and Mama Bear's beds were too big for Goldilocks. The small, slender Goldilocks slipped and slid around on those large theoretical surfaces. Katz and Raths see much of educational practice as a Goldilocks wandering around in search of a better fit. It was a happy circumstance for Goldilocks that she didn't run into the Greek mythic figure Procrustes, an infamous robber who captured unsuspecting travelers and placed them on his bed. If they were too tall, he cut off their limbs; if too short, he stretched them to fit. He gave new meaning to "one size fits all." In either case, the theory problem remains. If theory is too broad, practice rattles around in it. On the other hand, if theory is too rigid, then practice is made to fit

through drastic surgery. Of course, even though she irritated the bear family, Goldilocks did eventually find just the right fit. And in a separate story, Theseus eventually caught and killed Procrustes, ending his radical practices. Fitting theory and practice together, however, isn't quite that easy.

The distrust between theorists and practitioners often looms as an impossible chasm. Practice starts in the real world, moving from the bottom up, while theory moves from the top down. Each side stoutly maintains the correctness of its own viewpoint. Of course, neither side has a monopoly on the truth. Consider the case of Ted Williams, perhaps the greatest baseball hitter of all time. His natural swing, the result of hours of lonely practice in his backyard as a youth, in hotel-room mirrors off the field, and in the batting cages appears to be a prime example of gifted performance derived exclusively from practice. Such was not the case. Williams

said that as a result of his pilot training in World War II, he learned a theory that literally revolutionized not only his own batting but the practice of all baseball hitters ever since. In studying aerodynamics, he came across Bernoulli's theory, which focused on wind resistance and lift (Linn, 1993, p. 1985). He correctly concluded that bat speed, not weight, was the critical element in driving a baseball. He applied that principle of physics to his practiced swing with outstanding results. The 40-ounce "war-club" bats quickly went extinct. Lighter-weight bats, now the norm, thus emerged from a careful application of theory to practice. Ted Williams relied on both action and reflection.

Katz, L., and Raths, J. (1985). Dispositions as goals for teacher education. *Teaching and Teacher Education*, 1 (4), 301–307. Linn, E. (1993). *Hitter: The Life and Turmoils of Ted Williams*. New York: Harcourt Brace.

---

analytic theory is that it is based on a long series of assumptions that could not be tested—assumptions such as unconscious motivation, the suppression of libido drives, castration anxiety, penis envy, the Oedipus complex, homosexuality, paranoia, and the Electra complex. A theory is not parsimonious if we have to accept its suppositions on faith. The theory becomes more a set of beliefs or an ideology than a scientific basis for prediction. In order to make the theory fit, we are forced to add a number of qualifications. The theory remains interesting, yet it remains pure speculation.

A medieval philosopher, **William of Occam,** revolted against the wild theorizing of his day. You may have heard about a religious controversy con-

cerning how many angels could dance on the head of a pin. Highly speculative and elaborate theories evolved to resolve this controversy in Occam's time. He wrote a scathing treatise pointing out the need for parsimony. His work shook the scholastic world so severely that his thesis became known as Occam's razor, the tool to cut away needless elaboration and qualifications. Ideas had to be clear, concise, and to the point. Many a pseudotheory has been slashed by Occam's razor (Sabine, 1937).

This is not the whole story. Other theorists, heeding (or fearing) Occam's razor, decided to go in a completely different direction from the wooly-headed theorists of Occam's day by paring theory to its bare bones. They eliminated as many assumptions, qualifications, and suppositions as possible. In psychological theory the best example was early behaviorism. All known human characteristics such as learning styles, temperament, feelings, and stages of cognition, were eliminated. In fact, everything in psychological theory was cut away except one principle, the law of effect. In attempting to protect against meaningless elaboration, the drive to parsimony sometimes goes too far. In such instances parsimony is called *reductionism*. In seeking to streamline theoretical thought, too many ideas are dismissed. This is sometimes called "tossing the baby out with the bathwater."

Effective theory can be judged somewhere near the midpoint of an unusual continuum. The English scholar William of Occam sits in the middle, honing his razor; angels dancing on the head of a pin at one end; a baby in a tub of dirty water, about to be tossed, at the other. Naturally, as a new student to educational psychology you cannot realistically be expected to evaluate theories accurately on this continuum. However, you should realize that our current elaboration of theories for education does reflect our best estimates of the midpoint. The developmental approach provides a theory describing how students grow and change through a series of stages. This model for educational psychology incorporates many of the best features of earlier theories; in addition, it can and does change as new information is tested and found valid. We explain such a process in the following chapters. The theories we will be examining have direct relevance to practice. You will find contributions from many theories joined together in the developmental framework. You will also find aspects of earlier theories eliminated, ideas

that were either too speculative or too narrow (Jackson, 1990).

One final point: Do not expect a theory to tie together all loose ends. Our theories represent our best current understanding, not the final solution. Human behavior is not a closed but an open system. As we learn more and test more ideas, our understanding changes. Theory is dynamic. In the process of moving forward, it leads to successive approximations as our knowledge of human development slowly evolves. Theory can never be complete because of the nature of human beings. There is always a lack of total understanding and of closure. However, each new generation of educational psychologists does stand on the shoulders (not the face) of previous generations. You will become accustomed to the idea that although certain actions or activities represent our best current understanding, they do not come with an absolute guarantee. We act on the basis of informed judgment. In the words of Harvard psychologist Gordon Allport, we are "wholehearted but half-sure."

As we noted earlier, an increase in student diversity and negative environmental factors continue to make teaching even more complicated. By the year 2000 one-third of school-age youngsters will be nonwhite. The number of children with special needs will increase, and so will the number living below the poverty line. Physical violence, weapons, and drug use are alarmingly high and expected to grow. All these trends help to make the teaching-learning agenda more and more bewildering (*National education goals report*, 1994; Stallings, 1995).

Adding yet another dimension to the growing complexity of teaching, Wolfgang Althof and Fritz

Wooly-headed Thinking   Parsimony   Reductionism

Oser (1993) stress that effective teaching involves more than technical competence in classroom management and instruction. Student academic achievement is one, but not the only, objective. Professional competence needs to be expanded to include an ethical dimension. They note: "Beyond being good instructors, good teachers know they are role models, with a responsibility to foster students' social understanding, and a choice to help to facilitate or to destroy a willingness to find humane, cooperative, peaceful strategies of interpersonal negotiation and conflict solving" (p. 197).

Their view serves as an important reminder that a teacher in a democratic society not only teaches the 3 R's, so to speak, but also creates a classroom atmosphere that either promotes or delays human growth. Some years ago, this was called the hidden agenda or the implicit curriculum. In addition to teaching the formal curriculum, schools may reinforce and perpetuate social and educational differences among students, promote alienation, excessively reward obedience—to name a few of some of the unintended consequences that hinder pupil growth (Mosher and Sprinthall, 1970). Althof and Oser also call our attention to the role of the teacher in creating a democratic and humane classroom atmosphere as a necessary means of promoting not only academic but also human development. Children and teenagers are the potential human capital of our society. And we cannot afford to waste these valuable human resources.

EDUCATIONAL PSYCHOLOGY: FOUR PROBLEMS TO SOLVE SIMULTANEOUSLY

One cause of difficulty in understanding educational psychology is the hybrid nature of science and education. Both theoretical and practical concerns are intrinsic to each field. Now, to up the ante, we turn to the problems that educational psychology seeks to solve. What is the world on which we focus? The simple answer is the teaching-learning process. That has a nice clear ring to it—it couldn't be simpler. Yet, the moment we examine the issue more closely, we immediately confront four interrelated concerns: the students, the teacher, the classroom strategies, and the content to be taught. We can refer to this as the **four-way agenda of teaching** (see Table 1.1).

First we need to know what pupils are like. After all, we are not dealing with pieces of wood or rocks but with real, live, human beings. Each human is unique—and yet is like some other humans and like all other humans in some ways. You will find that both psychologists and educators make this statement quite often But when you listen carefully, you may also find that they quickly ignore their own words. It is a concept honored only in the breach. In other words, while offering three different versions of human behavior—the idiographic, which focuses on the uniqueness of individuals; the nomothetic, which looks for characteristics that all humans share;

TABLE 1.1   *THE FOUR-WAY AGENDA OF TEACHING*

STUDENT CHARACTERISTICS	*TEACHERS*
1. Physical	1. Attitudes to learning
2. Physiological	2. Attitudes to students
3. Cognitive	3. Attitudes to self
4. Personal	4. Understanding research
5. Moral/Value	
6. Motivations	
7. Individual and group behavior	
8. Special needs	
9. Cultural and gender	

TEACHING STRATEGIES	*SUBJECT MATTER*
1. Learning theories in practice	1. Structure of the disciplines
2. Teaching methods and models	2. Basic concepts of material being taught
3. Individual methods	3. Sequencing of subject matter
4. Lesson planning	4. Priorities in content selected
5. Variations in structure	5. Degree of specialized content
6. Student discipline	
7. Questioning	
8. Use of tests	

and an idiographic-nomothetic middle ground—both educators and psychologists all too often settle on one version. But you need to know about individual differences, group similarities, and the combination.

Marilyn Cochran-Smith (1995) has noted that there are no simple ways to respond to the increase in students' cultural diversity. We cannot, she asserts, solve the problem through gimmicks like "more lessons about basket-making and other customs in non-Anglo cultures" (p. 495). Teachers, she says, need to move beyond superficial color blindness in order to understand and respond effectively to the variety of legitimate pupil needs. "Show and tell" won't do; genuine discourse will.

The second part of the agenda shifts the focus from the pupils to you as a teacher, your own attitudes and understandings about learning. What are the goals for your classroom? What do you expect from your pupils? What is your level of self-understanding as a person and as a professional? The teacher's unspoken feelings about his or her role and the students are sometimes called the "hidden agenda" of the classroom. In fact, research has shown just how powerfully some of the unintentional behavior that results from this hidden agenda affects the pupils. So while you are learning about pupils in the classroom, they are most likely learning about you—"where you are coming from," as the saying goes.

The third part of the agenda is represented by the explicit set of teaching strategies, the actual classroom behaviors, you employ. Some years ago, during the so-called know-nothing period, when researchers kept bemoaning how little we knew about teaching, the solution as to which teaching methods to use was breathtakingly simple. Since the experts didn't know, you could "just do your own thing." "Be spontaneous and creative" was the dictum. As you might suspect, that is easier said than done. Flying by the seat of one's pants has always had an attractive, romantic aura about it. But in the classroom it often led to disaster. There is a series of very important specific teacher "moves" that must be learned. However, they cannot simply be applied like ingredients you would add as you follow a cooking recipe. Certain specific skills must be mastered before you can achieve true flexibility as a teacher.

The fourth part of the agenda is represented by the content of your teaching—that is, language arts, math, science, social studies, and so on. Undoubtedly, it's hard to teach history if you don't know the field. Knowing the field as a teacher also means knowing how to divide up the content and sequence

it in accordance with learning priorities. Clearly, content stands on a par with the other three parts of the agenda. All four are involved in the process of teaching.

In this book, we are focusing *only* on the first three parts: students, teachers, and strategies. That makes it just a three-ring circus, you may be thinking, as you review the enormous amount of material in those areas. This text will help you with three parts of the teaching-learning process. They are not the entire story, nor do they encompass all there is to know about teaching. Although we will not delve into the subject matter area, we do not see it as less important than the other three. There are four problems, and they must be solved simultaneously. Such has not always been the case. We will now turn to the history of educational psychology in order to give you a taste of its somewhat checkered past.

EDUCATION YESTERDAY AND TODAY

Yesterday: Trivia in the Classroom

In the late nineteenth century, a visitor to the public schools concluded that most classroom activity consisted of a game of recitation. The pupils and the teacher followed a systematic question-and-answer exercise. The teacher would ask a series of short, factual questions with the rapidity of a machine gunner: "Now class, pay attention . . . Tell me, who discovered America? What year? How many ships were there? What were their names? How long was the voyage?" Each question was followed by a brief pause, and then students with hands raised were called on, again with the speed of light, until one student gave the correct answer. At this point the teacher would fire the next question and skip around the class, calling on pupils whose hands were raised until the next right answer was called out. The 19th-century observer noted that the interaction between teacher and pupil seemed excessively mechanical. The process seemed to emphasize rote learning, the repetition of memorized facts from the textbook or given by the teacher. Inquiry was unknown. "In several instances when a pupil stopped for a moment's reflection, the teacher remarked abruptly, 'Don't stop to think, but tell me what you know'" (Rice, 1893).

These impressions of what we might call **trivia in the classroom** were echoed by other observers. An English educator in 1908 noted the "time-honoured" tradition in U.S. classrooms of question-and-answer recitation, in distinct contrast to the lecture method used in Europe. A study of classroom interaction

One researcher at the turn of the century found that over 80 percent of classroom talk consisted of asking and answering brief, factual questions.

further substantiated question-and-answer as the predominant approach to teaching in this country. Using stenographic notes of actual classroom discussions (this was in the days before tape recorders), a researcher in 1912 found that over 80 percent of all classroom talk consisted of asking and answering brief factual questions—questions that called for a good rote memory and an ability to phrase the answer in the same terms the teacher used. The teacher asked between one and four questions per minute, much as in today's TV quiz games in which contestants (pupils) are given a few seconds to come up with the right answer; if they don't have the answer at the tip of their tongue, they lose their turn, and the quiz master (teacher) moves on. The researcher noted:

> The fact that one history teacher attempts to realize his educational aims through the process of "hearing" the textbook, day after day, is unfortunate but pardonable; that history, science, mathematics, foreign language and English teachers, collectively are following in the same groove, is a matter for theorists and practitioners to reckon with (Stevens, 1912, p. 66).

William James, one of this country's first and perhaps greatest commentators on the problems of teaching and learning, provided the following example of the recitation quiz game in the classroom.

> A friend of mine, visiting a school, was asked to examine a young class in geography. Glancing at the book, she said, "Suppose you should dig a hole in the ground, hundreds of feet deep, how should you find it at the bottom—warmer or colder than on top?" None of the class replying, the teacher said: "I'm sure they know, but I think you don't ask the question quite rightly. Let me try." So, taking the book, she said: "In what condition is the interior of the globe?" and received the immediate answer from half the class at once: "The interior of the globe is in a condition of igneous fusion" (1958, p. 106).

WILLIAM JAMES

William James, American psychology's founding father, was born in 1842 in New York City. As a youth he showed little evidence of the academic brilliance that would follow. In fact, his early education was rather meandering and informal. He attended several private schools in this country and abroad. The only consistent educational experience he had was with his family at the dinner table. Conversation abounded there on every conceivable topic. All members had the opportunity to test their wits against the others. His multiple talents seemingly prevented him from settling on any one career. His brother, Henry James, became a famous novelist. It has often been said that William James was a psychologist who wrote like a novelist, and Henry James was a novelist who wrote like a psychologist. William studied art for a while in Newport, Rhode Island, before deciding to attend Harvard College and specialize in chemistry. However, he maintained his interest in art throughout his life.[1] After two years he switched his field again, transferring to comparative anatomy and physiology. At this point James wrote to a friend that the problem of career choice was limited to four alternatives, "Natural History, Medicine, Printing, and Beggary," and since he had sworn never to become a beggar, he settled on medicine. But once again he felt some discontent and decided to interrupt his studies, first to collect specimens from the Amazon River and later to spend time recuperating from illness by taking a trip to Europe. Finally, in 1869, he did complete his medical studies and was awarded the only academic degree he ever earned, an MD. A scholar commented that it "seems a strange one for a man who was to make his mark as a psychologist and philosopher." But William James's real education was not received in universities and did not lead to degrees. It had taken place in his home with his family.

When offered a position as instructor at Harvard at the age of 30, James jumped at the chance to drop the practice of medicine and to move into the classroom. For James this was an important step; for psychology, it turned out to be momentous. He thrived on academic life, worked hard at the craft of college teaching, and very early displayed a talent for both research and teaching. Once again, however, his enormous and restless talent stretched beyond the conventional and passed by the then-recognized academic disciplines. In 1876 he created and began teaching the first psychology course offered in this country. His originality and creativity burst forth, and the popularity of his lectures burgeoned. Essentially he was simultaneously creating a field of study, shaping the content, and outlining the sequence of topics. His monumental two-volume basic text for these courses, simply titled *Principles of Psychology,* is still

Today: Still Trivia in the Classroom?

Decades later, educational researchers studying classroom interactions between teachers and pupils made the following observations: (1) the teachers tend to do about 70 percent of all talking in the classroom; (2) most of this talk consists of question; (3) between 80 and 88 percent of all these questions call for rote memory responses; (4) the teachers typically ask two questions per minute; (5) pupil talk is almost exclusively a short response to the teacher's question; (6) inquiries and suggestions from pupils are virtually nonexistent (Bellack, Kliebard, Hyman, and Smith, 1966).

Similarly, a 1974 study of 156 randomly selected classrooms across the country found the same pattern in all but 5 percent of the classes (Goodlad and Klein, 1974, p. 51). And, unfortunately, studies in 1984 (Goodlad) and 1990 (Jeness) reached the same conclusion. In fact, Michael Cole has provided an interesting historical perspective. He found that pupils some 6,000 years ago were just as likely to have lists regarded as the single greatest work in American psychology. Here he outlined the basic tenets of psychology with such vision and clarity that even today this text has an incredibly modern flavor. Through this book, James established himself not only as the premier American psychologist but, in the minds of many, the founder of American psychology itself.[2] He started the first psychology laboratory in the United States and anticipated the theory of conditioning later demonstrated by Pavlov, as well as the importance of critical stages of learning and some of the principles of gestalt psychology. So substantial was his vision that his original book still provides modern readers with a relatively up-to-date version of psychology.

For the field of educational psychology James became both an educator and a philosopher. He saw the importance of tailoring educational material to fit the learner's true condition, not the condition that the teacher assumed the learner should be in. His pride in his own teaching enabled him to model effective instruction as well as tell others how to achieve it, a talent that few academic scholars can manage even today. In this way James devoted himself to the idea of improving all teaching. Education, then as now,

tended to be classed as slightly less respectable than certain other disciplines. James's independence of mind and his ability to go beyond the conventional once again were in evidence. As a Harvard professor, renowned scholar, and originator of the field of psychology, he devoted much effort and energy to improving the quality of classroom education. His famous lectures, *Talks to Teachers on Psychology*, are quoted briefly in the text to give you some sense of his flair with concepts as well as the significance of his thinking. His major point was that the entire enterprise of education is determined by the actual classroom teacher.

In these days of national curriculum projects and technological prescriptions for the classroom, we need to recall the central Jamesian theme: "Psychology is a science— teaching is an art; and sciences never generate arts directly out of themselves. An intermediary inventive mind must make the application, by use of its originality." James was convinced that the future of education depended directly on the quality of the intermediary inventive minds of the teachers. It was they who would do the job in the classroom and they who needed to apply psychological principles hu-

manely. James was convinced that understanding the nature of children and adolescents as behaving organisms was the key to improving teaching.

An educational theorist, Paul Woodring, probably summed up James's significance to education most succinctly. He noted that if James had been read carefully by teachers and teacher-educators over the past 50 years, many of our educational difficulties might have been avoided.

James's long and productive life ended in 1910 after some 35 years of teaching. The world lost that rare combination of talents—those of teacher, scholar, leader, and philosopher able to go well beyond current thinking. Not only did James have a personality so vivid that his sister described him as "born afresh every morning"; he has also been called "the most gifted writer of expository prose this country ever had."[3]

1. Leary, D. E. (1992). William James and the art of human understanding. *American Psychologist, 47,* 152–160.
2. Johnson, M. G., & Henley, T. B. (1990). *Reflections on the principles of psychology: William James after a century.* Hillsdale, NJ: Erlbaum.
3. Adelson, J. (1982). Still vital after all these years. *Psychology Today, 16,* 52–59.

of information to memorize as their modern-day counterparts. The content was different—for example, 84 different types of trees versus the 50 state capitals—but the process was the same (Cole, 1990, p. 96).

David Tyack and William Tobin (1994) have recently suggested that the overall system of schooling seeks to promote continuity at the expense of innovation. As a result, innovators become isolated and burn out (p. 477). In the meantime, the old forms— what is called the "grammar" of schooling—persist right up to the moment.

You may be struck by the remarkable similarity in the results of these studies—after so many years the same mode persists. This state of affairs raises two questions: Is the rapid-fire question-and-answer trivia quiz an effective educational method? If it isn't, then why does it persist?

Perhaps the best way to begin understanding the effect of rapid-fire question-and-answer procedures would be to ask you to remember such a situation in your own experience. You are in the third grade, sitting in a class of 30 children. The teacher towers over you physically, a difference exaggerated when she stands in front of the seated class. The class has been studying a unit on the American Indian. After a series of questions on Native American lore and myths, which you know about but don't get called on to answer (instead, the teacher has scolded you sternly for jumping up from your seat when you raised your hand), the teacher suddenly wheels around and looks directly at you: "What did the Navaho call their houses?" In the confusion (for you are still thinking about a previous question), you don't have the answer. The class falls silent. Twenty-nine children turn toward you. The teacher waits a few seconds that seem like years and then says, "Well?" "Tepee?" you say, hoping that it's right, but mostly wishing there were a place to hide. "Hogan," the teacher replies. "Hogan—oh, that is what I meant to say," you add in a near-whisper. The moment does pass as the girl two seats away from you expertly fields the next question about how a hogan is constructed. A few minutes later recess mercifully arrives, and you manage to sneak out as unobtrusively as possible. So much for the question-and-answer quiz and the promotion of learning.

A series of studies has shown, perhaps not as dramatically or as personally as the scenario sketched above, that the classroom trivia quiz does not promote learning unless we really think that the recitation of textbook facts is equivalent to learning. If we view the objectives of teaching and learning more broadly, then we can only conclude that a form of "Button, button, who has the button?" or "Hogan, hogan, what's a hogan?" does not help students learn except in a negative way. You do learn to play the game after a while; that is, you learn to say the right thing and to act out of reflex. You do remember the acceptable phrases and terms, whether they concern the kind of house a Navaho lived in or the state of igneous fusion in the center of the earth. But is this the process of inquiry we consider desirable? Is this the goal of human thinking? Does this generate the excitement of seeing new relationships among ideas? Is this the process through which we learn about ourselves?

EMERGENCE OF A THEORETICAL FRAMEWORK

Fundamentally, the problem faced by education and psychology has been to create a framework that is broad enough to provide working solutions to the four-part agenda of concerns we mentioned earlier. William James, this country's first psychologist, was also the first to grapple directly with the problem.

The scope and depth of his vision provided original and brilliant insights. Unfortunately, the field did not follow his views until very recently. Because of his importance we will describe his work in detail as well as some of the reasons for the long eclipse of his thinking and his current relevance. After that, we will look at the contributions of some other theorists: E. L. Thorndike, John Dewey, and Maxine Greene.

William James: The Early Promise

William James exerted tremendous early influence on the whole field of psychology and was probably this country's most significant educational psychologist. In the nineteenth century, psychology was considered part of philosophy, not a separate discipline. It was William James at Harvard in the 1880s who began to give systematic attention to psychology as a discipline in its own right and, more importantly for us, began to consider most seriously the question of applying psychology to the problems of the real world rather than leaving it in the laboratory.

James was concerned that the so-called scientific tradition would capture psychology and turn it away from its important purpose of helping us understand more about the processes of teaching and learning. He delivered a series of famous lectures (*Talks to Teachers on Psychology*) that are as relevant today as when they were first heard. At that time, "scientific" experiments were thought to be able to give us all the answers, including all the laws that govern human behavior. James feared the dangers of such an exclusive dependence on science. He warned that laboratory scientists "would go off by themselves and use apparatus and consult sources in such a way as to grind out in the requisite number of months some little peppercorn of new truth worthy of being added to the store of extant information on the subject" (1958, p. 38). Such efforts might produce a mountain of peppercorns but not necessarily truth.

James wisely saw that psychology had to look to the natural environment for much of its information. Laboratory studies, especially animal studies, might not be such a great help when it came to teaching children. He therefore launched the effort to examine and understand the process of teaching and learning in the classroom. He observed classrooms (remember his "igneous fusion" anecdote) and also suggested positive alternatives to the state of affairs he found there. For example, he pointed to the central importance of starting lessons at a point just beyond the pupils' present comprehension. The famous dictum "Start where the learner is and proceed" was derived from this insight of William James.

If the teacher is to explain the distance of the sun from the earth, let him ask . . . "If anyone there in the sun fired off a cannon straight at you, what should you do?" "Get out of the way," would be the answer. "No need of that," the teacher might reply. "You may quietly go to sleep in your room, and get up again, you may wait until your confirmation-day, you may learn a trade, and grow as old as I am— then only will the cannon-ball be getting near, then you may jump to one side! See, so great as that is the sun's distance!" (James, 1968, p. 333).

James's most important effort was to try to convince educators that the observations, thoughts, and questions they brought out of their work with pupils would be a significant source of "scientific" feedback. He was particularly concerned to retain the human mind, or as he called it, "mental life," as a proper object for psychology; in fact, he deliberately defined psychology as the "science of mental life." What goes on "inside" a person's head—thoughts, feelings, interests, values, sentiments—these were what James thought psychologists should study in order to shed light on human strivings and motivations.

James was the first to warn teachers and educators not to depend on psychology to provide all the answers, and the first to warn psychology not to present itself as a mirror image of physical science. He saw psychology as a natural science filled with uncertainty, an "open system" of questions concerning that most complex of all "systems," the human being. That was the problem, but it was also the challenge.

The difficulties of James's views were many. For example, to say that teaching is a process that we can never fully understand is unsettling to those in search of the truth. To say that we will have to be content with a series of approximations of good ideas and practices rather than perfect ideas or perfect practices is likewise unsettling.

Obviously it was, and still is, extraordinarily difficult to consider educational problems in such a broad perspective. James wanted educational psychology to study teaching and learning in the classroom in order to view educational problems in their real, or natural, environment. James wanted to focus on both the objective and the subjective nature of educational problems.

In rejecting James's views as too unwieldy, educational psychology headed in a logical direction. It seemed sensible when confronted with complexity to narrow the focus, to examine the effect of one variable at a time. And to add strength to this tendency, there was, at the time, an almost passionate desire

for psychology to pattern itself after the physical sciences and to search for the "molecules" of human behavior. This is sometimes referred to cynically as "physics envy." In fact the shift was so strong that Cahan and White (1992) found that the James view was considered as a "second psychology," a movement that became moribund with his death at the turn of the century. As a result, the emphasis shifted away from naturalistic studies of pupil and teacher behaviors in classrooms. There were too many uncontrolled variables operating in such settings; the open system of a classroom was not a scientifically researchable problem. The desire for precision in measurement and research design forced educational psychology into the laboratory. The era produced many useful pieces of information, especially about some aspects of learning. On balance, however, the focus was too narrow. Too much was left untouched. The classroom remained tragically similar to its 19th-century antecedent. To understand the impact of the new focus and its limitations, we will turn to the researcher whose name became synonymous with educational psychology, Edward L. Thorndike.

E. L. Thorndike: Scientific Education

The person most responsible for channeling education toward an emphasis on measurement was **E. L. Thorndike** (1913, 1932), a professor at Teachers College of Columbia University. Thorndike sought to eliminate speculation, opinion, and naturalistic investigation. In fact, he considered visiting a classroom an extraordinary waste of time. It was much more "scientific" to understand the learning process by experimenting on cats in a laboratory than by observing children in a classroom. And experiment he did. Thorndike studied the behavior of his famous cats in specially designed puzzle boxes. He was interested in discovering how long it took the cats to solve the puzzles (which usually involved getting out of the box) and in learning what rewards were the most effective in achieving the objective. (Will a hungry cat learn faster than a "fat" cat—or, in more scientific language, "an organism deprived of nutrition for 48 hours"—if food is the reward?) This procedure led to an almost endless number of empirical studies documenting how many trial-and-error sequences took place before the cat finally "learned" to stick a paw through the grating, lift up the latch to open the cage, and then stroll triumphantly over to the food. As you can see, Thorndike was focusing on one aspect of learning—that which takes place by trial and error. Putting a cat through this sequence

EDWARD L. THORNDIKE

Born in 1874 into the family of a Protestant minister and brought up in the mill towns of Massachusetts, E. L. Thorndike completed his undergraduate studies in classics at Wesleyan University. A somewhat singular and solitary person, he demonstrated early in his life a capacity for hard work, long hours, and precision. Almost a personification of the Protestant work ethic, Thorndike simply abhorred making even the slightest error and consequently was always striving for perfection in his work. He had enormous amounts of mental energy and virtually threw himself into the task of defining a scientific base for psychology.

At Columbia University's Teachers College he completed his doctorate in the department of philosophy, psychology, anthropology, and education in the late 1890s. At that time departmental specialization was not yet established. The field of educational psychology was amorphous and resisted a generic definition. Academic psychology and the so-called brass-instrument laboratories and physical measurements represented one stance. At the other end, William James at Harvard was lecturing on the art of teaching, separate from the science of psychology. In between there was a range of philosophers, educators, and psychologists all attempting to give definition and coherence to the field. This was educational psychology's moment of a "cultural revolution." Apparently Thorndike was not at all intimidated by the first-generation psychologists and educators. As a brand-new assistant professor at Teachers College in 1898, he took pleasure in attacking his elders. He referred to this period as his early assertive years. "It is fun to write all the stuff up and smite all the hoary scientists hip and thigh . . . My thesis is a beauty . . . I've got some theories which knock the old authorities into a grease spot." For such a fledgling— he was still in his twenties—to have the inner strength to attack the heroes of the day both in print and in association meetings was most unusual. Possibly within himself Thorndike transformed the Protestant ethic into a messianic vision not of religion but of scientific logical positivism. In other words, the dedication that a person might feel toward a religious mission was apparently shifted so that science became his religion.

For the entire 41 years of his professional life, Thorndike remained at Columbia Teachers College. He often enough would establish a stimulus-response connection in the nervous system, so that the cat would "remember" what to do.

It has been said that Thorndike was so influential that all subsequent research in education was merely a footnote to his work. His critics noted humorously of his influence that if one of Thorndike's cats behaved unpredictably, it would affect the curriculum for an entire nation.

On the positive side, Thorndike was an important influence because he exploded many of the educational myths of the day. The classical curriculum of the secondary school (four years of Greek, four years of Latin, and so on) had been justified on the grounds that such exercise would "train" the mind: spending time and effort on Latin, for example, would make it easier to learn French, while Greek would improve English usage. Using precise measurement procedures, Thorndike was able to show that little, if any, disciplining of the mind could be transferred from one subject to another. In an almost singular way, he could proclaim, "If you want to improve your English, study English, not Latin or Greek." Thorndike believed that transfer occurred only when elements in one situation were identical with or at least similar to elements in a second situation. Many a subsequent generation had Thorndike and his empirical research to thank for disposing of the mythical justification for the study of Latin and Greek. So Thorndike's contribution cannot be dismissed. However, his importance and influence were so great that educational psychology became defined educational psychology as essentially the psychology of laboratory experimentation. His lifework was to create a base of scientific knowledge through careful experiments, changing one variable at a time and using precise measures. He insisted that the operational definition was the only definition for science. If you couldn't see, measure, and directly record the phenomenon under investigation, then it was not scientific or even worthwhile. "Look, see, and collect data" were his words of advice for investigators. In fact, he really viewed himself more as an investigator than a scholar. He once noted that he had probably spent over 10,000 hours in reading and studying scientific books and journals, but he devoted even more time to his own experiments and writing. His bibliography runs to a prodigious 500 items. Science, he would say, was to be built by research, not by proclamation.

When Thorndike finished his classic work on measurement for educational psychology, he sent a copy to William James. The amusing dialogue that resulted went as follows:

Thorndike to James, with academic modesty: "I am sending you a dreadful book which I have written which is in no end scientific but devoid of any spark of human interest."

James's reply: "I opened your new book with full feelings of awe and admiration for your unexampled energy. It was just the thing I had hoped for when I was teaching psychology . . . I am glad I have graduated from the necessity of using that kind of thing any longer. I shall stick to 'qualitative' work as more congruous with old age!"[1]

Thorndike's work, as we have noted in the text, became almost an endless series of studies on trial-and-error learning. His famous cats in the puzzle box represented his observable data. He persuaded his university to create a psychology laboratory for him; and there he remained, building the wall of scientific knowledge brick by brick. Thorndike reached the pinnacle of his career in 1934, when he was elected president of the American Association for the Advancement of Science. No psychologist had ever been so honored. In fact, only one social scientist had ever been elected to head the professional organization that represented the entire scientific community.

For Thorndike, then, this was truly the moment of glory. The years of hard work, the struggle to create a scientifically respectable basis for educational psychology, had at last achieved the ultimate recognition. His biographer, Geraldine Jonçich, has noted that an editorial in the *New York Times* in January 1934 pleased him above all else when it said of him, "But first and last, he is a scientist."

1. Jonçich, G. (1968). E. L. Thorndike: The psychologist as a professional man of science. *American Psychologist, 23*(6), 444.

almost preoccupied by trial-and-error learning and measurement techniques. All other ideas, perspectives, and theories were practically abandoned. The field grew more narrowly scientific, objective, and empirical. We began to be able to measure educational problems more effectively, but the problems we were measuring were less and less significant. And the range of what we could know was limited to what we could measure.

This emphasis on empirical measurement was better suited to showing what was wrong than to showing what was right. This is not to say that educational psychology does not need rigorous measurement procedures and evaluation systems, but it cannot progress as a field if that is its only focus. The movement was more and more to the laboratory, for more and more replications and refinements of essentially the same studies. When William James warned of grinding out peppercorns, he was predicting the direction the field actually took. Literally thousands of studies have been produced that have had little influence on learning and the practice of teaching. Instead of a narrow focus, educational psychology needed to broaden its view to include once again studies in the natural environment.

John Dewey and Human Interaction

One of this country's most important theorists, **John Dewey,** always used the phrase "some organism in some environment" (1916). This was his way of em-

JOHN DEWEY

Without question one of this country's major educational theorists, John Dewey had a long and significant influence on the actual practice of both psychology and education. Born in Vermont in 1859, his life spanned almost a century, from just before the Civil War to 1952. During that time, the education of American pupils went through a transformation that paralleled the historical changes occurring in the United States, in large part because of John Dewey's ideas and his practice.

In some ways Dewey was a true product of nineteenth-century America. Naturally intelligent and serious about his educational mission, he wanted most of all to develop an educational philosophy that could be put into practice. The concepts had to be tested in the real world of schools and in the classrooms. Many psychologists were content to theorize about education and write learned essays, but for Dewey, this was not enough. If the ideas were not translated into action and tested, then the practice of education would forever remain overly theoretical. An American pragmatist, he had little patience with glossy educational rhetoric. He clearly was a doer.

Dewey's Yankee upbringing fostered in him a great respect for natural growth as well as for the critical relationship between person and environment. These themes recur throughout his educational writings. After graduating from the University of Vermont, he completed his Ph.D. at Johns Hopkins (under the tutelage of G. Stanley Hall) at the age of 25.

His first professorship was at the University of Minnesota, followed quickly by moves to the University of Michigan and then on to the University of Chicago in 1894, where he served as chairman of the department of philosophy and pedagogy. It was at Chicago that he established the first major educational laboratory school in the country. Here at last he had the natural learning environment he needed to test and revise his unique educational ideas. At that time the country's educators were convinced that children ought to sit quietly in a classroom and learn by rote a classical curriculum, an approach that has been labeled the "formal discipline theory." Instead of strengthening the mind, however, such a learning environment too often placed students in an exceptionally passive role. Anticipating the ideas of Piaget and the open classroom, Dewey developed learning envi-

phasizing that you could not study learning in the abstract and ignore the broader context—the environment in which that learning took place. Here is one of his sardonic comments on traditional education:

> The entire range of the universe is first subdivided into sections called studies; then each one of these studies is broken up into bits, and some one bit assigned to a certain year of the course. No order of development is recognized—it is enough that the earlier parts were made easier than the later. To use the pertinent illustration of Mr. W. S. Jackman in stating the absurdity of this sort of curriculum: "It must seem to geography teachers that Heaven smiled on them when it ordained but four or five continents, because starting in far enough along the course it was so easy, that it really seemed natural, to give one continent to each grade and then come out right in the eight years" (1956, p. 103).

Unfortunately, Dewey's important ideas were misinterpreted. He was thought to be advocating the so-called child-centered curriculum rather than the significant ecological concept of person-in-environment. Cafeteria-style education—in which a child was free to choose anything, even to play all day if he or she wanted—was supposedly the result of Dewey's work. However, these "progressive" views on education clearly missed Dewey's point. What he advocated was careful, guided experience for children, arranged according to their interests and caronments which ensured that children would actively engage in learning. His dictum of "learning through doing" became famous. Experience should precede or at least be concurrent with educational concepts and ideas. This was a revolutionary stance to the educators of the day, because it turned the educational process inside out. His objective was to create an experience-based curriculum to promote both more effective learning and greater competence in living.

By this time Dewey was easily the most widely known educational psychologist of his day. In 1886 he wrote an important textbook, titled *Psychology,* and in 1896 he published his famous paper on the nature of the reflex arc (which, though a strong statement of the Functionalist position, also foreshadowed some of Wertheimer's later ideas about the importance of the "Gestalt"). He constantly argued for a focus on the study of the *"whole* child and its *adaptation* to the environment." Clearly, Dewey became a psychological functionalist in the tradition of William James. In

1904 he moved to the center of educational thought on this continent, the famous Teachers College at Columbia University. While at Columbia he became an ardent supporter of women's rights, and even marched in parades supporting a woman's right to vote. During one of these parades he is said to have quickly picked up a placard without reading it, and apparently amused and puzzled the onlookers by carrying a sign that read: "Men can vote. Why can't I?"[1]

He remained at Columbia until his formal retirement, 26 years later. During that time he not only taught, but also authored many books and lectured throughout the United States. An innovator, he was one of those very rare educators who lived to see his ideas put into practice and become important educational doctrine.

Unfortunately, his most significant idea was also the most easily misunderstood. His concept of child-centered, progressive education was distorted in many instances into a laissez-faire curriculum, and in the late 1940s and early

1950s it became quite fashionable to criticize Dewey as soft-headed and to blame him for problems of classroom discipline. This misunderstanding has since been cleared up. Learning by doing finds expression in today's schools in a variety of ways. Learning laboratories and centers, workshops, lesson units, and school programs devoted to all aspects of human growth are reflections of his views in action. Perhaps Dewey's most important idea, or indeed vision, was the democratic ideal that always remained his goal. By developing significant education for all children, the American dream of free people in a free country might be realized. In his ninety-third year John Dewey died, the vision intact and, hopefully, the country closer to the goal. He saw developing significant education for all children as the way to realize the American dream of free people in a free country.

1. Hergenhahn, B. R. (1992). *An introduction to the history of psychology* (2d ed.). Englewood Cliffs, NJ: Prentice-Hall.

---

pacities. The importance of these concepts for educational psychology should not be missed.

The central idea of Dewey's work was that the child was not an empty vessel waiting patiently and quietly to be filled up with knowledge. In fact, Dewey's best writing took these traditional assumptions of education to task. For example, he tells of visiting a manufacturer of school furniture one day and having a difficult time finding what he wanted for his school. One dealer, apparently more intelligent than the rest, commented: "I am afraid we have not what you want. You want something at which the children may work; these are all for listening" (Dewey, 1956, p. 31).

In addition to the concept of active learning, Dewey stressed the idea of stages of growth and de-

velopment. In this he foreshadowed the now-classic work of Jean Piaget. Dewey noted that the child was often assumed to be a small version of an adult: "The boy was a little man and his mind was a little mind— in everything but size the same as that of the adult . . . Now we believe in the mind as a growing affair, and hence as essentially changing, presenting distinctive phases of capacity and interest at different periods" (1956, p. 102).

Finally, Dewey's most significant assertion was that teaching and learning interacted, that the pupil was as much a part of the learning environment as the teacher. He constantly battled against what he saw as the artificial separation between learning and the pupil.

Dewey's central view, then, was to promote a balance between experiential learning and careful, rational examination. He did not want pupils simply to experience in a vacuum. Supposedly, a teacher, in seeking employment at Dewey's laboratory school, said that he had 10 years of teaching experience. Dewey quickly retorted, "Was it really 10 years or was it one year 10 times!" In other words, what had the person learned from the experience? How much reflection, examination, and analysis of the experience had occurred? Thus, learning through experience includes what is commonly called "intellectual analysis." Dewey viewed this process as a means of promoting cognitive thought structures. In this area he essentially anticipated a second Piagetian concept of cognitive structures, or schemas, as the framework for understanding how children come to know and think. The classroom should be a natural environment in which living and learning occur together. In this way Dewey pioneered today's emphasis on education as an interactive process.

Constructivism: "The Good, the Bad, and the Ugly"

A central directing concept derived from both William James and John Dewey is the idea of **constructivism.** The major developmental theorists whom you will meet in the chapters on cognitive (Piaget and Vygotsky), personal (Erikson), and value and character development (Kohlberg) have all based their work on this concept. Unfortunately, like many concepts, such as creativity or even intelligence, the idea of constructivism has been misused to such an extent that it has become confusing, ambiguous, and downright contradictory. As D. C. Phillips (1995) has observed, the definition now seems to be "the good, the bad, and the ugly" all at once (p. 5).

As defined by James, Dewey, and the other theorists mentioned above, constructivism means exactly that: Each child creates, or builds, or constructs, meaning from experience. The child is the active agent, processing information and experience from the world. Using his or her mind like an erector set, the child builds an increasingly complex set of cognitive structures to figure out what is going on in the so-called real-world. The pictures of Suzanne and of Willy and Mikey have been posed to send the message. Each child is busily constructing (the equivalent of hammering, sawing, measuring) cognitions to extract meaning from the environment. Suzanne at the age of four, in tow with her parents, sits down at a posh restaurant. The adults order appetizers, entrees, and drinks. Her mother says quietly to the waiter that they will just give Suzanne a few tidbits,

so, "Bring her an empty plate." In a loud voice, Suzanne immediately pipes up: "What do you mean, an empty plate for me?" Similarly, Mikey, a four-year-old baseball addict whose favorite is Minnesota Twin Kirby Puckett, decides that all African-American ballplayers are named Kirby Puckett. After all, there are many Santa Clauses at Christmas, so why not have many Kirbys to cheer for? His older brother, Willy, a six-year-old, is more differentiated: he roots for all ballplayers named Willy.

In this text we will be using the concept of constructivism in its original sense, as the system of cognitions that each of us uses to create meaning. That cognitive system itself then forms a sequence of stages of development. Each stage is erected on the previous set of cognitions. Each new stage is more complex and represents a more efficient method of problem solving. Phillips refers to this as the traditional, or the "good" definition of the concept. Our knowledge, says Phillips, is not "acquired, ready-formed" (1995, p. 5). Learning may start with experience, but it is what we make it that determines meaning. The child is a youthful but natural scientist.

At the opposite end from this view is a definition that suggests that all knowledge is constructed not by individuals but by social political and economic power groups. This really means that knowledge is completely relativistic and reflects the views of the ruling class in a capitalist society. This is sometimes called **social constructivism** or **radical deconstructivism.** The idea is stark. All knowledge has been created by the ruling elite—for example, by DWEM (Dead White European Men)—to preserve their power through oppression of all others in society. Thus, stage and sequence cognitions are merely props for existing social and political oppression. Phillips cites Sandra Harding's view as an example: All knowledge created by the ruling classes is to be rejected as racist, sexist, and totally biased; the only true knowledge can be derived from those "at the bottom of such social hierarchies" (1993, p. 54). Otherwise the knowledge that each of us creates is already tainted and must be torn down, or pulled apart—that is **deconstructed**—before real learning can take place.

Phillips sums up his review by noting that the "good" represents the idea of active participation by the learner in the William James/John Dewey tradition, as well as the idea that such learning takes place in a social context; the "ugly" is the view based on political ideology; and the "bad" is closely associated with the "ugly," since it assumes a world of complete relativism or of situational ethics.

Clearly, it is important to understand and differentiate among the definitions of constructivism. The

Children as constructivists:
"Meaning is not given to us but by us."
Professor Eleanor Duckworth Harvard University

Suzanne

Willy

Mikey

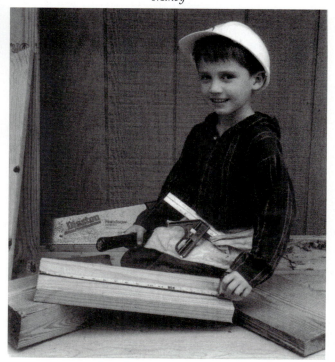

Sources: N. A. Sprinthall, W. Rankin, and H. E. Berry.

radical views (the "bad" and the "ugly") are versions of a Catch-22. The scientific method that we employ to study the process of growth and development is unscientific and biased, say the ideological deconstructivists. Thus, whatever findings we have researched and used to build a wall of scientific evidence must be discarded. This also means that we have no basis for discussion, since the methods of the James and Dewey constructivism are impossibly flawed. In contrast, our position is that the scientific method as a basis for knowing avoids empty theorizing, narrow empiricism, and political ideology. The process is slow, but in the long run the method is self-correcting. Humans create knowledge. Educational psychologists create knowledge about how each of us engages in the constructive process. The system is open; each wave of scientific evidence moves us closer to understanding just how complex is each individual and how to create effective learning environments.

Maxine Greene: The Teacher as Stranger

Perhaps the best way to close such a far-ranging chapter is to focus on the individual teacher. **Maxine Greene,** one of this country's leading educational philosophers, conceptualizes the role of teacher with a strikingly vivid image, "the teacher as stranger." That concept may be somewhat unsettling at first sight. Teaching is intensely personal. How is it possible to think of a teacher as separated from students, as an alien or foreigner in a land of pupils? Greene would be the first to agree that teaching is an interpersonal process. It must involve the heart and soul as well as the mind. Teaching is not divisible. Yet, the teacher cannot be one of the pupils. Instead, there is always a gulf, a separation. As a teacher you are the leader, the responsible adult. Our society grants a teacher special status. In fact, the pupils are not given the freedom of choice to attend school. Thus, there is fundamental asymmetry. Your purpose is clear—namely, to promote their growth. Their role is not to promote yours, even though it not only may but does occur. That is not, however, the primary agenda.

For the teacher the agenda is the pupils. Your role with the students is more that of a mentor than a colleague. You are constantly alert to individual differences, to signs of growth, to indicators of student interest, curiosity, or their need to know. This means you are with them, but part of you is separate. You can step back and review the process, ask yourself new questions, such as What strategy should I try with Carolyn? What's the best way to reach Douglas? How can I help Jane gain confidence as a

learner? Somewhat ironically, your increasing reflective ability is the key element in becoming Maxine Greene's "stranger."

By reflecting, you increase the depth of your understanding of teaching and children, and you come to appreciate your deepening wisdom. In the broadest sense Greene's teacher becomes a philosopher, but in a special way. We usually think of a philosopher as someone almost hopelessly lost in abstractions. That's not Greene's definition. She sees the crux of teaching in the actual art of doing philosophy. The teacher is not a mechanic but a seeker of truth. Learning philosophy by doing teaching is her way of connecting art and science. As you grow in effectiveness through such a process, you will then experience what she means by the word stranger, namely, a person who, by being somewhat removed from the others, has a clearer vision of the goals as well as the ability to stay on course.

In her recent work, *The Dialectic of Freedom* (1988), she stresses the importance of a broad definition of freedom that includes learning how to learn as well as social responsibility. Freedom is not rampant individualism, but rather helping each person become a self-reflective individual in full recognition of our common democratic goals of equality, an equality that includes sharing of the benefits as well as the burdens. Thus, she picks up the theme from Dewey that education is not only for intellectual development but also for human development. Freedom becomes, somewhat ironically, the exercise of human equality in interdependence. Greene puts the case more elegantly through metaphorical language. Read the lines below and see what images you experience. First, think of the times when you as a student truly experienced deeper teaching with a particular adult. Second, imagine yourself in the role of teacher surrounded by pupils, your charges:

> If the teacher is able to think and do while being vitally present as a person, then others may be aroused to act on their own freedom. Learning to learn, some of those persons may move beyond the sheltered places until they stand by their own choice in the high wind of thought.

She concludes, employing the metaphor of children as growing trees:

> The teacher, too, must raise shadowy trees and let them ripen. Stranger and homecomer, questioner and goad to others, the teacher can become visible to one's own self by doing philosophy. There are countless lives to be changed, worlds to be remade (1978, p. 298).

SPOTLIGHT ON TEACHING

The View from the Pupil's Desk

Reflective teachers ask questions that require reflective answers of their students.

As you consider your own goals for teaching, it is well to remember William James's comment about students: Their views are important too, particularly as a basis for understanding where they are coming from. A simple yet revealing exercise is to ask them three questions for written responses.

Some sample answers from a middle school were as follows:

Question 1: Why should children (or adolescents) attend school?

"To get involved in education and learn to get along with others."

"To learn and understand about different things and about life."

"To get a good education, get ready for high school, and have fun doing it."

"To get a good job and get along with others."

Obviously both the academic and the interpersonal were important goals.

Question 2: How do children learn best?

"By observing and by learning from friends."

"By studying and paying attention."

"By watching, observing, and doing. We do it over and over 'til we get it just right."

"Through the teacher. They teach us, and we do a lot of activities."

"We learn by having fun while we work."

"Children learn from teachers explaining how things work and what makes it work."

There are a variety of views, from teacher-directed learning to learning through observation and by doing.

Question 3: What is the teacher's job?

"To help children learn . . . not all the time, but to be there when help is needed."

"To teach us so we can become something good in life."

"To help us get a good education without boring us."

"To give us challenging assignments but explain it so we can do it."

"To make us feel special while we try to be good students, to believe we can do it, so we can believe it ourselves."

As you can see from these students' statements, the teacher's job is just about as complex as our theorists William James, John Dewey, and Maxine Greene have said. Perhaps the students say it more personally.

Note: We thank Stella Farrow from Lee County, North Carolina, for supplying us with these student comments.

MAXINE GREENE

After completing her undergraduate studies at Barnard College in 1938, with a liberal arts degree and a Phi Beta Kappa key, Maxine Greene began to follow what was then a traditional path: marriage, children, and a role as a suburban homemaker. However, in the late 1940s she made a mistake that changed the course of her life. She began graduate work at New York University in English, also a traditional area of study for females. The mistake was to take some work in philosophy with George E. Axtelle, whom she later described as a truly memorable teacher. It was the perfect match of person and ideas, and it provided a focus for the career she was to follow.

Combining philosophy with her intellectual interest in literary analysis, derived from her English studies, she soon saw philosophy as the master discipline. These two elements were the necessary foundations, but not the whole story. In addition, she had two other enduring interests, art and action. It was probably her interest in art as an aesthetic experience that provided the bridge between ideas and action. The result has been the careful development of a framework for educational philosophy that seeks to set forth a series of principles and actions, ideas and experiences, thoughts and feelings. In fact, the major goal of her publication record, which is quite vast, is to synthesize thought and action as a basis for a living philosophy.

Such was, of course, not the tradition of the so-called analytic school of philosophy. In that view, the goal of philosophy is analysis, in-depth and logical—the philosopher as critic. The difficulty with such a conception as a goal for philosophy is that it can too quickly lead to criticism for criticism's sake and, indeed, render the obvious obscure.

In breaking through the traditional career roles for women, Greene has also broken through the traditional framework for educational philosophy. She approaches philosophical goals quite differently and with a refreshing vigor. Instead of delving into levels of increasingly arcane meta-analyses, she always holds up ideas and goals to the real world of practice and action. There is a vivid existential quality to her work, and it is not the negative existentialism of the ``life is absurd'' school of thought. Instead, she produces a positive existentialism in her continued insistence on philosophy as thought in action. Her work began to enter the educational paradigm slowly at first. Analytic philosophy was, after all, the main school of thought, and it was not about to disappear overnight. But Greene's voluminous writings, coupled with her frequent, powerful conference presentations and keynote addresses, gradually created a major place for her ideas as a philosophy for education and educational psychology. In 1975 she was appointed to the endowed William F. Russell Professorship at Teachers College of Columbia University. A long series of honors and elections soon followed: Educator of the Year by Phi Delta Kappa, Best Educational Book of the Year from Kappa Delta Gamma, president of the American Educational Research Association, chairperson of the John Dewey Society, president of the Philosophy of Education Society, and election to the National Academy of Education.

For education the Greene philosophy becomes a set of guides to living the ``good life'' as a manager of child growth and development. As noted in the text, her idea of the teacher as stranger sets the role tasks clearly in the growth context. To act and reflect in the real world according to democratic ethical guides represent to her the means of living philosophy, of teaching as ``doing philosophy.'' She sees the educator's role as not simply to teach subject matter or skills or to maintain discipline. Those are only intermediate objectives. Instead, the framework suggests a far greater purpose, even though the purpose itself may be a paradox. As she says, ``How can one act on one's commitment and at once set others free to be?'' Her own career stands as the best answer.

Dewey developed learning environments that ensured children would actively engage in learning. His famous dictum of "learning by doing" became a byword.

THE ART AND SCIENCE OF TEACHING

We have pointed out the complexities of managing the four-way agenda of the teaching-learning process. We have also pointed out how, until recently, the science of educational psychology and the profession of education were more like ships passing in the night than interacting disciplines. We have shown how the scientific basis for psychology led to the laboratory and the professional basis for education to the classroom. The traditions of both promoted separation. Then we noted the reasons for optimism, primarily a growing cumulative basis for theory and practice that forms the content of this book. In the end, of course, whether any of this makes a difference will depend on you, the teacher. For teaching as practice is as fundamentally an art as any other human services profession, such as law,

medicine, or business management. In each case there are established scientific principles or, as one leading educational psychologist puts it, "the scientific basis for the art of teaching" (Gage, 1978). This means what it says. Art represents the skill, the art of putting it together in the real world of the classroom. Your own professional identity becomes the agenda for educational psychology.

By now you realize that our goal is to bridge the discipline of psychology and the practice of professional education. The solution is almost paradoxical: a theoretical practitioner, a practical theorist. To be successful in teaching requires both. There is the need for you to interact in the moment with students. There is also the need to reflect, to inquire, and to critique your own efforts.

In fact, if there is one common thread in all contemporary literature on teaching, it is the concept of a reflective practitioner. Virginia Richardson (1990) has commented that experience in teaching is only educative with careful and systematic reflection. This only increases the importance of both. And certainly given the enormous changes in store for schooling, particularly the increase in cultural diversity, teachers in all phases of their career will require greater sophistication in both cognition and action. Echoing John Dewey, Lampert and Clark (1990) noted that experience is not necessarily expertise. Although it is an overused concept, empowerment of teachers can be attained only through a balance or praxis of action and reflection.

One of the unique characteristics of teaching as a career is that you rarely practice in the company of other adults. The isolation comes with the territory. Supervision, collegiality, and the analysis of teaching with other adults are highly unlikely. This set of circumstances only increases the need to develop a reflective and a doing capacity. You cannot afford either as an exclusive mode. Acting and reflecting represent the key processes for professional growth, indeed, they serve as a kind of Rosetta stone for teacher effectiveness. So the struggle you embark on is highly significant and difficult, filled with frustration, apparent contradictions, and at times overwhelming complexity. However, the goal of becoming both artist and scientist is attainable.

SUMMARY

In introducing you to the field of educational psychology, this chapter has presented a series of major issues with which the field has struggled. As Snow noted in the metaphor of two separate cultures, the scientific and professional traditions more often than not go their own ways. The field of educational psychology attempts to bridge those traditions.

Both theory and practice are needed. Without theory, practice is aimless; without practice, theory is abstract speculation. Theory is nothing more than successive approximations that gradually increase our understanding. In arriving at theory, we must steer clear of the twin fallacies of wooly-headed thinking and reductionism. William of Occam expressed the ideal as one of parsimony: A theory should be neither more elaborate nor more abstract than it needs to be to explain the facts.

The teaching-learning process is a four-way agenda. That is, its four main concerns are pupils, teachers, teaching strategies, and subject matter. These elements must be considered together to account for the complexity of the enterprise.

Educational psychology did not gain a foothold in the classroom until relatively recently. In the early part of the century, William James and others noted the presence of trivia in the classroom. To a certain extent, this emphasis on learning facts continues today. But there is a growing consensus on the need for theory and practice for effective teaching and learning. Thanks to the pioneering efforts of James, Thorndike, and Dewey, teachers now have a firm theoretical foundation on which to base their practice.

The different definitions of constructivism were outlined to clarify the importance we attach to the positive concept (e.g., "good constructivism"). Children create or build meaning from experience, not the other way around. The idea originated by James and Dewey has received new emphasis as a basis for effective teaching and learning. The essence of good teaching, though, seems to be captured in Maxine Greene's metaphor of the "teacher as stranger"—the one who by reflective distancing learns to see the true needs of each student. That metaphor requires the teacher to become both scientist and artist.

KEY TERMS AND NAMES

constructivism
John Dewey
four-way agenda of teaching
Maxine Greene
William James

C. P. Snow
theory versus practice
E. L. Thorndike
trivia in the classroom
William of Occam

THEORY INTO PRACTICE: YOUR PHILOSOPHY AND ASSUMPTIONS ABOUT TEACHING AND LEARNING

Even though you have covered only one chapter, it can be helpful at this initial point to decide where you stand—what your philosophical orientation is. Certainly, reading about the views of humanists, empiricists, pragmatists, and existentialists gives you a sense of just how different those basic orientations are from one another. As a first step, then, in the process of becoming a self-reflective educator, you can start by rating some of the following statements about teaching and learning.

	VERY IMPORTANT	MODERATELY IMPORTANT	UNIMPORTANT
The role of the teacher is:			
1. To impart knowledge and skills, to transmit the culture.	_____	_____	_____
2. To employ a process approach, particularly learning how to learn.	_____	_____	_____
3. To provide an atmosphere that allows students to develop at an individualized pace.	_____	_____	_____
4. To understand the developmental needs of students and use an appropriate form of differentiated teaching.	_____	_____	_____
5. To focus on basic education for achieving literacy in the three R's as the building blocks for future learning.	_____	_____	_____
6. To view teaching and learning as a discovery activity.			
7. To be a resource person on call to meet the psychological and intellectual needs of students.	_____	_____	_____
8. To discern the developmental status of the students and select from my repertoire those teaching methods that best fit the students' needs.	_____	_____	_____
9. To make sure that the students master the facts prior to any individualizing of instruction.	_____	_____	_____
10. To help students understand the structure of the academic discipline under investigation.	_____	_____	_____
11. To help students experience close interpersonal relationships in the classroom.	_____	_____	_____
12. To combine doing and reflecting at different levels depending on the students' ability to draw meaning from the experience.	_____	_____	_____

This list will give you a picture of where you are now. Then we'd suggest you put it away and reexamine it near the end of the semester. Look for the similarities in attitudes as well as the areas in which you find you've changed your views. Reflect on the reasons for the areas of stability (the ideas and values in which you still believe) and the reasons why you have changed in other areas. This will also help you become aware of your own learning process. How much new theoretical and practical evidence does it take to confirm your "old" beliefs and how much does it take to convince you to give up some of your old beliefs in order to accept some new concepts?

Ratings of Very Important for items 1, 5, and 9 indicate that you have a strong preference for direct instruction as a method and a basic approach to subject matter as content; for items 2, 6, and 10, that you value an inquiry-discovery teaching method and process goals; for items 3, 7, 11, that you strongly value pupil-centered teaching as both method and content; for items 4, 8, 12, that you value developmentally based instruction as a method for promoting concept formation.

Naturally, your answers probably did not all fall exclusively either in or out of one of the four clusters. Most likely, your philosophy at this point is a blend of the four. Yet, it will be interesting to see how the emphases within this blend may change as you proceed to develop an understanding of how you learn and then how you may teach others.

If, after you've completed the exercise, there are some additional ideas you want to express, write them down here to preserve them for future reference.

The ratings indicate that my major initial educational beliefs are as follows:

_____

_____

_____

_____

_____

REFERENCES

Allen, J. S. (1992). Educating performers. *The Key Reporter, 57*(3), 5–9.

Althof, W., & Oser, F. (1993). Professional morality: Ethical dimensions of teaching. *Journal of Moral Education, 22*(3), 195–326.

Bellack, A., Kliebard, H., Hyman, R., & Smith, F. (1966). *Language of the classroom.* New York: Teachers College Press.

Cahan, E., & White, S. (1992). Proposals for a second psychology. *American Psychologist, 47*(2), 224–235.

Cochran-Smith, M. (1995). Color blindness and basket making are not the answers. *American Educational Research Journal, 32*(3), 493–522.

Cole, M. (1990). Cognitive development and schooling. In L. Moll (Ed.), *Vygotsky and education* (pp. 89–110). Cambridge: Cambridge University Press.

Dewey, J. (1916). *Democracy and education.* New York: Macmillan.

Dewey, J. (1956). *The child and the curriculum: The school and society.* Chicago: University of Chicago Press.

Gage, N. (1978). *The scientific basis for the art of teaching.* New York: Teachers College Press.

Goodlad, J. I. (1984). *A place called school.* New York: McGraw-Hill.

Goodlad, J. (1990). *Teachers for our nation's schools.* San Francisco: Jossey-Bass.

Goodlad, J. I., & Klein, M. F. (1974). *Looking behind the classroom door.* Worthington, OH: Jones.

Greene, M. (1978). *The teacher as stranger.* Belmont, CA: Wadsworth.

Greene, M. (1988). *The dialect of freedom.* New York: Teachers College Press.

Harding, S. (1993). Rethinking standpoint epistemology. In L. Alcoff & E. Potter (Eds.), *Feminist epistemologies* (pp. 49–82). New York: Routledge.

Heyns, B. (1988). Educational defectors. *Educational Researcher, 17*(3), 24–32.

Hyman R. T. (1971). *Contemporary thoughts on teaching.* Englewood Cliffs, NJ: Prentice-Hall.

Jackson, P. (1990). The functions of educational research. *Educational Researcher, 19*(7), 3–9.

James, W. (1958) *Talks to teachers on psychology and to students on some of life's ideals.* New York: W. W. Norton.

James, W. (1968). *Psychology.* New York: Macmillan.

Jefferson, T. J. (1816). Letter to Colonel Charles Yancey.

Jeness, D. (1990). *Making sense of the social studies.* New York: Macmillan.

Kozol, J. (1992). *Savage inequalities.* New York: HarperCollins.

Lampert, M. & Clark, C. (1990). Expert knowledge and expert thinking in teaching: A response to Floden and Flinzing. *Educational Researcher, 19*(5), 21–23.

Mosher, R., & Sprinthall, N. (1970). Psychological education in the secondary schools. *American Psychologist, 25,* 911–924.

The national education goals report (1994) (Vol. 1). Washington, DC: U.S. Government Printing Office.

Phillips, D. C. (1995). The good, the bad, and the ugly: The many faces of constructivism. *Educational Researcher, 24*(7), 5–12.

Rice J. M. (1893). *The public school system of the United States.* New York: Century.

Richardson, V. (1990). Significant and worthwhile change in teaching practice. *Educational Researcher, 19*(7), 10–18.

Sabine, G. (1937). *A history of political theory.* New York: Holt.

Shulman, L. (1978). *Review of research in teacher education* (Vol. 5). Itasca, IL.: Peacock.

Snow, C. P. (1963). *The two cultures: And a second look.* New York: Mentor.

Stallings, J. (1995). Ensuring teaching and learning in the 21st century. *Educational Researcher, 24*(6), 4–8.

Stevens, R. (1912). *The question as a measure of efficiency in instruction.* Contributions to Education No. 48. New York: Columbia University.

Thorndike, E. L. (1913). *Educational psychology* (Vol. 2), New York: Teachers College Press.

Thorndike, E. L. (1932). *The fundamentals of learning.* New York: Teachers College Press.

Tyack, D., & Tobin, W. (1994). The "grammar" of schooling: Why has it been so hard to change? *American Educational Research Journal, 31*(3), 453–479.

CHILD AND ADOLESCENT GROWTH

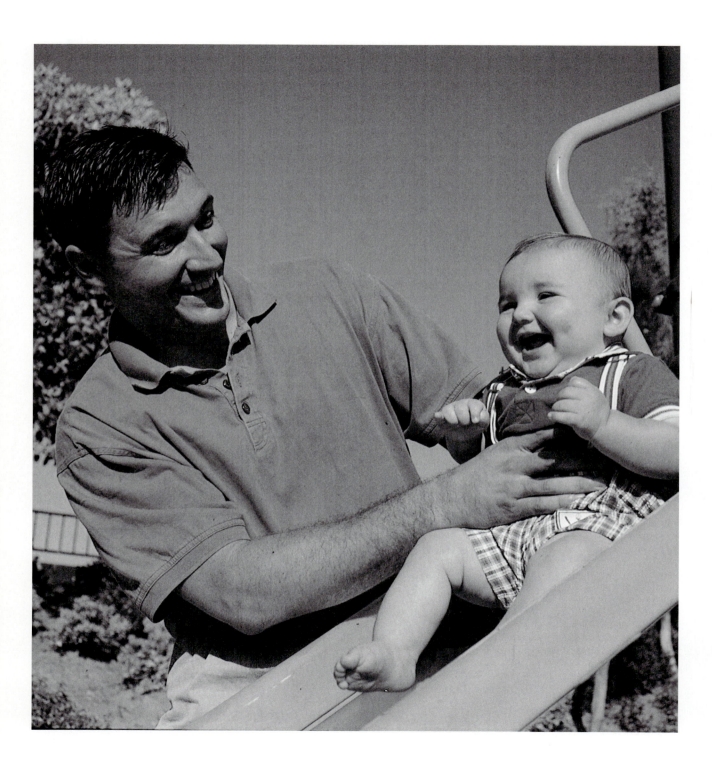

FUNDAMENTALS OF GROWTH AND DEVELOPMENT

Of all the species that inhabit the earth, the one whose growth and development is the slowest is Homo sapiens. The human being spends many long years in a state of physical immaturity, depending on the care and protection of others in order to survive. During the months that are required for the child to learn to walk and run with consistent steadiness, to communicate fears, joys, and needs, other species grow to full maturity. A two-year-old rhesus monkey has already attained sexual maturity, and a two-year-old rat may already be senile. In muscular development and the ability to achieve any degree of mobility, the two-year-old child is about at the same level as a chimpanzee of two months, a rabbit of two weeks, a colt of two hours, or a bird of a few minutes.

Some years ago a study dramatically illustrated the difference in growth rates between species: A husband-and-wife psychology team raised their infant son, Donald, along with a baby chimpanzee named Gua. Donald and Gua were treated as much alike as possible. They wore the same clothes, were fed the same food in the same way, and in general were given the same tender, loving care. They were also taught in the same way and given the same amount of practice in such things as standing, walking, eating with a spoon, and even toilet training (Kellogg and Kellogg, 1963).

The whole situation must have been a competitive nightmare for poor little Donald, because Gua outstripped him at everything. When Donald was barely able to pull himself into an erect position, Gua was walking, running, and pirouetting with the grace of a ballet dancer. When Donald still had difficulty even picking up a spoon, Gua was using the spoon to feed herself easily and with little spilling. When Donald was propped up and strapped to the seat of a swing, where he hung limply and loosely, Gua was performing like a trapeze artist on another swing.

The enormous difference in heredity and rate of maturation obviously allowed Gua to reach her genetic potential far sooner than Donald. Eventually, when Donald was nine months old (and the study was ended), he was beginning to catch up to Gua in certain areas, such as following verbal instructions, and to surpass Gua in others, such as speech development. But as for achieving physical mobility, Donald was still far behind.

Although the human infant in this picture may be the same chronological age as the cat, the cat is already capable of independent living, while the infant will be dependent on adult assistance for many years to come.

Donald may have lagged behind Gua in those developmental criteria based on physical strength and coordination, but human infants are far superior to other social animals in their ability to reflect on themselves, compare themselves to others, and then to self-correct (Shatz, 1994).

You may be wondering at this point why studies such as this are ever conducted. They may seem as absurd as the project of raising a human baby and an eagle together in a nest to see which one will be the first to fly. It may be obvious to you that different species mature at different rates and that chimpanzees achieve physical maturity more rapidly than humans.

It is easier to appreciate why such studies are conducted if you know something about psychology's brief but often stormy history. Against that historical background, the present state of our knowledge becomes more meaningful.

THE NATURE-NURTURE CONTROVERSY

Of all the great debates in the history of psychology—and there have been many—the one that has generated the most heat and caused the greatest division in the field is the controversy over the relative influences of nature and nurture.

The hereditarians, who favored nature, stridently claimed that all psychological traits were transmitted directly through the genes from generation to generation. Environment was of little consequence. If your father was a horse thief, you would be a horse thief, and if your mother's IQ was only 90, then you shouldn't make plans to go to medical school.

On the other side, the environmentalists as rigidly and shrilly claimed that a person's whole being was shaped by how and in what circumstances one was raised or "nurtured." Genetic endowment was a romantic myth, used to keep kings on their thrones, but of no use to science. The environmentalists held that all people were born genetically equal and that later differences among them were only a result of different environmental opportunities. Any baby could be molded into any kind of adult, provided the appropriate stimulus conditions were present.

A voice for the Hereditarians: Henry E. Goddard and the "Bad Seed"

In 1912 **Henry Goddard** published an account of the extremely damaging effects of an inferior genetic endowment, a "bad seed," on generation after generation of a family named **Kallikak** (Goddard, 1912). According to Goddard, who gleaned this material from books, newspapers, personal interviews, and other records, Martin Kallikak (a pseudonym chosen by Goddard to protect the family) was an American Revolutionary War soldier who was responsible for developing two completely different family strains. The "good" Kallikaks (whom Goddard traced through 496 descendants) resulted from Kallikak's marriage to a "worthy Quakeress." She bore him 7 "upright, worthy children," and from these 7 children came "hundreds of the highest types of human beings"—doctors, lawyers, business leaders, and even college presidents. Only 2 of the nearly 500 "good" Kallikaks were of below-average intelligence.

Goddard also traced the descendants of an amorous adventure that Martin Kallikak had with a feeble-minded tavern girl. The result of this affair was an illegitimate son, later known to his friends and neighbors as "Old Horror," who went on to father ten children of his own. Goddard identified 480 of these descendants, the "bad" Kallikaks, and found nothing but the lowest forms of humanity—horse thieves, prostitutes, alcoholics, and so on. Among the "bad" Kallikaks, he found only 46 who were of normal or near-normal intelligence. The rest, of course, were well below average.

Goddard wasted no time worrying about details, such as the dramatically different environments in which Kallikak's legitimate children and Old Horror grew up. The explanation was simple: The difference was hereditary.

Goddard's evidence, which was cited seriously in many psychology texts as late as the 1960s, is considered truly fantastic by modern geneticists. Even if intelligence were as directly and simply related to genotype as eye color is (which it isn't), there would still have to be far greater numbers of intelligent members of the "bad" Kallikaks, and vice versa. After all, Martin Kallikak was himself half responsible for Old Horror. But Goddard was out to "prove" his point of view, and a cherished belief clouded any scientific vision.

To understand the extreme stance taken by the hereditarians of years ago, let's go back in time and take a guided tour of Ellis Island during the spring of 1913, with Dr. Henry Goddard as host. Here are some of his words to take with us:

> Stated in its boldest form, our thesis is that the chief determiner of human conduct is a unitary mental process which we call intelligence: that this process is conditioned by a nervous mechanism which is inborn: that the degree of efficiency to be attained by that nervous mechanism and the consequent grade of intelligence or mental level for each individual is determined by the kind of chromosomes that come

Goddard's 1912 study of the two branches of the Kallikak family—the "good" strain, resulting from Martin Kallikak's marriage to a "worthy Quakeress," and the "bad" strain, resulting from an amorous adventure with a feeble-minded tavern girl—served to support the hereditarians' position.

> together with the union of the germ cells: that it is but little affected by any later influences except such serious accidents as may destroy part of the mechanism (Goddard, 1920, p. 1).

But Goddard was more than a man of words. He was far more than just an armchair, ivory-tower theoretician who merely pored over old genealogical records and created abstract definitions. He was also the pragmatic superintendent of New Jersey's Vineland School for the retarded, where Debbie Kallikak was confined (a doctored photo of her appears later in this chapter). He did his job at Vineland with the fervor and zeal of a dedicated patriot. He felt that he could protect his beloved country from intellectual erosion by confining those whose hereditary potential might menace the American gene pool. He called his mission "segregation through colonization."

Because of his work and reputation, Goddard was also called on to assist those U.S. officials who wanted restrictive immigration policies. Nobody carrying the "bad seed" of mental retardation or insanity was to be allowed into the United States. Government officials were determined to prevent any deterioration in the nation's collective IQ, and they did it in part by simply weeding out the undesirables on their arrival in New York. Although physicians examined these newcomers, and disallowed admission to those with obvious physical signs of mental deficiency, Goddard felt that too many were still slipping through, since many retarded individuals looked very much like other people. So Goddard and his "Moron Detection Team" from Vineland began wandering around the debarkation area at Ellis Island, picking out people who looked suspect, questioning them through an interpreter, and, if their answers were not good enough or quick enough, sending them to a room where they were given the Binet intelligence test, first translated into English by Goddard himself. Any immigrant who scored at or below the "moron" level (a term coined by Goddard from the Greek word *moros*, meaning "dull" or "foolish") was simply deported. This was what greeted many people as they emerged from a week in the cramped steerage section of a large ship, tired from the long voyage and undoubtedly frightened by the prospect of not being allowed into the country. In one encounter, Goddard reported,

We picked out a young man whom we suspected was defective, and, through the interpreter, proceeded to give him the test. The boy tested at only eight by the Binet scale. The interpreter said, "I could not have done that when I came to this country," and seemed to think the test unfair. We convinced him the boy was defective (Goddard, 1917, p. 105).

Not satisfied with simply weeding out defective immigrants, and colonizing those who were here, U.S. officials under Goddard's influence next turned their attention to eugenics. Largely on the basis of the evidence provided in Goddard's Kallikak study, the U.S. Eugenics Office concluded that anyone testing at or below the "moron" level should be physically and permanently prevented from doing any further damage to the nation's gene pool. The obvious and final solution was compulsory sterilization. A movement was launched to urge the states to pass laws requiring sterilization of all hereditary defectives, including, of course, the feebleminded and insane. In a "logical" extension of the extreme hereditarian stance, the list was quickly expanded to include tramps, beggars, alcoholics, criminals, epileptics, the physically deformed, the blind, and the deaf. One can only imagine what other groups might eventually have been included.

In 1927 the Supreme Court of the United States, in the case of *Buck v. Bell,* upheld the right of states to

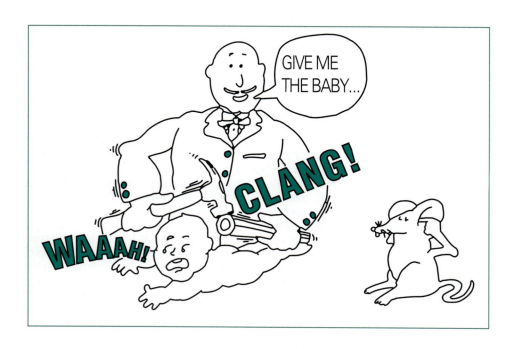

enforce compulsory sterilization of defectives. By 1938, 30 states had sterilization laws on the books and more than 27,000 compulsory sterilizations had been performed (Smith, 1985). In many instances, the persons chosen for sterilization were misled; in one celebrated case a young woman was told she was having her appendix removed. Even today several states retain these laws on their books, although apparently they are no longer enforced.

Goddard was not alone in urging sterilization programs during the 1920s. Many well-meaning Americans argued at that time that sensible programs of social reform should address the manner in which heredity and other biological factors affect human health, intelligence and opportunity. Even Margaret Sanger, venerated as a forerunner of today's woman's movement, endorsed laws for the forced sterilization of persons not measuring up to fixed IQ standards.

Even today, echoes of Goddard's original ideas can still be heard across the land. A recent newsletter from the Los Angeles chapter of the Mensa Society proclaimed that Americans must "face the concept of killing off the old, the weak, the stupid and the inefficient," that a "piece of meat in the shape of a man but without a mind is not a human being," and that perhaps the "homeless should be done away with like abandoned kittens" (Zamichow, 1995).

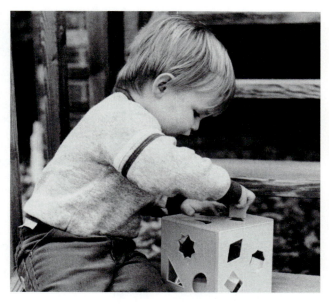

How much can children's cognitive development be shaped by the environmental stimuli presented to them? Could Watson have made this child into an engineer by manipulating the kinds of toys available to him?

A Voice for the Environmentalists: John B. Watson and "Give Me the Baby"

The strict environmentalists aligned themselves firmly against the position of Goddard and the hereditarians. This group subscribed to the ideas of the philosopher John Locke (1691), who asserted that the mind is a blank slate upon which experience writes. In the view of environmentalists, a human baby is nothing more than a lump of clay that can be molded and fashioned into any shape by that master artisan, the environment.

Perhaps the most eloquent advocate of the environmental position was the early behaviorist **John B. Watson.** It was Watson's belief that people are made, not born; that a baby can be shaped into any adult form—trapeze artist, musician, master criminal—through the judicious use of conditioning techniques. Watson began writing at about the time (1913) that Pavlov's work in Russia on the conditioning of dogs was beginning to be recognized in the United States. Watson reasoned that if a dog could be conditioned, so too could a baby. In a now classic study, Watson and his colleague, Rosalie Rayner, tested this theory by conditioning a nine-

month-old named Albert to fear a whole variety of objects (stimuli). This was done by presenting Albert with a certain conditioned stimulus (CS), a white rat, and then banging loudly with a hammer on a steel bar a few inches behind Albert's head. Watson assumed that the conditioned stimulus, the white rat, was originally neutral in its fear-inducing properties. He knew, however, that the unconditioned stimulus (UCS), the loud sound, would automatically produce a fear response in the baby. Because the CS was paired with the UCS, Albert formed an association between the two stimuli and reacted to the rat as he had originally responded to the loud sound. Albert had *learned* to associate the rat with the terrific din and, according to Watson, had thus learned to fear the rat. Later, Albert became afraid, through a process called stimulus generalization, of any stimulus that reminded him of the rat. By the time the study was completed, two months later, Albert was intensely afraid of white rats, rabbits, dogs, fur coats, Santa Claus masks, cotton, wool, and anything else that remotely resembled animal fur. Watson also tested babies for other fear responses and found, for example, that if they were dropped they exhibited a fear response.

JOHN BROADUS WATSON

One of American psychology's most vocal and most influential environmentalists, John B. Watson, was born near Greenville, South Carolina, in 1878. As a schoolboy, his performance was far from spectacular. He later attributed this lack of success to his own "laziness"—a rather subjective explanation from someone who would later demand so much objectivity from others. He attended Furman University, where he studied such topics as mathe-

matics, Greek, Latin, philosophy, and chemistry. In 1900 he went to the University of Chicago to study under the philosopher-psychologist John Dewey. He soon found Dewey "incomprehensible," so he changed majors and began studying with James R. Angell, a psychologist, and H. H. Donaldson, a biologist and neurologist. During these years, he said, his thinking was shaped by the works of the great British empiricists, David Hume and John Locke. Said Watson, "I got nothing out of Kant and least of all out of John Dewey."

In 1903 Watson received the first Ph.D. degree in psychology ever conferred at the University of Chicago. For the next five years he taught psychology there, and in 1908 went to Johns Hopkins University as a full professor. He immediately set up an animal laboratory, and in 1913 he shook the world of psychology with the publication of a paper titled "Psychology as the Behaviorist Views It." In this paper Watson attacked virtually all forms of psychology up to that time, and he announced a new school of psychological thought—behaviorism. He asserted that the only valid data

in psychology were the behaviors of organisms. He saw no room in psychology for mentalistic concepts such as "mind" or "consciousness." In this view, psychology needed introspection about as much as chemistry or physics did—that is, not at all. The data of psychology should be the observable response, and the best approach, in order to rule out any mentalistic overtones, was to study only the responses of organisms. He later wrote, "Belief in the existence of consciousness goes back to the ancient days of superstition and magic."[a] To be scientifically respectable, psychology must be behavioristic, objective, deterministic, mechanistic, and materialistic.

Watson then acquired a powerful ally. Reading about the Russian researcher I. P. Pavlov and Pavlov's work with the conditioned reflex, Watson pounced on this concept and made it a central feature of his own behaviorism. Like Pavlov, he became more interested in the search for specific stimuli that would control particular responses than he was in studying the response itself.[b] In 1919, in collaboration with one of his students, Rosalie Rayner, Watson began his

---

In order to "cure" Albert of these conditioned fears, Watson proposed, although he never actually tried, presenting him with the fear-provoking object again, while "stimulating the erogenous zones . . . We should try first the lips, then the nipples and as a final resort the sex organs" (Watson and Rayner, 1920).

Not everyone has found Watson's evidence for emotional conditioning thoroughly convincing.

It may be useful for modern learning theorists to see how the Albert study prompted subsequent research, but it seems time, finally, to place the Watson

and Rayner data in the category of interesting but uninterpretable results (Harris, 1979).

Mounting evidence is also beginning to cast some doubt on Watson's assumption that Albert's conditioning had taken place in a mechanical fashion, or that any stimulus Albert was able to detect could be linked to any response Albert could make. As we shall see later, it may be that Albert was more biologically prepared, or genetically sensitized, to learn to fear a live rat rather than, say, a picture of a rat (Bolles, 1980). The behaviorists have come under increasing attack because of their failure to incorporate now-famous study on the conditioning of baby Albert B. Together they showed how an apparently normal, healthy baby could be conditioned to fear virtually anything in its observable environment.

In 1920 Watson's career at Johns Hopkins abruptly ended. Amid great notoriety Watson was divorced by his wife and then asked by Johns Hopkins to resign his professorship. Later that year Watson married his research collaborator, Rosalie Rayner, and in 1921 he went to New York and spent the rest of his working life in the world of advertising. He soon became not only famous, but also rich and famous.

Although he had left the academic world, Watson continued to write books and articles that advanced his views on childrearing and teaching. In 1927 he thundered forth his famous demand, "Give me the baby." In 1928 his book *The Psychological Care of the Infant and Child* became an overnight best-seller (over 100,000 copies sold in the first two months). He rather cynically dedicated the book to "the first mother who brings up a happy child." In it he instructed the mothers of America never to hug or kiss their children and never to let them sit on their laps. "If you must, kiss them once on the forehead when they say good night. Shake hands with them in the morning." He also decried coddling remarks: "When I hear a mother say 'Bless its little heart' when it falls down, or stubs its toe, or suffers some other ill, I usually have to walk a block or two to let off steam." Watson offered warnings about maternal affection: "Remember when you are tempted to pet your child that mother love is a dangerous instrument, an instrument which may inflict a never healing wound which makes infancy unhappy, and adolescence a nightmare."[c]

Watson retired from the business world in 1946 and died in 1958, having exerted great influence on the fields of psychology and education. He made educational psychology more behavioristic, and he emphasized the importance of conditioning in the classroom and in childrearing practices. It was Watson who set the stage for the work of B. F. Skinner and the proponents of behavior modification in the classroom.

Watson's granddaughter, the actress Mariette Hartley, said that her mother's lack of physical closeness with Watson during childhood had filled her with a fear of getting too close to people. This fear was then passed on to Mariette. She feels that she has since worked out those repressed feelings (by turning to Freudian analysis for help) and now feels more comfortable with other people and even with the memory of her late grandfather, who within the family was known as "Big John" (Hartley, 1990). After recovering from her own father's suicide, Hartley made a sentimental pilgrimage back to her grandfather's exquisite stone house, where she "could still smell the whiskey in the carpets . . . and when I walked out back and remembered the picnics we had there I thought about [my grandfather] and of how much he had influenced my life."[d]

[a]   Watson, J. B. (1925). *Behaviorism.* New York: Norton.
[b]   McPherson, M. W. (1992). Is psychology the science of behavior? *American Psychologist, 47,* 329–335.
[c]   Watson, J. B., and Watson, R. R. (1928). *The psychological care of the infant and child.* New York: Norton, pp. 81–87.
[d]   Hartley, M. (1990). *Breaking the silence.* New York: G. P. Putnam's Sons.

those important variables that critics say didn't happen to fit their original hypotheses (Ahsen, 1990).

At the time, however, Watson believed that he had come upon ultimate truth in psychology—that, no matter what the genetic background, environmental stimulation in the form of conditioning could produce any behavior. Watson later said wryly:

The Freudians twenty years from now, unless their hypotheses change, when they come to analyze Albert's fear of a seal skin coat . . . will probably tease from him the recital of a dream which upon their analysis will show that Albert at three years of age attempted to play with the pubic hair of the mother and was scolded violently for it (Watson and Rayner, 1920, p. 14).

A few years later, Watson thundered his now-famous words, "Give me the baby," and this became the battle cry of environmentalists everywhere.

Give me the baby and I'll make it climb and use its hands in construction of buildings of stone or wood . . . I'll make it a thief, a gunman or a dope fiend. The possibilities of shaping it in any direction are almost endless. Even gross anatomical differences limit us

SPOTLIGHT ON HEREDITY

Does Apart Always Mean Different?

In the past few years, we have seen a large number of studies purporting to show the remarkable psychological similarities between identical twins reared apart (Bouchard et al., 1990). These studies all seem to assume that the only environmental influences are the families who raise the twins, and that if the twins have similar personalities despite differences in the families, these personality characteristics must have been inherited. Before jumping too quickly on the genetic bandwagon, however, we should consider whether MZs may be treated in like ways because of their *shared physical appearance*. Since the expectations of others are partly determined by one's physical

stimulus value, people who look the same are often treated in much the same way. Thus, the personalities of MZ twins may be similarly molded, regardless of what part of the country they were raised or now live in. Attractive MZs growing up in one part of the country may have social interactions, and thus shared experiences, more like those of their cotwins in another part of the country than those of their "close-in-age, same sex, but unattractive sibling living down the hall" (Ford, 1993, p. 1294). To be sure of the genetic explanation for these similarities, we should try to determine the effect of these very similar physical appearances on the personality development of

persons having no genetic linkage at all (Ford, 1993).

It is also important to realize that even family environments may not differ as radically as some hereditarians have assumed. Adoption agencies usually try to match natural and adoptive parents on a number of crucial variables, such as religion, race, educational level, socioeconomic status, and even region of the country. Furthermore, in some cases the twins, though reared in different families, actually still see each other, know the other is their twin, live nearby, and even play together. As Joseph Wyatt has said, "apart" does not necessarily mean "different" (Wyatt, 1993).

---

far less than you may think . . . Make him a deaf mute, and I will build you a Helen Keller. Men are built, not born (Watson, 1927, p. 233).

After reading about how Albert had been scared half to death by the sound of a steel bar being pounded behind his head and by being dropped, and how the way to "cure" him was to manipulate his genitals, the mothers of America did not line up to give Watson their babies.

Watson was striving to provide psychology with hard, scientific facts. His behaviorism was definitely not based on any humanistic view of human behavior or of society in general. Rather, he saw his mission as that of fact finder and cared little if his audience liked or disliked the facts. His approach was clinical and utterly detached. Even Watson's prescription for raising children was laced with the objectivity and detachment of cool science. Watson told American mothers to treat their toddlers as though the children were young adults: "Let your behavior

always be objective and kindly but firm. Never hug and kiss them; never let them sit on your lap. If you must, kiss them once on the forehead when they say goodnight. Shake hands with them in the morning" (Watson and Watson, 1928).

Even today, behaviorists exhibit a similar disinterest. They often see their ultimate goal as far too cosmic to be constrained by any feelings of sympathy for a particular child. B. F. Skinner, a more recent exponent of behaviorism, was once criticized for having allegedly said that if given a choice he would rather burn his children than his books. Skinner's self-righteous answer was that he had not used the word *burn*.

The word was *bury* . . . Much as I admire my children and grandchildren and as dearly as I love them, I still believe that my contribution through my books will prove to be greater than that through my genes. How could a thorough-going environmentalist say otherwise? (Skinner, 1975, p. 2.)

SPOTLIGHT ON LABELS

Beware the Labels

If an adult is reinforced for acting appropriately, we call it RECOGNITION.

If a child is reinforced for acting appropriately, we call it BRIBERY.

If an adult sticks to something, we call it PERSEVERANCE.

If a child sticks to something, we call it STUBBORNNESS.

If an adult is not paying attention, we call it PREOCCUPATION.

If a child is not paying attention, we call it ATTENTION DEFICIT.

If an adult tells her/his side of the story, we call it CLARIFICATION.

If a child tells her/his side of the story, we call it TALKING BACK.

If an adult raises his/her voice in anger, we call it OPEN EXPRESSION.

If a child raises his/her voice in anger, we call it TEMPER TANTRUM.

If an adult hits a child, we call it DISCIPLINE.

If a child hits a child, we call it CONDUCT DISORDER.

When adults behave in unusual ways, we call it UNIQUENESS.

When children behave in unusual ways, we rush them off for PSYCHOLOGICAL EVALUATION.

Author unknown. Reprinted from the *Colorado Society of School Psychologists Newsletter,* Fall/Winter 1991.

EDUCATIONAL PSYCHOLOGY: THE BATTLEGROUND

Nowhere were the lines between hereditarians and environmentalists more sharply drawn than in the field of educational psychology. In one camp were the measurement practitioners, who strongly subscribed to the value of testing IQ and achievement; in the other camp were the learning theorists. The measurement practitioners were, by and large, hereditarians. The learning theorists, with very few exceptions, were behaviorists, and behaviorists were environmentalists. Thus it was inevitable that these two groups, both solidly entrenched in the field of educational psychology, and with diametrically opposed views in the nature-nurture debate, would be in constant conflict.

The IQ Testers

The testers had traditionally emphasized heredity, at least on the subject of intelligence. The history of the testing movement goes back to England and **Sir Francis Galton,** Darwin's cousin. During the latter part of the nineteenth century, Galton created the first tests designed to measure intellectual potential. Galton believed that intellectual potential was a function of one's sensory equipment, one's power to discriminate among stimuli. He believed that sensory equipment was inherited. Parents who could detect slight differences among stimuli (could discriminate among subtle differences in tonal pitch, for example) were apt to have children with similarly keen powers. Furthermore, Galton believed, these sensory powers had survival value for the species. Cave dwellers who could detect the slight hiss of a rattlesnake were more likely to stay alive. **James McKeen Cattell,** who spent some time in Europe studying with Galton, brought this point of view back to the United States and, as Galton had done earlier, devised a series of sensorimotor tests (auditory range, visual range, reaction time, etc.) designed to measure a human's intellectual potential. Cattell was so enamored of this new area of study that he named his daughter Psyche. It was Cattell, in 1890, who first used the term *mental test*. Cattell was also the key figure in early studies of reading. "His work on letter and word recognition, legibility of letters and print types, and stimulus intensity formed the groundwork for most basic reading research of the next 30 years" (Venezby, 1977).

G. Stanley Hall, a distinguished psychologist and the first president of Clark University, had also studied in Europe, under Wundt, and had also concluded that intelligence is primarily inherited. Hall became

G. Stanley Hall was the foremost American advocate of intelligence as an inherited trait.

Lewis M. Terman, Hall's student, revised Binet's original scale and introduced the Stanford-Binet tests in 1916.

enormously influential among psychologists in this country for a variety of reasons. His doctoral students, who included Henry Goddard, Lewis M. Terman, and Arnold Gessell, became true believers in Hall's theoretical position and, armed with their own degrees, went out to spread the gospel. As the first president of the American Psychological Association and the editor of the *American Journal of Psychology*, Hall also had the power to influence psychology's agenda in very direct ways, for example, in deciding which articles would be published (Sokal, 1992).

The Stanford-Binet IQ test, which the testers used to obtain much of their data, was introduced into the United States by Lewis Terman. Starting with the original 1905 Binet scale, Terman created new norms based on U.S. standardizing groups and revised so many of the original items as practically to create a new test (1916). The data collected in his later studies of gifted children seemed to support a genetic explanation of intelligence.

The First World War gave tremendous impetus to the testing movement. Suddenly millions of men were available to U.S. government psychologists; moreover, the government was insisting that all these recruits be given intelligence tests. For the testers, the war became a golden opportunity both to demonstrate their testing skills and to gain public visibility. In the eyes of the testers, this opportunity was trans-

lated into an overwhelming triumph. James McKeen Cattell toasted the occasion when he chortled that the war had put psychology not only on the map but also on the "front page." Thus the testers, whose influence on psychology became increasingly powerful, used their front-page status to spread the genetic gospel they had "inherited" from Europe.

The Learning Theorists

The learning theorists, mostly Americans, were bound to be a strong influence on educational psychology. After all, what better contribution could psychology make to education than a more thorough understanding of the principles of learning? However, the major force among American learning theorists was behaviorism, and behaviorism was definitely an environmentalist position. Watson, the father of American behaviorism, sounded the clarion call when he wrote, "The data of psychology is behavior" (Watson, 1913, p. 160). And we have already seen ("Give me the baby"), Watson's extreme environmental stance. The behaviorists—Watson, Thorndike, Guthrie, Hull, and Skinner—spread a kind of mechanical-person gospel. They spent little time studying the organism's growth and development. The emphasis was on how the organism learned, regardless of its inherited potential, regardless of its stage of physical or psychological development, and often regardless of its species. In brief, they saw learning as a result of associations formed between stimuli and actions or impulses to act. These simple associations would accumulate and form larger groups of learned associations. Learning was seen largely as a result of conditioning, similar to Pavlov's dogs' learning to salivate at the sound of a certain tone. From his command post at Columbia Teachers College, E. L. Thorndike issued basic laws of learning that dominated the field of educational psychology, not to mention classroom practices, for more than 50 years.

And this influence took hold despite the efforts of those early psychologists to separate themselves as much as possible from the "lowly army of frontline teachers" (Powell, 1971). Many of these psychologists had an image of themselves as superscientists, their white lab coats symbolizing the purity of their endeavors. In fact, the goal of many of these early psychologists was to provide research that would substantiate their own previously authored educational systems.

Few American learning theorists ever studied children in the classroom or, indeed, ever studied any children at all. Thorndike and Guthrie worked primarily with cats, Hull with rats, and Skinner with rats and pigeons, but the principles of learning derived from these studies were generalized to human beings. Not that these generalizations were always invalid. They weren't! Children in a classroom can be conditioned to remain in their seats, just as rats can be conditioned to press a lever. But it is the solid contention of this book that there is much more to human learning than mere conditioning.

The learning theorists with their environmental bias had their day from 1920 until well after the Second World War, calling many of the shots in educational psychology in this country.

Why was the environmental position so attractive in the United States? There are at least five reasons:

1. American psychology was dominated by liberals, and almost all of them adopted an environmental stance. To their way of thinking, heredity doomed humans to a tooth-and-claw world, a racist society in which social change was impossible. The nature-nurture argument was rephrased in more "democratic" language as "instinct versus learning," or even as "beast versus man." An ideology, a cherished tradition, was getting between the psychologists and their data.

2. Even among psychologists who recognized the importance of genetic influences, the feeling was that heredity was fixed at conception and that there was no point in studying something that couldn't be changed. Environmental influences, however, could be manipulated, and heredity became unimportant simply because of its inaccessibility.

3. Genetics was a relatively new field, and very few psychologists were familiar with the information developing in that field (Plomin, 1990b). They were far more familiar with the related fields of sociology and cultural anthropology. The names Margaret Mead and Ruth Benedict, for example, were better known than names of important geneticists such as Thomas Hunt Morgan or even Charles Davenport.

4. The special field of behavior genetics had not yet evolved. Indeed, the relationship between genetic inputs and overt behavior remained largely unresearched until the 1970s (Plomin, 1990b), although a 1940 study by Robert Choate Tryon of the University of California at Berkeley set the stage for the current work in this area. Tryon had a large group of rats learn a maze, and then separated those animals that learned the maze quickly from those that learned slowly. By breeding the fast learners only with other fast learners, and the slow learners only with other slow learners, Tryon demonstrated that after seven generations he had created two significantly different groups of rats: maze-bright animals and maze-dull animals. Most breeding experiments like this, however, came after the heyday of behaviorism.

5. **Instinct theory,** so popular at the turn of the century, had done great damage to hereditarian claims. Now thoroughly discredited, instinct theory attempted to explain behavior by describing it in other terms: Why do people fight? Because they have an aggressive instinct. Why do people get together in groups? Because they have a gregarious instinct. Why do people twiddle their thumbs? Because they have a thumb-twiddling instinct. This kind of reasoning commits what is called the **nominal fallacy;** it confuses description with explanation. B. F. Skinner pointed out that such reasoning is extremely dangerous: If we assume that a redescription is an explanation, we may feel we have answers when in fact we don't; and we may give up the search (Skinner, 1953).

Do people have an inborn aggressiveness tendency that makes them fight? Yes, claimed the instinct theorists, who confused description with explanation, a nominal fallacy.

Today this insistence on the importance of environmental factors to the exclusion of genetic ones is giving way to a far more balanced view (Plomin, 1990a). Indeed, there may even be a danger that the current swing away from environmentalism could go too far and revive the tyranny of biological determinism (Plomin, 1989).

ETHOLOGY

Although it was easy for American psychologists to dismiss the views of instinct theorists as naive, they could not ignore the carefully detailed work of the European ethologists. Ethology is the study of behavior, especially animal behavior, in the natural setting (as opposed to a laboratory setting). Ethologists are primarily interested in discovering innate behavior patterns, or, as they are called in ethology, **innate releasing mechanisms (IRMs)**—patterns that many American psychologists overlooked, partly because they insisted on studying animals in antiseptic, arti-

ficial laboratories. Even worse, in most of their research the psychologists insisted on using rats that had been specially bred for many generations to be exceptionally timid and nonaggressive (for the protection of the researchers).

The following story, possibly apocryphal, nevertheless makes the point. It seems that a graduate student in experimental psychology, unable to obtain a group of specially bred, gentle white Sprague-Dawley rats, undauntedly captured some wild rats from the local dump. To the student's dismay, these rats, rather than learning the route through the complicated maze, simply ate their way through the wooden sides of the maze and quickly devoured the entire sack of food pellets. By the same token, it is highly unlikely that a Sprague-Dawley rat, its IRM reactions bred out of it hundreds of generations ago, could stay alive for five minutes at the city dump. One can only imagine a scene with this forlorn rat sitting passively, waiting to be presented with a lever to push.

Early in this century, a study was conducted that

bears directly on this issue. One of J. B. Watson's professors, Henry Donaldson, wanted to find out whether a group of well-bred lab rats might learn to survive in a natural environment, in this case a small island in Long Island Sound. In order to give the lab rats a fighting chance, Donaldson exterminated the island's native rat population. Upon returning a year later, Donaldson could not find a single lab rat still alive. He did, however, find the chewed-up remains of some of them. They had been bitten to death by the few native rats that had somehow survived the attempted extermination (Carnegie Institute, 1911).

Ethologists, in contrast, were interested in nature's animals: in how they survived in nature's own settings and how they were affected by natural *releasers*, the stimuli in an organism's environment that trigger unlearned behavior patterns. For example, if the male stickleback fish sees the color red, a rather violent attack response is released. This happens because during the breeding season all stickleback males develop bright red bellies, and if one red-bellied fish happens on another's nesting site, the intruder is roundly attacked and driven out of the nesting area.

CHERISHED BELIEFS AND SCIENTIFIC FACTS

As we have now seen, psychologists in general and educational psychologists in particular have battled for years over the question of the relative contributions of heredity and environment to behavior. Each side felt that it had the answer. As often happens when narrow or even single causes are sought to explain anything, the search for this single cause results more in the creation of controversy than in the accumulation of knowledge. Each side becomes rigid and dogmatic, and cherished beliefs begin to cloud scientific vision. If Watson had been less zealous in the cause of environmentalism, he could not possibly have overlooked the importance of heredity. Similarly, Goddard could not have disregarded the obvious difference in environmental influences on the "good" and "bad" Kallikaks had not his cherished opinion clouded his vision.

Nor was his clouded vision totally innocent. Stephen Jay Gould has discovered that in Goddard's original book on the Kallikaks, three of the photographs allegedly depicting "bad" Kallikaks were

SPOTLIGHT ON IMPRINTING

A Special Kind of Learning

Perhaps the most important factor in forcing American psychologists to reevaluate their position on the role of heredity in determining behavior was the work of the great German ethologist, Konrad Lorenz. Although it had been observed as early as 1873 that newly hatched chicks seem to follow the first moving stimulus they see, it was not until 1935 that Lorenz revived the term *imprinting* to describe this special form of learning (Lorenz, 1935). He also discovered that this phenomenon could occur only during one critical early period. Lorenz noted that goslings would

follow not just their mother but any moving stimulus that presented itself within the first few hours of life. Thus, if Lorenz presented himself during this critical period, the goslings would parade after him with a devotion usually reserved for their mother. This imprinting proved to be lifelong.

Although imprinting was first observed in organisms' natural environments, it has also been demonstrated in the artificial world of the laboratory, proving that psychology and ethology are not necessarily at cross-purposes (Hess, 1959). In fact, under

laboratory conditions it has been possible to determine the exact time when imprinting is strongest. Imprinting in ducks, for example, can occur up to 32 hours after hatching, although the optimal period is 13 to 16 hours.

Imprinting dramatically demonstrates the interactive importance of heredity, environment, and time in producing behavioral changes. Imprinting has been used as a model to explain the bonding process that typically occurs between mother and child.

KONRAD LORENZ

Konrad Lorenz was born in Vienna, Austria, in 1903. His father, Adolph, was a world-famous orthopedic surgeon and a professor at the University of Vienna. Even as a child, Lorenz avidly observed, studied, and sought to understand the ways of wildlife. During these years he learned to understand the signal code, or language, of various animal species, then learned to imitate this code in order to establish two-way communication. At the family's country home in Altenberg, where Lorenz spent the summer months, he explored the woods, set up his own microscope for studying the wondrous world teeming in the pondwater, and also raised a multitude of dogs, geese, and monkeys, as well as fish, crustaceans, and insects harvested from his favorite pond.

In 1928 Lorenz received his M.D. degree from the University of Vienna, but his love of animals continued along with his studies. In 1933 he earned a Ph.D. degree in zoology, and for the next four years he continued his research on the behavior of animals in their natural habitats. In 1937 he began his teaching career as an instructor of comparative anatomy and animal psychology at his beloved University of Vienna. That same year he also published his now-famous article "The Companion in the Bird's World." In this article Lorenz described the intricate biological mechanism of imprinting. During their first few hours of life, certain organisms become imprinted on the first moving stimulus object in their visual field—usually, of course, the mother—and then follow this object with slavish devotion and marching-band precision. This is how young organisms, especially birds, know which species they belong to, and it also accounts for their gregarious flocking behavior. Lorenz had revived the long-discredited instinct theory and made it scientifically respectable.

In 1940 he became a professor of psychology at the University of Königsberg in Germany. By this time the Second World War was raging through Europe, and Lorenz was called into the German army. In 1944 he was captured by the Russians and remained a prisoner until 1948, three years after the war had ended. He immediately returned to the University of Vienna, but in 1950 he again went to Germany, this time as the assistant director of the Max Planck Institute for Behavioral Physiology. Later he became director of the Institute for Behavioral Physiology, also in Germany. In October 1973 Lorenz won the Nobel Prize in medicine for his investigations of animal behavior in the wild. At the time of his death in 1989 he was survived by his wife, Margarethe, two daughters, Agnes and Dagmar, and a son, Thomas.

Lorenz wrote that "he who has once seen the intimate beauty of nature cannot tear himself away from it again. He must become either a poet or a naturalist . . . He may well become both." Lorenz did become both. His books and articles have an almost lyric quality. Among his numerous publications are *King Solomon's Ring* (1952), *Man Meets Dog* (1954), *Evolution and Modification of Behavior* (1965), *On Aggression* (1966), and *Studies in Animal and Human Behavior* (1970).

Lorenz established ethology, the study of animal behavior in the natural setting, as a serious and respectable discipline. The message of his research is: If you want to understand animal behavior, study the animal in its own environment, not in the artificial confines of the laboratory. In the field of educational psychology, this message translates as: If you want to understand schoolchildren, study them in the classroom, not just in the principal's or guidance counselor's office or in a college laboratory.

retouched. The pictures "were phonied by inserting heavy dark lines to give eyes and mouths their diabolical appearance" (Gould, 1981). If the bad Kallikaks hadn't really looked stupid and depraved enough, it now appears that Goddard saw to it that they would.

This problem is not confined to psychology or to education. In our long quest to gain knowledge about our environment and ourselves, we have often been blinded by cherished beliefs. Advances in astronomy were thwarted for centuries by our egocentric belief that the earth, our habitat, must be at the

These two photos of Kallikak family members are doctored. The mouths and eyes appear to have been altered in order to dramatize an illusion of feeble-mindedness.

center of the universe. Only slowly and grudgingly did we give up this notion, and then only on the understanding that the sun, at the center of our solar system, must be at the core of a revolving universe. Ptolemy's heliocentric view of the universe went virtually unchallenged for more than 1,000 years. Not until the sixteenth century did we finally accept our place in the universe: Ptolemy gave way to Copernicus, the earth was put in its proper place, and the ground was prepared for the later theories of Newton and Einstein.

We have been just as backward in other areas. Physiology did not really come into its own as a discipline until the nineteenth century (subjecting human bodies to the objective scrutiny of science seemed too threatening). Still more recently, psychology has insisted on probing our very inner being. Thus, the evolution of scientific disciplines has followed a fairly orderly sequence based on the degree to which each science has threatened our self-esteem. In every case, cherished beliefs have been hard to give up; and this is certainly true of educational psychology in the twentieth century.

NATURE-NURTURE: A MODERN SOLUTION TO AN OLD PROBLEM

It is now clear, near the end of the twentieth century, that the old question of heredity versus environment is unanswerable because it is meaningless. Behavior is the result not of a single cause, but of multiple causes. It is the result of heredity interacting with environment interacting with time (see Figure 2.1). Our hereditary potential can be nourished or stifled depending on the type, amount, and quality of our environmental encounters and depending on when these encounters occur. (They can occur too early or too late to be of optimum benefit.)

It is important to keep in mind that even traits that are highly heritable are still environmentally sensitive. For example, vocabulary size has a high heritability (and is also highly correlated with IQ), and yet every single word has to be learned through environmental inputs (Neisser et al., 1996).

FIGURE 2.1   Behavior is the result of heredity interacting with environment interacting with time.

Chapter 3 provides an overview of the biological basis of behavior. In the chapters that follow we outline some of the major considerations that have moved educational psychology beyond the nature-nurture controversy. Since human behavior is determined by the interaction of both (recall Dewey's phrase, "an organism in some environment"), we need to look at nature and nurture simultaneously. We can then begin to consider, not in a single- or narrow-minded way but within a broad context, how to educate children and adolescents. We need to know both how to strike and when the iron is hot. In Chapter 4 we discuss the significance and lasting effects of initial experience. In Chapters 5–7 we present the stages of cognitive and personal development to show, in our metaphor, just when the iron is hot. With this groundwork laid we can give our full attention in later chapters to arranging the environment for learning and teaching.

SUMMARY

The causes of behavior are multiple and complex, and it is dangerous to build a psychology of human behavior on the basis of animal studies alone. Growth rates differ markedly among species, and the rate of growth and development among humans is comparatively slow.

The nature-nurture controversy created a great division within the field of psychology. Henry Goddard's study of the Kallikak family attempted to "prove" that heredity was the most important factor in determining a person's psychological makeup. John B. Watson argued that environmental influences, through the process of conditioning, were paramount in determining psychological traits. In the field of educational psychology, the measurement practitioners (IQ testers) were typically strong believers in heredity, whereas the learning theorists were environmentalists. Also among the hereditarians were the instinct theorists, who early in the century tried to explain all behavior in terms of inherited instincts. In so doing, these psychologists made the error of confusing description for explanation (the nominal fallacy). By the 1930s, however, American psychologists generally took the view that environmental influences were more important than inherited traits.

Ethology, the study of animal behavior in the natural setting, made the study of certain types of instinctive behavior more respectable. The ethologists concentrated on studying responses that were attached to innate releasing mechanisms (IRMs). They also demonstrated a special form of learning called imprinting, which occurs only during a short and critical period in an organism's life.

Scientific objectivity has historically suffered as a result of the tendency, among scientists as among most of us, to maintain cherished beliefs and unbending attitudes despite clear contradictory empirical evidence. Psychology has been greatly affected by this tendency, for it is the discipline concerned with probing our inner beings and motivations. It is also the discipline for which many laypersons feel a certain familiarity and degree of expertise, even without professional training.

The modern solution to the age-old nature-nurture controversy is that neither heredity nor environment should be seen as the sole cause of behavior. Instead, behavior should be viewed as the result of heredity interacting with environment interacting with time. This final point is critical to an understanding of the rest of this text, and is considered today by most theorists to be one of psychology's most important principles.

KEY TERMS AND NAMES

James McKeen Cattell
ethology
Sir Francis Galton
Henry H. Goddard
imprinting
innate releasing mechanism (IRM)

instinct theory
Kallikak family
Konrad Lorenz
nature-nurture controversy
nominal fallacy
John B. Watson

THEORY INTO PRACTICE: ARE YOU A HEREDITARIAN OR AN ENVIRONMENTALIST AT HEART?

Although the issue of nature versus nurture can no longer really be considered an either/or proposition many of us have fundamental belief systems that strongly incline us to favor one over the other. One way to find out how strongly these beliefs or attitudes are embedded is to answer the questions posed on the next page, then compute the score and interpret its meaning.

To compute your score, code the responses on a scale of 4 to 1 points, beginning with 4 points for Strongly Agree. A hereditarian will strongly agree with items 1–6, 13, and 14; an environmentalist will strongly agree with items 7–12, 15, and 16. The maximum score on each set of eight items is 32 points.

The problem, or difficulty, with either extreme position is simply that it leads to attributions or interpretations of behavior that can be quite misleading. Thus, the belief of hereditarians that a person's potential is fixed at birth might lead them to be against programs for young children, such as Head Start. In contrast, an environmentalist might favor a policy of educating a profoundly retarded child in classes intended for the gifted and talented. To make a final check on these assumptions, go back and answer the questions in two modes. First answer the items as if you were J. B. Watson, then as if you were Henry Goddard.

	STRONGLY AGREE	AGREE	DISAGREE	STRONGLY DISAGREE
1. At a family reunion it is most important to look for personality traits handed down from grandparents to parents to children.	_____	_____	_____	_____
2. In deciding upon a choice of major in college, a most important factor would be how parents and/or relatives achieved in different areas.	_____	_____	_____	_____
3. In choosing between going to an opera or a football game, it would be wise to find out how earlier generations felt about opera versus football.	_____	_____	_____	_____
4. If a person is having a very difficult time learning mathematics, the first place to look for an explanation would be family history. Is there an uncle or aunt, father or mother who always had trouble with math?	_____	_____	_____	_____
5. To be really successful in life, the best path to follow would be in the family's footsteps. You can't make a silk purse out of a sow's ear.	_____	_____	_____	_____
6. The success or failure a person experiences is really "in the cards." After all, don't most juvenile delinquents come from delinquency-prone parents?	_____	_____	_____	_____
7. Anyone can succeed in any field with the right teaching and lots of motivation.	_____	_____	_____	_____
8. Show me a successful musician and I'll show you someone who's been positively reinforced every step of the way.	_____	_____	_____	_____
9. If you examine the background of any famous person, you will find somewhere a patient mentor or teacher who cultivated the achievement.	_____	_____	_____	_____
10. When a person fails, you can't really say he or she is to blame. Most likely you'll see a history of inadequate teaching or inadequate parenting. Don't blame the victim.	_____	_____	_____	_____
11. The problem with special education is not with the children at all. It is really the labels that are at fault. Since everyone believes that such a child is a slow learner, the child will act like one. It's a self-fulfilling prophecy.	_____	_____	_____	_____
12. Motivation and drive determine who excels. Aptitude makes very little contribution. After all, Thomas Edison said genius was 1 percent inspiration and 99 percent perspiration.	_____	_____	_____	_____
13. I find that it is important each day to check my horoscope, especially if I'm facing very important decisions.	_____	_____	_____	_____
14. Character traits such as introversion and extroversion are transmitted through a long evolutionary chain that is clearly fixed by the time of birth.	_____	_____	_____	_____
15. If you want to succeed, follow Horace Greeley's advice to go west; the climate is more conducive to achievement there.	_____	_____	_____	_____
16. People who spend all their time delving into the past, tracing family genealogy, looking for the Rosetta stone of their personalities, are just wasting their time.	_____	_____	_____	_____

REFERENCES

Ahsen, A. (1990). *Behaviorists' misconduct in science.* New York: Brandon House.

Bickerton, D. (1990). *Language and species.* Chicago: University of Chicago Press.

Bolles, R. C. (1980). Ethological learning theory. In R. A. Hinde & J. Stevenson-Hinde (Eds.), *Theories of learning.* Itasca, IL: Peacock.

Bouchard, T. J., Lykken, D. T., McGue, M., Segal, M. L., & Tellegen, A. (1990). Sources of human psychological differences: The Minnesota study of twins reared apart. *Science, 250,* 223–228.

Carnegie Institute of Washington (1911). *Yearbook No. 10,* **83.**

Ford, B. D. (1993) Emergenesis: An alternative and a confound. *American Psychologist, 48,* 1294.

Goddard, H. (1912). *The Kallikak family.* New York: Macmillan.

Goddard, H. H. (1917). The Binet tests in relation to immigration. *Journal of Psycho-Asthenics, 2,* 105–107.

Goddard, H. H. (1920). *Human efficiency and levels of intelligence.* Princeton: Princeton University Press.

Gould, S. J. (1981). *The mismeasure of man.* New York: Norton.

Harris, B. (1979). Whatever happened to Little Albert? *American Psychologist, 34*(2), 158.

Hartley, M. (1990). *Breaking the silence.* New York: G. P. Putnam's Sons.

Hayes, K. G., & Hayes, C. (1951). The intellectual development of a home-raised chimpanzee. *Proceedings: American Philosophical Society, 95,* 105–109.

Hess, E. H. (1959). Imprinting. *Science, 130,* 133–141.

Kellogg, W. N., & Kellogg, L. A. (1963). *The ape and the child.* New York: McGraw-Hill.

Lorenz, K. (1935). The companion in the bird's world. *Auk, 54,* 245–273.

McPherson, M. W. (1992). Is psychology the science of behavior? *American Psychologist, 47,* 329–335.

Neisser, U., Boodoo, G., Bouchard, T. J., Boykin, A. W., Brody, N., Ceci, S. J., Halpern, D. F., Loehlin, J. C., Perloff, R., Sternberg, R. J., & Urbina, S. (1996). Intelligence: Knowns and unknowns. *American Psychologist, 51,* 77–101.

Plomin, R. (1989). Environment and genes: Determinants of behavior. *American Psychologist, 44,* 105–111.

Plomin, R. (1990a). The role of inheritance in behavior. *Science, 248,* 183–188.

Plomin, R. (1990b). *Nature and nurture: An introduction to human behavioral genetics.* Pacific Grove, CA: Brooks/Cole.

Powell, A. G. (1971). Speculation on the early impact of schools of education on educational psychology. *History of Education Quarterly, 11,* 406–412.

Premack, D. (1971). Language in chimpanzees? *Science, 172,* 808–872.

Shatz, M. (1994). *A toddler's life: Becoming a person.* New York: Oxford University Press.

Skinner, B. F. (1953). *Science and human behavior.* New York: Macmillan.

Skinner, B. F. (1975). Bury not burn. *A.P.A. Monitor, 6* (November), 2.

Smith, J. D. (1985). *Minds made feeble: The myth and legacy of the Kallikaks.* Rockville, MD: Aspen Systems Corp.

Sokal, M. M. (1992). Origins and early years of the American Psychological Association. *American Psychologist, 47,* 111–122.

Sunderland, L. (1988). On interpreting photographs, faces, and the past. *American Psychologist, 43,* 741–744.

Tryon, R. C. (1940). Genetic differences in maze-learning ability in rats. *Yearbook of the National Society for Studies in Education, 39,* 111–119.

Venezby, R. (1977). Research on reading processes. *American Psychologist, 32*(5), 339.

Watson, J. B. (1913). Psychology as the behaviorist views it. *Psychological Review, 20,* 158–177.

Watson, J. B. (1925). *Behaviorism.* New York: Norton.

Watson, J. B. (1927). The behaviorist looks at instincts. *Harper's Magazine* (July), 233.

Watson, J. B., & Rayner, R. (1920). Conditioned emotional reactions. *Journal of Experimental Psychology, 3,* 8–34.

Watson, J. B., & Watson, R. R. (1928). *The psychological care of the infant and child* (pp. 81–82). New York: Norton.

Weller, S. (1988, November). Mariette Hartley is clicking on her own. *McCall's* (November), 56–66.

Wyatt, W. J. (1993). Identical twins, emergenesis, and environments. *American Psychologist, 48,* 1294–1295.

Zamichow, N. (1995, January 10). Newsletter articles stir furor in high-IQ group. *Los Angeles Times,* B1.

3

PHYSICAL GROWTH AND DEVELOPMENT

Each of us begins life as a tiny, watery speck smaller than the period at the end of this sentence. This speck, technically a zygote, contains the genetic background that will shape and direct our development for the rest of our lives. The zygote is formed at that magic moment of conception, when the sperm cell of the male fertilizes the egg cell of the female. Conception occurs after an incredible mad dash by tens of millions of sperm cells trying to find their way to a single egg. (Some have said, tongue in cheek, that so many sperm are necessary because not one of them will stop to ask for directions.) Thus, half of the genetic background contained in the zygote comes from the father, half from the mother, so that the baby will be like both parents, but not exactly like either one. The zygote contains the hereditary predispositions that will be constantly molded and modified through environmental interactions. And these interactions begin immediately. If the zygote were to be surgically removed from the uterus and placed in a foreign environment, such as a glass of water, it would soon perish. If the zygote remains in the uterus and the uterine environment remains healthy, then growth and development continue, and some nine months later a baby is born.

All during the nine-month period, environmental encounters are occurring. The uterine environment is relatively constant, but not totally so. Toxic agents in the mother's uterus can modify, damage, or even halt the development of the zygote. During prenatal development there are a number of critical periods when various harmful agents have important negative effects only at certain developmental times. For example, rubella (German measles) can have devastating effects during the first trimester, but apparently has little or no effect during the last trimester. Studies have also shown that expectant mothers who have two or three drinks of alcohol a day may produce neonates who have lowered arousal levels and who in later childhood may even show higher-than-average incidences of learning disabilities (Steinhausen, Willims & Spohr, 1993). It has also been shown that expectant mothers who use crack cocaine have babies with an increased risk of SIDS (Sudden Infant Death Syndrome), as well as a host of birth defects, including retardation (Brown & Zuckerman, 1991). Women who smoke during pregnancy also place the fetus at risk. By age four, the children of mothers who smoked during pregnancy showed shorter attention spans than did children who were not so exposed.

Another study even suggests that learning can occur in the uterus (Spelt, 1948). It has also been found that strong emotional arousal on the part of the expectant mother can be transmitted to the developing fetus. Although there are no direct neural connections between mother and fetus, a mother's emotionality in the form of specifically released hormones can pass through the placenta and change the physiology of the yet-unborn child. In short, our basic axiom that behavior is a result of the interaction of heredity, environment, and time covers one's entire life from the moment of conception.

THE ABCS OF GENETICS

Our knowledge of genetics is of very recent origin. The science of **genetics** is based on the study of heredity, the biological transmittal of characteristics from parent to offspring. The nature-nurture argument was based in large part on the fact that not enough was known about nature, and what was known about heredity wasn't fully understood by many psychologists, especially in the United States.

The fundamental unit of analysis in genetics is the **gene.** Genes are tiny particles that carry the hereditary characteristics. (For a more detailed coverage of the composition and function of the gene, see Nora and Fraser, 1989.) Inside each cell is the nucleus, and inside that is the spiraling ladder of DNA. The arrangement of the atoms on the rungs of the ladder are called bases, and it's actually this sequence of bases that we now call the gene (Pollack, 1995). The genes occur in pairs, one gene from each parent. Estimates of the total number of genes in any single human (the human genome) run anywhere from 5 million to 10 million. Since at conception each parent contributes to this vast number of genes, there is obviously room for great genetic variation in the resulting offspring. Except for identical twins, every individual is genetically unique. Because of this, scientists are now able to identify suspects in criminal investigations by the use of DNA "fingerprinting." The procedure involves extracting DNA from small bits of blood, hair, tissue, or semen found at the scene of a crime and then matching it to the DNA taken from the cells of a suspect.

Genes are composed of the rather large organic molecule **DNA (deoxyribonucleic acid)** and **RNA (ribonucleic acid)** (see Figure 3.1). These nucleic acids (DNA and RNA) are located in the **chromosomes,** which reside in the nucleus of every cell in the body. The DNA strand resembles a long, twisting rope ladder, with more than 2 million rungs. Each rung can be one of only four types, but how these rungs are ordered creates a code that preserves an individual's genetic uniqueness. A single strand of human DNA if stretched to its full length would measure a little over three feet in length, the height of the average preschool child. But when it is crammed into its proper slot in the heart of the cell, it measures only about a millionth of an inch across. The job of packing DNA into its tiny compartment is accomplished by the special proteins called *histones* that squeeze the DNA down to size. These histones also have the job of switching genes on and off along the DNA molecule in order to control its various functions.

In the nineteenth century, Darwin told the world that physical evolution is brought about by the survival of the fittest to procreate. If Darwin was right, the human body is the result of millions of years of DNA changes, changes that were shaped by selective forces that shout out one overpowering command: make more DNA. Therefore, as Angier has pointed out, we really have no choice. "No matter how much sex education we've had, no matter how many times we've been deeply wounded by a lover, no matter how much more relaxed things would be if we could just leave our hearts and pelvises out of the behavioral equation, we have to seek mates. Very few of us can transcend this biological imperative and choose a lifelong, monkish celibacy" (Angier, 1995).

Chromosomes are fairly long, threadlike bits of protein, and each cell in the human body contains 23 *pairs* of these chromosomes (see Figure 3.2). The only exceptions are the germ cells (sperm cells in the male, egg cells in the female), which carry only 23 individual chromosomes. At conception, then, the zygote receives half of its chromosomes from each parent, 23 from each, and thus achieves its full complement of 23 pairs.

The chromosomes direct the development of all structures in the body. One pair of chromosomes, the twenty-third, determines gender. If this pair is identical (both X chromosomes), the person will be female; if the pair is different (one X and one Y chromosome), the result is a male. Since the female carries only X chromosomes, the sex of the offspring is determined by the father; that is, it depends on whether the fertilizing sperm happens to carry the X or Y chromosome. In the average ejaculation there are more sperm carrying the X chromosome than there are carrying the male-spawning Y. Yet every year, ironically, more boys than girls are born, about 110 male births for every 100 female births. This is because even though there are fewer Y chromosomes to begin with, they end up penetrating more than half of all the eggs (Bean, 1990). Although the Y chromosome is smaller than the X, it seems to have more genetic "muscle." Dr. Barry Bean sees this as an indi-

FIGURE 3.1 DNA and RNA.

cation that there is a biological discrimination against women even before they are born. However, despite this initial male advantage, the difference is dramatically reversed as life progresses, to the point where there are far more older women alive than older men.

The DNA and RNA molecules are located within the nucleus of each cell, where the chromosomes are arranged. The DNA molecule contains chains of atoms and simpler molecules that code and store information about growth and development. Their arrangement allows the DNA molecule to reproduce

FIGURE 3.2 Human chromosomes.

itself exactly—that is, to achieve precise self-duplication. For this to occur, the chemical environment must be appropriate. DNA acts as a blueprint, or, as it is called by the geneticists, a template, for the formation of certain enzymes that help guide the development of the organism. The coded information contained in the DNA molecule is transmitted to other parts of the cell by the RNA molecules. DNA may be thought of as the architect's blueprint, while the RNA is the builder translating this blueprint into a finished home. These reactions, however, do not occur in a vacuum. The chemical environment must be appropriate for the DNA "architect" and the RNA "builder" to work effectively. Thus, the developing organism is both biological and psychological, and its biological nature should be constantly viewed as it relates to the whole organism in all its splendid complexity (Dewsbury, 1991).

Many human characteristics have a polygenetic background. Polygenetic inheritance is based on the involvement of a combination of many genes in setting the stage for the development of certain traits. It has been likened to the various instruments in a symphony orchestra, each producing an important component tone in the totality of sound that is en-joyed by the listener (McClearn et al., 1991). Researchers are currently involved in what is known as the Human Genome Project, an attempt to map out all 23 human chromosomes and to identify the individual genes that together are involved in even the most complex of inherited characteristics (Plomin 1990).

DOMINANTS AND RECESSIVES

One of the first discoveries in the field of genetics occurred over a century ago when the Austrian monk **Gregor Mendel** (1822–1884) learned an important fact about inheritance. In his study of the flower color of garden peas, Mendel discovered that organisms contain both **dominant genes** and **recessive genes.** Mendel found that if he crossed a red-flowered pea with another red-flowered pea, the resulting plant would have red flowers. Similarly, if he crossed a white-flowered pea with another white-flowered pea, the resulting plant would have white flowers. But if he crossed a red-flowered pea with a white-flowered pea, the resulting plant would have red flowers. Thus, the genes that determine flower color can be dominant or recessive, and in this case, red is dominant over white—that is, the trait carried by the dominant gene shows up in the flower. Crossing a red with a red, or a white with a white, produces a pure offspring, whereas crossing a red with a white produces a hybrid. When a dominant gene is paired with a recessive gene, the resulting hybrid always exhibits the dominant trait.

Among the human traits that follow this rule, perhaps the best example is eye color. Brown eyes are dominant over blue eyes. Thus, if both parents have blue eyes, their children must have blue eyes. This is because, for individuals to have blue eyes, they must be carrying only the recessive genes for eye color. If they were to have a dominant brown-eyed gene and a recessive blue-eyed gene, their eyes would have to be brown. If, however, both parents are brown-eyed but both are carrying a recessive gene for blue eyes, their children still might have blue eyes. Chances are greater, however, that they will have brown eyes.

Two hybrid parents, each with brown eyes, have only a one-in-four chance of producing a blue-eyed child. The trait that shows up is the **phenotype,** whereas the one that remains hidden is the **genotype.** A person with a phenotype of brown eyes may have a genotype of two brown-eyed genes or a genotype of one brown-eyed and one blue-eyed gene.

A trait like eye color, in which a single pair of genes determines the phenotype, is a fairly rare case in genetics. Most behavioral traits, such as measured intelligence, result from the combination of large numbers of genes. This **polygenic inheritance** allows for the enormous potential for genetic differences among individuals.

We can see from even this simplified excursion into genetics that heredity has lawful relationships, and it is certain that future discoveries in this field will uncover many more definite patterns and laws that influence physical traits and behavior. Studies have already shown that, in addition to motor skills and intelligence, schizophrenia and manic depression have rather strong hereditary components. This is not to deny that environmental influences are important; they are! But the genes do carry constitutional predispositions toward various behaviors that the environment may stifle or nourish.

DOWN SYNDROME

Normally each human carries 46 chromosomes in 23 pairs. Scientists have numbered each of the 23 pairs, and if anomalies in this arrangement occur, severe problems may follow. For example, an extra chromosome at the point of chromosome pair 21 results in a form of mental retardation called Down syndrome, which occurs in 1 out of every 600 live births and is said to be the most common chromosome anomaly

Many birth defects, such as the mental retardation indicated here, are the result of hereditary chromosome anomalies.

(Widerstrom et al., 1991). In over 95 percent of all cases of Down syndrome, the extra chromosome is contributed by the mother. Interestingly, chromosome 21 is also a strong suspect in Alzheimer disease, and it is known that people with Down syndrome who live until their forties have an above-chance likelihood of contracting Alzheimer disease (Cummings, 1985).

BEHAVIOR GENETICS

Psychologists are able to examine the possible effects of genetic endowment through both animal and human research. Though the results of animal studies cannot be directly generalized to humans, the animal data may be at least suggestive of hypotheses that might later be pursued when researchers attempt to understand the results of human studies. Studies in **behavior genetics,** both animal and human, have as their goal the discovery of lawful relationships between genetic endowment and observed behavior.

Animal Studies

The genetic studies of animals are typically of two types: inbreeding and selective breeding. Inbreeding studies usually involve the mating of brothers and sisters in order to obtain as much homozygosity in the population as possible. **Homozygosity** means that the gene pairs are identical. When animals are inbred, those of the same sex come to have the same, or almost the same, genotype. Inbreeding experiments are commonly carried out on such organisms as mice and fruit flies (*Drosophila*).

In selective-breeding studies, animals of a given strain are tested for some behavioral criterion, such as ability to run a maze. Then the animals demonstrating extremes of this behavior are selectively mated for generation after generation—the animals with the best performance on the maze, for example, are mated with one another, as are the animals with the poorest maze performance. In Chapter 2 we mentioned such a study by R. C. Tryon, who established that after seven generations two significantly different groups of rats had been created: maze-bright animals and maze-dull animals (Tryon, 1940). In another classic study, white mice were separated according to the amount of aggressiveness they exhibited. The most and least aggressive mice were then selectively bred. Again, after seven generations, dramatic differences in the aggressiveness displayed by the offspring became apparent (Lagerspetz, 1964).

Human Studies

Since social taboos would rule out breeding experiments at the human level, psychologists must rely on after-the-fact, or post hoc, data in studying human genetic endowment. In some studies lineage records are traced backward in an attempt to establish the possibility of direct ancestry, a method used by Henry Goddard (Chapter 2) in his study of the Kallikaks. The problem with this kind of research is that genetic background and environmental influences are easily confounded: Martin Kallikak's "good seed" descendants and the descendants of "Old Horror" were exposed to different environmental conditions. Sir Francis Galton, the father of intelligence testing, was the first to use this lineage technique when he compared the achievements of successive generations of his own brilliant family with those of a less fortunate family.

In another type of human research in genetics, adopted or foster children are compared with both their biological and foster parents. If the children are behaviorally more similar to their biological parents (whose influence on the child's environment is presumed to be zero) than to their foster parents, the similarity is attributed to heredity.

Perhaps the most popular technique at the human level is to examine for behavioral similarities identical twins who have been reared apart. Since identical, or **monozygotic (MZ), twins** reared separately still have precisely the same genetic endowment, any remaining behavioral similarities are presumed to stem from genetic causes. In one study, an attempt was made to discover whether or not there is a genetic component in schizophrenia (Gottesman, 1991). The researchers identified both MZ twins (called the probands) and fraternal, or **dizygotic (DZ) twins** who had been diagnosed as schizophrenic and then located their cotwins. The percentage of cotwins with the same trait—in this case, schizophrenia—is called the **concordance rate.** The study found the MZ concordance rate to be substantially higher than the DZ rate. Even in the case of MZ twins reared apart, the concordance rate was roughly 60 percent, a figure that certainly lends some support to the author's genetic interpretation. The role of genetics in diseases other than schizophrenia is only beginning to be understood.

Other studies have shown that heredity plays a significant role in many other traits and conditions including aggressiveness, alcohol dependence, emotionality, hypertension, epilepsy, several forms of mental retardation, nervousness, and extraversion (Wimer and Wimer, 1985; Loehlin, 1989). Thus, it is suggested that a baby might even be born with a predisposition to neuroticism. Could it be that a day-old neonate might start yearning for the "good old days"?

Delayed Effects: Genetics and Development

Many genetically determined outcomes don't show themselves until a certain level of development has occurred. For example, age of menarche, or the onset of menstruation, is largely genetically programmed, yet the trait itself will not appear until puberty. Likewise, certain types of male baldness, which are strongly linked to a genetic base, seldom appear until the thirties and forties. But we should not equate heredity with destiny. Environmental influences can substantially offset many biological potentials. For example, an adolescent boy who is biologically destined to be weak and skinny may turn to special diets, weightlifting, and perhaps even chemical enhancers to alter the predicted course of the genetic influence. A person born with the tendency to have a large nose can turn to a cosmetic surgeon for the environmental manipulation. Even the effects of certain inherited-disease tendencies, such as rickets, can be offset by dietary changes and sunbathing. Genes are important, but they are not the whole story.

Linkage Studies

Genetic linkage studies use molecular genetics, family relationships, and statistical methods to ferret out the causes of various inherited conditions. Linkage studies are based on identifying a family (the larger the better) with a particular disorder and then looking for similarities among the genetic markers that flank the suspected gene. Genetic markers are identifiable segments of DNA that are known to vary from family to family. Thus, DNA samples from family members with the condition are needed as a reference point for the genetic testing. If the family members are linked by the disorder *and* the specific gene markers, then the genetic linkage is statistically likely to be at that particular site. Another linkage technique utilizes DNA fragments, whose differences in length are known to be inherited. Linkage of these fragments to various phenotypic traits provides further direct evidence for a genetic basis for the condition being investigated. The researchers involved in the Human Genome Project are painstakingly tracing the exact genetic locations of a wide variety of human conditions, including color-blindness, male pattern baldness, and certain enzyme deficiencies.

PSYCHOLOGY'S FIRST PRINCIPLE

Psychology's first principle and most fundamental axiom is that the organism is a product of heredity interacting with environment and with time, as shown in the following formula:

$$O = H \leftrightarrow E \leftrightarrow T$$

It is meaningless to ask whether intelligence, introversion, or any other psychological trait is inherited or learned. It's like asking which is more important in running a car, the engine or the gasoline; or which is more important in determining the area of a rectangle, the height or the width.

Even something as seemingly directly inherited as physical height is profoundly influenced by environment and time. An individual with the inherited potential for tallness will still be short if the environment prevents physical exercise or proper vitamin intake, especially if this deprivation occurs in early childhood.

Keep this first principle constantly in mind through the rest of this chapter. When we discuss developmental stages, we will give various age norms. However, it is crucial to remember that they are only averages, that there are often large discrepancies between the averages and any individual case. For example, the averages show that children usually utter their first word at 12 months; but in fact some children say their first word at 8 months, some at 24 months. A great deal depends on the amount and quality of environmental stimulation.

Duke University's Greg Kimble has recast psychology's first principle by saying that behavior is the product of relatively enduring underlying potentials (both genetic and learned) and relatively *temporary* instigations to action (Kimble, 1990). In this statement Kimble uses the term *potentials* to mean any psychological outcomes that are possible for a person (a rather enduring capacity) and the term *instigation* to refer to all environmental conditions that provoke or prevent an action, where the timing may be both short and crucial.

Environmental influences in the form of nutrition are also of great importance. The undernourished child may lag in both physiological and psychological growth. This is especially true early in life. The nine months of prenatal life and the two or three years following birth are critical in the growth of brain tissue and are known to be the periods of greatest vulnerability to malnutrition. Mental deficiency is one possible result of an inadequate diet during this critical time period of development.

Though the time factor is given great importance

in the following discussion, it must be remembered that time is only one factor. Though it is a convenient factor to utilize in discussing physical development, it is only part of the total equation. The organism is a product of heredity, environment, and time in constant interaction.

LIFE BEFORE BIRTH

At birth the human baby is already about nine months old. As a matter of fact, during that first nine months, from conception to birth, more growth occurs than will ever occur again: That tiny speck, the zygote, has grown into a seven- or eight-pound baby by the time it emerges into what William James called the "blooming, buzzing confusion" of the external environment. And since the baby is born with a total of more than 100 billion neurons in the brain, it means that new neurons have been generating at a rate of 250,000 *per minute* over the course of the nine-month gestation period (Rakic, 1988).

The nine months of growth before birth can be conveniently divided into three periods: the zygote, the embryo, and the fetus.

The Zygote

The zygote, the cell formed by the union of two gametes, floats freely in the fluid inside the uterus. After about two weeks it attaches itself to the uterine wall and becomes a parasite, receiving all its oxygen and nourishment from the mother's body. By that time the zygote has already begun to differentiate into three parts: the outer layer, or ectoderm, which will form the brain; the middle layer, or mesoderm, which will form the heart; and the inner layer, or endoderm, which will form the liver.

The Embryo

The second stage of prenatal development, the embryonic stage, begins two weeks after conception, at the time the zygote attaches itself to the uterus. At this point the developing organism is called an **em-**

Actual size of fetus at 4 weeks, 8 weeks, and 12 weeks

bryo. The embryonic stage lasts until about eight weeks after conception, and during this time the organism increases its weight by 2 million percent. Some benchmarks during this period include:

Age 20 days: Heart begins beating, and sex organs are formed.

Age 40 days: Brainwaves can be recorded, indicating brain functioning.

Age 42 days: Hands and feet are formed and can be flexed, and fingers contain unique fingerprints.

Thus, by the end of the embryonic period, the organism is clearly identifiable as human.

The Fetus

From eight weeks after conception until birth the organism is called a **fetus.** Though the growth rate of the fetus is not as spectacular as the zygote's or embryo's, it is still extremely rapid by postnatal standards. The fetus is definitely a behaving organism, and its behavior can be studied. During this period, benchmarks include:

Age 10 weeks: Fingernails develop.

Age 16 weeks: Growth reaches 8 to 10 inches in length.

Age 24 weeks: Mother's voice is recognizable, and fetus can smile, frown, squint, and grimace.

Age 28 weeks: The brain's neural circuits are at the same maturational level as the newborn's.

Current medical techniques have established a fetal age of just over 20 weeks as the dividing line between whether or not the fetus can survive if prematurely born. At this age the fetus is capable of true breathing and can even vocalize a thin crying sound.

Modern medicine has made astonishing advances in the study and care of the newborn, a specialized field called neonatology. Doctors and nurses are now able to save the life of even a one-pound fetus, a fetus you could easily hold in just one hand. Because of the newly developed intensive-care techniques, these tiny "miracle babies" can live to a ripe old age of perhaps 80 years. This is especially true for the female fetus, who seems less susceptible to problems of prematurity, anoxia (abnormally low levels of oxygen in the blood), and maternal infection. Thus,

current medical techniques have been able to establish fetal age of just over 20 weeks as the dividing line between whether a given fetus can survive if prematurely born.

Reactions to stimuli   The fetus can react to stimuli as early as eight weeks after conception. At this time it is sensitive to stimulation of the nose, lips, and chin. The area of sensitivity gradually increases, and by the fourteenth week, the whole body is sensitive, except for the top and back of the head. The top of the head doesn't respond to stimulation until after birth.

Spontaneous action   Along with the ability to react to stimuli, the fetus can also act spontaneously. Certainly after the fourth month the mother is aware of fetal activity. This activity is quite diffuse—that is, movements are slow and involve several parts of the body at once.

All the preceding stages, from conception to birth, are collectively called the *prenatal stage of development.* Prenatal development is characterized by its rapidity and by a maturation rate that enables the fetus to perform certain functions well before they are actually needed. For example, the fetus can make breathing movements by the fourth month, walking movements by the fifth month, and sucking movements by the sixth month.

PHYSICAL DEVELOPMENT IN CHILDHOOD

The newborn baby, or neonate, is certainly not a miniature adult. Relative to other parts of the body, the baby's head and trunk are much larger than they will be at adulthood. For example, the head will only double in size from birth to adulthood, whereas the arms and legs may grow to five times their original length.

Although all normal babies follow the same overall patterns, the growth of girls seems to be more steady and constant than that of boys. Boys are more apt to show growth spurts, even though the general timetables are similar for both sexes (Kagan, 1984).

The Nervous System

In one sense the nervous system is complete at birth—that is, the number of typical nerve cells never increases after birth—but the size of these cells does increase. Also, although the neonate comes

Newborn babies spend most of their days asleep, averaging about 16 hours a day.

equipped with a fully structured nervous system, it is many years before this system can function efficiently.

Each nerve cell, or neuron, has two basic parts: fibers and cell bodies. Think of the neuron as a fiber with branches at both ends and a bulge (cell body) in the middle. The function of the neuron is to transmit messages (neural impulses) to and from all parts of the body. The branches, or fibers, pick up the messages and send them on their way. The receiving end of a neuron is the dendrite, and the transmitting end is the axon. In order not to short-circuit the electrically charged neural impulses, most of these fibers are insulated with a white sheath called *myelin*. The gray-colored cell body does not have this covering. Therefore the myelin-covered neural pathways are called *white matter* and the uncovered cell bodies are called *gray matter*. The myelinization of the nervous system is not complete at birth, so that a great deal of short-circuiting occurs among the baby's neural impulses. This accounts in part for the mass activity that is characteristic of a baby's physical reactions. Touching a baby's foot doesn't result in just a foot response but is usually followed by gross move-

ments of both feet, both arms, and even the trunk. It's as though you had no insulation on the wires leading to your electrical appliances, so that when you turned on the TV, the radio and stereo would go on, the alarm clock would buzz, the dishwasher would start, the coffee pot would begin percolating, and the doorbell would ring. Although the nervous system is structurally complete at birth, it is nowhere near functionally mature. The cerebral cortex, which is crucial for learning and complex behavior, doesn't become functionally mature until about age 2, and some maturation continues until about age 12 or 15.

Sleep

Newborns spend most of their days asleep, averaging about 16 hours a day. This time decreases rapidly until by age one they are sleeping only a little over 10 hours a day.

By the time they begin preschool most children are sleeping in the neighborhood of 10 hours a night, but a teacher faces a serious problem when a child comes to school already tired out because of a lack of sleep the previous night. Dr. John DeFrancesco has studied these conditions and says that sleep disorders, such as nightmares and sleep terrors, are often the culprits. Nightmares are bad dreams that tend to occur in the latter part of the sleep cycle. The child usually awakes from the nightmare, but, though frightened, is typically oriented and fairly alert. Sleep terrors, on the other hand, occur during deep sleep, and the child is found with eyes open, screaming, disoriented, terrified, and in some cases running around the room (DeFrancesco, 1995). Sleep terrors tend to run in families but are usually triggered by some stressful event. Most children outgrow the disorder, but for those who don't, brief treatment procedures, such as play therapy, have shown great promise.

Motor Development

One of the most dramatic features of infancy is the development of motor skills. Compared to the neonate, the two-year-old child is a study in grace and physical coordination. In one of psychology's truly classic studies, M. M. Shirley assembled a series of painstakingly detailed observations of the development of infants on a week-to-week basis. As can be seen from Table 3.1, Shirley's data suggest that there is a definite pattern to motor development: infants hold up their heads before they sit alone, sit before they crawl, and crawl before they walk. This pattern of development is almost exactly the same for every human baby, and each child passes through each of these physical stages at almost the same age (Shirley, 1931).

TABLE 3.1   STAGES IN MOTOR DEVELOPMENT

The skills listed here illustrate the progressive development of control over different groups of muscles. This development proceeds in an orderly fashion from the head region down the body and out to the ends of the limbs.

DESCRIPTION OF STAGE	NUMBER OF CASES	AGE, WEEKS MEDIAN
First-order skills (control of the neck muscles)		
On stomach, chin up	22	3
On stomach, chest up	22	9
Held erect, stepping	19	13
On back, tense for lifting	19	15
Held erect, knees straight	18	15
Sit on lap, support at lower ribs and complete head control	22	19
Second-order skills (control of the trunk and upper-limb muscles)		
Sit alone momentarily	22	25
On stomach, knee push or swim	22	25
On back, rolling	19	29
Held erect, stand firmly with help	20	30
Sit alone one minute	20	31
Third-order skills (beginning of body-limb coordination in prone position)		
On stomach, some progress	17	37
On stomach, scoot backward	16	40
Fourth-order skills (balance in upright position with support; locomotion in prone position)		
Stand holding to furniture	22	42
Creep	22	45
Walk when held	21	45
Pull to stand by furniture	17	47
Fifth-order skills (unsupported locomotion in upright position)		
Stand alone	21	62
Walk alone	21	64

Adapted from M. M. Shirley, The first two years: Postural and locomotor development, Vol 1 *(Minneapolis: University of Minnesota Press, 1931), p. 99, Copyright © 1931. Reprinted by permission of the University of Minnesota Press.*

The sequence of motor development.

Although many other studies since then have researched the age norms for infant motor development, with slightly different terminology and even slightly different age criteria, Shirley's data continue to remain valid.

Studies have also shown that motor development occurs according to at least three general rules.

1. *Cephalocaudal progression:* Motor ability develops from the head on down to the toes. The neonate's head is closer to the eventual adult size than is the rest of the baby's body. Also, the infant has more motor control of the head than of the muscles lower down the body. The progression of motor control follows this pattern: first the head; then the shoulders, arms, and abdomen; and finally the legs and feet.

2. *Proximodistal progression:* Growth and motor ability develop from the central axis of the body on outward. Trunk and shoulder movements occur earlier than separate arm movements. Control of the hands and fingers comes last.

3. *Mass- to specific-action progression:* The baby's first actions are global and undifferentiated. Slowly, the infant develops ability to make specific responses. Refined activity of the fingers and thumb usually doesn't occur until about one year.

Motor development is thus heavily influenced by biological maturation, though practice is certainly necessary for the full development of this inherited potential. Studies have clearly shown that for such activities as walking, for example, early practice is a key ingredient in the action's maintenance and further development. It has even been suggested that since unaided walking is under the influence of several environmental factors, it may be that an infant's true developmental status might better be determined by the assessment of a higher-order skill, such as walking, than by the more traditional testing of simple reflexes (Zelazo and Barr, 1989).

Sensory Development

Many studies have been done to determine what infants are able to receive through their sensory equipment. Since infants obviously cannot give verbal answers to questions, research in this area is much like animal research. If a researcher is trying to find out whether a rat can sense the difference between the colors red and green, the rat can be presented with a red light and some food in one goal box and a green light with no food in the other. After a number of trials, if the rat goes consistently to the red light, even when it is randomly switched to the goal box that has no food in it, the researcher will know that the rat can discriminate between red and green. (Studies have shown that rats, in fact, cannot make this discrimination between red and green colors when the amount of illumination is held constant.)

Newborn babies have been shown capable of discriminating between sweet and sour tastes, taste being the most highly developed of all the senses at birth. Responses to different smells have been observed within a few hours after birth.

Some babies respond to sound almost immediately after birth, whereas others may take a few days to gain this sense. This difference is a result of the time it may take for the amniotic fluid to drain out of the newborn's hearing mechanism. Once the fluid is drained, however, neonates can not only respond to sound but can also discriminate among certain sounds. Even neonates as young as three days old, for example, show a marked preference for the

mother's voice over the voices of others (DeCasper and Fifer, 1980).

Vision develops more slowly than many of the other senses. Response to light and darkness (the pupillary reflex) is functional within 2 days after birth, and by 10 days infants can follow moving objects with their eyes. The newborn's visual acuity is understood to be rather poor, however, and has been estimated to be in the range of 20/600, versus 20/20 among older normal children (Banks and Salapatek, 1983). Since neonates can still focus down to a distance of about eight to ten inches, nursing newborns can certainly see the mother's face (Smolak, 1986). They are also capable of imitating the mother's facial expressions, a fact that indicates that they not only are perceiving these expressions but have enough motor control to reproduce them. It is believed that this extremely early visual-motor coordination helps prepare the neonate for later cognitive growth (Bjorklund, 1989). There is even some evidence that the neonate's brain contains "grandmother cells," cells in the visual cortex that are so specialized that they respond to a specific face (Galluscio, 1990).

The specialization of cells may also be a function of environmental interactions. Some migratory cells in the developing cortex become specialized on the basis of the first stimuli that they are exposed to (Walsh and Cepko, 1992). Thus, young neurons can wander around the cortex, and then become functional as a result of *environmental inputs.* A cell becomes a visual neuron because it has roamed into the visual cortex and been exposed to signals from neighboring cells and from the optic nerve. If the same cell had happened to be in the auditory cortex when it was exposed to stimuli, it would have matured into a neuron involved in hearing. Thus, the environment can be seen as meshing with the genes to sculpt the brain. More and more, scientists are discovering the crucial importance of environmental stimulation on all parts of the developing organism.

By six months of age infants can discriminate between circles and triangles, and between the faces of parents and strangers. In fact, in one study it was found that infants as young as one month old could distinguish between familiar and unfamiliar faces (Maurer and Salapatek, 1976).

One classic study demonstrated that infants at six months can perceive depth and thus avoid situations in which they might fall (Gibson and Walk, 1960). In this study the babies were placed on a plate of glass that extended from a tabletop across a three-foot drop. When the babies reached what they perceived as the edge of the table, they refused to crawl across the rest of the glass. This perceived dropoff is called the **visual cliff,** and it has been observed not only in

Babies as young as six months can perceive depth.

infants but also in lower organisms such as cats and rats. The ability to perceive the visual cliff and act on that perception has obvious survival value for the species. Some researchers have even suggested an innate link between the visual and motor systems that tends to emerge at just about six months of age (Richards and Rader, 1981). By the time children reach first or second grade, they are typically learning to refine their basic visual-motor skills. After this they seldom develop many new basic skills, but they continue to improve the quality and complexity of the skills they already possess (Malina, 1982).

Emotional Development

Babies display different emotional behaviors and temperaments from the very day they are born (Goldsmith & Harman, 1994). The majority of researchers now generally believe that temperament and emotionality have large genetic components. For example, characteristics such as irritability, flexibility, and persistence seem to be stable from infancy through at least age eight (Pedlow et al., 1993). Harvard's Jerome Kagan has observed the same stability over time for shyness (Kagan & Snidman, 1991).

Neonates, of course, are unable to experience or express the full range of human emotions, but this ability begins to emerge very soon after birth. The earliest emotions seem to be only a general diffuse anxiousness or excitement, although even neonates have displayed a few very basic emotions. For example, in one study the faces of neonates showed different expressions for surprise, disgust, and distress (Trotter, 1983). Emotions such as happiness and anger tend to develop somewhat later. Feelings of shame and guilt arise much later because they depend on an understanding of social situations and relationships, the most obvious example being the ability to grasp the significance of social approval and disapproval (Lazarus, 1991).

Tests to determine how neonates experience emotions are difficult to conduct for two reasons. First, the researcher must try to resist the temptation to attribute adult feelings to the actions and expressions of the newborn. Second, as Lazarus has shown in numerous studies, the relationship between cognition and emotion is extremely intimate. Lazarus explains that all emotions begin with a diffuse and general arousal of the nervous system. Thus, the *situation* in which the child finds himself or herself when aroused may provide that child with direct cues as to how these diffuse feelings should be labeled. The developing baby has to learn the appropriate cues, usually from the caretaker, to use in order to identify which feelings are appropriate to which situation. Thus, the nature of emotional communication between infant and adult may be far more organized than was previously thought (Tronick, 1989).

Many psychologists argue that cognitive development and emotional development go hand in hand, and that emotions are actually cognitive constructions that have been formed on the basis of needs and values. Thus emotional constructions, like cognitive constructions, change considerably over the course of development (Dupont, 1994).

It is also important to remember that emotions are not only felt but expressed, and in fact there is mounting experimental evidence that the expression of the emotion affects the inner feelings. William James suggested this phenomenon over a century ago. According to what has become known as the James-Lange theory of emotion, we first react physically, and then we feel the emotion psychologically; that is, we run, then we feel the fear. Similarly, it has now been established that the act of smiling actually makes a person feel happier, leading some researchers to argue that without the facial expression the emotion cannot even be felt (Rinn, 1991).

Finally, the fact that the expression of basic emotions is universal among all humans, regardless of geography or culture, lends strong support to the notion that emotional expression, like virtually all other human behavior, has a genetic basis (Ekman & O'Sullivan, 1991).

SPOTLIGHT ON BONDING

A Mother-Child Connection

Some researchers believe that a process similar to imprinting among birds occurs among humans, specifically between mother and child. This is called maternal-infant bonding, and is said to produce a strong emotional attachment between the mother and her baby. The hypothesis is based on the view that women are "hormonally primed" to totally accept their infants for a short time after giving birth (Klaus & Kennell, 1982). The bonding process requires direct physical contact between mother and child and apparently must take place within the baby's first three days of life. Part of the reason for this is that during those first three critical days, the neonate is more alert and more able to respond than will be the case for the several days that follow (Brazelton, 1981).

The bonding process is important in building infant security that persists at least throughout childhood. Babies who had formed strong attachments to their mothers were found at age six to be more socially at ease, more persistent in solving new problems, and more willing to explore new areas of interest (Harris & Liebert, 1991). Researchers in this area have cited the failure to form this crucial psychological bond as a possible reason for later episodes of child neglect and even child abuse (Marano, 1985). This position is not without its critics, however, especially since it is said to place too heavy a responsibility on the mother for her child's development and relegates the father to only a secondary-caretaker role (Denmark, 1994).

Speech Development

At birth, speech is restricted to general, undifferentiated crying, yet by the second month the baby can communicate both discomfort and contentment through loud crying or gentle cooing. Of all the developmental factors covered so far, speech is obviously the one most influenced by learning. Yet even speech is built on a biological foundation. Studies of the various sounds made by infants throughout the world have found that certain sounds occur at about the same time and in about the same order in all infants. By listening to the sounds of a baby lying contentedly nearby, one can hear the basic sounds of all languages throughout the world, from the German guttural *r* to the singsong intonation of Chinese.

Learning theorists, such as B. F. Skinner, believe that babies keep some of these sounds—those reinforced by their parents—and slowly discard those that are not encouraged. By the ninth or tenth month they are able to imitate some of the sounds made by others around them.

Other theorists, such as Noam Chomsky, believe there is a heavy genetic component in language acquisition. Rather than learning language solely on the basis of reinforcement and imitation, Chomsky argues, children may acquire language as the result of an inborn "language acquisition device," which directs the infant's ability to learn (Chomsky, 1980). One researcher calls this inborn device a "biopro-gram," which is a specific genetically driven grammatical model that each child amends, probably through trial and error, to match the peculiarities of the native tongue. This genetically based machinery guides language acquisition, especially during the critical period between ages two and four, when youngsters develop from babblers into novice talkers (Bickerton, 1990). Maratsos agrees that language acquisition is genetically based, believing that the neonate enters the world with a built-in language "bias" that undoubtedly serves an evolutionary purpose (Maratsos, 1983). Furthermore, it is known that among adults language is processed in an area of the brain's left hemisphere (Geschwind, 1979) and that this left-hemisphere processing area is significantly larger than the comparable area of the right hemisphere. This cortical size difference is found not only among adults but also among neonates *and even among fetuses* (Wada et al., 1975). These facts lend further credence to the hypothesis that there is a genetic basis for language receptivity and acquisition.

From cooing to babbling　Children do not begin to speak meaningful language before they are about

SPOTLIGHT ON EBONICS (Black English)

Should Ebonics Be Taught in Schools?

For many years some educators regarded poor school achievement among black students as a product of inadequate language acquisition. Some experts now suspect that although such students have usually developed quite normally in their original language, Ebonics, they are being taught and evaluated in a second language, standard English, with which many of them are not as familiar. Linguists have been focusing increased attention on dialects, or variants of a language that differ in terms of vocabulary, grammar, and pronunciation. In fact, some dialects vary so markedly that they are scarcely recognizable as derivatives of a common language. In some countries, for example, speakers of one regional dialect may not understand a word spoken by someone using the dialect of another region. Black English, or Ebonics—literally, "Black Sounds"—is the dialect that many African-American children bring with them to schools. Until recently, this dialect was generally viewed as low-class, sloppy, or "poor people's talk," and children who spoke Ebonics often accepted and adopted this point of view about themselves. Their consequent feelings of inadequacy and lowered self-esteem then led them to become discouraged, defeatist, or even belligerent in school, usually in self-defense (Ogbu, 1978). Studies by certain linguists, however, have suggested that Ebonics is not a "substandard" dialect (Smith, 1994). Ebonics has its own structure and grammar, perhaps even as complex and complete as those of standard

English. Some words in Ebonics have been assimilated into standard English. "Tote," meaning to carry, and "dig," meaning to understand or admire, are examples. Differences in grammar and pronunciation have been traced to the West African languages that most black immigrants spoke when they were brought to America. Much in the same way that a German immigrant says "dis" for "this," because there is no *th* sound in German, a speaker of Ebonics says "tin" for "thin," or "raht" for "right." (The table below compares phrases and illustrates several grammatical differences.) Some of the vocabulary of Ebonics, such as "yam," "gumbo," and "joo joo" (magic), have a direct source in African dialects. Thus it has been argued that Ebonics is, in a sense, a foreign language and should be taught in the schools, just like Spanish. Although its grammar is often syntactically different from that of standard English, Ebonics is nevertheless richly expressive. For example, "He be sick" signifies a long-term illness, whereas "He sick" denotes a more transitory condition. "He don't be there" denotes extended absence: the person wasn't there yesterday, is not there now, and won't be there tomorrow. Or consider the following testimony to someone's rare ability to discriminate among various stimuli: "He so bad he can step on a wad of bubble gum and tell what flavor it is." Thus, Ebonics is seen as a legitimate language form with its own long history tracing its roots back to Africa, and perhaps even genetically based (Cook, 1997).

Several alternatives have been suggested to deal with black schoolchildren's problems in lower school achievement. The currently prevailing approach is that black students, like those from any other minority group, must learn the main language of the country in which they live. In contrast, proponents of Ebonics suggest that black children should be taught in their own language, much as many Spanish-speaking children are being taught in theirs, and that Ebonics should become part of the regular curriculum for black children. A third compromise approach urges that if black children are to be taught in standard English, at least their teachers should be given instruction in Ebonics so that they can better appreciate its richness and complexity. Since all schoolchildren in the United States must learn standard English, it is felt that a special burden is placed on black children, who are, in effect, forced to learn a second language (Delpit, 1988). As with most people who learn a second language, their level of proficiency may not be as great as it is in their native language. Even though socially and economically disadvantaged black children may use standard English when speaking with persons in authority ("the man"), they only use short sentences and simplified grammar. In these situations they speak with little expressiveness. When speaking with each other, however, their language is highly expressive and as grammatically complex as that used by any children of their age. Thus, it is argued that since poor school achievement among some black children results from inadequate language acquisition, allowing them to be taught and evaluated in their native language would be both fair and beneficial (DeFranz, 1994). It is seen as unfair to teach and evaluate students in their second language (one in which many of them are not as familiar) and to disregard totally their true, native language. This really places the children in double jeopardy, and too often the tragic result is underachievement. Proponents of Ebonics are hopeful that changing attitudes toward Ebonics in the classroom may promote an atmosphere more conducive to learning and personal growth for America's black children. One scholar suggests that an official policy of bidialectalism represents an ideal solution. She thinks black students should learn enough standard English to use it when necessary, but that teachers should learn enough about Ebonics to appreciate and understand its complexity and legitimacy (Hoover, 1990).

Opponents of the plan to teach Ebonics argue that children so taught will forever be at a disadvantage, that the continued use of Ebonics will stamp them as second-class citizens. Schools in England do not teach cockney children to drop their *h*'s; quite the contrary. Neither Martin Luther King nor Jesse Jackson ever used Ebonics, and in fact much of their success was due to their powerful rhetorical command of standard English. It is also argued that standard English is better able to capture complicated conceptualizations and has more variety, more synonym

STANDARD ENGLISH	EBONICS
He's working (regularly)	He be working
He's working (at the moment)	He working
He said he's coming	He say he be coming
Those boys	Them boy
Nobody knows it	Nobody don't know it

Table adapted from Seymour, 1971.

possibilities, and wider applicability. According to this position, since standard English offers the opportunity for richer, more precise communication, introducing Ebonics into the school curriculum—perhaps even teaching biology, algebra, and physics in Ebonics—may put already disadvantaged children at a greater disadvantage. Linguistic separation could almost predestine black children to fail. These youngsters are not Africans but Americans who intend to live in America, and should therefore be taught the language of their native land. A study that seems to lend support to this view found that bilingual children in New York City who took most of their classes in English became more proficient in English than those who were taught subjects in their primary language (Dillon, 1994).

Many believe that introducing Ebonics into the curriculum will further complicate our already complex society. A bilingual or bidialectical nation may prevent the kind of fusion among races and ethnic groups that a more or less homogeneous culture demands; adding more languages such as Ebonics, Spanish, and Indian tribal tongues in schools tends to

fragment a society rather than to bring it together. Yet others insist that in a pluralistic society such as ours, cultural diversity should be encouraged so that all of us can become more aware of our own cultural and racial values, past and present.

Cook, T. (1997, January 2). Should Ebonics be taught in schools? *CNN Crossfire.*

DeFranz, A. (1994). Coming to cultural and linguistic awakening: An African and African American Educational vision. In J. Frederickson (Ed.), *Reclaiming our voices: Bilingual education, critical pedagogy, and praxis.* Ontario, CA: California Association for Bilingual Education.

Delpit, L. (1988). The silenced dialogue: Power and pedagogy in educating other people's children. *Harvard Education Review, 58,* 15–27.

Dillon, S. (1994, October 21). Bilingual education effort is flawed, study indicates. *New York Times,* A20.

Hoover, M. (1990). *Successful black schools.* Oakland, CA: NABRLE Publications.

Ogbu, J. (1978). *Minority education and caste.* New York: Academic Press.

Seymour, D. (1971). Black children, black speech. *Commonweal, 19,* 46–62.

Smith, E. A. (1994). *The historical development of African-American language.* Los Angeles: Watts College Press.

a year old. Yet during this first year, babies do engage in a wide range of vocalizations. Although crying, as every parent knows, is the first sound, by three months most babies are engaged in cooing sounds, which are vocalizations composed of a series of soft, primarily vowel sounds that seem to be produced when the baby is relaxed and content. At this age, babies may also gurgle, emitting speech that involves consonant as well as vowel sounds. During these early months babies also become aware of the speech of others and will stop their own vocalizings to listen when other people are talking. By six months, a new phase—babbling—occurs. These babbling sounds, sometimes called "grunts" by specialists in the field, are laying a language foundation and will become the building blocks for later development (Dill, 1994). They may continue until the child is more than a year old.

Babbling differs from cooing in a number of ways. First, the child spends much more time making the babbling sounds, often while lying in the crib before going to sleep or upon awakening. Second, new combinations of sounds appear. Whereas cooing seems to be highly unstructured, babbling usually consists of both consonant and vowel sounds combined in a single syllable, such as "da," "knee," and "goo." Then at about eight months the infant begins to string these sounds together, repeating the same syllable patterns, such as "mi-mi-mi," "bah-bah-bah," and "noo-noo-noo." During this period of babbling, the baby will even begin to vary the pitch and volume of the vocalizations, in much the same manner as real speech (MacLachlan, 1981). Even deaf children babble, and since deaf children cannot be engaged in verbal imitation, this fact offers further evidence that language acquisition has a strong genetic basis.

Holophrases and telegraphic speech   After they have mastered their first word, babies increase their vocabularies slowly, using about 50 words by age 18 months. Each word, however, often conveys much more than just a single thought or concept. A single word that is used to express a whole phrase is called *holophrase.* "Down" can mean "Don't keep holding me; put me down" or "I want you to go downstairs" or "I want freedom; let me out of this stupid car seat" or "I want you to get down and play with me." Children also communicate very effectively through body language. They laugh, move toward and away from objects and people, and in general get the point across that they want something or don't like something (or somebody). The context, intonation, and body language all combine to create meaningful

holophrases. The infant who sees a bottle and says in a straightforward manner "bah-bah" seems to be simply identifying or labeling the bottle. If on another occasion his voice rises and he becomes agitated, "bah-bah" may mean he wants the bottle. If he bangs his hands on the tray of his high chair, picks up the bottle, throws it on the floor, and then says "bah-bah" in a complaining tone, it may mean he's had enough of the bottle or that its contents are not satisfying.

Infants' vocabularies increase slowly at first because at the same time they are devoting all their attention to learning the intricacies of walking. Once they have mastered walking, their language development speeds up. Speech recognition comes much earlier than speech production. It has been estimated that by 18 months of age babies can recognize up to six times as many words as they can produce (Siegler, 1991).

Sometimes babies will overgeneralize, or, as some experts say, overextend, a given word, using a single word to cover a whole host of similar ideas or things, such as "truck" for all rolling stock, whether it be a car, bus, or train. In fact to some extent people really never outgrow this phenomenon. To some adults all pasta is "spaghetti," as opposed to a gourmet chef who can rattle off 30 different kinds of pasta; or to the novice skier all frozen white stuff is simply "snow," whereas the ski instructor can recite what seems like an endless list of snow varieties, from packed powder to frozen granular to mashed potatoes. Or children may sometimes underextend, using words too specifically. Thus, a child may use the word "bottle" only for a baby bottle and not comprehend the meaning when it is applied to other bottles, such as soda bottles or water bottles; or a child may use the word "Mama" only for her mother and not comprehend that there can be other people in the world who are also mothers (Siegler, 1991).

At 18 months youngsters begin producing two- and three-word sentences, such as "I want car," which, depending on the context, might mean "I want to go with you in the car" or "I want to play with my toy car." Words and details of adult speech are omitted, and only the most important words are left, as in a telegram. This telegraphic speech is remarkably similar among children from many different cultures.

Language expert Eric Lenneberg has long argued that from infancy through adolescence there are critical periods for language development, and that language acquisition is largely genetic and therefore maturational in nature. The consensus seems to be that early language is especially timed and innately determined, but that as children get older the envi-

SPOTLIGHT ON CHILDREN

A Time to Play

As the great psychologist Erik Erikson (see biography in Chapter 6) said many years ago, the early years, especially ages three to six, are a period when playtime is extremely important in the developmental process. Play affords the child with a non-threatening opportunity to try out reciprocal social roles and even to learn cooperative strategies. William Damon (more on him in Chapter 7) has pointed out that playtime also provides a safe opportunity for the child to express thoughts and feelings that might otherwise remain bottled up and distorted. As an example, Damon cites the story of two preschool neighbors who were presented with baby sisters at about the same time. Although both children were overtly kind and affectionate to their new sibling, they often played a game with each other called "bad baby," in which a certain doll was used as a scapegoat for their natural jealousies and hostilities. The doll, that is, the "bad baby," was scolded, rejected, and severely punished during this emotionally releasing game. In another more telling example, a five-year-old named her "favorite" doll Allison, after her one-year-old baby sister. About every two weeks she would announce that she was going to play a game called "Let's Give Allison Away," and the doll would then disappear for a few hours or even days. On one occasion, the mother found the doll halfway down the toilet. Damon feels that this kind of play is developmentally healthy, since it allows children to discharge pent-up emotions and come to grips with their true inner feelings (Damon, 1983). David Elkind even argues that the "hurried child," the youngster who is not given enough playtime, who is pushed too hard and too soon to achieve, is at a developmental disadvantage, not only for emotional growth but, also for cognitive growth as well. (Elkind, 1981.)

---

ronment plays an increasingly important role. All children the world over don't speak the same language, and even within a single language grouping not all children learn the same pronunciations. In the United States alone, just compare the accents of Bostonians with those of midwesterners or southerners, all of whom are speaking English. There are also variations in idioms and other vocabulary: George Bernard Shaw once called the United States and Great Britain two countries separated by the common language.

The naming explosion stage   Between 18 and 24 months of age there is typically a fairly dramatic vocabulary spurt, called by many child psychologists "the naming explosion stage." The baby at 18 months begins wanting to name virtually every object in the visible environment and constantly looks around and asks, "What is that?" or, more typically, "Whatsat?" Whereas the child at 18 months is often able to produce up to 50 words, at 24 months that same child will probably be producing over 400 words. During this stage, the words often have unique pronunciations, which become clear only in context. One 18-month-old toddler (with whom I share a certain percentage of DNA) announced at a family gathering that his name was "Ham," the closest approximation to Sam that he could come up with. Since he had spent the previous 10 minutes going through a repertoire of what might be viewed as showoff behavior, his mother, my daughter-in-law, murmured softly that the name fitted him well.

By first grade, children may recognize up to 14,000 words; thus, from age 18 months to six years they are adding an average of nine new words a day, or about *one new word per waking hour* (Zimbardo, 1992). These figures are only averages; there are great individual differences. For example, children with high IQs begin talking as much as four months earlier than the average child. Also, girls begin talking sooner than boys, use more words in each sentence, and master larger vocabularies. Moreover, as they get older, girls have fewer speech problems than boys. Boys are more prone to stuttering, more apt to have difficulty articulating the consonants *l* and *r*, and more likely to fill up their speech with hesitation sounds such as "uh" and "er." Later in life

FIGURE 3.3 The adolescent growth spurt typically occurs earlier in girls than in boys.

there are still some dramatic speech differences between the sexes. Among stroke victims, for example, it is far more common for men to lose their ability to speak (Restak, 1979).

Speech and early experience Speech, like other developmental abilities, is a product of heredity, environment, and *time*. The sensitive-period hypothesis illustrates the importance of time. If environmental stimulation occurs too late, language acquisition will not proceed in a normal fashion. Evidence sup-

porting a sensitive-period explanation of language acquisition comes from a true "horror story" about a young girl reared in unbelievably impoverished circumstances (Curtiss, 1977). The girl, Genie, was locked by her father in a bare room when she was only 20 months old. During the day she was strapped naked to a potty chair, and at night she was tied into her crib. On those occasions when she was visited, by either her brother or her father, she never heard the sounds of human language. The father and brother would only bark or growl at her, in mock imitation of a dog. Any attempts by Genie to make any vocalization were severely punished by her father, who, as one author suggests, "lends renewed dignity to the notion of insanity" (Maratsos, 1979). Only after Genie was released, *12 years later,* did she learn to talk. Although she made great progress, given her earlier circumstances, her speech patterns remained below normal language ability, for example, "Want think about Mama riding bus." Genie never used pronouns and had no verb tensing, nor did her voice carry any inflections. In short, the study of Genie seems to indicate that at age 13, the critical period for language acquisition has passed.

PHYSICAL DEVELOPMENT IN ADOLESCENCE

Physical growth proceeds in fits and starts from age two to adolescence, but in adolescence another, really dramatic growth spurt occurs, and it occurs earlier in girls than in boys (see Figure 3.3). Although boys are typically taller and heavier than girls at age 10, by age 13 the girls are taller and heavier than the boys. By age 16, the boys are again taller and heavier.

At the risk of stating the obvious, body image is an important source of concern during adolescence. In fact, when teenagers are asked what they dislike most about themselves, fully one-half of the girls and one-third of the boys report "physical appearance" more than anything else (Conger & Peterson, 1984). Among those who overestimate their physical attractiveness, the vast majority are males (Gurman & Balban, 1990). Adolescents who are less satisfied with their body images tend to be more self-conscious and to have lower self-esteem (Adams & Gullota, 1983).

In girls, adolescence is signaled by **menarche,** or the first menstruation. This happens concurrently with breast development, usually by age 13, though it is also not uncommon for girls to reach menarche as early as age 10 or as late as age 16. The timing and variation in the onset of menarche are influenced in part by environmental factors such as nutrition and general health. Nutrition is especially important, since menarche occurs at both a fairly consistent weight, approximately 106 plus or minus 3 pounds, as well as percentage of fat to body weight, about 17 percent. Anorexic girls or girls who overtrain in athletics may not reach the required body-fat levels and therefore may retard the onset of menarche. Despite these environmental factors, the genetic age range for the onset of puberty is innately wired into the species (Scarr and Kidd, 1983).

Adolescence in boys does not have such clear-cut criteria. If we use such indices as the appearance of pubic hair, the first seminal ejaculation, or increase in the size of the penis and testes, adolescence in boys

Maturation rates for girls may vary substantially during early adolescence.

SPOTLIGHT ON MOOD DISORDERS

There is increasing evidence that very occasionally major depression can occur even in prepubertal children, with equal frequency among boys and girls. Among adolescents it is more common, and far more so among girls than boys. As for bipolar disorders, the mood swings so common among adult patients seem to have their origin at about the age of puberty. Unlike the adult version, the teenage bipolar exhibits the manic phase not by a euphoric mood, but by irritability and prolonged and aggressive temper tantrums. The alert teacher should look for the following problem behavior associated with mood disorders among elementary schoolchildren and adolescents:

1. Disruptive behavior, possible academic difficulties, and peer problems
2. Increased irritability and aggression, suicidal threats, and worsening school performance
3. Tendency of parents to say that nothing pleases their children, that they hate themselves and everything around them (Brown, 1996)

The following statistics confirm the importance of identifying mood disorders early: (1) up to 14 percent of children will experience an episode of major depression *before* age 15; (2) up to 30 percent of adult bipolar patients report having had their first episode before age 20; and (3) out of 100,000 adolescents, 2,000 to 3,000 will have mood disorders, and 10 of these will commit suicide (Brown, 1996).

usually begins between ages 11 and 17. Again, there is great variation in the age at which boys reach puberty.

Special Problems of Girls

Menarche can be a traumatic event for a girl who is psychologically unprepared, especially for the early-maturing (EM) girl. However, the girl who is secure in her sex identification and who has had adult support and guidance may regard her first menstruation with pride, as a sign that she is "grown up." The girl whose parents have prepared her for this new experience is less likely to be anxious about her menarche.

Breast development has special cultural overtones in Western culture. The United States has been described as a breast-oriented nation, and certainly the popularity of billboard ads for suntan lotion, TV ads for "the slightly padded bra," and the direct stares of males of all ages do much to validate this description. During adolescence, then, breast development becomes a symbol of approaching womanhood and sexuality. Typically, physical development of the breast from bud to full size occurs in about three years, from about age 11 to about age 14. The bud stage almost always precedes menarche and the first signs of pubic hair.

Special Problems of Boys

Boys who begin puberty relatively late suffer psychological distress for a variety of reasons. Late-maturing (LM) boys are apt to be shorter and physically weaker than the early maturers and are thus less likely to become outstanding athletes. Because social reinforcements are fewer, the late-maturing boy more often turns psychologically inward, becoming introverted.

The size of the penis is also of great concern to the adolescent boy. In the shower room after gym classes the adolescent quickly glances from boy to boy, to see whether he "measures up." The boy with the small penis is often openly ridiculed and his masculinity challenged. He worries that he will be an unsuccessful lover. The facts, however, as reported by William Masters and Virginia Johnson, are that the size of the penis is not highly correlated with the he-man physique or with great physical size. The largest penis they measured (without erection or stretching) was five and a half inches and belonged to a man only five feet seven inches tall. The shortest penis, just over two and a third inches, was found on a man almost six feet tall (Masters and Johnson, 1966).

Moreover, Masters and Johnson found little evidence for the widely held notion that the larger the penis, the greater the potential for giving sexual satisfaction. Because the vagina distends during sexual arousal in order to permit entry and then contracts around the penis in a snug grip, the size of the penis is of little importance.

Adolescent Sexuality

Perhaps the single most important developmental aspect of adolescence is the ability to produce sex cells and thus create new life. But although adolescents may be physically mature enough to create babies, in a society such as ours they are far from ready to take care of them. Even so, when the hormones are raging it is not easy to just say no. Teen pregnancies have become almost epidemic, involving almost 15 percent of all teenage girls, over 80 percent of whom are unmarried and unable or unwilling to identify the father (Alan Guttmacher Institute, 1990). This trend may reflect changes in societal values and social policies as well as teenagers' strong belief in their own invulnerability (Quadrel et al., 1993). A teenage girl is also more apt to get pregnant if she has an older sister who was pregnant as a teenager (East & Felice, 1992).

In his classic study on sexuality, Alfred Kinsey reached a series of conclusions concerning sexual behavior. Kinsey gathered his data in two major studies during the 1940s and 1950s. His findings included the following:

1. Men reach their greatest sexual activity (defined as sexual arousals leading to orgasm) at 16 to 17.

2. Women tend to be less easily sexually aroused at any age than men are, and seem less preoccupied with sex.

3. Fifty percent of women and 85 percent of men had intercourse before marriage.

4. Forty percent of women and 95 percent of men masturbated to orgasm (Kinsey et al., 1953).

In another study of human sexuality, Masters and Johnson combined interviews with observation of their subjects engaging in sexual activity (Masters & Johnson, 1966). (All subjects in the studies were volunteers.) In general, their conclusions tended to support Kinsey's findings. They said, for example, that masturbation is a common sexual practice and is not harmful. In addition, they found that women are capable of numerous climaxes in a relatively short time and that female orgasms occur in the clitoris and not in the vagina, as had been previously suggested. Probably their most significant conclusion was

that at least half of married adults suffer from some degree of sexual inadequacy. Masters and Johnson advocated effective educational programs to help reduce feelings of sexual anxiety and to eliminate popular misconceptions about human sexuality.

A more recent study, said by the authors to be the most scientifically valid study of sexuality ever conducted, involved 3,321 American men between ages 20 and 39 (Billy et al., 1993). The major results were as follows:

1. The median number of sex partners over a lifetime was 7.3.

2. The median age at which white men lost their virginity was 17.2 years; for black men it was 15.

3. The median frequency of sexual intercourse was less than once a week overall, and slightly more than once a week for married men.

4. Just over 2.3 percent of the men had engaged in homosexual activity during the previous 10 years, and just over 1 percent identified themselves as exclusively gay.

There is no question that a major concern of adolescents during junior and senior high school is human sexuality. Accurate information alone, of course, will not solve the complex issues of sexual inadequacy, but it can be an effective first step.

The Sissy-Boy Syndrome

That there may be developmental trends in the onset of adult male homosexuality has been suggested by psychiatrist Richard Green. Green asserts that he has identified a pattern of male development, called the sissy-boy syndrome, that seems to predict the later onset of homosexuality. Green first identified a large group of young boys on the basis of some or all of the following behavioral traits: dressing in girls' or women's clothes, playing with dolls, pretending to be a mommy, playing games almost exclusively with girls, and completely avoiding rough-and-tumble play. When contacted 15 years later (in their early twenties), 75 percent of these males acknowledged that they were either homosexual or bisexual. Of Green's control group, made up of men who had previously been found to have been typically masculine boys, only one had become bisexual (Green, 1987). It is possible that some of Green's subjects actually suffered from what psychiatrists call Gender Identity Disorder (GID), a condition that begins in childhood and is exhibited when a child insists on

SPOTLIGHT ON GENDER DIFFERENCES

Learned or Genetic?

Aside from the obvious anatomical differences between males and females, there is growing interest as to whether psychological differences between the sexes are learned or innate. The issue is indeed of momentous importance, for if the differences are learned, and if, as some suggest, they favor the male, then it is up to us, to society, to change the childrearing and educational practices that produce this inequality. For example, if boys are trained and shaped at an early age to be better equipped to succeed in our competitive society, then it's time the rules and norms were changed to give girls an equal opportunity to achieve success. If, however, physiological-psychological differences are in fact built into the species, then educational (and psychological testing) practices should be altered so that every member of each sex will be given full opportunity to make the most of his or her potential.

The following differences have been the most consistently noted over the years:

1. During the first few months of life, boys are less sensitive to and less often startled by sounds and do not turn as often toward them.
2. Girls show superior development of fine-motor coordination, not just with their fingers, but even in the small muscles of the larynx and pharynx; hence, they even sing in tune at an earlier age.
3. Girls learn to speak earlier, develop larger vocabularies, learn foreign languages more easily, and generally retain a linguistic superiority throughout life.
4. Boys suffer far more from speech difficulties such as stuttering, stammering, and the use of "um" and "er" interjections.
5. Boys are more overtly aggressive than girls, as children and especially as adolescents. Boys are also less able to sit still for long periods; thus, they are far more apt to be diagnosed as hyperactive when they reach school age.
6. Boys score higher than girls in tests of spatial relations, such as indicating which of four rotated shapes is identical to an original model or mentally traversing a maze.
7. On IQ tests, females consistently outperform males on a number of verbal subtests, especially those concerning vocabulary, whereas males do better in other areas, notably in those concerning arithmetic. David Wechsler has even provided a formula for a "masculinity-femininity" score, based on comparing a person's performance on subtests typically excelled in by males with those typically excelled in by females (Wechsler, 1958).

Environmentalists, on the one hand, explain all these differences as a result of the way our culture treats and differentially reinforces the sexes. No wonder little boys are more active and aggressive: they are told to be so by parents, teachers, and storybooks. Little girls are admonished not to run, jump, or be boisterous, because it simply isn't "ladylike." Through reinforcement, then, little girls condition themselves to sit more quietly and to develop their fine-motor coordination by drawing, learning to sew, or playing with dolls, all generally more passive pursuits. Boys are allowed to throw themselves into rough-and-tumble games, and because of their conditioning, they are less able to sit passively and exercise and develop their fine-muscle coordination. With language development, the situation is similar. Girls, having been conditioned to be more passive, are much better able to listen to language, imitate new sounds, and sit still long enough to read a book. Therefore, it's no wonder that they will acquire larger vocabularies. As for speech problems, again culture is the culprit. Society demands more of little boys, and when a three-year-old male mis-speaks, the

wearing the clothing and playing with the toys of the opposite sex. These children seem to be unable to accept their own masculinity or femininity.

Evidence obtained in another study, this one in-volving twins, points rather convincingly to a ge-netic basis for homosexuality (Bailey & Pillard, 1991). This study found that 52 percent of identical twin brothers (MZ twins) of homosexual men also parents make a major issue out of it. So much pressure is put on the male child to speak correctly that he becomes over-anxious. After all, isn't he eventually going to have to be the competitive breadwinner of the family? Anxiety then builds on anxiety, and a snowball effect is produced, with speech pathology as the result. As for spatial relations, boys are encouraged more to be curious about the world of nuts and bolts and hammers and saws. Therefore, it's no surprise that they learn to manipulate spatial concepts. They get more rewards for these activities. In short, the differences are due to cultural stereotyping, and the sooner we as a society do away with our preconceived notions, the better we'll all be. Girls will then be more able to reach their full potential—and boys will be, too, since they will be less wracked by pressures to perform.

The geneticists, on the other hand, insist that the cultural argument, though valid to some extent, has been generalized far beyond the physiological facts. For example, neurologist Richard Restak says that there are indeed fundamental differences, both chemical and morphological, between the male and female brains (Restak, 1979). The left hemisphere of the female brain is more heterogenous, more neurologically complex than the male's (Restak, 1988). (In righthanded people, and even in 60 percent of lefthanded people, the left hemisphere contains the language centers.) Doreen Kimura, a Canadian psychologist, has found that even among left-hemisphere stroke victims, far more women than men retain their ability to speak and to understand language (Kimura, 1986). Problems based on spatial relations, however, are controlled by the right hemisphere, and here the male brain is more complex. A difference in the size of part of the corpus callosum (the wide band of neural fibers connecting the two hemispheres of the brain) has been found between males and females, with females having a proportionately larger area (Whitelson, 1989). This may also help to explain why girls begin talking earlier than boys, since the stronger connection between the hemispheric areas that control speech may in fact speed up speech production and recognition. Kimura has also noted that a gender difference in the size of the two hemispheres, with the left hemisphere being relatively larger in women and the right hemisphere larger in men. She uses this physiological fact to explain the psychological fact that women tend to outperform men in language abilities (left hemisphere), whereas men outperform women in spatial tasks (right hemisphere). Kimura believes that the difference in hemispheric size between the sexes is due to hormonal influences occurring very early in prenatal life (Kimura, 1989), such as the masculinizing action of estrogen on the fetal brain (Nelson, 1995).

There are, say the geneticists, innate gender-based differences in brain organization, and to ignore them is simply to ignore reality. Society's task is really to adjust for these differences, not to deny them. Since boys tend to excel in right-hemisphere tasks, then tests such as the National Merit Scholarship Examination should be radically redesigned to ensure that both sexes have an equal chance. As things now stand, the tests are weighted with items (spatial relations and mathematics) that virtually guarantee superior male performance. Also, elementary grades should be restructured to allow boys more freedom of action and thereby help reduce the stress that might trigger such problems as hyperactivity, speech problems, and learning disorders. Sociologist Carol Tavris warns us that we should never confuse the very real differences in male and female experiences with the way culture translates these differences. Society must strive for equality of acceptance, a goal not of denying or exaggerating differences but of eliminating the unequal consequences that too often flow from them (Tavris, 1992).

were homosexual, compared with 22 percent for fraternal (DZ) twins and only 11 percent among genetically unrelated brothers (brothers by adoption). The researchers questioned 56 identical twins, 54 fraternal twins, and 57 adoptive brothers, and concluded that although these data seem to strengthen the case for a genetic component, they do not rule out all other factors, such as social conditioning.

SPOTLIGHT ON GENDER BIAS IN SCHOOL

Even as early as first grade, gender bias can be a problem for girls, and not just in the classroom but also out in the schoolyard or riding on the bus. First-grade "macho" boys have been heard taunting their female peers with remarks like "Let's do sexy," or taunts such as "Hey there, sexy babe," and this is said to have occurred in a school that was allegedly gender free, a school where even the four-year-olds don't play dressup or housekeeping, and the children are never segregated by types of play (Rubenstein, 1994). It is estimated that currently only about 10 percent of the nation's schools have serious programs in place to deal with gender issues. David and Myra Sadker have written a book detailing, among other things, how to spot gender bias in the schools.

Here is a list of things to look for (Sadker & Sadker, 1994):

1. Examine the textbooks in use and look for examples of gender bias.
2. Find out if teachers call on boys and girls with equal frequency.
3. Find out whether boys and girls have their work displayed equally on bulletin boards and in hallways.
4. Find out if boys and girls play together at recess and lunchtime.
5. Find out whether problems in the classroom produce equal treatment. Does the teacher assist boys and girls with equal frequency?
6. Find out whether in science classes the boys are doing the

work while the girls are told to sit around and watch.
7. Note whether teachers make up "boys only" and "girls only" teams for, say, spelling bees or athletic events.
8. Determine whether girls in the class get in trouble for the same actions as those displayed by boys. Does the reprimand include language such as "Suzie, that isn't ladylike"?
9. Note whether boys are allowed to insult each other by saying things like "You throw like a girl" or "You're crying over a little bruise like that? What are you, a girly-boy?"
10. Ask both boys and girls in the class if they can name 10 famous women from U.S. history. Incidentally, can you?

Another study examining a deep interior formation of the brain called the hypothalamus, found an anatomical difference between homosexual and heterosexual men. One specific node of the hypothalamus is nearly three times larger in heterosexual men than in homosexual men. In fact, the anatomical form of that node is remarkably similar in women and homosexual men, and substantially different in heterosexual men (LeVay, 1991). Even this anatomical difference, however, may not be inborn, but may be a result of environmental treatment and stresses, or even the individual's own reaction to that treatment. For example, among males in lower species, cells in the hypothalamus may become larger *as a result of behavior.* When male fish fight to obtain social dominance, the winner undergoes a series of physical changes, beginning with an increase in the release of a hormone called gonadotropin, which triggers the enlargement of both the hypothalamus and the gonads. Conversely, within days the defeated male shows a reduction in the size of the hypothalamus, as well as a shrinkage of the testes and

concomitant reduction of sperm production (Bond et al., 1991).

Finally, DNA linkage studies also suggest a connection between heredity and male homosexuality. Researchers have found that a DNA marker on the X chromosome is highly correlated with homosexuality (Hamer et al., 1993). As noted earlier in the chapter, the male receives only one X chromosome—and that from his mother.

In fact, Dr. Gunter Dorner has long argued that modern medicine now has the tools to prevent homosexuality. His evidence is based on research indicating that sexual orientation among males results from prenatal exposure to certain hormones and that the future homosexual can be detected through amniocentesis, a test of the uterine fluid that is already being used to predict such conditions as Down syndrome (Dorner, 1985). Dorner asserts that prenatal injections may reduce the hormonal influence that produces homosexuality.

None of the studies described above should be interpreted as indicating that biology should be

Adolescent boys are often concerned with penis size. According to researchers Masters and Johnson, the size of the penis is not highly correlated with physical size.

equated with destiny, but all do show significant genetic possibilities that cannot be ignored.

Early and Late Maturation

Much research has gone into discovering what differences, other than the rate of physical maturity, exist between early-maturing and late-maturing adolescents. One must be careful, in interpreting these studies, not to leap to the conclusion that these other differences between EM and LM adolescents are due only to the adolescent's changing biology. Personality variables, for example, are especially influenced by the way others perceive and, accordingly, treat us. A boy of 17 whose voice hasn't changed yet, whose body proportions are still as they were when he was 12, is all too often treated by those around him as though he were, in fact, still only 12 years old. Similarly, the 12-year-old boy who is speaking in a rich baritone, whose shoulders have broadened, and who shaves daily is more apt to be treated as if he were older.

Social psychologists tell us that the way people respond often depends on how others treat them. People who are treated like children very often respond in childlike ways, and those who are treated like adults respond with more maturity. Early maturity can itself be a problem, however. If teachers and parents see early maturity as a negative characteristic, the adolescent can be adversely affected. However, studies done over the years on early and late maturers (Jones, 1965; Wilson et al., 1969; Siegel, 1982; Simmons and Blyth, 1987) have been fairly consistent in revealing the following:

1. There are almost no differences in IQ, grade placement, or socioeconomic status between early-maturing (EM) and late-maturing (LM) adolescents. There is some evidence, that EM girls have somewhat lower grades in the fifth or sixth grades than their LM counterparts, but this difference seems not to persist into high school (Simmons and Blyth, 1987). This grade difference is somewhat difficult to interpret, however,

SPOTLIGHT ON ADOLESCENCE

The Workplace

A recent U.S. Department of Education Survey found that about half of all U.S. high school sophomores, two-thirds of all juniors, and three-fourths of all seniors held after-school jobs. At first glance, this may look like a very positive picture of American teenagers, showing them to be ambitious and ready to compete in the free-enterprise system. Aside from the monetary gain, it might seem that the teenager holding an after-school job would benefit in a variety of ways, building character, self-reliance, and good work habits. The evidence, however, is not nearly so positive. A study by Steinberg and Dornbusch (1991), found that compared to classmates who did not work at all, or who worked only a few hours a week, the working students received lower grades, spent less time on homework, cut classes more often, and were less involved in extracurricular activities. The workers also showed more physical complaints, higher rates of drug and alcohol use, more delinquent behavior, greater freedom from parental control, and lower levels of self-esteem. These behaviors were especially pronounced among students who worked more than 20 hours a week, but were significantly less likely among students working fewer than 10 hours a week. The issue, therefore, may not be simply whether or not a student works, but how much time she or he spends working. Finally, the authors caution that their findings may not reflect a genuine causal relationship. It may be that the workforce is especially attractive to youngsters who are already predisposed to some of those negative habits and who need extra money to pay for them.

since more of the EM girls became high school dropouts, a fact that changed the makeup of the group at large. Perhaps the girls who dropped out were the very ones who had weighted down the average of the EM girls in the first place. It is also known that children with extremely high IQs tend to be early maturers.

2. EM boys are rated by their peers as being physically more attractive and better athletes, and they are more often elected to student office.

3. On personality tests, EM boys show more self-control, more interest in girls, more extroversion, and higher levels of self-esteem.

4. EM girls are rated by adults as being below average on many social and personality traits, whereas LM girls are rated above average. In the fifth and sixth grades, the EM girl is significantly more satisfied with her body image. She is also aware that her new physical appearance is a source of much attention by the boys in her class as well as older boys. By the time they reach high school, EM girls tend to be shorter, stockier, and less satisfied with their figures, whereas LM girls are taller, thinner, and more satisfied.

5. EM girls date earlier and more frequently than the LM girls. They are also more likely to become sexually active, a pattern that extends into high school.

6. In peer ratings, EM boys are perceived more favorably on a variety of personal and social traits than are the EM girls.

Thus, when it occurs, early maturity is more apt to be an advantage to boys than to girls in our society.

GROWTH PERIODS AND EDUCATIONAL PROBLEMS

At each age and stage of development, children and adolescents need continued assurance from adults in order to accommodate themselves to and assimilate the effects of constant change. During adolescence, diversity and change are at peak intensity, and the differences between and within the sexes are at a maximum. The junior high school years are a period of especially great diversity in such areas as physical growth, glandular-sexual

SPOTLIGHT ON GENDER

"Suppose that when you wake up tomorrow morning, you discover that you have become the opposite sex. What do you think your life would be like?" This was one of the questions asked of both American and Swedish teenagers in an interesting study conducted by Margaret Intons-Peterson (1988). Before looking at the results, consider the background. About 30 years ago the government of Sweden passed legislation mandating that both parents share the responsibility of raising their children and that fathers be especially encouraged to participate in the childrearing process. One law provided that upon the birth of a baby one parent could have up to nine months' leave from work at 90 percent of his or her regular pay. In an attempt to discover if gender bias had changed as a result of this law, Intons-Peterson compared U.S. and Swedish children and adolescents on a number of gender-related variables. One of them was the sex-change question quoted above. Intons-Peterson found that although neither Swedish nor American boys of various ages saw any advantage in a sex change, most girls (in both countries welcomed the idea), but fewer Swedish girls than American ones responded positively.

changes, social changes, and cognitive shifts. Each individual student and each subgroup of students need extra support during this critical period. For example, the late-maturing boy needs help in developing confidence and needs assurance that before long he too will reach full maturity. Similarly, the early-maturing girl needs special support to withstand some of the intense pressures she is under from both adults and peers. Handling this situation can be extremely delicate. Class discussions may often do more harm than good, especially when they focus attention on specific students in the class. A public discussion of a particular student's problem may be a humiliating and destructive experience for the individual on whom the spotlight falls. Teachers need to develop an extra awareness of and sensitivity to those aspects of this often-hidden classroom agenda. Careful listening to student concerns and some judicious reading between the lines will provide the teacher with more than a few cues as to possible reasons for a student's sudden, "unexplainable" upset, mood change, or rapid attention shift.

In physical education and health classes, posting pictures and charts showing growth curves during adolescence may indeed be a case in which a picture is worth a thousand words. It should also be helpful to present the students with some facts of sexual growth and maturation. A few facts in this area may remove the mystery and correct some of the myths that students often pass on to one another. Information of this sort may often be followed by an audible and collective sigh of relief from the class. This is not to suggest that the teacher should deluge the seventh-grader with graphic illustrations from Masters and Johnson, for the student may confuse sex education with sexual encouragement. The object is to present information in a way that will help youngsters to feel comfortable with their own and their peers' physical, emotional, and sexual growth and less preoccupied by it. The goal is anxiety reduction, not sexual trauma.

The AIDS scare has added new impetus to the drive for sex education in the schools. The reasoning is that if youngsters are indeed going to be sexually active, then they had better know more about what they are doing. And the majority of today's teenagers are apparently sexually active. According to one survey, 60 percent of white males have had intercourse by age 18, 60 percent of white females by age 19, 60 percent of black males by age 16, and 60 percent of black females by age 18 (Hofferth & Hayes, 1987).

However, several studies have confirmed the nagging suspicion that sex education isn't automatically translated into any positive behavioral change. One study even found that teenagers' use of condoms declined after they had studied a sex education unit specifically designed to provide information on the risks of AIDS (Kegeles et al., 1988).

Because adolescents grow and mature in lags and spurts, fits and starts, worrying over each lag is an exercise in futility (as is doing a victory dance because of a sudden spurt). The vast majority of laggards eventually catch up, while the spurters eventually slow down (Lampl et al., 1992).

SUMMARY

Understanding of the biological basis of behavior is essential to understanding developmental psychology. An important component of this biological knowledge is the relatively new field of genetics, the study of how characteristics are biologically transmitted from parent to offspring. The basic unit of analysis in genetics is the gene, a tiny particle of heredity located in the nucleus of each of the body's cells. Genes are composed of DNA and RNA molecules. The DNA acts as a blueprint or template and contains the coded genetic information within the nucleus of the cell. RNA transmits this information to other parts of the cell. One of biology's most spectacular recent achievements was the deciphering of this genetic code. Since each offspring receives 23 chromosomes from each parent, the new individual is genetically unique, except in the case of identical twins, who begin life as only one cell. Psychologists are able to examine the effects of genetic endowment through both animal and human research.

Psychology's basic principle is that behavior is the result of heredity interacting with environment interacting with time. Before birth, the human organism goes through three basic stages of development: (1) zygote, (2) embryo, and (3) fetus. Tremendous changes occur during the prenatal period. The organism increases its size dramatically, from a tiny speck to a seven- or- eight-pound baby, in only nine months. Maturation both before and immediately after birth occurs on a schedule that is fairly consistent for all members of a given species. The maturation of various organs occurs safely ahead of the time when they must be used. Reflex and motor development, such as holding the head erect, sitting, crawling, and walking, is heavily influenced by biological maturation, though environmental encounters at the appropriate time are important for full development of the biological potential.

Sensory maturation shows functional development either at birth or within a few days of birth. Touch, smell, taste, and hearing develop slightly before vision. Bonding is a process that requires direct physical contact between mother and child and occurs within the first three days of life. It is said to produce a strong emotional attachment between the mother and child, and failure to form this bond may cause later episodes of child neglect or even child abuse.

Speech develops from the grunts and cries of the newborn to a recognizable word by the one-year-old. Once the child masters the intricate details of walking, the verbal repertoire increases dramatically. By age one, most children begin talking, using one-word sentences called holophrases. By age two, they are combining at least two words into a sentence. Children's language is obviously different from adult language, and proceeds through a number of developmental changes as children grow older. Using simple grammar, for instance, a two-year-old can combine many words into two-word sentences, many of which may be original. Over time, children combine more words together into telegraphic speech. Ever more complex grammatical forms continue to be acquired into middle childhood.

Adolescence marks the beginning of another growth spurt, a spurt that occurs earlier in girls than in boys. The early-maturing girl and the late-maturing boy may have special problems in our culture. Adolescents need extra support and understanding during this critical period of development.

Sex education must be handled sensitively and with compassion. If a teacher spends too much time attempting to detail the intricacies of sex education, adolescents may confuse education with encouragement, and their psychological problems may increase rather than decrease.

KEY TERMS AND NAMES

behavior genetics
bonding
chromosome
concordance rate
deoxyribonucleic acid (DNA)
dizygotic (DZ) twins
dominant gene
embryo
fetus
gene
genetics

genotype homozygosity
menarche
Gregor Mendel
monozygotic (MZ) twins
$O = H \leftrightarrow E \leftrightarrow T$
phenotype
polygenic inheritance
recessive gene
ribonucleic acid (RNA)
visual cliff
zygote

THEORY INTO PRACTICE: OBSERVING CHANGES IN GROWTH

To help you understand just how dramatic the process of physical growth and development is during the first few years of life, we suggest that you focus on the process of motor development.

1. Use Table 3.1, Stages in Motor Development, as a reference point.
2. Set up a series of visits in order to observe young children at different ages to:
    a. A newborn unit at a local hospital for infants up to two weeks old
    b. A day-care or home-care center for children 6 to 18 months old.
    c. A preschool program for children three to four years old.

Newborns: birth to two weeks　Starting with the youngest group, see if any of the newborns can hold up their chin or their chest. Since you'll probably have to observe from behind a glass wall, it may be difficult to see very much movement. If this is the case, ask the nurse in charge what range of motor activity the newborns demonstrate—such as grasping fingers, moving legs, and crying—and whether there are noticeable individual differences in the amount of motor activity. Spend a few moments taking in the entire scene, observing the tiny infants, most of them sleeping quietly; the activities of the nurses and attendants; and the general layout.

Day care or home care: 6–18 months　First notice the dramatic differences in motor activity compared to the newborns. Infants who are six months old will show all the first-order skills listed in Table 3.1. Many should also be demonstrating the second-order skills, such as sitting alone, rolling, and doing a kind of pushup.

Next, look for some one-year-olds. Notice how fast some can crawl and creep and especially how the coordination in getting the legs and arms working together has improved. If you happen to see a six-month-old lying stomach down, with arms and legs flailing but still not moving in any direction and nearby a one-year-old scooting along the floor with arms and legs coordinating, the differences will be readily apparent.

Then observe some eighteen-month-olds. Many will be mastering walking and running. You may be able to see some children in transition from crawling to walking. Notice how uncoordinated the first steps are, accompanied by lots of "unnecessary" motion, such as the waving of arms or tilting of the body. Then, gradually, the coordination improves, and the unnecessary movements drop away. The children begin to move about with deftness and grace.

A second point to notice during the transition from creeping to walking is regression. A child may take a few steps haltingly to obtain a desired toy across the room and then suddenly sit down and crawl rapidly. In Piaget's terms (Chapter 5), the child hasn't yet accommodated to the new skill of walking and so returns to an earlier method of problemsolving that is only temporarily a better solution. The last point to notice during the transition is the child's exclusive concentration on the new task of walking. During this phase, children often halt development in other areas. Thus, it is not uncommon for them to stop talking, or at least reduce the amount of talking, as they focus on mastery in locomotion. Since you may not be able to observe this directly in a single visit, you might ask the day-care workers for their observations on this point.

Preschool for three-to-four-year-olds　The first thing that will strike you is just how sophisticated the motor activity has become in such a relatively brief time. All the children now walk, run, and jump without hesitation. Compare what you see in this age group to the motor activity of the newborns and of the 6- to 18-month-olds. There is a quantum leap forward in ability. The basic physical work of such motor activity has been accommodated and assimilated so that it is part of the natural repertoire of activity.

Also notice that as a result of these skills, the style of play and interaction has changed. There is more grouping. Children gather in clusters for joint play rather than play in parallel. The groups coalesce around something of common interest and then quickly disband and reform with different members around a new object. If the classroom has a water table, note how the children pour water from large containers into smaller ones (without spilling too much), watch one another do it, and then disband, perhaps moving to the puzzle corner of the room and a new set of activities. What may appear as episodic or even perhaps aimless wandering is really an expression of the children's ability to explore freely and to enjoy the sense of mastery that bipedal locomotion provides. They are obviously more efficient and more effective than either the 6-month-olds who try to bump along on their bottoms or the 12-month-olds who crawl from place to place.

One final note   Observation of young children can become an extremely important part of a variety of professional roles: teacher, child-care worker, theorist, researcher. In fact, some of our major theories of development started with the seemingly mundane process of child watching. This Theory to Practice unit is only a first step in sensitizing you to the process. Here we have somewhat arbitrarily focused on locomotion. Other possibilities include sight, smell, language, and physical development itself. If you spent one day observing in any seventh-grade classroom, you would be struck by the enormous variability between girls and boys in size and physical coordination. Developing a keen sense of observation may well be one of the key attributes for anyone who is interested in the process of child and adolescent development as teacher, theorist, and/or researcher.

REFERENCES

Adams, G. R., & Gullota, T. (1983). *Adolescent life experience.* Monterey, CA: Brooks/Cole.

Alan Guttmacher Institute. (1990). *Adolescent sexuality.* New York: Alan Guttmacher Institute.

Angier, N. (1995, March). This can't be love. I feel this evolutionary spell. *New York Times Book Review, 7.*

Bailey, M. J., & Pillard, R. C. (1991). A genetic study of male sexual orientation. *Archives of General Psychiatry, 48,* 1089–1096.

Banks, M., & Salapatek, P. (1983). Infant visual perception. In P. Mussen (Ed.), *Handbook of child psychology.* Vol. 2: *Infancy and developmental psychology* (4th ed.). New York: Wiley.

Bean, B. (1990). Progenitive sex ratio among functioning sperm cells. *American Journal of Human Genetics, 47,* 351–353.

Benedict, H. (1979). Early lexical development: Comprehension and production. *Journal of Child Language, 6,* 183–200.

Bickerton, D. (1990). *Language and species.* Chicago: University of Chicago Press.

Billy, J. O. G., Tanfer, K., Grady, W. R., & Klepinger, G. (1993). The sexual behavior of men in the United States. *Family Planning Perspectives, 25*(2), 52–60.

Bjorklund, D. F. (1989). *Children's thinking, developmental function and individual differences.* Pacific Grove, CA: Brooks/Cole.

Bond, C. T., Francis, R. C., Fernald, R. D., & Adelman, J. P. (1991). Characterization of complementary DNA encoding as the precursor for gonadotropin-releasing hormone and its associated peptide from a teleost fish. *Journal of Molecular Endocrinology, 5,* 931–937.

Brandstadter-Palmer, G. (1982). Ontogenetic growth chart. In C. Kopp and J. Krakow (Eds.), *The child.* Reading, MA: Addison-Wesley.

Brazelton, T. B. (1981). Clinical issues of the Brazelton Neonatal Assessment Scale. In M. Coleman (Ed.), *Neonatal neurology.* Baltimore: University Park Press.

Brown, A. (1996, Winter). Mood disorders in children and adolescents. *NARSAD Research Newsletter (National Alliance for Research on Schizophrenia and Depression),* 11–14.

Brown, E. R., & Zuckerman, B. (1991). The infant of the drug abusing mother. *Pediatric Annals, 20,* 555–558.

Chomsky, N. (1980). The linguistic approach. In M. Piatelli-Palmieri (Ed.), *Language and learning.* Cambridge, MA: Harvard University Press.

Conger, J. J., & Peterson, A. C. (1984). *Adolescence and youth* (3d ed.). New York: Harper & Row.

Cummings, J. L. (1985). *Clinical neuropsychiatry.* New York: Grune & Stratton.

Curtiss, S. (1977). *A psycholinguistic study of a modern-day wild child.* New York: Academic Press.

Damon, W. (1983). *Social and personality development: Infancy through adolescence.* New York: Norton.

DeCasper, A. J., & Fifer, W. P. (1980). Of human bonding: Newborns prefer their mother's voices. *Science, 208,* 1174–1176.

DeFrancesco, J. J. (1995). Sleep terrors vs. nightmares. *First Steps, 2,* 8–11.

Denmark, F. L. (1994). Engendering psychology. *American Psychologist, 49,* 329–334.

Dewsbury, D. A. (1991). Psychobiology. *American Psychologist, 46,* 198–205.

Dill, S. (1994, January 16). Babies' grunts have meaning. *New York Times,* B6.

Dorner, G. (1985). Gonadotrophin secretion, sexual orientation and gender role behavior. *Endokrinologie, 86,* 1–6.

Dupont, H. (1994). *Emotional development, theory and applications: A neoPiagetian perspective.* Westport, CT: Greenwood.

East, P., & Felice, M. E. (1992). Pregnancy risk

among the younger sisters of pregnant and child-bearing adolescents. *Developmental and Behavioral Pediatrics, 13,* 128–136.

Ekman, P., & O'Sullivan, M. (1991). Facial expression: Methods, means and mores. In R. S. Feldman & B. Rime (Eds.), *Fundamentals of non-verbal behavior.* Cambridge: Cambridge University Press.

Elkind, D. (1981). *The hurried child: Growing up too fast, too soon.* Reading, MA: Addison-Wesley.

Galluscio, E. H. (1990). *Biological psychology.* New York: Macmillan.

Geschwind, N. (1979). Specializations of the human brain. *Scientific American, 241,* 180–201.

Gibson, E. J., & Walk, R. D. (1960). The visual cliff. *Scientific American, 202,* 2–9.

Goldsmith, H. H., & Harman, C. (1994). Temperament and attachment: Individuals and relationships. *Current Directions in Psychological Science, 3,* 53–56.

Gottesman, I. I. (1991). *Schizophrenia and genetics: The origins of madness.* New York: Freeman.

Green, R. (1987). *The sissy boy syndrome and the development of homosexuality.* New Haven: Yale University Press.

Gurman, E. B., & Balban, M. (1990). Self-evaluation of physical attractiveness as a function of self-esteem and defensiveness. *Journal of Social Behavior and Personality, 5,* 575–580.

Hamer, D. H., Hu, S., Magnuson V. L., Hu, N., & Pattatucci, A. M. (1993). A linkage between DNA markers on the X chromosome and male sexual orientation. *Science, 261,* 321–327.

Harris, J. R., & Liebert, R. M. (1991). *The child: A contemporary view of development* (3rd ed.). Englewood Cliffs, NJ: Prentice-Hall.

Hellige, J. B. (1990). Hemispheric asymmetry. *Annual Review of Psychology, 41,* 55–80.

Hofferth, S. L., & Hayes, C. D. (Eds.) (1987). *Risking the future.* Vol. 2. *Adolescent sexuality, pregnancy, and childbearing,* Washington, DC: National Academy of Science.

Intons-Peterson, M. J. (1988). *Gender concepts of Swedish and American youth* (p. 47). Hillsdale, NJ: Erlbaum.

Jones, M. C. (1965). Psychological correlates of somatic development. *Child Development, 36,* 899–911.

Kagan, J. (1984). *The nature of the child.* New York: Basic Books.

Kagan, J., & Snidman, N. (1991). Infant predictors of inhibited and uninhibited profiles. *Psychological Science, 2,* 4–44.

Kegeles, S. M., Adler, N. E., & Irvin, C. E. (1988). Sexually active adolescents and condoms: Changes over one year in knowledge, attitudes

and use. *American Journal of Public Health, 78,* 460–461.

Kimble, G. A. (1990). Mother nature's bag of tricks is small. *Psychological Science, 1,* 36–41.

Kimura, D. (1986, November). Male brain, female brain: The hidden difference. *Psychology Today,* 68–75.

Kimura, D. (1989, November). How sex hormones boost—or cut—intellectual ability. *Psychology Today, 62–66.*

Kinsey, A. C., Pomeroy, W. B., Martin, C. E., & Gebhard, P. H. (1953). *Sexual behavior in the human female.* Philadelphia: Saunders.

Klaus, M., & Kennell, J. (1982). *Parent-infant bonding.* St. Louis, MO: C. V. Mosby.

Lagerspetz, K. (1964). *Studies on the aggressive behavior of mice.* Helsinki: Suomalainen Tiedeakatemia.

Lampl, M., Veidhuis, J. D., & Johnson, M. L. (1992). Saltation and stasis: A model of human growth. *Science, 258,* 801–803.

Lazarus, R. S. (1991). Cognition and motivation in emotion. *American Psychologist, 46,* 352–367.

Lenneberg, E. (1967). *Biological foundations of language.* New York: Wiley.

LeVay, S. (1991). A difference in hypothalamic structures between heterosexual and homosexual men. *Science, 253,* 1034–1036.

Loehlin, J. C. (1989). Partitioning environmental and genetic contributions to behavioral development. *American Psychologist, 44,* 1285–1292.

MacLachlan, R. (1981). Language development. In R. C. Sprinthall & N. A. Sprinthall (Eds.), *Educational psychology: A developmental approach.* Reading, MA: Addison-Wesley.

Malina, R. M. (1982). Motor development in the early years. In S. G. Moore and C. R. Cooper (Eds.), *The young child.* Vol 3: *Reviews of research* (pp. 211–230). Washington, DC: National Association for the Education of Young Children.

Marano, H. E. (1985). Biology is one key to the bonding of mothers and babies. In H. E. Fitzgerald and M. G. Walraven (Eds.), *Human development* (pp. 85–86). Guilford, CT: Dushkin.

Maratsos, M. (1979). Is there language after puberty? *Contemporary Psychology, 24(6),* 456.

Maratsos, M. (1983). Some current issues in the study of the acquisition of grammar. In P. Mussen (Ed.), *Handbook of child psychology* (4th ed.), (Vol. 4). New York: Wiley.

Masters, W. H., & Johnson, V. E. (1966). *Human sexual response.* Boston: Little, Brown.

Maurer, D., & Salapatek, P. (1976). Developmental changes in the scanning of faces by young infants. *Child Development, 47,* 523–527.

McClearn, G. E., Plomin, R., Gora-Maslak, G., &

Crabbe, J. C. (1991). The gene chase in behavioral science. *Psychological Science, 2,* 222–229.

Nelson, R. J. (1995). *An introduction to behavioral endocrinology.* Sunderland, MA: Sinauer Associates.

Nora, J. J., & Fraser, F. C. (1989). *Medical genetics: Principles and practice.* Philadelphia: Lea and Febiger.

Pedlow, R., Sanson, A., Prior, M., & Oberklaid, F. (1993). Stability of maternally reported temperament from infancy to 8 years. *Developmental Psychology, 29,* 998–1007.

Pillard, R., & Weinrich, J. (1987). Cited in *Psychology Today* (April), 66. Also in *Archives of General Psychiatry, 43,* 808–812.

Plomin, R. (1990). The role of inheritance in behavior. *Science, 248,* 183–188.

Pollack, R. (1995). *The language and meaning of DNA.* Boston: Houghton Mifflin.

Quadrel, M. J., Fischoff, B., & Davis, W. (1993). Adolescent invulnerability. *American Psychologist, 48,* 102–116.

Rakic, P. (1988). Specification of cerebral cortical areas. *Science, 241,* 170–176.

Restak, R. M. (1979). *The brain: The last frontier* (p. 205). Garden City, NY: Doubleday.

Restak, R. M. (1988). *The mind.* New York: Bantam Books.

Richards, J., & Rader, N. (1981). Crawling-onset age predicts cliff avoidance in infants. *Journal of Experimental Psychology: Human Perception and Performance, 7,* 382–387.

Rinn, W. E. (1991). Neuropsychology of facial expression. In R. S. Feldman & B. Rime (Eds.), *Fundamental of non-verbal behavior.* Cambridge: Cambridge University Press.

Rubenstein, C. (1994, April 28). *New York Times,* C4.

Sadker, M., & Sadker, D. (1994). *Failing at fairness: How America's schools cheat girls.* New York: Charles Scribner.

Scarr, S., & Kidd, K. K. (1983). Developmental behavior genetics. In P. H. Mussen (Ed.), *Handbook of child psychology* (4th ed.). New York: Wiley.

Shirley, M. M. (1931). *The first two years.* Vol. 1: *Postural and locomotor development.* Minneapolis: University of Minnesota Press.

Shirley, M. M. (1933). *The first two years.* Vol. 3: *Personality manifestations.* Minneapolis: University of Minnesota Press.

Siegel, O. (1982). Personality development in adolescence. In B. B. Wolman (Ed.), *Handbook of developmental psychology.* Englewood Cliffs, NJ: Prentice-Hall.

Siegler, R. S. (1991). *Children's thinking* (2d ed.), Englewood Cliffs, NJ: Prentice-Hall.

Simmons, R. G., & Blyth, D. A. (1987). *Moving into adolescence.* Hawthorne, NY: Aldine.

Smolak, L. (1986). *Infancy.* Englewood Cliffs, NJ: Prentice-Hall.

Spelt, D. K. (1948). The conditioning of the human fetus in utero. *Journal of Experimental Psychology, 38,* 338–346.

Steinberg, L., & Dornbusch, S. M. (1991). Negative correlates of part-time employment during adolescence: Replication and elaboration. *Developmental Psychology, 27,* 304–313.

Steinhausen, H. C., Williams, J., & Spohr, H. (1993). Long-term psychopathological and cognitive outcome of children with fetal alcohol syndrome. *Journal of the American Academy of Child and Adolescent Psychiatry, 32,* 990–994.

Tavris, C. (1992). *The mismeasure of women.* New York: Simon and Schuster.

Tronick, E. Z. (1989). Emotions and emotional communication in infants. *American Psychologist, 44,* 112–119.

Trotter, R. J. (1983 August). Baby face. *Psychology Today, 44,* 12–20.

Tryon, R. C. (1940). Genetic differences in maze-learning ability in rats. *Yearbook of the National Society for Studies in Education, 39,* 111–119.

Wada, J., Clarke, R., & Hamm, A. (1975). Cerebral hemispheric symmetry in humans. *Archives of Neurology, 32,* 239–246.

Walsh, C., & Cepko, C. L. (1992). Widespread dispersion of neuronal clones across functional regions of the cerebral cortex. *Science, 255,* 434–440.

Wechsler, D. (1958). *The measurement and appraisal of adult intelligence* (4th ed.) (p. 150). Baltimore: Williams and Wilkins.

Widerstrom, A. H., Mowder, B. A., & Sandall, S. R. (1991). *At risk and handicapped newborns and infants.* Englewood Cliffs, NJ: Prentice-Hall.

Wilson, J. A. R., Robeck, M. C., & Michael, W. B. (1969). *Psychological foundations of learning and teaching* (pp. 188–189). New York: McGraw-Hill.

Wimer, R. E., & Wimer, C. C. (1985). Animal behavior genetics: A search for the biological foundations of behavior. *Annual Review of Psychology, 36,* 171–218.

Zelazo, P. R., & Barr, R. G. (1989). Do challenges to developmental paradigms compel changes in practice? An introduction. In P. R. Zelazo & R. Barr (Eds.), *Challenges to developmental paradigms: Implications for theory, assessment, and treatment.* Hillsdale, NJ: Erlbaum.

Zimbardo, P. G. (1992). *Psychology and life* (13th ed.). New York: HarperCollins.

4

EARLY EXPERIENCE

"As the twig is bent, so grows the tree." "You can't teach an old dog new tricks." "Train them during their formative years." These statements and others like them attest to the fact that we have long recognized the significance of early experience for growth and development. Yet it is only within this century that we have come to appreciate how important **early experience** really is. It is also only recently that we have begun to recognize in how many ways our psychological and physical beings are affected by the amount and quality of our early experience.

Psychologists have for some time recognized the importance of early experience for emotional growth. Freud, for example, argued in many papers at the turn of the century that personality development is a product of one's childhood. Many educators agreed with this view, and special schools were designed to enhance emotional and personal growth during those crucial years. In England, A. S. Neill established **Summerhill,** a boarding school at which the major emphasis is on encouraging healthy emotional adjustment (Neill, 1969). At Summerhill every student participates in school and curriculum decisions. No classes, books, or exams are required. Free expression of ideas and talent is encouraged, and

only minimal restraints are placed on the children in all areas of their lives.

Although maybe not as extremely permissive, there are many schools like Summerhill throughout the world, and it is safe to say that most schools today, not just the Summerhills, have been influenced to some degree by this alternative to the traditional, more authoritarian approach to education. The problem is that as psychologists learn more about human development, educators sometimes respond too zealously. When a new theory has been embraced indiscriminately, the resulting curriculum may emphasize one particular area but neglect other important areas. For example, some educators have argued that schools based on the Summerhill model may be nurturing emotional growth at the expense of intellectual growth. Some of the concepts underlying the Summerhill model are still with us today, in the arguments of some educators that children should have to learn only what they feel like learning and that the entire curriculum from kindergarten through graduate school should follow the inclinations of the children and not of their parents, teachers, or school administrators (Dultz, 1994).

Despite the fact that early experience has long

been considered critical in shaping emotional development, it wasn't until quite recently that psychologists began to recognize the importance of these same early years on intellectual development.

THE CRITICAL TIME HYPOTHESIS: THE KEY TO THE NATURE-NURTURE PUZZLE

The nature-nurture issue remained unresolved for many years because it was stated as an either/or proposition: the hereditarians emphasized the importance of inborn traits, while the environmentalists stressed the importance of external factors. And neither side fully recognized the importance of the third dimension, time. Konrad Lorenz's research on imprinting, described in Chapter 2, made it clear that learning, if it is to be effective, requires not only a hereditary potential and an environmental encounter, but an encounter at the appropriate time. If

There are critical, optimal periods when children can most easily be taught certain motor skills. For example, it is best to teach a child to roller-skate at the same time he or she is learning to walk. However, development of some motor skills is actually retarded by early training.

the encounter occurs either too soon or too late, no learning or minimal learning occurs.

Over 60 years ago, a forward-looking psychologist, Myrtle McGraw, did a comprehensive study of human development, using a pair of twin boys as subjects (McGraw, 1935). One of the twins, Johnny, was given a great amount of early training in a wide variety of activities. The other twin, Jimmy, was given no practice in these activities until months later. McGraw found that special, early practice had little or no effect on some behaviors, such as creeping, hanging by the hands, grasping objects, or even walking. Although Johnny was given stepping practice almost from birth, both twins took their first halting steps alone at 9 months, and both learned to walk almost simultaneously at 12 months. McGraw called behaviors such as these phylogenetic activities and concluded that they are not influenced very much by the environment or by special practice. However, with regard to certain special skills that McGraw called ontogenetic activities, the trained twin, Johnny, learned faster than his brother. Johnny began learning to roller-skate when he was 12 months old, just when he was learning to walk, and by 14 months he was both skating and walking with considerable grace. Jimmy did not begin skating lessons until he was 22 months old, and he did not profit nearly as much from this late training. Thus, delaying the training made it more difficult to learn this skill. The development of other motor skills, however, was actually damaged by early training. Johnny was given special training in tricycling when he was 11 months old and displayed little progress until he was about 19 or 20 months old, when he suddenly improved rather dramatically. Jimmy began tricycling when he was 22 months old, learned the skill quickly and efficiently, and became superior to his pretrained brother. The twin with the early training formed poor habits and was unable to develop the skill as well as the twin whose training was delayed. McGraw concluded that there are optimal periods during development when special training will assure the full acquisition of various motor skills.

McGraw was the first psychologist to conceptualize human development in terms of critical periods, and although her views were not widely accepted during the heyday of American behaviorism, they now have a decidedly commonsense appeal. In childrearing she advocated a middle road between constantly urging the child to practice new activities and just sitting back and allowing nature to take its own sweet time. Forcing children into activities before the critical period, when their nerves and muscles are simply not ready, is not only useless but,

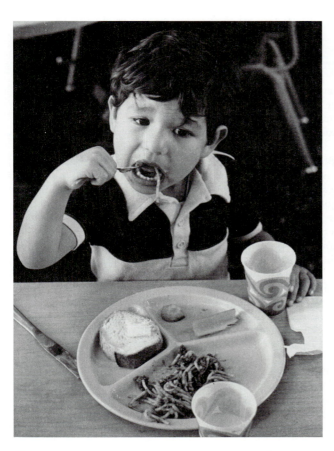

The teachable moment and readiness are central to the problems of growth.

more important, may even be damaging. McGraw died in 1988, but her insights into human development have proved to be an enduring legacy.

In another classic study, Josephine R. Hilgard provided a special 12-week practice period for a group of two-year-old children on such motor tasks as stair climbing and cutting with scissors. Another group of two-year-olds was given the training for only one week, the last week of the experiment. The children in the second group, older and presumably more mature when their training began, initially learned these tasks more quickly than did the other group, but they never fully caught up. The group with the early (and longer) training maintained superiority at the experiment's end (Hilgard, 1932).

Much research is still needed to provide hard data on precisely when the various critical learning periods occur. We do know, however, that critical periods generally coincide with the periods of most

rapid growth. John P. Scott has defined the critical period as a "time when a large effect can be produced by a smaller change in conditions than in any later or earlier period in life." Scott further maintains that "there must be changes taking place within the animal which are correlated with time and hence account for the existence of critical periods" (Scott, 1968). Thus, the concept of critical periods has profound importance in education. We must hope to catch the child at exactly that time when environmental encounters will most effectively allow his or her hereditary potential to flourish. Damage can be done, impairment can occur, if we are either too early or too late.

OBSERVATIONS AND THEORIES ON EARLY EXPERIENCE

The Berkeley Growth Study

In 1929, **Nancy Bayley,** another in the tradition of brilliant female psychologists specializing in growth and development, and her colleagues at the University of California at Berkeley began a longitudinal research project known as the *Studies in the Development of Young Children* (Bayley, 1940). In fact data are still being collected on the original subjects who are still alive, now in their mid-seventies. Although the study has contributed vast amounts of new data and fresh insights on the flow of human development, we will focus on only four specific observations.

1. *IQs are not constant.* Bayley's results have challenged the belief cherished by some psychologists that one's IQ is a unitary, immutable trait. Bayley found considerable variation in measured intelligence over long periods of time; in other words, IQ is not indelibly etched in the brain at birth but instead ebbs and flows as a result of environmental circumstances.

2. *IQ variability is greatest during the first few years of life.* By comparing correlations between IQs measured at various ages, Bayley found that the older the child, the greater the IQ stability. This evidence foreshadowed the central feature of Benjamin Bloom's hypothesis, discussed in the next section.

3. *Intellectual ability may continue to grow throughout life.* Bayley's data also indicate that intellectual ability does not top out in the late teens or early twenties but may continue to increase at least up to age 50. Again, whether an adult's intellect grows or declines seems to be a function of

NANCY BAYLEY

In 1966 Nancy Bayley became the first woman to win the American Psychological Association's prestigious Distinguished Scientific Contribution award. Her citation praised her for "the enterprise, pertinacity and insight with which she has studied human growth over long segments of the life cycle . . . Her studies have enriched psychology with enduring contributions to the measurement and meaning of intelligence . . . Her participation in a number of major programs of developmental research is a paradigm of the conjoint efforts which are essential in a field whose problems span the generations."[a]

Nancy Bayley was born in 1899 in a small town, called The Dalles, in northern Oregon. She attended local schools there, earned her B.S. and M.A. degrees from the University of Washington, and received her Ph.D. in psychology from Iowa State in 1926, just two years after completing her M.A. degree. For the next two years, she taught at the University of Wyoming, and in 1928 began teaching at the University of California at Berkeley. During the following year she began her famous longitudinal Berkeley Growth Study, starting with 61 healthy newborns. Testing and retesting this group over the years, both psychologically and physically, she produced many fresh and startling insights into the complex phenomenon of human growth.

Among her other accomplishments, Bayley developed a test of infant development, the Bayley Mental Development Index (BMDI), which attempts to measure both the intellectual and physical growth of infants from ages 2 to 30 months. BMDI scores at age one year correlate closely with IQ scores taken at age three years (Rose et al., 1989).

In 1954 Bayley became chief of the Child Development Section at the National Institute of Mental Health in Bethesda, Maryland, but she returned periodically to Berkeley to locate and test her sample subjects for the Berkeley Growth Study. In 1964 she returned to Berkeley to serve both as the administrator of the newly formed Harold E. Jones Child Study Center and as a research psychologist at the University of California. She retired in 1971.

In 1971 Nancy Bayley won the G. Stanley Hall Award, a special award presented by the American Psychological Association's Division of Developmental Psychology. She has written nearly 100 articles in her field, and it is clear that as her 1929 sample ages, it will continue to enrich psychology's book of knowledge.

[a]   *American Psychologist* (1966), p. 1191.

---

environmental stimulation. High school dropouts who spend all their working life in menial, undemanding occupations are less likely to experience intellectual growth than people who work in more mentally demanding occupations. More recent research has validated Bayley's findings. Older adults who remain intellectually curious and active typically maintain a high level of cognitive functioning (Datan et al., 1987).

4. *The components of intellect change with age level.* Perhaps Bayley's most provocative contribution is her suggestion that intellectual development in childhood occurs in qualitatively different stages. In her view, the fact that a child's growth score gradually shifts in strength from area to area supports the notion that changes occur in the organization of intellectual factors from one age to another. This view is consistent with those of Jean Piaget and others, presented in the next chapter.

Bloom's Hypothesis

Benjamin Bloom has sorted and analyzed countless studies on intellectual growth and, using the accumulated data, has plotted a negatively accelerated growth curve for intellectual development. He has

SPOTLIGHT ON PARENTS

The Parents' Turn

At parent-teacher meetings, parents are quick to ask what they can do to help. As the teacher you might start by pointing out that parents should take the time to talk to their children, even when they seem incommunicative. Ask the parent if the following is an all-too-common home scenario (Hellmich, 1994);

Parent: What happened in school today:
Child: I don't know. I guess nothin'.
Parent: Who did you play with?
Child: I don't know. I guess nobody.

If the parents respond with an embarrassed but knowing smile, urge them to try to catch their children when they are ready to chat (Craig, 1994). Also, gently remind the parents that they really have to ask the right questions, and then *listen* to the answers. Explain that right after school may not be a good time. Children are tired, and they want to play or watch TV. A better time is when children are having a snack, or at the dinner table, or even just before bedtime. Some children enjoy talking while in the car. When children are ready, however, parents shouldn't force the conversation into a police interrogation with general questions like "What happened in school today?" Show them how to be more specific, with questions like "How is Peter, the pet rabbit?" or with questions following up on something the child has talked about the day before, like "How is Billy's broken ankle? Did you sign the cast?" If the child gives some vague answers about the day, try asking funny questions like "You mean the zebra didn't visit you today at school?" The child might then say, "No Mommy, we played with blocks today." More specific questions can go on from there. Also, gently tell parents to pay some attention to what comes home in pockets or backpacks. Taking out the items in a backpack may reveal a treasure trove of information as to what's going on, such as whether there was a school assembly or a special class project. This can set the stage for questions about the items and events. Suggest to parents that when they are on a school visit they take note of the projects on the walls of the classroom or on the bulletin boards outside the classroom, then ask about them. One educator urges parents to use the following techniques for getting beyond the busy signal that so often occurs in parent-child communications (Greenspan, 1994).

1. Plan floor time with your child, that is, a special period of at least 30 minutes a day set aside for the parent and child. Follow the child's lead in spontaneous, unstructured talk or play.
2. Have problemsolving discussions. Help your child work through issues and problems. For a 6-year-old it might be that she wants to stay up until 11 o'clock. For a 10-year-old, you might talk about why he avoids homework. The point is to listen to your child and then offer your point of view. You can always pull rank, but giving a child the change to verbalize hidden thoughts can be helpful.
3. Practice empathy. If you can truly empathize, your child will discover that talking to you is an emotionally reassuring experience. Empathy doesn't mean always agreeing, but it does mean understanding.
4. Be firm about setting limits. Knowing the house rules helps the child feel secure, and a secure child will be a far better communicator.

found that, with increasing age, there is a decreasingly positive effect from a beneficial environment. Three-year-old children profit far more from enriching experiences than do seven- or eight-year-old children. Accordingly, Bloom argues that beneficial early experience is absolutely essential for cognitive growth. Almost two-thirds of our ultimate cognitive ability is formed by the time we are six years old, the age, incidentally, when most children are just entering school. By the time formal education begins, the child's potential for further intellectual development is beginning to slow. Bloom insists that earlier intervention is therefore required, especially among disadvantaged groups. Experience has its most profound effect very early in life, during the period of most rapid growth (Bloom, 1964).

This finding is consistent with Scott's argument regarding critical periods. Scott feels that critical periods occur when rapid organization of some kind is going on within the individual. Those mental changes that take place during a period of rapid development often occur easily and accidentally and then become a fixed and fairly permanent feature of the newly stabilized organization. Scott also reasons that any time we form new relationships, especially social relationships, can be a critical period for that relationship. Since most new relationships occur in early childhood, this is when most critical periods should occur. However, major new relationships also develop in adolescence and in adulthood. In fact, one of the most critical periods is adolescence, when young people may form their first sexual relationships. Sexual problems in adulthood may stem from events during adolescence. Probably another major critical period, for both parents, is the birth of the first child.

Bloom concludes that not only does lack of an enriched environment itself hinder a child's intellectual development, but the loss of precious time is especially harmful because there is no way to compensate for it later on. Just as in the case of Lorenz's goslings, there may be critical periods for intellectual development; once the period is over, new stimuli have less and less effect.

Stimulus Variety: The Basic Ingredient

After reviewing the literature on early experience, J. McV. Hunt concluded that early stimulus deprivation is more likely than early motor restriction to prevent normal motor development (Hunt, 1969). Hunt pointed out, for example, that Hopi children who are reared on cradleboards, and thus are carried about on their mothers' backs with their arm and leg movements almost completely restricted, walk as early as Hopi children reared with full use of their legs. Despite their early motor restriction, the children had a variety of rich sensory input. In a study confirming these findings, Wayne Dennis discovered children in an orphanage in Teheran who had been kept in conditions of extreme isolation; each child lived in a separate, almost soundproof, white cubicle. As a result of this severe sensory restriction, virtually all the children were mentally retarded, despite the fact that most came from literate families of Iran (Dennis, 1960). This finding, of course, is further evidence that intellectual development is a function of both environment and heredity. But the most re-

markable finding of Dennis' study is that these stimulus-deprived children, who had complete motor freedom, were also physically retarded: 60 percent were unable to sit up alone when they were two years old, and 85 percent could not walk when they were four years old.

As Hunt has been insisting for many years, the crucial ingredient in intellectual development is stimulus variety. The more the child hears, sees, and touches, the more the child will *want* to hear, see, and touch, and the more intellectual growth will occur. Motivation can therefore be generated from experience. However, Hunt cautions against suddenly overwhelming a child with stimulus variety. In what he calls the "problem of the match," Hunt points out that the variety of inputs must somehow be matched with the child's present level of growth. Too much stimulus heterogeneity, and the child withdraws in frustration; too little, and the child withdraws in boredom. Children naturally seek a level of optimum variety of stimuli; when they reach this level, children display joy, a spontaneous interest in learning, and continued cognitive growth. This is very similar to **Lev Vygotsky's** concept of the zone of proximal development, that some challenge is needed for maximizing intellectual development. The **zone of proximal development** is the distance between one's present developmental level and the level of potential future development (Vygotsky, 1978).

This growth can be seen in a variety of areas, including language acquisition. Studies of the rate of language development have found that the children who develop language skills earliest are those whose mothers spend the most time speaking directly to them (Smolak & Weinraub, 1983). However, the complexity of maternal speech should be matched to the child's current language level—complex enough to challenge the child, but not so complex that it overwhelms the child and perhaps even delays language development (Gleitman et al., 1984). Thus, intellectual abilities grow and are nourished by **stimulus variety.** The match is between stimulus inputs and the child's present position on the growth continuum, a position that itself results in large measure from the child's own past experiences and environmental encounters. These encounters begin at birth. There is even evidence that some learning takes place while the fetus is still in the uterus (Spelt, 1948). In another fascinating study of this type, babies whose mothers had read a certain passage to them during the last six weeks of pregnancy showed a decided preference for those same word sounds when tested after birth (DeCasper & Spence, 1986).

Bruner insists that a variety of stimuli and a changing environment are necessary for proper cognitive growth.

Bruner on Early Experience

Jerome Bruner, the great Harvard theorist, and one of the first American psychologists to adopt a cognitive point of view, also stresses the importance of early experience. Bruner maintains that cognitive growth depends on a process of model formation: the creation of rules and strategies for coping with the environment. As children develop, they should learn various techniques that will enable them to make maximum use of the information their environments provide. However, for proper cognitive growth to occur, youngsters must be exposed to a variety of stimuli, a shifting environment. Stimulus heterogeneity at an early age is the critical condition for continued cognitive growth (Bruner, 1969).

Piaget on Early Experience

Like Bruner, Jean Piaget (see Chapter 5 and the biography on page 110) was a strong supporter of the importance of rich childhood experience. He saw the developing child as analogous in many ways to a scientist performing experiments on the physical world and personally discovering the principles of mathematical and physical reasoning. That is, Piaget viewed the young child as *acting* on a rather *passive* environment. The more environmental encounters the child has, especially during the first few years of life, the richer the cognitive stage becomes. Some more recent cognitive theories take a more social approach and view the child as similar to an apprentice, learning through participation in problem-solving tasks under the tutelage of more skilled members of society (Rogoff, 1990). And just as the skilled tutor can affect the development of the child, so too can the child's responses alter the behavior of the tutor. Thus, the focus is increasingly on the *interactive* nature of the social contexts and on the manner in which they might be changed by the growing child (Winegar, 1989).

THE BIOLOGICAL BASIS OF EARLY EXPERIENCE

We have seen that psychologists such as Scott, Bloom, Hunt, and Bruner stress the importance of early experience in determining intellectual level. Now it is time to ask whether there is a biological basis for this argument. Are there corresponding physiological changes taking place as a result of a beneficial early environment?

The eminent physiological psychologist **Donald O. Hebb** outlined a theoretical model of the organization of neural activity in the brain (Hebb, 1949). Hebb contended that this organization depends on environmental stimulation, that proper development of the neural arrangements in the brain will not occur unless the developing organism has the opportunity to experience environmental changes.

The A/S Ratio

Hebb noted that there were significant differences among organisms in the proportion of association and sensory areas within the brain. For example, a rat has fewer association areas and more sensory areas than a human. Thus, the rat, that workhorse of American psychology, is more sensory-bound, more responsive to the stimuli in its environment than is the human. The human brain, with its greater number of association areas, is capable of far more and probably many different varieties of learning than the rat brain. Also, the relatively small sensory area makes the human less a creature of the moment, less apt to respond impulsively to every minute environmental change. As we go up the phylogenetic continuum, as the ratio of association areas to sensory areas **(A/S ratio)** increases, the developmental importance of pronounced stimulus heterogeneity also increases. Humans, for example, cannot perceive subtle changes in odor as well as some of the lower primates.

Hebb emphasized the critical importance of early experience on later development, especially on cognitive development. During infancy and early childhood, the human brain is unorganized and capable of only relatively simple forms of learning. As the child experiences more and more environmental stimulation, the brain slowly becomes organized. A group of neurons begins to work as a unit. Hebb called this organized pattern of brain cells a cell assembly. With the formation of a variety of cell assemblies, new learning takes place more quickly. As more and more cell assemblies are formed, a larger organization takes place, producing a series of cell assemblies, called *phase sequences*. Finally, as the phase sequences begin acting in concert, widespread organization of the brain results, and the child is now capable of extremely rapid learning. The difference between a young child in the cell-assembly stage, slowly and painstakingly learning a simple task, and an older child, with a series of smooth-functioning, integrated phase sequences already formed, quickly learning complex relationships and

concepts, is similar to the difference between a do-it-yourself carpenter and an experienced prefab team. The do-it-yourself carpenter may take months to construct a home that the professional crew could complete in days. Hebb was certain that children who spend their first six years in impoverished slum environments never fully make up for their crucial intellectual deficits (Hebb, 1978).

The Evidence from Krech

More direct and even more startling evidence supporting the importance of early experience has been supplied by the exciting and innovative research of David Krech (1969). Responding to evidence that certain drugs, such as Metrazol, may increase an organism's ability to learn, and that other drugs, such as magnesium pemoline, may increase the organism's ability to retain what has been learned (Grosser et al., 1967), Krech reasoned that the reverse might also be true—that is, if chemical agents could effect changes in the learning process, then environmental manipulation might bring about changes in the chemistry of the brain. By selecting 12 pairs of rat twins and randomly assigning them to two groups, Krech was able to control for possible genetic differences. One group of rats was raised in a stimulating environment, in a cage equipped with ladders, running wheels, and other rat toys. These animals were let out of their cages for 30 minutes each day and allowed to explore new territory. They were also trained to perform numerous learning tasks and in general received a rich and varied array of stimulus inputs. The other group of rats was raised in a condition of extreme stimulus homogeneity. These rats lived alone in dimly lit cages, were rarely handled, and were never allowed to explore areas outside the cage. All animals received exactly the same diet.

After about three months all the animals were sacrificed and their brains analyzed morphologically and chemically. If Hebb's theory were valid, the brains of the animals that had been exposed to a wide variety of learning situations should have been anatomically different from the brains of the deprived animals. That is, if the act of learning does indeed form neural cell assemblies and phase sequences, there should have been some physical evidence for this in the brains of the stimulated rats. In fact, the brains of the enriched rats were chemically and structurally different from the brains of their siblings. The cortex (gray matter) was larger, deeper, and heavier in the stimulated rats. Three components have been identified as contributing to this increase in brain size: (1) an increased number of glia cells (possible repositories of memory traces), (2) increased size of the cell bodies and their nuclei, and (3) an increase in the diameter of the blood vessels supplying the cortex.

Chemically, the brains also differed. The brains of the enriched animals showed greater quantities of an important enzyme, acetylcholinesterase, which readies the nerve cells for further neural transmissions. Thus, Krech demonstrated that providing stimulus and response variety during the early life of these animals caused chemical and structural changes in their brains and increased their ability to learn and to solve problems. In a very real sense he may have identified some of the physiological correlates of Hebb's constructs.

Environmental Stimulation for Physiological Development

It is now clear that for proper physiological development to occur, environmental stimulation is necessary; the nervous system and the perceptual apparatus do not mature automatically according to some preset internal clock.

Critics of the early-experience position often fall back on the neurological argument that since no new brain cells are added after birth, the central nervous system must remain unchanged, with or without environmental stimulation. They argue that the baby comes into the world with a full complement of typical brain cells and that, since no new cells are added, the baby must make do with the original equipment. However, as Krech showed, how this original equipment is organized and modified is definitely a function of environmental interactions. Krech proved that structural and chemical changes in the brain resulted from the type of early experience provided. We now know that the newborn brain comes genetically equipped with rules for how learning takes place and thus literally both shapes and is shaped by environmental experiences.

The genetic prewiring of the brain sets various developmental deadlines for the neural circuits to be formed; if the appropriate stimuli are missed at a crucial developmental time, these circuits never become fully formed, or perhaps even formed at all. For example, as we saw in Chapter 3 in the discussion of language acquisition, if the baby hasn't heard some of the sounds unique to the language by certain fixed times, then pronunciation becomes a lifetime problem. By age 10 we become somewhat more hard-wired, and the brain becomes less resilient. By age 10 we have also already created neural maps of perceptions, neural maps that come to reflect our culture and limit our freedom of action. To some ex-

tent we are prisoners of our genes, as well as prisoners of our environment. But whereas we cannot choose our genes, we can often choose our environments, seeking out more or less stimulation. As Hunt and Vygotsky have said, curiosity and discovery are intimately linked both to overall cognitive development and to momentary cognitive ability. As children become more acquainted with their stimulus surroundings, the threshold for the challenge of new stimuli begins to rise, and they search out ever more complex situations. If the stimulus pattern remains constant, they will lose interest. Thus, when the level of stimulus difficulty is just above threshold, children become increasingly energized by the curiosity drive, but when satiation occurs they withdraw in boredom (Loewenstein, 1994).

Some researchers in physiological psychology have challenged the traditional view that newborns have all the nerve cells they will ever get. For example, it has been discovered that tiny neurons (microneurons) do arise in the brains of young animals after birth. In addition, it has been found that in the adult mouse brain some immature neurons are held in reserve in case of neural damage to existing cells (Weiss & Reynolds, 1992). Technology has even advanced to the point where brain cells are now being produced in test tubes, hopefully for use as transplants in the event that normal brain cells later become damaged or perhaps even die.

Neurons send out branches—axons and dendrites—so that neural impulses can travel from one neuron to the next (see Figure 4.1). The junction between the axon of one neuron and the dendrite of the next is called the synapse. The neuron sends a message out along one axon, and the dendrite of the next neuron picks up the message at the synapse. Often the dendrite, the receiving branch, sends out a physical projection called a dendritic spine. This is something like adding another length to a TV antenna in order to get a better picture. Neurologists have found, however, that if these synapses are not used, the dendritic spines wither away and finally disappear. If a synapse is used frequently, new dendritic spines appear.

With increased use, the actual physical structures of the synaptic endings are altered so that they become more likely to transmit their neural messages. It's as though the size and complexity of the antenna were a function of how often the TV set was used. It has also been found that sensory apparatus must be stimulated by the environment in order to develop properly. Neurons on the retina of the eye may wither away unless they are given visual stimulation.

And what is behaviorism's answer to this wave of evidence in support of enriched early experience?

FIGURE 4.1   Neural impulses travel from one neuron to the next along the branches—the axons and dendrites—of the neuron.

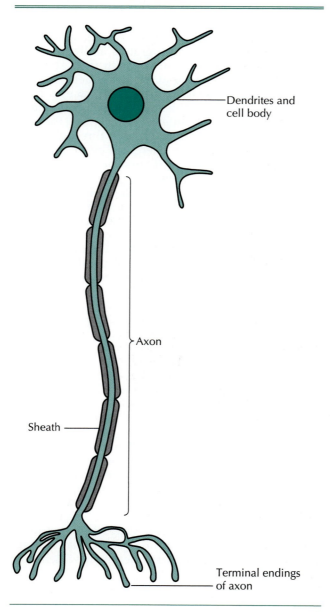

Dendrites and cell body

Axon

Sheath

Terminal endings of axon

Skinner's Air Crib: Healthful but Unstimulating

The late B. F. Skinner, still the world's most influential behaviorist, in 1968 urged parents to raise their children in his invention, the air crib. The air crib was an "air-conditioned, temperature-controlled, germ-free, sound-proof compartment in which the baby can sleep and play without blankets or clothing other than a diaper" (Rice, 1968, p. 27). While in this cubicle, the baby was less likely to catch cold or to suffer from heat rash. However, the air crib also created a constant environment, one unlikely to provide the enriching stimulus variety so important to intellectual development.

HEAD START'S SUCCESS

What proof do we have that these theories and studies of intellectual growth have any validity in the real world of the schoolchild? Hasn't the early-experience theory been tested in the Head Start program, and been found wanting? Let's look at the facts. Head Start, begun in 1965, has been providing educational, social, and nutritional benefits for children between ages three and five. About 750,000 children participate in this government-funded program each year (Kassebaum, 1994). Ninety percent of these children come from families living below the poverty level (Horn, 1990). The first director of Head Start, Edward Zigler, still believes that the program has had and continues to promise long-term positive effects (Zigler, 1990). Yet almost from its inception, Head Start has faced criticism. The Westinghouse Learning Corporation and Ohio University released a highly critical evaluation of Head Start as early as 1969. Later, there was general agreement with assertions such as H. M. Levin's that "good preschool programs are able to produce salutary increases in IQ for disadvantaged children, but these improvements are not maintained when the children enter the primary grades" (Levin, 1977). Since then, however, the evidence seems to suggest that the early critics may have spoken too soon.

The Head Start Synthesis Project of 1983 analyzed the outcomes from virtually all Head Start programs up to that time and concluded that Head Start could be isolated as a causal variable in improving intellectual performance (Hubbell, 1983). In fact, the report found that Head Start programs have produced improvements over the years, especially in terms both of the intellectual gains measured when the children entered regular school and, more important, in the tendency of those gains to persist.

The Perry Preschool Program

The Perry Preschool Program of Ypsilanti, Michigan, has reported the results of a longitudinal study of

Skinner's daughter Debbie is shown here in the air crib he invented.

Head Start participants there who have been followed over the years from ages 3 and 4 to age 19 (Berrueta-Clement et al., 1984). The curriculum for the program was especially designed to provide a wide variety of stimulus inputs without overwhelming the children. Most of the evidence presented here is based on the first two entering groups, from 1965 and 1966.

Although the experimental and control groups were measured at regular intervals over the years, most of the outcome data presented below are based on the measures taken when the participants had reached age 19. The main finding, in brief, is that Head Start has dramatic long-term effectiveness and that a quality preschool program can change the lives of low-income, educationally at-risk children and their families.

Increased school success   Youngsters who had attended the preschool program showed a significant increase in overall school success, as measured by the following factors:

1. Better academic grades.
2. Fewer failing marks.
3. Fewer absences in elementary school.
4. Fewer special-education placements.
5. Higher scores on the Adult Performance Level (APL) Survey, a standardized test developed by the American College Testing Program for assessing the skills needed for educational and economic success in modern society.
6. Greater likelihood of graduating from high school.

7. Greater likelihood of continuing education after high school. Individuals who were tested at age 27 were achieving more and were more apt to have gone to college (Schweinhart et al., 1993).

8. A more favorable attitude toward high school. This finding is particularly important, since it reinforces the claim that early childhood education increases the efficiency of later schooling.

IQ differences   Although preschool participants in the Perry Program showed significantly higher Stanford-Binet IQs on entering first grade, the difference narrowed by the time they reached fourth grade. It may be that ages three and four are too late to effect dramatic IQ improvement, but not too late to provide the enrichment for disadvantaged children to do better in school in the long run.

Socioeconomic success   Those who participated in the preschool program generally showed marked increases in socioeconomic success at age 19, as measured by two factors: (1) increased employment and (2) less reliance on welfare, food stamps, or other assistance programs.

Social responsibility   Another long-term consequence of the Perry Program was an increase in social responsibility. Those who participated in Head Start were found to have (1) fewer police arrests, both as juveniles and as adults, (2) fewer out-of-wedlock pregnancies, and (3) greater desire to undertake helping activities for family and friends, such as cooking meals, mowing lawns, making repairs around the house, and caring for children.

From these data the study's principal investigators build a strong case for the cost effectiveness of the preschool program. The cost of the Head Start program to taxpayers is more than offset by reduction in the later costs of special education, welfare, and especially costs associated with crime, both to the state and to the potential victims. For a small up-front investment, society can reap enormous and recurring dividends.

New Jersey and Oregon Studies

Another study of the effects of Head Start, conducted among black children in New Jersey and Oregon, found that although the immediate advantages in cognitive and analytic skills following exposure to the program were powerful, the effects tended to diminish over time. For example, follow-up tests showed that although the Head Start children maintained educationally substantive gains, the effects were not as large as those found immediately following the intervention (Lee et al., 1990). This lessening of the effects was attributed to the fact that the Head Start children, typically the poorest of the poor, usually go to the lowest socioeconomic public schools and are likely to receive less favorable treatment in such schools (resulting in reduced learning opportunities). Nor can we expect, as Zigler has said, to completely inoculate children in only one year against all the ravages of an early childhood of deprivation (Zigler, 1987).

The Milwaukee Project

The Milwaukee Project attempted to stimulate cognitive growth by providing systematic and structured training to low-IQ slum children. This training began early, as soon as mother and child returned home from the hospital. In 1981 the project directors reported that the significant IQ differences between the children involved in the program and a control group of children not enrolled were being sustained in favor of the preschool group, at least up to age 10 (Garber & Heber, 1981).

The Carolina Abecedarian Project

The Carolina Abecedarian Project has been providing enriched environments for children from early infancy up to preschool. The results have shown that at age 12, seven years after children left the program, the experimental group was still almost 5 IQ points higher than a matched control group (Campbell & Ramey, 1994).

Does School Attendance Matter?

Children who attend school regularly rather than intermittently score higher on IQ tests, and it has long been known that IQ scores tend to drop off during the summer vacation months and rise again in the late fall (Cecci, 1991).

It is now fairly certain that early experience is one of the key ingredients in cognitive growth. Had we known this years ago, the disparity between the "good" and "bad" Kallikaks might have been avoided, or at least ameliorated. But although it now seems fairly conclusive that stimulus conditions can be provided that will allow for maximum intellectual development, the importance of providing con-

SPOTLIGHT ON EARLY EXPERIENCE

The First Three Years

One of the most influential advocates of the importance of early experience in learning is Harvard psychologist Burton White. White has long insisted that intellectual and psychological competence are largely determined during the first three years (White, 1975). Indeed, White asserts that the critical period for proper psychological growth may be as short as the first 8 to 18 months. Growth during the first 8 months seems to take care of itself, for early development is so heavily influenced by biological factors that, aside from normal care, there is little the mother can do either to arrest or to facilitate this physiological process. From 8 to 18 months, however, the mother's personal resources are crucial to later cognitive and emotional growth. Mothers of competent children are alert and responsive to their infant's needs without being overly intrusive. The competent mother provides reassurance, guidance, and attention whenever the child needs them, but does not needlessly intervene just to prove to herself that she's a supermother. Although White recommends that the child be provided with suitable toys and materials in the home, he believes that the real key to sound growth is based on the quality of the child's interpersonal exchanges, especially with the mother. Finally, White even instructs mothers to encourage their children to adopt a certain amount of competitiveness by exposing the child to competitive situations where there is no implication of punishment.

ditions designed to promote emotional growth must not be overlooked.

Critical Perspectives

The early-experience school of thought has critics. Herrnstein and Murray, for example, have argued that if we do provide a uniformly beneficial environment for a number of children, we will simply make intelligence more susceptible to hereditary influence than it would otherwise be (Herrnstein, 1971; Herrnstein & Murray, 1994).

Admittedly, individual differences arising in a uniform environment would have to be due to heredity. But so would all individual differences arising in a uniformly bad environment. In the first situation, however, IQs would fluctuate around a high average value, whereas in the second, IQs would scatter around a low average value. Surely it would be more pleasant for the children themselves, and more beneficial to society in general, to let heredity decide differences among high IQs than among low ones (Grosser & Sprinthall, 1972).

A related theory argues that the "bottom half is always below average"; that is, if all IQs were raised by improved educational techniques, the lower half would still be at the bottom of the social order, and nobody's social status would be changed. This argument implies that society need not try to help the lower half by improving educational opportunities, for the result would only be to freeze present social arrangements. Such a line of reasoning requires comment.

A large factor in social status is occupation. Limitations of intelligence disqualify an individual from ever becoming a good engineer, physician, or attorney, for example. Suppose there were a threshold IQ for each occupation. Someone with a very high intelligence will have all the intellectual requirements for being everything from a ditchdigger to an engineer. Someone with a very low intelligence will not qualify for higher middle-status occupations. Therefore, the higher the IQ, the more occupations the individual is qualified to fill. But here we arrive at an interesting point. When we consider IQ as an occupational requirement, it is the absolute level of intelligence that matters, not the relative level. If the whole IQ scale were lifted above the threshold for the job of power lineman, those jobs requiring less intelligence would all share the same low IQ status, but social-class standing might not seem as important. Many occupational differences would be due not to limitations of intelligence but to differences in preference and interest, surely a more satisfying outcome.

A FINAL COMMENT

You may be wondering whether, if early experience is so significant in determining intellectual ability, there will be anything left for you to accomplish by the time the child reaches school age. Remember: The cognitive growth that takes place during those critical first six years simply provides the base for the intellectual structure the classroom teacher must build. The child should be allowed to begin formal schooling with the necessary background of cognitive skills so that she or he can take full advantage of the formal educational process. The goal of the early-experience theorists and practitioners is to prepare the child to profit fully from the educational experience. The job of the teacher, then, becomes more challenging, more stimulating, and less frustrating when the child enters school equipped with the necessary tools to learn. Educational experiences pick up where early experience leaves off, and studies have shown clearly that the quality of the educational experience influences both the rate and maximum level of cognitive growth achieved by an individual.

SUMMARY

Although psychologists have long pointed to the importance of early experience for emotional growth, only recently has the same attention been paid to cognitive or intellectual growth. McGraw's work in the 1930s showed that certain activities could best be learned during certain early critical periods. Similarly, Bayley's Berkeley Growth Study was aimed at pinpointing some of the changes that occur during the process of intellectual growth. Later, Bloom concluded that with increasing age, environmental influences have less and less effect on intellectual growth. Children at age three, for example, profit more from enriching experiences than children at age nine or ten. Almost two-thirds of one's ultimate cognitive growth occurs by age six.

Hunt sees stimulus variety as the crucial ingredient in cognitive growth. In the "problem of the match," Hunt points to the importance of matching the proper amount of stimulus variety to the child's present position on the cognitive-growth continuum. This is similar to Vygotsky's concept of the *zone of proximal development*—the distance between a child's present development level and that child's level of potential future development. According to Vygotsky, some degree of cognitive challenge is needed to maximize intellectual development.

In their explanatory systems of how and when cognitive growth occurs, both Piaget and Bruner have stressed the importance of sensory inputs and environmental encounters in the early years.

Hebb focuses on the internal physiological changes that occur during cognitive growth and development. He describes the neural organization that occurs in the brain as the child's ability to learn increases. At birth the brain cells are relatively unorganized, and the cellular organization occurs as a result of the child's own series of learning experiences. In support of this view, Krech's study of rats showed that the structure and chemical composition of the brain result in part from the quality and quantity of an organism's early experience. Physiological development requires early environmental stimulation.

Long-term evidence from the Head Start programs is just now beginning to surface. In one study, the Perry Preschool Program, 19-year-olds who had been in the program were compared with a control group of youths who had not. On virtually every measure the program had positive effects, ranging from an increase in academic ability and achievement to a decrease in criminal activity. Evidence from other studies, such as the Milwaukee Project, has raised cautious hopes that the use of innovative educational interventions during early childhood can maximize intellectual growth.

Early-experience theorists contend that providing a more beneficial environment during the preschool years can result in higher levels of intellectual functioning, especially among culturally deprived youngsters. Though providing more uniform environments does make hereditary effects more pronounced, the early-experience position is that intellectual differences among adults will still be reduced, and people will consequently have more occupational choices available to them.

The job of the teacher is in no way minimized by the efforts of the early-experience specialists. It is hoped that children will be better able to reach their intellectual potentials and thus better able to profit from the educational experiences provided in the classroom. The teacher's job should, accordingly, be more challenging and less frustrating.

KEY TERMS AND NAMES

A/S ratio
Nancy Bayley
Benjamin Bloom
cell assembly
critical periods
early experience
Head Start: Perry Preschool Program
Donald O. Hebb

Richard Herrnstein
Milwaukee Project
negatively accelerated growth curve
stimulus variety
Summerhill School
Lev Vygotsky
zone of proximal development

THEORY INTO PRACTICE: LEARNING THE CONCEPTS OF EARLY EXPERIENCE

This section aims at helping you to understand better the basic concepts and theories concerned with the development of young children.

Part I   The first phase is to identify the chief theorists with their ideas. Beside each name in the lefthand column, write the number of the correct concept from the righthand column.

	NAME		CONCEPT
_____	Myrtle McGraw	1.	A/S ratio
_____	Nancy Bayley	2.	Roller-skating twins and critical periods
_____	David Krech	3.	The air crib and controlling the environment
_____	Benjamin Bloom	4.	IQ variability is greatest during the first few years
_____	J. McV. Hunt	5.	The negatively accelerating growth curve
_____	D. O. Hebb	6.	Stimulus variety and stimulus deprivation
_____	B. F. Skinner	7.	Brain chemistry and environmental stimulation or deprivation

As you look down the list, probably the easiest and most vivid memory you'll recall is the picture of the child roller-skating (item 2 in the concept column) and the name of Myrtle McGraw. Next you'll probably think of the picture of the baby in the air crib (item 3) and imagine yourself as B. F. Skinner's daughter. For IQ variability, you will probably correctly choose Bayley if you associate her with the Berkeley Growth Study. If, instead, you selected Bloom for this item, you may also be correct, as long as your reasoning process has clearly demonstrated an overall *understanding* of the concepts involved. For example, if you remembered that Bloom's growth curve showed that the environmental stimulation of intellectual development is most influential during the early, formative years of life, then you may have correctly deduced that IQ variability must also be at its highest level during these critical early years. Of the four remaining choices, the problem now is to pick out three that you either know for

sure, or at least feel the most confidence about. Let's say you just can't recall anything about Bloom, but you're quite sure of Hebb and the A/S (associative/sensory) ratio of brain cells. This may then also remind you of that other brain researcher, David Krech, and the chemical changes in the brain. So now you're down to two names (J. McV. Hunt and Bloom) and two choices (the negatively accelerating growth curve or stimulus variety). At this point, the associative part of your brain remembers something about Hunt and the Hopi Indian children and you choose stimulus variety. This leaves Bloom's curve for your final correct answer.

Part II   The second phase of comprehension is to move from identification to description. You've been able to pick out or identify the concept and relate it to the theorist. Now the question is: Can you describe the connection in your own words? To try this out, pair the names and the concepts, for example,

McGraw/roller-skating twins and critical periods. Review the pairings and then think how you would describe each relationship and explain its significance: in other words, what would anyone who is interested in understanding children need to know about the findings?

Write one or two paragraphs on each of the pairs, using your own words. Then check your work with the descriptions in the glossary–study guide at the back of this book and/or the material in the chapter itself. Analyzing your own mistakes is the quickest way to unlearn the wrong connections and to replace them with the correct relationships. You will also be improving your ability to elaborate on the concepts so that you'll have a larger knowledge base to draw upon. To prove this point to yourself, cover up your answers to the identifications and go back and review Part I. Check how fast and accurately you can now spot the answers.

Part III This final part involves constructing an essay on the general topic of early experience. The question is usually phrased as follows:

> Discuss and critically analyze the major theorists and research findings that support the importance of early experience as a key to resolving the nature-nurture controversy. Outline implications for educational programming. (30 minutes)

After reading the question, you'll realize it has two parts. The first really calls for a presentation of the key concepts, theorists, and research findings. Hence, you would describe how experience in the first few years of life is the key to the nature-nurture puzzle by showing how "brain power" develops (Hebb, Bayley, Krech, Hunt) in a stimulating environment.

You can also point out the reverse, namely, the premature reduction of intellectual growth in environments that deprive a child of variety. Then you could mention Bloom's research, which demonstrated just how much brain power is developed before the first grade. You might add the critical-period concept (McGraw's roller skaters), which supports the idea that it is important to provide stimulation and growth opportunities that match the developmental sequence.

For the second part of the essay, you would want to point out the connection between theory and research as a basis for new educational practices. Stop for a moment and go back and review Table 4.1, which presents the findings of the Perry Preschool Program and other early-childhood educational programs. You'll quickly see how the first part of the essay relates to these programs. All the theorists predicted that a rich, stimulating environment with appropriate variety would promote intellectual development. In fact, the Perry follow-up studies on eight outcomes proved the point.

With this in mind, you can then wind up the essay by generalizing on the importance of educational experience during childhood. As Napoleon put it, "The hand that rocks the cradle rules the world."

REFERENCES

American Psychologist (1966), *21*, 1191.

Bayley, N. (1940). *Studies in the development of young children.* Berkeley: University of California Press.

Berrueta-Clement, J. R., Schweinhart, L. J., Barnett, W. S., Epstein, A. S., & Weikart, D P. (1984). *Changed lives: The effects of the Perry preschool program on youths through age 19.* Ypsilanti, MI: High/Scope Press.

Bloom, B. S. (1964). *Stability and change in human characteristics.* New York: Wiley.

Bruner, J. S. (1969). Cognitive consequences of early sensory deprivation. In R. C. Sprinthall & N. A. Sprinthall (Eds.), *Educational psychology: Selected readings* (pp. 34–36). New York: Van Nostrand-Reinhold.

Campbell, F. A., & Ramey, C. T. (1994). Effects of early intervention on intellectual and academic achievement: A follow-up study of children from low-income families. *Child Development, 65,* 684–698.

Cecci, S. J. (1991). How much does schooling influence general intelligence and its cognitive components? A reassessment of the evidence. *Developmental Psychology, 27,* 703–722.

Craig, J. (1994). *What happened at school today?* New York: William Morrow.

Datan, N., Rodeheaver, D., & Hughes, F. (1987). Adult development and aging. *Annual Review of Psychology, 38,* 153–180.

DeCasper, A. J., & Spence, M. J. (1986). Prenatal maternal speech influences newborns' perception of speech sounds. *Infant Behavior and Development, 9,* 133–150.

Dennis, W. (1960). Causes of retardation among institutional children: Iran. *Journal of Genetic Psychology, 96,* 47–59.

Dultz, R. (1994). *Educating the entire person.* Reseda, CA: Ron Dultz.

Garber, H. L., & Heber, R. (1981). The efficacy of early intervention with family rehabilitation. In M. J. Begab, H. C. Haywood, & H. L. Garber (Eds.), *Psychosocial influences in retarded performance.* Vol. 2, *Strategies for improving competence* (pp. 71–88). Baltimore: University Park Press.

Gleitman, L., Newport, E., & Gleitman, H. (1984). The current status of the motherese hypothesis. *Journal of Child Language, 11,* 43–80.

Greenspan, S. I. (1994). *Playground politics: Understanding the emotional life of your school-age child.* Reading, MA: Addison-Wesley.

Grosser, G. S., & Sprinthall, R. C. (1972, February). A rejoinder to Herrnstein. *Atlantic Monthly,* 38–39.

Grosser, G. S., Sprinthall, R. C., & Sirois, L. (1967). Magnesium premoline: Activation of extinction responding after continuous reinforcement. *Psychological Reports, 21,* 11–14.

Hebb, D. O. (1949). *The organization of behavior.* New York: Wiley.

Hebb, D. O. (1978). Open letter: To a friend who thinks the IQ is a social evil. *American Psychologist, 33*(12), 1143.

Hellmich, N. (1994, October 5) Gentle art of conversing with kids. *USA Today,* D8.

Herrnstein, R. J. (1971, September). I.Q. *Atlantic Monthly,* 43–64.

Herrnstein, R. J., & Murray, C. (1994). *The bell curve: Intelligence and class structure in American life.* New York: Free Press.

Hilgard, J. R. (1932). Learning and motivation in pre-school children. *Journal of Genetic Psychology, 41,* 36–56.

Horn, W. F. (1990). Psychology can help kids get a Head Start. *APA Monitor,* October, p. 3.

Hubbell, R. (1983). *Head Start evaluation, synthesis, and utilization project* (DHHS Publication OHDS 83-31184). Washington, DC: U.S. Government Printing Office.

Hunt, J. McV. (1969). Revisiting Montessori. In R. C. Sprinthall & N. A. Sprinthall (Eds.), *Educational psychology: Selected readings* (pp. 45–55). New York: Van Nostrand–Reinhold.

Kassebaum, N. L. (1994). Head Start: Only the best for America's children. *American Psychologist, 49,* 123–126.

Krech, D. (1969). The chemistry of learning. In R. C. Sprinthall & N. A. Sprinthall (Eds.), *Educational psychology: Selected readings* (pp. 152–156). New York: Van Nostrand–Reinhold.

Lee, V. E., Brooks-Gunn, J., Schnur, E., & Fong-Ruey, L. (1990). Are Head Start effects sustained? A longitudinal follow-up comparison of disadvantaged children attending Head Start, no preschool, and other preschool programs. *Child Development, 61,* 495–507.

Levin, H. M. (1977). A decade of policy developments in improving education and training for low-income populations. In R. H. Haveman (Ed.), *A decade of federal antipoverty programs: Achievements, failures and lessons* (pp. 521–570). New York: Academic Press.

Loewenstein, G. (1994). The psychology of curiosity: A review and reinterpretation. *Psychological Bulletin, 116,* 75–98.

McGraw, M. B. (1935). *Growth: A study of Johnny and Jimmy.* New York: Appleton-Century.

McGraw, M. B. (1939). Later development of children specially trained during infancy. *Child Development, 10,* 119.

Neill, A. S. (1969). The idea of Summerhill. In R. C. Sprinthall & N. A. Sprinthall (Eds.), *Educational psychology: Selected readings* (pp. 194–198). New York: Van Nostrand-Reinhold.

Rice, B. (1968, March). Skinner agrees he is the most important influence in psychology. *New York Times Magazine,* 17, 27 ff.

Rogoff, B. (1990). *Apprenticeship in thinking: Cognitive development in social context.* New York: Oxford University Press.

Rose, S. A., Feldman, J. F., Wallace, I. F. & McCarton, C. (1989). Infant visual attention: Relation to birth status and developmental outcomes during the first five years. *Developmental Psychology, 25,* 560–576.

Schweinhart, L. J. (1984). Preschool's long-term impact: Summary of the evidence. In J. R. Berrueta-Clement et al. (Eds.), *Changed lives: The effects of the Perry preschool program on youths through age 19* (pp. 95–105). Ypsilanti, MI: High/Scope Press.

Schweinhart, L. J., Barnes, H. V., & Weikart, D. P. (1993). *Significant benefits: The High/Scope Perry study through age 27* (Monograph of the High/Scope Educational Research Foundation, No. 10). Ypsilanti, MI: High/Scope Press.

Scott, J. P. (1968). *Early experience and the organization of behavior* (p. 68). Belmont, CA: Wadsworth.

Smolak, L., & Weinraub, M. (1983). Maternal speech: Strategy or response? *Journal of Child Language, 10,* 369–380.

Spelt, D. K. (1948). The conditioning of the human fetus in utero. *Journal of Experimental Psychology, 38,* 338–346.

Vygotsky, Lev (1978). *Mind in society.* Cambridge, MA: Harvard University Press.

Weiss, B. A., & Reynolds, S. (1992). Generation of neurons and astrocytes from isolated cells of the adult mammalian nervous system. *Science, 255,* 1707–1710.

White, B. L. (1975). *The first three years.* Englewood Cliffs, N.J.: Prentice-Hall.

Winegar, L. T. (1989). *Social interactions and the development of children's understanding.* Norwood, NJ: Ablex.

Zigler, E. F. (1987). Formal schooling for four-year-olds? *American Psychologist, 42,* 254–260.

Zigler, E. F. (1990). Letter. *Science, 248,* 1176.

COGNITIVE GROWTH

As we pointed out in Chapter 1, it is very important to gain an understanding of how children actually think in learning situations. This chapter takes a detailed look at the cognitive steps or plateaus of development that occur during childhood and adolescence. Since cognitive development depends on interaction between the child and the learning environment, we will also examine the problems of matching the child to the most appropriate learning tasks. This is another way of saying that we must have some informed basis for determining what we present to pupils and how we present it. Just as we know we cannot expect children to roller-skate before they can stand, we must also know when we can expect them to be ready to learn the various intellectual or cognitive tasks. If we understand how the cognitive systems develop, we can avoid both teaching children something before they are ready to learn it and missing a golden opportunity by waiting until they are well past the most sensitive moment.

Jean Piaget's work is featured throughout this chapter. In addition, we discuss the work of Patricia Arlin, who has expanded Piaget's cognitive stage theory through her concept of post-formal operations and wisdom and has thus provided a more complete picture of brain-power growth. We also consider the recent work of Lev Vygotsky, who has focused attention on the importance of group inter-

action as a method of promoting growth. His famous concept of the "zone of proximal development" offers a framework for effective teaching and learning. We discuss Vygotsky's similarities and differences with Piaget, as well as examples of Vygotsky matching and mismatching in classroom instruction. We examine the issue of possible gender differences largely through the multiple studies of Hyde and Linn, whose most recent research demonstrates an almost complete overlap between males and females across a wide variety of cognitive abilities; and we highlight the implications of these findings for teaching. In addition, we describe research by Robbie Case and his colleagues as a basis for the neo-Piagetian framework, which can comprehend both stage theory and recent work in information processing. Finally, we discuss a very broad framework for cognition offered by Robert Sternberg.

STAGES OF GROWTH AND DEVELOPMENT

Our understanding of cognitive growth has changed enormously in the past three decades (Case, 1992). Previously, the general view was that intelligence was, for all practical purposes, determined before birth. Even today this threadbare idea resurfaces

By understanding how and when cognitive systems develop, we can avoid, on the one hand, teaching children something before they are ready to learn it and, on the other hand, missing a golden opportunity by waiting to well past the most sensitive moment.

from time to time (Herrnstein & Murray, 1994). The implication was that there was nothing to do but accept those inborn differences as natural and provide different educational experiences depending on whether the child was a fast or a slow learner. On the basis of presumed differences in their speed of thinking, pupils were rated much as if they were on a track team and placed in the curriculum accordingly. (The word *curriculum*, by the way, is a Latin word meaning "a course to be run.") The same material was presented to all students but at different paces, since "slower" children were not expected to learn as much or to go as far as "faster" children. In any given period, the "slow" children would cover, say, half the material covered by the "fast" children, memorizing only half as much poetry, learning fewer spelling words and less arithmetic, and handing in shorter compositions in English. Since there was little or no recognition of major stages of cognitive growth, the differences between a first-grader and a twelfth-grader were largely differences in how

much they knew and how fast they learned it. In the same way, differences among first-graders (as among twelfth-graders) were also quantitative—how much material they learned and how fast they learned it. It has, unfortunately, taken us a long time to get away from these ideas.

Arnold Gesell (1940), who established the Institute of Child Development at Yale University during the 1930s, was the first to try to convince educators that growth and development occur in an unvarying sequence. Many of his ideas and theories were later discarded because they were oversimplifications, but this one concept lasted. Growth stages are major periods of change. Each child goes through periods of major reorganization followed by periods of integration during which a new stage is reached and the changes are assimilated. Although Gesell made a significant contribution with his idea of developmental growth stages, he erred in the details of his stages. He made the mistake of overgeneralizing from studying only a few children, and he presented an overly detailed "map" of development. For example, he made hard-and-fast statements about all two-year olds, all two-and-a-half-year-olds, all three-year-olds, and so on. This created much confusion in the 1930s and 1940s. Parents were literally measuring their children every six months or so against

"Actually, I'm a little too old to believe in you, but I don't want to take any chances."

From *The Wall Street Journal;* reprinted by permission of *Cartoon Features Syndicate.*

Arnold Gesell was one of the first to advocate that growth and development occur in an unvarying sequence.

Gesell's developmental graphs. Gross generalizations resulted: "All twos are terrible"; "The threes are terrific"; "At four and a half all children . . ." For a time, parental demand for Gesell's truths outran his ability to produce books: *The First Five Years of Life* was followed by *The Child from Five to Ten.* One mother was heard to comment despairingly, "I don't know what to do with my children anymore. They are 11 and 13, and Gesell stopped at ten!" Reading some of these books for their historical interest may help you understand some of the influences on your grandparents as they raised your parents.

The idea of sequential levels of development underpinned all the work of Gesell's institute. He demonstrated that growth took place in stages and that the stages themselves were like great leaps forward followed by periods of integration. The rest of this chapter explores the process of cognitive development, including the ages at which the major breakthroughs and periods of consolidation occur.

JEAN PIAGET: THE CONCEPT OF COGNITIVE GROWTH

Throughout the period 1930–1960, while efforts to break away from the idea of fixed and quantitative

intelligence were singularly unsuccessful (with the exception of Gesell's general concept of growth), **Jean Piaget** was working quietly and almost unnoticed at the J. J. Rousseau Institute for Child Study in Geneva. Using direct, careful, and systematic observation of children (including his own, the now-famous Jacqueline, Laurent, and Lucienne), Piaget began to form a view that would revolutionize our understanding of intellectual growth.

Although in the United States there was some brief interest in Piaget's work in the 1930s, it did not become widely known and appreciated until after the 1960s. There are two main reasons for such a long period of neglect. First, his ideas ran very much counter to the mainstream of educational psychology. He proposed that we start by investigating the child rather than following the official Thorndike view that we research "laws" of learning in the abstract. What went on in the mind of a child, so to speak, was considered either too complex to understand or simply irrelevant. Thus, while Piaget was carefully observing and noting how children thought, most of the establishment in psychology considered his model inappropriate.

Not all the blame lies on this side of the Atlantic, however. Piaget himself contributed somewhat to his neglect. Steeped in the tradition of European

JEAN PIAGET

Jean Piaget was born in Neuchâtel, Switzerland, in 1896. He was a curious, alert, studious, and extremely bright child. By age 10 he had published his first scientific paper, a description of an albino sparrow he had observed in a local park. From ages 11 to 15 Piaget worked after school as a laboratory assistant to the director of a natural history museum and in the process became an expert on mollusks and other zoological topics. When he was 15, he was offered the job of curator of the mollusk section at a Geneva museum. He received his degree from the University of Neuchâtel at age 18 and his Ph.D. in natural sciences three years later. Piaget had published more than 20 papers in the field of zoology before he was 21. In short, Piaget demonstrated a rare intellectual precocity during his childhood and adolescence.

In addition to his studies in natural science, the young Piaget read widely in sociology, religion, and philosophy. While studying philosophy he became especially interested in epistemology, the study of how knowledge is obtained. With his background in zoology, Piaget became convinced that biological scholarship, he seemed almost to enjoy writing his findings not only exclusively in French but in a style almost guaranteed to obscure rather than enlighten. Enough stories about him have circulated to suggest that he enjoyed the independence of his views and maintained a kind of lofty indifference to the problem of clearly transmitting his ideas to the wider world of psychology. To be fair, of course, most innovators who single-handedly move a field to a new level of understanding exhibit many of these same tendencies. But the important result was that during most of his adult life, his work was unknown here.

Today just the opposite is true: Piaget is among the first group of psychologists cited in academic references. John Flavell, one of this country's renowned experts on child development, offers this assessment: "Piaget's contributions to our knowledge of cognitive development have been nothing short of stupendous, both quantitatively and qualitatively" (1985, p. 4). Indeed, when Piaget made one of his rare visits to the United States in the late 1960s, the occasion was like an astronaut's reception (partly as a result of Flavell's excellent translation of his writings). As described by Maya Pines:

> It was a memorable occasion. With his fringe of long, straight white hair down the sides and back of his balding head, his high forehead, horn-rimmed glasses, gold watch chain and well-worn leather briefcase, he looked like a stock character—The Pro-

principles could be utilized in understanding epistemological problems. His search for a bridge between biology and epistemology brought him finally into the world of psychology.

After receiving his doctorate, Piaget sought training in psychology and so left Switzerland to study and gain experience at a number of European laboratories, clinics, and universities. During this time he worked for a while at Alfred Binet's laboratory school in Paris, where he did intelligence testing on French schoolchildren. He became fascinated, not by a child's correct answer to a test item, but by a child's incorrect response. He doggedly pursued the incorrect answers in the hope of learning more about the depth and extent of children's ideas and mental processes. His goal was to understand how children of various ages came upon their knowledge of the world around them. This became Piaget's lifework, to find out how children go about the business of obtaining knowledge.

Later Piaget took detailed, minute-by-minute notes of the mental growth of his own three children, Jacqueline, Lucienne, and Laurent.

In 1929 Piaget went to the University of Geneva, where he became the assistant director of the J. J. Rousseau Institute, and in 1940 he assumed the duties of director of the University of Geneva's psychology laboratory.

Piaget wrote a tremendous number of books and articles on cognitive growth in children. He believed that intellectual growth is a direct continuation of inborn biological growth. The child is born biologically equipped to make a variety of motor responses, which then provide the framework for the thought processes that follow. The biological givens impose on the developing a child an invariant direction to the development of cognitive processes. The ability to think springs from the physiological base. Clearly, Piaget kept his early training in natural science firmly in mind as he went on to develop his system of cognitive growth.

In his twilight years, Piaget actively sought answers to some of psychology's most fundamental questions. According to his biographer, friend, and former student, David Elkind, Piaget rose early, about 4 A.M., and wrote at least four publishable pages before teaching his morning classes. His afternoons were devoted to taking long walks and thinking about his current studies and research, and his evenings were spent in reading. As soon as his classes were over for the summer, Piaget went to his mountain retreat in the Alps. As fall approached, Piaget came down from the mountain, laden with new material for several articles and books. Piaget came down that mountain for over 50 autumns, and the volume of his writing was enormous. He died in Geneva in September 1980, in his eighty-fifth year.

Just as Freud has become synonymous with the study of emotional growth, Piaget has become known as psychology's foremost expert on cognitive growth.

fessor. On the platform, he commanded instant respect. Speaking in a booming voice, in French, he began by describing some of the key stages of children's intellectual development (Pines, 1970, p. 58).

Piaget's contribution to our understanding of mental growth as a process of interaction accounts for his significance. Through an intensive study of children over long periods—a painstaking process of almost endless observation—Piaget began to chart the unexplored territory of the human mind and to produce a map of the stages of cognitive growth. He proposed, first of all, that cognitive growth takes place in **developmental stages.** This means that the nature and makeup of intelligence change signifi-

cantly over time. The differences are not of degree (slow learners and fast learners) but of kind (qualitative). The transformation of the human mind as it develops can be compared to the transformation of an egg into a caterpillar and then into a butterfly. The stages of growth are distinctively different from one another, and the content of each stage is a major system that determines the way we understand and make sense of our experiences (particularly the experience of learning from someone else). Obviously, if we wish to provide experiences that will nurture and facilitate growth, we must take into account the intellectual system the child is using at the time. Piaget's work provides us with the broad outlines of the different cognitive systems children use at different periods in their lives. Each new, evolving system is a major qualitative transformation.

Research through Repeated Observations

It is important to know something about the way Piaget worked, how he was able to propose a system explaining such a highly complex process as intellectual development. You might think, in these days of supertechnology, that he would have used a complicated computer-based program and enormous research teams. But you would be mistaken. As we have already mentioned, Piaget's work was based on careful and detailed observation of children in natural settings, such as homes and schools. From a research methodology point of view, he was using repeated naturalistic observations. Thus, in some way his method is most like the kind of research a teacher or school counselor might do.

Starting almost like that other great "clinical" scientist, Sigmund Freud, Piaget very carefully examined the functioning of intelligence in a few children. On the basis of these subjective impressions, he began to ask himself some questions. Why, for example, did children become confused over family relationships? A child could readily acknowledge "I have a brother" but would still not understand that the brother also had a brother (or sister). He also found that children at certain ages seemed to have great difficulty in understanding "simple" ideas.

It seems hard to imagine that children don't understand that when they pour beans from a short, fat glass to a tall, thin glass, the number of beans remains constant. In one of his classic experiments, Piaget found that if he took two piles of beans, had a child actually count both piles to be sure they had the same number, and then left one pile spread out on the table, and bunched the second pile together, that—well, see if you can guess what the child would say. Remember, the child goes by what *seems* biggest. For example, if you ask children of four or five whether they would rather have a nickel or a dime, they are likely to name the nickel, "because it's bigger."

In yet another observation, Piaget asked preschool children to draw a picture of a glass half-filled with water. He then asked a child to draw the glass upside down. Figure 5.1 shows what one child drew.

At each point in each successive experiment, Piaget would carefully reexamine his own questions (hypotheses) and then develop some further ways of testing them. As a result, his research extended over almost an entire lifetime. At first his studies were

dismissed out of hand because he would try problems out on a single child or on three or four children. Also, because his sample was so small, he often did without statistics. (In this respect he resembled such theoretically disparate researchers as Freud and B. F. Skinner.) Nor did he follow a standard interview format: He wouldn't necessarily ask the same questions of each child, and so no two interviews were exactly comparable. It was almost too easy to criticize and dismiss his work on the grounds that his research designs were not standard.

Thus, partly because Piaget did not follow a standard research model and partly because his ideas, if understood, would have necessitated a major revision in our theories of cognitive growth, his work remained largely confined to Geneva. However, his findings were eventually noticed and have been widely accepted in the past 30 years. Scientific skeptics began to take notice of his work. Piaget continued to direct a series of studies, including some that used large samples. Essentially, however, it wasn't the sheer number of subjects that mattered but the emergence, over and over again, of the same principles of intellectual transformation. Through repetition, rather than the single critical experiment, Piaget accumulated sufficient evidence to become the major theoretician of intellectual development today.

The Meaning of Cognition: Piaget's Definition

Before we describe the stages of cognitive development, it is important to explain just what Piaget meant by the term *cognition*. Essentially cognition—thinking, or rational processing—is considered an active and interactive process. The mind in everyday language is not simply a blank sheet of paper on which the environment writes. But neither is it a totally separate apparatus that exists in splendid isolation. Flavell probably provides the clearest description: "Thus the mind neither copies the world, passively accepting it as a ready-made given, nor does it ignore the world, autistically creating a private mental conception of it out of whole cloth" (1985, p. 5).

Cognition, then, is the constant process of interaction between the person and the environment. In a real sense, it is the regulating mechanism that connects the person to the environment. The most important single point is that the cognitive process is active, not passive. A person affects the environment, and the environment affects the person at the same time. When we describe the specific implications of

FIGURE 5.1 Piaget's experiments with preschoolers: The first picture shows a child pouring beans from a short, fat glass into a tall, thin one. The second is a child's drawing of a half-filled glass of water—right side up and then upside down.

this definition, we will continually come back to this same basic point. The child is not an empty organism. Nor is learning the filling of an empty, passive vessel.

PIAGET'S STAGES OF COGNITIVE GROWTH

After examining the thinking patterns that children use from birth through adolescence, Piaget began to find consistent systems within certain broad age ranges. There are five major stages (see Table 5.1).

Since the five major stages are quite broad, each stage has subcategories. The important thing to remember, however, is that each major stage is a system of thinking that is qualitatively different from the preceding stage. Each stage is a major transformation in thought processes—compared to the preceding stage, a quantum leap forward, a breakthrough. It is also important to remember that the child must go through each stage in a regular sequence. It is impossible to skip or miss a stage or bypass it: The stages of cognitive growth are sequential and follow an invariant sequence. Children cannot overcome a developmental lag or speed up their movement from one stage to the next. They need to

have sufficient experience in each stage and sufficient time to internalize that experience before they can move on.

Our main concern as educators is to understand the major substance of each stage. Only then can we begin to consider what to teach and how to teach. Although the major substance of each stage is the main structure or scheme for the age span specified, these stages never exist in a pure form. There will always be some elements of the preceding and future stages mixed in. In other words, although a major intellectual activity does define each stage, bits and pieces of other stages will also be present.

In fact, there is universal agreement only about the starting point and the end of the sensorimotor stage, from birth to two years. Sandra Scarr-Salapatek

TABLE 5.1   STAGES OF COGNITIVE GROWTH

AGE	STAGE
0–2	Sensorimotor
2–7	Intuitive or preoperational
7–11	Concrete operations
11–16	Formal operations
16–Adulthood	Late formal operations

sums it up rather succinctly with the rhetorical question, "Do you know anyone who did not make it through the sensorimotor stage?" (1976, p. 185)

Beyond that point, however, the stage-to-stage differences are not as great, nor are the changes as abrupt as originally described by Piaget. Recent research, for example, has demonstrated that some symbolic thought, usually associated with later stages of development, actually occurs during the first stage. Similarly, research has indicated that children in the second stage have a greater ability to classify numbers than was previously suggested by Piaget's research (Flavell, 1992; Gelman, 1982).

Indeed, this overlap was confirmed by many of Piaget's observations just before his death in 1980. These have only recently been published. A recent publication in English, for example, indicates that children at each stage often use cognitive fragments of higher stages (Piaget & Garcia, 1991). Piaget had shown that a fully functioning adult can employ 16 methods of logical and formal thought. Young children use some of these methods, such as grouping, negation, and correspondence. These operations might be called "protologic," early but incomplete forms. Thus even though a child in the preoperational or concrete mode might make occasional use of higher-order thought, the child's primary method of problemsolving would still be in those earlier modes. The adage "One swallow does not a summer make" might describe this phenomenon. Thus, researchers who are still trying to disprove Piaget by showing a few early indicators of higher functioning either haven't stayed current with his studies or—to stay in the adage format—are making mountains of rejection out of molehills of cognitive fragments.

The important point to remember as you read and learn about stage characteristics is that there are no pure types. You will not find any single child who exhibits all the characteristics of a given stage, with the exception of the sensorimotor stage. Instead, you will see major trends and clusters of learning approaches that are truly consistent with the stage types. You will also see evidence of more-advanced-stage thinking at earlier stages. In other words, you can expect some overlap. Children during elementary school will exhibit very clear concrete thought, with some foreshadowing of formal and abstract reasoning. The same foreshadowing of a more advanced stage is seen in the preschool child as compared to the elementary school child. These two ideas, then, are not contradictory but rather deepen our understanding: Each stage has major characteristics of its own that describe in a consistent manner how a child processes experience; at the same time

the child will also exhibit some signs of the next stage as well as signs of prior stages.

In this regard, Rolando Garcia (Piaget & Garcia, 1991) maintains that the stages and sequences of Piaget are neither static nor complete. The path of cognitive development is an open system with no end point. Garcia notes that intuition of the type suggested by postformal operations or problem finding can never be truly formalized. Human cognitive systems are not finite but depend upon interaction. We do know, however, the inverse: Cognitive growth can be stopped. If we cut off exchanges with the environment, growth ceases. Garcia in rather strong words notes that for cognitions, "equilibrium is death" (p. 129). Each stage is a period of relative stability, of a preferred problemsolving strategy, not a static equilibrium.

In summary, recent research has shown that

1. The sequence of stage changes is in the order proposed by Piaget (Case, 1992).

2. Cross-cultural studies reconfirm the sequence, though the amount of time within a particular stage may vary (Ginsberg & Opper, 1988; Slone et al., 1994).

3. Transition periods between stages are broader and more flexible than predicted and therefore less abrupt (Flavell et al., 1993).

4. Elements of earlier-stage cognitions and later cognitions are more apparent, though the modal characteristics of each particular stage remain as the dominant scheme (Case, 1992; Flavell et al., 1995).

5. There are consistent changes in brain-wave patterns that correspond to Piagetian stages, with cycles of growth and stability reflecting the general Piagetian periods (Denton, 1987).

Despite the shortcomings in Piaget's original theory and a large number of studies critical of particular aspects of his work, John Flavell and associates (1993) have noted the lack of a new and satisfactorily comprehensive alternative theory to replace it. Thus, although development is not as "grand stagelike" as Piaget described it (Flavell, 1992, p. 1000), his theory remains our best approximation of the process of cognitive development. As we noted in Chapter 1, empirical studies by themselves can crossvalidate or cast doubt on theory, but only an entire new theory can replace an existing one. Piaget's relevance has been and will continue to be challenged, but the major tenets of the theory continue to inform practice in significant ways (Davidson, 1993).

SPOTLIGHT ON PIAGET

What If Piaget Had Studied Animals?

Since so much of Piaget's work has been repeated with children from different backgrounds and different cultures, sooner or later the question had to be raised: What about animals? Do animals, especially those who are quite advanced developmentally, such as a chimp (versus a slug), exhibit Piaget-like progressions in growth? The main experiments as the child reaches two years focus on the establishment of object permanence. The tests become quite sophisticated. The child may be shown a small toy cat. The examiner holds the cat in his or her hand, then moves the hand underneath three separate napkins. The cat is randomly deposited under one. The empty hand is opened in full view of the child. Usually the child smiles and then quite systematically looks under each napkin until the hidden cat is fully and triumphantly uncovered. This ability to track the events, so to speak, indicates the end of the sensorimotor period and the onset of internal and symbolic thinking.

So far, research with animals, using similar tests of object permanence, indicates that cats progress partway but stop short of full attainment. They can't track the shift from one hiding place to another. Monkeys, in contrast, can achieve the same level of functioning as a two-year-old human but then seem to top out. Chimps clearly reach this level as well as some measure of symbolic thinking at the next stage. In this sense, then, the research evidence does support the idea of intellectual development in humans and in animals. Careful observation of different species shows some of the same progressions during the sensorimotor period. Thus far, it appears that chimps and apes are the only species besides humans that clearly make it all the way through the sensorimotor period.[a]

As we noted in Chapter 2, chimps can learn sign language and thus can communicate at a more nearly human level than other animals. This development of language is the hallmark of the preoperational stage. In fact, for a while in the 1970s it was suggested that chimps could master some of the elementary rules of grammatical sentence structure, a clear parallel to human development during the preschool years. At present, however, there is no firm evidence that the chimps can really create original sentences. Instead they apparently imitate adult repetitions.[b] Additional research may be able to locate a point somewhere in the preoperational period at which chimps cease further cognitive-stage growth, leaving the field of further cognitive development exclusively in the province of the human species.[c]

---

[a] Flavell, J. H. (1985). *Cognitive development* (p. 37). Englewood Cliffs, NJ: Prentice-Hall.
[b] Kalat, J. W. (1988). *Biological psychology.* Belmont, CA: Wadsworth.
[c] Barber, T. X. (1996). Restrictive versus open paradigms in comparative psychology. *American Psychologist, 51*(1), 58–59.

Sensorimotor Experience (Birth to Two Years)

Cognitive activity during the **sensorimotor stage** is based primarily on immediate experience through the senses. The major intellectual activity of the stage is the interaction of the senses and the environment. Activity is practical. Without language to label experiences or to symbolize and hence remember events and ideas, children are dramatically bound to immediate experience: They see what is happening and feel it, but they have no way of categorizing their experience. Responses are almost completely determined by the situation. For example, a hungry child will figuratively scream the house down for food. It does no good to "tell" a six-month-old, "Now just wait a minute; I'm warming your bottle." The child has no way to represent the idea that in one or two minutes a nice warm bottle of milk will appear, and obviously the baby doesn't know what a minute is or, for that matter, what any of those other words mean. It's like speaking in English to someone who understands only Armenian. The child cannot, so to speak, go to the mental equivalent of an instant replay and say, "Oh, when she says that, it means something good is coming, so I won't be hungry much longer, and my yelling isn't going to make it come faster."

Being tied to immediate experience during this stage also means that there is almost nothing between the child and the environment. Because mental organization is raw, the quality of experience is unusually significant. Thus, what and how the child learns will remain immediate, as vivid as any first experience. It would be fair to say that learning in the sensorimotor stage is a continuous peak experience. It is something like going through each day as if it were the first day of school, the opening night of a play, your first final exam, your first date, your first encounter with death, the first time you found yourself completely alone, and so on—all in the same day.

To give you some idea of how easily children at this age are bound by experience and can be victimized by it, we need only think of six-month-olds. This is the age at which children begin to be able to follow an object with their eyes (visual pursuit). Their eyes swing back and forth, following the path of a shiny object, 50 to 100 times. They literally can't take their eyes off the moving object. Because this is the "first" time they have seen an object move from side to side, they will follow its visual path almost indefinitely unless we wisely choose to change the environment.

The development of visual pursuit (a sensorimotor behavior) is critical to mental development. Visual pursuit has to be learned before a very important concept called *object permanence* can be learned. As children begin to grow intellectually, they understand that when an object disappears from view, it still exists even though they can't see it. Whether it's a button hidden under a pillow, a person leaving the room, or a boy or girl hiding behind a door, children who have developed the concept of object permanence know the disappearance is only temporary and are thus liberated from endless visual pursuit.

Some of the most recent research on object permanence indicates that some aspects of such symbolic representation may appear as early as year one, but are short-lived. The child's attention is usually quickly overpowered by any visual distraction (Flavell et al., 1993, p. 59), and the object in question disappears from the child's attention. If, however, the child is aided through cuing, then by at least 13 to 15 months there is some evidence of an early memory for events. Such memory must be inferred from nonverbal behavior, since the child's verbal ability is severely limited (Bauer, 1996).

The ability to notice and follow objects might be likened to a first stage of recognition. The growth of object permanence is almost like the beginning of an elementary memory. Children can "hold" in their minds a picture of the missing object; no longer is out of sight out of mind. The experience of seeing things in the first few months of life and then of seeing those same things disappear and reappear plays an important role in mental development. Piaget compared sighted babies with those born blind and noted: "The inadequacy of the initial scheme [mental organization] leads to a lag in development of three to four years and more" (Piaget, 1970, p. 30). Lacking visual experience during the critical period of senso-

Intuitive preoperational reasoning. "If cars A and B get to the finish together, they go at the same speed."

Preoperational child's drawing of a house on a hill.

A child who is thinking at a preoperational level and is asked to draw an upright pencil falling usually cannot draw the sequence of steps shown here. Similarly, if asked to draw a picture of someone dropping a ball, the child will usually draw the beginning and the end, but not the ball in the process of falling, as pictured here.

rimotor learning (birth to two years) prevents the growth of mental structures.

The adage "There's no substitute for experience" best summarizes the sensorimotor period of cognitive development. This is so true of children from birth to age two that it accounts for the recent trend of providing babies with interesting crib mobiles and is also responsible for bringing back the popularity of some of the old-fashioned baby toys like rattles to shake and suck and blankets to hug. Linus, from the Peanuts cartoon, learning with his blanket in tow, stands as the prototype of a child in the sensorimotor stages. A rich and responsive sensory environment is the best means of developing the young child's intelligence. Note how this relates directly to some of the research findings mentioned in Chapter 4 concerning the development of "intelligent" animals by exposing them to "creative" toys and "interesting" cages. The quality of experience during this first stage prepares the child to move to the next stage.

Babies during this stage are primarily learning through their senses and are most strongly affected by their immediate environment. However, since object permanence develops in this stage, especially between year one and year two, we now know that babies are also capable of some representational thought much like that of the next stage. Young babies can store information, even though their ability to do so may seem quite crude. We would be wrong to assume that because their talk, gestures, and manipulations are so poor, there is no thought during the sensorimotor period. As Flavell puts it,

"They just *look* incompetent to the naked eye" (1985, p. 39).

Intuitive or Preoperational Thought (Two to Seven Years)

During the **preoperational stage,** the quality of thinking is transformed. Children are no longer bound to their immediate sensory environment. They started to develop some mental images in the preceding stage (object permanence, for example), and in this stage they expand that ability by leaps and bounds. Their capacity to store images (words and the grammatical structures of language, for example) increases dramatically. Vocabulary development, including the ability to understand and use words, is especially noteworthy. The average two-year-old understands between 200 and 300 words, while the average five-year-old understands 2,000 words—a huge percentage increase.

During this stage, then, there is a major breakthrough in the use of language. Since this is the time when children are maximally ready to learn language, adults who talk a great deal to children, read to them, teach them songs and nursery rhymes—in other words, use language to communicate with them—have a significant effect on their language development.

The predominant learning mode at this stage is intuitive; preoperational children are not overly concerned with precision but delight in imitating sounds and trying out lots of different words. They

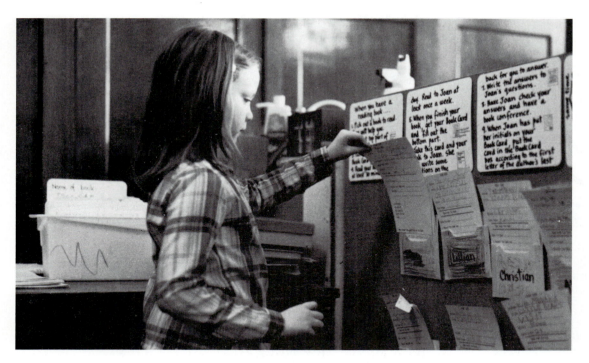

Piaget's second stage involves intuitive, or preoperational, thought. Oral vocabulary development is especially significant during this stage.

are also unconcerned about the consequences of language. This is the time, for example, when preschoolers regard "bathroom" language as hysterically funny, taking great glee in using choice expressions such as "poop face."

Obviously, the richer the verbal environment at this time, the more likely it is that language will develop. This is not to suggest that we should force-feed language teaching. In fact, teaching is almost unnecessary. The advantage of the intuitive mode is that children are capable of free associations, fantasies, and unique illogical meanings. They can pretend that stuffed toys are real, they can have imaginary friends, tell wild stories about their parentage, have whole conversations with themselves as well as with inanimate objects—these are all ways children have of trying language out, of teaching themselves. Intuition frees them to be experimental regardless of reality.

From the adult's point of view, the spontaneous nature of a child's language may have its drawbacks. Since the child doesn't worry about logic or reality, if talking to a tree, a dog, or a stranger in the street "feels" OK, you can be sure the child will do it. How many stories have you heard about children who

suddenly say something like, "Hey Daddy, look at that fat guy standing next to you." We have to remember that such comments are for the purpose of practice. In spite of embarrassing moments, the more extensive the practice, the greater the future verbal facility and competency. Studies have shown that children who are deprived of speech to any significant degree during this period suffer a developmental lag that may be irreversible.

Piaget, in studying the use of language during this period, found that children seem to talk at rather than with others. We have all had the experience of realizing that other people weren't really listening to us; that they were talking over, around, and through us, mostly to hear themselves talk, as the old saying goes. Among three-to-seven-year-olds this is the predominant mode. Piaget called it *collective monologue.* If you ask a group of children to tell you a story, together, you will find as many different stories as there are children. Their speech patterns are egocentric; each child's remarks bear little relationship to what the others are saying. However, in terms of practice, the collective monologue is another means children have of trying out words without having to wait their turn.

The intuitive period is truly a golden opportunity for facilitating language development. But we should also make it clear that preoperational thought is a general mode during this time. This is why a child at this level will choose a tall, thin glass of water rather than a short, wide one. Intuitively, the tall glass seems to have more water in it because it's taller. "Let's not worry that it's thinner," the child might say, "because being taller is enough. It looks bigger to me!" You may think this is a cavalier disregard of the facts, and that's just the point—it is. And it will do absolutely no educational good to tell a child of this age the "real" reasons why the amount of water is the same in both glasses. All you would accomplish would be to get the child to parrot back what you say, without the slightest understanding. There are literally thousands of uproariously funny stories that illustrate children's failure to understand abstract concepts despite their rapidly advancing mastery of language. Ask a six-year-old to say, and then explain, the pledge of allegiance to the flag ("the republic of Richard Stands and one naked individual") or some biblical references ("Pontius the pilot on the flight to Egypt"; "The Father, Son, and Holy Smoke"). The child is not a midget-sized adult. A child's understanding is qualitatively different from an adult's.

Piaget also showed that children at this age have difficulty realizing the reversible nature of relationships. He illustrated this fact with the following interview. A four-year-old girl was asked:

Have you got a sister?
Yes.
And has she got a sister?
No, she hasn't got a sister. I am my sister (1964, p. 85).

We can say, then, that the mental structures at the preoperational stage are largely intuitive, freewheeling, and highly imaginative. Do not assume, however, that because the process seems illogical it is necessarily inferior as a mode of thought. Indeed, much work in the area of creativity suggests that intuition and free association are important aspects of creative or original problemsolving. Intuition allows us to break out of the constraints imposed by reality. Inventors, artists, and other creative people commonly find that many of their ideas come to them intuitively or, as it is sometimes called, preconsciously. When we say "From the mouths of babes . . . " we are testifying to the importance of intuitive thinking.

Thus, we can say that the system of thinking that children typically employ during this period is creative and intuitive. Puff the Magic Dragon lives. Yet

during this time there are some few signs of an impending shift toward a greater recognition of reality. Recent research has shown a greater ability among preschoolers to distinguish between the real and the imaginary and to understand number sequences than was originally thought. This means children can learn to count better than "one, two, three, ten zillion" and can learn letters better than "*l* and emma *p*." There is also evidence that children at this stage can show some signs of self-discipline (Mischel, 1981). Their increased language ability essentially means that children can talk to themselves about resisting temptation. Some instruction in a formal sense will not damage children. This does not mean, however, that a teacher should structure any substantial portion of a preschool day on learning letters and numbers. As in the case of the sensorimotor period, although some attributes of the next stage are evident, these new characteristics are very fragile.

The major significance of the period is best summed up by Flavell, who notes that while sensorimotor learning is slow, step by step, concrete, and tied to immediate experience, preoperational learning is lightning fast and mobile. It is the beginning of symbolic thinking, with ideas replacing concrete experience. The child's ideation can range over the past, present, and future in a wink. The greatest single difference is, of course, the level of communication. Children can now share their cognitions socially. Sensorimotor experience is much more private and uncommunicative. "Each baby is imprisoned in her own separate cognitive world" (1985, p. 28).

Concrete Operations (7 to 11 Years)

Piaget's next stage represents another major reorganization of mental structure. In the preoperational stage children are dreamers, with magical thoughts and fantasies in abundance. Now, in the **concrete operations stage,** they are young logical positivists who understand functional relationships because they are specific, because they can test the problems out. For example, if we show children at this age two piles of beans or two glasses of water, they will tell us there is no change in volume. This time around they understand the specific, or concrete, aspects of the problem. Now they can measure, weigh, and calculate the amount of water or number of beans so that an apparent difference won't "fool" them.

The most recent research on the shift between intuitive and concrete operations indicates a less abrupt shift. A six- or seven-year-old does not wake up one day having moved from the previous stage to the new one. Nevertheless, over a broader time span

"You said we could paint anything we wanted to!"

© 1967 *NEA Journal.*

the shift becomes readily apparent. Flavell and associates (1995) conducted some 14 studies with over 400 children between 2.8 and 9 years to assess their understanding of the concept of thinking. The preschoolers in general considered thinking as isolated and mysterious mental events floating randomly in their heads, unrelated to causes or outcomes. The opposite was true for children in grades one through three. One researcher characterized the shift as a "sharp difference," perhaps another way to describe a qualitative change (Harris, 1995).

In their wholehearted abandonment of magical thinking, fantasies, and imaginary "friends," youngsters at this stage become almost too literal-minded. Their ability to understand the world is now as "logical" as it once was "illogical." For example, they can easily distinguish between dreams and facts, but they cannot separate hypothesis from fact. Five-year-olds usually describe a dream as something that happens in their bedroom, that they watch like a movie, while 9-year-olds describe dreams as mental images inside their heads. Also, once a 9-year-old's mind is made up on a question, new information will not easily change that point of view. In one study, 7-to-10-year-olds were presented with a number of reasons for concluding that Stonehenge (a prehistoric site in England) was a fort rather than a religious center. See the Spotlight for the outcome.

In humor we also find evidence of the literal-mindedness of this stage. This is the time when children delight in using explicitness and literalness as a basis for their jokes. Slapstick and pie-throwing

reach their zenith during this period. "When am I going to get my just desserts?" asks the fall-guy comedian plaintively. "Are you sure you want it now?" says the partner, holding a cream pie behind his back. You can fill in the balance of the dialogue and imagine the screams of delight from an elementary-age audience.

Whereas in the previous stage children play around with fantasies, during the concrete operations stage they play around with literal-mindedness. One researcher illustrates this juvenile sophistry with the following story (again, a favorite at this age). An eight-year-old boy comes to the table with his hands dripping wet. When his mother asks him why he didn't dry his hands, he replies, "But you told me not to wipe my hands on the clean towels." His mother throws up her hands and replies, "I said not to wipe your *dirty* hands on the towels." Another reported the following as a most popular story: "A mother loses her child named Heine. She asks a policeman, 'Have you seen my Heine?'" (Wolfenstein, 1954). Usually by this time children are laughing so hard that we never hear the punch line. We must admit, that, compared to the previous period, when the simple term "poop face" was considered hilarious, concrete-stage humor is more sophisticated, if not more appealing, to adult tastes.

Schooling and concrete operations   In many ways schooling at the elementary age seems to fit the pupils' cognitive stage rather well. A curriculum that emphasizes skills and activities such as counting, sorting, building, and manipulating will nurture cognitive growth. Field trips to historical sites and science through "kitchen physics" are additional examples. Activities can now have rules. In fact, you could almost say during this time that making the rules for a game or classroom activity is more significant than the activity itself. Whereas the preschool child will obey rules without understanding why we have them, the elementary school child understands rules because of their functional value. You cannot play real baseball without following the rules. However, we must also remember that they have a literal understanding of the concept of rules: Rules are given laws that cannot be changed. Adults understand that rules are a system of regulations that can be replaced by another system, but children see them as fixed, necessary, and arbitrary. The danger, then, is that we will exploit the children's literal-mindedness in order to manipulate rather than educate them.

Difficulties to avoid   Although schooling at this age is generally successful when it emphasizes skills and concrete activities, certain other aspects are not

SPOTLIGHT ON STONEHENGE

A Fort or a Religious Temple?

David Elkind, a leading Piagetian scholar, teaches a discovery unit in elementary school social studies to illustrate the inability of concrete-thinking pupils to distinguish between facts and theories.[a] He shows a series of pictures of Stonehenge. He points out a large number of facts—the huge size of the stones, their placement in an open field, the circular trenches of outer and inner "defense" lines, and similar bits and pieces of information from which it is possible to conclude that Stonehenge was a prehistoric fort. He is careful to list a very large number of facts to back up the conclusion. He then presents just a few facts, such as the open field and the two stones (the heel and the altar) that line up perfectly with the sunrise on June 21 each year, thereby suggesting that the site was really a religious temple. This second conclusion has fewer facts behind it, yet it is essentially more logical. The children, however, will not change their minds. To them, the large number of concrete facts, a quantitative difference, is more important than the smaller number of facts that "prove" the religious nature of the site. Essentially, for children at this age, there is no difference between theories and facts. What is important is the quantity of evidence. The basis for complex scientific and logical reasoning is not yet available to elementary-age children.

You can try similar activities with children this age. Pile up many facts on one side of an argument versus a more abstract set of reasons on fewer facts. In history this could be the defeat of the British at Yorktown (the importance of strategic position and the flanking by the French fleet, versus sheer numbers of soldiers, cannons, rifles, supplies, etc.). In science it could be whether the earth or the sun is the center of our system (the earth is more important, with people, technology, civilization, etc., versus orbits). In any case, the idea is to clarify student opinion to understand the difference between concrete facts and abstract theories.

---

a   Elkind, D. (1970). *Children and adolescents* (p. 54). New York: Oxford University Press. Copyright © 1981 by D. Elkind. Used by permission of Oxford University Press, Inc.

useful. For example, there is increasing interest in teaching elementary-age children the structure of knowledge in the various disciplines—math, English, history, science—through the entire elementary school sequence. Thus, we no longer teach history as facts or events but as a way of thinking. How does a historian think? What is the process whereby he or she knows, say, that Stonehenge was a religious site? Given this broad objective of teaching structure, we then try to develop a spiraling curriculum. At each grade we present the concepts in a more sophisticated manner.

This process breaks down at the children's level of cognitive understanding. Since their mode of think-

In Piaget's third stage, concrete operations, activities now can have rules; schooling at this age should emphasize skills and concrete activity.

ing is concrete and they don't have the mental equipment to grasp abstractions, they translate the abstractions into concrete and highly specific terms. Boys and girls at this stage develop their own way of understanding the subjects in accordance with specific everyday experience. They learn addition in the first grade, subtraction in the second grade, fractions in the fifth, and so on for each subject and each teacher. In the case of subjects in the new curriculum, the same situation prevails but the words have changed. For example, in the "new" math they learn set theory in the second grade, rational and irrational numbers in the fourth, and so on. In other words, the compartments the children use are a reflection of the concrete operations they learn to perform every day in school. All they have learned, in the meantime, is a new set of rote responses. Mary Alice White (1968), a renowned school psychologist, observed the same

situation when it came to the question of what parts of the curriculum are considered most important by the children. You can guess by now that they chose the subjects having the most tests and the most homework. Obviously, from a concrete point of view, that is the way to judge the importance or value of a subject. Even though teachers may say that all the subjects are important, actions speak louder than words, especially during this stage.

Parents of these children also get caught in the trap of the literal-minded thinker. Many parents report being upset and frustrated when they try to help their children with schoolwork. Children comment, "But that's not the way Teacher wants us to do it! She wants us to make the plus sign this way, not that way." "Teacher says we have to do spelling first, then arithmetic." "Fractions come before decimals." Usually neither the parent nor the teacher realizes that the difficulty lies in the child's cognitive level. Instead, parents frequently get angry with their children for not realizing, for example, that decimals and fractions are equivalent. And they get annoyed at the teacher for teaching in such simplistic black-and-white terms. At the same time, the teacher gets annoyed at reports of such literal-minded parents. The children are caught in the middle between two equally arbitrary systems, neither of which they understand.

During the prior stage of intuitive reasoning, children exhibit a small amount of ability to reason concretely. So too, during the concrete stage, children exhibit some fragile ability to reason abstractly, especially when the learning task is simplified. Thus, there is some foreshadowing of the next stage. This does not mean, however, that it is worthwhile to spend large amounts of academic learning time attempting to promote formal thinking during the elementary school. When such attempts were made in the 1960s, the programs did not succeed. Elementary-age children could not develop the ability to think abstractly in learning concepts such as culture or society.

Some cognitive-developmental researchers have attempted to find evidence of a potential for abstract thought in elementary-age youngsters. By simplifying the task and then intensively training the children, it is possible to "prematurely" bring about some aspects of growth. However, as Eleanor Neimark points out, these same training or teaching methods have vastly different effects on adolescents as compared to elementary-age pupils. She notes "a clear change in the quality and power of thought" between ages 11 and 15 (1982, p. 493). Prompting elementary-age children to verbalize (that is, memorize) abstract definitions such as love, country, or parent will not cause the children to generalize what they have learned. It is much better to wait for the onset of puberty and the start of formal operations to begin instruction designed to promote abstract concept formation.

Formal Operations (11 to 16 Years)

The shift to the **formal operations stage** brings remarkable differences in the characteristics of thinking. Table 5.2 outlines the four main differences.

Possibilities and hypothesis testing To an elementary-age child the difference between a possibility and a probability is not particularly strong. This point can be illustrated by the findings of studies in which students played what is sometimes referred to as "The Las Vegas Game." It involves an apparatus with three buttons—red, yellow, and blue. When the correct button (red) is pressed, a reward or prize drops into a small chute. The catch is that the machine is adjusted so that it pays off only 66 percent of the time. Thus, the most efficient strategy is to push the red button repeatedly. Both elementary children and adolescents have been tested on the game, and researchers have discovered marked differences from age to age in how the children approach the game.

In one study conducted with this game, elementary-age children were puzzled by the fact that no matter which of the three buttons they pushed, the prize came out only part of the time. For example, Lisa, age nine, concluded that the best strategy was shift from button to button—for example, "If you win, you shift, and if you lose, you shift." Once she and other nine-year-olds had settled on a strategy, they stuck with it, even when it was apparent that their strategy did not always lead to success. As a result, they received many fewer prizes than they would have had they simply pushed the red button repeatedly. Fifteen-year-old Angie also entertained the idea that the strategy might be a complex one.

But once Angie saw that the strategies she tried were not successful, she abandoned them and fairly quickly came to the conclusion that the most efficient way to play the game was to push the red button repeatedly. Her score was much higher than Lisa's.

Essentially, then, Lisa had decided that since there were three buttons, somehow all had to be pushed at one time or another. The teenager recognized the variety of possibilities and then logically focused on the sequence with the highest probable payoff. To put it another way, elementary-age children tend to think about what is; adolescents, about what might be (Sprinthall & Collins, 1995).

Such testing of hypotheses is another characteristic difference. Thus, the teenager has a greater potential for examining logical evidence before reaching closure. A classic demonstration of this characteristic of thought involves the task of finding the combination of five colorless chemicals that will produce a solution of a particular color. Most adolescents know immediately that the right answer is one of the logically possible combinations of colorless chemicals. Most of them proceed to solve the problem by simply trying each possible combination in turn until the right color shows up. Younger children, however, are less likely to conceive the possible combinations of so many liquids, nor can they proceed systematically through the possible combinations in search of the correct ones (Inhelder & Piaget, 1958).

Expanded thought: Metathinking Another extremely important shift is adolescents' ability to think about their own thinking and the thoughts of others. This kind of reflection, known as *metacognition,* allows for wide-ranging use of the imagination. Ideas can be tried out in the mind. In addition, teenagers can become aware of *how* they know as well as what they know. Being conscious of a variety of possible learning strategies means the opportunity for self-correction in problemsolving is much greater. Teenagers can talk to themselves, a process sometimes called an internal dialogue, and reach

TABLE 5.2   COMPARISON OF CHILDHOOD AND ADOLESCENT THOUGHT

CHILDHOOD	*ADOLESCENCE*
Thought limited to here and now	Thought extended to possibilities
Problemsolving dictated by details of the problem	Problemsolving governed by planned hypothesis testing
Thought limited to concrete objects and situations	Thought expanded to ideas as well as concrete reality
Thought focused on one's own perspective	Thought enlarged to perspective of others

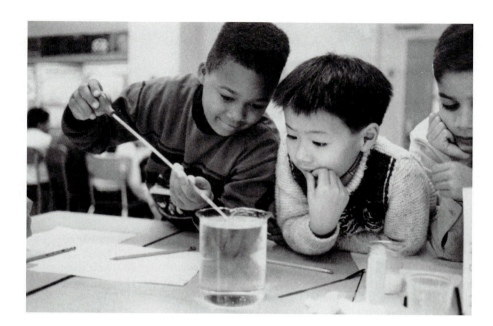

In Piaget's fourth stage, formal operations, children can develop formal patterns of thinking and are able to attain logical, rational strategies.

new insights without actually needing to test each solution in concrete reality.

Perspectival thought   Closely related to meta-thought is the new awareness that different people have different thoughts about the same idea or situation. In other words, a kind of relativism develops. There is no longer one single and correct point of view. Not everyone understands in the same way. Piaget demonstrated repeatedly that young children tend to think that everyone views situations as they do. He described these young children as egocentric because they were centered or focused on their own view. Adolescents, however, are more likely to recognize that other people's interests, knowledge, and ways of thinking are different from their own.

Formal operations: A social invention or a real state?   Some critics have challenged the shift from concrete to formal operations as an invention fabricated by intellectual elitists. These critics view formal operations and abstract thinking only as aspects of a narrow academic and pedantic superiority unrelated to the real world. This is termed by D. C. Phillips (1995) as a type of rampant sectarianism, or more familiarly as social and political *de* constructionism. In other words the stage is only an invention of an obscure and self important learned class either in this country or elsewhere (Smagorinsky, 1995). And indeed, some impressive research studies

by Richard Haier (reported by Hostetler, 1988) has provided a succinct defense of formal operations. Haier presented his research subjects with nonverbal tasks of varying levels of complexity. He then studied the amount of brain energy used (glucose burned) in solving the puzzles. The subjects who functioned at more complex and abstract cognitive levels not only solved more puzzles but also burned less glucose, especially with the more difficult puzzles. Formal operations were more efficient both intellectually and physiologically in solving complex problems such as figuring out intricate designs. Haier concluded that "smart brains" work *better, not harder* on difficult tasks. The less complex thinkers had much greater error rates with the difficult problems and also burned much more glucose. Thus we can conclude that formal operations are not simply a culturally bound delusion espoused by an overly educated upper class, but rather an effective and efficient method of solving complicated problems.

There was also a very interesting corollary to the Haier study. When confronted with a boring, rotelike learning task, a test of visual vigilance in identifying a sequence of zeros, the abstract thinkers burned more glucose than did the concrete thinkers. In terms of this result, the Haier research cuts two ways: Abstract thinking is more efficient for complex tasks, while concrete is more functional for less complex, rotelike tasks. We will discuss the implications of this finding for teaching and learning in the next section.

Cross-Cultural and within-Culture Differences:—"No More than Skin Deep"

Certainly an important issue for education is the universality of the stage system. Can we safely assume that the stage and sequence outline is valid both across and within cultures? Generally, research conducted in different countries over the past 30 years has found consistent support for the existence of learning stages (Ginsberg & Opper, 1988; Slone et al., 1994). Although stylistic differences (impulsive, reflective, visual, auditory, inductive, deductive, and so on) may exist, the system of making meaning via stages is highly similar both across and within cultures. Development is determined largely by interaction with the environment. Thus, whether African-American children or African children exhibit stage growth depends on the quality of their educational environment at home and at school, not on whether they live here or in Africa. The same is true for other ethnic groups. David Rowe and his colleagues, basing their conclusions on evidence from U.S. black, Hispanic, white, and Asian ethnic and racial groups, found the developmental differences "no more than skin deep" (Rowe et al., 1994, p. 396). Their complex statistical analysis produced nearly identical matrices. All children have the potential for stage growth if the environmental conditions can be tailored to meet them at their current stage. In our world today, differences in environmental conditions will inevitably show themselves in noticeable differences in motivation, self-confidence in learning, and openness to new ideas. We address these issues in detail in the chapters on teaching effectiveness (Chapters 12–14).

EDUCATIONAL IMPLICATIONS OF PIAGET'S THEORY

Intelligence: Action and Reflection

A significant educational implication of cognitive development is that growth in any one stage depends on activity. In other words, the development of brain power is not fixed at birth but is a function of appropriate activity during any particular stage. In order to learn, children must engage in appropriate activities. These do not include merely sitting and listening to or observing others. In speaking of development in the first two years, Piaget has said: "Sensorimotor causality does not derive from perceptive causality; to the contrary, visual perceptive causality is based upon a tacticokinesthetic causality that is itself dependent upon the activity proper"

(1970, p. 34). This quote, while demonstrating how difficult it can be to understand a passage from Piaget, also indicates the significance of his equation: Intelligence = activity. Anthropological studies, especially studies of prehistoric humans, have indicated that our brain power increased after the invention of tools. The manipulation of tools such as axes, knives, and primitive shovels, induced the brain to grow. In a sense, primitive men and women, as they began to use tools, were almost challenged to come up with new uses for tools and to invent more efficient and effective tools. The effect of rising to the challenge posed by this activity, the manipulation of tools, itself increased our capacity to understand and become more sophisticated cognitively—the activity developed our mind. The critical point for us is the key phrase in all of Piaget's writings, that *activity produces cognitive growth*. Thus, over and over in his writings to educators, Piaget calls for the active school.

The American Question: Can We Speed Up Growth?

In a technologically oriented society such as ours, someone inevitably asks what Piaget called the American question: How can we speed up development? "The first question which I am always asked in the United States is, 'Can one accelerate these stages?'" The answer obviously is no; we cannot speed up the process of intellectual growth.

Barnaby Barratt (1975), an English psychologist, actually researched the question. He selected students aged 12, 13, and 14 from the top tracks in math and presented them with difficult reasoning tasks. Then he quite systematically instructed the students in how to solve similar problems. He taught them the steps to use and the reasons. The results indicated that the training "took" with the 14-year-olds but was ineffective with the 13-year-olds and even less effective with the 12-year-olds. The improvement was a result of two factors: the critical teaching *and* the stage of cognitive development. The students had to be far enough along developmentally in order to grasp the reasoning process and generalize it to similar problems.

The study also substantiated a second aspect of learning: the "trained" 14-year-olds performed better than their same-age cohorts in the top math tracks, showing a higher level of reasoning. This is sometimes called the "other side of the American question": If we can't speed up growth, should we simply let students mature at their own pace? Barratt's results indicate that if left alone adolescents will not necessarily develop to their potential in employing formal operations.

In fact, a series of studies at the University of Oklahoma demonstrates convincingly that educational programs can be effective at all ages (Renner et al., 1976). For example, the researchers in those studies created materials to emphasize the concrete aspects of **conservation** among first- through third-graders. At this time children are at the transition between preoperational and concrete patterns. It is difficult for them to hold their perceptions constant on tasks such as transfer of liquid or solid amount (for example, the spread-out versus bunched-up beans). The researchers systematically instructed such children by employing many hands-on experiences in six types of conservation: numbers, liquid amount, solid amount, weight, length, and area. In most of these categories, the results indicated that such careful teaching did improve the children's ability to conserve in problemsolving.

Thus, the answer to the American question is to nurture the process of growth at particular stages rather than simply attempt to accelerate constantly. Teachers do not need to carry the banner "Onward to Formal Operations." Rather, it is important to follow the suggestion of Piaget: "Present the subject to be taught in forms assimilable to children of different ages in accord with their mental structures" (1970, p. 153).

Patricia Arlin: Beyond Piaget— Late Formal Operations

One of the criticisms of Piaget's theory is that the end point of cognitive development, formal operations, may be too limited. A focus on logical reasoning may exclude thought in other areas such as wisdom and/or creativity. In fact, it is Robert Sternberg's opinion (1986) that traditional Piagetian theory is really not concerned with individuals of exceptionally high levels of cognitive talent. The reason for the lack of attention to additional stages of development may be that Piaget first concentrated heavily on the thought process of children and then on early adolescence. Recently, a researcher at the University of British Columbia, **Patricia Arlin,** has explored the possibility of postformal operations as a new and more advanced stage (1986). According to Arlin, this stage is characterized by the ability to develop new solutions, devise programs based on broadened visions, and formulate the "productive questions" that enable individuals to expand the knowledge base and gain fresh insights.

Arlin specifies that this advanced stage represents an expansion—not a rejection—of Piaget's theory. Indeed, the ability to define concepts and to reason abstractly is a platform upon which problem-finding ability may rest. Arlin notes, however, that most assessments of Piaget's formal-operational period involve asking a person to solve a problem. Finding a new problem or discovering new questions is simply not accounted for in the Piagetian scheme.

Arlin's work in postformal operations has continued (1993). She has recently identified specific cognitive elements that represent the process of problem finding. These include:

1. Complementarity

2. Detecting asymmetry

3. Openness to change

4. Redefinition of limits

5. Intuition and taste for levels of significance

6. Preference for creativity/originality

Complementarity has a special meaning in that it is the ability to connect unrelated or even contradictory ideas in a new format. For example, Piaget himself brought two ideas together, assimilation and accommodation, to form a larger theory of how we learn. Before Piaget, the general view was that learning was either inductive or deductive. He joined two apparent contradictions and formed a new synthesis; each previous idea was an equal partner in contributing to the new idea. Here is another way to think of this process: Elements that are added together more than increase the total. The metaphor of 1 plus 1 equals 3 represents the complement. (Note that *complement* does not mean the same thing as the similar-sounding word *compliment*.)

The process of detecting asymmetry is almost the opposite of complementarity. While most observers would accept an idea or problem solution as accurate, the problem finder would notice perhaps a subtle difference. It was, of course, Piaget himself who noticed differences in children's thinking. Before, many thought that children were simply mini-adults in cognitions. Piaget spotted the asymmetry and launched his inquiry. Just think how many persons saw apples fall from trees before Isaac Newton, and yet did not detect gravity.

Openness to change means simply the ability to remain cognitively flexible. Knowledge development is seen as the process of successive approximations. The problem finder creates solutions yet does not close the door on new theory and practice. Erik Erikson's revision of his theory of psychosocial development, described in Chapter 6, is an example.

In pushing the limits, the problem finder is willing to change current theories. Behavioral scientists always operate from a particular model or paradigm. By testing out the cases or instances where the information doesn't fit, the finder may uncover weaknesses. For example, some of Piaget's critics found instances in which children's thought was more than one stage past their preferred mode. Such a challenge created the need for more research and theory change.

To some degree it is difficult to define the intuition involved in maintaining a bedrock view of what is fundamentally important. In everyday language we often speak of those who get so focused on the trees that the forest disappears. The problem finder can maintain a broad perspective even when it is necessary to focus on small and intricate details. For example, Kohlberg (see Chapter 7), while spending countless hours developing an exact coding scheme for his interview method, never lost sight of the larger philosophical issues of moral judgment.

The final element is a preference for particular conceptual modes involved in exploration and temporary closure. Perhaps the best example is that of famous but fictional detectives, such as Sherlock Holmes or Jane Marple. They use both quantitative and qualitative methods. In fact the hallmark in all their stories is the period of reflection. Holmes is often staring off into the wilderness or playing the violin, cognitively rearranging the empirical facts. Marple, on the other hand, reviews all the facts and then sees a theoretical resemblance to characters from her own small village, St. Mary Mead, for the clues. She often undergoes such a process silently while knitting. In the process of sorting through ideas, the facts are often rearranged to reach novel solutions.

All six elements, then, are involved in the postformal operations stage in adulthood. Arlin's work also demonstrates that elements or fragments of postformal cognitions will appear in adolescence and young adulthood, foreshadowing their more complete emergence later in the life cycle. The problem for the educator at this point is to enhance such abilities to prepare for the transition beyond formal operations, by providing experiences in each of these elements. Arlin quotes Louis Pasteur, the famous French scientist, who noted that new discoveries don't just happen by chance but come to a "prepared mind" (Arlin, 1986). Arlin's research may help us to understand the stage framework more clearly and create teaching strategies to enhance such growth. Her work, then, can be considered as a new map for the journey beyond our current understanding, itself perhaps the best of wisdom as the art and science of problem finding.

In addition to her contribution to basic research, Arlin has noted some important implications, particularly for teaching. She conceptualizes wisdom as a more complex level than professional expertise in teaching. She has found an empirical relation across wisdom, postformal operations, and teaching effectiveness. The "wise" teacher knows when to employ his or her expertise (professional competence) and when to set it aside if it is getting in the way of student learning. The wise teacher is also an expert. But the expert teacher is not always wise (Arlin, 1993; Arlin & Fung, 1995).

Accommodation and Assimilation

In broad outline the stages of cognitive growth—sensorimotor, intuitive or preoperational, concrete, formal, and possibly postformal—represent major transformations of mental organization. Each stage is qualitatively different from the one preceding and is a new means of dealing cognitively with the world. However, it is important for educators to understand how cognitive growth occurs. We have already noticed the critical importance of activity. Equally significant are Piaget's concepts of **accommodation** and **assimilation.** Children at particular stages are maximally able to assimilate particular kinds of experiences. This means, for example, that sensorimotor experiences can be most fully taken in from birth to two years, preoperational from two to seven, and so on. Conversely, it is difficult to assimilate experiences beyond the level of mental development. Thus, as teachers, we can get children to say they know, or force them to memorize, but we should not be fooled into believing that they really understand. Piaget might say, "To know by heart is not to know."

According to Piaget, the activity of assimilating certain experiences from the environment forces the child to accommodate, or internalize, them. Internalizing experiences is critical to cognitive growth and cannot take place if experiences are allowed, in effect, to go in one ear and out the other. Piaget suggested that the most complete development takes place when children assimilate experiences from their environment, since only then will they be able to accommodate, or internalize, those learnings. As we have indicated, the major challenge facing edu-

SPOTLIGHT ON GENDER DIFFERENCES

Real or Artificially Created?

There is long-standing controversy concerning the possible significance of gender differences in cognition, cognitive developmental stages, and academic achievement, particularly in scientific thinking and performance. Recent research by Janet Hyde and Marcia Linn on overall differences and by Gail Jones and Jack Wheatley on classroom atmosphere sheds light on this important question.

Many early investigations of conceptual complexity (Dulit, 1972) and of academic achievement in math and science concepts (Eccles, 1986) concluded that males were superior to females in aptitude and achievement. These findings were often used both to justify the small number of female scientists and to "cool out" aspiring females in secondary school. Using meta-analysis, which permits compiling large numbers of studies simultaneously, Hyde and Linn (1988) reviewed studies involving millions of subjects over multiple years and found that gender differences in math and science

areas had been disappearing since 1970. Although there had been systematic bias in the early research, with underreporting of gender similarities and overreporting of gender differences, more recent studies reported progressively smaller differences, accounting for only 1 to 5 percent of overall variation. To avoid bias themselves, Hyde and Linn also reviewed 165 studies of gender differences in verbal ability involving more than 1.5 million subjects. This time they found that the early studies generally reported higher scores for females and lower scores for males. However, after correction for the early bias, their meta-analysis revealed that gender differences in vocabulary, analogies, reading, writing, anagrams, and the SAT verbal were about zero. Given the ratio of males to females in the population, there is less than 0.1 percent difference between them (Weinberg, 1993). The most recent research on cognitive stages (Case, 1992; Flavell et al., 1995) and other aspects of scientific cognitions

(Voyer et al., 1995) likewise indicates that gender differences are increasingly minimal.

Some math and science studies, however, continue to suggest that males show superiority at the highest level of mathematical thinking (Murray, 1995). Before we assume that genetics in the form of a male math gene is responsible for this difference, we need to take into account the possible influence of classroom interactions in schools.

Jones and Wheatley (1989) investigated teacher-student interactions in 60 math/science classrooms at the secondary school levels, involving 17 male and 43 female teachers and more than 1,300 students almost equally divided by gender. They found that classroom atmospheres and teacher-student interaction played a significant role in gender differences in performance.

Classroom atmospheres:

Of the 196 graphic displays in the classrooms, 93 percent were of male scientists.

---

cators is to develop an array of such experiences to provide maximal cognitive development.

Piagetian scholar **Hans Furth** (1995) has suggested another way to think of the two processes. Furth notes that assimilation by itself means that the person simply takes all new experiences into his or her mind without worrying in the least whether they really do fit. Thinking as assimilation is more like daydreaming or imagining. We don't check out our views. We take in new experiences, but our understanding does not change. Furth calls taking in experiences and ideas from the outside world without

changing what they mean an *inside process.* Accommodation by itself is, of course, just the opposite. We may think about a new experience or idea, but we do not try to take it into our consciousness. We keep the new information at arm's length, so to speak. A student who dutifully memorizes a string of abstractions without any understanding performs pure accommodation. The words are said, but the meaning isn't there. In fact, psychologists every once in a while run across a human being who exhibits monumental feats of memory such as reciting an entire Shakespearean play, reeling off the names of all the

When females were depicted, the roles were limited and stereotyped (veterinarian, wearing an apron, or the astronaut Sally Ride).

Teacher-student interaction:

In the lab, males carried out demonstrations twice as often as females.

In the classrooms, males were allowed to volunteer four times as often as females.

Males spoke out more often and were allowed to dominate every teacher-student interaction.

Males received more praise and more criticism than females.

Teachers referred to females by appearance but not to males.

Teachers referred to scientists and scientific work as "he," "him," or "his."

Although the study did not examine nonverbal behavior (eye contact, body movement), both classroom atmospheres and teacher-student interactions revealed a distinct pattern of male favoritism and encouragement. Males did science amid pictures of male scientists. They volunteered. They talked. Females watched and for the most part remained passive and quiet. The pattern was the same *whether the teacher was male or female*. The Jones and Wheatley study also confirmed findings of bias in classroom interactions previously found at the elementary and middle school levels. It thus seems clear that classroom socialization is a continuing factor in producing even the extremely small gender differences that are still reported. Given the negative classroom experiences documented so clearly by Jones and Wheatley, it is surprising that females do as well as Hyde and Linn have found. Anyone interested in teaching mathematics or science at any level should be careful not to ascribe differences in outcome to gender until socialization and teaching have been shown to be unbiased.

Case, R. (1992). *The mind's staircase.* Hillsdale, NJ: Erlbaum.

Dulit, E. (1972). Adolescent thinking à la Piaget: The formal stage. *Journal of Youth and Adolescence, 1,* 281–301.

Eccles, J. (1986). Gender roles and women's achievement. *Educational Researcher, 15*(6), 15–19.

Flavell, J., Green, F., & Flavell, E. (1995). Cognitive processes: comprehension, thinking, and introspection. *Monographs of the Society for Research in Child Development, 60* (1, pp.1–196).

Hyde, J., & Linn, M. (1988). Gender differences in verbal ability: A meta analysis. *Psychological Bulletin, 10*(4), 53–69.

Jones, J. G., & Wheatley, J. (1989). Gender influences in classroom displays and student-teacher behaviors. *Science Education, 73*(5), 535–545.

Murray, B. (1995, November). Gender gap in math scores is closing. *APA Monitor 26*(11), p. 43.

Voyer, D., Voyer, S., & Bryden, M. P. (1995). Magnitude of sex differences in spatial abilities: A meta-analysis and consideration of critical variables. *Psychological Bulletin, 117*(2), 250–270.

Weinberg, S. (1993). The Hedges and Friedman Index: Two-tailed significance. *Review of Educational Research, 63*(4), 627–529.

Roman emperors, or itemizing all the Köchel numbers of all Mozart's work. When quizzed more closely, we realize that these people do not really comprehend the meaning of any of the material they spout forth. Some persons with this ability are called *idiot savants,* which means literally stupid-wise people. The learning may reflect rote repetition or a photographic memory. The information remains separated from understanding, a kind of splendid isolation, not to be confused with genuine learning.

If assimilation and accommodation remain as separate, isolated experiences, then no real mental growth occurs. In a manner similar to the way two-year-olds play in parallel, the two processes don't interact. When they do interact, however, a most significant learning activity takes place, the process of equilibration.

Equilibration: Perturbation and Knowledge Disturbances

As illustrated in Figure 5.2, **equilibration** is the process of balancing what we already know (assimilation) and what we may be asked to learn that does-

FIGURE 5.2 Piaget's learning interaction. Equilibration is the process of balancing assimilation and accommodation.

Assimilation

Fitting experiences into our present stage of cognitive development. One of William James's children at approximately two years of age, on seeing an orange for the first time, insisted that it was a ball. When he saw a corkscrew for the first time, he called it "bad scissors."

Accommodation

Changing our present stage of cognitive processing to incorporate new experience. Any child after being sprayed by a black-and-white furry animal: "That kitty can't be a kitty!"

Equilibration

Assimilation

Continuity with past perceptions. Stability.

Accommodation

New perceptions. Revising previous understandings. Change and growth.

Equilibration is the balancing act between the "old" and the new—between perceptions and experiences. It is a dynamic process that attempts to reduce dissonance.

An eight-year-old "equilibrating" on the volume conservation task:
"It sure looks like there is more water in the tall, thin glass, but when I pour it back into the short, fat glass, it's the same—I wonder . . ."

A secondary school pupil "equilibrating" during a rereading of *Moby Dick*:
"When I read this as a kid I thought it was just a neat whaling story—how to harpoon, the dangers of the sea. Now it seems different. Why is the captain so obsessed with this whale? Does it have some special meaning?"

n't quite fit (accommodation). Furth calls this a process of *knowledge disturbances*. There is an important developmental assumption about the propensity to know, variously termed "curiosity drive," "competence motivation," "the intrinsic need to master the environment," or "personal efficacy." Studies have shown that monkeys will "work" for long hours on interesting puzzles. So too will human babies. In fact, Flavell (1992) mentions recent research that shows that babies will also "work" in order to get at interesting pictures, sounds, and puzzles. In other words, humans appear to have an intrinsic drive, motivation, or personality disposition to learn new things. As we interact with the environment, we become curious about any new event or unfamiliar idea. That is what Furth means by

knowledge disturbances. Our natural bent doesn't allow us to be content just to exist; so when new things don't fit our past assimilations, we ask why. Such is the basic learning motivation to master problematic situations. We learn by balancing the old information *and* the new—the process of equilibrating.

But how does the process work? Do we simply continually expose children to a wide variety of new experiences, a kind of force-feeding, to move them to higher stages? Clearly not, because growth occurs slowly. New information and experiences are balanced (equilibrated) slowly so that the scales never dip too far. This is called "learning by exposure to a moderately discrepant environment." Another way to describe it is as a slight mismatch—new information not quite fitting with our old views. The end result of such experiences is the gradual development of more complex cognitive structures, or learning sets. First growth occurs within a particular stage as a result of small discrepancies and slow equilibration. Then there is movement to the next stage, followed again by a new set of mismatches and the slow incorporation for growth within the new stage. The slight imbalance on the accommodation side creates an adapting intelligence—not a fixed but an ongoing process. In this sense intellectual growth is the gradual development of more complex and more efficient rational problem-solving capacities that we can generalize to new problems.

Furth provides an interesting description of a seven-year-old German boy starting to accommodate new information. Furth's example demonstrates that once the new information is taken in through equilibration, the boy thinks in a new way. The boy learns that churches have steeples. Then, during a bike ride, he overhears a number of adults entering a house say they are going to church. The boy muses. A regular house can't be a church. It doesn't have a steeple. It seems nearly impossible to consider a simple house as a real church. His father tells him not to ride his bike near the house on Sundays because of the traffic. Soon he hears other people nearby talking of attending services there. He continues to deny the validity of the new insights. Gradually, however, the moderate discrepancy pushes him to reconsider his earlier impossibility. After talking, listening, seeing (and perhaps even peeking inside during a service), he comes to a new understanding of the idea of a church with or without special architecture. In Furth's description he very carefully points out that no one tried to argue with the boy, nor did the situation become stressful. In fact, he pointedly notes that the boy was "in a relaxed state of mind" when he began to think through the discrepancies (1981, p. 267).

It's clear that accommodation should not be forced. Equilibration takes place when there is a threshold of new awareness, or curiosity. There is some sense of uneasiness, an awareness that might be expressed as "Somehow my thinking doesn't quite handle the new information. Gradually I'll need to change my mind."

One final illustration: A small child in the first grade reported with a broad smile on arriving home each day, "I'm going to get a present for going to school!" After a few more days a parent asked, "Are you sure you're going to get a present?" "Oh, yes," came the answer brightly. "She said when she called our name you could say 'here' or 'present.'" So in time we come to know when a house is a church and when a present isn't a present. When such an accommodation takes place, there is a qualitative shift in thinking. We cannot go back to our old way of thought once the change is really incorporated.

Under conditions of accommodation and equilibration, we sense that a new explanation is better, or we intuitively begin to feel that a new level of understanding is starting to dawn. We are not quite sure, and in fact may be a bit apprehensive, about exploring an unknown; part of us may be attracted to the change, while another part (our old, comfortable way of thinking) resists. The feelings gradually have to be worked through during equilibration. Some of the old must be relinquished to make room for the new, a process that can involve anxiety.

As a teacher introducing new concepts, slightly better problem-solving methods, or somewhat more comprehensive theories, remember that you are inducing some equilibration process in the pupils. They will need extra psychological and personal support during such transition periods.

In addition to giving extra personal support during new learning, also remember that there is little sense in teaching preoperational or early concrete thinkers to think abstractly. If for the sake of equilibration we present information that is over the heads of the pupils, new learning will not take place—there will be no reconciliation of new ideas. In fact, the only notable increases may be in pupil frustration, anxiety, and perhaps rote memorization.

To sum up the phases of the learning of new concepts (that is, how we accommodate and then assimilate knowledge disturbances), Table 5.3 outlines a seven-step process that includes both the thoughts and feelings that the learner experiences. Gradual-

TABLE 5.3 PHASES OF DEVELOPMENTAL LEARNING

EQUILIBRATING THE NEW AND THE OLD

1. Awareness of a moderate discrepancy arises in understanding the meaning of an event or idea.
2. A feeling of puzzlement ensues: curiosity, uneasiness, affective arousal.
3. More new information accumulates that doesn't fit the prior understanding.
4. During periods of relaxed reflection, one tries to fit the new pieces of information into the old scheme; talking to oneself.
5. A new balance is reached. The new information moves from accommodation to assimilation.
6. After sufficient time the new information becomes "old" information and can be generalized to similar situations.
7. A new moderate discrepancy arises, and the process continues.

ness, curiosity, and relaxed reflection lead eventually to mastery of the new concept, self-confidence as a learner, and the ability to generalize the idea to other similar circumstances. This learning process is quite obviously different from rote memorization.

One of the criticisms of Piagetian theory has been that it views the mind as a kind of cold, aloof, disembodied cognitive mechanism and fails to take into account the emotional or affective side of learning. Although Piaget's style makes his own description nearly impossible to interpret, his disciple Furth (1995) has shown precisely where affect/emotion enters the learning process, between points 1 and 2 in his scheme (Table 5.3). The disorganization of our no-longer equilibrated system triggers our feelings. The disruption or perturbation creates a variety of emotions from puzzlement to uneasiness. How the teacher responds to such affective arousal will determine in a significant way how the student moves through Furth's phrases of equilibration. We will address this issue at greater length in the next section.

LEV VYGOTSKY: TEACHING FOR GROWTH

As we have noted, Piaget, if not actively opposed to educational applications, was at least ambivalent. A Russian researcher, **Lev Vygotsky,** validated and in some cases anticipated Piaget's early work on stages. More important, however, was Vygotsky's willingness to insist that those insights focus on application. In a sense that was an easy transition for him to make, as he was a teacher before becoming an educational psychologist. In the 1920s he also worked directly with another major Russian psychologist, Alfred Luria, soon after the Bolshevik revolution. Before that time Russia's huge peasant population had been kept illiterate. The new government under Lenin confronted a major and fundamental educational challenge. Luria and Vygotsky worked to create educational methods to teach these people not only how to read but, more importantly, how to understand what they were reading (Blanck, 1990). As a result of their efforts the two men found four stages of cognitive growth that paralleled those of Piaget. Thus, subjects in Uzbekistan would answer the following question in accord with their stage of development:

> In Siberia all bears are white. My friend Ivan was in Siberia and saw a bear. What color was it?

At an abstract level the subject would immediately answer correctly. At the concrete level the an-

swers were quite different; for example, "I've never been to Siberia so I don't know" or "Ivan is your friend, ask him."

These results convinced Vygotsky that learning to read without comprehension was fruitless. His experiences led to a series of extremely important instructional principles.

1. Effective teaching marches just ahead of the current developmental stage of the learner.

2. The child must be actively involved in learning, not a passive receptacle.

3. Education includes a major social interactive component with parents, teachers, and peers. Learning activity should include reflective discussion with others.

4. Stages of cognition are a series of radically transformed systems that undergo restructuring and reorganization.

5. Each stage is qualitative, and transitions involve disintegration prior to a new and more complex integration. Without appropriate interaction no growth occurs.

6. The cerebral cortex undergoes neurological reorganization (similar to Hebbs's cell-assembly concepts; see Chapter 4) during stage growth.

Vygotsky's view of the basic structural components of cognitions and stages is clearly similar to Piaget's. For example, he regarded memorization as a dead end, "fossilization" (1985). He also saw the higher-order cognitive process as the essential building block for logical thought, comprehension, and generalization. (In fact, it was probably this view that caused his work to be banned in the Soviet Union from the early 1930s until the late 1950s; Vygotsky refused to tailor his research to the demands of the Stalinist regime.) Clearly, the overlap between Piaget and Vygotsky is substantial. The main difference between them is the degree to which interpersonal or social interaction causes development. Although Piaget seemed to view the learner as a solitary figure (Charles Lindbergh or Amelia Earhart) and Vygotsky emphasized the value of interaction (learning in groups), neither would claim that we learn exclusively either alone or with others.

The Zone of Proximal Development

Vygotsky was careful to distinguish between effective development instruction and traditional classroom learning. He asserted: "The only good kind of

Two theories of developmental learning
Vygotsky as a social interacter: "Groupie" learning
Piaget as a lone eagle: Amelia Earhart or Charles Lindbergh

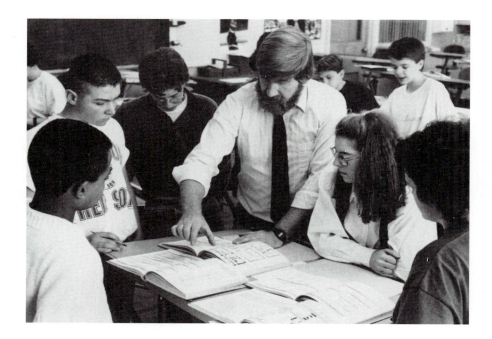

According to Vygotsky, meaningful learning occurs when the teacher is able to engage students in problem-solving activities that are just beyond their current level of functioning. He called this the "zone of proximal development."

instruction is that which marches ahead of development and leads it: It must be aimed not so much at the ripe as at the riping" (1962, p. 104). That is, education should lead development but be only slightly ahead of the learners' current preferred mode. He embodied this concept in the term *zone of proximal development.*

With these insights Vygotsky solved "the American question." Vygotsky does not call for acceleration but rather for a slow and careful sequencing of instruction. The teacher should not and cannot do the cognitive work on behalf of the child. Instead the teacher can present problems to be solved, and then must be willing to provide substantial time and place for the discussion process. The problems selected, of course, should be only slightly beyond the present competence while a new means of problem-solving is demonstrated. This is both active teaching and active learning through meaningful activities. The students are not told what to say or asked to memorize lists of facts but rather to engage in problem-solving activities and then to try to draw out reflective meaning through discussion. Insights are not given by the adults but rather are created and tested out by the children. The bottom line in all this is Vygotsky's emphasis on comprehension. Learning without comprehension borders on the fraudulent because it creates the illusion that education has somehow taken place. Vygotsky was so committed

to the dynamic process of cognitive problemsolving that he viewed standardized IQ tests as measuring merely static and fossilized knowledge. It is interesting to note in this regard that the current revisions in national tests such as the National Teacher Examination and perhaps even the Scholastic Aptitude Test are moving in the Vygotsky direction of presenting more problem-solving questions and less testing of memorized recognition of facts.

Peer Interaction and Vygotsky's Zone: Three Studies

One of the first studies of the effects of group interaction was undertaken by Jonathan Tudge (1990). He formed dyad groups of elementary students. The experimental dyads were mismatched by stage, a concrete level student was paired with a student at the preoperational level. The control group dyads were matched by stage. Each of the dyads worked on the Piaget water jar problem and gave a solution, including the reasons for their answer. His mismatched pairs (the experimental group) achieved an 80 percent rate of conservation, the control group only a 50 percent rate.

In a more comprehensive study along the same lines, Gail Jones and Glenda Carter (1994) divided 83 elementary students into four groups of approxi-

SPOTLIGHT ON RICHARD LIGHT

Vygotsky-Piaget Groups at Harvard

Richard Light has been assessing the approaches to college teaching through a series of seminars at Harvard University. Although he did not set up a direct experiment on the developmental approach, his work clearly points in the direction of peer interaction. He selected one of the most terrifying subjects, statistics, for his work. Rather than follow the conventional lecture-and-demonstration method, he used peer-led small groups. On an intuitive basis he selected group leaders who were slightly ahead of their peers in background and leadership. He then met with the leaders on a regular basis to review the content and the demonstration procedures. The leaders in turn met with small groups (five to eight students) for instruction. The atmospheres became more relaxed as the term progressed. Fear, anxiety, and mutism were replaced by increasing interaction. The noise level went up as the participation increased. Thus all the elements of the Piaget-Vygotsky model were present. And, as you've most likely guessed, the outcome was also positive. The students did better in statistics under the peer-led interaction than with conventional large-group instruction. In fact Light, who is a very dynamic and highly rated teacher himself, was so impressed by the findings that he recommended this approach for the teaching of any subject from statistics to moral reasoning. To be sure, faculty guidance was important. Light termed it *mentored small groups*. The socially isolated students actually gained the most from the peer interaction.[a]

You can try the Light method by setting up small groups with a student teacher for each. The format looks like the diagram.

Don't forget to meet regularly with the group leaders to supervise their techniques and keep the content valid.

[a] Light, R. J. (1990). *The Harvard Assessment Seminars.* Cambridge, MA: Harvard University.

Traditional Section

Mentored Cluster

- Group of 20 to 25 students meets with teaching fellow each week.

- Group meets same time, same place each week.

- Discussion is led by teams of two or three students with teaching fellow present.

- Groups of five students meet without a teaching fellow each week.

- Teaching fellow acts as resource between section meetings.

- Teaching fellow meets with student discussion leader before and after each session.

- One student acts as discussion leader each week.

mately the same size, two with matched ability levels (Low-Low and High-High groups) and two with mismatched ability levels (Low-High and High-Low groups). The central feature was a process study of actual verbal interactions over a three-week period, bracketed by a pretest and post-test analysis of academic achievement on a national assessment test. The results from the testing, presented in Table 5.4, indicate that only in the matched Low-Low ability groups were there no significant gains. In the other groups the gains were essentially the same, 2.5 points. This result was to be expected in the High-High group. In what is sometimes called the "Matthew effect," high-ability students generally gain in positive learning environments. On the other hand, it was somewhat surprising to find that in both mismatched groups, as long as one partner was high, all benefited.

Seeking an explanation for these outcomes, Jones and Carter next examined the children's discussion groups as they attempted to solve a series of balance-beam problems in lab meetings. When a low-ability student was matched with another low-ability student, the focus of discussion was mostly random, with large amounts of off-task behavior ("Let's group the blocks by color"), competition on irrelevant aspects of the task, and an interest in completing the worksheet as neatly as possible. These activities indicated that no real learning was taking place, simply random mindless experience. When a low-ability student was mismatched with a high-ability partner, the interaction was dramatically different, though *not at the outset*. At the beginning, the low-ability student behaved in much the same fashion as in the Low-Low groups. The high-ability student gradually helped the partner develop an interest and focus on the task. In taking turns the low-ability partner improved in the understanding of the problem and could verbalize in his or her own words important aspects of the process. The sharing of cognitions helped the low-ability student develop a

cognitive blueprint or map of the activity, not just the activity itself. It turned out that the high-ability students in the mismatched groups used many of the techniques of teaching effectiveness, such as positive reinforcement, nonverbal encouragement, and "wait time" in asking questions. Most important, both partners in the dyad gained in achievement.

In the High-High dyads the verbal interactions were on-task immediately. There was some competition but mostly cooperation. There was also a careful equality as to how much work each contributed.

On the overall basis then, the mismatched and matched High-High groups gained from the experience. The problems in the Low-Low groups confirmed the Vygotsky notion of the importance of a constructive mismatch or manageable dissonance to promote growth. Also, and perhaps equally important, was that high-ability students do not either lose ground or stagnate if paired with a low-ability partner. However, the teachers in the study had prepared interesting and novel learning activities that required a manipulation/demonstration activity, rather than some dreary rote memory problem, in order to challenge the learner within the zone of growth. The authors emphasized the importance of preparing the learning activity to maximize learning, just as Vygotsky suggested. We now turn to another study in this format, but with older students.

Dimant and Bearison (1991) had observed that not all college students were functioning at the level of formal operations. In fact some estimates run as high as 50 percent that certain students are still functioning at a concrete level in some subject areas. Dimant and Bearison set up three groups of dyads from a pool of 45 college students. One grouping had seven pairs of formal and concrete thinkers (the mismatched group). The second group was composed of eight pairs of concrete thinkers (the matched group). The third group consisted of 15 students as a control, receiving standard instruction. All groups studied the same problem-solving activities over a six-week period, figuring out how to combine liquids in a chemical mixture. The dyads were instructed to discuss the procedures and the solutions between themselves ("Talk out loud as you explore the problem") while attempting to answer the questions posed for each problem.

The dyad instruction, then, followed the Piagetian model. The learning was activity-based and inductive. The dyads engaged in the mixing tasks. Also there was substantial reflection through discussion as the pairs sought to figure out and agree on the reasons. The Vygotsky zone was also created for the mismatched pairs in which one member was slightly ahead of the other. The results were most interesting.

TABLE 5.4   GAIN SCORES IN CONCEPTUAL COMPLEXITY BY ABILITY GROUPINGS

DYAD GROUPINGS BY ABILITY	NUMBER OF CHILDREN	MEAN GAIN
Low-Low	13	0.77
High-Low	14	2.62
Low-High	16	2.64
High-High	40	2.58

Source: *Carter & Jones (1994)*, p. 616ff. Copyright © 1994. Reprinted by permission of John Wiley & Sons, Inc.

1. The mismatched pairs achieved the greatest gains in formal operations.

2. Both members of the dyad in the mismatched group gained.

3. The matched concrete pairs showed no gains and were similar to the controls.

The Dimant and Bearison study, then, confirms the approach used with elementary-age children but also extends the implications. Their study indicates that the mismatched group used more planning strategies, reasoned out loud more, and interacted more frequently than the others. They were noisier, yet with a purpose. Perhaps most surprising was the second finding, namely that both sides of the dyad benefited. It is perhaps easier to see why the concrete thinker improved, but why would the formal thinker benefit? The program does not rob Patricia or Peter to pay Pauline or Paul. The answer probably lies in the interaction. The formal thinker would improve by the activities of explaining and seeking consensus. This outcome reminds us of the old truism that one who teaches, learns. It also reminds us that conventional instruction and peer interaction by themselves are not particularly effective.

Vygotsky and Affect

Vygotsky, like Piaget and Furth, was also concerned about both the cognitive and affective aspects of learning. In his model, sarcasm, hostile questioning, poking fun at student error, and the like are at least as destructive if not so more so. Periods of relaxed reflection in group activity are important, with the teacher or a peer modeling respect for thoughtful pupil contributions. The zone of proximal growth in fact has a heavy affective component. Just think for a moment of the positive and excited feelings you've experienced when you have been just on the verge of new understanding. Such breakthroughs are the best examples of your self-concept as a learner. It is the feeling that comes from a realization that fragments of ideas and concepts are now being reorganized and restructured into a more meaningful whole. The glimpse is the first step in the zone as the positive feelings build. In education it is almost a truism to distinguish between extrinsic and intrinsic motivation. The extrinsic is learning in order to receive some kind of an external reward (money, a grade, a gold star). The intrinsic is vastly different, the enjoyment that comes from learning and problemsolving itself. The zone creates the framework for such intrinsic motivation. On the other hand, it does require

careful observation and understanding by the teacher. If the teacher is too far ahead, then the experience is just as meaningless as when the level of teaching is too far behind. In fact one developmental scholar has commented somewhat ironically that often teachers get trapped in between stages: "Either we are too early and they can't learn it or we're too late and they already know it" (Duckworth, 1996).

Vygotsky's Contribution

Tragically, Vygotsky died at the relatively early age of 37. Apparently he had been aware of his failing health for a number of years, which may have accounted for the almost-frenzied pace of producing over 180 written contributions in a very short time. Much of his research was conducted in remote villages, and he was forced to spend a good deal of time earning a living by teaching. Somehow he was able to integrate these many activities while turning out a huge number of scholarly papers. Today his work stands as a major contribution, especially for educational psychology. He was clearly interested in basic research, yet he was even more committed to the translation of these ideas into practice. In Chapter 1 we spoke about the four corners of teaching and learning; Vygotsky's concept of social interaction within the zone of proximal growth shed important light on the problem. His brief and meteoric career in the 1920s and 1930s has very significant implications for educational practice.

BRAIN PHYSIOLOGY AND STAGES: WHAT'S KNOWN AND WHAT ISN'T

As our technological ability to assess brain functions increases, particularly through the use of electroencephalograms (EEGs), a question arises: Is there any relation between changes in the brain and the stages of cognitive development? Piaget made such a claim without the benefit of such advanced technology. Appropriate interactive experiences produce stage growth up to a point, and then transformation (a qualitative shift) occurs. The person employs a new and more sophisticated system of cognitive process. Recent EEG work by William Hudspeth at the University of Northern Colorado and Robert Thacher at the University of Maryland has shown changes that coincide with those assumed by Piaget (Denton, 1987). The process of brain maturation was found to be discontinuous rather than linear. This meant that there were growth spurts that lined up with the sensorimotor, preoperational, concrete, and formal stages. The only significant differences between these findings and Piaget's estimates were that the sensorimotor stage may extend from birth to three and a half years rather than to two years. In addition, the EEGs revealed the possibility of a fifth stage. Formal operations matured between 11 and 15 years. The EEGs of young adults suggest a postformal period much as Patricia Arlin's work has outlined. These studies are preliminary but may well represent major new findings. At this point, what is known about the physiology of changes in the brain does suggest a clear relationship in the organization of the brain between stagelike cognitive growth and structural change.

Brain changes, however, do not occur automatically. Important differences take place according to interaction. Recent research has shown that a rich and stimulating environment for rats produces brains with a heavier cortex, larger neurons, more connectors, and more support cells. This is another reminder of the developmental truism of appropriate "hands-on" experience as the engine for growth. To prove the point, one study placed adult rats in a stimulating environment (a cage loaded with rat toys). Baby rats as well were placed in the same cage. Unfortunately, the adults dominated the scene. They played actively with all the toys. The babies watched on the sidelines. You may guess who benefited from the interactive experience. The baby rats did not develop. Robert Sylvester drew some apt parallels. How many times do adults organize activities for children that only play out adult fantasies (Little League baseball, ballet, piano for tots) and do not provide children with growth opportunities? A second parallel even closer to the classroom is the continued reliance on memorization, drill, and workbooks. Sylvester suggests such busywork provides an environment like that of rats in "culturally impoverished" cages with only one running wheel. He said those rats didn't develop either; "shades of continual drudgery with workbooks and long division problems" (1986, p. 93).

The research, then, has two related implications. Brain physiology exhibits changes in general accordance with Piaget stages. Appropriate hands-on active learning experiences are important to nurture such growth. Dull, passive experiences don't help. Adult experiences somewhat watered down also don't help.

At the same time, it is just as important to underscore what the recent brain research does not show. Some have suggested that brain changes called periodizations are directly relevant to teaching. In this view, periods of rapid growth may be followed by periods of no growth. Children may not be capable of learning much of anything when growth ceases (Epstein, 1978).

At this point we must remember that no evidence supports such a position. As Kurt Fischer and Marvin Lazerson summarize the findings, "They suggest that there is only a broad, nonspecific relation between brain development and Piagetian periods. They do not support the argument that children cannot learn new skills during times when their brains are growing slowly" (1985). Thus, it is important to be alert to any indication that a child may be like a computer and be "down" and unable to learn just after the growth-spurt periods. Growth depends on appropriate interaction before, during, and after stage shifts.

PIAGETIAN THEORY: NEW DIRECTIONS

By far the most important research program in the post-Piaget era is the work of Professor **Robbie Case** and his colleagues, both at the Ontario Institute for Studies in Education and at Stanford University. Case has systematically set out to examine the Piagetian model one step at a time through an impressive series of linked studies. In this manner he avoids the difficulties experienced by the first wave of anti-Piagetians, who would conduct studies in a narrowly focused area of information processing, find exceptions to the stages, and pronounce an end to the theory. Case found, for example, that some evidence of advanced thought in young children could be produced only under extreme testing conditions. A second problem was that such early competence was very task-specific and different from the tasks used to assess the same competence later on. A third problem was the inability of young children to generalize. For example, while some might show an indication of conservation before age five or six, there was, in Case's words, "massive failure" to promote the general competence of conservation at an earlier age. The overall problem, then, is that the researchers critical of Piaget themselves overgeneralized from their findings. Those researchers, Case noted, "sacrificed too much of the original Piaget" (1992, p. 376).

In order to right the balance, Case carried out a long series of research. Certainly one of the major weaknesses of the interpretation of Piaget's early work was an assumption that each stage was a generalized set of mental operations that was very broad across a wide variety of intellectual, interpersonal and value domains. In the language of technical research this is called the *question of synchronous versus asynchronous development*. Is the progression across

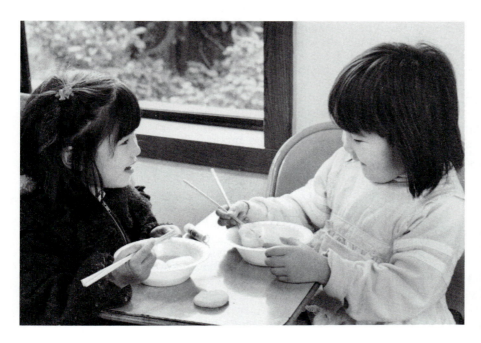

Robbie Case's research validated Piaget's earlier findings that cognitive growth occurs in stages and that, while individual differences occur within stages, the sequence of stages seems to remain intact for all humans.

domains even or uneven? If it is uneven, that is, a systematic gap in development (also called *décalage*), then do we eliminate the concept of qualitative stages? Also, it was clear that the research studies supported the idea of uneven growth versus a single-stage model.

As a result, Case accepted the idea of different domains and then set out to test whether stage growth occurred *within* specific competencies. Usually he and his associates set up problem-solving activities for children in different groupings—generally 4, 6, 8, and 10 years of age—and in some studies added groups of adolescents or even younger children. Moreover, some of the studies were conducted cross-culturally. The domains assessed included

1. Physics problems: some standard Piaget tests of conservation

2. Social tasks: sharing gifts and juice at a birthday party

3. Numerical concepts: telling time and changing money

4. Empathy: feelings of happiness, sadness, anger, etc.

5. Storytelling: completing stories for intentionality

6. Spatial concepts: relationships in children's drawings

7. Motor development: the use of utensils with yogurt, peas, carrots, etc.

The children were drawn from a variety of intellectual levels. Most studies were conducted with children with normal range IQs and were then cross-validated with other groups such as high-IQ gifted or learning disabled (LD) children. Perhaps the most remarkable feature of these studies is the care and patience of the researchers in questioning the children to determine their cognitive structure. The researchers didn't lead but rather clarified and supported as the answers were given. Imagine, for a moment, what was involved in studying motor development, watching and tracking an 18-month-old's attempts to scoop yogurt, keep peas on a spoon, mash a banana with a fork. The room must have been awash with food fragments, yet the researchers intrepidly continued. Or imagine the researcher who traveled to an extremely rural area in Africa's Upper Volta, translated the material into the local language (Ewe), and then negotiated intensively with the local chiefs for consent to travel from house to house (shades of Vygotsky and Luria in their treks to Uzbekistan).* Of course, at least as im-

---

* Ironically and tragically, this particular researcher, Thomas Fiati, withstood all the rigors of rural Africa, only to be killed in an auto accident near home, just after submitting the final draft of his doctoral thesis.

portant as the process was the outcome of these investigations.

With normal-range IQ children, the results supported the following conclusions:

1. Growth in each of the seven domains progresses in a stage sequence.

2. Individual differences are always within each stage and never exceed two substages.

3. The different domains do not constitute a single larger stage but are parallel and somewhat independent, e.g., a multilevel conception of domains.

4. Stage of complexity is more important than the information-processing working memory in solving problems.

Case's studies, then, confirmed that the amount of unevenness, asynchrony, or individual differences in information processing remains *within* each stage and does not span stages. Thus, individual differences in, say, working memory will vary among six-year-olds but will not explain variations in the problem-solving competency of eight-year-olds in the various domains under investigation. This also means that we cannot think of concrete operations as a single stage but rather as concrete operations in different domains. An earlier study by Sprinthall and Burke (1985) compared groups of 8-, 9-, and 10-year-olds across three domains—physics, interpersonal, and emotional—and obtained similar results. The age trend confirmed a developmental stage sequence, yet there was a very low intercorrelation (relationship) across the domains. The children were growing at different rates across the domains.

Case and associates also conducted rigorous tests of individual differences versus stage differences in studies with three groups of gifted children: high verbal, high performance, and high on both measures. They examined performance on nine different measures and found very few differences from same-age average-ability peers in a wide variety of domains such as storytelling, story complexity, art, counting, and speed. These results indicate that the stage of development was by far the most important variable. The one interesting exception occurred with learning tasks that involved providing cues and feedback. The high-IQ children were much more likely than others in their age group to employ the cues in modifying their solutions. On the other hand, when Case compared the high-IQ youngsters with a group of older children with the same "mental" age on seven tests, the high-IQ group scored lower than

their same-mental-age peers. This outcome appears to confirm that stage is more important than other factors and that development in those domains was for the most part equal. Giftedness seems more likely to be an indicator of rapid learning within a stage and not an indicator of rapid development through successive stages.

Two additional studies added validity to Case's neo-Piagetian model. The LD children showed no major differences across domains from non-LD children. Although the children were slower in their processing rate, they were not more than one substage lower. In the cross-cultural study comparing city-schooled children with nonschooled rural youngsters from the Upper Volta River in Africa, the results also indicated the importance of the stage domain sequence. Assessments in four domains with three age groups revealed only one exception to the stage progression: for the completely nonschooled rurals, numerical representation lagged behind the performance of their schooled urban peers; otherwise the sequence remained intact.

Case and his associates have cross-validated some of Piaget's basic concepts, changed some aspects of the model, and provided a framework for incorporating information processing with the redesigned theory. As their work continues, further clarifications will emerge. Even now, however, the conclusions and implications are significant. The concept of **qualitatively** different stagelike cognitive structures has been reconfirmed. There are variations of performance within each stage according to information-processing concepts of working memory and speed of learning, for example, **quantitative** differences. Rather than global stages, there is a series of different domains of stage and sequence in problemsolving. Educators should continue to employ the stage-and-sequence model from Piaget along with the modifications supplied by Case. For developmental researchers, there will always be a tension between the question of the span of the stage concept from one global or grand stage versus a series of overlapping domains that are highly specific. Lewis has recently suggested that a central conceptual structure (CCS)— that is, the self—actually organizes both specific contexts and a general scheme and are two sides of the same coin (Lewis, 1994). As we shall see, however, this is not the final word on needed modifications.

Cognitive Development: Too Narrow a Focus?

Psychologist **Robert Sternberg** (1986) at Yale University has cautioned that an exclusive focus on cognitive development may be misleading. He argues that both laypeople and professionals tend, wrongly, to equate cognition with logical reasoning, problem-solving, and speed of learning. He also notes that most standard measures of intelligence (see Chapter 16) assess only a very limited aspect of cognitive ability. As a result of his surveys, he now concludes that in addition to the domain of intelligence, there are two areas of equal importance, wisdom and creativity. He defines *wisdom* as involving concepts such as judgment, fairness, sagacity (willingness to consider advice from others as well as interpersonal sensitivity), perceptiveness, and information seeking. Intelligence and wisdom may overlap in some areas, but the domains also have some distinct differences. Sternberg sees *creativity* as imaginative, unconventional, aesthetic, flexible, a novel integration of information, and similar processes. In his view, however, current measures of creativity are trivial.

Sternberg maintains that a three-factor model of brain power provides us with a more accurate framework for understanding the process of cognitive growth. Also, at least implicitly, he is suggesting that the goals of schooling ought to be broadened. A focus on intelligence and achievement abandons the other aspects of development either to random forces or to oblivion. Thus, a longitudinal study of the famous "Quiz Kids," children of unusually high intelligence who performed in a radio program of that name in the 1940s, determined that they appar-

ently lacked creativity as adults (Sternberg & Davidson, 1985). And, a careful and systematic study of superior academic achievers at Johns Hopkins University, conducted by Paul Janos and Nancy Robinson, classified the Phi Beta Kappa graduates as "stable, stodgy, and unoriginal," intelligent but not creative (1985). Finally, the recent study of talented youth by Benjamin Bloom (1985) could find no adequate definition of interpersonal competence, and so the area was dropped from further study. Sternberg, of course, would say that an extremely important aspect of wisdom was overlooked. Imagine for a moment the brilliance of the late Dag Hammarskjold in his leadership at the United Nations (1981). With diplomatic skill, a vision of international justice, and an ability to deal with culturally diverse world leaders, he would stand as a prime example of wisdom. Similarly, if we examined the skill of Eleanor Roosevelt in her work at the conference on human rights for women or her work on behalf of civil rights for African-Americans, we would see a different kind of intelligence at work (Hareven, 1968). It will be important, as Sternberg's work progresses, to follow this line of inquiry. In line with his claim that "three heads are better than one," a fully functioning person would ideally possess all three traits: intelligence, wisdom, and creativity. This viewpoint implicitly diminishes the importance of Piaget's work by calling attention to its scope, which is limited to intelligence.

SUMMARY

According to the definition of cognitive developmental stages presented here, growth is qualitative rather than quantitative. It is characterized by great leaps forward, followed by periods of integration, rather than by linear, step-by-step changes in degree. Piaget came to this conclusion on the basis of repeated observations of children in natural settings.

Piaget's work created a new and significant stage theory regarding the process of cognitive growth. The stages are defined by the system of thinking employed and by modal age. In the sensorimotor stage, from birth to 24 months, learning is tied to immediate experience; object permanence is learned at this stage. In the preoperational stage, from 2 to 7 years of age, language development allows the child to free-associate and fantasize; creativity is a characteristic of this age. Children from 7 to 11 years of age are usually in the concrete operations stage, when literal-mindedness reigns. Finally, children reach the

stage of early formal operations, from 11 to 16 years, when thought enlarges to include possibilities, hypotheses, ideas, and the perspective of others. Although children usually operate at the stage appropriate to their age, they are sometimes capable of next-stage-up thinking, and teachers should encourage such development.

Piagetian theory emphasizes activity as a central ingredient of intelligence at all stages. Active learning experiences tend to promote cognitive growth, while passive and vicarious experiences tend to have minimal impact.

To the American question—Can we speed up growth?—Piaget's answer is that constant acceleration of learning is not possible because of the limitations of thought processes at various ages. But the process of growth can be nurtured.

The promotion growth requires attention to accommodation and assimilation. When new information is presented that does not fit the learner's current understanding, a knowledge disturbance is created. Taking in such new information involves accommodation. The next phase involves making the new concept fit with previous knowledge, or assimilation. Equilibration involves a balancing of accommodation and assimilation.

Furth has pointed out not only how this process works but also the feelings of anxiety and worry that go along with the struggle between the old way of thinking and the changes needed to grasp the new concept. When the previous balance is upset, emotions such as anxiety and exhilaration come into play. Vygotsky demonstrated how to promote growth within the zone of proximal development through carefully managed peer interaction.

A new addition to the model has been provided by Patricia Arlin. She has shown how the problem-finding stage is actually a prototypical fifth stage in the scheme. She outlined the elements in this stage, which may define higher-order cognition as wisdom. Robert Sternberg, like Arlin, has found the Piaget model lacking in the domain of wisdom; he also suggests adding creativity as a separate domain, with the result being a triad model. In his extensive research, Robbie Case has substantial evidence to cross-validate Piagetian theory. Case, however, has also pointed out the need to view stages of growth according to different domains.

For teachers, the most important result of all these studies is the implication that children are not adults and should not be treated like miniature adults in the classroom. Activity should be a major mode of learning. The hands-on approach has much greater educational merit than passive watching, listening, or rote memorization.

KEY TERMS AND NAMES

accommodation
active school
the American question
Patricia Arlin
assimilation
Robbie Case
conservation
developmental stage
equilibration
Hans Furth
Arnold Gesell

periodization
Jean Piaget
   sensorimotor stage
   preoperational stage
   concrete operations stage
   formal operations stage
Robert Sternberg
qualitative development
quantitative development
Lev Vygotsky

THEORY INTO PRACTICE: APPLYING PIAGET

In this section, we provide a series of Piagetian tests that you can use to assess some levels of cognitive development. The first set provides a means of measuring concrete operations. The second set assesses abstract reasoning (formal operations). The tests can be administered individually or to small groups. The students' answers, particularly their reasons and explanations, will provide insight into their present cognitive functioning. Remember, however, that a developmental stage, by definition, is completely different from a traditional IQ score or a special-education label, which are permanent classifications. A developmental stage is only a picture of current functioning. Do not make the mistake of assuming that current-stage functioning is fixed at any particular age.

Measuring Aspects of Concrete Operations*

The following tests are designed to assess elementary-age children's ability to conserve and to classify.

---

*   The items in this section and item 3 in the next section were developed by Pisila Taufé Ulungaki, a specialist in tests and measurements at the University of Minnesota.

Instructions: (1) Read each item carefully. (2) Answer all the items. (3) Mark the correct answer. (4) Explain your answer.

Practice item: Before you begin, look at the practice item below. Study it carefully to see how you are to find the right answer.

Shown below are two sets of fruit.

Set A has oranges. Set B has apples.

Set A: ☺☺☺☺☺☺☺☺

Set B: 🍎🍎🍎🍎🍎
🍎🍎🍎

A. Of the two sets, which set has the most fruit?

☐ a. Set A has the most fruit.
☐ b. Set B has the most fruit.
☑ c. They have the same number of fruit.
☐ d. None of the above answers is correct.

B. Explain your answer. *Set A has 8 oranges. Set B has 8 apples. Therefore, both sets have the same number of fruit. (or) Set A = 8. Set B = 8. Therefore, Set A = Set B.*

---

1. Shown below are two groups of marbles. Each circle represents a marble.

Group A: ○ ○ ○ ○ ○ ○ ○ ○ ○

Group B: ○○○○○○○○○

A. Of the two groups, which group has more marbles?

☐ a. Group A has more marbles.
☐ b. Group B has more marbles.
☐ c. Both groups have the same number of marbles.
☐ d. None of the above answers is correct.

B. Explain your answer. _____

_____

_____

_____

---

2. Shown below are nine wooden blocks.

A. Two ways to sort the blocks into groups that are alike would be

☐ a. By color and by groups of two blocks.
☐ b. By shape and by groups of four blocks.
☐ c. By color and by shape.
☐ d. None of the above answers is correct.

B. Explain your answer. _____

_____

_____

_____

3, 4. Shown below in Picture A is a bottle half full of water.

A   B   C

A. Suppose the bottle is tilted as shown in Picture B, and then placed flat as shown in Picture C. Draw the water levels on the bottles in Picture B and in Picture C.

B. Explain your answer. _____

_____

_____

_____

5. Shown below is a bowl half full of water. Beside it is an iron ball.

A. Suppose the iron ball is placed into the bowl of water. Will the water in the bowl go up or down, or will the water level remain the same?

☐ a. Remain the same.
☐ b. Go up.
☐ c. Go down.
☐ d. None of the above answers is correct.

B. Explain your answer. _____

_____

_____

_____

6. There are three girls named Jane, Mary, and Susan. Suppose Jane is taller than Mary and Mary is taller than Susan. Is Jane taller than Susan?

☐ a. Yes.
☐ b. No.
☐ c. Both are the same height.
☐ d. Not enough information is given.

Explain your answer. _____

_____

_____

Answers: 1. c; 2. c; 3, 4. B   C   5. b; 6. a

Measuring Aspects of Formal Operations

The following test items represent different approaches to measuring formal operations. The ability to think abstractly is the major element that separates people at this level from those at the prior stage.

---

1. *The meaning of proverbs and aphorisms.* Ask students to describe the meaning of any sayings such as:

Still water runs deep.

A stitch in time saves nine.

A rolling stone gathers no moss.

Make hay while the sun shines.

Let no good deed go unpunished.

Penny wise and pound foolish.

The louder he proclaimed his honor, the faster we counted the silverware.

Don't look a gift horse in the mouth.

In my beginning is my end.

Concrete thinkers will give literal descriptions tied very closely to the content: "When the water is very still, it means it's very deep," as opposed to "A quiet person often observes and understands the complexities of life." Or, "A farmer should gather in the hay before it rains" versus "When a good opportunity is at hand, act."

2. *Logic problems: The bean, bird, fish, snail islands puzzle.** This puzzle is about four islands in the ocean. People have been traveling among these islands by boat for many years, but recently an airline started in business. Students must listen carefully to the clues given about possible plane trips. The trips may be direct or they may include stops on one of the islands. When a trip is possible, it can be made in both directions between the islands. Here is how the puzzle should be presented:

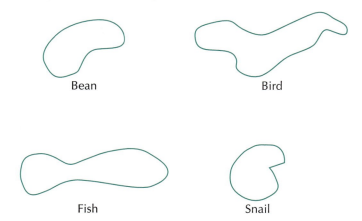

Bean

Bird

Fish

Snail

This is a map with the four islands, called Bean Island, Bird Island, Fish Island, and Snail Island. You may make notes or marks on your map to help you remember the clues. Raise your hand if you have questions about the clues.

First clue: People can go by plane between Bean and Fish Islands.

Second clue: People cannot go by plane between Bird and Snail Islands.

Use these two clues to answer Question 1.

---

*   This item is from J. W. Renner, D. G. Stafford, A. E. Lawson, J. W. Mckinnon, F. E. Friot, & D. H. Kellogg, *Research, Teaching and Learning with the Piaget Model.* Copyright © 1976 by the University of Oklahoma Press. Reprinted by permission.

QUESTION 1: Can people go by plane between Bean and Bird Islands?

☐ a. Yes
☐ b. No
☐ c. Can't tell from the two clues.

Explain your answer. _____

_____

_____

Third clue: People can go by plane between Bean and Bird Islands.

Use all three clues to answer Questions 2 and 3. Don't change your answer to Question 1.

QUESTION 2: Can people go by plane between Fish and Bird Islands?

☐ a. Yes
☐ b. No
☐ c. Can't tell from the two clues.

Explain your answer. _____

_____

_____

QUESTION 3: Can people go by plane between Fish and Snail Islands?

☐ a. Yes
☐ b. No
☐ c. Can't tell from the two clues.

Explain your answer. _____

_____

_____

Concrete thinkers will have difficulty remembering the combination of clues. Usually their explanations will indicate their inability to consider all the clues simultaneously.

Answers:　1. Can't tell; 2. Yes—take plane from Fish to Bean and Bean to Bird;
　　　　　　3. No—the second clue makes that impossible.

3. *Physical properties problems:* Ask students to answer the following physical science questions.

(a) The diagram below represents a scale. Beside it are several rings representing balls of different weights for balancing the bar of the scale.

A. Suppose a four-ounce ring was placed on the scale as shown at point 4 in the diagram. By using one of the weights below, show how the bar could be balanced.

☐ a. Place the 8-ounce ring on 2.
☐ b. Place the 4-ounce ring on 5.
☐ c. Place the 2-ounce ring on 2.
☐ d. None of the above.

B. Explain your answer. _____

_____

_____

_____

(b) Shown below is a pendulum made in the form of an object hanging from a string. Also shown are pendulums with different string lengths and different weights.

A. A science class made some trials to see if the pupils could find out what made the pendulum swing faster or slower. The following is a record of the class observations of swing.

Length	Weight	Rate	Comment
short	light	slow	false
short	heavy	fast	true
long	light	fast	false
long	light	slow	true
short	heavy	slow	false
short	light	fast	true
long	heavy	fast	false
long	heavy	slow	true

By studying the above table of observations, select the choice that seems best.

☐ a. It is the weight.
☐ b. It is the length.
☐ c. It is the combination of both.
☐ d. None of the above.

B. Explain your answer. _____

_____

_____

_____

Answers: 3(a). a, 3(b). b

REFERENCES

Arlin, P. K. (1986). Problem finding and young adult cognition. In R. Mines & K. Kitchener (Eds.), *Adult cognitive development* (pp. 22–33). New York: Praeger.

Arlin, P. K. (1993). Wisdom and expertise in teaching: An integration of perspectives. *Learning and Individual Differences, 5,* 341–349.

Arlin, P. K., & Fung, L. (1995, April). *Wisdom and expertise in teaching: Searching for developmental indicators.* Paper presented at the annual meeting of the American Educational Research Association, San Francisco.

Barratt, B. (1975). Training and transfer in combinational problem-solving: The development of formal reasoning during early adolescence. *Developmental Psychology, 11*(6), 700–704.

Bauer, P. (1996). What do infants recall of their lives? *American Psychologist, 51*(1), 29–41.

Blanck, G. (1990). Vygotsky: The man and his cause. In L. C. Moll (Ed.), *Vygotsky and education* (pp. 31–58). Cambridge: Cambridge University Press.

Bloom, B. (1985). *Developing talent in young people.* New York: Random House.

Carter, G., & Jones, G. (1994). Relationship between ability-paired interactions and the development of fifth graders' concept of balance. *Journal of Research in Science and Teaching, 31*(8), 847–856.

Case, R. (1992). *The mind's staircase.* Hillsdale, NJ: Erlbaum.

Davidson, P. (1993). Revising the logic of operations as a relevance logic: From hypothesis testing to explanation-commentary. *Human Development, 36*(3), 147–149.

Denton, L. (1987). EEG's bolster Piaget theory. *APA Monitor, 18*(8), 27.

Dimant, R., & Bearison, D. (1991). Development of formal reasoning during successive peer interactions. *Developmental Psychology, 27,* 277–284.

Duckworth, E. (1996). *"The having of wonderful ideas."* New York: Teachers College.

Elkind, D. (1970). *Children and adolescents.* New York: Oxford University Press.

Epstein, H. (1978). Growth spurts during brain development: Implications for educational policy. In J. A. Chall & A. F. Mirsky (Eds.), *1978 Yearbook of the National Society for the Study of Education.* Chicago: University of Chicago Press.

Fischer, K., & Lazerson, A. (1985). Research: Brain spurts and Piagetian periods. *Educational Leadership, 41*(5), 70.

Flavell, J. H. (1985). *Cognitive development.* Englewood Cliffs, NJ: Prentice Hall.

Flavell, J. H. (1992). Cognitive development: Past, present, and future. *Developmental Psychology, 28,* 998–1005.

Flavell, J., Green, F., & Flavell, E. (1995). Cognitive processes: Comprehension, thinking, and introspection. *Monographs of the Society for Research in Child Development 60 and 82.*

Flavell, J., Miller, P., and Miller, S. (1993). *Cognitive development* (3d ed.). Englewood Cliffs, NJ: Prentice Hall.

Furth, H. (1981). *Piaget and knowledge* (2d ed.). Chicago: University of Chicago Press.

Furth, H. (1995). Self in which relation? *American Psychologist, 50*(3), 176.

Gelman, R. (1982). Basic numerical abilities. In R. J. Sternberg (Ed.), Advances in the psychology of human intelligence (Vol 1). Hillsdale, NJ: Erlbaum.

Gesell, A. (1940). *The first five years of life.* New York: Harper & Row.

Ginsberg, H., & Opper, S. (1988). *Piaget's theory of intellectual development.* Englewood Cliffs, NJ: Prentice Hall.

Glassman, M. (1994). All things being equal: The two roads of Piaget and Vygotsky. *Developmental Review, 14*(2), 186–214.

Hammarskjold, D. (1981). *Markings.* New York: Knopf.

Hareven, T. (1968). *Eleanor Roosevelt: An American conscience.* Chicago: Quadrangle Books.

Harris, P. (1995). The rise of introspection. *Monographs of the Society for Research in Child Development, 60*(1, pp, 97–103).

Herrnstein, R., & Murray, C. (1994). *The bell curve.* New York: Free Press.

Hostetler, A. (1988). "Smart" brains work better not harder. *APA Monitor, 19*(5), 15.

Inhelder, B., & Piaget, J. (1958). *The growth of logical thinking from childhood to adolescence.* New York: Basic Books.

Janos, P., & Robinson, N. (1985). Psychosocial development of intellectually gifted children. In F. D. Horowitz & M. D. O'Brien (Eds.), *The gifted and talented: Developmental perspectives* (pp. 149–196). Washington, DC: American Psychological Association.

Jones, G., & Carter, G. (1994). Verbal and nonverbal behavior of ability-grouped dyads. *Journal of Research in Science Teaching, 31*(6), 603–619.

Lewis, M. (1994). Reconciling stage and specificity in neo-Piagetian theory: Self-organizing conceptual structures. *Human Development, 37*(3), 143–169.

Light, R. J. (1990). *The Harvard Assessment Seminars.* Cambridge: Harvard University.

Maccoby, E. (1990). The role of gender identity and gender constancy in sex-differentiated development. In D. Schrader (Ed.), *The legacy of Lawrence Kohlberg* (pp. 5–20). San Francisco: Jossey-Bass.

Mischel, W. (1981). Metacognition and the rules of delay. In J. H. Flavell and L. Ross (Eds.), *Social cognitive development*. New York: Cambridge University Press.

Neimark, E. D. (1982). Adolescent thought: Transition to formal operations. In B. B. Wolman (Ed.), *Handbook of developmental psychology*. Englewood Cliffs, NJ: Prentice Hall.

Piaget, J. (1964). *Judgment and reasoning in the child*. Paterson, NJ: Littlefield Adams.

Piaget, J. (1970). *Science of education and the psychology of the child*. New York: Viking.

Piaget, J., & Garcia, R. (1991). *Toward a logic of meanings*. Hillsdale, NJ: Erlbaum.

Pines, M. (1970). *A revolution in learning*. New York: Harper & Row.

Phillips, D. C. (1995). The good, the bad, and the ugly: The many faces of constructivism. *Educational Researcher, 24*(7), 5–12.

Renner, J., Stafford, D., Lawson, A., McKimmon, J., Friot, F., & Kellogg, D. (1976). *Research, teaching, and learning with the Piaget model*. Norman: University of Oklahoma Press.

Rowe, D., Vazonyi, A., & Flannery, D. (1994). No more than skin deep: Ethic and racial similarity in developmental process. *Psychological Review, 101*(3), 396–413.

Scarr-Salapatek, S. (1976). An evolutionary perspective on infant intelligence: Species patterns and individual variations. In M. Lewis (Ed.), *The origins of intelligence: Infancy and early childhood*. New York: Plenum.

Slone, M., Dixon, J., & Bokhorst, F. (1994). Physical knowledge of sugar water solutions: Cross-cultural data. *Journal of Genetic Psychology, 155*(1), 65–75.

Smagorinsky, P. (1995). The social construction of data. *Review of Educational Research, 65*(3), 191–212.

Sprinthall, N. A., & Burke, S. (1985). Intellectual, interpersonal, and emotional development during childhood. *Journal of Humanistic Education and Development, 24,* 50–58.

Sprinthall, N. A., & Collins, W. A. (1995). *Adolescent psychology: A developmental view*. New York: McGraw-Hill.

Sternberg, R. J. (1986). Intelligence, wisdom, and creativity: Three is better than one. *Educational Psychologist, 21*(3), 175–190.

Sternberg, R. J., & Davidson, J. E. (1985). Cognitive development in the gifted and talented. In F. D. Horowitz & M. D. O'Brien (Eds.), *The gifted and talented: Developmental perspectives* (pp. 37–74). Washington: American Psychological Association.

Sylvester, R. (1986). Synthesis of research on brain plasticity: The classroom environment and curriculum enrichment. *Educational Leadership, 44*(1), 90–93.

Tudge, J. (1990). Vygotsky, the zone of proximal development. In L. C. Moll (Ed.), *Vygotsky and education* (pp. 155–174). Cambridge: Cambridge University Press.

Tudge, J., & Winterhoff, P. (1993). Vygotsky, Piaget, and Bandura: Perspectives on relations between the social world and cognitive development. *Human Development, 36*(2), 61–81.

Vygotsky, L. (1962). *Thought and language*. Cambridge: MIT Press.

Vygotsky, L. (1985). *Pensée et langage*. Paris: Editions Sociales.

White, M. A. (1968). The view from the pupil's desk. *Urban Review, 2,* 5–7.

Wolfenstein, M. (1954). *Children's humor*. Glencoe, IL, Free Press.

PERSONAL GROWTH

Although this chapter concentrates on personal development during childhood and adolescence, it is important to remember that the various stages of growth are not separate from one another. We indicated earlier that the mind is not a discrete entity, any more than the body. Mind and body function together and are intimately interconnected. In the same way, we cannot really separate personal development (the growth of personality) from cognitive development (the growth of intellectual skills). For example, a basic part of our personality resides in our self-concept; how we perceive and think about ourselves, especially in relation to other people, will certainly affect our personal development. Therefore, as you read this chapter, be careful not to assume that personal growth takes place in a vacuum.

The ideas of growth and development presented here are based largely on Erik Erikson's elaboration of Sigmund Freud's original work. It was Erikson who transformed Freud's theories of emotional growth into a major development scheme as a means of understanding the process of healthy personal growth.

Following a description of the Erikson stages, we focus on recent research and theory detailing the importance of identity formation during adolescence. The work of James Marcia and Alan Waterman outlining four different identity statuses provides a sig-

nificant understanding of these developmental pathways. We will also examine the dual identity problem faced by ethnic minorities and the work by Sally Archer on gender identity. Finally, we discuss the importance of identity achievement as both an index of psychological maturity and a necessary precondition to the first stage of adulthood, intimacy.

THE PRE-FREUDIAN VIEW OF MINDLESS CHILDREN

Before the earthshaking discoveries of Sigmund Freud, at the turn of this century, it was generally assumed that, until they reached the age of six or seven, children were mindless creatures, more like animals than humans. It was important to meet their physical needs, but beyond that they were thought to be in a kind of incubation period, too young to know or feel anything. There was little reason to take the early years seriously as a time when anything significant could occur.

Interestingly enough, this view of young children is common to many cultures throughout the world. In both modern and primitive societies, many practices are based on the notion that children are unthinking creatures, with no minds of their own or emotions of any consequence. These cultures sharply demarcate the beginning of the juvenile period (at about age seven) from the age of mindlessness (birth to age six). English common law and Catholic canon law, for example, both assume that children do not know anything before their seventh year. In non-Western cultures, a variety of initiation rites, performed between the ages of six and seven, are based on similar assumptions. In fact, one culture actually killed children who became seriously ill before the age of six, in the belief that they were not really children at all but snakes masquerading as humans (S. White, 1968).

In this country, one of the pioneers in establishing childhood as a significant era in human development was **Lawrence K. Frank.** A child psychologist of particular eminence, he devoted his entire professional life to pointing out those practices within and across cultures that were designed to meet adult needs and that ignored the needs of children. He documented the entire array of childrearing practices that assumed children were little more than pieces of clay to be molded into any shape by adult "master craftsmen." Molding and shaping had everything from physical to psychological manifestations. In some cultures heads are flattened, feet are bound, necks are stretched, skin is punctured or tattooed. In other cultures natural physiological functions, such as breathing, feeding, and sleeping patterns, are altered. The array of psychological practices is even greater, especially in the realm of what we could call character building. Using extreme forms of punishment, from severe scolding to beatings, adults have tried for centuries to defeat and deflect the process of personal growth. As Frank put it, "Civilized man has survived *despite,* not because of, these methods of child care." The methods were too often created to suit the adult, not the child, and were based on an almost absolute ignorance of the special nature of childhood. As a result, "In the area of conduct and belief there apparently are no limits to the grotesque, the cruel and brutal, the diabolical ingenuity of man in warping and twisting human nature" (Frank, 1969, p. 71).

The theoretical justification for all this beating, scolding, and molding is detailed by Rolf Muus (1988). The idea that a young child is a midget-sized adult is termed *preformationism.* In that view—also called the *homunculus view*—there are no qualitative or stage differences between or among children, adolescents, or adults; a baby is simply a preformed little adult and therefore should be treated like one. The preformationist approach to teaching is illustrated by the copybook of the youthful Timothy Orne, laboriously written in 1738.

This background allows us to appreciate what a shock wave was set off by the works of Sigmund Freud.

SIGMUND FREUD'S DISCOVERY OF CHILDHOOD

In searching for the causes of adult emotional difficulties, **Sigmund Freud** created a revolutionary view of childhood that in no way resembled the prevailing view of childhood as a time of benign emptiness. Freud, using the methods of clinical research, hypnotized his clients or asked them to free-associate ("Tell me the first thing that comes to mind") or to recount their recent dreams. He found, over and over again, that major aspects of his clients' personal development originated during the first six years of life. In fact, Freud discovered that he could understand the adult personality only by examining the kind of experiences and personal relationships the adult had had in childhood (before entering school). To know an adult, Freud would say, know the child. Hence the famous expression, "The child is father of the man." In early experience could be discovered the foundations of later personal development. Uncovering significant childhood experiences is the essence of **psychoanalytic theory.**

Freud, with a kind of possessed genius, had to withstand enormous vilification as his theories became known. He was literally hated and feared, almost like the messenger in ancient times who was executed for being the bearer of bad news. Freud's bad news was simple: Adults must stop treating children as if they were too young to know or experience anything. There could be no justification whatsoever for childrearing practices that mangle, distort, inhibit, and break the young spirit.

FREUD'S VIEW OF EMOTIONAL GROWTH DURING CHILDHOOD

Freud discovered that during their first years children go through a sequence of emotional stages, much as Piaget found them to go through a sequence of cognitive stages. In charting the course of emotional growth, Freud named three major stages of development from birth through age seven: the **oral stage** (birth to 18 months), the **anal stage** (18 months to three years), and the **phallic stage** (three to seven years).

According to Freud, this sequence of major emotional transformations leaves an indelible imprint on

Fingers firmly gripping the thin shaft of a quill pen, many a student in an early American school labored over his copy book, tracing the elaborate dips and swirls of the ABCs and struggling with the accompanying writing exercises.

Each page of the large, clothbound text contained examples of the exacting script of the teacher. On blank lines below the teacher's writing, the students meticulously sought to achieve the same effect, repeatedly tracing garnished letters of the alphabet and copying sentences of a relentlessly uplifting tone. Hour after hour they toiled, and some of the more gifted among them ultimately went on to achieve calligraphy so ornate as to be virtually unreadable.

The reward for this drudgery was the book itself, page upon page of the most elegant penmanship, often cherished for years by such scholars as Timothy Orne.

the adult personality. Also, as with cognitive growth, certain dimensions of personality are maximally affected at each of these stages. During the oral stage, for example, the quality of nurturing that children receive, especially as related to feeling, will maximally affect their later feelings of dependence and trust in the world. During the anal stage (the name is derived from the universal requirement for bowel training), independence and control are at the forefront of development. In the phallic stage, sexual identity is the major aspect of personality formation.

Freud suggested that a period of latency (7 to 12 years) follows, in which the oral, anal, and phallic dimensions are integrated and no new elements are added. However, during adolescence (the genital stage), the period of so-called *Sturm und Drang* (a German expression meaning a period of extreme stress and strain), all the previous elements—oral, anal, and especially phallic—are brought back into play. During adolescence the basic elements are reworked into an adult character. This is a time for recapitulation, for going back over the issues of de-

pendence (oral period), independence (anal period), and identity (phallic period) to prepare for a fully functioning adulthood in which, according to Freud, we can love and work productively—a simple but profound human objective.

Freud established once and for all that extremely significant personal and emotional aspects of our development are determined during the first six years of our lives. It was no longer possible to assume that the young child had no mind or any significant emotions. Instead, Freud's theory provided valid information to buttress an old adage, "As the twig is bent, so inclines the tree." The adult personality is affected in major ways by the emotional experiences of childhood.

In other words, the interactions between the child and significant adults during the first six years determine whether or not the adult will be able to function efficiently. Inadequate or negative childrearing practices will result in a personality that is flawed. The person may function adequately but will show major deficiencies.

SIGMUND FREUD

If there is a single name in all psychology that is synonymous with personality theory, it is Sigmund Freud. Born in Freiberg, Moravia, in 1856, he spent his early years as a member of a tightly knit family in Central Europe. Reportedly, his youth was marked by severe bouts with depression and anxiety. These difficulties apparently started him on a journey of discovery aimed at understanding the roots of personality and gaining insight into the relationship between personality structure and actual behavior. It was to be a long and productive professional journey, beginning with his graduation from medical school at the University of Vienna in 1881. His career extended all the way to the beginning of World War II in 1939.

After completing his medical studies, Freud became increasingly interested in diseases of the nervous system. Instead of continuing to look for physical and physiological reasons, he shifted his attention toward a new arena, the mind. If diseases such as hysteria, high-anxiety states, and deep personal depression were not connected to a physical cause, then the usual types of medical treatment, from actual operations on nerves to prescriptions for drugs, were bound to fail. Such activities merely treated the symptoms. Often, after these treatments, patients simply developed a new set of symptoms. As a result of these ideas, Freud decided to study with Josef Breuer, a physician famous for his treatment of hysteria through hypnosis. Freud found that inducing hypnotic trances was somewhat limited as a treatment of choice. Some patients could not be successfully hypnotized, and others simply shifted symptoms.

Freud began to experiment with unique treatment methods, primarily asking patients to free-associate and to report on their dreams. In some ways this seemed an outrageous procedure for a physician to use. Imagine Freud asking a patient to stretch out on his soon-to-be-famous couch, then suggesting that he or she say whatever came to mind. (The first rule of psychoanalysis was to speak out and not repress any hidden thoughts.) All the while Freud himself was sitting behind the couch, quietly jotting down notes, rarely speaking. Such a procedure seemed the work of a mad genius at best or of a charlatan at worst. Not only did Freud break with the traditions of his time completely, but he even went so far as to carry on psychoanalytically oriented treatment by mail: In the famous case of "Little Hans," he successfully treated a young boy by writing to the father and explaining, step by step, how to cure the patient of a severe case of horse phobia. Since horses provided most of the transportation in those days, Hans's malady can be compared to that of a child today who would run and hide at the sight of an automobile.

Always an innovator, Freud continued to evolve creative treatment techniques throughout his life; however, his major contribution

ERIK ERIKSON: THE SEQUENCE OF STAGES AND TASKS OF PERSONAL DEVELOPMENT

Erik Erikson, one of Freud's students, has done more than any other theorist to modernize Freudian theory and make it into a more complete theory of child and adolescent development. In a sense, one of the major difficulties with Freud's view was that it was too deterministic. According to Freud, by the time we are six or seven years old, personal growth is essentially all over. Our basic personality structures are already set. As shown in Table 6.1, Erikson (1982) expanded the ideas of stages of development into a broader framework—a life cycle—and outlined the positive and negative dimensions of each period. This helped clarify and balance Freudian theory as a means of understanding personal growth.

was his insight into the causes of behavior. Through hours of quiet listening to patients' free associations and descriptions of dreams, he began to construct a theory of personality. He heard the same themes repeated over and over again and in time created his theory of infant sexuality. Adult patients were helped to gradually recall early feelings, thoughts, and sexual fantasies from their childhood. To suggest to the world that innocent little children had such sexual feelings was almost too much for the Victorian age to accept. Nevertheless, despite the enormous criticism generated and the departure of some of his closest associates, Freud continued to expand on the importance of sexuality as a determinant of personality during the early years of life. His three-part typology of the mind—the id, the ego, and the superego—combined with his three layers of thought—conscious, preconscious, and unconscious—led to his famous dictum that all human behavior was overdetermined. His clinical approaches demonstrated that our present behavior is related to a whole series of "causes." The task of the psychologist is to uncover great amounts of psychic material and then gradually help the patient understand how many of the factors from the past have been regulating his or her present behavior. In fact, Freud said that the psychologist is like an archaeologist—carefully and systematically digging through the past in order to uncover the intrapsychic traumas of a person's early history. Here he found the structure of the past influencing present behavior; here was the repository of events, feelings, disconnected ideas, fantasies rooted in the unconscious.

The unconscious, according to Freud, is the key to human behavior. Even though individuals may try to suppress or repress inner thoughts and feelings and push them into the unconscious, the repressed material sneaks out in disguised form. Slips of the tongue, unfortunate "accidents," forgetting important events, getting names of familiar people mixed up, and similar unusual behavior are not just incidental activities or randomly determined. He was able to show that such events are instead a direct expression of an individual's unconscious motivation. For example, a guilt-ridden criminal might "accidentally" leave a trail from the scene of a crime in order to bring about his own punishment. Other examples abound in everyday life.

The insights of Freud changed our level of understanding in dramatic ways. It has been said that his greatest contribution was to end, once and for all, the age of innocence. Some have also remarked that it would have been impossible to understand the horrors of the twentieth century without his theories of why and how people react. These theories demonstrated the importance of both sexual and aggressive human drives. The adverse interpersonal relationships so common in this age are current reminders of this insight. The desolation created by two major world wars, the total annihilation of innocent populations, the use of ultimate weapons from A-bombs to gas chambers—these products of a so-called advanced civilization can be better understood through his views. It is to be hoped that his insights will teach the world the importance of recognizing and gradually developing control over these destructive human drives.

Freud spent many of his last years in Nazi Germany, as a captive of one of the most demonic regimes in human history. During his final year of life, in England in 1939, he watched the world he knew collapse in a paroxysm of hatred, tragic testimony to his deepest fears for humanity.

Whereas Freud had emphasized the negative and pathological aspects of emotional growth, Erikson directed the theory into a broader context. He saw development continuing throughout one's life, but gave special significance to childhood (birth to 6 years), the juvenile era (6 to 12 years), and adolescence (12 through the college years). Although he has suggested stages of development well into adulthood, we will concentrate on these three categories.

As if to underscore the significance of Erikson's theory as a positive outline of stages of personal and emotional growth, Daniel Goleman (1995) has suggested that educators and psychologists have ignored this facet of development for too long. In fact, he has coined the term emotional quotient (EQ) to highlight the issue. He has been able to demonstrate that such emotional intelligence is a central component of effective human communication. The highest

TABLE 6.1   ERIKSON'S GROUND PLAN FOR PSYCHOLOGICAL GROWTH

AGE	*BIPOLAR CRISES AT EACH STAGE*				
Birth–24 months	Basic trust vs. mistrust	Early autonomy, etc.	Early initiative	Early mastery	Early identity
2–3 years	Later forms of hope, etc.	Autonomy vs. shame	↓	↓	↓
4–6 years	↓	Later forms of will	Initiative vs. guilt	↓	↓
6–12 years	↓	↓	Later forms of purpose	Mastery vs. inferiority	↓
13–18 years	↓	↓	↓	Later forms of competence	Identity vs. diffusion
18 years through college	↓	↓	↓	↓	Identity (moratorium and achievement) vs. continued diffusion
Resolution:	Hope	Will	Purpose	Competence	Fidelity

levels of negotiation skills by diplomats and mediators are determined by their level of emotional development. Thus, personal growth has been revalidated through Goleman's work. Erikson's framework spells out the specific importance of particular emotional and personal themes at different points on the development scheme.

The Epigenetic Principle: The Engine for Growth

You may recall that Piaget discussed the importance of equilibration as the mechanism that promotes cognitive development. There is a built-in drive to acquire more complex systems of thinking. In a parallel sense, Erikson says much the same for personal growth. His terms are different, but the assumptions are the same. Erikson refers to the **epigenetic principle.** Personality itself goes through structural elaborations in accord with a ground plan. Development is not random but proceeds according to the outline. Nor is development automatic; the ground plan is really a map of potential. If the child's interaction with the environment is healthy and the basic crisis of each stage of development is resolved, then the child will be ready for the next stage. We do not have to force a child to grow as a personality. The epigenetic principle means the potential for growth already is a given.

Originally Erikson posed his framework in terms of stages of crises, with bipolar definitions of the crisis at each stage—for example, trust versus mistrust. More recently, he has suggested that each of these opposites can be combined. During the first years the child wrestles with the problem of how trustful or distrustful to become. Under appropriate conditions of nurture, these opposites are resolved into a new condition called "hope." Thus, as the first two years of life end, the child's personality can be disposed toward a basically positive outlook. Similarly, the resolution to the second stage, autonomy versus shame, is now termed "will." Apparently Erikson was quite uneasy about denoting the resolutions in terms such as hope, will, purpose, competence, and fidelity. He was worried that such "old-fashioned" terms might lead psychologists to dismiss his work as more philosophy than behavioral science. However, such terms actually clarify the goals of each stage as a meaningful synthesis, a new combination. For example, under the old system it was difficult to resolve the trust-versus-mistrust polarity as trust. Hope, however, represents more a resolution of two opposite tendencies than an either-or choice. The same is true of the other stages, as you will see in the following descriptions.

Childhood (Birth to Six Years)

Trust versus mistrust (birth to 24 months): Hope

Erikson subdivided childhood into three categories that almost precisely duplicate Freud's. The first of these categories, from birth to 24 months, he labeled the stage of trust versus mistrust. In Freudian terms, this is the oral period, in which there is great emphasis on feeding, sucking, biting, drooling. The quality of nurture—the quality of care and affection that go into feeding, cuddling, bathing, and dressing the child—will develop feelings of trust or mistrust. The extent to which a baby's first experience of the world is of a dependable, warm place will create a general outlook, ranging from positive and trusting to negative and mistrusting. We are not talking about the old controversy of breast feeding as opposed to bottle feeding, but rather about the need for affectionate physical contact and comfort during feeding and other childrearing activities. A cold, tense mother breastfeeding could be as lacking in good nurture as a bottle prop (a device that allows no human contact in feeding the baby).

Evidence for the importance of early experience has been provided by several researchers. Harry Harlow's research has supported the concept of the importance of early nurturing patterns. Harlow raised baby monkeys under different conditions of nurturing for numerous studies. Figure 6.1 depicts two types of substitute monkey "mothers": one, a warm, soft cloth; the other, a cold, harsh wire. Both are capable of providing milk, but as you might expect, the wire mother's babies manifested substantial bizarre behavior as adults. They were unable to mate, to relate to strange or novel objects, and in fact showed many behaviors reminiscent of schizophrenia. The cloth mother's babies, however, were able to explore strange and terrifying situations and demonstrated an ability to master their environment (Harlow & Harlow, 1962).

Equally dramatic was a study conducted by René Spitz (1946). He studied the effects of orphanage experiences on very young children. Even though the children were given adequate physical care, washed, fed, and kept in warm, clean rooms, there was an almost complete lack of human warmth and contact. During an epidemic, the orphanage children were dramatically less able to withstand disease than were children of nearby families. In fact, when the figures were published, they were very hard for people to accept—34 of 91 orphanage children died, compared to almost none of the other children in the area.

Extreme cases of early deprivation of nurturance indicate that the failure to develop could result in actual physical death or a kind of psychological death in the form of emotional withdrawal from the world (so-called anaclitic depression).

Erikson notes that maternal warmth and care teach children through the senses (as Piaget might say) that they can depend on the world. The mother is practically the entire world for very young children. Through her they learn that, although she disappears at times, she also always reappears. From the regularity as well as the quality of the experience, children develop their outlook on life and prepare to move to the second stage. As with the stages of cognitive growth, the stages of personal development are sequential. If children's basic dependency needs are met during their first 24 months, they will be ready to move to the second stage of personal development. However, if these needs are not properly met, children may not be able to move on.

Nearly all the early research and theory focused on mothering rather than parenting or the specific role of a father. Barbara Risman (1986) studied a sample of males (custodial parents) and found that they performed so-called mothering and nurturing tasks with high levels of effectiveness. This is really confirmation of the developmental view that concepts such as a "maternal instinct" that reserved parenting to females are inaccurate and misleading. Risman was able to document that males in the role of a single parent can provide the necessary support and challenge in the process of childrearing. Generic parenting, then, may be a much more accurate description of effective child development practice.

For a while it was thought that the primary caregiver had to be the child's natural parents. The experience of young children in England during the 1940 bombing blitz was often cited as evidence. Because of the physical danger, many children were moved from the cities and placed in model child-care centers directed by experts, including Anna Freud and Dorothy Burlingham. Despite the best efforts of these experts, the children separated from their natural parents showed definite developmental lags. The problem, of course, is with the interpretation of causes. Wartime separation from parents for extended periods (sometimes parents could visit only once a month because of travel restrictions) is not really a fair test of substitute parenting. In an atmosphere of high anxiety and extended separation, it may be more significant that the children didn't regress more markedly. The caregivers were responsible for the children's well-being 24 hours a day, week after week, and the ratio of adults to children was far from ideal.

More recent evidence—namely, a careful review

Erikson's periods of childhood almost duplicated Freud's. He labeled his first stage trust versus mistrust and felt that good nurturance would develop feelings of hope in the child.

FIGURE 6.1   Harlow gave baby monkeys two kinds of substitute "mothers": one was a warm cloth and the other was a cold wire. The wire mother's babies manifested bizarre behavior as adults: for example, they were unable to mate, and they exhibited characteristics similar to those of schizophrenia.

of early-childhood programs—seems to indicate that although babies are extremely sensitive to experience, they are also resilient. In other words, the negative effects of early deprivation are not quite as longlasting or as indelible as originally thought. The idea of critical periods was borrowed too directly from studies of ducks and other animals. Human babies are more adaptable and can overcome the negative effects of deprivation (Zigler & Berman, 1983). However, this evidence in no way negates the importance of providing infants with positive environments. The primary caregiver does not have to be the natural mother. As long as the primary caregiver provides the child with a consistent, sensitive, and nurturant environment, the child will have a good chance to resolve the polar conflict between trust and mistrust as personal hope.

Autonomy versus shame (two to three years): Will

During this second period of childhood, emotional and personal development move into what Erikson calls the stage of autonomy versus shame. This is when children emerge from their almost total dependence on a primary caregiver and begin, literally and figuratively, to stand on their own two feet. The physical maturation that allows them to crawl, walk, run, and climb provides the means for a great leap into personal autonomy. This is a time of intense exploration, when they seem to be actively involved in almost everything. Physical maturation also frees them from dependence on the bottle or the breast and enables them to learn how to control their bowels and bladders. Thus, the positive aspect of this period is a fundamental sense of self-direction.

Erikson makes it clear, however, that there can be negative emotional development, too. Whereas in the first stage children are particularly sensitive to the way in which their dependency needs are met, in this second stage they need to be independent, and the way in which that need is met will maximally affect their sense of personal autonomy. If children at this stage are punished excessively for exploring their house or neighborhood, if they receive particularly harsh and punitive bowel training, or if they are so overprotected that they are almost "smothered," then the major emotional lesson from this period will be personal shame. The growing sense of self-control ("I can do it myself!") can be impaired as easily as it can be nurtured during this second period of childhood.

It may be difficult for adults to learn not to interfere but rather to support the child's desire for freedom and autonomy. For example, if you watch a boy of three trying to tie his shoes, you may see him work with extraordinary motivation even though the loops aren't matched, and well over half the time as he tries for the final knot, he ends up with two separate laces, one in each hand. Then watch parents as they watch their children attempt a task like this. Too often the parent will step in and take over, tie the shoes the "right way," and defeat the child's growing attempt at self-mastery. The same goes for putting on boots, coats, and even playing with toys. It is exceedingly easy to fall into the trap of almost always responding negatively to a child at this age. Commonly, a parent might say "no" up to 200 times a day at this stage. Such nagging is not only aversive in the extreme, but also a constant reminder to the child of his or her lack of self-control.

This is also the time when language begins, and here again the child's sense of independence is clearly in the balance. Adults need to understand that the child's first attempts to speak will always be halting. All children stutter somewhat during this time, just as all tumble constantly as they learn to walk and run. Attempts to speak need encouragement and modeling. Adults should not baby-talk back to a child, nor should they overcorrect a child's use of language. The surest way to promote stuttering at this stage is to harp on the misuse of language. It will definitely promote a sense of personal shame if, when children first try to talk, they are criticized for not talking the "right way."

Burton "Bud" White (1987), formerly of Harvard, has shown that patterns of mothering and fathering at this stage are clearly related to the child's sense of personal mastery, independence, and self-control. Even at this early stage, certain patterns of interaction between parents and children can accurately predict competence and future mastery. The most successful patterns are found in homes where the parents do substantial indirect teaching. Effective parents talk clearly and do a great deal of "labeling" ("This is a dog," and then, gradually, "This is a big dog," and so on). Children in these homes are also allowed substantial initiative in selecting activities; there is a balance between activities initiated by a parent and activities initiated by the children. A mother or father may ask for children's ideas and ask questions to help them understand the activity (for example, "Now, what do you suppose will happen if I put the piece in the puzzle this way?" or "if you pour all the water from the big glass into this little cup?" and "What will Little Red Riding Hood find when she goes into the bedroom?").

White has shown, then, that parents who provide an interesting, stimulating environment, talk frequently to their children, give them some initiative, and do a great deal of indirect teaching by asking questions and drawing out their perceptions and

SPOTLIGHT ON EARLY EDUCATION

Is Day Care as Good as a Mother?

An issue of major importance is the effect of day care on infants, especially in their first two years. On the one hand, both Freud's and, more directly, Erikson's theories strongly imply that there is no satisfactory substitute for a close bond between an infant and one primary caregiver—either a parent or another adult. In addition to theory, both experimental research (Harlow's monkeys) and clinical observations (the English children during World War II) support that view.

On the other hand, there have been major changes in child care both since World War II and since the experimental studies were completed. And from a sociological standpoint, in the great majority of families in this country both parents now work outside the home. Thus, the question of parenting takes on new theoretical and practical importance. As a result, Jerome Kagan and his colleagues at Harvard decided to test the effects of day care in a highly formal way.[a] They set up two matched groups of infants between three and six months old. During the two-year study, day care (from 8

ideas have the most positive effect on their children's developing sense of competency. Their sense of being "doers" and being able to control and affect the environment receives a major boost during this time.

Recently, White's research has been applied in a special preschool project. His studies show that developmental delays in personal growth can be identified reliably as early as two years. He and other experts have concluded that effective programs to unlock growth can be started at the same time. In

this sense his research has two sets of implications, one for parents in general and one for school systems. There is strong support for the idea that school-based projects can teach principles of effective parenting, and the results of a current longitudinal study provide further support for the concept. Parents who participated in the special preschool project were able to learn to encourage healthy personal development. From the point of view of this chapter, the most significant finding is that the project helped parents to work effectively during the au-

A.M. to 5 P.M.) was provided for one sample, while the other sample was reared exclusively at home. The parents were largely from working-class backgrounds.

A wide variety of measures of child development indicated no major or even minor differences between the two groups of children. In fact, some clinical evidence indicated that the day-care experience was somewhat better. The researchers noted a subtle difference. On the one hand, the natural mothers tended to be somewhat overly emotionally involved with their own child (all of whom were either first or second children). The carefully selected and trained day-care workers, on the other hand, seemed able to provide a less intrusive yet not overly detached experience.

Before you conclude, however, that all previous research and theory were wrong, there are some important factors to consider. In the first place, the program was truly ideal. The day-care workers were all carefully screened. Rather than relying on academic qualifications, the experts directly observed how sensitive the staff applicants

were in handling real children. In addition, the workers were carefully trained in the latest techniques, and the program materials and physical space were state-of-the-art. All the staff members selected also had prior experience in raising their own children. Continuous supervision and staff development were also part of the program. Perhaps most important was the staff-to-baby ratio. Each worker was responsible for three babies for the first 15 months. The ratio for toddlers was one to five. In a sense the most significant finding, then, was that there is no appreciable difference in development for babies between 3 and 15 months as long as there is one effectively trained worker for every three babies. Any further generalization to either higher ratios or less than ideal conditions is not warranted during Erikson's trust-versus-mistrust stage. In fact, Kagan was mightily impressed by these workers. They were truly gifted in providing just the right amount of nurturance to each of their three charges. When feeling distressed, such babies would immediately pick out their own worker for com-

fort. When feeling pleased, they would do the same for contact.

Did such surrogate mothers actually replace the natural mothers? The results here also indicated no real differences between the two groups. The day-care children still viewed their mothers as the most "salient adult figure," and so the program did not interfere with that process. From this we can conclude, at least tentatively, that an ideal or model program can provide young babies with a trust-enhancing psychological experience. Working parents who place their children in such programs do not have to feel pangs of guilt that somehow their baby will miss out on the resolution of trust-mistrust as a precursor of hope.[b]

---

[a] Kagan, J., Kearsley, R., & Zelazo, P. (1980). *Infancy*. Cambridge, MA: Harvard University Press.
[b] Naturally enough, such research doesn't really settle such an issue. Ignoring the Kagan results, Deborah Fallow has written extensively to prove the point that there is no effective substitute. See Fallow, D. (1985). *A mother's work*. Boston: Houghton Mifflin.

tonomy-versus-shame stage to promote a resolution toward "will." Will is not willfulness, in the sense of stubbornness. What Erikson is referring to is a stage of initial independence. Children learn to think for themselves as they shift from sensorimotor to symbolic thought. There is a similar potential change in their understanding of themselves as individuals. Will really means "self-direction" and "individuality" and, in fact, is the beginning of a sense of identity. The tension between autonomy and shame can be resolved. As Erikson puts it, "In balancing these

two tendencies, rudimentary willpower supports a maturation both of free choice and of self-restraint" (Erikson, 1959, p. 78).

As you work with older children you may find some who have not adequately resolved the dependence-independence polarity and who alternate between willfulness and excessive compliance. In such cases it is very important to help the children develop appropriate self-control and direction. You may be sorely tried at times, but remember the epigenetic principle: The ground plan for growth is a

ERIK ERIKSON

Born at the turn of the century, Erik Erikson spent his early years in Europe. As a son of well-to-do parents, he received an education that was both formal and informal. Like other upper-class children, when he finished his regular school work, he traveled the European continent. He described this period as his *moratorium*—a term he used in his later theory of human development to describe a temporary life space that adolescents go through between the completion of general academic education and the choice of a life career. He noted that at the time of his own young adulthood, it was fashionable to travel through Europe, gaining a perspective on civilization and one's own possible place in it. He chose the avocation of portrait painting as an activity during this time. It permitted maximum flexibility for travel and yielded some productive output as well. Obviously talented, he soon gained a reputation as a promising young artist, especially for his portraits of young children.

The turning point in his life came when he was invited to a villa in Austria to do a child's portrait. He entered the villa and was introduced to the child's father, Sigmund Freud. There began a series of informal discussions as he completed his work. A few weeks later, he received a written invitation from Freud to join the Psychoanalytic Institute in Vienna and study child analysis. Erikson recalled that at this point he confronted a momentous decision: the choice between a continued moratorium, with more traveling and painting, and a commitment to a life career. Fortunately for psychology and particularly for our eventual understanding of children and adolescents, Erikson ended the moratorium.

After completing his training, he came to the United States, working from 1936 to 1939 at Yale as a research associate in psychiatry and at Harvard with Henry Murray, who developed the Thematic Apperception Test. After serving as a professor from 1939 to 1951 at the University of California, he moved to the Austen Riggs Clinic in Pittsburgh. With each move, his reputation grew. In 1950 his theoretical framework was adopted in toto by the White House Conference on Children. The conference report, a national charter for child and ado-

given. We need to nurture each positive type of growth at each stage.

Initiative versus guilt (three to six years): Purpose

Personal development during the third stage of childhood takes place in the areas of initiative and guilt. This is the time when the child's identity as a boy or as a girl is maximally affected. In the preceding stage the child discovers that he or she can be a person with self-direction. Now the task is to discover what kind of a person he or she is, especially with regard to a sense of maleness or of femaleness. Children at this stage begin to identify with the appropriate adult and to model, or copy, aspects of the adult's behavior. This can be seen most readily in families that allow children to express themselves without a lot of censoring. In such an atmosphere boys will directly express their growing maleness by becoming unusually interested in their mothers. They engage in what becomes almost a rivalry with their father for their mother's attention and affection. The same is true of girls who, in discovering their femaleness, become very attached to their fathers. Many families report the humorous comments their children make at this age. A boy may say how happy he feels when daddy isn't home, all the while glancing rather obviously toward his mother. Similarly, a girl may wish to go off with daddy in the car. There are often pointed remarks concerning marriage: "I'm not going to marry anyone," a five-year-old boy might declare, "I'm going to stay home and take care of mommy when daddy gets too old!" These comments reflect questions of sexual identity that are surfacing for the first time.

lescent development in the United States, was almost a paraphrase of his thoughts. In 1960 Erikson accepted a professorship at Harvard. Thus the career that had started so informally at Freud's villa culminated in almost unprecedented eminence in a professorship in one of the country's oldest and most prestigious institutions of higher education—all without the benefit of a single earned academic degree. Whereas in 1950 Erikson was offered only associate status in the American Psychological Association, in 1955 he was elected a fellow of the Division of Developmental Psychology without ever having been a member.

Erikson's work has made a major contribution to our understanding of healthy psychological growth during all aspects of the life cycle. In addition to the high quality of his insight, Erikson possessed a genuine flair for linguistic expression, both spoken and written. In fact, one could almost compare his command of the English language with the benchmark established in this century by Winston Churchill. Erikson's genius was his ability to see the threefold relationship among the person, the immediate environment, and historical forces: Each human is partially shaped by environmental and historical events, but each human, in turn, also shapes the environment and can change the course of history.

The only shortcoming in Erikson's overall framework is his differentiation between the sexes. Conditioned and shaped by the major historical and psychological forces of his own time, he followed in the tradition of a predominantly male-oriented theory of psychology. Though able to break with many of the limiting traditions of his time, particularly in moving the concept of development from an exclusive pathological focus to a view that emphasized the positive and productive aspects of growth, he was unsuccessful in breaking with the cultural stereotypes regarding female growth.

After his official retirement, Erikson continued to be an active leader in the cause of healthy development for all humans. In 1983 he addressed the annual meeting of the American Psychiatric Association on the broad and compelling issue of survival in the nuclear age. Closing with a call for civilization to turn back from the brink of nuclear holocaust and "learn to use our technological genius for the development rather than the destruction of mankind," he received a standing ovation. Even in retirement his life epitomized the life cycle completed, the stage of wisdom.

Erikson personified his own theory of development in his achievement of personal and professional integrity. He reached the end of life with "an acceptance of his own responsibility for what his life is and was and of its place in the flow of history." These factors include his limitations as well as his many successes. He died in 1994 at the age of 91 (Erikson, 1982, p. 70).

Adults often have difficulty understanding the importance of such issues. It seems, on the face of it, rather absurd for a four- or five-year-old girl to proclaim that she would like her mother to go away. But if adults punish such statements, the child is left with strong feelings of guilt concerning her identity. To punish her for expressing her natural desire to establish herself as a female will have lasting negative effects. And ridicule or sarcasm will be just as damaging as physical punishment, for it will make her feel very small and insignificant, guilty at having expressed some of her inner feelings about what kind of a person she hopes to become. As we have seen, particular aspects of personality are unusually affected during each stage. Between three and six years, it is the personal identity that is most affected. Thus it is especially important for children at this time to be reassured that they will become full-fledged adults and not to be made to feel guilty over these wishes. Erikson notes:

> Both the girl and the boy are now extraordinarily appreciative of any convincing promise of the fact that someday they will be as good as father or mother—perhaps better, and they are grateful for sexual enlightenment, a little at a time, and patiently repeated at intervals (1959, p. 78).

In school itself, especially in kindergarten and the first grade, many of these same issues are plainly visible. Boys often become so enamored of their teacher that they forget and sometimes call their own mother by their teacher's name. "Some kids really know how to hurt a mother," one mother remarked, half

Promoting initiative instead of guilt in children is a key task between 3 and 6 years.

humorously, when this happened to her. Recently, a first-grade teacher invited her class to her wedding. This happens every so often, but this particular wedding was featured in a television news broadcast. And there, for all the world to see, was the class—little girls in crinkly party dresses, bubbling over with excitement as they focused all their attention on the groom; and the boys, in coats and bow ties, weeping as the beaming bride swept down the aisle. This makes the point, perhaps melodramatically, that emotions and feelings at this stage are genuine, legitimate, and need to be accepted.

Research summarized by Eleanor Maccoby (1990) indicates that Erikson was correct about the formation of gender constancy during this age range. For example, three- and four-year-olds will say that a cat could become a dog if its whiskers were cut off, a boy wouldn't be a boy if he wore a dress, a girl would no longer be a girl if her hair were cut off, and so on. Gender identity is not yet firm. Gradually, with cognitive growth, the child "constructs" a solid and constant picture of a boy or a girl regardless of superficial external characteristics. The gender identity as a boy or girl then promotes exactly the behaviors that Erikson noted, namely a strong imitation of the same sex. Gender constancy is not a result of ex-

ternal reinforcement, but the other way around. A boy seeks out activities and boy "things." Girls do the opposite. As is the case for development in general, gender constancy is not imposed but rather constructed during the onset of concrete operations (Piaget). The research now indicates that this is a developmental process. Erikson was incorrect in attributing this initiative stage so strongly to family dynamics.

Children's physical size in relation to adults can also increase any anxieties they may have at this age. In a world of seeming giants, children may fear that they will never grow big enough to be adults. At this age they need reassurance that they will not only grow to become full-fledged adult men and women but will also surpass their parents. We can imagine nothing worse than growing up to be 30- or 40-year-old "pseudoadults" who still live in the shadow of our parents. As in childrearing, so too in teaching—the ultimate test of how effectively we assist the formation of personal identity is the extent to which we help children outgrow their need for us. By deliberately reinforcing and nurturing children's male or female identities at this stage, we will help build a firm foundation for the next stage of emotional growth. And we will help them continue their general progress from dependence to independence.

Erikson is particularly concerned that at this stage of development children have ample time to play. In fact, he calls this time the *play age.* From a cognitive viewpoint, preoperational, freewheeling fantasy thinking peaks at this age. Erikson says that the child can well use this time to develop a sense of humor, the beginning of an ability to laugh at oneself. "The play age, furthermore, 'occurs' before the limiting advent of the school age, with its defined work roles." Thus, Erikson seems to caution against moving too far in the direction of early formal education during this stage. Extensive structured and basic education in reading, math, and writing may inhibit the child, reduce a sense of healthy purpose, and constrain the growth of creativity. Some parents, oversold on the idea of infant stimulation, have begun formal instruction at home well before even this stage. Armed with flash cards for numbers and letters, such parents seem to be drilling their children into premature socialization as students. In a vain attempt to raise a child's IQ score through such artificial drill and practice, the parents may instead inhibit successful resolution of purpose. As Erikson says:

This long childhood exposes adults to the temptation of thoughtlessly and often cruelly exploiting the child's dependence by making him pay for the psychological debts owed to us by others, by making him victim of tensions which we will not or dare not correct in ourselves or in our surroundings. We have learned not to stunt a child's growing body with child labor; we must now learn not to break his growing spirit by making him victim of our anxieties (1959, p. 77).

Probably the most persuasive research on the validity of Erikson's theory for this age comes from the follow-up of the Brookline (Massachusetts) Early Education Program (BEEP) (Hauser-Cram et al., 1991). The researchers employed a Piaget type of active learning program for young children. The focus was on promoting initiative and competence motivation through a variety of large-group, small-group, and individualized experiences. Social, emotional, motoric, and cognitive activities were carefully planned. No one domain was dominant. Further, the approach in each area was on child-centered activity with minimal didactic instruction. On the other hand, the program was not simply unstructured "play." There was an educational purpose embedded in such activities. The teachers themselves (in concert with our definitions of effectiveness—see Chapter 13) varied the amount of structure and support in accord with the developmental needs of the children.

In addition to the school program, a parallel plan was established to educate the parents. The researchers set up three levels of programs according to the observed competence of the parents. They were seeking to reduce possible dissonance between home and school and, for those parents who needed it, provide help in becoming more effective. The program was broad, with nearly 300 children, almost 40 percent from minority backgrounds, including almost 20 percent from non-English-speaking homes.

The results were dramatic. The BEEP children over a one- and three-year follow-up outperformed controls in both academic and social development. The highest success rates were with the children initially "at risk." A careful analysis of the program indicated that it was the developmental nature of the activities that promoted such growth. In fact a comparison indicated that a preschool oriented toward academic achievement that employed behavior modification techniques actually harmed initiative and competence: A 12-year follow-up found higher rates of school behavior problems and delinquency (Schweinhart et al., 1986), just as Erikson would have predicted.

These results were further confirmed by another longitudinal study by Frances Campbell and Craig T. Ramey (1995). Over a 7- to 10-year period with a sample composed exclusively of low-income (98 percent African-American) children, the results again demonstrated the power and significance of preschool programs. A three-way comparison clearly found that the preschool program was more effective during the Erikson stage of initiative than either a delayed program that was started during elementary school or for a control group, during mastery. A high-quality environment not only produced substantial academic gains but also prevented most of the experimental-group children from being assigned to special education—12 percent versus 47 percent for either the delayed group or the control group. This stage, then, is not a time to force-feed an academic program through behavior modification, but rather to provide a broad set of flexible learning experiences. Children from impoverished backgrounds are particularly helped by such model developmental approaches.

Not only can children from economically impoverished backgrounds be helped by preschool programs; research by Margaret Hibbert and Norman Sprinthall (1995) has also shown positive effects for children with special needs (emotionally vulnerable). A model program was designed for equal numbers of special needs and normally developing children. The program included a variety of learning centers as well as individualized attention. There were, however, no "pullouts," or removals of special-needs children to resource rooms (see Chapter 20). All children remained in the same classroom throughout the class time. The results indicated that both groups improved on measures of emotional growth and academic competence. These improvements were greater than in comparable "mainstreamed" preschool classes. These results support Erikson's contention about the vital importance of emotional development during the initiative stage. A model inclusion program can be viewed as a means of promoting such growth for both normally developing children and children with special needs.

The Juvenile Period (6 to 12 Years)

Mastery versus inferiority: Competence   During the elementary school years, Erikson indicates that personal and emotional development turns outward. Children enter a new world—the classroom, the neighborhood, the gang. These become the arenas for growth. The home remains an important base of operations, but the other arenas have special significance. In sheer number of hours, children now spend much more time (excluding sleeping) away from home than ever before. As juveniles they can fully participate as members of a same-sex gang. We may recall from Piaget that not until they are six or seven years old can children genuinely listen to or talk with other children. Now that "collective monologues" have been replaced by genuine discussion, important new groups can be formed.

During this time neighborhood and classroom gangs become major socializing agents. As opposed to adolescent cliques, the juvenile gangs are almost always made up of boys only or girls only. Occasionally a boys' gang will allow a particularly talented tomboy to join, but in general the juvenile world is stable and neatly stereotyped. That world is divided into two camps on everything: boys versus girls, good guys in white hats versus bad guys in black hats; all infants are "babies"; all adults are always right (including all teachers). There is no room for relativity in anything. In the Piagetian framework, this is the stage of concrete thought. From the personal point of view, this factor provides for a period of considerable emotional stability. The juvenile usually stands in an unambiguous relationship at home. He or she may have considerable freedom to roam the neighborhood. Adults are not overly concerned about academic performance in school, although children at this age are, in fact, interested in learning many of the skills that are taught. At a concrete and functional level it is "fun" to decipher words, learn to write, add, and subtract, since each

of these skills makes a whole new realm of experience available to them—reading for comic books, writing for notes to pass around, adding for figuring out how much a new bike will cost, and so on. There is no need to lecture children at this age about the importance of learning these skills.

In addition to the many school-oriented skills, children during this period also develop a general sense of personal mastery. The sheer number of new activities and games they learn at this age is enormous—swimming, riding, sailing, skiing, roller skating, camping, boating, baseball, basketball, football, hockey, kick-the-can, sewing, cooking, collecting things (look in any child's pockets at this age!)—the list is almost endless and is testimony to the raw amount of energy and **competence motivation** that exists at this age. The old saying that a child has 10,000 muscles that want to move and only one set to sit still is most appropriate. At the same time, we should understand Erikson's major point: This tremendous amount of energy can be put to the service of personal competence motivation. If children are not encouraged to engage actively with the surrounding world, their sense of personal industry will give way to personal inferiority. In other words, this is the time when the child's need to function and actively acquire multiple skills will *maximally* affect his or her sense of personal industry.

Erikson's term *competence,* to reflect the resolution of that industry, is unusually appropriate. In fact, it's

The period from ages 6 to 12 (Erikson's stage of mastery versus inferiority) presents a special challenge to both teachers and parents. During this period children have a natural desire to master new goals and control their environment. Robert White called this attribute "competence motivation."

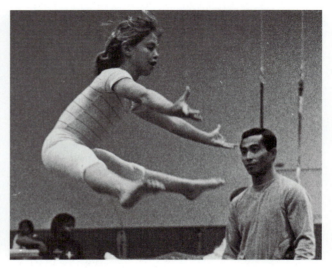

possible to guess that Erikson's choice came from his association with another Harvard psychologist, Robert W. White. White (1959) coined the term *competence motivation* to describe what he considered a universal attribute of humans and other species. White reviewed all the major theories and research evidence for personal development and concluded that there is an inborn "drive" to master the environment. This drive is in our very bones, so to speak. We humans—and other animal species as well—are not the empty organisms, or so-called black boxes, that classic stimulus-response theory would suggest, nor are we passive agents who merely react to but never act on the world, as classic psychoanalytic theory would say. White found, to the contrary, that humans and animals are naturally curious and seek to master and control the world around them. Just watch a child in a supermarket for a while, and you will see a perfect example of the need to explore and master the environment.

The reason the idea of competence is so important for educators is perhaps obvious by now. Personal and emotional development from 6 to 12 years of age takes place largely in school. Children of this age spend more time in school than anywhere else. Thus, the classroom situation will be a major influence on their development at this stage. We too often overhear teachers making comments such as "What can we do with a child who comes from a bad home environment?" The point is, we should not assume that we cannot have a positive effect on personal development and especially on the competence motivation of our pupils. In fact, elementary school teachers are in a particularly strategic position to emphasize activities that can both nurture and, in some cases, restore a sense of mastery. Our elementary schools are gradually shifting away from rote learning, passive listening, and neatness ("Always color inside the lines!") and are moving toward the open, active classroom. The so-called open classroom emphasizes many different activities and individual projects and absorbs great amounts of energy. By stressing doing instead of listening, the active school will do much to promote the pupils' sense of personal mastery. Erikson says that children are maximally ready for active learning between the ages of 6 and 12. Our task as educators is to respond to this natural tendency so as to facilitate rather than impair healthy personal growth. We shouldn't worry so much about creating quiet, orderly, neat, and polite pupils. That objective will work directly against the opportunity to affect personal industry and mastery.

A challenge during mastery is to ensure that the growing sense of competence does not become channeled along stereotyped gender lines. Jacqueline

Eccles and colleagues (1993) found that most children entered the first grade with positive competent beliefs (PCBs) about themselves. By grade four, however, boys were more positive to *sports* and *math* with girls more positive to *reading* and *music*. Such an early differentiation does not serve to promote broad PCBs across a variety of activities.

A second challenge at this stage concerns the problem of early drug abuse. Randall Jones (1992) studied over 500 children in grades three and four and found that about 25 percent ($N = 131$) had been involved with drug abuse (cigarettes, smokeless tobacco, alcohol, glue, marijuana, and cocaine) over a five-month period. He then compared their scores on Erikson's stage with those of the nonabusing group. The abusers had lower psychosocial scores on *trust* and *industry,* while the nonabusing group gained on all the measures of psychosocial stages. There were no gender differences. Jones speculated that the effects of drug abuse at this stage may impair the process of healthy development. Lacking trust and industry, such children may not be prepared for the next stage of identity formation.

Adolescence (13 through the College Years)

Identity versus diffusion: Fidelity Adolescence, in which the major issue is identity versus diffusion, is perhaps the most famous of Erikson's stages. The changes that take place during adolescence bring about a major shift in personal development. We have already seen (Chapter 5) that cognitive development in this period gives the adolescent a completely new way to understand and think. We also have noted (Chapter 3) that the very substantial glandular changes at this time represent a major new system. Puberty obviously marks a major qualitative departure from the past. Changes of this magnitude in cognitive and physiological areas will by themselves create major psychological change. "How do I understand what is happening to me when so much is different?" someone in this stage might ask. It is no understatement to say that of all the stages of personal development, none is more radical than adolescence. Change is the name of the game during this period.

Early adolescence and self-concept The changes in physiological, glandular, and psychological systems experienced during early adolescence constitute the most substantial shift a human being undergoes. The adolescent can now experience the world in a major new way. He or she begins to think in relativistic terms and can appreciate the difference between objective reality and subjective perception. In

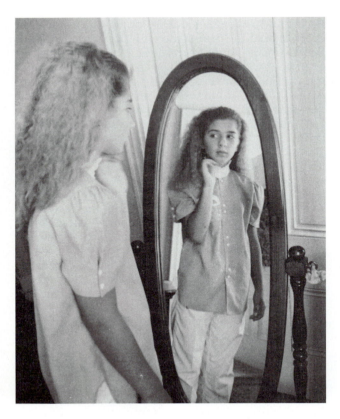

Self-consciousness and social conformity often accompany the first stage of identify formation.

addition, the adolescent develops the important ability to perceive feelings and emotions both in self and others, as well as the ability to take the perspective of another person (figuratively to place oneself in another person's shoes). And finally, he or she is now able to understand as-if situations and to distinguish between symbolic and literal meaning. In short, the thinking system that begins to develop during this period provides the adolescent with a new and sophisticated mechanism for making meaning from his or her own experience, particularly in reference to understanding one's own identity as a person. To summarize, as an adolescent begins to think about self and identity, he or she can perform the following operations:

1. Differentiate feelings and emotions in self and others

2. Distinguish between objective and subjective reality

3. Adopt the perspective of another person

4. Understand symbolic meaning, and role-play as-if situations

In one sense, then, it seems that personal development during adolescence represents a great leap forward, since one can now be more complex, comprehensive, empathic, and abstract and can now maintain a broad perspective on self and others. However, as one distinguished psychologist, **David Elkind** (1978), points out, just the reverse occurs. The more complex thought system raises the adolescent to new heights of mental operations, yet lowers him or her to new depths. On first entering this new stage, the teenager tends to become excessively egocentric in thought. The external world is no longer viewed as permanent and unchanging, but rather as relative, subjective, and phenomenological. Accordingly, the teenager may begin to perceive himself or herself as the center of the universe.

This egocentrism, unfortunately, is accompanied by excessive self-consciousness. The teenager is unusually vulnerable to pressures to go along with the crowd. The extent of social conformity in junior high was demonstrated in a well-designed study specifically employing a developmental-stage framework. The researchers predicted the level of conformity on the basis of stage of ego development. Their results indicated that eighth-graders of both sexes had the highest scores on social conformity as well as on ego stage—the equivalent of Lawrence Kohlberg's Stage III (see Chapter 7). Both younger students with lower-stage scores and older students with higher-stage scores were less other-directed. Those with Stage III scores were the most strongly concerned with how others perceived them and with going along with the group (Hoppe & Loevinger, 1977).

The influence, of peers, then, continues to be highly significant. A massive national survey by Schultz (1989) clearly demonstrated that during adolescence, peers replace others as the main source for discussions about important decisions. The rank order was (1) peers, (2) parents, (3) relatives, and (4) teachers/advisors. Peers were chosen almost as frequently as all other groups combined.

In another, less formal study, researchers interviewed junior high students on their personal perceptions of self and others. The results can be summed up in the words of one of the subjects. When asked, "What is the most real thing to you?" her unhesitating reply was, "Myself" (Kohlberg & Gilligan, 1971).

Elkind on adolescence   Elkind (1970) has noted that how an adolescent views his or her "self"—that is, the self-concept—can be described along two ba-

SPOTLIGHT ON ASCRIBED COMPETENCE IN HIGH SCHOOL

A 10-Year Study

Many years ago, James Coleman published what is now a classic study of teenagers, *The Adolescent Society*. Among a large sample (almost 8,000) he found that the main personal values were based largely on externals such as good looks, clothes, and athletics. Academic achievement was always far down the list. There were some gender differences, namely, girls valued academic achievement even less than the boys (1 percent versus 10 percent). What about today, some 30 years later? Are the patterns the same or different?

A study by Jill Suitor and Rebel Reavis (1995) of almost 500 students over a 10-year period provides an interesting picture of how much has changed and how much has remained the same. For girls, there was one important shift, they sought prestige more through sports and less through cheerleading; otherwise, physical appearance and sociability remained most important, with academic achievement again farther down on the list. For boys, prestige was still determined primarily by sports and physical appearance; academic achievement remained less important. As the authors note, "football and fast cars" continued to be the arena for prestige for males, and physical attractiveness continued to be of paramount interest for females. Their findings indicate that teenagers' sources of identity remain focused on externals such as athletics and appearance instead of on individuation and personal autonomy.

Coleman, J. (1960). *The adolescent society*. New York: Free Press.

Suitor, J., & Reavis, R. (1995). Football, fast cars, and cheerleading: Adolescent gender norms, 1978–1989. *Adolescence*, *30*, 265–272.

sic dimensions of egocentric thinking: the personal fable and the imaginary audience.

The personal fable is a deep-rooted belief in one's personal uniqueness—the notion that no one else in the world can possibly understand how "I" really feel. As Elkind notes, the complex beliefs create an aura—"only he can suffer with such agonized intensity or experience such exquisite rapture." To retain this image an adolescent may create a personal fable, "a story which he tells himself (and others) and which is not true" (1978, p. 130).

Possibly the best example of sexual fantasies and egocentrism can be found in the novel, Catcher in the Rye, by J. D. Salinger (1964). Holden Caulfield, "everyperson as an adolescent," describes a classic dialogue with one of his near friends, "Old Ackley," in which the two are discussing sexual prowess. Holden narrates that he listened silently as Ackley described in monotonous detail how he "made it" with a girlfriend the previous summer. Holden is patient to a point, but he has heard Ackley's story at least a hundred times. The trouble is, each time the story is different. In Elkind's terms this is Ackley's personal fable—an untrue story repeated ad infinitum (and ad nauseam, one might add).

Essentially, the imaginary audience refers to the belief that everyone else in the world is preoccupied with the personal appearance and behavior of the adolescent—as if the entire world paused each morning to see how the teenager was dressed for school or waited with hushed anticipation for the adolescent to speak his or her lines. In front of such imaginary audiences adolescents can swing from excessive self-criticism (admiring one's own martyrdom) to the other extreme—self-admiration to the point of boorishness. Elkind cites the famous passage from *Tom Sawyer* of Tom witnessing his own funeral as a universal fantasy of adolescents: "They will really miss me when I'm gone and be sorry too for all the mean things they said."

On an optimistic note, Elkind finds that adolescents can be helped to gradually distinguish between real and imaginary audiences, as well as to differentiate between themselves and others in both thoughts and feelings. Given the support of adult understanding, both the personal fable and the imagined audience are progressively modified and diminished. It is to be hoped that as adults, we can retain some of the positive aspects of this stage, namely, a healthy respect for our own individuality.

SPOTLIGHT ON TEACHING

Adolescent Crushes

Adolescent identity development occurs alongside a major physiological change, the onset of puberty. Psychologist Robert Kegan wryly observes: "Sex to teenagers is a world of extraordinary allure, unexplored possibility, scaring but thrilling— Sex is what God gives to teenagers when the appeal of Disneyland starts to fade" (1994, p. 8). He goes on to observe that when Disneyland starts to fade, teachers may find themselves the new objects of attention.

As a result of the emergence of sexuality during the later grades in middle school, it is quite common for teenagers to have crushes on movie stars, rock singers, and young adult teachers and especially student teachers. From a developmental point of view this is understandable. It is relatively safe for the early adolescent to imagine such a romantic encounter, whereas an actual encounter with a peer would be in most cases too real and too scary. In psychological terms such a shift is termed a displacement of feelings and needs from one person to another (Anna Freud, 1958). The signs are just about impossible to miss. Verbal and nonverbal behaviors are overdone,

almost like those in a grade B movie or a daytime TV soap opera. They may include hanging around after class, constantly offering to help, dropping some not-so-subtle hints, and perhaps even leaving notes. For example, one very attractive young male gym teacher was leading his seventh-grade class through a series of increasingly difficult floor exercises. Since at that grade level girls are usually much more physically mature and coordinated than boys, by the time he reached the last set, there were only females left in the competition. They moved closer and closer to him. By the end of the exercise he literally had no elbow room at all and was beset by the cluster to help him carry out all the equipment. Laughter, broad smiles, and eye contact were flowing back and forth. Meanwhile, a sullen group of boys sitting on the sidelines quietly eased themselves out of the gym.

The problem in such scenarios is how to handle the issues yet avoid the extremes of ignoring or ridiculing the feelings or, even worse, playing into the fantasy. Ridicule is a way of demanding that the teenager deny the reality of her or his feelings. On the other

hand, a coy and seductive response will easily be misread as one of actual interest. Teenagers at this time derive sexual implications from practically everything they see anyway (a tendency already encouraged by TV and music videos). Thus, it requires great tact to explain that you do understand that a student may have strong feelings of liking for a person just a bit older. These feelings mean that the teenager is growing up toward adulthood. And, although you do appreciate the attention and the offers of extra help, you really can't play favorites with some students. Also explain that eventually the student will develop such feelings to someone closer in age. Dealing with the emergence of tenderness and caring, though not part of the formal agenda of teaching, is nonetheless a most important aspect of the emotional and personal atmosphere in teacher-student interaction.

Kegan, R. (1994). A rationale for guiding adolescents' sexual behavior from the perspective of developmental psychology. *Moral Education Forum, 19*(2), 7–17.

Freud, A. (1958) Adolescence. *Psychoanalytic Study of the Child. 13,* 225–276.

Although many of Elkind's ideas about egocentrism have been supported by research (Sprinthall & Collins, 1995), there do remain some questions concerning the imaginary audience, the fable, and the transition to formal operations. Dan Lapsley (1993) prefers to conceptualize both the audience and the fable as a result of the teenager's increased ability to imagine such situations, that is, as a new and over-active imagination rather than as egocentrism. Whichever explanation is more valid, the overt behaviors are highly similar.

The crisis of personal identity   Because adolescence represents such a major discontinuity in growth, Erikson has singled out one critical issue as the major task of this stage—resolving the crisis of personal identity. Our definition of self—how we see ourselves *and* how others see us—forms the foundation of our adult personality. If that foundation is firm and strong, a solid personal identity results; if not, the result is what Erikson calls a diffuse identity. Identity diffusion is something like suffering from amnesia or like perpetually wandering over a landscape, trying to "find" a selfhood. With no sense of past or future, the diffuse personality is like a stranger in his or her own land, with no roots, no history. The sense of personal alienation prevents the establishment of a stable core for the personality.

Western societies have made it extremely difficult for adolescents to come through this stage with a firm sense of personal identity. Industrialized societies have exaggerated the marginal status of adolescents by grossly overextending the period of dependency. This is justified by the amount of special learning and training that is needed to survive in our complex world. However, it is easy to forget the negative personal effects of keeping a 21-year old, or even an 18-year-old, in a position of dependency. To make matters worse, adults seem to be unable to decide just when it is that an adolescent becomes an adult. The age of legal adult responsibility is extremely inconsistent in this country: The legal age for marriage differs not only by gender (girls are permitted to marry without parental consent earlier than boys) but also by state residency, with some states permitting legal marriage as early as 14. And there are similar discrepancies in the legal age for going to work, driving a car, entering into a legal contract, voting in elections (for most of this nation's history adolescents were old enough to die for their country in war before they were old enough to vote in elections), drinking alcoholic beverages, and enlisting in the military services.

These few examples highlight the problem of identity formation. Erikson notes that adolescents are caught between two major systems, both of which are in flux. They have to cope with internal, cognitive, and glandular changes at the same time that they are confronting a series of inconsistent and changing external regulations. And they go through all this while simultaneously discarding the identity they had in the previous stage, the age of mastery. Playing kick-the-can, riding a bike, participating in the Boy or Girl Scouts, enjoying the antics of the Three Stooges on TV, acting like a tomboy, and, most important, viewing adults as almost always correct because they are older and bigger—these dimensions of personal development during the elementary age all have to be discarded. Adolescence is almost like entering a foreign country without knowing the language, the customs, or the culture;

only it's worse because the travelers don't even have a guidebook. It is truly a major shock during adolescence to find that adults are not always right and, in fact, are often working very hard to cover up their mistakes. The discovery of relativism, especially in the moral behavior of adults, further exaggerates the difficulties of personal development. On the one hand, adolescents learn that some police officers take bribes, some professors plagiarize, some teachers copy lesson plans, some major corporations "fix" prices, some elected officials solicit bribes, some professional athletes play under the influence of drugs, and so on. On the other hand, these same adults have a tendency to lecture adolescents on the subject of responsibility, the importance of obeying rules, and, above all, showing respect to adults. The resulting overreaction is well known. If you can't rely on some adults, don't trust anyone over 30! If some businesspeople are overly materialistic, all businesspeople are Babbitts! If some adults are unfaithful, all marriages are institutionalized hypocrisy! The list is endless, and serves as a poignant reminder of how difficult it is to understand the highly complicated problems of living and personal development in a modern society.

JAMES MARCIA: THE FOUR FACES OF IDENTITY STATUS

The major contribution of **James Marcia** (1966, 1976) has been to focus attention on the specific phases of identity formation during the college years and to chart the actual transitions.

In interviews Marcia asked questions in three areas of concern common to college students: (1) occupation, (2) religious ideology, and (3) worldview. The format allowed students to talk at length about their own thoughts. For example, he asked: "How would you compare your own political ideas with those of your folks?" (political ideology). On religion, he asked: "Is there any time you've doubted any of your religious beliefs?" On occupation, he asked: "How have you become interested in —— career?" Of course, whether such an approach yields informative data depends on the skill of the interviewer in not leading respondents to specific answers but in stimulating reflective thought. Fortunately, Marcia and his staff were highly skilled counselors who were comfortable with silences and could ask a wide variety of open-ended questions until they were convinced that they had a good sample of each students' worldviews.

On the basis of a series of studies with this technique, Marcia found that he could group students'

SPOTLIGHT ON SEXUAL ORIENTATION AND IDENTITY

With the onset of puberty, identity formation and gender constancy change in significant ways. Biological changes and the potential for procreation add new and powerful dimensions to identity as a male or female. There is an increase in the absolute levels of hormones (androgens) for both sexes. These changes, combined with socialization patterns, sometimes called "social scripting," result in differentiated sexual behavior. Sexuality begins in biology but ends in culture. For example, heterosexual males involved in date-raping have associated with other males who place a high value on sexually aggressive experiences and who may have experienced a history of family violence. Thus, the current peer group and past history are contributing factors in how their heterosexuality is expressed (Stets, 1992). Similarly, heterosexual females are influenced by peers and socialization and are much more likely than males to report their first sexual experiences in the context of an emotionally significant relationship (Jones & Dembo, 1989).

What about identity among those teenagers with a same-sex orientation? Although the research base on this topic is small, it is clear that feelings of being different in sexual orientation emerge during adolescence, but are not the result of a single encounter. The same-sex orientation involves persistent feelings over long periods and consistent reactions (negative to the opposite sex and positive to the same sex). It is not a transitory set of feelings. The process of identity formation is difficult for all teenagers, but for those whose orientation is different, it is doubly so. Teenagers with a same-sex orientation face a host of negative reactions, including rejection by parents and friends, physical and verbal abuse, and other forms of discrimination. As a result, there is a high incidence of attempted suicide, emotional distress, and substance abuse among them (Remafedi, 1991).

Both the American Psychiatric Association and the American Psychological Association, after examining all the research, have concluded that homosexuality and lesbianism are the result not of psychopathology but of biological dispositions interacting with cultural scripting (Sprinthall & Collins, 1995). In fact, a recent study of young adult lesbians (Morrow, 1993) clearly indicates that they exhibit the same characteristics of ego development as their heterosexual peers, including the same stage levels. It is important to note, however, that Morrow's sample was composed of those who had made it through adolescence.

Teenagers tend not to discuss these questions with their parents but may well see a teacher as a major resource for assistance. If you become a secondary school or community college teacher, counselor, or youth worker, you will certainly be confronted with the issues of heterosexual and homosexual orientations and identity formation, perhaps in the form of an overly aggressive heterosexual male, a male or female with persistent feelings of being different from most peers, or a female trapped in an excessive focus on appearance and flirting. None of these behaviors are indices of pathology but instead are attempts to resolve sexual identity. You will need both tact and understanding to separate the issues and help to resolve them in a psychologically healthy manner.

Jones, G., & Dembo, M. (1989). Age and sex role differences in intimate friendships during childhood and adolescence. *Merrill-Palmer Quarterly, 35,* 445–462.

Morrow, D. (1993). Lesbian identity development through group process. Unpublished doctoral dissertation, North Carolina State University, Raleigh.

Remafedi, G. (1991). Adolescent homosexuality. In R. M. Lerner, A. C. Peterson, & J. Brooks-Gunn (Eds.), *Encyclopedia of Adolescence* (Vol. 1, pp. 504–507). New York: Garland.

Sprinthall, N. A., & Collins, W. A. (1995). *Adolescent Psychology.* New York: McGraw-Hill.

Stets, J. F. (1992). Interactive processes in dating aggression. *Journal of Marriage and the Family, 54,* 165–177.

thought according to four distinct aspects of identity formation. Essentially, he uncovered two intermediate phases between extremes of the bipolar identity and diffusion. He labeled and described the phases as follows.

Identity Diffusion

A state of suspension from life is a predominant mode in **diffusion.** There are few, if any, commitments to anyone or to any set of beliefs or principles.

James Marcia found that identity formation among college age students moved from a very diffuse sense of identity, where social roles are tried and abandoned quickly, to a gradually more permanent sense of self, which often emerged following a period of intense experience-gathering and self-reflection.

Instead, there is a major emphasis on relativity and living for the moment. No area of personal gratification is relinquished; all things are possible. There seems to be no core to the person; social roles are tried on and quickly abandoned. The person seems egoless, directionless, and wandering.

Identity Foreclosure

The main aspect of **foreclosure** is the avoidance of autonomous choice. The person is other-directed rather than inner-directed. There is very little questioning: The person largely accepts whatever role authority figures or influential friends prescribe. There seems to be little dissonance. The person accepts somewhat fatalistically what adults say about career, religion, and politics. The struggle to establish the self as an independent and autonomous person is avoided. It is as if the person were fearful of the responsibility that goes with personal freedom.

Identity Moratorium

A **moratorium** is often a result of a painful and deliberate decision to take time off from current pressure, such as school, college, or a first job. The goal is to create some breathing space in order to explore more fully both one's own psychological self and objective reality. The surface difference between moratorium and diffusion may appear subtle; yet underneath, the difference is substantial. In moratorium there is a genuine search for alternatives, not simply a biding of one's time. There is a major need to test oneself in a variety of experiences to increase one's in-depth knowledge of self. Commitments are temporarily avoided for legitimate reasons: "I need more time and experience before I can commit myself to a career such as medicine" or "I am not ready to go for a Ph.D. in history. There are too many unknowns I need to explore first." A moratorium is not simply a cop-out so that the person can drift aimlessly. It is an active process of searching, with the major goal of preparing for commitment. Erikson's own life, as the biography points out, contained a very significant moratorium, as well as an even greater commitment. One flowed from the other, Erikson would say.

Identity Achievement

The final phase of identity formation results in identity **achievement.** Erikson's definition is the clearest: "the accrued confidence that one's ability to maintain inner sameness and continuity is matched by the sameness and continuity of one's meaning for others" (1959, p. 89). The person gradually incorporates each successive childhood identification, yet goes beyond those earlier forms. A new personal entity is formed as a unique individual. The process, however, is reciprocal, as we noted earlier. The emergence of such individuality and self-direction on the part of the person (the core personality) is acknowledged by others. It is this aspect of identity formation that can be the most troubling and troublesome, since such recognition is neither automatic nor necessarily universal. In fact, many people now recognized as great had a major crisis during which their emergent achieved identity was not immediately recognized by adult society in general. Erikson's biography of Martin Luther (*Young Man Luther*) contains the most complete account of this phenomenon, and similar episodes can be found in the personal histories of major figures such as Malcolm X, George Bernard Shaw, and Marie Curie.

Marcia found, most importantly, that identity achievement almost always contains elements of personal crisis, confrontation, and thoughtful decisionmaking. The person was aware of the variety of tough choices life offers, and the choice selected was accompanied by commitment, that is, a personal pledge that the psychological resources the individual possessed would be placed in the service of the goal.

Cycles in Identity Development

The phases of identity formation described above illustrate that, rather than marking a critical decision point, for most adolescents identity formation probably means successfully meeting a long series of small, relatively minor challenges. James Marcia (1991) has recently proposed that these cycles of challenge and adaptation continue throughout the life span. Marcia describes these cycles as recurring patterns of moratorium and achievement. He refers

to these patterns as MAMA cycles. In Marcia's own words:

> Similar to development in cognition and moral reasoning, identity development proceeds via a kind of assimilation–disequilibration–accommodation process. Life events unanticipated by the initial late adolescent identity . . . can disconfirm that identity . . . and lead to its reformulation. Hence, identity has its initial, but—at least for (individuals who can be categorized as) Achievements and Moratoriums—not its final, form at adolescence (p. 531).

Building on Marcia's findings, Alan Waterman and other researchers have provided a model of the multiple possible pathways taken by college students during identity formation.

The theoretical model, diagrammed in Figure 6.2, illustrates the twists and turns in the developmental process during the college years. It also clearly illustrates that the progression from identity diffusion to achievement and fidelity does not necessarily proceed in a straight line—and that students have several possible options they may follow. For example, a student can remain in diffusion or move to foreclosure or moratorium. A student in foreclosure can remain there, slip back to diffusion, or move up to moratorium. Similar possibilities hold for students in the other phases, particularly for those in the achievement phase. Students who have reached achievement are not assured of the ultimate emergence of fidelity. They may instead shift to either moratorium or even diffusion. The diversity of college environments can aid in promoting growth, yet psychological growth is not automatic, and it is not guaranteed. Further longitudinal research, including intensive case studies, may help clarify who chooses which path and under what conditions.

Recent Research on Identity Status

There has been a major increase in identity status research in the last decade, some of which validates and some of which challenges Marcia's original views. At the most general level, the research consistently finds a clear relationship between the more advanced statuses—that is, moratorium and achievement—and a wide variety of measures of development. Identity achievement in particular is positively linked with the following:

> Ego development level (Loevinger), Formal operations (Piaget), Ethical reasoning (Kohlberg), Locus of control (Rotter), as well as Psychological well-being,

FIGURE 6.2 The sequence of identity development. Waterman takes the position that a moratorium cannot be maintained indefinitely. He also suggests that one cannot regress from moratorium to foreclosure once the crisis stage has been reached during a moratorium.

Phase One (Starting at Diffusion)

Phase Two (Starting at Foreclosure)

Phase Three (Starting at Moratorium)

Phase Four (Starting at Achievement)

Adapted from A. Waterman (1985), p. 18. Copyright © 1985 by Jossey-Bass.

healthy psychological adjustment, coping, personal efficacy, and low status of anxiety (Waterman, 1992, p. 63).

In addition to positive relationships between achievement and general measures of maturity and self-direction, the opposite was also found. College students in foreclosure demonstrated highly stereotyped personal relationships and low levels of personal expressiveness, personal efficacy, and cognitive complexity. It is interesting to note, however, that students in foreclosure had high levels of self-es-

teem and goal directedness. In a sense this suggests that their self-esteem and career goals are tied directly to their unquestioned acceptance of their parents' wishes. This is also a reminder that a variable like positive self-esteem should not be considered as a goal of development unless we know the context. Otherwise we would be caught in a developmental contradiction: positive self-esteem as an outcome of sacrificing the drive toward self-direction and autonomy. Also the rigidity and authoritarianism that are associated with foreclosure may account for Randall Jones's finding (1992) that students in foreclosure were twice as likely to become substance abusers as were those in the comparison statuses. Even the motivation for drug abuse was different: "bored" for the students in foreclosure versus "exploration" for the others.

As you can surely guess, the most troublesome status for college students was diffusion. Such students displayed low levels of personal expressiveness, goal-setting ability, and cognitive complexity but high levels of impulsivity; they were least effective in helping and had the greatest difficulty with intimacy. Certainly all these results confirm Erikson's original claim about the positive nature of identity achievement and the psychological problems associated with either foreclosure or diffusion. Moratorium tends to be rated as similar to identity achievement in almost all domains except anxiety. The consistent difference between these two statuses is affective: The achievers are not anxious, whereas students in moratorium experience high levels of anxiety (Waterman, 1992). Active exploration apparently does exact some emotional toll during the process.

As a result, the achieved identity status is very important. The correlations are always positive with other domains, such as an internal locus of control, self-direction, and high levels of moral judgment. The most recent research on this general index finds no differences by gender (Balistreri et al., 1995). In addition, a recent cross-generational comparison by Michael Zuschlag and Susan Kraus Whitbourne (1994) on the sequence of identity status in college found a striking similarity in stage and sequence among undergraduates from 1969, 1977, and 1988, even though there were many changes in the general environment of the country over that 20-year span. We must also remember, however, the importance of other contextual or environmental factors, particularly in terms of identity development. Joaquim Coimbra and Bartolo Campos (1990) point out the significance of any specific life context (social class, rural/urban setting, and so on) in either promoting or retarding identity formation.

Both Waterman and his colleagues and a recent

study by John Wires, Ralph Barocas, and Albert Hollenbeck (1994) have shown the relevance of identity status theory as applied to school teenagers. The overall framework indicates that the younger teenagers can be classified accurately on the earlier statuses of foreclosure and diffusion with a few at the later statuses of moratorium and achievement. Thus, the stages of identity formation can be applied to secondary school students as well as to those of college age.

Identity and Moral Development: Ahead and Behind

As noted in the previous section, there are positive correlations between identity and moral development. John Snarey (1995), however, has provided an interesting insight into how these domains vary according to life stage. In an overlapping longitudinal study of 600 subjects over a 10-year period he traced scores on two measures, ego/self development and moral development. He found that during adolescence the two aspects were parallel and thus correlated; the correlation coefficient was +.65 and can be considered as positive and significant. But he also found that ego/self development was always more advanced than moral judgement: self-development is "the first order of business during adolescence" (p. 9). Certainly almost every theoretical description of adolescence as a time of change, introspection, and concern about self in relation to others would bear out his empirical research. Thus, as a teacher you can expect teenagers to show greater concern with self than with issues of character and value development. Technically this can be referred to asynchronous development, uneven growth with moral judgement lagging behind. In fact, Snarey was able to chart the relationship throughout the life span: During adolescence the ego stage is higher than the moral stage, in middle adulthood (ages 30–49) ego and moral stage are about equal, and in mature adulthood (50 years plus) the moral stage exceeds ego level.

Identity Formation and Minority Status

At the turn of the century, W. E. B. DuBois eloquently stated that African-Americans faced not one but two identity issues: How should one resolve "two warring idols in one dark body" (1963, p. 17)? The same holds true for other adolescents from devalued ethnic backgrounds. Yet the issue of minority status and identity has only recently emerged as a focus of psychological research.

All adolescents face the development of an achieved identity, but this challenge is compounded by the issue of ethnic identity. For teenagers from socially favored ethnic backgrounds, ethnicity is not a particularly salient problem, since they do not encounter racial prejudice; in fact, they may even feel a sense of entitlement. For racially distinct minorities from devalued backgrounds, however, the story is completely different. During the elementary school years, the identity question is usually resolved in an awkward and nonfunctional manner. At this age children often exhibit a very low ethnic awareness or a preference for the majority culture. In the now famous Supreme Court case of *Brown vs. Board of Education* (1954), African-American children expressed exactly this view. Jean Phinney and Doreen Rosenthal (1992) have found a similar trend during early adolescence: either a preference for the majority culture or an unexamined acceptance of an ethnic identity.

The rise of consciousness about ethnic/color differences, however, emerges in a major way during adolescence. This awareness of difference also carries with it a realization that difference is often devalued by the majority culture. One theorist, Don Locke, refers to the process as the dominant culture placing those from, say, an African-American background on ethnic probation (1992, p. 4).* Being on probation means that as a person you don't quite make it. You don't quite fit in. You are not quite legitimate. This can lead to a vain attempt to be accepted by the majority. Malcolm X stands as a vivid example of just how far a teenager might go in attempting to identify with the majority culture (see Spotlight). Other ethnic minorities have used other means to achieve similar goals, such as changing family names or facial characteristics in an attempt to gain acceptance. Such instances may recede as the majority culture becomes more mature in respecting cultural diversity and as the emerging minority groups continue to develop self-affirmation and pride. For example, Japanese-American ethnic identity is no longer as salient as for other Asian groups (Phinney & Rosenthal, 1992, p. 163). Similarly, among African-American females, the importance of skin color and adolescent identity has changed. Being "whiter" is no longer desirable; a middle ground, not too white and not too black, is the currently desired skin color (Robinson & Ward, 1995). This rather precise middle ground is still a color designation,

---

* Not so many years ago, whenever an African-American demonstrated a great achievement (Marion Anderson's arias, Jackie Robinson's baseball prowess, Wilma Rudolph's running), the comment would follow, "a credit to her or his race" . . . still on probation.

SPOTLIGHT ON ETHNIC IDENTITY

Malcolm X and Self-Esteem

One of the ironic consequences of racism is that the victim often tries to identify with the groups who are the oppressors. For example, Bruno Bettlehein, recalling his years in a Nazi concentration camp, described how a few of the Jewish prisoners tried to make over their garb to resemble the SS uniforms and played some of the same games as their guards, such as punching each other as hard as they could. In a similar vein, Malcolm X, an African-American reformer who was assassinated in 1965 at age 40, described an incident during his adolescence when he became ashamed of his African traits, particularly his kinky hair.

Making himself over was no easy task. It involved what was called "conking" to straighten his hair. The method was crude: Apply lye, the kind plumbers use to open clogged drains. The result would be hair more similar to the majority white population and different from his natural look. He asked his friend "Shorty" to help him. They mixed lye, thin-sliced potatoes, and eggs in a mason jar. He could feel the jar heat up. After applying a thick coat of petroleum jelly, Shorty administered the hot mixture to Malcolm's hair. Suddenly his head was afire, the lye dripping down his cheeks; his eyes watered and his nose ran as Shorty worked furiously to spray and rinse. "The first time's always worst. You get used to it better before long," said Shorty. "You got a good conk." Malcolm recalled, "How ridiculous I was! Stupid enough to stand there simply lost in admiration of my hair now looking 'white.'" (1964, p 54).

A recent study by Jean Phinney and Linda Line Alipuria (1990) shows how strongly this last point of view has taken hold in our society. Ethnic identity is a most important component in self-esteem for students from minority backgrounds. Such students show a strong need during adolescence to find out about their ethnic backgrounds and to make a commitment to that identification. Accepting and feeling proud about one's ethnic roots are central to self-respect and self-esteem. Such students feel no need to apply burning lye to their heads to change their appearance.

Malcolm X (1964). *The autobiography of Malcolm X.* New York: Grove Press.
Phinney, J., & Alipuria, L. L. (1990). Ethnic identity in college students from four ethnic groups. *Journal of Adolescence, 13,* 171–183.

however, and indicates that there is still some psychological ambivalence about accepting one's ethnic background. But such ambivalence is common among many adolescents.

Thus, ethnic minorities face a more difficult process of identity formation. In general, they have fewer opportunities for open exploration when in fact they need more time and support to "sift through two sets of cultural values and identity options" (Markstrom-Adams, 1992, p. 177). The lack of such exploration will result in premature foreclosure, and this only increases the risk of the teenager's joining a cult, gang, or some other extremist group.

The one issue that exemplifies the problem most clearly is ethnic minorities' lack of academic achievement in secondary school. The terms may vary—"acting white," "being an Anglo," "trying to pass," and so forth—but the message is the same: If you succeed in school, you will be rejecting your ethnic heritage. This attitude creates a no-win situation. The choice seems to be to reject the majority culture and join a gang or to become raceless. As a college student, Eric Watts recently wrote about his experiences as an African-American in secondary school. He was particularly discouraged when his peers deprecated his studying or his use of standard English with comments such as "Eric, stop talking like a white boy" (Watts, 1992, p. 48). One who strives for such academic achievement is regarded as a "square" or, even worse, as a "preppie." The alternatives, as John Ogbu (1988) points out, at least for inner-city youth, fall into three categories: (1) act *cool*—streetwise, (2) play the *jester*—prankish, or (3) be the *antagonist*—the fighter. None of these identity choices will serve the long-term interests of minority adolescents.

When ethnic minority adolescents are provided with the psychological and social support to resolve their dual-identity issues, the outcomes are unusually positive. Once they have learned to withstand the negative peer pressure and the negative influence of some community adults, minority teenagers and college students actually reach more advanced levels of psychological development than their majority-culture peers. In a study of college-age Mexican, Asian, and African-Americans, those who had successfully resolved the identity-achievement question had significantly higher scores on four measures of psychological adjustment. The result was validated at the high school level (Phinney & Rosenthal, 1992). These results confirm Erikson's truism that the teenager has to coordinate his or her own emerging identity while interacting with an environment of peers and adults that has increasingly potent influence. Leaving the relative safety of elementary school, the adolescent from an ethnically devalued background has fewer resources and a greater task. School programs can help. Research by Don Locke and Marie Faubert (1993) demonstrates what modifying the classroom environment can do. They have shown that minority youth can both develop a positive ethnic identity and achieve academically in a school that is developmentally oriented. Otherwise, as Courtland Lee (1990) points out, the ethnic adult community has to compensate for the lack of acknowledgment and affirmation by the school in particular or by the adult society in general.

In a study of rural minority teenagers, Lee found multiple examples of discrimination and prejudice by school and community adults that may have been unintentional, and yet the effect was the same. The national *Quality Education for Minorities Project* (1990) found the same unfair treatment in schools across the country. Certainly minority youth deserve more positive help in resolving their identity.

Janet Helms: Racial Identity Formation

Janet Helms (1994) has provided the most systematic research on racial identity formation by African-Americans. She suggests that the dual-identity problem is only one phase in a larger process. She found that the awareness of racial differences proceeded along a sequence of forms depending upon the salience of the issues and the process of internalization. Table 6.2 presents the successive phases of identity formation for African-Americans. The descriptions show widely different responses to the experience of racism and prejudice. For example, in the *preencounter* phase, the individual is basically unaware of racial differences and naively believes that differences in ethnicity and skin color do not exist or, perhaps even worse, tries to pretend that he or she is white. In the *immersion/emersion* phase, the consciousness of being oppressed/rejected by the white culture leads to calls for a new type of segregation, a separate African-American nation/region or black nationalism. These phases are part of a movement to the final phase of internalization, in which the individual African-American has come to terms with experiences of having the "race card" used against him or her. The hatred of self learned from the oppressors has given way to a new level of consciousness. Rage has subsided, but a commitment to seek equality and racial justice remains. In fact there is a parallel between this stage of personal identity development and Kohlberg's level of principled value stage (Chapter 7).

Identity Formation and Gender

As is the case with ethnicity, a substantial new research base is helping clarify and extend gender identity status. The traditional dichotomy between males as instrumental and females as caring puts the same limitation on identity formation as we have shown in the domain of moral development. In fact some of the earlier research on identity suggested

---

TABLE 6.2   *JANET HELMS'S PHASES OF RACIAL IDENTITY FORMATION AMONG AFRICAN-AMERICANS*

Preencounter	Idealization of the majority white culture. Racism is desired. The individual tries to separate himself or herself form ethnic/racial background. Overidentification with white culture.
Encounter	Growing consciousness of being different from the white culture. The salience of skin color emerges. There is a recognition of effects of prejudice on the self.
Immersion/emersion	The polar opposite of the preencounter stage. Overidentification with "black power" and "black nationalism." There is a desire to avoid white culture and seek separation. Integration is not possible. Total enmeshment with African-American culture is sought.
Internalization	Acceptance and valuing of one's own racial identity as well as the majority culture. Biculturalism—the ability to live in both cultures—achieved. Individual differences are recognized in both cultures.

that foreclosure was more adaptive for females than the movement to achievement, self-direction, and personal efficacy. It was felt that a foreclosed identity would protect women from conflicts over personal achievement—the syndrome denoted as "fear of success." During the 1970s a series of studies underscored the worries that achieving females experienced in college (Horner, 1972; Larkin, 1987). This research presents an eerie parallel to the behavior of peers and of society in general in sending a message to minorities about "acting white." Similar message was sent to women about "acting male." The context of the message in the form of rigid societal expectations clearly created a major psychological conflict. If a female wanted to become an M.D., would she lose her chance to become an "M-r-s"? It wasn't feminine to hit the books or to achieve success in "hard" science. A young woman who did so would probably remove herself from the marriage pool.

As is the case for minorities, society in general may perpetuate the stereotypes, sending the social "you can't succeed in 'male' domains" message to females. Jacqueline Eccles (1986) has laid the blame with mothers who believed the myths of female incompetence in math and science, Gail Jones and Jack Wheatley (1989) with female and male science teachers. Karen Arnold (1987) found a major decline of female identity as an academic achiever in a sample of former high school valedictorians.

Two recent studies, a large-scale cross-sectional and a small-sample longitudinal, continue to call our attention to the problem of self-confidence and gender during adolescence. Reporting in the American Psychological Association's *Monitor,* Freiberg (1991) found a noticeable decline in confidence and assertiveness by females. Table 6.3 presents the results. Females moved from about a 60 percent confidence level to 29 percent between elementary and senior high school. The males also declined, but by far less. Jack Block and Richard Robins (1993) report similar findings in their study of almost 100 boys and girls over a 10-year period, assessed at ages 14, 18, and 23

years. Females continued to decrease in self-confidence while boys showed particular gains by the end of college.

Given these findings, then, it is no wonder that a foreclosed identity appeared to be a safe means of avoiding conflict. The problem, of course, for young women is that in this case such a solution relegates over half the population to a subservient role. Research in psychological development demonstrates clearly that females have the same potential for development as males. It is clear, however, that neither *foreclosure* nor *diffusion* is adaptive in the long run. Foreclosure will obviously not work, since the majority of women in this country will become the head of household and main breadwinner for the family as a result of divorce, abandonment, or death of a spouse. To carry out such responsibility competently without achieving a firm sense of an individual identity would be close to impossible. Similarly, to remain in *diffusion* would be maladaptive. Ruthellen Josselson (1987) has shown that adult women in diffusion have little sense of direction and cannot make commitments, that they are distant and estranged from their families, and that they cannot maintain firm and stable interpersonal relationships—hardly a psychological state conducive to mental health.

Sally Archer (1992a, 1992b, & 1994) has taken the lead in revising the stereotyped views of identity formation for females. She does not suggest that we can simply transform the male model *in toto* into a female model. Identity formation involves the same levels of development for both males and females, but for some time to come it will remain more difficult and painful for females because of external barriers to development. For example, Archer finds that gender differences are the exception now rather than the rule in identity status. There are no differences by gender and identity by vocation, religion, sex roles, values, and dating.

A study by Eva Skoe (1991) confirms the lack of gender differences. In a college sample, she found no differences between males and females on *identity status, moral judgment,* and a specially constructed *care interview.* The higher stages, in general, correlated positively for both groups, cross-validating Waterman's earlier findings. For example, higher identity scores were related to higher moral judgment scores and, in this case, higher scores on the care interview.

The major continuing difference is in the family-career priorities (Archer, 1992a). Males in grades 6, 8, 10, and 12 see almost no connection between career and family and do not make any mention of the problems of child care, the psychological or economic impact on children, or the need to facilitate

TABLE 6.3   SELF-ESTEEM SURVEY

	Confident and Assertive	
	Females (N = 2,400)	Males N = 600
Ages 8–9	60%	67%
Ages 16–17	29%	46%
Decline	31%	21%

Data Source: *Freiberg (1991).*

the development of their spouse. Archer's sample of high school seniors responded as follows to the question "How concerned are you about the issue of balancing career and family demands?"

	GREAT CONCERN	SOME CONCERN	NO CONCERN
Males	0%	25%	75%
Females	42%	42%	17%

As a result, Archer points out that a most crucial issue, career and family, remains a singular struggle for females even though they have now entered the workforce in huge proportions. Who, she asks rhetorically, will help them resolve this aspect of *identity achievement*? Must such women wait for the departure of children before they can pursue identity commitments of their own? In fact, some research indicates that it is only the women who maintain continuous employment who also follow the stepwise sequence. This, at least, indicates that context rather than outdated notions of biology is a critical factor in identity development (Patterson et al., 1992).

In summarizing, Archer points out that the failure of society in general to support the process of identity formation creates an unfair burden. Females bear the costs of such invisibility. "There is a remarkable dearth of investment in the recognition of these identity concerns by parents, peers, school counselors or classroom instructors" (Archer, 1992a, p. 98). Thus, while there are no major differences by gender in most of the identity domains either in this country or cross-culturally (Costa & Campos, 1992), the area of career and family remains largely a female concern, with females left to their own singular resources for resolution. Unfortunately, Archer's interviews reveal a major naïveté in some of their current reflections. The identity correlates of realism are low when a high school female brightly announces that she will complete college, get married, go to medical school, take a few years off to have children, and resume her career—all without help from anyone. Archer concludes that too often females are caught up with such "fairy tales." "Like all other toys, they must eventually be stored away; but in this case before they do irreparable damage" (Archer, 1992a, p. 99).

EDUCATIONAL IMPLICATIONS

As educators, we need to take special note of the challenges posed by the immensely complex years of adolescence. There are no easy solutions. But this does not mean that nothing can be done. For years it was fashionable to say that adolescence is a tough period, but everyone outgrows it eventually, so all you can do is grin and bear it. We now realize that such advice is mere rationalization and in no way excuses us from responsibility. The number of psychological casualties during adolescence is now too obvious to permit such an attitude. For example, we now realize that adolescent drug abuse is a symptom of the problem of personal identity formation or, in Erikson's terms, an attempt to solve the problem of identity diffusion. It is only an attempt because it is a nonsolution. The moment the drug wears off, the same problems are still there, waiting to be attended to.

Educators are by definition in a strategic position to help guide personal growth. Adolescents feel a need to pull away from their own parents, and so other adults can be of special significance. It is therefore our responsibility to develop effective ways to make this influence work. Erikson makes it obvious that to assist growth we need to provide adolescents with increasing amounts of independence and responsibility. In the previous stage—mastery—activity was the key. In this stage our objectives as educators should be to provide real experience and genuine responsibility.

Thus, the variety of school programs, especially at the secondary level, involving peer and cross-age teaching, community internships, peer counseling, and teenage health "consultants," is important primarily because such role-taking can involve genuine responsibility. In these programs teenagers learn to teach, counsel, and care for younger classmates. Such responsibility stimulates their own leadership development and psychological maturation. Thus, the potential for empathic understanding and human caring that is available for development during adolescence can be capitalized on in the service of healthy personal growth.

The problem, of course, is that to achieve developmental goals, the learning experiences need for the most part to be "real world" activity plus a careful balance of introspection, readings, and reflection. When done well, the results are impressive. For example, James Leming (1992) found that the most positive of all approaches to drug-abuse prevention in high school was the use of carefully trained peer counselors. Another study has shown that training high school females as math tutors to aid fifth-grade females was successful on three counts: (1) the teenage tutors developed a greater level of psychological/identity growth toward independence, (2) the elementary school females improved in actual math achievement, and (3) the fifth-graders also learned to attribute their success to their own effort. In a control class of teenage teacher aides, without weekly readings and discussions, there was no change in development, no change in math achievement, and a decline in success attribution to self (Sprinthall & Scott, 1989).

A third recent study demonstrated the positive impact of a peer counseling program with high school students as group leaders of middle school pupils whose families were going through a divorce. The high-schoolers spent one semester in an elective course in peer counselor training and then led the "divorce" groups for a semester. The results again were threefold: (1) the leaders moved to higher levels of psychological/ego development, (2) the middle school students improved in their "locus of control" and ego development, and (3) the middle school students also indicated a greater ability to adjust/cope with the family disruption (Sprinthall et al., 1992). The controls showed no change. Similarly positive results have been found with college students as peer helpers (Zimmerman, 1989; Mann, 1992).

Thus, peer influence can be channeled into important educational and developmental activity. It does require a comprehensive educational plan, namely weekly classes to discuss the issues involved and training in the use of teacher or counselor skills. Peer programs without the reflection review component either have no positive results or in some cases move toward negative results. A study by Paul Adams (1988) with college students involved in unguided small-group discussions indicated that students at higher stages of development actually lowered their level of reasoning to match that of a peer. This reminds us that social conformity in a developmental sense may peak in middle school but continues to exert substantial influence even in college. Adolescent peers do represent a potential resource for identity development, but not if left to themselves.

IDENTITY ACHIEVEMENT: WHAT'S NEXT?

An important issue for the identity framework concerns the issue of stage and sequence—what follows identity achievement? We have pointed out on the basis of Waterman's work, the positive nature of this status—higher self-direction, value development, more complex social perspective taking, and a whole series of other positive attributes. Recall, however, that the Erikson model is a series of stages and that adequate resolutions of each stage have major implications for the next. Remember also that development is not automatic, so age alone is *not* an index of

increasing psychological maturity (Levit, 1993). Thus, from an Eriksonian viewpoint, identity achievement becomes a critical stepping-stone to the next stage, *intimacy* versus *isolation*.

Gerald Adams and Sally Archer (1994) have examined this issue carefully and conclude that identity achievement is a major prerequisite for genuine intimacy during early adulthood, for both males and females. In contrast to earlier suggestions that females were different—that they could move into intimacy without developing their own identity, autonomy, and individuation—Adams and Archer take a firm stand based on research and theory that identity achievement is "of equal importance to the individual's psychological and social functioning regardless of gender." They point out that such individual autonomy and identity "is predictive of depth, quality, and intimacy in social relationships" (p. 209). This means that both males and females need to achieve a sense of individuality. As Erikson says, identity precedes intimacy. Such development changes the behaviors of both males and females. Both become capable of mutual interdependence, or, as another theorist puts it (Bakan, 1966), of *agency* (self-direction) and *communion* (equality in connectedness).

Adams and Archer also point out the negative effects, especially on women who move into intimate relationships without reaching an achieved identity. In line with Eriksonian theory, such change merely postpones the identity issue until sometime later in adulthood. The entire question can be summed up in the words of the famous Brazilian educator Paolo Freire, "Locality before universality," meaning you need to know who you are as a person before you can reach out to others as an equal.

ERIKSON'S CONTRIBUTION

Each stage in personal development is characterized by certain aspects that can be maximally affected either positively or negatively. For too long, personal and emotional development was considered out of bounds for educators and as the exclusive province of child guidance clinics and of those specially trained to deal with pathological problems. Erikson's great contribution was to integrate the problems of personal growth into the overall process of healthy personality development. Erikson spells out the major personal issues for us so that we can understand much more about our pupils at each of the various stages. We hope that such insight will guide us to more effective ways of helping children and adolescents during important, indeed critical, times.

Perhaps Erikson's greatest contribution to development is yet to come. Very recent theory by John Snarey (1995) suggests that Erikson's framework of ego development is in fact a general theory of development. In Chapter 1, we described three main faces of growth, the cognitive, the value, and the personal, as representing a three-sided pyramid. In an ideal sense this perspective would suggest that growth can and should take place across the three faces or domains. Instead, Snarey is promoting the idea that Erikson's ego theory, supported by increasing amounts of empirical research, can become a unifying concept. Otherwise, he fears that developmental stage theory will gradually disintegrate. There will be a proliferation of domains—social, altruistic, forgiveness, interpersonal, artistic, psychomotor (athletic), and so on—to the point where stage theory will disappear amid a mist of infinite domains. To avoid such stage proliferation, he views Erikson's ego as an overall personality concept that is composed of such subdomains as cognitive (Piaget) and moral (Kohlberg). Erikson's ego then becomes like a busy executive, managing different departments within the company and the external relations with rivals and friends. At higher stages of ego development the person is increasingly competent in managing internal and external problems across the different subdomains. The more complex stage of ego development thus becomes a core stage of problem-solving. We often speak of a person being "centered." Erikson describes ego as "an age-old term which in the scholastics stood for the *unity* of body and soul, and in philosophy in general for the permanency of conscious experience" (1982, p. 147). Thus, it is the whole person as a unifying element struggling and growing in the ability to "put it all together" that defines a general stage and sequence of overall psychological maturity. It is, of course, a difficult task at each level to achieve such integration, yet it is essential as a basis for a healthy identity. As Erikson wrote:

> Indeed in the social jungle of human existence there is no feeling of being alive without a sense of ego identity . . . The danger of this stage is identity diffusion . . . Youth after youth, bewildered by some assumed role, a role forced on him by the inexorable standardization of American adolescence, runs away in one form or another, leaving schools and jobs, staying out all night, or withdrawing into bizarre and inaccessible moods (1959, pp. 90–91).

SUMMARY

Personal development should not be regarded as a process separate from other aspects of development. There is a common tendency to pay lip service to the idea that aspects of development are not really separate but then to talk about these domains as if they were compartmentalized.

Before Freud, children under six were generally assumed to be empty, literally mindless creatures. Accordingly, little was expected of them. Freud was a pioneer in emphasizing the importance of sensitive growth periods for personal development during childhood.

Erikson's elaborated Freud's thought into a theory of a series of stages extending over the life cycle. Each stage is marked by psychosocial crises that require the resolution of opposite, or bipolar, traits. How adequately a person resolves the crisis of each stage helps determine and promote strength for succeeding stages. The stages are linked together in an interdependent manner:

Trust versus mistrust, resolved as hope

Autonomy versus shame, resolved as will

Initiative versus guilt, resolved as purpose

Mastery versus inferiority, resolved as competence

Identity versus diffusion, resolved as fidelity

Evidence supports the importance of the specified major issue at each stage. For example, Harlow's work, Spitz's research, and Anna Freud's studies all suggest the critical importance of careful, warm, and consistent parenting in the first 24 months to establish hope in the infant.

White's studies detail the significance of patterns of parenting during preschool years as a means of building competence, autonomy, and initiative in young children. During the juvenile years, it is important for educators to encourage and facilitate personal competence.

Newer evidence on the process of identity formation during adolescence—the phases of foreclosure, diffusion, moratorium, and achievement—has emerged from the work of Marcia and Waterman. The sequence of identity formation appears to be the same for minority youth and females, for males in general, but it is more difficult because of particular societal barriers. Janet Helms has provided a framework for identity formation among African-Americans. The paths of growth from preencounter, encounter, immersion/emersion, to internalization represent different levels of consciousness about one's own identity and a means of getting off "ethnic probation."

Among educational programs designed to promote development, peer helping methods in schools and colleges have had the most positive outcomes.

Finally, John Snarey has recently proposed Erikson's theory as a general theory of psychological growth across personal, cognitive, and value domains.

KEY TERMS AND NAMES

Sally Archer
David Elkind
Erik Erikson
    competence motivation
    epigenetic principle
Lawrence K. Frank
Sigmund Freud
    oral stage
    anal stage
    phallic stage
    psychoanalytic theory

Janet Helms
James Marcia
    diffusion
    foreclosure
    moratorium
    achievement
Alan Waterman

THEORY INTO PRACTICE: IDENTITY FORMATION PHASES— AN INTERVIEW GUIDE

To increase your understanding of Marcia's phases of identity formation, we suggest that you either ask yourself the following questions or interview a friend or colleague. We have provided some prototypical examples of answers that represent the different phases. The main point of such questions is not to obtain any one specific answer but rather to help the person elaborate on the reasons for any specific choice. If you interview someone, be sure to remain nonjudgmental about the person's reasoning. The process involves asking open-ended questions with no right or wrong answers; the interviewer must remain value-neutral during the questioning. Your goal is to find out how the person really thinks and feels about the questions without the influence of any evaluation by the interviewer.

Sample Questions in One Domain: Occupation

How have you gone about choosing a career for yourself? Have you had this in mind for a long time?

What factors or persons have been most important in influencing you?

How sure are you about your choice?

What other fields have you considered?

How do you feel about your choice or choices?

The point of the questions is to provide a great deal of scope to the person being interviewed so that you can listen for themes and reasons. Sometimes much information can be solicited simply by asking, "As you think about choosing a career, what stands out?"

Marcia's approach involves asking similarly open-ended questions about religious orientation, worldview, or politics. Depending on how much time you have, you can switch to those areas for further elaboration after you complete the occupational questions.

A final point: You may not find such pure types as in the sample answers, so be prepared to listen for shades of meaning. The probe questions should help to clarify the person's thinking, but do expect some overlap in responses.

Sample Responses to Occupation Questions

Foreclosure   "Well that's easy. I've always known from elementary school on that I wanted to be a civil engineer. My dad is one, and he always told me that engineering work is for me. Even when I had trouble in high school math and began to find an art course much more enjoyable, my dad hired a math tutor for me, and I made it through.

"So when it came to college, it was pretty clear where I'd go. Actually, I visited only one kind of college. Also, it turned out I had to take an extra year in prep school to get my SAT math score up high enough for admission.

"The work itself is a real grind, but my dad always said, 'College is like a bank account. You can't make withdrawals until you make deposits.' So I'll keep plugging along. I'm just below a graduation grade point average, but I'm getting tutored in two subjects, so I think I'll squeeze through. My family have all said how proud they'll be when I become an engineer. I'm sure I'll be proud, too. Everybody I know wants to see me succeed in engineering."

Diffusion   "I don't really think about it much. I mean, I know I'm supposed to be in college to become something, but if I'm honest, I'd have to say that the whole thing is a drag. I change my mind so often. Last week, I met this guy who is an audio-engineer in charge in recording sessions for one of the top record companies. He's got it made—money, a great car, a wardrobe—the works. So I said, Yeah that's for me. But you know, just before that I got all charged up about being an anthropologist after watching a special on Jane Goodall. I guess what I'm going to do is just wait and see what develops. After all, college is a lot of fun, so why worry? Maybe something will come along and motivate me, but for now I'm really here just to have a good time. I'm sure sooner or later something will happen."

Moratorium   "You know, that's one of the most interesting questions you can ask. I used to think of the square peg in the square hole. There is one perfect job for me; find it. Now what I've been realizing is that I keep discovering new interests and even new abilities here in college. I'm not the same as I was in high school. I'm taking a course in geology— you know, 'Rocks for jocks'—and its very interesting. The field trips. Even the reading. I'm doing extra work, even though some of my friends think I'm crazy to work that hard, but it is interesting and then the same is happening in a course in music—you know, 'Clapping for credit'—but I find all kinds of interesting information. I actually listen to music differently. I can analyze how the compositions are put together.

"I used to think college, the study part, would be a drag, but it's not. I'm learning, yet I'm [also] learning that I had better keep my choices open. It's too soon to choose. And you know I used to envy these people who could tell you from day one, "I want to be a flight surgeon' or something like that. Now I say that's maybe OK for them but not for me. I've got lots of things I want to explore first."

Achievement   "It has taken me a long time to figure out where I want to go now that I'm finishing college. All through high school and in the first two years here, I must have changed my mind a hundred times. First, it was a teacher-coach in the tenth grade, then an English teacher in the eleventh, then a business executive, and so forth. Gradually, however, I found that more and more of my attention and interest was on foreign-policy questions. I joined two clubs, spent a summer in central America, and started taking all the electives I could in international relations. I even talked the poli. sci. department into creating an interdisciplinary major for me. Every time I turned around I found myself pointed in that direction. I mean, what could be more exciting than to become a diplomat, represent the country, and work toward international understanding? I know it will be frustrating. There are still lots of myopic people. But that's also a real challenge.

"So I'm off to graduate school in international relations after I finish a two-year stint with the Peace Corps. I figure some real experience is called for, not just striped pants and high tea."

REFERENCES

Adams, G., & Archer, S. (1994). Identity: A precursor to intimacy. In S. Archer (Ed.), *Interventions for adolescent identity development* (pp. 193–213). Thousand Oaks, CA: Sage.

Adams, P. S. (1988). Peer influence and moral decision-making in undergraduate cliques. *Moral Education Forum, 13*(3), 9–15.

Archer, S. (1992a). Females at risk: Identity issues for adolescents and divorced women. In C. Vandenplas & B. Campos (Eds.), *Interpersonal and identity* _development: New directions_ (pp. 87–102). Porto, Portugal: University of Porto.

Archer, S. (1992b). A feminist's approach to identity research. In G. R. Adams, T. P. Gullotta, & R. Montemayor (Eds.), _Adolescent identity formation_ (pp. 215–249). Newbury Park, CA: Sage.

Archer, S. (1994). An overview. In S. Archer (Ed.), _Interventions for adolescent identity development_ (pp. 3–11). Thousand Oaks, CA: Sage.

Arnold, K. (1987, July). _Retaining high-achieving women in science and engineering._ Paper presented at the AAAS Symposium on Women and Girls in Science and Technology, University of Michigan, Ann Arbor.

Bakan, D. (1966). _The duality of human existence._ Chicago: Rand-McNally.

Balistreri, E.; Busch-Rossnagel, N.; & Geisinger, K. (1995). Ego identity process questionnaire. _Adolescence, 18_(2), 179–192.

Block, J., & Robins, R. (1993). A longitudinal study of consistency and change in self-esteem from early adolescence to early adulthood. _Child Development, 64_(3), 909–923.

Campbell, F., & Ramey, C. (1995). Cognitive and school outcomes for high-risk African-American students at middle adolescence. _American Educational Research Journal, 32_(4), 743–772.

Coimbra, J., & Campos, B. (1990). Organization of interpersonal experience and organization of interpersonal action-related thought. In C. Vandenplas-Holper & B. Campos (Eds.), _Interpersonal and identity development: New directions._ Porto, Portugal: University of Porto, pp. 35–46.

Costa, M. E., & Campos, B. (1990). Socio-educational context and beginning university students' identity development. In C. Vandenplas-Holper & B. Campos (Eds.), _Interpersonal and identity development: New directions_ (pp. 79–86). Porto, Portugal: University of Porto.

Costanzo, P. R., & Shaw, M. E. (1996). Conformity as a function of age level. _Child Development, 37_, 967–975.

DuBois, W. E. B. (1963). _An ABC of color._ Berlin: Seven Seas.

Eccles, J. (1986). Gender roles and women's achievement. _Educational Research, 15_(6), 15–19.

Eccles, J.; Wigfield, A.; Harold, R.; & Blumenfeld, P. (1993). Age and gender differences in children's self- and task perceptions during elementary school. _Child Development, 64_(3), 830–847.

Elkind, D. (1970). _Children and adolescents._ New York: Oxford.

Elkind, D. (1978). Understanding the young adolescent. _Adolescence, 13_, 127–134.

Erikson, E. (1959). Identity and the life cycle. _Psychological issues_ (vol. 1). New York: Norton.

Erikson, E. (1982). _The life cycle completed._ New York: Norton.

Faubert, M.; Locke, D.; Sprinthall, N. A.; & Howland, W. (1996). Promoting cognitive and ego development of African-American rural youth. _Journal of Adolescence 19_, (3) 533–44.

Frank, L. K. (1969). Quoted in Sprinthall, R. C., & Sprinthall, N. A., _Educational psychology: Selected readings._ New York: Van Nostrand.

Freiberg, P. (1991) Self-esteem gender gap widens in adolescence. _APA Monitor, 22_(4), 29.

Freud, A. (1958). Adolescence. Psychoanalytic study of the child, 13, 225–276.

Goleman, D. (1995). _The emotional quotient._ New York: Bantam Books.

Harlow, H. F. & Harlow, M. K. (1962). Social deprivation in monkeys. _Scientific American, 207_, 136–146.

Hauser-Cram, P.; Pierson, D.; Walker, D.; & Trinan, T. (1991). _Early education in public schools._ San Francisco: Jossey-Bass.

Helms, J. (1994). _Black and white racial identity: Theory, research, and practice_ (2d ed.). Westport, CT: Greenwood Press.

Hibbert, M., & Sprinthall, N. A. (1995). Promoting social and emotional development of preschoolers: Inclusion and mainstreaming for children with special needs. _Elementary School Guidance and Counseling, 30_(2), 131–142.

Hoppe, C., & Loevinger, J. (1977). Ego development and conformity. _Journal of Personality, 41_, 497–504.

Horner, M. (1972). Toward an understanding of achievement-related conflicts in women. _Journal of Social Issues, 28_, 157–175.

Jones, G., & Wheatley, J. (1989). Gender influences in classroom displays and student-teacher behaviors. _Science Education, 73_(5), 535–545.

Jones, R. (1990). _Black adolescents._ Berkeley, CA: Cobb & Henry.

Jones, R. M. (1992). Ego identity and adolescent problem behavior. In G. R. Adams, T. P. Gullotta, & R. Montemayor (Eds.), _Adolescent identity formation_ (pp. 216–233). Newbury Park, CA: Sage.

Josselson, R. (1987). _Finding herself: Pathways to identity development in women._ San Francisco: Jossey-Bass.

Kohlberg, L., & Gilligan, C. (1971). The adolescent as a philosopher. _Daedalus, 100_(4), 1051–1086.

Lapsley, D. (1993). Toward an integrated theory of adolescent ego development: The "new look" at adolescent egocentrism. _American Journal of Orthopsychiatry, 63_, 562–571.

Larkin, L. (1987). Identity and fear of success. _Journal of Counseling Psychology, 34_, 38–45.

Lee, C. (1990). Black male development: Counseling the "Native Son." In D. Moore and F. Leafgren

(Eds.), *Problem solving strategies and intervention for men in conflict* (pp. 125–137). Washington: American Psychological Association.

Leming, J. (1992). The influence of contemporary issues curricula on school-aged youth. *Review of Research in Education, 18,* 111–161.

Levit, D. (1993). The development of ego defenses in adolescence. *Journal of Youth and Adolescence, 22,* 493–512.

Locke, D. C. (1992). *Increasing multicultural understanding.* Newbury Park, CA: Sage.

Locke, D. C., & Faubert, M. (1993). Getting on the right track: A program for African-American high school students. *The School Counselor, 41,* 129–133.

Maccoby, E. (1990). The role of gender identity and gender constancy in sex-differentiated development. In D. Schrader (Ed.), *The legacy of Lawrence Kohlberg* (pp. 5–20). San Francisco: Jossey-Bass.

Mann, A. (1992). *A quantitative and qualitative evaluation of a peer tutor-training course.* Unpublished doctoral dissertation, North Carolina State University, Raleigh.

Marcia, J. (1966). Development and validation of ego identity status. *Journal of Personality and Social Psychology, 3,* 551–558.

Marcia, J. (1976). Identity six years after. *Journal of Youth and Adolescence, 5,* 145–160.

Marcia, J. (1991). Identity and self-development. In R. Lerner, A. Peterson, & J. Brooks-Gunn)Eds.), *Encyclopedia of adolescence* (Vol. 1), pp. 529–533). New York: Garland.

Markstrom-Adams, C. (1992). A consideration of factors in adolescent identity formation. In G. R. Adams, T. P. Gullotta, and R. Montemayor (Eds.), *Adolescent identity formation* (pp. 173–192). Newbury Park, CA: Sage.

Muus, R. (1988). *Theories of adolescence.* New York: Random House.

Ogbu, J. (1988). Cultural diversity and human development. In D. Slaughter (Ed.), *Black children and poverty* (pp. 11–28). San Francisco: Jossey-Bass.

Patterson, S. J.; Sochting, D.; & Marcia, J. (1992). In G. R. Adams, T. P. Gullotta, & R. Montemayor (Eds.), *Adolescent identity formation* (pp. 9–24). Newbury Park, CA: Sage.

Phinney, J. S., & Rosenthal, D. A. (1992). Ethnic identity in adolescence: Process, context, and outcome. In G. R. Adams, T. P. Gullotta, & R. Montemayor (Eds.), *Adolescent identity formation* (pp. 145–172). Newbury Park, CA: Sage.

Quality Education for Minorities Project. (1990). Cambridge, MA: Massachusetts Institute of Technology. Author.

Risman, B. (1986). Can men "mother"? Life as a single father. *Family Relations, 35,* 95–102.

Robinson, T. R., & Ward, J. V. (1995). African-American adolescents and skin color. *Journal of Black Psychology, 21*(3), 256–274.

Salinger, J. D. (1964) *The catcher in the rye.* New York: Bantam.

Schweinhart, L.; Weikart, D.; & Larner, M. (1986). Consequences of three preschool curriculum models through age 15. *Early Childhood Research Quarterly, 1,* 15–45.

Schultz, J. B. (1989). AHEA's survey of American teens. *Journal of Home Economics, 81,* 27–28.

Skoe, E. E. (November 1991). *Identity, care-based and justice-based moral reasoning in women and men.* Paper presented at the annual conference of the Association for Moral Education, Athens, Georgia.

Snarey, J. (November 1995). *Ego development and the ethical voices of justice and care: An Eriksonian interpretation.* Paper presented at the annual conference of the Association for Moral Education, New York.

Spitz, R. A. (1946). Hospitalism: A follow-up report. In *Psychoanalytic study of the child* (Vol. 2). New York: International University Press.

Sprinthall, N. A., & Collins, W. A. (1995). *Adolescent psychology: A developmental view.* New York: McGraw-Hill.

Sprinthall, N. A., & Scott, J. (1989). Promoting psychological development, math achievement, and success attribution of female students through deliberate psychological education. *Journal of Counseling Psychology, 36*(4), 440–446.

Sprinthall, N. A.; Hall, J. S.; & Gerler, E. R. (1992). Peer counseling for middle school students experiencing family divorce. *Journal of Elementary School Counseling, 26*(4), 279–294.

Waterman, A. (1985). Identity in adolescence: Processes and contents. In *New directions for child development.* San Francisco: Jossey-Bass.

Waterman, A. (1992). Identity as an aspect of optimal psychological functioning. In G. R. Adams, T. P. Gullotta, & R. Montemayor (Eds.), *Adolescent identity formation* (pp. 50–72). Newbury Park, CA: Sage.

Watts, E. A. (1992). The color of success. *Brown Alumni Monthly, 92*(7), 47–48.

White, B. L. (1987). *Educating the infant and the toddler.* New York: Heath.

White, R. W. (1959). Motivation reconsidered: The concept of competence. *Psychological Review, 66,* 297–333.

White, S. (1968). *Changes in learning processes in the late preschool years.* Paper presented at the American Educational Research Association convention, Chicago.

Wires, J.; Barocas, R.; & Hollenbeck, A. (1994). Determinants of adolescent identity development: A cross-sequential study of boarding school boys. *Adolescence, 29,* 361–378.

Zigler, E., & Berman, W. (1983). Discerning the future of early childhood intervention. *American Psychologist, 38*(8), 894–906.

Zimmerman, N. (1989). *Effects of a role-taking curriculum on the psychological maturity of college students.* Unpublished doctoral dissertation, North Carolina State University, Raleigh.

Zuschlag, M., & Whitbourne, S. (1994). Psychosocial development in three generations of college students. *Journal of Youth and Adolescence, 23*(5), 567–577.

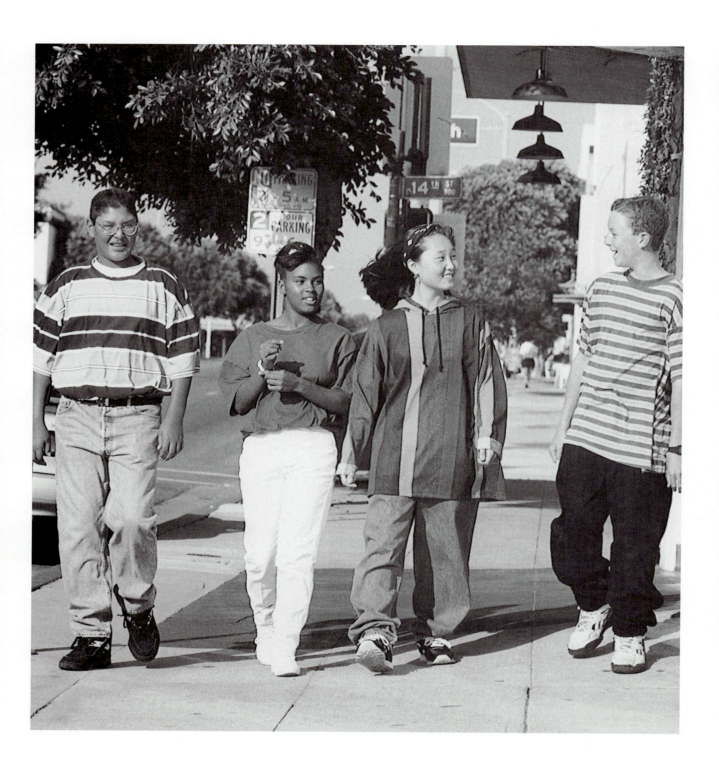

VALUE
DEVELOPMENT

It is perhaps ironic that in the area of value and moral development, there has been major disagreement between professional educators and psychologists. On the one hand, from the very beginnings of the public or common school, educators have insisted that a pupil's character and values should be the proper object of teaching. Horace Mann, considered the architect of free public education, maintained stoutly in the early nineteenth century that veracity, probity, and rectitude were the significant goals of education. "Train up a child in the way he should go, and when he is old he will not depart from it" (Cremin, 1957). Character and citizenship were viewed as major objectives of schooling. Practically every public school had a printed curriculum objective extolling the virtues of character development. The Boston Public Schools' guide in the 1920s was typical of many:

We are unfit for any trust till we can and do obey.

Honor thy father and mother.

True obedience is true liberty.

The first law ever God gave to man was a law of obedience.

On the other hand, psychologists have maintained, at least for the last 50 years, that attempting to inculcate traits and virtues is almost totally ineffectual. In other words, while educators were stoutly maintaining that schools mold character, psychologists were busily denying that values could be taught.

Today this debate has taken on more urgency. Many schools across the country have formed "character education" committees. Radio and TV talk shows are filling the air with suggestions. Character education and values have assumed first place in many public opinion polls as an appropriate focus for public education.

In this chapter, we review why educational psychologists have been reluctant to jump on this bandwagon. Also and more importantly, we present a developmental framework based largely on Larry Kohlberg's theory that does have implications for educational practice. Though controversial, the latest research strengthens the developmental approach. We outline the stages, review the gender and cross-cultural issues, and then describe a series of promising approaches to guide the slow and often halting process of value and character education.

EXPLODING THE MYTH OF CHARACTER EDUCATION

In the 1920s two researchers, **Hugh Hartshorne and Mark May** at the University of Chicago, conducted a long series of studies, which they replicated again and again (1928–1930). Their results were a bombshell. In every study they arrived at the same conclusion: Formal character instruction had no positive effect. After studying over 10,000 children and adolescents in regular school classes in character education, special Sunday-school classes, Boy Scout classes, and others, they found no correlation at all between character education/virtue training and actual behavior (such as cheating). They also found that character education produced essentially no consistent moral behavior in the same person from one situation to another. This seemed to imply that people who cheat in one situation may or may not cheat in the next situation. (The sample honesty test in the accompanying illustration may help demonstrate such an assertion.) In general, moral behavior seemed unpredictable and moral character traits mythical. If ingrained character traits such as honesty or dishonesty did exist, then it would be possible to predict behavior accurately.

Hartshorne and May were as dismayed by these results as everyone else, To make matters worse the researchers also found no relationship between what people said about morality and the way these same people acted. People who expressed great disapproval of cheating or stealing actually stole and cheated as much as anyone else. Hartshorne and May concluded that the risk of detection was the single most important factor in deterring cheating. They also found that it was meaningless to divide people into simple categories and label them as either honest or dishonest. Like so many other aspects of human nature, cheating is normally distributed around a level of moderate cheating. (Results that have a normal distribution can be fitted to a bell-shaped curve. The distribution will look the same as that for measured intelligence, height, weight, or coin flipping for heads or tails. See Chapter 15 for further discussion of normal distribution.) Hartshorne and May found that what was true for supposed pairs of traits such as honesty/dishonesty was also true for traits such as altruism/selfishness and self-control/impulsiveness. These results, of course, called into the question the entire concept of character traits.

One of the criticisms of Hartshorne and May's research was that the situations set up in tests such as eye-hand coordination and memory did not really create a battle of conscience. In other words, the stakes were low, so maybe the students didn't really care and merely opened their eyes out of curiosity or some other motive. Such a finding, if proved, would of course undermine their whole argument. In a quite ingenious study, (e.g., high stakes) the researchers, Kohlberg & Candee (1984), built a special computerlike ray gun complete with video screen. The game was rigged to yield a score just below the level needed to win a special prize as a sharpshooter. In the first test, over 80 percent of the students cheated on their reported score, thus confirming the original research findings. In a second study, however, the critical findings were completely different. More gadgetry was added to increase the battle of conscience—or at least that was the intention of the researchers. With additional computer equipment, a new sequence was rigged. Now the students would reach the very brink of success; then they would miss. Under these new conditions only 15 of the 100 children cheated. What happened? This was a total reversal of all previous findings—or was it? Interviews revealed that the students in the second study thought that the machine was indeed wired into a real computer that kept the actual score. Therefore, there was no point in cheating.

One problem seems to be that attempts to inculcate particular virtues amount to only superficial add-ons. Reading stories about virtuous people—in the 1930s it was *The Book of Courage*, by Hermann Hagedorn; today it is *The Book of Virtues*, by William Bennett—is at best a vicarious experience. Likewise, lectures or exhortations on virtuous behavior will almost always go in one ear and out the other.

Another problem involves the question of which virtues are to be inculcated, and how any particular group of adults defines them. Certainly the lists will almost inevitably change over time. In the 1970s the virtues included spontaneity, openness, authenticity and "do your own thing." In the 1990s they included trust, respect, responsibility, and fairness. Perceptions and definitions change with the times.

In our view, the specific-virtue approach misses the key concept that children and adolescents as well as young adults and adults themselves are all in the process of development.

KOHLBERG'S THEORY: A DEVELOPMENTAL VIEW

Lawrence Kohlberg (1968), working first at the University of Chicago and then at Harvard, revolutionized our understanding of moral development. He

The Hartshorne and May Technique

This is a sample honesty test as well as an eye-hand coordination and memory test. At the signal for each trial, place your pencil at point X. Study the circles, then close your eyes and write the number 1 in the first circle, the second circle, the third circle, and so on. For the second trial, open your eyes, place your pencil at point X, close your eyes and write the number 2 in the first circle, the second circle, and so on. For the third trial, follow the same procedure and write the number 3, and so on. Proceed for five trials.

After each trial, put a check mark in the score box for each time you hit the correct circle. Count the checks and enter the total in column T. After the last trial, add up column T. This is your total score. The maximum is 50.

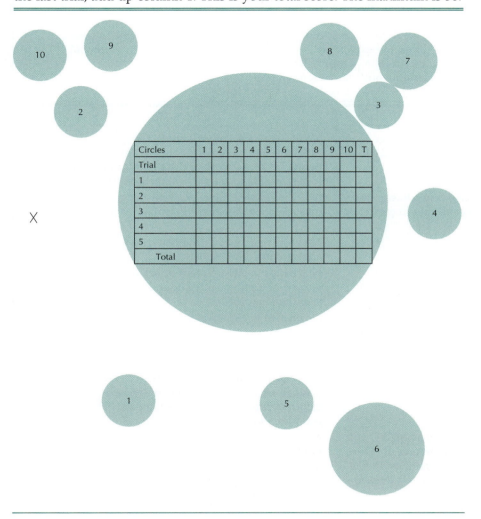

Circles	1	2	3	4	5	6	7	8	9	10	T
Trial											
1											
2											
3											
4											
5											
Total											

found that people cannot be grouped into neat compartments with simplistic labels, such as "This group is honest" or "This group cheats" or "This group is reverent." Instead, he found that moral character develops. This idea, that moral growth occurs in a developmental sequence, has completely changed our basic assumptions.

After conducting a long series of studies with chil-

SPOTLIGHT ON CHARACTER EDUCATION

Boon or Boondoggle?

One topic that is ever-present in today's educational concerns is character education. Community leaders, local school boards, professional groups, state and national legislatures alike are calling for schools to adopt programs in character education. The Association of Practical and Professional Ethics, founded in 1991, embodies the explosion of interest. Each day the media headline yet another example of immoral/unethical behavior. In all walks of life the sense of urgency for new programs increases. The hole in the moral ozone layer is large and expanding. As actress Lily Tomlin quipped, "I may be cynical, but I can't keep up."

However, the urgent call for programs can lead to simple-minded solutions that in the long run will only fail. In our haste to respond to a complex need, it is easy to grab for magical solutions. The following table lists some examples of such solutions.

PROGRAM	*OUTCOME*
"Scared Straight": Promote character through fear. Expose predelinquents to adult prisons and talks from hardened "lifers."	No change between experimental and control groups in follow-up delinquent behavior. Instead, visiting the prison became a mark of distinction among the teenagers (Finkenauer & Kuhmerker, 1979).
"Boot camp" sentences for teenage drug abusers and dealers: Harsh living conditions in rural camps; heavy emphasis on discipline.	No change: Boot camp programs have a random effect on subsequent behavior (Freeman, 1993).
DARE programs to build character in order to resist drug abuse.	No positive effect on drug behavior with early adolescents (Ennett et al., 1994).
"Values Clarification": Explore and identify each person's value structure. Singular units.	No change in either values or behavior. Program is viewed as highly relativistic and at best only a first step (Leming, 1981).
Ethics through readings: Examine lives of moral exemplars, read virtuous accounts of historical figures (e.g., George Washington and the cherry tree).	No change in either values or behavior. Academic classes are too vicarious, separated from real life. Films, excerpts, short stories, etc. fail to promote moral development (Rest, 1986).
Direct instruction of common virtues, such as honesty and truthfulness, through lectures, exhortations, and classroom rules.	No positive effects upon attitudes or behavior. Some positive effects on acquisition of information. The lecture-recitation approach is too passive to affect complex attitudes and behavior (Leming, 1992).
Religious education versus secular education: Religious schools emphasize the importance of values through scripture and other spiritual writings. Public schools are proscribed from direct religious education.	No major differences in level of ethical development or behavior between teenagers from religious schools and public schools. Amounts of cheating, lying, and stealing are highly similar (Josephson Institute, 1992). Self-ratings and self-reports of altruism are highly inaccurate (Krebs & Van Hestern, 1994).

dren and adults, Kohlberg found that moral development occurs in a specific sequence of stages regardless of culture or subculture, continent or country. This means that we can no longer think of moral character in either/or terms, or assume that character is something we do or do not have. Instead of ex-

PROGRAM	OUTCOME
Character education: "Packaged" curriculum units focus on an array of virtues, such as honesty and truthfulness.	No hard evidence as to positive effects; only anecdotal and opinion survey information (Edwards, 1995; Leming 1995)
Volunteer experiences: Students engage in a variety of helping activities in community service, such as collecting canned goods, chopping wood, tutoring, and coaching.	Without careful guided reflection, readings, and discussions, there is no change in levels of development (Sprinthall, 1994).
Student part-time employment, such as sales clerk or fast food-worker.	No positive effects from work experience by itself. A series of negative outcomes is most common: greater cheating, drug use, skipping school (Steinberg & Dornbusch, 1991).
Character education through genetic influence: In this view, character is determined at birth; education is irrelevant. Identify and reward those favored at birth.	Henry Goodard's "bad seed" theory (see Chapter 2) was thoroughly discredited, as is the current thinly veiled attempt to revive genetic determinism (Herrnstein & Murray, 1993) and their "bell curve" argument.

As long as educators ignore the reality that character development is a slow developmental process, quick-fix or simple-minded solutions will be proposed, and fail.

Edwards, R. (1995, March). Character education: Popular but effective? *American Psychological Association Monitor, 26*(3), p. 42.

Ennett, S., Tobler, N., Ringwalt, C., & Flewelling, R. (1994). How effective is drug abuse resistance education? A meta-analysis of Project DARE outcome evaluations. *American Journal of Public Health, 84*(9), 1394–1399.

Finkenauer, J. O., & Kuhmerker, L. (1979). Scared straight. *Moral Education Forum, 4,* 1–7.

Freeman, L. W. (1993). Boot camp and inmate moral development: No significant effect. *Journal of Offender Rehabilitation, 19*(3–4), 123–127.

Herrnstein, R., & Murray, C. (1994). *The bell curve.* New York: Free Press.

Joseph and Edna Josephson Institute of Ethics. (1992). *Ethics in action.* Marina del Rey, CA: Author.

Krebs, D., & Van Hestern, F. (1994). The development of altruism: Toward an integrated model. *Developmental Review, 14,* 103–158.

Leming, J. (1993). Synthesis of research: In search of effective character education. *Educational Leadership, 51*(3), 63–71.

Leming, J. (1995). Reflections on thirty years of moral education research. *Moral Education Forum, 20*(3), 1–9.

Rest, J. (1986). *Moral development.* New York: Praeger.

Sprinthall, N. A. (1994). Counseling and social role taking: Promoting moral ego development. In J. Rest & D. Narvaez (Eds.), *Moral development in the professions* (pp. 85–100). Hillsdale, NJ: Erlbaum.

Steinberg, L., & Dornbusch, S. (1991). Negative correlates of part-time employment during adolescence: Replication and elaboration. *Developmental Psychology, 27*(2), 304–313.

isting as fixed traits, moral character occurs in a series of developmental stages. In other words, what Piaget identified as stages of cognitive development, and what Erikson suggested to be stages of personal development, Kohlberg described as stages of moral development. Developmental stages, by definition, have several components. Each stage has the following features:

1. It is qualitatively different from the preceding stage.

2. It represents a new and more comprehensive system of "mental" organization.

3. It occurs in an invariant sequence.

4. It is age-related within general groupings.

With these points in mind, we can now examine some of the specific aspects of Kohlberg's theory.

KOHLBERG'S SIX STAGES OF MORAL GROWTH

Kohlberg identified six distinct stages of moral growth. He formulated these stages by studying the system of thinking people actually employ in dealing with moral questions. By asking people from different backgrounds and of different ages to respond to problems involving moral dilemmas, he found that their responses fell into six judgmental systems, on which he based his six categories. The following example illustrates the type of problem he used:

> In Europe, a woman was near death from a special kind of cancer. There was one drug that the doctors thought might save her. It was a form of radium that a druggist in the same town had recently discovered. The drug was expensive to make, but the druggist was charging ten times what the drug cost him to make. He paid $200 for the radium and charged $2,000 for a small dose of the drug. The sick woman's husband, Heinz, went to everyone he knew to borrow the money, but he could only get together about $1,000 . . . He told the druggist that his wife was dying and asked him to sell it cheaper or let him pay later. But the druggist said: "No, I discovered the drug and I'm going to make money from it." So Heinz got desperate and broke into the man's store to steal the drug for his wife. Should the husband have done that?

As you can see, the problems are complex; they have no single, correct answer. In fact, the least significant part of the response is the direct answer yes or no. Most significant are the reasons given for why the person should not behave in certain ways. In other words, the way in which suggested behavior is justified defines the respondent's level of moral development.

Preconventional Morality: Stages I and II

Stage I obedience and moral decisions are based on very simple physical and material power—"Big fish eat little fish"; "Might makes right"; "The survival of the fittest." Stage I behavior is based on the desire to avoid severe physical punishment by a superior power.

Stage II actions are based largely on satisfying one's own personal needs, or "looking out for number one." The idea is to figure out ways to make trades and exchange favors—"You scratch my back and I'll scratch yours"—but to come out a little bit ahead on each trade. The orientation is materialistic in that moral discussions are expressed in instrumental and physical terms. If, for example, a person is caught stealing a car, punishment is determined by how much the car cost. This also means that it is perfectly permissible to use influence to fix any so-called wrongdoings. Fixing traffic tickets, bribing people, stealing from the boss, and similar misdemeanors are OK as long as you get away with it. If students alter their report cards, it's a Stage II response, provided they are successful. The clever con man or flim-flam artist is another example. In philosophical terms this category of moral thinking is referred to as *instrumental hedonism*, characterized by little human regard for the other person ("Nice guys finish last"). Genuine empathy is lacking.

In spite of the obvious shortcomings as a system of moral thinking, Stage II—"Let's make a deal"—does represent an advance over Stage I. Gypping people financially, ignoring other's feelings, cheating at elections, and similar behaviors are not as bad as physical torture or death. Thus, Stage II thinking represents a more adequate method of problemsolving, but only when compared to Stage I, where right and wrong are determined by the fastest gun, the quickest fist, or the biggest bomb.

These first two stages are sometimes classified together as the preconventional stage of moral development. The reason for calling it "preconventional" will be obvious when we look at Stages III and IV.

Conventional Morality: Stages III and IV

The next two stages are classified as the conventional stage of moral development.

Stage III is characterized by social conformity. At this stage a person makes moral judgments in order to do what is nice and what pleases others. At the same time, Stage III thinking is more comprehensive and more complex than Stage II. At this level a person does begin to take into account how others gen-

Kohlberg's Stage II actions are based largely on satisfying one's own personal needs.

uinely view the dilemma situation. The egocentrism of Stage II is replaced by the ability to empathize, to feel what others may be feeling, or, as it's called, by an increase in social-role-taking perspective.

The problem with this stage, however, is that individuals may have great difficulty in resolving the conflicting feelings of all those involved in a dilemma situation. Thus, in the Heinz case mentioned above, a Stage III response would probably conclude that it was wrong to steal because almost all the people in the community say that stealing is wrong. "I will go along with the majority consensus, or social convention. I understand that most people

hold that view, and I would feel very uncomfortable going against the wishes of the majority." Thus, moral judgment is equated with following the crowd.

Stage III moral thinking depends on the existence of distinct stereotypes and sharp differences. Relativism and complexity are absent. In this sense, moral behavior is other-directed. Stage III behavior conforms strictly to the fixed conventions of the society in which we live. We don't look inward to the "self" and attempt to work through a decision independently. Kohlberg often illustrates Stage III behavior by referring to the comic-strip character Charlie Brown. Charlie is usually caught in a hopeless predicament because of his trying to please everyone. His pleading with the iron-willed Lucy is both a comic and a poignant illustration of what it is like to try to live life always looking to other people for direction.

At *Stage IV,* the individual looks to rules, laws, or codes for guidance in dilemma situations. In one sense, civil- and criminal-law codes in our society represent a more stable and comprehensive system of resolving moral dilemmas than attempting to solve such questions on the basis of social conventions, community popularity, and what the leading crowd decides is the "nice" thing to do. Laws and rules as codified wisdom can be viewed as a positive glue, providing a society with stability and cohesion by guarding against rampant fads, quickly changing social customs, and societal anarchy or mob rule. The laws or rules represent society's attempt to set the same standards of conduct for all its citizens. Moral judgments are made by individuals in accordance with those rules. A person thinking at this level, then, does not simply look out for number one (Stage II) or follow the crowd (Stage III), but rather makes decisions that square with the existing legal codes.

Difficulties arise, however, with this rigid, law-and-order orientation. What do we do when the laws conflict or are unclear? Lawyers have a saying that difficult and complex social problems make for "bad" laws. In the Heinz case, for example, the law protects the druggist against stealing, but what about the wife's right to life? It is always possible to come up with exceptional cases to any comprehensive fixed law. For example, there are a few cases each winter in which an electric or gas company has turned off the customer's power service for nonpayment. Contract law is clear: If a person doesn't pay the bill, then the provider of the service is not obligated to continue service. But what happens when the nonpayor dies of the cold? This may be an overly dramatic example, but such exceptional cases do oc-

LAWRENCE KOHLBERG

Born in 1927 to eminently successful parents, Kohlberg started life in a very conventional world of material comfort and followed a path of academic achievement in elite private schools. In fact, that period may have been the only conventional one in his life. Before entering college, he took a three-year moratorium in the Eriksonian sense, yet with a moral purpose. He served as a junior engineer on a ship smuggling Jewish refugees into Israel. Unlike the movie *The Exodus*, he was caught by the British and imprisoned, an early experience upon which he noted he could ponder serious questions of justice and fairness. After his release, he enrolled at the University of Chicago and obtained his degree in only two years.

Kohlberg then enrolled as a Ph.D. candidate at the same university, and completed his doctorate in 1958; after spending only two years for his undergraduate studies, it took him nine years for the Ph.D. He remarked wryly that it only proved you couldn't accurately predict human behavior in all cases.

Kohlberg's concern for the welfare of others did not diminish in graduate school. Assigned for clinical internship to a mental hospital, he soon noticed that the resident staff, including his own supervisor, were using electric shock therapy, not as a treatment but as a means of punishing uncooperative patients in a manner that foreshadowed the classic film *One Flew Over the Cuckoo's Nest*. All his colleagues looked the other way. It was left to him, an intern with the lowest status on the medical hierarchy, to challenge his superiors. He did and was promptly dropped from the placement.

His research inquiry in graduate school was less volatile personally but turned out to be almost as provocative. Instead of accepting the then current notions of a psychoanalytic model for child development, he began to evolve an alternate set of ideas to explain the process of growth, and particularly the concept of moral reasoning.

What started as a traditional thesis on the relationship between the superego (the Freudian term for conscience) and moral behavior was transformed into a remarkably original framework for moral development in stages. His uniquely creative dissertation forced an almost complete revision of moral development theory.

In 1962 Kohlberg became an assistant professor at the University of Chicago. Six years later he was offered and accepted a full professorship at Harvard University, where he formed an innovative graduate program in human development. He was also awarded a special five-year Research Career Award by the National Institute of Mental Health to promote his longitudinal study on stages of moral development in adults, children, and adolescents.

Kohlberg's center at Harvard became the focal point for two decades of research and development. He attracted established national and international scholars as well as an extraordinary crop of eager students. Yet he never lost sight of the importance of both theory and practice. Thus it was not surprising to find him working as hard at application as at developing new theory. He spent three years on a weekly basis working with female prisoners and their guards to create a humane and rehabilitative atmosphere on site. He spent even more time creating high schools based on his concepts in an urban ghetto, a blue-collar community, and a suburban district. Few researchers have been as willing as Kohlberg to subject their best work to the acid test of practice.

In 1987 Larry Kohlberg died after a long, debilitating illness. Perhaps the best tribute to his work is the huge number of scholars, whom he always regarded as genuine colleagues, who have continued the inquiry. These disciples have provided a dynamic legacy by developing new ideas and practices related to his work.

Boyd, D. (1988). In honor of Lawrence Kohlberg: Some directions of current work. *Journal of Moral Education, 17*(3), 167–245.

Kuhmerker, L. (1991). *The Kohlberg legacy*. Birmingham, AL.: REP.

Schrader, D. (1990). The legacy of Lawrence Kohlberg. *New Directions for Child Development, 47*, 1–16.

cur. To handle such questions more comprehensively, we need recourse to a higher stage of reasoning.

Postconventional Morality: Stages V and VI

In the Kohlberg scheme, an individual at the stage of postconventional morality, the highest stage of moral development, behaves according to a social contract (Stage V) or according to a universal principle such as justice (Stage VI). Moral thinking and judgments are complex and comprehensive. Diverse points of view are considered. Each situation is examined carefully in order to derive general principles to guide behavior appropriate for all. There are never any easy solutions to complex human problems and moral dilemmas. Judgments and decisions are neither simply situational and conveniently relative, nor easy and fixed in their application of a rule. At this level, we have to account simultaneously for all the situational aspects, motivations, and general principles involved.

The system of thinking at this level, then, represents a more adequate method of problemsolving. Laws are viewed as a system of governance: Each law can be judged in terms of the extent to which it squares with the principles of the system.

At *Stage V* the principles are usually written as a document of assumptions or a declaration of ideas. For example, the U.S. Constitution sets forth a series of principles as the basis for judging the adequacy of each law. The key issue is to resolve dilemmas and conflicting laws by interpreting the intent of these written principles—justice, freedom, liberty, and equality of opportunity, to name a few.

It is important to realize that problemsolving on moral questions, social justice, or squaring my freedom with your freedom is not necessarily simpler at Stage V. Reasoning at this level requires the ability to think abstractly (to view laws as a system of governance), to weigh competing claims, to take into account both the logical and emotional domains, to take a stand and yet remain open to future, more adequate interpretations of social justice.

At Stage VI the principles of social justice are universal, yet not necessarily in written form. It is always difficult to explain the exact difference between Stage V and Stage VI because in some ways both systems are based on similar concepts. Philosophers themselves are unclear as to the distinctions. The "official" definition of Stage VI is that the principles are abstract, ethical, universal, and consistent. As Kohlberg notes, "At heart, these are universal principles of justice, of the reciprocity and equality of human rights, and of the respect for the dignity of human beings as individual persons" (1975).

Comparing the Stages

One way to appreciate the different levels of complexity involved in judgments at each stage is to examine and compare the different response patterns associated with the preconventional (Stages I and II), conventional (Stages III and IV), and postconventional (Stages V and VI) levels. Let's look at some typical responses, at different levels, to the Heinz case.

A Stage I or II response (preconventional) would say that it was OK for Heinz to steal the drug because the druggist was himself a robber, or simply because Heinz needed it. However, he should be smart enough not to get caught. A Stage III or IV response (conventional) would say that Heinz was wrong in breaking into the store. Either it isn't nice to steal ("What if everyone went around just taking things?"), or the law must always be obeyed regardless of circumstance ("What happens to a society if we all break laws according to our own whims?"). In either case, the social convention or the rule says unequivocally, "Thou shalt not steal." Heinz should be judged the same way an escaped convict would be judged. There is no difference between Heinz and Clyde Barrow of *Bonnie and Clyde* fame. A Stage V or VI response (postconventional) would weigh Heinz's behavior against universal principles. How does the value of life compare to the value of property? What general rights do all people have? What constitutional provisions are there for such behavior? Also, what are the provisions for changing laws? Since there may be bad laws, what avenues are available for seeking redress? Is the law that allows the druggist to make whatever profit he can such a bad law? If so, does this justify, or does it simply rationalize, Heinz's theft? These are essentially Stage V considerations. Moral decisions are based on a system of laws themselves judged on the basis of the common good and social utility. This means that at Stage V we view the problem not in terms of a single law, but in terms of the entire system.

At Stage VI the consideration would be based not so much on a system of laws (such as a written constitution), but on unwritten, moral, and universal principles. A moral principle would be something like the Golden Rule ("Do unto others as you would have them do unto you"), or it would be an ethical principle like Immanuel Kant's categorical imperative ("Act only as you would be willing that everyone should act in the same situation"). Stage VI principles apply across all social classes and cultures and, in fact, can be considered genuine principles only if they can be applied universally.

The idea of universal application is really the other half of "Love thy neighbor as thyself." In this case, then, it is irrelevant whether the woman in the Heinz dilemma is his wife. At Stage VI the concept of justice means that no matter who she is, rich or poor, friend or stranger, the respect for human life requires action to save her. Such a requirement, the philosopher John Rawls (1971) argues, is based on the concept of justice as equity. This means that in a democratic society—where our creed calls for life, liberty, and the pursuit of happiness—each person has a responsibility to all others. We are not, at this level, individuals concerned only about ourselves or those whom we know well.

Thus, at Stage VI, decisions are made on the basis of a universal law, a "higher" law that may not be written or even codified. However, the principles are implicit: value for human life, equality, and dignity. These are distinguished from static virtues and character traits because the values and principles are universal and dynamic. This also distinguishes such principles as "justice" from narrow and prescribed rules, such as "Thou shalt not steal." Stage VI requires that we consider the circumstances and the situation, as well as the general principles and the reasons behind the rules.

Thus, in the Heinz case, a Stage VI response might consider Heinz to be justified in stealing the drug since the value of human life is greater than the value of property—a universal principle. At the same time, Heinz should also be willing to accept legal punishment for stealing. The key here is the reasoning that makes it clear that Heinz deliberately challenged the law that allowed the druggist to make large profits and that he committed an act of civil disobedience and was willing to accept society's punishment for stealing. Socrates' refusal to alter his principles even to save his own life is an example of a Stage VI response. This is an important distinction. A certain behavior in and of itself is not necessarily an indicator of high-moral-stage thinking.

There needs to be a logical relationship between a person's behavior and the reasoning behind it. On the one hand, to steal the drug to please my neighbor is clearly not principled reasoning. On the other hand, to say that life is more important than property and yet not steal is just as clearly not principled behavior.

The Research Evidence

A series of cross-cultural studies conducted by Kohlberg in the 1960s shows constant trends. Stage I and II behavior becomes less frequent as age increases, and Stage IV, V, and VI behavior increases over the same span. Thus, we can say the that sequence is developmental and invariant. Moral behavior develops from lower to higher stages, and no stages are skipped. In this sense, moral growth is similar to cognitive growth.

Since Kohlberg's original set of studies in the 1960s, a substantial amount of research evidence has lent support to the stage and sequence framework. These studies will be detailed throughout the chapter in the appropriate sections discussing the new longitudinal results, the relation between moral behavior and stage, the cross-cultural evidence, and the question of gender differences.

CURRENT ISSUES IN MORAL DEVELOPMENT

Age Trends

In 1979 all the longitudinal data that formed the basis for the six-stage theory were rescored as part of a large-scale effort to improve both the reliability and validity of the scoring system. An extensive measurement manual now permits a much more exact assignment of student responses. There are more detailed examples of interview answers and more systematic rules for assigning "mixed" responses—that is, answers that contain different stage levels. The new scoring manual is a response to critics of the earlier, more or less intuitive scoring system. However, even more significant than the manual is what the new results say to the educator. The new norms substantially change some of the basic program goals. Essentially, the single most important change is a revision downward as to when postconventional Stage V and Stage VI reasoning occur in general.

In fact it now appears that so few subjects ever reach Stage VI that the stage itself can be considered only as a theoretical possibility. None of the longitudinal studies in three countries provided empirical evidence for Stage VI (Kohlberg, 1984, p. 270). As a result, Kohlberg suspended his claim for the stage except through case specific studies or from his longitudinal subjects. The only living example of such reasoning and behavior is described by Kohlberg as the "Case of Joan," a young female social worker who defends the rights of a delinquent teenager from the arbitrary rules of her case-work manager and a judge's legal ruling. Both her reasoning and behavior represent the highest level of justice and respect for human personality (1984, p. 486).

Figure 7.1 presents the age trends based on the rescoring of the research subjects' "old" responses—that is, their answers at 10, 13, and 16 years of age—plus their "new" answers during their early and late

FIGURE 7.1   New norms: Percentage of moral reasoning at each stage.

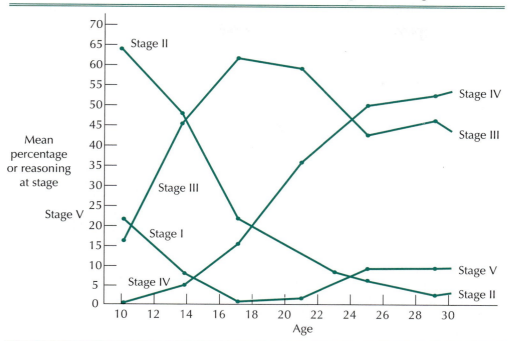

twenties. Remember that the key to a longitudinal study is that the researchers work with the same subjects over a long time span—in this case, over a period of 20 to 25 years. The change in the system of reasoning, then, is based on the answers that the same subjects gave to the Heinz dilemma and to similar stories after being tested every three or four years (Colby et al., 1979).

The age trends, in general, are similar to those in the earlier studies previously discussed; that is, the sequence remains the same. There is no skipping of stages. The lower stages always precede the higher. However, it is now clear that principled reasoning (Stage V) does not emerge in any substantial way during the secondary school years. Earlier estimates suggested that 30 to 35 percent of moral reasoning during the period from 16 to 18 years could be classified as principled, that is, based on a clear understanding of the universality of democratic principles such as freedom and justice for all, the right to due process, the necessity of free speech, majority will and minority rights, and equality before the law. It is now clear that such reasoning is more complex than the earlier scoring system was capable of detecting.

The new norms indicate that at the junior high level, the two most common modes of reasoning are

Stage II and Stage III—almost 45 percent each. Stage I accounts for about 7 percent, and Stage IV for about 4 percent. This means that students have moved substantially beyond Stage I (almost 25 percent at age 10). Also, it is apparent that Stage II thinking is declining rapidly, while Stage III thinking is increasing in a major shift. The junior high youngsters are in the process of giving up an exclusive concern with their own materialistic rewards. Instead, more of the moral and value judgments are governed by a conformity to group norms. This finding indicates, in a manner similar to those for personal development outlined in Chapter 6, that the value choices are increasingly other-directed during this time.

During senior high school, the shifts that are apparent at ages 13 to 14 continue. Stage II declines further, to less than 20 percent—almost equaling the rise in Stage IV to 15 percent. The major increase is clearly the emergence of Stage III. This form of moral reasoning now accounts for 60 percent of judgments at ages 16 to 18. That is the peak. The power of the peer group and of other reference groups is strongest at this time.

It is important to remember the second part of this point. It is almost folk wisdom that the peer group during middle adolescence helps mold value orientations. James Coleman's classic *Adolescent Society* clearly indicates the extent to which the high school "leading crowd" determines the value content. Most teenagers follow the dictates of the group. However, Kohlberg's results indicate that such direction can come from sources other than the peer group. In other words, many teenagers are other-directed in general. The source of direction may be the leading crowd of the peer group or certain charismatic adults. The power of pseudoreligious cults, gurus, and other adult-directed extremist groups has enormous appeal during this stage. The weakness of Stage III reasoning is particularly apparent under these conditions. Although it may not be the most important event of a lifetime for a teenager to process moral judgment according to the leading crowd in high school, there is no assurance that the adolescent would not be equally vulnerable to the exhortations of a cult that demanded shaved heads, public begging, and participation in drug-induced, religiouslike rituals.

During the early 20s, the shifts noted at junior and senior high school continue. Stage I virtually disappears, and Stage II declines to less than 10 percent. Similarly, Stage III begins to decline at 16 to 18 years. The most significant shift is the major increase in Stage IV judgment. By ages 24 to 26, reasoning in accord with democratic laws becomes the major mode. At this time there is also a small but highly significant development of principled reasoning to almost 10 percent. The overall trends remain the same, but usage at the higher, more complex stages occurs much later than was previously reported. If anything, this indicates the need for more effective developmental programs to help stimulate the process of moral judgment. The new data on Piaget's norms indicated that secondary pupils were capable of but not using formal operations. The situation in moral reasoning is similar. Students are capable of Stage IV reasoning at the secondary level, yet most do not use that mode. Similarly, students at the college level are capable of Stage V reasoning yet rarely employ it. The potential, however, is there. It appears that more effective developmental experiences are needed in order for children to become informed citizens, as required by a democratic society.

Modal Stage plus One: A Preference for More Complex Reasoning

While the rescored norm results may be discouraging because the base rates are lower, there is a very important and optimistic point. Two of Kohlberg's graduate students (now professors), James Rest (1973b) and Eliot Turiel (1966), demonstrated that

Moral development—like both cognitive and personal development—appears to proceed in an invariant sequence of developmental stages. A child cannot skip stages in moral development but, interestingly, will prefer moral judgments one level beyond his or her own. This fact has significant implications for the classroom teacher.

students who reason in a modal sense at one particular stage actually understand and value reasoning at the next level up on the scale—that is, modal stage "plus one." At the end of the chapter we will discuss what implications these findings have for teaching. At this point, however, the main idea is to note that students usually reason in their modal stage about 40 to 50 percent of the time. Part of their reasoning is at a lower stage but part is higher; no one is totally in one stage at any single time. The higher reasoning component exerts a kind of pull and can gradually draw the student to a more complex level. Thus, it is important to remember two things about stage reasoning: First, the modal level is simply the most common system and is employed about half the time; there is variation. Second, there is a built-in preference for the stage next higher in the sequence. Table 7.1 summarizes both the modes and the plus-one stages.

An Invariant Sequence

There is an important point to remember about the concept of development. To qualify as a develop-

TABLE 7.1   VARIATION IN STAGE USAGE BY AGE GROUP (Modal Stage Circled)

KOHLBERG STAGE	AGES			
	10	13–14	16–18	20–22
Stages I and II (Mix)	(47.6)%	8.1%	2.2%	0%
Stage II (Specific)	33.3	16.2	11.1	0
Stages II and III (Mix)	14.3	(56.8)	17.8	9.4
Stage III (Specific)	4.8	16.2	(44.4)	31.3
Stages III and IV (Mix)	0	2.7	24.4	(40.6)
Stage IV	0	0	0	18.8

mental change, as we may recall from Chapter 5, a change can take only one direction: up. A developmental change can occur only from a lower to a higher stage. As Figure 7.1 suggests, not all people end up at Stage VI with Gandhi, Martin Luther King, Mary McCloud Bethune, Jane Addams, Harriet Tubman, or Abraham Lincoln. However, with a few extreme exceptions (such as schizophrenics and other institutionalized patients), the researchers have found that major regressions in moral growth do not occur (Rest, 1973a, 1983). In fact, longitudinal results, show a downward shift in scores only 8 percent of the time. Since the subjects had been tested six times over a 30-year period, the downward shifts noted fall within the acceptable error of measurement. The retesting also indicated that every case of reversal at one age was more than made up at the next. These results provide firm evidence supporting the direction of growth as a graduated sequence from less to more complexity. The results also show quite clearly that the growth is systematic—one stage at a time. While there were no genuine reversals, neither did any of the subjects bypass or skip a stage (Kohlberg, 1984).

These same trends of stage and sequence without reversals/regressions have also been documented by substantial research in other countries and cultures. This information is detailed in the Spotlight on Cross-Cultural Similarities.

Moral Judgments and Moral Action

A key element so far missing from this discussion is the connection between stages of moral growth and actual behavior in the "heat of battle," so to speak. This is an important issue, given that thinking about issues is no substitute for acting in real situations. The evidence for moral maturity and moral behavior comes from a series of studies. Naturally, if the theory of moral development has any meaning, we would predict significantly different behavior according to significantly different levels of moral judgment. For example, we would expect that almost all who responded to the Heinz dilemma at Stage I or II ("It's all right to steal, especially if you get away with it") would themselves cheat or steal if given any chance at all. And, at the opposite extreme, we would expect that almost no one who responded at Stage V or VI would cheat or steal.

To put this expectation to the test, a series of studies using "cheating" tests has been conducted. In these studies the situations were varied. Some were traditional classroom experiments on tests, similar to the Hartshorne and May approach, such as taking a vocabulary test, an aptitude test, or coding a foreign language. Other situations were more situation-specific, such as a problem of returning an important questionnaire or a whistle-blowing situation (that is, willingness to report obvious cheating). The results are summarized in Table 7.2 and clearly show almost a linear relationship between stage and behavior. The higher the stage, the greater the ability to resist the temptation to cheat.

In another, more dramatic, study of behavior the tests of moral judgment were administered to subjects who participated in the famous experiments of Stanley Milgram, in order to rate their level of moral maturity. In the Milgram experiments, research subjects were told to "follow orders" exactly as specified by a scientific investigator. The subjects were told that they were going to administer a series of strong electric shocks to an innocent "victim" in the next room. The subjects could hear the "victim" pounding on the door, wincing, and screaming every time they pushed a button marked "high voltage." The experiment was set up to test how long subjects would follow orders and continue to administer increasing amounts of electricity to another human be-

SPOTLIGHT ON CROSS-CULTURAL SIMILARITIES

When Kohlberg's dilemmas were first published, there was almost an immediate reaction: The stories and issues were culturally specific and relevant only to the United States. His response to these doubts was predictable: Let's do some cross-cultural research and check out the results. Soon the research studies mounted, with some adaptations. The standard dilemma content would be scrutinized by local ethnologists in order to avoid context problems. For example in the version in Kenya, the druggist in the Heinz dilemma was changed to "chemist" and the "dollars" became shillings. In the Turkish version, the problem involved a spouse dying from hunger and a grocer demanding full payment. Such research has now been conducted in almost 50 countries. The results cross-validate both stage and sequence in all settings for Western and Eastern industrialized nations, with no gender differences (Snarey, 1995). The only area of difference was in tribal-rural cultures organized around feudal concepts, where individualism and democracy were categorically rejected.

The same results were reported in studies with an objective version of the moral judgment system by James Rest and Darcia Narvaez in over 40 countries (1994) and by Georg Lind (1995) in studies in western and eastern Europe with the Lind measure of moral competence. Thus, there is major empirical support for the cross-cultural validity of moral stages and sequences.

To give you some appreciation of the cross-cultural similarities, we present a case study of responses of two 12-year-old boys, one from a midwestern city in the United States and the other from a city in southwestern China. Both were responding to the Heinz dilemma, with some adaptations from the Chinese version, as follows:

In the southwestern part of China, a woman was very sick because of overworking in an orange orchard, which she and her husband grew in order to make their life better. It seemed that only one kind of medicine, a thing called "ginseng," native to the northeastern part of China, could bring her back to life. Their neighbor, a businessman in the village, bought some ginseng from northeastern China. He paid 3,000 yuan for it, but he was charging 10,000 yuan. The woman's husband, Cheng Jing-long, borrowed money from everyone in the village, but he couldn't get together 10,000 yuan. So he begged the businessman to sell him the ginseng for 3,000 yuan, because his wife was dying and they were neighbors. But the businessman said, "No, I have traveled a long way to get this precious ginseng, and I cannot sell cheaper, and I'm going to make money from it." Without any way out, Cheng Jing-long broke into the businessman's house to steal the ginseng for his wife.

Should Cheng Jing-long have done that? Why or why not?

For both boys, respecting the community law was most important (Stage IV). Second most important was the husband's love for his wife or whether he was stealing to help someone else (both Stage III). In third place was the issue of the greatest good for society as a whole (stages V and VI). Thus, despite major differences in background (it is hard to imagine two giant industrialized nations more different than the United States and China), the youngsters selected the same issues of moral judgment and in the same order.

This case study of responses to the Heinz dilemma serves as an example of a large number of research studies in nearly all parts of the globe. In general, they lend support to Kohlberg's claim that value and character development proceed through a sequence of stages that has validity across many different cultures.

We are indebted to Dr. Jerene Mortenson for the cross-cultural case study.

Lind, G. (1995). *The psychology of moral competence,* Hillsdale, NJ: Erlbaum.

Rest, J., & Narvaez, D. (1994). *Moral development in the professions,* Hillsdale, NJ: Erlbaum.

Snarey, J. (1985). Cross-cultural universality of social-moral development. *Psychological Bulletin, 97*(2), 202–232.

ing. (In fact, of course, the supposed victim was part of the experiment and was not actually hooked up to the electric current.) The study itself caused a tremendous stir because the results revealed that, in general, fully 65 percent of all subjects, regardless of age, background, or educational level, were willing to obey orders, no matter what! Figure 7.2 shows various phases of this classic experiment.

TABLE 7.2 CHEATING STUDIES (Percentage of Cheating at Each Stage)

1a.   Vocabulary Test

Stage V	17
Stages I–IV	53

(*N* = 35, college students)

1b.   Coding a Foreign Language

Stage IV	43
Stage III	64
Stage II	80
Stage I	73

(*N* = 302, adolescents)

1c.   Krebs-Kohlberg Tests of Honesty

Stage V	20
Stage IV	55
Stage III	78
Stage II	64
Stage I	81

(*N* = 123, adolescents)

1d.   Failing to Return an Important Questionnaire

Stage V	0
Stage IV	9
Stage III	60
Stage II	66

(*N* = 31, college students)

2.   A College Aptitude Test

Stage V	5
Stages III and IV	14
Stages I and II	27

(*N* = 154, college students)

3.   Remaining Quiet in Whistle-Blowing Situation

Stage V	12
Stages I-IV	65

(*N* = 25, college students)

Sections 1a-d from Kohlberg & Candee (1984), pp. 498–581. Copyright © by Lawrence Kohlberg. Section 2: Lonky & Reihman (1989). Reprinted by permission of E. Lonky. Section 3: Braebeck (1984). Reprinted by permission of Academic Press.

The results of the moral judgment testing showed that only 13 percent of the subjects rated at Stages I to IV refused to obey the orders, while 75 percent of those rated at Stages V and VI refused to obey. This outcome, of course, very closely fits the concept of moral maturity at the postconventional level. Only

at that level would we expect a person to refuse to follow the rules and say, in effect, "I really don't care what the experiment is all about or whether a scientist tells me I must do what he says. I will not deliberately inflict harm on that guy in the next room. He is more important than any experiment." In other words, only at that level could a person distinguish between obeying the law and valuing human life. We might recall at this point the number of times in history that humans have been willing to exterminate helpless victims on the grounds that they were "just following orders."

Another study of particular interest in detailing the relationship between moral thought and action was conducted by Shari McNamee (see Table 7.3). Sometimes referred to as a test of the Golden Rule and the parable of the Good Samaritan, her experiment was conducted with college students, who were told they were to participate in a "psychology subject" program. She describes it as follows:

> Undergraduates who agreed to be interviewed on the standard moral dilemmas were led to a testing room. As they were entering the room they were intercepted by a student presenting himself as the next subject for the experiment. The student stated that he had just taken drugs and was having a bad time. He had come to the experiment because he thought that the experimenter, being a psychologist, could help him. The response of the experimenter was that she was a research psychologist, not a therapist. The drug-user persisted in soliciting aid, hoping that the experimenter could refer him to help. The experimenter replied that she had no experience with drugs and did not know what facility could help him. She told him to reschedule his testing session. The drug-user slowly left the room. The subject was faced with the choice of whether to remain an uninvolved bystander or whether to intervene (1977).

TABLE 7.3 PERCENTAGE OF STUDENTS HELPING A DRUGGED STUDENT, BY MORAL STAGE SCORE

KOHLBERG STAGE SCORE	NUMBER	HELPED BY REFERRING VICTIM	THOUGHT THEY SHOULD HELP
II	11	9%	36%
III	29	27%	77%
IV	17	38%	69%
V	29	73%	83%

Data from McNamee (1977).

FIGURE 7.2   Various phases of Milgram's classic experiment: (a) a shock generator; (b) a subject being strapped into place; (c) a subject refusing to obey orders; (d) an obedient subject being introduced to his unharmed "victim." The chart relates Kohlberg's stages to the results.

(a)

(b)

(c)

(d)

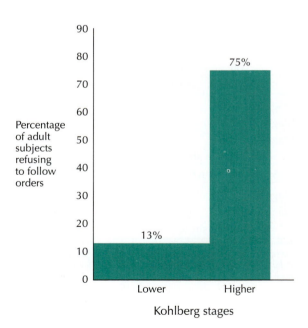

Percentage of adult subjects refusing to follow orders

75%

13%

Lower   Higher

Kohlberg stages

Photos © 1965 by Stanley Milgram. From the film *Obedience*, distributed by the New York University Film Library.

Almost three-fourths of the students who were rated at the principled level (Stage V) offered to help the victim. There was a linear relationship between stage score and willingness to help: 38 percent of Stage IV, 27 percent of Stage III, and 9 percent of Stage II subjects offered assistance. Thus, the relationship between stage score and actual behavior in a high-stress dilemma situation was clearly established. Two other points of interest: In McNamee's study the authoritative scientist was a female and in Milgram's experiment the scientist was a male, yet the outcomes were similar. Both studies used equal numbers of male and female subjects, and there were no gender differences in response by stage.

One final point on the McNamee study: In addition to observing actual helping behavior, McNamee also asked the subjects if they thought that they should help a distressed person. This is a kind of lip-service test to see if some of those who said they should help actually didn't. The results are most interesting. The greatest discrepancy occurs among those at Stage III. More than three-fourths of the subjects at that level said they ought to help, but just over one-fourth actually did. This is a 50 percent difference between lip service and helping behavior. If you review the major characteristics of Stage III reasoning, you will see that the theory would predict exactly such an outcome. Since obedience to social conformity peaks at this stage, such subjects would agree to a socially acceptable statement yet be unable to resist the authoritative role of the scientist's social pressure. These results, then, further validate the Kohlberg theory.

In a major review of more than 80 studies of the relation between moral behavior and reasoning, Gus Blasi (1980) examined the research design, the results, and the theoretical assumptions. Although not all the studies were well designed, Blasi concluded that overall the interrelation between moral behavior and moral reasoning was strongly supported. Even more important was his conclusion that at higher levels of reasoning humans behave in a more consistent and altruistic manner than at lower levels of reasoning. The strongest finding of all was that at higher stages there was a much greater resistance to following the crowd or to going along in order to get along. Table 7.4 summarizes the results of four studies of the ability to resist authoritarian commands.

From the meta-analysis and a specific look at individual studies, we do find convincing evidence of the stage-behavior relationship. You may have noticed, however, that the outcomes aren't perfect. For example, a few persons assessed at the principled level cheated on exams, wouldn't "blow the whistle," or refused to help the "victim." Also the opposite occurred. At least a few at lower stages behaved

TABLE 7.4   RESISTING AUTHORITARIAN COMMANDS (Percentage Resisting at Each Stage)

1. Refusing to Administer "Electric Shocks"	
Stage V	75
Stage I–IV	13
(N = groups of 30, adults)	

2. Under Duress, Helping a Bystander	
Stage V	73
Stage IV	38
Stage III	27
Stage II	9
(N = 86, college students)	

3a. Arrested for Civil Protest	
Stage V	73
Stage IV	44
Stage III	31
Stage II	10
(N = 339, college students)	

3b. Follow-up Study: Arrested Protesters (15 years later)	
Stage V:	
Free Speech Leaders	69
Student Leaders	43
Random Comparison	17
(N = 77, adults)	

Note: Studies 1 and 2 were laboratory studies of human behavior. Studies 3a and 3b were natural-setting investigations.

Source: Sections 1, 3a: Kohlberg (1984), pp. 415-422. Copyright © 1984 by Lawrence Kohlberg. Reprinted by permission of HarperCollins Publishers, Inc. Section 2: McNamee, (1977). Reprinted by permission of Carfax Publishing Company. Section 3b: Nassi (1981). Copyright © 1981 by the American Psychological Association. Adapted with permission.

in a principled manner. In addition to the stage of moral reasoning, then, there must be other factors involved. One researcher, Blasi (1990), now suggests we need to focus on moral motivation as an important factor. Rest (1986) suggests that the process includes at least four components:

1. Identification of the problem as a moral issue
2. Understanding the problem at an emotional level
3. Willingness to set aside personal nonmoral motives
4. Ego strength to act despite public opposition

The last component, which demonstrates that actions speak louder than words, may be the greatest challenge for anyone. Thus, if you find yourself in a dilemma, and later on you discover that your actions were not in concert with principled judgment, you can use the Rest model. By understanding the stage level and feelings of the participants, examining your own motives, and developing the strength to act (whether or not it pleases others), you will experience firsthand the problem of consistency, stage, and behavior. The question as a whole is among the most complex that behavioral scientists study.

Gender Differences: Gilligan's Critique

When the Kohlberg theory was first validated, there were two studies, one in Canada (Sullivan et al., 1970) and one in the United States (Turiel, 1976), that specifically examined the relationship between gender and stage. Both studies indicated that there was no gender difference, and the topic was largely dropped as a matter of research interest. **Carol Gilligan,** however, challenged these findings in a 1977 journal article that was soon expanded into a book. Her *In a Different Voice*, published in 1982, created a major controversy. Relying mostly on historical evidence, case studies, and small-scale empirical research presented with a flair for the dramatic, she proclaimed that the Kohlberg theory was gender-biased. Not only did the scoring system penalize females, in her view, but his description of postconventional (Stages V and VI) reasoning systematically left out a concern for human caring. In other words, she claimed the Kohlberg theory defined principled reasoning as too objective and narrowly rational. Human compassion was absent from his system. Gilligan also pointed out that the original longitudinal sample was all male. Quoting from source material ranging from Portia in *The Merchant of Venice* and Nora in *A Doll's House* to characters from Mary McCarthy's novel *The Group*, she made a most persuasive case. She claimed that psychological theory was only one instance of pervasive sexism from a male-dominated society:

> As we have listened for centuries to the voices of men and the theories of development that their experience informs, so we have come more recently to notice not only the silence of women but the difficulty in hearing what they say when they speak. Yet in the different voice of women lies the truth of an ethic of care, the tie between relationship and responsibility, and the origins of aggression in the failure of connection (1982).

Gilligan's views had an immediate impact not only on psychology but also on the larger community. In 1984 she was named Woman of the Year by a leading national feminist magazine. Soon many theorists and researchers began to review their prior studies. How could so many have missed such an obvious bias? Could it really be true that all of Kohlberg's work was valid for only one-half of the population?

One of the first comprehensive reviews was published by James Rest, a professor at the University of Minnesota, where the tradition of precise measurement is extremely strong (1986). In fact during the early days of Kohlberg's interview-rating approach, Rest had created an objective paper-and-pencil test of Kohlberg's theory. Researchers used his instrument with teenagers, college students, young adults, and professionals. The samples were large and represented both genders. Rest's quite startling finding was that there was no empirical evidence to support Gilligan's charge. By far the most frequent finding was that there was no difference between male scores and female scores, regardless of the sample. Further, he found that when gender-based differences were found in a few studies, the differences were in favor of the females, as shown in Table 7.5.

Although Rest's written-test method had been validated, the interview approach was still suspect. Gilligan had been especially critical of the interview method, claiming that whenever the raters came across comments suggesting the importance of love, caring, sympathy, and the like, those ideas were immediately classified as Stage III (social conformity).

Lawrence Walker (1984) published a major analysis of both approaches to judgment, the Rest objective method and the open-ended Kohlberg dilemma system. When his methodology was criticized (Baumrind, 1986), he redid his analysis and ex-

TABLE 7.5   PRINCIPLED REASONING BY AGE AND GENDER ON DEFINING ISSUES TEST (N = 2,886)

GRADE	FEMALES	MALES
Junior High	19.8	19.1
Senior High	30.4	28.7
College	45.9	44.1
Graduates	63.0	61.0

Data Source: *Rest & Narvaez (1994).*

Note: *These same differences with females demonstrating slightly higher scores than males was true for studies of professions, e.g., medical and veterinary doctors, certified accountants, and dentists.*

panded the research base to include about 10,000 subjects. The results were exactly similar to those of James Rest; no differences were recorded from either method according to gender (Walker, 1986). Mary Braebeck's reviews (1982, 1987) reached similar conclusions. All these studies, however, were cross-sectional; only the original Kohlberg sample followed the same subjects over time. Without findings from longitudinal research as well, it was still possible that Gilligan's claim was valid.

The major longitudinal study, including 225 males and more than 400 females from a variety of educational backgrounds, was analyzed by Loren Lee and John Snarey (1988). They reviewed not only life-span changes in moral judgment but also changes in the related domain of ego development. They found no differences by gender on an overall basis. On the other hand, they did find that females tended to have slightly higher ego development scores than men. In either case, however, the results did not favor males. Of course, it is important to remember that in all these studies males and females were also compared on the basis of equal education and/or career opportunities. An earlier study by Constance Holstein (1976) had shown that males who had completed college and had begun working had higher moral judgment scores than their spouses who had less education and did not work outside the home. Behavioral scientists do not think that such differences as Holstein found can be attributed to either a gender difference or a biased scoring system, since those differences disappear when education and job status are controlled (Kohlberg, 1984).

Care, Gender, and Ethnicity

Perhaps the most trenchant criticism of the Gilligan dichotomy comes from a careful review of Gilligan's work at the Emma Willard School, a private school for girls (Gilligan et al., 1989). Diane Scott-Jones (1991), a leading expert in ethnic identity formation during childhood and adolescence, pointed out an extreme irony in the study. The Gilligan group had reported at length on the special, caring orientation of the small sample of predominantly white female teenagers raised in the elite private school atmosphere. Scott-Jones noted that the limitations of the care orientation were evident when one considered the experience of black girls at the school. She reports that seven black students experienced continuous racial discrimination and exclusion and soon developed their own organization for mutual support. Apparently, the caring orientation of the white girls did not extend to those whose only difference was skin color. Scott-Jones concludes that "maximizing and romanticizing differences between males and females may be appealing . . . but it may have the long-term effect of maintaining a women's traditional subordinate status (p. 32).

To a major degree, then, the charge of gender bias has not been proved. To an even greater degree, Gilligan's claims continue to be puzzling.[1] It is true that Kohlberg's sample was male, but there have been an enormous number of studies since that time (including cross-cultural replications) with both sexes. The results are highly consistent with the claim of a universal sequence for both sexes. This does not mean, however, that there is nothing of substance to Gilligan's view. She has served as a valuable reminder that issues of caring and compassionate concern for others are important components of moral judgment. She has also correctly pointed out that the content of many of the standard dilemmas themselves (such as Heinz) routinely depict males as the key actors. As we move toward genuine sexual equality, fairness would require more females as the main figures.

Kohlberg himself was certainly sensitive to Gilligan's position and noted that the revised scoring manual avoids automatically classifying "caring" content as Stage III. Perhaps a less obvious but, in the long run, a more significant change is the definition of postconventional (Stages V and VI) reasoning. In his most recent writings, Kohlberg described the Golden Rule as having two elements: (1) Do unto others as you would have them do unto you, *and* (2) love thy neighbor as thyself. The first part has been routinely mentioned in all his earlier writings and linked to the philosophy of Immanuel Kant. The focus on the second clearly reflects an ethic of caring, which is really Gilligan's central point.

In Kohlberg's own words, "Our theory recognizes affect in appeals to respect for the dignity of persons as well as in appeals to caring and responsibility between persons" (1984, p. 291).

The most recent research only confirms the outcomes from previous findings. Judith Daniels, Michael D'Andrea, and Ronald Heck (1995) specifically employed Gilligan's technique of basing interview questions on Aesop's fables to avoid content contamination in a cross-sectional study of children

---

[1]   They appear even more puzzling in light of her own earlier research. Gilligan et al. (1971) found no sex differences in moral judgment in a sample of teenagers. Gilligan and Belenky (1980) reported a positive correlation ($r = +.61$) between moral judgment on the Kohlberg scale and improved life circumstances with a sample of adult females. Thus, her own earlier research showed no bias in the Kohlberg theory.

SPOTLIGHT ON MORAL DEVELOPMENT, INTELLIGENCE, AND BEHAVIOR

There is often confusion about the relationship of moral development, intelligence, and behavior. Critics often assail moral judgment as a code word for verbal intelligence. Since the assessment requires verbal reasoning, the argument goes, moral judgment assessment is really confounded; therefore, it follows that any relationship between judgment and behavior is really explained by ability or IQ levels. There are two studies that illuminate both these questions.

Mary Howard-Hamilton (1991) and Philip Vincent (1991) investigated the relationship between IQ and moral judgment with two separate samples of teenagers. Their combined results, shown in the table below, indicate quite clearly that, in a sample of 235 academically gifted adolescents (all above the 95th percentile), moral judgment using Rest's Defining Issues Test ranged all the way from the bottom to the top of the scale. There were no gender differences. Thus, there was no relationship between the IQ scores and moral judgment. On average, the judgment scores were the same as those in Rest's national sample, only the range was broader.

MORAL DEVELOPMENT SCORES OF 235 ACADEMICALLY GIFTED ADOLESCENTS

MORAL DEVELOPMENT STAGE	NUMBER	PERCENTAGE
Low (0–29 points)	58	25
Moderate (30–49 points)	107	44
High (50 points and above)	70	30

Sources: Howard-Hamilton (1991) and Vincent (1991).

Whereas Howard-Hamilton and Vincent have shown the independence of intellectual ability and moral judgment, a study by Krebs and Kohlberg (reported in Kohlberg, 1984) illustrated the two-way relationship of intellectual ability, moral judgment, and cheating behavior. They grouped a sample of 107 adolescents according to IQ and Kohlberg stage after presenting the teenagers

and adolescents (ages 10 to 18). They also used Gilligan's scoring system for rating care versus justice responses for the "porcupine and the mole" and the "dog in the manger" stories. There were no gender differences in either the spontaneous responses or the choice of the best solution. Both male and females choose the same responses, often a balance of care and justice. Similarly, Kimberly Schonert-Reichl (1994) found no gender differences in her study of middle school children. At the same time she reported positive general relationships for both genders between higher moral judgement and prosocial behaviors and conflict resolution, while lower levels of judgment were related to excessive submissiveness and easy victimization. Finally, Dennis Krebs and his colleagues (1994) in a study of college stu-

dents reported no gender differences on moral judgment or on moral orientation (care). They changed the key figures in the dilemmas so that instead of asking what should someone named Heinz do to help his spouse, the question was more direct, "What would *you* do in such a situation?" and then examined responses across nine dilemmas. The conclusion was: "Care is no more of a province of females than justice is of males, and optimal moral development requires attention to both" (p. 25).

Altruism, the Integration of Justice and Care

Although the research clearly does not support the Gilligan claim, the general Kohlberg scheme does

	Ability	
	High IQ (N = 27)	Low IQ (N = 33)
Moral Stage — I and II (Preconventional) (*N* = 22)	82%	85%
III and IV (Conventional) (*N* = 41)	49%	67%

with the opportunity to cheat on a test. The quadrant above presents the results. The most interesting and most startling outcome was the virtually identical percentage of cheaters who were assessed at Stages I and II (preconventional). Almost all at those stages, 82 percent and 85 percent, regardless of IQ, were likely to cheat. Thus a high-IQ but low-moral-stage student is just as willing to cheat as a low-IQ and low-moral-stage student. The students least likely to cheat were, in order, Stage III and IV low IQ followed by Stage III and IV high IQ. These results, then, confirm that IQ and moral judgment are not simply different sides of the same coin. Therefore, teachers and student teachers should not assume that high-IQ students will refrain from cheating simply because they are intelligent.

Howard-Hamilton, M. (1991). *The effects of a DPE program on the moral reasoning, identity formation, and achievement motivation among gifted adolescents.* Unpublished doctoral dissertation, North Carolina State University, Raleigh.

Kohlberg, L. (1984). *The psychology of moral development.* New York: Harper & Row.

Vincent, P. F. (1991). *The teaching of ethics as a means to facilitate moral development in gifted adolescents.* Unpublished doctoral dissertation, North Carolina State University, Raleigh.

not directly address the question of how caring for others can be conceptualized in a developmental sequence. For example, the idea of helping/caring for a victim clearly shifts, as we have seen in the Mc-Namee study. Nearly all the students at Stage III said they should help, but few actually did, in contrast to those at the higher levels of judgment. In all instances, however, there still is a gap between behavior and judgment. Rest's theory would suggest that such a gap stems from the need to assess more than judgment/reasoning. Dennis Krebs and Frank Van Hestern (1994) have recently constructed a framework that seeks very deliberately to integrate caring for others as an important developmental domain through the concept of altruism. By altruism they mean thoughts and behaviors that enhance the welfare of others as an end in itself. Their research had indicated a consistent drop in judgment scores when the dilemmas shifted from the general (Heinz et al.) to one's own personal/immediate life issues. Also they found that affect (emotions) was more aroused by such a shift from the third- to the first-person problems, but that caring by itself was too global and too undifferentiated. Altruism, on the other hand, could be conceptualized as a stage and sequence concept. For example, civic-mindedness at early stages would be quite simply "What happens to me if I help someone?" An intermediate level might be "What will others think of me if I help or not?" An advanced level would likely be "What happens to the general welfare if I help or not?" In each case, one's own feelings are more likely to be aroused by such questions than in processing third-party dilemmas. They correctly point out that development in one domain does not and cannot assume synchronous or even development in another domain. "A moral retrograde may as easily become an expert in physics as a dolt in science may be a saint" (p. 115).

Altruism, then, is viewed as a developmental sequence and is related to stages of moral judgment. Persons at higher stages are more likely to behave altruistically. However, by adding a specific focus on altruism as a complement to moral reasoning, we are more likely to close the gap between stage level and predictions of actual behavior. Krebs and Van Hestern specifically include how each of us processes and interprets our emotional reactions to help-requiring situations—that is, feelings connected to prosocial behaviors in us versus feelings that may be misattributed to nonaltruistic responses. In fact, they clearly state that the *quality of empathy* is determined not only by judgment but also by social perspective taking. This more inclusive approach, then, broadens how each person understands moral/ethical issues as a conceptual or reasoning process and includes both the social perspective and emotional process.

Through altruism, care manifests qualitatively different stages in how each person understands cognitively and affectively another person's needs. Obviously, the most important part of the integration of justice and care through altruism is the narrowing of the competence-performance gap. Developmental competence is represented by stages of cognition, while performance is actual behavior. Although predictions can never be, nor should they be, perfect, we can reduce the inconsistencies through more adequate theory. Altruism represents an advance toward this goal. Otherwise cognitive developmental theory will be subject to withering criticism as intellectual game-playing. In the words of a nearly vituperative critic, cognitive development can be viewed as merely, "Reified adulterations of intellectualized restatements of interactional morality—the intellectuals' phobic reactions to social uncertainty" (Haan, 1983, p. 246). By reducing the systematic discrepancy between judgment and behavior, the Krebs and Van Hestern theory guards against such intellectual navel gazing.

The research of Sally Powers into the effect of family atmosphere on children's moral development supports the commonsense notion that an atmosphere of support and encouragement promotes moral development while an atmosphere of hostility and authority stunts such development.

Family Influences and Moral Judgment

One aspect of moral development that remains largely unresearched is the influence of the family on the growth of values. Sally Powers (1988) found a real dearth of studies in this area. One reason, of course, is that it is a most difficult research problem since it involves adults and children all interacting at different stages. Most prior research had been inconclusive. Such a daunting task, however, did not stop Powers. She created a category system to analyze family dialogue as family members attempted to resolve moral dilemmas. She found three negative modes and three positive ones associated with moral development during adolescence. Families that used *focus, challenge* (but not conflict), and *sharing* promoted growth; families employing *distraction, distortion,* and *rejection* inhibited development. Powers also found that the emotional atmosphere of the family was crucial. Atmospheres of praise, encouragement, and noncompetitive humor promoted open participation. Sarcasm, hostility, threats, and devaluing contributions promoted tension and conflict and inhibited participation and development. It may seem obvious that if we want adolescents to increase in their ability to reason, participation, support, and clarifying discussion are central; yet too often Powers found the opposite atmosphere. Picture an early adolescent haltingly presenting a somewhat controversial defense of Heinz stealing the drug. Then the father, a practicing attorney, takes the argument apart piece by piece, sarcastically putting down lawbreakers as anarchists and ridiculing his child's attempt. The contest is so one-sided that the discussion ceases. The young teenager is chastised and quickly learns to keep such ideas out of the family dialogue. In fact, Powers discerned that conflict and tension with the father were associated with lower levels of moral judgment. Mothers at high levels of moral judgment were more supportive and more able to tolerate clarifying differing opinions. They were less defensive and hostile to teenagers who initially took a different point of view.

What Powers has not been able to discern is the differential question: Is there an ideal environment for children and adolescents at different developmental stages? She does think that we cannot specify one best environment because the proportions of focus, challenge, and sharing in a supportive atmosphere probably will shift by age and stage. We do know that distraction, distortion, and rejection in a conflictual atmosphere inhibit growth. Those atmospheres are not as bad or as extreme as the violence in the Irish and Lebanese study discussed later in the text; however, verbally humiliating a teenager in a dilemma discussion does have negative long-term consequences, an opportunity for development missed.

SYSTEMATIC METHODS FOR MORAL DEVELOPMENT

In this section we turn from the question of basic research to application. What are some of the current educational methods designed to effect moral/ethical reasoning and behavior? We will describe a variety of methods as well as some research findings on the outcomes. These methods include: Classroom dilemma discussions, social role-taking programs, and Just Community schools.

Classroom Dilemma Discussions

By far the most common technique for promoting value growth at both the junior and senior high school levels is to present a sequence of open-ended moral dilemmas for discussion and analysis. In this approach the instructor's role is critical. The instructor is to clarify and encourage the students to verbalize their reasons for choice. Especially during the initial periods of group discussion, it is extremely important for the instructor not to step in, take over, and start lecturing and correcting. The students need time and support in order to articulate their own reasoning. Also, the instructor needs to facilitate the process in order to clarify the different levels of reasoning within any class or group. Remember that there is a modal stage for age groups, but there is also a range both above and below the mode.

First, the leader must be able to identify the variety of reasoning levels. To do so, the leader may have to ask clarifying questions. For example, suppose you are running a discussion on a dilemma like Heinz and the drug, and a pupil says, "Heinz should steal because I would." At this point you don't have enough information to assess the level of reasoning. So you go on and ask, "OK, but why would you?" This question might lead to another dead end, such as "Well, I think it's OK to steal, sometimes." Then further clarification would be needed, such as "Well, how do you decide when it's 'sometimes'?" At that point the pupil might present some reasons, such as "Well, a person's life is more important than . . . " And then you could identify the judgment level.

A second phase of group discussion involves teaching the students to listen to one another's different levels—in other words, to have them respond to one another. In the example above, for instance, one or two might say that life is more important than property (stages V and VI), others might say it's against the law to go around ripping off stores (stage IV), and still others might say, "Well, it's OK to steal if he can figure out a way to pin it on someone else" (stage II). Then it would be important to help the students listen and understand the different answers and different sets of reasons. Often a leader can use role-reversal techniques at this point—asking a pupil who takes one position to discuss the question from someone else's viewpoint. Occasionally, this technique is called moral musical chairs, since it involves changing positions in the discussion (but without leaving anyone out!) (Vincent, 1994).

TABLE 7.6   LEADING MORAL-DILEMMA DISCUSSIONS: THE QUESTIONING METHOD

Starting the Discussion	Continuing the Discussion	Reaching Closure

Getting the facts straight.
  Be sure the content is accurate.
  Paraphrase what the issues are.
  Make sure all are tuned in.
 	
Use open-ended questions to survey the group:
  "What should Person X do? Why, or what are the main reasons?
 	
Ask clarifying questions:
  "Would you say a little more . . . ?"
  "Do you mean . . . ?"
  "Let me see if I can paraphrase . . . ?"
                OR
Ask others in the group if they understand Person X's reasons.
  Make sure everyone has a chance to make an opening statement. Use "wait time" if needed.
	The following techniques are helpful in developing greater elaboration.
	Alternative consequences:
	  "What might happen if the person did A, or B, or C?"
	Role switch:
	  "What would your reasons be if you were Person X, Y, or Z? Put yourself in the shoes of the other person."
	Feelings and emotions:
	  "How do you suppose Person X is feeling? How might you feel in such a situation? What might be some consequences of those feelings?"
	Personal experience:
	  "Has anything like this ever happened to you? What were your thoughts, feelings, actions? Looking back, is there anything you would change?"
	Change a key element:
	  "Let's say that the person in the situation is someone you didn't even know, rather than someone very close to you. How might that change things?"
	"Some people say":
	  "Some say there is never a good reason to break a law. How would you answer that view?"
	Have discussants talk back and forth to each other:
	  "Henry how would you answer Amy?" "Jill and Troy seem to be on opposite sides . . ."
		Issue-related questions:
		  "Now that we viewed it from so many different positions, what are the key elements, or most persuasive issues? Is there any particular element that would cause you to switch your view?"
		Justice-related questions:
		  "From a justice-and-fairness-to-all perspective, what solution would be best?"

Source: *Berkowitz (1984).*

Role reversal plus one   The role-reversal technique is useful, but it has limits. A series of studies has shown that, in general, people tend to process value issues most of the time at one particular level, their modal response. Through active listening and clarifying, that level can become evident. Also, people can comprehend the level of reasoning at all stages below their modal stage but at only one stage above it (Rest, 1986). This point is crucial. Reasoning that is more than one stage above people's most common system is essentially beyond their comprehension. As a result, an individual might pay lip service to such reasoning, but it would not influence behavior.

The questioning method for leading moral-dilemma discussions is presented in Table 7.6, which summarizes both the different phases of the discussion approach and some suggested teaching methods. Marvin Berkowitz (1984) has found that the leader needs to do more than just clarify students' answers. He or she must also challenge statements in order to guide participants' thinking to more complex levels. If a favorable balance can be maintained between support and challenge, discussion, it has been shown, is an effective method of enhancing value development.

In the chapter on teaching effectiveness (Chapter 12) we will discuss at greater length this approach to inductive teaching. This will include further examples of exactly how to ask open-ended questions and how to follow up for greater elaboration of the students' thoughts and feelings, all central to the process of cognitive development.

Development of values versus values clarification

Another educational method designed to promote moral growth is known as *values clarification*. The value-clarification method is substantially different from the value-development approach. The goal of values clarification is to raise consciousness, yet in a highly relativistic, individualistic manner. Because this approach is not based on the concept of development stages, there is no standard for judging the adequacy of reasoning except in process terms. Thus, if a student publicly declares that, after careful reflection and consideration of alternatives, he or she firmly believes that African-Americans, Hispanic Americans, Native Americans, and other minorities are inferior and deserve to be discriminated against, the goals of clarification have been met. In fact, one very awkward moment occurred in a clarification session with a group of white law-enforcement officials who considered getting away with violent acts of racism to be their "proudest moments."[2] Values clarification, obviously, is not related to a theory of democratic justice, and the techniques may in some cases only reinforce lower-order racist, sexist, or ethnocentric reasoning.

Several comparative studies have explored whether the values-clarification approach is superior to the value-development discussion method as a means of fostering moral behavior. James Leming (1981) compared 33 studies of values clarification

TABLE 7.7 EFFECTS OF MORAL-DILEMMA DISCUSSION COMPARED TO OTHER CLASSES

	NUMBER	CORRELATION[a]
Moral-dilemma discussions	23	+.41
Control classes	17	+.09
Academic classes	9	+.09
Control classes	7	+.16

[a] *A measure of the amount of positive change or level of moral judgments.*

Source: *Rest (1986), p. 81.*

and 26 of value development and found little evidence that values clarification supports value development. Another review of 56 studies has yielded important information as to what works in the classroom and what doesn't. As Table 7.7 shows, overall these studies found that students in value-dilemma programs learn more complex reasoning than do students in control classes. The discussion-group students, for example, develop a greater ability to see important issues from a variety of points of view. Also and most important, such students show a greater awareness of basic democratic values, such as individual rights and responsibilities. Thus, if we think of the goals of education as nurturing the ability to reason and understand higher-order concepts, the research clearly supports the discussion method (Rest & Narvaez, 1994).

For middle school children, a somewhat more structured approach has been employed. Mary Braebeck and her colleagues (Braebeck et al., 1994) have reported on a middle school curriculum, "Facing History and Ourselves." The program includes films and readings on the Holocaust as well as the discussion-oriented dilemma method of instruction. The program also examined other examples of prejudice/discrimination/genocide through the same approach. The research sample included almost 200 students, and the results indicated an eight-point gain in moral judgment. Even though the material was very dramatic and in some cases distressing (few students had any prior knowledge of the Holocaust), there were no negative effects upon self-esteem or the psychological well-being of the students. Thus the dissonance created by the material did not inhibit psychological discussions toward positive moral judgment. Also there was no difference between males and females at either pretest or posttest. Both genders gained equally.

---

[2]   This incident was related to the first author in a moment of candor by one of the leaders of the values clarification method.

Social Role-Taking Programs

A second method involves a series of educational conditions mostly focused on adolescents and college students. In these programs, teenagers participate in a significant helping/altruistic role such as a peer counselor/tutor or a cross-age counselor/tutor to a younger child. There is a genuine participatory role, not role-playing, in which the teenager actually takes on the responsibility of helping a peer or younger child.

In one program (Sprinthall & Scott, 1989), the goal was to involve high school females as math tutors for elementary age females. There has been so much information concerning female fear of success and erosion of confidence in math skills that the choice of participants and focus was obvious. What might happen to the self-confidence and academic achievement of fifth-grade females if they received tutoring by adolescent females? And what might be the developmental impact upon the high school helpers?

The teenage helpers met each week as a group for training in tutoring methods (the heavy use of concrete manipulative materials for the elementary students). In addition to the skill training, the teenagers discussed their own feelings and thoughts about such helping and wrote weekly reflection entries in their journals. There were two sets of noteworthy results for both the elementary-age tutees and the senior high tutors.

For the elementary females, the tutored group (about 40 minutes per week) improved in both skills and attitudes. They raised their national score on the California Achievement Tests from the fiftieth to the sixty-first percentile. A control group improved only four points. In addition, the tutored group became more confident as self-directed learners. In psychological attribution theory, it has been found that males attribute success to their own effects and failure to the environment. "If I get an A," a male might say, "it's because I earned it. If I get a D, either the test isn't fair or the teacher couldn't teach the stuff." Self-confidence as a learner is retained. Females, on the other hand, tend to attribute success to luck and failure to self-inadequacy (Fennema et al., 1979). The elementary-age females in this study changed positively in their attributions of success and failure. They felt more in charge of their own learning and reduced the tendency to blame themselves when faced with learning difficulties. Quite importantly, the girls in the control group showed a decrease in self-confidence and an increase in self-blame over the 6-month period. In that relatively short time, the erosion of perceiving one's self as an active learner in math had begun.

The senior high females involved in helping also benefited. As one research colleague put it, "We did not rob Patricia to pay Pauline." The tutors improved on measures both of moral development and conceptual complexity. They became more self-directed, less peer-dominated, more complex in problemsolving, and more principled in moral judgment. On the other hand and most tellingly, a control group who participated in a helping experience as teachers' aides did not change. This group did not meet for discussion or engage in reflective journal writing. This outcome indicates that so-called service learning or various kinds of volunteer work may not have any noticeable developmental impact without guided reflection.

A second study (Sprinthall et al., 1992), patterned on the role-taking model, involved high school students as leaders of small discussion groups for middle school students. All the early adolescents came from families that had recently experienced a divorce. Mavis Hetherington (1989) found that such family disruption had the greatest negative effect upon middle school pupils. Probably as a result of so many psychosocial changes, those students reacted the most negatively when parents separated. Early adolescence has often been considered the weakest link in the chain of development, and the added stress of divorce probably accounted for the greater stress, anxiety, acting-out, and withdrawal moods of that age group.

At the same time, some recent research (Ersone, 1990) has shown at least retrospectively that secondary school students experiencing a family divorce are reluctant to seek out professional school counselors. The vast majority of students in that sample remembered experiencing distress yet avoided counseling assistance for fear of some stigma, such as being labeled crazy. They also reported in retrospect that it would have been helpful to talk with somebody to gain some perspective and support.

The model peer-assistance program was set up on the basis of these two findings. The high school students were trained for one semester in small-group techniques and reviewed the emotional issues that arise when parents separate. After training they worked in pairs leading weekly meetings. Some 40 early adolescents had been identified by the school counselors in the stress of a divorce. Eight small groups of 5 students each were formed and met for a semester. The high school leaders continued to meet with their supervisor for continued skill training in discussion techniques, planning, dialogue, and reflection through journal writing. The combination of action and reflection was continually stressed in these "seminars."

The results were positive for both groups. The early adolescents made gains in self-concept and self-esteem. They were less morose and withdrawn. The discussions helped them realize that they were not responsible for the divorce, a common misperception at that age. Also they improved in their ability to get along with the separated parent and in some cases with their new blended family. Teachers and counselors reported improved school performance. By far the most positive impact, however, was from the relationships they formed with their new "big" brothers and sisters. Certainly anytime high school juniors and seniors pay positive attention to sixth- and seventh-graders, those squirrely teenieboppers are transformed. This study was no exception. There were clear signs in the journals and in verbal and nonverbal behavior that the middle schoolers felt important, significant, and affirmed by such contact.

The high school group leaders also demonstrated significant psychological growth on measures of value development and of ego level. Signs of psychological maturity were evident, derived from the leadership experience. It was, however, more than the experience itself. As in the small-group counseling course, these students also reflected on their learnings each week both in the seminar and in their journal entries. The students would comment particularly on their different feelings associated with being a teacher versus their usual role in secondary school classes. Like the control group in the math tutoring study, a control group of peer leaders minus the reflection sessions showed no similar gains in maturity. Another outcome of these reflection seminar groups for the high school students was a sense of community. The high school students in both the math project and the model peer-counseling program all mentioned their positive feelings from group participation. For the first time they felt that they had gotten to know and understand their peers during the training classes. For example, one student commented, "I really like coleading the group of students. Mostly I just feel good and comfortable about this class. I feel closer to the students in here than to anyone else in school." Another wrote: "Seems like I communicate better with these middle school students than with some of my high school friends" (Sprinthall et al., 1992, pp. 291–292). Such reflections helped deepen the group counseling experiences for the high school leaders. The usual subgroups, cliques, and isolates that Coleman (1961) documented many years ago as endemic to secondary school, disappeared. The class of helpers became unified not only in purpose but also in relationship to one another. Those single classes, then, serve as small examples of what secondary schools can become, a place for development through a community with values different from good looks, fast cars, and athletics.

Table 7.8 presents a meta-analysis of findings from social role-taking studies. The average effect size for both measures of development was about plus 1 standard deviation for the experimental groups compared to the control classes. From a statistical viewpoint, this is a very significant difference (Sprinthall et al., 1991).

In addition to those studies, there have been other investigations both in this country and in Europe confirming these findings. For example, Judith Boss (1994) found that a one-semester community-service program that included weekly discussions, reading, and journalizing produced a greater positive effect than did the discussion method by itself. She suggested that the need to participate in a helping activity created more intellectual and personal disequilibrium than the other method. If we recall the material on both Piaget and Vygotsky (Chapter 5), then it is understandable why the participation and reflection requirements would cause more of a perturbation, or cognitive dissonance. Then the professor's role was to help the students through the zone of proximal growth, as Vygotsky would say, to a higher level of development. Boss's students, in the experimental class, improved an average of 8.6 points on the measure of moral judgment, while the control class (discussion only) remained unchanged. These findings are highly congruent with studies reported by Ruggenberg (1993), Mason and Gibbs (1993), and Armon and Slaboda (1995). The last study was unusual in that the college students worked as peer helpers in an inner-city school. Their results indicated an increase not only in moral judgment but also in cultural sensitivity, an appreciation of cultural differences.

Two studies in Europe provide further confirmation of the power of the role-taking approach. Campos (1991) reported on the positive effects of role-taking on psychological maturity in studies of adolescents in Portugal. Lind (1995) studied these same effects with German college students. He was able to classify the amount of formal and informal role-taking/reflection opportunities in a sample of almost 300 students. His results indicated (like Boss's findings) an eight-point gain for high levels of both versus no change for either role-taking alone or reflection by itself.

As a result of these studies, then, it should come as no surprise that James Leming (1992) found, through a meta-analysis of almost 500 different programs, that peer-led activity and discussion oriented

TABLE 7.8   SOCIAL ROLE-TAKING: A META-ANALYSIS OF MORAL JUDGMENT AND EGO DEVELOPMENT EFFECTS

Study		KOHLBERG MJI OR REST DIT			LOEVINGER SCT OR HUNT CL		
		Posttest Mean	Posttest S.D.	Effect	Mean	S.D.	Effect
Dowell (1971)	E	350	—	MJI	5.3	—	SCT
	C	280	82	+.85	3.3	1.09	1.83
Rustad & Rogers (1975)	E	401		MJI	5.7		SCT
	C	295	55	+1.97	4.3	.89	1.57
Mosher & Sullivan (1976)	E	345		MJI	7.21		SCT
	C	272	36.5	+2.02	5.57	1.40	1.17
Tucker (1977)	E	44.2		P	6.00		SCT
	C	41.3	16.7	+.18	5.70	1.26	+.23
Hedin (1979)	E	40.2		P	5.48		SCT
	C	35.3	6.8	+.72	4.05	1.06	1.35
Cognetta (1980)	E	39		P	6.05		SCT
	C	38	12.3	+.08	4.46	1.16	+1.37
Exum (1980)	E	No available data			7.06		SCT
	C				5.83	.98	1.25
Satterstrom (1980)	E	48		P	2.0		CL
	C	48	19	.00	1.8	.42	+.47
Sprinthall & Scott (1989)	E	34.8		P	1.72		CL
	C	26.2	9.7	+.87	1.39	.27	+1.22
Sprinthall, Hall, & Gerler (1992)	E	33.3		P	6.70	SCT	SCT
	C	22.3	12.9	+.85	5.58	1.20	+.93
Reiman & Parramore (1993)	E	56.9		P	1.9		CL
	C	46.4	13.4	+.93	2.0	.61	−.16
Average Effect Size		(N = 10)		+.85 MJI or DIT	(N = 11)		+1.10 SCT or CL

Note: MJI = Kohlberg scale (100 = Stage I, 200 = Stage II etc.).
DIT = Rest scale (percentage of principled reasoning, 0% to 95%).
CL = Hunt scale (conceptual complexity, a 3 pt.scale 1.0, 2.0, 3.0).
SCT = Loevinger scale (ego development, a 10 pt. scale).
Data Source: Sprinthall, N. A. (1994). (Article contains all the research references.)

drug and alcohol programs were "by far the most effective in reducing drug/alcohol abuse . . . and [demonstrated] a definite superiority over the other approaches" (p. 120). We now know from this research that such programs have two positive effects upon both the teenage leader-helpers and the members of the programs themselves.

James Rest has specified four components of moral behavior: empathy, comprehension, motivation, and ego strength. The fact that the role-taking method involves many of these components helps explain why such programs have consistently

shown such a positive effect upon moral judgment and helping behavior.

Just Community Schools

A third method is by far the most comprehensive and the most complex to implement. Whereas the dilemma-discussion method and the social role-taking procedures generally involve classroom-size programs, the Just Community involves a school-within-a school of some 200 to 300 students and 6 to 10 teachers and counselors. The idea was originated by Larry Kohlberg and his colleague Ralph Mosher and was tried out in a number of high schools (inner-city, urban, and suburban). The key idea is that the teachers and students become a single community on the model of the New England town meeting. Gradually the rules and policies of the school, or the school governance, become the focus for all school meetings and discussions.

There is, of course, more to the democratic school than the governing process. The academic program provides for instruction, but there is great emphasis on interaction and dialogue versus the passive lecture-workbook routine. The community-meeting atmosphere does change the academic-classroom climate. The adult teachers are seen as authoritative in subject areas but not as authoritarian. They are viewed as consultants more than as truth givers. Clearly, the democratic high school approach is vastly different from that of the conventional secondary school. The schools are smaller (from 200 to 300 students), the rules are set by the community, and the instruction is highly interactive. See Table 7.9.

A number of studies have focused on different outcomes: general cognitive development, practical everyday interactions and school atmosphere, and behavioral outcomes.

Cognitive development On formal measures of cognitive development, students in the democratic schools demonstrated a greater advancement in moral stage. Generally, students enter the school in the stage II to III range and are close to stage IV when they finish. This outcome should not be surprising, given that much of the discussion in town meetings is similar in format to that involving moral dilemmas. Different views are presented in seeking resolutions

to, say, the drug problem, smoking, or fighting. The emphasis is always on the reasons for making a decision. Such an educational approach clearly can cause students to recognize and appreciate decisions based on fairness to both the majority and minority points of view. Compared to students in conventional schools, the differences favor the democratic schools by about one stage (Mosher et al., 1994).

Practical everyday interactions A second index of outcomes was derived from a series of practical or real school life dilemmas, such as "Would you drive a classmate whom you don't really know to a nearby town for an important college entrance on a Saturday morning?"

A typical response by a regular school student would be:

It doesn't mean I shouldn't give him a ride, but if I don't know them well enough, I think just out of protection for myself and my property, I wouldn't. I think people may say that being responsible to yourself is more important than other people. I think there is an extent where you put yourself first. And when you believe in putting yourself first, like I do, or try to at least, I don't feel I should be obligated to do somebody else's work, especially if I don't know them, I don't think I should give them a ride (Kurtines & Gewirtz, 1984, p. 91. Copyright © 1987. Reprinted by permission of John Wiley & sons, Inc.).

Students from the democratic school were more likely to say something like:

Yes, they should because Cluster is a community. Because you have a responsibility to the kids in this school, even if you don't like them all that much,

TABLE 7.9 THE ORGANIZATIONAL STRUCTURE OF A JUST COMMUNITY PROGRAM

INSTITUTION	MEMBERS	TASKS
Agenda committee	8–12 students and 2–3 teachers	Deciding on issues: putting together the agenda
Advisory group	1 teacher/adviser and 10–15 students	Creating an informal atmosphere for discussing personal problems; having a moral discussion on the one or two important agenda issues
Community meeting	All students and teachers	Discussing and resolving moral issues; making rules and appealing violations
Discipline committee	6–8 students and 2 teachers	Hearing cases of rules violations and interpersonal problems of disrespect; giving sanctions; enhancing interpersonal understanding

Source: *Kurtines & Gewirtz (1987), p. 108. Copyright © 1987. Reprinted by permission of John Wiley & Sons, Inc.*

SPOTLIGHT ON A JUST COMMUNITY

School Rules

In Just Community high schools, a Fairness Committee, consisting of both students and faculty, meets to discuss and create school rules. The following list, compiled by one such committee, serves as an example of the rules and sanctions jointly developed:

1. Stealing: Offender will be confronted by a subcommittee (the Fairness Committee) for restitution, community service, and possible police notification.
2. Vacation homework: Adequate time should be provided by teachers either before or after the vacation, in most cases.
3. Fines of $1.00 per day will be assessed for overdue equipment or classroom materials.
4. All school clocks should be synchronized.
5. Vandalism: All members of the school will participate for one day each quarter for clean-up.
6. No radios, tapes, or headsets are allowed in the school.
7. Student-faculty lounge will be open each day (9:00 A.M. to 1:20 P.M.). Thereafter the room may be used by the Ping-Pong club.
8. Teachers have the option, after conferring with department heads, not to give midterm exams.
9. Sexual harassment is not acceptable. Investigative and punishment procedures are detailed in the student handbook.

It is evident that the range of issues is enormous, from one-dollar fines to sexual harassment, from time for the Ping-Pong club to student vandalism and a community cleanup.

Mosher R. L., Kenny, R. A., & Garrod, A. (1994). *Preparing for citizenship: Teaching youth to live democratically.* Copyright © 1994. Reprinted by permission of Greenwood Publishing Group, Westport, CT.

---

you are in school and you're with them everyday, you know, you are supposed to think of them as part of the school and part of the community, so you should do it (ibid., p. 93).

Over a series of such dilemmas the results were always the same. Yet these measures are still somewhat hypothetical; what about more direct measures of behavior?

Behavioral outcomes   The programs had a noticeable effect on behavior: fighting was reduced (there was only one incident in five years), stealing ceased, attendance increased, drug and alcohol use was virtually eliminated, and an honor code was instituted, in addition to which voluntary steps were initiated by students to integrate the schools more fully (Power, 1988). As if this weren't enough, further study demonstrated clear differences in unobtrusive measures: greater reading of newspapers and current-affairs magazines and viewing of TV newscasts, more political discussions, a greater feeling of internal political efficacy (the feeling that an individual citizen can make a difference) and less political cynicism, and a greater respect for society's laws (a

corollary to the increase in stage IV). The researchers concluded that "those schools that most stimulate authentic democratic participation among students show the largest increase in students' political development" (Nadeau & Burns, 1989, p. 57). The Spotlight provides an example of school rules created by student-faculty participation in democratic decision-making.

In contrast, to all these outcomes is what happens and what doesn't in regular high schools. Regular high school classes in civics as well as other formal curriculum programs have an insignificant effect, and students tend to become more politically cynical over the school years. Since research has shown that high school students' political orientations influence their adult orientations more than any other factor, clearly an opportunity for development is missed. Mosher, Kenny, and Garrod (1994) provide the most complete description of the findings from these three dimensions of moral judgment, moral atmosphere, and moral behavior. They have also researched the effects according to racial/ethnic and class differences in African-American, Asian American, and working class Irish-American teenagers. They report that despite initial difficulties arising from the well-known cliquishness of teenagers, within one or two semesters the Just Community welded these diverse groups together (pp. 129 ff).

SELF-ESTEEM AND MORAL DEVELOPMENT

Most humanistic psychologists consider the concept of self-esteem a most important variable in development. Certainly every day we hear references to the importance of self-esteem as critical to positive growth; conversely, lack of achievement, delinquency, social isolation, and similarly negative outcomes are attributed to lack of self-esteem. Research, however, fails to support these views. The first difficulty is that self-esteem is usually conceptualized as a unitary and quantitative trait. The problem here is perhaps obvious: A successful delinquent may have very positive self-esteem from activities such as stealing cars, shoplifting, and beating up his rivals. On the other hand, a successful academic achiever or "overachiever" may be racked by worry and self-doubt about the next examination or term paper.

Clark Power (1995) has suggested that we revise our conception of self-esteem toward the idea that as a personality trait, self-esteem by itself is *amoral*, or nonmoral. There is no empirical research bridge across self-esteem moral judgment and moral behavior. As a result, Power is now researching the concept of self-esteem from a developmental perspective. What are the different types of self-esteem associated with different stages of development?

In this effort to map stages of self-esteem, we may be able to understand how each of us "constructs" the issues and experiences that make up our current esteem. Professor Fritz Oser offers a version of an Aesop fable to illustrate this constructivist process. A traveler from a rural Greek village was traveling to Athens and asked a stranger what kind of people lived in that great city. "What are people like where you come from?" was the reply. "Oh," said the traveler, "they cheat, steal, and drink heavily." "You will find the same things in Athens," said the stranger. Shortly thereafter came a second traveler with the same question and who received the same inquiry from the stranger. "Oh," said the second traveler, "they are fine citizens who care for each other and who seek justice." "You will find people in Athens who are fine citizens, who care for each other, and who seek justice," came the reply.

SUMMARY

Kohlberg's theoretical breakthrough revolutionized our understanding of moral development. His work parallels Piaget's and Erikson's in that it includes specific, age-related stages of growth. Each stage represents a system of thinking defined by how we process moral/ethical and value questions. Each stage is also part of an invariant sequence and represents a qualitatively more comprehensive system of understanding than the previous one.

Kohlberg's framework emerged from interviews with his research subjects. By presenting moral dilemmas to people from different backgrounds, he was able to sample the system of reasoning, thinking, and judging—the reasons behind their decision. In analyzing these reasons, Kohlberg formed the six-stage category system. Then he set out to validate the system both cross-sectionally and longitudinally. Recent research has not supported Gilligan's critique of the system as gender-biased. Krebs and Van Hestern are now working on the concept of stages of altruism as a direct theoretical and practical connector between justice and caring.

Kohlberg's stages are defined by the major set of assumptions a person uses to think through and rationalize, or justify, an important ethical decision. Each stage is "better" than its preceding one; higher stages take into account an increasingly broader perspective, represent more complex and abstract thought, contain more personal empathy, and "solve" social problems more on the basis of principles. Thus, the direction of the system is highly congruent with the principles of a democratic society— values and ethics based on principles of justice. At higher stages, behavior is more consistent with democratic principles.

Cross-cultural research with both the interview method and the objective test method supports the universality of Stages I through IV. In tribal cultures, however, there appears to be an absence of emphasis on individual rights as denoted by Stages V and VI.

In behavioral terms, there is not an exact one-to-one relationship between moral stage and actual behavior. However, the trends in practically all studies are consistent with the theory, whether it be performance on "cheating" tests or behavior in the Milgram and McNamee studies.

Classroom dilemma discussions, social role-taking programs, and Just Community schools all offer examples of effective strategies to promote moral development. They stand in striking contrast to the weaknesses of some current and fashionable quick fixes for character education.

Teaching for moral development needs to be understood as a slow and complex process. On the one hand, we cannot really accelerate moral development beyond the limits set by the stage concepts. On the other hand, we cannot just sit by and beg the value question.

Undoubtedly the most important aspect of the issue of moral growth is that it confronts educational psychology with questions of character education in the form of stages of moral maturity. For almost half a century such questions of moral education and general education have been avoided or not considered a legitimate area for inquiry. Kohlberg has changed all that. We now must think through the value questions as part of a developmental sequence.

KEY TERMS AND NAMES

Marvin Berkowitz
  dilemma discussions
character education
cross-cultural validity
Carol Gilligan
Hugh Hartshorne and Mark May
Invariant sequence

Lawrence Kohlberg
Ralph Mosher
  just communities
Clark Power
  self-esteem
James Rest
Social role-taking

THEORY INTO PRACTICE: LEADING A DILEMMA DISCUSSION

Without doubt, the best way to understand the dilemma approach is to practice leading a small group of friends or students in discussing an actual dilemma. The content can vary according to the composition of the group. For example, if you were working with a group of junior high or middle school students, you might try the following dilemma.

Middle School: Caught in the Middle

You've just moved to a new school. You hated to leave your old school. You had many close friends, and even many of the teachers were all right. Your father has just started a new job with lots of pressure, and he travels more now, too. Your mother has decided to work, since your two older brothers are now in college and the expenses are increasing. You're not exactly miserable, but you are not happy at all. You don't know anybody at school. It's a lot bigger, and the kids don't seem very friendly. You've told your parents how awful things are, but they are busy and say you will outgrow it anyway. What's worse is that it's the middle of the year, and your courses are all different, and you're behind in all your subjects.

One day as you walk home from school, alone as usual, four kids who are really the "in crowd" (you know because you've seen them practically running the school) stop you and ask if you would like to join them. You say, "Why not?" to look cool and try not to show how much you want to be in with somebody. All of you stop at one of the homes. Both parents there work, too. After a while you are really starting to enjoy it. It's a really neat house, and the kid has all the latest rock videos, and there's a lot of good-natured kidding around. It reminds you just how bad things have been. These kids are really cool, and they accept you.

After some cokes and pizza from the microwave, one of the kids pulls out a funny-looking hand-rolled cigarette. After lighting it, the kids take turns, and everybody seems to be having more and more fun. Suddenly, it's your turn. All your new friends are saying, "Listen, this won't hurt you" and "Look at adults; they're always drinking and smoking, and this stuff doesn't even give you a hangover. Besides, we all do it and it hasn't hurt us." You don't know what to do. Would you go along?

We suggest very strongly that you tape-record the discussion. Then, after the session, replay the tape and make a tally mark for each time you followed one of the Berkowitz elements.

1. Getting the facts straight by asking the students to state the dilemma
   _____ a. Checking for understanding by paraphrasing
   _____ b. Use of open-ended questions
2. Elaborating and clarifying
   _____ a. Alternatives and consequences
   _____ b. Role-switches
   _____ c. Feelings
   _____ d. Personalizing
   _____ e. Key element changes
   _____ f. "Some people say . . ."
   _____ g. Student-to-student talk
3. Closure
   _____ a. Review key issues
   _____ b. Raise the issue of justice for all questions

As you review the findings, regard them as a picture of your own currently preferred mode of discussion leading. If you find very few, or no, marks in certain areas, then consider running a second discussion with that (those) element(s) in mind. In all probability, you may be responding inadequately in the area of feelings and emotions. Often teacher education, unfortunately, does not acknowledge the importance of emotions in learning. In fact, one researcher found that, on the average, teachers clarified students' feelings once out of every 1,000 interactions. In dilemma discussions, almost by definition, there should be strong feelings on the issues. Examining and exploring emotions is central to the growth process. Some continual practice may be necessary.

The second activity is to listen for the structural content of the positions the pupils take. What types of reasons do they give on their own? Below is a list of reasons students may offer in trying to figure out a solution. Alongside each statement is the Kohlberg level for the reason.

After you have tried out a dilemma discussion with school students, you might consider someone closer to home. If you are about to do student teaching, gather a small group of colleagues, turn on the tape, and try the following:

A Student Teacher: Caught in the Middle

You and your cooperating teacher have been working hard this term to help one of your students, the principal's child. He has been marginal, and his grade will determine whether he graduates. Without being overbearing, the principal has sent a clear signal that you will receive an extra-strong recommendation if all goes well.

The cooperating teacher has noted that the student is really working well for a change; assignments are on time, and quality is up to a C–. You are pleased with his progress.

The student's final term paper is handed in. The cooperating teacher grades it as a C+, enters the

STAGE	REASON
I	What are the chances of being caught?
III	How important are the new friends?
II	Will you lose a lot of privileges at home if you are found out?
IV	You might be arrested and charged in juvenile court.
III	Even though it's risky, you will be "in" with the group.
III	You are being tested by the new group to prove you would fit into their life style. You need to go along to get along.
III	What will happen to your reputation if you say no, and they spread it around? Will you be isolated as a "goody two-shoes"?
IV	How important is it to stand up for yourself and obey the law?
VI	You understand the issue of societal values for mental and physical well-being for yourself.
V	You think about yourself, your new friends, and responsibility for the good of everybody.
II	Your parents have just promised you your own video and an increased allowance for tapes if you don't experiment with drugs.

DISCUSS IN SEQUENCE

RESPONSE

1. What are the issues?
   What are the feelings?
2. What are possible actions?
   (Brainstorm; don't judge.)
3. Outline the possible consequences.
4. What would the best solution be in fairness to all involved? Is that what you would do?

grade, and with a sigh of relief says, "Well, we both deserve credit. He made it. Take a look at the paper. It's not great, but it is solid. Meanwhile I'll report the grade and tell the principal."

That night you glance at the work. You are halfway through the paper when you suddenly realize that much of the work has been lifted from a just-published anthology.

Instructions   At the end, replay the tape and do an analysis of discussion leading. Examine your checklist as a guide for your own further development. Also, consider rating the reasons by Kohlberg level.

Additional resources   See K. A. Strike and J. F. Soltis (1985), *The ethics of teaching* (New York: Teachers College Press). This work has an excellent discussion of the philosophical issues, basically the conflict between Stage V consequentialism and Stage VI reciprocity, that is, with the Golden Rule as a framework. Then the authors present a series of very challenging ethical dilemmas that teachers often face. We would suggest employing these case studies for teacher education, particularly with a small-group discussion method in the Berkowitz mode.

THEORY INTO PRACTICE: IDENTIFYING STAGES—KOHLBERG LEVELS AND THE CASH MACHINE

A recent headline story proclaimed the honesty of two middle school boys who turned in the $10,000 they found in a large envelope next to an automated teller machine (ATM). Apparently the ATM worker had carelessly set the bundle down on the floor, forgotten about the package as he filled the machine, locked the door, and left the scene. The boys received major national attention, including TV and newspaper interviews. They were extolled as exemplars of good citizenship and character, exactly what the nation so desperately needs, as role models for other teenagers. But were they really role models of virtue and character? What reasons did they give for their altruistic actions? The following list represents a sample of their reasons. See if you can classify by Kohlberg level as an insight into their actual stage of development.

1. "Maybe we should keep it. It would be great to get that set of drums I want, and you [his buddy] could get that set of amp speakers."

2. "But maybe we had better return it. It is really too much dough. It sure will be noticed, and then we might get caught, so we better give it back."

3. "Some of our friends said we were stupid, but probably we did the right thing. We did get a reward [$500], some free concert tickets, and lots of interviews and stories in the paper."

Bearing in mind that reasons for and against keeping the money can be on different sides of the same stage, you can see that the main reason to keep the money was materialism (Stage II) in the first statement. In the third statement, there is still an element of Stage II—a smaller monetary reward plus concert tickets—but also a balance of Stage III in the social-conformity concerns: "Our friends thought we were stupid" versus "We received lots of compliments and notice." In the second statement, however, the reasons were clear-cut stage I: "If we keep the money, it is so much that it will be noticed, and we'll be caught and punished."

There will always be a need to examine both actions and reasons before proclaiming virtue or character as a permanent fixture. After all, how might you react to a possible $10,000 windfall? At the end of the interview one of the boys commented almost as an aside, "I still think about those drums."

REFERENCES

Armon, C., & Slaboda, M. (1995, November). *Mutual, authentic relationships that encourage self-reflection: An evaluation of a university-high school mentor program.* Paper presented at the annual meeting of the Association of Moral Education, New York.

Baumrind, D. (1986). Sex differences in moral reasoning: Response to Walker's (1984) conclusion that there are none. *Child Development, 57,* 511–521.

Bennett, W. (1993). *The book of virtues.* New York.

Berkowitz, M. (1984, April 23), *Process analysis and the future of moral education.* Paper presented at the annual meeting of the American Educational Research Association, New Orleans.

Berkowitz, M., & Gibbs, J. (1983). Measuring the developmental features of moral discussion. *Merrill-Palmer Quarterly, 2*(4), 399–410.

Blasi, A. (1980). Bridging moral cognition and moral action. *Psychological Bulletin, 88*(1), 1–45.

Blasi, A. (1990). Kohlberg's theory and moral motivation. *New Directions for Child Development, 47,* 51–57.

Boss, J. A. (1994). The effect of community service work on the moral development of college ethics students. *Journal of Moral Education, 23*(2), 183–198.

Braebeck, M. (1982). Moral judgment: Theory and research on differences between males and females. *Developmental Review, 3,* 274–291.

Braebeck, M. (1984). Ethical characteristics of whistle blowers. *Journal of Research in Personality, 18,* 41–53.

Braebeck, M. (1987). Editorial. Feminist perspectives on moral education and development. *Journal of Moral Education, 16,*(3), 16.

Braebeck, M.; Kenny, M.; Stryker, S.; Tollefson, T.; & Sternstrom, M. (1994). Human rights education through the "Facing history and ourselves" program. *Journal of Moral Education, 23*(3), 333–347.

Campos, B. (1991). Psychological development and personal and social education in schools. In H. Starkey (Eds.), *Socialization of school children* (pp. 53–56). Amsterdam: Swets & Zeitlinger.

Colby, A.; Kohlberg, L.; & Gibbs, J. (1979). The measurement of stages of moral judgment. *Final report to the National Institute of Mental Health.* Cambridge, MA: Center for Moral Development and Education.

Coleman, J. (1961). *The adolescent society.* New York: Free Press.

Cremin, L. A. (1957). *The republic and the school* (p. 100). New York: Teachers College Press.

Daniels, J.; D'Andrea, M.; & Heck, R. (1995). Moral development and Hawaiian youths: Does gender make a difference? *Journal of Counseling and Development, 74*(1), 90–93.

Ersone, D. (1990). *Parental divorce during childhood.* Unpublished master's thesis, North Carolina State University, Raleigh.

Fennema, E. (1990). Justice, equity, and mathematics education. In E. Fennema & G. Leder (Eds.), *Mathematics and gender* (pp. 1–9). New York: Teachers College Press.

Fennema, E.; Wolleat, P.; & Pedro, J. (1979). Mathematics Attribution Scale. Catalog of Selected Documents in Psychology (ms. no. 1837).

Gilligan, C. (1982). *In a different voice* (p. 173). Cambridge, MA: Harvard University Press.

Gilligan, C., & Belenky, M. (1980). A naturalistic study of abortion decisions. In R. Selman and R. Yando (Eds.), *Clinical-developmental psychology: New directions for child development* (Vol. 7). San Francisco: Jossey-Bass.

Gilligan, C.; Kohlberg, L.; Lerner, M.; & Belenky, M. (1971). *Moral reasoning about sexual dilemmas: Technical report of the U.S. Commission on Obscenity and Pornography.* Washington, DC: U.S. Government Printing Office.

Gilligan, C.; Lyons, N.; & Hammer, T. (1989). *Making connections: The related worlds of adolescent girls at Emma Willard School.* Troy: Emma Willard School.

Gilligan, C.; Ward J.; Taylor, J.; & Bardige, B. (1988). *Mapping the moral domain: A contribution of women's thinking to psychological theory and education.* Cambridge, MA: Harvard University Press.

Gregg, V.; Gibbs, J.; & Basinger, K. (1994). Patterns of developmental delay in moral judgment by male and female delinquents. *Merrill-Palmer Quarterly, 40*(4), 538–553.

Haan, N. (1983). *Social sciences as moral inquiry.* New York: Columbia University Press.

Hagedorn, H. (1930). *The book of courage.* Chicago: Winston.

Hartshorne, H., & May, M. (1928–1930). *Studies in the nature of character* (Vols. 1–3). New York: Macmillan.

Hetherington, E. M. (1989). Coping with family transitions: Winners, losers, and survivors. *Child Development, 60,* 1–14.

Higgins, A. (1995). Understanding the moral self: Research goals for the next five years. *Moral Education Forum, 20*(2), 30–35.

Holstein, C. B. (1976). Irreversible, stepwise sequence in the development of moral judgment: A longitudinal study of males and females. *Child Development, 47,* 51–61.

Howard-Hamilton, M. (1991). *The effects of a DPE program on the moral reasoning, identity formation, and achievement motivation among gifted adolescents.* Unpublished doctoral dissertation, North Carolina State University, Raleigh.

Kohlberg, L. (1968). The child as a moral philosopher. *Psychology Today, 7,* 25–30.

Kohlberg, L. (1975). The cognitive-developmental approach to moral development. *Phi Delta Kappan, 56*(10), 671.

Kohlberg, L. (1984). The meaning and measurement of moral judgment. In L. Kohlberg (Ed.), *Essays on moral development* (Vol. 2, pp. 415–422). New York: Harper & Row.

Kohlberg, L., & Candee, D. (1984). The relationship of moral judgment to moral action. In L. Kohlberg (Ed.), *Essays on moral development* (Vol. 2, pp. 498–581). New York: Harper & Row.

Krebs, D., & Van Hestern, F. (1994). The development of altruism: Toward an integrated model. *Developmental Review, 14,* 103–158.

Krebs, D.; Vermeulen, S.; Denton, K.; & Carpendale, J. (1994). Gender and perspective differences in moral judgment and moral orientation. *Journal of Moral Education, 23*(1), 17–26.

Krebs, D.; Wark, G.; & Krebs, D. (1995). Lessons from life: Toward a functional model of morality. *Moral Education Forum, 20*(2), 22–29.

Kuhmerker, L. (1991). *The Kohlberg Legacy.* Birmingham, AL: REP.

Kurtines, W., & Gewirtz, J. (1984). *Morality, moral behavior, and moral development.* New York: Wiley.

Kurtines, W., & Gewirtz, J. (1987). *Social development and interaction.* New York: Wiley.

Lee, L., & Snarey, J. (1988). The relationship between ego and moral development: A theoretical review and empirical analysis. In D. Lapsley & C. Power (Eds.), *Self, ego, and identity: Integrative approaches* (pp. 151–178). New York: Springer-Verlag.

Leming, J. S. (1981). Curricular effectiveness in moral/values education. *Journal of Moral Education, 10*(3), 147–164.

Leming, J. S. (1992). The influence of contemporary issues curricula on school-aged youth. In G. Grant (Ed.), *Review of Research in Education, 18,* 111–162.

Lind, G. (1995, November). *Opportunities for role-taking and guided reflection in higher education.* Paper presented the annual meeting of the Association for Moral Education of New York.

Lonky, E., & Reihman, J. (1989, August). *Self-regulation and moral reasoning as mediators of moral behavior.* Paper presented at the annual convention of the American Psychological Association, New Orleans.

Mason, M. G., & Gibbs, J. C. (1993). Role-taking opportunities and the transition to moral judgment. *Moral Education Forum, 18*(3), 1–12.

McNamee, S. (1977). Moral behavior, moral development, and motivation. *Journal of Moral Education, 7*(1), 27.

Mosher, R. L.; & Kenny, R. A.; & Garrod, A. (1994). *Preparing for citizenship: Teaching youth to live democratically.* Westport, CT: Praeger.

Nadeau, G., & Burns, N. (1989). *Democratic schooling: High school structure and socialization.* Cambridge, MA: Harvard Graduate School of Education.

Nassi, A. (1981). Survivors of the Sixties: Comparative psychological and political development of former student activists. *American Psychologist, 36,* 753–761.

Power, F. C. (1988). The just community approach to moral education. *Journal of Moral Education, 17,* 195–208.

Power, F. C. (1995, April). *The development of self-worth in adolescence: A moral perspective.* Paper presented at the annual meeting of the American Educational Research Association, San Francisco.

Powers, S. I. (1988). Moral judgment development within the family. *Journal of Moral Education, 17,* 209–219.

Rawls, J. (1971). *A theory of justice.* Cambridge, MA: Belknap Press of Harvard University Press.

Rest, J. R. (1973a). Patterns of preference and comprehension in moral judgment. *Journal of Personality, 41,* 86–109.

Rest, J. R. (1973b). The hierarchical nature of moral judgment. *Journal of Personality, 41,* 86–109.

Rest, J. R. (1983). Morality. In P. Mussen (Ed.), *Handbook of Child Psychology* (4th ed, pp. 556–629). New York: Wiley.

Rest, J. R. (1986). *Moral development.* New York: Praeger.

Rest, J. R. & Narvaez, D. (1994). *Moral development in the professions.* Hillsdale, NJ: Erlbaum.

Ruggenberg, J. (1993). Community service learning: A vital component of secondary school education. *Moral Education Forum, 18*(3), 13–19.

Schonert-Reichl, K. (1994). The interrelations of moral reasoning, empathy, and age among adolescents with behavior disorders. *British Columbia Journal of Special Education, 18*(3), 248–262.

Scott-Jones, D. (1991). From "voice" to "fugue" in females' development. *Educational Research 20*(2), 31–32.

Skoe, E., & Diessner, R. (1994). Ethic of care, justice, identity, and gender: An extension and replication. *Merrill-Palmer Quarterly, 40*(2), 272–289.

Snarey, J. (1985). Cross-cultural universality of social-moral development. *Psychological Bulletin, 97*(2), 202–232.

Sprinthall, N. A. (1994). Counseling and social role taking. In J. Rest & D. Narvaez (Eds.), *Moral development in the professions.* Hillsdale, NJ: Erlbaum, 85–100.

Sprinthall, N. A., & Collins, W. A. (1995). *Adolescent psychology: A developmental view.* New York: McGraw-Hill.

Sprinthall, N. A.; Hall, J.; & Gerler, E. (1992). Peer counseling for middle school students experiencing family divorce. *Journal of Elementary School Counseling, 26*(4), 279–294.

Sprinthall, N. A., & Scott, J. (1989). Promoting psychological development, math achievement, and success attribution of female students through deliberate psychological education. *Journal of Counseling Psychology, 36*(4), 440–446.

Sprinthall, R. C., Schmutte, G. T., & Sirois, L. (1991). *Understanding educational research.* Englewood Cliffs, NJ: Prentice-Hall.

Sullivan, E.; McCullough, G.; & Stager, M. (1970). A developmental study of the relationship between conceptual, ego, and moral development. *Child Development, 41,* 399–411.

Turiel, E. (1966). An experimental test of the sequentiality of developmental stages in the child's oral judgment. *Journal of Personality and Social Psychology, 3,* 611–618.

Turiel, E. (1976). A comparative analysis of moral knowledge and moral judgment in males and females. *Journal of Personalty, 44,* 195–208.

Vincent, P. V. (1994). *Developing character in students.* Chapel Hill, NC: New View Publications.

Walker, L. K. (1984). Sex differences in the development of moral reasoning: A critical review. *Child Development, 55,* 677–691.

Walker, L. K. (1986). Sex differences in the development of moral reasoning; A rejoinder to Baumrind. *Child Development, 57,* 522–526.

LEARNING THEORY

LEARNING BACKGROUNDS

The study of learning has been at the very heart of psychology, especially American psychology, since its origin about a century ago. In the 1890s the great Harvard psychologist William James saw the importance of learning, which he called "that enormous fly-wheel of society, its most precious conservative agent . . . It keeps the fisherman and deckhand at sea through winter; it holds the miner in his darkness . . . It keeps different social strata from mixing" (James, 1890, p. 79). James felt that learning, especially during childhood's critical stages, shapes and directs our later lives: "Could the young but realize how soon they will become mere walking bundles of habits, they would give more heed to their conduct while in the plastic state" (p. 83). We might paraphrase James by saying that if society realized how soon its children would become walking bundles of habits, that society would give more heed to the importance of its early childhood education programs.

Though the study of learning has been one of the the core areas of American psychology, the pursuit of this study has been anything but serene. Great debates, full of sound and fury, over the nature and process of learning all but shattered the foundation of the fledgling discipline. Some psychologists, rigid behaviorists like John B. Watson, felt that learning in-

volved the patterning of overt responses. Knowledge, in their view, resides in muscular reactions, not in cerebral exercise. As you drive to your favorite restaurant, it would be your arms and legs that "know" the route, not your head. These psychologists were correct to some extent. Certain kinds of learning do occur as a result of response patterning. For example, try explaining to a youngster how to tie a necktie. It is almost impossible to transmit this knowledge through words alone. You will find that you have to demonstrate, and even then, you will stand behind the child, since your responses are so restricted and rigid that you can't tie a necktie while facing it. In playing the piano, knowledge of certain intricate passages seems to reside in your fingers. You may have forgotten a certain tune, but after fiddling around on the keys for a few minutes, your fingers suddenly "remember." Or in sports like skiing and golf, despite hours of verbal instruction, you ultimately have to learn a certain "feel," a certain muscular patterning.

In fact, many psychologists now believe that we have at least two separate modes of learning and memory, one called declarative and the other called procedural (Alper, 1986). Declarative learning stores information about names, dates, past events, episodes in one's life, and facts, whereas procedural learning is made up of motoric patterning and conditioning. This theory is used to explain why Alzheimer victims may still recall motoric patterns, such as tying shoes, riding a bicycle, or hitting a golf ball, but are not able to activate such declarative memories as the names of their children. More will be said on this important issue in Chapter 11.

Other psychologists, cognitive theorists like Max Wertheimer, Wolfgang Kohler, and Kurt Lewin, felt that learning required thinking and insight. Thus, as you drive to your favorite restaurant, your arms and legs won't be any help without a more general cognitive map, probably located in your brain. To the cognitive theorists, teaching children by drill or rote is like training a bunch of parrots. Children really learn only when they discover solutions for themselves, only when they "understand."

ASSOCIATION LEARNING AND COGNITIVE LEARNING

Now that the dust has settled on some of the great theoretical debates of the past, two main schools of thought on learning have emerged, though many variations still exist. These two main schools of thought are **association learning** and **cognitive learning.** Association theorists, on the one hand, see learning as the result of connections (associations) between stimuli (sense impressions) and responses. Dogs salivating when they hear the can opener opening their food, babies waving "bye-bye" on cue from their mothers, and fifth-graders saying "72" to the stimulus "9 times 8" are all examples of association learning. A bond has been formed between two elements, a stimulus and a response.

Cognitive theorists, on the other hand, view learning as a reorganization of a number of perceptions. This reorganization allows the learner to perceive new relationships, solve new problems, and gain a basic understanding of a subject area. A fifth-grader suddenly realizing that multiplication is successive addition, an ape suddenly understanding that by putting two short sticks together it can obtain a banana that was out of reach, and an eighth-grader discovering a way to calculate the area of a parallelogram are all examples of cognitive learning.

These two views of learning parallel the two sides of another controversy that has historically split the field of psychology: **behaviorism** versus **gestalt psychology.** The behaviorists have typically been associationists, whereas the gestaltists have been cognitive theorists.

THE ORIGINS OF PSYCHOLOGY: WILHELM WUNDT

Wilhelm Wundt is credited with setting up the first experimental psychology laboratory in Germany around 1879. He was strongly influenced by philosophy, but he was also influenced by physiology, having begun his career as a physician and later becoming a physiologist. In a sense, then, psychology as a separate discipline resulted from a marriage between philosophy and physiology, with Wundt performing the ceremony. Like the philosophers who preceded him, Wundt was interested in studying conscious experience, and he sought to do this by analyzing consciousness into its smallest components. He was looking for the basic elements of psychology, the smallest parts of analyzable consciousness. This was analogous to the work of physicists who, at roughly the same time, constructed the atomic table. As physics had its elements, so, too, thought Wundt, would psychology. Wundt felt that by analyzing consciousness into these tiny elements, or "atoms," he could make psychology as respectable a science as physics.

The main thesis of Wundt's work was that these basic individual elements of the mind, or atoms of experience, are linked by associations. The problem was to ferret out these elements for study. To accomplish this, Wundt used the technique of **introspection.** He trained subjects to look within themselves and report all their most fleeting and minute feelings and sensations (Wundt, 1910). Both behaviorism and gestalt psychology began in reaction to Wundt.

The Gestaltists Attack Wundt

A group of psychologists, led by Max Wertheimer, got together around 1910 at the University of Frankfurt and began the school of psychology known as gestalt psychology. The gestaltists felt that in trying to produce a neat atomic chart of psychology, Wundt had lost sight of the reality of human experience. They felt that by analyzing experience into its smallest parts, Wundt had, in effect, destroyed the total experience. He was like a musician analyzing each note separately and never hearing the melody. "The whole is more than the sum of its parts," thundered Wertheimer. You must study the whole, the totality, the entire configuration, or, to use the German word, the *Gestalt.* "To dissect is to distort" became the gestaltists' central message. The gestaltists felt that the study of the associations formed between tiny elements, whether they are elements of consciousness or stimuli-response connections, is misleading be-

SPOTLIGHT ON THE EXPERIMENTAL STUDY OF LEARNING

Ebbinghaus the Pioneer

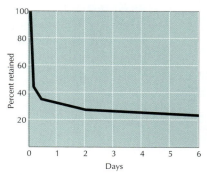

Ebbinghaus's retention curve. Most of the learned material is lost very rapidly and the rest more and more slowly.

The experimental study of learning had quiet beginnings. In Germany during the 1880s, Hermann Ebbinghaus carried out the first of these studies, and produced pioneering work that eventually earned him the title "father of learning psychology." Because he wanted to study learning in its pure form, he chose to control for the influence of meaningfulness. In order to do this, Ebbinghaus used long lists of nonsense syllables (*cay, lek, hum,* etc.), which he felt allowed him to control for original difficulty. Since so many words have past associations or inherent interest, they might be easier for some people to learn than for others, whereas all lists of nonsense syllables should be of comparable difficulty and would have to be learned from scratch. At first, Ebbinghaus was his own subject,

and he spent many long and lonely hours learning these meaningless words. His work led him to draw two major conclusions:

1. Once something is learned, it is not forgotten at an even rate. Most of what is forgotten is lost very quickly, and the rest is lost at a slow and fairly stable rate.
2. In order to learn new material, it is more efficient to space the practice sessions than to mass them. For example, if you had one hour to learn something, you would retain more by taking four 15-minute practice sessions spread over a few days than by spending one full hour working without a break.

The results of these studies, though interesting to the learning

theorist, seemed to have limited practical use in the classroom. Laws governing the learning of meaningless information may not always be directly generalized to the learning of meaningful material. Information learned in the classroom should, of course, be meaningful, although unfortunately students are still made to memorize vocabulary, long passages from poems, and arcane grammatical rules— material that at the time may be no more meaningful to them than were the nonsense syllables to Ebbinghaus. More recent studies, however, have added considerable strength to Ebbinghaus's contention that several practice sessions well-spaced is a more efficient learning strategy, especially when studying vocabulary lists, than is one long massed session (Dempster, 1987).

MAX WERTHEIMER

Max Wertheimer was born in Prague in 1880, the son of a school-teacher. As a student, young Wertheimer had far-ranging interests. He studied law for a while, then switched to philosophy, and finally began to study psychology. After attending a number of schools and universities, Wertheimer received his Ph.D. degree at Wurzburg in 1904. For the next six years he continued his work in psychology at Prague, Vienna, and Berlin. Wertheimer had been schooled in the structuralist psychological tradition, which held that all psychological phenomena could be broken down and analyzed into their smallest parts, or elements. In 1910, while traveling by train from Vienna to a Rhineland vacation resort, Wertheimer was suddenly struck by an idea. As the train raced along, he gazed out the window and was fascinated by the apparent movement of the poles and trees, and even distant mountains. What he knew were stationary objects appeared to be moving along with the train, and whereas his mind told one story, his eyes told another. He began rethinking the structuralistic viewpoint, and the more he pondered, the more he doubted. Suddenly he decided to forget his planned vacation and left the train at Frankfurt. He rushed to the nearest toy store and purchased a child's stroboscope. This was in the days before motion pictures, and a stroboscope was a device that, when turned at a constant speed, exposed a series of still pictures that appeared to move. In his hotel room Wertheimer examined his new purchase. He spun the stroboscope, fascinated by the apparent movement that the device produced, and in one of the history of psychology's great examples of insight, thought, "Aha, Wundt and the structuralists must be wrong." Here was a psychological perception, apparent movement, which simply could not be explained or understood by analyzing the individual still pictures. When the elements of this perception were studied individually, the total phenomenon of perceived movement was lost. The whole must be more than just the sum of its parts. In order to understand this perception of movement, one had to study all the parts together in their particular *Gestalt*, a German word that means

cause elements often act and look differently when they are taken out of context. For example, Wertheimer would say that if you were to study each frame in a motion picture, you would never see movement, which is what a motion picture is all about.

The Behaviorists Attack Wundt

The school of behaviorism was born under the aegis of John B. Watson at Johns Hopkins University. The behaviorists attacked Wundt because of his use of introspection as a scientific tool. The behaviorists believed in elements, but they didn't like the way Wundt went about finding them. In the now-classic article, "Psychology as the Behaviorist Views It," Watson (1913) proclaimed that behaviors constitute the real data of psychology. According to Watson, introspection is as useless to psychology as it would be to chemistry or physics. The only thing that is really observable, and therefore the only thing that really allows for the use of the scientific method, is the subject's overt behavior. Watson also announced to the world what would and what would not be proper areas for psychologists to study. If consciousness can be studied only through introspection, and if it has no behavioral correlates, then throw it out of psychology. Unlike Wundt, Watson didn't care if you talked the talk, unless you also walked the walk. As we will continue to see, Watson was not one to equivocate.

"whole," or "totality," or "configuration."

Wertheimer went to the University of Frankfurt and began a series of controlled experiments. His first subject was Wolfgang Kohler, who was later joined by Kurt Koffka. Early in 1912 Wertheimer explained to Kohler and Koffka the results and meaning of his studies. Gestalt psychology had been born. Both Kohler and Koffka became zealous advocates of this new school of thought, and both went on to produce many experiments, articles, and books in support of it. Both became famous gestalt psychologists in their own right.

In 1912 Wertheimer published his now famous article "Experimental Studies of the Perception of Movement." As a result of this single revolutionary article, a tremendous new movement in psychology was launched and thousands of articles and books were written and are still being written on this important subject.

In 1916 Wertheimer joined the faculty at the University of Berlin, where he worked with another soon-to-be-famous gestalt psychologist, Kurt Lewin. In 1933 Wertheimer came to the United States, where he taught at the New School for Social Research in New York City. He remained at the New School until his death in 1943.

Wertheimer was a man with a cause, but he was not arrogant or authoritarian. He was a gentle, warm, deep-thinking man. He had a close personal relationship with Albert Einstein, and he was deeply concerned with the social and ethical issues of his times.

Wertheimer was also interested in education and the techniques of good teaching. He pointed out the importance of gestalt principles as they apply to learning in the classroom. He criticized the use of repetition and rote memorization, explaining that such procedures lead only to blind, nonproductive learning on the part of students. He insisted that educators should teach for understanding, and that under-

standing is made possible when the teacher arranges the material so that the student can see the "whole," or the *Gestalt*, and not just a series of seemingly unrelated parts. In his book *Productive Thinking*, Wertheimer stressed the importance of gestalt theory in the practical problem of educating children.

Whereas Watson and Guthrie were concerned with overt responses, stressing always what the student *did*, Wertheimer emphasized the child's process of mental organization, stressing instead what the student *understood*.

Today the Wertheimer tradition lives on. His son, Michael, also a distinguished psychologist, has served as president of four different divisions of the American Psychological Association, is currently teaching at the University of Colorado, and in 1991 was presented with the APA's prestigious award for "distinguished education and training contributions."

Behaviorists and Gestaltists Attack Each Other

Although these two powerful schools of psychology began by fighting independent battles with Wundt, the scene of battle soon shifted, and they began fighting each other. Watson fell in with a powerful ally, Ivan Pavlov, the Russian whose work on the conditioned reflex was being recognized at about the same time Watson was preparing for combat. Watson found just what he needed when he needed it: the conditioned reflex, something observable to replace Wundt's nonobservable elements. Watson soon felt that all learning could be explained on the basis of conditioning, that is, the association of stimuli with responses. A new unit of analysis had been found

that was both observable and consistent with the principle of association. Watson was ready to take over American psychology, and through his direct influence and through the indirect influence of those who followed—Edwin Guthrie, Clark Hull, E. L. Thorndike, and B. F. Skinner—Watson certainly did shape and direct the course of American psychology. Learning was a matter of accumulating a series of stimulus-response associations. There is no need to study insight, or even thinking in the traditional sense, for conditioning pretty much explains it all. The gestaltists did not agree. Wertheimer, and later Kohler and Lewin, felt that learning could not be dissected into little stimulus-response associations and still be consistent with what they saw as reality. Children could be conditioned *ad nauseam*, trained to recite the multiplication tables, the state capitals, the major agricultural products of each country, but without insight or real understanding, the information would be virtually useless. According to the gestaltists, if you want children to learn nonsense, go ahead and condition them; but if you want them to learn meaningful relationships, then a different approach is needed—a cognitive approach.

We now turn to a discussion of how the association-learning and cognitive-learning positions were formed and eventually translated into action. We begin with those theories that dominated the first half of the twentieth century, spotlighting the early associationists Thorndike, Pavlov, and Guthrie. As will become clear, Watson, though not singled out for independent coverage here, influenced or was influenced by the work of the other three. The discussion of the early cognitive theorists focuses on Wertheimer and Kohler, two gestaltists who made important contributions to our current knowledge of cognitive learning. In Chapter 9 we examine in some detail the two most influential spokespersons for each position: B. F. Skinner and Jerome Bruner. The present chapter provides a background for appreciating the significance of Skinner and Bruner in education today.

THE EARLY ASSOCIATION THEORISTS

E. L. Thorndike

In 1898 **Edward L. Thorndike** published a paper entitled "Animal Intelligence" and was thereby catapulted to the forefront of the emerging field of learning psychology. From his headquarters at Columbia Teachers College, Thorndike issued his concepts and laws of learning for many years thereafter. For most of the first half of the twentieth century, he was truly Mr. Educational Psychology in the United States. His studies of cats learning to escape from puzzle boxes are now legendary. Thorndike viewed learning as a series of stimulus-response (S-R) connections, or bonds. His theory of learning described the ways in which these S-R connections could be strengthened or weakened. He felt that learning was basically a trial-and-error enterprise, and he paid little attention to the possibility of concept formation or thinking.

Thorndike postulated three major laws of learning:

1. **The law of readiness:** When an organism is in a state in which the conduction units (S-R connec-

tions) are ready, then the conduction is satisfying. If the conduction unit is not ready, then conduction is annoying. Thorndike was referring here to a brief, neurological readiness, not the kind of maturational readiness that, as we saw in Chapter 4, was of concern to Myrtle McGraw. Thorndike was referring to a more momentary phenomenon, a kind of neurologically teachable moment.

2. **The law of exercise:** This law, also called the law of use and disuse, states that the more an S-R connection is used, the stronger it will become; the less it is used, the weaker it will become. This law is obviously based on the old maxim about practice making perfect. Thorndike, especially in his later writings, made it clear that practice led to improvement only when it was followed by positive feedback. Blind practice, with no knowledge of the consequences of the act, had no effect on learning.

3. **The law of effect:** This was by far Thorndike's most important law. It states that an S-R connection followed by satisfaction (reward) is strengthened, whereas a connection followed by annoyance (punishment) is weakened. In later years Thorndike played down the importance of the second part of the law. He came to feel that reward strengthened learning far more than punishment weakened it.

There is no doubt that Thorndike had a dehumanizing effect on American education. His first work involved the study of how cats solve problems. He saw little basic difference between animal and human learning, with no regard for the qualitative differences in learning that Piaget insisted occur at different periods during human development. Thorndike spread a kind of mechanical-person gospel that viewed animals and children as akin to robots.

Thorndike's contribution to education, however, cannot be minimized. He was, through his law of effect, the first psychologist to stress the importance of motivation in learning. When an individual is rewarded for learning, then learning is far more apt to occur. This aspect of learning seems to have been overlooked by Ebbinghaus. Since he was so close to his experiments (he was, after all, his own subject), Ebbinghaus could hardly take note of his own fantastically high motivation. (If you have any doubts about the strength of Ebbinghaus's motivation, try spending a few months doing virtually nothing but learning lists of nonsense syllables.)

In addition to stressing the importance of motivation in learning, Thorndike also made much of another crucial concept, that of transfer. His law of identical elements states that the learner is better able to confront new problems if these new problems contain elements similar to those the learner has already mastered. This, after all, is largely what schooling is all about. If we learned how to use an encyclopedia while we were in school, we are more likely now to be able to diagnose what is wrong with our car by looking it up in our owner's manual, or to prepare a gourmet meal from the directions in a cookbook, or to plan an advertising campaign by making use of appropriate library resources. Transfer will be discussed in greater depth in the next chapter.

Ivan Pavlov

The laboratory work of the Russian physiologist Ivan Pavlov was of great importance to the study of learning. Though most modern physiological psychologists consider his theory of the neurological process of learning a historical curio, his laboratory techniques and findings are still of great significance. In 1904 Pavlov won the Nobel Prize in medicine for his work on the digestive activity of dogs. His lasting fame, however, resulted from what at the time were incidental and chance observations regarding digestion in his dogs. Pavlov noted that the dogs salivated not only when meat powder was placed directly in their mouths, but also well before that (for example, when they heard the trainer's footsteps coming down the stairs). Pavlov later coined the term *conditioned reflex* to describe this phenomenon (Pavlov, 1927).

A reflex must have an identifiable stimulus that automatically elicits the response, even though no learning has occurred. For example, when a bright light shines directly into a person's eyes, the pupils automatically contract. No learning or training is required for this to occur. Similarly, when food is placed in a dog's mouth, salivation automatically occurs. Reflexes are therefore directly caused by an unconditioned stimulus, much as pulling the trigger of a loaded gun automatically causes the gun to fire.

Pavlov also noted that if a neutral stimulus—one that does not elicit a certain response—is repeatedly paired with an unconditioned stimulus—one that does automatically elicit a certain response—the neutral stimulus will eventually take on the power to elicit the response. This is now called **classical conditioning,** and an example will illustrate. When meat powder is placed directly in a dog's mouth, the dog automatically salivates. This is a reflex action and does not have to be learned. However, if a 2,000-cycle tone is presented immediately before the meat powder is given, the tone soon comes to evoke the salivation. Through association with the meat powder, the tone begins to act as a signal that meat powder will follow, and the dog eventually learns to respond to the signal the same way it used to respond only to the meat powder. Technically, the meat powder is called the **unconditioned stimulus** (UCS), since responding to it does not depend on prior experience or learning. The tone or signal is called the **conditioned stimulus** (CS), since the response to it must be learned. For the same reasons, salivation to the meat powder is called the **unconditioned response** (UCR), and salivating to the tone is called the **conditioned response** (CR).

When John B. Watson studied the acquisition of fear in baby Albert, this was the technique he used (see Chapter 2). When Watson first presented Albert with a white rat, Albert showed no sign of fear. Then Watson struck a steel bar right beside Albert's head, and this loud sound (unconditioned stimulus) automatically made Albert cry (unconditioned response). After repeated pairings of the white rat and the loud sound, Albert began crying as soon as the rat came in view, even when he heard no loud sound. The rat (conditioned stimulus) took on the power to elicit the crying (conditioned response). Note that the conditioned and unconditioned responses are the same: salivation in the case of Pavlov's dogs and crying in the case of Watson's baby. The difference is what brings them about. The conditioned response is one that is elicited by a stimulus that has to be learned through association.

One reason educators must know about conditioning is that a great number of autonomic reflexes can be conditioned while the child is still in school. Just as Albert was conditioned to fear a rat, so the schoolchild may be conditioned to fear math, science, spelling, or any other school subject. Autonomic responses, such as sweating, rapid heartbeat, or general feelings of anxiety, may be conditioned by certain cues that come to be associated with various aspects of the school setting. Children who have been conditioned to such an extent that they are literally paralyzed by fear at the mere sight of a math problem are unlikely to be able to learn much math. They might sincerely try to learn the subject, but because of a great and crippling discomfort, they are not able to.

This is not to say that teachers deliberately create these fears, but they can unwittingly set the stage for such conditioning. For example, a math problem is presented, followed by some other action of the teacher that may already be associated in the child's past experience with feelings of tension, and now the math problem itself triggers autonomic reactions of anxiety on the part of the child. After a few associations of this kind, the mere presentation of the math problem (CS) begins to elicit anxiety (CR). Sometimes this process occurs because teachers themselves have a conditioned fear of math and unwittingly transmit it to their students in the form of scolding, bullying, or a generally "uptight" approach to learning the subject.

Pavlov found that reflex conditioning had some extremely important by-products. For example, once a dog was conditioned to salivate to a 2,000-cycle tone, it would also salivate to a 1,300- or 2,700-cycle tone, even though these new stimuli had never been used in training. In other words, once a given conditioned stimulus is associated with a reflex, other similar stimuli also take on the power to elicit the response. This is called **stimulus generalization.** The original conditioned stimulus becomes generalized, and the organism begins responding to other stimuli that are in some way similar to the original one. Once Watson's young subject, Albert, was conditioned to fear the rat, he was also afraid of a Santa Claus mask, a sealskin coat, human hair, a dog, a rabbit, and cotton wool. The point is, reflex conditioning has wide-ranging effects. A child who is conditioned to fear math problems may generalize this fear to many other school subjects, perhaps even the entire school situation. Phobic reactions can be understood in this way. Suppose an unruly child is punished by being locked in a closet. The conditioned stimulus may be generalized so that the child becomes fearful of any enclosed area. The result, claustrophobia, could carry over into adulthood, and the person so afflicted might live a severely restricted life.

Pavlov found that the only way to break the association between a conditioned stimulus and a conditioned response was through a process called **extinction.** Extinction is achieved when the CS loses its power to evoke the CR; it is accomplished by repeatedly presenting the CS without following it with the UCS. If the 2,000-cycle tone is consistently presented without the meat powder, the dog eventually stops salivating upon hearing it. It is important to note that for extinction to occur, the conditioned stimulus must be repeatedly presented by itself. Unfortunately, when the conditioned reflex is fear, the afflicted individual naturally avoids the conditioned stimulus, and extinction is never allowed to occur. Joseph Wolpe, a famous psychotherapist, uses techniques of classical conditioning and extinction in treating phobias.

Edwin Guthrie

The last of the early associationists we will cover here is **Edwin Guthrie.** Guthrie was the behaviorist-associationist par excellence. Following directly in Watson's footsteps, he rejected any psychological concepts that might have "mentalistic" overtones. He postulated one law of learning: learning by association, or, as he called it, *contiguity.* According to Guthrie, if a certain stimulus (or pattern of stimuli) is followed by a response, then the next time that stimulus appears, the same response will follow. That's all there is to it—stimuli and responses in sequence. There is no need to call on reward, reinforcement, or "effect" in order to explain how learning occurs. He also believed that learning occurs the first time the stimulus and response become associated (Guthrie, 1935). To create conditions that will promote learning, Guthrie believed that the teacher should provide the stimulus, and the student should respond. For example, the teacher might point to a map and the students would then reply with the name of the city. The important thing was for the appropriate stimulus to be presented before the desired response occurred.

A frenzied mother once brought her child to Guthrie. The child had been in the habit, on coming home from school, of opening the door of his home, taking off his coat, and throwing it on the floor. The mother told Guthrie that no matter how many times she told her child to pick up the coat and hang it in the closet, the child continued this behavior. Guthrie did not reach for any deep psychological explanation, like finding out what throwing the coat on the floor symbolized, what it "meant" to the child. He simply told the mother to rearrange the stimulus-response sequence. When the child threw his coat on the floor, he should not be told to hang it up. He should instead be told to put the coat on, to go back outside, to come through the door, and, only then, to hang up the coat. Thus hanging up the coat could become a response to the stimulus of entering the house rather than to the stimulus of the mother's command, "Take your coat off the floor and hang it up."

The advice apparently worked, for from then on the child hung up his coat correctly. Fortunately for Guthrie, and especially for the child, a longer sequence of S-R associations did not form. That is, according to Guthrie's system, the child might have forever learned to come home, open the door, throw the coat on the floor, pick it up, put it on, go back outside, come back in, then hang up the coat!

THE EARLY COGNITIVE THEORISTS

Max Wertheimer

As mentioned earlier, **Max Wertheimer** founded the school of psychology called gestalt psychology. He insisted that it was misleading to study small parts of psychological concepts like perception or learning. Studying parts in isolation was unjustified, because changing any single part necessarily changes the whole. Similarly, the whole may remain, even when all the parts have changed. For example, if we play a tune in two different keys, even though the individual notes are different each time, the tune retains its integrity.

Wertheimer was concerned with the way children learn, particularly in school. He was against the use of rote memorization, especially when it so often

seemed to be an end in itself. Above all else, he wanted children to achieve understanding, to have insight into the nature of the problem.

Wertheimer explained that there are two kinds of solutions to problems, type A and type B. Type A solutions are those which use originality and insight, whereas type B solutions are those which make use of past associations in a rigid, inappropriate way. Wertherimer used the example of teaching a child how to find the area of a parallelogram (see Figure 8.1).

The child is first taught how to find the area of a rectangle, not by memorizing the formula but by understanding why the formula works. The rectangle is divided into smaller squares, and the child sees that the total area is composed of the number of squares in a row times the number of rows. Wertheimer then cut a parallelogram out of paper and asked the child

FIGURE 8.1   Wertheimer's parallelogram problem.

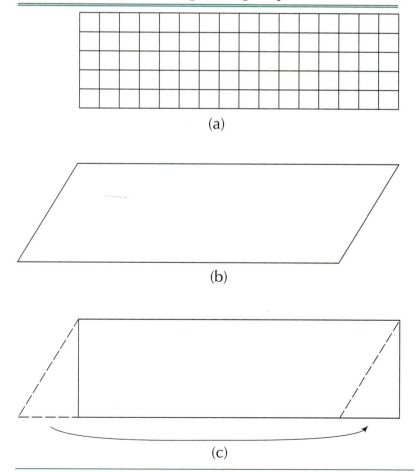

(a)

(b)

(c)

to determine its area. Some children persisted in multiplying the length times the height, a type B solution. Others used type A solutions, like cutting off one of the triangular ends and fitting it against the other end. At this point, the child had created a rectangle and could correctly utilize the previously learned formula. Another type A solution involved bending the parallelogram into a loop with the two angular ends abutting each other, then making one vertical cut which would also create a rectangle. The children using type A solutions had obviously discovered a real geometric relationship (Wertheimer, 1945).

Wolfgang Kohler

Wolfgang Kohler, like Koffka (see box), had also worked with Wertheimer at Frankfurt. Later, however, during World War I, he spent several years on the island of Tenerife, off the coast of Africa. There he performed gestalt psychology's most famous animal studies. Kohler arranged an ape's cage so that there were bananas hanging from the top and a couple of boxes on the floor. In order to reach the bananas, the ape had to stack one box on top of another and then climb to the top. The ape's solution to the problem appeared to Kohler not to be one of blind trial and error. Instead, the ape seemed to size up the situation and then, almost in a flash, to understand the problem and "see" the solution. The ape displayed what Kohler called insight, and Kohler felt that this was more typical of learning, especially human learning, than Thorndike's concept of blind trial and error.

In another experiment, Kohler put food outside the cage, beyond even an ape's long reach. Inside the cage, however, there were some sticks. At first the apes would throw the sticks at the banana. Then they "realized" that by using the stick as a kind of tool they could reach out and rake the banana in. One especially intelligent ape, named Sultan, was even able to join two short sticks together to rake the food in.

Kohler's explanation was that the apes were able to see the problem as a unified whole. In the box-stacking problem, the ape did not see the boxes and bananas as separate elements but came to realize that they belonged together as part of a whole. Similarly, the sticks and bananas were perceived as belonging together, and it was only after this reorganization of perceptions that insight into the solution to the problem occurred.

Insight has been called the "a-ha" phenomenon. Kohler made much of the concept of insight, perhaps too much. He felt that insight learning did not depend on past experience, that it was not just a special

case of transfer. As we shall see in a later chapter, Harry Harlow's studies on learning sets have since cast some doubt on the validity of Kohler's interpretation.

Recently, not only has Kohler's interpretation been challenged, but also his motivation. An American psychology professor, Ronald Ley, visited the island of Tenerife in hopes of finding the ape research station where Kohler first conducted his classic experiments during World War I. He uncovered instead the long-kept secret that while doing his learning studies on apes, Kohler may have also been engaged in a far more dangerous activity—that of wartime spying for Germany, using his laboratory as a cover for espionage activity (Ley, 1990).

NEW DIRECTIONS IN PSYCHOLOGY AND EDUCATION

You may now be wondering why nobody tried to bridge the gap between the two learning theory traditions, for both positions evidently have some merit. The behaviorists did have a strong case for insisting that overt responses are the appropriate data for psychology. If you were trying to judge people's attitudes toward some issue, you would, in all probability, be more influenced by what they did than by what they said. For example, if your boss constantly bragged of being an equal opportunity employer but never hired African-American applicants, you might rightly feel that "actions speak louder than words."

Yet you probably feel equally sure that the gestaltists also had a good case; learning, understanding, discovering new relationships must be more than just the mere conditioning of certain responses. Some reorganization of perceptions, something going on within the organism, must account for understanding and discovery.

In fact, some psychologists did attempt to bridge the gap. **E. C. Tolman,** for example, produced a theory called *purposive behaviorism*. It was called purposive because Tolman insisted that, far from being random and chaotic, learning is goal-directed. The learning organism is a striving organism, striving to give meaning to behavior. Yet Tolman's theory was also behavioristic because he believed that scientific validity could be achieved only by observing objective behavior.

Tolman stated that both rats and humans learn by forming cognitive maps of their environment (Tolman, 1948). This explains how organisms get from place to place. They form hypotheses, see relationships, and then select appropriate responses on the basis of their cognitive maps. Although Tolman did

SPOTLIGHT ON KURT KOFFKA

Gestalt's Foreshadowing of Modern Cognitive Psychology

Kurt Koffka, who had worked under Wertheimer at the University of Frankfurt, extended many of his mentor's ideas and produced a theory that in this age of the cognitive revolution has an extraordinarily modern ring. He talked about learning as resulting from what he called the memory process, which is the brain activity that accompanies incoming stimulation. Thus, an environmental experience produces a memory trace that can be permanently etched in the mind of the learner. As Koffka saw it, the brain could carry an internal representation of the stimulus information, a phenomenon that is today called encoding. (See Chapter 11.) The various traces, resulting from the myriad of similar experiences that occur over time, form interrelated aggregates, or internal gestalts, that come to govern both our perceptions and our continued learning. These interrelated traces, called by Koffka trace systems, allow the child to become an increasingly more efficient problem solver. For example, the child may develop trace systems that correspond to a class of objects or events, such as books, cars, games, boys, girls, and so on.[a] As learning expert B. R. Hergenhahn says of Koffka,

> These trace systems will be a kind of neurological summation of all our experiences with objects in a certain class, such as cows, or clowns . . . If we look at an individual elephant, the process aroused by that elephant will be influenced by the trace system that resulted from all our other experiences with elephants. The resulting experience will be a combination of the two influences, with the trace system being the most important. Our memory of that event, then, will be one of "elephantness" that has little to do with any particular elephant but has more to do with what they have in common.[b]

As we shall see in Chapter 11, this process is virtually identical with what the current cognitive psychologists are calling concept formation, or the schema. Thus, the gestaltists viewed the learner as not just a repository of discrete stimulus-response associations, but as the beneficiary of abstractions and learning strategies that allow for the development of higher levels of reasoning and learning.

---

[a] Koffka, K. (1935). *Principles of Gestalt Psychology.* New York: Harcourt Brace.

[b] Hergenhahn, B. R., & Olson, M. H. (1993). *An Introduction to Theories of Learning.* Englewood Cliffs, N.J.: Prentice Hall. p. 267.

---

mphasize stimulus-response connections as the units of analysis, he was still an associationist use he saw learning as a result of bonds formed ng a number of stimuli. The learner forms an as- ion between some new stimulus, or sign, and a usly encountered and therefore meaningful , or "significate." Tolman's behaviorism is an S-S (sign-significate) psychology, rather atsonian S-R psychology.

olman was more responsive to the work of the developmental psychologists than were most of the behaviorists. He postulated his famous H-A-T-E variables (heredity, age, training, endocrine) as of crucial importance in understanding and predicting behavior. Heredity sets certain limits on what environmental manipulation can accomplish. Age deter-

mines how much impact training can have. Training is, of course, vital, since learning cannot occur in a static environment. Endocrine, or internal physiological, factors also play an important role in learning. Thus Tolman, perhaps more than any other learning theorist, understood the importance of individual differences. And in many ways the ensuing years have been kind to Tolman's position. It is now known that rats and other animals have far more flexibility in making choices and solving problems than could be explained by the orthodox Watsonian and Pavlovian models of straight S-R conditioning (Domjan, 1987).

With all its sophistication and thoroughness, Tolman's system never exerted the influence on teaching that Thorndike's or Watson's did. Though he

SPOTLIGHT ON THE STUDY OF LEARNING

The All-Time "Greats"

The importance that psychologists have attached to the study of learning can be seen in the results of a poll conducted among psychology's historians to name the all-time greats in their field. The results were as shown.

Notice that among the top 10, 6—James, Watson, Pavlov, Ebbinghaus, Piaget, and Skinner— are identified primarily with the study of learning. Even the

Rank	Individual
1	Wundt
2	James
3	Freud
4	Watson
5	Pavlov
6	Ebbinghaus
7	Piaget
8	Skinner
9	Binet
10	Fechner

remaining 4—Wundt, Freud, Binet, and Fechner—all spent some time addressing the issue of learning.

Korn, J. H., Davis, R. & Davis, S. F. (1991). Historians' and chairpersons' judgments of eminence among psychologists. *American Psychologist, 46,* 789–792.

---

may be rediscovered in the next decade, and in the long run may have more influence than Thorndike, that is not yet the case.

Why was Tolman so ignored by the field of education during his lifetime? There are a number of reasons, but it is primarily because he never translated theory into practice. The teacher might learn from Tolman that a rat at a choice point in a maze hypothesizes a solution before acting, but this hardly helps the teacher in the classroom. The teacher wants answers to specific questions regarding learning and discipline in the classroom, not sophisticated and elegant theorizing. Further, Tolman failed to develop his theory to its fullest potential. He didn't do

enough experiments to generate precise predictions. As Winfred Hill, a modern expert in the field of learning, has said of Tolman, "His system is more a road sign or a pious hope than it is an accomplished fact" (Hill, 1971).

And so educational psychology turned away from the old-line theorists and toward psychology's "new breed" theorists, psychologists who talked to teachers, who told teachers what to do in given situations, who told teachers how to produce desired behavior changes or set up conditions that aid discovery. Educational psychology turned to B. F. Skinner and Jerome Bruner.

SUMMARY

The study of learning has been of utmost importance in psychology for over a century. Though psychologists agreed on the importance of learning as an object of study, they disagreed on the mechanics of how the learning process occurred.

The major schools of thought were:

Behaviorist-associationists: Those who viewed learning as a result of the forming of connections between stimuli and observable responses

Cognitive-gestaltists: Those who believed that learning results from the reorganization of perceptions and the forming of new relationships

Both the behaviorists and the gestaltists began their schools of thought as reactions to Wundt's associationist-introspectionist brand of psychology. The gestaltists, led by Wertheimer, challenged Wundt's associationist position, while the behaviorists, led by Watson, attacked Wundt's use of introspection.

Wertheimer and the gestaltists argued that psychological phenomena could not be understood by studying simple associations among tiny elements but must be viewed as a total configuration, or *Gestalt*. Wertheimer argued that the whole is more than just the sum of a group of separate parts. Learning was seen as the understanding of a total, meaningful relationship, and the only acceptable approach to the study of learning was a cognitive one. Watson and the behaviorists, though not objecting to the study of separate parts, did denounce Wundt's use of introspection. Watson argued that the only true scientific data in the field of psychology were observable responses. Thus, if a concept such as consciousness could not be seen, touched, or observed in any way, it should be thrown out of psychology. Watson believed that learning could be thoroughly understood on the basis of Pavlov's principles of classical conditioning.

The first experimental studies of learning were conducted by Ebbinghaus in the late nineteenth century. In order to control for past associations, Ebbinghaus studied the learning of nonsense syllables. He discovered that most learned material is forgotten very quickly, and that later the rate of forgetting slows to a fairly even pace.

Thorndike, an early associationist, posited three major laws of learning: (1) the law of readiness, showing the importance of neurological anticipation; (2) the law of exercise, showing the importance of practice; and (3) the law of effect, indicating the importance of motivation.

Pavlov, a Russian psychologist, discovered some lawful relationships between stimuli and responses. He showed how learning could take place through conditioning, a trained association among stimuli and a certain response. Pavlov's system is now called classical conditioning and applies only to reflex activity. Pavlov also introduced such concepts as extinction, stimulus generalization, and discrimination learning.

Guthrie, a psychologist in the behaviorist-associationist tradition, felt that all learning was a result of stimuli and responses in sequence. Guthrie saw no need to use concepts such as motivation or reinforcement to explain learning.

Wertheimer, the first of the cognitive-gestalt psychologists, was concerned with how the learner achieved understanding and insight when confronted with a problem. He felt that rote memorization did not lead to real understanding.

Kohler, also of the cognitive-gestalt school, performed several important animal studies. His studies on apes led him to conclude that learning was a result of a series of insightful solutions, not blind trial and error.

Tolman attempted to bridge the gap between behaviorists and gestaltists by creating a type of psychology called purposive behaviorism. Tolman thought that striving toward a goal gave meaning to the resulting behavior. Learning occurs when a new stimulus (or sign) is associated with a previously encountered and therefore meaningful stimulus (significate).

The two basic positions, behaviorist-associationist and cognitive-gestaltist, have their proponents in B. F. Skinner and Jerome Bruner. Skinner (the behaviorist) and Bruner (the cognitive theorist) are especially important in educational psychology today, for each devotes a great deal of time to talking directly to the classroom teacher.

KEY TERMS AND NAMES

association learning
behaviorism
cognitive learning
gestalt psychology
Edwin Guthrie
Hermann Ebbinghaus
Kurt Koffka
Wolfgang Kohler
   insight
Ivan Pavlov
   classical conditioning
   conditioned response
   conditioned stimulus

extinction
stimulus generalization
unconditioned response
unconditioned stimulus
stimulus-response learning
Edward L. Thorndike
   law of effect
   law of exercise
   law of readiness
E. C. Tolman
Max Wertheimer
Wilhelm Wundt
   introspection

THEORY INTO PRACTICE: LEARNING BACKGROUNDS— FOCUSING YOUR THINKING

Exercise A

A more complete understanding of the historical roots of current views of the learning process can be facilitated by adopting a more focused approach to these background issues. The two major precursors of today's positions are the behaviorist-associationist and the cognitive-gestaltist theories. Both carry other theoretical positions with them, and these may help illuminate the differences between the two contemporary viewpoints. For example, as was stated in Chapter 2, the behaviorist-associationists tended to ally themselves with the blank-slate position of John Locke, whereas the cognitive-gestaltists felt strongly that the neonate came into the world equipped with some biological givens.

Using these distinctions, indicate whether the following psychologists would tend more toward explaining behavior on the basis of nature or on the basis of nurture:

1. Wertheimer

2. Watson

3. Kohler

4. Guthrie

5. Tolman

Exercise B

Thorndike insisted that learning occurs as a result of the formation of stimulus-response connections in one direction. If, for example, you are studying a foreign language by first being presented with the foreign word (stimulus) to which you are then to respond with the English word, the learned association will go largely in that direction; that is, you will then find it difficult to reverse the association and respond with the foreign word when the English word is given as the stimulus. For example, try learning the following paired associates by looking first at the German word and then repeating the English word:

GERMAN	ENGLISH
Sagenhaft	Mythical
Ruckzug	Retreat

GERMAN	ENGLISH
Klug	Clever
Jux	Fun
Heikel	Tricky
Funken	Radio
Fremd	Strange
Adler	Eagle
Antwort	Answer
Ubel	Nasty

Once you feel you know the words well enough to go through the list with few if any errors, try reversing the process. Covering the column of German words, read the English word and attempt to respond by giving the German word. You will find, as Thorndike suggested, that this is not an easy task. Hence, Thorndike felt that he had explained why children who have learned the alphabet from A to Z find it virtually impossible to repeat it backward. If you don't believe him, try it yourself! Or try repeating the Pledge of Allegiance backward.

The cognitive gestaltists, however, believe that we learn not just on the basis of an S-R sequence, but, instead, as a result of forming a new whole that has an underlying coherence and meaning. Thus, Wertheimer believed that instead of learning unidirectional relationships between items, we learn on the basis of whole units.

How might Wertheimer explain why we are apparently able to learn the German-English sequence in only one direction at a time, or why we have great difficulty repeating the alphabet backward?

Exercise C

As we have seen, Wertheimer argued that a child who knows how to find the area of a rectangle by multiplying its base by its altitude may have great trouble trying to apply that type B solution when a parallelogram is substituted for the rectangle. Wertheimer felt that the child who used a type A solution, however, could easily solve the problem by creatively snipping off the triangular ends of the parallelogram and then attaching these leftovers in such a way as to recreate the rectangle (see Figure 8.1).

How might Thorndike show that his theory of

learning is still needed in explaining how a child might attain the numerical solution to the parallelogram problem? How might Wertheimer reply?

Exercise D

Ebbinghaus, the father of the experimental study of learning, produced evidence that indicated how quickly we forget what we've just learned. To some, the Ebbinghaus data have been used to suggest that learned material is extremely fragile, so fragile—in fact, that much of what a child learns in school will largely disappear soon afterward.

Let's use the Ebbinghaus approach to gain a more focused view of this seeming dilemma.

Take the following list of nonsense syllables and try to commit them to memory: *mum, wen, sed, hom, dod, hur, wuz, fon, cam, tel, sik, pam, und*. Once you feel you have it, wait about an hour (without using the time to rehearse) and then see how many of the 13 syllables you can recall. Write the number down. If you're like most people, your recall even after as short a time as one hour will be severely limited.

Now let's rearrange the list of syllables and present them as follows: *pam, cam, hom, wen, hur, mum, tel, fon, und, sed, dod, wuz, sik*. Next, read the following sentence: "Pam came home when her mom telephoned and said dad was sick." Rehearse the sentence for a few minutes and try again to list all 13 syllables. You should discover that your recall has dramatically increased. Wait an hour, and try again. Write down the number of syllables you correctly remembered, and compare this with the number you had previously written down.

Why has the rearrangement of the syllables and the accompanying sentence aided you in preserving the content of the list?

Model Answers

Exercise A   (1) Nature, (2) nurture, (3) nature, (4) nurture, (5) both nature and nurture.

Notice that in order to answer the items correctly you needed an underlying understanding of the differences between the behaviorist-associationists and the cognitive-gestaltists. However, you also needed a background of facts in order to determine which psychologist represented which view. In this case, as in most learning situations, the background of facts and the deeper understanding form a reciprocal relationship. You need some facts to reach understanding and, with understanding, the facts themselves become more organized and easier to recall.

Exercise B   Wertheimer and other cognitive-gestaltists might suggest that these tasks were rigged in order to validate answers that the behaviorist-associationist had already deduced. For example, it is of course easier to produce the English word as a response to the German word. The English word is already an integral part of your working response repertoire. It is always easier to produce a verbal response you already possess than one that is not in your vocabulary. Also, the alphabet has no coherent unity to begin with. There is no opportunity in such a task to utilize the principles of understanding or insight. The alphabet has no more internal coherence than would be found in a list of digits drawn from a random number table.

Exercise C   Thorndike might argue that no matter how creatively you cut up the parallelogram, if you didn't possess the ability to multiply, learned largely through associative conditioning, you would have great difficulty applying the creative solution in such a way as to correctly calculate the area. Wertheimer would then add that even if learning to multiply was originally based on type B conditioning, the number facts inherent in multiplication will become far more meaningful, and thus easier to recall, when they are used in producing type A solutions.

Exercise D   The rearrangement of the list to conform to the sequence of words in the sentence increased your ability both to commit the syllables to memory and to retain them for future use. Thus, although the Ebbinghaus forgetting curve may be valid for nonsense syllables that remain nonsensical, once the syllables are given even the slightest hint of meaning, the learning becomes far more long-lasting. As a teacher you should remember this lesson well. Presenting facts (names, dates, mathematical operations, etc.) in the absence of any underlying schema or theme forces the pupil to operate at the level of Ebbinghaus and his nonsense syllables. The pupils may seem to learn the material, but sometime in the near future—the next hour, the next day—the learning will be gone. If, however, you can weave these facts into an overall unified structure, a structure that allows the pupil to reach some degree of understanding (the more the better), the material may become truly consolidated into a coherent whole that could possibly last a lifetime.

REFERENCES

Alper, J. (1986, July–August), Our dual memory. *Science, 86,* 44–49.

Dempster, F. N. (1987). Effects of variable encoding and spaced presentation on vocabulary learning. *Journal of Educational Psychology, 22,* 1–21.

Domjan, M. (1987). Animal learning comes of age. *American Psychologist, 42,* 556–564.

Ebbinghaus, H. (1913; originally 1885). *Memory: A contribution to experimental psychology,* trans. H. A. Ruger & C. E. Bussenius. New York: Teachers College.

Guthrie, E. R. (1935). *The psychology of learning.* New York: Harper.

Hill, W. F. (1971). *Learning: A survey of psychological interpretations* (p. 129). Scranton, PA.: Chandler.

James, W. (1890). *The principles of psychology.* New York: Henry Holt.

Ley, R. (1990). *A whisper of espionage.* Garden City Park, NY: Avery.

Pavlov, I. P. (1927). *Conditioned reflexes.* London: Oxford University Press.

Thorndike, E. L. (1898). Animal intelligence. *Psychological Review, Monograph Supplement,* 2(8).

Tolman, E. C. (1948). Cognitive maps in rats and men. *Psychological Review, 55,* 1–4.

Watson, J. B. (1913). Psychology as the behaviorist views it. *Psychological Review, 20,* 158–177.

Wertheimer, M. (1945). *Productive thinking.* New York: Harper.

Wundt, W. (1910). *Physiological psychology* (5th ed.). New York: Macmillan.

Now that we have had a look at some of the positions learning theorists have taken over the years, you may be questioning whether there is anything in all these theories for you, the future classroom teacher. If the study of learning has generated so many different and often conflicting explanations, how can the prospective teacher begin to understand the learning process, let alone stand up in front of a roomful of children and help them learn? Is the study of learning really as complicated as the controversies that we have outlined seem to indicate?

Part of the reason that there are so many theoretical positions is that learning means so many different things to so many different people: a child memorizing a poem, a rat finding its way through a maze, a baby trying to imitate an adult saying bye-bye, a consumer choosing one brand of toothpaste over another, a teenage boy fearing and thus avoiding all contact sports, a young geometry student suddenly seeing the solution to a difficult problem, and on and on. Almost all our thoughts and behavior have been learned. Learning may be adaptive or maladaptive, conscious or unconscious, overt or covert. Feelings and attitudes are learned just as certainly as facts and skills. Learning means so many different things that controversies sometimes result merely because different theorists are studying different aspects of learning. Like the blind men feeling the elephant, each theorist describes only that part with which he or she happens to come in contact. And yet, our present knowledge of learning is neither so incomplete nor so complicated that the classroom teacher can't profit from it. There are scientific principles of learning that can be translated into classroom use in order to make learning more efficient and productive.

In this chapter the spotlight falls on two important theorists, B. F. Skinner and Jerome Bruner. Each has a dramatically different philosophical lineage: Skinner, until his death in 1990, was still the most important behaviorist-associationist, and Bruner has been considered the most influential cognitive-gestaltist. In fact, it was Bruner's foresight, back in 1960 when he established the Center for Cognitive Studies, that set the stage for the important new work in learning called *information processing*. Also, both Skinner and Bruner have had a great deal to say to the practicing classroom teacher.

Part of the problem in the past was that some learning theorists were of virtually no help to the educator. It may have been glorious to contemplate the elegance of Clark Hull's "oscillation of reaction potential" or Kenneth Spence's paper on the transposi-

BURRHUS FREDERICK SKINNER

B. F. Skinner was born in Pennsylvania in 1904; his father was a lawyer. Young Skinner attended the local schools, graduating from high school in 1922. He was a quiet child, and was known for not having much to say. He then went to Hamilton College in New York, where he majored in English. During his senior year he sent some poetry he had written to Robert Frost for comment and evaluation. Frost's response was so flattering that, following college graduation, Skinner took time out to do what he felt would be some serious writing. He was not pleased with the result. Said Skinner of this experience, "I discovered the unhappy fact that I had nothing to say, and so I went on to do graduate study in psychology, hoping to remedy that shortcoming." And remedy it he apparently did, for Skinner was not at a loss for something to say for the rest of his life.

Skinner showed an early interest in utopian societies. He had been born only a short distance from where Joseph Smith had written the *Book of Mormon*, and as a young man he had read *Walden Pond*, Thoreau's classic about getting away from the world as it is and creating a world of one's own.

In 1928 Skinner entered Harvard, where he found himself attracted to the ideas of John B. Watson. Watson, though not at Harvard himself, was very influential in American psychology at that time. Skinner pursued a degree in experimental psychology and received his Ph.D. in 1931. He remained at Harvard under various research fellowships until the fall of 1936. At that time he joined the faculty at the University of Minnesota, where he stayed until after World War II. During the war Skinner participated in an extremely provocative government research project, the results of which were not made public until 1959. He had been conditioning pigeons to pilot missiles and torpedoes. The pigeons were so highly trained that he said they could guide a missile right down into the smokestack of a naval destroyer.

In 1945 Skinner went to the University of Indiana as chairman of the psychology department, a job he held until 1948. During this time he developed the now-famous "air crib," a soundproof, air-conditioned, germ-free, glass-enclosed box for raising children in a scientifically controlled environment. One of his daughters, Deborah, spent much of her first two years in an air crib. Skinner later attempted to market the box as the "Heir Conditioner," but the device was not widely acclaimed by the mothers of America. Skinner's grandiose plans for mass-producing the box were quietly dropped. Deborah was also toilet trained by another of Skinner's contraptions—a music box that was placed inside the toilet and played the "Blue Danube" whenever it got wet.

In 1948 Skinner was appointed to the faculty at Harvard, and from his command post in Cambridge he influenced a whole generation of students in the experimental study of learning. In order to study learning among rats and pigeons, he developed the experimental chamber, or as it is now affectionately called, the "Skinner box." This device has enabled American psychologists to study animal responses with a precision and ease never before possible. While the animal is in the chamber, its every movement can be recorded and made ready for analysis by automated equipment.

tion controversy, but neither offered practical advice to the teacher trying to find out why Johnny couldn't read.

This chapter focuses on the theories of Skinner and Bruner. Another important theoretical model of learning, information processing, will be covered in Chapter 11.

B. F. SKINNER AND RESPONSE ANALYSIS

No other psychologist ever dominated American behaviorism to the extent that B. F. Skinner still does today. John B. Watson maintained that behaviors are the data of psychology, and thought that responses,

After visiting his daughter's arithmetic class in elementary school, Skinner became extremely interested in educational psychology. He says of that visit that he had been witness to "minds being destroyed."[a] He felt that human beings should be trained in much the same fashion as the rats and pigeons in his lab. Children, too, could be conditioned, step by step, each correct response followed by reinforcement, until they acquired complex forms of behavior. He developed and tested his first "teaching machine" in the 1950s and as a result has been credited with creating a revolution in the technology of education. Many teachers saw the teaching machine, or programmed instruction, as a threat to their jobs. Skinner took great pains to assure teachers that programmed instruction is a learning aid, not a substitute teacher. He also assured educators that the children trained with this device would not become mechanized little robots but instead would be more likely to reach their intellectual potential.

Skinner's division of the learning process into operant responses and reinforcing stimuli also led to the development of behavior modification techniques in the classroom. Under this system, teachers are trained to wait for their students to emit appropriate responses and then to reinforce these responses speedily and consistently. Behavior

modification is the second revolution in teaching technology attributed to Skinner.

Skinner was a most prolific researcher and writer. His best-known works are *The Behavior of Organisms* (1938); *Walden Two*, a novel about a utopian society in which everyone's behavior is shaped according to conditioning principles (1948); *Science and Human Behavior* (1953); *Verbal Behavior* (1957); *Schedules of Reinforcement* (1957); *The Technology of Teaching* (1968); and *Beyond Freedom and Dignity* (1971). Skinner also wrote a lively autobiography, *Particulars of My Life* (1976), followed (1979) by a second autobiographical account, *The Shaping of a Behaviorist.*

Skinner is now recognized as having been America's most important and honored behaviorist psychologist. Skinner died in August 1990, only days after having addressed the American Psychological Association's national convention in Boston. He may have been a quiet child, coming in like the proverbial lamb, but at age 86 he went out like a lion. During this final address, he scathingly derided psychology's new emphasis on cognitive psychology:

So far as I am concerned, cognitive science is the *creationism of psychology*. It is an effort to reinstate that inner initiating-originating-creative

self or mind which, in a scientific analysis, simply does not exist . . . this association [the APA] has been through a recent trial just because of this difference. It has . . . suffered a secession by cognitive psychologists who are unhappy when they associate with so many practitioners . . . I would regard it not as a secession, *but as an improvement* . . . it is time for psychology as a profession and as a science to realize that the science which will be most helpful is not cognitive science searching for the inner mind or self, but selection by consequences represented by behavioral analysis.[b]

On August 10, 1990, in a final tribute, the APA presented Skinner with a citation for his outstanding lifetime contribution to psychology. And shortly after Skinner's death, the president of the APA called Skinner "the greatest contemporary psychologist . . . whose contributions helped shape modern psychology and who continued decade after decade to refine and develop his powerful concepts."[c]

---

[a] Skinner, B. F. , Why Teachers Fail, Lecture to Philosophy of Education Society, New York, 1965 (also appeared in *Saturday Review* October 16, 1965). p. 164.
[b] *APA Monitor* (1990), 21, 6.
[c] Fowler, R. D. (1990). In memoriam. *American Psychologist, 45,* 1203.

---

not conscious experiences, should be studied and analyzed. Skinner wholeheartedly agreed, and in 1938, with the publication of *The Behavior of Organisms*, he outlined a system of response analysis that was far more thorough and detailed than anything ever seen before. Although behaviorists were already preoccupied with response analysis up through the mid-

1930s, Skinner's arrival changed this preoccupation to a near obsession. To the Skinnerians, every little squiggle on the cumulative recorder may be fraught with profound significance.

Skinner's work is not concerned with what goes on inside the organism, the organism's motivational or emotional state, or even its neurology. Skinner's psychology is an "empty organism" psychology, a psychology of environmental conditions (stimuli) associating with and affecting the organism's response repertoire.

To Skinner, the mind (or, indeed, any internal factor) is irrelevant to an understanding of why people behave as they do. Skinner's philosophical lineage, back through Watson, Thorndike, and the other early associationists, is clear and direct. He views *learning* as an association between stimuli (S) and responses (R), though not always in that order. He emphasizes R-S associations as much as S-R associations; that is, he has found that conditioning takes place when a response is followed by a reinforcing stimulus.

Skinnerian psychology is based on a totally environmental view of behavior. Since the consequences of a response influence further action and since these consequences occur in the outer environment, it is the environment that causes changes in behavior. All that a person does or can do in the future is a direct result of that person's own unique history of reinforcements and punishments.

Throughout our discussion of Skinner's system, we focus on the conditioning of rats and pigeons. Although his data were derived primarily from work with these animals, Skinner's findings are, nonetheless, relevant to education. Many of his results have also been found valid when classroom children became the experimental subjects. A fairly thorough knowledge of Skinner is essential to the classroom teacher, for as we shall see later, Skinner believes that his techniques do work in the classroom just as surely as in the aseptic confines of the Skinner box.

Reinforcement

Skinner picked up the behaviorist-associationist tradition about where Thorndike left off. You may recall that one of Thorndike's three major laws of learning was the law of effect, which stated that learning is an association between a stimulus and a response as a result of the *consequences* of an act. If the S-R sequence is followed by a satisfying state of affairs, the association is strengthened; that is, learning takes place.

Skinner borrowed the law of effect, streamlined it somewhat, and called it **reinforcement.** Thorndike had spent considerable time defending his law of effect against the charge that it was subjective and mentalistic (a charge leveled by behaviorists who were even more tough-minded than Thorndike). Skinner's concept of reinforcement needs no such defense. He totally stripped his concept of any subjective or mentalistic overtones. Reinforcement neither offers a reward nor creates a feeling of satisfaction in the learner. Reinforcement, like all Skinner's concepts, is defined strictly in operational terms, that is, in terms of the way it is observed or measured. Thus, a **positive reinforcement** is any stimulus that, when added to the situation, increases the likelihood that the response will occur. Similarly, a **negative reinforcement** is any stimulus that, when removed from the situation, increases the probability that the response will occur. That is all there is to it. There is no mention of subjective feelings, only a description of observed events. If a pellet of food is a positive reinforcer to a hungry rat, it is only because the rat pressed a lever to get another pellet. Reinforcement is defined as something that is observed to increase the likelihood that a response will recur. Skinner is no hedonist basing his concepts on the search for pleasure but an objectivist defining his concepts in operational terms.

Skinner insists that reinforcement *always* strengthens learning, whether the reinforcement is positive or negative. The response rate always increases following a reinforcing stimulus; otherwise it is simply not considered a reinforcer. Think of positive reinforcement in terms of a plus sign (+), that is, a stimulus that is "added" to the situation, like adding a pellet of food when the lever is pressed. Think of a negative reinforcer in terms of a minus sign (−), that is, a stimulus that is "subtracted" from the situation, like turning off (subtracting) an electric shock when the lever is pressed.

Responses: Two Types

Skinner, like the earlier behaviorists, based his system on the observation of overt responses. He divided all responses into two categories: respondents and operants. Respondents are those responses that can be automatically triggered by a specific unlearned or unconditioned stimulus; Pavlov called them *reflexes.* Pavlov and, later, Watson based a whole system of learning on the fact that reflexes can be conditioned. Skinner accepted the fact that **respondents** (his name for reflexes) can be conditioned in precisely the manner Pavlov described, but he didn't consider respondent conditioning to be nearly as important as Pavlov and Watson had. The reason is that many living organisms have very few respondents. To generalize the laws of classical conditioning to the whole range of human behavior is to carelessly overwork a fairly restricted formula. As Skinner pointed out, a human being is far more than a mere jack-in-the-box with a list of tricks to be elicited by pressing the correct buttons. The bulk of an individual's response repertoire takes another form.

All those responses that cannot be classified as respondents are known as **operants.** An operant is a response that occurs spontaneously, without having to be triggered by an unconditioned stimulus. For example, when you stretch your legs, raise your hand, or shift in your seat, there are no known unconditioned stimuli that automatically force those responses.

An operant is therefore a response for which the original stimulus is either unidentified or nonexistent; it may be loosely thought of as voluntary behavior. The consequences of operant behavior, however, can be observed, even though the stimulus is not known. In operant conditioning, reinforcement is contingent on the operant's first being emitted. Thus, the organism must "operate" on the environment in order for the reinforcement to follow. Before Skinner came along, psychologists called operant responding "instrumental responding." Skinner strongly believed that most human behavior is of the operant type.

Some responses we first think are respondents turn out not to be when they are subjected to further analysis. For example, putting your foot on the brake pedal to the stimulus of a red traffic light is not a reflex. You had to learn the significance of a red traffic light. You didn't come into the world already equipped to press your foot down automatically at the sight of a red light. This response is an example of a conditioned operant.

Operant Conditioning

The best way to understand operant conditioning is to examine the experimental situation Skinner used so successfully over the years. Figure 9.1 is an illustration of what has become known as the "Skinner box," a term Skinner himself carefully avoided; Skinner always referred to it as the "experimental chamber" (Wiener, 1996). It is a small box, the sides and top of which are made of clear plastic. A lever protrudes from one side, and there is a tube that empties into the food cup next to the lever. The experimenter decides which operant to condition; in this case it will be pressing the lever. The experimenter then simply waits while the rat explores the cage. Since there aren't that many things to do in a Skinner box, the rat eventually presses the lever. A pellet of food (a reinforcing stimulus) immediately drops down the tube into the food cup. The rat pounces on the food, and conditioning has begun. When the rat chances to press the food-producing lever, the response is not a reflex action triggered by a particular unconditioned stimulus. Skinner said that operants are emitted by the organism, whereas reflexes or respondents are elicited by unconditioned stimuli.

Thus, the sequence of events for **operant conditioning** is as follows.

1. The emitting of the free operant (the rat chancing to press the lever) followed by

FIGURE 9.1 The experimental chamber, often called the Skinner box.

2. The presentation of a reinforcing stimulus (the rat is given a pellet of food) followed by

3. An increase in the probability that the response will occur again

The response is now becoming controlled, or predictable. Note that the events must follow in the order specified above. The food must come after the response is emitted. How long after? The sooner the better. For optimum conditioning, the reinforcement should immediately follow the response. This is an important Skinnerian principle. Skinner believed that in the classroom the student should be reinforced as soon as the appropriate response is emitted.

Unlike the case of reflex or **respondent conditioning,** the experimenter cannot force the response to occur. The experimenter may have to wait a while until the rat chances on the lever and emits the appropriate operant. Pavlov had no such wait, for he could automatically trigger the desired response (salivation) by simply presenting the unconditioned stimulus (meat powder).

In operant conditioning, although the experimenter might have to wait as long as 15 or 20 minutes before the rat presses the lever for the first time, after a few reinforced responses the rat begins pressing ever more frequently. It is not unusual to see a conditioned animal pressing the lever 300 to 400 times in the space of one hour. With a highly conditioned rat, the sound of lever-pressing emanating from the Skinner box is reminiscent of the sound of a high-speed typist.

We may now state Skinner's general principle: If the occurrence of the operant is followed by a reinforcing stimulus, the rate of responding, for that particular operant, will increase.

Remember that the free operant originally had no connection with a stimulus. In operant conditioning, the response produces the reinforcing stimulus, or, in Skinner's terms, the reinforcement is contingent upon the occurrence of the response. In this case, then, a response-stimulus connection is formed, not a stimulus-response connection.

We have said a number of times that as conditioning proceeds, the rate of responding increases. Increases over what? The rate increases over what is known as the **operant level,** or the frequency with which the response typically occurs in the untrained animal. For conditioning to take place, a response must occur before it can be reinforced. The experimenter must therefore select a response that the animal is apt to make on its own, such as rising on its hind legs, stretching its neck, or, more commonly, pressing a lever. When first placed in the experimental chamber, the naive rat may happen to press the

lever three or four times in the course of an hour, even though the lever is not producing any food. That is, the animal will occasionally press the lever even without positive reinforcement. The operant level is, therefore, the rate at which the free operant is typically emitted prior to conditioning.

Extinction

Extinction may be loosely thought of as a kind of forgetting process. Consider the animal that has been conditioned to the point that it is pressing the lever 400 times per hour. Similarly, the response may be extinguished, or the animal *deconditioned* to the point that it will press the lever only 3 or 4 times per hour. The technique is simple: Allow the conditioned response to occur, but do not reinforce it. With the Skinner box, this means that pressing the bar no longer produces a food pellet. After enough nonreinforced lever presses, the animal "gives up," and the rate of response returns to its preconditioned, or operant, level.

Extinction requires that the animal emit the response and that the response not be reinforced. If the animal were somehow prevented from making the response, extinction would not occur. For example, if a conditioned animal were removed from the Skinner box and returned to its home cage, where there was no lever to press, the animal would retain the conditioning. If the animal were returned to the Skinner box, even a year later, lever-pressing would be resumed.

The first time a conditioned animal's response is extinguished, **spontaneous recovery** of the response will occur. This requires time, though sometimes as little as an hour. If the animal whose behavior has been extinguished is taken out of the Skinner box for an hour or so and then returned to it, lever-pressing will resume, even though no new training has taken place. These spontaneously recovered responses will extinguish more quickly, however, than did the original extinction. Several extinction-spontaneous recovery sequences may be necessary before extinction is complete, that is, the animal remains at the operant level with no further evidence of spontaneous recovery.

Discrimination

Although in its original state the free operant is not attached to a stimulus, it may become so through training. This technique is called **discrimination training,** and the operant that has become associated with the stimulus is called a *discriminated operant.*

Discrimination training is accomplished in the following manner: We introduce a new stimulus to an animal that has been conditioned to press the lever, such as a light that we turn off and on in a random sequence. We now reinforce the animal only for pressing the lever when the light is on. Since any lever-pressing that takes place when the light is off is not reinforced, the response is extinguished as far as periods of no light are concerned. The animal emits the response only when the light is on; that is, the operant has become attached to the stimulus "light on." At this point the operant is no longer free, but is firmly controlled by the stimulus.

Technically, the stimulus for which responding is reinforced is called the *discriminated stimulus*, or the S^D—in this case "light on." The stimulus for which responding is extinguished is called the stimulus delta, or the S^Δ—in this case, "light off." A response to the discriminated stimulus (pressing the lever) is followed by reinforcement (food pellets). The following sequence of events is crucial to the development of discrimination: (1) stimulus, (2) response, and (3) reinforcement.

The same techniques used to teach the rat to respond differentially to the S^D and S^Δ can also be applied to humans in a variety of situations, including remediation programs. For example, in one study of severely dyslexic male children, all of whom had been (among other problems) confusing *d*'s with *b*'s and *p*'s with *q*'s, Stan Deno was able to eliminate all the children's identification errors by using a combination of reinforcement and extinction procedures (Deno & Chiang, 1979).

Teachers who decide to use discrimination techniques, however, must be aware that the children should not be reinforced only for the correct response, since children also have to know when and why their responses are incorrect. The most effective feedback strategy involves not only praising the child for the right answer, but also providing information to the child when the answer is wrong (Getsie, 1985). Also, more important than the amount of reinforcement is the way the reinforcers are delivered. The use of praise in the classroom is most effective when it is (1) contingent on the behavior to be strengthened, (2) specific to behaviors the child can understand, and (3) believable to the child (Nafpaktitis et al., 1985). Verbal praise, for example, is hardly believable if it is being contradicted by the teacher's tone or general body language. This is especially true when using conditioning techniques to improve disruptive behavior in social situations. Even such human activities as cooperation and social facilitation have been explained as examples of operant conditioning (Guerin, 1994), and problems as diverse as obsessive-compulsive disorders and poor penmanship have been treated with Skinnerian behavioral therapies (Steketee, 1993).

Stimulus Generalization

Once discrimination training has been completed—that is, once the animal has attached an operant to a certain stimulus—the stimulus may become generalized. **Stimulus generalization** has occurred when other stimuli similar to the one used in training take on the power to produce the response. If the animal has been trained to respond to a bright light, through generalization it may also respond to a dim light, even though the dim light was never used in training. Or perhaps a buzzer was used as the stimulus; through generalization, the animal may also be found to respond to a clicking sound or even a bell.

When generalization is noted, further discrimination training may be used to train the animal to respond only to a fairly specific stimulus magnitude. For example, if the original discrimination training used "light on" as the S^D and "light off" as the S^Δ, the animal will eventually respond only when the light is on. However, because of generalization, responses will occur at many different light intensities. Perhaps the original S^D was a fairly bright light, but because of generalization the animal also responds to a dim light. We may now "correct" for this generalization by a new discrimination series in which the bright light is the S^D and the dim light is the S^Δ. That is, we continue reinforcing responses to the bright light, while extinguishing responses to the dim light. This procedure allows the experimenter to determine the animal's capacity for distinguishing between rather subtle stimulus differences. For example, we can probe such questions as how small a difference in light intensity the animal is capable of identifying. Experiments have even been carried out in which the S^Δ was a card printed with the words "Don't Press," and the S^D a card with the word "Press." The experimental animal, in this case a pigeon, then displays the seemingly uncanny ability to "read" by rushing over to the lever and pecking whenever the "Press" card is shown. The pigeon reacts on cue, much in the way that a studio audience on a TV show frantically claps when the "Applause" sign is presented. As one TV narrator said in describing such an experiment, "It gives new meaning to the term *birdbrain*." And if training birds to discriminate between written letters seems amazing, listen to this. At Reed College, Dr. Allen Neuringer, noting that pigeons have extremely sharp acuity for sounds, trained them to differentiate between musical selections from Bach and Stravinski. The birds accomplished this with ease. Then the pigeons were exposed to music by five other composers, which they had to classify as sounding like either Bach or Stravinski. Neuringer says that of the five composers used, the birds correctly categorized all but one. They incorrectly grouped Vivaldi with Stravinski (*New York Times,* 1991). On further reflection, maybe the birds had that one right too.

Conditioned Reinforcement

A stimulus that is not originally reinforcing may take on reinforcing power through repeated presentation with one that is. For example, if lever-pressing produces both a light and a food pellet, the light, by association with the food, will take on the power of reinforcement. The sequence of events for establishing **conditioned reinforcement** is (1) response; (2) neutral stimulus, such as a light or buzzer; followed by (3) the primary or unconditioned reinforcement. It is important that this order of events be followed, for if the neutral stimulus is presented before rather than after the response, discrimination, and not conditioned reinforcement, will result. If a light is presented before the response has been emitted, the light will become an S^D, whereas if it follows the response, it becomes a conditioned reinforcer. In a sense, discrimination training teaches the rat to respond to the light, whereas conditioned reinforcement teaches the rat to respond *for,* or in order to get, the light.

Schedules of reinforcement   The way in which the reinforcers are arranged determines in large measure the strength of the resulting conditioning. Responses that are reinforced periodically, rather than each time they are emitted, tend to be conditioned more strongly and are thus more difficult to extinguish. Though there are many variations on the major themes, Skinner has identified five major schedules of reinforcement:

1. *Continuous reinforcement (Crf):*   As the name implies, the Crf schedule provides for reinforcement each time the operant is emitted. For example, a rat in a Skinner box will receive a pellet of food every time the lever is pressed.

2. *Fixed ratio (F.R.):*   Under the F.R. schedule the reinforcement occurs only after a fixed number of operants have been emitted. For example, on an

Although the teacher may sometimes use primary reinforcers such as candy, conditioned reinforcers such as good grades, promotions, prizes, and teacher approval are usually more appropriate.

F.R. schedule of 3:1, the rat in a Skinner box must press the lever three times in order to get one pellet of food. Skinner has demonstrated that the ratio can go as high as 196:1 and still maintain the conditioning.

3. *Fixed interval (F.I.):* Instead of being based on the number of responses being emitted, the F.I. schedule is keyed to a fixed *time* interval. That is, a given period of time must elapse, regardless of what the organism is doing, before the reinforcement is presented. For example, on an F.I. schedule of 30 seconds, 30 seconds must be allowed to elapse before the organism's next response will be reinforced.

4. *Variable ratio (V.R.):* Like the F.R., the V.R. schedule is based on the number of responses being emitted. Under the V.R. schedule, however, the ratio is constantly being varied so that the organism never knows which response will be reinforced. The rat might be reinforced after 5 responses, then after 15 responses, then after the very next response, and so on.

5. *Variable interval (V.I.):* On this schedule the time periods, rather than the number of responses, are varied. The rat may have to wait thirty seconds, then 5 seconds, then 50 seconds, and so on before pressing of the lever will deliver the reinforcement.

Analysis of the reinforcement schedules Each of the reinforcement schedules creates differences in the way the resulting conditioning is exhibited. The Crf schedule, though extremely useful for the acquiring of new behavior, does not result in a great deal of perseverance. Extinction can occur rather rapidly when a response has been conditioned on the continuous schedule. Parents in the United States may be guilty of using too much reinforcement in bringing up their children, and consequently nurture such qualities as a lack of perseverance, low frustration tolerance, impulsiveness, impatience, and a generally low level of ego strength.

Children at home, or rats in the Skinner box, tend to give up easily (have a low resistance to extinction) when the reinforcers are continuous. This is especially true in a highly industrialized nation in which continuous reinforcement is built into the society. Coke machines, television sets, automobiles, and many other devices yield rewards quickly and consistently for a minimum of effort. Indulgent parents, who readily provide their children the means for making life easy and convenient, should not be surprised to find that their children lack some of the

old-fashioned traits that the parents were taught to admire in their early lives (Carpenter, 1974, p. 28).

The other schedules, F.R., F.I., V.R., and V.I., are all of the intermittent type: They require that the organism learn to wait out the hard times. Responses conditioned in this way become highly resistant to extinction. Intermittent reinforcement does condition perseverance and perhaps hope.

Life outside the Skinner box creates many conditions that are analogous to the various intermittent schedules. For example, factory workers or farm laborers who are paid on a piecework basis are being conditioned on an F.R. schedule. In piecework one's pay is based on a set number of items produced or, in the case of produce, picked. Workers who are paid by the hour or by the week illustrate the F.I. schedule. An example of the V.R. schedule might be a door-to-door encyclopedia salesperson who is paid on a commission basis. The salesperson knows that he or she must emit a number of responses but never knows which response is going to lead to a payoff. Slot machines and other forms of gambling are set up on a V.R. basis. Because the V.R. schedule creates responses that are highly resistant to extinction, people can often become addicted to gambling. This helps explain why the gambler can persevere through long, dry spells and still go back to the game. The V.I. schedule also creates strongly conditioned responses that are maintained at a rapid rate and are highly resistant to extinction.

In one example of the V.I. schedule, a person fishing watches a bobber float on the water. At varying time intervals, however, the bobber disappears below the surface, sometimes, alas, just because of the pull of tide or current, but, happily, at other times because a fish has grabbed the hook. The person fishing remains encouraged and hopeful as a result of this variable payoff.

The variable schedules are typical of most social situations. Human interaction is characterized by inconsistent reinforcement, and the result is a repertoire of responses that may become almost extinction-proof. Habit, as William James has told us, that great flywheel of society, keeps people doing the same things over and over again, even when the habits are self-destructive.

THE ENGINEERING OF SOCIETY

Skinner suggests that through the judicious use of reinforcement schedules, a society free of war, crime, poverty, and pollution could be behaviorally engineered. The individuals in the society could be shaped to reflect the best of human traits: honesty, al-

Even though Skinner's data came primarily from working with rats and pigeons, he thought the results could be applied to humans.

truism, ambition, and so on. It was Skinner's conviction that this not only could be but should be done. A culture should be designed in which the behavior of the individuals is systematically controlled. As Skinner has said, "A refusal to use the knowledge we have could mean the difference between the survival and the destruction of our civilization or even the species" (Skinner, 1978).

Skinner felt that a democratic society cannot provide true justice because it must ignore minority opinion. A society should be planned and managed by someone who is interested in the good of all. Skinner does not seem overly concerned about who will decide which behaviors are to be reinforced and which are to be extinguished.

> The relation between the controller and the controlled is reciprocal. The scientist in the laboratory, studying the behavior of a pigeon, designs contingencies and observes their effects. His apparatus exerts a conspicuous control on the pigeon, but we must not overlook the control exerted by the pigeon. The behavior of the pigeon has determined the design of the apparatus and the procedures in which it is used (Skinner, 1971).

Thus, just as the scientist in the laboratory is to some extent under the control of the pigeon, so too

will the controller of a society be influenced by the members of that society. Despite Skinner's view on the apparent equality between the controller and controllee, some of you may feel you'd prefer the role of experimenter to that of pigeon.

Verbal Behavior

Skinner uses his system to explain all animal and human learning. For example, Skinner believes that learning to talk follows the principles of operant conditioning. Picture for a moment a one-and-a-half-year-old baby contentedly lying in a crib. The baby is cooing, gurgling, uttering a whole series of disconnected sounds. Suddenly, from out of the babble, and surely by accident, the baby chances on the sound *da-da*. The parents, who have been listening intently, are beside themselves with joy. They heap praise on the baby and, sure enough, the baby soon says "da-da" again.

In technical Skinnerian terms, from the entire repertoire of possible verbal operants, the baby has emitted the operant "da-da." This is immediately followed by positive reinforcement, increasing the probability that the operant will be repeated. After more "da-da" responses are followed by more reinforcements, the baby will emit the operant at a fairly

SPOTLIGHT ON THE ENVIRONMENT

The Master Controller

The heart of Skinner's message is that we are all at the mercy of environmental controls. What we do, who we are, what we become, all result from the particular set of environmental stimuli that have impinged on us and that will continue to impinge on us. We humans are yoked to our environments just as rigidly as animals are to theirs. Environment and only environment controls behavior, and whoever controls the environment controls the people. People are directed not by cherished ideals, strong emotions, or the forced will of profound ideas, but by the environment.

Humans and animals differ not because of varying complexities of perception or ideation, but only because of varying environmental complexities. Skinner spent his professional lifetime insisting that the environment and the reinforcement schedules provided by the environment are the true and only prime movers.

For Skinner, then, the one who controls the reinforcers is the one who ultimately controls behavior, and this may not be as bad as it first sounds. The Skinnerian argument is essentially that our behavior is constantly being shaped by reinforcers, regardless of whether we are aware of that fact. As Hergenhahn has said, it is not a "question of whether behavior is going to be controlled, but who or what is going to control it."[a] Parents may wish to guide their child's emerging personality by reinforcing certain behaviors they deem appropriate, or they can step aside and let society rear their children by leaving the reinforcers in the hands of peers, baby sitters, and the TV set.

[a] Hergenhahn, B. R., & Olson, M. H. (1993). *An introduction to theories of learning.* Englewood Cliffs, NJ: Prentice Hall.

---

frequent rate. Conditioning of the operant has occurred. Now, however, the parents' expectations are raised so that reinforcement no longer follows every utterance of the magic word. The parents begin teaching the baby to discriminate, so that only when the father himself is presented as the stimulus does the baby get reinforced. When the baby says "da-da" to the mother's presence, no reinforcement follows, and the response to that stimulus is extinguished. In this case the father is the S^D, the stimulus for which responding will be reinforced, and the mother is the S^Δ, the stimulus for which responding will be extinguished.

This discrimination will occur quickly, but because of stimulus generalization, the family may be in for an embarrassing moment. A few days later the postman arrives at the door with a delivery. The baby, seeing the male figure, proudly calls out "da-da." Obviously, further discrimination training is in order. When the baby says "da-da" to other male figures, reinforcement is withheld. Finally, the father is perceived as the only appropriate S^D for that operant, and the family perhaps breathes a sigh of relief.

Skinner's contention that verbal behavior is learned strictly through operant conditioning has not gone unchallenged. As we saw in Chapter 3, spe-

cialists in the field of psycholinguistics believe that language acquisition is not a mere matter of conditioning. **Noam Chomsky,** for example, sees the child as genetically prewired, born with biological givens that direct the course of language development. In this way Chomsky feels he can explain how children learn sentence structure and the complex grammatical sequencing of words—both of which he says children learn far more easily and *quickly* than the principles of operant conditioning can explain. Evidence in support of Chomsky's notion has been provided in a number of studies.

Operant Conditioning in the Classroom

Only Skinner's general approach to the problem of classroom teaching will be treated in this section. Specific techniques, such as teaching machines and the arrangement of reinforcements to promote student control, will be covered in the next chapter.

Education is the learning of certain responses that will be useful later in life. How can this best be accomplished? The teacher, says Skinner, should use the techniques that produce meaningful behavioral changes. Though the teacher may sometimes use pri-

Skinner is against aversion techniques since punishment in school always leads to attempts to escape the classroom situation.

mary reinforcers such as M&M candy, conditioned reinforcers such as good grades, promotions, prizes, and the generalized social reinforcement of approval are usually more appropriate. One of the real problems with the use of conditioned reinforcers, however, is that they are often too distant. As we have seen, operant conditioning is most effective when reinforcement is immediate. This is one of the reasons why Skinner strongly favors the use of the teaching machine. It can provide immediate reinforcement and help bridge the gap between student behavior and the most distant conditioned reinforcers such as promotion or grades. Skinner is against the use of punishment in the classroom, not because it won't control behavior—it will—but because it may produce a host of negative emotional reactions. Negative emotional reactions, conditioned through the use of punishment, may prevent further learning and even further school attendance. Punishment always leads to attempts to escape, and when children do escape from the classroom situation, formal learning in the classroom is obviously impossible.

Just what is the goal of education according to

Skinner? Skinner believes that education should maximize knowledge. This is done through operant conditioning, through building up a student's repertoire of responses. Understanding a subject, such as history, is simply the result of having learned a verbal repertoire. Skinner insists that when students can answer questions in a given area, and speak and write fluently about the area, then, by definition, they understand that area. A verbal repertoire is not a sign of knowledge—it is the knowledge. In order to teach a knowledge of biology, one must teach the specific behavior from which the knowledge is inferred. That is, in order to say that students know something, we must observe certain responses: how they speak, the diagrams they draw, the equations they can solve, and so on. These, then, are the very responses that should be trained into the students who don't display this knowledge.

Good teaching is thus the ability to arrange the proper sequence of reinforcements and to make sure that these reinforcements are contingent upon students emitting the appropriate responses.

BEHAVIORISM TODAY: THE FUNCTIONAL VIEW

Traditional behaviorism generally adhered to three underlying principles:

1. Organisms enter the world, come into any new situation, as virtual blank slates. Under the leadership of Watson, behaviorists as a group were extremely strong environmentalists. They clung to the cherished belief, previously espoused by English philosopher John Locke, that the mind was a "blank slate upon which experience writes," or "nothing in the intellect not first in the senses." And in a way they clung to this belief in a manner that probably would have made Locke blush, since Watson most certainly would have considered Locke a mentalist for having used such terms as *mind* and *intellect*. Behaviorists paid little attention to internal cognitive structures and even less, of course, to genetic predispositions.

2. There are few important differences in learning and/or conditioning styles across species. An understanding of rat and pigeon behavior could be easily extrapolated to the human condition.

3. Any response an organism is capable of producing could be linked through training with any stimulus the organism could be made aware of. Learning was seen as occurring in an automatic

fashion, and the learner was typically seen as a recipient of environmental stimuli, not a selector of stimuli.

Given these premises, it is little wonder that behaviorism had to adhere to a robot model of learning and that the twin concepts of growth and development had to play, at most, a secondary role. In large measure the behaviorists painted themselves into a corner. Because of their almost slavish insistence on these three fundamental principles, they had to overlook, or attempt to explain away, empirical data that ran counter to their position. Anomalies began to appear, and traditional behaviorism went into what Thomas Kuhn would call a "crisis" stage (Kuhn, 1970). Attempts to stem the flow soon gave way in the face of a virtual torrent of new evidence.

The Challenge Today

More recent work in conditioning is offering a strong challenge to the traditional behaviorist position. Martin Seligman, for example, has shown that responses to some stimuli are much easier to condition than responses to others. Seligman's position is that each organism comes into the world biologically prepared to be conditioned more quickly to certain environmental stimuli than to others and that this preparedness differs from species to species. Birds, for example, are conditioned easily to visual stimuli, whereas human infants are conditioned more quickly to verbal stimuli. Seligman says that the organism carries within itself "certain equipment and predispositions [which are] more or less appropriate to that situation" (Seligman, 1970).

Seligman believes, therefore, that since organisms have evolved a variety of adaptive behavior sequences over millions of years, it is unlikely that today's conditioning procedures can countermand these built-in predispositions. For example, was Watson's conditioning of little Albert really as automatic as it appeared, or was Albert already biologically prepared to learn to fear the white rat? In one study, usually overlooked by the behaviorists, Elsie Bregman at Columbia Teachers College attempted to replicate this experiment of Watson's. Her finding—an obvious anomaly for orthodox behaviorism—was that fear in a child could indeed be conditioned if the CS was a live animal, but conditioning did not take place if the CS was an inanimate object (Bregman, 1934). It is therefore highly likely that humans are born biologically prepared to suspect that live animals might do them harm and, because of that tendency, learn quickly to fear and avoid them. Selig-

man also believes that common phobias, such as the fear of snakes, enclosed places, or speaking in public, undoubtedly have biological roots in an evolutionary survival system (Seligman, 1972). Although few of us have ever actually been bitten by a snake, locked in a closet, or pelted with stones by an angry crowd, these extremely common phobias are too easily acquired to be explained on the basis of the traditional principles of conditioning.

Keller and Marian Breland have also discovered serious anomalies in the behaviorists' paradigm (1961). Using operant conditioning techniques, the Brelands trained raccoons to pick up coins and deposit them in a slot in order to receive a food reinforcer. Although the raccoons dutifully learned this routine rather easily, the conditioning soon decayed and literally drifted into a different behavioral sequence. The raccoons, despite continued reinforcement, soon began rubbing the coins together as part of an instinctive washing ritual (as though preparing to eat them). This action broke up the conditioning sequence. The Brelands called this phenomenon *instinctive drift* and stated that many of the artificial conditioning routines produced so easily in the laboratory will soon drift back toward the organism's natural behavioral repertoire.

Could it be that the behaviorists have consistently been lucky in arranging their studies in such a way that the conditioning environment just happened to meet the organism's preparedness? As we have seen, Watson was certainly lucky in choosing a live rat as a CS, since Albert would not have been conditioned nearly as easily, if at all, to a stuffed rat or a picture of a rat. Were Thorndike and Skinner also as lucky? Certainly a rat can be conditioned quickly to press a lever for food. But what if one of Thorndike's cats were substituted for one of Skinner's rats? Cats, although they can learn that pressing a lever delivers food, soon stop pressing and simply sit and wait— and the hungrier they get, the more they crouch down and wait. The difference is in the types of food-gathering techniques utilized by the two species. Rats actively seek out food in their environment, whereas cats are great ambushers that normally crouch patiently while awaiting their prey. Also, note that the lever in a Skinner box is always made of metal, not plastic or wood; nonmetallic levers would probably simply be eaten by the rats rather than pressed.

With pigeons, the typical Skinnerian arrangement is to substitute a small, lighted key *to be pecked*, rather than a lever to be pressed. High-speed photographs of this pecking response show clearly that the pigeons are, in fact, not simply pecking the key but trying to eat it (Moore, 1973).

JEROME BRUNER

Jerome Bruner was born into a successful upper-middle-class family that fully expected him to become a lawyer. Bruner, however, had other ideas. He graduated from Duke University in 1937 and then went to Harvard, where in 1941 he earned his Ph.D. degree in psychology. When Bruner first arrived at Harvard, his interest was focused on the investigation of perception in animals. Harvard had only recently (1933) created an independent department of psychology, and under its chairman, the brilliant E. G. Boring, the research emphasis was directed toward animal learning and perception. Bruner chose to study under the great Harvard researcher and physiological psychologist, Karl S. Lashley. With the outbreak of World War II, Bruner's interests shifted to social psychology, and he wrote his doctoral dissertation on the techniques of Nazi propagandists. During the war, Bruner joined the Army and worked on psychological warfare at General Eisenhower's headquarters in Europe. After the war he returned to Harvard and in 1947 published a significant paper on the great influence of needs on perception. In this study he showed that poor children are more likely to overestimate the size of coins than are well-to-do children. From this study he concluded that values and needs strongly affect human perceptions and also that people create meaning out of their perceptions by making them consistent with their past experiences. People are thus able to reduce the possibility of mental strain by viewing the world in such a way as to minimize environmental surprises. These findings led to what became known as the "new look" in perception theory and also laid the groundwork for an American school of cognitive psychology. Cognitive psychology deals with the human being's abil-

Critics of Skinnerian behaviorism have not totally disavowed behaviorism as a viable system. When the Brelands first started writing about species-specific conditions, they simply wanted the world to know that the conditioning techniques that worked with a pigeon did not necessarily work with a raccoon, and vice versa. Marian Breland (now Marian Breland Bailey) has since stated that psychologists who took the "misbehavior of organisms" as a blanket disavowal of Skinnerian behavior analysis are wrong (Bailey & Bailey, 1993). Skinnerian principles, she insists, are valid, but must be seen in the context of the instinctive differences that occur naturally among various species. Also, John Garcia points out that Skinner's lasting fame stems from his marvelously efficient operant methodology, even though he overlooked the importance of the biological basis of behavior (Garcia, 1993). Once, when showing off cumulative records generated by a rat, a pigeon, and a monkey, all working on an F. I. schedule, Skinner asked rhetorically, "Which is which?" and then answered "It does not matter" (Skinner, 1959). The Brelands, Garcia, and others, however, have responded (with data in hand) that it surely does matter, and that to ignore the dramatic genetic differences among various species is to deny an obvious reality.

A Message to Educators

What should we, as educators, derive from this evidence? Traditional behaviorism should no longer be accepted at face value. What seemed like an almost noninteractive model of conditioning should now, most assuredly, be viewed as extremely interactive. The environmental manipulations that produce conditioning interact decidedly with the particular or-ity to obtain knowledge and develop intellectually. Although the field of cognitive psychology had been important in Europe, America, under the heavy influence of the behaviorist tradition, had turned a deaf ear to anything as subjective and "unscientific" as the study of thinking. Bruner changed all that. In 1960 he established Harvard University's Center for Cognitive Studies, and although he didn't invent cognitive psychology, he certainly went a long way toward making it a respected scientific discipline. Bruner was the "Minuteman" who fired the first shot in what is now called the "cognitive revolution."

Always the empiricist, Bruner kept science's basic rule clearly in mind: Begin by observing the data from which the conclusions are to be drawn. Once, when several academic psychologists were debating the possible impact a certain film might have on children, Bruner was brought in as a consultant. After listening to this group of armchair speculators for a while, Bruner suddenly interrupted them and said, "Why not get a child, show him the film, and then we'll ask him what he thought of it."

This is also Bruner's approach to the problems of educational psychology. If you want to know how children go about the business of learning in the school situation, then study children in the classroom rather than rats and pigeons in cages. In 1962 Bruner published an extremely important book, *The Process of Education*. As Harper's magazine said, "To people starved for reasonable comments on education in intelligible English, Bruner's writings are above reproach." In this book Bruner developed three important points. First, schools should strive to teach the general nature, or structure, of a subject rather than all the details and facts of a subject. Second, any subject can be taught effectively in some intellectually honest form to any child at any stage of development. And finally, Bruner stressed the importance of intuition in learning. Intuition is a problem-solving technique whereby a child relies on insight or immediate apprehensions rather than on the planned steps of formal analysis.

Bruner's work has not gone unnoticed by his colleagues. In 1963 the American Psychological Association awarded him the Distinguished Scientific Award, and in 1965 Bruner was elected president of the American Psychological Association.

Jerome Bruner has made things happen in educational psychology. Says *Harper's*, "He is the first person to come along in years—perhaps the first since John Dewey—who can speak intelligently about education to his fellow scholars as well as to educators."

---

ganism's innate predispositions. Again, we see behavior as resulting from the interplay of heredity and environment. Conditioning should not be seen as completely automatic in its nature, nor as permanent in its result, as the behaviorists have led us to believe. Instinctive drift can override and even countermand conditioning sequences that attempt to compete with innate predispositions. Just as with the raccoons, children who have been conditioned to act in a particular way through the use of tokens or whatever may quickly "drift" out of that conditioned behavior, *especially if the situation changes.*

Conversely, we should not glibly use the instinctive drift argument to give up on changing behavior we can't seem to control. It becomes all too easy to say "This kid was born to be bad" when his or her disruptive behavior continues despite efforts to change it. We must keep in mind that whatever the genetic basis might be for a particular set of responses, the innate predisposition is still being expressed in *learned ways.*

Perhaps the most provocative of the new research is the work relating learning and conditioning to what we now know of age-related changes in capacity. No longer can we afford to smugly set forth universal laws of associative learning; we must, instead, attempt to identify the adaptive importance of particular instances of learning found at particular stages of development. The human organism is, after all, biological as well as psychological.

JEROME BRUNER AND THE PROCESS OF THOUGHT

Whereas Skinner presents a behaviorist-associationist account of learning, borrowing heavily from Watson and Thorndike, the position of **Jerome Bruner** is

Teenagers playing in a high school orchestra exemplify two motivating factors: a drive to achieve competence and a need to work with others cooperatively.

more consistent with the cognitive-gestaltist position. For example, Bruner insists that the final goal of teaching is to promote the "general understanding of the structure of a subject matter" (Bruner, 1962). When the student understands the structure of a subject, he or she sees it as a related whole. "Grasping the structure of a subject is understanding it in a way that permits many other things to be related to it meaningfully" (Bruner, 1962, p. 28). He sees children as "makers of meaning in the ordinary conduct" of their lives; that is, they shape and are shaped by their home culture (Bruner, 1990, p. 19). These are hardly the words of a behaviorist-associationist. Bruner stresses the importance in learning of forming global concepts, of building coherent generalizations, of creating cognitive gestalts. Bruner tells the teacher—and he constantly aims his message at the working classroom teacher—to help promote conditions in which

the student can perceive the structure of a given subject. When learning is based on a structure, it is longer-lasting and less easily forgotten. The student who once studied biology, for example, may forget many of the details over the years, but these details can be more easily and quickly reconstructed if the general structure is still there.

Bruner calls his position a theory of instruction, not a learning theory. He feels that a learning theory is *descriptive;* that is, it describes what happens after the fact. A theory of instruction, on the other hand, is prescriptive: it prescribes in advance how a given subject can best be taught. If a learning theory tells us that children at age six are not yet ready to understand the concept of reversibility, a theory of instruction would prescribe how best to lead the child toward this concept when he or she is old enough to understand it.

Bruner's theory has four major principles: motivation, structure, sequence, and reinforcement.

Bruner's First Principle: Motivation

Bruner's first principle, **motivation,** specifies the conditions that predispose an individual to learn. What are the critical variables, especially during the preschool years, that help motivate and enable the child to learn? Implicit in Bruner's principles is the belief that almost all children have a built-in "will to learn." However, Bruner has not discarded the notion of reinforcement. He believes that reinforcement, or external reward, may be important for initiating certain actions or for making sure they are repeated. He insists, however, that it is only through intrinsic motivation that the will to learn is sustained. Bruner is far more concerned with intrinsic motivation than with what he believes to be the more transitory effects of external motivation.

Perhaps the best example of intrinsic motivation is curiosity. Bruner believes that we come into the world equipped with a curiosity drive. He feels this drive is biologically relevant, that curiosity is necessary to the survival of the species. Bruner suggests that young children are often too curious; they are unable to "stick with" any one activity. Their curiosity leads them to turn from one activity to another in rapid succession, and the curiosity must therefore be channeled into a more powerful intellectual pursuit. Games like Twenty Questions help develop a sense of disciplined curiosity in the child.

Another motivation we bring into the world with us is the drive to achieve competence. Children become interested in what they are good at, and it is virtually impossible to motivate them to engage in activities in which they have no degree of competence.

Finally, Bruner lists reciprocity as a motivation that is built into the species. Reciprocity involves a need to work with others cooperatively, and Bruner feels that society itself developed as a result of this most basic motivation.

Bruner has been using a variant of the transactional model to describe language acquisition, which he feels depends strongly on the myriad of small but continuing interactions between mother and child. Through these interactions, the child not only learns the words but also what language is used for. A child may learn to utter a request perhaps up to a year before the request can be properly phrased as a sentence. Because of these mother-child transactions, the child who is learning language is also learning the cultural conventions that are so important to the process of socialization (Bruner, 1983).

According to Bruner, the intrinsic motivations are rewarding in themselves and are therefore self-sustaining. How can the teacher take advantage of this in the classroom situation? Bruner's answer is that teachers must facilitate and regulate their students' exploration of alternatives. Since learning and problem solving demand the exploration of alternatives, this is at the very core of the issue and is critical in creating a predisposition to the long-term pursuit of learning.

The exploration of alternatives has three phases: activation, maintenance, and direction.

Activation   In order to activate exploration, in order to get it started, children must experience a certain level of uncertainty. If the task is too easy, they will be too bored to explore alternatives; on the other hand, if it is too difficult, they will be too confused to explore alternatives. This is similar to J. McV. Hunt's problem of the match or Vygotsky's zone of proximal development, already discussed in Chapter 4. The teacher must provide students with problems that are just difficult enough for the children's intrinsic curiosity motivation to itself activate exploration.

Maintenance   Once activated, exploration must be maintained. This involves assuring children that exploration is not going to be a dangerous or painful experience. Children must view exploration under the guiding hand of the teacher as less risky, less dangerous than exploration on their own. The advantages of exploration must be made greater than the risks.

Direction   Meaningful exploration must have direction. The direction of exploration is a function of two factors: knowledge of the goal and knowledge that the exploration of alternatives is relevant to the achievement of that goal. Children must know what the goal is and how close they are to achieving it.

Thus, Bruner's first principle indicates that children have a built-in will to learn. Teachers must manage and enhance this motivation so that children will see that guided exploration is more meaningful and satisfying than the spontaneous learning they can achieve on their own. In short, Bruner's first principle is a justification for formal schooling.

Bruner's Second Principle: Structure

Bruner's second principle, structure, states that any given subject area, any body of knowledge, can be organized in some optimal fashion so that it can be

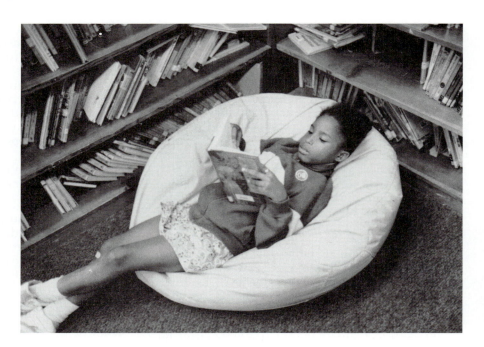

During the symbolic stage the child can translate experience into language.

transmitted to and understood by almost any student. If appropriately structured, "any idea or problem or body of knowledge can be presented in a form simple enough so that any particular learner can understand it in a recognizable form" (Bruner, 1966). This is not to say that all the nuances of Einstein's theory of relativity can be fully mastered by a six-year-old. It does mean, however, that if properly structured, Einstein's general position could be understood by the child, and that under questioning the child could convey to a physicist a recognizable account of the theory.

According to Bruner, the structure of any body of knowledge can be characterized in three ways: mode of presentation, economy, and power.

Mode of presentation   Mode of presentation refers to the technique, the method, whereby information is communicated. One of the reasons a teacher may fail to convey some fundamental point to a seemingly uncomprehending child is that the teacher's mode of presentation simply does not fit with the child's level of experience. The child will remain uncomprehending as long as the message is incomprehensible. Bruner believes that a person has three means of achieving understanding: enactive, iconic, and symbolic representation.

Enactive representation is needed for very young children, who can understand things best in terms of actions. For example, children can demonstrate their understanding of the principles of a balance beam by referring to their experiences on a seesaw. If the child on the other end is heavier, you compensate by sliding farther back on your own end; if the other child is lighter, you push yourself farther forward. Young children also define words in terms of the actions that are associated with them: A chair is to sit on, a spoon is to eat with, and so on. When children are in the enactive stage of thinking, it is important that the teacher's messages somehow make contact with their muscles. Even adults may revert to enactive representation when learning something new, especially a new motor skill. Teaching an adult to ski is best accomplished wordlessly. A skilled ski instructor doesn't just tell students to "edge into the hill" but will instead ask them to imitate her own stance. In short, when young children are in the enactive stage of thinking, the best, the most comprehensible messages are wordless ones.

Iconic representation may be used with somewhat older children. They learn to think at the iconic level when objects become conceivable without action. Children can now draw a picture of a spoon without acting out the eating process. They may even be able, at this stage, to draw a diagram of a balance beam, for they now possess an image of it

SPOTLIGHT ON THE LEARNER

Challenging through Impasses

Some theorists believe that for children to discover and learn new concepts, they must first confront an impasse, or a more difficult problem that just can't be solved in the usual way.[a] That is, if you don't constantly supply the child with new and difficult challenges, discovery learning and cognitive growth will be impeded. As we saw in Chapter 4, this is essentially the position taken by Hunt and Vygotsky. Both researchers felt that cognitive growth depends on the child's always reaching for somewhat more difficult levels of thinking and being challenged by ever-increasing stimulus complexity.

Others take the more moderate view that although impasse learning may account for many childhood discoveries, it doesn't cover them all.[b] For example, Siegler has shown that in Piaget's number conservation, young children solve problems by counting and comparing the number of objects in the two rows. Even though this approach produces consistently correct answers, older children shift away from it and base their answers on the reasoning that the act of merely spreading out or contracting a row could not possibly change the number of objects.[c] Similarly, in language acquisition, children shift from the incorrect use of verbs ("I falled down") to the correct use ("I fell down") without confronting any apparent impasse and often without any external pressure at all.[d]

---

[a] Van Lehn, K. (1988). Towards a theory of impasse driven learning. In H. Mandl & A. Lesgold (Eds.), *Learning issues for intelligent tutoring systems* (pp. 19–41). New York: Springer-Verlag.
[b] Newell, A. (1990). *Unified theories of cognition: The William James lectures.* Cambridge, MA: Harvard University Press.
[c] Siegler, R. S. & Jenkins, E. (1989). *How children discover new strategies.* Hillsdale, NJ: Erlbaum.
[d] Bowerman, M. (1987). Commentary. In B. MacWhinney (Ed.), *Mechanisms of language acquisition* (pp. 443–466). Hillsdale, NJ: Erlbaum.

---

that no longer depends on action. This is a significant breakthrough in the development of intellect, for the use of pictures or diagrams allows children at this stage to be tutored in simpler ways.

Symbolic representation can be used at the stage at which children can translate experience into language. The balance beam can be explained through the use of words rather than pictures. Symbolic representation allows children to begin making logical derivations and to think more compactly. Bruner says that through symbolic representation "powerful representations of the world of possible experiences are constructed and used as search models in problem solving" (1966, p. 14).

Which of these modes should the teacher choose in order to facilitate the learning process? It depends on the learner's age and background and on the subject matter itself. For example, Bruner believes that teaching a problem in law demands symbolic representation, whereas geography is well suited to the iconic. New motor skills are often best communicated by enactive representation, especially at first.

Mathematics can, and often should, be represented by all three modes.

Economy of presentation   Economy in communicating a body of knowledge depends on the amount of information the learner must keep in mind in order to continue learning. The fewer bits of information, the fewer facts the learner must bear in mind, the greater the economy. The best way to provide economy in teaching is to give the learner concise summaries. For example, Bruner feels that it is more economical to "summarize the American Civil War as a battle over slavery than as a struggle between an expanding industrial region and one built upon a class society for control of federal economic power" (1966, p. 46).

Power of presentation   Bruner believes that nature is simple; hence, to be powerful, a presentation of some aspect of nature should reflect nature's simplicity. Teachers often make difficult what is inherently easy. A powerful presentation is a simple presentation, one that is easily understood. It allows the learner to see new relationships, to find connections between facts that may at first seem quite separate. Bruner feels that a powerful presentation is especially important in the field of mathematics.

Bruner's Third Principle: Sequence

The extent to which a student finds it difficult to master a given subject depends largely on the sequence in which the material is presented—Bruner's third principle. Teaching involves leading the learner through a certain sequence of the various aspects of the subject. Since Bruner believes that intellectual development is innately sequential, moving from enactive through iconic to symbolic representation, he feels it is highly probable that this is also the best sequence for any subject to take. Thus, the teacher should begin teaching any new subject with wordless messages, speaking mainly to the learner's muscular responses. Then the student should be encouraged to explore the use of diagrams and various pictorial representations. Finally, the message should be communicated symbolically, through the use of words.

Bruner's Fourth Principle: Reinforcement

Bruner's fourth principle is that learning requires reinforcement. In order to achieve mastery of a problem, we must receive feedback about how we are doing. The timing of the reinforcement is crucial to success in learning. The results must be learned at the very time a student is evaluating his or her own performance. If the results are known too soon, the learner will become confused and his or her explorations will be stifled. If they are known too late, the learner may have gone beyond the point at which the knowledge would have been helpful, and by this time the child may have incorporated false information. The teacher's role is indeed sensitive. If the learner has gone on to incorporate false information, this must now be unlearned in order for the learner to get back on the right track.

Discovery Learning

Though it is possible to memorize a poem, the multiplication tables, or the state capitals, meaningful learning often requires actual discovery. The facts and relationships children discover through their own explorations are more usable and tend to be better retained than material they have merely committed to memory. Teachers can provide the conditions in which **discovery learning** is nourished and will grow. One way they can do this is to guess at answers and let the class know you are guessing. The students can then analyze the teacher's answer. This helps prove to them that exploration can be both rewarding and safe, and it is thus a valuable technique for building lifelong discovery habits in the students.

Bruner is not saying that discovery learning is the only form of learning. Nor is he saying that students must discover for themselves the solutions to every problem in a given field. That would be extremely wasteful, even if it were possible, for it would mean that each generation would have to rediscover the ideas and technology of its culture. Beginning physics students, for example, shouldn't have to discover the technology of radio transmission, as Marconi once did. Students can, however, through insightful questioning and prompting by the teacher, discover for themselves some of the basic principles that account for radio transmission. Learning through such discoveries enables the student to reach a level of understanding that far surpasses the rote memorization of a radio chapter in an electronics book.

Discovery learning is more conceptual, and studies have repeatedly shown that conceptual learning has longer-lasting consequences than nonconceptual activities. For the teacher, however, teaching ideas rather than facts is a more intellectually demanding undertaking, and it is said that these teachers should be allowed extra time to engage in reflective thought and curriculum design, both with colleagues and with outside consultants (Prawat & Floden, 1994).

The process of learning the strategies of discovery is also important in nourishing creative thinking, a mode of thinking Bruner finds crucial to the well-developed mind. Creative thinking supplies the poet, the storyteller, the innovator (who lurk within all of us) with the potential to break away from the formal rules of logic. Thinking, after all, is not just an exercise in formal logic. Thinking is nested in a person's total sphere of awareness, including beliefs, desires, expectations, emotions, and intentions. In fact, Bruner rails against some of the cognitive psychologists of the 1980s, especially those who rely solely on the computer model to explain thinking. These psychologists, Bruner tells us, actually impoverish psychology, since they emphasize only the logical mode of thinking (Bruner, 1987).

Teaching for discovery is obviously not easy. The teacher must be bright and flexible and must really know the subject matter. In order to communicate knowledge, the teacher must have mastery of that knowledge. Finally, the good teacher is a patient teacher, for discovery teaching cannot be hurried. It is often frustratingly slow, but the goal of real student understanding is well worth the wait.

A FINAL COMPARISON

At times it may seem that Skinner and Bruner are from two different worlds, that they discuss entirely different concepts. In part, this is true. Skinner's data came primarily from his work with rats and pigeons; Bruner's, from his observations of children in learning situations. Skinner is an associationist; Bruner, a cognitive theorist. Skinner is an avowed behaviorist; Bruner speculates on events occurring within the child's mind. Yet both are discussing learning, and both are talking to working teachers. Skinner speaks of the laws of conditioning, and Bruner, acknowledging that the teacher is a potent reinforcer, insists that the teacher should know these laws.

Piaget maintained that there are really two kinds of learning, P learning and LM learning. **P learning** is physical learning, learning that takes place when physical things act on us. **LM learning** is logico-mathematical learning, learning that results from our actions on things (Piaget, 1959).

Piaget's distinction is similar to the distinction between associative and cognitive learning. P learning is, in effect, conditioning, and it's the kind of learning that has been so thoroughly analyzed by Watson, Thorndike, and Skinner. P learning is externally motivated; it is made up of the properties of the physical objects that act on us (the sweetness of candy or the aversive properties of a slap on the hand) that have a potential reinforcing effect. This, of course, is precisely the way the behaviorists have described motivation in learning; and indeed this is exactly the way they should have described it, since they have been describing P learning almost exclusively. When Skinner, on the one hand, tells us that learning is the result of a given response followed by a reinforcing stimulus, he is in effect defining P learning—a physical event acting on the learner. LM learning, on the other hand, has been more the province of the cognitive-gestaltist theorists. LM learning is the result of our continuous experience of organizing and reorganizing our actions as we proceed toward the goal of understanding. Piaget says that LM learning is intrinsically motivated—that is, the discovery of a new relationship is self-rewarding. When children experience new LM relationships that they have discovered through their own actions, they feel pleasure, a joy that swells up from within.

After examining the positions of Skinner and Bruner, can we now say which one is right—which theory says it all? The answer, of course, is that both are right, though neither one is likely to have the supertheory. Skinner's laws of conditioning are certainly valid. The evidence with regard to operant conditioning overwhelmingly supports his position. Skinner has much to teach us about how to teach. He has simplified and made more efficient the learning of the informational background children need in order to think creatively. It must be remembered that P learning, though perhaps not as glamorous as LM, is crucial to intellectual growth. Skinner has given us invaluable aids for transmitting this P-learning base.

Bruner, too, has made an extremely important contribution, but at a different level. In his theory of instruction he has pointed out ways of carrying children beyond mere conditioning, or P learning. Bruner's interest is more in the area of cognitive organization, understanding, LM learning. To some extent, Bruner's theory may be more speculative than Skinner's, but exciting advances in science have often in the past been foreshadowed by sophisticated speculation. This isn't to imply that Bruner's position is not founded on an empirical base. After all, Bruner has spent long hours watching children going about the business of learning.

Now, in the 1990s, there seem finally to have occurred some elements of real compromise between the behaviorists and the more cognitively oriented theorists. In fact, an approach called *cognitive-behavior modification* has recently been gaining more and more adherents. These theorists accept much of what Skinner expounded over the years, but they utilize the Skinnerian methods within a context of cognitive reorganization. For example, instead of just having the child reinforced for emitting the appropriate operants, the child is also taught to mentally repeat phrases over and over, such as "I know I can be quiet and stay in my seat while the teacher is talking" (Meichenbaum et al., 1989). In this way, there is a stronger possibility that the external reinforcers will be linked to the child's internal cognitions.

Not all the answers are in on this complex phenomenon called learning, but Skinner and Bruner have pointed us in the direction of knowing more about what the questions are.

SUMMARY

Two major theorists in educational psychology are spotlighted in this chapter: Skinner, representing the behaviorist-associationist tradition; and Bruner, representing the cognitive-gestalt tradition. Both Skinner and Bruner discuss learning issues that are of practical importance to the classroom teacher.

Skinner based his view of learning on the data gathered from his experimental laboratories, with little in the way of any theory building or deductive interpretations. Operant conditioning occurs when a response is followed by a reinforcing stimulus. The rate of responding then increases. Skinner distinguishes between operants (responses that need no stimuli to set them off) and respondents (responses that do need unconditioned stimuli to be activated). Skinner uses the term *respondent* to describe the same kind of behavior that Pavlov had previously described during his conditioning studies on dogs—that is, Skinner's respondent is synonymous with Pavlov's reflex.

The operant conditioning system also includes such other concepts and techniques as extinction, spontaneous recovery, discrimination, stimulus generalization, and conditioned reinforcement.

Skinner also conducted research into the schedules of reinforcement—that is, the methods by which reinforcers are arranged. Responses that are reinforced periodically, on the basis of either time or the number of responses emitted, are conditioned more strongly and are thus more difficult to extinguish.

Skinner maintained that language is learned via the principles of operant conditioning. Also, such cognitive-sounding concepts as understanding and knowledge are really examples of operant conditioning. In order to gain knowledge, one must be equipped with the specific set of responses from which that knowledge may be inferred.

Good teaching, according to Skinner, is the ability to arrange the proper sequences of reinforcements for the student and then to be certain that the presentation of these reinforcers is contingent on the student's emitting the correct response.

Behaviorism today faces two important challenges, one due to internal, experimental anomalies (experimental results that are not consistent with the theory), and the other due to the rise of a more ethological and functional interpretation of behaviorism's known facts. Any theory faces a severe test when another theory can predict outcomes with more accuracy and entails fewer assumptions.

Bruner's position regarding learning is in the cognitive-gestalt tradition. His goal is to create a theory of instruction that will allow a teacher to prescribe how a given subject can best be taught.

Bruner's theory has four major principles: motivation, structure, sequence, and reinforcement. These four principles are aimed at producing a learning based on understanding and meaning, rather than on the conditioning of facts and details.

Bruner insists that meaningful learning requires the child to search actively for solutions. Such discovery learning is far longer-lasting and more useful than learning based on memorization and conditioning. Good teaching demands that the student be encouraged to explore alternatives and discover new relationships. Bruner also insists that when presented appropriately, any subject matter can be understood by almost any child.

The theories of Skinner and Bruner, though seemingly diametrically opposed, share a common framework when viewed from the position of Jean Piaget. Piaget distinguishes between P learning, learning that takes place when physical things act on us, and LM learning, learning that results from our actions on things. Skinner's position seems consistent with Piaget's P learning, while Bruner may be discussing Piaget's LM learning.

KEY TERMS AND NAMES

Jerome Bruner
  discovery learning
  enactive representation
  iconic representation
  LM (logico-mathematical) learning
  motivation
  P (physical) learning
  structure
  symbolic representation

Noam Chomsky
B. F. Skinner
  conditioned reinforcement
  discrimination training
  extinction
  negative reinforcement
  operant conditioning
  operant level
  operants

positive reinforcement
reinforcement
respondent conditioning
respondents

schedules of reinforcement
spontaneous recovery
stimulus generalization

THEORY INTO PRACTICE: LEARNING THROUGH UNDERSTANDING*

The behaviorist-associationists, Skinner, Thorndike, and Guthrie, all insist that learning results from the associations that are developed through the combining of stimuli with responses. In contrast, the cognitive-gestalt view stresses that learning should be based not on blind trial and error but instead on an overall understanding at a conceptual level. As a result, some cognitive theorists have perhaps gone too far in downgrading the learning of facts and rote memorization. Such expressions as "mere facts," which appear frequently in the cognitive literature, attest to the disdain the cognitivists feel for this type of learning. Jerome Bruner, however, though certainly a cognitive theorist, acknowledges that the memorization of facts may still provide important components to the learning process. Some facts and specifics are essential in the development of meaningful understanding. For example, it would be difficult to solve an inertia problem in the physics lab, regardless of how much "understanding" is involved, if the student doesn't yet know how to multiply fractions. Bruner calls these facts the *stuff* of learning. Without some data to process, discovery learning and concept formation are difficult indeed. However, Bruner insists that one must go beyond just the facts (names, dates, events) for a cognitive reorganization to occur. In this exercise, we will attempt to put some of Bruner's notions to the test. The focus will be on both the development of concepts and the use of the iconic mode of representation.

If possible, select some younger children. (If that's not possible, ask your roommate or friends to help.) Present them with the following example:

Assume that plane flights in the south are limited to serving just five cities: (1) Charlotte, North Carolina; (2) Atlanta, Georgia; (3) Daytona, Florida; (4) El Paso, Texas; and (5) Birmingham, Alabama. Further assume that the flights occur in such a way that one can fly only from

Birmingham to Charlotte

Daytona to Charlotte

Atlanta to Birmingham

Atlanta to El Paso

Charlotte to Daytona

Charlotte to El Paso

Birmingham to Atlanta

Charlotte to Atlanta

Allow the subjects to study the list and, if they wish, even to memorize it. When they feel comfortable with the background of factual information, ask them to tell you the shortest way, or the most efficient route, to take in order to make a round trip between Atlanta and Daytona. Now despite having memorized the information, the subjects will soon see that it is virtually impossible to come to a solution just by trying to process all that information in their heads.

Next, provide some conceptual help by introducing a more efficient method of holding the information in storage. Rewrite the list so that the five cities are now presented in alphabetical order: A—Atlanta, B—Birmingham, C—Charlotte, D—Daytona, and E—El Paso. Tell your subjects to categorize this information as follows:

Atlanta to Birmingham (A to B)

Atlanta to El Paso (A to E)

Birmingham to Charlotte (B to C)

Birmingham to Atlanta (B to A)

Charlotte to Atlanta (C to A)

Charlotte to Daytona (C to D)

Charlotte to El Paso (C to E)

Daytona to Charlotte (D to C)

Although the solution now becomes somewhat easier to imagine, it is still extremely difficult to keep all those sequences in mind and to move them around into a coherent model.

Finally, ask your subjects to diagram the various route combinations by using arrows to indicate the possible directions, such as:

---

* We are indebted to Jerome Bruner and J. Richard Hayes for the idea behind the example we use in this exercise.

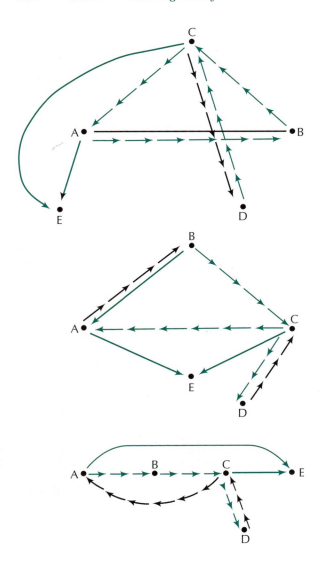

Notice the various diagrams that result. Some, such as the one at the bottom, produce a picture of the problem that represents the information in an extremely powerful form. The diagram at the top, though consistent with the parameters of the problem, does not show the same economy of thought. At this point, the problem begins to solve itself, and it becomes readily apparent that there is only one way to make a round trip between Atlanta and Daytona: from Atlanta to Birmingham, from Birmingham to Charlotte, from Charlotte to Daytona, from Daytona back to Charlotte, and, finally, from Charlotte back to Atlanta. It then becomes apparent that El Paso is just a trap.

The diagram has provided a cognitive map of the entire problem, and through the use of this symbolic representation the subject was able to process the information more economically. As shown, the subject did need some facts to work with, but the facts alone, without a cognitive reorganization, were not sufficient to produce a valid solution. The symbolic representation provided the driving force for the final understanding.

REFERENCES

APA Monitor (1990), *21,* 6.

Bailey, M. B., & Bailey, R. E. (1993). Misbehavior: A case history. *American Psychologist, 48,* 1157–1158.

Bregman, E. O. (1934). An attempt to modify the emotional attitudes of infants by the conditioning response technique. *Journal of Genetic Psychology, 45,* 169–178.

Breland, K., & Breland, M. (1961). The misbehavior of organisms. *American Psychologist, 16,* 681–684.

Bruner, J. S. (1962). *The process of education.* Cambridge, MA: Harvard University Press.

Bruner, J. S. (1966). *Toward a theory of instruction.* Cambridge, MA: Harvard University Press.

Bruner, J. S. (1983). *Child's talk.* New York: Norton.

Bruner, J. S. (1987). *Actual minds, possible worlds.* Cambridge, MA: Harvard University Press.

Bruner, J. (1990). *Acts of meaning.* Cambridge, MA: Harvard University Press.

Carpenter, F. (1974). *The Skinner primer.* New York: Free Press.

Deno, S. L., & Chiang, B. (1979). An experimental analysis of the nature of reversal errors in children with severe learning disabilities. *Learning Disabilities Quarterly, 2,* 40–45.

Fowler, R. D. (1990). In memoriam. *American Psychologist, 45,* 1203.

Garcia, J. (1993). Misrepresentation of my criticisms of Skinner. *American Psychologist, 48,* 1158.

Getsie, R. L. (1985). Meta-analysis of the effects of type and combination of feedback on children's discrimination learning. *Review of Education Research, 55,* 9–22.

Guerin, B. (1994). *Analyzing social behavior: Behavior analysis and the social sciences.* Reno: Context Press.

Kuhn, T. S. (1970). *The structure of scientific revolutions* (2d ed.). Chicago: University of Chicago Press.

Meichenbaum, D., Price, R., Phares, E. J., McCormick, N., & Hyde, J. (1989). *Exploring choices: The psychology of adjustment.* Glenview, IL: Scott, Foresman.

Moore, B. R. (1973). The role of directed Pavlovian reaction in simple instrumental learning in the pigeon. In R. A. Hinde & J. Stevenson-Hinde (Eds.), *Constraints on learning.* New York: Academic Press.

Nafpaktitis, M., Mayer, G. R., & Butterworth, T. (1985). Natural rates of teacher approval and disapproval and their relations to student behavior in intermediate school classrooms. *Journal of Educational Psychology, 77,* 362–367.

New York Times (1991, April 9), C9.

Piaget, J. (1959). Apprentissage et connaissance (première partie). In P. Greco & J. Piaget (Eds.), *Etudes d'epistémologie génétique* (Vol. 7, pp. 21–67). Paris: Presses Universitaires de France.

Prawat, R. S., & Floden, R. E. (1994). Philosophical perspectives on constructivist views of learning. *Educational Psychologist, 29,* 37–48.

Seligman, M. E. P. (1970). On the generality of the laws of learning. *Psychological Review, 77,* 410.

Seligman, M. E. P. (1972). Phobias and preparedness. In M. E. P. Seligman & J. L. Hager (Eds.), *Biological boundaries of learning.* New York: Appleton-Century-Crofts.

Skinner, B. F. (1959). A case history in scientific method. In S. Koch (Ed.), *Psychology: A study of a science.* New York: McGraw-Hill.

Skinner, B. F. (1971). *Beyond freedom and dignity* (p. 169). New York: Knopf.

Skinner, B. F. (1978). Why don't we use the behavioral sciences? *Human Nature, 1*(1), 32.

Skinner, B. F. (1988). Whatever happened to psychology as the science of behavior? *Counseling Psychology Quarterly, 1,* 111–122.

Steketee, G. S. (1993). *Treatment of obsessive compulsive disorder.* New York: Guilford Press.

Wiener, D. N. (1996). *B. F. Skinner: Benign architect.* Boston: Allyn & Bacon, Longwood Division.

10

LEARNING IN THE CLASSROOM 1: THE BEHAVIORAL VIEW

"In an American school, if you ask for the salt in good French, you get an A. In France you get the salt" (Skinner, 1953). This statement by B. F. Skinner illustrates perhaps the major feature of the educational process. The concepts, skills, and techniques we teach are not only useful in the present, but, more important, they will also be useful at some later time. One of the major goals of education is to equip us to transfer what we learn in the classroom to future situations. Learning to add, subtract, and spell results in the immediate advantage of good grades, a gold star, a promotion to the next grade, or perhaps a teacher's or parent's general approval. Eventually, however, the advantages become more compelling. In later life we learn that our ability to spell or multiply or derive square roots has enormous practical consequences, for example, in helping us earn a living. Some of us learn this too late. "If only I had paid more attention in school," we moan. And, we might add, we might have paid more attention if our classroom experience had been structured differently.

TRANSFER

Transfer is the key to classroom learning. Transfer takes place when learning task A influences learning task B. Transfer may be positive or negative. When learning A facilitates learning B, **positive transfer** is said to have taken place; conversely, when learning A inhibits learning B, **negative transfer** has occurred. Here are a few examples of positive transfer: Learning to ride a motorcycle is easier if you already know how to ride a bike; learning Italian is easier if you already know Latin; writing a letter to Santa Claus is easy if you have learned your second-grade spelling. Here are some examples of negative transfer: Learning to lean forward while snow-skiing may cause you to fall on your face when you learn to water-ski; learning to keep your elbows away from your body to hit a baseball may cause a disastrous slice when you learn to hit a golf ball; studying a French assignment until the wee hours may wreak havoc with the Spanish exam you take the next morning.

There is also a special case of negative transfer in which the influence works in reverse. You successfully learn A and then learn B; when you try to recall A, you draw a complete blank. This is called *retroactive inhibition,* and it happens when the second task works retroactively to inhibit recall of the first task. More will be said on this important topic when we discuss information processing in Chapter 11.

Formal Discipline

Current theories of transfer can be traced back to the early Greek notion of formal discipline. According to this view, the role of the school is to discipline the student's mind. It was thought that the mind, like an athlete's muscles, must be systematically exercised until it becomes so strong it can learn and understand virtually any new material. The theory of formal discipline remained in vogue until the early twentieth century. Subjects such as logic, Latin, and Greek were taught not for their practical value, but because they were thought to strengthen the student's mind to the point at which all later problem-solving would be easy.

The theory of formal discipline was challenged around the turn of the century by three important psychologists. The first, William James, put the theory to the test (1890). He spent 132 minutes, over an 8-day period, memorizing a long segment of poetry (Victor Hugo's *Satyr*). He reasoned that if the theory of formal discipline was correct, exercising the mind by memorizing another poem would make further memorization easier. He therefore spent the next 38 days memorizing book 1 of Milton's *Paradise Lost.* Finally, he tried to memorize another segment of the *Satyr,* equal in length to the first segment he had memorized, only to find that it took him even longer than it had previously. The results of this rather informal test led James to suspect the validity of the theory of formal discipline.

The second challenger, E. L. Thorndike, had subjects practice estimating the length of lines one-half to one-and-one-half inches long (Thorndike & Woodworth, 1901). When the subjects achieved a certain degree of accuracy in the task, Thorndike introduced a different, though similar task: estimating the length of lines 6 to 12 inches long. Thorndike found that there was little, if any, improvement on the second task as a result of the practice gained from the first task. Although he believed that he had thoroughly refuted the theory of formal discipline, Thorndike still maintained that transfer could occur. Thorndike based his explanation of transfer on the existence of certain elements in the second task that were identical with those in the first task.

The Learning Curve

Many studies of the learning process have shown that the acquisition of new information or of a new skill proceeds in a predictable fashion. When first confronting a new subject, we begin learning slowly and then pick up speed rather dramatically. Finally, our pace slows down and begins to level off.

Figure 10.1 shows a typical **learning curve.** It is said to be negatively accelerated because as the number of trials increases, there is less and less increase in the amount learned. After the first few trials, in which the learner is "catching on" to the basic procedures, rather huge chunks of new learning are quickly assimilated. As time goes on, however, improvement becomes less and less pronounced and finally levels off. This leveling off is called a *plateau.* Novice golfers may score 150 their first few times around the course, but after their fourth or fifth round they may be down to around 120. At this point they may feel that it's easy to excel at golf and that, if they can continue lopping 30 strokes off their score, they will soon be ready for "the tour." They soon learn, however, that lowering their score from 100 to 90 is far more difficult than lowering it from 120 to 110.

Students learning a new skill may reach a whole series of plateaus. Typing students, for example, may proceed fairly rapidly at first and then level off. Perhaps they were learning the keyboard letter by letter. Suddenly, they notice another increase in performance, for now they have learned certain letter sequences like *ing,* or *tion,* or *the,* which can be rattled off as though they were single letters. This is actually an example of positive transfer, in which the previous learning finally builds up to the point at which a sharp increase in new learning has become possible.

FIGURE 10.1   A typical learning curve.

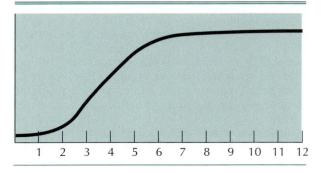

Learning Sets

Harry Harlow has done some important research in learning, using monkeys as subjects. Harlow coined the term **learning set** to describe the phenomenon of learning how to learn. He found that with practice his monkeys became increasingly skilled at solving discrimination problems. They improved not only on the previously learned problems but on novel problems as well. The fact that the monkeys developed these learning sets freed "them from the restrictions of the slow, trial-and-error process of the original attempts" (Harlow et al., 1971).

Using straightforward reinforcement techniques, Harlow trained monkeys to respond to an odd item among a set of three items. For example, the monkey would be presented with three geometric shapes, two circles and an "odd" item, in this case a triangle. Once the monkey learned to respond to the triangle, a different three-item set was presented, say, two knives and a fork. With enough previous training, the monkeys would show the ability to select the fork, the new odd item. In short, the monkeys had learned a rule or a relationship rather than a simple discriminated response to the triangle.

Harlow feels that his concept of learning sets explains what the gestalt psychologists labeled as insight. He sees the sudden spurt in learning, the so-called "a-ha" phenomenon, as just another extension of the theoretical concept of transfer.

Students can also be trained in learning how to learn. Through instruction, students have demonstrated an increased ability to learn relationships, which aid them in the retention of both classroom and textbook materials (Brown et al., 1981).

Massed versus Distributed Learning

If you had four hours to parcel out any way you wished, how could you make the most of this time to learn a new skill? In learning new motor skills, the evidence is fairly clear—distributed practice of, say, 16 15-minute segments is more efficient than a **massed learning** dose of four straight hours. When learning to skate, ride a bike, or perform a new skill in a physical education class, this distributed practice prescription is indeed sound advice. Not only are the shorter sessions less fatiguing, but, by their very nature, motor skills are best learned a step at a time.

The Spacing Effect

The value of spaced learning over massed learning is now called the **spacing effect,** and documentation of this phenomenon goes back more than 100 years. In 1885 Hermann Ebbinghaus stated that "with any considerable number of repetitions a suitable distribution of them over a space of time is decidedly more advantageous than the massing of them at a single time" (Ebbinghaus, 1885). A few years later, in 1901, the great Harvard psychologist William James, in his talks to teachers and students, advised that it is better to learn new material over many different days than "again and again on just a few days" (James, 1901).

Since those early days, the literature in educational psychology has been filled with studies in support of the facilitative nature of the spacing effect. (For an impressive summary of the research, see Dempster, 1988.) And the studies continue to mount. For example, it has been found that students exposed to a short course in statistics learned more when the material was spread out over several sessions than when the same material was covered in a single long session (Smith & Rothkopf, 1984). Also, in learning and understanding the main points of a certain text, it was found that well-spaced presentations were significantly more effective than a single, longer presentation (Reder & Anderson, 1982). Finally, in a study concerned with the learning of word definitions, acquisition was shown to be definitely enhanced by the spaced presentations, and learning held up whether the words were presented with or without sentence context (Dempster, 1987).

On the strength of such a long and solid record of documentation, teachers should make more of an effort to include the spacing effect in their presentations and curriculum plans. One fairly straightforward approach could be based on increasing the amount of class time spent on review, with a special emphasis on spacing these review sessions. Also, the teacher might encourage students to space their study times, and also warn students about the deleterious effects of cramming for exams.

The question of whether the material to be learned should be carved up and doled out in small units or whether it should be presented as an integrated whole, if only sketchily, is of great concern to educators. Is it more efficient for you, the reader, to try to master the material in this chapter by reading three pages a day or by reading through the whole chapter first and then going back and attempting to iron out the details? The message from Jerome Bruner is clear: the more meaningful the material, the easier it is to learn. Therefore, breaking it down into parts is a risky venture, unless the material to be learned is something like Ebbinghaus's nonsense syllables. To learn a simple problem or a short passage of poetry, working on it as a whole is probably best, since breaking that kind of material down into tiny units makes it less meaningful and might even destroy its meaning completely. Bruner has stressed the importance of keeping a subject internally coherent and meaningful when setting up efficient learning conditions. When a larger volume of material must be learned, a compromise can be worked out; the material can be divided into meaningful units and then learned as separate wholes.

The trouble with learning material in parts is that the parts eventually have to be pieced back together, and that can be extremely time-consuming. In many learning situations the best approach is to work first on the whole and then go back to the various parts. When presenting a new unit in, say, social studies, the teacher should spend some time discussing the general point of the whole unit before introducing the details. Giving the student an overview first makes even the use of a teaching machine more effective.

SOCIAL LEARNING OR MODELING

Albert Bandura, an important contemporary psychologist, has suggested that a significant part of what a person learns occurs through imitation or modeling. Bandura has been called a social learning theorist in that he is concerned with the learning that takes place in the context of a social situation. During social interactions an individual may learn to modify his or her behavior as a result of how others in the group are responding.

Bandura's **social learning theory** is truly an all-inclusive psychology, borrowing as much from behaviorists as from cognitive theorists. Bandura sees behavior, internal cognitive structures, and the environment as interacting so that each acts as an interlocking determinant of the other (1978). People are to some extent products of their environments, but they also choose and shape their environments. It's not simply a one-way street.

Bandura suggests that learning takes place on the basis of OIR: observation, imitation, and repetition (Bandura, 1986).

Modeling versus Operant Conditioning

Though recognizing the importance of Skinner's operant conditioning, Bandura insists that not all learning takes place as a result of the direct reinforcement of responses. People also learn by imitating the behavior of other people, or models, and this learning takes place even though these imitative responses are not themselves being directly reinforced. For example, young children may stand up when the "Star-Spangled Banner" is played because they see their parents stand. A child's response in this instance is not immediately followed by an M&M candy or any other primary reinforcer. The child simply imitates the response made by the parents.

Learning new responses In the previous example, the child's ability to stand up was, of course, already a part of his behavioral repertoire. Bandura further says that people can also learn new responses simply by observing the behavior of others. A child learns to ski or an adult learns a tennis stroke simply by imitating the behavior of the instructor. The language-lab method of teaching a foreign language is based on the premise that people can efficiently learn to imitate the electronically reproduced sentences and phrases they listen to. The list of new forms of behavior that can be learned through **modeling** is virtually endless, and though the previous examples stress positive forms of learning, modeling may also create undesirable responses. A child may learn to become overly aggressive or deceitful and dishonest through the modeling mechanism.

In a now-classic study, Bandura subjected a group of young children (ages three to six) to the improbable spectacle of watching adult models punch, kick, and yell at a large, inflated Bobo doll (Bandura et al., 1963). When later allowed to play with Bobo themselves, these children displayed twice as many aggressive responses as a control group of children who had not witnessed the adults' performance. The form of imitation in this study was indeed direct. The children even yelled the same phrases the adults had used: "Kick him," "Sock him in the nose," and so on. One might speculate that had the adults danced with Bobo rather than punching it, the children, too, would have behaved in this gentler fashion.

Reinforcement and modeling Although learning through modeling does not require direct and immediate reinforcement, Bandura has suggested that reinforcement may still be involved. In the first place, many of the significant models in the child's world, parents and teachers, are also in charge of the child's reinforcement schedule. The parent not only may provide the modeling stimulus but also may reinforce the child when the behavior is imitated. Second, Bandura has demonstrated that a child is more apt to imitate an adult model's response when the adult is being reinforced for that response (Bandura & McDonald, 1963). In other words, the child who observes an adult being praised for a certain action is more likely to respond in the same way than a child who views the action but not the subsequent reinforcement. Bandura calls this vicarious *learning,* since the learner in this instance is not being reinforced but is merely witnessing the reinforcement.

Thus, reinforcement and modeling can together create very potent conditions for behavior change. Many of our most persistent habits and attitudes are a result of this combination of powerful forces.

Significance in the Classroom

Other than the parents, the classroom teacher may be the most important model in the child's environment. Many children have been known to model their teacher's behavior so closely that they in a sense "become" the teacher when interacting with younger brothers and sisters at home. In some cases, these children demand that the younger siblings call them by their teacher's name—"I'm not Debbie, I'm Mrs. D." The teacher's likes and dislikes regarding subject matter may become obvious to the students and result in imitative attitudes. The teacher who loves music but hates math may, through vicarious learning, transmit these feelings to the class. So-called math blocks may be created in this way, and the student can be permanently affected.

Other types of negative teacher behavior may also be imitated by the students. A first-grade teacher was having a very difficult time maintaining what she considered to be proper discipline in her classroom. She began spending more and more time screaming at the children. The parents of one of the children found that each day, after school, the child would shut herself up in her room and scream at her dolls (even using the same words the teacher had used). A teacher's attitude toward minority-group students can also have a significant effect, both on how the minority student learns to perceive himself or herself and on how the student is perceived by the other members of the class. In short, teachers provide conditions for learning in the classroom not only by what they say, but also by what they do.

OPERANT CONDITIONING IN THE CLASSROOM: BEHAVIOR MANAGEMENT

As we saw in the previous chapter, Skinner's principles of operant conditioning can be translated into specific classroom techniques. The Skinnerians feel that colleges have failed to equip prospective teachers for the actual day-to-day job of educating chil-

dren. The new teacher, no matter how knowledgeable in educational theory, is usually at a complete loss when it comes to putting theory into practice. The teacher may understand the importance of recognizing individual differences, and may know full well that learning requires motivation and that students' interest must be captured, but then what? What happens when, in order to motivate students, the new teacher proudly displays the best student's written work on the bulletin board, only to find the next day that the essay is on the floor and the thumbtacks have been stolen? What happens when the new teacher, steeped in the philosophy of fairness, leaves the room and asks the students to cover their eyes so that the one guilty child can come discreetly forward and return a dime that has been stolen from another child? Not only is the dime not returned, but one young philanthropist, missing the teacher's point entirely, loudly offers to contribute a dime to the aggrieved child so that the class can go on to important matters. What happens when the new teacher demands that an unruly child sit down and be quiet, only to have the child stare back coolly and say, "Make me!"? What happens when . . . and on and on.

The popularity of operant conditioning techniques is due in large measure to the fact that operant conditioning offers the teacher a precise prescription for handling specific classroom situations. The Skinnerians do not resort to such clichés as "seizing the teachable moment" or being an "educational provocateur." The Skinnerians are specific, and they urge the teacher to be just as specific.

The Case for Behavior Modification

Some of the essentials of this thing we now call behavior modification have probably been with us since time immemorial. As soon as people "discovered" that their behavior could be affected by environmental conditions, some aspects of behavior modification came into being. Many of today's college students, on hearing their first lecture on behavior modification, respond with a smug yawn and ask, "So what else is new? I learned that from my grandmother, she used to call it bribery." The fact is, however, that despite its apparently long history and its obvious overtones of "mere common sense," **behavior modification** as it is technically understood and used today is of fairly recent origin. It is a powerful technique that has been derived from both learning theory, especially as suggested by B. F. Skinner, and from the cumulative results of numerous learning studies from the laboratories of experimental psychologists.

As we survey the behavior modification literature, the prospective teacher should be aware that the American Psychological Association strongly urges that behavior modification be used only in the pursuit of positive goals, such as reducing human suffering and increasing human functioning. It should not be used as a method for imposing dictatorial conformity or slavish rituals. It is also important to remember that a particular problem child does not exist in a vacuum. The child is not just a member of your class but also a member of various outside peer and social groups and, especially, a member of a family. Positive intervention is far more successful when accomplished through teamwork, with members of the child's family as part of the team. "Parent and family priorities and needs, as well as their values and beliefs, will continually influence the content and style of intervention" (Widerstrom et al., 1991, p. 132). Finally, it should be pointed out that behavior modification, unlike Freud's theory of psychoanalysis, assumes that the most important forces affecting any individual are the current life experiences, not the memories of childhood events and traumas.

Defining objectives   Every teacher has a general idea of educational goals for the class as a whole or for individual students. It is crucial that these goals be specifically stated in objective, behavioral terms, so that both the teacher and the students know what the goals are and when they have been reached. Furthermore, goals should be specified not just for the term but for each day of the term.

Behavioral terminology avoids words such as *understanding*—that is, words that do not describe a demonstrable behavior. A behaviorally formulated objective is one that describes the behavior that will result when the objective is attained. For example, students can be said to have learned multiplication when they can recite the multiplication table with no errors. In terms of daily goals they may be expected to make no more than five errors the first day, no more than two the second day, and none at all the third day. Each time a goal, or **terminal behavior,** is reached, a new goal is set so that the first goal becomes just a step in a continuing process toward a larger overall goal.

Say the goal, or the terminal behavior, for a certain child is to develop better study habits in the classroom. This must then be defined in behavioral terms. Perhaps the teacher wants the child not to gaze into space, to talk and fidget less, and to read and write more. When the goal is objectified in this way, the teacher can accurately judge whether or not the terminal behavior is achieved, and, if it is, exactly when.

Reading skills can be objectified as the ability to recognize correct definitions for 100 selected words. Music appreciation can be objectified as the ability to identify the composers of 20 musical compositions. The proponents of behavior modification argue that anything that can be taught can be objectified, and that all educational goals can be stated in behavioral terms. Critics may argue that being able to recognize 20 composers "isn't what we mean by musical appreciation" or that recognizing definitions of 100 selected words "isn't what we mean by reading skills." If so, the Skinnerians would say that it is up to the critics to state clearly what they do mean so that these goals can be knowingly reached:

> Mathematical behavior is usually regarded, not as a repertoire of responses involving numbers and numerical operations, but as evidences of mathematical ability or the exercise of the power of reason. It is true that the techniques which are emerging from the experimental study of learning are not designed to "develop the mind" or to further some vague "understanding" of mathematical relationships. They are designed, on the contrary, to establish the very behaviors which are taken to be evidences of such mental states or processes (Skinner, 1954, p. 86).

Establishing the operant level   Once the goal has been defined (and nobody says this is easy, but then, good teaching is not easy), the teacher must observe the student and establish the operant level, or the rate at which the behavior occurs naturally in the classroom. Since student responses are so often specific to the stimulus situation, it is important that the operant level be established by observing the classroom. Many children who are disruptive in class are as good as gold in the counselor's or principal's office. If unruly students are sent to the psychologist's office, they are not as likely to display their disruptive behavior, since the releasers for this behavior remain back in the classroom.

Let's visit a fifth-grade classroom and observe the behavior of an 11-year-old boy, Walter S. An art lesson is in progress. As the teacher begins giving the directions for today's project, Walter stands on top of his desk and calls out his own name, "Wally, Wally, Wally," and makes strange, grunting sounds for two minutes. After the teacher's tenth request, Walter sits down and remains silent for just over one minute. The students then file toward the front of the room to pick up their supplies. Walter spends the next 2 minutes running back and forth, occasionally sliding, as though going into home plate. The teacher brings Walter's supplies to his desk, where Walter remains seated quietly for almost 3 minutes. Among the art supplies are some elastic bands which he suddenly discovers can be put to use in an aggressive way. He flicks them at the other students for the next 30 seconds, or until he runs out. One girl receives a direct hit and calls loudly to the teacher, who is three rows away helping another student. Walter laughs at the girl's discomfort but immediately takes his seat when the teacher comes over to investigate the uproar. Walter finally gets down to work and remains quietly at his seat for almost 10 minutes. Suddenly, he discovers that a certain piece of cardboard, which he had previously cut, doesn't quite fit where he had planned to glue it. He leaps back on top of his desk, makes loud noises, and contorts his face. The class seems to enjoy his performance, and despite the teacher's pleas, he remains on top of his desk for almost 3 minutes.

Out of 22 minutes of class time, Walter has now spent just over 7 minutes engaging in disruptive behavior. His operant level for disruptive behavior is, thus, a little over 34 percent.

What should be done with Walter? Behavior modification experts, such as Charles and Clifford Madsen, say that the teacher has the responsibility to help Walter. He is obviously a problem child. In testing Walter, the school psychologist discovers that Walter's home life is extremely bad: He has no father, his older siblings engage in delinquent behavior, there is no supervision in the home at all, and so on. Walter's test scores show him to be "precariously adjusted." Perhaps the teacher now feels a sense of compassion toward Walter and even some guilt for having disliked him so. Walter is probably headed for real trouble and may someday spend a great deal of time in a more structured institution than a school. Should the teacher give up on trying to interact meaningfully with Walter? The proponents of behavior modification say no.

In discussing the problem child, in this case the proverbial "Johnny," Madsen and Madsen say:

> The truly pathetic situation is that no one will teach Johnny. The one place where there is some hope for Johnny is the school. Yet, many teachers quickly abdicate responsibility once his history is known. Johnny can discriminate. He can be taught new responses to deal with that world outside the home. He can learn to read, write, spell; he can learn new rules of social interaction and thereby break the cycle of the past. If cooperation (with the home) is impossible, he can even learn these responses in spite of a bad home. It is not easy to deal with the Johnnies [or the Walters]. They take time, energy and a disciplined teacher. All the Johnnies do not survive; yet for these children the school is their only hope.

Who has the responsibility of discipline?—The teacher (Madsen and Madsen, 1970, p. 14).

The modification of behavior   Once the educational goals have been defined behaviorally and the operant level assessed, one can begin the job of modifying behavior. The techniques used are those outlined in Chapter 9. In order to change responses, in order to modify behavior, we must allow the operant to occur and then provide an appropriate stimulus situation. For example, if we wish to strengthen a certain response (i.e., increase the rate of a given operant), the response must be allowed to occur and then be followed by positive or negative reinforcement. Recall that a positive reinforcement is a stimulus that, following a given response, increases the rate of that response. A negative reinforcement is a stimulus that, when removed, increases the response rate. Both positive and negative reinforcement increase rather than decrease the strength of a given response. Punishment, however, is an aversive stimulus that reduces the rate of the response. We will discuss punishment in detail later in the chapter, but it is important to note now that punishment and negative reinforcement are very different kinds of stimulus situations that have exactly opposite effects on response rates.

The Use of Reinforcement

Positive reinforcement   In the classroom, positive reinforcement may be provided by a primary reinforcer, such as milk, cereal, or candy, or it may be a conditioned reinforcer, such as gold stars, high grades, social approval, or, in the case of younger pupils, physical contact.

> A certain student, John D., would not remain attentive or even attempt to do his numerical reason problems. The teacher set the behavioral goal of nineteen correct solutions out of twenty problems. Observation of the student indicated that his operant level was zero; he simply would not do the work. After a conference with his parents, the boy was sent to school each morning without any breakfast. The teacher used milk and cereal as the positive reinforcers for correct math solutions. The student reached the desired goal on the fourth day.

> Tommy L., a third-grade student, was boisterous and noisy in class and prevented other students from concentrating on their own work. The first behavioral goal was set at thirty minutes of complete silence. Tommy was presented with an M&M candy

SPOTLIGHT ON CONDUCT DISORDERS

Is Behavior Modification the Answer?

The American Psychiatric Association's *Diagnostic and Statistical Manual of Mental Disorders* (DSM IV) identifies a conduct disorder when the child's behavior aggressively impinges on the basic rights of other children (and adults). Most schoolchildren with this disorder are overly aggressive, were or maybe still are bed wetters, have been cruel to animals, and are likely to have set fires. According to DSM IV, a diagnosis of conduct disorder is based on the child's showing three of more of the following criteria during the previous year:

1. Bullies, threatens, or intimidates others
2. Initiates physical fights
3. Uses a weapon that could cause serious harm to others
4. Is physically cruel to people or animals
5. Has stolen or destroyed others' property
6. Has broken into someone's dwelling or car
7. Has engaged in fire setting with the intention of serious damage
8. Lies and breaks promises to obtain favors or avoid obligations
9. Stays out late at night despite parental prohibitions, beginning at least by age 13
10. Has run away from home at least twice and is constantly truant at school, also beginning by age 13[a]

Estimates of the prevalence of this condition ranges from 4 to 10 percent of American children,[b] and the gender difference is about four to one in favor of boys.[c] Gender studies indicate that although boys typically begin to show signs of this condition by age 10, girls don't exhibit symptoms until the early teen years.[d] Unless treated, this condition has been shown to remain stable over at least a 30-year period and can lead to severe adult antisocial problems.[e]

Although there are strong hints that conduct disorders have a genetic component,[f] poor parenting and severe family problems also play a key role.[g] Even so, some school systems have initiated programs aimed at helping to prevent conduct disorders from ever emerging. In one such study, showing promising results, sixth- and seventh-graders were trained in problemsolving, impulse control (through behavior modification), and family coping skills. As adolescents, they appeared to show reduced aggressiveness and alcohol use. Whether these changes can be sustained without also providing programs for parental training is currently in doubt.

[a] American Psychiatric Association (1994). *Diagnostic and statistical manual of mental disorders* (4th ed.). Washington, DC: Author.
[b] Martin, B., & Hoffman, J. A. (1990). Conduct disorders. In M. Lewis & S. M. Miller (Eds.), *Handbook of developmental psychopathology.* New York: Plenum.
[c] Earls, F. (1994). Oppositional-defiant and conduct disorders. In M. Rutter, E. Taylor, & L. Hersov (Eds.), *Child and adolescent psychiatry.* Oxford: Blackwell Scientific Publications.
[d] Kazdin, A. E. (1990). Conduct disorder in childhood. In M. Hersen & C. Last (Eds.), *Handbook of adult and child psychopathology: A longitudinal perspective.* New York: Pergamon.
[e] Eron, L. D., & Huesmann, L. R. (1990). *The stability of aggressive behavior—even into the third generation.* In M. Lewis & S. M. Miller (Eds.), *Handbook of developmental psychopathology.* New York: Plenum.
[f] Wicks-Nelson, R., & Israel, A. C. (1991). *Behavior disorders of childhood* (2nd ed.) Englewood Cliffs, NJ: Prentice Hall.
[g] Caplan, M., Weissberg, R. P., Grober, J. S., Sivio, P. J., Grady, K., & Jacoby, C. (1992). Social competence promotion with inner-city and suburban young adolescents: Effects on Social adjustment and alcohol use. *Journal of Consulting and Clinical Psychology, 60,* 56–63.

each time he remained quiet for forty-five seconds. On the eighth day the goal was reached. At this point a new goal was set for sixty minutes of silence. Also the reinforcement schedule was altered so that Tommy had to remain silent for two minutes in order to receive the M&M reinforcement. The new goal was reached in only three days.

Such primary reinforcers as food for the child who has had no breakfast or candy for the child who loves sweets are obviously of a positive nature. When it comes to conditioned reinforcers, however, the teacher must observe the situation closely, for, what the teacher or school department may consider a positive reinforcer will not necessarily be such for each student or even each student's parents. For example, schools have been awarding automobile bumper stickers to proud parents advertising that "My Child Is an Honor Student." This practice has been greeted with a degree of ambivalence, and even scorn, by some children and their parents, especially parents whose children did not accord them the honor of displaying that sticker. These students felt left out, and their parents complained that the stickers were elitist and undemocratic. A countersticker has now been produced that announces to the world that "My Kid Beat Up Your Honor Student"—hardly a technique for combatting conduct disorders among children or their parents.

If we think of a particular child as having the goal of teacher attention (just as the rat in the Skinner box has the goal of obtaining the food), then the actual conditioning is based on learning that a specific behavior leads to the attainment of a specific goal (Rescorla, 1987). Usually, however, the teacher can select from conditioned reinforcers. Madsen and Madsen suggest the following (1970):

1. Words—spoken and written
2. Expressions—facial and bodily
3. Closeness—nearness and touching
4. Activities and privileges
5. Things—materials, awards, toys.

Some theorists are now arguing against the use of extrinsic, conditioned reinforcers of any kind. Perhaps the most popular current spokesperson for this position is Alfie Kohn (1993), who is attempting to convince the world of education that grades, gold stars, and other conditioned reinforcers harm children by, among other things, encouraging cheating and destroying the rapport between student and teacher. To Kohn, reinforcement actually becomes another form of punishment and thus should be avoided at all costs.

Negative reinforcement   Negative reinforcement —the removal of an aversive stimulus in order to increase response rate—has been used in a variety of school settings. One fairly common use of this is the so-called time-out procedure, a technique that is also commonly used by parents in the home (Sears et al., 1957). In a study conducted at the University of Kansas on preschool children with poor cognitive, language, and social skills, the time-out procedure has produced some dramatic results. A child who exhibits low self-control is placed for brief periods in a small room next to the classroom. When the child's

behavior becomes more positive and less hyperactive, he or she is allowed to return (aversive stimulus is removed) to the regular classroom. This technique is especially potent when it is later combined with the use of various positive reinforcers, which can then be used to build up a repertoire of desirable responses. In fact, one of the reasons the time-out procedure has proved to be so effective is that while the child is in isolation there are few if any positive reinforcers for maintaining the child's undesirable behavior (Brantner & Doherty, 1983).

Negative reinforcement has proved successful in shaping a variety of desired responses. In one instance a student who had not done his homework assignment was placed in a time-out room and told to complete the work. Only when the assignment was finally completed was the student allowed back into the classroom. In this case, the removal of the aversive stimulus (escape from the isolation room) acted to strengthen the behavior (doing the assignment).

Negative reinforcement should be used only with great caution. An example cited by Madsen and Madsen involved a second-grade boy whose teacher made him wear a girl's ribbon in his hair until he began acting in a more controlled fashion. Whenever his behavior improved, the hair ribbon was removed. Madsen and Madsen question the advisability of this particular technique on the grounds that it might affect the child's perception of his sex identification.

A teacher should examine carefully the possible disturbing consequences whenever considering the use of negative reinforcement. There is a real difference between placing children in a time-out room, where they have the opportunity to finish their work, and shoving them into an unlighted closet with the door closed. It is obviously very easy for the teacher's intended negative reinforcement to become simple punishment. When that occurs, as Skinner has pointed out, the whole purpose of reinforcement is defeated (Skinner, 1969). Control by aversive means may provoke a counterattack; daydreaming, dropping out, vandalism, refusal to learn assignments are all common indications of an attempt to avoid aversive control.

Consistency   Perhaps the major premise underlying the technique of behavior modification is that consistency should be observed at all times. Once a child is placed on a reinforcement program, the teacher must not waver. As Skinner's research on animals has shown, behavior that is intermittently reinforced is the most difficult to extinguish. If children are told that every time they act in a certain way they will be sent to the principal's office, they must be sent to the office every time they act that way. There can be no exceptions. Inconsistency teaches just that—inconsistency. As Madsen and Madsen point out,

> The child does not remember the 1,321 times he went to bed at 8 P.M., he remembers the two times he got to stay up. The third grader does not really believe that the teacher will send him to the time-out room (isolation) for ten minutes. This is already the sixth time the teacher has threatened and nothing has happened yet. The ninth grader cheated before and didn't get caught; why should he get caught this time? The college student has turned in late papers before; why should this professor be such a hard nose? (1970, p. 34).

Consistency is a key ingredient in the success of any behavior modification program. The cute little student who pleads, "Can't you make an exception just this once?" may be hard for the teacher to resist, but resist the teacher must. Once the teacher breaks the rules, the children learn only too well that the rules are there for the breaking.

> A ninth-grade creative writing class was slowly but surely getting out of control; assignments were not being turned in, the students were becoming increasingly boisterous and rude both to the teacher and to each other. The teacher, Miss W., pleaded with the students to be fair and meet her halfway, but this had no effect. It was suggested to Miss W. that reinforcement principles might be applied. She thereupon informed the class that if they behaved well for two successive days, they would go on a trip downtown to see the movie *Hamlet*. The next two days found the class no different, just as rowdy, just as out of control. Virtually every five minutes Miss W. shouted (to those who could hear her) that if they didn't behave, the trip would be canceled. In fact, she actually canceled the trip three times, but on the third day, the class pleaded with her and she relented. They saw the movie, and the next day the classroom situation deteriorated even more. Miss W. was beside herself. "I've tried everything, even behavior modification, and nothing works." She went back to class and pleaded with the students to be fair.

In her discussion of discipline in the classroom, one educator has suggested two basic rules:

1. Be consistent.
2. Know your subject matter.

From personal experience, that educator discovered those rules as she went through her first year of teaching. She found that initially children will not give back kindness for kindness; they must be shown rules, and these rules *must never be relaxed.* Nor can a threat of punishment be made unless it will be carried out—every time. As she notes,

> That second year of teaching, I began the first classes with a quiet statement of the rules: no one could leave his or her seat without permission; no one could communicate with a fellow student without permission; no one could call out an answer without first being recognized. The penalty for the smallest infringement of the rules was to remain after school in my room from three until five o'clock. No exceptions would be permitted. Invariably, some inoffensive student would open his mouth by mistake. He would be given a note on his desk, unobtrusively, to report at three. The next morning, after a dull session of gazing at me or resting his head on the desk, the student "got the word around." "She's tough, be careful." Two or three students slipped—and suffered utter, long boredom. The result was a quiet room, not of surly students, but of careful, somewhat surprised young people (Spettel, 1983).

Thus, the teacher in the classroom, like a first-rate sports referee, must be an absolutely consistent enforcer of the rules. When a referee calls a foul, the player can't stop the game to negotiate a better deal, or beg for an exception just this once, or promise not to do it again. Once the rules have been explained, the teacher should not be put off by the child who constantly asks why. "Why" isn't always a question; it can also, as every parent knows, be a subterfuge, a stall, or an opening salvo in a new barrage of negotiations.

Timing   To modify behavior effectively, the reinforcement must be timed to occur after the desired response has occurred. The teacher should never, never deliver the reinforcement on the promise that the behavior will occur later. For example, a teacher asks the students in his class to turn in their assignments at the beginning of each class period. At the start of the next class period no assignments are handed in. The teacher then tells them that if they promise to begin turning in their assignments the following Monday, they can have a record party for the last half hour of today's class period. The class quickly promises, has the record party, and the teacher is still waiting for the homework.

A seven-year-old boy enters his house muttering an innocuous swear word. His mother becomes upset and urges the boy never to say that word again. In exchange for his promise to obey her, the mother gives him a quarter. An hour later he returns demanding a dollar, saying, "If you think that word was bad, wait till you hear this!"

Reinforcement must follow actual behavior. We learn by doing, not by talking about doing or by promising to do. As the behavior modifiers argue, the reinforcement must be made contingent on the appropriate response.

Punishment

The use of **punishment** to control behavior has been a controversial issue among both learning theorists and educators. Thorndike, for example, changed his position on the question of punishment. His original law of effect stated that reward and punishment had equal but opposite effects, with reward strengthening and punishment weakening a learned stimulus-response connection. Later Thorndike revised this law drastically, saying that reward was far more effective in reinforcing learning than punishment was in weakening it. Later still, the Skinnerians demonstrated that if a rat was reinforced, say, 100 times for pressing a lever and thus had a rather large buildup of responses waiting to be emitted, punishment would temporarily slow the response rate but would not reduce the number of responses that would be emitted once the punishment was removed.

The typical experiment used a rat in an experimental chamber. The rat was reinforced with a food pellet for each lever press, until lever-pressing became highly resistant to extinction. (The rat's lever-pressing response was strengthened until the animal would emit, say, 200 responses without being further reinforced.) The lever was then electrified so that the rat now received a punishing shock every time it pressed the lever. The rat learned very quickly to stay away from the lever. However, once the shock was removed, the animal went determinedly back to the lever and all 200 responses were finally emitted. Punishment had merely held the responses in abeyance, suppressing them until the aversive stimulus was removed.

Because of Thorndike's changed position, the rat data from the Skinnerians, and other studies and theoretical positions, many psychologists and educators assumed that punishment had no real effect on learning. This scientific news was greeted with some skepticism, especially by older teachers who recalled the effect of the hickory stick on class control. Many parents and grandparents also found it difficult to mesh this "scientific breakthrough" with their own experiences in raising children.

More recent psychological studies, especially those carried out in the past 30 years, have shown that punishment is indeed an effective technique for controlling behavior. The problem with the previously mentioned rat study was that it was an extremely artificial situation. In the first place, the rats were exceptionally highly motivated to press the lever—the lever was the route to life-sustaining food. In the second place, no alternative response would produce the reinforcement. If a rat is given another response option during the time the punishment is in force, the original lever-pressing response does indeed weaken very rapidly. Punishment may not be a humane conditioning technique, and it may create some serious side effects, but it does control behavior. Even the most humanitarian parent seems to know this in moments of crisis. A child who is playing on a busy highway is quickly punished and then shown another area where he can play safely. A baby is not "reasoned with" when she is found poking her fingers into a light socket.

Punishment in the classroom usually takes the form of disapproval or of withholding a positive reinforcer. Severe disapproval by the teacher may often be an effective form of controlling behavior, but it does not instill a love of learning. Withholding a positive reinforcer, if the rule of consistency is religiously followed, is also an extremely effective behavior modifier. This method of aversive control takes such forms as the loss of privileges, objects, or pastimes the students value. The purist should note that withholding a positive reinforcer when used as punishment is not the same as extinction.

> In extinction, consequences that ordinarily follow the behavior are simply discontinued; in punishment, behavior results in the application of aversive consequences through forfeiture of positive reinforcers. Thus in extinguishing aggression sustained by peer attention, the behavior is consistently ignored; under the punishment contingency, however, the rewards of peer attention are pitted against the negative effects of confinement to one's room, loss of television privileges, or some other type of negative outcome (Bandura et al., 1963, p. 338).

Proponents of behavior modification have made extensive use of punishment in psychotherapy. For example, male homosexuals have been treated by showing them slides of nude men and women. While viewing the slides of male nudes, the patient receives an unpleasant shock through electrodes attached to his leg. While viewing the female nudes, no such punishment is administered. The proponents claim this technique has been successful in changing the sexual orientation of a number of subjects (*Time,* August 13, 1990, p. 72).

Children who suffer from stuttering have also been treated by the administration of electric shock whenever they begin stammering. Fairly dramatic recovery rates, within two weeks or less, have been attributed to the use of this technique (Craig & Cleary, 1982). Successful treatment of stuttering has also been claimed for techniques using positive reinforcement.

Punishment has proved effective with severely disturbed and developmentally disabled children, children who unless restrained might bang their heads against hard objects, tear and bite off pieces of their own flesh, pummel their own faces, and so on. Despite the fact that these children might appear to be enjoying the pain, they apparently don't enjoy pain when it is inflicted by others. Research in this area indicates that the use of shock, administered whenever severe self-injurious behavior (SIB) is observed, can drastically reduce and even eliminate many self-destructive responses. The use of punishment in these special cases has even been automated and is called the SIBIS (Self-Injurious Behavior Inhibiting System). SIBIS automatically detects self-injury, such as a blow to the head, and then delivers electrical shock to the arm or leg while recording the entire event. The sensor module is worn on the head and includes an impact detector and radio transmitter (Linscheid et al., 1990). In one study, self-injurious behavior was treated with SIBIS and was virtually eliminated, even during a follow-up observation six years later (Williams et al., 1994).

Twenty years ago a plea was advanced that if a person who may not have the capacity to give full and informed consent is to be subjected to such aversive conditioning procedures, then an outside, objective advocate should be called in to determine the person's best interests. Thus, retarded or psychotic children and adults will be protected from possible abuses arising from the indiscriminate use of a painful shock as an aversive stimulus.

Does punishment cause long-term emotional damage? This question has not yet been fully answered. The traditional, almost legendary view is that punishment is very much involved in the origin of behavioral disorders. One theorist has outlined a long series of punishment-provoked problems, including rigidity, social deviance, poor adjustment, and regression (Maurer, 1974). However, other psychologists are not so sure. Some experts argue that many punishment procedures produce no negative long-term emotional outcomes, and in fact one researcher suggests that positive side effects occur (Linscheid et al., 1994). Perhaps the real question is

not whether some forms of aberrant behavior can be produced by certain punishment procedures, but whether these reactions are typical results of punishment. "The answer to this question is clearly 'no,' although specific circumstances can be contrived to produce such effects" (Walters & Grusec, 1977).

Many of the experts in behavior modification now lean toward the view that most of the alleged negative side effects of punishment can be eliminated or at least minimized if the punishment is administered correctly and if alternative behaviors are available and encouraged. Teachers and parents, however, should never rely on punishment as the behavior modifier of choice. The overuse of punishment can produce in children the feeling that they are always doing something wrong. Eventually, the child may even begin to desire punishment in order to alleviate these feelings of guilt.

Aversive Stimuli

The use of aversive stimuli in the classroom, whether as negative reinforcement or as punishment, should be viewed with extreme caution. Though certainly an effective means of controlling behavior, it rarely instills a joyful attitude toward learning. Aversive stimuli can also act to classically condition emotional responses that can cause "blocks" to future learning (see Chapter 9). Punishment's effect on behavior, though possibly very depressing in the presence of the aversive stimulus, may not generalize at all beyond that stimulus. As we have seen, punishing a student for a certain behavior does not necessarily ensure that the student stops engaging in the behavior. This has been the message of punishment expert H. T. Hurt, who has long said that punishment does not always eliminate inappropriate behavior; "rather, the student may simply learn not to engage in that behavior in the presence of the teacher" (Hurt et al., 1978, p. 32). Thus, though not shown in front of the teacher, the behavioral pattern may remain with the student in all other situations.

Some students expect to be physically punished by their teachers or principals, probably because this type of punishment is so widespread in American homes. Data from two national surveys indicate that physical punishment, in the forms of slapping and spanking, is a way of life in U.S. households (Straus, 1994).

One result of punishment is that the child may learn to lie in order to avoid painful negative consequences. Unless accompanied by pathology, as in a conduct disorder, the lying will typically lessen when the child realizes that it is safe to admit to his or her various transgressions. There are situations, however, when our society tends to excuse lying, especially when it is used to promote social harmony or to prevent an even more immoral act, such as Europeans lying to the Gestapo over whether they were housing Jews (Saxe, 1991). Lying can be a symptom of a deeper problem, and is usually accompanied by feelings of fear and inferiority, self-doubt, a poor self-image, or guilt. Some children are forced to lie by parents who are overly harsh or inconsistent, and the habit is then brought to school. In this situation the lying becomes a defensive form of self-preservation. Some children, however, seem to be inveterate liars, at times even confusing fantasy with reality. Fantasy involves spending too much time living internally in a make-believe world, whereas lying is a mode of overt behavior. Children, however, sometimes convince themselves that their lies are true, weaving a fantasy around behavior that they perceive to be socially acceptable. The new teacher should not be dismayed to discover that identifying a lie or a lying child is not easy. Even veteran teachers are often surprised by the seemingly innocent child who has suddenly been caught in a flagrant lie. In fact even professionals in the field, such as judges, police officers, psychiatrists, lie detector experts, and Secret Service agents, are often unable to spot a liar. One study involving professionals from all these fields presented a series of 10 videotapes and asked the subjects to identify those who were telling the truth. Only the Secret Service agents were able to make consistently accurate determinations (Ekman & O'Sullivan, 1991). Of course, viewing a video is not the same as seeing a living, breathing, squirming little suspect sitting in front of you, but the evidence still points to the difficulty of making accurate judgments when it comes to lying.

If punishment is to be used, it should be used sparingly and only in conjunction with a positive reinforcement of some alternative response. That is, while the punishment is suppressing an undesirable response, positive reinforcement should be used to strengthen a socially approved alternative response. Punishment has only a short-lived effect on people who have few response options. This is why it is so often ineffective in the case of criminals—they have few, if any, socially approved means of achieving the material things our society values. In short, behavior modification brought about through positive reinforcement is more likely to be lasting and, eventually, self-perpetuating than that brought about through the use of aversive controls.

Psychologist Bruno Bettelheim has long opposed the use of punishment as a method for changing behavior. Taking a humanistic position, he argues that punishment may traumatize the child and/or make the child become more devious. The best way to discipline a child, Bettelheim asserts, is to tell the child that "we are sure that had he known he was doing wrong he wouldn't have done so" or that "we disapprove of what he has done but are convinced that his intentions were good" (Bettelheim, 1985). Treating children in this manner, Bettelheim believes, can promote a healthy sense of moral discipline, rather than destruction of self-esteem.

Extinction

A basic principle in learning is that behavior that is not reinforced will slowly be extinguished. A rat that has learned to press a lever 400 times per hour will eventually press it only 4 or 5 times per hour if its lever-pressing response ceases to be reinforced. Learned responses are abandoned when they no longer result in a payoff.

Studies of extinction in rats and humans have uncovered an interesting phenomenon. During extinction the rate of responding initially increases before it begins to peter out. The teacher who discovers that her display of anger toward a certain student somehow positively reinforces his undesirable behavior decides that she will simply ignore the student in order to extinguish his behavior. To her dismay, the teacher notes that the student's disorderly behavior increases rather than decreases. At this point consistency may be difficult, but it must be maintained if the extinction technique is to be successful. The student who is suddenly denied reinforcement for his undesired behavior tries even harder before finally realizing that the situation has really changed.

Extinction techniques will work only if the teacher can

1. Identify what is reinforcing the student's behavior
2. Eliminate that reinforcer
3. Remain faithful to the program

Shaping

Shaping is the technique of reinforcement by **successive approximation** until the desired response is emitted. For example, a rat newly introduced into an experimental chamber doesn't immediately rush over to the lever and start pressing it in order to receive the reinforcer. If left completely on its own, the rat may take an hour or even longer to stumble upon the lever. In order to speed up the conditioning process, the experimenter will shape the rat's behav-

SPOTLIGHT ON SELF-DIRECTED LEARNING

Behavior Modification in Action

Virtually all the behavior modification techniques described so far can in fact be used by individuals wishing to change their own behavior.[a] In effect, you can act in the dual role of both subject and experimenter. You choose the responses you want to reinforce, and you choose the reinforcers and even the scheduling of the reinforcement. You must select your own behavioral goals, and as your own controller, you must discipline yourself so that you will not violate the law of consistency no matter what the distractions might be. For example, suppose you decide that you want to lose 10 pounds. Next, decide what the reinforcer should be, and in this you must be totally honest with yourself and choose something that you really do want. Let's say that you are an ardent fan of your school's basketball team. Next, set up a schedule that is realistic, such as 2 pounds per week. Don't try for the whole 10 pounds all at once. Remember, there are such things as successive approximations and shaping. Now comes the hard part: Don't allow yourself to go to next week's home game unless the 2 pounds have been lost! Continue this procedure each week until the shaping has changed your shape.

This is just one example in a general area called self-regulated learning (see Chapter 19). Behaviorists, as in the example above, like to say that they are concerned only with tangible goals and outcomes,[b] not with the less obvious process outcomes sought by some of the cognitive psychologists, such as self-actualization or reduced cognitive dissonance.[c]

---

[a]   Watson, D. L., & R. G. Tharp, R. G. (1985). *Self-directed behavior* (4th ed.). New York: Norton.
[b]   Mace, F. C., Belfiore, P. J., & Shea, M. C. (1989). Operant theory and research on self-regulation. In B. J. Zimmerman & D. H. Schunk (Eds.), *Self-regulated learning and academic achievement: Theory, research and practice* (pp. 27–50). New York: Springer-Verlag.
[c]   Zimmerman, B. J. (1990). Self-regulated learning and academic achievement: An overview. *Educational Psychologist, 25,* 3–17.

---

ior by reinforcing it first for simply facing the lever; then, each time the rat makes a new response that results in a further approach to the lever, the behavior is immediately reinforced. The point is to get the animal winning as quickly as possible even if the ultimate behavioral goal has not been exhibited.

In the classroom, this shaping technique is an important aspect of behavior modification. It is important, especially in the younger grades, that children attain success *quickly and often.* Later, the number of reinforcements may be stretched over longer periods and thereby reduced. With young children, the use of food is extremely effective. As time goes by, the food may be paired with social stimuli such as smiling, nodding, praising, so that later on conditioned reinforcers may replace the primary reinforcers.

Madsen and Madsen provide an excellent example of shaping in which M&M candy is used to reinforce the responses of young children on the first day of school.

The teacher may start the very first class with an M&M party. While the children are eating, the teacher says, "We will have another M&M party if everyone is quiet while I count to ten." The teacher counts aloud quickly, making sure they win. After giving the candy the teacher says, "If everyone is quiet for five minutes we will have another party, but if someone talks we will not get to have one." Now the teacher sits back and waits; in all probability someone will talk, whereupon the teacher says, "Oh, I'm very sorry. Mary talked before our time was up; now we will not get to have a party. Maybe tomorrow we may have one if everyone is quiet." Some children will think this is not fair. Because the teacher does not get angry at Mary, Mary cannot give her problem to the teacher (Madsen & Madsen, 1970, p. 26).

The Token System

Another behavior modification technique that is being used more and more is the **token system,** or the token economy. In this system, individuals receive various tokens for emitting desired responses, and

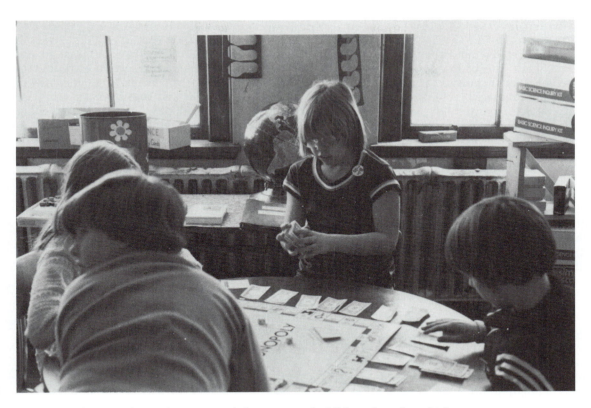

The game of Monopoly, in the context of play, can teach children the value of token money.

these tokens are later exchanged for prizes or privileges (just like the use of money). The token system is simply another method for employing a work-payment incentive program. Rather than keep a large refrigerator stocked with tasty food and drink beside the desk, the classroom teacher can set up a token economy.

Tokens, or conditioned reinforcers, can be virtually anything the teacher has available: pieces of colored cardboard, colored wool, gold stars, or poker chips, for example. The tokens are assigned point values and may eventually be turned in for some treasured prize, privilege, or desired activity. Tokens are awarded for desirable student behavior: accurate spelling, a certain number of correctly solved math problems, learning a specified number of lines of poetry, participating in class discussions, whatever. The colored pieces of cardboard may be set so that a red piece is worth, say, five points, a blue piece three points, and a white piece one point. Point values are assigned to the prizes so that a child can accumulate enough points in one day to earn a moderately val-

ued prize, but may have to spend an entire week working toward a particularly desirable prize. This system has two advantages: It maintains a high daily rate of desirable responses, and it teaches delayed gratification, or an ability to think in long-range terms.

Some psychologists have questioned the use of the token system for two reasons. First, since the token system relies for its effect on extrinsic reinforcement, it may in the long run decrease a student's intrinsic motivation to learn. Second, once the tokens are withdrawn (and a student cannot be kept on a token system forever), the resulting behavior changes may be extinguished.

Perhaps token systems in school settings are best employed when they are viewed from the outset as temporary arrangements. According to one educator, token systems in the classroom should be started only, "when teachers know how and plan to remove the system. Books and things learned from exciting teachers maintain interest, not the tokens" (Stephens & Cooper, 1980).

The Premack Principle

The **Premack principle** states that behavior that occurs at a naturally high rate of frequency may be used to reinforce behavior that occurs at a naturally low rate of frequency (Premack, 1965). For example, if left to their own devices, many children will spend far more time watching TV than reading. According to Premack, when such children have finished a given amount of reading, allow them to watch TV for a while. The teacher should carefully observe the children during free-choice periods and note the behaviors that naturally occur most frequently. These behaviors can then be used as positive reinforcers for low-probability responses. Teachers usually find that academic behavior has a low natural frequency, meaning that, when given a choice, most children prefer not to do schoolwork.

BEHAVIORAL TECHNOLOGY AND THE THREE R'S

Since the publication of such critiques of American education as the Coleman report (1966), the Jencks et al. report (1972), and, *A Nation at Risk* (National Commission on Excellence in Education, 1983), concerned citizens are loudly wondering what is wrong with our educational system and even whether schools really do make a difference.

The answer from the behaviorists is that, yes, schools can make a difference, *if only professional educators would utilize the technology that is now available to them.* In fact, this behavioral technology has been around for several decades—at least since the publication of Skinner's seminal 1954 article, "The Science of Learning and the Art of Teaching." So why aren't educators taking advantage of these tried-and-true techniques? Wayne Piersal, in a provocative article, has suggested that our reluctance to implement behavior modification programs is rooted in our culture's insistence on blindly clinging to tradition. He cites evidence to indicate that this has always been true, at least in Western cultures. Thus, the discovery that lemon or lime juice could cure scurvy occurred in 1601, but it took another 180 years for the British navy to act on this knowledge and use lime juice on a regular basis (Piersal, 1987).

As evidence that behavior programs are effective in solving many of the substantive problems of the classroom, Piersal has offered data on learning spelling, handwriting, oral reading, and mathematics.

Spelling

A number of studies, dating back at least to the 1960s, indicate that strict adherence to a specific reinforcement approach can facilitate an increase in spelling ability. To cite just one study, a group of fourth-grade children, all of whom had had spelling difficulties, was put on a reinforcement plan that set a success criterion of 100 percent. The reinforcements were all based on preferred activities (Premack effect), such as listening to records. Within a short time, 64 percent of the children attained the criterion measure (Axelrod, 1982).

Handwriting

Regarding handwriting, the evidence produced over the years also seems to be clearly indicative of a positive effect for behavior programs. In one example, a program of self-instruction and self-correction led to a higher level of performance in both copying paragraphs and writing lists of words (Kosiewicz et al., 1982).

Oral Reading

Studies in the area of oral reading also suggest the efficacy of behavior programs. Teachers used positive reinforcers, including candy, to train a group of moderately retarded girls in oral reading by (1) pronouncing aloud a word the student missed, (2) instructing the student to point to the given word and repeat it aloud a number of times, and then (3) asking the student to read the entire sentence all over again. The results showed that this procedure produced a marked increase in each student's oral reading ability (Singh et al., 1984).

"Earning by learning" is an approach to the teaching of reading that is unabashedly capitalistic in nature, and yet totally true to Skinnerian principles. Begun in Georgia, the program offers children, especially poor and at-risk children, monetary payments for reading. A child is paid two dollars for each book that is read in a given month (as long as a few simple questions are answered to prove that the book has been read and understood). The program is now operating in 17 states. The goal is achievement, not process. The children are paid, not by the hour, nor on the basis of some amorphous measure of effort or feeling of self-esteem, but by whether they can prove they have read and understood a book (Gingrich, 1995). Students in the program have shown dramatic increases in reading comprehension scores.

Mathematics

In the area of mathematics, especially number facts, behavior programs have a long history of positive results. Setting up a program in this area is relatively easy, since the correct response is self-evident. In just one example, reinforcement in the form of praise produced a solid increase in arithmetic performance (Schunk, 1981). In this study, reinforcement that followed modeling (a demonstration by the teacher of how to solve division problems) was more effective than reinforcement that followed didactic instruction alone.

In examining this rather impressive list of solid results, we must again be reminded that the implementation of these programs was always energized by a live, human hand. It takes a caring teacher to breathe warm life into the cool technology of behavior modification.

PROGRAMMED INSTRUCTION

The general concept of **programmed instruction** is probably as old as formal schooling itself. Each grade level has a certain small portion of our accumulated knowledge allotted to it, and each child is expected to master that segment before being allowed to proceed to the next grade. Children who don't keep up with the rest of the class are held back and repeat the year. Children who are not challenged by the content in their grade are skipped ahead to a level more consistent with their ability. The proponents of behavior modification agree with this practice in general (except in cases in which the pressure of the social promotion pushes all the children ahead, regardless of achievement), but they argue that the practice is too general and not tailored to the needs of the individual child. The individual child, they urge, needs a system of precision teaching, an educational prescription written just for him or her.

Programming is the arrangement of the material to be learned in a sequence of steps designed to lead students to the final goal. The steps are usually quite close together, ensuring a gradual increase in difficulty. The material being presented is broken down into small units called *frames,* which can be presented to students by mechanical means (the teaching machine). The entire program may have hundreds of frames, and the frames are written in such a way as to maximize the possibility of success. They may sometimes seem repetitious, but this is the result of a deliberate attempt to prevent any misconceptions from forming in the student's mind. A good

program is one in which the students make very few errors, no more than 5 percent. This means, of course, that the students are constantly experiencing success or that they are on what is close to a continuous reinforcement schedule. Teachers can add their own reinforcers (such as prizes or desired activities) for the completion of, say, every 25 items. This puts the students on an intermittent schedule of reinforcement (fixed ratio) for the external reinforcers while they remain on a continuous reinforcement schedule for the intrinsic success reinforcer.

Almost anyone with some degree of literacy can go through a program. Not all students will proceed at the same rate, but that, after all, is the story of individual differences. The first frame is always very easy, and the students are led by small steps into more complicated frames until the unit is completed or until the students have achieved the desired *terminal behavior.*

Programs may be written in book form, with the questions on one page and the answers on the facing page. The students cover the answers, respond, and then uncover the answers as a self-check. Programs may also be placed in machines that are set so as not to move from one frame to the next until each one in turn has been successfully completed. Some machines are even equipped with a buzzer or bell that sounds when a correct response has been given. The buzzers and bells act as further conditioned reinforcers for correct responses.

Programmed instruction has several key advantages.

1. The student must pay attention, for if the program is to continue, responses must be given. The student is therefore an active participant in the learning process, not a mere passive observer.

2. Each student proceeds at his or her own rate. One student may finish in one hour a program that takes another student five hours to complete.

3. Reinforcement, to use Skinner's term, or feedback, to use Bruner's, is immediate. There are no delays between the response and knowledge of results.

4. Learning that takes place in a programmed setting is always by positive reinforcement. Aversive techniques are never used. Machines don't shout, or hit, or "tell parents."

5. Machines can be set automatically to keep track of errors. These can be discussed later with the

SPOTLIGHT ON TECHNOLOGY

Computers in the Classroom

As of 1997 there were roughly 2.8 million computers in the nation's 100,000+ schools, or about 1 for every 15 students. Along with the various add-ons and peripherals, such as modems, disk drives, and printers, the estimated cost to the schools has been somewhat over $4 billion. With all that time and money spent on this powerful educational technology, why are our schoolchildren still performing at lower academic levels than was promised by the rosy forecasts of the computer advocates? Why are we continuing to show rising rates of illiteracy, declining math scores, and lower levels of reading comprehension? Although it may go without saying, it must be stressed that computers are most effective when good teachers are involved. So much of the early promise of computers in the classroom has now faded, not because they don't work, but because they are not the panacea that the early propagandists had predicted. However, some of the current critics of computers in the classroom are now using the same hyperbole that characterized the rhetoric of the early proponents. For example, to criticize computers on the basis that "everything was better in the good old days when I was a kid" is nothing more than a glittering generalization. Flash cards were not the most sensitively humane of pedagogical exercises (nor, of course, are some of the drill and kill computer programs used today). But compared to some of the old "Talking Head" models of instruction, which were based on an "I send, you receive" model of teaching, today's computers do allow for interaction between the electronic tutor and the flesh-and-blood learner. As has been shown, interaction is essential for engaging students more deeply in their own learning experiences. It may be that to a large degree education is a solo enterprise, but for those who see it as working best as a group activity, the computer allows for interactions without the social baggage of extraneous chatting that so often accompanies group learning.

Most studies of computer-assisted instruction (CAI) show that the new systems can work. Computer-driven practice programs seem to make children better spellers, and the integrated learning systems, which deliver entire curricula to students, offer guarantees that grade averages will go up. There is also clear evidence that the use of word processors has had an educational benefit. Because the rigors of editing and rewriting have been made so much easier, students can now produce written work that

student, and in this important student-teacher dialogue, any misconceptions about the subject matter can be eliminated.

Probably the main disadvantage to programmed instruction is that many students report finding it boring. "If that same question is asked one more time, I'll scream," said one student facing the seventeenth successive frame making the same point. In their zeal to increase frame difficulty ever so slowly, certain programmers have simply not increased the frame difficulty at all for long periods in the program. This is often resented by the alert student.

Computer-Assisted Instruction

Even the teaching machine is being phased out and replaced by what is called **computer-assisted instruction (CAI).** With the advent of the microcomputer, CAI has taken a great leap forward. In past years CAI was restricted to fairly wealthy school districts. It consisted of using a computer (usually just one) together with TV screens and typewriters to allow groups of students to try their hands at programming in BASIC or to go through fairly stilted preprogrammed lessons. These earlier computers were expensive and had very limited internal memory. During the 1980s this somewhat cumbersome surpasses much of the work done just a few years ago. Also, motivated students using some of today's math programs learn about algebraic equations, powers, and logarithms far more quickly than when everything had to be done longhand. But one of the real problems is that despite having the new technology available to them, teachers have not always been prepared enough to take full advantage of this electronic opportunity. Even though teachers are allegedly being instructed in the most effective use of CAI, this process is too often cursory, incomplete, and frustrating. Too many teachers have had to go through painful and personally expensive self-education. One result is that there are now dramatic differences among teachers in computer expertise as well as in their ability to communicate this knowledge to students. This fact is especially critical, because, after all, good teachers will always be the heart and soul of good education. All of this has led to 6 important rules for gaining the most benefit from the new technology:

1. Give computers to teachers before placing them in the classroom.
2. Move the machines out of the computer labs and into the classrooms.
3. Provide at least one computer for every three students.
4. Give teachers the time and freedom to restructure their curriculum around the technology. Although CAI has the potential to radically transform how teaching and learning occur in the public schools, preservice teacher preparation plays an important role in whether this transformation will actually occur.[a]
5. Give teachers instruction in the basics of computer networking. This is especially useful for the teacher who is at all research-oriented. The tools of research are no longer based on library card catalogs. A computer network allows the user to electronically browse through and retrieve articles and documents essential for the research process.[b]
6. Don't expect overnight miracles. It may take up to a few years before any significant gains are apparent.

---

[a]   Ashburn, E. A., & Cilley, D. M. (1992, March). Teaching and learning to teach through technology. *IBM Higher Education* (a supplement to *T.H.E. Journal*), 32–36.
[b]   Hoh, J. H. (1992). Creation of an information infrastructure. *AAHE Bulletin, 8,* 2–4.

technology was gradually replaced by the inexpensive yet powerful microcomputer.

The increase in capacity and decrease in cost of computers has been dramatic. Not too long ago, one of the major mainframe manufacturers was selling a computer called the Century 200 for what was hailed as a breakthrough price of only $250,000. There were a few necessary extras, such as a $95,000 "clean room," a special, dust-free environment with built-in monitors for constant temperature, pressure, and humidity control. The machine's internal memory was 64K (kilobytes), or about the same memory capacity as today's $100 microcomputer. It has recently been estimated that had automobile technology advanced at the rate of computer technology over the past 35 years, a Rolls-Royce would now cost $2.50 and would get 2 million miles per gallon of gas (Rochester & Gantz, 1983).

The microcomputer, the small, stand-alone, desktop computer with its own central processor, has now found its way into virtually every school system in the country. To be sure, some microcomputers are still being used to promote computer literacy and programming skills (see the Spotlight on Computer Literacy), but many have become supplemental teaching tools in such traditional subjects as math, geography, history, and English grammar. Thus the microcomputer has taken on the role of personal tu-

"I want you to interface your homework before you download the TV."

tor, aiding students in sharpening their skills and increasing their understanding of basic curriculum mainstays. And, as with any personal instructor, the student can proceed at his or her own pace.

The earliest software programs were designed to promote drill and practice; that is, they were much like flashcards on a screen. Then came the software tutorial, a program for taking a student through a discrete lesson unit. The latest software has as the final goal the mastery of global concepts. The student makes many choices throughout the running of the program and, in effect, is prodded into discovering a concept for himself or herself. A student's error automatically triggers a program review of the material not fully comprehended. Thus, CAI is constantly interactive, forcing the student to respond, to make

choices, to participate. Unlike TV instruction, CAI does not allow the student to become a passive recipient of information.

When teachers have been properly prepared, the research findings on CAI have been largely positive. Children are learning more and liking it better. In a meta-analysis of over 50 studies, James Kulik and colleagues (1983) have shown the striking effectiveness of CAI in grades 6 through 12. Computer-based teaching raised final exam scores from the fiftieth to the sixty-third percentile, and these gains were maintained in follow-up examinations given several months after the completion of instruction. CAI was also found to be more efficient than traditional instruction in that it significantly reduced the amount of time the students needed for learning. In addition,

CAI was shown to be more effective at the secondary level than it had proved to be among college students. Because of this, Kulik wondered if CAI might be even more effective with elementary-age children than with older students.

A study performed by the Educational Testing Service (ETS) appears to lend substance to Kulik's suspicion. Using a sample of several thousand elementary-age children divided into CAI (experimental) and non-CAI (control) groups, the ETS found that at the end of the first year CAI students scored at the sixty-fourth percentile while the control groups scored at the fiftieth percentile on a standardized math test. At the end of the second year, the CAI students had jumped to the seventy-first percentile, and after the third year to seventy-sixth. "In other words, the increase in their test scores was steady over several years" (Ragosta, 1983).

It may very well be that learning through computer interaction has both developmental and cumulative effects. The earlier the child begins, the better the learning strategies being incorporated; hence CAI may have a snowball effect as training continues. CAI has also been shown to be especially beneficial to homebound students—students who, for a variety of reasons, cannot attend school in the normal fashion. In one report, from Maryland, homebound students from kindergarten through grade 12 were provided with home computers and the skills

to use them (by teachers who had been thoroughly trained in a National Science Foundation summer-long workshop). These students demonstrated not only that they could keep up with their in-school peers, but that in many cases they could surpass the schoolchildren (Copper, 1991). Finally, aside from the achievement outcomes, CAI has been shown to have produced other important effects.

Affective-motivational outcomes   Gerald Bracey reported that from kindergarten through grade 12 students consistently display positive attitudes toward computers (Bracey, 1982). Students almost unanimously report that they enjoy working at their own pace and appreciate the elimination of public embarrassment over making mistakes. Students are more willing to try, to take chances in the secure knowledge that a wrong guess is never going to expose them to public scorn. In Jerome Bruner's analysis of learning, for true discovery learning to occur, the student must be willing to take chances and explore new areas. This can take place only when the student knows that exploration is both rewarding and safe (Bruner, 1966).

Because students feel more in control of their educational destinies when CAI is involved, they are less likely to explain away poor performance as just a matter of bad luck. They gain a feeling of mastery, which may be at least as important an outcome as

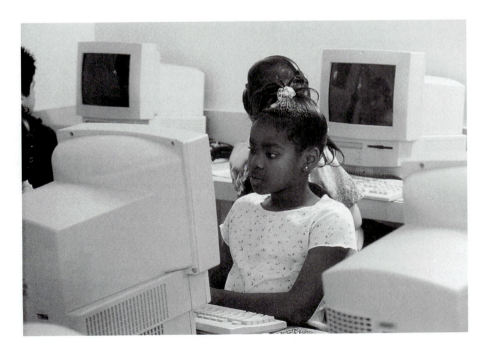

Microcomputers now make computer-assisted instruction (CAI) a possibility for all students.

SPOTLIGHT ON COMPUTER LITERACY

How Much Is Enough?

Without a doubt, the computer revolution is here. Computers and their "magic" chips do everything from making out the payroll and scanning income-tax returns to running cars, watches, cameras, and corporations. It's little wonder that educators have begun insisting that every educated person should become "computer literate" and that no self-respecting classroom should be without at least a couple of these electronic miracles. Even first-graders are being introduced to computers and being taught some elementary programming skills. They are also learning what not to do, such as never to remove the disk while the little drive light is still on. Thrilled parents bask in the reflected glory of their children's computer accomplishments and secretly dream of the day when their children will be winning Nobel prizes for having achieved some new and exotic technological breakthrough. In short, "computer literacy" has become the catchword of the end of the century. To argue against computers is viewed as akin to seeing the first automobile roll down the road and saying, "I'd rather have a horse" or "The only accelerator I'll ever need is a buggy whip."

What has made the computer revolution even more compellingly dramatic has been the advent of the microcomputer, that incredible little desktop machine. The micro is a stand-alone computer with its own input device (the keyboard), internal memory (RAM), central processor, memory storage system, and output display (the screen).

The memory capacity of even the least expensive of today's PCs exceeds that of many of the mainframes of just a few years ago. But the question is not whether today's computers are extraordinary marvels of electronic wizardry. They are. It is whether every child should become computer literate, and, if so, how literate. Computer literacy seems to have several definitions, but most are some variation of the following: By computer awareness and literacy is meant a general understanding of computers, their uses and applications to every-day living. Knowing what [computers] can and cannot do, how they are used in today's world, and how they may affect our lives are central themes which run throughout a program in computer awareness and literacy.[a] Problems begin, however, as soon as we begin to operationalize the generalities in this definition. For example, to some experts, knowing what computers can and cannot do demands expertise in programming. "To tell a computer what you want it to do, you must be able to communicate with it. To do that, you will need to learn a language for writing your ideas down . . . If you can tell a computer how to do the things you want it to do, you are computer literate."[b] To others, learning to program the computer is not essential: "Computer literacy is a familiarity with a device that enhances one's ability to live in and cope with the modern world. This does not mean, however, that students must acquire the ability to program, but rather the ability to manipulate

computer technology."[c] The issue of whether or not to include programming in the definition of computer literacy is, therefore, one that divides the experts. Some, mercifully of the minority, claim that computer literacy is virtually synonymous with achieving a degree in computer science. The student should have courses in everything from machine language to FORTRAN, from computer architecture to advanced Pascal, and much, much more. Admittedly, some students should probably follow this rigorous path, but all students? A more modest goal of those advocating programming is that each student learn at least one programming language, usually either BASIC or LOGO. Their argument is not that learning to program is an end in itself but that it teaches the student how to think. Learning to create logical algorithms and translate them into a programming language is alleged to produce, in a sense, a strong and disciplined mind. A certain amount of elementary programming in LOGO or BASIC might also be introduced in the early grades. However, there is danger in carrying this strategy too far. Without competent, informed computer teachers, students often pick up very bad programming habits that must be broken later. It may therefore be better to postpone the bulk of programming instruction until students reach a junior high class taught by a specialist.

Advocates of programming also urge that students be taught the binary numbering system. Since computers can respond only to on-off commands, to understand what a computer goes through, one must learn to convert base 10 to base 2, and at least be able to add and subtract in base 2. A thorough knowledge of the binary system, it is felt, is essential for understanding the rudiments of any programming technique. Others feel that programming skills are not necessary, that computer literacy is like automobile literacy: You only have to learn how to make it go, not the physics or engineering involved. Those who hold this view define computer literacy as being able to turn on the machine, insert a disk, and follow a "user friendly," menu-driven program. And since the use of a computer demands entering data of some sort, they argue that the student is far better off taking a course in typing than one in base 2 math. A parallel argument is that taking courses in BASIC is like taking a course or two in French. It might be fun to then go to a French restaurant and order your meal directly from the menu, but if you need a highly accurate translation of more difficult material, you'd better hire an expert. Besides, in programming, a little learning can be dangerous: If you start breaking into a prepackaged program in order to change a line or two, you might ruin the whole program. This position also sees the learning of base 2 as a waste of time. The machine may have to "think" in on-off terms, but the student doesn't. A final antiprogramming argument is that in a few years BASIC and LOGO may well be dead languages, important

historically but of little relevance to students entering the twenty-first-century job market. The computers of tomorrow will still be programmable, "but nobody except the experts will do the programming . . . The final custom-fitting of all commercial programs will be done by the user, but in English, not in BASIC."[d]

What can we expect of students in the year 2000 in the way of computer literacy? The consensus among those holding the middle-ground view is that minimal computer literacy should include:

1. Knowing a little about the history of computers, from the giant, vacuum-tubed mainframes of yesterday to the miniaturized microcomputers of today.
2. Knowing the basic parts of the computer, from input to output.
3. Knowing how to handle, format, and copy disks as well as how to protect them from damage.
4. Knowing at least one word-processing program and one math program.[e] Research strongly suggests that the use of at least these two types of programs enhances students' writing and math skills.
5. Knowing how to handle the computer safely and intelligently and, as much as possible, learning the basic damage-prevention techniques.
6. Knowing enough about how to get along with a computer that you can then use the

computer itself to learn more about the computer.[f]

Obviously, some students should be provided with more than just these minimal competencies. The choice of what to include should also take into account each student's own special aptitudes and interests. Students interested in science, for example, should be exposed to laboratory simulations on the computer, whereas those preparing for an office career should be trained in database and spreadsheet techniques.

In short, the ultimate goal of computer literacy should be to provide students with skills they can use in all their traditional courses so that they may be better students today and better citizens tomorrow. In the words of one expert, "The schools, relying primarily on computers and teachers for instruction, will play a central role in the moral and intellectual development of U.S. youngsters."[g]

[a] Watts, N. (1981, April). A dozen uses for the computer in education. *Educational Technology*, 20.
[b] Luehrmann, A. (1984, April). The best way to teach computer literacy. *Electronic Learning*, 39.
[c] Scher, R. (1984, January). The computer backlash. *Electronic Learning*.
[d] D'Ignazio, F. (1983, September). Beyond computer literacy. *Compute*.
[e] Bracey, G. (1982, November–December). Computers in education: What the research shows. *Electric Learning*.
[f] Steinberg, E. R. (1991). *Teaching computers to teach*. Hillsdale, NJ: Prentice Hall.
[g] Wagschal, P. (1984, December). A last chance for computers in the schools. *Phi Delta Kappan*.

academic achievement itself (if indeed the two can be separated).

Social outcomes

The dire warnings that CAI will dehumanize the classroom, usually issued by an educational philosopher who has never seen students busily working *together* on a personal computer, are beginning to appear groundless. Bracey reported that CAI often fosters a cooperative group atmosphere. When two or three students are working together on a single computer, there is more "collaboration, or cooperative problem solving, than there is anywhere else in the school" (1982, p. 54). The students are typically immersed in trying to get the program to run and are not flagrantly competing to be the first person with a hand in the air, signaling the teacher that "I won."

The prevailing consensus is that CAI is an asset in the classroom. It tends to promote achievement, motivation, and a spirit of cooperation—an extremely powerful academic mix. Also, as a teaching aid CAI can provide simulations of activities the student otherwise might never experience. This is probably most pertinent in science courses, where laboratory supplies might be scarce or where running a particular experiment could be too dangerous, expensive, or time-consuming. Perhaps CAI simulations can reverse the trend, reported by the National Science Foundation, of students' dropping out of science and science-related courses (Lepper, 1985).

A note of concern has recently been sounded by Cole and Griffin, who found that CAI may not always be used on a fair and equitable basis. They say that more computers are being placed in the hands of America's affluent children than of its poor children, and even when the poor children do get computers, the equipment is used almost exclusively for rote drill instead of cognitive enrichment (Cole & Griffin, 1987).

Obviously, a great deal more research is needed in this important area. As M. R. Lepper points out, the influence of this new technology "is likely to have more important effects on the lives and the social and psychological functioning of children than any other technological advance in the past century" (Lepper, 1985).

The Teacher's Role

Although computers have proved effective in transmitting facts and, to some extent, even concepts, the teacher is needed to tie these facts and subconcepts into more global abstractions. The teacher can use current examples of certain principles, thus helping to make the computer lesson seem more alive and thus more effective. Bruner has said that the student must have a background of facts, the "stuff of learning," before discovery learning can take place. A computer can obviously supply that "stuff." Knowing a few names and dates does allow for a certain level of understanding, which will aid a student in further exploration and discovery. A student who thinks that John Dewey and Aristotle were classmates together at Columbia, for example, may find it difficult to appreciate the significance of the historical succession of philosophical ideas. There are, however, some areas that simply can't be fully taught by the computer. History and literature would be reduced to a pile of bits and pieces (or perhaps even bits and bytes) without the teacher to integrate the material into a living picture.

School systems should not be misguided into spending large portions of their budgets buying ever-more-sophisticated computers in the fond belief that CAI alone will turn our schoolchildren into budding rocket scientists. This is especially true when the computer purchase comes at the expense of teacher salaries. One of the most glaring problems facing American education today is the failure to pay teachers a decent wage. "We will not attract the brightest and best people into the teaching field until we treat this profession as the priority we believe it to be" (De Concini, 1988, p. 117).

As we saw at the beginning of this chapter during the discussion of whole versus part learning, when material is learned in discrete units, the parts must be put back together. No programmer can ever anticipate all the ways in which children may misinterpret how the separate parts should be glued back together into a meaningful whole. The teacher must be there, on the spot, guiding, motivating, doing the real job of teaching in its true sense.

SUMMARY

Learning in the classroom involves the concept of transfer. What is learned in class is thought to transfer into later-life situations, and thus will enable the learner to earn a living and enjoy a fuller life.

Theories of transfer date back to the early Greek notion of formal discipline, in which the mind, considered comparable to an athlete's muscles, was thought to require systematic exercise if it was to grow. Even as late as the early twentieth century, proponents of this position created academic curricula that stressed such subjects as logic, Greek, and Latin not because these subjects had any practical value, but because they "strengthened" the mind.

Formal discipline theory was seriously challenged by a number of psychologists, including William James, E. L. Thorndike, and Charles Judd. All of their studies pointed to the fact that "training the mind" had little if any lasting benefits.

Educators today are no longer concerned with the theory of mental discipline, but they are concerned with promoting positive transfer between learning in the classroom and living effectively in later life.

The learning curve, a plotting out of one's learning speed, typically shows negative acceleration; that is, when confronted with a new subject, students learn a great deal of the material in a relatively short time and then, with increased practice, add less and less new learning.

Harlow coined the term *learning sets* to explain what gestalt psychologists had previously labeled as insight.

Massed versus distributed practice involves the question of how the learner should allocate his or her time for maximum efficiency. In learning a new physical skill, distributed practice (an hour a day for a week) is more efficient than massed practice (seven straight hours in one day). On intellectual tasks, however, distributed practice may destroy the meaning of the material. In this case it is best to divide the material into meaningful units and then work on each unit in a massed-learning session.

The efficiency of spaced learning over massed learning is now called the spacing effect, and its documentation as a valid phenomenon goes back at least as far as the seminal work of Hermann Ebbinghaus in the first decade of this century.

Whole versus part learning involves the question of whether learning is most efficient when the material is broken down into small, discrete units or left in a total, organized whole. The best method seems to be to work first on the whole in order to gain a general overview of the material and then go back and work on the various parts.

Albert Bandura has suggested that a large part of what a person learns occurs through imitation, or modeling. This is called social learning theory, since it is concerned with learning that takes place within a social situation. Bandura has shown that learning that occurs through modeling need not be based on direct reinforcement of the response. Other than the parents, the teacher may be the most important model in the child's environment. Conditions for learning are thus established not only by what the teacher says but also by what he or she does.

The current popularity of operant conditioning in the classroom is due in large part to the fact that the teacher is presented with a very precise prescription for handling specific classroom problems. Changing a student's behavior through the use of conditioning techniques is called behavior modification.

To use behavior modification techniques, the teacher must first define the educational objectives in behavioral terms, that is, determine exactly *what* the student should learn and *how* the student is to show that the learning has taken place. The teacher can infer that learning or understanding has taken place only by observing the *behavior* of the student.

Once the objectives have been defined, the teacher observes the student's initial rate of response, or operant level, for the activity in question. The operant level, or base rate, for the given activity should be observed in the classroom situation.

After the behavioral goal is set and the student's operant level is established, the teacher can use reinforcement to strengthen (condition) some student behavior and withhold reinforcement of (extinguish) other student behavior. Reinforcement always increases response rate. Positive reinforcement occurs when the response rate increases by adding the reinforcer (giving the student M&M candies, gold stars, or high grades), and negative reinforcement occurs when the response rate increases by taking away the reinforcer (removing an aversive stimulus when the desired behavior is emitted). Aversive stimuli should be used as negative reinforcement or punishment only with great caution, since they can result in the student's acquiring not only the goal behavior the teacher intended but also other, potentially damaging responses.

The key to the successful use of behavior modification techniques is *consistency*. The teacher must follow through on the established reinforcement schedule without exception.

Reinforcement must *follow*, not precede, the student's response. Usually, the sooner the reinforcement follows the response, the more impact it will have in changing behavior.

Behavior modification proponents also make use of the token system, a system based on the use of conditioned reinforcers, or tokens. The token system has two main advantages: (1) It maintains a high daily rate of desirable responses, and (2) it teaches delayed gratification.

The Premack principle states that behavior that naturally occurs at a high rate can be used to reinforce behavior that occurs at a naturally low rate. Thus, one set of responses may be used to reinforce another set of responses. If a student has a higher rate of TV-viewing responses than reading responses, then viewing TV can be used as reinforcement for a certain amount of reading. Success in using behavioral modification techniques has been shown in the following basic-skills areas: spelling, handwriting, oral reading, and mathematics.

In programmed instruction the material to be learned is arranged in an orderly sequence of steps designed to reach a certain goal. A good program is one in which the level of difficulty increases very slowly, so that students make very few errors (less than 5 percent). The material to be learned is broken down into small units, or frames, and can be presented to students by mechanical means (the teaching machine). The basic advantage of programmed instruction is that each student can proceed at his or her own rate. However, brighter students may become bored with the long succession of similar items. Also, when material is learned in bits and pieces, it is often hard for the student to integrate the discrete parts into a meaningful whole.

Teaching machines are being phased out in favor of computer-assisted instruction. With the advent of the microcomputer and the recent upgrading of instructional software, CAI has proved to be an important teaching adjunct. Research findings indicate that CAI has been effective in increasing academic achievement. It appears also that CAI has other personal benefits, especially in the affective-motivational and social areas.

Despite its apparent success as a "private tutor," CAI can never replace the teacher. He or she must remain as the major component in the total educational enterprise. The teacher's role becomes even more critical during this technological age of bits, bytes, and chips. Without the teacher to explain relationships and integrate concepts, CAI's long-term success may turn out to be shallow. Critics suggest that CAI may be in danger of producing a generation of child robots whose knowledge base, though admittedly large, will be superficial and perhaps even random.

KEY TERMS AND NAMES

Albert Bandura
    modeling
    social learning theory
behavior modification
computer-assisted instruction (CAI)
learning curve
learning set
massed learning
Premack principle
programmed instruction

punishment
shaping (successive approximation)
spacing effect
teaching machine
terminal behavior
token system
transfer
    negative transfer
    positive transfer

THEORY INTO PRACTICE: OPERANT CONDITIONING

Since an operant is any response an organism can emit without the presentation of an identifiable stimulus, operant conditioning can be easily demonstrated in a variety of situations. You don't need rats or pigeons or fancy automated equipment in order to show how a freely emitted operant can be conditioned. The operant will condition as long as it is consistently followed by a reinforcer. For demonstration purposes, we will focus on the freely emitted eye blink (not an eye blink response that is elicited by the presentation of a puff of air). It is important to remember that the same response may be both an operant and a respondent, depending on what produces it. For example, a tap on the patellar tendon will act as an unconditioned stimulus in producing a knee jerk. However, if you happen to kick up your

leg in the absence of any known stimulus, that same response would have been emitted and therefore classified as an operant. Similarly, the blink of an eye as a response to a puff of air would be a respondent, whereas that same blink in the absence of any stimulus would be an operant.

First, prepare two tally sheets. On each sheet write the numbers 1 to 150 in neat, straight columns. Next, select someone from your class, give him or her one of the tally sheets, and instruct the subject to make a check mark next to a number, beginning with the number 1, every time a tap of the pencil is heard. You must then carefully watch your subject's eyes, and each time you observe an eye blink, lightly tap your pencil on the desk. Thus, the tap will be *contingent on the blinking response* and will, therefore, act as a reinforcer. In short, each time your subject blinks, you tap. The subject's column of check marks will become a running tally of the number of blinks he or she emitted. Continue this procedure for two minutes. *Be sure not to let the subject know that his or her blinking behavior is influencing your taps.* Then take a one-minute break. After the break, provide the subject with the second tally sheet and continue the same procedure for another two minutes. At the end of this time, count the number of check marks that the subject has made on each tally sheet. Compare the results. If conditioning has occurred, there will be a significant increase in the number of check marks on the second sheet. This will indicate that the rate of operant responding has increased as a result of the operant's having been paired with a reinforcing stimulus. The reinforcer, of course, is the tap.

Why is the tap reinforcing? The fact that the tap acts as a reinforcer actually needs no further explanation as long as the operant rate showed an increase during the second time period. After all, Skinner insists that no internal inferences need be made. If the stimulus that follows a response results in an increased response rate, the stimulus is, by definition, a reinforcer. If you must speculate further, however, you might question your subject. It could be that when someone is told to respond (make a check mark) only after hearing a certain signal, then that person may begin to want to hear the signal (since not hearing it could be frustrating).

It must be pointed out again that the response being conditioned here is the eye blink, not the inscription of the check mark. The reinforcing stimulus, the tap, is presented *after each eye blink.* If you want further proof, you might set up a third trial in which you never tap your pencil, no matter how often the subject blinks. Thus, you would be running your subject through an extinction period, during which the rate of blinking should decrease. Of course, as with any conditioned operant, we cannot expect to cause blinking to cease completely. But we can expect that the response rate will eventually return to its operant level (that is, its preconditioned rate).

If possible, you might try this procedure with children in a classroom. Remember to send the chosen subject out of the room while you explain the real purpose of the study to the child who will do the tapping. Also, explain to the other children in the room the importance of not divulging the actual purpose of the demonstration to the subject.

REFERENCES

Axelrod, S. (1982). *Behavior modification for the classroom teacher* (2d ed.). New York: McGraw-Hill.

Bandura, A. (1978). The self system in reciprocal determinism. *American Psychologist, 33,* 344–358.

Bandura, A. (1986). *Social foundations of thought and action: A social cognitive theory.* Englewood Cliffs, NJ: Prentice Hall.

Bandura, A., & McDonald, F. J. (1963). Influence of social reinforcement and the behavior of models in shaping children's moral judgments. *Journal of Abnormal and Social Psychology, 67,* 274–281.

Bandura, A., Ross, D., & Ross, S. A. (1963). Imitation of film-mediated aggressive models. *Journal of Abnormal and Social Psychology, 66,* 3–11.

Bettelheim, B. (1985, November). Punishment versus discipline. *Atlantic Monthly,* 51–59.

Bracey, G. (1982, November–December). Computers in education: What the research shows. *Electronic Learning.*

Brantner, J. P., & Doherty, M. A. (1983). A review of timeout: A conceptual and methodological analysis. In S. Axelrod & J. Apsche (Eds.), *The effects of punishment on human behavior.* Orlando, FL: Academic Press.

Brown, A., Campione, J., & Day, J. (1981). Learning to learn: On training students to learn from texts. *Educational Researcher, 16,* 14–21.

Bruner, J. S. (1966). *Toward a theory of instruction.* Cambridge, MA: Harvard University Press.

Cole, M., & Griffin, P. (1987). *Contextual factors in education.* Madison: Wisconsin Center for Education Research.

Coleman, J. S. (1966). *Equality of educational opportunity.* Washington, DC: U.S. Department of Health, Education and Welfare, Office of Education.

Copper, L. R. (1991). CAI with home-bound students proves successful in model program. *T.H.E. Journal, 18,* 68–69.

Craig, A. R., & Cleary, P. J. (1982). Reduction of stuttering by young male stutterers using EMG feedback. *Biofeedback and Self-Regulation, 7,* 241–255.

De Concini, D. (1988). America's little red schoolhouse: Is it holding up today? *American Psychologist, 42,* 115–117.

Dempster, F. N. (1987). Effects of variable encoding and spaced presentation on vocabulary learning. *Journal of Educational Psychology, 22,* 1–21.

Dempster, F. N. (1988). The spacing effect: A case study in the failure to apply the results of psychological research. *American Psychologist, 43,* 627–634.

Ebbinghaus, H. (1913; originally 1885). *Memory: A contribution to experimental psychology* (p. 89). Trans. H. A. Ruger & C. E. Bussenius. New York: Teachers College Press.

Ekman, P., & O'Sullivan, M. (1991). Who can catch a liar? *American Psychologist, 46,* 913–920.

Gingrich, N. (1995). *To renew America* (p. 264). New York: HarperCollins.

Harlow, H. F., McGaugh, J. L., & Thompson, R. F. (1971). *Psychology* (p. 301). San Francisco: Albion.

Hurt, H. T., Scott, M. D., & McCroskey, J. C. (1978). *Communication in the classroom* (p. 32). Reading, MA: Addison-Wesley.

James, W. (1890). *The principles of psychology.* New York: Henry Holt.

James, W. (1901). *Talks to teachers on psychology and to students on some of life's ideals.* New York: Holt.

Jencks, C., Smith, M., Acland, H., Cohen, D., Gintis, H., Heyns, B., & Michelson, S. (1972). *Inequality: A reassessment of the effects of family and schooling in America.* New York: Basic Books.

Kohn, A. (1993). *Punished by rewards: The trouble with gold stars, incentive plans, A's, praise, and other bribes.* Boston: Houghton Mifflin.

Kosiewicz, M. M., Hallahan, D. P., Lloyd, J., & Graves, A. W. (1982). Effects of self-instruction and self-correction procedures on handwriting performance. *Learning Disabilities Quarterly, 5,* 71–78.

Kulik, J. A., Bangert, R. L., & Williams, G. W. (1983). Effects of computer-based teaching on secondary school students. *Journal of Educational Psychology, 75,* 19–26.

Lepper, M. R. (1985). Microcomputers in education: Motivational and social issues. *American Psychologist, 40*(1), 18.

Linschied, T. R., Iwata, B. A., Rickets, R. W., Williams, D. E., & Griffin, J. C. (1990). Clinical evaluation of the Self-Injurious Behavior Inhibiting System (SIBIS). *Journal of Applied Behavior Analysis, 23,* 53–78.

Lincheid, T. R., Pejeau, C., Cohen, S., & Footo-Lenz, M. (1994). Positive side effects in the treatment of SIB using the self-injurious behavior inhibiting system (SIBIS): Implications for operant and biochemical explanations of SIB. *Research in Developmental Disabilities, 15,* 81–90.

Madsen, C. H., & Madsen, C. K. (1970). *Teaching discipline.* Boston: Allyn & Bacon. Quotations are reprinted by permission.

Maurer, A. (1974). Corporal punishment. *American Psychologist, 29,* 614–626.

National Commission on Excellence in Education (1983). *A nation at risk: The imperative for educational reform.* Washington, DC: U.S. Department of Education.

Novak, J. (1980). *Handbook for the learning how to learn program.* Ithaca: New York State College of Agriculture and Life Sciences.

Piersal, W. C. (1987). Basic skills education. In C. A. Maher & S. G. Forman (Eds.), *A behavioral approach to education of children and youth.* Hillsdale, NJ: Erlbaum.

Premack, D. (1965). Reinforcement theory. In D. Levine, *Nebraska symposium on motivation* (pp. 123–180). Lincoln: University of Nebraska Press.

Ragosta, M. (1983). Computer-assisted instruction and compensatory education: A longitudinal analysis. *Machine Mediated Learning, 1*(1), 108.

Reder, L. M., & Anderson, J. R. (1982). Effects of spacing and embellishment on memory for the main points of a text. *Memory and Cognition, 10,* 97–102.

Rescorla, R. A. (1987). A Pavlovian analysis of goal-directed behavior. *American Psychologist, 42,* 119–125.

Rochester, J. B., & Gantz, J. (1983). *The naked computer* (p. 15). New York: Morrow.

Saxe, L. (1991). Lying: Thoughts of an applied social psychologist. *American Psychologist, 46,* 409–415.

Schunk, D. H. (1981). Modeling and attributional effects on children's achievement: A self-efficacy analysis. *Journal of Educational Psychology, 73,* 93–105.

Science engineering education for the 1980s and beyond (1980) (National Science Foundation Report). Washington, DC: National Science Foundation of the Department of Education.

Sears, R. R., Maccoby, E., & Levin, H. (1957). *Patterns of child rearing.* Evanston, IL: Row, Peterson.

Singh, N. N., Singh, J. S., & Winton, A. S. (1984). Positive practice overcorrection of oral reading errors. *Behavior Modification, 8,* 23–37.

Skinner, B. F. (1953). *Science and human behavior* (p. 402). New York: Macmillan.

Skinner, B. F. (1954). The science of learning and the art of teaching. *Harvard Educational Review, 24,* 86–97.

Skinner, B. F. (1969; originally 1965). Why teachers fail. In R. C. Sprinthall and N. A. Sprinthall (Eds.), *Educational psychology: Selected readings* (pp. 164–172). New York: Van Nostrand-Reinhold.

Smith, S. M., & Rothkopf, E. Z. (1984). Contextual enrichment and distribution of practice in the classroom. *Cognition and Instruction, 1,* 341–358.

Spettel, G. B. (1983, February). Classroom discipline now. *The Clearing House,* 267. Reprinted with permission of the Helen Dwight Reid Educational

Foundation. Published by Heldref Publications, 4000 Albemarle St., N.W., Washington, DC 20016. Copyright © 1983.

Stephens, T. M., & Cooper, J. O. (1980, November). *Educational Forum, 17,* 112.

Straus, M. A. (1994). *Beating the devil out of them: Corporal punishment in American families.* New York: Lexington Books/Macmillan.

Thorndike, E. L., & Woodworth, R. S. (1901). The influence of improvement in one mental function upon the efficiency of other functions. *Psychological Review, 8,* 247–261, 384–395, 553–564.

Walters, G., & Grusec, J. (1977). *Punishment* (p. 158). San Francisco: Freeman.

Widerstrom, A. H., Mowder, B. A., & Sandall, S. R. (1991). *At-risk and handicapped newborns and infants: Development, assessment and intervention.* Englewood Cliffs, NJ: Prentice Hall.

Williams, D. E., Kirkpatrick-Sanchez, S., & Crocker, W. T. (1994). A long-term follow-up of treatment for severe self-injury. *Research in Developmental Disabilities, 15,* 487–501.

11

LEARNING IN THE CLASSROOM 2: THE COGNITIVE VIEW

The cognitive theorists, using the computer as their basic model and E. C. Tolman as their ancestral hero, have provided another important theory of learning and memory called **information processing.** Tolman, as we have already seen, was essentially a behaviorist, but a behaviorist with a decided difference. He held that maze learning could not be explained as a mere collection of tiny S-R connections but must instead be based on the organism's internalization of a cognitive map of its environment. Even a rat could therefore incorporate a picture of its surroundings and find its way through the maze on the basis of that picture. The cognitive map, then, was viewed as an internal representation of environmental *information*. Information regarding the organism's expectancies (or the anticipation of what leads to what) were then incorporated into the organism's cognitive map. Therefore, for Tolman, learning was based more on information that was stored by the organism rather than on information just fed from muscle twitches. These are clearly not the thoughts of a Watsonian behaviorist.

Although at first glance the information processing model may seem like a step backward into the era of Wilhelm Wundt, who attempted to analyze consciousness into its various components, it is in reality far more empirically based. Wundt presumed to be using empirical techniques when he instructed his subjects to look within themselves at the elements of their own conscious awareness. Wundt called this technique *experimental introspection,* but from the viewpoint of science it was far too subjective and unreliable. Introspective reports varied from subject to subject and, worse, from laboratory to laboratory. The data were too inconsistent to provide psychology with anything resembling a firm foundation. The information processing theorists, in contrast, analyze mental events in terms of their behavioral effects—effects that can be reliably observed and measured. Such overt measures as reaction times (chronometric measures) and verbal recognition of various stimuli can be and are used to verify inferred mental constructs.

Although the information processing theorists take a behavioral stance with respect to measurement, they have traditionally leaned toward the gestalt orientation when it comes to theory. They have been addressing such issues as the organization of thinking, the role of meaning in learning, cognitive strategies in problem solving, the structure of human awareness—in short, most of the same areas that had earlier been studied by such gestaltists as Max Wertheimer, Wolfgang Kohler, and Kurt Koffka. This "new look" at learning and memory does not deny the evidence from the behavioral studies of classical and operant conditioning. Skinner's functional relationships between stimuli and responses are accepted as established facts. But the information processing theorist wants to know not just that an organism can be conditioned, but *how* the pigeon learns to discriminate among stimuli, *how* the rat learns its way through the maze, and *how* the child learns to recognize words on the printed page. What learning *rules* underlie these regular relationships? Because of its cognitive-gestaltist orientation, however, some psychologists, especially the behaviorists, have not looked kindly on this new approach. For example, Skinner said:

> The cognitive revolution is a search inside the mind for something that is not there. You can't see yourself process information; information processing is an inference from behavior and a bad one at that. If you look carefully at what people mean when they talk about the mind, you find it just refers to how they behave (Skinner, 1987).

In a speech to the American Psychological Association's annual meeting in 1990, delivered just days before his death, Skinner heaped even more criticism on cognitive science by calling it, not a science but the "creationism of psychology . . . an effort to reinstate that inner initiating-originating-creative self or mind which, in a scientific analysis, simply does not exist." And to those cognitive scientists feeling oppressed by the APA and threatening to leave the meeting, Skinner bade them good riddance and said that he would regard their departure "not as a secession, but as an improvement." Skinner asked the question "Can psychology be a science of the mind?" and then answered his own query with a resounding no. Instead, he insisted, psychology is and always will be the *study of behavior.*

Despite Skinner's criticisms, the torrent of new studies and fresh insights from the cognitive laboratories makes the information processing model too important to be overlooked by the educational psychologist of the late 1990s.

LEARNING AS INFORMATION PROCESSING

Information processing theory is loosely modeled on the way in which computers process information. The assumption is that in order for information to be remembered, it must move through several stages and that these stages proceed sequentially. The goal is to understand the "architecture with which the child is innately equipped and explain how this architecture interacts with environmental stimulation to yield changing mental representations" (McShane, 1991, p. 13).

Just as data to be entered into a computer must be encoded in a form that the computer can store and process, information that flows through the sensory receptors and is attended to must also be encoded before it can be stored and processed. At the psychological level, **encoding** involves the creation of memory traces, which are abstractions based on the salient features of the incoming information. It is also thought that at the physiological level the nervous system adopts an internal code that represents the external stimulus. In this way, the encoded representation of the external object or event becomes internal information and is thus readied for storage.

Although there are several variations in the specifics of how the information processing model of learning appears to work, the consensus view is that learning and remembering are based on the flow of information that passes *within* the organism. The sense organs respond to and pass along incoming information, which is encoded in the memory and nervous system. The encoded information is then stored and processed in a manner that allows it to be retrieved and acted on. Thus, as with the computer, the information processing model consists of input of encoded information, storage and processing, and finally, output, or retrieval.

Cognitive theorists have suggested that there are at least two modes of information processing: one that operates automatically, incidentally, and without any real voluntary control; and another that is deliberate, intentional, and under a person's full, volitional control. One of the implications of this theory is that the automatic processing of information occurs at the preconscious or even at the unconscious level, whereas the intentional mode is at the conscious level (Kihlstrom, 1987). The model to be presented in this chapter will focus on the intentional mode, that is, on intentional learning, which fits more closely with the major mission of the schools.

Storage refers to internal memory, or the persistence of information over time. In one form, it is analogous to the computer's use of disks or tape to

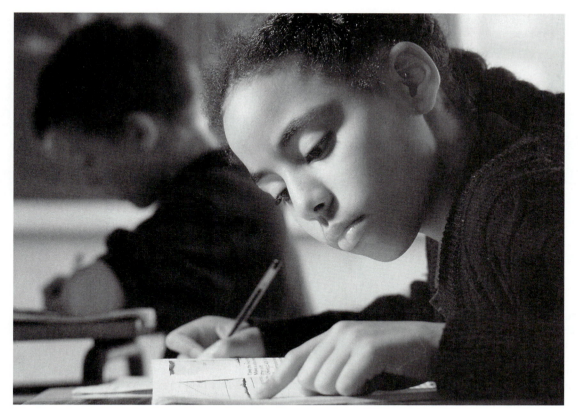

The first phase of information processing is encoding, which involves the formation of memory traces that may entail physiological changes.

save information for future use. Unless damaged, of course, a computer's disk stores information that does not change over time, whereas there is considerable debate over whether human memory possesses that type of etched-in-stone immutability.

Retrieval is the output end of the memory process. It refers to the utilization of the stored information, loosely comparable to accessing the computer's database. To be retrieved, stored information must be not only available but also accessible to the individual. That is, although stored information may be theoretically available, it may not always be easily located and utilized.

With this brief analogy in mind, we will now turn to how learning is acquired in the view of information processing theorists. Figure 11.1 shows in diagram form the main features of the information processing model of learning.

The Sensory Register

When information from the environment first impinges on a receptor (sense organ), there is an extremely brief moment—half a second to perhaps as many as four seconds—when it is held in sensory memory. This memory, also known as the **sensory register,** is called *iconic memory* for visual items and *echoic memory* (or sometimes acoustic memory) for auditory items. The visual representation is called an *icon* because of its pictorial quality, and a stored auditory item is called an *echo* because of its sound quality. Echoic memory endures long enough to enable us to piece together a series of sounds, as when listening to music or to someone speaking, whereas iconic memory seems to fade in as short a time as a few milliseconds. Regardless of how long they last, the icon and the echo play the important role of

FIGURE 11.1   THE INFORMATION PROCESSING MODEL OF INTENTIONAL LEARNING.

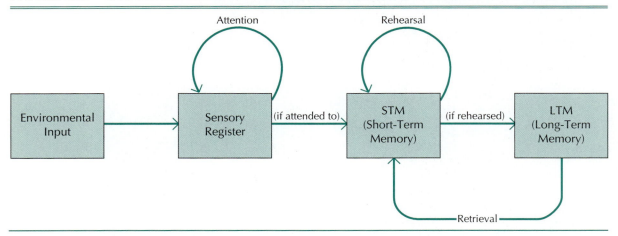

holding information in the sensory register until (or if) further processing is to occur.

Because the sensory memory holds only raw, unprocessed sensory information, it is sometimes seen as a sensory buffer, or waystation, situated between the external environment and internal memory. Although both iconic and echoic memory are based on neural traces (electrochemical changes in neurons) in the receptors and the nerves leading from the receptors to the brain, it seems that the traces are held for a slightly longer period in echoic memory than in iconic memory (Kolers, 1983). Other sensory memories may also exist, such as touch, taste, and smell, but the evidence regarding sight and sound is now more direct. Regardless of the sensory mode involved, the activation produced by incoming information may create a recognition pattern, or an internal connection between the external stimulation and previously encoded information. The brief and volatile sensory memory trace disappears almost immediately unless it is attended to, recalling to us the old adage "in one ear and out the other."

If the individual is paying attention to the incoming stimulation, the information is encoded and moved along from the sensory memory register into storage. A critical component here is attention, for if the information is not attended to immediately, it most likely will be lost. For example, if you are introduced to someone at a party and don't really pay attention to the introduction, moments later you may not even recall the person's name.

Some theorists do suggest, however, that under certain conditions it is possible to activate a kind of incidental-acquisition process whereby some information from the environment may be automatically encoded in the sensory register without either attention or intention (Hasher & Zacks, 1979).

Short-Term Memory

The first of the two main systems for storing the information encoded in sensory memory is **short-term memory (STM)**—sometimes called *working* or *active* memory. It appears that short-term memory can encode only about seven separate items (plus or minus two) and can hold them for only a limited time (Miller, 1956). Estimates of how long information may be retained in STM vary from about a few seconds to almost a minute (Broadbent, 1984). Since seven is the typical number of separate items in a telephone number, STM is often referred to as *telephone number memory*. Thus, if you were verbally given a phone number, you could most probably hold it in STM long enough to pick up the phone and dial the number. However, if the other party didn't answer the ring or there was a busy signal, you probably couldn't recall the number long enough to dial a second time.

Even though STM is restricted to about seven items, the items may be grouped together, or **chunked.** In this way, several items may be packaged together and processed as a single element. For example, you might be asked to repeat a series of nine digits, a number that is pushing the limit of the "magical" value of seven plus or minus two. By chunking the digits into groups of three, however, you then have to hold only three separate items in

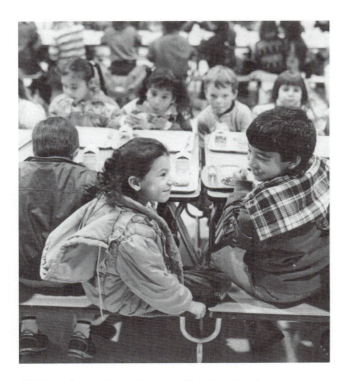

Sight and sound are the most direct routes for sensory input.

mind, not a difficult task. The same is true for letters. Whereas a random set of 17 letters pushes STM far beyond its limit, by chunking the letters, retention can be made easy. Take the letters OPECIBM-SONARRADAR, which is a total of 17 letters. If you chunk them into OPEC, IBM, SONAR, and RADAR, the task of remembering them falls far short of STM capacity. Radio and TV commercials make use of this strategy, especially when giving telephone numbers. They tell you that telephone operators are standing by to receive your call. Rather than present you with 11 separate numbers to dial in order to get your volume of *Art Treasures of the World*, you are told to dial 1-800 ART INFO, which is at most only three separate units. The toll-free 1-800 part has probably already been chunked and encoded by the listener, leaving only ART and INFO to be retrieved when getting to the phone. It has also been shown that chunking, especially around gestalt laws of perception, can aid in the recall of visual as well as auditory stimuli.

The magic 7 ± 2 value that has been placed on STM could easily create a bottleneck in the transfer of information from sensory storage, on through STM, and finally to LTM. Immediate memory is, therefore, like the narrow end of a funnel, opening into the vastness of LTM. That is, tremendous amounts of information can be stored in LTM, but the corridor leading in can get quickly jammed up. The bottleneck would be a severe constraint if all information were processed serially, that is, in the form of a series of processes occurring one at a time with no overlaps. Today, however, cognitive theorists talk of parallel processing, in which two or more processes occur simultaneously. During parallel processing, LTM, STM, and even sensory storage interact and work together in concert. It is clear, however, that STM is easily disrupted by distractions.

Long-Term Memory

The information from STM can be passed along to be processed and consolidated into **long-term memory (LTM).** Encoding into LTM can typically take up to about 20 minutes, but this interval can be dramatically shortened in certain situations, such as in "flashbulb" storage (Squire, 1987). LTM has the potential to hold encoded information for a lifetime. However, not all information from STM enters LTM. The key to LTM storage is being motivated enough to engage in rehearsal of the items from your STM.

This is yet another example of one of E. L. Thorndike's major laws of learning, the law of exercise, or the idea that under the right conditions practice helps make perfect. A story is told about a visitor to New York City who asked a cab driver if he could tell her how to get to Carnegie Hall, and the cabbie replied, "Practice, madam, practice." If at a party, you were introduced to an extremely attractive person, your level of motivation might automatically be high enough to prod you into saying over and over again to yourself, or aloud, not only the person's name but also the vital phone number (if you were lucky enough to get it). Also, when being introduced to someone new, force yourself to think only of that person and his or her name. Don't divide your attention by concentrating on yourself and the kind of impression you're making. Make every effort to use that person's name during the conversation—"I like your tie, Jim" or "That's a nice dress, Lisa."

When listening in class, you should *always* take notes. Not only do you have the notes to refer to later, but the act of note taking itself is a rehearsal strategy. Persons remember more after taking notes, even if they lose the notes, than do those who simply sit and listen (probably because the act of writing also engages procedural memory).

Rehearsal: Two Types— Maintenance and Elaborative

Maintenance rehearsal is the rote repetition of the information in STM, like repeating the above-mentioned phone number a few dozen times. **Elaborative rehearsal,** on the other hand, is not based on mere repetition but occurs when the information is expanded, embellished on, and related to other items or concepts already in LTM. Most theorists now believe that elaborative rehearsal plays the more important role in the transfer of information from STM to LTM and leads to greater depth of processing (Ashcraft, 1989).

Two Long-Term Memory Systems?

Researchers in the areas of both cognitive and brain science are now suggesting that we may have at least two long-term memory systems: declarative memory and procedural memory (Alper, 1986).

Declarative memory represents the brain's storehouse of names, dates, facts, places, faces, and past experiences. It is called "declarative" because it can be brought to mind and stated or declared in terms of a fact, proposition, or image. Most theorists today are convinced that there are two types of declarative memories: episodic (sometimes called *autobiographical* memory) and semantic (Tulving 1985).

Episodic declarative memory, as its name implies, consists of memory for past episodes in one's life. It is made up mostly of images from personal experiences organized on the basis of when and where they occurred. It's as though our lifetime experiences were on a long reel of movie film, and we rewind the reel to go back and look at the images on a few frames. Your ability to recall what you did last night or last week (or even years ago) is based on your retrieval of episodic memory. Try to remember your childhood home, its color and shape, your bedroom, its wallpaper or paint, and whether you got out of bed to the right or left and where your parents slept. Or can you recall your first-grade school, the classroom you were in, the area you played in at recess, your first fight with a neighborhood bully? According to the model, first proposed by Atkinson and Shiffrin (1968), these memories are stored as images and are related to one another by space and time, and so if you shut your eyes and relax, you can probably recall many of those childhood scenes.

Semantic declarative memory contains our storehouse of words and the meaning of words, facts, general information, concepts, and rules and strategies for learning—most of the things that we were supposed to learn in school. Since words are stored in semantic memory, some children with reading problems, for example dyslexics, are thought to be less efficient in retrieving verbal labels from their memory cores. One study, however, found that dyslexics with rather severe retrieval problems for words did demonstrate deficits in their abilities to process verbal material, but had no accompanying semantic memory problems (Murphy et al., 1988). Nor is semantic memory just a matter of school-facts material. Many of the principles and rules that we learn on the playground or in social situations, so-called street smarts, are also stored in semantic memory. The organization of this memory is grounded, not on an ordered-time basis, but on networks of interconnected relationships and ideas called *schemata,* as a plural, or **schema** in the singular. For example, you might have a schema that covers virtually everything you know about football: that there are referees, that there are 11 players on each side, that players may get injured, that a touchdown counts for six points, and so on. That is, any body of information related to a central core concept represents a schema.

The typical schema is domain specific; that is, it is concerned with only a single overall theme. Some theorists have suggested that children only have to learn where information can be found, such as learning to use a computer to search the Internet, rather than storing an information base themselves. Cognitive psychology, however, teaches us that children can't learn how to learn about some subject area without building on previous knowledge in that area. The more books a child reads about computers, for example, the easier the books become simply because the main points are getting increasingly familiar. But the ability to understand one area, such as computers, doesn't automatically translate into the ability to read and understand books on the Civil War, the poetry of Robert Frost, or the fundamentals of football. These areas have their own vocabularies and conceptual bases.

The organization of a schema can be rather complex, but this very complexity may later be of enormous help during retrieval. It allows you to try several retrieval routes to your goal. As you associate around the fact or principle you're searching for, first trying one network then another, you continue to increase the likelihood of finding the target. This is because as you activate one thought or concept, a number of other related concepts will be activated through what is called the *spread of activation.* For example, a student was trying to remember the name of Alexander the Great's horse, and he dug diligently into his Alexander-the-Great schema. He kept searching, much of the time out loud, talking about Alexander—that he was from Macedonia, that his father was named Philip, that Aristotle was his tutor, and so on. Then all of a sudden, as though out of the blue, he triumphantly shouted "Bucephalus!" The spread of activation is similar to a fishing net being pulled in: with the first pulling of a single strand, all the other strands are eventually drawn up behind until the entire net is clearly exposed. Cognitive theorists believe that the idea of the spread of activation is fundamental to an understanding of recall from long-term memory.

Any attempt to fully understand memory must also take into account the importance of social forces (discussed in more detail in Chapter 17). A culture's values and customs have profound effects on people's schemata in particular and their overall memory in general. What people with good memories are able to recall may vary among cultures and often depends largely on what a given culture sees as important (Mistry & Rogoff, 1994).

Procedural memory contains traces of motor skills, typically learned through repetitive practice and/or conditioning. Procedural memory can be displayed, as when an expert skier gracefully descends a mountain, but is difficult to declare, or put into words. You can generally describe to someone how to ski, but actually learning to ski requires doing it, feeling it, and then practicing it. A person relies on procedural memory when tying shoes, playing scales on the piano, riding a bicycle, hitting a golf ball, and so on. Anyone who doubts that procedural memory is real should try asking typists where certain letters are on the keyboard. Watch as their fingers flex out the answer. That this memory system is separate from declarative memory is evidenced by a series of reports on individuals who have undergone brain surgery and have apparently, on occasion, lost one type of memory but not the other. Also, patients with Alzheimer disease often show no impairment of their procedural memory, but can't recall the names of their children. In one case, a golfer who was suffering from the disease retained his perfect golf swing, but only seconds after hitting the ball, he couldn't remember where the ball had landed.

Because verbal representations play such an important role in our LTM, some theorists believe that we can retain few, if any, memories of events that occurred prior to our acquisition of language. This view is not universally held, however; a growing body of research seems to show that children have much more understanding of their environment, and its implicit social rules, than was previously thought. This cognitive skill appears to begin early, even before there has been any language development and certainly before children can verbalize any memory of their understanding (Lazarus, 1991). Either way, with or without language, we all have long-term memories that seem to be permanently stored.

Permastore   Psychologists are using the term **permastore** to describe these permanently etched long-term memories, since the durability of these memories is analogous to permafrost, or "the unchanging nature of the permanently frozen state of the soil a few feet beneath the ground in Arctic regions" (Baddeley, 1990, p. 239). One study found that some aspects of a foreign language, Spanish, are retained in some cases for up to 50 years, despite not being rehearsed or even used at all (Bahrick, 1991).

It has even been suggested that every experience a person has, especially when emotions are involved, leaves a permanent memory trace on the brain and therefore that our freedom to act or think might be forever compromised if at one time we happened to participate in or even witness a particularly dreadful scene (Johnson, 1990). Such memories remain indelibly inscribed in the permastore and continue to influence our lives.

Thus, some memory experts maintain that all memories stored throughout the lifetime of an individual are permanent and, given the right cues, potentially retrievable (Spear & Riccio, 1994). Sometimes hypnosis can be used as an aid in bringing to the surface material that is embedded in long-term memory (Woodard, 1996).

Retrieval from long-term memory   Once information has been stored in LTM, it is available but, not always easily located and utilized. John P. Houston, an expert in learning theory, gives the example of the student who knows (has stored) the names of all the states of the Union but, at any given moment, may not be able to retrieve all of them (Houston, 1991). Even though the information is in storage and available, it may not always be accessible. The student may know the names of all the states abutting, say, Indiana, but explains forlornly that he just doesn't seem to have them handy or that they have momentarily escaped him or, in more recent vernacular, that he can't locate the exact track on the hard disk of his memory. Theorists have drawn a distinction between availability and accessibility (Tulving, 1983):

1. A memory may not be accessible because it was never fully stored in the first place or because it

SPOTLIGHT ON THE GIFTED

The Context of Behavior

It is sometimes difficult to distinguish between attention deficit-hyperactivity disorder ADHD children and those who are gifted. The table below indicates how important context is in making the distinction.

Given these similarities, it is

BEHAVIOR ASSOCIATED WITH ADHD[a]	BEHAVIOR ASSOCIATED WITH GIFTEDNESS[b]
Poorly sustained attention in almost all situations.	Poor attention, boredom, daydreaming in specific situations.
Diminished persistence on tasks not having immediate gratification.	Low tolerance for persistence on tasks that seem irrelevant.
Impulsivity, poor delay of gratification.	Judgment lags behind development of intellect.
Impaired adherence to commands to regulate or inhibit behavior in social situations.	Intensity may lead to power struggles with authorities.
More active, restless than normal children.	High activity level, may need less sleep.
Difficulty adhering to rules and regulations.	Questions rules, customs, and traditions.

[a]   R. A., Barkley, (1990), *Hyperactive children: A handbook for diagnosis and treatment* (2d ed.), New York: Guilford.
[b]   Webb (1993),
Source: *Adapted from J. T. Webb & D. Latimer (1993, July), ADHD and children who are gifted*, ERIC Digest, 1–2.

important that the teacher examine pupil behaviors in context. Although both types tend to be risk-takers, the gifted child is more risk-specific and typically will not exhibit this or other ADHD-like symptoms in all situations. The gifted child may appear to be ADHD by one teacher but not by another, or in the classroom but not, say, in gym or music activities. The true ADHD child, on the other hand, will display the same behavior in virtually all situations (except when playing computer games or watching TV). The gifted child gets off task not because of an inability to attend, but because of boredom or a curriculum mismatch. The gifted child is usually spending large amounts of time waiting for the rest of his or her classmates to catch up. A final major distinction between the two groups is that in most situations gifted children tend to be consistent in the quality of their performance, especially if they like the teacher and feel intellectually challenged. ADHD children, on the other hand, are usually extremely inconsistent in their performance. Finally, all these conditions may come together in that singular child who is both ADHD and gifted.

---

was stored but has long since faded away. Such a memory is simply no longer available.

2. There are memories that are not currently accessible but are still being retained, and if these memories are given the right set of circumstances or a changed situation, they may come tumbling forth.

3. Certain memories are both retrievable and accessible. Prompting, by providing cues, aids storage search and eventual retrieval. This is why, when meeting a long-ago acquaintance, you may find it so much easier to remember the person's face than his or her name.

All people have a better memory for faces than for names. Remembering the face is a recognition task (the face is right there in front of you), but the name is strictly a matter of recall. Also, it's been shown that recognizing a face that is in some way unusual is even easier (Bartlett et al., 1984).

Recognition is also the reason why multiple-

SPOTLIGHT ON THE TOT

The Tip-of-the-Tongue Phenomenon

Everyone at one time or another is beset with a word retrieval problem, a problem that has the potential for both stress and embarrassment. We become literally stuck in midsentence as we search for a word or name. Memory researchers say that this occurs as a result of a temporary retrieval failure in our long-term semantic memory systems, and they have even given a technical-sounding name to this problem, calling it the "tip-of-the-tongue phenomenon," or TOT. Psychologists have found that TOTs increase with age, but it is also clear that all of us, including elementary-age children, are subject to them. Psychologist Alan Brown has found that young adults report having a TOT experience at least once a week, whereas older adults acknowledge having them about two to four times as often. Brown believes that these self-reports, however, may underestimate the real frequency of the problem, since many TOTs may seem so trivial that they are simply not important enough to be tracked down or, more likely, to be publicly announced to the researchers. People say that their TOTs occur most often when they are trying to remember names of friends, acquaintances, or famous persons. Brown suggests, however, that perhaps we are more apt to remember the TOTs that involve friends because they can often produce the most embarrassment. Certainly, if you were at a family gathering and suddenly couldn't remember the name of one of your relatives, it might prove more unsettling than if you couldn't think of the name of some actor in a movie you just saw. You could always change the subject and talk about a different movie, but you can't very well come up with a synonym for your dear aunt's name.

The TOT phenomenon is certainly largely a retrieval problem, but it may also be a function of how the information was stored in the first place. Why is stored information momentarily not usable? Brown feels that the answer to that question may someday uncover some of the answers to questions involving the entire memory process: how information is stored in general and how the retrieval process works in particular, that is, how information is accessed from LTM. Brown believes that if psychologists can look at that very moment when the gears of memory are out of mesh, the study of TOTs may make it easier to get a good look at the entire memory system. Sometimes, after an extremely frustrating TOT, you might simply give up and at a conscious level forget about it. Then later, suddenly, in the midst of doing or thinking about something else, the word or name seems to pop right up out of your head. Perhaps the retrieval process is not always at the fully conscious level. One hint when this tormenting syndrome occurs is to do a little free associating, no matter how farfetched the associations may seem. Think of everything you can that is in some way associated with the lost word or thought. By massaging the engram in this way, the word you're looking for is more likely to come bubbling to the surface.

Source: Brown, A. A review of the tip-of-the-tongue experience. *Psychological Bulletin* (1991), 109, 204–223.

---

choice and true-false tests are easier than exams that require unaided recall. For example, compare the following items:

1. Who was president of the United States immediately after Franklin D. Roosevelt?

2. True or false: Harry S Truman was president of the United States immediately after Franklin D. Roosevelt.

Item 2 should be easier because you are being offered more ways to search your memory. Item 1, the recall item, demands that you access your memory of Franklin Roosevelt and then search for Truman. But for item 2, the recognition item, you could search from Truman to Roosevelt, even if you could not access it the other way around, from Roosevelt to Truman.

Finally, according to Robert S. Wyer and Thomas

SPOTLIGHT ON LONG-TERM MEMORY

Episodic versus Autobiographical Memory

Researchers on long-term memory have typically taken two views on the manner in which studies should be conducted. The term *episodic memory* refers to a form of long-term memory that is based on the storage of past scenes, images, and lifetime experiences. Semantic memory, on the other hand, contains the storage of words and verbal information and labels. Researchers who use the term episodic memory prefer to conduct their studies under the controlled conditions of the university laboratory, where, hopefully, most of the extraneous variables are ruled out. Usually, the experimental task is low in the amount of meaning provided to the subject, and the to-be-remembered words are deliberately made difficult to associate with past experience. Just as was true with the Ebbinghaus studies, this is done to ensure that each subject starts out on a level playing field. In contrast, researchers who use the term *autobiographical memory* base their work on the study of past events that are laden with meaning and may even have verbal overtones. In this approach, which bridges the gap between pure episodic and semantic memory systems, no attempt is made to either restrict meaning or any connections with the subject's past experience. For example, in one study of autobiographical memory, college graduates were selected from the classes of 1979, 1969, 1959, 1949, and 1939 and sent a 20-item questionnaire. As a partial test of the "flashbulb memory" theory, the items were designed such that 10 were concerned with emotionally charged events, while the other 10 were judged to be neutral. For example, one of the "emotional" items was "your first significant male/female relationship," whereas one of the "neutral" items was "the subjects you took as a college freshman." Respondents were asked to rate on a scale of 1 to 10 how well they remembered the event. Statistical analysis showed that the emotional items were recalled significantly more often than the neutral items. It may be that what college graduates remember best about their first year of college is not, alas, classroom assignments, but the onset and ending of affairs of the heart.

Conway, M. A. (1995). *Flashbulb memories*. Hove, England: Erlbaum. Sprinthall, R. C., & Burns, P. (1991). Flashbulb memory among college graduates. *A.I.C. Alumni News, 24,* 9. Tulving, E. (1983). *Elements of episodic memory.* New York: Oxford University Press.

K. Srull, three stages of long-term memory retrieval have been identified (1989). First, the individual must identify the correct storage bin in memory and then search for the appropriate schema (and then the item within that schema). Second, those schemata that have been most recently used will be at or near the top of the storage bin and will therefore be easier to find and use again. Third, when a person has an integrated and coherent schema, the recall of odd or "expectancy-inconsistent" information will precede the recall of more consistent items.

Concept formation   Information processing is more than just the shuffling of stimulus inputs from sensory memory to short-term memory to long-term memory and then retrieving the bits of information. Information is also processed into conceptual form and becomes part of our semantic memory in a process known as **concept formation.** It is based on identifying the typical characteristics of stimuli, often called the *prototypes*, and then organizing them in such a way as to provide encoded meaning (Ashcraft, 1989). Since memory for the meaning of events lasts longer than memory for specific, physical details, once information is processed into concepts, it is not only more easily stored in LTM but, perhaps more important, more easily accessed for retrieval.

As children learn to increase their verbal-conceptual bases, their ability to comprehend written material also increases. One expert in the area of reading, Joanne Carlisle, has found that children can be trained in the use of strategies designed to increase reading comprehension (1983). Carlisle's technique is based on a "learning how to learn" approach, in which children are provided with numerous examples and lots of practice in forming abstractions, looking for relationships, and then retrieving the concepts. In short, the children are deliberately provided with learning sets.

It seems clear that individuals who have formed learning sets will acquire and be able to use new information more efficiently than those who haven't, a fact that partially explains the difference in acquisition speed between the novice and the expert in a given cognitive area.

Another, related difference between the novice and the expert is in their backgrounds of chunked material (Walberg, 1988). Chunked material, as we have seen, is the representation of linked groups of items, even abstract groups, as clusters that can be processed as a single ensemble. This background of chunked items is stored in LTM and can be called upon when new material is entering STM to dramatically increase STM's storage capacity. Thus, rather than information flowing in a stage-by-stage, or serial, manner (100 percent of processing occurring in each stage before the next stage can kick in), STM may be interacting with LTM early on with incoming stimulation. The processing may therefore be parallel rather than linear and/or serial. This allows the expert to size up a situation with a "practiced eye," such as when a master chess player can look for a few seconds at a complicated board arrangement of 20 pieces or more and then later reproduce it perfectly. Interestingly, when chess pieces are laid out in random fashion, the expert doesn't do much better at remembering them than the beginner. But when game situations are involved, the expert far surpasses the beginner. The expert has already encoded thousands of possible chess arrangements, some say as many as 50,000, and so the encoding process involved in memorizing the new arrangement can be done in only two or three parallel chunks (Baddeley, 1990). Says Herbert Walberg, "Such chunks may underlie mental processes ranging from childhood stages of cognitive development as identified by Jean Piaget, to new scientific discoveries" (Walberg, 1988, p. 77).

Emotions and Memory

Emotions are known to play an important role in memory, sometimes inhibiting memory and sometimes enhancing it. Many of us have probably been in situations in which our emotions were so strong that we barely remembered our own names. Students have even been known to panic during exams, and then complain that although they had spent much time studying, at the moment when the blue books were passed out, so did they. "My mind drew a blank" is the often-heard plea to the wary instructor.

Two things are important in this connection. First, the better the material is learned, perhaps even overlearned, the less anxiety will be generated. People are less nervous doing things they do well. Second, self-conscious efforts at relaxation (especially deep muscle relaxation) may often reduce the amount of felt anxiety, thus mitigating its crippling effects.

There is also, however, a phenomenon called **flashbulb memory,** which is an extremely vivid recollection of an event or situation that was etched into memory because the individual was then in a highly charged emotional state (Brown & Kulik, 1977). For example, we may have almost total recall of the moment we heard the news of some close relative's death or, for those old enough, the moment we heard that President Kennedy had been assassinated, or the moment we learned of the Challenger space shuttle disaster. Flashbulb memories seem to be most enduring when they involve death, accident, or sex (Rubin & Kozin, 1984). Thus, events in one's life that are emotion-arousing can sear a lasting impression on the memory. The arousal system that triggers this flashbulb effect is apparently the same one that alerts the person to react to life-threatening situations by either fighting or fleeing. This "fight or flight" reaction is the one that makes your heart beat faster, readies your muscles for action, and puts your whole body in its most primitive survival mode. What causes this is the release of a group of hormones: ACTH, vasopressin, and opioid peptides (McGaugh, 1990). Two other important emotion-arousing hormones, adrenaline and noradrenaline, are also released. As one memory expert phrased it, "There is a distinct class of memories that are emotional and personally important and, sometimes, surprising. These memories are more detailed and long-lasting than most everyday autobiographical memories" (Conway, 1995, p. 126). It is also believed that this aspect of the human memory system probably evolved because it had enormous survival value, ensuring that our distant ancestors would vividly remember the events and circumstances that were most threatening to them (Cahill et al., 1994). Thus, the emotional side of the flashbulb memory phenomenon has become fairly well understood, and recent work on this topic has largely confirmed Brown and Kulik's original ideas (Winograd & Neisser, 1992).

THE INFORMATION PROCESSING THEORY OF FORGETTING

Forgetting, to the cognitively oriented information theorist, is defined as the inability to retrieve infor-

SPOTLIGHT ON HOW WE THINK

Is Computer Thinking Like Human Thinking?

Artificial intelligence is predicated on the belief that human thinking can be simulated by computer programs. Typically, a theory on thinking is first devised, and then a computer program is written that simulates the theory. Allen Newell and Herbert Simon wrote a program called The Logic Theorist, which attempted to simulate a series of rules for solving problems in formal logic.[a] The program worked well enough to solve most of the complicated problems advanced by the logicians Alfred Nash and Bertrand Russell in their 1925 masterpiece, *Principia Mathematica.*

Some theorists, such as Simon, feel that computer programs have actually been shown to think, and even, on occasion, to show flashes of insight.[b] Others such as Michael Wertheimer (son of gestalt founder Max Wertheimer), take a decidedly different view: "All of the requisite thinking, insight and understanding go into the writing of the program; once the program

is running, neither the computer nor the program nor the combination of hardware and software thinks: all the thinking has been done beforehand, and was used in constructing the program."[c] Even a washing machine can be programmed to carry out an intricate series of instructions, from wash cycle to rinse to dry; yet no one would claim that a washing machine can think.

The question at issue, however, is not really whether computers can think, but rather whether computers can be programmed to parallel, even roughly, the human thought process. So far, the answer is a decided no. Despite more than 20 years of research, no program yet written approaches the human ability to extract meaningful information from the environment and to form abstractions and high-order cognitive structures. Top chess masters can still (as of this writing) beat the computerized chess programs, even though chess

is one of the better programs to have been developed.[d] But despite their elegance, computer chess programs still cannot incorporate information and abstractions about the environment as well as the average 2-year-old child. To some extent this lack of progress is due to the fact that even the most technologically sophisticated computer is no match for the intricacies of the human mind. It is also due to the fact that we still do not fully understand how human intelligence is organized.[e] Although computers have long been likened to the human brain, they are in fact far different. A computer has a central processor acting on meticulously programmed instructions. It breaks a task into tiny components and acts on them very rapidly, but always in a preset sequence. The brain has billions of neurons, each of which is connected to thousands of other neurons, and they operate as a group. Thus, the power of the brain comes not just from its sheer

---

mation. The two major reasons for forgetting, according to these theorists, are decay and interference.

Decay

Decay is the passive loss of the memory trace due to inactivity or lack of rehearsal. Actually, this is not a new idea. Thorndike, an early S-R theorist, postulated as one of his three major laws of learning the law of exercise. In this law, Thorndike stated that the more an S-R connection is used, the stronger it becomes; conversely, the less it is used, the weaker it becomes. Hence, through inactivity, the S-R connection simply atrophies over time.

The information processing theorists accept decay as an important influence on forgetting, especially at the input stage of the processing sequence. Sensory memory, you will recall, decays in a matter of less than a few seconds, and information in STM, if not rehearsed, is lost in less than about a minute. But what about LTM? Here the evidence is not totally clear. Some theorists claim that once information is brought into LTM, it is stored quite permanently. For example, Wilder Penfield believed that the brain is like a recording tape and that all its memories are *permanently* stored (1969). While performing brain surgery, Penfield stimulated various areas of a patient's cerebral cortex with a slight electric current. (The patient was conscious.) As long as it persisted, numbers of neurons, but from the multiple interconnections among these neurons. Also, as one mathematician has said, human thinking cannot be equated to the action of some very complicated computer, since the computer lacks consciousness, emotions, and motivations. The computer cannot "perceive poetry or the beauty of an evening sky or the magic of sounds; it cannot hope or love or despair."[f]

One computer-driven device did seemingly demonstrate motivation. Called the "tortoise," the little robot would scurry around the floor until its batteries ran low, at which point it would rush over to the nearest power socket, plug itself in, and recharge its own batteries. When thoroughly charged (satisfied?), it would detach itself from the socket and go off on its way. Another group of programmers tried to teach a computer both a motivational sequence and what to do when hungry. The computer was

instructed to react in a variety of ways to hunger instructions. Finally, when asked what it would do when it wanted a midafternoon snack, the computer replied that it would go to the nearest pizza stand. When asked what it would do when it got there, the computer responded that it would "eat the pizza stand." Another group of programmers prepared a Pentagon computer to answer questions to be posed by a visiting four-star general. When the general arrived, he typed in "Will it be peace or war?" and the computer answered "Yes." "Yes what?" asked the general. "Yes, sir," answered the respectful computer.[g]

A critical difference between artificial intelligence and human intelligence is that although computers can obviously compute better than humans, they are much worse than humans at matching. The computer can match incoming words against those stored in its memory only if those words are exact counterparts. As Morton

Hunt says, "Any two-year-old child could do better."[h] Can the computer ever be expected to approximate the complex patterning and economy of the human mind?

---

[a] Newell, A., & Simon, H. A. (1972). *Human problem solving*. Englewood Cliffs, NJ: Prentice-Hall.
[b] Simon, H. A. (1986). The information processing explanation of gestalt phenomena. *Computers in Human Behavior, 2,* 241–254.
[c] Wertheimer, M. (1985). A gestalt perspective on computer simulations of cognitive processes. *Computers in Human Behavior, 1,* 20.
[d] Best, J. B. (1989). *Cognitive psychology* (2d ed.). St. Paul: West.
[e] Anderson, J. R. (1980). *Cognitive psychology and its implications*. San Francisco: Freeman.
[f] Penrose, R. (1989). *The emperor's new mind: Concerning computers, minds, and the laws of physics* (p. 447). New York: Oxford University Press.
[g] Jennings, K. (1990). *The devouring fungus: Tales of the computer age*. New York: Norton.
[h] Hunt, M. (1982). *The universe within*. New York: Simon & Schuster.

---

each stimulation produced in the patient extremely vivid memories of long-past events. When the stimulation ceased, so too did the memory. The images and memories reported by the patient were so dramatically distinct that the patient felt as though they were being relived. The patient also believed that these memories had been completely forgotten. Thus, Penfield argued that the memories had remained organically intact and would remain so for life but that under normal circumstances the patient simply couldn't retrieve them.

This experiment, provocative though it may be, doesn't absolutely close the book on the case for permanent LTM. Critics suggest that Penfield's patient may not have been recalling actual events but instead was experiencing new sensations that only resembled past events (Houston, 1991).

Other theorists believe that decay does take place in LTM, but at a much slower rate than in STM. Estimates of the decay rate in LTM vary somewhat, but most theorists concede that once in LTM, information will probably remain relatively intact for many years. Memories such as these are said to reside in permastore.

Interference

Forgetting also occurs because of interference, which takes place when the recall of one event is inhibited by the incursion of another event. Again, this is not a brand-new explanation. For example, S-R theorist Edwin Guthrie, in his 1930s learning theory, put forth interference as the sole reason for forgetting. Interference is viewed as being of two types: proactive inhibition and retroactive inhibition.

Proactive inhibition   When you learn A, then later learn B, only to discover that your previous learning of A has in some way disrupted your recall of B, **proactive inhibition (PI)** has occurred. The previously learned, older material (A) has worked forward in time to hamper your efforts to retrieve that newer material (B). You might take a French course one semester and a Spanish course the next. On the Spanish final, your recall might well be disturbed by the interference effects produced by having previously taken the French course.

Retroactive inhibition   When the learning of new material (B) prevents the recall of older material (A), **retroactive inhibition (RI)** has occurred. To use the foreign language example again, after finishing the Spanish course you might now find your recall of French disrupted. You might very well confuse your *estars* with your *êtres*. Your knowledge of French would have remained more solidly intact had you not spent the intervening semester working on Spanish. Some students cram for a final until they drop off to sleep in the early morning hours in a state of exhausted confusion. On awakening, just before the exam, the material suddenly seems less confusing and more understandable. Some students attribute this to the fact that they have continued learning in some mysterious fashion while asleep. Though this theory is admittedly seductive, a simpler explanation is that sleeping helped to prevent retroactive inhibition. Going to sleep, rather than adding to the store of knowledge, may simply prevent a large degree of interference. Also on awakening, the student is obviously less tired and more alert for the retrieval process. In general, the best way to take a break while studying for an exam is to do something as different as possible from the exam material. For example, if you are studying for an educational psychology exam, it is better to take a 15-minute Ping-Pong break than to spend the time reading over your sociology notes.

There is even some evidence that the brain may continue to process information during periods of sleep. Since virtually no new stimulations are being added, the brain tends to rework the information it already contains (Evans & Evans, 1983). Also, dreaming itself may be involved in the memory process. Francis Crick (of DNA fame) has suggested that a sleeper's dreams are part of a natural house-cleaning system, ridding the mind of unwanted, false, or nonsensical memories and thereby clearing the way for new information (Crick & Mitchison, 1983). As a Nobel laureate, Crick still casts a long shadow down the corridors of science, and the Crick "dreaming-clears-the-mind" hypothesis continues to receive great attention.

Houston (1991) has prepared an exercise that should give you a quick, firsthand impression of how retroactive inhibition works. Cover the three telephone numbers on the right side of Table 11.1, and concentrate on the number to the left. Spend about 30 seconds looking at and rehearsing that number. When you're satisfied that you know it, cover the entire table and wait for about 45 seconds. During this waiting period, *do not rehearse the number.* Think of other things, such as how many different brands of soft drinks you can name. After the 45 seconds have elapsed, try to recall the phone number. You will probably be able to repeat it correctly. Now prepare yourself for the demonstration of retroactive inhibition by covering the number that you just learned. Concentrate on memorizing the three numbers on the right side. When you think you have them down pat (it should take about a minute), try to recall the old number. Unless you encode and process information at a level far beyond the ability of the average person, that first number is now virtually impossible to retrieve.

Offsetting the effects of interference   The process of storing information (learning), then, can disrupt both past and future learning. Says Houston, "The very act of learning itself constitutes an ironic source of forgetting" (1991, p. 226). Don't make too much of this accurate, though somewhat restricted, statement, however. You needn't assume that you'd better not learn too much now or it will make it that much more difficult to learn new material later. Nor should you be wary of tackling new material for fear

TABLE 11.1   *TESTING RETROACTIVE INHIBITION*

NUMBER TO BE LEARNED FIRST	NUMBERS TO BE LEARNED SECOND
562-7201	617-5317
	413-2096
	783-0301

of forgetting what you've already learned. As we shall soon see, the facilitative action of positive transfer may more than compensate for the inhibitory effects of interference. In fact, it has been shown that a background of information, especially when that information is *organized,* can offset the effects of interference (Reder & Ross, 1983).

Even the so-called memory experts must work to keep their information intact. In one celebrated case, Stephen Pawelson memorized all 24 books of Homer's *Iliad,* an absolutely monumental task. The *Iliad* consists of almost 16,000 lines, and none of these lines is really very easy. For example, the first line is, "The wrath do thou sing, O goddess of Peleus's son, Achilles," and reciting the entire epic takes all day long, from "rosy fingered dawn to dark-browed night." Pawelson, a former accountant, said that each time he'd memorize a new book his recall of the previous book would start to fade, a classic example of retroactive inhibition. To overcome this loss, he'd have to go back and reweave his memory of the material that was unraveling. He said that this was like filling a leaking bucket, since only by constantly going back over the previous books could he plug all those leaking memory holes (Galvin, 1988).

Aids to Retrieving Learned Material

Processed information is of little use unless it can be retrieved. What, therefore, can be done to increase a student's ability to recall and utilize processed information and to compensate for interference?

Overlearning   Studies show that retention is longer and retrieval easier when material is overlearned—that is, learned to a point beyond which it appears to be mastered. Teachers should encourage students to keep at it, even though the students feel the material has been fully learned. Overlearning is especially valuable with those areas that students find difficult. The alert teacher will spend extra time going over such material.

Understanding   Teachers should stress the understanding of concepts rather than concentrate only on the repetition of facts. When provided with categories of understanding, students are more likely to learn new information quickly and efficiently. When equipped with a conceptual framework, students are more apt to be able to deduce solutions to new problem areas. Also, abstractions are easier to develop when an underlying understanding of a concept has been incorporated. Conceptual learning becomes self-perpetuating, since each new concept provides

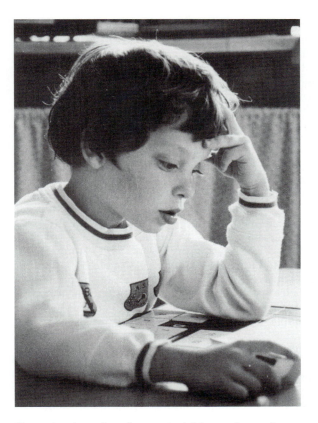

Retention is easier when material is overlearned.

an anchorage that makes the acquisition of new information and new concepts more efficient. It's as though entering new information into a computer literally expands the computer's internal memory. Learning then requires less effort and becomes more enjoyably efficient. Also, as a myriad of studies have shown, the more meaningful the material is, the greater the likelihood of both its acquisition and retrieval. It is virtually impossible to teach for understanding if the material seems random and meaningless. For example, suppose you were given the following sequence of numbers to memorize: 100816449362516941. Since this series is far beyond the STM limit of seven, as a random sequence it is virtually impossible to recall. With understanding, however, it becomes a relatively simple task, since it is composed of the squares of the numbers from 10 to 1 in that order.

Building an organized knowledge base   The acquisition and retrieval of new information can be made easier when it builds on previously incorporated information. Studies on positive transfer as well as Harry Harlow's data on learning sets show that acquisition improves when it is built on an existing knowledge base. Just as new motor skills are improved by positive transfer (learning to ride a bike aids in learning to ride a motorcycle), so too are more cognitively based skills. Concepts build on facts, and *concepts build on concepts*. Knowing how to add, subtract, multiply, and divide is obviously helpful to the student taking a course in algebra. Having taken algebra, in turn, makes a course in physics more understandable. The ability to access and utilize information is a direct function of the number of previously incorporated categories available to a student. Recalling that Truman succeeded Roosevelt is facilitated by stored information about Truman, Roosevelt, and any other facts relating to the United States at the end of World War II. These encoded facts also increase the likelihood of a student's acquiring a schema, or the organized concepts relating to that historical time period. It is clear from the research that the more organized associations one has, the deeper the processing. These concepts, in turn, help ensure a more complete understanding of such concepts as the restructuring of the postwar economy or of the sociopolitical justifications for the establishment of the United Nations. Thus, as students acquire more different *organized* categories into which information may be processed, the information becomes ever more accessible to retrieval and use.

The main message here is that the better we organize information and relate it to what we already remember, the better we can recall it. An expert chess player remembers the pieces on the board better than the beginner not because of a better inherent memory, but because the expert understands the entire situation as an organized and coherent whole. The beginner, in contrast, is trying to remember the individual pieces as separate units, a much more difficult task.

Relating new material to the existing knowledge base   The teacher should always strive to interweave new material with relevant existing learning. When new material is tied into the student's existing knowledge base, teaching effectiveness is increased (White & Gagne, 1976). Part of the reason for this is that information is then stored in several categories, and each of the associations then serves as a cue to a source of retrieval. Thus, the more categories under which new information is indexed, the more readily it can be retrieved. The student should constantly be reminded of these related categories as new information is presented.

Using cue associations   When attempting retrieval, the student should be taught to work on actively producing as many cue associations as possible. Since retrieval of stored information is often cue-dependent, an *active* search of all relevant cues often brings the information back into working memory. For example, in trying to retrieve the name of Abraham Lincoln's assassin, the student should think of as many things as possible about Lincoln, perhaps the fact that he was assassinated at a play, the name of the theater, or even the quotation *"Sic semper tyrannis."* The more associations the better, since eventually one of them might cue the name John Wilkes Booth. This technique is often called *associative searching*, since it usually makes use of less commonly employed pathways among the various concepts and facts related to the information being retrieved. Its opposite is *active searching*, in which information is accessed along more practiced pathways (Klatsky, 1984). Obviously, the student should be encouraged to utilize the associative search only if a direct search comes up empty.

Mnemonics

Mnemonic devices (Mnemosyne was the Greek goddess of memory) are techniques for aiding both the acquisition and retrieval of learned material. An example of a mnemonic would be the simple rhyming scheme "Thirty days hath September, April, June, and November." Mnemonic devices may be either visual or verbal. Suppose you wanted to remember to pick up some ice cream, bread, and milk. As an aid to memory, you might attempt to produce a vivid visual image of your grocery list, perhaps by imagining a gigantic ice cream cone soaking in milk and surrounded by slices of bread. With that bizarre picture fixed firmly in mind (in fact, the more outlandish the image, the better), your grocery list should be secure.

The reason for using bizarre associations is that in creating them, and perhaps even visualizing them, you force yourself to pay attention, and anything that focuses attention becomes an extremely potent factor in both the encoding and retrieval of learned material. Furthermore, anytime you force yourself to focus your attention, the physical arousal activates certain brain chemicals, which can then help to promote learning. With adolescents or adults, such stimulants as the caffeine in coffee can artificially produce an increased arousal level that then aids memory (Blum, 1984).

Or, instead, you might choose a verbal mediator and simply think of the letters IBM—ice cream, bread, and milk. Just don't make the mistake of forgetting what the letters stand for and inadvertently bring home instant coffee, bananas, and margarine.

The ancient Greek and Roman orators used to employ imagery to help them memorize the key points in their speeches. The orator would imagine himself strolling down some well-known path and then tie the image of a passing landmark to each successive rhetorical point. This is now known as the *method of loci*, and as many after-dinner speakers will attest, it still works today as well as it did millennia ago. You might even use it on your way to take an educational psychology exam. Suppose, you need to do some last-minute cramming on Thorndike's three major laws of learning. As you leave the dorm, the flagpole is on your left, and on top of the pole you picture a gymnast going through an "exercise" routine. Next, as you pass the library, you visualize a large cat at the main entrance poised to pounce on a mouse; the cat appears to be coiled in "readiness." Finally, before entering the building where the test is to be given, you walk by the campus snack bar and remember the "effect" the cold french fries had on you the last time you were there. As you mentally rewalk the route during the test, you recall the laws.

Verbal mediators are also used as mnemonics. Fifth-graders, for example, may learn the acronym HOMES in order to remember the names of the five Great Lakes: Huron, Ontario, Michigan, Erie, and Superior. Such acronyms are called *first-letter mnemonics*, since the peg word, HOMES, contains the first letters of all the items to be recalled. Research in this area has shown rather convincingly that if the peg word itself is not too complicated, the use of the first-letter mnemonic definitely aids recall (Nelson & Archer, 1972). The novice handling a boat might learn to use the mnemonic "red, right, returning" in order to recall that the red buoys should be kept to the right when returning to the harbor. Many so-called memory experts utilize long and intricate mnemonic devices when performing their amazing feats of recall.

Some teachers are now updating the mnemonic technique by using it in rap-style rhymes in the classroom. The hope is that rap's current popularity can be harnessed as an educational vehicle for imprinting rote lessons on developing minds. Students are encouraged to join in the fun by exercising their creative talents by writing their own educational raps. The only rules are they have to rhyme and they can't be too gross. For example, to learn the state capitals, fourth-graders in Atlanta have created their own capital rap, which includes "South Carolina has sun and sand; Columbia sits on very flat land"; "Let's all sing New Jersey's praise; Trenton town is where we

gaze"; "Massachusetts, where the British ran; Boston's where it all began"; and "North Carolina is never going to falter, because they have Raleigh, named after Sir Walter."

Mnemonic devices, however, may be so complex that recalling the original stimuli is even more difficult than it might otherwise have been. One college student had learned a long poem that was designed to ensure the memorization of all the U.S. presidents in order. The first letter in each word of the poem corresponded to the first letter in the last name of the president. Sometimes, however, the student would forget a word or line from the poem, and at other times he would forget the name the letter had designated. For example, once when asked who the thirteenth president was, he paused, repeated the poem to himself, and then proudly answered, "Franklin" (Instead of Fillmore).

Another use of the peg word mnemonic combines the verbal mediator with a visual image. The following example, one of the simplest peg systems, uses rhymes for numbers (Kantowitz & Roediger, 1980). First, rehearse and put into memory storage the following words:

1	Gun	6	Sick
2	Shoe	7	Heaven
3	Tree	8	Gate
4	Floor	9	Wine
5	Hive	10	Hen

Now have some other person give you a verbal list of ten items, slowly and in order, such as

1	Book	6	Orange
2	Football	7	Track meet
3	Bathtub	8	Rose Bowl
4	Coke	9	Professor
5	Candle	10	Dice

As each item is announced, create a mental picture associating the item with the peg word. Here's an example, although you can probably do this far more creatively yourself.

1. Gun—a *book* that has been hollowed out and contains a gun

2. Shoe—a large shoe kicking a *football*

3. Tree—a *bathtub* perched high in the limbs of a large tree

4. Floor—a bottle of *Coke* spilled all over a kitchen floor

5. Hive—a beehive with flaming *candles* inserted in it

6. Sick—eating an *orange* and becoming violently sick from it

7. Heaven—a *track meet* in heaven, with angels competing in each event

8. Gate—a large gate at the entrance to the *Rose Bowl,* festooned with admission tickets

9. Wine—your *professor* drinking too much wine and acting in a foolish fashion

10. Hen—a large hen laying a dozen *dice* instead of eggs

Once you've stored these images, the other person can either give you a number, say, 4, and you'll respond with "Coke"; or an item, say "track meet," and you can respond with the number 7. It's not hard to do, and you'll definitely impress your friends and relatives with your "amazing" powers of memory.

Mnemonic devices are unquestionably effective in aiding the recall of specific information. They may be troublesome at the start of a learning sequence, since they take time to initiate, but once in place they allow information to remain systematically stored—like an office filing system.

Yodai mnemonics, first introduced in Japan, literally means "essence of structure" and makes use of virtually all the mnemonic techniques mentioned so far, such as vivid imagery, poems, and even songs. In one study using the Yodai technique, it was found that third-graders in the United States learned to manipulate fractions in a few hours—a feat that typically takes two to three years. According to the study, once these manipulative math procedures are acquired, understanding naturally follows (Higbee & Kunihira, 1985). The use of songs as memory enhancers, such as having first-graders sing "ABCDEFG," has long been a part of most elementary school curricula in the United States. After all, what child can't sing all the words to the latest soft-drink commercial or the most current Michael Jackson hit? In the teaching of reading, great success has also been claimed for the "Hooked on Phonics" method, which uses audiotapes to teach children how to associate letter sounds with musical tones (Gateway, 1988). However, even though the phonics approach can be of great benefit to the beginning reader, sooner or later the child must begin to sight-read, rather than forever continue the slow and sometimes painful process of sounding out each word.

The learning of certain set procedures or algorithms can also be aided by the use of mnemonics. As pointed out by Carol Spafford and George Grosser, the mnemonic FOIL can be used for multiplying two sets of variables. Example: $(b + c)(d + e)$ = FOIL. In sequence multiply (1) F, the First letter of each term, b times d; (2) O, the Outer numerals, b times e; (3) I, the inner numerals, c times d; and (4) L, the last numerals, c times e. Finally, all the products are added for the total answer $(bd + be + cd + ce)$ (Spafford & Grosser, 1996).

This seemingly bright picture has another side, however. Too much reliance on mnemonics may actually prevent understanding and especially creativity. Advocates of this view believe that mnemonic devices are merely tools for rote memorization, better used for training parrots than children. Material learned in this fashion is difficult to relate to larger concepts. As one critic notes, "Mnemonics may help children learn arbitrary associations but are likely to be less helpful when the material to be learned has conceptual links not expressed by the mnemonic cover story (Kilpatrick, 1985).

IQ AND INFORMATION PROCESSING

Studies dating back to the 1920s have consistently shown that IQ and the acquisition and retention of new material are highly correlated. A child with an IQ of 130 will typically learn and retain more information than a child whose IQ is only 100. But what about forgetting? In a series of studies, first reported in 1959 by Herbert Klausmeir and John Feldhausen, children with high, average, and low IQs were shown to retain about the same *proportion* of what they had learned (Klausmeir et al., 1959). That is, although in absolute terms the high-IQ children learned and retained the most, the percentage of what was retained over time remained the same for all three IQ groups. Thus, the proportion of information retained seems to be a constant across a wide range of IQ values (Gentile et al., 1982).

Yale psychologist Robert Sternberg has also studied intelligence as it relates to information processing. Sternberg (1982) has found that people who score highest on IQ tests are not necessarily the ones who are the fastest responders at all stages of the information processing sequence. In fact, the highest IQs are registered by people who spend *more time* encoding the relevant cues in a given problem and then *less time* in strategically processing the information during the solution phase. The greater time spent during the early encoding stage is, thus, compensated for by a lessening of the time spent later in the sequence and in an increased likelihood of finding the correct solution.

DEVELOPMENTAL ASPECTS OF INFORMATION PROCESSING

There are, of course, obvious differences between the infant's and the adult's abilities to process information. And once again, we find the nature-nurture controversy arising. At the two extremes, one view states that cognitive development is a straight function of genetic unwinding (nature); the other view is that it is based solely on experience. The position that we will take falls between these two poles—that is, that the human information processor develops increasingly sophisticated strategies as a result of the overall interaction of heredity, environment, and time. Cognitive maturity thus depends on a genetic predisposition interacting with environmental encounters occurring within a range of specific age levels. The developing child acts on and reacts to his or her environment, and, as a result, the quality of the child's information processing system is transformed.

On average, older children obviously have better memories than younger children. Much of this has to do with language. As language acquisition progresses, the older child has more categories of verbal representations to use to encode and retrieve information. Also, as we have seen in our discussion of Jean Piaget, qualitative differences in the child's cognitive style and level develop over time. As the child's cognitive base broadens and matures, higher and more abstract levels of thought processing typically become the rule. In fact, the latest studies indicate that the child goes through critical periods in the development of processing capacities (Kail, 1991a). Each passing day brings fresh evidence demonstrating the linkage between the information processing model and the currently accepted parameters of cognitive growth. Let's now examine some of the developmentally related components of the information processing model.

Differences in Processing Input

Earlier studies had suggested that younger children were able to take less information into their sensory registers (or hold it as long) than were older children and adults. But doubt is now being expressed about this finding. More recent studies have indicated that five-year-olds do not differ from adults in the amount of information they perceive or the time they hold it in the sensory register. What the earlier studies interpreted as a sensory difference now appears to be a difference in how much information can be encoded into STM before it simply decays in the sensory register. It is at this stage of the process that older children show superiority. Nor can this advantage be explained solely on the basis of language differences (Solso, 1995). The mature learner's apparent superiority in the amount of information recorded in sensory memory may actually be due to a more refined strategy of sensory rehearsal. In fact, the literal sensory image (icon) is believed to persist even longer in the young child than in the adult. Thus, at least with regard to visual memory, the infant is simply processing the information more slowly, even though the icon may in fact remain intact somewhat longer (Lasky & Spiro, 1980).

Processing speed   Again, although earlier studies seemed to indicate that processing speed was a direct function of age, the current view is more cautious. In the earlier studies investigators had typically presented the subjects with a simple stimulus, then measured the time it took for recognition to occur. But what had at first appeared to be a difference in processing speed may instead have been an artifact of the experimental methodology. Perhaps older children were more willing to take a guess at what the stimulus might be and, because of their broader knowledge base, were more accurate when they did guess.

Thus, the evidence on processing speed is still unclear. Its importance from a developmental point of view, however, should not be minimized. As Robert Solso states, "If children indeed process individual stimuli more slowly, the cumulative effect of this deficit across large numbers of stimuli could be substantial" (1995, p. 369).

Attentional processes   Since the ability to attend to or focus on relevant stimuli is a key element in the transfer of information from the sensory register to STM, the study of the growth of attentional processes is of major significance to developmental psychologists. Researchers are especially interested

SPOTLIGHT ON READING FOR UNDERSTANDING

Metacognition in Action

It's one thing to learn to read, but it's even more important to learn how to understand what is being read. Comprehension difficulties are often related to the reader's failure to participate actively in the reading process. We have all been told many times that teaching students to read more strategically not only increases their understanding of important textual information but also their motivation. Too often, however, teachers are not told how to teach these strategies. The Nolan technique, described here, has been used many times in different teaching environments and has proved to be invaluable, especially with children who are below average in comprehension ability.

The Nolan technique is based on combining two cognitive strategies: self-questioning and prediction. Previous research on the use of strategy and reading comprehension has typically focused on the effects of a single technique. However, relatively little has been done with the combination of two cognitive strategies in a single intervention.

Children using the combined metacognitive strategies are given a series of short passages to read, and then, while reading, are taught to utilize the following steps, called self-questioning with prediction, or SQWP.

1. Identify the main idea.
2. Write down the main idea.
3. Think of a question based on main idea and write it down.
4. Answer your question.
5. Predict what will happen next.

Results show that after as few as a half-dozen sessions, students who used self-questioning with prediction scored significantly higher on measures of reading comprehension than those who used only self-questioning or a more traditional vocabulary-development intervention. Combining two cognitive strategies in a single intervention encourages students to actively monitor their states of reading. Self-questioning directs the student's attention to critical aspects of the text, thereby increasing understanding of important textual elements. The prediction component stimulates a purpose for reading because the student is forced to anticipate coming events in the passage. Motivation is increased by the anticipation of discovering whether one's guess will be confirmed. Importantly, the combined metacognitive strategies benefited both students whose reading comprehension was slightly below grade level and those whose comprehension was severely below grade level.

Further, in follow-up studies students have reported that they continued to use the combined metacognitive strategies months after the training period has ended. Here are some of their comments:

Using a strategy helps me in social studies to find important facts in the paragraph.

I'm more in charge of what I'm doing when I use a strategy during reading.

I feel good when I use a reading strategy since it helps me in my classes to answer questions about what I read.

Finally, because metacognitive strategies facilitate reading comprehension, they may be applicable not only across content areas but also across skill areas, such as creative writing and artistic endeavors.

Source: Nolan, T. E. (1991). Self-questioning and prediction: Combining metacognitive strategies. *Journal of Reading, 35*(2), 132–138.

---

in two aspects of the attentional process—actually two sides of the same coin—selective attention and divided attention.

Selective attention involves homing in on one source of incoming information, while ignoring other possible distractors. Can the child continue to listen to the teacher while tuning out a peer conversation in the back of the classroom? Can the child pick out the salient features in a workbook problem without getting lost in the extraneous details? In one study of the way first-graders solve arithmetic word problems, it was found that performance increased when the stimuli, in this case *pictures* of the objects to be quantified, were different rather than the same.

For example, the children were better able to add five stegosaurs plus one brontosaur than when presented with five stegosaurs plus one stegosaur. The use of different objects to represent these quantities provided a more interesting and novel visual array and thus increased the child's ability to attend selectively to the important information in each question (Sprinthall & Nolan, 1991).

For dyslexics (children with severe reading problems), selective attention may be difficult to sustain because they are receiving too many incoming stimuli. The distribution of visual receptors on the dyslexic's retina has been shown to differ from that of the nondyslexic (Grosser & Spafford, 1990). Dyslexic children have significantly more receptors for detailed vision (called *cones*) in the peripheral region of the retina, and as a result they are receiving stimuli from a wider-than-normal visual field. This may be an asset in certain athletic endeavors, but it presents problems to the child trying to attend selectively to a word or words on a printed page. The fact that the dyslexic child sees letters and colors at greater peripheral distances than the normal reader suggests that the visual process needed for reading, certainly an extremely complex visual task, may be compromised by the presence of so many competing stimulus distractions occurring in the child's peripheral visual field (Dautrich, 1993). Thus, being able to see out of the corner of one's eye may be great for playing basketball, but a decided disadvantage when learning to read.

Although conventional wisdom has estimated that dyslexia occurs at a ratio of four to one in favor of boys over girls, recent studies have challenged that assumption. For example, Lubs et al. (1991) report that among siblings dyslexia occurs as frequently in girls as in boys. Lubs suggests that the disproportionate reporting of boys by teachers and school officials is due more to the tendency of boys to be more disruptive in the classroom than to their dyslexia. Another study found that among a large group of children in kindergarten through grade three, the number of boys and girls who could be objectively (based on psychological tests and DSM-IV criteria rather than classroom histrionics) classified as dyslexic was just about even, despite the school system's original classification of four boys for each girl (Shaywitz et al., 1990).

For most children, however, the ability to attend selectively tends to increase naturally with age (Kail, 1991b). For example, many teenagers say they are able to study and comprehend, despite the seeming distraction of loud music blaring from a nearby radio.

The other side of the coin is called **divided atten-tion,** and is shown when the child can listen to the teacher *and also* pick up the peer conversation in the back of the room or when the teenager is studying a history lesson with the radio on, and is able to attend to both sources of incoming information. This ability is also developmentally based, with adolescents being much better at this than are younger children (Shiff & Knopf, 1985). This isn't to say that adolescents should be encouraged to study while the television or radio is on. It's just that they are better able than younger children to perform that kind of information balancing act.

Thus, the evidence in this area is fairly straightforward. The research clearly shows that older children are indeed better able to focus and control their attentional processes than are younger children. Unless affected by other conditions, such as health problems, emotional problems, or learning disabilities such as ADHD, a child's potential ability to attend to relevant cues and ignore the irrelevant seems to be a direct function of growth and development.

Because they typically cannot focus their attentional processes, ADHD children often become social isolates, spurned by both teachers and classmates. Among the classmates the ADHD child is the "last one picked" and the "first one picked on." And for most teachers the evaluation of ADHD children is that they "can't sit still; don't pay attention; mess around and get into trouble; they try to get others into trouble; they are rude; they get mad when they don't get their way and say they can beat everybody up" (Henker & Whalen, 1989, p. 216). Fortunately, medication has proved effective with these children. Stimulant medication such as methylphenidate (Ritalin) is not only the most widely used therapy for ADHD children, but also the most effective (Henker & Whalen, 1989). Ritalin apparently activates the child's attention-focusing centers. Once the child is able to fully attend to incoming information, the hyperactivity seems to lessen, often in dramatic fashion (Barkley, 1990). There is no evidence that Ritalin is either addictive or more apt to promote later drug use (Levine, 1993). Parent training has also been shown to be an invaluable aid in alleviating much of the ADHD symptomatology (Anastopolous et al., 1993). Parents can become part of the remediation process, which has the side effect of increasing the self-esteem and reducing the stress levels of the parents themselves.

There is growing suspicion that the ADHD diagnosis is being overused and now covers many more conditions than was originally suggested. One problem the ADHD critics have with the diagnosis is that it now seems as though the whole process falls into the nominal fallacy category, that is, confusing de-

SPOTLIGHT ON A LEARNING PROBLEM

Attention Deficits

One extremely perplexing problem, common among learning-disabled children,* is a condition known as attention deficit-hyperactivity disorder, or ADHD.[a] The child who suffers from this syndrome is simply unable to concentrate for a sustained period or even to pay much attention to incoming information, as when trying to listen to the teacher in class. This is, of course, extremely troublesome to the learner, since the information can not get processed at all if it never enters STM in the first place. Children who suffer from this condition are said to show impulsive rather than reflective thinking.[b] Among preschoolers, and even among some older children, some of the symptoms associated with this condition are fairly common and should not be viewed as especially dangerous. At very early ages they may signal only a temporary developmental lag. But by grades four and up, this syndrome can become an extremely incapacitating condition for the developing learner and may indicate that the child is learning-disabled. ADHD children have great difficulty attending to instructions, even in game situations, especially games of concentration like "Simon Says." To be diagnosed as having ADHD, the child must exhibit a large number of specific criteria. Since inattention and hyperactivity are so often combined with impulsivity, the criteria to follow will define the combined type. The criteria listed (in descending order of discriminating power) by the American Psychiatric Association

But he was here a second ago.

Portrait of a typical ADHD child.

for ADHD (combined type) are as follows:

Inattention
a. Fails to pay attention to details or makes careless mistakes in schoolwork and other activities.
b. Has difficulty sustaining attention in tasks or play
c. Has difficulty listening to what is being said when being spoken to directly
d. Has difficulty following through on instructions
e. Cannot organize tasks or activities
f. Avoids and dislikes engaging

in tasks that require sustained mental effort

g. Often loses things needed for activities at school or at home
h. Is easily distracted by extraneous stimuli
i. Is forgetful in daily activities

Hyperactivity
a. Fidgets with hands or feet or squirms in seat
b. Has difficulty remaining seated when asked to do so
c. Runs about or climbs excessively
d. Has difficulty playing or engaging in leisure activities quietly
e. Is "on the go" or acts as if "driven by a motor"
f. Talks excessively

Impulsivity
g. Blurts out answers to questions before they are completed
h. Has difficulty awaiting turn in games
i. Interrupts or intrudes on others[c]

Since it is the rare child indeed who hasn't shown many, or even all, of these behaviors at one time or another, the American Psychiatric Association carefully points out that to receive a valid diagnosis of ADHD, the child must display at least six of *each* of the nine listed criteria, must show the onset before age seven, and must exhibit these symptoms for six months or longer. When this condition is suspected, the teacher should notify the school psychologist.[d] Although many ADHD children seem to grow out of this condition when they reach midadolescence, by that time much of the damage is done. Later effort may not compensate for lack of early learning.

As with many conditions listed in DSM-IV, there is controversy over the etiology of ADHD. Since there are heritability studies that show the possibility of a genetic linkage, some advocates for the ADHD child (such as an organization called CH.A.D.D.—Children with Attention Deficit Disorder) have taken the position that there is *always* a genetic basis for this condition. Others take the environmental view that ADHD can be learned, and that the conditions for this disorder are largely imposed by current childrearing practices. They maintain that childrearing philosophies have changed over the past 30 years and that parents today have become overly interested in providing not just time for their children, but quality time. Quality time has come to mean an hour or so when parents are paying total attention to the child, as opposed to the child paying attention to the parent. Thirty years ago, children were taught to pay attention to their parents, and this shift has prevented today's children from learning how to pay attention to adults. Therefore, when they do get to school it should come as no surprise that so much of their behavior is considered "off task." This view, so that argument goes, can explain the increase in the number of ADHD children in the nation's schools over the past several years. Another view is that the number of ADHD children hasn't really increased, but that teachers and psychologists have become more sensitive in identifying the ADHD child.

The alert teacher should also be aware that attention deficits are not always accompanied by great bursts of hyperactive energy. The condition called attention deficit disorder, or ADD, without hyperactivity can be even more insidious, especially because ADD children are less apt to advertise their struggles.[e] The ADD child does not display the overt and dramatic symptoms of ADHD and is thus more difficult to identify, at least at first. In fact sometimes a teacher may even welcome such a nondisruptive child. The careful observer, however, might notice a faraway look in the child's eyes as though the child had "spaced out." The ADD child simply cannot maintain a well-organized thought pattern or a clear focus on incoming information. The ADD child may be able to do the first few word problems correctly, but then starts making errors on the next few problems even though they are no more difficult.[f] However, the child who daydreams or who displays indifferent, seclusive, and withdrawn behavior is showing symptoms that may be warning signs of a more serious problem than ADD. The withdrawn child who begins not acknowledging other people, who displays rigid thinking patterns, and who even starts using a private language (often muttering meaningless phrases) may be drifting off onto the lonely road to unreality. The caring teacher can often detect these prepsychotic signs. This does not mean that all teach-

Attention Deficits (concluded)

ers must train to be professional psychologists, but, like it or not, we all do psychologize whenever we make inferences about how or why people behave as they do. Aside from the parents, perhaps nobody else has the opportunity to observe the child for so many hours and in such a variety of situations.

*The term *learning-disabled* is used to refer to a child who has normal or near-normal intelligence but also displays a baffling variety of learning and

behavior problems, such as an IQ-achievement discrepancy, possible central nervous system dysfunction, information processing difficulties, learning problems not due to an impoverished environment, and even some emotional problems, as defined in D. P. Hallahan & J. M. Kauffman (1991), *Exceptional Children: Introduction to special education* (5th ed.), Englewood Cliffs, NJ: Prentice-Hall.
[a] Henker, B., & Whalen, C. K. (1989). Hyperactivity and attention deficits. *American Psychologist, 44,* 216–230.
[b] Hallahan, D. P., & Kauffman, J. M. (1991). *Exceptional children: Introduction to special education* (5th ed.). Englewood

Cliffs, NJ: Prentice-Hall.
[c] American Psychiatric Association (1994). *Diagnostic and statistical manual of mental disorders* (4th ed.). Washington, DC: Author.
[d] McKinney, J. D., & Speece, D. L. (1986). Academic consequences and longitudinal stability of behavioral subtypes of learning disabled children. *Journal of Educational Psychology, 78,* 365–372.
[e] Jordan, D. R. (1992). *Attention deficit disorder* (2d ed.). Austin, TX: Pro-Ed.
[f] Jordan, D. R. (1991). Whatever happened to ADD without hyperactivity? *CH.A.D.D. ER* (1991), *4,* 4.

---

scription for explanation: "Why doesn't Johnny pay attention, stay in his seat, or complete his work?" "Because he has an attention deficit." "How do you know he has an attention deficit?" "Because he doesn't pay attention, stay in his seat, or complete his work" (Goodman & Poillion, 1992).

Encoding   The ability to internally encode incoming information also seems to have a substantial developmental component. A stimulus may be encoded on the basis of its size, distance, density, color, shape, texture, name, and so forth. Whereas young children typically incorporate only a small number of stimulus dimensions, sometimes only one or two, older children engage in what is called **multiple encoding** (Solso, 1995, p. 370), using a large number of encoding alternatives.

Differences in Storing Information

Rehearsal strategies   Age-related differences have also been found in rehearsal strategies. This is an obviously important factor, since rehearsal allows STM codes to be processed into LTM. The major findings in this area indicate that as children get older, they develop more organized rehearsal strategies, which, because of their cumulative effects, allow significantly more information to be consolidated into LTM. Younger children, though still attempting to

rehearse, do so in a less systematic fashion than older children.

Chunking techniques   Closely related to rehearsal strategies are **chunking** techniques, since both depend on organizational skills and the ability to form abstractions. A list of words—such as *airplane, train, bus, couch, table, chair, piano, guitar, trumpet*—is easy to remember when chunked into the three categories of modes of transportation, furniture, and musical instruments. If the list is encoded as nine separate and seemingly random items, retrieval becomes far more difficult. Younger children, even when prompted as to the obvious chunking categories, have difficulty memorizing this type of list. Up to about third grade, children seem not to do any better on easily categorized items than they do on unrelated items.

Retrieval skills   Retrieval skills have also been found to be based on age-related strategies. As children mature, they develop what appears to be an almost spontaneous increase in the use of retrieval strategies. This, after all, should not be surprising. Since the developing child is encoding and organizing information in an increasingly sophisticated manner, it is little wonder that he or she can access the processed information more efficiently. The older child utilizes more categories, more information storage bins, and because of this is better able to use retrieval cues to facilitate the search. It has also been suggested that older children possess more knowledge about their own memory skills and thus are better equipped to know when certain retrieval skills are appropriate. This concept of having internal knowledge about memory has been called *metacognition,* or *metamemory,* by John Flavell and others (Flavell, 1985). Thus, young children may not use as many retrieval aids as older children, either because the younger children don't yet have the aids or, if they do, don't know that they have the aids—or even that the aids might be helpful in retrieval. The difference between cognition and metacognition is in the students' self-awareness and control. Cognitive processes often grow over time, with little awareness or effort on the part of learners. Metacognition involves definite awareness, and even conscious monitoring and control. Elizabeth Bondy puts it this way: "A student who summarizes the chapter he/she has just read exercises cognitive skills. When the student constructs a summary as a means of obtaining feedback on his/her understanding of the material, the student engages in metacognition" (Bondy, 1984, p. 236).

Metacognition is thus defined as thinking about thinking, and Bondy believes that these metacognitive strategies can be taught, that classroom teachers can promote the development and use of metacognitive abilities. Among other strategies she suggests are

1. Providing opportunities for feedback

2. Having students keep a daily learning log

3. Providing instruction in self-questioning techniques

4. Teaching students to rate their own abilities to comprehend

Studies aimed at the direct instruction of children on the use of these metacognitive strategies have consistently reported increases both in their usage as thinking tools and in *memory performance* (Lodico et al., 1983).

Finally, retrieval sometimes requires a rather concerted effort on the part of the learner, and younger children may not be as willing to exert themselves in the search for cues. Also, retrieval takes more effort when the incoming information is relatively new and unorganized. The younger child probably has to exert more effort in retrieving information simply because it is not as easily accessed.

In summary, the evidence emerging from the information processing studies has confirmed the developmental aspects of this important theory.

THE PHYSICAL LOCUS OF MEMORY

In Search of the Engram

Before closing this chapter, we should take a brief look at the physical side of the learning organism. As prospective teachers, your appreciation of the overall information processing model in general and the learning child in particular should be enhanced by developing some awareness of recent research into the biological correlates of learning and memory. How does a memory form in the physical sense? And if we can find out how it is formed, can we also discover its physical location? Finally, are there any physiochemical procedures available for enhancing one's memory capabilities?

Even though psychologists have studied memory for more than a century, most of the studies have focused on how the memory system works, not on what the functions of memory are or what the memory system does for us—questions that William James certainly would have asked. Rather than concentrate solely on analogies from physics and computer science, some of today's theorists want to remind us of the Jamesian message of functionalism and nudge us more into the area of biology, where a clearer picture of these matters of *function* may emerge. These researchers insist that biology, as opposed to physics, is better able to apply population thinking and therefore to help us recognize the importance of individual differences and variation (Bruce, 1991).

Implicit in all discussions of the memory process is the ghost of the "black box," or the notion that explanations that are based on physical or physiological analogies are merely hocus-pocus illusions and are therefore really no explanations at all. Even today, behaviorists often charge physiological and cognitive psychologists with "stuffing" the black box, or creating internal, neural explanations to cover their own ignorance. But even the most ardent behaviorist cannot allay the gnawing thought that when learning is identified at the behavioral level, even as a new squiggle on a Skinnerian cumulative record, somewhere, someplace, somehow changes are taking place within the organism's nervous system. The actual, physical location of the memory trace has been called the **engram.**

During the height of behaviorism, in the 1940s and 1950s, those researchers who dared to voice these nagging thoughts, such as the great Harvard physiological psychologist Karl Lashley, usually spoke of electrical reverberating circuits and saw the brain as a direct analog of the electronic computer. When these researchers failed to find the precise lo-

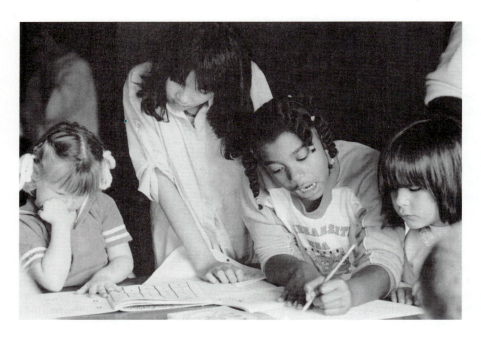

Students can be helped to develop their metacognition, or their ability to think about thinking.

cation of these reverberating circuits within the nervous system, Lashley uttered his plaintive though tongue-in-cheek comment, "Learning is just not possible" (1950, p. 480).

Beginning in the mid-1950s, however, a different approach was taken, one based on a biochemical model. Theorists began to focus on chemical changes. The Swedish biochemist Holger Hyden was one of the first, in 1959, to put forth the **RNA theory** (Hyden, 1959). In order to support a biochemical account, it seemed essential to find molecules large enough and complex enough to store the millions of memories that an individual might accumulate over the years. Logic seemed to dictate, therefore, that the enormously large, life-controlling nucleic acids, RNA and DNA, might be the storage sites. Hyden suggested that since we are born with roughly 10 billion brain cells (the accepted number at that time), and that within each of these cells there are millions of RNA molecules, then the RNA theory could logically account for trillions of images and memories that humans can store over a lifetime. Hyden then did an experiment and found that changes in the RNA within nerve cells could occur as a direct result of environmental stimulation. Although this, of course, did not prove that memories are all encoded in RNA molecules, it certainly suggested that RNA might play a role, perhaps as a link in the memory chain. Since Hyden's study was completed, physiologists now estimate the number of brain cells

to be over 100 billion, with 100 million more supporting cells, such as the nonconducting glial cells. And since each brain cell reaches out through its axonal pipeline to up to 1,000 other cells, there are probably more synaptic connections within a single human brain than there are stars in the universe.

About the same time as Hyden's early work, James V. McConnell began reporting some astonishing findings that aroused skepticism among many of his colleagues (McConnell et al., 1959). McConnell, working with flatworms, or Planaria, had first succeeded in training these tiny organisms to respond to a conditioned stimulus. He then cut the worms in half, allowing the heads to regenerate new tails and the tails to regenerate new heads. Both "new" flatworms retained the conditioned response, indicating that memory might be chemical in nature. If this were the case, McConnell reasoned, then it might be possible, in effect, to transplant a memory from one organism to another if the right chemicals from the trained worm could be injected into an untrained worm. This approach simply did not work. McConnell then recalled that under certain conditions flatworms will eat one another, and since they have only a rudimentary digestive tract, it might even be possible that tissue from one worm could pass into the body of the cannibal worm in a relatively unchanged state. The new experiment was a success: After grinding up trained worms and feeding them to untrained worms, McConnell found that the untrained worms responded to the conditioned stimulus. He felt sure that memory had been chemically transferred from one organism to another.

Also working from a biochemical model, William Corning and E. Roy John (1961) trained a group of flatworms, cut them in half, and allowed the halves to regenerate, some in normal pond water and some in a solution of ribonuclease, an enzyme that is known to break up RNA. Under both conditions, pond water and ribonuclease, the heads that regenerated new tails retained the conditioning. However, only the pond-water tails that regenerated new heads retained the learning. The tails that had regenerated heads in the ribonuclease failed to show evidence of conditioning.

This finding demonstrated a direct link between RNA and learning. Since the heads of flatworms contain about 75 percent of their nervous systems, the fact that the RNA inhibitor did not affect them is not surprising, since most of the coded RNA was simply retained in the head. However, the tails, which had to regenerate the bulk of their nervous systems, were affected by the ribonuclease. The ribonuclease apparently prevented the coded RNA from being duplicated in the new head cells. Although these results furnish no definite proof that memory resides in the RNA molecule, they do indicate at least that RNA is involved in the memory process. John further believes that memory is not localized to one section of the brain but is more probably spread throughout the brain (John, 1976).

The Two-Stage Memory Process Revisited

During the late 1950s and early 1960s, it became increasingly evident that memory could not be explained on the basis of a single process and that the engram was not a single unit, like a computer's silicon chip or a bank's safe-deposit vault. Some researchers today avoid the term *engram* completely because of its localized connotation (Allison, 1992). Even Lashley's own studies, imprecise though they may seem by today's standards, seemed to indicate that memories were not just localized into neat little pockets, but were probably spread throughout the brain. But although Lashley's concept of the reverberating electrical circuits was vulnerable as an explanation of long-term memory, it was clear from our knowledge of the neural impulse that its electrical properties were somehow involved.

The **two-stage memory process** system was foreshadowed by the work of William James. (What, in modern psychology, was not?) James had said that consciousness occurred in two stages, transitive and substantive. James hypothesized that all ideas first enter consciousness in a transitive state, that is, as fleeting will-o'-the-wisps of only marginal existence. The idea then *may* or *may not* proceed into substantive form. If it does, the idea gains stability because of its transformation into a physical substance (James, 1890). Much later, in 1949, D. O. Hebb set forth his famous dual-trace memory theory. As Hebb stated it:

> The conception of a transient, unstable reverberatory trace is therefore useful, if it is possible to suppose also that some more permanent structural change reinforces it. There is no reason to think that a choice must be made between the two conceptions; there may be traces of both kinds and memories which are dependent on both.

As we have seen, current theories imply that memory is governed by at least two stages, short-term and long-term, and that perhaps, as James and Hebb suggested, these stages are qualitatively different. Short-term memory is probably largely electrical, whereas long-term memory may be largely chemical. STM may be fleeting because no permanent change takes place within the organism. The short-lived electrochemical process decays rapidly. But sometimes, before the short-term trace disappears, a second series of events occurs in the brain that may involve the production, as Hyden has suggested, of new proteins. Thus, although STM is accompanied by transient electrical changes in the brain, LTM may be accompanied by the physical production of new, permanent brain proteins. Thus, permanent learning may exist in the form of a protein molecule (Lynch, 1984).

This theory is not inconsistent with the previously mentioned RNA theory, in that the RNA is needed for protein synthesis. Further, even the prime mover of the RNA theory back in the late 1950s, Holgar Hyden, has since suggested that the retrieval of stored information depends on, among other things, the presence of unique *proteins* in the neuron (Hyden, 1970).

Some familiar phenomena seem to support this position. People who suffer head injuries with loss of consciousness usually sustain a loss of memory for events just preceding the trauma. This **retrograde amnesia** indicates that when the brain is jolted, a long-term memory may somehow be prevented from consolidating (Crovitz et al., 1983). Some experimental evidence was supplied by Murray Jarvik and R. Kopp (1967). In a series of studies, they demonstrated that if organisms are given a jolt of electric current to the brain, a current just strong enough to scramble the brain's electrical circuitry, the organisms are unable to recall the training that preceded the shock. Other studies, however, have raised some questions concerning the interpretation of these data. For example, is the memory permanently gone, or is it simply currently irretrievable as a result of emotionally induced interference factors? It has been found, for example, that human amnesia patients may sometimes have their seemingly lost memories restored under conditions of sedation. Using a different approach, Bernard Agranoff, another advocate of the two-stage memory theory, has worked with the antibiotic puromycin, which inhibits the formation of new proteins (Agranoff, 1965). When puromycin was injected into the brains of trained organisms just prior to learning, they showed no memory impairment at first. However, when tested a few hours later, they evidenced far less retention of the task than did a control group that had not received puromycin. The action of the puromycin, it appears, prevents the short-term memory from consolidating into the more permanent long-term memory. Other researchers have validated this finding, and the general phenomenon is now called the *puromycin effect* (Flexner & Flexner, 1970).

Because so many studies have demonstrated that protein inhibitors can block the formation of memory, it's becoming increasingly apparent that the synthesis of new proteins is clearly involved in the consolidation of at least some memories (Davis & Squire, 1984). In addition, just as some chemical agents have been shown to inhibit memory, others (such as Metrazol and magnesium pemoline) have been shown to facilitate the consolidation process (Grosser et al., 1967).

And the search goes on. In 1983 James V. McConnell reported on a study conducted by Ewen Cameron in which elderly senile patients were found to have significantly higher levels of ribonuclease in their bloodstreams than did the nonsenile elderly. Since ribonuclease is an enzyme that breaks up and destroys RNA, an attempt was then made to lower the ribonuclease levels in the senile patients by injecting them with yeast RNA. It was hoped that the ribonuclease would then destroy the yeast RNA rather than the RNA produced in the brain. Also, in order to enhance RNA production in the brain, other patients were given the drug magnesium pemoline. The results in both cases proved promising. Some of the patients given yeast RNA did recover memory, though not all. The patients who had been injected with magnesium pemoline also showed improved memory, but as soon as they were taken off the drug, memory deterioration again set in (McConnell,

1990).

In an animal study conducted by Michael Warren, two groups of "elderly" mice were kept in dramatically differing environments. One group was constantly stimulated, trained, and handled, whereas the other group was confined to sensory isolation chambers. The stimulated mice proved to be better problem solvers and also had *more RNA in their brains*. Warren, extrapolating this finding to the human level, suggested that older people who continue to lead an active and challenging life have less chance of developing intellectual impairments than do those who sit around in gloomy silence (Warren et al., 1982).

Memory and Physiology: from Proteins to Calpain

Neuroscientist Gary Lynch believes that the two long-term memory systems, declarative and procedural (outlined earlier), are based on qualitatively different physiological principles. Lynch says that these two forms of memory reside in different structures of the brain and are even under different biochemical controls. Lynch sees the protein model as best fitting the data on procedural knowledge, and, as we have seen, the studies mentioned above, by McConnell, Corning and John, and Jarvik, were all based on learning through conditioning. Regarding declarative memory, Lynch postulates a somewhat different mechanism. When a neural impulse travels from one neuron to the next, it must cross a small gap called a synapse. At this point, the impulse releases tiny amounts of certain chemicals called neurotransmitters. When these neurotransmitters bind to the next neuron (to its dendritic spines), permanent changes take place in the responsiveness of the synapse and in the shape of the postsynaptic neuron. The key to this permanent change is an enzyme called *calpain*, which is activated in the postsynaptic neuron as a result of the release of the neurotransmitters from the presynaptic neuron. The calpain increases when nerve cells are stimulated and consequently exposes more receptors. This sequence promotes new synapses on the nerve cell which, in turn, facilitates new learning. It is also known that this mechanism functions most efficiently in those areas of the brain involved in declarative memory. Thus, there are major differences in the biochemistry of the two long-term memory systems, declarative and procedural, and there are also differences in their physical locations. Procedural memory, though primarily dependent on activity of the cerebellum, seems to be more widespread in the brain (including even the brain stem), whereas declarative memory is, at least originally, more focused. The current position is that declarative memory is first stored in the hippocampal region (an area located near the base of the brain) and then later becomes integrated into regions of the cortex where the higher levels of brain functioning take place. For example, visual information is stored mostly in the occipital lobe, while auditory and verbal memories tend to be in the parietal and temporal lobes. Thus, human memory is probably not a broad power of the mind, but is made of separate abilities, carried out in different brain locations with the hippocampus as the command center linking the various brain sites. When a hippocampal nerve cell is electrically stimulated, new synaptic nerve connections are formed in seconds (Lynch, 1986). Also, when the hippocampus is damaged or removed, only the memory for facts and events (declarative memory) is lost. The memory for physical skills, that is procedural memory, remains untouched (Squire & Zola-Morgan, 1991).

Thus, the old electrical model of learning and retention, which was most vulnerable in attempts to explain long-term memories, has been revived to explain short-term memories in a way that fits the empirical data. Permanent, possibly lifelong memories, however, are better explained via the biochemical model.

Friendly Rivals

As we have now seen, students of memory seem to have formed two distinct groups. On one side, there are the cognitive psychologists (which include the information processing theorists and artificial intelligence experts), who have built complex systems modeled after the general field of computer science. On the other side are the neuroscientists, the brain experts, who are looking for the physiological correlates of human behavior. For the past decade, these two groups, cognitivists and neuroscientists, have to some extent been friendly rivals. Neuroscientists have criticized the cognitivists for relying too heavily on computer analogies while ignoring the most important clues to the workings of the mind: the actual functioning of the brain (Ambros et al., 1990). Cognitivists, on the other hand, have felt that the neuroscientists have ignored the thinking process and become hopelessly mired in the billions of connections among the neurons. The neuroscientists have even begun using the term *wetware*, presumably because the brain is moist as it sits in the cranium, as opposed to the software and hardware analogies used by the cognitive scientists. The two groups, however, are beginning to join theoretical forces and even in some cases to collaborate on stud-

Researchers have suggested that there is a qualitative difference between short-term memory, which we may use to remember a phone number just recited to us, and long-term memory, which we may use to recall an experience from the past as we glance at a photo. Short-term memory probably involves fleeting electrical changes in the brain, whereas long-term memory involves more permanent chemical changes.

ies in memory and learning. Several cognitive theorists have suggested the term *cognitive neuroscience* to denote this new hybrid (Granger et al., 1989; Gardner, 1991).

Serenity, however, does not prevail in the field of cognitive research. For example, one researcher has complained that the concept of the memory trace, so near and dear to the hearts of information processing theorists, is merely a metaphor, a figure of speech rather than an empirical fact. Because the memory trace has been *reified* (the fallacy of treating an abstraction as though it were a concrete reality), it is alleged that cognitive scientists have been confusing psychology with physiology and, worse yet, attempting to integrate cognitive psychology with neuroscience and even artificial intelligence. We are warned that this may produce even greater confusion in the near future (Watkins, 1990).

However, despite this warning, the merger of educational psychology, cognitive psychology, and neuroscience has come of age in the 1990s and has made David Krech's prophecy even more compelling:

> Both the biochemist and the teacher of the future will combine their skills and insights for the educational and intellectual development of the child. Tommy needs a bit more of an immediate memory stimulator; Jack could do with a chemical attention-span stretcher; Rachel needs an anticholinesterase to slow down her mental processes; Joan, some puromycin—she remembers too many details and gets lost (Krech, 1969).

The physical aspects of memory are still being revealed. Physiological psychologists are now looking for answers within the organism, and the old admonition to avoid "stuffing the black box" is today as anachronistic as a portrait of George Washington seated happily in front of a computer terminal.

SUMMARY

The information processing model of learning and memory has a cognitive-gestalt orientation and is based on a computer analogy. The theory attempts to correlate the psychologist's understanding of thought processes with what is known of computer technology. Learning and remembering are seen as resulting from the flow of information that passes through various stages within the organism.

The model presented in this chapter is focused on intentional learning. Incoming information is encoded within the organism both at the psychological level (in the form of a conceptual representation) and at the physiological level (in the form of the neural memory trace). The stimulus information first enters the sensory register, where it is held for only a few seconds. If the learner is paying attention to these stimuli, they enter the first of the two main storage compartments, short-term memory, or STM. STM has only a limited capacity, about seven (plus or minus two) items, and only a limited duration, less than a minute. If the learner is motivated enough to rehearse the contents of STM, the information may then be passed along into the second storage bin, called long-term memory, or LTM. LTM has the potential for holding information for up to a lifetime. Rehearsal can take two forms: maintenance, in which the learner uses rote repetition; and elaborative, in which the learner relates the new information to other concepts and therefore expands his or her conceptual base. LTM provides for two different systems, declarative and procedural. Declarative memory represents the brain's storehouse of names, dates, and past experiences, whereas procedural memory contains traces of motor skills, typically learned through repetitive practice. Further, declarative memory has two components: episodic, which consists of memory for past episodes in one's life, and semantic, which involves the memory of words and the meaning of words. Semantic memory also contains what researchers call schemata (the plural of schema). A schema is any body of information that is related to a central concept. Because LTM can be so long-lasting, the term *permastore* has been used to describe permanently etched long-term memories. On the output side, information becomes available for retrieval when it can be located and accessed. A variety of retrieval strategies are available to aid in the storage search, but in general, the greater the number of organized categories into which information has been placed and the more meaningful these categorizations, the more accessible the information becomes. Memory for the general meaning of information is both longer-lasting and more easily accessed than is memory for specific and unrelated details.

Emotions can play a role in the memory process. Strong feelings of fear or anxiety may act to hinder memory, whereas the impact of an emotional event, such as hearing the news of the death of a loved one, may be permanently etched in what is called a flashbulb memory.

Forgetting occurs as a result of both decay and interference. Decay is thought to occur passively over time. Two important interference factors are proactive inhibition (PI), in which past learning interferes with the processing and recall of new information; and retroactive inhibition (RI), in which new learning interferes with the recall of past learning.

Studies have shown that retrieval can be facilitated by the following: (1) overlearning, (2) understanding new information, (3) building an organized knowledge base, (4) relating new material to an existing knowledge base, (5) using cue associations, and (6) using mnemonics. Mnemonic devices, such as visual imagery, peg words, and rhyming, can be used as memory aids both for learning new information and for retrieving already processed information. But some critics warn that mnemonic devices should not be overused, since material learned in this way may not be easily related to other concepts in a meaningful way.

Studies of the relation of IQ to information processing show, not surprisingly, that those with higher IQs learn and retain more information than those with lower IQs, though the percentage of what is retained over time remains about the same. Also, those with high IQs spend more time encoding and less time processing information than those with lower IQs.

The sequencing of information processing has extremely important developmental aspects, and researchers are now proposing a number of age-related correlates of the processing model. The developing child is seen as both acting on and reacting to his or her environment, and as a result, the quality of the child's information processing system is transformed. The processing system is also enhanced as the child incorporates metacognitive skills, or the ability to understand one's own memory and learning strategies.

Since the entire processing model is based on incoming information's getting through STM and into LTM, and since this step requires the *attention* of the learner, a great deal of research has gone into the problem of attention deficits. The most dramatic example of an attention deficit problem is the child suffering from ADHD, attention deficit–hyperactivity disorder. Theorists describe two forms of the attentional process: selective attention and divided attention. Selective attention is shown when the child is able to focus on one source of incoming information while ignoring other possible distractors. Divided attention occurs when the child can tune in on more than one source of incoming information, such as reading a book and listening to the radio. Studies show that this ability seems to be developmentally based, with teenagers much more adept than younger children.

The material presented up to this point comes from the theories and research of the cognitive psychologists. Another group of researchers, called neuroscientists or brain scientists, are also working on unraveling the mysteries of learning and memory. These scientists are examining the physiological components of the learning model. The search for the biological underpinnings of memory has led researchers to believe that the production of cortical ribonucleic acid (RNA) and the synthesis of new brain proteins are important links in the internal chain of neurologically grounded memory events.

Most neuroscientists now believe that the two long-term memory systems, procedural and declarative, involve different physiological processes. The protein theory seems more consistent with the data involving procedural memory, whereas permanently induced changes in both the synapse and postsynaptic neuron fit best with the facts obtained for declarative knowledge. These researchers now suggest that chemical agents may soon be used to enhance the information processing abilities of both children and adults.

KEY TERMS AND NAMES

attention—selective and divided
attention deficit–hyperactivity disorder (ADHD)
chunking
concept formation
declarative memory—episodic and semantic
dual-code theory
encoding
engram
flashbulb memory
information processing

intentional learning
long-term memory (LTM)
mnemonic devices
multiple encoding
permastore
proactive inhibition (PI)
procedural memory
protein synthesis
rehearsal—maintenance and elaborative
retrieval

retroactive inhibition (RI)
retrograde amnesia
RNA theory of memory
schema

sensory register
short-term memory (STM)
storage
two-stage memory process

THEORY INTO PRACTICE: IMPROVING YOUR MEMORY

Now that you've been exposed to the major theories of memory and information processing, it's time to put some of these ideas into the well-lit arena of practicality. Let's focus on some of the topics in the area of memory, and see if you can both improve your own processing skills and also, perhaps, discover some fresh insights of your own.

Mnemonics

First, we'll look again at those encoding devices known as mnemonics. Several mathematicians, who also happen to be memory experts, have demonstrated what seem to be amazing feats with regard to retrieving enormously long strings of digits. Some are able to recall the value of pi out to thousands of decimal places. In fact, one recent pi champion is Hideaki Tamoyori of Japan, who proved that he could remember pi out to 40,000 places. Part of the fascination with memorizing pi seems to be its transcendental quality: the virtually random sequence of digits following the decimal point seems to be infinite. To find out how it is done, let's try to memorize *pi* as far as ten decimal places, which equals 3.1415926536.

Although it's clearly possible to chunk these digits and then memorize them as numbers, an easier technique (and also the one the memory experts use) is to learn a simple series of sentences—the more meaningful, the better—then count each letter of each word in the sentence and retrieve the digits on the basis of the number of letters per word. An example for pi might be

How I want a drink. Yesterday my thirst would not quench.

Breaking it down, we have HOW (three letters), I (one letter), WANT (four letters), A (one letter), DRINK (five letters), and so on. Within a few minutes, you'll have it—the astonishing ability to rattle off pi to 10 places. For 20 places, try

How I wish I could enumerate pi easily, since all these [censored] mnemonics prevent recalling any of pi's sequence more simply.

To prove the efficiency of this method, select a few pupils or friends and ask some to memorize the sequence as simply a series of random digits. For a second group, ask others to memorize the sequence by chunking the digits, that is, to learn 314, 159, 265, and 36. For a third group, teach them the sentences shown above. Time the individuals in each group on the basis of how long it takes to repeat the sequence three times with no errors. A day later, check them a second time.

Meaning

As you have read, the more meaningful any information is, the easier it is to encode and retrieve. One way to increase the meaningfulness of information is to categorize it on the basis of an organized knowledge base. Let's say you want to memorize the following list of a dozen items: trombone, bicycle, footstool, piano, chair, car, skateboard, tuba, couch, clarinet, bus, and end table.

First, organize the items into categories that are already known to you, that is:

Musical Instruments	*Furniture*	*Modes of Transportation*
clarinet	couch	car
trombone	end table	bus
piano	chair	bicycle
tuba	footstool	skateboard

Then, within each category, reorganize on the basis of the size of each item, from, say, largest to smallest.

Musical Instruments	*Furniture*	*Modes of Transportation*
piano	couch	bus
tuba	chair	car
trombone	end table	skateboard
clarinet	footstool	bicycle

Now, see how many items on the list you can repeat. Try this list with a group of students or friends, as a random list for some, as organized by category for others, and as organized by size and category for a third group. This time, let each person hear the items just once, and then the next day, find out the number of items each person can correctly recall.

Finally, take the following sentences (which were read aloud at an AERA meeting in California by Professor David Rumelhart):

Mary heard the ice cream truck coming. She remembered her birthday money and ran into the house.

Read the sentence to a friend, and then a few hours later ask the friend to repeat what you had said. This should provide you with a dramatic example of how memory is shaped by past associations. This is what you can expect to hear:

A little girl, I think her name was Mary, ran home to get her birthday money, or was it her allowance, to

buy some ice cream. She bought the ice cream and was happy.

In looking at the original sentences, nowhere are we told that Mary is a young girl or even that she wanted to get her money to buy ice cream. We simply assume these extra facts on the basis of inferences we made that were shaped by our past associations. Mary may have been a college student, who heard the ice cream truck all right but who at that moment was merely going into the house to get money for a textbook. Or, as Professor Rumelhart suggests, read the sentence again, changing only a couple of words, *ice cream truck* to *bus*, or *birthday money* to *gun*. With these not-so-subtle changes, you may find incredible differences in interpretations.

REFERENCES

Agranoff, B. W. (1965). Molecules and memories. *Perspectives in Biological Medicine, 9,* 13–22.

Allison, M. (1992). New research in the neurobiology of learning. *Headlines, 3,* 2–11.

Alper, J. (1986). Our dual memory. *Science, 86,* 44–49.

Ambros, I. J., Granger, R., & Lynch, G. (1990). Simulation of paleocortex while performing hierarchical clustering. *Science, 247,* 1344–1348.

Anastopolous, A. D., Shelton, T., DuPaul, G. J., & Gouvremont, D. C. (1993). Parent training for attention-deficit hyperactivity disorder: Its impact on parent functioning. *Journal of Abnormal Child Psychology, 21,* 581–596.

Ashcraft, M. H. (1989). *Human memory and cognition.* Glenville, IL: Scott, Foresman.

Atkinson, R. C., & Shiffrin, R. M. (1968). Human memory: A proposed system and its component processes. In K. Spence & J. Spence (Eds.), *The psychology of learning and motivation.* New York: Academic Press.

Baddeley, A. (1990). *Human memory: Theory and practice.* Needham Heights, MA: Allyn & Bacon.

Bahrick, H. P. (1991). A speedy recovery from bankruptcy for ecological memory research. *American Psychologist, 46,* 76–77.

Barkley,. R. A. (1990). *Hyperactive children: A handbook for diagnosis and treatment* (2d ed.). New York: Guilford.

Bartlett, J. C., Hurry, S., & Thorley, W. (1984). Typicality and familiarity of faces. *Memory and Cognition, 12,* 219–228.

Blum, K. (1984). *Handbook of abusable drugs.* New York: Gardner.

Bondy, E. (1984), (March/April). Thinking about thinking. *Childhood Education,* 234–238.

Broadbent, D. E. (1984). The maltese cross: A new simplistic model for memory. *Brain Behavior Science, 7,* 55–94.

Brown, R., & Kulik, J. (1977). Flashbulb memories. *Cognition, 5,* 73–99.

Bruce, D. (1991). Mechanistic and functional explanations of memory. *American Psychologist, 46,* 46–48.

Cahill, L., Prins, B., Weber, M., & McGaugh, J. L. (1994, October 20). Andrenergic activation and memory for emotional events. *Nature, 371,* 702–704.

Carlisle, J. F. (1983). Training in reading comprehension. *Annals of Dyslexia, 33,* 187–202.

Conway, M. A. (1995). *Flashbulb memories.* Hove, England: Erlbaum.

Corning, W. C., & John, E. R. (1961). Effect of ribonuclease on retention of conditioned response in regenerated planaria. *Science, 134,* 1363–1365.

Crick, F., & Mitchison, G. (1983, July). The function of dream sleep. *Nature, 304,* 111–114.

Crovitz, H. F., Horn, R. W., & Daniel, W. F. (1983). Interrelationships among retrograde amnesia, post-traumatic amnesia, and time since head injury: A retrospective study. *Cortex, 19,* 407–412.

Dautrich, B. R. (1993). Visual perceptual differences

in the dyslexic reader: Evidence of greater visual peripheral sensitivity to color and letter stimuli. *Perceptual and Motor Skills, 76,* 755–764.

Davis, H. R., & Squire, L. R. (1984). Protein synthesis and memory: A review. *Psychological Bulletin, 96,* 518–559.

Evans, C., & Evans, P. (1983). *Landscapes of the night.* New York: Viking.

Flavell, J. H. (1985). *Cognitive development.* Englewood Cliffs, NJ: Prentice-Hall.

Flexner, J. B., & Flexner, L. B. (1970). Further observations on restoration of memory after treatment with puromycin. *Yale Journal of Biology and Medicine, 42,* 235–240.

Galvin, R. M. (1988, January–February). Stephen Pawelson's amazing memory. *Harvard Magazine,* 113–116.

Gardner, H. (1991, February 8). Mind explorers merge their maps. *New York Times,* C30.

Gateway Educational Products. (1988). *Hooked on phonics.* Orange, CA: Gateway Press.

Gentile, J. R., Monaco, N., Iheozor-Ehofor, I. E., Ndu, M., & Ogbonaya, P. K. (1982). Retention by fast and slow learners. *Intelligence, 6,* 125–138.

Goodman, G., & Poillion, M. J. (1992). ADD: Acronym for any dysfunction or difficulty. *Journal of Special Education, 26,* 27–56.

Granger, R., Ambros, I. J., & Lynch, G. (1989). Derivation of encoding characteristics of layer II cerebral cortex. *Journal of Cognitive Neuroscience, 1,* 61–87.

Grosser, G. S., & Spafford, C. S. (1990). Light sensitivity in peripheral retinal fields of dyslexic and proficient readers. *Perceptual and Motor Skills, 71,* 467–477.

Grosser, G. S., Sprinthall, R. C., & Sirois, L. (1967). Magnesium pemoline: Activation of extinction responding after continuous reinforcement. *Psychological Reports, 21,* 11–14.

Haber, R. N. (1983). The impending demise of the icon: A critique of the concept of iconic storage in visual information processing. *Behavioral and Brain Sciences, 6,* 1–11.

Hasher, L., & Zacks, R. T. (1979). Automatic and effortful processes in memory. *Journal of Experimental Psychology, 108,* 365–388.

Henker, B., & Whalen, C. K. (1989). Hyperactivity and attention deficits. *American Psychologist, 44,* 216–230.

Higbee, K. L., & Kunihira, S. (1985). Cross-cultural application of Yodai mnemonics in education. *Educational Psychologist, 20,* 57–64.

Houston, J. P. (1991). *Fundamentals of learning and memory* (4th ed.). San Diego: Harcourt Brace Jovanovich.

Hyden, H. (1959). Biochemical changes in glial cells and nerve cells at varying activity. In O. Hoffman-Ostenhoff (Ed.), *Biochemistry of the central nervous system.* London: Pergamon.

Hyden, H. (1970). The question of a molecular basis for the memory trace. In K. H. Pribram (Ed.), *Biology of memory.* New York: Academic Press.

James, W. A. (1890). *The principles of psychology.* New York: Holt.

Jarvik, M. E., & Kopp, R. (1967). An improved one trial passive avoidance learning situation. *Psychological Reports, 2,* 221–224.

John, E. R. (1976). How the brain works. *Psychology Today, 9,* 48–52.

Johnson, G. (1990). *How we build the world inside our heads.* New York: Knopf.

Kail, R. (1991a). *The development of memory in children* (3d ed.). New York: Freeman.

Kail, R. (1991b). Processing time declines exponentially during childhood and adolescence. *Developmental Psychology, 27,* 259–266.

Kantowitz, B. H., & Roediger, H. L. (1980). Memory and information processing. In G. M. Gazda & R. J. Corsini (Eds.), *Theories of learning: A comparative approach.* Itasca, IL: Peacock.

Kihlstrom, J. F. (1987). The cognitive unconscious. *Science, 237,* 1445–1452.

Kilpatrick, J. (1985). Doing mathematics without understanding it: A commentary on Higbee and Kunihira. *Educational Psychologist, 20,* 65.

Klatzsky, R. (1984). *Memory and awareness: An information-processing perspective.* New York: Freeman.

Kolers, P. A. (1983). Perception and representation. *Annual Review of Psychology, 34,* 129–166.

Krech, D. (1969). The chemistry of learning. In R. C. Sprinthall & N. A. Sprinthall (Eds.), *Educational psychology: Selected readings* (p. 156). New York: Van Nostrand-Reinhold.

Lashley, K. S. (1950). In search of the engram. *Society of Experimental Biology Symposium, 4* (pp. 454–482). Cambridge: Cambridge University Press.

Lasky, R. E., & Spiro, D. (1980). The processing of tachistoscopically presented visual stimuli by five-month-old infants. *Child Development, 51,* 214–225.

Lazarus, R. S. (1991). Cognition and motivation in emotion. *American Psychologist, 46,* 352–367.

Levine M. D. (1993). *Developmental variation and learning disorders.* Cambridge, MA: Educators Publishing Service.

Lodico, M. G., Ghatala, E. S., Levin, J. R., Pressley, M., & Bell, J. A. (1983). The effects of strategy-monitoring training on children's selection of effective memory strategies. *Journal of Experimental Child Psychology, 35,* 203–277.

Lynch, G. (1984). A magical memory tour. *Psychology Today, 18.*

Lynch, G. (1986). *Synapses, circuits, and the beginnings of memory.* Cambridge, MA: MIT Press.

McConnell, J. V. (1990). *Understanding human behavior* (5th ed.). New York: Holt, Rinehart & Winston.

McConnell, J. V., Jacobson, A. L., & Kimble, D. P. (1959). The effects of regeneration upon retention of a conditioned response in the planaria. *Journal of Comparative and Physiological Psychology, 52,* 1–5.

McGaugh, J. L. (1983). Hormonal influences on memory. *Annual Review of Psychology, 34,* 297–324.

McGaugh, J. L. (1990). Significance and remembrance: The role of neuromodulatory systems. *Psychological Science, 1,* 15–25.

McShane, J. (1991). *Cognitive development: An information processing approach.* Oxford: Blackwell.

Miller, G. A. (1956). The magical number seven plus or minus two: Some limits on our capacity for processing information. *Psychological Review, 63,* 81–97.

Mistry, J., & Rogoff, G. (1994). Remembering in cultural context. In W. W. Loner & R. Malpass (Eds.), *Psychology and culture* (pp. 139–144). Boston: Allyn & Bacon.

Murphy, L. A., Pollatsek, A., & Well, A. D. (1988). Developmental dyslexia and word retrieval deficits. *Brain and Language, 35,* 1–23.

Nelson, D. L., & Archer, C. S. (1972). The first letter mnemonic. *Journal of Educational Psychology, 63*(5), 482–486.

Newman, R. S., & McVey, K. A. (1982). Learning the functional significance of mnemonic actions: A microgenetic study of strategy acquisition. *Journal of Experimental Child Psychology, 34,* 490–509.

Nolan, T. E. (1991). Self-questioning and prediction: Combining metacognitive strategies. *Journal of Reading, 35*(2), 132–138.

Paris, S. G., Lorayne, H., & Lucas, J. (1974). *The memory book.* New York: Stein & Day.

Penfield, W. (1969). Consciousness, memory and man's conditioned reflexes. In K. Pribram (Ed.), *On the biology of learning.* New York: Harcourt Brace Jovanovich.

Reder, L. M., & Ross, B. H. (1983). Integrated knowledge in different tasks: The role of retrieval strategy on fan effects. *Journal of Experimental Psychology, 9,* 55–72.

Rubin, D. C., & Kozin, M. (1984). Vivid memories. *Cognition, 16,* 81–95.

Safire, W. (1991, July 7). There's no wearware. *New York Times Magazine,* 6.

Shaywitz, S. E., Shaywitz, B. A., Fletcher, J. M., & Escobar, M. D. (1990). Prevalence of reading disability in boys and girls. *Journal of the American Medical Association, 264,* 998–1002.

Shiff, A. R., & Knopf, I. J. (1985). The effects of task demand on attention allocation in children of different ages. *Child Development, 56,* 621–630.

Skinner, B. F. (1987, August 25). Quoted in *New York Times.*

Skinner, B. F. (1990). Can psychology be a science of the mind? *American Psychologist, 45,* 1206–1210.

Solso, R. L. (1995). *Cognitive psychology* (4th ed.). Boston: Allyn & Bacon.

Spafford, C. S., & Grosser, G. S. (1996). *Dyslexia: Research and resource guide.* Boston: Allyn & Bacon.

Spear, N. E., & Riccio, D. C. (1994). *Memory: Phenomena and principles.* Boston: Allyn & Bacon.

Sprinthall, R. C., & Nolan, T. E. (1991). Efficacy of representing quantities with different pictures in solving arithmetic word problems. *Perceptual and Motor Skills, 72,* 274–276.

Squire, L. R. (1987). *Memory and brain.* New York: Oxford University Press.

Squire, L. R., & Zola-Morgan, S. (1991). The medial temporal lobe memory system. *Science, 253,* 1380–1386.

Sternberg, R. J. (1982). Who's intelligent? *Psychology Today, 16,* 30–39.

Tulving, E. (1983). *Elements of episodic memory.* New York: Oxford University Press.

Tulving, E. (1985). How many memory systems are there? *American Psychologist, 40,* 385–398.

Walberg, H. J. (1988). Synthesis of research on time and learning. *Educational Leadership, 45,* 76–85.

Warren, J. M., Zerweck, C., & Anthony, A. (1982). The effects of environmental stimulation on old mice. *Developmental Psychobiology, 15,* 13–18.

Watkins, M. J. (1990). Mediationism and the obfuscation of memory. *American Psychologist, 45,* 328–335.

White, R. T., & Gagne, R. M. (1976). Retention of related and unrelated sentences. *Journal of Educational Psychology, 68,* 843–852.

Winograd, E., & Neisser, U. (1992). *Affect and accuracy in recall: Studies of "flashbulb" memories.* New York: Cambridge University Press.

Woodard, F. J. (1996). Hypnosis and phenomenological-perceptual psychology. *Journal of Clinical Psychology, 52,* 209–218.

Wyer, R. S., & Srull, T. K. (1989). *Memory and cognition in its social context.* Hillsdale, NJ: Erlbaum.

TEACHING EFFECTIVENESS

Oh, city kids are skipping
and their tricks are really neat.

METHODS
AND MODELS
OF TEACHING

As we noted in Chapter 1, research into teaching effectiveness has expanded rapidly in the last decade. In this chapter we will review and generalize the research suggestions. We will also show how these results can be incorporated into a broad framework to guide your practice. A model of teaching basically represents a specific cluster of teaching strategies designed to reach a particular type of learning outcome with pupils. However, no single model represents the best way to teach. Instead, overall effectiveness will depend on your ability, first, to master specific techniques and, second, to combine them within a particular model. Finally, you must develop the ability to use a variety of models. When you have reached that point, you will be on your way to mastery of a repertoire of teaching models.

In Chapter 13 we will switch focus from the teacher to the students, addressing the question of how to apply the different models according to your goals as well as the needs of the students. Here we will concentrate first on discrete teacher skills and then on models. We start with a review of elements of teaching effectiveness and then look at the use of a system of analyzing teaching as a bridge to the more general models.

ELEMENTS OF TEACHING EFFECTIVENESS

The most comprehensive review of elements of teaching effectiveness has been completed by **Herbert Walberg** from the University of Illinois. Using the techniques of statistical meta-analysis, he compiled more than 3,000 studies, then carefully analyzed them to determine just how important each particular element was in student learning (Walberg, 1986). More recently, he was part of an Australian-U.S. team that assessed 134 reviews of 7,827 field studies and several large-scale U.S. and international surveys of learning (Fraser et al., 1987). From his results, he compiled a list of weighted factors. Table 12.1 is a selection from his list of the elements most closely related to teacher behavior in the classroom—in other words, the kind of procedures a teacher may actually employ. Each of the selected teaching processes listed in Table 12.1 will be discussed here in turn: engaged academic learning time, use of positive reinforcement, cues and feedback, cooperative learning activities, classroom morale, higher-order questioning, and use of advance organizers. In this and the next two chapters

HERBERT J. WALBERG

If you were to ask any educational psychologist to list the 10 most productive and influential scholars in the field, you would be sure to find Herbert Walberg's name in that select group.

Walberg is an eminent scholar and a prolific writer. His manner is quiet and unassuming. His particular genius has been his policy research and his mastery of educational psychology's three components of theory, research, and practice. Thus, his work speaks to all educational psychologists. The theorists see in his work a synthesizing of ideas, a means of combining previously separate conceptual frameworks into a more cohesive cluster of directing concepts. The researchers follow very carefully his new system of meta-analysis as a means of combining empirical results from a wide variety of studies. No longer are educational studies dependent on one or a dozen or even 100 studies. Walberg has

shown the field how to review 2,000 to 3,000 studies and end up with meaningful conclusions. In the pre-Walberg era, many reviews of the research literature would suggest that there was little in the way of substantial knowledge and (often with a whimper) conclude that "more research is needed." A few years later, another review would be published with similar results and end with the same call.

To some degree the most important aspect of Walberg's work may be its implications for practice. His recent summarization of the research on teaching effectiveness is a clear example of just how practical research can be in the hands of such a brilliant man. He avoids any allegiance to a particular school of thought and instead reviews all studies on the basis of parsimony both theoretically and empirically. One of the continuing complaints about educational psychologists in general is that if you know the

we will also focus on related teacher behaviors and classroom interaction patterns that contribute to and differentially affect the learning of students of different ethnicity, economic status, and gender.

Engaged Academic Learning Time

Although it may seem too obvious to note, academic learning time in the classroom has emerged as an important variable. Studies have shown that the amount of on-task behavior can vary as much as 40 percent from one classroom to the next (Walberg, 1988). Even how quickly a teacher calls the class to order can vary all the way from one to 10 minutes. Thus, how efficiently you plan your lessons, how long you take to get started, how you handle digressions, off-task behavior, and discipline, and how you handle transitions will have an effect on student learning.

Important as academic learning time is, there is not an exact relationship between time on task and learning outcome. Moreover, it is difficult, if not impossible, to measure what is going on in a student's mind at a specific moment. In fact, one study showed that students who appeared to be paying attention (engaged in academic learning time) were actually thinking about nonacademic issues (Peterson & Swing, 1982). Students soon learn the importance of putting on a good face in order to protect their privacy. As a result of these and other factors, time is an important necessary condition but far from the whole story. In measurement terms the efficient use of instructional time has an impact equal to 38 percent of one standard deviation. Basically, academic achievement is moderately affected by the efficient use of time (Dempter, 1987).

Some teachers structure academic learning time differently for different groups of students on the basis of the students' previous level of academic theoretical framework of the researchers, you can safely predict their conclusions without even looking at the data. Walberg, however, stands apart from any specific tradition and lets the actual analysis of the findings determine what elements really make a difference in distinguishing effective from ineffective teaching.

Shortly after completing his Ph.D. at the University of Chicago in 1964, he joined an outstanding team of researchers at the Harvard Graduate School of Education in Harvard Project Physics. Over a three-year period the group developed and evaluated an innovative approach to teaching physics in secondary schools. While at Harvard he authored or coauthored 34 journal articles, and 13 were immediately reprinted by other authors. He was much sought after as a speaker, consultant, and editor. A midwesterner at heart, he soon accepted a professorship at the University of

Illinois, Chicago Circle, and was rapidly appointed a research professor. In fact, one of the difficulties in reporting on Walberg's progress is how quickly any comment is outdated. As we go to press, he has written or edited 53 books and more than 350 articles, chapters, and monographs.

In a recent conversation, he shared with us two current endeavors from which he derives a great deal of satisfaction. First, he recently accepted appointments to the boards of two charter schools in the Chicago area, to his knowledge, the smallest and largest charter schools in the United States. The smallest school consists of 50 alcoholic and drug-abusive teenagers. This charter school is designed to be small so that it can foster more intense, enduring relationships with adults as well as consistency of adult interactions with students over time. This charter school hopes to be the academic

and emotional salvation for these at-risk students. The other charter school has 5,000 students in several sites in Chicago. The goal is for these urban students, who typically don't do well on standardized tests, to take and pass three advanced placement examinations. Walberg will help evaluate the progress of these two charter schools in meeting their aims. Second, in recent work with the National Society for the Study of Education, the research arm of national and regional accreditating agencies, Walberg is focusing on accreditation based not on fads in education, but on empirical research and particularly meta-analysis of research on best practices in education. We look forward to the results forthcoming from these important studies. With Herbert Walberg involved, the results will undoubtedly encompass and synthesize both prior and current research.

achievement (Reynolds & Walberg, 1992) or their race, gender, ethnicity, and socioeconomic class. We discuss the research on these issues and the effects of teachers' expectations in Chapter 14.

Use of Positive Reinforcement

By far the single, most significant discrete instructional variable in Table 12.1 was the use of positive reinforcement. The careful and consistent use of Skinnerian reinforcement techniques, both verbal and nonverbal, had an effect greater than one standard deviation. This means that if one class, for example, scored an average of 80 points on a 100-item test and the standard deviation was 10 points, then a similar class without positive reinforcement would score one standard deviation below, or an average of 70 points. The reinforced class on the average would be at a B level, versus a C level for the other class.

Does this mean, then, that the teacher should apply principles of positive reinforcement to all students all the time? As was the case with academic learning time, it's not quite that simple. The relationship between positive reinforcement and achievement is nonlinear. You must be selective; indiscriminate praise doesn't work. The effect will wear out if the students hear you praise all activities and products, even those of marginal competence.

Table 12.2 gives some important guidelines for the effective use of praise. Jere Brophy has carefully outlined and compared different methods (Brophy, 1981). To add to the complexity, it turns out that the effect of praise, even when properly applied, varies according to student characteristics. Students from middle-class backgrounds are not as susceptible to praise as are students from lower- or working-class backgrounds. The method still works but not as powerfully. Lower- and working-class parents tend not to use positive reinforcement as frequently as middle-

TABLE 12.1 THE EFFECTS OF SELECTED TEACHING TECHNIQUES AND PROCESSES

TECHNIQUE OR PROCESS	SIZE OF EFFECT ON ACADEMIC ACHIEVEMENT[a]
Engaged academic learning time	+ .38
Use of positive reinforcement	+1.17
Cues and feedback	+ .97
Cooperative learning activities	+ .76
Classroom morale	+ .60
Higher-order questioning	+ .34
Use of advance organizers	+ .23

Source: Data from H. Walberg, "Synthesis of Research on Teaching," in M. C. Wittrock (Ed.), Handbook of research on teaching, *3d ed. (New York: Macmillan, 1986). Copyright © 1986 by American Educational Research Association.*

[a] *The size represents units of standard deviations; for example, in the case of "cues and feedback," teachers employing this mode had students whose achievement scores averaged almost one standard deviation higher than those in control classes.*

class parents. As a result, their children are more affected by praise. Praise by itself, then, has to be used carefully in order to produce the desired effects.

In addition, the quantity and quality of reinforcement given to students seem to vary according to student characteristics. For example, girls receive significantly less attention from classroom teachers than do boys, and African-American girls have fewer interactions with teachers than do white girls, despite evidence that they attempt to initiate interaction more frequently (**AAUW** Report, 1992). Another example of differential reinforcement according to gender was found by Myra and David Sadker and Susan Klein, who reported that when boys called out, teachers listened, but when girls called out, they were told to raise their hands if they wished to speak (Sadker et al., 1991). Boys also get more precise teacher comments about both their scholarship and conduct. In Chapter 14, we discuss more of these findings.

Reinforcement is important in helping determine to what students attribute their successes and failures. Teachers need to consider what they are reinforcing—ability, effort, conformity, risk taking, the right answer, neatness, cooperation, and so on. It is important to examine whether the amount and type of reinforcement vary according to gender, race, and class.

We discuss motivation extensively in Chapter 18, but here we want to mention two more of Herbert Walberg's collaborative studies in relation to the notion of reinforcement. First, using evidence from 61

educational research experts, 91 meta-analyses, and 179 handbook chapters and narrative reviews, Margaret Wang, Geneva Haertel, and Herbert Walberg (1993) found that the actions and daily efforts of the people who are most involved in students' lives (that is, other students, teachers, and parents) is what mattered most to students' learning in school. In contrast, policies at the program, school, district, state, and federal levels were found to have limited effect on learning. Second, Steven Brown and Herbert Walberg (1993) report on a study in which students from three public elementary schools (grades three, four, six, seven, and eight, all homogeneously grouped) were assigned to two groups and given different instructions before taking the mathematics section of the Iowa Test of Basic Skills. The control students were given the ordinary standardized test instructions. The other students were given special instructions to do as well as possible for themselves, their parents, and their teachers. On average, the students given special instructions did significantly better. The motivational effect of the special instructions was constant across grade levels and gender, but differed significantly across schools. The average effect was moderately large, implying that the special instructions raised the typical student's score: from the fiftieth to the sixty-second percentile.

Cues and Feedback

To some extent the use of cues and feedback is related to the process of questioning and reinforcing. Through cueing, the teacher provides some help to students in answering questions. In the so-called good old days, many a famous university professor would earn a reputation for tearing students apart in the process of questioning. In the now-classic movie *The Paper Chase*, Professor Kingsfield is shown again and again carefully dissecting a quivering student. Intimidation and sarcasm were the stock-in-trade. In contrast, current research in teaching effectiveness shows that good teachers cue their students, helping them to develop an answer. Such a teacher will pick up part of an answer and then ask for clarification or elaboration—for example, "Yes, Columbus did lead the expedition in 1492, and do you remember who sponsored the voyage?" Such prompting can reduce the anxiety of the classroom trivia methods (Chapter 1) and expand the students' thinking. Given the finding that teachers are more likely to prompt and encourage boys than girls, even when the boys do not volunteer to give an answer or opinion, you will want to try to use prompts equitably among all your students.

A second component of effective cueing is some-

TABLE 12.2   GUIDELINES FOR EFFECTIVE PRAISE

EFFECTIVE PRAISE	INEFFECTIVE PRAISE
1. Is delivered contingently	1. Is delivered randomly or unsystematically
2. Specifies the particulars of the accomplishment	2. Is restricted to global positive reactions
3. Shows spontaneity, variety, and other signs of credibility; suggests clear attention to the student's accomplishment	3. Shows bland uniformity, which suggests a conditional response made with minimal attention
4. Rewards attainment of specified performance criteria (which can include effort criteria, however)	4. Rewards mere participation, without consideration of performance processes or outcomes
5. Provides information to students about their competence or the value of their accomplishments	5. Provides no information at all or gives students information about their status
6. Orients students to better appreciation of their own task-related behavior and thinking about problemsolving	6. Orients students to comparing themselves with others and thinking about competing
7. Uses students' own prior accomplishments as the context for describing present accomplishments	7. Uses the accomplishments of peers as the context for describing present accomplishments
8. Is given in recognition of noteworthy effort or success at difficult (for *this* student) tasks	8. Is given without regard to the effort expended or the meaning of the accomplishments (for *this* student)
9. Attributes successes to effort and ability, implying that similar successes can be expected in the future	9. Attributes success to ability alone or to external factors such as luck or easy task
10. Fosters endogenous attributions (students believe that they expend effort on the task because they enjoy the task and/or want to develop task-relevant skills)	10. Fosters exogenous attributions (students believe that they expend effort on the task for external reasons, to please the teacher, win a competition or reward, etc.)
11. Focuses students' attention on their own task-relevant behavior.	11. Focuses students' attention on the teacher as an external authority figure who is manipulating them
12. Fosters appreciation of and desirable attributions about task-relevant behavior after the process is completed	12. Intrudes into the ongoing process, distracting attention from task-relevant behavior

Source: *J. Brophy (1981). Copyright © 1981 by American Educational Research Association, Washington, DC. Reprinted by permission.*

times called wait-time, which gives the student some time to think about the question. By providing time and then helping a student elaborate an answer, the teacher will increase academic achievement and decrease anxiety.

Providing constructive (also called corrective) feedback is the other part of this strategy. Ever since the famous Ellis Page study, it has been shown conclusively that feedback improves academic achievement. Page demonstrated this by systematically providing brief written comments on assignments (Page, 1958). When teachers merely collect assignments and then either say nothing or simply make a check mark, an opportunity for growth has been missed. The same is true for homework. In fact, Walberg found that graded homework with comments was 50 percent more effective than homework by it-

self. Constructive feedback obviously provides the student with information on which to build learning. Walberg summarizes: "the effects of cues, engagement, reinforcement, and corrective feedback on student learning are enormous" (1990, p. 471).

Cooperative Learning Activities

There are many ways of organizing classrooms of students. When doing so, use a range of organizational configurations (one-on-one with the teacher and individual seatwork, small groups, group projects, whole class). There is a strong interest in today's schools in many types of **cooperative learning** activities. Walberg's meta-analysis found that the use of cooperative learning activities activities had an effect equal to about three-quarters of one standard deviation (refer to Table 12.1). Noreen Webb and Annemarie Sullivan Palincsar further specify these group learning activities into categories such as peer tutoring, cooperative learning, collaboration, peer response groups in writing, and peer learning in whole-class contexts, and they present the research findings about when and how these types of cooperative activities influence learning and other outcomes in the classroom (1996). Individual differences and learning styles among children, as well as cultural and family backgrounds, may influence how comfortably and effectively children participate.

Research by Dorothy Buerk, Elizabeth Fennema, and others on the factors associated with women's success in mathematics classrooms, for instance, is quite consistent in showing that girls may learn more effectively in cooperative rather than competitive situations (Buerk, 1985; Barnes & Coupland, 1990; Fennema & Leder, 1990; Isaacson, 1990). "Girl-friendly" classrooms are described as having "low levels of competition, high levels of cooperative learning or individualistic learning structure, high levels of teacher communication . . . [about] the intrinsic value of math and the link between math and various interesting occupations" (Eccles, 1987, p. 158). Charlotte Morrow (1996) describes the highly successful SummerMath program for girls and teachers at Mount Holyoke College, which uses a cooperative learning approach. SummerMath objectives include developing a learning community, using the connected mode of communication and questioning, taking on the challenge of difficult mathematics problems in an atmosphere of support, developing one's mathematical voice, and becoming a confident and competent knower and constructor of knowledge.

Research in Native American communities also strongly suggests the importance of cooperative learning strategies. Competitive and individualistic learning strategies appear to violate the norms within the Native American culture. **K. Tsianina Lomawaima** (1995) cautions us, however, that "too much research has been predicated on the hope that one teaching method . . . will serve all Native Americans equally well." She urges teachers to "acknowledge the diversity of native cultures . . . and work locally to develop relevant content and methods" (p. 342). Later in this chapter we will discuss further the need for all teachers to be flexible in their teaching models and methods, and this includes the use of cooperative learning strategies.

We will discuss this approach in greater detail in Chapter 20. Here we want to stress the importance in the classroom of employing small-group techniques with cooperative objectives. Cooperative activities encourage student participation and result in improved academic performance through a blend of techniques.

Classroom Morale

Like cooperative learning, promoting good classroom morale is not strictly a teaching strategy. Nevertheless, classroom atmosphere has a significant impact on learning. Walberg's research found that the old approach of strict discipline and tight control is not effective, nor is the casual, "laid-back" approach. Instead, feelings of cohesiveness, satisfaction, goal direction, and student perceptions of a friendly atmosphere make a positive difference in learning. These findings were cross-validated by Thomas Good's research (Good, 1983). He found that one main element of effective teaching is the creation of a relatively relaxed learning environment within a task-oriented focus. We will have more to say on this when we move to models of teaching that illustrate the relation between class morale and methods. At this point it is clear that positive class morale cuts across specific techniques as a general factor producing student achievement.

Essential to an equitable and effective classroom environment for all students are the acceptance and appreciation of similarities and differences among members of the classroom (and school) community. Differences in ethnicity, race, class, religion, gender, primary language, sexual orientation, learning style, ability and disability, family configuration, and

lifestyle must all be respected and acknowledged for classroom morale to be positive for all. We can identify the elements of classroom morale that are important to achieve an optimum learning atmosphere. These are discussed further in Chapter 13.

Higher-Order Questioning

Since teacher questioning has an unusually long history, examining its use as a strategy is clearly important (Redfield & Rousseau, 1981). Generally, as we illustrated in the opening chapter, the common questioning approach is more like a game of Trivial Pursuit than education. But asking rapid-fire questions calling for rote, almost robotlike answers does not increase achievement. How the questions are posed obviously makes a difference.

Recently there has been a remarkable upsurge in the "teaching of thinking." Such a process, which involves logical analysis and argumentation principles, is most encouraged by higher-order questioning. A higher-order question is basically a query that requires the student to analyze and produce a reasoned response, not a mimicking of the teacher's words. In other words, there is not an already prescribed factual answer to the question. Asking a student to name the year of the Columbus expedition is clearly a low-order question. Asking the student to explain why Columbus was able to convince the monarchy of a country different from his own to support his voyage calls for greater intellectual work, and thus qualifies as a higher-order question. Formal instruction designed to promote "thinking" will be discussed in detail in the next chapter.

One of the continuing issues in the research on classroom questioning is the problem of wait-time. Perhaps the effectiveness of higher-order questions is determined not so much by their actual frequency but how much time is provided for them. Students obviously need reflection time to process a complex question. The research of Mary Budd Rowe (1986) has shown that simply increasing wait-time by a few seconds both after the question is posed and after the student has responded has a very positive effect upon student learning. She says to the teacher, "Slowing down may be a way of speeding up!" (p. 43).

Kenneth Tobin (1986) has likewise shown the positive effect of wait-time. In this case, the teachers in an experimental sample waited an average of three to five seconds in teaching math concepts. The results were dramatic. On all 12 measures of outcome, the results favored the experimental group of teachers. Teacher "talk" declined, and student achievement increased. The most interesting finding was that the students' answers changed. Instead of mim-

SPOTLIGHT ON PROCEDURES

Teaching Tip

As a teacher, you can alleviate some of the artificiality of classroom discussions by acknowledging right off that classrooms have their own rules, which are unlike real exchanges or dinner-table talk. Students must be assured that silence is not only okay, but valued. Preface your questions with a statement such as, "This will require a bit of thinking time. Raise your hands when you have a response. After 10 hands are up, I will call on someone to share." Or ask students to respond to questions by first talking to their seat mates. This way they can work out the kinks in their emerging ideas in a less threatening forum. Say, for example, "Take one minute to reflect on this question with the person sitting next to you." Or ask students to write out their responses, then invite several to read aloud what they have written.

Wait at least three seconds after asking a question before you take any responses at all. Research shows that when wait-time is increased to three seconds or more, the amount of elaboration and the chance of being correct are greater. Finally, ask students to come to class with three questions that they have prepared in advance. After all, if one can pose a question, one is on the edge of understanding it.

One classroom study shows that teachers average 200 questions per class, whereas students do not average one question each. Teachers pose 11 questions for every student inquiry. Remind yourself that *you* do not need to display your knowledge, for it is the students, not teachers, who need opportunities to practice the skills of posing and answering questions. Do not apologize for the silence in your classroom if you judge it as educational silence.[a]

---

[a]   Pritchard, Ruie Jane (1992, January). North Carolina State University, College of Education and Psychology. *Emphasis: Teaching and learning, 1*(11) (NCSU). Reprinted by permission of the author.

---

icking the teacher or mindlessly repeating a memorized phrase, students gave longer, more thoughtful answers. Also, there was an increase in their comprehension. In short, the expanded wait-time helped the students think more deeply about the concepts being taught. Tobin concluded that for subjects such as mathematics and language arts, in which higher-order cognitive outcomes are desired, the wait method is highly recommended. Of course, from the standpoint of this book, we would not limit such goals exclusively to those two disciplines. Certainly, higher-order questions and thinking are appropriate for all adolescents and all school subjects. Wait-time, however, is not a straight-line variable. This means that if 3 to 5 seconds is good, then 10 to 15 is not better, and on and on. Excessively long periods of wait-time can be almost as bad as too brief periods. Too much dead air in the classroom is to be avoided just as much as the rapid-fire trivia approach.

Use of Advance Organizers

The final skill involves the use of the deductive approach. The student is told in advance the main point or the main concepts to be covered. On the one hand, such advance organizers have been shown to help students focus attention on key points. On the other hand, the effect is positive but not particularly strong, representing about a 25 percent improvement in the standard deviation. In all probability, then, an advance organizer is a good method to get a class clued in. Since some learners need a clear road map of the main points in a lesson in advance, the method should not be ignored (Gage, 1985).

In fact, research by William Doyle suggests that a more careful application of advance organizers can improve the impact on student learning. He has shown that in some of the earlier research studies, a major problem was created. Often, it could be shown that the teacher never clearly established the advance organizer. Thus, if the first step in the system was not always in place, it is small wonder that some of the studies showed no positive effects. In his own study, he assessed the effect or the outcome after he had determined that the organizer was in place (Doyle, 1986). When the students understood the organizer, there was significant transfer of learning over a seven-day period. Naturally, this one study does not prove the point. It certainly suggests, however, that the use of organizers is positive. More to the point, however, is the need to pay attention to how well the students can grasp the concept. Taking a developmental perspective, Doyle notes that intellectually complex advance organizers that assume the students are already using formal abstract reasoning may fail if such concepts are not closely matched to the appropriate level of cognitive development. We will say more about this problem of matching and mismatching concepts and developmental level in the next chapter. For now, in using organizers, it is important to remember the need to attend to comprehension by the students. If the point of the advance organizer is a mystery to the students, confusion and ambiguity will follow.

TEACHING EFFECTIVENESS: DIRECT INSTRUCTION EXCLUSIVELY?

As a result of meta-analysis of teaching, there was a growing tendency to view effective instruction as synonymous with direct instruction. The Center at the Institute for Research on Teaching at Michigan State University, in particular, generated large numbers of studies supporting the contention that gains in academic achievement are often associated with this method. Essentially, direct instruction is highly structured. The teacher presents the material in small steps, uses advance organizers, checks for understanding, has students answer turn by turn in an ordered fashion, and provides immediate feedback on their answers. Furthermore, the teacher accomplishes all this at a brisk and businesslike pace (Rosenshine, 1987). By implication, the teacher would spend very little time, if any, on other methods, such as inductive or discovery teaching. The research seemed to support the idea that effective teaching is a sequence of carefully and constantly monitored actions. In fact, the claim was that the direct method was appropriate for all subjects at all grade levels.

Finally, the claim was that not only will academic achievement improve across the board but also affective and personal development will be promoted. In assessing the validity of these conclusions, it is important to understand the many limitations. The main research base was elementary school classrooms rather than secondary schools. Further, the research has been limited to a few specific subject areas at an introductory level, and there was no attempt to involve a true cross-section of school types, for example, urban, rural, high and low socioeconomic status, majority and minority. Thus, doubt can be cast upon the claim of generalization. Finally, the

greatest problem is that effective teaching cannot ever simply reach the point of prescribing a single set of teacher behaviors good for all pupils, for all subjects, and for all time.

As a result, we take the position that the direct method represents only a partial picture of the teaching process, and we caution against some of the generalizations. Certainly, we agree with both Larry Cuban's (1988) critique and Lee Shulman's (1986, 1987) much more moderate views calling for a broader conception. The research tried to focus on one variable at a time as if it were possible to freeze teaching frame by frame. Teaching is too interactive and involves a synthesis of many variables rather than success with just a single variable. Also, followup showed that not all the trained behaviors continued to correlate with achievement gains, that some of the experimental teachers did not always use the prescribed pattern, and that not all the prescribed behaviors were necessary for improved achievement. In other words, a fine-grained analysis of the claims could not support the contentions of the direct school of teaching. The final, most telling point was the complete absence of theory to explain the findings. Without theory, as we noted in Chapter 1, there is little to guide practice, and there is no systematic way to explain the inconsistencies in the behavioral observations. A fair conclusion is that direct or active teaching does provide some but not all the answers to the complex problems of teacher effectiveness.

In Chapter 13 we present an alternative to direct teaching called teaching for higher-level understanding. This model adds to our understanding of the complex problems of teacher effectiveness.

THE FLANDERS SYSTEM: BRIDGING TO MODELS

One weakness of such a massive meta-analysis as Walberg's is that the result cannot depict actual patterns of teaching. A robot could be programmed to use certain elements in a sequence, but student learning wouldn't necessarily be affected. Classroom interaction between teacher and students would be frozen while the machine cranked through its program. To understand how the elements fit together more clearly, we turn to the work of **Ned Flanders** (1970). He and his associates did extensive classroom observations of teachers at different levels and across different content areas. He found that teacher talking behavior could be clustered into seven categories (and student talk into three), as shown in Table 12.3. In Table 12.4 you can also see how much of his sys-

NED FLANDERS

Born in 1918 and raised on the West Coast, Ned Flanders completed an A.B. degree in chemistry at the University of California in 1940 and received a B.S. in electrical engineering from Oregon State College in 1944. He then shifted to educational psychology, earning both a master's degree and a Ph.D. at the University of Chicago. After teaching at Chicago for a brief period, from 1949 to 1962 he served as an assistant and then associate professor of educational psychology at the University of Minnesota.

During this period at Minnesota Flanders' research focus matured. He began to crack one of the most difficult problems in education—creation of a theoretical and practical model to define teaching effectiveness. Hundreds of earlier research studies had been conducted in this area, almost always yielding insignificant results. Researchers had tried to correlate personality characteristics, temperamental traits, personal interests, cultural backgrounds, social and economic status, marital state, birth order, and similar variables with effective teaching performance. Attempts had also been made to relate measures of a teacher's "warmth" or knowledge of subject matter to effective performance in the classroom. These so-called characteristic studies produced inconclusive and often contradictory results. One study might find a small but statistically significant correlation between a trait such as friendliness and teaching effectiveness; the next study was just as likely to show no relationship.

When Flanders began to develop the concept of direct versus indirect teaching, he also started a series of field studies to test the possible relationships. His central findings remained consistent through a long series of studies. With various subject matters, at different grade levels, and in different school settings, teachers employing indirect teaching styles were producing higher levels of academic learning in their pupils than were those using direct methods.

As we move toward educational accountability, with the general public demanding increasing documentation of teaching effectiveness, the Flanders system gives evidence of becoming a major index of effective teaching. In 1962 Flanders moved from Minnesota to the University of Michigan, where he continued his work. He published *Teaching with Groups* and *Analyzing Teaching Behavior,* as well as numerous articles reporting his research on teacher interaction analysis. In 1970 Flanders returned to California, where he worked at the Far West Laboratory doing research in teaching. Since leaving the Far West Laboratory, Flanders has been primarily interested in preservice and inservice teacher education. His most recent projects involve teachers forming partnerships, so each can observe the others' classroom and where each teacher chooses his or her own self-improvement priorities. In between assignments in this country and others overseas, Flanders has been trying to learn how to retire. Meanwhile, he enjoys a beautiful view straight across San Francisco Bay and through the Golden Gate. The vivid sunset colors are often magnificent.

TABLE 12.3   CATEGORIES FOR FLANDERS INTERACTION ANALYSIS

TEACHER TALK	**INDIRECT INFLUENCE**	1. **Accepts feelings:** Accepts and clarifies the tone of feelings of the students in an unthreatening manner. Feelings may be positive or negative. Predicting or recalling feelings are included.
		2. **Praises or encourages:** Praises or encourages student action or behavior. Jokes that release tension, but not at the expense of another individual; nodding head and saying "um-hm?" or "go on" are included.
		3. **Accepts or uses ideas of students:** Clarifies, builds, or develops ideas suggested by a student. As teacher brings more of his or her own ideas into play, shift to # 5.
		4. **Asks questions:** Asks a question about content or procedure with the intent that the student answer.
	DIRECT INFLUENCE	5. **Lecturing:** Gives facts or opinions about content or procedure; expresses his or her own ideas, asking rhetorical questions.
		6. **Giving directions:** Directions, commands, or orders that students are expected to comply with.
		7. **Criticizing or justifying authority:** Statements intended to change student behavior from unacceptable to acceptable pattern; bawling someone out; stating why the teacher is doing what he or she is doing; extreme self-reference.
STUDENT TALK		8. **Student talk—response:** Talk by students in response to teacher. Teacher initiates the contact or solicits student statement.
		9. **Student talk—initiation:** Talk initiated by students. If "calling on" student is only to indicate who may talk next, observer must decide whether student wanted to talk.
		10. **Silence or confusion:** Pauses, short periods of silence, and periods of confusion in which communication cannot be understood by the observer.

Source: *Flanders, (1970), p. 34. Reprinted with permission.*

tem, developed in the 1950s and 1960s, still relates to current research on teaching behaviors.

The seven categories represent the most commonly observed teaching behaviors, which brings us to the next question: What is the relation between these behaviors and student achievement? Actually, a major analysis of the Flanders studies was done by Nathaniel Gage (1978) in his book *The Scientific Basis for the Art of Teaching.* Instead of examining one element at a time, however, Gage grouped the system into two broad categories: indirect teaching—types 1, 2, 3, and 4; and direct teaching—types 5, 6, and 7. You can see that the main difference between the two modes is basically whether teaching is viewed as asking questions or as giving directions and lecturing.

In comparing the modes Gage also wanted to examine possible differences according to grade level, elementary versus secondary. He found very clear evidence that teachers who employed the indirect mode at the secondary level produced greater academic gains than did teachers who used the direct mode. This means that the academic performance of teenage students will be enhanced through the effective use of questioning and open inquiry. The finding held true across subject matter. However, this re-

search does not mean that the secondary teacher must stay exclusively in the indirect mode. The evidence is based on ratios of time expended in one mode versus the other. At the high school level effectiveness is increased if the teacher uses the indirect mode more than half the time. Obviously, there will be times for giving careful directions, lecturing, and criticizing students for misbehavior; yet for the most part, employing questioning, reinforcing, cueing, and responding to feelings will produce academic gains to a greater degree.

To further buttress this approach to teaching and learning, researchers conducted a series of independent studies at the college level. Although the actual Flanders system was not used, the overall results were quite similar: Professors who provided time for student questions, allowed students to question one another, and encouraged them to make statements in class fostered cognitive growth and greater complexity of thinking (Chickering & McCormick, 1973). So, results from both high school and college students indicate the advantage of the indirect mode with older students. Certainly if you think about Piaget's work, you will remember that during adolescence students can develop greater capabilities for abstract reasoning and greater independence in thinking

TABLE 12.4   A COMPARISON OF TEACHER EFFECTIVENESS: FLANDERS AND WALBERG

FLANDERS' TYPE	WALBERG'S ELEMENTS OF TEACHING EFFECTIVENESS
(6) Gives clear directions	Academic learning time
(2) Praises or encourages	Use of positive reinforcement
(3) Accepts and builds on student ideas	Use of cues and feedback
A combination of indirect modes plus (6), gives clear directions	Cooperative learning
(1) Accepts feelings	Classroom morale
(2) Praises	
(3) Accepts ideas	
(4) Asks questions	
(3) Accepts and builds on student ideas	Higher-order questions
(6) Gives clear directions	
(5) Lectures	Advance organizers
(4) Asks questions	

than earlier in their development. This is probably a main factor favoring the indirect mode. We will have more to say about the interaction between teaching method and pupil development in the next chapter.

At the elementary level, Gage's review yielded somewhat different results. He found less of a relation between the indirect modes and pupil learning. There were some positive outcomes in the indirect mode but also many in the direct mode. In fact, research, especially at the elementary level, seems to indicate that the more directive approach can be quite significant in producing student achievement (Gage, 1985). For example, in elementary school instruction in both reading and mathematics, the teacher-directed approach yielded stronger gains. Actually it took reading teachers and researchers a very long time to finally understand that young nonreaders need to be taught to "break the code" and learn the letter symbols (instead of learning through the ask-and-guess technique). Similarly, direct methods in math are necessary to teach the rudiments of the number system. Again it is important to underscore the point of these findings. The results indicate that a ratio is desirable—spending more time on direct methods, but not focusing exclusively on them. The effective elementary teacher needs to ask questions, praise, build on ideas, and respond to feelings. However, the elementary teacher may well use the more direct methods more than half the time. The careful use of advance organizers and a low level of ambiguity provide younger students with helpful guidance for learning.

A recent analysis of teaching effectiveness at the elementary level cross-validates the findings of the importance of using a ratio of Flanders' indirect and direct teaching categories to increase students' learning. The analysis was based on a review of 16 studies of reading comprehension at the elementary level (Rosenshine & Meister, 1994). All the studies were using a new instructional procedure called reciprocal teaching. Although the actual Flanders system was not used, the results were similar. Teachers used strategies such as summarization, question generation, clarification, and prediction. Teachers modeled and sometimes explicitly taught these strategies to their students. In dialogue between teachers and students, the students were encouraged to generate questions, summarize, predict what might next happen, and clarify as they tried to make meaning of their reading texts. The use of these strategies (similar to Flanders' indirect categories) increased students' achievement in reading. The median effect size ranged from .32 on standardized tests of comprehension to .88 on experimenter-developed comprehension tests. This study also cross-validates Walberg's findings in Table 12.1.

With this background we can now move to the next level of generality in regard to teaching, namely, comprehensive models of teaching. A model is a cluster of strategies that is logically consistent with a certain set of assumptions about how students best learn. Another way to view it is as a "school of thought" regarding how best to manage the development of the pupil. So now to models.

Teaching is interactive, and the teacher's job is to manage and direct the instructional process, not the telling process.

MODEL ONE: THE TRANSMITTER OF KNOWLEDGE

Probably the most common teaching model, and certainly the one with the longest tradition, is that which views teaching as the transmission of knowledge. This view assumes that there exists a well-known and finite body of knowledge from which the teacher selects certain facts and concepts to pass on to pupils. In a metaphorical sense, the teacher looks over all the knowledge "stored" in the Library of Congress, pores through books and pamphlets, reads and digests everything, and takes some of it to school, where it will be disseminated.

This model emphasizes the need to give pupils basic facts and information before they can be expected to think for themselves. They must learn what is already known before they can come up with any new ideas that might fit in with the existing knowledge.

The assumptions are clear. Learning new information is essentially a linear, step-by-step sequence. The teacher's expertise is needed to arrange both the content material to be mastered and the method of presentation. Probably the most obvious distinguishing characteristic of this model is the high degree of structure employed.

In Model One, the teacher uses advance organizers (Ausubel & Sullivan, 1970). At the outset of a lesson the teacher presents the pupils with the general rule, the generalization, or the main "point" of the activity. For example, a social studies unit might start with "Today we are going to study about the origins or beginnings of civilization—the early settlements on the banks of two rivers in the Middle East." Thus, at the outset, the goal of the lesson is described at a generalizable, conceptual level—learning about the origins of civilization. This technique helps the students tune in immediately to the overall objective. It creates, at least theoretically, a set of expectations that is clear and explicit. The pupils are ready.

Immediately following the presentation of the generalized idea, the teacher changes the level of abstraction to concrete examples. Stating the rule or principle at the outset creates a readiness in the pupils. Their cognitive attention is focused. The concrete examples help them understand the connections between the facts and the general point. Thus, in the social studies example, the teacher would now present a series of concrete facts and examples: "For many thousands of years tribes would wander from place to place; food was gathered as it grew naturally; as the seasons changed, the tribes would pick up and move on, seeking less hostile climates." These examples would set the stage for the understanding of the generalized idea. The teacher would proceed to a presentation of a long series of facts: "Gradually, as groups of tribes were settling temporarily all over the globe, the group that settled in Mesopotamia happened to hit upon a most fortuitous set of circumstances—a benign climate and incredibly rich soil. These circumstances, together with a series of other factors, led to the permanent establishment of cities and government, to economic specialization, to the beginning of architecture, even to the establishment of schools—in short, to all the elements of what we call civilization."

Finally, the presentation of examples is followed by the restatement of the generalized principle. In this sense, the transmission-of-knowledge model is often called *guided discovery*. Through various examples, all pupils are led to the same generalization. Ambiguity is low. It is clear from the outset what the goal is; concrete examples are carefully selected to support the point; and at the end, the pupils are reminded what rule or generalization they have learned.

Probably the strongest example of this model of transmitting information is the lecture format. Although it can be used with other teaching strategies, this model is most effectively used as a format for lectures, or for minilectures. If you recall your own experience as a pupil, you will readily remember instances of hopelessly disorganized lectures that did not follow this model. Look back at your own notes, or the lack of them, from these lectures. You may find a few random comments in your own writing, lots of questions and false starts, perhaps even a scribbled memo to yourself: "But what's the point of today's lecture? He can't seem to make up his mind. Where is it all going? He must have 18 hands—on the one hand this, on the other hand that. I hope the period ends soon!"

Thus the transmission-of-knowledge model, through the use of advance organizers, can provide a clear and systematic approach to teaching. One of the disadvantages of the model is that so much of the work of learning is controlled and directed by the teacher.

This is why the effective use of advance organizers and teacher-led instruction also requires much attention to maintaining pupil activity. If teachers aren't careful, then pupil passivity can increase markedly for some students, particularly the low achievers. One study found that low achievers did not understand the directions, spent most of their time watching their peers speed through the assignment, turned in incomplete work, and were frequently criticized. Such a cycle was repeated, often to the distress of both the students and the teacher (Good, 1983; Berliner, 1984). Also, it is clear that some students will do better under learning conditions that are less teacher-directed and controlled.

MODEL TWO: INDUCTIVE INQUIRY

Another common teaching model that came into vogue in the 1960s suggests that the teacher's role is to reveal or unveil the fundamental structure of a discipline. The idea here is to teach concepts or the process of inquiry, not facts. In some ways this is like teaching for problemsolving, whereby we learn to solve problems by understanding the framework or the structure of the concepts. For example, pupils used to learn to cross-multiply fractions to solve a division problem. In Model Two, the teacher focuses on the concepts of fractions and divisions so that the pupils understand that cross-multiplying is really dividing both sides of an equation by a common number. Similarly, in a social studies class, or what used to be called geography, pupils are no longer asked to memorize the principal cities and products of a state. Rather, they might be given a blank map showing topographical features such as hills, mountains, valleys, rivers, and lakes, and then they might be asked to figure out where cities might be located. In other words, they go through an inquiry process that helps them understand why big cities grow in certain locations. The Model Two teacher produces minischolars in the various disciplines.

According to this model, the sheer intellectual excitement of discovering the reasons behind events—for example, the logic a historian or a mathematician actually uses—motivates the pupils to further activity and exploration. Teaching and learning resemble an archaeologist's uncovering of one fragment after another of some mysterious object. The archaeologist's curiosity about the fragments naturally makes him or her want to make sense of the puzzle; this curiosity produces both activity and excitement. The *discovery* method of teaching is based on this model. The teacher, by analyzing material and asking questions but not giving answers, spurs pupils to learn by helping them discover the answer. The experience and the insight resulting from having put the puzzle together nurture the entire educational process.

There are a variety of specific methods that enhance discovery learning, such as the inductive-thinking strategy of Hilda Taba, the inquiry-training method of Richard Suchman, and the scientific-inquiry technique of Joseph Schwab (see review in Joyce, 1978). These methods are related to John Dewey's original project method, which emphasized the process of inquiry rather than content acquisition as central to learning. In each case, the teacher arranges material that is open-ended in order to stimulate the processes of asking questions and exploration by the pupils.

It is, of course, possible to overemphasize learning

by discovery. It can be exasperating never to have any of your questions answered. It isn't necessary to discover everything for yourself in order to learn. Most important, however, it is difficult to know, especially at the elementary level and in junior high, exactly how much the pupils genuinely understand about the structure of a discipline taught in this way. The idea of a structure is itself abstract and therefore beyond the comprehension of the concrete stage of thinking in which most of these children are. To understand such concepts and such processes, substantial cognitive sophistication is necessary. For example, to learn how a historian "thinks," we must understand concepts such as fact, opinion, values, cultural relativism, subjectivity, and objectivity—to name a few.

A major debate has been going on between those who advocate this approach and those who hold other views. Jerome Bruner, formerly a professor at the Harvard Center for Cognitive Studies, is a leading advocate for teaching for the structure of knowledge. One of his most provocative statements promotes this view: "Any subject can be taught effectively in some intellectually honest form to any child at any stage of development" (Bruner, 1966, p. 44). Thus, according to Bruner, the six-year-old minischolar can learn to think like a historian or a mathematician.

We have already mentioned (Chapter 5) some of the problems inherent in the so-called spiraling curriculum, a system that teaches children the same concepts, with increasing sophistication, throughout their entire schooling. The difficulties, especially at the elementary level, are enormous. Because elementary-age children find it difficult to understand abstract concepts, they tend to translate the abstractions into concrete terms and miss the connections altogether. Jean Piaget said that Bruner's statement always filled him with wonder. Imagine, for a moment, trying to teach a seven- or eight-year-old the structure of algebra or the idea that historical knowledge is relative and biased.

Nor is the educational problem limited to the elementary ages. Much secondary school material is based on the assumption that all teenagers are already well into formal operations, which we know is not the case. Model Two teaching, though it has a laudable objective, rests on a doubtful assumption. There is a difference between assuming the ability to think abstractly and carefully creating a series of experiences that will nurture and promote the development of this ability. Teaching to reveal the abstract structure of the disciplines may often result in a mismatch between curriculum and pupils.

Thus, an important component of the inductive method is to work at developing the student's potential to reason more openly and independently. This means, in addition to substantial cueing in questioning, that use of structure and advance organizers may also be necessary, especially at the outset.

MODEL THREE: INTERPERSONAL LEARNING

While the first and most common teaching model emphasizes learning the facts and the second stresses the discovery of concepts, the third model, interpersonal learning, stresses the development of warm human relationships between teacher and pupil. If the teacher can convey a genuine affection and empathy, a warm, facilitative classroom climate will be created, and the pupils will take it from there. The quality of the human interaction, especially the degree to which the teacher treats the pupils with sincerity and honesty, is the key to creating the best environment for learning.

A leading exponent of this third model was **Carl Rogers.** According to Rogers, teaching as deliberate instruction is a vastly overrated function. The educator should, instead, devote much more attention to creating the conditions that will promote experiential learning. Rogers emphasized experience and feeling rather than thinking or reading as the proper pathway to knowledge—an odd thought, no doubt, as you sit reading a textbook! Rogers was convinced that traditional learning is so impersonal, cold, and aloof that it really goes in one ear and out the other. According to him, we learn only what is really important and relevant to us as people. In his classic work *Freedom to Learn,* Rogers (1969) presents three necessary and sufficient conditions for the promotion of learning: empathy, unconditional positive regard, and congruence, or genuineness. **Empathy** allows us to communicate to our pupils that we really understand the emotions they are experiencing and permits us to "read" their feelings accurately. **Unconditional positive regard** allows us to accept our students for what they are without passing judgment. This acceptance is unconditional and involves none of the usual bargaining ("If you do this for me, then I will like you"). Rogers repeatedly said that teachers must place no conditions on these relationships and must accept students without reservation. **Congruence,** or genuineness, means being "real," honest. Going through the motions and pretending we like children or listening to their feelings and emotions halfheartedly is not enough.

If teachers provide these conditions, then, according to Rogers, the children will be free to learn. The

CARL R. ROGERS

Born at the turn of the century in a Chicago suburb, Carl Rogers spent his early years deciding how to focus his career. In 1919 his first interest at the University of Wisconsin was scientific farming. Simultaneously he was extremely active in church work, including attendance at a Christian youth conference in Beijing, China. Upon his return to this country he shifted his undergraduate major to history. He felt that such a change was more in line with his emerging desire to go into evangelical work. He received an A.B. in history in 1924 from Wisconsin. Ironically, in view of his subsequent eminence in the field, he had but a single academic course in psychology as an undergraduate, and that by correspondence.

To prepare for the ministry, Rogers attended Union Theological Seminary in New York. There he began to change his emphasis once again, from the dogma of religion to more general questions concerning the nature of the helping relationship. His interest in the healthy personal and psychological development of each person as an individual became more important than the formal, organized practice of religion. It was here that one of his key concepts took shape, the unique and special nature of "personhood." Much later, this idea was actualized with the establishment of his famous Center for Studies of the Person. With this shift in focus, Rogers transferred from Union to Columbia University Teachers College. He received his Ph.D. in 1931, having spent much of his time doing fieldwork in Rochester, New York, with the city's department for the prevention of cruelty to children.

His lifelong interest in preventive treatment for mental health problems had its roots in this early work. One of the major difficulties that proponents of psychological treatment as a concept have grap-

pled with almost from its inception has been this matter of preventive treatment. To provide help after a person becomes emotionally upset—that is, treatment after the fact—had been a major model of psychotherapy. It was really borrowed from the practice of medicine. Psychological help, then, in this view, takes the form of diagnosis, prognosis, treatment, and cure. People with problems would be classed into categories of mental illness, become patients, and, if the psychotherapy was successful, would be cured. Rogers felt almost from the beginning that this approach had severe limitations. Diagnostic categories easily became negative labels. Focusing on mental disturbance could cause therapists to overlook the positive forces for growth inside each person. Treatments designed to help people often encouraged dependency or became a purchase of friendship. Rogers waged a long battle with the traditional psychological and psychiatric establishment on these issues. In his view, it was most important to prevent personal problems from being treated as long-term mental illness. An ounce of prevention is always worth more than a pound of cure. In this vein,

natural makeup of children and teenagers is such that if we remove the inhibitions imposed by outside direction, then self-directed learning will follow.

Model Three teaching is not as concerned as Model One with disseminating appropriate information, nor does it worry too much about understanding concepts or discovering the structures of a discipline. Model Three teaching is concerned primarily with human interaction. This may also be its major drawback.

We realize that classroom atmospheres are important; clearly, pupils have difficulty learning anything

if the anxiety level is high. Under such conditions our perception, how much we can "see," becomes narrow. Studies have shown that nonsupportive, critical, and negative classroom climates have adverse physiological and psychological effects on the pupils: heartbeats increase, the galvanic skin response (a scientific term for sweaty palms, etc.) goes up, the resistance level (measured in ohms) increases. In the psychological domain the pupil's self-concept as a learner decreases, and self-direction in learning declines. Also, as one might expect, negative attitudes toward the teacher increase. Finally, he tried to develop counseling techniques that would encourage the positive growth forces within each person. To grow psychologically strong people was his answer to the treatment question.

Essentially, Carl Rogers' entire career was a pilgrim's progress toward the goal of personhood for all. After almost a decade at the Rochester Clinic, he moved into the university setting, first at Ohio State from 1940 to 1945 and then at the University of Chicago. At Chicago he created a now-famous client-centered counseling agency for the university. With this as a laboratory, he began to provide not only a significant new approach to college counseling but also a research base to document his work. He was the first counselor therapist to record his sessions on tape. By analyzing the actual transcripts of the counseling interactions, he was able to dispel many of the myths surrounding psychological treatment. He was not well received by the more orthodox establishment. His openness in providing a public record of counseling challenged therapists to examine their own work and attest to its effectiveness. Up to that time, treatment failures were almost always blamed on the patient. If patients didn't get well, there were three possible explanations: They might be too disturbed, they might be untreatable, or they might have a chronically weak ego. Rogers was able to show that many treatment problems were actually derived from the therapists.

Research on the counseling process began to show that particular conditions were absolutely essential if the person was to be helped. In a series of significant research studies started first in Chicago and then moved to Madison, Wisconsin, Rogers concluded that three conditions represented the core of the therapeutic relationship: unconditional positive regard, empathy, and congruence. (These are explained in the text.) The famous Rogerian triad became the central ingredient in the helping process. What was true for psychotherapy, he felt, applied equally to counseling and teaching.

Throughout his career, Rogers stressed the importance of the quality of interpersonal relationships, that how we relate to each other as human beings is central to the development of the person. Too often, he would say, we neglect this fundamental truism. Just as John Dewey can be thought of as the major proponent of education as a democratic ideal, so Carl Rogers can be viewed as a lifelong fighter for the democratization of counseling and psychotherapy. He saw the need to develop equal and genuine relationships between people. The ability to help and care, according to Rogers, is an important resource within each human being, and we all have a responsibility to use it, as part of our mutual human interdependence. His work was always focused on that goal.

In an address to the American Psychological Association in 1972, he once again challenged psychologists to move out of a narrow scientific and even narrower professional stance and teach the principles of healthy growth to all people. "If we did away with 'the expert,' the 'certified professional,' the 'licensed psychologist,' we might open our profession to a breeze of fresh air, to a surge of creativity, such as it has not known for years."

In 1987, after an exciting but demanding visit to Russia, Carl Rogers died during an operation for a broken hip at the age of 85. His goal of world peace seems closer now as a result of his efforts.

and perhaps most important, academic achievement declines in a stressful directive-critical teaching atmosphere. Even pupils' voices—both the content of what they say and how they say it—reveal differences clearly in favor of supportive classroom atmospheres. Thus, the quality of the interpersonal relationship between the teacher and pupils does have an impact on many facets of classroom interaction and on how the pupil actually learns (Flanders & Morine, 1973).

Greta Morine-Dershimer (1985) described further the elements of the complex interpersonal communication environment in the classroom between teachers and students, and among peers. In one study in a multiethnic community, she found that students with higher academic status participated more frequently and were listened to by their peers more carefully. Ethnic minority students in these classes had lower academic status and received significantly less attention than the other students. One interesting finding is that the use of nonstandard English in interpersonal communication was not a causal factor in school achievement, whereas negative teacher expectations based upon students' usage of the language may influence how much a student learns.

We cannot necessarily conclude that teaching and learning can be explained exclusively by the three Rogerian conditions. We can all think of examples from our own experience in which ideas, directions, and other types of academic content were important, and a skeptic might be quick to conclude that love alone is not enough. We are not suggesting either extreme. Obviously, unconditional positive regard is not sufficient; but just as obviously, such facilitating conditions are important and necessary.

One final point: Recall that Walberg's massive summary of pupil achievement outcomes denoted classroom morale as a key factor in learning. In this sense, the atmosphere or climate can enhance morale or do just the opposite. If pupils feel prized as persons instead of feeling unworthy, then the learning outcome is positive. There are always exceptions, of course. Someone is bound to say, "I really felt put down all the time in that class, but I learned the material." Individuality is such that a few can learn even under the worst possible conditions. But, these are exceptions, not the rule.

SYNTHESIZING TEACHING

From a developmental view, each of the three general models of teaching we have discussed has assets as well as liabilities. It would be a great mistake to settle exclusively on any one of these methods. There is something to be said in favor of each one, as well as something to be said against each one. Certainly, from the point of view of the pupil, the deficits are clear. **Bruce Joyce,** one of the country's leading researchers in the teaching-learning process, has commented that the actual teaching styles of most teachers are extremely limited. As a result, it is most important to "add and blend" a repertoire of models—that is, synthesize teaching—in order to enhance effectiveness. In other words, the old advice that advocated finding your own model, learning it, and sticking with it no longer holds. Joyce notes a series of personal experiences to underscore the need for variety. His account illustrates how a teacher may so overuse one approach that the student soon becomes sick of the subject matter:

When I was in high school, I was one of the poorest members of a good swimming team. The coach used drill-and-practice methods to teach us the strokes and how to increase our speed. He was tremendously encouraging to all of us, including those who

really were not doing the team that much good. We loved him, enjoyed each other, and felt good about ourselves. As my body matured in college, I showed some promise as a long-distance swimmer and was taken under the wing of a fairly genial but hard-driving coach who emphasized practice rather than instruction. Given the academic demands of college, our little group had keys to the pool and were asked to swim for four to six hours sometime during each evening or night. It was, of course, not his fault that he couldn't be there to provide variety, but one of the side-effects of that experience is that I have not swum five consecutive laps since I was 20 years old. I love to play in the water, but I have an incredible aversion to anything remotely resembling swimming practice (1978, p. 18).

Avoiding Rigidity

Having learned to use the various Flanders categories outlined in Table 12.3, you will be able to combine clusters that will most naturally fit the major teaching models presented at the outset. Employing advance organizers in the transmission-of-knowledge model (Model One) means that category 5 (lecturing) would be the most common technique used. Similarly, the inductive modes associated with Model Two would rely heavily on category 4 (asking open-ended questions) plus categories 2 and 3. The interpersonal model (Model Three) would include a strong emphasis on category 1 (accepting feelings) as well as on categories 2 and 3. The goal, then, is to learn to apply these models with skill in order to increase the variety of learning experiences for the pupils (Joyce et al., 1987). Joyce warns that it is very important to avoid a heavy-handed reliance on any one model day in and day out. Recent research has shown that the effective use of a blend of models does yield consistent increases in student achievement.

When I am working with my classes, there are certain days when I simply have a terrific urge to get things clarified or when I want to express myself and the way I think about material. On those days, I am very likely to lecture with the use of advance organizers. There are other days when I would be bored silly by that same approach, and use another to stay lively and help the students stay with me. Pretending that we are not people would be a serious error in teaching, and our intuition about what feels right on any given day should be listened to, even though we select models on an analytic basis much of the time (Joyce, 1978, pp. 18–19).

All three models—the transmittal of knowledge, inductive inquiry, and interpersonal learning—are important to the classroom teacher, and effective teaching demands a combination of the three. Certainly it would be a mistake to depend exclusively on any one.

Enhancing Flexibility among Models

Good teachers work at avoiding rigidity and enhancing their flexible use of different models of teaching. **Kathy Carter,** past president of the Division of Teaching and Teacher Education of the American Educational Research Association, summarized the research on teachers' knowledge and learning to teach. In her 1990 review are helpful examples of teachers who attempt to be flexible within their preferred primary models of teaching. She presented the following two examples, drawn from case studies of four teachers by Tom Russell and his colleagues Phyllis Johnston, Hugh Munby, and Charlotte Spafford (1990) who examined how teachers' images of teaching helped or hindered their ability to learn from their experiences, to increase their flexibility in using the different models of teaching, and to synthesize or construct their own genuine teaching style appropriate to the students' needs.

> For example, the teacher who appeared to be constrained the most by her image of teaching and learned the least from her experience was Wendy, a high school science teacher who saw herself as a transmitter of knowledge. During her first 2 years of teaching, she came to explore methods of helping students participate more fully in classroom work, but she was not able to reframe her experience in ways that resulted in notable changes in her teaching actions. She did modify and improve a number of her teaching techniques, but her teaching stayed largely consistent with the transmitter view, despite her expressed wish to change.
>
> In contrast, Roger, a fifth-year science teacher of seventh and eighth grades, came to teaching with a strongly held belief in the inquiry approach, but he learned from watching his students that, although they enjoyed working with science in this fashion, their *learning* of the content and concepts of science was sometimes questionable. Roger began to read criticisms of the inquiry approach to teaching that he had supported, but he initially greeted these criticisms with anger and resentment. Later he experimented by using his own blend of inquiry and content knowledge in science, and, seeing that his students were constructing much-improved meaning about the subject of science, he altered his original view of teaching and continued to construct his own interpretation of teaching from his classroom experiences and from his reading of theory about how children learn. (Carter, 1990, p. 301).

Development toward greater flexibility in teaching starts when teachers become aware of the teaching strategies with which they are most comfortable, and act on refining these strategies. Teachers attempt to look at their practice from different perspectives and increase their flexibility among the models of teaching. They initially maintain a coherent framework for their teaching and often ignore feedback from students that doesn't fit into this framework. (In a Piagetian sense of new learning, we could call this part of the pattern *assimilation,* as we discussed in Chapter 5). At the next level of awareness, teachers become more attentive to students' reactions and feedback. The teachers then reflect on puzzling situations, and do start to reframe their teaching practices to *accommodate* the new, disequilibrating information. Joyce and his long time collaborator and co-author, Beverly Showers, researched the concept of peer coaching study teams as a way for teachers to learn from each other while planning instruction, developing support materials, watching one another work with students, and thinking together about the impact of their behavior on students' learning (Joyce and Showers, 1995; Showers and Joyce, 1996). In their redefinition of peer coaching, the 'coach' is the one teaching and 'the coached' is the one observing in order to learn from her or his colleague. Building shared goals and strong collaborative bonds between the teachers in peer coaching study teams is more important than technical feedback as teachers work at enhancing their flexible use of different models of teaching.

NONVERBAL BEHAVIOR

In addition to the need for blending in Joyce's sense, there is yet another important component of teaching effectiveness. To an ironic degree the nonverbal aspect of being human is so obvious that we often overlook it. In fact, until the work of theorists such as Charles Galloway (1977), of Ohio State University, and a few others, the area of body language, or nonverbal communication, was largely ignored in teaching and teacher education. This happened in spite of earlier and pioneering research work that indicated most clearly just how significant the phenomenon was.

From 75 to 90 percent of a message's impact is transmitted nonverbally. The actual verbal content turns out to be far less important than tone of voice, facial expression, and posture. In the classroom, how you stand or sit, move, gesture, and raise and lower your voice, for example, will convey what you really mean to your students. But unfortunately, as Galloway points out, too often we are almost totally unaware of our own nonverbal modes. We rarely see ourselves in interaction and hence do not really understand what impact we may be having on others.

Perhaps even more important is the extent to which we convey how we really feel about others without words. Studies have shown that teachers who have positive attitudes toward the world actually employ an important set of facilitating nonverbal cues to encourage student participation and involvement. Those with negative attitudes display **nonverbal behavior** designed to discourage and inhibit student involvement (Smith, 1981). Researchers could predict what type of nonverbal behavior a teacher would use if they knew the teacher's attitude set. Moreover, it is obvious that the children understand the meaning of the different body language systems.

As a result Galloway and his colleagues devel-

TABLE 12.5   NONVERBAL BEHAVIORS: THE GALLOWAY SYSTEM

		Congruent	Incongruent
DIRECT INFLUENCE	1, 2	**Congruent** Nonverbal behavior is consistent with words. No "mixed messages" are given. Body language demonstrates an appropriate range of feelings.	**Incongruent** Behavior contradicts words; for example, smiles when annoyed. Body language is overcontrolled. Feelings are rarely if ever shown.
	3	**Implement** As teacher uses ideas of pupils, nonverbals are consistently encouraging; for example, leans toward, smiles.	**Perfunctory** Nonverbal behavior indicates no genuine interest in student ideas; for example, bored posture or facial expression.
	4	**Personal** Teacher maintains face-to-face eye contact, is "connected" with the class, maintains a comfortable "psychological" distance.	**Impersonal** Teacher avoids eye contact; for example, talks to the floor or ceiling or maintains excessive distance.
INDIRECT INFLUENCE	5	**Responsive** Tone, pace of talk are designed to keep student interest.	**Unresponsive** Teacher drones on and on, with little variation in tone, and screens out student cues.
	6	**Involve** Nonverbal behavior encourages student participation in clarifying directions and rules.	**Dismiss** Nonverbal behavior cues students to avoid participation.
	7	**Firm** Nonverbal behavior is consistent with firm language in controlling misbehavior.	**Harsh** Nonverbal behavior is severe, aggressive, genuinely intimidating.

oped a nonverbal version of the Flanders system. Instead of coding verbal messages, however, they rated the body language of the teachers. Table 12.5 outlines the main elements of the patterns of communication, divided into two main areas: nonverbal behavior that (1) facilitates students' development or (2) constricts their growth. He has also organized the nonverbal categories according to indirect methods and direct approaches.

The results of Galloway's research have two major implications. First, there is a clear connection between a teacher's nonverbal behavior and the classroom atmosphere. We noted both in the teaching model focused on interpersonal relationships and from the meta-analysis on the importance of classroom morale that such elements have an important effect on learning. Essentially, your nonverbal behavior will set the tone in the classroom.

Second, teachers need to make a deliberate attempt to become more aware of their own basic repertoire of nonverbal behavior. This doesn't mean you need to enroll in a method acting school. It does mean you should recognize and improve areas in which your nonverbal behavior may be inhibiting student growth. Obviously, the use of videotapes of classroom performance is one major way of gaining awareness and seeing the effect of a new behavior. Another is to ask a good friend to observe and write down examples of how your behavior fits into the **Galloway system.**

The most difficult problem is that there can be no exact prescription of how to behave. You need to find a comfortable middle ground between a cold, aloof, restricted set of behaviors and their opposite—a rushing, gushing, overpowering, and hectic nonverbal repertoire. If you are naturally inclined to be quiet and to limit your nonverbal behavior, then you will want to work on adding to your repertoire. If, however, your nonverbal behavior seems to indicate that you are running the class as if you were con-

SPOTLIGHT ON TEACHER ENTHUSIASM

Regular Education and Special-Education Classrooms

Whenever we think of teaching effectiveness, a question frequently asked is: What about enthusiasm? Doesn't it make a difference if the teacher is genuinely interested in and eager to convey the subject matter? Certainly Thomas Good's concept of active teaching seems to indicate the need for well-paced instruction.[a] Obviously, a teacher who labors over each point in a slow, pedantic manner must have a negative effect. Such a teacher, humorless, plodding, and somewhat out of touch with reality, represents almost a Hollywood version of an ineffective educator.

It was Jacob Kounin who first formalized a framework to help understand the concept of **teacher enthusiasm**.[b] How alert, wide awake, or "with it" a teacher is does make a major difference, particularly in handling discipline and in moving from one subject to the next. In other words, one of the keys to a good learning environment is the avoidance of "down time," when nothing seems to be happening in the classroom. Thus,

managing a group involves a pace or tempo.

From a logical viewpoint, then, teacher energy is clearly important. What does the research say?

The first series of studies was done by Barak Rosenshine through careful observation of actual classroom instruction. Through such naturalistic study, Kounin's ideas were validated. The enthusiastic, "with-it" teachers outperformed their cohorts. The pupils gained in academic achievement. The positive correlations to achievement ranged between .30 and .60.[c] But since such findings weren't particularly surprising, they received only modest notice in the educational psychology literature. It remained for a new group of researchers to put the concept at the forefront through a series of provocative and somewhat controversial studies, the "Dr. Fox studies."

Every once in a while, a group of behavioral scientists will come up with a startling new approach to a phenomenon. D. H. Naftulin, J. E. Ware, and F. A. Donnelly de-

cided to push the study of enthusiasm to the limit.[d] At a professional conference they hired an actor to give a lecture. Introduced with all the appropriate (though "fake") expert credentials, the actor used charisma, enthusiasm, and style in delivering a basically meaningless talk. At times, it even verged on double-talk. Of course, by now you may have guessed the outcome. The audience solemnly proclaimed through evaluations that the talk was well organized, clearly presented, and "stimulated thinking." The redoubtable Dr. Fox had indeed outfoxed his audience. National newspapers and the media quickly picked up the study.

Naturally, there is and has been much debate about what such a study actually proves. It does not suggest that in a real classroom over the course of an entire school year students will learn meaningful content from meaningless lectures. After all, you can't fool all the people all the time. Further studies have shown that when real content is included, the "expressiveness" of the teacher continues

ducting a fire drill, then you'll want to relax more and express less of yourself nonverbally. Incidentally, this also holds even in the area of discipline. The old truism used to be "Don't smile until Christmas" if you were a new teacher (Ryan, 1970). The idea was to keep the students in line right from the start through stern composure. We now know that's wrong. Effective teachers are skillful not only in stating their expectations but also in demonstrating a genuine interest in listening to and working with the students, thus conveying an atmosphere of mutually

shared expectations. They can even smile before Thanksgiving.

Communicating Expectations

Teachers communicate expectations to students verbally and nonverbally. It is important to be aware of the way you communicate expectations nonverbally because students' performance is often influenced by a teacher's subtle, as well as not-so-subtle apto have a significant effect not only on student ratings but also on achievement. So what is now being referred to as "an extended visit with Dr. Fox in the classroom" essentially supports Kounin's original contention and Rosenshine's first series of naturalistic studies.[e] The experimental studies help to cross-validate the original findings.[f] Enthusiasm makes a difference.

A recent study by Frederick Brigham, Thomas Scruggs, and Margo Mastropieri focused on teacher enthusiasm in learning disabilities classrooms. Students with learning disabilities in two junior high school special-education classrooms were given instruction in science over a two-week period with levels of teacher enthusiasm manipulated in a crossover design. Results suggested that more enthusiastic presentations resulted in significantly higher academic achievement as well as lower levels of off-task behavior. The authors cite two possible theories to explain why enthusiasm produces such positive changes in students.

The first theory was based on Rosenshine's earlier work, which suggested that enthusiastic "with-it" teachers, with their varying positions, voice tones, and gestures, attract high levels of attention from students and consequently excellent cognitive engagement and achievement. These authors suggest a second possible explanation: Students consciously or unconsciously model the enthusiastic attitude that the teacher exhibits toward the content, and consequently concentrate more, think more about the subject, and achieve more than they would have with a less enthusiastic teacher.[g] Further research could lend support to one or more of these ideas to explain why enthusiasm continues to make a difference.

---

[a]   Good, T. L. (1983). Recent classroom research: Implications for teacher education. In D. C. Smith (Ed.), *Essential knowledge for beginning educators* (pp. 55–64). Washington, DC: American Association of Colleges of Teacher Education.

[b]   Kounin, J. (1970). *Discipline and group management in the classroom.* New York: Holt, Rinehart & Winston.

[c]   Rosenshine, B. (1970). Enthusiastic teaching: A research review. *School Review, 78*, 499–514.

[d]   Naftulin, D. H., Ware, J. E., Jr., & Donnelly, F. A. (1973).The Dr. Fox lecture: A paradigm for educational seduction. *Journal of Medical Education, 48*, 630–635.

[e]   Williams, R. G., & Ware, J. E., Jr. (1977). An extended visit with Dr. Fox: Validity of student satisfaction with instruction after repeated exposure to a lecturer. *American Educational Research Journal, 14*(4), 449–458.

[f]   See Larkins, A. G., McKinney, C. W., Oldham-Bass, S., & Gilmore, A. C. (1985). Teacher enthusiasm: A critical review. In H. S. Williams (Ed.), *Educational and psychological research.* Hattiesburg: University of Southern Mississippi. This is an excellent, comprehensive review of the concept of enthusiasm, including a detailed examination of the research design employed.

[g]   Brigham, F. J., Scruggs, T. E., & Mastropieri, M. A. (1992). Teacher enthusiasm in learning disabilities classrooms: Effects on learning and behavior. *Learning Disabilities Research and Practice, 7*, 68–73. The article includes a summary of research on teacher enthusiasm in regular education and special-education classrooms.

---

proaches. What personal convictions or opinions a teacher communicates about a student's competence has a powerful effect on student performance, and sometimes teachers have "reference group" expectations about an entire category of people that can have an impact on all members of that group. We can add school, societal, and family expectations to our discussion of communicating expectations (see Chapter 14).

A study of teachers' nonverbal behavior yielded some interesting as well as distressing results. The researchers studied three groups of experienced teachers—preschool, remedial, and elementary—by viewing video clips of the teachers' classroom behavior. The ratings yielded two general patterns of nonverbal behavior: pattern 1 behavior was flexible, democratic, and warm; pattern 2 was hostile, condescending, and dogmatic (Babad et al., 1987). There were, however, very few differences in other aspects of teacher behavior, particularly at the verbal level. At the nonverbal level, it was a different story. First, there was a major difference associated with teaching

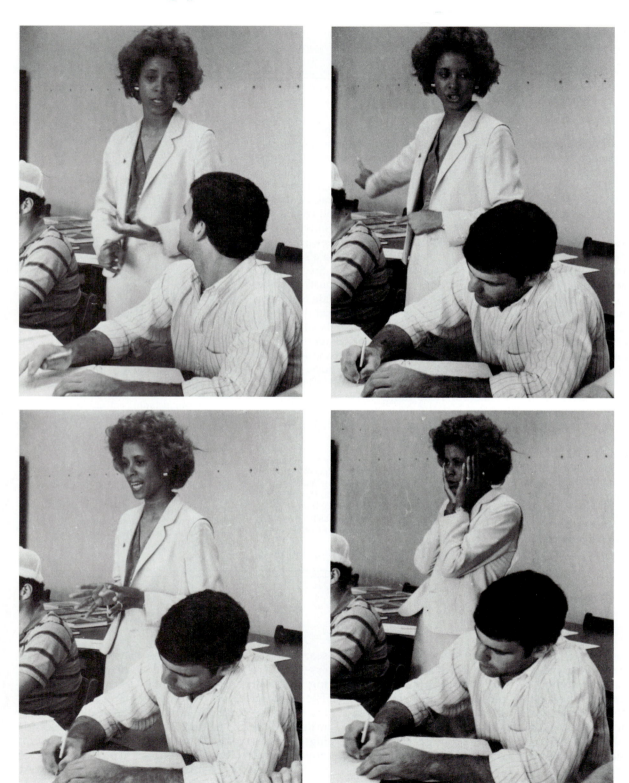

As Galloway's research on nonverbal behavior points out, actions speak louder than words in the classroom.

area. Pattern 1—flexible, democratic, and warm —was highest for the preschool group, second for the remedial teachers, and lowest for the elementary teachers. Thus, there is major variation in nonverbal behavior. The second finding of importance was that the main nonverbal channel for conveying the negative feelings of hostility, condescension, and dogmatism was facial expressions. The face, more than body posture, voice tone, or other elements of nonverbal behavior, was the main channel. It is also interesting to note that those who rated the video clips—the research judges—showed the greatest reliability in rating the facial dogmatism messages. If the results of this study are replicated, they may well provide us with a very significant clue about the importance of classroom atmosphere, morale, and affective states as they relate to pupils' feelings. In short, it is your facial expression that transmits the affective message. This may explain why actors in training spend so much time practicing their routines in front of a mirror.

If teachers' nonverbal behavior influences students, is the converse also true? As you've probably guessed, it does work both ways. Teachers can be clearly influenced by a student's physical appearance, posture, and tone of voice (Woolfolk & Brooks, 1983). As a result some students receive frequent approval while others receive not only less approval but also less eye contact, fewer smiles, and more disapproval. We'll comment more on this when we discuss the personal aspects of teaching (Chapter 14), since it relates very much to the basic attitudes a teacher may have toward pupils and the self-fulfilling prophecies that result.

Cross-Cultural Differences

If you think about it, you will quickly realize that body language varies considerably according to a person's cultural background. Some nonverbal behavior may have a very different meaning in different cultures. As a result, when the cultural background of the child and the teacher vary widely, nonverbal messages may be misinterpreted. Two examples illustrate the point. Some Native American children are taught not to maintain steady eye contact with an adult. In some tribes an adult who looks straight into another person's eyes is seen as untrustworthy. This does not mean that you can't look at Native American children; however, if you force the child to look directly into your eyes, you may be sending a very mixed message. Similarly, the amount of physical space that is psychologically comfortable varies considerably among cultures. A newly arrived student from Great Britain may require more "personal space" than a student from Mexico. At the same time, however, it is most important not to overgeneralize. Many English children and Mexican children would welcome either closer or more distant contact. What they are accustomed to may also depend on how Americanized their family has become.

In dealing with children from culturally different backgrounds, it is wise to watch for signs of incongruity. When the children's behavior is incongruent, it may indicate that whatever you are attempting to communicate nonverbally is being misunderstood. In other words, they may be decoding your nonverbal message in a way you didn't intend. Because of the enormous complexity of cross-cultural differences, it may be impossible for research to develop a definitive list of them. As a teacher, you should be sensitive to their existence and observe the nonverbal responses to your own behaviors as an index of effective communication. In addition, you should actively seek to find out more about these differences by asking other school personnel, parents, and community members, and by further reading and attending cultural events. Cross-cultural differences can be discussed in class (or privately) with students; it is an important area of study and understanding.

SUMMARY

Research on teaching effectiveness based on meta-analyses conducted by Walberg indicates that the following factors are key elements: engaged academic learning time, positive reinforcement, cues and feedback, cooperative learning, positive class atmosphere, higher-order questioning, and advance organizers. The system of instruction developed by Flanders shows how these elements fit together in actual classroom interaction.

Teaching elements can also be grouped into general models of teaching. In Model One the emphasis is on the transmission of knowledge. Use of advance organizers and direct teaching methods are the main features. Model Two involves inquiry or discovery-based teaching. It emphasizes the indirect methods of open-ended questioning and of building on student ideas. The focus of Model Three is the quality of interpersonal relations. A positive classroom atmosphere is a central component of the model.

Joyce emphasizes the need for a variety of teaching models. Instead of relying exclusively on any single model, he suggests synthesizing methods. Teachers thus need to practice the different skills involved with each method in order to achieve teaching effectiveness.

One of the main criticisms of the teaching models has been the absence of any emphasis on teacher nonverbal behavior. Based on Galloway's system, a new method of analyzing teacher nonverbal behavior has been developed that parallels Flanders'

framework. Galloway's work underscores the importance of teacher awareness of how actions often do speak louder than words in the classroom. In the area of cross-cultural differences, there are few, if any, consistent nonverbal differences. It is important, however, for teachers to become aware of possible incongruities between pupil words and body language. Thus, teachers need to learn about not only their own nonverbal channels of communication but also those of their pupils.

KEY TERMS AND NAMES

AAUW
Kathy Carter
cooperative learning
Ned Flanders
Galloway System
    nonverbal behavior
    teacher enthusiasm
K. Tsianina Lomawaima
Bruce Joyce

Greta Morine-Dershimer
Carl Rogers
    congruence
    empathy
    unconditional positive regard
Herbert Walberg

THEORY INTO PRACTICE: VERBAL AND NONVERBAL BEHAVIOR

In developing your own awareness of your verbal and nonverbal teaching behavior, you will need to practice single elements at first. The method has been called *microteaching,* which means to divide the complex process of instruction into smaller-sized components and then practice each skill separately. Basically, this is the format we have followed in the chapter. We presented some very concrete elements, such as positive reinforcement, cues and feedback, questioning, praise, and advance organizers. Then we showed how these elements can be blended into a more general system (Flanders) and finally into models. So to practice, we suggest going back to the Walberg components or the Flanders outline. Do not start with the models.

The second aspect of the method emphasizes relatively short practice on one skill. The practice is then followed as soon as possible by a review playback as a check. This way you will reduce the likelihood of maintaining any ineffective teaching skill under development.

For Verbal Behavior

1. Select one microskill from either the Flanders or Walberg list.

2. Prepare a brief unit or lesson plan to teach to a small group of students (peers or volunteers).

3. Set up an audiotape recorder so that it is relatively unobstrusive.

4. Teach the unit for 10 to 15 minutes or so. Specifically try to use the designated microskill. For example, if you want to practice positive reinforcement, use a unit that will allow you to pose a number of questions. Then, when students respond, you'll have the opportunity to reinforce. The same holds true for areas such as cues or responding to feelings.

5. When you've finished the unit, turn off the tape. Before starting the playback, make a chart such as the one on the opposite page, to organize your analysis. To reduce defensiveness, plan to do this kind of review and playback *by yourself* at least for the first few times. It can be disconcerting, especially at the outset, to hear the difference between what you intended to do and what actually happened. Also, you'll need time to become less self-conscious. Keep it to yourself at the start.

VERBAL MICROTEACHING CHART: AUDIO PLAYBACK

Focus Area: Use of Audio Playback Positive Reinforcement

1. How many questions were asked? _____
2. How many questions were answered correctly? _____
3. How many times did I offer a positive reinforcer to correctly answered questions? _____
4. List examples of the words and phrases used as positive reinforcers.
5. Review the ratio between correct answers (item 2) and positive reinforcers (item 3).
   a. Are you satisfied with the number of times you followed the correct answer with a reinforcer?
   b. If not, then recycle the unit (or another one) and try again.
6. Review the content of your verbal reinforcers as listed in item 4.
   a. Are you satisfied that you have enough variety in your responses, or are you relying on one or two "pet" expressions?
   b. If not, then repeat the exercise after writing down some additional phrases in your own words that you could use.

For Nonverbal Behavior

1. Select one microskill, such as eye contact, voice tone, or body stance.

2. Prepare a brief unit or lesson plan to last 10 to 15 minutes.

3. Set up a video camera. Since this can be somewhat complex the first time, allow yourself some extra time to become familiar with the equipment. Set the camera in a corner with the wide-angle lens focused on the place where the small group will be sitting. Check the recording level to be sure the sound is being picked up. Then turn on the equipment.

4. Teach the unit to the group and consciously try to emphasize the particular nonverbal behavior you selected for practice.

5. When done, turn off the equipment and rewind the tape. Before playback, prepare a chart, in the same manner as before, for use in analyzing what you observe on the tape.

   After reviewing your performance, you may decide to recycle. It is important, however, to continue to concentrate on one specific skill. Do not fall into the trap of trying all the components at once. That will overload your learning circuits, so to speak.

Only after you have mastered a number of these individual teaching skills should you consider evaluating yourself on the entire Flanders scale. That would be the next step toward synthesis.

For further information on this approach, see S. Rogers (1987), "If I Can See Myself, I Can Change," *Educational Leadership, 45*(2), 64–67.

NONVERBAL MICROTEACHING CHART: VIDEO PLAYBACK

Focus Area: Eye Contact

1. How many times did I look up at the students as a group? _____
2. How many times did I maintain eye contact of at least two seconds with a specific pupil during the unit? _____
3. Review the ratio of times you looked up (item 1) to times you maintained contact (item 2).
   a. Are you satisfied with the number of general glances at the class compared with individual contacts?
   b. In reviewing the tape, how would you characterize the quality of the eye contact? Was it friendly or staring? How did the students react? Review their body posture and compare their attention during times when you glanced at them in a general way versus times of specific contact.
   c. Did you feel uncomfortable throughout the unit, or did you find yourself becoming less self-conscious by the end of the session?

REFERENCES

American Association of University Women (1992). *How schools shortchange girls.* Washington, DC: AAUW Educational Foundation.

Ausubel, D. P., & Sullivan, E. V. (1970). *Theory and problems of child development* (2d ed.). New York: Grune & Stratton.

Babad, E., Bernieri, F., & Rosenthal, R. (1987). Nonverbal and verbal behavior of preschool, remedial, and elementary school teachers. *American Educational Research Journal, 24*(3), 405–415.

Barnes, M., & Coupland, M. (1990). Humanizing calculus: A case study in curriculum development. In L. Burton (Ed.), *Gender and mathematics* (pp. 72–80). London: Cassell.

Berliner, D. C. (1984). The half-full glass: A review of research on teaching. In P. L. Hosford (Ed.), *Using what we know about teaching* (pp. 51–77). Alexandria, VA: Association for Supervision and Curriculum Development.

Brophy, J. (1981). Teacher praise: A functional analysis. *Review of Educational Research, 51,* 5–32.

Brown, S. M. & Walberg, H. J. (1993). Motivational effects on test scores of elementary students. *Journal of Educational Research, 86*(3), 133–136.

Bruner, J. (1966). *Toward a theory of instruction.* Cambridge, Mass.: The Belknap Press of Harvard University Press.

Buerk, D. (1985). The voices of women making meaning in mathematics. *Journal of Education, 167,* 59–70.

Carter, K. (1990). Teachers' knowledge and learning to teach. In W. R. Houston (Ed.), *Handbook of research on teacher education* (pp. 291–310). New York: Macmillan.

Chickering, A., & McCormick, J. (1973). Personality development and the college experience. *Research in Higher Education, 1,* 43–70.

Cuban, L. (1988). Researchers advising policymakers: A word to the wise. *Educational Psychologist, 23*(3), 287–293.

Dempter, F. (1987). Time and the production of classroom learning. *Educational Psychologist, 22*(1), 1–22.

Doyle, W. H. (1986). Using an advance organizer to establish a subsuming function concept for facilitating achievement in remedial college mathematics. *American Educational Research Journal, 23*(3), 507–516.

Eccles, J. (1987). Gender roles and women's achievement—Related decisions. *Psychology of Women Quarterly, 11*(2), 135–171.

Fennema, E., and Leder, G. (Eds.). (1990). *Mathematics and gender.* New York: Teachers College Press.

Flanders, N. A. (1970). *Analyzing teacher behavior.* Reading, MA: Addison-Wesley.

Flanders, N. A., & Morine, G. (1973). The assessment of proper control and suitable learning environment. In N. L. Gage (Ed.), *Mandated evaluation of educators.* Stanford: California Center for Research and Development in Teaching.

Fraser, B. J., Walberg, H. J., Welch, W. W., & Hattie, J. A. (1987). Synthesis of educational productivity research. *International Journal of Educational Research, 11,* 73–145.

Gage, N. L. (1978). *The scientific basis for the art of teaching.* New York: Teachers College Press.

Gage, N. L. (1985). *Hard gains in the soft sciences.* Bloomington, IN: Phi Delta Kappan.

Galloway, C. M. (1977). Nonverbal: Authentic or Artificial. *Theory into practice, 16*(3), 129–134.

Good, T. L. (1983). Recent classroom research: Implications for teacher education. In D. C. Smith (Ed.), *Essential knowledge for beginning educators* (pp. 55–65). Washington, DC: American Association of Colleges of Teacher Education.

Isaacson, Z. (1990). They look at you in absolute horror: Women writing and talking about mathematics. In L. Burton (Ed.), *Gender and mathematics* (pp. 20–28). London: Cassell.

Joyce, B. R. (1978). *Selecting learning experiences: Linking theory to practice.* Washington, DC: Association for Supervision and Curriculum Development.

Joyce, B. & Showers, B. (1995). *Student achievement through staff development: Fundamentals of school renewal,* 2nd ed. White Plains, NY: Longman.

Joyce, B., Showers, B., & Rolheiser-Bennett, C. (1987). Staff development and student learning: A synthesis of research on models of teaching. *Educational Leadership, 45*(2), 11–23.

Lomawaima, K. T. (1995). Educating Native Americans. In J. A. Banks & C. A. Banks (Eds.), *Handbook of research on multicultural education* (pp. 331–347). New York: Macmillan.

Morine-Dershimer, G. (1985). *Talking, listening, and learning in elementary classrooms.* New York: Longman.

Morrow, C. (1996). Women and mathematics: Avenues of connection. *Focus on Learning Problems in Mathematics, 18*(1,2,3), 4-18.

Page, E. B. (1958). Teacher comments and student performance. *Journal of Educational Psychology, 49,* 173–181.

Peterson, P., & Swing, S. (1982). Beyond time on task: Students' reports of their thought processes during classroom instruction. *Elementary School Journal, 82,* 481–491.

Redfield, D. L., & Rousseau, E. W. (1981). Meta-analysis of experimental research on teacher questioning behavior. *Review of Educational Research, 51*(2), 237–246.

Reynolds, A. J., & Walberg, H. J. (1992). A process model of mathematics achievement and attitude. *Journal for Research in Mathematics Education, 23*(4), 306–328.

Rogers, C. R. (1969). *Freedom to learn.* Columbus, OH: Merrill.

Rosenshine, B. (1987). Explicit teaching and teacher training. *Journal of Teacher Education, 38*(3), 34–36.

Rosenshine, B. & Meister, C. (1994). Reciprocal teaching: A review of the research. *Review of Educational Research, 64*(4), 479–530.

Rowe, M. B. (1986). Wait time: Slowing down may be a way of speeding up! *Journal of Teacher Education, 37*(1), 43–50.

Russell, T., Munby, H., Spafford, C., & Johnston, P. (1990). Learning the professional knowledge of teaching: Metaphors, puzzles, and the theory-practice relationship. In P. P. Grimmett & G. L. Erickson (Eds.). *Reflection in teacher education* (pp. 67–90). New York: Teachers College Press.

Ryan, K. (1970). *Don't smile until Christmas.* Chicago: University of Chicago Press.

Sadker, M., Sadker, D., & Klein, S. (1991). The issue of gender in elementary and secondary education. In G. Grant (Ed.), *Review of research in education* (pp. 269–334). Washington, DC: American Educational Research Association.

Showers, B. & Joyce, B. (March 1996). The evolution of peer coaching. *Educational Leadership, 53*(6), 12–16.

Shulman, L. E. (1986). Paradigms and research programs in the study of teaching. In M. C. Wittrock (Ed.), *Handbook of research on teaching* (p. 12). New York: Macmillan.

Shulman, L. E. (1987). Knowledge and teaching: Foundations of the new reform. *Harvard Educational Review, 57*(1), 1–22.

Smith, H. (1981). Nonverbal communication in teaching. *Review of Educational Research, 49*(4), 631–672.

Tobin, K. (1986). Effects of teacher wait time on discourse characteristics in mathematics and language arts classes. *American Educational Research Journal, 23*(2), 191–200.

Walberg, H. J. (1986). Synthesis of research on teaching. In M. C. Wittrock (Ed.), *Handbook of research on teaching* (pp. 214–229). New York: Macmillan.

Walberg, H. J. (1988). Synthesis of research on time and learning. *Educational Leadership, 45*(6), 76–81.

Walberg, H. J. (1990). Productive teaching and instruction: Assessing the knowledge base. *Phi Delta Kappan,* 470–478.

Wang, M. C., Haertel, G. D., & Walberg, H. J. (1993). Toward a knowledge base for school learning. *Review of Educational Research, 63*(3), 249–294.

Webb, N. M., & Palinscar, A. S. (1996). Group processes in the classroom. In D. C. Berliner & R. C. Calfee (Eds.) *Handbook of Educational Psychology,* 841–873. New York: Simon & Schuster Macmillan.

Woolfolk, A. H., & Brooks, D. M. (1983). Nonverbal communication in teaching. *Review of Research in Education, 10,* 103–150.

13

TEACHING OBJECTIVES

Sooner or later all those involved in the educational enterprise confront the question of teaching objectives. What is the point and purpose of the curriculum content? Is it content mastery, or academic skills acquisition? Is it personal growth? Or are attitudes, beliefs, and dispositions the ultimate purpose? The basic problem involves examining the question, education for what? And, as you may have guessed, there are as many proposed purposes as there are questions. In this chapter we will discuss the problem in a global sense, and then outline a framework that provides significant guidance for the choices that teachers face.

We will also present information on the general principles involved in lesson planning. Such planning can become an important vehicle for attaining specified objectives.

OBJECTIVES: THE PROBLEM OF WHAT TO TEACH

What objectives do we want to achieve in teaching anybody anything? Years ago this very question was given perhaps its best portrayal in *The Saber-Tooth Curriculum,* a book written under the pen name of J. Abner Peddiwell. It was a spoof, but it made its point most dramatically and effectively. In Paleolithic times a tribe developed an educational curriculum based on survival needs. The young were taught how to scare away saber-toothed tigers with firebrands, how to club woolly horses for clothing, and how to fish with their hands. However, as time passed and the Ice Age began, the survival needs changed: The tigers caught cold and died, the woolly horses ran away, and the fish disappeared in muddy water. In their places came big, ferocious bears that weren't scared by firebrands, a herd of antelope that could run like the wind (the woolly horses had been slow and clumsy), and new fish that hid in the muddy water. It soon occurred to the tribe that their educational curriculum was, in today's parlance, not relevant. Scaring tigers, clubbing horses, and catching fish by hand were relics of the old days. The tribe now needed to learn how to trap bears, snare antelopes, and make fishnets. However, the "educational establishment" of the tribe declared in august tones:

> Don't be foolish . . . We don't teach fish-grabbing to grab fish; we teach it to develop a generalized agility which can never be developed by mere training (in net-making). We don't teach horse-clubbing to club horses; we teach it to develop a generalized strength in the learner which he can never get from so prosaic and specialized a thing as antelope-snare setting. We don't teach tiger-scaring to scare tigers; we teach it for the purpose of giving that noble courage . . . (Peddiwell, 1939, pp. 42–43).

The debate on educational objectives has a long history. The controversy usually covers the same terrain; namely, advocates of teaching skills for survival are in opposition to those who would teach for intrinsic and general education. Each side has some merit. We certainly do need to learn survival skills, but if that is all we learn, it is obvious that our skills are destined to become obsolete. Critics compare this approach to training a generation of dinosaurs—animals that, because of their inability to adapt to changing times, were unable to survive.

In addition to the criticism of the time-limited nature of specific skill training, a second aspect is almost always raised by critics of the skills-for-survival curriculum. Memorizing facts and mastering information generally have almost no long-term effects. In a series of classic studies conducted in the 1930s, Ralph Tyler demonstrated quite clearly that pupils unlearn almost as fast as they learn. He studied the amount of content retained. After one year the pupils "forgot" almost 50 percent of the content taught. The figure shot up to 80 percent after two years. As an aside, he ironically noted that most pupils in this country in the 1930s thought that all banks paid 6 percent compound interest, since that was the figure commonly used in arithmetic word problems (Tyler, 1933). So much for the argument that the goals of education should be to inculcate specific skills and content! When Jean Piaget said that "to know by heart is not really to know," he neatly summarized the fundamental flaw in this educational goal.

However, proponents of learning for its own sake claim that a "classical education" will train the mind for disciplined thought. Mind training can never become obsolete, because skills we have developed can be brought to bear on any problem we meet in life. However, as you may recall from Chapter 1, E. L. Thorndike conducted a series of studies showing that the theory of mind training through the study of Greek and Latin was false. Such learning could not be generalized. Such a classical general education for the disciplining of the mind seemed as nebulous a goal as memorizing specific concrete skills.

What should the goals of education be?

EDUCATIONAL GOALS: BLOOM'S TAXONOMY

Education has always been unable to decide between those who advocate a curriculum of relevance and those who desire a program of general education. In the mid-1950s, a team led by Benjamin S. Bloom of the University of Chicago bravely decided to settle the matter once and for all, and developed the now famous taxonomy, or classification, of educational objectives (Bloom, 1956).

Bloom felt that one of the major difficulties confronting anyone interested in education was the definition of goals, that is, what we want to strive for as teachers, counselors, or educational administrators. If you ask any of your friends to define their goals as teachers, you are likely to receive either an impossibly abstract statement ("I want to help students realize their full potential as individuals—to become self-actualizing") or some very explicit and narrow statement ("My job is to teach the multiplication tables").

Bloom examined this problem of considering educational objectives from either an impossibly cosmic or hopelessly trivial point of view. He came up with a scheme that classifies educational objectives and relates each objective to specific classroom procedures. Bloom's approach can be helpful in that it initially forces teachers to specify their goals and the means of getting there; it fits procedures and materials to instructional strategies. Bloom's system also specifies a sequence of six stages or levels of objectives that are matched to a sequence of assessment strategies. We will describe each level of his system by defining its content and briefly discussing its associated assessment procedures.

Level One: Basic Knowledge

Definition   Students are responsible for information, ideas, material, or phenomena. They have to know specific facts, terms, and methods.

Assessment   Direct questions and multiple-choice tests are applicable. The object is to test the students' ability to recall the facts, to identify and repeat the information provided. The teacher doesn't ask the students to form new judgments or to analyze ideas; he or she simply tries to find out how much material they can recall.

Level Two: Comprehension

Definition   Students must show they understand the material, ideas, facts, and theories.

Assessment   A variety of procedures are applicable. Students can restate the material in their own words, reorder or extrapolate ideas, predict or estimate. In other words, at this level students are assessed on the basis of their capacity to act upon, or process, information. Assessment at this level requires more activity from the pupils than assessment at level one. Objective or multiple-choice questions can still be used, but they would be of a different order, since they must provide evidence that the pupils have some understanding or comprehension of what they are saying.

Level Three: Application

Definition Students must be able to apply their knowledge to real situations. At level two we are satisfied if they understand the ideas. At level three we want them to demonstrate that they can actually apply their ideas correctly.

This particular level has been one of the stumbling blocks of educational psychology itself. In Chapter 1 we raised the question of why, after 50 years, the mode of classroom teaching has changed so little. We also cited the research showing the predominance of what we called trivia in the classroom. Educational psychology, as a field, contains much basic knowledge (level one) and understands much of it (level two) but has been unable to apply the ideas to real situations (level three). The application of knowledge is critical because it means putting knowledge into action, rather than merely talking about what might be done.

Assessment We have to go well beyond the usual procedures in order to assess how well students apply what they learn. If, for example, we are teaching them to play volleyball, the test would be obvious: Put them on either side of a net and evaluate their performance. It is easy to see whether children can apply their knowledge of addition or subtraction: Just give them some money, have them "buy" things in a mock store, and see if they end up with the correct change. In geometry, have them construct a right-angled triangle out of wood and then measure the length of each side. In physics, children can wire a bell and see whether or not it will ring. However, the one drawback to tests of this sort is the possibility that pupils may learn by rote how to apply the information. The teacher needs to be aware of this possibility and to vary application tests to ensure that pupils can genuinely put their knowledge into practice.

Level Four: Analysis:

Definition Analysis is essentially a more advanced aspect of level two (comprehension). Analysis requires that pupils classify or break material down into its components, understand the relation-ship among the components, and recognize the principle that organizes the structure or the system. (As you can see, it becomes increasingly difficult to describe the levels as we move from the simple and the concrete to the complex and abstract.)

Assessment The ability to analyze material can be assessed in a number of ways. For example, we might see whether students can identify the assumptions behind an argument or a debate. Thus, an advocate of the use of preventive nuclear war might argue that "in times of extreme danger, with national survival at stake, a country has to defend itself by striking at and destroying the enemy before the enemy attacks it." Students would be asked to identify the assumption from which this person's argument is constructed. In order to analyze the statement, students would have to ask some of the following questions: How extreme is the danger? Does the end (survival) justify the means (a nuclear war)? In everyday language, this kind of analysis is called *critical thinking*. Critical thinking allows us to separate fact from opinion and to compare theories so that we can take a position based on logic. Piaget's stage of formal operations involves just this kind of logical thinking.

Level Five: Objective Synthesis

Definition The educational objective at level five is to learn to synthesize material. This means making something new, bringing ideas together to form a new theory, going beyond what is now known, providing new insights. This is a tall order, since it means guiding pupils beyond our own level of understanding to help them create new ideas for themselves, and perhaps outgrow ours!

Assessment Assessment should be designed to produce new ideas, methods, or procedures. Some obvious examples might be writing an original short story, play, or poem; painting a picture; composing music. In other areas, term papers or essays might be vehicles for synthesis. Unfortunately, it is often difficult to judge whether an essay or term paper is a genuine synthesis, one that is indeed a novel or creative approach to a topic. Creativity itself is a highly subjective matter and very difficult to measure. You might just see whether or not you find yourself saying, "Now, why didn't I think of that?" One of the major rewards of teaching comes when we realize that one of our pupils is breaking new ground, advancing our knowledge.

Level Six: Objective Evaluation

Definition   Level six, the learning of value judgments, involves all the previous levels to some degree. Pupils are developing the ability to create standards of judgment, to weigh, to examine, to analyze, and most of all, to avoid hasty judgment. Evaluation requires a lengthy process of scholarly care, of minute examination.

Assessment   Although it may sound circular, it is possible to evaluate evaluation—there are standards for judging the way others pass judgments. For example, we can judge the performance of an umpire at a baseball game (the fans, managers, and players do so all the time). In the same way we can judge the performance of a trial judge or a labor arbitrator or a newspaper editor. It is possible, but it is also difficult.

The basic principle of assessment at level six, then, consists of developing critical evaluation skills. Essay exams, especially at the college level, often ask for a critique of a particular theory, literary work, or historical interpretation. To do this successfully students need a comprehensive, logical framework as a basis for judgment. In writing such an essay they provide a sequence of reasons extensively spelled out so that the reader can follow a train of thought each step of the way to the conclusion. Thus, the judgment cannot remain intuitive. To say that a painting by a master such as Picasso is great because it makes you feel more deeply is not an adequate basis for your conclusion. In a critique you must consciously describe the standards you use for such a judgment call.

Table 13.1 summarizes the different Bloom levels and provides examples of questions that best reflect each level. Critics of Bloom's notion of a hierarchy of levels of thinking want to leave it up to the teacher to determine the difficulty or intellectual challenge of the task, and not depend solely on the form of the question (Schrag, 1989). Of course, we agree that at all levels teachers need to be thinking as well about students' prior knowledge, the materials accessible to students to answer the questions, and the responses desired from students.

Taxonomy and Developmental Stages

Although Bloom and his associates did not directly connect their objectives to developmental and Piagetian cognitive stages, there is an implicit relationship. Bloom's levels one, two, and three—basic knowledge and facts, comprehension, and application—are all clearly within the grasp of concrete thinkers. When we reach levels four, five, and six, we are moving toward the need for symbolic and logical thinking in Piaget's formal-operations sense. As you read the descriptions of the style of thinking required at these levels, you realize the importance of a careful instructional sequence to promote the growth of abstract thinking. We cannot assume that adolescents are automatically able to use formal operations at Bloom's levels four to six without deliberate teaching that is aimed at this objective.

EDUCATIONAL OBJECTIVES AND DEVELOPMENTAL STAGES

David Hunt: Conceptual Stages

The work of **David Hunt** represents a more direct connection between educational objectives and developmental stages. Hunt has been able to specify the interaction between the conceptual level of the pupils and the expectations, learning atmospheres, and conceptual level of the teachers. We have stressed throughout this text that a developmental approach to education means that we have to look both ways, so to speak: at the pupils and their levels of development, and at the teachers. Hunt suggests that if it is important to assess the levels of the pupils, it is equally important to assess the levels of the teachers (and, as we will note later, the level of the curriculum material itself). Thus, Hunt (1974) presents a three-stage framework for educational objectives and instructional strategies.

Conceptual level proceeds through three general stages.

Stage A: Low conceptual level   Generally, thinking is concrete and stereotyped. There is a single "right" way to learn. Rules are fixed and unchangeable. Obedience to authority is unquestioned. Problemsolving tends to be rigid. Social desirability and pleasing others are strong motivations. Students are anxious for closure and seek highly structured learning activities.

Stage B: Moderate conceptual level   Students exhibit some evidence of toleration for uncertainty and ambiguity and awareness of alternatives. There is some openness to new ideas, increased independence in thinking (inner-directedness), awareness of emotions, and increased inductive inquiry.

TABLE 13.1   BLOOM'S TAXONOMY: KEYING QUESTIONS TO LEVELS

BLOOM LEVEL	QUESTIONS
Level One—Factual knowledge: Questions require factual recall of material.	How much is . . . Who is . . . What is . . . When was . . . How did . . .
Level Two—Comprehension: Questions require the student to think more broadly, to show more in-depth understanding, to explain using his or her own words.	Demonstrate the meaning of . . . Paraphrase, in your own words, . . . Give an example . . . How are these ideas similar to . . . Explain the meaning of (the story, a graph, etc.). . .
Level Three—Application: Questions ask the student to apply learning to a new situation or to develop a product.	What would happen if . . . Apply the formula to the following problem . . . Teach your friend the meaning of . . . Using your knowledge of angles, build a toothpick tower . . . Using the story as a basis, write . . .
Level Four—Analysis: Questions are designed to ask the student to take the material apart and examine the pieces.	How are _____ the same, and how are they different? List the basic assumptions . . . Describe the variety of motives . . . Distinguish between theory and facts . . . Separate the major and minor themes . . .
Level Five—Synthesis: Questions attempt to get the student to go beyond our present knowledge.	Describe the three major theories, and show how they may be combined . . . Write an essay proposing a new solution to the problem of . . . Write a play (paint a picture, do a musical score, construct a formula, etc.) that best illustrates a new way to understand . . .
Level Six—Evaluation: Questions are designed to require the student to evaluate ideas according to an explicit and detailed set of reasons. The system of judgment employed must be clearly explained.	Write a careful critique of _____ theory. Detail the strengths and weaknesses. Justify your conclusion. Evaluate the recent decisions by _____, according to democratic versus expedient principles. Compare and contrast the approaches to _____ according to the following ethical principles . . . Detail the logical inconsistencies in theory X as an example of an inadequate scientific paradigm.

Stage C: High conceptual level   Students exhibit evidence of integration and synthesis in complex intellectual and interpersonal arenas. They weigh and balance alternatives and can simultaneously process their own view and those of others. Closure is temporary. Students employ successive approximation and principles in decisionmaking, and they will not compromise those. They accept full responsibility for the consequences of their own behavior.

Young children tend to think very concretely (stage A) and need careful and explicit directions. Pupil "growth" proceeds in a developmental sequence from concrete to abstract, from simple to

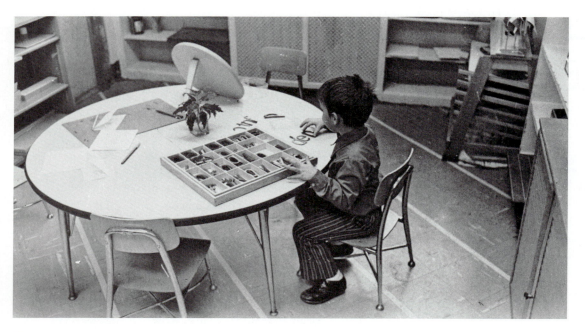

Young children tend to think concretely.

complex, and from being dependent on others toward self-direction. Most important, Hunt shows that such developmental growth does depend on how the teacher structures the learning experiences. To facilitate the pupils' achieving increased levels of intellectual complexity, teachers need to match the learning tasks with the actual developmental functioning of the pupils. Thus, for stage A pupils, teachers need to provide high structure, explicit assignments, frequent feedback, and consistent and concrete rewards. For stage C pupils, of course, a significantly different environment, characterized by low structure, substantial freedom for pupils to develop their own assignments, less frequent feedback, and more abstract and intrinsic rewards, would be required.

Attribute-Treatment Interaction

The idea of matching teaching goals and methods to pupils' level of development is called the **attribute-** (or aptitude-)**treatment interaction (ATI)** model. The current system of thinking (a pupil's attribute) interacts with the teaching method (the treatment). The outcome of the experience, then, does not result from one or the other by itself. In a sense, what this means is that no generic teaching methods can be ap-

plied across the board. Some pupils learn more material and develop positive attitudes with one particular method, while other pupils do better with a different method. In this model, neither teaching nor learning is a one-way transaction. This also explains why a teacher-proof or pupil-proof curriculum is impossible. The experiments with specified national curricula content and methods in the 1960s showed the inadequacy of the single-mode approach. However, where attribute and treatment meet and match, the interaction determines the end result.

To illustrate the different effects of a learning environment and pupils' conceptual level (CL), Hunt demonstrated some aspects of variation. Figures 13.1 and 13.2 indicate that learning outcomes vary, especially for low-CL pupils. Both figures show that stage A pupils understand learning material in significantly greater amounts when teachers employ advance organizers and the rule-example-rule sequence. Stage C pupils, in contrast, learn best under methods using **low structure** (examples only) and discovery. They also comprehend under high structure, but composite concept learning declines under the rule-example-rule sequence. Also—and this doesn't show in either of the figures—the stage C pupils are less motivated under either condition of **high structure.** Thus, according to Hunt, the teacher employs variable structure in order to achieve sig-

FIGURE 13.1 Integration and comprehension of academic content.

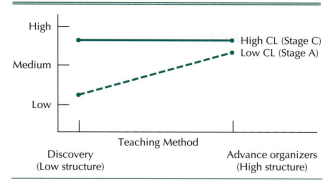

nificant educational objectives. He uses the term **accessibility channels** to denote the meaning of developmental stages. The teacher tunes up the material and method in accordance with the different channels the pupils prefer to use.

Some students need a great deal of structure, concrete directions, immediate feedback, and so on; others don't (Hunt, 1981). Table 13.2 summarizes some of the main differences according to the stage of development of the pupil. With pupils at the concrete level of cognitive functioning (low conceptual level), a systematic sequence carefully directed by the teacher is appropriate. With pupils at a less concrete and more abstract level, a more interdependent approach is appropriate.

When ATI was first proposed by Hunt, the research base was thin (Cronbach & Snow, 1977). However, more recent research, especially that of Penelope Peterson and her associates at the University of Wisconsin and Michigan State University, has provided a solid basis for Hunt's view. In a number of classroom investigations Peterson found a definite trend of interaction between pupil characteristics (such as different levels of ability, levels of anxiety, and attitude) and teaching method (Peterson et al., 1980; Levin & Peterson, 1984; Peterson et al., 1989). She also found an interaction between pupil attributes and the kind of examination employed.

Thus, the whole approach to teaching effectiveness and educational goals needs to include the concept of ATI. A single approach to teaching is obviously not justified. For pupils of high ability, low anxiety, and positive attitudes, an approach more consistent with small-group instruction, open-ended questioning, and greater student initiative is called for. The opposite is true for those of lower ability, greater anxiety, and less positive attitudes. Such pupils much prefer a more highly structured and teacher-directed method. Although her work did not explicitly employ Hunt's conceptual-stage assessment of pupils' attributes or characteristics, Peterson's research (1988) does support the general ATI model.

The most comprehensive review specifically of the Hunt model was conducted by Alan Miller (1981). Like Peterson, he examined different teaching methods, particularly variation in levels of structure, as the "treatment." His measure of aptitude, however, was a direct assessment of the students' stage of conceptual development; thus, his summary provides more direct support for the ATI theory. Basically, his conclusions are similar to Peterson's. Pupils who process information and experience at a more advanced conceptual level prefer greater involvement in learning, more exploratory "indirect" teaching, and participation in discussions; they can resist premature closure (or coming to a conclusion) in problemsolving. However, such an open-ended or low-structured approach does not foster learning with pupils who are at a less advanced conceptual level.

At the college level the importance of varying the structure according to the cognitive-developmental level of the student was demonstrated by Widick and Simpson (1978). Concrete "dualist" college students required all the elements outlined in column 2 of Table 13.2. Students operating on a more abstract level benefited from open-ended inquiry. (More support for varying the structure according to the cognitive-development stages of the student is found in Chickering, 1981.)

David Lohman's work supports both the Hunt position and the work of Penelope Peterson. In synthesizing all the research, he concludes that "more able, older, and less anxious students may better profit from less externally structured activities

FIGURE 13.2 Composite concept learning.

TABLE 13.2 DIFFERENTIATION OF STRUCTURE

FACTORS	HIGH STRUCTURE	LOW STRUCTURE
Concepts	Concrete	Abstract
Time span	Short	Long
Time on task	Multiple practice	Single practice
Advance organizers	Multiple use of organizers	Few if any advance organizers
Complexity of learning tasks	Learning tasks divided into small steps and recycled	Learning tasks clustered into "wholes"
Theory	Concretely matched with experiential examples	Generalized, including collaborative classroom research
Instructor support	Consistent and frequent	Occasional

such as discussion groups and guided discovery learning episodes" (Lohman, 1986). These findings have been supported by the work of Mayer (1988), who found that thinking skills need to be closely related to specific subject matter. He also found that high-CL students do not benefit from the high-structure approach employed in the study. The low-CL students, however, not only improved their comprehension but also could transfer the new learning strategies to other situations. Snow, Corno, and Jackson (1996) suggest that using Hunt's approach may bring teacher decisionmaking about teaching strategies back to the centerstage of teaching, especially at a time when there are many external teaching styles being imposed on teachers. Teachers' own sense of their classrooms and their determination of the high-CL or low-CL of their students need to be given greater priority. Teachers can choose appropriate low or high structure teaching strategies to match students' CL levels and, consequently, do not have to rely on only one teaching strategy for all students.

Matching or Mismatching: The Art of Teaching

As we indicated in the opening chapter, the goals of education almost always include a reference to enhancing human development. Indeed, a developmental view clearly suggests growth as an outcome. If we view the ATI model from this perspective, then an immediate question arises. Suppose we match teaching methods to the pupils' conceptual level and the short-term outcome is improved academic achievement and positive attitudes. Does this **matching** aid the process of growth? Or does such a match

keep a pupil in place, so to speak? Particularly for students who enter your class with low-CL styles, wouldn't the continued use of a high-structured approach rob them of initiative? Wouldn't there also be times when even high-CL students would need a more directive approach? In answering such questions, there are two important points to keep in mind: how CL is defined and how growth can be encouraged.

The initial preferred style   In the first place CL refers to the **current preferred style of learning;** it is not a permanent classification. In Chapter 5 we indicated that Piaget described learning as a process of equilibrium, balancing the old (assimilation) and the new (accommodation). At any stage of development, we use a relatively coherent system to maintain consistency, or a steady state of equilibrium. Even when "knowledge disturbances" occur (recall the boy who was trying to reconcile his idea of church with a building that looked like a house), we try to maintain our present system. This is what we mean by a preferred method. We are used to thinking and problem solving in particular modes. These modes work best when matched with appropriate learning environments. To match pupils' preferred style of learning, then, is another way to say, "Start where the learner is." This also means starting with and accepting the pupils' current methods of problemsolving—starting with how they think, not what they think. Hence, the first rule from ATI is to match, or start teaching in concert with, the pupils' level of development.

Graduated mismatching   The second principle is **mismatching**—the process of shifting to a slightly more complex level of teaching in order to help the student develop. Recall that students have a potential or an intrinsic drive to learn, as Robert W. White and others have shown us. However, they will not shift quickly or suddenly to higher levels of conceptual development. Remember how long it took the boy to accommodate to the new concept of church, and that was a relatively simple "new" learning. You need to be prepared to present and review new material in a recycled manner, listening carefully to your students' questions. In this way you will understand who is "getting it" (accommodating to the new material and methods) and who needs further experience at his or her current level.

Another way to view the problem of matching and then mismatching is to recall Kohlberg's research on modal stage plus one, discussed in Chapter 7. In moral-dilemma discussions, leaders found that under relaxed conditions (a nonpunitive atmosphere) pupils would gradually understand and support reasoning just slightly ahead of their current preferred mode. The slightly higher level of complexity creates a kind of knowledge disturbance, or dissonance. In resolving the dissonance, the pupils end up with a more complex level of thinking; in other words, they experience developmental growth. So we can answer the first part of the earlier question: In dealing with pupils whose current conceptual levels and styles are low, the teaching strategy is to match the low level with high structure and very gradually shift. What about other students, those further along? Do we just stick with the low-structure approach? Not quite—and we'll describe why.

Two qualifications   Certainly, the general rule with students who function at more complex levels would be to use less structure, more participation, more discovery, and so on. However, there are two important qualifications. First, development varies according to domain. A particular student may be an advanced thinker-reasoner in one area, yet not in another. When we discussed Piaget's stages of cognitive growth, we cited examples of adults not always thinking like adults. An advanced thinker in history or agronomy may be at a more concrete level in statistics, art, or music. Variations also exist within any subject matter. In psychology some students may quickly understand a variety of theories of personality at an abstract level yet have problems understanding, say, physiological or experimental psychology. So even with so-called more advanced students, you may have to deviate from the general rule of low structure in your teaching because of systematic gaps in students' understanding of different subjects as well as different topics within one subject.

When you discover such gaps, it's a sign to shift the teaching to higher structure and more direct instruction.

The second qualification has to do with pupil anxiety. Under stress, many students will lower their preferred style of solving problems. This is certainly understandable when we realize that when stress is too high, humans tend to narrow their perceptual field; that is, they screen out more and more information and experience. An extreme example is the story of a victim being quizzed by detectives immediately following an armed robbery. "All I saw was the barrel of the gun pointed at my face," he said when asked to describe the assailant. Of course, a classroom should never be quite that stressful. Yet in introducing new material and/or new learning strategies, pupils can be quite anxious. In specific cases, such as students who face excessive parental pressure for achievement, the anxiety level may be even higher. Under such conditions it is highly appropriate to shift modes and provide more advance organizers, more explicit directions, and quicker feedback.

One final point: Anxiety can also be quite high during specific developmental transitions. In other words, changes taking place within the pupil can be as anxiety producing as any changes you make in the teaching material and problemsolving work. In discussing Erik Erikson's work (Chapter 6), we noted particular psychological-personal milestones of development. During each of these transition stages of personal growth, anxiety tends to be higher than usual. The most obvious example is puberty, accompanied by egocentrism, the personal fable, and the magical audience. Yet starting the first grade, leaving home, and shifting to the stage of mastery is also an important transition with its own anxieties, the "little worries" common to children. Certainly the same is true for entrance to high school and to college. Resorting to a more structured approach to teaching at such times is simply another way to start where the learner is. You will soon be able to move to a more open-ended approach, especially as the anxiety from the personal transition subsides and the student becomes better accommodated to the new level of psychological maturity.

To summarize, then, the general rule of using a low-structure approach with abstract thinkers has some important qualifications: (1) There is variation across and within academic subject matter; pupils may not excel in all areas. (2) Pupils may experience high levels of anxiety when confronted with new material and/or when going through transitions in personal growth. In any of these situations, switching to higher structure in teaching will not impede pupils' growth. You need not worry that you are robbing students of their chance for initiative by more adequately matching your method to their temporary need for more structure. Instead, you are more likely to find that students experience a sense of relief. They can get back on the learning track and then resume their growth toward a more complex mode.

In an overall sense, then, the ATI model, by suggesting flexibility in teaching mode, helps you avoid two kinds of educational failure. First, you avoid the prospect of boring the students with a single "tried and true" teaching method. Second, you avoid the problem of either overmatching or undermatching. Overmatching, on the one hand, is teaching at a level well beyond the pupils' current preferred mode, such as expecting fourth-grade children to understand the symbolic meaning of Ahab and the white whale in *Moby Dick* or succumbing to the current fad of infant stimulation with flashcards for six-month-old babies. Undermatching, on the other hand, presents not "plus one" but "minus one" material to students: ideas and problems they already know and techniques that require "old" learning methods. Asking students to memorize long lists of material when they should be learning to draw inferences is an example of undermatching. With either over-matching or undermatching, growth is not an outcome. Effective teaching from an ATI perspective requires a quite different approach, one that is more responsive to pupils' needs and is more likely to nurture their growth and achieve the general educational goals of Bloom's taxonomy.

Mary Belenky, Blythe Clinchy, Nancy Goldberger, and Jill Tarule: Educational Objectives and Connected Teaching

Belenky, Clinchy, Goldberger, and Tarule focused on possible differences as well as similarities in the cognitive processes of men and women. These researchers chose to study women's experience because the traditional research in ways of thinking had most often focused on men (see, for example, William Perry's original study, 1970). Their study *Women's Ways of Knowing* (1986) has helped us understand women's developing ability to speak up and speak out. The importance of being involved and active in the learning process emerges as central to development.

The four researchers were knowledgeable and well versed in the research on cognitive processes and intellectual development and also in the emerging work in psychology of women. Their research analysis presents a progression of five perspectives that women used to view reality, organize their thinking, and draw conclusions. These five perspectives are: silence, received knowing, subjective knowing, procedural knowing, and constructed knowing. They are ways of knowing that women have learned to cultivate and value. *Voice* is used as a metaphor that applies to all aspects of women's experiences; it represents the intertwined development of a sense of voice, mind, and self.

What kind of structure would Hunt recommend for each of the five ways-of-knowing perspectives? The first perspectives include characteristics of low conceptual level, while the later perspectives include characteristics of higher conceptual level. Note that connected teaching practices can match all levels to ease anxiety, improve attitudes, and enhance learning, especially for women students. Do you think connected teaching practices should be limited only to women students? Are the five ways of knowing limited only to females?

Silence   Some individuals live in silence with "extreme denial of self and . . . dependence on external authority for direction" (Belenky et al., 1986, p. 24). The individual feels powerless. Silence connotes not being able to speak. Words of others are heard as weapons that diminish the self. From this first perspective it is not possible for the individual to express thoughts or feelings. Both Belenky and Goldberger are currently focusing on the characteristics of this position of silence. Belenky is founder of the Listening Partners Program, in Marshfield, Vermont. This program focuses on how poor, marginalized women can be empowered to gain a public voice without abandoning the standpoint, language, and values of women engaged in mothering. Goldberger is on the faculty of psychology at the Fielding Institute. She is focusing on gender, race, class, and power; she is also investigating silence as an imposed burden—the process of "being silenced" as contrasted with a person's "choosing of silence" in specific situations, even though one had developed a public voice earlier. For further discussion, see Goldberger et al. (1996).

Received knowledge   In this second perspective, knowing comes from listening to others who are the authorities. Knowledge comes from outside the self. It is a view of the world that is concrete and dualistic, right or wrong, black or white. Facts are to be memorized and regurgitated. The received knower believes it is beyond one's capacity to create one's own knowledge. Feelings of low self-esteem and lack of originality prevail. The individual at this position accumulates facts, and the words of others become one's own.

Subjective knowledge   At the third perspective a major change in knowing occurs. Power is recognized as coming from within the self. The source of knowing now comes from one's own personal experience. The subjective knower begins to listen to her inner voice, and, as it comes alive, she becomes her own authority. Her gut feelings seem infallible. The awareness of other people's experiences rests with the right of others to have an opinion, too. The trust in an outside authority is lost.

Procedural knowledge   The fourth perspective marks another shift. Here the self actively listens and carefully speaks after observing and evaluating various perspectives. The voice of reason permeates one's attitudes about authority, the world, and oneself. Reason coupled with intuition and feeling predominates. Two categories evolve at this position, separate and connected knowing. The separate way of knowing functions under standard rules and conventions of rational thought, and the separate procedural knower is more concerned with principles and critical thinking procedures. In the connected way of knowing, knowledge and reason are gained through personal experience and relationships, caring, empathy, and patience.

Constructed knowledge   At the fifth perspective speaking and listening are used equally in active dialogue with others. Knowledge is constructed by persons who experience each other as equals. Here one "finds a place for reason and intuition and the expertise of others" (Belenky et al., 1986, p. 133). The individual is aware that truth is based on the context in which it is embedded. It is one's frame of reference that directs one's knowledge and understanding. Constructed knowers are able to weave together reason and emotion, the objective and the subjective.

Connected teaching for knowledge construction
In traditional education, the student tries to look at the material through the teacher's eyes. In contrast, the data from women's experience describes the connected teacher who "receives and accepts the student's feelings toward the subject matter, looking at the subject matter and listening to it through the student's eyes and ears" (Noddings, 1984, p. 177). In **connected teaching** the student is treated from the start not as a subordinate but as a colearner whose

Recent research indicates that for most women meaningful learning of abstract concepts is enhanced if the concepts to be learned are somehow connected to their own personal experiences.

opinions are valued. Throughout *Women's Way of Knowing,* the interviews demonstrate the importance of "connected education." Teaching practices that foster connected knowing are described in the Spotlight on Connected Teaching. Individuals value personal individual experience; nurture each other's thoughts to maturity; construct truth through consensus, not conflict; bridge private and shared experience; accord respect for each other's unique perspectives; and base authority on cooperation, not subordination.

Connected knowing comes from personal experience and is grounded in the personal and the particular. Separate knowing refers to reasoning in which there is distance between the knower and the object. It can be argued, of course, that students need models of impeccable reasoning and that it is through imitating such models that students learn to reason. But none of the women interviewed named this sort of learning as a powerful experience in their own lives. Instead, students need models that show thinking as a human, imperfect, but attainable activity.

The dominant pedagogy in education is based on separate knowing and direct teaching; however,

SPOTLIGHT ON CONNECTED TEACHING

Connected teaching outlines an educational context constructed from interviews with 135 women as they described important learning experiences. Presented here are some of the key phrases that distinguish the practices of connected versus separate teaching.

1. *Incorporating personal individual experience:* Connected learning is based on personal individual experience while acknowledging existing uncertainties. It is strongly influenced by the Deweyan notion of significant experience followed by self-reflection and discussion. Connected teaching accords respect to and allows time for the understanding that emerges from firsthand experience.

2. *Nurturing each other's thoughts to maturity*: The connected classroom provides a culture for growth—a "yogurt" kind of class. It is something like the actors' studios where dialogue and plot are created as a scene progresses; it is not like a movie theater where people are mere spectators. The connected teacher tries to create groups in which members can nurture one another's thoughts to maturity. Sometimes these take the form of triads or working small groups. In a connected class no one apologizes for uncertainty. It is assumed that evolving thought will be tentative.

3. *Constructing truth through consensus, not conflict:* The connected class constructs truth not through conflict but through consensus, defined as a feeling or sensing together.

4. *Bridging private and shared experience:* Consensus implies not necessarily agreement, but a crossing of the barrier between one person and another, which can also be described as bridging private and shared experience.

5. *Respecting each other's unique perspectives:* Connected teachers welcome diversity of opinion in class discussion. Teachers and students collaborate in constructing a new interpretation. In a connected class, like a community, people get to know one another. They do not act as representatives of positions or as occupants of roles but as individuals with particular styles of thinking.

6. *Basing teacher's authority on cooperation, not subordination:* Connected teachers are careful not to abandon themselves to their students' perspectives. A connected teacher is not just another student; the role carries special responsibilities. It does not entail power over the students; however, it does carry authority, an authority based not on subordination but on cooperation.

7. *Using participant observation methodologies:* A form of connected knowing used in investigations is called participant observation. Teachers participate with students in order to undergo experiences similar to those of the students. In this way teachers use their own reactions to formulate hypotheses about the students' reactions. A teacher trusts each student's experience, although as a person or a critic the teacher might not agree with it. To trust means not just to tolerate a variety of viewpoints, acting as an impartial referee. To trust means to try to connect, to enter into each student's perspective.

8. *Emphasizing belief over doubt:* Connected teachers are believers; they trust their students' thinking and encourage them to expand it. Yet an adversarial doubting model predominates much of education. Only a handful of the women interviewed described a powerful and positive learning experience in which a teacher aggressively challenged or doubted their notions. On the whole, women found the experience of being doubted debilitating rather than energizing.

9. *Midwife education versus banker concept of education:* Connected teachers educate through a problem-posing model. The connected teacher helps students articulate and expand their latent knowledge; more like a midwife teacher. Midwife teachers are the opposite of banker teachers. It seems that the banker concept of education is dominant today. Whereas the bankers deposit knowledge in the learner's head, the midwives draw it out. Connected teachers assist students in giving birth to their own ideas, in making their tacit knowledge explicit, and in elaborating it. They encourage students to use their knowledge in everyday life. Connected teachers use their own knowledge to put the students into conversations with other voices, past and present.

Belenky, M. F., Clinchy, B. M., Goldberger, N. R., & Tarule, J. M. (1986). *Women's Ways of Knowing* (chap. 10). New York: Basic Books.

many teachers do use connected teaching practices. Also, some research methodologies are more attuned to connected knowing than others, for example, collaborative action research, which will be discussed further in Chapter 14. Jill Mattuck Tarule, Dean of Education at the University of Vermont, is currently focusing on collaborative learning and its relationship to the characteristics of the position of "constructed knowledge."

The concepts of connected teaching enable us to further examine strategies that better match in an ATI framework the intellectual development needs of all students, and particularly women students. Connected teaching provides for the inclusion of life experiences. With connected teaching strategies, learning becomes more engaging. Blythe McVicker Clinchy, a professor at Wellesley College, is currently investigating the extent to which both men and women recognize and use their abilities for connected knowing when this epistemological perspective is explored in interviews. (See, for example, Clinchy, 1989.) We think that good teaching includes the flexibility to teach in the connected mode. The connected mode includes a number of the indirect teaching categories from Flanders, the characteristics of inquiry (Model Two), and interpersonal teaching (Model Three). The more traditional separate mode has more characteristics of direct teaching and Model One.

PLANNING: THE VEHICLE FOR EDUCATIONAL GOALS

So far in this chapter we have been stressing the need for a careful analysis of pupils' conceptual level as a basis for selecting particular modes or models of teaching. We have focused on the interaction between teaching as a process and the students' effort at drawing meaning from the teacher's strategies. There is, in addition to this ATI, another important part of teaching—namely, lesson planning. Sometimes it is best to think of planning as similar to drawing a road map. The purpose of the plan is to provide you with a sequence of routes or steps to follow as you teach the material. Naturally, there is no single best way to organize a lesson or unit in a plan. Research and practice have shown, however, that some basic steps are effective. These fundamental steps are components of a good plan; they are based on the work of **Madeline Hunter** (1984).

As you read through Hunter's model think about whether it is an example of high or low structure. Would low-CL students or high-CL students profit more from Hunter's model? Are some steps a more appropriate match for low-CL learners?

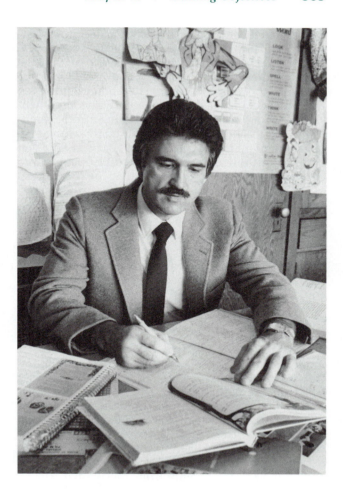

Careful lesson planning involves, among other things, starting with developmentally appropriate objectives.

Step one: Anticipatory set The first step is to increase the students' interest in and motivation to learn the material. It's an attempt to get the students to "lean toward" you with an orienting question. For example, in a high school unit on social studies, the teacher might say, "Today's topic will focus on the question of what the Native Americans experienced during the period of manifest destiny. Why do many Indians regard Thanksgiving as a national day of shame?" Hunter suggests a relatively brief yet somewhat provocative beginning to gain attention.

Step two: Objective and purpose The initial rhetorical question sets the stage. The teacher now moves to tell students what the point of the unit is and why it's important. This is particularly necessary for concrete thinkers, those at low to moderate conceptual levels. Surprising as it may seem, discussions with pupils at the end of a class often reveal rather poignantly that they completely missed the point of the lesson. Presenting the objective is no guarantee of comprehension. Hunter says, however, that you will increase the probability of comprehension by being quite explicit in spelling out the goals. Thus, the teacher who raised the Native American question might then explain, "The goal is to help you understand how differently a group of people in a country may interpret the meaning of a historical event. Most of us have been brought up to understand that Thanksgiving is a national holiday celebrating . . ." Hunter says you can reduce the ambiguity by describing the goals.

Step three: Input   Essentially, this is where you select and apply your specific teaching strategy. It could be a lecture (Model One), a small-group discovery (Model Two), an interpersonal discussion (Model Three), or a blend of direct and indirect methods. Teachers have often misinterpreted Hunter on this point and felt that they must use a direct model. Such is not the case. In fact, you need to decide (your best guess) which of a variety of models best suits the particular day, the material, and other available resources, including student presentations of information, filmstrips, video material, overheads, and even the blackboard. The idea is to select an input method that is keyed to the outcomes noted in step two. Thus, if your goal is to help students understand historical events from the Native Americans' point of view, you would not have them memorize long lists of tribes.

Once again it may seem obvious, but Hunter did find that one of the most common errors in teaching was the failure to link input with teaching objectives.

Step four: Modeling   Think of modeling as a demonstration accompanied by verbal description of what you want the students to do. Sometimes, for example, if the students are to work in small groups, you set a small group up in a "fish bowl" for a brief demonstration. If you want students to look up Latin roots in a dictionary, you might put a dictionary entry on an overhead and talk the class through the process. The point of modeling is to ensure that the students employ the process in a manner that facilitates their understanding of the input.

Step five: Checking for understanding   Hunter makes it clear that effective planning of lessons is interactive. Thus, some time should be set aside for questions to check student understanding. Every

once in a while a teacher is absolutely floored when the questions reveal how far off task a particular student is. Most students will not ask what may appear to be a "dumb" question. Your role is to maintain a class atmosphere supportive enough to encourage students who aren't sure to ask for help. You can increase the likelihood of students' feeling free to say that they do not know and to ask questions by using the strategies for connected teaching.

Step six: Guided practice   By this Hunter means that the students do the activity under your direct supervision. Guided practice precedes the last step, independent practice. Before you move to independent practice, either in class or as homework assignments, you should have the students perform some part of the task and show you their products. Suppose, for example, you are teaching a grammar unit on the period (the punctuation mark). Have the students practice writing a paragraph and then compare their work to an overhead with correct punctuation. The idea is simply to prevent too many errors from occurring before you set them free to work on their own. It is clearly easier to correct errors early than to allow a student to do an entire assignment incorrectly. Unlearning bad habits is always more difficult than learning the correct procedure at the outset.

Step seven: Independent practice   The final step, either as seatwork or homework, occurs when students work on the material alone or in small groups without your direct supervision. This is basically a test of the first six steps. If the process has been successful, then you will see evidence in the student products that they have learned the material. Remember that the outcome of this independent practice can be keyed to any level on the taxonomy from basic knowledge to synthesis and/or evaluation. You start by keying the outcomes of independent practice to students' current level of functioning, and then gradually increase the level of complexity. Such building on success encourages and motivates students each step of the way.

Criticisms of the Hunter approach   While there is general acceptance of the Hunter approach, there is continuing controversy about some aspects of step two (objective and purpose) and step four (modeling). The problem with step two arises from a concern about how much structure is appropriate. Do all students need to be told the point of the lesson in advance? We have seen in the ATI section that such explicit identification can reduce the possibility of inquiry-discovery. Students, especially the higher-CL thinkers, may find that such statements of objectives at the outset reduce their motivation as well as the excitement that goes with not quite knowing what to expect. After all, how engrossing would a Sherlock Holmes mystery be if we knew in advance . . . ?

The problem with step four is similar in kind. By modeling the steps involved in the learning activity, there is the possibility of reducing some student initiative in problemsolving. Remember that Lohman (1986) found that, on the one hand, the advanced thinkers in math actually learned less when taught through a concrete sequence. On the other hand, the careful stepwise sequence was helpful to the concrete thinkers. This means your modeling needs to be presented in a relativistic manner. You might say, "Many students have found this sequence helpful in solving the problem"; then present the model. Afterward, you can add, "You may decide to use all of these steps or you may use your own system." In either case, the test of effectiveness will come during the final phase of independent practice. The critical point, of course, is that a prescriptive model fits the needs of some learners but not all. For a more extensive discussion, criticism, and response to the Hunter method, see Gibboney (1987), followed by Hunter's response and Gibboney's reaction.

In Hunter's defense, we should add that at least part of the problem results from literal interpretations of her model. Her stepwise approach should never be applied every day, across the board. In her original article, she said it was a teaching decision whether to include or exclude each element. Variations were not only permitted but encouraged. The point was to examine the learning outcomes and to use them as a guide for choosing an approach.

NEW EDUCATIONAL GOALS FOR ALL: TEACHING FOR HIGHER-ORDER UNDERSTANDING

Partly as a result of the discouraging findings reported by national assessments of educational progress and partly as a result of the new demands for a highly literate work force presented by a postindustrial society, there was an upsurge of interest in teaching for critical inquiry (Ravitch & Finn, 1988). Ironically, the national tests have shown that basic skills in elementary school are improving but that comprehension and critical thinking in secondary school have not improved at all—in fact, if anything, such higher-order skills have declined. Coming at a time when national leaders have designated educational development as a priority for the

1990s, the decline has prompted major rethinking of educational goals. Thus, in the past few years, there have been multiple calls for a thinking skill curriculum. The work of Arthur Costa (Costa, 1985; Costa & Margano, 1987) represents a very popular video-based staff development program for teachers, published by the Association for Supervision and Curriculum Development.

Costa takes the position that teachers must concentrate greater attention on the process of instruction. Rather than focusing on standard classroom procedures, he encourages teachers to use a different vocabulary to promote critical reasoning by students. It is pointless to continue to remind them to think. That's too broad, too vague, and too overused. Instead, he suggests the use of careful questioning phrases such as:

> Let's compare [not "look at"] these two pictures.
>
> What do you predict [not "think"] will happen when . . . ?
>
> How can you classify [not "group"] these materials . . . ?
>
> What evidence do you have to support . . . [not "How do you know it's true that . . . "]?

If you return briefly to Bloom's taxonomy in this chapter, you will quickly realize that some of the current rhetoric on thinking skills can be considered as an updated version of the higher levels of objectives in the cognitive domain. Compare, for example, Costa's list above with questions of comprehension (level two), analysis (level four), synthesis (level five), and evaluation (level six).

Keeping the relationship of thinking skills and Bloom's taxonomy in mind, we review a variety of conceptions of thinking. Then we focus on some current approaches to teaching for higher-level thinking.

Conceptions of Thinking

In the 1970s and 1980s, researchers investigated generic teacher skills and behaviors like use of praise and wait-time (see the discussion in Chapter 12) to increase student learning. The emphasis was on student acquisition and retention of knowledge, focusing on academic achievement in a traditional sense, with a dependence on standardized achievement test scores as the measure of success in student learning. In the 1990s, however, less investigation is being done in the format of process-product research on knowledge, retention, or generic teacher behaviors (like wait-time and praise), and more research is focusing on case studies of the relationship between teaching and learning in specific subjects. Major researchers on direct-teaching "effectiveness" suggest that the process-product research of the 1970s and 1980s established a good knowledge base for the case studies now being conducted (Brophy, 1992; Shulman, 1992; Good, 1996). The current research has moved (1) from simplistic knowledge acquisition, simple concepts and ideas, to complex forms of understanding of theories and generalizations; (2) from studies of generic teaching and learning to indepth studies of teaching and learning in specific subject areas; and (3) from individualist models of learning to the social context in which learning takes place.

Perhaps future generations will judge that the 1990s were a decade when we Americans really looked carefully at the education of *all* children in our schools, not just the elite. Lauren Resnick (as quoted in Nickerson, 1988, p. 7) focused on the historic distinction between mass education and elite education as she also looked to the research of the future.

> "Mass education was, from its inception, concerned with inculcating routine abilities: simple computation, reading predictable texts, reciting religious or civic codes. It did not take as goals for its students the ability to interpret unfamiliar texts, create mate-

rial others would want and need to read, construct convincing arguments, develop original solutions to technical or social problems" (Resnick, 1987, p. 5). What is new about the current growing interest in the teaching of higher-order cognitive skills in the public schools, Resnick suggests, is not the inclusion of thinking, problem solving, and reasoning in someone's school curriculum but the idea that these things should be included in everyone's curriculum. "It is a new challenge to develop educational programs that assume that all individuals, not just an elite, can become competent thinkers" (p. 7).

Socially Constructed Knowledge

Current research on teaching and learning indicates that more teachers see students as active participants in their own learning. Teachers recognize the need for more detailed knowledge of what students bring to the learning tasks in which they are engaged. In discussing what research on learning has to say about teaching, Gaea Leinhardt (1992) points to three elements that she views as fundamental to new approaches to the research on learning: (1) multiple forms of knowledge, (2) the role of prior knowledge, and (3) the social nature of knowledge and its acquisition. The student's job is to connect thinking skills (explaining, interpreting, posing problems or solutions) with specific content knowledge of a field like

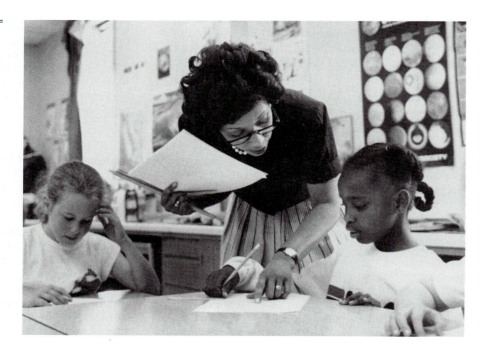

Current views of learning and teaching focus on how students actively process new information on the basis of prior knowledge they bring to the learning task. Teachers are seen as change agents who help students actively modify their existing knowledge.

history or mathematics. Her point is that understanding depends on the learner's ability to process various types of knowledge specific to the domain or topic or subject. Leinhardt suggests that we think of prior knowledge as an issue of "access," "interconnectedness," and "depth." Research described in Jere Confrey's (1990) review of the research on student conceptions in mathematics and science shows how prior knowledge can help or hinder new learning.

In addressing the assets and limitations of prior knowledge, teachers can assist students in recognizing their own beliefs and in assessing and revising these beliefs as new learning occurs. Classroom discussion (with ground rules to counteract possible negative personal verbal attacks) can use the children's energy and creativity to pose ideas and refute misconceptions.

Shared knowledge or socially constructed knowledge is as important as one's individual knowledge. This concept is built upon modern assumptions about learning: "(a) learning is an active process of knowledge construction and sense-making by the student; (b) knowledge is a cultural artifact of human beings: we produce it, share it, and transform it as individuals and as groups; and (c) knowledge is distributed among members of a group, and this distributed knowledge is greater than the knowledge possessed by any single member" (Leinhardt, 1992, p. 23). This seems basically to be an extension of Piaget's and Vygotsky's notions of the importance of social interaction in new learning (see Chapter 5). Teachers who understand the social nature of knowledge provide time in class for talk, public reasoning, shared problem solving, and shared projects. This is a form of connected teaching (see Spotlight).

Restructuring Teaching for Higher-Order Thinking

Higher-order thinking can be related to formal operational thought; postconventional moral thought; categories of analysis, synthesis, and evaluation; high conceptual level; connected teaching; and constructed knowledge. There are a number of current approaches to fostering students' higher-level thinking and understanding. All include some balance of focus on the following components: (1) in-depth knowledge of a subject or topic (Glaser, 1984; Prawat, 1991), (2) critical thinking skills (Beyer, 1987; deBono, 1983), and (3) dispositions of thoughtfulness (Dewey, 1933; Siegel, 1988). Although most researchers agree that all these components are needed, there is disagreement on the degree of emphasis to be given each of the three components

when developing good thinkers. As you read, do you think each component is equally important, or is one more important than the others?

Fred Newmann, director of the National Center on Organization and Restructuring of Schools, describes the differences among in-depth skills in a subject, critical thinking skills, and intellectual dispositions. In-depth knowledge of a subject area includes knowing domain-specific content such as solving quadratic equations in mathematics, using laboratory equipment in science, or jurisprudential reasoning in social studies. Thinking skills include the ability to identify and pose problems, interpret information and find new sources of information, offer evidence and detect bias, construct alternative solutions, and generalize from data. **Dispositions of thoughtfulness** include curiosity and confidence to explore new questions, a tendency to be reflective and think things through for oneself, and willingness and flexibility to take risks to entertain alternative and original solutions to problems.

Richard Prawat (1991), of Michigan State University, contrasts four kinds of approaches to teaching higher-order thinking: (1) teach thinking skills directly; (2) embed skills in the subject matter; (3) focus on concepts and ideas, and the skills will naturally follow; and (4) teach dispositions directly. In the first method, the *stand-alone* approach, thinking skills like comparing, ordering, classifying, and making inferences are taught separately from the subject matter. In the second method, an alternative called the *embedded* approach, thinking skills are embedded into the subject matter, and teachers focus on both the thinking skills and the subject content, trying to keep a balance between the two. In the third, more recent *immersion* approach, teachers assign the highest priority to the subject matter content of students' thoughts, and the subject matter ideas become the central factor in promoting higher-level thought. Although no recently articulated program exists to teach *dispositions* directly, we wonder if concepts of connected teaching might enhance this fourth approach and encourage dispositions of thoughtfulness in all students.

Principles and practices of good subject matter teaching for the goals of understanding and higher-order thinking are summarized in Table 13.3. In writing about the elementary school level, Jere Brophy asserts that teachers will need to go beyond presenting information and modeling skills. They also will need to "structure a great deal of thoughtful discourse by using questions to stimulate students to process and reflect on the content, recognize relationships among, and implications of, its key ideas, think critically about it, and use it in problem-solv-

TABLE 13.3   TEACHING FOR UNDERSTANDING AND HIGHER-ORDER APPLICATIONS

1. The curriculum is designed to equip students with knowledge, skills, values, and dispositions useful both inside and outside school.

2. Instructional goals underscore developing student expertise within an application context and with emphasis on conceptual understanding and self-regulated use of skills.

3. The curriculum balances breadth with depth by addressing limited content but developing this content sufficiently to foster understanding.

4. The content is organized around a limited set of powerful ideas (key understandings and principles).

5. The teacher's role is not just to present information but also to scaffold and respond to students' learning.

6. The students' role is not just to absorb or copy but to actively make sense and construct meaning.

7. Activities and assignments feature authentic tasks that call for problemsolving or critical thinking, not just memorization or reproduction.

8. Higher-order thinking skills are not taught as a separate skills curriculum. Instead they are developed in the process of teaching subject matter knowledge within application contexts that call for students to relate what they are learning to their lives outside school by thinking critically or creatively about it or by using it to solve problems or make decisions.

9. The teacher creates a social environment in the classroom that could be described as a learning community where dialogue promotes understanding.

10. The teacher maintains sustained examination of a few topics rather than superficial coverage of many.

11. The lesson displays substantive coherence and continuity.

12. Students are given an appropriate amount of time to prepare responses to questions.

13. The teacher asks challenging questions and/or structures challenging tasks.

14. The teacher is a model of thoughtfulness.

15. Students offer explanations and reasons for their conclusions.

Sources: *From Brophy, J., "Probing the Subtleties of Subject-Matter Teaching" in* Educational Leadership 49, 7, 4–8, *and Onosko, J. J., "Exploring the Thinking of Thoughtful Teachers" in* Educational Leadership 49, 7, 40–43. *Adapted by permission of the Association for Supervision and Curriculum Development. Copyright © 1992 by ASCD. All rights reserved.*

Note: Items 1 through 9 are from Brophy (1992), and items 10 through 15 are from Onosko (1992). The items complement one another; Brophy's work derives mostly from the elementary level and Onosko's work from the secondary level.

ing or decision-making applications" (Brophy, 1992, p. 6). Brophy summarizes research from the Center for the Learning and Teaching of Elementary School Subjects at the Institute for Research on Teaching at Michigan State University. This research focuses on instruction in reading, writing, mathematics, science, and social studies aimed at challenging students to engage in higher-order thinking.

How do elementary teachers teach for understanding and higher-order thinking? They use a technique called scaffolding. Barak Rosenshine and Carla Meister (1992) suggest the use of instructional processes called *scaffolds* to teach cognitive strategies at the elementary level: "Although scaffolds can be applied to the teaching of all skills, they are particularly useful, and often indispensable, for teaching higher-level cognitive strategies, where many of the steps or procedures necessary to carry them out cannot be specified. Instead of providing explicit steps,

one supports, or scaffolds, the students as they learn the skill" (p. 26). (See the Spotlight on Scaffolding.)

How do secondary teachers teach for higher-order thinking? Joe Onosko, social studies professor and supervisor of practicing teachers in the University of New Hampshire Five-Year Teacher Preparation Program, worked on the Higher-Order Thinking in the Humanities Project with Fred Newmann. The study included numerous observations and interviews with teachers from 16 secondary schools across the United States. Onosko and Newmann (1994) identified six of the most fundamental indicators of secondary classrooms where students are encouraged to do higher-order thinking. These are listed as items 1–15 in Table 13.3. Onosko reported that outstanding teachers unanimously listed the development of students' thinking as a fundamental goal of their instruction. Outstanding teachers were willing to reduce content coverage to pursue the

SPOTLIGHT ON SCAFFOLDING

The instructional term *scaffolding* (see item 5 in Table 13.3) was introduced by Jerome Bruner in the 1970s. It complements Vygotsky's notion of the zone of proximal development (ZPD) and Hunt's notion of optimal mismatch. As you remember from Chapter 5, the ZPD is the zone between pupils' assisted level of learning (the intended goal) and their unassisted level of learning (their independent current level).

Elena Bodrova and Deborah Leong describe and model three types of scaffolding: *mediators, language,* and *shared activity.* Each of the following types of scaffolding provides a way to get a child from his or her independent current level to an assisted intended level of learning. The three types are, of course, interconnected and interdependent.

Mediators are tools (or clues) to help a child perform a more complex behavior. Mediators could be cue cards, clocks, alphabet strips, signs, slogans, or the like. Language is a second type of scaffolding. Both Piaget and Vygotsky emphasize the relationship between language and thought. Language is public and private. Private speech (e.g., saying the new concept or reading aloud), inner speech (e.g., saying the new concept silently to oneself), written speech (e.g., drawings, numbers, symbols, and letters) are all ways children use language as scaffolds to bring new concepts into their minds. Publicly exchanging concepts and ideas and sharing with others is also a part of language as a scaffold to new learning.

A third type of scaffolding is shared activity, with a teacher, an older or younger peer, or, in the case of a preoperational child, an imaginary friend. In this type of scaffolding the learner adopts the strategies of the more or equally knowledgeable partner and gradually makes them his or her own. And by helping a less knowledgeable partner the learner solidifies his or her knowledge. So in peer teaching both the older and younger, or more advanced and less knowledgeable, peers benefit each other through shared activity.

Leong, D. & Bedrova, E. (1995). *Tools of the mind: The Vygotskian approach to early childhood education.* © 1995. Adapted by permission of Prentice Hall, Upper Saddle River, NJ.

---

goal of understanding because they believed that stressing content coverage impedes students' thinking. They acknowledged the difficulty of getting students to higher-order thinking, yet they did not become frustrated with students. Outstanding teachers were also able to describe lengthier, more elaborate, and more precise perspectives on what thinking skills entail. For example: the student understands the relevance of data to a central theme, interprets information, determines points of view and identifies their effects, formulates hypotheses, and subjects some to criticism. Outstanding teachers identified a greater number of intellectual dispositions associated with thinking, like curiosity, confidence, a thirst for reasons, and willingness to take risks.

The social studies teachers at Aragon High School, San Mateo, California, developed a successful design for unit plans that promote active, cohesive, in-depth student learning (Onosko & Swenson, 1996). The components of the plan include (1) a problem-based central question, (2) an "introductory grabber" to draw students into the content and thinking skills, (3) rich detail coming from students'

in-depth exploration and research of the material, and (4) a culminating activity wherein students share their findings, debate ideas, exhibit their accomplished learnings, and demonstrate their understandings focused on the central question. Elizabeth Wood (1992), a student teaching intern, used this plan to design and teach a unit titled "The Treatment of Native Americans. Could the U.S. Have Done Better?" In the Spotlight on Designing Thoughtful Issue-Based Units: An Inquiry Approach, we include her unit plan introduction and two of the seven lesson plans for the unit (4 and 5) as an example of an inquiry approach to designing thoughtful units aimed at developing students' higher-levels of cognitive understanding.

One of the questions you may have is: How do we measure development of student's higher-order thinking? The difficulty of assessment is a barrier to the more prevalent use of indirect teaching techniques and inquiry approaches to teaching and learning (Onosko, 1991). We think that the emphasis on designing performance-based assessments will help teachers plan for and assess higher-order think-

SPOTLIGHT ON DESIGNING THOUGHTFUL ISSUE-BASED UNITS

An Inquiry Approach

E. B. Wood

INTRODUCTION

This unit was developed to introduce students to the history of the Native Americans in the United States. I facilitated this unit after the students had studied Jacksonian America and the Civil War in order that they be familiar with the backdrop of both the Removal Act of 1830 and the Indian Wars of the 1870s and 1880s. The unit follows a chronological organization, but is focused solely on the experience of the Native Americans from the early 1800s to present day. The unit is broken down into seven distinct lessons, with the intention that each lesson encompasses more than one class period. The entire learning sequence can fill up two weeks of class time, depending on the depth of study. The focus of the unit is to encourage students to complete an in-depth study of the interaction of the Native and Euro-Americans through American History and to make personal judgments about the justness of the situation. In the course of the unit, students will design and evaluate alternative solutions to the persistent issue of how to accommodate inherent differences between minority and dominant cultures. By looking at the current conditions of the Cherokee Nation, students will understand the current manifestation of past governmental policies and will gain insight to the relevance of historical knowledge. . . .

LESSON FOUR

Lesson Focus: Indian Removal: A National Security Measure?

For students to begin thinking about alternative solutions to the "Indian problem" of the 1830s;

For students to understand that there are usually many factors that one must consider when developing public policy;

For students to gain an appreciation of Andrew Jackson's personal beliefs about Native Americans;

For students to understand the importance of re-assessing ideas in light of new information.

Procedure: Review lesson three in small groups. Review the previous discussion of the cultural differences leading to the Native American/Euro-American conflict over land. If possible, keep list of values and definitions on blackboard overnight.

Divide class into new small groups, creating equal numbers of *Little Tree* experts and Lockean experts in each group. Allow the groups approximately 15 minutes to discuss ways that both sets of values could co-exist mutually. Encourage groups to be creative with solutions to the land conflict by reminding them that the United States was only fifty years old at the time of the Removal and that restructuring its political or social frameworks would not be out of the question. Ask all students in the group to keep notes on ideas and possible solutions.

Give brief overview of President Andrew Jackson. Reconvene class for short lecture (approx. 10 minutes). Provide students with a biographical sketch of Andrew Jackson (remind them of what they learned in previous units), focusing on his interaction with Native Americans; give background information about the expansion of the United States and the "need" for border protection; utilize maps.

Whole-group discussion: Based upon assigned readings, small group discussions and the mini lecture, discuss the following questions:

1. According to Jackson's letter, what were the President's reasons for removing the Native Americans?

ing. We need more research on assessing hands-on science, how to create tests worth taking, what the differences are between authentic and performance assessments, how to evaluate problemsolving in mathematics, and how to use portfolios for assessment in writing, literacy, mathematics, and computing. "The use of new performance measures, including portfolios, seems promising, but they must not be viewed as a new *answer* to educational problems," cautions Tom Good (1996, p. 648). His review of new

2. Do you think this was the only reason for Jackson's actions? What other ideas influenced his policy decisions?
3. Should national security influence whether the US government honors its treaties?
4. Discuss this question in terms of "might makes right." Why was the Euro-Americans' security more important than the Native Americans' security?

Re-assessing alternative solutions: Have students return to their small groups and ask them to re-evaluate their earlier solutions in light of the problem of national security. Do your initial solutions increase or decrease national security for Euro-Americans? Should they be amended in light of the new concern of security? Can you come up with any new solutions?

Conclusion/Assignment: Conclude the lesson by sharing with students the overview of the next day's activities and assigning for homework a second reading from *The Education of Little Tree* (second excerpt, pp. 38–46).

LESSON FIVE

Lesson Focus: Indian Removal of the 1830s—The Best Option?

For students to gain an appreciation of the power that the United States' federal government had over the Native Americans in the 1830s;

For students to understand why many opposed the removal of the Native Americans;

For students to create and assess alternatives to the removal of the Native Americans beyond the Mississippi.

Procedure: Review earlier lessons. Prior to class, write basic provisions of the Indian Removal Act of 1830 on the blackboard. Once class assembles, open discussion and ask students for their "expert" opinions on whether the legislation was the best way for the U.S. government to "solve" the conflicts between Native Americans and Euro-Americans.

Small-groups brainstorm alternatives. Allow small groups to reconvene for 5–10 minutes to review their proposed solutions from Lesson Three. Ask them to decide on the best alternative to the Removal Act. If they agree that the Act was actually the best solution, ask them to come up with a defense.

Redirect attention to the central

blackboard and ask each group to present their solution; record proposals on the board. Through class discussion, record support and objections on the board for each solution.

Assessment/Culminating Activity: Give students time to work individually on their final assignment, a letter to President Jackson either supporting or rejecting the 1830 legislation. If the student decides to support the Act, s/he must give reasons why s/he rejected the other options; if s/he rejects the Act, s/he must explain why s/he supports an alternative proposal.

Conclusion/Assignment: Conclude the lesson by discussing the length and scope of the final paper (minimum of a 5-paragraph essay, in a formal-letter format) and setting the due date (2–3 days later). Homework for the next day will be a reading on the attempted flight of the Nez Perce and Chief Joseph.

The introduction and Lessons Four and Five are excerpted from the entire lesson plan in E. B. Wood (1992), The treatment of Native Americans: Could the U.S. have done better? *Horizons, 14*(1), 42–50.

approaches to assessment finds few studies that focus on theory and implementation. Good urges teachers to experiment with these progressive ideas. He urges us to ask questions such as: what types of assessment, for what audience, and for what purpose? But before advocating teachers' extensive use of portfolios, he suggests the importance of funding to support exploratory research and development concerning students' use of portfolios, as well as parents' and policymakers' reactions.

Clearly, there is a substantial overlap between higher-order thinking and the higher levels of Piaget's stages of formal reasoning (Chapter 5). The new emphasis on thinking represents a major opportunity to reintroduce cognitive-developmental goals into the school curriculum, particularly at the junior high and high school levels.

There is an obvious theoretical linkage not only to Bloom, Piaget, and Vygotsky, but also to the instructional strategies in the work on attribute-treatment interaction. We have shown that older, able, nonanxious learners benefit from the inductive, low-structured approach. For the process to succeed, however, the teacher needs to understand that he or she must consider the learning stage of the pupil and the particular lesson goal before launching an all-out drive for critical thinking. For example, in teaching for higher-order thinking skills in mathematics, students whom we would term concrete thinkers achieved better under conditions that provided careful step-by-step modeling. The directions were clear and to the point. Ambiguity was deliberately reduced. However, such concrete teaching actually impaired the performance of students who were at the abstract, self-directed stage. This second group of students, whose inner direction was high, learned better with open-ended inductive and discovery-type questions (Lohman, 1986). Thus, the problem of any single approach to teaching, which ignores the developmental characteristics of learners, carries the danger of helping some and harming others. The warning, then, to the new calls for teaching for higher-order cognitive skills and understanding (from kindergarten to graduate school) is that teachers need to vary the questioning method and then gradually mismatch. The success of the lesson or unit will be determined by the amount of structure and the development of the questions asked.

Restructuring Schools

As we move into the twenty-first century, schools are being restructured to support teaching for *all* students' higher-order understanding. Federal, state, and local education agencies are developing policies and supporting model programs for school organizational change. This is quite an undertaking. The message is clear. To produce real change, the framework of schools and classrooms needs to be fundamentally changed. James Comer, Professor at Yale University, is one of the major contributors to models of school change. The Comer process for reforming education (for example, Comer et al., 1996) is based on 26 years of experience and nationwide success.

Comer's School Development Program builds a community of healthy students, parents, teachers, and administrators. Comer's theory of school reform is an outgrowth of his understanding of social psychology, community health, and psychiatry. In Comer's plan, adults work creatively and enthusiastically with each other and with children to set a powerful model for the children's attitudes toward school, society, and the future. The schools are opened up to parent participation. Teachers have the time to plan together.

University-school partnerships play a crucial role in Comer's continuing school development programs. Teachers and students from elementary and secondary schools and the university combine forces to learn collaboratively and creatively. This means that future teachers get the experience of teaming with teachers, working with parents, learning with pupils, while they are confronting the dilemmas of learning to teach. In school-university partnerships, experienced teachers and administrators in the school are learning alongside the university professors. This is a form of professional development school. Other recent research is related to preparing culturally competent teachers for urban schools (Haberman, 1996), professional development schools (Book, 1996), and leadership in restructuring schools, colleges, and departments of education (Zimpher & Sherrill, 1996).

The lessons learned from Comer's process are applicable to other school restructuring efforts in rural, urban, and suburban settings.

1. The evaluation plan must take into account the unique circumstances in school districts and schools.

2. Quantitative research must be accompanied by carefully structured ethnographic studies to derive rich information.

3. Measuring program outcomes, such as improved student performance on standardized tests, is meaningless unless there is also careful measurement of the level and quality of program implementation.

4. Evaluation of the program becomes an intervention in itself; for example, as a result of the very activity of surveying parents, the parents begin to understand that the school does want their involvement.

The premier lesson learned, writes Comer, is that schools can be transformed. Comer refers to himself and coworkers as servant leaders: "We serve the needs of the entire school community. We have seen superintendents, principals, teachers, parents, and

JAMES P. COMER

Dr. James P. Comer is a study in contrasts. He was born into poverty; his mother worked as a domestic and his father at any job he could find. He was one of five children and exemplified Courtland Lee's findings: He succeeded in spite of the educational programs. He was often targeted in school because of his skin color. Even in 1952 at Indiana University, the hostility continued. At one point during orientation a sudden rainstorm forced the students to jump into the cars sent to pick them up. He rode alone; no one else would get into the same car. Other incidents, small and large, followed: He was refused service at a local ice cream parlor, and a professor reading his paper as a model to a class ripped it to shreds when he discovered that Comer was an African-American. The schools and colleges worked to denigrate him and to teach him self-hatred. He said it was the un-usual support of his family that kept him going. And go he did, through Indiana, through medical school, and eventually to a tenured full professorship with a chair in psychiatry at Yale University.

It was clear that Comer was on the fast track to academic prestige with all the comforts and "perks" of an Ivy League existence, complete with dialogue, theoretical models, and the gentility of tweed jackets. Like his colleagues, he could now live in the fashionable New Haven suburbs and, by careful choice of roads, avoid seeing what was happening to African-American children in the inner city. He did not, however, put on such blinders or forget his own past. Instead, he chose a remarkable path for his own work—tackling the seemingly endemic problems of inner-city schools.

Imagine an M.D. and psychiatrist literally taking off his white coat, giving up extremely lucrative individual therapy and all those posh surroundings—for what? To take on the renovation of schools with 99 percent minority enrollment, where more kids went to jail than graduated, with drugs everywhere and resources practically nonexistent. By then Comer made it clear he was in for the long haul. This was not to be one of those brief, hit-and-run encounters, in which a university type hits the school, briefly gathers some data, and promptly runs to the campus for publication and promotion. Comer stayed. Through long hours and a steady commitment to his vision, he was able to achieve the impossible. He developed teams of effective professionals and gradually won the support of the community, and slowly but surely the students began to learn. After 15 years, the recognitions arrived. He now sits on the boards of the MacArthur, Carnegie, and Field Foundations, consults nationally, and has networked his approach to some 50 other schools. He always remembers, however, how many of his childhood friends, who were just as smart as he was, went downhill. Comer's work serves as a prime example of what another eminent African-American psychologist, Kenneth Clark, calls *America's Shame: America's Hope.* Comer's publications are now widely disseminated as models of reform. No professors are ripping up his papers now!

Sprinthall, N. A. & Collins, W. A. (1995). *Adolescent psychology: A developmental view.* New York: McGraw-Hill, p. 346.

community members transforming the children in their schools and districts as a result of their actions. Islands of despair have been turned into places of hope because of the servant leaders in the schools" (Comer et al., 1996, p. 166).

Comer started with the worst schools in the system, those with the lowest scores and the highest absentee rate. Over time the students in Comer's schools equaled or surpassed the national average standardized test scores even though 70 percent of the students come from families on welfare. In addi-

tion to evaluating test scores, Comer's School Development Program studies the real-life situation of the school. Staff members also collect data on school climate and children's self-concept, behavior, and social acceptance. They analyze data and report summaries back to the school in a timely fashion, so the school community can revise, plan, and continue its efforts. The number of schools participating in Comer's School Development Program has grown from 2 in 1968 to more than 550 in 1995.

SUMMARY

Objectives remain a topic of interest to educational psychologists. The spoof *The Saber-Tooth Curriculum* continued the debate about general education versus skill-based education that has been with us for centuries. Focusing on Bloom's taxonomy, we attempted to show how this classification system could be most useful in the selection of educational goals at different levels.

Hunt's scheme illustrates the different levels and modes of thinking that students typically employ. Through his framework of ATI, Hunt tries to bridge the gap between teaching strategies and pupils' preferred learning strategies (CL stages). By attributes Hunt means the characteristic learning style of the pupil. By treatment he means the instructional method. Whether learning really takes place will depend on the interaction between the two. He further specifies that such interaction can follow a mode of matching (a strategy that fits the learner's current mode) followed by graduated mismatching (teaching at a level just beyond the current mode). There are some important qualifications, however, for using a highly structured strategy, even for students who generally function at higher conceptual levels. Belenky, Clinchy, Goldberger, and Tarule's study has added information about the ways in which women understand and make meaning from their educational experiences. A teacher's plans to match and

constructively mismatch instruction to all students needs should consider these five positions, or ways of knowing. Particularly important at the procedural position are two modes of learning, connected and separate.

Besides paying attention to the interaction between teaching style and student modes of learning, teachers must learn how to effectively organize their material through lesson planning. Hunter has suggested a system for lesson planning that can and should be keyed to learning outcomes. By following the steps she outlines, teachers can reduce the likelihood that students will misunderstand either the point of the unit or the learning activities expected of them. By preventing students from going down the wrong road, teachers can thus increase the amount of academic or on-task learning time.

Scaffolding and issue-based unit planning can help teachers focus on students' higher-order thinking. When teaching for higher-order thinking and understanding, teachers focus on in-depth knowledge in the subject, critical thinking skills, and dispositions of thoughtfulness. The Comer School Development Program is a model partnership of parents, community members, school and university teachers, and administrators working side-by-side to support teaching that develops all students' higher-order thinking.

KEY TERMS AND NAMES

accessibility channels
   attribute-treatment interaction (ATI)
   conceptual level
James Comer
connected teaching
current preferred style of learning
dispositions of thoughtfulness
higher-order thinking

David Hunt
Madeline Hunter
low and high structure
matching and mismatching
Penelope Peterson
Saber-Tooth Curriculum
socially constructed knowledge
Women's Ways of Knowing

THEORY INTO PRACTICE: A DETECTIVE APPROACH TO LESSON PLANNING

Since we have outlined the Hunter method and the issue-based planning method in some detail, we will present an example of the inquiry approach to lesson planning. In this method, sometimes called the *detective approach,* you do not reveal the main point of the lesson content at the outset. You provide information in the form of a scenario of a problem to solve, but you do not solve the problem. Instead, your role is to continue to ask clarifying questions to promote greater inquiry.

Step one: Explain your own role   For example, say to the class, "I'm going to present a problem along with a series of facts. Your task will be to figure out which of the variety of explanations seems most logical and reasonable. Even though I have a good idea as to what the most logical answer might be, I'm not going to reveal it. I will give you the pieces of the puzzle, but you'll need to put them together yourselves."

Step two: The discrepant event—The lost colony
Present the facts of a puzzling situation, for example, the famous case of North Carolina's lost colony. The facts are these:

1. There had been two previous attempts to establish a colony on Roanoke Island. In 1585, a group of 100 people, led by Ralph Lane, had stayed for one year. Discouraged by a lack of food and deteriorating relations with the local Native Americans, Lane and his group attacked and killed the local chief and others before evacuating the colony and returning to England. Shortly afterward, another English expedition landed. A small party of men was left to hold the island until a larger number of colonists could be brought over.

2. In 1587, the second group of more than 100 colonists arrived, but they found no trace of the small group. The colonists, however, worked hard to build their homes in the new world while warding off attacks from the Native Americans. Also, the colonists themselves mistakenly attacked a group of friendly Native Americans. The situation remained tense.

3. Food was scarce. After a few weeks, the colonists implored Governor White to return to England for supplies. He left in August 1587.

4. As a result of the activities of the Spanish Armada (1588), it was three years before White returned. There was no trace of the colony except for the word "CROATOAN" carved in a tree. By a prearrangement, a cross was to have been carved as a distress sign. No cross was carved. The fort, in fact, was relatively intact.

5. A search of nearby Croatoan Island a few years later revealed no sign that the colonists had reached the island or indeed that they had even attempted to head in that direction. In fact, no trace was found at all. There was very little food on the island.

Step three: Review and verify the basic information   Make sure the students understand the facts. Often, the best way to do this is to ask the students to state the facts and the problem in their own words, that is, check for understanding. This is similar to questioning at Bloom's levels one and two.

Step four: Explore and identify relevant pieces of information   In this case, there are a number of excellent accounts, including some of the original documents. (See the reference to Parramore and Parramore at the end of this practice unit.)

1. There was no evidence of a massacre.

2. The distress sign was not used.

3. There had been Indian attacks and counterattacks prior to Governor White's return to England.

4. The colonists' fort was well built.

5. There was a history of tribal warfare among different groups of nearby Native Americans.

6. Food was scarce on Croatoan Island.

7. A Spanish ship in 1588 reported no sign of the colonists in the area.

8. There was no evidence of severe hurricanes in the area.

9. There were rumors later on of a small number of English living at the other end of Pamlico Sound, yet this could not be confirmed.

Step five: Trial explanations   Be sure not to move too quickly to the theorizing. Remember that students may be uncomfortable with such an open-ended problem and seek to push for one right answer quickly. Your role here is crucial. You'll need to prevent early closure by paraphrasing, refocusing, and challenging. "What's the evidence for that position?" "How does the view that the colonists were all killed compare with the view that they moved to another part of the country and intermarried?" Or "What about the possibility that another European power, Spain, attacked the colony and decided to keep the attack secret?" Or "Could the colonists have tried to return to England?" Or "If the colonists settled with an Indian tribe, why was there no record or signs, or could they have been killed along with their friendly Native Americans by a hostile tribe?"

This is sometimes called synthesizing at Bloom's level five, or putting the facts together for the most logical and defensible explanations.

Step six: Temporary closure   After a thorough discussion of the different theories, you move to what appears to be the best solution. One way of helping students understand the temporary nature of the conclusion, for example, what a successive approximation means, is to evaluate the competing theories, marshal the evidence, and conclude with what appears to be the best enlightened guess.

You end, however, by noting, "What new evidence which could come to light in the future might cause us to change our best theory today?"

An archaeological dig in shallow water reveals the remains of colonists and Indians, canoes and rafts, all apparently drowned, caught by a rogue wave.

Some Spanish records unearthed near St. Augustine, Florida, indicate the intention to drive the British out of North Carolina.

A scuba diver 50 miles down the coast finds artifacts of a colony buried in shallow water and evidence of a plague.

A stone is uncovered in Chowan County with the name "Virginia Dare" and the inscription "Gone to Heaven 1591." She was the first child born in the colony.

In this manner, you will help the students to begin to think like historians, to make logical interpretations after examining all sides of the issue, and to reach a conclusion while remaining open to further evidence.

Finally, of course, the goal is to turn student inquiry away from you as the teacher with the right answer to you as a person who models a process approach for promoting critical inquiry.

For a more detailed account of the lost colony, including examples of the actual reports and maps of the area, see T. Parramore and B. Parramore (1984), *Looking for the "Lost Colony"* (Raleigh, NC: Tanglewood Press). For copies write to Tanglewood Press, 5012 Tanglewood Drive, Raleigh, NC 27612. This is an excellent example of how information can be structured to promote inquiry and concept attainment through discovery.

An additional example can be found in M. Weil and B. Joyce (1978), *Information Processing Models of Teaching* (Englewood Cliffs, NJ: Prentice-Hall), pp. 156–173. It contains an actual classroom transcript of students' attempts to solve the puzzle of a now-deserted island's culture. The elements are in a suggested sequence that is to be employed flexibly. Quite unfortunately, some school districts have adopted the Hunter model and rigorously enforced its use: if even a single step is skipped, the teacher is marked down. It is important to recall that Hunter has called for a flexible interpretation.

Our view is that learning outcomes and educational objectives can be achieved through the use of a modifiable sequence of lesson-planning steps. Since the overall goal is to increase the students' independence as learners, lesson planning is a means of achieving the goal of helping students learn to think for themselves. Such planning helps to liberate pupils rather than feeding their dependence.

REFERENCES

Belenky, M. F., Clinchy, B. M., Goldberger, N., & Tarule, J. (1986). *Women's ways of knowing: The development of self, voice, and mind.* New York: Basic Books.

Beyer, B. K. (1987). *Practical strategies for the teaching of thinking.* Boston: Allyn & Bacon.

Bloom, B. (Ed.) (1956). *Taxonomy of educational objectives, Handbook 1: Cognitive domain.* New York: McKay.

Book, C. L. (1996). Professional development schools. In J. Sikula, T. J. Buttery & E. Guyton (Eds.), *Handbook of research on teacher education* (2nd ed.) (pp. 194–210). New York: Macmillan.

Brophy, J. (1992). Probing the subtleties of subject-matter teaching. *Educational Leadership, 49*(7), 4–8.

Chickering, A. W. (Ed.). (1981). *The modern American college.* San Francisco: Jossey Bass.

Clinchy, B. M. (1989). The development of thoughtfulness in college women: Integrating reason and care. *American Behavioral Scientist, 32*(6), 647–657.

Comer, J. P., Haynes, N. M., Joyner, E. T. & Ben-Avie, M. (Eds.) (1996). *Rallying the whole village: The Comer process for reforming education.* New York: Teachers College Press.

Confrey, J. (1990). A review of the research on student conceptions in mathematics, science, and programming. In C. Cazden (Ed.), *Review of Research in Education, 16* (pp. 3–56). Washington, DC: American Educational Research Association.

Costa, A. L. (1985). Toward a model of human intellectual functioning. In A. L. Costa (Ed.), *Developing minds: A resource for teaching thinking.* Alexandria, VA: Association for Supervision and Curriculum Development.

Costa, A. L., & Margano, R. (1987). Teaching the language of thinking. *Educational Leadership, 45*(2), 29–33.

Cronbach, L., & Snow, R. (1977). *Aptitudes and instructional methods.* New York: Irvington Press.

Cross, W. E., Jr. (1991). *Shades of black: Diversity in African-American identity.* Philadelphia: Temple University Press.

deBono, E. (1983). The direct teaching of thinking as a skill. *Phi Delta Kappan, 64*(10), 703–708.

Dewey, J. (1933). *How we think.* Boston: D. C. Heath.

Gibboney, R. A. (1987). A critique of Madeline Hunter's teaching model from Dewey's perspective. *Educational Leadership, 44*(5), followed by Hunter's response, 51–53, and Gibboney's answer, 54–55.

Glaser, R. (1984). The role of knowledge. *American Psychologist, 38,* 93–104.

Goldberger, N., Tarule, J., Clinchy, B., & Belenky, M. (1996). *Knowledge, difference, and power.* New York: Basic Books.

Good, T. L. (1996). Teaching effects and teacher evaluation. In J. Sikula, T. J. Buttery, & E. Guyton (Eds.), *Handbook of research on teacher education* (2d ed.) (pp. 617–665). New York: Macmillan.

Haberman, M. (1996). Selecting and preparing culturally competent teachers for urban schools. In J. Sikula, T. J. Buttery, & E. Guyton (Eds.), *Handbook of research on teacher education* (2d ed.) (pp. 747–760). New York: Macmillan.

Hunt, D. E. (1974). *Matching models in education.* Toronto: Ontario Institute for Studies in Education.

Hunt, D. E. (1981). Teachers' adaptation: Reading and flexing to students. In B. Joyce, C. Brown, & L. Peck (Eds.), *Flexibility in teaching* (pp. 59–71). New York: Longman.

Hunter, M. (1984). Knowing, teaching and supervising. In P. L. Hosford (Ed.), *Using what we know about teaching* (p. 175). Alexandria, VA: Association for Supervision and Curriculum Development.

Leinhardt, G. (1992). What research on learning tells us about teaching. *Educational Leadership, 49*(7), 20–25.

Levin, J., & Peterson, P. (1984). Classroom aptitude by treatment interactions: An alternate analysis strategy. *Educational Psychologist, 19*(1), 43–47.

Lohman, D. F. (1986). Predicting mathematic effects in the teaching of higher-order thinking skills. *Educational Psychologist, 21*(3), 191–208.

Mayer, R. E. (1988). *Teaching for thinking: Research on the teachability of thinking skills.* Paper presented at American Psychological Association Convention, Atlanta, Georgia.

Miller, A. (1981). Conceptual matching models and interactional research in education. *Review of Educational Research, 51*(1), 33–85.

Nickerson, R. L. (1988). On improving thinking through instruction. In E. Z. Rothkopf (Ed.), *Review of research in education.* Washington, DC: American Educational Research Association.

Noddings, N. (1984). *Caring: A feminine approach to ethics and moral education.* Berkeley: University of California Press.

Onosko, J. (1991). Barriers to the promotion of higher-order thinking. *Theory and Research in Social Education, 19*(4), 341–366.

Onosko, J. (1992). Exploring the thinking of thoughtful teachers. *Educational Leadership, 49*(7), 40–43.

Onosko, J. J., & Newmann, F. M. (1994). Creating more thoughtful learning environments. In J. N. Mangieri & C. Collins Block (Eds.) (pp. 27–49). *Creating powerful thinking in teachers and students: Diverse perspectives.* New York: Harcourt Brace College Publishers.

Onosko, J. J. & Swenson, L. (1996). Designing issue-based unit plans. In R. Evans & D. Saxe (Eds.) *The handbook on teaching social studies.* Washington, DC: National Council for the Social Studies, pp. 89–98.

Peddiwell, J. A. (1939). *The saber-tooth curriculum.* New York: McGraw-Hill.

Perry, W. (1970). *Forms of intellectual and ethical development in the college years.* New York: Holt, Rinehart and Winston.

Peterson, P. (1988). Selecting students and services for compensatory education: Lessons from aptitude-treatment interaction research. *Educational Psychologist, 23*(4), 313–352.

Peterson, P., Fennema, E., Carpenter, T., & Loef, M. (1989). Teachers' pedagogical content beliefs in mathematics. *Cognition & Instruction, 6*(1), 1–40.

Peterson, P., Janicki, T., and Swing, S. (1980). Aptitude-treatment interaction effects of three social studies teaching approaches. *American Educational Research Journal, 17*(3), 339–360.

Prawat, R. S. (1991). The value of ideas: The immersion approach to the development of thinking. *Educational Researcher, 20*(2), 3–10, 30.

Ravitch, D., & Finn, C. (1988). *What do our 17 year olds know?* New York: Harper & Row.

Resnick, L. (1987). *Education and learning to think.* Washington, DC: National Academy Press.

Rosenshine, B., and Meister, C. (1992). The use of scaffolds for teaching higher-level cognitive strategies. *Educational leadership, 49*(7), 26–33.

Schrag, F. (1989). Are there levels of thinking? *Teachers College Record, 90*(4), 529–534.

Shulman, L. (1992). In R. Brandt, On research on teaching: A conversation with Lee Shulman. *Educational Leadership, 49*(7), 14–19.

Siegel, H. (1988). *Educating reason.* New York: Routeledge and Kegan Paul.

Snow, R. E., Corno, L., & Jackson, D. (1996). Individual differences in affective and conative functions. In D. C. Berliner & R. C. Calfee (Eds.) *Handbook of Educational Psychology,* New York: Simon & Schuster Macmillan, pp. 243–310.

Tyler, R. (1933). Permanence of learning. *Journal of Higher Education, 4,* 203–204.

Widick, C., & Simpson, D. (1978). Developmental concepts in college instruction. In C. Parker (Ed.), Encouraging development in C. Parker (Ed.), *Encouraging development in college students.* Minneapolis: University of Minnesota Press.

Zimpher, N. L. & Sherrill, J. A. (1996). Professors, teachers, and leaders in SCDEs. In J. Sikula, T. J. Buttery, & E. Guyton (Eds.), *Handbook of research on teacher education,* 2nd ed. New York: Macmillan, pp. 279–305.

TEACHING: THE PERSONAL DIMENSION

Thus far in our discussion of teaching effectiveness, we have focused on teaching from the standpoint of strategies, objectives, student characteristics, and planning. We now shift to the teacher as a person. How do you as an individual understand yourself in the teaching role? That is the basic question—a quite broad one, encompassing your attitudes toward yourself, the subject matter you are teaching, and, finally, your students. These three dimensions of knowing yourself make up the core material in this chapter. Without question, the person of the teacher exerts a telling influence on the classroom. You set the limits, you establish the tone, you model acceptable behavior, you make the rules, you translate the material, you organize the schedules—in short, you orchestrate the class.

How you think and feel about teaching, the material, and the pupils sets an atmosphere or climate. Since your attitudes and perceptions do exert considerable influence, even though it may be subtle, it is important to examine them. The early Greek philosophers knew the significance of self-knowledge. To know oneself as a teacher, then, represents a key sensitivity and necessary awareness.

THE TEACHER AS A PERSON: THE ELUSIVE QUESTION

One of the most elusive questions in education is what human qualities make an effective teacher. One long-standing myth is that teachers should manifest all the noble virtues and have no human frailties. The problem is that no human can possibly live up to the myth. Even worse, teachers soon realize the impossibility of such a goal but have to keep busy preventing other people from finding out. A more realistic perception of the teacher would dispense with both the myth of human virtues (all teachers love all children all the time) and the assumption that teachers are not responsible for the failure of children to learn.

What Is Teaching Really Like?

If done well, teaching is really hard, and it can't be done single-handedly. Good teachers consistently reflect on their practice, study their impact on students, and reevaluate their goals and methods. They

SPOTLIGHT ON TEACHING

Be Everything at Once

Job Opening

Looking for a SELF-starting, SELF-propelled, SELF-confident, SELF-supporting, SELF-sufficient, SELF-promoting, SELF-cleaning, SELF-less individual.

MINIMUM wage guaranteed. Hours: 7:30 A.M.–4:00 P.M., plus evenings and weekends.

Average 60 stimulating hours per week—no overtime pay. Summers off (unless you have a mortgage or need a degree).

Must be able to work independently in a chaotic, cooperative/competitive environment.

Applicant must have skills and knowledge in the following areas:

Diplomacy	Crowd control	Social work
Risk taking	Family therapy	Systems management
Communications	Time management	Motivational techniques
AV operation and repair	First aid	Bulletin board design
Community building	Interior decorating	Clerical procedures
Cooking	Plumbing	Administration
Aerobics	Legal affairs	Acrobatics
Acting	Pest control	Accounting
Carpentry	Current affairs	Psychology
Geography	Computer literacy	Writing
History	Math (new and old)	Foreign languages
Science	Literature	Art appreciation
Health	Music	Behavioral management

Some light housekeeping required. Sense of humor, compassion, and caring mandatory. Diplomatic, paramedic, and military experience helpful.

Prior seminars in stress reduction useful. Flexibility and courage a must! Interested applicants should apply to:

Your Local Public School

From Frances Morse, Nancy Frane, and Esther Kattef, teachers at Edward Devotion Elementary School, Brookline, MA, who compiled these ideas from a faculty meeting where 60 staff members discussed the topic "Teaching as a Profession." Previously published in the *Boston Globe* (1991) and in *The Teachers' Network News* (Cambridge: Harvard Graduate School of Education, 1990).

---

try to improve their expertise and their interactions with parents and coworkers, broaden their knowledge base, meet students' individual needs, and examine their own assumptions about children, families, and education. (See the Spotlight on Teaching.)

What teachers need to do to become better teachers can be physically, intellectually, and emotionally exhausting. In order to continue this rigorous work, teachers need opportunities to solve problems collaboratively with colleagues, share frustrations and satisfactions, consult other resources, engage in peer supervision, and take a day occasionally to observe in other schools.

A number of popular accounts have presented both the humorous and the tragic aspects of what it is really like to teach. Bel Kaufman's *Up the Down Staircase* (1964), Jonathan Kozol's *Death at an Early Age* (1967), Kevin Ryan's *Don't Smile until Christmas* (1970), and *Biting the Apple* (Ryan et al., 1979) are first-person accounts that reveal the disparity between the myth and the reality of school. They depict harried teachers trying to live up to some idealized version of patience, love, and total responsiveness all the time, every day. Sometimes teachers are like overpermissive parents who try to fulfill the perfect mother or father ideal by withholding all genuine feelings ("Don't smile until Christmas!") and finally "boil over," screaming out and hitting their children. Teachers are no better than parents at holding in their genuine feelings. Some incident inevitably

The teacher: A model of perfection or a human being?

opens the floodgate, and all the pent-up anger and personal disappointment break loose. The class learns just what it has suspected all along and may, in fact, have been testing: The teacher was putting on an act of always being "nice."

Unfortunately, the teacher usually feels guilty about having lost control and therefore never realizes the impossibility of living up to the myth that sets the entire process in motion. Instead of developing more realistic perceptions of teaching and learning, teachers who have tried and failed often adopt a set of attitudes that justify and rationalize their failures.

The Hidden Agenda

One of the most important—and discouraging—findings from recent research is the extent to which teachers' true feelings about children (as opposed to their idealized version) affect their ability to be effective educators.

We need to realize that our attitudes are not always clearly known to us. Because we develop our attitudes slowly over a long period, we are often not conscious of what they are or of how our attitudes and expectations influence our behavior. This is why we can say one thing and do another. We may pay lip service to one set of goals, yet a careful examination of how we act may reveal a completely different set. This discrepancy has been called the **hidden agenda** or the implicit curriculum of teaching.

The hidden agenda has special significance for the teacher. We have to be honest with ourselves in determining how much we act without consciousness. Our own attitudes will determine the conditions we create for learning in the classroom. Because of how powerfully these attitudes affect what we convey to students we have an obligation to become more fully aware. It has been shown that adults are poor at identifying the nonverbal messages they convey, and so we must have someone else help us identify the attitudes and expectations we may be transmitting.

For example, if we feel that learning requires that there be no ambiguity, that the "right" answers be presented, and that the pupils know exactly what to say, you can imagine what sort of classroom environment we would provide. Our attitude would affect the way the desks would be arranged, the choice of books and readings we would use, and the way we would manage the discussion time. And this environment would have a very definite influence on the pupils' learning "set." In other words, we affect the attitudes the pupils themselves develop toward learning. There is truth to the old saying "Actions speak louder than words"; our attitudes, motives, and perceptions influence the way we act, and they are transmitted to our pupils through our actions, thereby affecting their attitudinal development.

The Medium and the Message

Marshall McLuhan (1964) has suggested one of the ways our attitudes influence our communications. McLuhan's famous statement "The medium is the message" expresses the idea that the verbal content of a message is interpreted, or given its true meaning, by the way it is delivered.

Our view is less extreme: Content is important, yet we do wish to emphasize the importance of the way messages are transmitted. We have all had the experience of being put down by someone. It isn't so much what that other person says as the *way* it is

"Oh, my teacher and I communicate, all right . . . she looks at me in a certain way and I understand what I'd better do!"

said (the medium). The real message lies in the person's tone, inflection, facial expression, demeanor. It is the nonverbal visual and auditory cues that deliver the real message. A poor attitude in the classroom is reflected in a bad medium, which in turn creates an atmosphere in which learning and growth cannot take place.

Teachers' attitudes can be grouped into three related categories: attitudes toward teaching and learning, attitudes toward pupils, and attitudes toward self.

ATTITUDES TOWARD TEACHING AND LEARNING

We have often mentioned that the way teachers perceive teaching and learning is crucial. Is "knowledge" a finite list of facts for students to memorize? Do we tend to encourage "correct answers" and focus on outcome, or do we consider the process of learning important? Do we consider teaching to be more like training, so that we "tell" pupils what to do? There are widely divergent assumptions about teaching and learning, and our own attitudes and the way we actually behave in class are molded by those assumptions.

If we had to single out one major attitude that

pervades schools, it would be the cherished belief that knowledge equals truth. Teachers and pupils tend to believe that there is an answer for every question, that the truth is known, and that the teacher's voice is like the voice of God. In Chapter 1 we discussed classroom trivia, a form of rapid-fire question-and-answer interaction. Obviously, this kind of teaching reinforces the concept of knowledge as truth and puts the teacher in charge of deciding whether the pupil is "right." The teacher is the center of the classroom, the decisionmaker. "That's absolutely correct" means a bull's-eye. "That's almost right" means a near-miss. A scowl ("teachers' dirty looks") means the student was completely and absolutely wrong.

This view of knowledge as truth also has unfortunate consequences from a developmental standpoint. During elementary school, children move into Jean Piaget's stage of concrete operations (see Chapter 5) and are extremely literal-minded. They also, at this age, tend to divide the world into two camps, the "good guys" and the "bad guys" (see Chapter 7). In other words, children already have a built-in personal and cognitive bias in favor of "truth." If we then consider the special influence of initial learning experiences—recall how strongly we are affected the first time we experience something (see Chapter 4)—we begin to realize how easy it is for the pupils to accept the notion that there is only one answer. The main problem for teachers is the temptation to exploit this situation. It's very easy for them to become the fountainhead of all knowledge, the expert who knows the truth and then decides how close or far away the pupils' answers come. In fact, pupils actually encourage such behavior by the teacher. And teachers may enjoy their presumed omniscience.

In this way the teacher's authority can easily become authoritarian. The confusion of authority and authoritarianism is perhaps the basic dilemma teachers face. This is partly our own fault, especially if we are guilty of confirming the pupils' view of knowledge as fixed and unchanging. Many poignant examples come to mind. Think of the number of times students of all ages ask questions like "What are you going to cover on the next exam?" "How much will this count toward the final grade?" "Do we have to read all the assigned pages?" If you listen closely, you will hear exactly what such students have learned: To please the teacher, you only have to mouth the "right answer."

These attitudes have been learned for the most part in school. Don't blame the students if they are expert apple polishers. That is the behavior that has received the most positive reinforcement throughout their school life.

The teacher should avoid the "knowledge as truth" syndrome and should discourage black-and-white thinking.

Conceptual Levels of Teachers

We pointed out in Chapter 13 that how students understand knowledge is related to their conceptual level. The research and theory of David Hunt detailed how pupils at lower levels of conceptual development would prefer concrete to abstract concepts, high rather than low structure, immediate and concrete rather than delayed and intrinsic feedback and rewards. We discussed this as the ATI approach. What are the implications for teachers as persons and their attitudes toward learning? David Hunt has applied his research method to teachers themselves. Through the use of a test that assesses an individual's conceptual level (CL), he has found that teachers, like students, also have different conceptual systems in regard to teaching and learning. We've asked you to look and listen carefully to your students in order to understand how they understand the process. Hunt's work also suggests that with regard to yourself you look and listen just as carefully.

Hunt's research has indicated that teacher attitudes toward teaching and learning can be clustered into one of three stages. Bruce Joyce, Clark Brown, and Lucy Peck (1981) provide an extended discussion and detailed examples of Hunt's research. Table 14.1 outlines the three stages.

As an example, a study examined the natural, un-coached teaching style of student teachers according to their stage of development on conceptual level. Using the Flanders index of direct versus indirect teaching modes, researchers found a significant difference between the high-CL and low-CL student teachers, even though no difference showed up in grade-point achievement.

As Table 14.2 shows, the high-CL student teachers used all seven teacher strategies with a ratio of direct to indirect modes of close to 50 percent. The low CLs, in contrast, were much less flexible and used the indirect categories much less frequently, less than 33 percent of the time. This study is highly similar in outcome to numerous other investigations. The higher-stage teacher is less dependent, more flexible, and essentially more competent as a teacher.

Does Conceptual Level Make a Difference?

Naturally, a most important question is the empirical one: What is the relation between the teacher's conceptual level and actual teaching behavior? Is this just another case of an interesting and perhaps elegant set of ideas that doesn't translate to the real world of the classroom? In fact, a definite relationship has been found between the CL stage and teacher behavior. This research has been summa-

TABLE 14.1   TEACHER ATTITUDES TOWARD LEARNING AND TEACHING

(Based on Hunt's Conceptual Level Model)

Stage A

Shows strong evidence of concrete thinking
Sees knowledge as fixed
Employs a single "tried and true" method
Exhibits compliance as a learner and expects the same from pupils
Is low on self-direction and initiative; needs detailed instructions
Doesn't distinguish between theory and facts
Relies almost exclusively on advance organizers
Believes teaching is "filling the students up" with facts
Stays at Bloom's levels one and two regardless of student level
Enjoys highly structured activities for self and for pupils
Is very uncomfortable with ambiguous assignments
Does not question authority
Follows a curriculum guide as if it were "carved in stone"
Verbalizes feelings at a limited level; has difficulty recognizing feelings in pupils
Is reluctant to talk about own inadequacies; blames pupils exclusively

Stage B

Shows growing awareness of difference between concrete versus abstract thinking
Separates facts, opinions, and theories about teaching and learning
Employs some different teaching models in accord with student differences
Gives evidence of teaching for generalization as well as skills
Shows some evidence of systematic "matching and mismatching"; can vary structure
Is open to innovations and can make some appropriate adaptations
Shows sensitivity to pupils' emotional needs
Enjoys some level of autonomy and self-directed learning as a goal for self and for the pupils
Employs Bloom's levels one through four when appropriate
Uses evaluations that are appropriate to assignments

Stage C

Understands knowledge as a process of successive approximations
Recognizes that today's theories may be tomorrow's anachronisms
Shows evidence of originality in adapting innovations to the classroom
Is comfortable in applying all appropriate teaching models
Is most articulate in analyzing his or her own teaching in both content and feeling
Has high tolerance for ambiguity and frustration; can stay on task in spite of major distractions
Does not automatically comply with directions—asks examiner's reasons
Fosters an intensive questioning approach with students
Can use all six of Bloom's levels when appropriate
Responds appropriately to the emotional needs of all pupils
Can "match and mismatch" with expert flexibility
Exhibits careful evaluations based on objective criteria according to level of assignment

rized by Miller (1981). At stage C teachers do the following:

Allow constructive student expression

Allow students to raise questions

Allow students to hypothesize

View the student as a participant in learning

View knowledge as an open-ended process

Vary the structure and pace according to learner need

Use a variety of teaching models

TABLE 14.2 CONCEPTUAL LEVEL OF STUDENT TEACHERS AND CLASSROOM INTERACTION

	FLANDERS RATIO 1, 2, 3, 4
	1–7
High CL (N = 16) GPA = 3.1	45% indirect modes
Low CL (N = 13) GPA = 3.0	31% indirect modes

Source: *Data from L. Thies-Sprinthall (1980). Supervision: An educative or miseducative process?* Journal of Teacher Education, 31(2), 17–30. Data reprinted with permission. Copyright by the American Association of Colleges for Teacher Education.

Note: *Based on over 6,000 teacher-pupil interactions. N = number of student teachers. GPA = grade-point average.*

Exhibit empathy toward nearly all students

"Read and flex" with the students

In other words, the stage C teachers can manage group instruction and respond to individual and small-group differences. The results indicated that academic performance in such classrooms was higher than in other classrooms. Diane Lee (1993) suggests that stage C teachers are more competent and "wise," and, in a recent review of studies on teacher professional development, we note that stage C teachers seem better able to adopt and implement strategies for higher-order thinking and cognitively guided instruction (Sprinthall, Reiman, and Thies-Sprinthall, 1996). The key seems to be the concept of "reading and flexing." By that, Hunt means the ability of the teacher to be affected by the pupils and adjust the lesson accordingly. Some students need high structure, others less. The stage C teacher modifies the approach to meet the students' needs. Such flexibility in teaching is not random. Instead the teacher systematically selects different approaches in the best sense of matching and mismatching as described in the previous chapter.

The stage A teachers, on the other hand, hold quite strongly to the view that there is only one correct way to teach. Their concept of subject matter is just as singular. All material has to be boiled down to a group of facts that the students memorize. Stage A teachers give out large amounts of information almost exclusively in a directive fashion. The students are not allowed to raise questions. Rather, they are asked a succession of precise factual questions, resembling our metaphor of classroom trivia. Such

teachers also draw nearly all the conclusions for the students, regardless of the students' levels of development. In other words, everyone "gets" the same method whether they need it or not. In contrast, the stage C teachers also use a highly managed approach with some, but they use an interdependent approach with students who are ready to exercise more self-direction and autonomy in learning.

In philosophical terms Hunt's framework reminds us of the importance of understanding our own assumptions and beliefs about the purpose of teaching. At one level of complexity, students are grouped together as basically the same, as passive receptors of knowledge. The teaching methods are few, largely "tried and true." The outcomes indicate that students don't learn much, except that teaching and learning involve mostly passive memorization. In contrast, teachers who understand the process of teaching and learning at a more complex level, who essentially can apply all levels of Benjamin Bloom's taxonomy to their own teaching, are more likely to have a positive impact on a much broader cross-section of pupils.

ATTITUDES TOWARD PUPILS

Teachers' attitudes toward the pupil are also important in determining classroom atmosphere. Learning climates are subjective, and we were all adept as children in determining whether a teacher "likes kids." The feeling is readily apparent. Does the teacher feel we are competent? Does she or he expect us to do well? Do we feel that the teacher really wants us to be successful?

Teacher Expectations

The importance of teacher expectations, attitudes, and feelings about children has been demonstrated dramatically in a series of studies by Robert Rosenthal, a social psychologist. He has shown that the teacher's expectations determine to a considerable extent how much pupils, or for that matter almost any animal, will learn. His studies have demonstrated, for example, that if experimental psychologists are told that the rats in their study are especially bred for intelligence, those rats will learn the mazes more quickly than the "control" rats, even though no such special breeding was carried out. In other words, Rosenthal has shown that when experimenters expect their rats to do well, those rats outperform their rivals. If the experimenters expect a good performance, they encourage the rats, handle them more carefully, pat them frequently, root for them—in short, treat them with concern and great care because they are expected to do well. If that is so for rats, what about pupils?

In the now-famous Oak Hall School experiment, Rosenthal and coworker Lenore Jacobson (1968) told a group of schoolteachers at the beginning of the school year that particular pupils would have a "growth spurt" during the coming term. In order to lend credence to this prophecy, the researchers said that a special test, "The Harvard Test of Inflicted Acquisition," had been administered to all the children in the elementary school. The results of the test became the basis for their alleged prediction. They identified some pupils as "growth spurters" even though the selections had been random: the identified pupils as a group were not any "smarter" than the others.

At the end of the school term, the results showed that the pupils originally identified as in the growth-spurt group did much better on a series of tests than the other pupils. Their academic performance had improved and, especially in the early grades, their measured IQs were significantly higher than the other pupils'. Also, all the designated children received glowing comments from their teachers. Thus, a major research study has substantiated the effect of the self-fulfilling prophecy. When teachers expected some pupils to experience a growth spurt, the pupils improved in academic performance and intelligence.

A second major finding of this study—and one that is rarely reported—concerns the teachers' attitudes toward the other children. Rosenthal selected a subgroup of pupils in his control group, pupils who showed intellectual gains during the term but who hadn't been identified ahead of time to the teachers. He found that the teachers regarded these children as less well adjusted, less interesting, and less affectionate than the others. In other words, the pupils who made it on their own, who gained intellectually in spite of the prediction, were perceived negatively by the teacher.

Thus, the **Rosenthal effect** is threefold: (1) Pupils who are expected to do well tend to show gains; (2) pupils who are not expected to do well tend to do less well than the first group; and (3) pupils who make gains despite expectations to the contrary are regarded negatively by the teacher. What the effect of those negative expectations may be on such pupils the next time around has not been determined. We can guess, however, what negative expectations in general will produce. Rosenthal quotes Eliza Doolittle from George Bernard Shaw's famous play *Pygmalion*:

You see, really and truly, . . . the difference between a lady and a flower girl is not how she behaves, but how she's treated. I shall always be a flower girl to Professor Higgins, because he . . . treats me as a flower girl, . . . but I know I can be a lady to you, because you always treat me as a lady, and always will (Rosenthal & Jacobson, 1968, p. 183).

At the time of the original study, serious objections were raised concerning technical aspects of the research design. Very rarely can a researcher design a single study that is fail-safe. Rosenthal's response to the criticisms has been instructive. Rather than engage in an endless debate on details, he has instead sponsored a large number of continuing studies. In fact, 10 years after the Oak Hall School experiment, he had reviewed some additional 345 studies on the topic. He was able to show the cumulative significance of how our expectations unintentionally affect the outcomes of our studies (Rosenthal & Rubin, 1978).

The self-fulfilling prophecy of teachers' expectations has also been criticized on the grounds that it fails to take into account such factors as students' background experiences, malnutrition, and parental involvement. Rosenthal (1987) replied to these criticisms with the validity of the original research and subsequent evaluations of similar research studies that show the striking effect of low expectations. It is important to underscore the unintentional nature of the influence. The adult (teacher, researcher, professor) does not consciously seek to affect the outcome, yet nonetheless our attitudes and perceptions shape how we interact.

Evaluations of the Rosenthal effect   Perhaps the best summary with regard to the validity of teacher expectations comes from an independent source. In their evaluation, **Jere Brophy and Thomas Good** (1974) avoided too close an identification with either the original Rosenthal work or the host of critics. Their somewhat dispassionate summary concludes:

Regardless of where one stands concerning the original data, work by a large number of investigators using a variety of methods over the past several years has established unequivocally that teachers' expectations can and do function as self-fulfilling prophecies (p. 32).

In fact, Good and Brophy (1997) are careful to separate two different strands of research on the question. In his earlier studies Rosenthal focused on experimental factors. He attempted to produce the effect by telling teachers that subgroups of children in their classes had different levels of learning potential. The teachers were misled by an experimental manipulation of their knowledge. There is, however, a quite different second strand of research. Observers evaluate natural teacher behavior in the classroom either directly or with video. No faked information is given to the teachers. Instead, teachers are simply watched. Then, if the observed and recorded teacher behavior reveals differences among the children, the characteristics of the children are analyzed. The second method may not be as experimentally pure from a research design perspective, but it is less fraught with interpretative problems. If, for example, a series of observational studies demonstrates that a large number of teachers treat high achievers positively and low achievers negatively, then we don't have to worry about whether the teachers understood or misunderstood the meaning of any of the research procedures in an experimental study. The differences in teacher behavior toward high and low achievers can be taken as an index of the normal repertoire of instructional differences. Also, we don't have to be concerned about the validity of the specific measure of academic outcome. Thus, the two biggest threats to research validity are removed. A series of replicated observational studies outlines a pattern of differences. No false information is provided. Most important, as we shall outline in the next section, the pattern of teacher behavior toward some pupils is exactly the opposite of the Walberg meta-analysis list of effective behaviors. Classroom observations reveal major differences in the use of these behaviors according to the status of the pupil.

Perhaps we should recall that the whole question of the self-fulfilling prophecy first came to light some 70 years ago. A horse in Germany who came to be known as "Clever Hans" gained notoriety for his ability to add, subtract, multiply, and divide by tapping his foot. A psychologist named Pfungst, after long study, figured out that the questioners were unintentionally cueing the horse by lifting their heads up just before the horse reached the correct number of taps. He found that most humans who questioned Hans gave some cue without meaning to—raising their heads, lifting an eyebrow, or even dilating their nostrils. Pfungst concluded that he had spent far too much time "looking for, in the horse, what should have been sought in the man."

How expectancy messages are transmitted   Since most teacher expectations are not conscious intentions, how are the messages conveyed? So far it

seems that nonverbal communication channels are a main mode of transmission. Charles Galloway's work, cited in Chapter 12, pointed out the importance of nonverbal behavior. Rosenthal, following this lead, has provided a creative series of studies detailing just how the expectations are communicated. He masks the verbal content of a statement so that those tested can't quite make out the words. Then he asks them to guess the meaning of the statement. His test, called Profile of Nonverbal Sensitivity (PONS) (Rosenthal, 1979), assesses the ability to read between the lines, so to speak, and understand quite accurately what the person really means, even with the exact content obscured.

In a recent study Rosenthal and colleagues (Babad et al., 1991) involved students as judges of teachers' verbal and nonverbal behavior. The judges in this study included students of differing ages as well as teachers differing in experience. These judges were shown very brief videotaped examples of unfamiliar teachers who were talking about or talking to pupils for whom (unbeknownst to the judges) the teachers held high or low expectations. The judges did not see or hear the pupils on the videotape clips. The results showed that when teachers were involved with the pupils for whom they held high expectations, the raters judged the unseen pupil more positively than when teachers were involved with the pupil for whom they held low expectations. This study is interesting because it demonstrated that students can serve as observers and judges of unfamiliar teachers and that accurate detection of these teachers' expectancy levels can be made on the basis of brief videotaped exposure to these teachers. There has been relatively little research focused on students' perceptions except for that of Rhona Weinstein and her colleagues, whose research studies established that children are indeed highly sensitive to their own teachers' differential behaviors; see descriptions and results of these studies in Weinstein (1989).

The work on teacher expectations clearly indicates that people can't really hide their true attitudes. Perhaps highly skilled actors, after disciplined practice, can successfully mask their real feelings, but most teachers, like everyone else, cannot do so: most students can read their teachers almost like a book. Yet "most teachers believed that their students would *not* know at all about the existence (and identity) of their pets and favorites" (see Babad et al., 1991, p. 230). Tone of voice, facial expression, body stance, eye contact, and similar aspects of body language act as channels, sending clear messages about our real expectations. From research findings we know, first, that our expectations represent a self-fulfilling prophecy, and second, that our body language sends the message, either in a positive or negative mode. Thus, the findings help us understand how the process works. One highly surprising finding, however, is most important to note. Especially in Rosenthal's U.S. samples, adults were highly inaccurate in judging their own nonverbal behavior. The correlations were close to zero on the self-ratings. This should remind us of Robert Burns's famous line about our lack of power "to see ourselves as [others] see us." The research lends further credence to the notion that our expectations as well as the way they are communicated are unintentional. Rosenthal's findings suggest that we ask *not* ourselves how well we are doing but rather those with whom we are working.

Cultural Differences and Student Characteristics

The next question concerning teacher expectations shifts the focus to cultural differences and student characteristics. Is there any pattern or cluster of student characteristics that may be associated with positive or negative expectations? Rosenthal, remember, looked only at one variable in his original study, namely, student ability in terms of "readiness for a growth spurt." But, as it turns out, other student characteristics do have an impact on teacher expectations. And, in turn, student characteristics affect how students understand and interpret teachers' verbal and nonverbal expectations. For example, Lisa Delpit (1988) reminds us that "members of any culture transmit information implicitly to comembers. However, when implicit codes are attempted across cultures, communication frequently breaks down" (p. 283). Delpit describes Shirley Brice Heath's (1983) examples of veiled teacher commands that are misinterpreted by students of diverse backgrounds and different linguistic traditions. For example, while the veiled command "Is *this* where the scissors belong?" may be understood by some students as a direct command to put away the scissors, other students may regard it as a real question and not as a direct command. If veiled commands are ignored, the child could be viewed as disobedient. So the attempt by the teacher to express herself in less powerful indirect terms removes the explicitness that the child may need to understand the rules of the new classroom culture.

Research with minorities at school provides very limited access to cultural assumptions underlying the pupils' distinctive attitudes and behaviors. To learn about cultural diversity it is necessary for teachers to learn about the home communities by

reading about them and getting into them (Ogbu, 1995). Shirley Brice Heath (1995) suggests that the following five types of contemporary communities will provide an increasingly larger proportion of America's public school students: (1) a Puerto Rican barrio in New York City; (2) a pre–World War II Japanese fishing community in California and its current extended community; (3) a rural-oriented African-American community of the 1970s and its current extended connections; (4) a community-based youth organization in a high-crime inner-city area; and (5) a community of street youth in a university neighborhood. She presents ethnographic portrayals of these five different contemporary communities. The portrayals include community members' collective views of learning through formal and nonformal education and descriptions of the communities' ways of socializing individuals into their membership. The portrayals can help teachers to better understand students' diverse backgrounds and what happens when students from these communities come to school and undergo socializations to new affiliations and new self-identities. Understanding students' community backgrounds may help teachers understand students' interpretations of the teachers' verbal and nonverbal expectations.

It is important for teachers to reflect on their own expectations about cultural differences and students' characteristics. In Table 14.3 Hilda Hernandez (1989) summarizes four different perspectives that teachers may hold about why students in a cultural minority may fail to do well in school. Each of the four perspectives, *genetic inferiority, cultural deficit, cultural mismatch,* or *contextual interaction,* attributes blame differently for the academic achievement levels that are different among cultural groups. Each of the four perspectives suggests different solutions to equalize academic achievement among different cultural groups. The fourth perspective of "contextual interaction" is the most likely to result in positive change in a way that doesn't devalue any one culture or exalt any culture.

You may wonder what the research has shown about these different perspectives on cultural differences and school learning.

Shortly after the process of desegregating the public schools began in 1954, with the "deliberate speed" akin to that of a glacier, a few minority children began appearing in the classrooms of previously segregated white schools. Often the transition was marked by riots, federal marshals, bomb threats, stonings, and the use of electric cattle prods. These were the outward and visible signs of massive resistance. With a few exceptions, that era has ended. The public schools became integrated. However, lack of

*TABLE 14.3   PERSPECTIVES ON DIFFERENTIAL ACADEMIC ACHIEVEMENT
AMONG CULTURAL GROUPS*

PERSPECTIVE	ATTRIBUTION OF BLAME	PRIMARY SOLUTIONS
Genetic inferiority: Minorities fail to do well because they are genetically inferior.	The groups themselves, not society	No solutions are possible because little can be done to change heredity.
Cultural deficit: Minorities fail to do well because their culture is viewed as deficient.	The groups themselves, as well as social prejudice and discrimination	Train minorities to be less deficient and eliminate prejudice and discrimination.
Cultural mismatch: Minorities fail to achieve because their cultural traits are incompatible with those in the U.S. mainstream.	No one factor; cultures just happen to be different	Change groups so that they can participate in the mainstream, but also change schools in order to better accommodate and ameliorate the mismatch.
Contextual interaction: Minorities fail to achieve because of unfortunate interactions of many factors.	No one factor, group, or institution; outcomes produced through the interaction of many factors such as circumstances, cultural values, etc.	Change one or more of the factors or the context to alter interactions and thereby change the outcomes.

Source: *Hernandez (1989), p. 37. Reprinted with the permission of Merrill, an imprint of Macmillan Publishing Co. Copyright 1989 by Merrill
Publishing Co.*

integration between city and suburb, and increasing segregation of inner-city schools is an ensuing problem.

The resistance to cultural pluralism, however, did not officially end with the removal of the last police dog, the breakup of the final gathering of white supremacists at the curbstone of the school, or the mapping out of new bus routes. The legal guarantees ended physical resistance. As the reality changed and increasing numbers of African-Americans, Native Americans, and Latinos actually sat at the desks, a new set of barriers was erected. As we shall see in the chapter on intelligence, a new series of studies attempted to show just how inferior black children were because of an inadequate pool of inherited genes. (Shades of the "good" and "bad" Kallikaks!) The implication was direct: Desegregation would fill the schools with inferior humans of limited potential. Teaching procedures would have to be adjusted—downward.

Because the inferior-gene-pool theory could not be supported scientifically, a second theory was proposed: The problem was not poor genes; it was that most minority children came from psychologically deprived environments, for example, "the Negro family." The cause was different, but the result was the same: minority children entering schools were still viewed as significantly less competent. As was the case with the genetic theory, careful reexamination of the so-called family deficit theory has shown

that such a conclusion was a dangerous oversimplification. Certainly, some minority children do experience an inadequate home environment and come from economically weak families with parents who are incompetent and/or violent. Such families, however, are the exception, not the rule. Malnutrition, crowding, excessive noise, premature autonomy, and similar environmental problems will impair any student from any background. Yet to claim that all or nearly all minority children live in such disorganized families creates an unwarranted stereotype. Rather than attribute the difficulty to the minority status of the parents, it would be far more accurate to link such environments to economic poverty rather than to ethnicity.

Thus, we have evidence that indicates that minority children do not inherit from an inferior gene pool, nor are minority families deficient as home environments. What about learning styles such as impulsiveness or concrete versus abstract thinking? A massive review of such learning style differences concluded in no uncertain language that cognitive styles varied as much within ethnic, racial, socioeconomic status and language groups as they did between these groups (Shipman & Shipman, 1985).

Two major factors, however, do distinguish minority and nonminority children in a school situation. The differences are explained not by genes, by home environments, or by learning styles, but rather by psychological variables—attitudes. Minority children are systematically treated differently—namely, as less competent, with lowered achievement goals—and receive less adequate teaching strategies. Thus, one major factor is the difference in educational treatment, not in the children themselves. Minority children tend to receive less. While as a group they may enter the first grade slightly behind majority students, the longer they remain in school, the further behind they fall. In other words, the school experience itself does not produce growth.

A second factor, which is even broader, has to do with the general social and economic goals available to all students. Putting it harshly, minority students ask, "What's the use of studying in school?" Not only is the daily experience more often negative than positive, but in the long run there may also be few opportunities for advancement. **John Ogbu,** a cultural anthropologist, has done a careful study of the origins of human competence in different countries (Ogbu, 1978). Each country had easily identified minority members regarded as "outcasts." These outcasts for a number of generations, indeed for centuries, were systematically denied full participation in society. They were taught, often through violent means (beatings and murder), to remain in their "place." After so many years of harsh repression, such outcast minorities did learn their lesson. No matter how hard they worked in school, their future opportunity was extremely limited. Each new generation had ample evidence of their own prospects from what had happened to the previous generation.

A good example is the famous Supreme Court case *Griggs* v. *Duke Power.* Blacks working as laborers in a coal mine were barred from becoming miners unless they made a certain score on an IQ test. Those new rules virtually prevented promotion of any black laborers. Since the test score had no relationship to actual job performance, the Court ruled against Duke Power. The selection procedure was systemic discrimination—in the words of the Court, "Built-in headwinds for minority groups." The system ensured that a disproportionate number of minorities would be excluded.

Ogbu's point is that the apparent "failure" of African-American, Hispanic, Native American, and other minority students to complete their schooling has been a functional adaptation to reality. Until recently, the virtual exclusion of African-American, Hispanic, and Native American workers from any high-status and highly paid employment that required a formal education sent a strong message: If you want to get ahead in this society, don't waste your time studying. There has been, in Ogbu's words, a "job ceiling." Most of the adults whom minority youth knew were in low-wage, low-skill jobs

for which a high school diploma was hardly a ticket to upward mobility. This has resulted in a situation that might be called a combination of fantasy and reality. A minority youth may say on one hand, "Yes I'd like to be a doctor or a lawyer," then turn around and take whatever low-paying job he or she can get.

What this means is that any differences between minority students and majority students in school performance are most likely not due to specific (or inborn) cultural differences. Characteristics that minority students are supposed to possess, such as short attention span, hyperactivity, and verbal deficits, are simply stereotypes. There is no major evidence that identifies a unique cultural trait that either promotes or prevents learning. Instead, the differences you may observe are most likely a result of social conditions such as direct prior experience in negative schooling or a deep-seated feeling rooted in history that school achievement is not a pathway to a better life. Of course, since the enactment of civil rights legislation and the slow integration of schools, the atmosphere is changing. It may be years, however, before the majority culture can honestly and genuinely convince previously oppressed minorities of a real change in educational opportunity. Each time a teacher, even unintentionally, negatively reinforces a minority student, employs less eye contact, praises majority students more frequently, or uses different cues, that teacher reconfirms the suspicion in the minority student's mind and heart of unequal and unfair treatment. Each time the society as a whole uses what is called *systemic discrimination* to prevent access to better-paying occupations, to higher education, and to professions, the job ceiling effect is reawakened.

The only meaningful difference, then, between minority and majority students in school situations is in motivational patterns. The motivation to learn has been redirected for many minority students. In the past such children received a strong message in the school itself as well as from the larger society. Their "place" was not with books and learning and upward economic mobility, but with physically demanding, backbreaking, low-wage, and low-status roles. Educationally related career achievement was a road to nowhere.

The publicity concerning a successful New York businessman, Eugene Lange, seems to prove Ogbu's point quite dramatically. In 1980 he visited his old elementary school (P.S. 121). Instead of giving the usual Horatio Alger sermon to the ghetto sixth-graders, he promised the 61 students free college tuition. With the help of a concerned counselor, Johnnie Rivera, and the financial incentives, 48 of the original 61 graduated from high school. Rather than the anticipated 40 to 50 percent dropout rate, almost 80 percent completed high school. Even more encouraging were the 25 students who enrolled in college. As a case study, then, Lange's money and Rivera's guidance dramatically raised Ogbu's ceiling.

These findings have two implications. If you are from a majority background, as a teacher you will need to become particularly sensitive to the motivation issue. In fact you may have to go "the extra mile," at least in the beginning, to convince minority students that you will treat them in the same respectful manner and with the same effective methods as the other children. Remember that such children and adolescents have every right to be suspicious and guarded. Too many prior generations have suffered at the hands of so-called white benefactors. Do not expect immediate acceptance, and do not push too hard. Gushing over a student's first halfhearted product will be viewed as a phony performance. Also, do not attempt to "buddy up" by quickly adopting any form of minority verbal expressions or vernacular. That, too, will be seen as false. Expect a period of legitimate testing to clear the air. Minority students, like all others, are fair and generous interpersonally, after you show them fairness and generosity in concrete ways. It's the actions they will look for, not the words.

How about the case of the minority member as teacher? If you are in that category, should you expect instant rapport? Yes and no. Obviously, it will be easier for you to understand the legitimate emotional and motivational needs of minority students. Most likely such issues are close to you personally. This doesn't mean, however, that you will have an automatic acceptance level with those minority students whose backgrounds may be different from your own. Thus, you will need to exercise some care if you begin to notice some mistrust. Also, and especially with adolescents, you may notice some hints or subtle feelings that your own educational attainment is only a case of "tokenism" and that you "sold out" to the white establishment. Such doubt on their part, while genuine, is apt to disappear quite rapidly as your humanity and care become more evident. So, on the one hand, you will start with minority students in a far stronger position than do teachers from majority backgrounds. That's a real plus. But on the other, you will have another set of very difficult problems. Quite unfortunately, as the expectancy research shows, almost half of all teachers (your colleagues) do not accept their pupils on an equal basis. These are some of the teachers who believe the stereotype that any difficulty in classroom learning is caused by the skin color of the child. Failure is laid at the doorstep of the student. This can be a highly distressing situation for you. Such teachers, thoughtlessly, may start a practice of asking you to give those students "a good talking to," or they may make a series of increasingly disparaging comments in front of you about some of their minority students. In pointing a finger at such students, they are often unaware that they may be pointing the remaining three fingers at themselves. In any case, there are certainly no quick solutions to the problems of prejudice and racism. You can remind such teachers that their attitude can become a self-fulfilling prophecy and that no relationship exists between ability and ethnicity. It will also serve as yet another reminder of just how far we still have to go on the road to equity and full participation for all students.

Student Characteristics That Affect Teacher Expectations

Social class **Howard Becker,** a sociologist, demonstrated the primary importance of the social class of the pupil a number of years ago in a now-classic study. He found that most teachers in the large urban school system he examined could be grouped as lower middle class on a socioeconomic scale (Becker, 1969). In general, these teachers valued conformity, obedience, neatness, cleanliness, punctuality, hard work—highly conventional values. He then interviewed more than 60 such teachers to find out how they perceived their pupils. He found three sets of perceptions that closely followed class lines. The teachers perceived children from their own class (lower middle class and blue-collar working class) as the "best" pupils. They were neat, orderly, clean, and followed directions.

Teachers felt that pupils from lower-class backgrounds (essentially poor blacks) were, in general, morally unacceptable: The teachers reported being shocked by the "awful" language and upset because "they" (the lower-class students) were perceived as not really valuing education or wishing to improve themselves. It is not difficult to imagine how such attitudes affected the teachers' expectations regarding the pupils they described in those terms.

Finally, the teachers had a third set of attitudes toward children from upper-class, well-to-do homes. They found these children to be very fine students, bright, clever, quick—but very difficult to teach: "They are too unruly—have no manners—interrupt me—are quick to correct my mistakes," noted one teacher. Another said, "They all have maids and servants at home. They won't pick things up that they drop. One student said to me 'If I picked that up, there wouldn't be any work for the janitor to do.'"

SPOTLIGHT ON DEMOGRAPHICS

Discontinuity between Teacher and Student Diversity

Data analysis by Carl Grant and Walter Secada on diversity in the student population and a summary of data on gender, race/ethnicity, and age of the teaching force from Linda Darling-Hammond and Eileen Mary Sclan demonstrate the discontinuity between the U.S. student population and teaching force. Whereas the student population is increasingly diverse, the teaching force is homogeneous, and is likely to remain so into the next century. How will you deal with diversity in your classrooms and schools?

Race/ethnicity in the student population: In 1976, 24 percent of the total student enrollment in U.S. schools was nonwhite; by 1984, the figure had risen to 29 percent. In the 20 largest school districts, the respective figures were 60 percent and 70 percent. By the year 2000, between 30 and 40 percent of the total school enrollment will be children of color. One in four students is poor. One in five lives in a sin-

gle-parent home. One in seven is at risk of dropping out of school.

The intercorrelation among these various demographic characteristics has been well documented. For example, poverty and race are correlated. Of white children between one and three years old in 1968, 25 percent experienced some period of poverty over the next 15 years. Among black children, the share was 78 percent. The experience of poverty is more intense for black children. Of white children experiencing poverty, 20 percent lived in poverty for more than 4 years of their childhood; among black children similarly situated, the comparable statistic was 59 percent.

Increasing numbers of children from minority language backgrounds are entering school with little or no competence in English. Although Spanish is the predominant first language for most of these children, and is likely to remain so into the next century, in-

creasing numbers of children are entering school with language backgrounds such as Arabic, Chinese, Hmong, Khmer, Lao, Thai, and Vietnamese.

Gender of teachers: In 1991 the average public school teacher was 42 years old, white, married to an employed spouse, and a parent. The large majority of teachers continue to be women—almost 90 percent at the elementary level and just over half (56 percent) at the secondary level. The concentration of women in teaching has increased from 67.7 percent in 1961 to 72.1 percent in 1991. Very few men teach English/language arts, special education, bilingual/English as a second language, and in the elementary grades; they continue to outnumber women in mathematics, science, social studies, and vocational education.

Race/ethnicity of teachers: Minority teachers are underrepresented in teaching generally, and in mathematics and science particu-

---

The teachers also tended to be fearful of reprisal from the parents of the third group. Although the children from the ghetto could be dealt with severely if necessary (including being subjected to corporal punishment), the children from well-to-do backgrounds were immune from direct punishment. The teachers were obviously worried about "influential" parents calling the school board or going directly to the superintendent with complaints about the teachers' actions toward their children.

More recent and psychologically oriented research has validated Becker's work on the importance of social class. When the social classes of the teacher and the pupils differ, especially if the pupils come from a lower socioeconomic class than the teacher, then there is a real possibility that the teacher systematically expects less from and does

less effective teaching with such children. For example, studies have shown that low-income and minority students continue to be much more likely than white or upper-income students to be placed in remedial and low-level courses (Oakes, 1992). The current discontinuity between teacher and student diversity is shown in the Spotlight on Demographics.

Ethnic background—race   The first major study detailing the achievement outcomes of students whose racial or ethnic background was different from the teacher's was done by Eleanor Leacock and her associates (1969) at the Bank Street School in New York. Leacock's researchers, unlike Rosenthal or Becker, actually went into the classroom. They observed the teacher's behavior and checked student achievement. As a result, they found a fairly systemlarly. The percentage of African-American and Hispanic college students who majored in education at the bachelor's degree level declined steadily between 1972 and 1987. Even with more recent increases, African-Americans represented only 8 percent of public school teachers in 1991, approximately the same as two decades earlier. Other minorities increased their representation to 5 percent of public school teachers by 1991, although numbers are still small. The 13 percent of the public school teaching force that is minority compares to about one-third (33 percent) of all public school students who are members of minority groups.

Minority teachers are much more likely to teach in central cities and in schools with a large population of minorities. African-American teachers make up 16.1 percent of the teaching force in central cities, and Hispanic teachers constitute 6.6 percent of urban teachers, substantially higher than their representation nationally. Whereas one out of five public school teachers in the 1987–88 school year taught in schools where more than half the students were minorities, the majority of Asian, African-American, and Hispanic teachers taught at schools with a predominantly minority student body.

Age of teachers: The teaching force has aged considerably since the 1970s, when the last major hiring boom occurred. The percentage of teachers under age 30 declined sharply from 37.1 percent in 1976 to 11.1 percent in 1986, where it has held steady since. Meanwhile the proportions of teachers in their forties and fifties has increased since the mid-1980s. Nearly 23 percent were older than 50 in 1991. This means that large numbers of teachers will be retiring around the turn of the century, many of them in fields such as mathematics and science, where there are already shortages. This trend, along with rising student enrollments, contributes to the projection that at the end of the 1990s and the beginning of the twenty-first century, more than 200,000 teachers will need to be hired annually.

Grant, C. A., & Secada, W. G. (1990). Preparing teachers for diversity. In W. R. Houston (Ed.), *Handbook of research on teacher education* (pp. 403–404). New York: Macmillan. Excerpted with permission of Macmillan Library Reference, USA, a Simon & Schuster Macmillan Company. Copyright © 1990 by the Association of Teacher Educators.

Darling-Hammond, L., & Sclan, E. M. (1996). Who teaches and why: Dilemmas of building a profession for twenty-first century schools. In J. Sikula (Ed.), *Handbook of Research on Teacher Education* (2d ed., pp. 69–70). New York: Simon & Schuster Macmillan. Excerpted with permission of Macmillan Library Reference, USA, a Simon & Schuster Macmillan Company. Copyright © 1996 by the National Association of Teacher Educators.

atic pattern of negative attitudes and expectations toward most lower-class ghetto blacks. Teachers universally expected less of those pupils, even in the very first years of elementary school, than of other children. In addition, teacher expectations declined the longer the pupils were in school. Fifth-graders were seen as less capable and less competent than second-graders in the same school. Leacock found that the schools in this study in the areas where poor blacks lived were neither in continual rebellion nor were they a "blackboard jungle." Rather, the schools were populated by overworked, ineffective, and frustrated teachers and bored, uninterested, and withdrawn children. There were one or two "troublemakers" in each class, but the majority of pupils were quiet and listless. Leacock also compared teacher-pupil interaction in the lower-class black schools with that in middle-class schools (with both black and white children) and found less than half as much interaction in the lower-class schools. This low rate of interaction meant that the "poor" children were being ignored, that most of the time they spent in class was passed in quiet boredom, and that their teachers displayed a genuine lack of interest. Also, the interaction that did take place tended to be twice as negative as that in the middle-class schools; teachers tended to undermine the children, were very derogatory about the children's work, and were supercritical of their attempts to read, do math problems, and do blackboard work.

Another classroom observation study by Brophy and Good (1974) gave a detailed account of the different teacher behaviors according to the ethnic background of the children. They watched for

LINDA DARLING-HAMMOND

In *What Matters Most: Teaching for America's Future* (1996) Linda Darling-Hammond reminds us that new teachers are still given the most challenging teaching assignments and left to sink or swim with little or no support. Her efforts as director of the National Commission on Teaching and America's Future have resulted in a report that many believe to be the single most important strategy for achieving America's goals: A blueprint for recruiting, preparing, and supporting excellent teachers in all of America's schools. This is not the first time that Darling-Hammond has been in the forefront of reform efforts in teaching and teacher education. Her extensive publications include six books and more than 150 journal articles, book chapters, and monographs on educational policy and practice. In the *Handbook of Research on Teacher Education* (1996) Darling-Hammond confronts the dilemmas in the changing context of teacher education and the increasing diversity of race and ethnicity in the student body compared to the increasing homogeneity of the teaching force. In the *Handbook of Research on Multicultural Education* (1995) she addresses the inequalities for minorities in access to knowledge and resources, resulting in barriers to educational opportunities. In her most recent book, *The Right to Learn* (1997), Darling-Hammond calls for a system of democratic education that empowers *all* children for the twenty-first century, a system based upon the hard-won lessons learned about equality in education and excellence in teaching.

Linda Darling-Hammond is a well-spoken, passionate, and caring supporter of teaching quality and educational equity. Her early work as a public school teacher awoke her concerns about and commitment to reform and restructuring in the teaching profession. Supportive versus destructive learning environments in schools often depend on the teacher. She saw how much difference a teacher can make. She experienced the contrasts and inequalities within the family, the community, and the school.

Dr. Darling-Hammond was born and schooled in Cleveland, Ohio. Serving as a teacher's aide in the Cleveland public schools in 1969 triggered her zeal for teaching and sealed her fate. She earned a B.A. degree *magna cum laude* from Yale University in 1973 and pursued a teaching certificate in English at Temple University. She completed her student teaching in an underfunded high school where, like many novices, one of her assigned classes consisted entirely of 12th-graders who had failed English the year before. She went on to her first job as an English teacher and tried to talk the principal into restructuring her classes so that she might have the high school students two years in a row in an English/social studies block in order to ensure more powerful learning for them, but she was refused because of the constraints of scheduling. These experiences fueled her fire for reform. During this early period of her career her commitment to urban education was supported by Bernard Watson, former deputy superintendent of Philadelphia schools, who was her faculty adviser at Temple and a mentor with great enthusiasm for teaching in the public schools. With support from a scholarship and a research assistantship, she pursued further work and a

---

teacher eye contact and the frequency of goal-setting behavior by teachers and pupils. The results are summarized in Table 14.4.

Recent findings at other levels of education are also negative. A study of higher education using the same Brophy and Good observational instruments revealed patterns of professional behavior that differed according to the ethnic status of the students. Professors took more time to answer questions asked by nonminority students, asked less complex questions of minority students, and provided fewer cues and feedback to the latter. The results were the same in undergraduate and graduate classes. There was no difference in the general participation rates between nonminority and minority status (Trujillo, 1986).

career in urban education. She continued study at Temple University and earned a doctorate degree in urban education, with highest distinction, in 1978.

Linda Darling-Hammond is currently a professor at Teachers College, Columbia University, where she is also codirector of the National Center for Restructuring Education, Schools, and Teaching (NCREST). Before joining the Teachers College faculty in 1989, she was senior social scientist and director of the RAND Corporation's Education and Human Resources Program. She earlier served as director of the National Urban Coalition's Excellence in Education Program, conducting research on exemplary city school programs and urban school finance issues. Her work in New York in urban education is so important that at one point she turned down the invitation of a deanship at Harvard University.

Dr. Darling-Hammond has assumed leadership on numerous national advisory boards, commissions, and professional organizations dealing with educational reform issues, including the National Board for Professional Teaching Standards (NBPTS) and the National Academy of Education. She is past president of the American Educational Research Association. As chair of New York State's Council on Curriculum and Assessment,

she helped fashion a comprehensive school reform plan that supports curriculum and assessment for more challenging learning goals linked to professional development and greater equity in opportunities to learn. As chair of the Model Standards Committee of the Interstate New Teacher Assessment and Support Consortium, (INTASC), she helped develop licensing standards for beginning teachers that reflect current knowledge about what teachers need to know to teach diverse learners to these higher standards.

Amid an impressive array of editorial boards, publications, awards, and other professional activities, Darling-Hammond still relishes opportunities to work with students and their teachers in elementary and secondary schools. As codirector of NCREST, she takes this opportunity often. One recent delight was her discovery that the Children's Community School in Silver Spring, Maryland, a progressive preschool and elementary school that she helped start in the 1980s, is now assisting the work of other such progressive community schools. Darling-Hammond's continued enthusiasm comes from collaborative work with colleagues and beginning and experienced teachers at Teachers College who are motivated and committed to improving education.

When reflecting on her career and what stands out in her accomplishments and contributions to teacher education and the teaching profession, she suggests that two of her publications serve as bookends on 12 years of work. In 1984, while working at the RAND Corporation, she published *Beyond the Commission Reports: The Coming Crisis in Teaching*, a 19-page best-selling monograph calling for policy attention to the importance of teaching. In 1996 the fruition of her significant efforts was the publication of *What Matters Most: Teaching for America's Future*, which outlines the path to a strong teaching profession.

Dr. Darling-Hammond has played a principal role in focusing our attention on NBPTS standards as the benchmark for accomplished teaching; student standards linked to teaching standards; extended teacher-preparation programs providing a year-long internship in a professional development school; mentor programs for beginning teachers; a professional career continuum that rewards teachers' continuous improvement; and restructured schools to support student and teacher learning. What matters the most, she says, are educational equity, quality teaching, and caring for all students.

The message is clear for inner-city children from lower-class backgrounds: They are either ignored, criticized, or undermined in their attempts to learn. This suggests that teachers in ghetto schools are teaching their children not to learn. Sometimes this behavior is deliberate, most often it is inadvertent, reflecting unconsciously held assumptions about the abilities of inner-city children. It therefore comes as

no surprise to find that pupil achievement in such schools is significantly lower than in ethnically similar nonghetto schools. The teachers' unfortunate attitudes toward their pupils pervade some schools and doom those children to failure. Other research has indicated that such children end up not only with lowered academic achievement but also with a negative concept of themselves as learners. They have

TEACHER 14.4   TEACHER RESPONSES ACCORDING TO PUPILS' ETHNIC BACKGROUND

Eye Contact	Teacher Response Rate
Initiated by white pupils	57% (14 to 8)
Initiated by black pupils	11% (35 to 4)
Teacher Goal Setting with Pupils*	
White middle-class school A	43 (12.3 instances/hour)
White middle-class school B	46 (15.3 instances/hour)
White lower-class school	18 (6 instances/hour)
Black lower-class school	15 (5 instances/hour)

* Based on three-hour-long observations.

lower self-confidence in problemsolving situations. For such children, "formal" education in school may be worse than no education at all.

Family composition   A third factor that affects teacher expectations and also is beyond the control of the individual pupil is family background. Whether the pupil comes from a two-parent or a single-parent home makes a significant difference in teacher predictions. In a comprehensive review of the literature, Diane Scott-Jones (1984) found that even when teachers viewed videotapes of children demonstrating precisely the same behaviors, their predictions differed. For children denoted as from one-parent homes, the teachers expected *both* lower academic performance and greater psychological problems. When children were said to be from intact homes, the attitude changed markedly despite the behavioral similarity. Further (almost to prove Rosenthal's point), another study indicated that both single and dual parents were accurate in their predictions of the different teacher expectations. In other words, the message did get through that teacher expectations differed just on the basis of family makeup.

Scott-Jones also noted that when social class is controlled as a variable, research studies indicated no difference in either intelligence or academic achievement between children from single-parent and from intact homes. Since the number of single-parent homes has grown dramatically, she was concerned about this teacher bias, with good cause. Ac-

cording to some estimates, as many as 60 percent of all children may at one time or another live in a single-parent family. Such estimates do vary with both ethnic background and family income. Unfortunately, the likelihood of living in a single-parent home is much greater among economically poor and ethnically different children; such children may be doubly impaired as learners because of negative expectancies. Teacher expectations are also affected by other nontraditional household arrangements involving adoptive families, legal families, communes, same-sex households, common-law unions, and neighbors or relatives.

Student temperament   The fourth area of significance is students' basic personality temperament: At the broadest level, research has shown that teachers can be affected by the general social skills of children. Pupils with "easy" temperaments (that is, likable personalities) who were quick to adapt to the teacher's requests and were pleasant to be around were consistently overrated as to their actual abilities. "Slow to warm up" children, who were less likable, moodier, less quick to adapt, and more "emotional," were rated lower on the same estimates. In fact, one study suggested that such temperamental differences were more significant than IQ or socioeconomic status as factors influencing teacher expectations. There is insufficient evidence to back up such a claim. In any case pupil temperament does have an influence (Woolfolk & Brooks, 1983). Teachers are unintentionally more positive to likable children and less positive to the "slow to warm up" ones. As in the case of Brophy and Good's research, the teacher expectations were assessed at a nonverbal level. Their tone of voice was different, and they maintained less eye contact with those they considered difficult to teach.

Gender differences   The influence of gender is a fifth area of concern. People may assume that a lot has improved in equitable treatment of students on the basis of gender because there have been some political changes in the area of gender equity (most notably Title IX). And, in fact, some students are very able to analyze stereotypes from their own gender socialization; see, for example, the Spotlight on "Fairer Tales." The AAUW report (1992) shows, however, that there are many subtle and not-so-subtle factors operating in classrooms to the educational detriment of females. Years ago, the standard view was that gender differences, particularly in elementary school, favored girls. Boys tended to be more hyperactive, noisier, shorter on attention span, and less "academic" than girls. As a result, it seemed natural to conclude that the teachers favored girls as more docile, easier to teach, and quicker to learn how to behave like good pupils. But a case can be made for the converse. In the 1970s, for example, careful classroom observations in preschool indicated that teachers were responding to the sexes differently and to the disadvantage of girls (Maccoby & Jacklin, 1974). Teachers encouraged assertiveness, autonomous problemsolving, and independence in boys but were likely to devalue the very same behavior in girls. The girls were getting a different message—to show less activity and more docility in learning.

Evidence in the 1980s confirmed those findings. Jeanne H. Block showed that a large array of different expectations almost always favors boys. Teachers interact more favorably with boys and give them more positive feedback while directing more criticism at girls. In one study, Block (1984) reported that high-achieving girls received the lowest level of supportive feedback, significantly fewer statements of praise, and significantly more disparaging statements. She also noted that such negative expectancies can be found from nursery school to college. In preschool, boys receive more attention. In college, female intellectual aspirations are taken less seriously by professors. Nine reports published since 1982 focused on the chilly college classroom climate for nonminority and minority women. Their researchers note that faculty call on men by name, coach them toward more complex answers, wait longer for them to formulate an answer, credit their answers by name, and often address the class as though no women were present (Hall & Sandler, 1982, 1996). These expectations and the discouragement and denigration of female academic effort may well have, in Block's words, "pernicious effects."

Elizabeth Fennema and colleagues, in studies of math teaching at both elementary and secondary levels in the United States and around the world, indicate similar differences (Fennema & Leder, 1990; Burton, 1990). Boys were encouraged and girls discouraged even though no major differences in ability were evident. Thus, there seems to be reasonable evidence that the gradual decline in mathematical achievement by females, which doesn't start until adolescence, is brought on in part by lowered teacher expectations (Hyde et al., 1990).

Some teachers may not have accommodated their expectations to today's greater emphasis on educational equity, which stresses factors such as independence and self-direction as opposed to conformity and docility. The main point is that gender can result in different expectations (Sadker & Sadker, 1994).

There are many checklists and activities that allow teachers to investigate and monitor their treatment of female and male students. Some can be used in the privacy of one's own classroom with audio- or videotape. Others can be used and discussed with colleagues. Teachers don't intentionally set out to treat students differently on the basis of characteristics such as gender. Differential treatment occurs because we are unaware of how our biases and assumptions are acted out in the classroom. Any remedy for inequitable treatment of students must include developing awareness of and reflection on our biases and teaching behavior.

It is important to remember that gender *combines* with other factors that influence teachers' expectations of students. As we have mentioned previously, ethnicity and racial background are predictive of the level of classroom interaction. For example, "Majority males are more likely to interact with the teacher than minority males, and majority females are more likely to interact [with the teacher] than minority females." (Sadker et al., 1991, p. 299).

Effects of Student Differences in Academic Achievement on Teachers' Behavioral Responses

Teachers' behavior in class differs according to their perception of students as low achievers or as high achievers. The most recent summary by Good and Brophy (1997) identifies 18 differences. For low achievers, teachers provide

Less wait-time

Fewer cues or rephrased questions

Inappropriate reinforcement

Greater criticism for failure

Less praise for correct responses

Less public feedback

Less interaction in instruction

Fewer opportunities to answer questions

Seating farther away from the teacher

Less demanding experiences

Interaction in private

Less benefit of the doubt in grading

Less friendly interaction

Briefer feedback

SPOTLIGHT ON FAIRER TALES

"Cinder-Ella to the Rescue"

Jessica Kogan

In a course Ellen Silber and Jeanne Bodin teach at Marymount College, students are asked to rewrite fairy tales. Here is an edited excerpt from one submission, along with the student's comments on her story.

One day an announcement came that the king was having a ball to welcome his son home after a long journey and all the young people in the kingdom were invited. Cinder, her mother and sisters talked late into the night trying to figure out a way to clothe the girls.

Finally, Cinder said to her sisters, "If you want to go to the ball don't let anything stop you."

"But how can we go to the ball without evening gowns?" the sisters cried in unison.

Cinder replied, "We have velvet curtains in our house and silk bedsheets. We have beads, pearls and buttons from old

dresses. We can make the gowns together."

"That is wonder idea, but you have to promise to come to the ball with us," cried the sisters. Cinder told her sisters she would see, and then she started to design the gowns. Cinder had a flair for design and knew how to put fabrics together. She knew how to design clothes taking one's physical appearance into consideration. She was determined to create comfortable clothes. "Why should they bind themselves into the male concept of beauty and squeeze into some tight-fitting gown that made it almost impossible for them to move?" she asked. So instead, Cinder created free flowing and comfortable gowns that complimented her sisters' looks. Each gown was uniquely designed for the sister who would be wearing it. Then the girls and their mother started to cut fabric and sew the gowns together. They worked long hours

and the gowns started to take shape.

The sisters continued to beg Cinder to go to the ball with them, and she finally agreed and started to work on her own gown and slippers. On the day of the ball, the sisters got dressed and helped comb each other's hair. They looked lovely in the gowns that Cinder had designed. They were dignified and well dressed, and each sister definitely had her own unique style. The best part was that the sisters couldn't believe how comfortable the gowns were.

The sisters were ready to leave for the ball when they realized that they had no coach to take them to the palace. "Oh well," Cinder said, "I guess we will have to walk the mile to the palace." And so they did. When they got to the ball, all the women wanted to know where they bought their gowns. The prince came over to Cinder and expressed his sympathy over her father's death. Cinder and

---

Less eye contact and less generally responsive nonverbal behavior

Less use of effective but time-consuming instructional methods

Less acceptance and use of ideas

More emphasis on repetition, facts, and drill and practice

It is both interesting and professionally depressing to realize that when Good and Brophy began their research on teacher expectations and academic achievement, they reported only four main differences—essentially the first four in the new list. Obvi-

ously, more focused and extensive research since that time has uncovered a much greater list of differences, and this is only in respect to academic achievement. What might be the outcome of more intensive research on teacher expectations with respect to social class, ethnicity, family background, and gender differences? On the one hand, would the list of differences continue to multiply in a fashion similar to the list for academic achievement? On the other hand, could teacher training programs focus more directly on the problem of expectations? Recent studies may point the way.

For example, Dorene Ross and William Smith's (1992) case study of preservice teachers' perspectives the prince talked about the kingdom and world affairs, and he was glad to see how well versed she was on so many topics. He asked her many questions about business and politics, and their discussions went on late into the night. The prince respected Cinder's independence and intelligence and enjoyed talking to her.

Soon after the ball, Cinder, her mother and sisters opened the dress design shop and called it "Cinder-Wear." Cinder's sisters and mother soon developed into good business persons just like Cinder. They worked very hard and were determined to become successful, and they did. The Ellas used unique marketing ideas, but the most beneficial practice they used to increase business was "networking." Soon, throughout the kingdom, women started to open many different types of businesses, and through networking and supporting each other, they became successful.

Cinder, her mother and sisters lived very full and rewarding lives and were very happy. Cinder continued to see the prince, and their relationship developed into one of mutual trust and respect. The prince and Cinder often discussed the changes that were taking place in the world. At the time this story was written, the prince and Cinder were discussing the possibility of getting married. One thing for sure is that if they get married, it will be a true partnership, and they will live with love and respect for many years.

Jessica comments:

In my rewrite, I made Cinderella's relationship with her mother and sisters a positive one. I tried to show that by supporting each other they achieved success and fulfillment as women. I didn't mention Cinderella's looks but instead concentrated on her strengths. I wanted her to be independent and resourceful. I did not want her success and happiness to be based on her getting married. I wanted her relationship with the prince to be based on mutual respect, and I didn't want the prince's main qualities to be that he was handsome, charming and rich. I wanted him to be a man of substance who was interested in more than a pretty face. I tried to create in Cinder a character who would be viewed by men and women alike as being admirable and strong. "Cinderella to the Rescue" is the type of story that could give young women an alternative to the hopeless, helpless princess stories.

Kogan, J. (Summer 1996). Cinder-Ella to the rescue. *Equity Newsletter, 2*(1), 12. Reprinted with permission of the publisher, Dr. Ellen Silber, Director of the Marymount Institute for the Education of Women and Girls, Marymount College Tarrytown, 100 Marymount Avenue, Tarrytown, NY.

on diversity describes an elementary education course in which preservice students in their first field experiences are helped to identify and examine perspectives about the problems that confront diverse students in classrooms, their commitment to teaching diverse learners, and their beliefs about the causes of failure for diverse learners. The course emphasizes ethical issues related to educational equity.

Another interesting study was conducted to test procedures designed to change teacher expectations about physically or mentally challenged children. Teachers viewed a series of videotapes consisting of three 10-minute segments. The third segment demonstrated a highly interactive teaching method with two children who had moderate to severe mental handicaps. The results indicated quite clearly that teacher attitudes changed very significantly after the interactive teaching (Delcos et al., 1987). As opposed to the teachers in the control group, those who viewed the dynamic approach gave the two children much more positive ratings both in learning potential and in learning the specific task. Actually seeing how an expert teacher works interactively with such "different" children had a positive effect upon the novice teachers' attitudes. This should remind us that expectations are not immutable. Modeling more effective approaches in teaching groups of children

SPOTLIGHT ON PREJUDICE

Learning Shame

Dick Gregory

I never learned hate at home, or shame, I had to go to school for that. I was about seven years old when I got my first big lesson. I was in love with a little girl named Helen Tucker, a light-complected little girl with pigtails and nice manners. She was always clean and she was smart in school. I think I went to school mostly to look at her. I brushed my hair and even got me a little old handkerchief. It was a lady's handkerchief, but I didn't want Helen to see me wipe my nose on my hand. The pipes were frozen again, there was no water in the house, but I washed my socks and shirt every night. I'd get a pot, and go over to Mister Ben's grocery store, and stick my pot down into his soda machine. Scoop out some chopped ice. By evening the ice melted to water for washing. I got sick a lot that winter because the fire would go out at night before the clothes were dry. In the morning I'd put them on, wet or dry, because they were the only clothes I had.

It was on a Thursday, I was sitting in the back of the room, in a seat with a chalk circle drawn around it. The idiot's seat, the troublemaker's seat.

The teacher thought I was stupid. Couldn't spell, couldn't read, couldn't do arithmetic. Just stupid. Teachers were never interested in finding out that you couldn't concentrate because you were so hungry, because you hadn't had any breakfast. All you could think about was noontime, would it ever come? Maybe you could sneak into the cloakroom and steal a bit of some kid's lunch out of a coat pocket. A bite of something. Paste. You can't really make a meal of paste, or put it on bread for a sandwich, but some-times I'd scoop a few spoonfuls out of the paste jar in the back of the room. Pregnant people get strange tastes. I was pregnant with poverty. Pregnant with dirt and pregnant with smells that made people turn away, pregnant with cold and pregnant with shoes that were never bought for me, pregnant with five other people in my bed and no Daddy in the next room, and pregnant with hunger. Paste doesn't taste too bad when you're hungry.

The teacher thought I was a troublemaker. All she saw from the front of the room was a little black boy who squirmed in his idiot's seat and made noises and poked the kids around him. I guess she couldn't see a kid who made noises because he wanted someone to know he was there.

It was on a Thursday, the day before the Negro payday. The eagle al-

who have traditionally been on the short end of positive expectations can be a positive step.

How Widespread Are Negative Expectations?

Having established the importance of teacher expectations, how they are communicated, and the different forms they take, we come to the final point. How broad is the phenomenon? Does it happen only infrequently and then only to a small proportion of pupils? Naturally, it is difficult to derive a firm index. One group of researchers estimates that as many as 33 percent of all teachers show highly differentiated teaching behaviors toward children perceived differently according to academic potential. This is a highly conservative estimate for two reasons. First, only teachers who were clearly (indeed almost blatantly) highly different were included. Second, the expectations were based on only one student characteristic, learning potential. If we add in the other findings indicating a bias due to social class, race, ethnicity, family configuration, temperament, and gender, we would have to conclude that negative expectations are probably operating in more than half the classrooms in the country.

It is clear that for all who plan to teach, systematic awareness of expectations represents a crucial learning. The ability to relate in a positive and constructive manner to all children is not easily achieved; however, it can be developed. It is critical. How many of those factors known to bias teachers are within the student's current power to change—ability, social class, race, temperament, family, prior academic achievement? Should such unchangeable elements influence over half of those currently in ways flew on Friday. The teacher was asking each student how much his father would give to the Community Chest. On Friday night, each kid would get the money from his father, and on Monday he would bring it to the school. I decided I was going to buy me a Daddy right then. I had money in my pocket from shining shoes and selling papers, and whatever Helen Tucker pledged for her Daddy I was going to top it. And I'd hand the money right in. I wasn't going to wait until Monday to buy me a Daddy.

I was shaking, scared to death. The teacher opened her book and started calling out names alphabetically.

"Helen Tucker?"

"My Daddy said he'd give two dollars and fifty cents."

"That's very nice, Helen. Very, very nice indeed."

That made me feel pretty good. It wouldn't take too much to top that. I had almost three dollars in dimes and quarters in my pocket and held onto the money, waiting for her to call my name. But the teacher closed her book after she called everybody else in the class.

I stood up and raised my hand.

"What is it now?"

"You forgot me."

She turned toward the blackboard. "I don't have time to be playing with you, Richard."

"What is it now?"

"My Daddy said he's . . ."

"Sit down, Richard, you're disturbing the class."

"My Daddy said he'd give . . . fifteen dollars."

She turned around and looked mad. "We are collecting this money for you and your kind, Richard Gregory. If your Daddy can give fifteen dollars you have no business being on relief."

"I got it right now, I got it right now, my Daddy gave it to me to turn in today, my Daddy said . . ."

"And furthermore," she said, looking right at me, her nostrils getting big and her lips getting thin and her eyes opening wide, "we know you don't have a Daddy."

Helen Tucker turned around, her eyes full of tears. She felt sorry for me. Then I couldn't see her too well because I was crying too.

"Sit down, Richard."

And I always thought the teacher kind of liked me.

Gregory, Dick (with Robert Lipsyte) (1964). *Nigger: An autobiography.* New York: E. P. Dutton, pp. 43–46. Copyright © 1964 by Dick Gregory Enterprises, Inc., and E. P. Dutton, a division of New American Library.

---

teaching? As you review this material, try not to see it as just a litany of complaints about teachers. Instead, consider it an important agenda for change so that pupils may have a better chance to learn.

A fine example of a teacher's progress in learning to deal more openly with her own assumptions and behavior about racial and social differences among her students can be found in *White Teacher,* by Vivian Gussin Paley (1989). In their foreword to the book, James P. Comer and Alvin F. Poussant write:

Paley is effective in helping people appreciate themselves because she respects human differences but is always mindful of human similarities. It was a relief, and a basis for hope, to discover that she didn't start out that way; that she grew to be comfortable with differences through a personal commitment to fairness and a determined effort to understand herself and culturally different people . . . the fact that she was able to grow and change is what is most significant (p. ix).

The lesson here is that we need to raise expectations and standards for all students. We can no longer conduct business as usual. We can achieve high standards in a great variety of ways and through a multitude of materials by finding and using culturally, multiculturally, and linguistically relevant materials in developing students' basic skills. We can also use a variety of approaches, from peer tutoring to dramatizations, in instruction. "Raising standards and expectations does not mean homogenizing instruction but creating new and different opportunities for learning for all students" (Nieto, 1992, p. 262). **Sonia Nieto** also reminds us that "good

SPOTLIGHT ON MULTICULTURAL EDUCATION IN PRACTICE

Good Intentions Are Not Enough

Students' achievement is based on subtle and not-so-subtle ways in which teachers expect. The research (Rosenthal self-fulfilling) had mixed receptions from educators—some supporters, some not. But teachers' expectations were finally taken seriously. Prior to that, students' failure in school could be attributed wholly to individual or family circumstances. The continuing research also adds the effects of teacher attitudes and behaviors and school expectations. The significant factor is the manner in which teachers, schools, communities, and society often interact to produce failure.

Sonia Nieto writes:

Expectations are bound up with the biases we have learned to internalize. If we expect children who come from economically poor communities to be poor readers, we may reflect it in modifications we make in the way we teach them. Similarly, if we expect girls to be passive and submissive, we may teach them as if they were. Although our teaching approaches are either frequently unconscious or developed with the best of in-

tentions, the results can be disastrous. Having good intentions or even caring deeply about students is not enough. We need to consider our biases, which even the most enlightened teachers carry with them, every day that we set foot in the classroom. We are sometimes shocked when others point out to us, for instance, that we call on the girls in our class less often than the boys or that we accept slovenly work from some students and not from others. African-American and Latino students have often stated that teachers were happy with a C from them in math, say, whereas they expected higher grades from other students in the class. We cannot mandate, of course, that teachers develop high expectations for all students or that schools become antiracist, antisexist institutions overnight, but we can suggest changes in the educational environment that help promote these processes.[a]

Nieto suggests a number of specific changes teachers can make in each of the following areas:

I. Countering racism, sexism, and low expectations
   - Promoting and actively working toward creating a diverse staff
   - Making difference and similarities an explicit part of the curriculum
   - Making racism and discrimination an explicit part of the curriculum
II. Changing schools: Restructure and renewal
   - Investigating the effects of school organizational structures like tracking, testing, and disciplinary policies; the curriculum and pedagogy, as well as the physical structure of the school
   - Increasing the role of students; teachers, parental and community involvement
III. Respecting and affirming cultural differences
IV. Perceiving linguistic diversity as a resource.[b]

---

[a]   Nieto, S. (1992). *Affirming diversity: The sociopolitical context of multicultural education* (p. 286). New York: Longman.
[b]   Ibid., pp. 284–301.

---

intentions are not enough" (see the Spotlight on Multicultural Education in Practice).

Denny Taylor and Catherine Dorsey-Gaines (1988) provide a dramatic example from their case study of poor, inner-city, black families with academically successful students. They found that these children consistently did their homework, made the honor roll, and had positive attitudes about school. Their parents motivated them to learn and study, communicated high hopes for their education, spoke

optimistically about the future, and in fact considered literacy an integral part of their lives. These high parental and home expectations were prevalent in spite of such devastating conditions as family deaths; lack of food, heat, and hot water; and a host of other hostile situations. These researchers concluded that the fragmentation that takes place as these successful children move from the hopes of their families through an education system that "disconnects their lives" is overwhelming. When these

One of the characteristics associated with both successful schools and successful teachers is the ability to project high expectations for all their students. In such an environment, minority and lower-class children have demonstrated much higher academic success rates.

children are successful, it is often in spite of, rather than because of the school system. Beverly Daniel Tatum (1992a) examined the experiences of black families in white communities from the viewpoint of the families themselves. On the basis of interviews with black families who are living, working, and raising children in the midst of a predominantly white community, Tatum highlights not only the struggles these families face but the strategies they used to overcome the obstacles they encountered. These researchers concluded that the family context was strong. Why wasn't that family strength being represented in the school experience of these children? If educators were better able to recognize strengths of all kinds in their students, then negative expectations might change, thus positively affecting the achievement of all students.

There are positive examples of children from the most economically disadvantaged families who have reached unparalleled levels of success in school in spite of the tremendous odds against them. Research on effective schools found a substantial number of schools in which poor children demonstrated academic achievement as high as their peers in middle-class schools (Levine & Lezotte, 1995). The Success for All program reported by Robert Slavin et al. (1990), is a comprehensive inner-city program designed to bring all children to grade level by third grade. It provides another positive example. The re-

sults from the first year of the program showed substantially enhanced language and reading skills compared to children who were involved in other programs.

ATTITUDES TOWARD SELF

We humans have known about the importance of self-knowledge for a long time. Socrates said that the unexamined life is not worth living. It is obvious that the way teachers perceive and feel about themselves is a major determinant of classroom atmosphere and student performance. Self-confidence, poise, self-control, an eagerness to lead a class of children will obviously set the tone for cooperation and learning in the class. Similarly, a superanxious, trembling, insecure teacher will set the opposite tone. How we see ourselves is a most important component in determining classroom atmosphere.

A Concerns-Based Approach

Frances Fuller, of the University of Texas, pioneered an approach to the personal aspects of teaching effectiveness (1969). She found that almost all student teachers and beginning teachers experience a similar sequence of phases of personal growth. She was able to chart the phases and called her approach the

CBAM method (concerns-based adoption model). Table 14.5 outlines the central components of the scheme.

The phases can be grouped into three general categories: self-concerns, management, and impact on students. In the early phases teachers are worried about whether the students really like them, how they are being evaluated, how they feel as teachers, and how they fit with the more experienced teachers in the building. Fuller has shown that such initial concentration on self is normal. During the first phases, then, a heightened self-consciousness is the mode. After all, the situation is new. As a beginner, you are an outsider. The process is strange and the role unfamiliar. In Piaget's terms, the need to accommodate, to learn a new role, to adjust to an unfamiliar environment creates a classic disequilibrium. Recall, from Chapter 5, the outline of the process of knowledge disturbances (perturbations) that occur in pupils when new learning is required. Basically, this same process applies to you as a beginning teacher. During such a period of disequilibrium, then, you can expect some preoccupation with yourself, your appearance, and relationships. This outlook will narrow your perceptions at the outset. Given a reasonable amount of support and time, you will find yourself moving to the middle group of Fuller phases.

In the management phase, the beginner is focused on teaching behaviors and strategies. The self-consciousness of the first phases gradually gives way to concerns about method. This means you will find yourself asking questions such as, Are the assignments on target? Are my instructions clear? Where can I find more planning time to revise some units? Am I using positive reinforcement or am I reinforcing inappropriate behavior? In a sense, the focus is still on self but it is also on teaching behavior. Learning how to manage the class, to operate smoothly, handle the transitions, maintain order, and do it all with enthusiasm is obviously a major concern during this phase.

The impact phases include consequences, collaboration, and refocusing. It is notable that beginners proceed from self to management *before* they can become greatly concerned over impact. After you feel comfortable with the students in a reasonably controlled environment, you will be able to concentrate on teaching outcomes. At that point, you will be able to set aside the earlier concerns almost entirely and attend to what happens to the pupils. In our terms, you may begin to recognize individual differences, modify teaching methods, flex with and "read" the pupils, and vary the structure to meet student needs. In short, you will be on your way to becoming a competent teacher. You will be able to analyze and change your practice. Careful reflection will occur as a natural part of your work.

Unfortunately, Fuller's work has shown that student teachers and beginning teachers generally do not reach the level of impact. Instead, some remain at the personal level, while the majority reach management. The problem, however, is not the beginner's fault. It has been shown that novice teachers all too often do not receive adequate professional support and supervision. The National Commission on Teaching and America's Future (1996) reports that "new teachers are typically given the most challenging teaching assignments and left to sink or swim with little or no support" (p. 39). It is not unusual for the newest teacher to receive the toughest assignment, the most difficult-to-reach children, the worst room, and an inadequate orientation. It is hardly surprising that under these conditions a novice has difficulty moving beyond survival (self).

Quite recently, the question of more adequate support and guidance for beginners has received new attention. Yvonne Gold (1996) provides the details on many states now taking the question of beginning teacher induction seriously. One major example has been set up in North Carolina to provide special training in supervision (Thies-Sprinthall & Sprinthall, 1987; Reiman & Thies-Sprinthall 1993; 1998). Such mentor programs provide the novice with on-site help on a continuous basis. Research has shown that novice teachers in these programs do proceed more quickly through the Frances Fuller phases of concern. This means that the beginner can attend more quickly and more competently to the needs of the students. We noted in Chapter 1 that classroom teaching involved four "corners": self, pupils, strategies, and content. Student teaching as traditionally organized and beginning to teach without adequate mentoring do not provide the conditions for professional growth. However, with recognition of the legitimate needs for guided assistance, both student teachers and novice teachers can reach competent levels of practice.

Reflective Inquiry

There are many ways for teachers to become reflective practitioners. The following suggestions may help you to identify and maintain an awareness of your unconscious biases and differential behavior toward students, your attitudes toward self, and phases of concern.

1. Videotape a teaching session and rate your behavior as observed in the tape.

TABLE 14.5   PHASES OF CONCERN: TYPICAL EXPRESSIONS

PHASE	EXPRESSION	FEELINGS
6. Refocusing	I've started to modify some of the standard techniques to promote inquiry and it works.	Competent, excited
5. Collaboration	I tried out a new unit on creativity that I'll share with a colleague. My colleague has been helpful to me.	Successful, confident
4. Consequence, impact	Are all my students learning enough? How can I match and mismatch? Are my expectations fair to all?	Positive, puzzled, occasionally apprehensive
3. Management	How can I control the class? Which management techniques work best?	Frustrated, discouraged, occasionally pleased
2. Personal	How do I look to the students? How am I in coming across to them? Do they like and respect me?	Anxious, self-conscious, scared
1. Information	There are an awful lot of ideas and teaching methods I need to find out about.	Curious but somewhat apprehensive
0. Awareness	I'm not really concerned even though I don't know how to teach.	Apathetic

2. Have a colleague, student teacher, or student keep track of certain of your teaching behaviors for a designated period. Design a checklist to keep track of who goes out of the room for special services, whose artwork you hang up, which parents you invite to come into the classroom.

3. Write narratives about your teaching experiences.

4. Focus on one issue, such as how you plan groups for instruction, and then research it further with a group of interested colleagues.

5. Investigate your own stages of racial identity.

Let us focus on an in-depth discussion of the last three items for teacher portfolios: teacher narratives, collaborative action research, and racial identity stages.

Teacher narratives   The creation of and contemplation on teachers' stories contribute to professional growth. Teachers' narratives represent attempts by teachers to reflect upon incidents in their lives and classrooms. Teachers' stories invite reflection and are, in themselves, a metaphor for change. They form one part of a **portfolio.** Nancy Frane wrote this short beginning of a narrative as one of her experiences in teaching first grade.

I remember teaching first grade the year that Nate was in my class. I clipped a little microphone onto my shirt and hooked the transmitter box onto my belt. Nate put the receiver around his neck, hooked the box to his belt, and switched one of his hearing aids to a different setting. "Testing, testing, are we on?" I would say. If Nate grinned and shook his head, I would generally groan, and change any variable I could think of to make it work. After a while, the other children would help. "Nate, are you sure you are on Channel A?" "Did you remember to turn it ON, Ms. Frane?" they would ask. When we triumphed, we could all talk and hear about why some of the marigolds died, and why eleven is an odd number. When the darned thing would not work, there was an undercurrent of tension in the room, as I strained my voice and pantomimed everything I could. The other children waited patiently (and not so patiently) for me to repeat everything, and Nate strained to follow the discussion. In the middle of a heated conversation about whether or not 53 is a "five number" (a multiple of five) because, "after all, it has a five in it," Nate announced that we were "off." In fact, his whole hearing aid was off. Never minding about the five numbers, I flipped the old battery out of the hearing aid and passed it around. Under a pile of file cards and erasers in my desk, I found a new battery and passed that around. Nate passed his hearing aids around. I showed the transmitter box, and all the children took turns wearing the microphone. We talked about batteries, microphones, and ears of all kinds. After that, I noticed how easily the other children wore the microphone to talk with Nate during show and tell. At group time, the children on either side of Nate leaned in toward him, sometimes resting a head on his shoulder, to hear the sounds through his transmitter, and Nate would generously turn up the volume so that the others could hear the transmitter more clearly (Frane, 1992, unpublished).

Another short narrative recounts Vivian Gussin Paley's experience with a student teacher.

Janet, my student teacher, was more sensitive to the feelings of children than the most experienced teachers I know. She instinctively understood the nature of objectivity and involvement. Her involvement did not encourage dependency and her objectivity could never be interpreted as indifference.

She liked every single child. This is a great comfort to children, having a teacher who likes everyone and knows how to show it. When you have a teacher who likes some and not others, you must keep maneuvering for her approval. This interferes with the more important business of learning to relate to your own peers.

Stuart was in our class that year, and he had a bad stutter. Stuttering, like skin color, is a characteristic most teachers prefer to ignore. Even after I could comfortably discuss color, I could not easily refer to a child's stuttering. I would look intently at the child and not let anyone interrupt, even in the natural way children always interrupt each other. I felt as though I was holding my breath.

Janet, by her example, showed me that I was afraid of the stuttering. My behavior revealed an inability to accept this stuttering child. After she had been in our class a few days, Janet was reading a story about a boy going to the Central Park Zoo in New York. Stuart excitedly tried to say that he had been there, but got stuck on the word "my" and could not extricate himself. Janet said, "Stuart, I see you have trouble with certain words, like 'my.' Some people call that stuttering. When you get older you'll figure out what to do about those words. But we don't mind waiting for you to say them. Not a bit. Take your time."

Larry was in the group listening to the story. "No, we don't mind. Not a bit," he repeated. Susan picked it up. "Sure. Just take your time." I realized what was going on. Janet had shown everyone it was all right to talk to Stuart about his stuttering. The message they had got from me was that it was not all right. And to Stuart, she was saying, in effect, "You don't have to try to keep this problem a secret."

Janet was interested in Stuart's problem, for one of her own children stuttered. She would say things like, "Stuart, you're having trouble with 'give' right now. Try saying, 'Let me have it' or 'I need it' instead of 'give it to me.'" She was showing him that the

stuttering did not have to control him. He could manipulate a little, change a few words, make a game out of it. She was not acting like a speech therapist. She was just putting herself in his shoes and figuring out what *she* would do if she stuttered. He knew that and he felt good about it (Paley, 1989, pp. 40–41).

Nona Lyons (1990) suggests that teacher narratives reveal how teachers' attitudes toward knowledge, themselves, and their students enter into their teaching. Reviewing and rethinking issues in the narratives can be part of your continuing development. Kathleen Casey (1995) has reviewed the new narrative research in education and concludes that "the repertoire of stories still waiting to be told (and studied) is practically limitless. What better way to grapple with making sense of our rapidly changing world than through the study of stories?" (p. 240).

Collaborative action research   This is an inquiry process in which teams of teachers and university researchers study some aspect of their work in an effort to promote improved practice, develop staff, and contribute to theory in their field. It is based on the premise that those who are involved in the process of discovering the need and direction for change will be able to successfully carry it out. Action research was developed in the 1940s and 1950s (see Corey, 1953) as a means of applying the scientific method to social science and improving school practices. In the 1970s and 1980s, it was instrumental in effecting educational reform in England and Australia (Elliot, 1991; Kemmis & McTaggart, 1988) and has gained respect and usage in the United States (Holly, 1991).

Collaborative action research is grounded in practice. The specific focus of the research grows out of issues that are immediately relevant to teachers. The research is conducted within the school and revised, when warranted, to meet the needs of the situation or the students or the teachers. For example, suppose that, in the course of collecting data on peer teaching, it is discovered that the chosen peer teaching format is too unwieldy for the number of students in a classroom. Rather than waiting to discover whether an unrealistic teaching strategy will yield good results, the action researcher can revise the format of the new peer teaching strategy immediately and resume the research. The findings can be readily applied to the real-life setting.

Teachers and university faculty working collaboratively complement each other. In some projects teachers may direct the process while the university personnel act as consultants and offer technical support. In others, the university researchers can facilitate the overall action research process while the teacher researchers determine the specifics of the study. Leadership and involvement will shift naturally depending on what skills and expertise are necessary at various points in the project; yet the process should always remain democratic (Oja & Smulyan, 1989). Best results occur when communication between participants is open and frequent, and all are involved in every aspect of the process.

The exact procedure for a collaborative action research study will vary depending on the nature of the group and the research question. However, the following provides a rough model:

1. *Choose a research focus.* This may come about when members of a group identify a problem to be solved or a situation to be understood better (for example, the development of higher-order thinking skills). Then they choose a specific research question or questions (for example, What percentage of the teacher questioning currently stimulates higher-order responses? or Will peer teaching produce greater results in accurate formation of concepts?). At this point, the team may choose to gather some baseline or current status data for later comparison or for more insight into the current situation by identifying specific ideas and questions to focus on.

2. *Review information related to research focus or question.* This can stimulate the development of specific research questions or provide in-depth understanding of questions already chosen. It can also serve to familiarize the group with possible approaches to conducting the study.

3. *Develop a plan to answer the specific research question.* This includes determining the kinds of data to be collected, from whom or what will be collected, research methods to be employed, and project length. It may also involve implementing an experimental practice for comparison or evaluation. Precisely defined research questions will be easiest to work with.

4. *Conduct the research.* Plans are modified and revised as needed.

5. *Analyze the data and apply the findings.* Findings may create impetus for action or warrant further study. Findings may be applicable beyond individual classrooms, and a plan for their dissemination (discussion, school meeting, report) may be formed. In this way the team members guide their own practice and contribute theory to the broader education community.

6. These five steps are repeated in a process or cycle of continued planning, action, observing, re-

flecting, and replanning to investigate a classroom or school problem in a systematic way.

The process of collaboration and the opportunity to reflect on and experiment with practice are vehicles for both professional and personal growth. Collaboration offers opportunities to exchange ideas and consider other perspectives; it requires creating and acting upon group decisions. Through these, educators can become more flexible in thinking, increase their repertoire of action research and problemsolving skills, develop better communication skills, and strengthen bonds of collegiality. Time for reflection enables teachers to evaluate practice. You may become clearer in your own educational philosophy and its connection to your actions in the school and classroom. Creating a context in which experimentation is the norm frees you to consider and test ideas without fear of criticism.

When teachers work together in collaborative action research, they increase their capacity to reflect on their values, assumptions, and attitudes and improve their teaching practices. Teachers gain in their cognitive flexibility to meet students' learning needs. Teachers who advance in postconventional stages of development prefer the collaborative action research team for solving school and classroom problems because it is nonhierarchical and self-managed, it has norms of experimentation, it involves shared decisionmaking, and it provides a context in which teachers can develop their own tasks, roles, and responsibilities in the process. Marilyn Cochran-Smith and Susan Lytle maintain that "research by teachers represents a distinctive way of knowing about teaching and learning that will alter, not just add to, what we know," and that teacher research represents "a radical challenge to our current assumptions of theory and practice, schools and universities, and inquiry and reform" (1996, p. 92).

Additionally, teachers who work with their students in action research describe their classes as more alive. The teacher models inquiry methods and reflective practice, and the students become an increasing part of the classroom evaluation procedures. A spirit of inquiry permeates the classroom and school. Classrooms become restructured so that students' roles change. Students become less passive and more involved in planning, evaluating, and introspection. Pride is developed in the classroom, and trust between teachers and students increases.

People who have participated in and studied the collaborative action research process have suggested various criteria for successful projects.

1. Choosing a question for inquiry that is important enough to warrant the time spent studying it

2. A willingness to examine one's own practice and an openness to the perspective of others

3. Effective group collaboration, including shared commitment to the process and project, opportunity for all voices to be heard, and good facilitation

4. Support of the school administration in terms of time and encouragement

The climate of education is increasingly supportive for teachers to become action researchers on school and classroom problems (Calhoun, 1994). Efforts to improve schools are changing administrative policies to allow teachers to be more active in the school. As a result collaborative action research is seen as an advantage and not as a threat to administrative decisionmaking. Although time is a concern, school improvement programs encourage administrators to structure the day to provide more time for teachers to solve problems together. Successful collaborative action research requires a climate of trust. As collaboration among teachers grows, the traditional barriers and closed-door policies among teachers will change.

Networking is a way that teacher-researchers can turn to each other for ideas and advice; networking provides teachers an opportunity to reflect upon their practice with peers. Teacher networks can be local, regional, or national in scope. Teachers in the networks can communicate through electronic mail. Some networks focus on specific subjects, while others focus on topics like diversity, assessment, and bilingual education. Joanna Richardson (1996) describes the following teacher networks. We list their names and e-mail addresses here for your information.

AERA Special Interest Group on Teacher as Researcher, **http://www.ilstu.edu/depts/labschl/tar** on the World Wide Web

Bread Loaf Rural Teachers Network, **info@bread-net.middlebury.edu**

California Subject-Matter Projects, **robert.polkinghorn@ucop.edu**

Collaboratives for Humanities and Arts Teaching, **dennis@info.csd.org**

Diversity & Excellence Working for the Education of Youth; **er44@columbia.edu**

Foxfire National Programs, **foxfirefnd@aol.com**

Geography Alliance, **gep@nationalgeographic.com**

History Teaching Alliance, **compston@cc.wwu.edu**

Impact II, **teachnet@teachnet.org**

National Writing Project, **nwp@garnet.berkeley.edu**

Urban Mathematics Collaboratives, **merling@lasalle.edu**

Racial identity stages   As we have shown, racism is an unfortunate fact of life in society that profoundly affects people's aspirations and experiences. Talking about race, learning about racism, and using the racial identity development models may help make you more conscious of your own expectations about race and culture and help you teach *all* students more effectively.

It is also important to be able to evaluate your students' positions along the continuums of racial, cultural, and gender-based identity stages. Like all the stage theories written about in this book, your place on these racial identity stages affects your ability to teach effectively.

Beverly Daniel Tatum (1992b) compares the stages of white racial identity development by Janet Helms with William Cross's model of black racial identity development. The two models of racial identity development are outlined briefly here.

Janet Helms (1990) describes the evolution of a positive white racial identity as involving both abandonment of racism and the development of a non-racist white identity. She identified six stages in a model of white racial identity development. The first stage is the *contact* stage; one is unaware of cultural and institutional racism, and of one's own white privilege. There is often naive curiosity about or fear of people of color, based on stereotypes from media, family, or friends. Stage two is called the *disintegration* stage because the bliss of ignorance at stage one is replaced by the shame, guilt, and sometimes anger at the recognition of one's own advantage because of being white and the role of whites in the maintenance of a racist system. Stage three, *reintegration,* and the person's desire to be accepted by one's own racial group may lead to a reshaping of the person's belief system to be more congruent with an acceptance of racism; the guilt and anxiety of the previous stage may be redirected in the form of fear and anger toward people of color (particularly African-Americans), who are now blamed as the source of discomfort. At stage four, the *pseudoindependent* stage, one abandons beliefs in white superiority, but may still behave in ways that unintentionally perpetuate the system. At the fifth stage, *immersion/emersion,* the white individual begins a search to replace racially related myths and stereotypes with accurate information about what it means and has meant to be white in U.S. society. At the final stage, *autonomy,* a newly defined sense of oneself as white is internalized, and the person is energized to confront racism and oppression in daily life.

Cross (1991) describes five stages in the development of black identity. In the first stage, *pre-encounter,* the African-American has absorbed many of the beliefs and values of the dominant white culture. The individual seeks to assimilate and be accepted by whites, and actively or passively keeps a distance from other black people. Movement into the *encounter* stage begins with an event that forces the individual to acknowledge the impact of racism in one's life. One is forced to focus on his or her identity as a member of a group targeted by racism. In the third stage, *immersion/emersion,* there are simultaneous desires to surround oneself with visible symbols of one's racial identity and to avoid symbols of whiteness. The fourth stage, *internalization,* begins when one feels secure in one's own sense of racial identity. The individual at this stage is willing to establish meaningful relationships with white people who acknowledge and are respectful of his or her self-definition. At *internalization-commitment,* the final stage, people have found ways to translate their personal, internalization of blackness into a plan of action for a sense of commitment to the concerns of African-Americans as a group, and sustain this commitment over time. Movement through the five stages may be described as a spiral motion. In new situations or as a result of new encounters, the person may go back to an earlier stage to recycle through the later stages and deal with the new experience.

Tatum suggests that for other students (Asian, Latino, Native American), the process of racial identity development may be similar to that described for African-Americans.

Values and Teaching

One very common approach to the dilemma of values and teaching has been to say that teaching is like indoctrination. "Face it, teaching is a form of brainwashing," or so this view proclaims. Since adults know more than kids, it is right and just for the adults to induct each new generation of children into the ways of the adult world. There is no need to be upset by this indoctrination; it's simply the way things are—a natural law. This is something like saying, "Well, so what's wrong with teaching middle-class values? After all, that's the majority view. And almost everybody would like to be middle class anyway!" The fact that such rhetoric makes the shabby rationalizations seem palatable to some raises more questions than it answers.

Another, more elegant, solution to the value dilemma has been to suggest that teaching should be value-free—that is, teachers really should express no genuine personal values. They should present all sides of any question fairly and impartially. Like anthropologists studying another culture, teachers would be trained for neutrality. Their only values would be plurality and relativism; all views would have merit and receive equal treatment. Not only would there be freedom for all views, but teachers would also be expected to pursue and embody all views with equal vigor.

Asa G. Hilliard III (1992) reminds us that "no academic content is neutral" or "universal in and of itself" (p. 13). Perhaps the most adequate means of conveying the impossibility of value neutrality in teaching is to offer a brief example. A social studies teacher who was supervising a group of teacher trainees had become embroiled in this very controversy. His trainees insisted that the pupils were to be "free." They, as future teachers, had no right to impose their views on the children. At this point the social studies master teacher gave up on the dialogue and invited the teachers-in-training to observe his next class. To make his point as dramatically as he knew how, he decided to teach his pupils about the disadvantages and advantages of the concentration camps of World War II. After listing the obvious disadvantages, he proceeded "objectively" to list the advantages—the creation of jobs (guards, dog trainers, searchlight makers), the uncrowding of cities, the increase in availability of housing, and even the production of certain goods almost too grisly to mention. The horrified practice teachers immediately protested that the master teacher was being unfair. How was it possible to even consider a concentration camp as an advantage to anyone? The master teacher had reduced the idea of value-free teaching to an absurdity. To say that he was merely presenting evidence from a "different point of view" was simply a means of begging the question of values.*

TEACHING GOALS AND STRATEGIES: A DEVELOPMENTAL MODEL

It is apparent that teaching can hardly be considered as brainwashing and that relativism just as obviously leads in a circle. We need to return to the ideas from prior chapters on strategies and goals as a framework for our role concepts. The attitudes we hold toward the role of the teacher bear a direct relationship to the strategies we employ and the goals we seek to achieve. If we examine the question from

---

* This case example was provided by Bernard Seiderman, formerly of the Great Neck, Long Island, school system.

the student's point of view as well as in terms of the goals of a democratic society, we can begin to formulate an answer.

All children enter school with potential for development. Such development takes place in the cognitive, personal, and value domains. By viewing students developmentally, we gain a picture of how they currently function *and* their potential for developing increasingly more complex systems of thinking, self-development, and value judgment. Whether or not such growth takes place depends on an appropriate match between where the learner is and what level he or she is moving toward. The teacher's role is to arrange the learning environment in all subject areas to stimulate the natural process of development. Each child brings to us a natural desire to learn, an innate urge to grow. Of course, as a result of past experience, this desire may not be as obvious with some pupils as it is with other, more openly eager learners. Yet all have the potential. We've called this the process of accommodation, the need to learn more about the world and find better ways to solve problems.

On one side of the teacher, then, we have a group of youngsters whose developmental needs are ready to be met in the service of their own growth. But consider a different perspective—the teacher as an agent for the democratic goals of the adult society. Without going into the deep philosophical questions, it is clear that the goals of a democracy absolutely demand effective education for its young people. The purpose of education in its broadest sense is to teach them how to think, especially about democratic principles. To function successfully as citizens, adults must know not only how to work and contribute to the general welfare but also how to weigh questions, vote intelligently, understand equity and the generic meaning of democratic freedom and responsibility, and appreciate differences among people. For that to happen, for such broad societal goals to be achieved, the schools' role is critical. An informed public is the keystone to anyone's definition of democracy. Without development, our children will remain in prejudice, ignorance, and self-centeredness. Thomas Jefferson (1816) stated the issue most succinctly: "If a nation expects to be ignorant and free, in a state of civilization, it expects what never was and never will be."

The daily activity of the classroom can be a vehicle to accomplish this admittedly lofty goal. Mouthing great phrases and calling on eternal virtues will not do it. In fact, Lawrence Kohlberg's research has shown that talk and moral behavior do not go hand in hand. Thus the day-to-day process of gradual development in the classroom is very significant. We can't hurry the process; acceleration too often leads to low-level memorization. Thus, the goals and strategies of teaching aim to promote the developing potential of each child through a sequence from less complex to higher-order, more complex thinking, self-development, and value judgment.

Where does the teacher come into this picture? Learning more intensively about children outlines their potentials for growth. Learning more about your own attitudes and stages outlines your potential. So we can hold up the same mirror. Your own growth as a professional teacher is a central consideration. As the orchestrator of the classroom, you determine much of what transpires. We have shown how negative teacher expectancies adversely affect student growth. We have also shown how a limited range of strategies has similarly negative outcomes. Only the teacher who gradually develops to higher levels of complexity as an individual can also increasingly master the art of teaching. Matching and mismatching require a substantial ability to engage in *reflective teaching*. Teaching cannot be reduced to a series of robot moves. Reflective teaching means the ability to analyze the process of what you are doing and have an impact on children simultaneously. Sometimes this is called on-the-spot decisionmaking.

Research has shown that even experienced teachers are not particularly adept at considering alternatives while teaching (Shavelson & Stern, 1981). Instead, the norm seems to be quick closure even though the research also indicates that such a limited ability to choose and select reduces student learning. The reason we point this out is that a strong tendency exists in all of us when we become aware of the developmental approach to expect that we can quickly go through a "growth spurt." In other words, we can accept the idea of gradual development, of slow but sure growth in others, but not in ourselves. We can take the "fast track" and get on with the process. The developmental method is for others. We make the point in this chapter that it is all right to "be" where you are right now, yet still understand that you can grow slowly.

Research has demonstrated that teachers who try out their current methods, master those, and systematically increase their repertoire of strategies show definite evidence of developmental growth (Thies-Sprinthall, 1984). An important component is cognitive reflection, that is, the ability to analyze your own teaching (Glassberg & Sprinthall, 1980). The two go hand in hand. You try a new approach and then review and analyze the results, make changes, and try again. To act without reflection leads to unguided fads, but reflection by itself leads to excessive introspection and inaction. Both action and reflection are needed.

Fritz Oser (1986), a Swiss educator, has commented that teachers who actively engage in the process of *metareflection* will develop a **discourse perspective.** This means a growth in complexity of thought and an increase in confidence to express views or, in other words, to engage in discussions (discourse) with colleagues concerning the teaching-learning process. One of the exciting results of Oser's research is that "students think that discourse-oriented teachers are not only more trustworthy, caring, and just persons but that they are also didactically better teachers" (1994, p. 116).

SUMMARY

The personal side of teaching involves teacher attitudes in three general areas: (1) attitudes about teaching and learning, (2) attitudes toward pupils, and (3) attitudes toward self.

Teachers' attitudes toward learning sometimes harden into the belief that knowledge is truth; with this belief teachers expect pupils to look for the single correct answer to the problems posed in the classroom. Hunt has found that teachers' conceptual level influences how they teach. Teachers at a low conceptual level tend to be more authoritarian than teachers at higher levels, and the former use a single method of teaching with all students.

Teachers' attitudes toward students also influence teaching style. The early and now classic study of the importance of a self-fulfilling prophecy by Rosenthal and Jacobson illustrates the importance of such attitudes. A review of recent research documents the wide variety of student characteristics that "cause" teachers to treat some pupils negatively, reducing the possibility of academic achievement. Student so-cial class, race, family background, temperament, gender, and academic achievement are among the important factors that influence teacher attitudes.

Teachers' attitudes toward themselves are also important. Fuller catalogued seven phases of concern that teachers pass through in their personal growth in teaching. A continued reflective approach to teaching encourages teachers to think about attitudes toward self and the impact on practice. Methods for continued reflection on teaching include teacher narratives, collaborative action research, and investigation of racial identity stages. Teachers cannot be value-free in their interactions with students. They must strive to incorporate in their teaching a genuine developmental model designed to promote pupil growth both in subject matter competency and in the values needed for future citizenship in a democratic community that affirms diversity. By nurturing their own capacity for reflective teaching, teachers can play a major role in pupil growth.

KEY TERMS AND NAMES

Howard Becker
Jere Brophy and Thomas Good
collaborative action research
developmental model
discourse perspective
Elizabeth Fennema
Frances Fuller
hidden agenda

networking
Sonia Nieto
John Ogbu
portfolio
racial identity stages
reflective inquiry
Rosenthal effect
teacher expectations

THEORY INTO PRACTICE: THE PROCESS OF LEARNING SELF-REFLECTION

The most important dimension of the personal aspects of teaching concerns your ability to reflect upon experience. There is an old saying, "Ten years of experience or one year ten times," meaning, did the person learn anything new during the ten years of experience or was it just the same year after year? Reflection is not an automatic process. Like nearly everything else in education, reflection requires development. One way to begin the self-reflection process is to record your teaching experiences in a journal. Here are some general guidelines:

1. The journal is to contain a focused account of your ideas and feelings before, during and after a series of teaching experiences.

2. The experience can be an individual tutorial, a small-group activity, or the teaching of an entire class. In other words, the experience itself must be real rather than a simulation.

3. Generally, it is best to regard the journal as your own private and confidential account so that there will be a greater tendency for you to be honest with yourself. The result should be an uncensored account of your ideas and feelings. (However, if you have a professional supervisor or mentor whose role it is to facilitate your development, you will find it helpful to share your journal with that person in order to obtain continuing feedback and suggestions to deepen your understanding.)

4. You'll need to keep the journal over a reasonable period, during student teaching, for example. Such a record will be meaningless if you use it either sporadically or just at the beginning and the end. Continuity is crucial.

5. A journal is not a mere recording of running commentary or stream of consciousness. Nor is it simply a content description of your activities (the so-called laundry list approach). You should keep the writing focused on the issues at hand.

6. The goal of the journal is to provide you with an increasingly complex account of your cognitions and emotions. Such reflections under appropriate conditions can become a rich source of private information for self-development as a teacher.

7. At the outset, expect some personal dissonance unless you have done this activity once or twice before. Do not become too critical of your initial accounts. Description without analysis is the approach most people use.

8. Often, beginning teachers find it helpful to use a checklist for their initial journalizing experiences. Others find that such structure is helpful

for getting started and then branch off into their own approach.

The checklist includes a series of directive questions such as:

1. What are at least five feelings I experienced during the teaching episode?

2. What teaching strategies did I employ?

3. What are the main learnings I got from teaching this episode?

4. What questions do I still have after reviewing my feelings, strategies, and learnings?

5. What were the notable student actions or reactions during the episode?

6. What concerns me most at the moment?

7. Were my experiences in this episode inadequate, marginal, or excellent?

The journal entry should be longer than one page but less than four. Too brief an account will not give you enough feedback, while writing very extensively may become so burdensome that after an initial week or two you'll start skipping.

After you've made three or four entries, you might wish to check on your level of analysis. If so, go back to the section on Bloom's levels (Chapter 13) and review the characteristics. See if you are becoming more analytic in your commentary.

How are the feelings changing? How are they the same and how different?

How are the strategies changing? Are you more aware of differences in effectiveness with some content, or with some pupils?

Are you beginning to understand how the basic assumptions relate to different strategies?

Remember, these questions are only to serve as a means to focus your reflections on the personal experience of teaching. You may find the checklist approach too confining. If so, follow your own method. The point is to promote a regular and systematic approach to the subjective side of teaching. In so doing you will be making the first steps toward becoming a reflective practitioner. The goal is to make your expectations of yourself and of individual pupils more complex.

THEORY INTO PRACTICE: ASSESSING PHASES OF CONCERN

In addition to learning how to reflect in general through journalizing, you can reanalyze the content of your journal by applying Fuller's phases. After you've made a series of entries, examine what you've noted as the major questions and what you've written down as your major feelings.

To practice identifying phases and feeling, see if you can classify the following statements, using the codes (phase numbers) that follow this table.

EXPRESSION	PHASE	FEELINGS
1. I don't have enough time to organize my class activities.	_____	_____
2. The students don't seem to think that I'm "with it."	_____	_____
3. I feel absolutely drained after every class.	_____	_____
4. My planning period was interrupted again. I had a hard time trying to get all materials.	_____	_____
5. I keep hearing about how important clothes are in sending different messages—power colors—but I'm more comfortable in jeans.	_____	_____
6. A friend told me about a new curriculum guide in the library about teaching for thinking.	_____	_____
7. I noticed during the cooperative learning groups that I can see the different levels of student questions much more clearly.	_____	_____
8. I just came out of the teachers' room. Nobody paid any attention to me. They all seem so confident.	_____	_____
9. I just heard that I'm to be evaluated through a "surprise" visit.	_____	_____
10. At parents' night, I found out that three of my pupils who are doing very well in class were originally classified as mildly retarded and hated school.	_____	_____
11. Somebody said the assistant principal was spooking around. I don't know who that person is, and what's more I don't care.	_____	_____
12. We are trying a new approach. It's called team planning and teaching. I've learned a lot, and many of my own ideas were received very positively by the other members of the team.	_____	_____

CODE	PHASE	FEELINGS*
3	Management	Frustrated
2	Personal	Self-conscious
2	Personal	Anxious, exhausted
3	Management	Annoyed
2	Personal	Confused, worried
1	Information	Curious
4	Consequence	Pleased, gratified
2	Personal	Scared, isolated
2	Personal	Apprehensive
4	Consequence	Proud, competent
1	No awareness	Apathy
5	Collaboration	Confident and accepted

* These should be considered as only a sample of feelings that may be generated and is in no way the complete range.

REFERENCES

American Association of University Women. (1992). *How schools shortchange girls.* Washington, DC: AAUW Educational Foundation.

Babad, E., Bernieri, F., & Rosenthal, R. (1991). Students as judges of teachers' verbal and non-verbal behavior. *American Educational Research Journal, 28*(1), 211–234.

Becker, H. (1969). Social class variation in the teacher-pupil relationship. In R. C. Sprinthall & N. A. Sprinthall (Eds.), *Educational psychology: Selected readings* (pp. 300–308). New York: Van Nostrand-Reinhold.

Block, J. H. (1984). *Sex role identity and ego development.* San Francisco: Jossey-Bass.

Brophy, J. E., & Good, T. L. (1974). *Teacher-student relationships: Causes and consequences.* New York: Holt, Rinehart & Winston.

Burton, L. (Ed.). (1990). *Gender and mathematics: An international perspective.* Exeter, England: Cassell Educational Limited.

Calhoun, E. F. (1994). *How to use action research in the self-renewing school.* Alexandria, VA: Association for Supervision and Curriculum Development.

Casey, K. (1995). The new narrative research in education. In M. W. Apple (Ed.), *Review of Research in Education* (pp. 211–253). Washington, DC: American Educational Research Association.

Cochran-Smith, M., & Lytle, S. L. (1996). Communities for teacher research: Fringe or Forefront. In M. W. McLaughlin & I. Oberman (Eds.), *Teacher Learning: New Policies, New Practices* (pp. 92–112). New York: Teachers College Press.

Corey, S. (1953). *Action research to improve school practices.* New York: Teachers College Press.

Cross, W. E., Jr. (1991). *Shades of black: Diversity in African-American identity.* Philadelphia: Temple University Press.

Darling-Hammond, L., & Sclan, E. M. (1996). Who teaches and why: Dilemmas of building a profession for twenty-first century schools. In J. Sikula (Ed.), *Handbook of Research on Teacher Education* (pp. 67–101). New York: Simon & Schuster Macmillan.

Delcos, V., Burns, M. S., & Kulewicz, S. (1987). Effects of dynamic assessment on teachers' expectations of handicapped children. *American Educational Research Journal, 24*(3), 325–336.

Delpit, L. D. (1988). The silenced dialogue: Power and pedagogy in educating other people's children. *Harvard Educational Review, 58*(3), 280–298.

Elliot, J. (1991). *Action research for educational change.* Philadelphia: Open University Press.

Fennema, E., & Leder, G. C. (Eds.) (1990). *Mathematics and Gender.* New York: Teachers College Press.

Fuller, F. (1969). Concerns of teachers: A developmental conceptualization. *American Educational Research Journal, 6,* 207–226.

Glassberg, S., & Sprinthall, N. A. (1980). Student teaching: A developmental approach. *Journal of Teacher Education, 31,* 31–38.

Gold, Y. (1996). Beginning teacher support: Attrition, mentoring, and induction. In J. Sikula (Ed.), *Handbook of Research on Teacher Education* (pp. 548–594). New York: Simon & Schuster Macmillan.

Good, T. L., & Brophy, J. E. (1997). *Looking in classrooms.* New York: Longman.

Hall, R. & Sandler, B. R. (1982, 1996). *The classroom climate: A chilly one for women?* Project on the Status and Education of Women. Washington, DC: Association of American Colleges.

Heath, S. B. (1983). *Ways with words.* Cambridge, MA: Harvard University Press.

Heath, S. B. (1995). Ethnography in communities: Learning the everyday life of America's subordinated youth. In J. A. Banks & C. A. McGee Banks (Eds.), *Handbook of Research on Multicultural Education* (pp. 114–128). New York: Simon & Schuster Macmillan.

Helms, J. E. (Ed.). (1990). *Black and white racial identity: Theory, research, and practice.* Westport, CN: Greenwood Press.

Hernandez, H. (1989). *Multicultural education: A teacher's guide to content and process.* Columbus, OH: Merrill.

Hilliard, A. G. (1992). Why we must pluralize the curriculum. *Educational Leadership, 49*(4), 12–16.

Holly, P. (1991). Action research: The missing link in the creation of schools as centers of inquiry. In A. Lieberman & L. Miller (Eds.), *Staff development for education in the 90's: New demands, new realities, new perspectives* (pp. 133–157). New York: Teachers College Press.

Hyde, J. S., Fennema, E., & Lamon, S. J. (1990). Gender differences in mathematics performance: A meta-analysis. *Psychological Bulletin, 107*(2), 139–155.

Jefferson, T. (1816, January 6). A letter to Colonel Charles Yancey.

Joyce, B., Brown, C., & Peck, L. (Eds.). (1981). *Flexibility in teaching.* New York: Longman.

Kaufman, B. (1964). *Up the down staircase.* Englewood Cliffs, NJ: Prentice-Hall.

Kemmis, S., & McTaggart, R. (1988). *The action research planner.* Victoria, Australia: Deakin University Press.

Kozol, J. (1967). *Death at an early age.* Boston: Houghton Mifflin.

Leacock, E. (1969). *Teaching and learning in city schools.* New York: Basic Books.

Lee, D. M. (1993). The place of wisdom in teaching. *Learning and individual differences, 5*(4), 301–317.

Levine, D. U., & Lezotte, L. W. (1995). Effective schools research. In J. A. Banks & C. A. McGee Banks (Eds.), *Handbook of Research on Multicultural Education* (pp. 525–547). New York: Simon & Schuster Macmillan.

Lyons, N. (1990). Dilemmas of knowing: Ethical and epistemological dimensions of teachers' work and development. *Harvard Educational Review, 60*(2), 159–180.

Maccoby, E., & Jacklin, C. (1974). *The psychology of sex differences.* Stanford: Stanford University Press.

McLuhan, M. H. (1964). *Understanding media.* New York: McGraw-Hill.

Miller, A. (1981). Conceptual matching models and interactional research in education. *Review of Educational Research, 51*(11), 33–85.

National Commission on Teaching and America's Future (1996). *What matters most: Teaching for America's future.* New York: Author.

Nieto, S. (1992). *Affirming diversity: The sociopolitical context of multicultural education.* New York: Longman.

Oakes, J. (1992). Can tracking research inform practice? Technical, normative, and political considerations. *Educational Researcher, 21*(4), 12–21.

Ogbu, J. U. (1995). Understanding cultural diversity and learning. In J. A. Banks and C. A. McGee Banks (Eds.) *Handbook of research on multicultural education* (pp. 582–593). New York: Simon & Schuster Macmillan.

Ogbu, J. (1978). *Minority education and caste: The American system in cross-cultural perspective.* New York: Academic Press.

Oja, S., & Smulyan, L. (1989). *Collaborative action research: A developmental approach.* London: Falmer Press.

Oser, F. (1986). Moral education and values education: The discourse perspective. In M. C. Wittrock (Ed.), *Handbook of research on teaching* (pp. 917–941) (3d ed.). New York: Macmillan.

Oser, F. (1994). Moral perspectives on teaching. In *Review of Research in Education* (pp. 57–127). Washington, DC: American Educational Research Association.

Paley, V. G. (1989). *White teacher.* Cambridge, MA: Harvard University Press.

Reiman, A. J., & Thies-Sprinthall, L. (1998). *Supervision and mentoring for teacher development.* New York: Addison-Wesley Longman.

Reiman, A. J., & Thies-Sprinthall, L. (1993). Promoting the development of mentor teachers: Theory and research programs using guided reflection. *Journal of Research and Development, 26*(3), 179–185.

Richardson, J. (August, 1996). Networking. *Teacher Magazine, 7*(9), 40–44.

Rosenthal, R. (1979). *Sensitivity to nonverbal communication: The PONS test.* Baltimore: Johns Hopkins Press.

Rosenthal, R. (1987). Pygmalion effects: Existence, magnitude, and social importance. *Educational Researcher, 16*(9), 37–44.

Rosenthal, R., & Jacobson, L. (1968). *Pygmalion in the classroom.* New York: Holt, Rinehart & Winston.

Rosenthal, R., & Rubin, D. (1978). Interpersonal expectancy effects: The first 345 studies. *The Behavioral and Brain Sciences, 3*, 377–415.

Ross, D. D., & Smith, W. (1992). Understanding preservice teachers' perspectives on diversity. *Journal of Teacher Education, 43*(2), 94–103.

Ryan, K. (1970). *Don't smile until Christmas.* Chicago: University of Chicago Press.

Ryan, K., Newman, G., Mager, J., Applegate, J., Lasley, T., Flora, R., & Johnson, J. (1979). *Biting the apple: Accounts of first-year teachers.* New York: Longman.

Sadker, M. P., & Sadker, D. M. (1994). *Failing at fairness.* New York: Macmillan.

Sadker, M., Sadker, D., & Klein, S. (1991). The issue of gender in elementary and secondary education. In G. Grant (Ed.), *Review of Research in Education* (pp. 269–334). Washington, DC: American Educational Research Association.

Scott-Jones, D. (1984). Family influences on cognitive development and school achievement. In E. W. Gordon (Ed.), *Review of research in education* (pp. 259–306). Washington, DC: American Educational Research Association.

Shavelson, R. J., & Stern, P. (1981). Research on teachers' pedagogical thoughts, judgments, decisions, and behavior. *Review of Educational Research, 51*(4), 455–498.

Shipman, S., & Shipman, V. (1985). Cognitive styles: Some conceptual, methodological, and applied issues. In G. W. Edmund (Ed.), *Review of Research in Education* (Vol. 12). Washington, DC: American Educational Research Association.

Slavin, R. E., Madden, N. A., Karweit, N. L., Livermon, B. J., & Dolan, L. (1990, Summer). Success for all: First-year outcomes of a comprehensive plan for reforming urban education. *American Educational Research Journal, 27*(2), 255–278.

Sprinthall, N. A., Reiman, A. J., & Thies-Sprinthall, L. (1996). Teacher professional development. In J.

Sikula (Ed.), *Handbook of Research on Teacher Education* (pp. 666–703). New York: Simon & Schuster Macmillan.

Tatum, B. D. (1992a). *Assimilation blues: Black families in a white community.* Northampton, MA: Hazel-Maxwell. First published in 1987 by Greenwood Press.

Tatum, B. D. (1992b). Talking about race, learning about racism: The application of racial identity development theory in the classroom. *Harvard Educational Review, 62*(1), 1–24.

Taylor, D., & Dorsey-Gaines, C. (1988). *Growing up literate: Learning from inner-city families.* Portsmouth, NH: Heinemann.

Thies-Sprinthall, L. (1984). Promoting the developmental growth of supervising teachers: Theory, research, programs, and implications. *Journal of Teacher Education, 35*(3), 53–60.

Thies-Sprinthall, L., & Sprinthall, N. (1987). Experienced teachers: Agents for revitalization and renewal as mentors and teacher educators. *Journal of Teacher Education, 169*(1), 65–75.

Trujillo, C. M. (1986). A comparative examination of classroom interactions between professors and minority and nonminority college students. *American Educational Research Journal, 23*(4), 629–642.

Weinstein, R. S. (1989). Perceptions of classroom processes and student motivation: Children's views of self-fulfilling prophecies. In R. Ames & C. Ames (Eds.), *Research on motivation in education: Goals and cognitions* (vol. 3) (pp. 187–221). New York: Academic Press.

Woolfolk, A. E., & Brooks, D. M. (1983). Nonverbal communication in teaching. *Review of Research in Education, 10,* 103–150.

INDIVIDUAL DIFFERENCES: MEASUREMENT AND RESEARCH

15

MEASUREMENT AND INDIVIDUAL DIFFERENCES

The material presented in this chapter is aimed at giving you a general introduction to some of the techniques employed by statisticians and educational researchers. Though as a working teacher you may never have to compute the reliability or the validity of a measuring instrument, your understanding of these vital concepts will be greatly enhanced if you roll up your sleeves and "dirty your hands with the data." If you can calculate the standard deviation and Pearson r, you will not necessarily be a master statistician, but you will be better able to evaluate the statistical analyses of researchers in the field. In this chapter you will see how researchers use some of these techniques to achieve a better understanding of the facts and theories of educational psychology.

As a prospective teacher you will be expected to read and understand the literature in your own field. If you wish to further your studies and someday become an educational psychologist, you will have to spend considerable time honing your assessment skills. It has recently been stated that "the expanded role forecast for the educational psychologist in the twenty-first century is based on new approaches to assessment, clearly focusing on the purpose of assessment, and the validation of assessments in the context of use" (Tittle, 1991, p. 163). In any event, a basic introduction to statistical and research proce-

dures will enhance your ability to understand workshop and conference presentations as well as the research articles that you will be expected to read.

MEASUREMENT

As you look within yourself and at the people around you, you realize that you are a very special and unique being. Nobody else in the world is quite like you. Nobody else in the world has the same physiological equipment, the same genetic endowment (unless, of course, you are an identical twin), or has experienced the same sequence of life situations. Nobody else uses the identical blend of defense mechanisms that you use when encountering stress, and nobody else is guided by the exact mixture of motives, attitudes, and feelings. Thus, one of the basic themes of psychology is that of **individual differences:** No one is exactly like anyone else.

It is, however, impossible to avoid drawing comparisons as you look at the people around you. Perhaps you notice many similarities. You have a friend who seems to enjoy the same things you do. You play chess with someone who beats you just about as often as you beat her. You and your best friend spend about the same amount of time studying for an exam, and you make similar grades on that exam. Perhaps you have been pleasantly surprised to discover, during a conversation with someone you have just met, how similar your abilities, goals, tastes, and feelings really are. In many ways you are surprisingly like many other people. In some ways you are just like all other people—that is, you eat, drink, breathe, sleep, exercise, and have the same physiological needs. Therefore, it can be said that in some ways all people are exactly alike.

In order to assess how much you resemble and how much you differ from other people, you must in some way be measured. Meaningful comparisons cannot be made without meaningful measurements. **Measurement** is the assignment of a number to an object or event according to rules. This may represent something physical, as when you step on the scales and note, with dismay or pleasure, the number that indicates your weight. Or it may be more subtle, as when you take a vocational aptitude test and receive your score in mechanical aptitude. You have, in fact, been measured hundreds of times in hundreds of areas. In order to buy new clothes you

must know your size. When you visit a physician, your temperature and blood pressure are taken. Before entering college, you probably took an aptitude test. Hundreds of numbers have been assigned to you, from shoe size to that first quiz grade you received in elementary school.

The importance of understanding testing techniques and the analysis of the measures they afford cannot be overemphasized to anyone contemplating a teaching career today. Whether one agrees or disagrees with the recent proliferation of educational testing, it has become an obvious fact of American life. In 1988 almost 60 million primary and high school students took more than 100 million standardized tests, and even this number doesn't factor in the countless teacher-made tests to which America's schoolchildren are exposed (Fiske, 1988).

Reliability and Validity

To permit meaningful comparisons, measurements must be meaningful. In order to have meaning, all

Measurement of progress is important in the classroom.

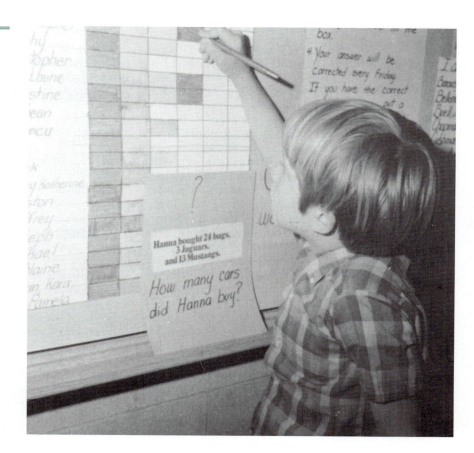

measurements must satisfy two basic criteria: They must be reliable, and they must be valid.

Reliability

Reliability is an indication of the consistency of a measurement; that is, if we measure something that is not itself changing dramatically, we should assign roughly the same number to it over repeated measurements. If you stepped on the scales and read 140 pounds one day, 240 pounds the next day, and 40 pounds the day after that, your faith in the precision of the scale would be severely shaken. The numbers would be meaningless. The same is true of psychological tests. If you took an IQ test one day and received a score of 140, then took the same test the next day and received a score of 50, you would undoubtedly feel bewildered. In order to have any meaning, our measurements must, on the one hand, be consistent over repeated measurements—that is, reliable.

On the other hand, a test cannot be so consistent as to be rigid and misleading. A good test yields roughly the same scores over repeated measurements as long as the thing being measured does not change dramatically. Suppose, however, you went on a crash diet, and every day your friends commented on how much weight you had lost, and after a few weeks you found your clothes no longer fit you. If, in this instance, you still found the scales were reading the same weight, it would be obvious that the measurements were too consistent to be an adequate reflection of reality.

Validity

Measurements must also be valid. **Validity** is an indication of the extent to which a test measures what it is supposed to measure. When you step on the scales you want to know your weight, not your IQ or mechanical aptitude or some unknown quality. One way to assess validity, called *predictive* validity, is to compare a set of test scores against some separate or independent observation of the thing being measured. For example, if we were trying to establish whether or not a certain test of flying ability is valid, we might give the test to a large group of student pilots and then compare their test scores with the flight instructor's ratings of each person's actual ability to fly a plane. If those with the highest test scores also turn out to be the best pilots, the test is considered valid. The validity of such a test is important, because it allows us to predict on the basis of a person's test score whether or not that person will profit from flying lessons. Similarly, a valid test of college aptitude would predict whether an individual will be able to profit from the college experience. Thus, measurements must be an accu-

rate reflection of what they are intended to measure—that is, they must be valid.

When using a test for a particular educational objective, it is up to the test publisher to supply the school with information regarding the way the test was validated and its level of validation. However, it is the responsibility of the user of the test, in this case the teacher, to become familiar with this information and to make the final determination regarding whether or not the test is appropriate for the job at hand (Geisinger, 1992).

Correlation

In order to give precise statements about reliability and validity, a statistical technique called correlation may be utilized. Although correlation does not allow for direct cause-and-effect statements, it does allow the scientist to make predictions.

Correlation is a statement about the strength of the association between two (or possibly more) variables. If the correlation between two variables is high, the variables will tend to vary together; that is, wherever one of the traits is found, chances are good that the other trait will also be found. If we observed that people with blond hair usually have blue eyes, then we would say that there is a correlation between the variables hair color and eye color. This is not to say that having blond hair causes one to have blue eyes, but it does allow us to predict, whenever we know that certain individuals have blond hair, that they are also likely to have blue eyes.

Correlation is one way to assess reliability. If a certain test is given to a large group of subjects on two separate occasions, and if those individuals who score high on the test the first time also score high the second time and those who score low the first time also score low the second time, the two sets of measurements are said to correlate and the test is considered reliable. A high correlation between the two sets of scores indicates reliability because it demonstrates that the test is yielding consistent scores. The two variables, that is, the scores on the first administration of the test and the scores on the second, are in fact occurring together, or correlating.

Correlation can also establish validity. To establish validity we would give a test measuring some ability or trait to a group of individuals and then correlate their scores with actual performances by these same individuals on the ability or trait being measured. For example, we might compare scores on a sales aptitude test with actual performance in selling a certain product. If, in fact, there is a correlation between the two variables (the test scores and the number of sales achieved), the test has been shown to be valid—it is indeed measuring what it is intended to measure.

**TABLE 15.1
UNORDERED IQ
SCORES**

75
100
105
95
120
130
95
90
115
85
115
100
110
100
110

**TABLE 15.2
DISTRIBUTION
OF IQ SCORES**

130
120
115
115
110
110
105
100
100
100
95
95
90
85
75

Reliability and validity are only two ways to apply this extremely useful technique. Later in this chapter we will cite other applications of correlation in educational psychology, and we will present a simple mathematical procedure for computing correlation.

Distributions: Tables and Graphs

Since a picture can often be well worth the proverbial 1,000 words, data can be described very effectively through the use of graphs and tables. In creating one type of table, the first step is to form a **distribution,** an arrangement of any set of scores in order of magnitude. Table 15.1 presents a set of IQ scores. Arranging these scores into a distribution means listing them sequentially from high to low. Table 15.2 is a distribution of the IQ scores from Table 15.1.

A distribution allows the observer to see general trends more readily than the unordered set of raw scores does. To further simplify our inspection of the data, they can be presented as a frequency distribution. A frequency distribution is a listing of each score achieved, together with the number of individuals receiving that score. Table 15.3 is a frequency distribution of our IQ scores.

The X at the top of the first column stands for raw scores (in this case, IQs), and the f over the second column stands for frequency of occurrence. As can be seen, of the 15 people taking the test, 2 received scores of 115, 2 received 110, 3 scored 100, 2 scored 95, and everyone else made a unique score.

Tables can also be set up as summary statements and often provide a rich visual recap of what the data are showing. For example, in comparing two sample groups, A and B, with respect to performance on the verbal section of the Scholastic Assessment Test, group A having been coached, the tabled values might look like those shown in Table 15.4. The table immediately informs us that the coached group did perform at a somewhat higher level than the uncoached group and, further, that both groups are displaying similar amounts of variability, and were of similar size.

In addition to presenting frequency distributions in tabular form, statisticians often present their data in graphic form. It is customary to indicate the raw scores, or actual values of the variable, on the horizontal, X axis, called the *abscissa.* The frequency of occurrence is presented on the vertical, or Y axis, called the *ordinate.*

When graphing data, two of the most popular approaches involve setting up the data in the form of either a frequency histogram or a frequency polygon. Before using either of these, however, you must first set up a frequency distribution. Assume that we had a set of scores from a group of first-graders be-

**TABLE 15.3   IQ SCORES PRESENTED
AS A FREQUENCY DISTRIBUTION**

X (RAW SCORE)	f (FREQUENCY OF OCCURRENCE)
130	1
120	1
115	2
110	2
105	1
100	3
95	2
90	1
85	1
75	1

TABLE 15.4   BREAKDOWN VALUES

	GROUP A (COACHED)	GROUP B (NOT COACHED)
Number of students	425	434
Average SAT score	490.05	470.86
Range of scores	522	510

TABLE 15.5 FREQUENCY OF DISTRIBUTION OF WISC-III SCORES AMONG 86 STUDENTS

SCORE, X	FREQUENCY OF X, f
15	1
14	0
13	4
12	11
11	16
10	20
9	15
8	12
7	5
6	1
5	1

FIGURE 15.2

SCORE	FREQUENCY
15	*
14	
13	****
12	***********
11	****************
10	********************
9	***************
8	************
7	*****
6	*
5	*

ing evaluated on the arithmetic subtest of the WISC-III. The scores range from a high of 15 to a low of 5. Using the procedure described previously, the frequency distribution should look like that shown in Table 15.5.

Now, to create the **histogram,** place all the scores on the *X,* or horizontal, axis (abscissa) at equal intervals and run the scores from the lowest on the left to the highest on the right. Then, indicate all the frequencies on the *Y,* or vertical, axis (ordinate), again using equal intervals and beginning with zero, and place a rectangular bar over each score up to the point where the score intersects the frequency. (See Figure 15.1.)

Another method for displaying histograms that has become increasingly popular, especially in statistical computer programs, is to express the frequencies horizontally rather than vertically, with each asterisk representing an individual score (Sprinthall et al., 1990). (See Figure 15.2.)

We can also use the same data to illustrate another commonly used graphic form, called the frequency polygon. For the *frequency polygon,* place a dot over each score, again at the point where the score intersects the frequency. Then, connect all the dots with a series of straight lines (see Figure 15.3).

FIGURE 15.1 Histogram.

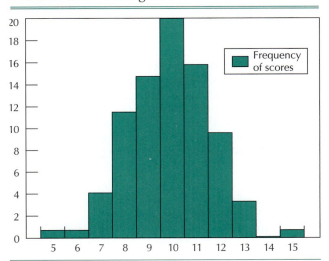

FIGURE 15.3 Frequency polygon of WISC-III scores among 85 students.

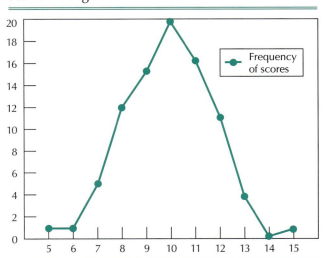

FIGURE 15.4

STEM	LEAF
6	035
7	13578
8	04455569
9	00145
10	0

Finally, a very economical way of graphing data, called the **stem-and-leaf display,** presents only the first digit in the stem column, while in the leaf column we find the trailing digits. For example, if we were to graph the scores on a certain reading test, where the values range from a low score of 60 to a high score of 100, the stem column would present the digits 6 through 10, with the 6 representing scores in the sixties, the 7 representing scores in the seventies, and so on. The leaf column would then include the trailing digit, so that a 0 next to the 6 would indicate a score of 60, the 3 a score of 63, and the 5 a score of 65. (See Figure 15.4.)

Note that in this example, most of the scores were in the eighties, and were specifically 80, 84, 84, 85, 85, 85, 86, and 89. Also, notice that there was only one score of 100.

In both the histogram and the frequency polygon, it is essential that the base of the ordinate represent a

FIGURE 15.5   Data that are correctly plotted.

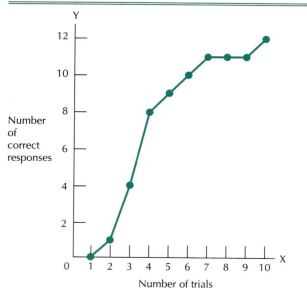

FIGURE 15.6   Here, the base of the ordinate is not set at zero. Such graphs can easily lead to a false interpretation of data.

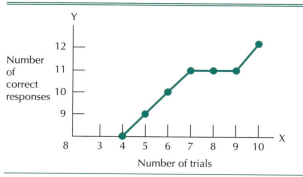

frequency of zero—if not, the graph may tell a very misleading story. For example, suppose we are graphing data from a learning study that shows how increasing the number of learning trials increases the amount learned. Let us plot the number of trials on the abscissa and the frequency of correct responses on the ordinate (Figure 15.5). Our graph shows that by trial 4 the subject made 8 correct responses and that by trial 10 the subject made 12 correct choices. These data are typical of the results obtained in learning studies; that is, a great deal of learning usually occurs during the first few trials, but, as the number of trials increases, further increase in learning lessens.

Suppose, however, the statistician wished to give a false interpretation of the data. He or she could simply focus on one small area of the graph (see Figure 15.6). Now the same data tell a very different story about how learning takes place. It looks as if no learning took place before trial 4 and that the great bulk of learning took place between trials 4 and 10. We know from the previous graph that this is incorrect. In fact, most of the learning took place during the first 4 or 5 trials, and between trials 4 and 10, the learning was actually beginning to top out or level off. This is one instance of how statistics can be used to distort data—if the audience is naive about statistical techniques. Whenever a graph is presented in which the base of the ordinate is not set at zero, be on the alert. The stage has been set for a possible sleight-of-hand trick.

Measures of Central Tendency

To help us understand how individuals differ and how they are alike, we have some useful techniques for finding the *average,* or typical score, in a distribution. Knowing the average IQ for a certain class may help us plan the curriculum, decide how extensively certain topics should be covered in class, or choose books for the library. Information about the typical score in a distribution allows us to interpret more meaningfully all the scores in the distribution.

Statisticians have three methods for obtaining the average, and each is designed, when used appropriately, to give us the most accurate picture possible of the distribution. The averages are called **measures of central tendency** because they describe the typical, middle, or central score in a distribution; they tell us about our average or typical person's score. Choosing the appropriate method can be tricky because the interpretation of the data may vary widely, depending on how the average has been obtained.

The mean   If you were given a set of IQ scores and asked to find the average score, you would most likely compute the mean. That is, you would add all the IQ scores together and divide by the total number of scores. The **mean** is thus the arithmetic average; it is certainly the most commonly used measure of central tendency.

$$M = \frac{\Sigma X}{N}$$

The Greek letter Σ (sigma) is a symbol that tells us to add; it is read as "summation of." N stands for the number of cases. Thus, the equation tells us that the mean (M) is equal to the summation (Σ) of the raw scores (X) divided by the number of cases (N). The mean of our distribution of IQ scores would be computed as in Table 15.6.

As it happens, the mean is an appropriate measure of central tendency in the preceding example because the distribution is fairly well balanced; that is, there are no extreme scores in any one direction. Since the mean is computed by adding together all the scores in the distribution, it is not easily influenced by extreme scores unless the extreme scores are all in one direction. The mean is typically a stable measure of central tendency.

Interpreting the mean can sometimes be very deceptive, especially in groups in which the population itself or the size of the population changes. For example, the mean IQ of the typical freshman class in a college is usually about five points lower than the mean of the same class when the students later become seniors. Does this indicate that students increase their IQs as they proceed through college? No, because the size of the senior class is almost always smaller than the size of the freshman class, the two populations are no longer the same. Those with the

TABLE 15.6   CALCULATION OF THE MEAN FROM A DISTRIBUTION OF RAW SCORES

X	CALCULATION
130	
120	
115	
115	
110	
110	
105	
100	
100	
100	
95	
95	
90	$M = \frac{\Sigma X}{N} = \frac{1545}{15}$
85	
75	$M = 103$
1,545	

lowest IQs in the freshman class are apt to leave college and never become seniors.

The median   In some situations, however, the use of the mean can lead to an extremely distorted picture of the "average" in a distribution. For example, look at the distribution of annual incomes in Table 15.7. One of the income scores ($10,000,000) is so ex-

TABLE 15.7   SKEWED DISTRIBUTION OF INCOME SCORES SKEWED TO THE RIGHT

	$10,000,000
	45,000
	45,000
	34,600
	34,500
	34,500
(Median)	34,400
	34,300
	34,000
	33,500
	33,000
	33,000
	32,600
Total =	$10,428,400
Mean =	$ 802,184.60
Median =	$ 34,400.00

SPOTLIGHT ON TESTING

The Lake Wobegon Effect: Can All Children Be above Average?

Garrison Keillor, during his national public radio show, used to conclude each of his stories with the words: "That's the news from Lake Wobegon, where all the women are strong, the men good-looking, and the children above average." It was a clever and gently cynical comment suggesting that in his town there simply were no below-average children, even though by definition half of the children, of course, had to be below one important average—the median. In the mythical town of Lake Wobegon, "the town that history forgot," such logic was irrelevant. But in the real world of schools and nationally standardized tests, no such flagrant inconsistencies could even be possible. Or could they?

Some time ago, a West Virginia physician, John Cannel, had been treating teenagers for a variety of problems and noticed that many of his young patients were performing far below grade level on a variety of nationally normed tests. When he inquired of the local school officials, he found that each of the administrators was simply reporting from a different set of norms. The discrepancy bothered the doctor. He began to expand his inquiry beyond his own district and state. Eventually he collected achievement test scores from all 50 states. The results were shocking: 49 of the 50 states reported that

their students were "above average." Only Mississippi was different. Here the students were reported as having average scores, right at the fiftieth percentile. In short, *no state had any below-average children.* The question, then, is what happened to the bottom half? Did it disappear into the never-never land of statistical skullduggery?

As one might guess, Dr. Cannell's findings caused a great stir as well as a variety of responses. The national test publishers were obviously put on the defensive, lamely saying that the problem was probably caused by "old" norms. This meant that the proper interpretation of these data should have been that if the present students were in fact above the fiftieth percentile, it merely indicated that they were higher than the original normative sample (Flynn effect?). Such rhetoric, however, seemed only to add to the confusion. If the test norms were out of date, and if the local students did not have the same characteristics as the original normative sample, then what was the point of calling the tests "nationally standardized achievement tests"? In fact, Dr. Cannell suspected, though could not prove, that some test publishers deliberately used initially misleading norm groups. Then school districts could buy and proudly use their

test scores as indicators of educational excellence.

The real problem, of course, is that in valid nationally standardized tests, by definition one-half of the students must be in the lower half of any normal distribution. If students all across the country receive a quality education and their scores continue to improve, then by the rules of standard norm-referenced testing procedures, new norms should be published and new averages announced. The average score is then moved up or down depending on the performance of a currently relevant and representative national sample, as is now being done with the SAT.

Dr. Cannell is continuing his fight for more honesty in testing at the national level. He has shifted from general practice to psychiatry, where he hopes to be of greater service to troubled teenagers. He has warned test publishers that part of that service will also include his insistence upon honesty in test score reporting.

Cannell, J. J. (1989). Nationally normed elementary achievement testing in America's public schools: How all 50 schools are above the national average. *Educational Measurement: Issues and Practices, 7,* 123–149.

Denton, L. (1988). Real-life Lake Wobegon no joke. *APA Monitor, 19*(8), 8–9.

tremely far above the others that to use the mean income as a reflection of the average income would give a misleading picture of high prosperity for this distribution. A distribution that is unbalanced as a result of a few extreme scores in one direction is said to be *skewed.*

A much more accurate representation of central tendency for a skewed distribution is the **median,** or middlemost point in a distribution. Whereas the mean income in Table 15.7 was found to be $802,184.60, the median would be only $34,400, a far more accurate reflection of the typical income for this

TABLE 15.8   CALCULATION OF THE MEDIAN WITH AN EVEN NUMBER OF SCORES

120
118
115
———114.5   (Median)
114
114
112
693

$M = 115.50$

distribution. Since income distributions are usually skewed, you should be on the alert for an inflated figure whenever the mean income is reported. The median is generally a more appropriate value when reporting incomes. To calculate the median, be sure the scores are in distribution form, that is, arranged in order of magnitude. Then count down through one-half of the scores. For example, in Table 15.7 there are 13 income scores in the distribution. We therefore count down 6 scores, and the seventh score coincides with the median. (There will be the same number of scores above the seventh score as there are below it.) If there is an even number of scores in a distribution, as in Table 15.8, the median is found by determining the point that lies halfway between the two middle scores—in this case, 114.5. Unlike the mean, the median is not affected by an extreme score in one direction. In Table 15.8, for example, the median would still be 114.5 even if the low score were 6 instead of 112, whereas the mean would be an unrepresentative 97.83 (see Table 15.9).

Figure 15.7 shows what skewed distributions look like in graphic form. In the positively skewed distribution, most of the scores are found at the low end of the distribution, whereas in the negatively skewed

TABLE 15.9   CALCULATION OF THE MEDIAN WITH AN EVEN NUMBER OF SCORES AND A SKEWED DISTRIBUTION

120
118
115
———114.5   (Median)
114
114
6
587

$M = 97.83$

FIGURE 15.7   A graphic presentation of skewed distributions: (a) negatively skewed; (b) positively skewed.

(a)   (b)

distribution, most of the scores are at the high end. We label this according to the direction of the tail. When the tail goes to the right, we call the curve positively skewed; when it goes to the left, it is negatively skewed.

The mode   The third measure of central tendency is called the mode. The **mode** is the score that occurs most frequently in a distribution. In a frequency polygon the mode is located at the highest point of the curve; in a histogram it is located at the tallest bar. Some distributions, called *bimodal,* have two modes (see Figure 15.8). Distributions of this type occur if scores are clustered in two separate places, or if the group being measured probably breaks down into two subgroups.

Assume that the distribution in Figure 15.8 represents the running speed (in seconds) in the 70-yard dash for a large group of seventh-graders. There are two modes: one at 13 seconds and the other at 18 seconds. Since there are two scores sharing the same high frequency, it is probable that two subgroups are being portrayed. For example, the running speeds for boys may be clustering around one mode while the speeds for girls are clustering around the other.

VARIABILITY

Measures of central tendency give us information about the similarity among measurements; **measures of variability** give us information about how

FIGURE 15.8   A bimodal distribution.

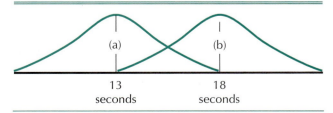

(a)   (b)

13   18
seconds   seconds

scores differ or vary. Measures of variability are crucial in education because they give us vital information about one of psychology's basic themes—individual differences.

The Range (*R*)

One way to describe variability in any distribution of scores is to compute the range (*R*). The range is the difference between the highest and lowest scores, and it is a measure of the width of the total distribution. The range is given as a single value. For example, if the highest score in an IQ distribution is 140 and the lowest score is 60, then *R* would equal 80.

The Standard Deviation (SD)

The standard deviation is the absolute heart and soul of the variability concept. Although the range is important in giving some meaning to a set of scores, it does have one fairly significant limitation: It is based on only two scores, the highest and the lowest. The standard deviation, in contrast, takes into account *every single* score in the entire distribution. The **standard deviation (SD),** therefore, is a measure of variability that indicates how far *all* the scores in a distribution deviate from the *mean.* The higher the numerical value of the SD, the more the scores vary around the mean, or the more the scores spread out around the mean. The smaller the value of the SD, the less the scores spread out from the mean—the more tightly they cluster around it. A distribution with a small standard deviation tells us that the group being measured is homogeneous, whereas a distribution with a large standard deviation describes a heterogeneous group of scores. This standard or typical deviation is always expressed as a single value.

To calculate the SD, follow the steps given with Table 15.10. After arriving at an answer for the standard deviation, always check its value for statistical logic. First, the standard deviation may never be negative, since you can never have less than no deviation. The smallest possible value for the standard deviation is zero, and this will occur only if every score in the distribution is the same. Second, the value of the standard deviation can never be greater than one-half the value of the range. In the example in Table 15.10, in which the range is equal to 15 – 2, or 13, the standard deviation cannot be greater than 13/2, or 6.50. Suppose you had forgotten to take the square root of 12.50 and mistakenly assumed that to be the standard deviation. By knowing that 12.50 is too high (greater than 6.50), you would have found

TABLE 15.10 CALCULATION OF THE STANDARD DEVIATION FROM A DISTRIBUTION OF RAW SCORES

X	X2	CALCULATIONS
15	225	$M = \dfrac{\Sigma X}{N} = \dfrac{72}{8} = 9.00$
12	144	
10	100	
9	81	$SD = \sqrt{\dfrac{\Sigma X^2}{N} - M^2} = \sqrt{\dfrac{748}{8} - 9.00^2}$
9	81	
8	64	$= \sqrt{93.50 - 81.00} = \sqrt{12.50}$
7	49	
2	4	$SD = 3.535 = 3.54$
72	748	

1. Add the *X*'s to obtain ΣX.
2. Divide by *N* to obtain *M*.
3. Square each *X* to obtain X^2.
4. Add these squares to obtain ΣX^2.
5. Divide the ΣX^2 value by *N* and subtract the squared mean, M^2.
6. Take the square root to obtain the SD.

the error because you would undoubtedly have checked your work. It is wise always to check your standard deviation values even if you're using a computer. After all, even the most powerful computer programs have been known to have bugs in them, and even very bright students have been known to have pressed an incorrect function key.

Figure 15.9 shows two IQ distributions, both of which have the same range (60) and the same mean (100). The distributions are different because they have different standard deviations. Distribution *b* has a relatively large standard deviation, indicating that the scores deviate widely from the mean. Distribution *a* has a smaller standard deviation, indicating

FIGURE 15.9 Two IQ distributions with different standard deviations.

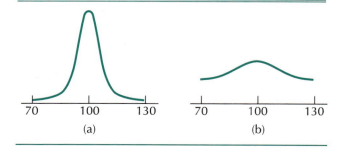

(a) (b)

that the variability is much less, that is, most of the scores are clustering rather tightly around the mean.

The Normal Curve

Many behavioral measures in educational psychology conform to what statisticians call the **normal curve** (see Figure 15.10). The normal curve is actually a theoretical distribution, but so many measurements come so close to this ideal that it is of utmost importance. The normal curve is a frequency-distribution curve with scores plotted on the *X* axis and frequency of occurrence on the *Y* axis. However, it has a number of interesting features that set it apart from other frequency-distribution curves. First, in a normal curve most of the scores cluster around the center of the distribution, and as we move away from the center in either direction, there are fewer and fewer scores. Second, it is symmetrical, that is, the two halves of the curve are identical. It is in perfect balance. Third, the mean, median, and mode all fall at the same point, the midpoint of the distribution. Finally, the normal curve has some constant characteristics with regard to the standard deviation.

The mean divides the normal curve into two equal halves, with 50 percent of the scores falling above the mean and 50 percent falling below it. The area between the mean and a point one standard deviation above the mean includes 34 percent of the scores. Since the normal curve is symmetrical, 34 percent of the cases also fall between the mean and a point one standard deviation below the mean. Thus, between the two points that are one standard deviation away from the mean, that is, ±1 SD, there are 68 percent (just twice 34 percent) of all the cases. As we go away from the mean another full standard deviation, 13.5 percent of the distribution is added to each side. Thus, approximately 95 percent of the cases fall between ±2 SD units. Similarly, since going out a third SD from the mean adds 2.5 percent in each side, 99 percent, or virtually all the cases, fall between ±3 SD units. Less than 1 percent of the scores lies beyond ±3 SD units.

These facts relating percentage of cases to units of the standard deviation are constants; that is, the facts are true regardless of the size of the standard deviation. These constants hold as long as the curve is normal.

If the distribution of scores is normal, then the standard deviation will take on a value that is equal to approximately one-sixth of the range. Thus, in a normal distribution of IQ scores, in which the range is equal to 90, the standard deviation will be equal to approximately 15. If when calculating the standard

FIGURE 15.10   The normal curve is a frequency-distribution curve with scores plotted on the X axis and frequency of occurrence on the Y axis.

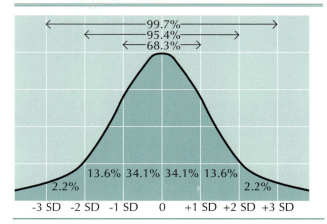

deviation on a large group of scores, you find that its value is less then one-sixth of the range, you can assume that there is less than the normal amount of variability among the scores and that the group being measured is rather homogeneous. If, however, the standard deviation turns out to be greater than one-sixth of the range, you may surmise that the group is heterogeneous.

Standard Scores (*z* Scores)

It is difficult to compare scores on different tests without knowing the mean and standard deviation for each test. For example, if you were to get a score of 72 on a certain math test and 64 on an English test, you wouldn't know on which test your performance was higher. The mean on the math test might have been 85, and the mean on the English test might have been 50, in which case you scored higher on the English test even though your raw score was lower. The point is that information about the distribution of scores must be obtained before raw scores can be interpreted. For this reason, we use *z* **scores,** or **standard scores,** which take the distribution into account. This allows us to understand an individual's test performance relative to others taking the same test. The *z* score is equal to the difference between the raw score and the mean, divided by the standard deviation.

$$z = \frac{X - M}{\text{SD}}$$

The z score indicates, in units of standard deviation, how far above or below the mean a certain score lies. If the mean of the math distribution (85) were subtracted from your math score (72) and divided by the SD (10), your z score would be –1.3.

$$z = \frac{72 - 85}{10} = \frac{-13}{10} = -1.3$$

Thus, on the math test you fell 1.3 SD units below the mean. A negative z score always indicates that the score is below the mean, while a positive z score shows that the score is above the mean. A score of 64 on the English test minus the mean of 50 and divided by the standard deviation, again of 10, yields a z score of 1.4.

$$z = \frac{64 - 50}{10} = \frac{14}{10} = 1.4$$

Since the sign in this case is positive, your score on the English test falls 1.4 SD units above the mean. Though your raw score on the English test is lower than your raw score on the math test, your actual performance on the English test, compared to all other performances on the same test, is considerably higher. Thus, by converting raw scores into z scores, comparisons can be made between an individual's performance on various distributions that have different means and standard deviations.

Percentiles (Deciles and Quartiles)

A raw score can be described very precisely by converting it into a percentile. A **percentile** is that point in a distribution at or below which a given percentage of scores fall. For example, a score at the ninety-fifth percentile means that 95 percent of the scores in the distribution are at or below that point, whereas a score at the fifth percentile means that only 5 percent of the scores fall at or below that point. Knowing the percentage of cases falling between various SD units on the normal curve allows you to calculate the percentile. In the distribution for the normal curve (Figure 15.10), for example, 34 percent of the cases fall between the mean and –1 SD. Since 50 percent of the cases fall below the mean, and since 34 percent of these cases fall between the mean and –1 SD, we can

see that 16 percent of the cases must fall below –1 SD. A z score of –1, meaning a raw score one full SD below the mean, would yield a percentile score of 16. Or, a z score of +1, indicating a raw score of one full SD above the mean, would mean a percentile score of 84 (the 34 percent falling between the mean and 1 SD plus the 50 percent falling below the mean).

Statisticians can determine the percentile for any z score, not just those for whole numbers. For example, a z score of 1.52 shows that about 44 percent of the cases fall between the mean and 1.52 SD units above the mean. Thus, the percentile for that z score would be 94 (the 44 percent falling between the z score and the mean plus the 50 percent lying below the mean). Statistical tables are available that indicate the exact percentage of cases lying between the mean and any z score (Sprinthall et al., 1990).

Assume that we are working with an IQ distribution whose mean is 100 and whose SD is 15. A student with an IQ of 122 would have a z score of 122 – 100, divided by the SD of 15, or 1.47. The student with an IQ of 122 would fall 1.47 SD units above the mean. A z-score table indicates that 43 percent of the cases fall between a z of 1.47 and the mean. Adding that to the 50 percent below the mean, we now know that the student with an IQ of 122 is at the 93rd percentile.

Other variations on the percentile theme include (1) deciles, each worth 10 percentile units, and (2) quartiles, each worth 25 percentile units. The table below illustrates the comparison, where D_1 = the first decile and Q_1 = the first quartile. Notice that the fiftieth percentile is equal to the fifth decile as well as the second quartile.

T Scores

T scores are also based on the normal curve and can easily be converted from z scores by simply setting the mean at 50 and the standard deviation at 10. This ensures that all T scores have positive values (unlike z scores, which are negative whenever they are below the mean). To calculate a T score, simply multiply the z score by 10 and add 50. Like the z score, the T score can be used as a measure of an individual's performance relative to the mean and, of course, to the rest of the distribution. When raw scores are converted into T scores, they give us a measure of how

Percentiles	0	10	15	20	25	30	35	40	45	50	55	60	65	70	75	80	85	90	95	100
Deciles		D1		D2		D3		D4		D5		D6		D7		D8		D9		
Quartiles					Q1					Q2						Q3				

far the raw score is from the mean of 50 in standard deviation units of 10. Thus, a *T* score of 60 is one full standard deviation above the mean, and a *T* score of 40 is one standard deviation unit below the mean. *T* scores run from a low value of 20 (3 standard deviations below the mean) to a high of 80 (3 standard deviations above the mean). Thus, *T*-score values range from 20 to 80, which gives us a range value (*R*) of 60.

Normal Curve Equivalent (NCE)

Another increasingly popular standardized score is called the **Normal Curve Equivalent (NCE) score.** Like the *T* score, the NCE is based on the normal curve and is calculated by setting the mean at 50 and the standard deviation at approximately 21. Because of its larger standard deviation, the range of NCE scores is wider than for *T* scores, and approximates 0 to 100.

Stanines

Stanines, like *z*, *T*, and NCE scores, are based on the normal curve, but unlike the others, stanines divide the distribution into units of nine intervals (whereas *z*, for example, divided the distribution into six intervals). The mean of the stanine distribution must equal 5 and the standard deviation must equal approximately 2. By examining Table 15.11, one can see that stanine 5 (the middlemost interval) contains 20 percent of the cases, stanines 4 and 6 contain 17 percent, stanines 3 and 7 contain 12 percent, stanines 2 and 8 contain 7 percent and, finally, stanines 1 and 9 contain the remaining 4 percent. A child who scored in the 6th stanine, for example, would have performed better than 60 percent of those taking the same test. Many standardized tests in the field of educational psychology report scores on the basis of stanines.

To help you convert scores from one form to another, Table 15.11 shows equivalents among several popular scales. It includes raw score equivalents for the Scholastic Assessment Test (SAT), Normal Curve Equivalent (NCE) scores, and the Wechsler IQ (WIQ) tests (which include the WAIS, WISC, and WPPSI).

TESTING

Norm-Referenced and Criterion-Referenced Testing

The various tests used in psychology and education use either norm-referenced or criterion-referenced scoring systems. The difference is fundamental. In a **norm-referenced test** an individual's performance is *compared* to the average performance of the entire test-taking population. For example, for an IQ test, an individual's score is reported not in terms of the absolute number of correct answers given but instead on the basis of a comparison between the individual's absolute performance and the average performance of all the individuals of the same age who have taken the test. This procedure, in fact, is precisely the same as that used back at the turn of the century by that giant in the field of intelligence testing, Alfred Binet. Binet used the term *mental age* to describe his scoring technique, and this early system is an example of norm-referenced scoring. In order to establish a student's mental age, Binet would give his intelligence test to large numbers of children of various ages. The average performance for a given age became the benchmark for evaluating a given student's performance. For example, after testing thousands of eight-year-olds, he discovered how many items the average eight-year-old could answer correctly. As a result, a child of *any age* who answered the same number of items was assigned a mental age of eight. The mental-age technique, like all other norm-referenced scoring systems, provides information regarding a person's relative standing. Most of the mass-produced tests used in psychology and education today are of this type. Intelligence tests, achievement tests, aptitude tests, and so on are accompanied by national norms with which an individual's performance can be compared.

The **criterion-referenced test** is based not on relative performance but on absolute performance. For this reason, it is also called a *mastery test,* since the focus is on what absolute fraction of the material covered on the test the student has conquered. For example, the Federal Aviation Administration gives a test to each prospective pilot before that pilot is allowed to solo. The applicant must get at least 70 percent of the questions correct before taking to the air without the instructor. Thus, the FAA demands that the pilot know the vast majority of the material on the test, regardless of how others have performed. The FAA reasons that it's not enough to have a high relative standing on the test, since it's possible that the majority of those taking the test are so ignorant of flying techniques and procedures that they would probably all kill themselves.

Most teacher-made tests—and these account for most of the educational tests given each day throughout the country—are criterion-referenced. The teacher makes up a history test and scores it on the basis of the absolute percentage of a student's correct answers, not on the basis of what percentage

TABLE 15.11

PERCENTILE	Z	T	STANINE	SAT	NCE	WIQ	
1	−2.41	25.90	0.18	259	1.0	63.85	
2	−2.05	29.50	0.90	295	6.7	69.25	
3	−1.88	31.20	1.24	312	10.4	71.80	
4	−1.75	32.50	1.50	325	13.1	73.75	(1st Stanine)
5	−1.65	33.50	1.70	335	15.4	75.25	
6	−1.56	34.40	1.88	344	17.3	76.60	
7	−1.48	35.20	2.04	352	18.9	77.80	
8	−1.41	35.90	2.18	359	20.4	78.85	
9	−1.34	36.60	2.32	366	21.8	79.90	
10	−1.28	37.20	2.44	372	23.0	80.80	(1st Decile)
11	−1.23	37.70	2.54	377	24.2	81.55	(2d Stanine)
12	−1.18	38.20	2.64	382	25.3	82.30	
13	−1.13	38.70	2.74	387	26.3	83.05	
14	−1.08	39.20	2.84	392	27.2	83.80	
15	−1.04	39.60	2.92	396	28.2	84.40	
16	−1.00	40.00	3.00	400	29.1	85.00	
17	−0.95	40.50	3.10	405	29.9	85.75	
18	−0.92	40.80	3.16	408	30.7	86.20	
19	−0.88	41.20	3.24	412	31.5	86.80	
20	−0.84	41.60	3.32	416	32.3	87.40	(2d Decile)
21	−0.81	41.90	3.38	419	33.0	87.85	
22	−0.77	42.30	3.46	423	33.7	88.45	
23	−0.74	42.60	3.52	426	34.4	88.90	(3d Stanine)
24	−0.71	42.90	3.58	429	35.1	89.35	
25	−0.67	43.30	3.66	433	35.8	89.95	(1st Quartile)
26	−0.64	43.60	3.72	436	36.5	90.40	
27	−0.61	43.90	3.78	439	37.1	90.85	
28	−0.58	44.20	3.84	442	37.7	91.30	
29	−0.55	44.50	3.90	445	38.3	91.75	
30	−0.52	44.80	3.96	448	39.0	92.20	(3d Decile)
31	−0.50	45.00	4.00	450	39.6	92.50	
32	−0.47	45.30	4.06	453	40.1	92.95	
33	−0.44	45.60	4.12	456	40.7	93.40	
34	−0.41	45.90	4.18	459	41.3	93.85	
35	−0.39	46.10	4.22	461	41.9	94.15	
36	−0.36	46.40	4.28	464	42.5	94.60	
37	−0.33	46.70	4.34	467	43.0	95.05	
38	−0.31	46.90	4.38	469	43.6	95.35	
39	−0.28	47.20	4.44	472	44.1	95.80	
40	−0.25	47.50	4.50	475	44.7	96.25	(4th Decile and Stanine)
41	−0.23	47.70	4.54	477	45.2	96.55	
42	−0.20	48.00	4.60	480	45.8	97.00	
43	−0.18	48.20	4.64	482	46.3	97.30	
44	−0.15	48.50	4.70	485	46.8	97.75	
45	−0.13	48.70	4.74	487	47.4	98.05	
46	−0.10	49.00	4.80	490	47.9	98.50	
47	−0.08	49.20	4.84	492	48.4	98.80	
48	−0.05	49.50	4.90	495	48.9	99.25	
49	−0.03	49.70	4.94	497	49.5	99.55	
50	−0.00	50.00	5.00	500	50.0	100.00	[Median (5th Decile)]
51	0.03	50.30	5.06	503	50.5	100.45	
52	0.05	50.50	5.10	505	51.1	100.75	

TABLE 15.11 (continued)

PERCENTILE	Z	T	STANINE	SAT	NCE	WIQ	
53	0.08	50.80	5.16	508	51.6	101.20	
54	0.10	51.00	5.20	510	52.1	101.50	
55	0.13	51.30	5.26	513	52.6	101.95	
56	0.15	51.50	5.30	515	53.2	102.25	
57	0.18	51.80	5.36	518	53.7	102.70	
58	0.20	52.00	5.40	520	54.2	103.00	
59	0.23	52.30	5.46	523	54.8	103.45	
60	0.25	52.50	5.50	525	55.3	103.75	(6th Decile and Stanine)
61	0.28	52.80	5.56	528	55.9	104.20	
62	0.31	53.10	5.62	531	56.4	104.65	
63	0.33	53.30	5.66	533	57.0	104.95	
64	0.36	53.60	5.72	536	57.5	105.40	
65	0.39	53.90	5.78	539	58.1	105.85	
66	0.41	54.10	5.82	541	58.7	106.15	
67	0.44	54.40	5.88	544	59.3	106.60	
68	0.47	54.70	5.94	547	59.9	107.05	
69	0.50	55.00	6.00	550	60.4	107.50	
70	0.52	55.20	6.04	552	61.0	107.80	(7th Decile)
71	0.55	55.50	6.10	555	61.7	108.25	
72	0.58	55.80	6.16	558	62.3	108.70	
73	0.61	56.10	6.22	561	62.9	109.15	
74	0.64	56.40	6.28	564	63.5	109.60	
75	0.67	56.70	6.34	567	64.2	110.05	(3rd Quartile)
76	0.71	57.10	6.42	571	64.9	110.65	
77	0.74	57.40	6.48	574	65.6	110.10	(7th Stanine)
78	0.77	57.70	6.54	577	66.3	111.55	
79	0.81	58.10	6.62	581	67.0	112.15	
80	0.84	58.40	6.68	584	67.7	112.60	(8th Decile)
81	0.88	58.80	6.76	588	68.5	113.20	
82	0.92	59.20	6.84	592	69.3	113.80	
83	0.95	59.50	6.90	595	70.1	114.25	
84	1.00	60.00	7.00	600	70.9	115.00	
85	1.04	60.40	7.08	604	71.6	115.60	
86	1.08	60.80	7.16	608	72.8	116.20	
87	1.13	61.30	7.26	613	73.7	116.95	
88	1.18	61.80	7.36	618	74.7	117.70	
89	1.23	62.30	7.46	623	75.8	118.45	(8th Stanine)
90	1.28	62.80	7.56	628	77.0	119.20	(9th Decile)
91	1.34	63.40	7.68	634	78.2	120.10	
92	1.41	64.10	7.82	641	79.6	121.15	
93	1.48	64.80	7.96	648	81.1	122.20	
94	1.56	65.60	8.12	656	82.7	123.40	
95	1.65	66.50	8.30	665	84.6	124.75	
96	1.75	67.50	8.50	675	85.9	126.25	(9th Stanine)
97	1.88	68.80	8.76	688	89.6	128.20	
98	2.05	70.50	9.10	705	93.3	130.75	
99	2.41	74.10	9.82	741	99.0	136.15	
100	3.00	80.00	11.00	800	100.00	145.00	

Note: *All conversions are based on the formula: Score = (z) (SD) + mean. Since SAT scores come only in units of 10 points, a 608 rounds to a 610, a 482 to 480, and so on.*

of the class did worse than that student. The algebra teacher who wants to know how a given student is doing with reference to *instructional objectives* in a particular classroom is going to use a criterion-referenced test. It is even possible for the same test to be both norm- and criterion-referenced (Lyman, 1991).

Test specialist Arthur Bertrand identified three crucial components of good criterion-referenced testing (Bertrand & Cebula, 1980):

1. Learning behaviors to be demonstrated by students must be clearly stated prior to the learning experience (e.g., the child will be able to punctuate a four-sentence paragraph).

2. Acceptable levels of success must be stated explicitly (e.g., punctuation must be done with 80 percent accuracy).

3. Test situations or conditions must be made available in order that the students can demonstrate whether or not they have met the criteria.

According to Lorrie Shephard (1979), norm-referenced tests should be used for monitoring pupil (and program) progress over the long run, from fall to spring or from year to year. Criterion-referenced tests, however, are preferred for day-to-day testing in the classroom. These tests are more easily keyed to current instructional objectives.

Studies indicate that students show higher levels of academic achievement in classes in which teachers use tests, and use them often, than in those that rarely test or don't test at all. Frequent testing is even more effective when the students are of only modest ability (Bangert-Downs et al., 1986). Testing can now be accomplished in a very systematic fashion with the use of computer programs. No longer do professional, and often expensive, national testing firms have to be called on for the laborious job of scoring the tests and summarizing the results. Ready-to-run computer programs, which can be used on inexpensive personal computers, are now available for schools and/or school districts to do in-house standardizing. In this age of accountability, in-house testing has become increasingly popular, since it gives schools an economical way of determining the areas in which their students need extra help. It has been shown that when teachers are given clear and understandable data on student progress, student achievement levels increase (McKinnon, 1987).

Teachers typically prefer not to use standardized, norm-referenced tests, usually saying that their particular instructional activities should not be narrowed to those areas sampled by the norm-referenced tests. This reluctance seems to be based on the fact that the content of the course cannot be under teacher control when standardized tests are being used as judge and jury of both the teacher and the students. In fact, some educationists insist that the fastest and most efficient way to change a curriculum is to change the tests (Sykes, 1995).

Measurement-Driven Instruction (MDI)

Some critics allege that enforcing national standards on the public schools will lead to standardized testing (Sizer, 1996). As they are fond of saying, we should be "teaching the child, not the subject." They argue that standardized testing creates an artificial classroom, since it forces teachers to "teach to the test," especially when the children's test scores are used not just to evaluate the children but also the quality of the teacher's work. The general term now used for this is measurement-driven instruction, or MDI (Popham, 1987). In fact, there have even been charges that teachers have gone one step further and, instead of just teaching to the test, have taught the test itself (Bracey, 1987). When the teaching is too narrowly focused on the direct answers to test questions, trivialization of the curriculum would surely occur. But if the general content of the domain under question is being taught, the test evaluation could still be fair and also remain valid. One educationist maintains that standardized tests are actually fairer than the more subjective assessments, such as portfolios (Hirsch, 1996). In fact it has been argued that standardized multiple-choice tests, such as the SAT, rather than being biased against minorities may in fact be biased in favor of some minorities by consistently overestimating the educational achievements of these children (Breland, 1979). In any case it is true that over the years teachers admit that they have consistently taught to their own tests, and probably should. It may really be an issue of whose test is being taught to whom. To test students on material they haven't yet been exposed to would be an exercise in folly.

Ethnic bias can creep into standardized tests. Several years ago the word *regatta* was used in one of the College Board tests. This resulted in a storm of protest, since that is not a word that is often bandied about in minority neighborhoods. Since that time, the Educational Testing Service has been careful to review each word for any such signs of cultural bias. But as the ETS insists, "test results cannot be judged in isolation from the unequal outcomes produced by our educational, economic and social systems" (Educational Testing Service, 1991, p. 3). In other words, a fair and accurate test will in fact reflect the quality of academic preparation, and if it doesn't, it will not

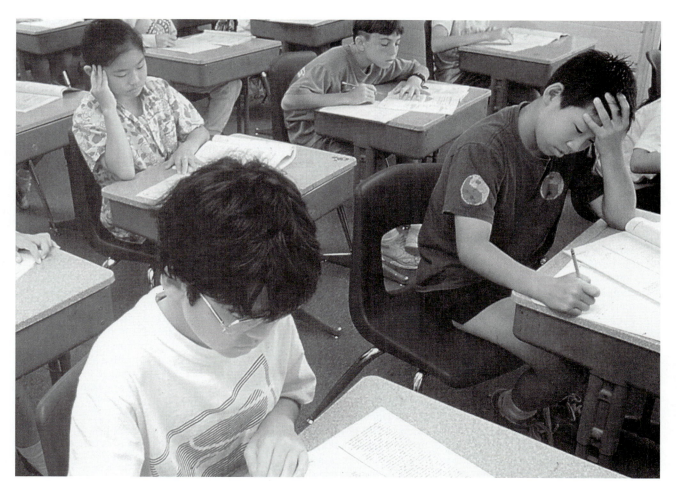

Research indicates that frequent testing closely tied to classroom instruction not only increases student achievement levels, but provides teachers with valuable data with which to plan their instruction.

be a true indicator of educational accomplishments for any test taker, no matter what the student's educational or economic background might be. The concerns of minorities have also been addressed through the use of what is called *race norming*, in which test scores within minority groups are compared only with those from the same minority population rather than across the board.

Race norming is especially important when dealing with any of the cognitive ability tests, as opposed to aptitude or personality tests. Proponents insist that it is the only fair way to evaluate test scores in the absence of equal environmental and cultural backgrounds. This, of course, means setting up separate racial and ethnic norms for the groups under study. For example, on the WISC-III, one item asks:

"What is the right thing to do if a fellow (girl) much smaller than yourself starts to fight with you?" Critics contend that black children answer this item incorrectly because they are taught by their families and neighborhood peers that the appropriate response is "hit him back." Thus, since some test items are assumed to generally favor white culture over the culture of blacks and other minorities, test score adjustments should be used to compensate for the cultural imbalance that is built into these tests (Helms, 1992).

Multiple-Choice Tests or Essays?

What about multiple-choice tests or, as many poorly prepared students like to call them, "multiple-guess

SPOTLIGHT ON EVALUATION

The Portfolio Approach

Another testing technique currently gaining in popularity is called the "PEP," for Project, Exhibits, and Portfolios. Just as an aspiring artist or model carries samples of past work to a prospective employer, so too does the student who selects examples of his or her best work over a term or even an entire year of study. It is said that the portfolio approach places more emphasis on a student's overall accomplishments than on the ability merely to score well on a single battery of tests. As one reviewer put it, "Asking students to select and reflect on examples of their own work provides rich products for assessments."[a] Typical portfolios include original poetry, plays, short stories, essays, and art projects. Even in math, a student might produce a series of fractions, showing their relationships to decimals, or an arrangement of dice to illustrate probabilities, or even an essay on the life of Blaise Pascal. At the end of the year, the student hands over the portfolio to the teacher for evaluation. Portfolios are especially popular among those educationists who favor OBE, "outcome-based education," and when used in this context usually fall under the heading of "Authentic Assessment." The basic concept is that these techniques measure what the student can really do, not what he or she allegedly knows. There is also evidence that portfolio testing may assist students diagnosed as dyslexic.[b]

The development of a uniform scoring system for the portfolios, however, has so far been extremely difficult to accomplish. Teachers at this point are too often grading the same portfolio very differently; indeed, teachers' scores on writing portfolios have agreed with one another less than half the time.[c]

Teachers preparing for the twenty-first century should be made aware of this approach and should be given workshop preparation in learning to better calibrate the scoring procedures. Perhaps the scoring could never be worked out on a 100-point scale, but it is not beyond the realm of possibility that ordinal scores, say 1 to 5, could be implemented. If Olympic judges can learn to do it, so too, it would seem, should professional educators.

These methods are now being used to evaluate teachers, and even the curriculum itself. A portfolio could be constructed to include a teacher's lesson plans and materials, videotaped teaching episodes, and the teacher's reflections on his or her own teaching. Such an exhibit "can provide direct evidence of what a teacher knows and can do."[d]

Whether the portfolio approach will prove as valuable as its early promises suggest is still in question. There is no doubt, however, that new testing methods will be explored into the twenty-first century. Innovative testing procedures are on the horizon, procedures intended to bridge the gap between cognitive psychology and psychometric methods. New formats will undoubtedly appear, "along with a renewed interest in performance testing, to permit assessment of higher-order cognitive skills and important performance tasks such as writing, oral communications and problemsolving."[e]

[a]   Tittle, C. K. (1991).Changing models of student and teacher assessment. *Educational Psychologist, 26*(2).
[b]   Spafford, C. S., & Grosser, G. S. (1996). *Dyslexia: Research and resource guide.* Boston: Allyn & Bacon.
[c]   Rand study points to problems in Vermont's portfolio assessment program (1993, February). *Executive Educator, 11.*
[d]   Wolf, K. (1991, October). The schoolteacher's portfolio: Issues in design, implementation, and evaluation. *Phi Delta Kappan,* 129–136.
[e]   Hambleton, R. K. (1991). Meeting the measurement challenge of the 1990s: New psychometric models, methods and tests. *The Score, 14,* 9.

---

tests"? One of the criticisms of the multiple-choice test is that it rewards rote memorization rather than true understanding. This can certainly happen if the test is poorly designed, but when thoroughly researched and carefully prepared, the multiple-choice test can assess a person's ability to apply concepts to problem-solving situations. Rather than breaking up the unity of knowledge and isolating the pieces, as the critics typically charge, *a well-designed* multiple-choice test, such as the SAT, demands that the student be able to understand concepts and bring facts together. This is especially true of the SAT's reading comprehension section. Research evidence clearly shows that the SAT verbal score shares much in com-

SPOTLIGHT ON COMPUTER-ASSISTED TESTING

Assessment in the 1990s

The computer age has led to a high-tech form of testing called **computer-assisted testing (CAT).** Here the individual sits at a computer keyboard, and the questions are presented on the screen. The testing becomes personalized since the testing is interactive with the computer, in effect, custom designing the test to each student's skill level. For example, the questions may get progressively more difficult until a level is reached. When a student begins to get the questions wrong, an easier set of questions suddenly appears. This branching of easier and harder questions, called going "up the ladder" or "down the chute," continues until the student's true level of competence is reached. The Educational Testing Service is currently putting both the SAT and the Graduate Record Exam (GRE) on a computer format. Supporters of this approach claim that CAT is viable, cost-effective, and a big improvement over paper-and-pencil testing (Vale, 1990).

Vale, C. D. (1990). The future of computerized testing: Technology, economics, and marketability. *The Score, 13,* 6–7.

mon with IQ, the correlation between them being an extremely high +.80 (Flynn, 1987). What about essay questions? There is the fear that standardized tests based only on essay questions and writing samples may have an adverse effect on cultural bias (*Science Agenda,* 1990). Verbally adept but uninformed students may bluff their way through an essay exam (Aiken, 1997), and this tactic is used less often by minorities.

Although essay exams can often illuminate the student's thought process in more detailed form, the teacher with a large class of widely varying abilities, interests, and needs may have to rely on the multiple-choice test. It not only ensures reliability of testing, but, more important it permits more free time to work with individual students and parents. It is often all too easy to blame standardized multiple-choice testing for deteriorating academic skills and overlook the more immediate culprits, overcrowded classrooms and underpaid teachers.

Gender Equity Testing

There still seem to be gender-based differences in a number of standardized ability and aptitude tests. Most researchers have found little difference among children up to age 10, some slight differences in junior high, and the major differences occurring in high school and college (Sadker et al., 1991). For example, on the SAT, females score lower on the math section than do males, and until very recently females have traditionally scored higher on the verbal section (Wainer & Steinberg, 1992). In fact, it is felt that the verbal abilities of females on the SAT are almost certainly now being *underestimated.* Before 1980 the high school dropout rate for girls was significantly higher than for boys, but now that trend has been reversed, with more boys currently dropping out. The inclusion of more below-average girls in high school and fewer below-average boys may be the reason for this underestimate of female verbal superiority (Halpern, 1989). Also, on tests of vocational aptitude there are a wide variety of significant differences between the genders (Connor & Vargas, 1992). It may be that the current test formats are producing gender differences that are more apparent than real. For example, research has shown that girls outperform boys on essay tests, whereas boys tend to do better on multiple-choice tests (Mazzeo et al., 1991). Research has actually been conducted to show that items concerning such things as batting averages tend to favor boys, whereas question in the general area of child care favor girls (Pearlman, 1987).

These performance differences have led to a call for gender equity testing, that is, the creation of tests that, though revealing individual differences among boys and girls, are designed to show no significant differences between the scores of girls *as a group* and boys *as a group.* If this proves to be impossible, perhaps gender norming the current tests might be the next step. In any event, proponents of this view are anxious to provide testing that does not reveal any major differences between the sexes.

SPOTLIGHT ON GRADE-EQUIVALENT SCORES

A Note of Caution

Grade-equivalent scores are based on relating a given student's score on a test to the average scores found for other students in a particular grade, at the same time of year, and of roughly the same age. For example, assume that in September a large, representative sample of third-graders (called the norming group) produced an average score of 30 on a certain arithmetic test. If a given student is then tested and receives a score of 30, that child would be assigned a grade-equivalent score of 3.0. If the child did somewhat better than that and had a score of, say, 3.4, it would indicate a performance equal to that of a third-grade student in the fourth month (December) of the school year. Grade-equivalent scores are typically reported in tenths of a year, so that a score of 5.9 refers to the ninth month (June) of the fifth grade, and a score of 0.0 to the first day of

kindergarten. Thus, the scores range from 0.0 (or sometimes K.0.) through 12.9, representing the thirteen years of school from kindergarten through grade 12. The first of September is given on the scale as 0, whereas the end of September as 0.1, the end of October as 0.2, and so on until the end of June, as 0.9. Grade-equivalent tables are provided for the major nationally standardized tests, and although they are quick and easy to figure (simply look up the raw score in the test publisher's table), they must be interpreted with some caution. First, as we have seen over and over again, children do not all grow and develop at the same yearly rate, never mind the same monthly rate, so don't be overly concerned when a seemingly bright child suddenly underperforms the norms by a few months. That same child may quickly catch up and even outperform the norms

several months later. Second, don't be too quick to use a precocious child's high score in some area as a reason to have that child skip a grade or two.[a] A third-grader might even get a grade equivalent of 7.0 on a given test. This doesn't mean that the child is now ready for a fast promotion to junior high. What it does mean is that the third-grader has certainly mastered third-grade material and has done as well as a seventh-grader when measured on a *third-grade test*. However, there are undoubtedly many things the seventh-grader has learned and is expected to know which are not even part of a third-grader's consciousness and which, of course, don't appear on a third-grade test.

[a]   Aiken, L. R. (1997). *Psychological testing and assessment* (9th ed.). Boston: Allyn & Bacon.

The New SAT

In 1994 the ETS changed the rules of the SAT by (1) allowing calculators and (2) including some items that don't give multiple-choice alternatives, but demand that the student provide the answer. In 1995 the SAT was renamed and recentered. Instead of calling itself the Scholastic Aptitude Test, it is now called the Scholastic Assessment Test, a name change that is intended to deemphasize the intelligence-measuring connotation of the test. Also, a score of 500 became the mean score for both the verbal and math sections. The SAT was originally standardized in 1941 on a much smaller group of college applicants (about 10,000, mostly white males), and the mean at that time was set at 500 and truly reflected the academic potential of that particular group of

test takers. Today the number of students taking the SAT has grown to almost 1.5 million, making the new norms far more representative of today's population of high school students than was the 1941 group, against which all students have long been compared. In 1993 the mean score on the verbal portion of the test was 424, and the mean on the math section was 478, for a combined average of 902. In 1995 the combined average was therefore jumped by 92 points to 1,000. It did not, of course, mean that post-1995 students were suddenly that much smarter, since the relative rankings (percentiles) remained the same, but the scoring system did add a constant to everyone's score in order to reflect the new mean. For pre- and post-1995 comparisons one can convert the SAT scores into standard (z) scores, where

$$z = \frac{\text{SAT}-500}{\text{SD}}$$

Thus, the 1995 student who has a combined score of about 900 will still have a *z* score of −1.00 (sixteenth percentile), just the same as the 1993 student whose combined score was only about 800.

Grade Inflation?

During the past few years, there have been strong suspicions that academic grading in schools and colleges has risen even though today's students are not achieving noticeably more in real terms. The evidence seems to confirm these suspicions, since long-term comparisons of grade-point averages (GPAs) have shown a systematic increase. Actually, even had there been no increase in grades it could still be argued that grade inflation has occurred. This argument is based on the fact that since SAT scores, which do correlate significantly with GPAs, have been declining, it follows that GPAs should not have either stayed the same or risen but *should also have declined.*

Curriculum Testing

Virtually any curriculum that is more that five years old requires a thorough evaluation. This is most obvious in fields such as science, but it should probably be done in all areas. Although it has been traditional to use pupil achievement scores as a means for assessing the quality of the curriculum, student scores are useful only insofar as the tested curriculum matches both the planned and taught curriculum. Curriculum expert Jurg Jenzer points out that curriculum evaluation can be a positive tool for evaluating students, teachers and, of course, the school. This type of testing should answer the following:

1. To what degree have the curriculum's goals been reached?

2. Has the overall mission of the curriculum project been reached?

3. Is the curriculum content appropriate in view of the mission objectives?

4. Has the instruction been truly based on the curriculum?

5. Have the assessment procedures measured the taught curriculum *and* the planned curriculum? (For more on these important testing issues, see Jenzer, 1992).

Correlation: A Useful Tool for Making Predictions

Although correlation does not imply causation, it is a useful tool for making predictions. A *correlation* is a statement about the relationship between two variables; it tells us the extent to which the two variables are associated, or the extent to which they occur together. There is, for example, a correlation between College Board scores and college grades. This means that the two variables, College Board scores and college grades, tend to occur together: People with high College Board scores tend to have higher college grade-point averages than do people with low College Board scores.

The Sign of the Correlation

Correlations come in three general forms: positive, negative, and zero. Positive correlations are produced when individuals who score high on the first variable also score high on the second, and those who score low on the first variable also score low on the second. For example, a positive correlation between height and weight means that those individuals who are above average in height are also above average in weight, and those who are below average in height are correspondingly below average in weight. Negative correlations are produced when individuals who score high on the first variable tend to score low on the second, and those who score low on the first, score high on the second. A negative correlation between college grades and number of absences means that those who are above average in college grades tend to have fewer absences, whereas those who are below average in college grades tend to have more than the average number of absences. Finally, zero correlations are produced when individuals who score high on the first variable are as likely to score high on the second variable as they are to score low, or when individuals who score low on the first variable are as likely to score low on the second variable as they are to score high.

Correlation Values and Their Interpretation

In order to express the degree to which two variables are associated, or correlated, a single number is used. This number may vary from +1 through zero to −1. A value of +1 indicates a maximum positive correlation. A maximum relationship is obtained when two measures of a group of individuals, for example, height and weight, associate perfectly. There can be

SPOTLIGHT ON CORRELATION AND CAUSATION

The Chicken and Egg Riddle

Suppose a researcher found a correlation between the amount of exercise a person indulged in and the amount of money that person had in the bank. The correlation would probably be negative; that is, people who are involved in heavy exercise programs might tend to have smaller bank accounts. This would not necessarily mean that persons who exercise regularly don't have enough time left over to earn and save money, since it may well be that another variable, age, is being overlooked. Elderly persons who have had a lifetime in which to acquire money are probably less apt to jog five miles a day than a high school student who is still on a family allowance. Other studies of this type have found a strong positive correlation between the amount of time teachers spend smiling and the achievement level of their students; that is, the more the teachers smiled, the higher the students' grades. One cannot conclude that smiling teachers cause students to achieve more, since, for one thing, we don't know which came first—the smiles or the achievement. Perhaps the teachers are smiling as a result of the high level of student achievement, apparently basking in reflected glory. Or it might be that a *third* variable is influencing both the smiling and the achievement. Perhaps some smiling teachers are happy optimists who see only the best in their students and therefore are more apt to award higher grades.

The important message here is that we should never leap to a cause-and-effect conclusion on the basis of the correlation alone. It is especially easy to look at a two-variable correlation and mistakenly assume that the variable that came first (preceded) somehow caused a change in the variable that followed. That type of conclusion commits what the scientists call the *post hoc fallacy*, which is written in Latin as post hoc, *ergo propter hoc* (translated as "because it came after this, therefore, it was caused by this"). Many examples of this fallacy come readily to mind. We have all heard someone complain that it always rains right after the car is washed, as though washing the car caused it to rain. Or the traffic is always especially heavy when you have an important exam to take, as though all the other drivers know when the exam has been planned and gang up in a contrived conspiracy to force you to be late. Or perhaps while watching a sporting event on television, you have to leave your TV set for a few minutes. When you return, you discover that your favorite team has finally scored. You angrily hypothesize that the team deliberately held back until you weren't there so you would not be able to enjoy the thrill of victory. Some correlation conclusions have been very similar to these rather extreme examples.

Of what use, then, is correlational research? Prediction! Even though causal factors may be diffi-

cult to isolate, correlational studies do allow the researcher and/or teacher to make better-than-chance predictions. As for the correlation mentioned above between wealth and exercise, regardless of the reason, the negative correlation between exercise and bank account still allows for a better-than-chance prediction of the bank account value on the basis of exercise patterns—the more the exercise, the smaller the bank account. If, in a two-newspaper city, there is a dependable relationship between which newspaper a person buys (liberal or conservative), and the political voting habits of that person, then one might predict the outcome of certain elections on the basis of the newspapers' circulation figures. We can make the prediction without ever getting into the issue of what causes what. That is, did the liberal stance of the newspaper cause the reader to cast a liberal vote, or did the liberal attitudes of the reader cause the selection of that particular newspaper? We don't know, nor do we even have to speculate on causation in order to make the prediction. In short, accurate predictions of behavior do not depend on the isolation of a causal factor. One need not settle the chicken-egg riddle in order to predict that a certain individual might choose an omelet over a dish of cacciatore. But in making that prediction we must not allege that a cause-and-effect relationship has been established.

FIGURE 15.11 Scatterplot diagrams showing three kinds of relationships between two variables.

no exceptions when the correlation is +1. Thus, every single individual in the group who is higher than another in height is also higher in weight. A value of zero indicates no relationship at all, or a zero correlation. A value of –1 indicates a maximum negative correlation. A correlation of –1 between college grades and number of absences would mean that every single individual in the group who is higher than another in college grades is also lower than that other in number of absences. Most correlations found in the literature fall somewhere between these perfect correlations of +1 and –1. The closer the correlation is to ±1, however, the more accurate the resulting prediction; and prediction, after all, is the major goal of correlation research. For example, if the correlation between height and weight is +.65, we can more accurately predict a given individual's weight, knowing the person's height, than if the correlation is only +.25.

Scatterplot Diagrams

In order to get a visual representation of how two variables might correlate, statisticians use a graphic device known as a scatterplot diagram. A scatterplot diagram is a correlation graph in which each dot represents a pair of scores: one for the distribution of one set of scores and the other for the distribution of the other set of scores. Figure 15.11 shows the three kinds of relationships that can exist between two variables. The scatterplot diagram on the left portrays a positive correlation: The array of dots goes from lower left to upper right, telling us that as one variable increases, so too does the other. The scatterplot diagram in the middle portrays a negative correlation: The array of dots goes from upper left to lower right, telling us that as one variable increases, the other decreases. Finally, the scatterplot diagram on the right portrays a zero correlation, or no relationship at all: As one variable changes, there is no related change in the other.

The Pearson *r*

One of the most frequently used correlation coefficients is the **Pearson product moment correlation** or, more simply, the **Pearson *r*.** This measure was developed by Karl Pearson, a student of Sir Francis Galton.

$$r = \frac{\Sigma XY/N - (M_X \times M_Y)}{(SD_X)(SD_Y)}$$

If you have learned to calculate a standard deviation, computing a Pearson *r* will be fairly easy. Assume that we are interested in testing the hypothesis that there is some relationship or correlation between

Karl Pearson, a student of Sir Francis Galton, devised the Pearson product moment correlation, the Pearson r, *which indicates the strength of the possible association between two variables.*

TABLE 15.12   CALCULATION OF THE PEARSON r

	MATH SCORE			SPELLING SCORE		
STUDENT NUMBER	X	X²		Y	Y²	XY
1	4	16		6	36	24
2	12	144		10	100	120
3	2	4		3	9	6
4	5	25		4	16	20
5	9	81		5	25	45
6	6	36		10	100	60
7	2	4		3	9	6
8	10	100		10	100	100
9	6	36		9	81	54
10	9	81		10	100	90
	10)65	527		10)70	576	525

$M_x = 6.50$

$$SD_x = \sqrt{\frac{\Sigma X^2}{N} - M^2}$$

$$= \sqrt{\frac{527}{10} - 650^2} = \sqrt{52.70 - 42.25}$$

$$= \sqrt{10.45}$$

$SD_x = 3.23$

$M_y = 7.00$

$$SD_y = \sqrt{\frac{\Sigma X^2}{N} - M_y^2}$$

$$= \sqrt{\frac{576}{10} - 7.00^2} = \sqrt{57.60 - 49.00}$$

$$= \sqrt{8.60}$$

$SD_y = 2.93$

$$r = \frac{\Sigma XY/N - (M_x)(M_y)}{SD_x SD_y} = \frac{525/10 - 6.5 \times 7}{3.23 \times 2.93} = \frac{52.50 - 45.50}{9.46}$$

$$r = \frac{7}{9.46}$$

$r = .739$, which is rounded to

$r = .74$

math ability and spelling ability among fifth-grade students. We administer a 12-item math quiz and a 12-item spelling quiz to a group of fifth-graders. Let the math scores be represented on the X distribution and the spelling scores on the Y distribution. Then the Pearson r is calculated as follows:

1. Calculate the mean for each distribution. In Table 15.12, ΣX (or 65) divided by N (or 10) equals 6.5. Similarly, ΣY (or 70) divided by 10 equals 7.

2. Compute the standard deviation for each distribution. Square each score and add the squares. Thus, for the X distribution, the first score, 4, when squared equals 16. Next, the score of 12 is squared, yielding 144, and so on. These squared scores are then added, yielding 527 for the X distribution. The Y distribution is treated in exactly the same way: Square the first score, 6, and get 36. Add all the squares and get 576. Each of

these values is used to obtain the standard deviation for each distribution. For X, divide ΣX^2 (527) by N (10) and get 52.70. From that, subtract the square of the mean (52.70 – 42.25). For the resulting value, 10.45, extract the square root, 3.23, which is the standard deviation. For the Y distribution, divide 576 by 10, which equals 57.60. Subtract the square of the mean (57.60 – 49.00) and get 8.60. Extract the square root, 2.93, to obtain the standard deviation.

3. Multiply each raw score in the X distribution by its corresponding score in the Y distribution. Thus, 4 times 6 equals 24; 12 times 10 equals 120; 2 times 3 equals 6; and so on. These XY values are then added, yielding a total ΣXY of 525.

4. Divide ΣXY by N, and then subtract the product of the means. Thus 525/10 minus the product of 6.50 times 7 equals 7.

5. This value is then divided by the product of the

ANNE ANASTASI

Anne Anastasi was brought up in New York City. She attended Public School 33, where she was awarded a gold medal for general excellence. She then entered public high school, but after two frustrating months she dropped out. Although she had found her stay at P.S. 33 to be happy and productive, she found high school to be a total waste of time. Her high school was overcrowded, and she resented both the 15-minute trolley-car ride and the fact that her teachers were remote and impersonal.

During her dropout phase, there were many family discussions about her academic future. Finally, a friend suggested that she should simply skip high school completely and go to college. Thus in 1924, at age 15, Anastasi became a freshman math major at Barnard College. As a freshman, she took an introductory psychology course, and although she found the course interesting, it was not until her sophomore year, when she took a course in developmental psychology, that she decided

psychology was to be her lifework. Psychology gave her the opportunity to have the best of two worlds. She could satisfy her interest in mathematics through the study of psychological statistics and also her emerging interest in human development and behavior.

She graduated from Barnard at 19 and immediately entered the Ph.D. program in psychology at Columbia University. She received her doctorate two years later. The high point of her short tenure as a graduate student came during the summer of 1929. She began that memorable summer as research assistant to the famous American geneticist Charles B. Davenport. Next she took a six-week course with the illustrious learning theorist Clark Hull. Finally, as the summer ended, she attended the International Congress of Psychology at Yale University. There she saw and heard great psychologists from all over the world, including Ivan Pavlov, Charles Spearman, and William McDougall.

In 1930 Anastasi joined the faculty at Barnard College, where she remained until 1939. She then went to Queens College in New York as chairman of the psychology department, and in 1947 she joined the faculty at Fordham University.

Anastasi considers herself to be a "generalist" in the field of psychology. Her interests range widely, and she has published in such diverse areas as the psychology of art, memory, personality, intelligence, emotion, statistics, language development, test construction, cultural differences, creativity, male and female differences, and the nature-nurture controversy. The bibliography of Anastasi's papers and books reads like a compendium of the whole field of psychology. There are few areas in psychology to which

this talented woman has not devoted some of her time and energy.

In 1971 Anastasi was honored by her professional colleagues by being chosen as the president of the American Psychological Association, a group at that time of over 31,000 members.

Anastasi is a firm believer in the influence of early experience on intellectual growth and development. She urges a program of concentrated effort on improving environmental conditions at early life stages, especially for disadvantaged groups. She feels that early in life the cumulative effects of an impoverished environment can be minimized. She is also a firm believer in intelligence testing, when the tests are administered properly and evaluated fairly. She feels that IQ tests should not be discontinued just because some children receive lower scores than others. This would be like asking a physician to throw away her or his thermometer just because children who are ill register an undesirable deviation from the norm. Measuring instruments don't produce social discrimination; only people do.

In 1958, in her paper "Heredity, Environment and The Question 'How?'" Anastasi argued that people should stop asking the question about which component, heredity or environment, is more important in determining individual differences. A better question is how heredity and environment interact in the development of behavioral differences. The focus should be on the mechanism of the interaction, because behavior is the result of the interaction. Anne Anastasi, the generalist, specifically recommends here that we take a new look at one of psychology's oldest and most often debated problems.

standard deviations of *X* and *Y*. Thus, 3.23 times 2.93 equals 9.46. Dividing 7 by 9.46 gives us a Pearson *r* of .739, which can be rounded to .74.

Since the highest possible correlation is 1.00, which is a perfect positive correlation, the Pearson *r* of .74 indicates a fairly strong association between the two variables, math scores and spelling scores. Thus, our sample of fifth-graders provides data that tell us that students who perform well on the math quiz are also likely to perform well on the spelling quiz. Since the correlation is not 1.00, we cannot say that every student who is high in math ability is also high in spelling ability. Our correlation of .74 indicates that there will be some exceptions but that in general the relationship will be dependable. Thus, knowing a student's math score allows us to predict his or her spelling score, and because the correlation is fairly strong, we will be right in our predictions far more often than we will be wrong. Although correlation does not imply causation, it does allow for accurate predictions. We can't say that an individual is a good speller because he or she has high math ability, but we can say that, given information about the pupil's math ability, we can predict fairly accurately how well he or she will spell.

SAMPLING: GENERALIZING FROM THE FEW TO THE MANY

Perhaps you have been told never to generalize, never to leap to conclusions on the basis of a few observations. An old proverb states that one swallow does not make a summer. Statisticians say, "Never generalize from an *N* of one." Someone once said that no generalization is absolutely true, even that one.

This is certainly all good advice. It prevents us from committing the **inductive fallacy**—that is, automatically assuming that all members of a class have a certain characteristic because one member of that class has it. It would be fallacious to say, "I once met a Mongolian who was a liar; therefore, all Mongolians are liars."

However, under certain prescribed conditions—that is, using certain strategies or rules of the game—it may be appropriate to generalize on the basis of a limited number of observations. Certain statistical techniques allow us to generalize to a whole group after observing some part of that group. The key to these techniques is that the small groups must be representative of the entire group: they must reflect the traits and characteristics of the entire group. If we want to predict political attitudes of Americans in general, we cannot interview just men, or just women, or just Democrats, or just people who are receiving social security. We must interview a group that represents all these traits and many more.

The entire group, or the total number of people, things, or events having at least one trait in common, is called a *population*. Any group selected from the population is called a *sample*. In order to ensure that the sample is representative of the population, statisticians usually use the technique of random sampling. *Random sampling* gives every single member of the entire population an equal chance of being selected for the sample. If you wanted to select a random sample of the population of students at your college, you could not do it by selecting every third person in the college cafeteria. Perhaps some students never eat in the cafeteria, and they would not be represented in the sample. Nor could you choose a random sample by selecting every *n*th person who enters the library. Again, some students avoid the library and would not be represented in the sample. To be sure to have a random sample, to be sure that every student in the college has an equal chance of being chosen, you would take the names of every student enrolled in the college, drop the names in a barrel, and, blindfolded, pick out, say, 50 or 100 names. In this way the group selected would be truly random, and because the group was selected on a chance basis, it would likely be representative of the entire population. Random sampling allows the statistician to legitimately generalize to the population.

SUMMARY

Measurement is the assigning of a number to an observation (object or event) according to certain rules. To give meaning to these numbers, all measurements must satisfy two basic criteria: They must be reliable and they must be valid. Reliability indicates the consistency of a measurement, while validity is the extent to which a test measures what it is intended (and purports) to measure.

To make meaning out of the chaos of raw data from any study, the researcher typically arranges the raw scores in order of magnitude, called a distribution of scores. When the scores are presented beside another column, listing the frequency of occurrence for each score, a frequency distribution is created. Educational psychologists also use graphs to present data in a more meaningful form. The actual scores are indicated on the horizontal axis, or abscissa, and the frequency of occurrence is presented on the vertical axis, or ordinate. Another method of portraying frequency distribution data is the stem-and-leaf display, in which only the first digit(s) is (are) shown in the stem column and the trailing digits are shown in the leaf column.

In order to aid in our understanding both of the ways in which individuals differ and the ways in which they are alike, methods are employed for finding the average or typical score in a distribution. These techniques, called measures of central tendency, include the mean, which is the arithmetic average; the median, which is the middlemost point in an ordered distribution; and the mode, which is the most frequently occurring score in a distribution.

Just as the measures of central tendency give us information about similarity among measurements, measures of variability provide information about how scores differ or vary. Two important measures of variability are the range, which is the difference between the highest and lowest scores in a distribution; and the standard deviation (SD), which is a measure of how much each score generally varies or deviates from the mean. In addition, many behavioral measures in psychology conform to what is called the normal curve, a theoretical distribution that shows the majority of scores as falling around the center of the distribution, and fewer and fewer scores as we move away from this center in either direction. A standard score, or z score, is a translation of a raw score into units of standard deviation. The z distribution has a mean of zero and a standard deviation of 1.0. Similarly, a T score, also based on the normal curve, is derived by setting the mean at 50 and the standard deviation at 10. T scores range in value from 20 (three standard deviations below the mean) to 80 (three standard deviations above the mean). NCE scores, or normal curve equivalents, are also standardized on the normal curve and are based on a mean of 50 and a standard deviation of approximately 21. Finally, stanines are also translated from the normal curve and divide the curve into units of nine intervals. The stanine distribution has a mean of 5 and a standard deviation of approximately 2. A percentile is that point in the distribution at or below which a given percentage of cases fall. Variations on the percentile theme include (1) the decile, every 10 percentile units; and (2) the quartile, every 25 percentile units.

Tests can be scored by being criterion-referenced and/or norm-referenced. Criterion-referenced tests evaluate an individual's performance on the basis of a comparison with some arbitrarily fixed standard. Norm-referenced tests judge the individual's performance on the basis of a comparison with the average performance of all the individuals who took that same test.

The correlation coefficient, first developed by Karl Pearson, is a numerical statement describing the strength of the association between two (or possibly more) variables. Though correlational statements should not, in and of themselves, be used to imply causation, they can be used to make better-than-chance predictions.

By using scientific sampling techniques, such as random sampling, the researcher can legitimately generalize the results of a few measurements taken on a small group to a much larger group. Thus, the educational psychologist may measure only a sample and yet is able to accurately generalize these measures to an entire population. The key issue in these sampling procedures is that the sample must be representative of the population to which the results are to be extrapolated.

KEY TERMS AND NAMES

Anne Anastasi
computer-assisted testing (CAT)
correlation
criterion-referenced test
distribution
grade-equivalent scores
histogram
individual differences
inductive fallacy
measurement
measurement driven instruction (MDI)

measures of central tendency
   mean
   median
   mode
measures of variability
   range (R)
   standard deviation (SD)
normal curve
Normal Curve Equivalent (NCE) score
norm-referenced test
Pearson r (product moment correlation)

percentile
portfolio approach
random sampling
reliability
stanine

stem-and-leaf display
T scores
validity
z score (standard score)

THEORY INTO PRACTICE: STATISTICAL EVALUATION

Exercise 1   You have been assigned to work with a classroom teacher to help in the interpretation of test grades. The teacher has prepared a 50-item multiple-choice test to be used on a group of 30 students after they complete a social studies unit on the causes of the Civil War. The test was timed and scored on the basis of the number of items a student correctly answered. The scores were as follows:

31, 20, 23, 29, 30, 31, 34, 35, 44, 31, 31, 32, 21, 45, 39, 21, 37, 22, 31, 31, 35, 25, 36, 29, 29, 30, 29, 35, 34, 30

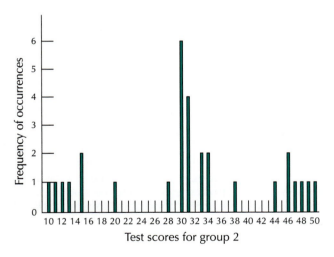

Calculate the following measures of central tendency: the mean, the median, and the mode. Next, calculate the following two measures of variability: the range and the standard deviation.

On the basis of your calculations, indicate whether the test has produced any indication of centrality among the scores. Also, write a statement regarding your views on whether the test showed the group to be homogenous or heterogeneous.

Exercise 2   The teacher you have been assigned to also decided to use the same exam with another

class, also following the presentation of the Civil War unit. This class was also composed of 30 students, and their scores were as follows:

15, 33, 46, 31, 10, 12, 50, 31, 31, 13, 11, 20, 30, 30, 44, 48, 49, 15, 30, 47, 30, 46, 30, 38, 30, 34, 34, 33, 31, 28

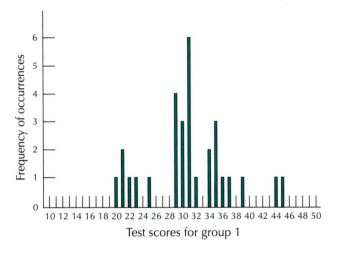

As before, calculate the mean, the median, the mode, the range, and the standard deviation.

Is there any noticeable difference between the performances of the two groups? Compare both the centrality and variability of the scores in the two distributions. Do the groups show the same degree of homogeneity or heterogeneity? Or are the two distributions about even in the amount of variability shown?

Is there anything you might tell the teacher regarding your overall evaluation of the two groups?

Exercise 3   Draw two histograms, one for each set of scores. Indicate the raw scores on the horizontal axis (abscissa), and the frequency of occurrence on the vertical axis (ordinate). As shown in the text, use a series of rectangles over each score in order to indicate frequency.

Exercise 4 You have been given a large amount of student information from a local school district. Among the data, you find some measures that were obtained from a random sample of children selected from the K–12 population (ages 5 to 18). The measures were as follows:

STUDENT'S NUMBER	SHOE SIZE (IN INCHES)	READING ACHIEVEMENT SCORES
1	5	10
2	8	12
3	11	21
4	13	22
5	13	20
6	10	20
7	11	18
8	10	20
9	9	19
10	7	16
11	9	23
12	10	16
13	7	13
14	11	21
15	12	30

A friend suggests to you that from a quick inspection of the data it looks as if there is a rather strong correlation between the variables; that is, the high scores on the reading test seem to be associated with larger foot sizes and the lower reading scores seem to be associated with smaller sizes. To find out if there is such an association, you are asked to calculate a Pearson *r* correlation coefficient between the two variables.

What is the correlation?

What does this tell us about the relationship between these two variables?

Does the analysis prove that forcing children to wear larger shoes might cause an increase in reading ability? If so, why, and if not, why not?

Answers *Exercise 1:* The mean is 31.00; the median is 31; the mode is 31; the range is 25; and the standard deviation is 5.99. The scores seem to indicate that the group is relatively homogeneous and that there are definitely indications of common centrality, since the mean, median, and mode all occur at the same point.

Exercise 2: The mean is 31.00; the median is 31; the mode is 3; the range is 40; and the standard deviation is 11.69. In this group, although the measures of centrality have virtually the same values as those in the first group, the variability is significantly larger; that is, in this group the scores are more heterogeneous and are thus producing higher values for both the range and standard deviation. The teacher should be aware, and probably already is, that the job of teaching the second group will be more difficult. Material that is understandable for the lower-achieving student may at the same time seem overly easy for the higher-level students (who might then become bored). Similarly, setting the level to accommodate the higher-level students may totally frustrate and confuse the lower-level students. The extremes of ability levels shown in this group will probably make the teacher's job more demanding in terms of teaching skills as well as social sensitivity and personal understanding.

Exercise 3: The histograms should look something like those on the previous page.

Exercise 4: The Pearson *r* correlation is +.85. The size of the correlation shows that there is a dependable relationship between foot size and reading ability among the pupils in the chosen sample; that is, children with larger feet tend to read at a higher level than children with smaller feet. Correlation, however, should not be used in an attempt to prove a cause-and-effect relationship. In this example, an extremely important third factor was left out of the two-variable analysis, and that was the age variable. Obviously, older children will tend to have bigger feet and should also, because of experience and maturation, be better readers. The problem of the "third factor" is one that haunts much correlational research. Despite this limitation, the correlation could still be used for predictive purposes. In this case, for example, knowing a given child's shoe size should allow the researcher to make a better-than-chance prediction regarding the same child's score on a test of reading ability.

REFERENCES

Aiken, L. R. (1997). *Psychological testing and assessment* (9th ed.). Boston: Allyn & Bacon.

Bangert-Downs, R. L., Kulik, J. A., & Kulik, C. L. (1986). *Effects of frequent classroom testing.* Paper presented to the American Educational Research Association, San Francisco.

Bertrand, A., & Cebula, J. (1980). *Tests, measurement, and evaluation: A developmental process.* Reading, MA: Addison-Wesley.

Bracey, G. W. (1987). Measurement-driven instruction: Catchy phrase, dangerous practice. *Phi Delta Kappan 68,* 683–686.

Breland, H. M. (1979). *Population validity and college entrance measures.* Princeton, NJ: College Board.

Connor, K., & Vargas, E. (1992). The legal implication of gender bias in standardized testing. *Berkeley Women's Law Journal 7,* 13–89.

Educational Testing Service (1991). *Sex, race, ethnicity and performance on the GRE general test.* Princeton, NJ: Author.

Fiske, E. B. (November 13, 1988). America's test mania. *The New York Times.*

Flynn, J. R. (1987). The ontogeny of intelligence. In J. Forge (Ed.), *Measurement, realism, and objectivity: Essays on measurement in the social and physical sciences.* Boston: D. Reidel.

Geisinger, K. F. (1992). Metamorphosis in test validation. *Educational Psychologist 27,* 197–222.

Halpern, D. F. (1989). The disappearance of cognitive gender differences: What you see depends on where you look. *American Psychologist 44,* 1156–1158.

Helms, J. E. (1992). Why is there no study of cultural equivalence in standardized cognitive ability testing? *American Psychologist 47,* 1083–1101.

Hirsch, E. D. (1996). *The schools we need and why we don't have them.* New York: Doubleday.

Jenzer, J. (1992). Curriculum process and design. In *Mathematics curriculum resource handbook.* Millwood, NY: Krauss International.

Lyman, H. B. (1991). *Test scores and what they mean* (5th ed.). Englewood Cliffs, NJ: Prentice Hall.

Mazzeo, J., Schmitt, A., & Bleistein, C. (1991, April). *Do women perform better, relative to men, on con-structed response tests or multiple choice tests? Evidence from the Advanced Placement Examinations.* Paper presented at a meeting of the National Council on Measurement in Education, Chicago.

McKinnon, G. (1987). In-house standardized test scoring has numerous benefits. *Electronic Learning 7,* 46.

Pearlman, M. (1987, April). *Trends in women's total score and item performance on verbal measures.* Paper presented at the annual meeting of the American Educational Research Associates, Washington, DC.

Popham, W. J. (1987). The merits of measurement-driven instruction. *Phi Delta Kappan 68,* 679–682.

Sadker, M., Sadker, D., & Klein, S. (1991). The issue of gender in elementary and secondary education. *Review of Research in Education 17,* 309–315.

Science Agenda (August–September, 1990). New directions in educational testing. *Science Agenda,* 14.

Shephard, L. (1979). Norm-referenced versus criterion-referenced tests. *Educational Horizons 68*(1), 26–35.

Sizer, T. R. (1996). *Horace's hope: What works for the American high school.* Boston: Houghton Mifflin.

Sprinthall, R. C. (1997). *Basic statistical analysis* (5th ed.). Boston: Allyn & Bacon.

Sprinthall, R. C., Schmutte, G. T., & Sirois, L. (1990). *Understanding educational research.* Englewood Cliffs, NJ: Prentice Hall.

Sykes, C. J. (1995). *Dumbing down our kids: Why America's children feel good about themselves but can't read, write, or add.* New York: St. Martin's Press.

Tittle, C. K. (1991). Changing models of student and teacher assessment. *Educational Psychologist 26*(2), 157–165.

Wainer, H., & Steinberg, L. (1992). Sex differences in performance on the mathematics section of the Scholastic Aptitude Test: A bidirectional validation study. *Harvard Educational Review 62,* 323–336.

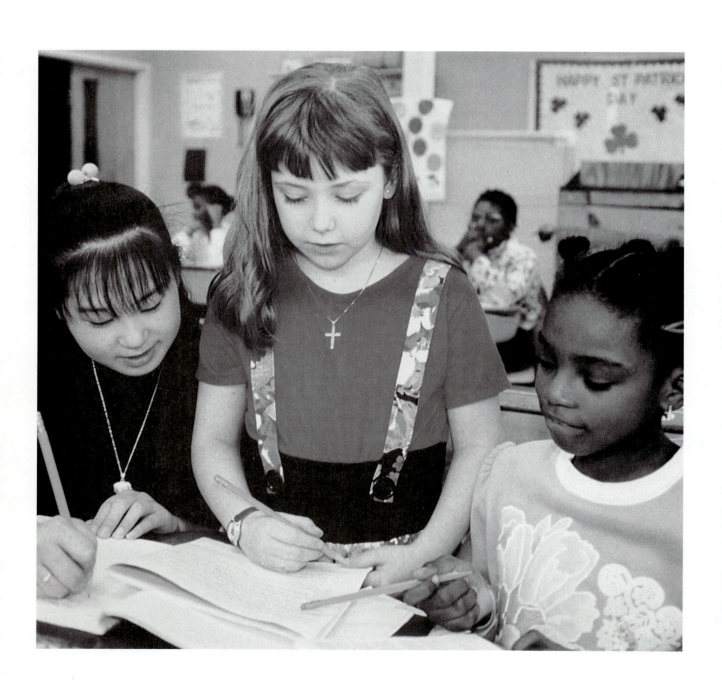

INTELLIGENCE: CONCEPTS AND MEASURES

Among the lay public, the term intelligence is probably the most widely used psychological concept of all. The media constantly bombard us with stories of new theories and studies, often anecdotal, on the topic of intelligence. Historians estimate the IQs of important persons from the past. People talk about whether they or others are intelligent enough for this job or that college or to marry this or that person. Politicians have even legislated immigration quotas on the basis of their versions of intelligence. Hardly a day goes by without our hearing the term mentioned at least once, but what does it mean? What is intelligence? Does it even exist, and if it does, is it displayed differently among different people engaged in different tasks?

WHAT IS INTELLIGENCE?

If you could step back in time and observe those first humans living among large and ferocious beasts, you probably wouldn't have given those weak, skinny, hairless creatures much chance for survival, never mind even an outside chance of taking over the planet. In a tooth-and-claw world, the human being would not have appeared to be "fit" enough to survive. But we humans did survive and did take charge of our world. Why? Undoubtedly because of our wits. We had no claws, no fangs, no protective

shells. Our only armament was our intelligence. Our ability to size up new situations, learn from past mistakes, and create new patterns of thought all contributed heavily to our overall capacity to *adapt to new situations* and then *transmit our learning to new generations*. Intelligence had and continues to have survival value. Sandra Scarr has said that from the point of view of biology, intelligence has evolved as a primary adaptive mechanism and as such shows typical patterns of individual variability (Scarr, 1981).

Toward the end of the nineteenth century, the eminent psychologist Sir Francis Galton (younger cousin of Charles Darwin) assumed from his research that intelligence was a unitary trait and could be measured as a single value, like height or weight. Further, he assumed that intelligence was a function of the quality of a person's sensory apparatus, and he devised a series of tests of reaction time and sensory acuity in order to measure this ability. In fact, Galton was attempting to use Darwin's theory of evolution as an explanation for human intellect. The Galton argument is essentially this: if intelligence is based on one's sensory-motor apparatus, and if sensory equipment evolved on the basis of survival value, then intelligence must be highly heritable. In 1882 he set up a testing booth in a London museum and charged people a fee to have their hearing, vision, reaction time, and other sensorimotor equipment measured. Perhaps the most significant fact to emerge from his data was the concept of individual differences: Galton found that people varied widely in their abilities to perform on simple sensorimotor tests. Despite their seeming simplicity, one thing is certain about Galton's tests—they were definitely not culturally biased.

Galton's willingness to stress the hereditarian side of the intelligence issue may have been partly due to the fact that he had some extremely bright relatives. But he also felt that he needed even more objective evidence. He collected data on assumed intellectual relationships between pairs of twins. Virtually all later studies of intelligence are based on Galton's idea of studying relationships in the context of individual differences. As we saw in the last chapter, one of Galton's students, a mathematician named Karl Pearson, actually worked out the basic equation for the correlation coefficient, and thus furnished the statistical groundwork for the data analysis that has proved so useful in the study of intelligence. As a result Galton is considered to be the "father of intelligence testing."

Although Galton's tests seem naive by modern standards, his emphasis on the relationship between sensory ability and intellect foreshadows much of today's research on the importance of sensory stimulation in determining cognitive growth. Although Galton certainly stressed the importance of heredity, he also acknowledged the influence of environmental factors: "success would become an equal measure of both ability and the favourableness of environment" (Galton & Schuster, 1906, p. xxv). Despite the interactionist tone of that quote, Galton never missed the opportunity to stress the importance of the genetic argument, even though he carefully framed it within the context of environmental inputs. For example, Galton insisted that being born to intelligent parents does not guarantee that the child will be a success in later life. The child might even be "stupid, eccentric or downright mad . . . but . . . the child of illustrious parenthood has an enormously greater chance of turning out gifted to a higher degree" (p. 64). Galton also invented what he called the index of co-relation to be used in analyzing his test data. However, it was left to one of students and colleagues, Karl Pearson, to work out the mathematical details of this index, which is now known as the Pearson *r* or product moment correlation.

Individual Differences and Correlation

Galton and Pearson were impressed by the fact that individuals varied so greatly in such characteristics

as height, weight, and intellect. Because of this variety, the measurements of these characteristics would be more useful if they reflected the frequency with which the characteristics could be expected to occur in the population on the basis of chance, rather than their own absolute units of measurement, such as feet or pounds. The idea of relative standing is of great importance in psychology. It is more important to know that a man's height places him in the relative position of exceeding 50 percent of the adult male population than to know that he stands five feet, nine inches tall.

The concept of individual differences also makes it possible to find a common ground of comparison between different kinds of measurements. Even though height and weight cannot be compared directly because different units of measurement are used, they can be compared in terms of how much each varies from its own average. In effect, this means that apples and oranges can be compared on the basis of whether, say, a given orange and a given apple are both larger or smaller, or juicier or riper, than the average orange and apple. Thus, the relationships between two measurements can be expressed in quantitative terms, and this value is called the *correlation coefficient*. As we saw in Chapter 15, correlations range in value from +1 through zero to −1. The stronger the relationship, the greater the deviation from zero.

Although he emphasized nonintellectual factors in his search for the substrate of intelligence, it now seems likely that Galton was onto something, even back then. He sensed that reaction time and sensory acuity must be components of intelligence, but he offered little in the way of solid proof. Studies being conducted today, however, seem to be confirming Galton's intuition, for they show that people with higher IQs tend to perform more quickly on perceptual as well as cognitive tasks; they scan, comprehend, retrieve and respond more quickly than those with lower IQs (Deary, 1995).

Since Galton's time, however, most psychologists have turned away from the sensory-motor approach to intelligence and have concentrated more on intellectual factors. For example, just after the turn of the century, **Charles Spearman,** a friend and colleague of both Pearson and Galton, used Pearson's correlational technique as the basis for studying what he believed to be the components of intelligence. He theorized that intelligence was made up of several factors, an underlying general factor *g* and a series of very specific factors *s*'s. According to Spearman's **factor approach,** the *g* factor acted as a driving force that would power a set of special skills unique to specific situations, such as verbal ability, mathemati-

TABLE 16.1   SPEARMAN'S INTERCORRELATIONS OF INTELLIGENCE AND SUBJECT AREAS

	CLASSICS	FRENCH	ENGLISH	MATH	PITCH	MUSIC
Classics	—	.83	.78	.70	.66	.63
French	.83	—	.67	.67	.65	.57
English	.78	.67	—	.64	.54	.51
Math	.70	.67	.64	—	.45	.51
Pitch	.66	.65	.54	.45	—	.40
Music	.63	.57	.51	.51	.40	—

cal ability, and even musical ability. The g factor, however, provided the main thrust for activating the s factors. According to Spearman's model, g was a form of dynamic brain energy that would set in motion the "specific engines" of ability. Spearman began by looking at the academic grades English prep school students received in six of their scholastic subject areas, those presumed to comprise intelligence: classics, French, English, math, pitch, and music. He then calculated Pearson r values among the various grades and came up with the intercorrelations shown in Table 16.1.

By placing these intercorrelations in matrix form, Spearman could note the ordering of the correlational strengths, known as "loadings," by looking down any column or across any row. Further, since all the correlations were positive, he assumed that there must be some underlying factor that had to be shared by all of them. He called that common factor g for general intelligence. By looking at the ordering of the correlations, he could see that classics had the highest g loading and music the lowest. Those areas with low g values were said to represent specific s talents. Thus, to Spearman, intelligence was made up of two main factors, a single general factor g and a number of specific factors s. Spearman firmly believed that although g was largely inherited, the specific factors were far more amenable to environmental inputs.

Recently there has been renewed interest in Spearman's g. On the basis of an extensive survey of the evidence to date, some researchers now argue that Spearman may have been right all along, that there does exist a general g factor that, in varying degrees, dominates most of the specific types of cognitive skills that have lately been claimed (Carroll, 1989). "No one can deny that the g factor exists as a functional entity. It predicts future academic behavior, job success in the work-place, and it correlates in interpretable ways with a host of other variables" (Green, 1992, p. 331).

A challenge to the g theory was issued from the work of **L. L. Thurstone.** Thurstone, from the 1920s through the 1940s, worked diligently on an attempt to refine Spearman's factors but did not add supportive evidence for the g concept. Thurstone suggested, instead, that intelligence was always a composite of special factors, each peculiar to a specific task. He identified seven different factors, or what he called "vectors of the mind." These, he said, were the major components of intelligence, and he labeled them the "primary abilities" (Thurstone, 1935).

Thurstone's Seven Primary Abilities of Intelligence

In his book *The Vectors of the Mind* (1935), Thurstone postulated that intelligence consisted of a series of seven specific "primary mental abilities." This, of course, was in opposition to Spearman's view that intelligence was composed of one general factor, g, surrounded by a group of specific factors. Thurstone's seven Primary Mental Abilities (PMAs) were:

V for verbal comprehension

W for word fluency

N for number and computational abilities

S for spatial visualization

M for associative memory

P for perceptual speed

R for reasoning ability

Thurstone believed these Primary Mental Abilities (PMAs) to be free of any overriding, dominant general factor and in fact were independent of one another. His research was based on a technique, originally utilized by Spearman, called "factor analysis," which, as we saw above, uses a correlation matrix to

SPOTLIGHT ON INTELLIGENCE

The Sternberg View

Yale psychologist Robert Sternberg approaches intelligence from an information processing perspective, and he calls his position a triarchic theory of intelligence; that is, it is based on three major types: componential, experiential, and contextual.[a]

1. Componential intelligence is based on a person's ability to learn how to do new things, acquire new information, absorb the explicit knowledge taught in schools, store and retrieve that information, and carry out tasks speedily and effectively. In fact, Sternberg argues that most IQ tests typically focus only on componential intelligence, whereas in his view it only occupies one-third of the total.
2. Experiential intelligence is based on a person's ability to solve new problems, to act creatively, and to use insight. This form of intelligence also allows the person to process past information quickly, freeing the mind for the more important work of seeking creative solutions to new problems. As examples of

some experiential items consider the following:[b]

A. "A woman who lives in a small town married 20 different men in that same town. All of them are still living, and she never divorced any of them. Yet she broke no laws. How could this be?"
B. "Susan gets in her car in Boston and drives toward New York City, averaging 50 miles an hour. Twenty minutes later, Ellen gets in her car in New York City and starts driving to Boston, averaging 60 miles an hour. Both women take the same route, which extends a total of 220 miles between the two cities. Which car is nearer to Boston when they meet?"
3. Contextual intelligence is based on a person's ability to use practical knowledge and common sense. Individuals high in contextual intelligence are typically called "street smart," are able to get along with other people, and usually able to stay out of trouble. Such individuals can adapt to

their environments and even reshape them to accommodate their strengths and minimize their weaknesses. Sternberg calls this practical aspect of intelligence *tacit* knowledge (out of which contextual intelligence is formed). He sees tacit knowledge in general as made up of all the important things you aren't formally taught in school but were able to pick up yourself on the basis of what works and what doesn't. He is convinced that success in life depends as much on tacit knowledge as the explicit knowledge you might obtain from more academic pursuits. As examples of contextual knowledge Sternberg offers the following, all of which may have more than one possible answer:[c]

C. Your cafeteria typically provides very poor food, and all agree that the food is so bad it is barely edible. Nobody, however, can agree on a solution. Should you:
(1) Select their fruit and yogurt because that is impossible to ruin?

---

ferret out those groups of variables, or fundamental factors, that are relatively independent of one another. Those individual variables that correlate highly are said to have high factor loadings, and, of course, when the correlations are low, so too are the loadings.

Many years later, **J. P. Guilford,** using this factor approach, argued that intelligence may be composed of up to 120 separately identifiable traits (Guilford, 1967). Similarly, since the 1980s psychologists such

as Howard Gardner and Robert Sternberg have created new theories of intelligence that seem to provide an almost humanistic perspective. As one psychologist has said, the creators of these new theories, "mindful of the pitfalls of IQ, borrow from cognitive psychology and neuroscience to define smartness as a complex web of abilities" (McKean, 1986).

In a famous claim, first articulated in 1969, the noted psychologist P. E. Vernon suggested three basic meanings for the concept of intelligence:

(2) Start a petition for a new food service?

(3) Eat at the diner across the street?

D. You have been selected by your department chair to serve on a committee that will select students to be admitted as graduate students in the psychology department at your university. You have been thinking about what leads to later success in the field of psychology. Rate the importance of the following student characteristics to later success in the field of academic psychology:

(1) scholastic aptitude

(2) ability to set priorities according to the importance of the task

(3) interpersonal skills

(4) a tendency to try to do everything perfectly

(5) broad-ranging interests and hobbies

(6) full knowledge of the psychology literature

Answers appear at the end of this spotlight.

The difference between compo- nential (explicit) knowledge and contextual (tacit) knowledge (and also, perhaps, different stages of moral development) may be illus- trated by the following story: Two young men, one a graduate stu- dent in higher mathematics, the other a high school dropout who is known for his "street smarts," are out hiking. The two enter an aban- doned tunnel, and when about halfway through, they suddenly see a large and ferocious bear en- tering the tunnel behind them. The graduate student whips out his cal- culator, estimates such values as the distances involved and the speeds at which the bear and they might run, and then does some quick calculations. In the mean- time, the dropout is taking off his hiking boots and lacing on his sneakers. "It's no use," says, the graduate student. "My equations make it clear that we can't outrun that bear." The dropout replies, "That may be, but the way I figure it, we don't have to outrun that bear. All I've got to do is outrun you."

Finally, Sternberg believes that highly intelligent people, as evalu- ated on his triarchic measures, tend to be more creative and more willing to take risks than those with lower measured intelligences.[d]

Sternberg's Answers

A. The woman is a minister.

B. When the cars pass, they are next to each other and thus equally distant from Boston.

C. A good choice would be (1) if you like fruit and yogurt and are not comfortable starting petition drives; (2) if you don't like fruit and yogurt, but you are comfortable organizing a petition; or (3) if you don't like the first two options.

D. Professional psychologists rate (1), (2), (5), and (6) as more im- portant than (3) or (4).

---

[a] Sternberg, R. J. (1985). *Beyond IQ: A triarchic theory of human intelligence.* New York: Cambridge University Press.
[b] Sternberg, R. J. (1986). *Intelligence applied* (pp. 214, 215). Orlando, FL: Harcourt Brace Jovanovich.
[c] Adapted from ibid., p. 318.
[d] Sternberg, R. J., & Lubart, T. I. (1992). Buy low and sell high: An investment approach to creativity. *Current Directions in Psychological Science, 2,* 1–5.

Intelligence as a genetic capacity: This part of intel- ligence is due to the "luck of the genes," and is based on the understructure that is part of one's inherited equipment. D. O. Hebb once referred to this as intelligence A, the genotypic form of intel- ligence. According to Australian geneticist Gillian Turner (1996), there are a large number of genes that provide for the genetic basis of intelligence, and these genes appear to be located on the X chromosome. In fact they seem to be arrayed along the entire length of the X chromosome. Because the Y chromosome is so much smaller than the X, it does not contain a matching gene for each gene on the X. Thus, a female baby, who al- ways receives two X chromosomes, has the bene- fit of having her possibly low IQ genes compen- sated for by a second set of genes from another X chromosome. A male baby, on the other hand, gets only one X chromosome, and if it's not normal, the impact cannot be diluted by the pres-

ANTHROPOMETRIC
LABORATORY

For the measurement in various ways of Human Form and Faculty.

Entered from the Science Collection of the S. Kensington Museum.

This laboratory is established by Mr. Francis Galton for the following purposes:—

1.   For the use of those who desire to be accurately measured in many ways, either to obtain timely warning of remediable faults in development, or to learn their powers.

2.   For keeping a methodical register of the principal measurements of each person, of which he may at any future time obtain a copy under reasonable restrictions.   His initials and date of birth will be entered in the register, but not his name.   The names are indexed in a separate book.

3.   For supplying information on the methods, practice, and uses of human measurement.

4.   For anthropometric experiment and research, and for obtaining data for statistical discussion.

Charges for making the principal measurements:
THREEPENCE each, to those who are already on the Register.
FOURPENCE each, to those who are not:— one page of the Register will thenceforward be assigned to them, and a few extra measurements will be made, chiefly for future identification.

The Superintendent is charged with the control of the laboratory and with determining in each case, which, if any, of the extra measurements may be made, and under what conditions.

H & W. Brown, Printers, 20 Fulham Road, S.W.

SIR FRANCIS GALTON

In 1822 Francis Galton was born into a wealthy and highly educated English family. Among his relatives were many of England's most intelligent, accomplished, and gifted citizens, including Charles Darwin, who introduced the modern theory of evolution, and Arthur Hallam, the subject of Tennyson's "In Memoriam." Galton's wife also had "connections": her father had been headmaster of Harrow and a brilliant educator.

In 1838 Galton began his studies in medicine, but two years later he shifted to mathematics. Following college, Galton traveled several times to Africa, trekking into areas of that continent that had not been explored before. In 1854, he received the Royal Geographical Society's gold medal for these adventurous forays.

After his marriage in 1853, Galton turned to writing. His first book, *The Art of Travel,* was a practical guide for the explorer. His second, on meteorology, was one of the first attempts to set forth precise techniques for predicting the weather.

During the 1860s Galton became impressed with his cousin Charles Darwin's book, *On the Origin of Species.* He was fascinated with Darwin's notion of the survival of the fittest through adaptation, and he attempted to apply this concept to human beings, thus founding the field of *eugenics,* or the study of how the principles of heredity could be used to improve the human race.

In 1869 Galton published his first major work, *Hereditary Genius,* in which he postulated the enormous importance of heredity in determining intellectual eminence. He felt that "genius" ran in certain families, and he was eager to point to his own brilliant family as "exhibit A." He also became impressed with the wide range of individual differences that he found for virtually all human traits, physical as well as psychological.

Following the publication of *Hereditary Genius,* Galton wrote other major works, including *English Men of Science, Natural Inheritance,* and *Inquiries into Human Faculty.* His range of interests in psychology was extremely wide, embracing such topics as imagery, free and controlled associations, personality testing, and, of course, the assessment of intellect. Certainly Galton takes his place in history as a hereditarian, but he did not overlook environmental influences completely. To gain understanding of the possible interaction between heredity and environment, Galton performed psychology's first research studies on twins.

In 1909, just two years before his death, Galton was knighted. Galton's place in the history of psychology is assured. More than any other person, he set psychology on the road to quantifying its data, and the whole testing movement in educational psychology owes a major debt to Galton's early work.

ence of a second X chromosome. Thus, the evidence seems to be mounting that boys receive the bulk of their inherited intellectual potential from the mother, while girls share in fairly equal measure the inherited potential passed on by both parents.

Intelligence as observed behavior: This second meaning, called by Hebb intelligence B, is based on observations of what the individual does. This is the phenotypic form of intelligence and is a result of the interaction of genes and the environ-ment. In this sense intelligence becomes an adverb, and we define it on the basis of whether or not the individual acts intelligently.

Intelligence as a test score: The third meaning of intelligence, Hebb's intelligence C, is based on a strict operational definition. Intelligence is what the intelligence test measures. Though this seems to be a straightforward, no-frills definition, it creates a meaning of intelligence that can differ from what the majority of individuals would regard as intelligent behavior.

THE BEGINNINGS OF IQ TESTING

Alfred Binet and Mental Age

In 1904 the minister of public instruction in Paris, France, appointed **Alfred Binet** to a special commission that was to study the problem of educating mentally retarded children. The commission concluded that separate schools should be established to educate those children who could not profit from the regular classroom situation. Binet and his colleague, Theodore Simon, developed the first real intelligence test for the express purpose of identifying these children. Binet discarded Galton's notion of measuring intelligence through the use of sensorimotor tasks and assembled instead a series of intellectual tasks. It was Binet's belief that intelligence was the ability to make sound judgments. The various tasks were arranged in order of difficulty and presented to a group of French children. Binet's test was an individual test of intelligence; that is, the test was given to one child at a time and administered by a trained examiner. Binet later used the concept of **mental age** to score the test. He discovered, for example, how many of the tasks the average six-year-old could pass, and then any other children who passed the same number of tests were assigned a mental age of six years. Thus, Binet defined mental age in terms of the age at which a given number of test items are passed by an average child. This means that from the very beginning the measurement of intelligence has been a relative measure of mental growth. Binet's intelligence scores were not absolute, for they were based on how well a given child does compared to the average child of the same age. As we saw in Chapter 15, this is a clear example of a norm-referenced system. Binet's scores were assigned relative to the performance shown by children of the *same age,* taking the *same test.*

Binet tried to define intelligence in terms of an individual's ability to make sound judgments. "To judge well, to comprehend well, to reason well, these are the essentials of intelligence. A person may be a moron or an imbecile if he lacks judgment, but with good judgments he could not be either" (Binet & Simon, 1905). But, unlike many of the theoreticians who followed, Binet spent little time fretting over the intricacies and possible embellishments of his definition. Binet's goal was to measure intelligence, not merely to talk about it. He understood intelligence in terms of what it enabled children to do, in much the same way an electrician understands electricity. Binet's test worked. With it, he could predict reasonably well which children would do well in school and which ones would have difficulties. Of course,

there were exceptions, but these were fewer and fewer as the test improved. Sometimes a bright but disobedient child would do worse in school than his intelligence test score would predict, and sometimes a dull but docile child would do better. This outcome, however, may have been due as much to faulty teacher evaluation as to inaccurate test scores.

The Early Stanford-Binet

Binet continued working on his 1905 scale, creating new items to improve the test. He revised the whole test twice, in 1908 and in 1911. In 1916 an American psychologist, **Lewis M. Terman,** of Stanford University, published an American revision of the Binet test. Terman's test was standardized on American children and introduced so many new items that it was virtually a new test. He called it the **Stanford-Binet test,** and it soon became immensely popular in this country. In scoring the test, Terman introduced the concept of the **intelligence quotient,** or **IQ.**[*] IQ was determined by dividing mental age (MA) by chronological age (CA) and multiplying by 100 to get rid of the decimals. Thus,

$$IQ = \frac{MA}{CA} \times 100$$

A six-year-old scoring a mental age of nine years would have an IQ of $9/6 \times 100$, or 1.5×100, or 150; a six-year-old scoring a mental age of five years would have an IQ of $5/6 \times 100$, or $.833 \times 100$, or 83. Since the test was standardized in such a way that the mental age was determined by how well the average child in a given age group did on the test, the average IQ for each age group had to be 100. That is, a six-year-old child scoring a mental age of six years (as the average six-year-old had done), would have an IQ of $6/6 \times 100$, or 100. Since the IQ expresses a child's rate of mental growth, the child whose IQ is 100 is progressing at an average rate.

IQ TESTS TODAY

The Current Stanford-Binet

The Stanford-Binet test was revised in 1937, 1960, and again in 1985. The 1960 revision used a different method of computing IQ, a method previously used by **David Wechsler** and called the **deviation IQ.** The

---

[*]   Terman borrowed the term IQ from a German psychologist, William Stern, who published a paper describing its use in 1913.

ALFRED BINET

Alfred Binet was born in Nice, France, in 1857. He went to secondary school in Paris and received a law degree in 1878. Practicing law did not appeal to Binet, and he soon decided to go back to school. In 1890 he received a degree in the natural sciences, and in 1894 he earned his Ph.D. in science, with a dissertation that focused on the nervous system of insects. During the time he was working on his doctorate, Binet became deeply interested in suggestibility, and in 1886 he published a book on hypnosis that showed the effect of different suggestions on subjects in both the hypnotic and waking states. He published another book in 1886 on the general topic of reasoning and intelligence. Later he would devote all his time to the pursuit of knowledge in this field.

In 1903 Binet wrote a book titled *The Experimental Study of Intelligence,* using as his basic data the thinking processes displayed by his two daughters. He would give a logic problem to his daughters and analyze the steps they took to reach a solution. Though he found

that they attacked and solved some problems in the same way, he noted marked differences in their approach to other problems. In his own immediate family, Binet thus observed the pervasiveness and importance of individual differences, as well as various cognitive growth patterns.

When in 1904 the French minister of public instruction announced his wish to identify and place in special schools those children who were mentally retarded, Binet took on the challenge. This was a situation made to order for a student of individual differences. He asked for and was granted an appointment to the special committee being set up for this purpose. If children who could not seem to profit from regular schooling were to be placed in special classes, a device or technique had to be developed to identify these children. Binet argued that the diagnostic technique should be intellectual, not medical. It had been the practice in France to use physicians to diagnose mental retardation, since retardation was believed to be a physical condition. Binet pointed to the errors and inconsistencies that occurred in these medical diagnoses. If a child was seen by three different physicians on three successive days, three completely different medical diagnoses could result from these examinations.

In 1905 Binet, with a collaborator named Theodore Simon, published the first real intelligence scale. For their test, Binet and Simon assembled a series of intellectual tasks, rather than the sensorimotor tasks that Galton had used. Binet believed that intelligence was displayed in one's ability to make sound judgments rather than in one's ability to react quickly to a

physical stimulus. Thus Binet took intelligence out of the medical-physiological realm and placed it squarely in the intellectual-psychological area. He wanted to test complex higher-order thinking processes that tend to vary with age.

In 1908 Binet revised his original test, retaining the best items from the 1905 scale and adding a number of new tasks. In scoring this 1908 test, Binet utilized a new term, *mental age.* The test would not be scored simply on the basis of the number of items a child passed but rather with reference to age standards. Binet's scoring technique thus defined intelligence as a *developmental* rather than as a static concept.

In 1911, shortly before Binet's untimely death, a second and final revision of the Binet-Simon test was published. This test was a further refinement of the original scale, again substituting new items for previous items that had shown low validity.

Binet's death in 1911 shortened a career just reaching full bloom. It is certain that many of the controversies that erupted in the field of intelligence would have been lessened had he lived long enough to complete his work. For example, Binet believed that intelligence was not just a fixed, immutable individual trait, but rather a developing, trainable, dynamic cluster of abilities that could be nourished or stifled as a result of environmental inputs.

Binet's contribution to educational psychology was enormous. If a person's work can be measured on the basis of the amount of research the work has generated, Binet must stand near the top of his field.

Binet defined mental age in terms of the age at which a given number of test items are passed by an average child. In 1916 Lewis Terman of Stanford University introduced the Stanford-Binet test. The latest version of the test, last revised in 1985, uses a different method of computing IQ. The method is particularly important in measuring the IQs of individuals.

The Wechsler tests—those for both children and adults—measure IQ as a function of verbal as well as performance abilities. Wechsler's tests also perform another valuable function, that of personality evaluation.

problem with the original method of calculating IQ was that by about age 13, the ratio began to break down. The mental age of teenagers no longer continued to increase as it had when they were younger. Nor do adults add to their mental age from year to year. Thus, the ratio of mental to chronological age could be used only with fairly young children unless statistical corrections were added in. The deviation IQ avoids this problem by using the percentage of cases in each age-group achieving a given score. The Stanford-Binet has a standard deviation of 16 IQ points. Thus, a 17-old scoring at the eighty-fourth percentile for that age group (that is, equaling or exceeding 84 percent of all 17-year-olds taking the test) would have a Stanford-Binet IQ of 116. Statistical tables are used to find what percentages of cases fall below the various standard deviation unit points.

The Wechsler Tests

David Wechsler has produced a number of individual intelligence tests. Like the Stanford-Binet, these tests are administered individually by trained examiners and take about an hour. Wechsler introduced his first test, then called the Wechsler-Bellevue, in 1939. This was an adult test, standardized on an adult sample group. In 1955 he revised his adult test,

calling it the Wechsler Adult Intelligence Scale **(WAIS)**. The adult test was revised again in 1981 and is now called the **WAIS-R** (the R for "revised").

In 1949 Wechsler published the Wechsler Intelligence Scale for Children (WISC). In 1963 he published the Wechsler Preschool and Primary Scale of Intelligence (WPPSI), which was designed for children from ages four through six and a half. Since 1949, the WISC has been revised twice, in 1974 as the WISC-R and in 1992 as the WISC-III.

The Wechsler tests mark a significant departure from the tradition of the Binet tests. Wechsler believed that the Binet tests were too heavily loaded with verbal items. According to Wechsler, "Intelligence . . . is the aggregate or global capacity of the individual to act purposefully, to think rationally, and to deal effectively with his environment" (Wechsler, 1944). Thus, not only is the poet with high verbal facility able to score well on the WAIS-R, but so too is the garage mechanic who can expertly reassemble a four-barrel carburetor, even though he or she cannot quote long passages from Shakespeare. The Wechsler tests, which use a deviation IQ, produce three IQ scores: a verbal IQ, a **performance IQ,** and a full-scale IQ score. Thus, the garage mechanic may receive a verbal IQ of only 105, but with a performance IQ of 126 he or she would achieve a full-scale IQ of 115, which is at the 84th percentile.

DAVID WECHSLER

David Wechsler was born in Lespedi, Romania, in 1896, one of seven children. His family moved to New York City when he was six years old. He attended the New York public schools and in 1916 graduated from the College of the City of New York. He immediately enrolled in the graduate psychology program at Columbia, completing his master's thesis under R. S. Woodworth in 1917. With America's entry into World War I, Wechsler was drafted into the Army. While awaiting his induction, he joined the great Harvard psychologist E. G. Boring at Camp Yaphank on Long Island and helped administer and score the recently developed Army Alpha intelligence test. Because of his training in psychology, and especially because of his work with Boring on the Alpha test, he was assigned to Fort Logan, Texas, where his duties included testing thousands of recruits on the Army Individual Performance Scales, the Yerkes Point Scale, and the Stanford-Binet IQ test.

During this time, Wechsler became increasingly impressed by the disparity often shown between a man's tested intelligence and the quality of his previous work record. Often a man would test at a very low level on the various assessment devices, yet his past history indicated that he had been quite successful in his civilian job. The same man often proved later to be extremely competent in performing his military duties. Wechsler began to question the validity of some of these tests, especially the Stanford-Binet with its high verbal content. Perhaps the test did predict success or failure in school, but it was apparently less effective in predicting performance in the military. Wechsler concluded that by emphasizing the intellectual component, the Stanford-Binet was perhaps missing other aspects of a person's intellect that may contribute to overall intelligent behavior. It wasn't until 1939, however, with the publication of Wechsler's own intelligence test, that he was able to put these ideas into practice.

In 1919 the Army sent Wechsler to Europe, where, at the University of London, he had the opportunity of working with both Spearman and Pearson. From Spearman, Wechsler learned of the two-factor theory of intelligence, *g* and *s*, and from Pearson he was schooled in statistical techniques, especially the techniques of correlation.

After Wechsler was discharged from the Army in August 1919, he won a fellowship for study at the University of Paris and at the Laboratory of Psychology at the Sorbonne. During this time he met both Theodore Simon and Pierre Janet.

In 1922 Wechsler returned to the United States, where he became both a part-time graduate student in psychology at Columbia and a staff psychologist at the Bureau of Child Guidance. In 1925 he received his Ph.D. from Columbia.

From 1925 to 1932 Wechsler worked in private practice as a psychologist. During this period he also worked part-time for the Psychological Corporation, the company that later published the tests that bear his name.

In 1932 he became chief psychologist at New York's Bellevue Psychiatric Hospital, and in 1933 he also joined the faculty of New York University's College of Medicine. From this point on, Wechsler devoted much of his energy to the creation of a new intelligence test, a test that would be suitable for adults and that would tap a wide variety of intellectual and performance abilities. After trying out many items from previous tests and adding new items of his own, Wechsler produced, in 1939, the now famous Wechsler-Bellevue Intelligence Scale. Concurrently, he published *The Measurement of Adult Intelligence,* a book that brought together all his ideas on the question of intelligence and the manner in which it should be measured. He defined intelligence as the global capacity of an individual to act purposefully, to think rationally, and to deal effectively with his environment. Thus, he saw intelligence not as a narrow ability or single factor but as a global capacity that includes many components. Wechsler did not separate intelligence from other personality factors.

Wechsler's name has become synonymous with intelligence testing in America. He is truly one of the great psychologists of our time, and up to the year of his death, 1981, he continued his contributions to our understanding of intelligence and its measurement.

SPOTLIGHT ON IQ TESTING

The WISC-III

The most recent version of the Wechsler Intelligence Scale for Children (WISC), called the WISC-III, was introduced in 1991. It was an attempt to improve the original rather than to redesign the instrument completely. Like its predecessors, the mean IQ on the WISC-III is still 100, and the standard deviation is 15. Those trained to administer the WISC-R will find the transition easy and straightforward. In fact, some of the scoring rules have been simplified and the testing materials modified to make them more user-friendly. Some examples of items from the verbal scale are:

Information: Where does milk come from?

Comprehension: Why do we put food in the refrigerator?

Arithmetic: If you had two crayons, and the teacher gave you two more, how many would you have altogether?

Similarities: How is a cow like a horse?

The WISC-III has introduced a new subtest, called Symbol Search, that was designed to tap a child's cognitive processing speed. In fact the subtests for the WISC-III can be categorized on the basis of the four factors shown below (Wechsler, 1991).

The standardizing group for this update was composed of 2,200 children, ages 6 to 16, who were 70 percent white, 15 percent black, 11 percent Hispanic, and the rest "other." These percentages are virtually identical with those shown for the population at large according to the 1990 U.S. Census.

FACTOR I: VERBAL COMPREHENSION	FACTOR II: PERCEPTUAL ORGANIZATION	FACTOR III: FREEDOM FROM DISTRACTIBILITY	FACTOR IV: PROCESSING SPEED
Information	Picture completion	Arithmetic	Coding
Similarities	Picture arrangement	Digit span	Symbol search
Vocabulary	Block design		
Comprehension	Object assembly		

The verbal subtests   On the WISC-III, the verbal IQ is calculated on the basis of the following subtests:

1. *Information:* A series of orally presented items that test the child's general storehouse of information about the world.

2. *Similarities:* A series of orally presented pairs of words for which the child attempts to discover how the two things are alike. This test appears to measure a child's ability to think in abstract terms.

3. *Arithmetic:* A set of arithmetic problems that the child solves mentally. This test is designed to test the child's powers of mathematical reasoning.

4. *Vocabulary:* A set of orally presented words,

which can be used to predict the size of the child's vocabulary.

5. *Comprehension:* A series of orally presented situations that evaluate the child's level of practical information, general ability to utilize past experience, and understanding of social rules and concepts.

6. *Digit span (optional):* A test of short-term memory in which the examiner reads a series of digits and asks the subject to repeat them, some verbatim and some in reverse order.

The performance subtests   The performance IQ is computed on the basis of the following:

1. *Picture completion:* The child is shown a set of colorful incomplete pictures and is asked to

SPOTLIGHT ON INTELLIGENCE

Howard Gardner's View

Harvard's Howard Gardner, the creator of what he calls the theory of multiple intelligences, originally identified *seven* separate kinds of intelligence:[a]

Linguistic: based on the intelligence of words, spoken and written

Logical-mathematical: the intelligence of numbers and reasoning

Spatial: the intelligence of pictures, images, and diagrams

Musical: the intelligence of tones, rhythms, and timbre

Bodily-kinesthetic: the intelligence of visual-motor (bodily) coordination

Interpersonal: the intelligence of dealing with other people and demonstrating social understanding

Intrapersonal: the intelligence of self-knowledge, including metacognition

For each of these basic seven types, Gardner has identified a cluster of dedicated neural brain tissues, thereby providing a mind-brain profile that he assumes resulted from biological evolution. Gardner is now talking about an eighth intelligence, called "naturalistic intelligence," which he defines as the ability to view and understand the natural environment with a keen eye and a high level of interest, a talent that Darwin must have possessed. He is also talking about possibly adding a ninth, which he is calling "existential intelligence," a talent for pondering the meaning of our lives, our origins, our reasons for being here on this earth, and so forth. This ninth intelligence is still in embryonic form because so far Gardner has not found its correlate in the brain.[b]

Why do we need another theory of intelligence? Gardner says that the problem with the previous theories is that the traditional measures used in their support really accounted for only the first two of his seven types, that is, verbal and mathematical abilities. He insists that intelligence must involve more than that, and must include "a set of skills for problem solving that enable the individual to resolve genuine problems or difficulties that he or she encounters and, when appropriate, to create an effective product—and must also entail the potential for finding or creating problems—thereby laying the groundwork for acquisition of new knowledge."[c] Gardner also suggests that the term *genius* may apply to differing intelligences. For example, whereas Einstein may have been strong in logical-spatial areas, he was weak in the personal spheres, or whereas Freud may have been strong in linguistic and personal areas, he was weak in spatial and musical categories.[d] Gardner has even suggested getting rid of traditional IQ tests altogether, even though he admits they are good predictors of school success and some job successes. The previous theories created a "dipstick" view of intellect. The examiner looks at the dipstick and says, "Aha, 95. Maybe you can get through high school, but forget about college" or, "Aha, 120. Maybe you can be a pharmacist, but forget about medical school." Gardner argues that despite their predictive accuracy, IQ tests have

name the missing part. This is a test of visual recognition.

2. *Coding:* The child must associate certain symbols with specific numbers, or shapes. The child draws the symbol (or shape) in squares containing the associated number. This is a test of speed of movement, processing speed, and memory.

3. *Picture arrangement:* A set of pictures that, when arranged properly, tell a logical story. This is an attempt to measure the child's ability to size up and understand a total situation.

4. *Block design:* The child is presented with a number of small blocks that must be put together to match a number of prearranged patterns. This is a test of perceptual analysis as well as visual-motor coordination.

5. *Object assembly:* The child must arrange various puzzle parts to form a certain object. This is a

too often had destructive social consequences.[e]

Teachers have been trained to link Gardner's basic intelligences into a single teaching unit, so that each new activity combines words, numbers, pictures, music, the body, social skills, and personal understanding. Thus, the various forms of intelligence are brought together into a single overall lesson plan. In one example, first-grade children were taught to tell time by (1) being told a story about a kingdom that had no time. (2) In this kingdom there lived 12 children named "one," "two," "three," up to "twelve," who sat around in a clocklike circle holding up their respective hourly numbers. (3) These students then had to act out a scene in which they all pointed to the highest point in this mythical kingdom, which became a reference point from which a child would (4) sing a "timely little chime" every hour. (5) The children then danced around an imaginary clock, while the teacher provided a musical background, which in this example consisted of Bill Haley's "Rock around the Clock." (6) The children then

went back to the circle and shared their educational experience, using both pictures and words. Finally, (7), they were told to keep a personal diary indicating special times in their day, like 3:30 P.M., when school lets out (Armstrong, 1994).

Not only students are being trained in this way. Teachers themselves are taught at multiple-intelligences (MI) workshops to utilize all of the seven intelligences in the classroom. In one program, teachers were presented with the chapters from Gardner's *Frames of Mind* by interacting with each other using all of the seven modalities, such as physical exercises to study bodily kinesthetics, graphics and visual puzzles to understand spatial intelligence, songs to learn musical intelligence, and so on.[f] It has even been proposed that special MI schools should be established that focus on promoting individuality and nurturing the various intelligences.[g]

Gardner has also explored what he calls "genuine understanding" and how this ability might be demonstrated.[h] This can be accomplished at the intrapersonal level,

for example, by having students show that they have understood the concept of self-regulation by creating and initiating their own projects and setting their own time frames. They may also learn to set their own standards of evaluation, learning how to judge for themselves when their various projects are ready for display.

[a] Gardner, H. (1983). *Frames of mind: The theory of multiple intelligences*. New York: Basic Books.
[b] Gardner, H. (1996, November 1). *Multiple intelligences*. Workshop presentation at American International College, Springfield, MA.
[c] Gardner, H. (1985). Human intelligence isn't what we think it is. In F. Linder & J. H. McMillan (Eds.), *Annual editions: Educational Psychology*. Guilford, CT: Dushkin.
[d] Gardner, H. (1993). *Creating minds*. New York: Basic Books.
[e] Gardner, H. (1985).
[f] Hoerr, T. R. (1994). How the new city school applies the multiple intelligences. *Educational Leadership, 52*(3), 29–31.
[g] Haggerty, B. A. (1995). *Nurturing intelligences*. Reading, MA: Addison-Wesley.
[h] Gardner, H. (1991). *The unschooled mind*. New York: HarperCollins.

test of manual dexterity and powers of recognition. There are also two optional performance subtests, Symbol Search and Mazes.

As can be seen from the outline of the various subtests, all have been selected to tap many different abilities. The Wechsler tests were not designed to establish IQ as a unitary factor but, consistent with current thinking, as a general series of abilities made up of many factors. Some of the subtests home in on a

person's memory, some tap perceptual and motor skills, some call for the child to be able to reason abstractly, and so on.

In addition to being important instruments for measuring intelligence, the Wechsler tests have useful diagnostic capabilities that enable a skilled examiner to evaluate such personality characteristics as defense mechanisms, the ability to cope with stress, and the general mode of handling life's situations. Such well-documented procedures as the Personality Assessment System (PAS) have shown truly remarkable results in ferreting out important personality factors from Wechsler profiles (Couchon, 1983). Thus, a Wechsler test gives a three-dimensional picture of the subject, and can often tell us not only that a given child lacks motivation, but also why.

Group Tests of Intelligence

Though the Stanford-Binet and Wechsler tests have made an extremely important contribution to the field of intelligence testing, the fact that they are individual tests means that they are time-consuming and therefore rather expensive to administer. During World War I there was suddenly an urgent need to test huge groups of men quickly, and a new approach to testing was introduced. Two **group tests of intelligence** were devised in 1917: the Army Alpha test, for the men who could read; and the Army Beta test, a nonverbal test for illiterates. Though the nonverbal Beta test proved to be less effective than the Alpha, the success of the Alpha led to the development of a great number of group tests. These are also referred to as paper-and-pencil tests, and they usually consist of a series of multiple-choice items. They must be administered and timed precisely as stated in the directions. D. O. Hebb has even suggested that those giving IQ tests should be rigorously trained and strictly licensed, just as physicians are. IQ tests placed in the wrong hands can have tragic consequences (Hebb, 1978).

Despite the numerous versions of intelligence, and even despite the controversies that have arisen over the use of IQ scores, few psychologists today would advocate completely abandoning intelligence testing. Since intelligence is ultimately based on observed behavior, a good IQ test is one way through which one's behavior can be objectively observed in a controlled situation. A test such as the **Wechsler Intelligence Scale for Children (WISC-III),** in the hands of a skilled examiner, samples a large variety of behaviors all of which are assumed to be indicators of various kinds of intelligence. Without question, IQ correlates more highly with virtually every measure of social and occupational success than does any other available assessment technique. As Charles Locurto says, "If we were limited to making one measurement of a seven-year-old child to predict that child's eventual success . . . the one best measure would be that child's IQ" (Locurto, 1991, p. 160). Most psychologists agree that intelligence tests, even with their limitations, have made valuable contributions to the decisionmaking process in schools, clinics, and in-

dustry. Despite the empirical evidence, however, some psychologists still urge that IQ tests be abandoned. At least one researcher has even suggested that the use of intelligence tests may not be ethical, since the tests are artificial procedures that measure everyone with the same yardstick, even though children are different (Messick, 1980). But then again, if children weren't different, there would be no need for the yardstick in the first place. It seems somewhat ironic to be talking about outlawing tests for the very reason for which they were designed—"to prevent subjective judgments and prejudice from being the basis for assigning students to special classes or denying them certain privileges: (Weinberg, 1991, p. 101).

Despite the interesting and innovative work of Howard Gardner and Robert Sternberg, many test experts argue that neither of these theorists has produced any measures or operations that possess the internal coherence or the external validity achieved by the more traditional psychometric tests, such as the Stanford-Binet or the various Wechsler tests (Brody, 1992). In fact, Nathan Brody advocates that in our search for this fuzzy concept we call intelligence we should use *g* as the starting point. He suggests that we should research the biological basis of psychometrically identified *g*, which he sees as the predisposing factor that is at least partly, if not primarily, genetic, as well as the environmental factors and conditions that somehow moderate the relationship of measured intelligence and observable behavior (Brody, 1992). This, of course, is not a view held by Sternberg (Sternberg & Wagner, 1993).

Though not stressing the importance of *g*, Sternberg does not rule it out. The first part of his triarchy is similar in nature to what Spearman referred to as *g*. Gardner, however, denies the existence of *g* and argues instead that there are seven distinct forms of intelligence. Although intercorrelations do exist among these seven intelligences, Gardner appears to assume that these correlations are due to the methods of testing rather than to the realities of intelligence. Since tests tend to put heavy emphasis on linguistic and logical ability, individuals with these skills are "likely to do well even in tests of musical and spatial abilities, while those who are not especially facile linguistically and logically are likely to be impaled on such standardized tests" (Gardner, 1983, p. 17).

Emotional Intelligence

Psychologist Daniel Goleman (1995) maintains that emotional intelligence (EI) may matter more in life than IQ. Emotional intelligence is based on one's "ego resilience," and includes self-awareness, impulse control, persistence, motivation, empathy, and social deftness. Goleman uses the concept of EI to explain why some people of high IQ are not successful and yet others, of more modest IQ, may do surprisingly well. In fact, a lack of emotional intelligence may even negatively affect one's cognitive abilities and is said to have ruined both careers and marriages. Deficits in emotional intelligence produce outcomes that run the gamut from depression and eating disorders, to aggressiveness and violent crimes. Goleman believes that EI is neurologically based, probably in the amygdala, and feels that behavioral and cognitive retraining can be of use in repatterning one's neural pathways, which will then increase the ego mechanisms necessary for continued EI development.

WHAT DO IQ TESTS PREDICT?

Academic Achievement

The evidence gained since 1905 is generally consistent with Binet's early results. More than 90 years and hundreds of studies later, it is now clear that IQ tests do predict scholastic success. The correlation between IQ and grades in school averages a little over +.50, with the correlations being at their highest during kindergarten through grade four and decreasing in high school and college as the student groups become more homogeneous. The correlation between IQ and total years of education is +.55; that is, the higher the IQ, the longer the child is likely to remain in school. The correlation between IQ and job performance across a wide range of occupations is +.54 (Neisser et al., 1996).

Since the highest possible correlation is 1.00, IQ scores are obviously not infallible predictors in every case. There are children whose IQ scores are lower than other children's but whose grades are higher, because a number of nonintellectual factors also influence scholastic success. Physical illness, emotional upset, and lack of motivation, for example, can interfere with success. Research suggests that lack of ego strength is another related factor. Academic achievement has been shown to be largely a result of a student's reality orientation, or ego strength. That is, successful students possess strong egos, are willing to postpone pleasure, are not so easily distracted, and are generally more able to pursue tasks in an organized fashion. Underachievers, in contrast, have low ego strength, are less able to control their impulses, and are especially unable to postpone gratification (Hummel & Sprinthall, 1965).

On the other side of the correlational coin, however, are the negative correlations that occur between IQ and a wide range of juvenile offenses. Even when social class is controlled, IQ correlates negatively with many socially undesirable outcomes, including teenage pregnancy and felony arrests (Neisser et al., 1996).

Success in Life

Although IQ tests predict academic achievement with some degree of accuracy, this fact in and of itself may not seem all that important. After all, IQ is measured by means of tests, and grades are determined exactly the same way, by performances on tests. Perhaps all that this proves is that children who do well on one test also do well on other tests. How well does an IQ score predict success or failure in other areas of one's life? Do children with high IQs and high school grades also succeed in later life, financially and emotionally?

To help answer these questions, Terman in the 1920s began a monumental study of 1,500 California schoolchildren (Terman, 1925). All the children had tested IQs of 140 or more. Terman followed these subjects for the next 25 years in order to find out whether there were any significant adult correlates of a high IQ in childhood. Many of Terman's original subjects are still being studied today as part of a gerontology project (Cravens, 1992). Thus, whereas Binet had focused on identifying children who were "unintelligent," Terman's focus was on the gifted child. One recent Terman scholar has wondered how their lives might have turned out had they not been continuously reminded of their glitteringly brilliant status (Shurkin, 1992).

First, Terman dispelled the myth that very bright children are physically fragile and undersized. Terman's subjects were above average on many physical characteristics, including height, weight, physical development, and general health. Also, the gifted children tended to be heavier at birth, cut their first tooth two months earlier than average, walked and talked two months earlier than average, and reached puberty earlier.

While in school, the gifted children received significantly higher marks than their classmates and were more likely to be skipped ahead to a higher grade. In fact, by the end of elementary school, all 1,500 children had averaged a skip of one full grade. Perhaps this is how the myth of the undersized and puny genius originated. Since children with high IQs were skipped frequently, they were likely to end up in classrooms with children who were larger because they were older.

On tests of emotional adjustment the gifted children were found to be better adjusted than the average child. They were also more socially adaptable and more likely to be leaders among their peers.

As adults, Terman's group continued to be successful. They earned more money, had more managerial jobs, and made far more literary and scientific contributions than the average adult. When checked in 1959, the group had published more than 2,000 scientific papers and 33 novels and had taken out 230 patents. A great number of them were listed in *Who's Who* and in *American Men and Women of Science*.

Finally, they had fewer divorces than the average adult, and criminal convictions and alcoholism were rare. Even the death rate was about 33 percent lower than that for the general population.

Another study found that IQ has a significant correlation with income. In fact, IQ predicted a person's income better than such other measures as parents' education or parents' income (Duncan et al., 1972). Two more recent studies have come to the same general conclusion: IQ test scores are the single best predictor of job performance, regardless of the job (Ree & Earles, 1992). Further, these results were not flawed by such uncontrolled variables as social economic status, nor were they biased against minorities (Barrett & Depinet, 1991).

It is obvious that the IQ test predicts more than just elementary school grades. It must be pointed out, though, that not all Terman's subjects attained the great success of the majority. It is also true that many highly successful people do not have IQs of 140 or more. High IQs are associated with a wide range of achievement in a wide variety of areas, but they do not tell the whole story. Personality variables such as ego strength and motivation, and physical variables such as health or accidents, also play a vital role in determining one's ability to live effectively and achieve success.

HEREDITY, ENVIRONMENT, AND TIME

In earlier chapters of this book, especially in Chapter 3, we pointed out that all human behavior, including intelligent behavior, is a product of heredity interacting with environment interacting with time. This is one of psychology's basic axioms, and nowhere is the validity of this axiom more compelling than in the area of intelligence.

Hereditary Factors

Heredity limits the extent to which intelligence can be influenced by environment and time. It is now fairly certain that intelligence has a genetic component. The genetic component sets the limits to how any given trait will respond to environmental stimulation. This genetically constrained range is the *reaction range* and can be most clearly shown in the case of human height. Despite the fact that one's height, a polygenic trait, can be greatly influenced by environmental factors such as nutrition, there are some pygmy groups in Africa whose height could never approach that of the average American, regardless of environmental influences. Geneticists are now studying an array of genes, located on the X chromosome, that seem to be involved in the biological substrate of intelligence (Turner, 1996).

As long ago as 1937, it was demonstrated that the more closely two people are related genetically, the more similar are their IQs (Newman et al., 1937). This study was one of the first to show that identical twins reared apart still had similar IQs. A review of the major IQ studies revealed the correlations shown in Table 16.1 (Erlenmeyer-Kimling and Jarvik, 1963; Locurto, 1991). These data make it clear that genetic factors are indeed involved in determining IQ. The closer the genetic relationship, the higher the reported IQ correlations.

A study conducted at the University of Minnesota showed that identical twins reared apart displayed marked similarities not only on such measures as intelligence, but also achievement and a number of personality factors. Even the brain-wave tracings of these monozygotic (MZ) twins showed an extremely high degree of resemblance. The genetic prewiring for MZ twins appears to be significantly more simi-

TABLE 16.1   AVERAGE IQ CORRELATIONS

RELATIONSHIP	r
Monozygotic twins raised together	.85
Monozygotic twins raised apart	.76
Dizygotic twins	.56
Siblings raised together	.55
Siblings raised apart	.47
Parents and children	.40
Adopted siblings (youngsters)	.37
Grandparent and grandchild	.27
Adopted siblings (adolescents)	.00

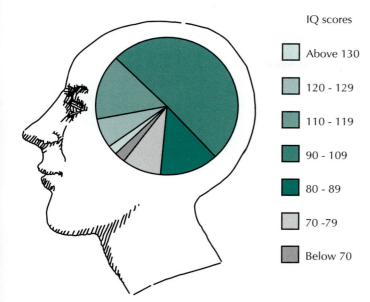

IQ scores

☐ Above 130

☐ 120 - 129

☐ 110 - 119

☐ 90 - 109

☐ 80 - 89

☐ 70 -79

☐ Below 70

FIGURE 16.1   According to the Wechsler Adult Intelligence Scale, 2.2 percent of Americans have an IQ over 130, and a corresponding 2.2 percent are mentally retarded. The majority are in the middle range, with IQs between 90 and 109.

lar than could be accounted for on the basis of a straight environmental explanation (Bouchard et al., 1990).

Genetic inputs can be clearly seen in the early stages of language development. For example, in comparing 12-month-old adopted children with both their natural and adoptive mothers, it has been found that infant language development correlates more highly with the natural mother's cognitive skills than with those of the adoptive mother (Hardy-Brown et al., 1981). Genetic inheritance also plays a part in the development of nonintellectual traits. In a study on infant shyness, it was found that among 24-month-old adopted children, the less sociable the adoptive mother was, the shyer was the child; but when both the adoptive *and* natural mothers scored low in sociability, the child was even shyer (Daniels & Plomin, 1985).

Environmental Factors

The IQ correlation chart also shows the importance of environmental factors. For example, when identical twins are reared together in the same environment, their IQs are more similar than when they are

raised apart. Note, too, that when unrelated children are reared together, there is a significant correlation between their IQs. In this instance, where there is no genetic linkage at all, similar IQs result from the similar environment.

Home environment   The HOME (Home Observation for Measurement of the Environment) index has shown that children from the most intellectually stimulating homes tend to have the highest IQs. Researchers visit each child's home for no less than an hour and rate the environment on a number of important variables, such as socioeconomic status (SES), parental education, whether the parents read to the child, how much time is spent watching TV, and how many books are in the house (Caldwell & Bradley, 1984; Bradley, 1989). The following list is a typical subscale of the HOME scale:

1. Emotional and verbal responsiveness of the mother; example, mother kisses or caresses the child at least once during the visit.

2. Acceptance of child; example, mother does not interfere with child's actions or restrict the child's movements more than three times during the visit.

3. Organization of physical and temporal environment; example, child's play area appears safe and free of hazards.

4. Provision of appropriate play materials; example, mother provides toys or other play materials during the interview.

5. Maternal involvement with child; example, mother tends to keep child within visual range and to look at the child often.

6. Opportunity for variety in daily stimulation; example, child eats at least one meal per day with mother.

Other studies have noted a strong relationship between IQ and the socioeconomic status of the family. It is clear that the higher the family's SES, the more possibilities there are for intellectually advantageous home conditions, which of course affect the child's IQ (Gottfried, 1984).

Interesting and important as these results are, we must keep in mind that the child's IQ is a product of the environmental interactions, the timing of these interactions, and the parental IQs. Perhaps more intelligent mothers pass on superior genes and are also themselves intelligent enough to create a more stimulating home environment for their children.

The transactional model   The interplay between mother and child, in which each, in effect, shapes the other's environment, has given rise to a view of general development called the **transactional model** (Sameroff, 1975). These reciprocal influences affect not only the child's cognitive growth, but also the formation of the child's temperament. In a study of the development of temperament among infant males, Eleanor Maccoby discovered that if a mother perceives her son as having a difficult temperament, she may become so influenced by this perception that she begins withdrawing her efforts at socialization. The child, in turn, begins showing less and less self-control, and the frequency of temperamental outbursts increases (Maccoby & Martin, 1983). This may, of course, lead to the development of an emotional set that could make the child virtually uncontrollable by the time he reaches kindergarten (Smolak, 1986).

Nutrition   Chronic long-term malnutrition has severe intellectual effects, as shown in studies of African and certain Central American villages (Ricciuti, 1993). However, long-term malnutrition is usually accompanied by other negative social conditions. Although this level of malnutrition rarely occurs in the United States, studies have been done on U.S. children in which experimental and control groups were compared after vitamin and mineral supplements were supplied to the experimental group and only a placebo to the control group. The experimental groups later achieved significantly higher IQ scores (Schoenthaler et al., 1991).

Lead and alcohol   There is considerable evidence that long-term exposure to lead has a negative impact on the IQs of children (Baghurst et al., 1992), as does the mother's use of alcohol. Heavy drinking on the part of the mother during pregnancy can result in a condition known as fetal alcohol syndrome, a condition that includes retardation as well as a variety of physical symptoms (Streissguth et al., 1989). Even when the full syndrome is absent, evidence shows that moderate drinking tends to lower the IQ of the child.

TV and IQ   Since children seem to be reading less and watching more, TV has been blamed for declining scholastic achievement scores. But at least one study, this one on preschoolers, found no significant correlation between the amount of time a child watches TV and that child's IQ score (Plomin et al., 1990). In fact, some studies have shown that TV can have important positive effects on children, such as when they learn the alphabet (*Sesame Street*) or learn the essentials of nutrition and good health by watching TV (Calvert & Cocking, 1992).

Stimulus variety   Another important environmental factor in intelligence is stimulus variety, especially in early childhood. As we saw in Chapter 4, important figures in the field of psychology such as J. McVicker Hunt, Jerome Bruner, Benjamin S. Bloom, and David Krech feel that stimulus variety is perhaps the most important ingredient in intellectual development. Hunt states that the more we see, hear, and touch in early childhood, the more we will want to see, hear, and touch later on. The key to cognitive growth, according to Hunt, is matching the child's current intellectual ability with just the right amount of stimulus variety to bring out the natural desire to continue learning.

As was mentioned in Chapter 4, Vygotsky insists that cognitive growth is directly related to the challenge inherent in new experiences. Vygotsky speaks of the zone of proximal development, or the distance between one's present developmental level and one's potential level, which he believes can best be accomplished by what he calls *scaffolding*, such as adult guidance or working with advanced peers (Vygotsky, 1978). In order to reach higher stages of intellectual development, students should work within this zone. Therefore, since they don't go a bit beyond a child's present ability, many homework assignments that simply review well-practiced activities may even act as deterrents to cognitive growth (Clifford, 1991). Also, Bruner tells us that infants must be exposed to a wide variety of stimuli and a shifting environment if normal intellectual growth is to be maintained. Bloom says that an abundant early environment is the key to full development of intelligence. And Krech has shown, at least in animals, that without stimulus heterogeneity, animals are less able to learn, and their brains never develop fully.

Past experience in learning situations is another crucial environmental ingredient in intellectual development. Children who learn to master one problem are able to transfer this knowledge to other problems they may encounter later. The knowledge gained from past experience may begin to snowball and provide the child with a solid base for future understanding. Harry Harlow has shown how this works with monkeys. Monkeys that were trained to solve a certain problem (the oddity problem) were far better at solving complex discrimination problems presented to them at a later time than monkeys that were not so trained. Through training, the monkeys had developed what Harlow called a *learning set*. They had, in effect, learned how to learn. As Harlow says, "Learning to learn is no doubt an essential feature of the intellectual development of monkeys, apes, and children growing up in their natural environments" (Harlow et al., 1971, p. 353).

INFANT INTELLIGENCE

Attempts to measure the intellectual potential of infants dates at least as far back as the work of Nancy Bayley (see the biography on p. 90). Recently, **Marc Bornstein** has been conducting studies with an **infant intelligence test** in which 6-month-olds were measured on the basis of how long it took them to process information concerning moving stimuli (Bornstein, 1985). Bornstein hypothesized that the more intelligent the baby, the sooner he or she would lose interest in the stimuli, since the more intelligent infant would process the information about the stimulus more quickly in the form of an internal stimulus representation. When these children were four years old, they were given the Wechsler Preschool and Primary Scale of Intelligence (WPPSI) IQ test. Bornstein found significant correlations ($r = .54$) between how well the subjects scored at six months and how they scored as four-year-olds. This correlation is especially noteworthy, given the fact that both measures were taken only on the child and were independent of other predictors, such as parental education or the family's SES. The latter two measures have typically produced correlations as high as .60 (Zelazo, 1989). It has also been shown that a baby's loss of interest in the stimuli is a true test of processing speed, and not just a reflection of neuronal fatigue (Zelazo et al., 1991). Bornstein also found a correlation between the children's IQ and the quality of the interactions between mother and child, assessed when the children were one year old. To be sure, the amount and quality of mother-baby interactions can vary with either party in the relationship. Do intelligent and responsive babies induce more parental responses, or are highly responsive parents responsible for the response levels of their offspring? The best guess is that the most important factor is the interaction itself, with both mother and baby playing critical roles in the quality of the interplay.

More recently, Bornstein has found significant correlations between infant IQs (as measured on the basis of how long it took them to process and habituate to new stimuli) and WISC IQs taken at age 6 (Bornstein, 1989). Other studies have found that these correlations persist at least up to age 11 (Rose & Feldman, 1995).

Finally, Bloom lists three environmental variables that he feels are important in developing a child's intellectual abilities:

1. The amount of stimulation children receive for verbal development

2. The amount of affection and reward children receive for verbal-reasoning accomplishments

3. The amount of encouragement children receive for "active interaction with problems, exploration of the environment and the learning of new skills" (Bloom, 1964, p. 190)

Again we see that environmental factors, especially the timing of these factors in either stimulating or retarding development, play a key role in determining how the genetic blueprint will be expressed (Farber, 1981).

Time

We have seen the importance of hereditary and environmental interactions for intellectual development. It is also vital to understand the nature of this interaction from the point of view of time. Chapter 4 was devoted entirely to the importance of early experience on psychological development. Let us now look at some of the highlights.

Most psychologists today are convinced of the profound importance of early experience for proper cognitive growth. Bloom states the case forcefully in saying that environmental effects on intelligence are most pronounced during a child's first few years of life.

The heavy line in Figure 16.2 shows Bloom's famous negatively accelerating curve for intellectual growth. Notice that as age increases, intellectual development increases less and less. By age four we have already achieved 50 percent of our adult intelligence, and by age eight we have achieved 80 percent. The shaded area surrounding the main curve indicates the potential for changes in intelligence. You will notice that as age increases, there is less and less potential for changes in intelligence. Therefore, during the first few years, a beneficial environment is most effective in increasing intellectual development, but as time goes on this beneficial environment comes to have less effect. The younger the child, the more opportunity there is for change, but by age 10 IQ tests tend to predict adult levels very well. For example, in a search of the literature it was found that the average change between ages 12 and 17 was less than 7 IQ points (Neisser et al. 1996). Clearly, a stultifying environment is most damaging during those early, critical years. Bloom feels that the difference between a beneficial and a stultifying environment in early childhood can produce IQ differences of 20 points or more.

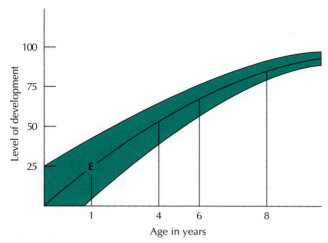

FIGURE 16.2   Bloom's negatively accelerating curve for intellectual growth.

Bloom's estimate may be too conservative, however. Wayne Dennis' study (1960) of a Teheran orphanage in which the children were kept in a condition of extreme sensory deprivation also showed that stimulus variety at an early age is critical for cognitive growth (see Chapter 4). Almost all of those sensory-deprived children were intellectually retarded. In another study (1969), Dennis described a Lebanese orphanage where environmental conditions were so dismal that mental retardation was the rule. The average IQ of the 133 children tested was only 53. This is probably the lowest average IQ ever reported for a group of children who were otherwise considered normal. Some of these children were later adopted by middle-class families and in every case dramatically increased their IQs. The more stimulating home environments provided an average gain of 28 IQ points. Despite the improvement, however, the mean IQ of the adopted children was still only 81, again showing that improved environmental conditions at a later age cannot compensate fully for a deprived environment during the first few years of life. As Hebb says, "There are fundamental aspects of a baby's learning that must occur at the proper time if they are to have their full value as the basis of later learning" (1978, p. 1143). Thus Hebb is fully endorsing the early-experience position regarding mental growth. In fact, he says that you cannot take even a six-year-old out of the slums and expect to undo the damage already inflicted by that environment. "In a word, the child from a seriously deficient environ-

ment is an intellectual *cripple,*" and this damage is no longer reparable (p. 1144).

The Mix

It cannot be overstressed that the results of the various studies of intelligence should be interpreted on the basis of all three of the components of intelligence, namely, heredity, environment, and time. The interplay among these factors, though certainly complex, is of crucial importance in understanding the overall parameters of human behavior. As Sandra Scarr keeps reminding us, even a person's genetic predispositions are involved in shaping the person's environment, and the environment, in turn, may nourish or stifle the unfolding biological messages. Highly active children, for example, tend to seek out activities and friends that may be more stimulating than (or at least different from) those selected by a low-activity child (Scarr & McCartney, 1983). Thus, heredity, environment, and time do not act out their roles in independent vacuums. Highly intelligent children may actively surround themselves with the kinds of environmental influences that tend to maintain and strengthen their maturing intellectual abilities.

THE FLYNN EFFECT

James Flynn, after a careful analysis of worldwide IQ scores, has found an increase in IQ scores in every successive year after a test was first standardized (Flynn, 1980). For example, on a test standardized in say, 1932, persons today do better than the original standardizing group. Could it be that word gets around on how to answer some of the questions? Or could it be that today's students have generally more test sophistication? It has also been pointed out that there has been a corresponding gain in height during that time period, and this gain has been attributed to better nutrition (Lynn, 1991). Perhaps better nutrition is responsible for the higher test scores. At this time, nobody knows the answer to this seeming paradox.

The average IQ of all high school graduates is 103; among college graduates, the figure increases to 114 (Herrnstein & Murray, 1994). This difference is not based on the fact that the college experience is worth 11 IQ points, comforting though that thought might be. It is based instead on the selection process that weeds out the people with lower IQs for admission to college and throughout the four-year educational experience.

Gender Differences in IQ

The full-scale IQs of males and females of a given age are almost identical. This result is partly due to the averaging out of differences that occur among various subtest scores. In the past, a number of studies seemed to suggest that males typically scored higher on spatial, mechanical, and numerical tests, whereas females scored higher on verbal tests and tests involving quick, manual movements and attention to detail. More recently, however, evidence demonstrates a definite decline in these cognitive-gender differences. The only exception to this now appears to be the gap (still favoring males) that exists in numerical abilities, especially high school mathematics (Feingold, 1988).

The development of IQ also reveals certain gender-based differences. The mean IQ of males increases slightly after age six, while that of females tends to go down (Haan, 1963). This difference may have a cultural explanation. If society demands more achievement from males than females (and this apparently is the case), and if achievement motivation and IQ correlate at all, then perhaps society's emphasis on inculcating the achievement motive more in males than females accounts for this difference. As social psychologists continually remind us, people tend to behave as others around them expect them to behave.

Are There Genetic Differences in Intelligence among Racial Groups?

Studies of the educational performance and attainment of black students typically show them as lagging behind white students as early as the second grade (Alexander and Entwistle, 1988). However, it is clear that this gap has narrowed over the past 20 years (Nelson-LeGall, 1991). Further evidence for this trend comes from the work of Ken Vincent, whose data show only a 7-point difference in IQ points among a sample of 12-year-olds (Vincent, 1991). SAT data also show a narrowing of the gap (Wainer, 1988). As was recently stated, "Black SAT takers improved substantially more in scores than white SAT test takers, and neither the changes in the pool of test takers nor the well-advertised national decline in SAT scores was responsible" (Herrnstein & Murray, 1994, p. 292). Not only has the gap in educational performance narrowed, but so too has the gap in educational attainment. Since 1960 the average level of educational attainment for black students has increased from the completion of eighth grade to the completion of high school (QEM, 1990).

Research on the reasons for the black-white intellectual and educational differences that still exist tend to focus on three general areas. First, it has been found that individual characteristics tend to play a role, primarily psychological characteristics, such as the typical black student's lower level of motivation (Graham, 1989) or lack of self-esteem (Powell, 1989). Second, it has been shown that black children, especially poor ones, may be getting fewer educational resources and are subjected to lower teacher expectations (Fine, 1991). Finally, it has been argued that lower levels of school performance are related to structural-societal conditions that tend to exclude blacks from full participation in the dominant white economy and culture. It has even been suggested that the educational system is organized in such a way as to deliberately provide an inadequate education to black children in order to perpetuate their low social and economic status (Ogbu, 1990).

It is worth noting that these three arguments are not totally independent. For example, if black children are subjected to inferior educational resources and low teacher expectations, it follows that their behavior might then conform to these conditions and expectations—resulting then in a lowered self-concept and a loss of motivation. And if Ogbu is anywhere near right in his theory, it would certainly follow that black children, who are seen by Ogbu as the objects of a societal conspiracy, might well assimilate negative self-perceptions, a loss of motivation, and a concomitant lack of academic achievement.

Within-group differences do, of course, appear among black school children, and the research clearly shows that the most important variable separating the group is gender. In educational settings, black females consistently outperform black males, and this gender lead continues all the way to college, especially among blacks attending predominantly white colleges (Mikelson, 1989). The most persuasive explanations for this difference seem to be that (1) males are more apt to leave school in order to get jobs and help support their families, and (2) males are perceived by their teachers as more threatening, which then translates into the teacher misjudging the males and offering them little in the way of educational encouragement (Pollard, 1993). Thus, studies on racial differences consistently show that there is more variation *within* the groups designated as races than *between* such groups (Zuckerman, 1990).

Some have attributed differences in IQ to genetic causes. **Arthur R. Jensen,** of the University of California at Berkeley, has interpreted the difference between the tested IQs of blacks and whites as implying that white children are genetically superior to black children. This argument claims that IQ has an extremely high genetic factor (about 80 percent) and that there must therefore be racial differences in intelligence (Jensen, 1969). Jensen says that differences in intelligence are "predominantly attributable to genetic differences, with environmental factors contributing a minor portion of the variance among individuals in IQ" (p. 4).

Jensen has based his argument on the concept of heritability. **Heritability** (*H*) is the proportion of the total variability in a population that is due to genetic, as opposed to environmental, factors. Thus, if all the variation in IQ scores in a given population is due to genetic factors, the heritability of IQ would be 1.00. If all the variability is due to environmental factors, then the heritability of IQ would be zero. Since, as we have seen over and over again, IQ is the result of heredity, environment, and time, the heritability value for IQ lies somewhere between 0 and 1.00. Jensen argues that the actual value is around .80. Even if Jensen were correct in saying that the heritability of intelligence is .80, this does not mean that 80 percent of an individual's IQ is due to genes. Actually Sir Francis Galton made this point back in the 1860s when he did his genetic studies on the correlation between the heights of fathers and sons. Even though the heritability of adult height approaches 90 percent, it does not mean that an individual who is 72 inches tall can attribute 61 of those inches to heredity and the other 11 inches to both the environment and the interaction between heredity and environment. Instead, it means that 90 percent of the variation in height within a specified group of people can be attributed to heredity.

Behavior geneticist Jerry Hirsch has said that heritability explains variation only "in some particular population at a single generation under one set of conditions" (Hirsch, 1971, p. 244). Thus, since heritability applies only to a specific environment, it really matters very little what the estimate of the actual heritability value is in the discussion of a given black child's IQ. "High or low heritability tells us absolutely nothing about how a given individual might have developed under conditions different from those in which he actually did develop" (Hirsch, 1971, p. 244).

Jensen appears to accept this definition when he says that heritability is a population statistic that has "no sensible meaning with reference to a measurement or characteristic of an individual . . . Estimates of *H* are specific to the population sampled, the point in time, the manner in which the measurements were made, and the particular test used to obtain the measurements" (Jensen, 1969, p. 42). Despite the clarity and precision of this definition, Jensen then presents a case that goes far beyond the bounds of his own

careful restriction. Jensen's estimated *H* value of .80 is generated by a review of identical-twin studies done exclusively on white American and English children, and yet he applies this value to both black and white children alike—hardly identical populations. As a matter of fact, in a study conducted by Scarr of over 1,000 twins of differing economic and racial backgrounds, it was found that the heritability of IQ is always higher among economically advantaged than among lower-class children (Scarr, 1971). Thus, it is not an unreasonable hypothesis that the value of *H* increases as a function of an increase in the socioeconomic backgrounds of the populations being studied. As one reviewer put it: "In other words, 'native talent' may manifest itself conspicuously in people who grow up in favorable environments and remain suppressed in adverse environments" (Piel, 1975). In fact Scarr argues that this is precisely how the nature-nurture interaction works. "When the environment is good, heredity exerts a strong influence on IQ," stronger than when the environment is impoverished (Scarr and Weinberg, 1978b).

IQ comparisons between the races are made even more difficult to evaluate because of the possibility that IQ scores reflect the race of the examiner. A number of studies have suggested that the IQ scores of black children are underestimated by white examiners or perhaps overestimated by black examiners. In one experiment a single group of black children was tested by both black and white examiners. By the use of different forms, L and M of the Stanford-Binet, the children were tested in a counterbalanced design, first by an examiner of one race and then by one of the other. The mean IQ score of these black children when tested by the black examiner was 105.7, but it dropped to a mean of 101.9 when tested by a white examiner. This difference was statistically significant (Forrester & Klaus, 1964). Since both black and white examiners were equally trained and equally competent, the difference in IQ scores probably resulted from either differing expectations on the part of the examiner or differing motivational sets on the part of the children.

The high correlation obtained between the IQs of parents and children overemphasizes the genetic explanation. An impoverished home environment has an adverse effect not only on the intellectual development of the children raised in it but also on the way those children eventually raise their own children. The childhood experiences of the second generation are a function of the childhood experiences of the previous generation:

Such handicaps combine to sustain the very conditions from which they are derived, so the vicious cir-

SANDRA SCARR

After graduating with high honors from Vassar, Sandra Scarr worked first as a case aide in a family clinic and then as a research assistant at the National Institutes of Health. It soon became obvious to her that, on the one hand, her career pattern could continue in the same direction—serving as a helper and facilitator for other people's work. On the other hand, given her inquiring mind, it also became obvious that alternatives were possible. Youthful women honors graduates of liberal arts colleges did not necessarily have to be content to perform minor, ancillary roles as helpers and assistants. Such persons, as well as anyone, could aspire to leadership roles. There were very few women of eminence who had entered the competitive and heretofore male-dominated area of research psychology. With this in mind, she entered Harvard University, completed her M.A. degree in 1963, and entered the Ph.D. program in social relations.

Under the somewhat quaint Harvard tradition, Scarr was assigned to a sponsor, John Whiting, a world-renowned anthropologist, and to a thesis adviser, Irving Gottesman, an equally renowned genetic psychologist. She clearly thrived in the atmosphere of the Harvard program in social relations, with its diverse faculty which read like a *Who's who* in psychology: Gordon Allport, Roger Brown, Jerome Bruner, Eric Erikson, Jerome Kagan, David McClelland, Thomas Pettigrew, B. F. Skinner, and Robert Whit. She quickly mastered the fundamentals of such a broadly gauged psychology, and she completed her Ph.D. in just two years with a research thesis titled "Genetics and Human Motivation."

Graduation was followed by a series of academic and administrative appointments at Bryn Mawr, the University of Maryland, the Carter Foundation for Child Development, and the University of Pennsylvania. Her talent was obvious and her scholarship promising. Promotions were rapid. She moved to Minnesota in 1972 as an associate professor in the School Psychology Training Program. Just two years later, she accepted a full professorship at the university's Institute of Child Development. She was elected a Fellow of the American Psychological Association and a fellow of the American Association for the Advancement of Science, and she was also received into numerous other scientific and professional organizations.

She left Minnesota in 1977 and became the first woman to be named to a full professorship in the department of psychology at Yale University. In 1983 she was selected as the Commonwealth Professor of Psychology at the University of Virginia, where her students refer to her affectionately as "Sandra Scarr Super Star." She also served as the editor of the American Psychological Association's journal *Developmental Psychology* and as president of the Society for Research in Child Development. She is at present the editor of the the American Psychological Society's journal *Current Directions in Psychological Science.*

---

cle tends to be repeated for generation after generation. Clearly the correlations between IQs of parents and children are bound to be high, and give a superficial impression of genetic determination (Rose & Weinberg, 1976).

One way to lessen the impact of a genetically based interpretation of the similarity between the IQs of parents and children is to study the mental development of black children who are reared by so-cially advantaged white parents. Sandra Scarr conducted just such a study (Scarr & Weinberg, 1976). She analyzed 101 white, middle-class families who had adopted 176 children, 130 of whom were black and the rest of whom were Asian and American Indian. The mean IQ of these adopted black children was 106, which was 21 points higher than the national mean for blacks. More important, however, was the fact that the mean IQ for the black children who had been adopted as infants was 110. This latter group, of course, was in the advantaged cultural environment all through the early, critical periods of intellectual growth (Scarr & Weinberg, 1978a).

The Cumulative Deficit in IQ

A classic study of white children from a deprived rural area in Virginia found the average IQ of 6-to-8-year-olds to be 84 and the average for the 10-to-12-year-olds to be only 53 (Sherman & Key, 1932). Thus, under conditions of stimulus deprivation the negative impact of the environment tends to accumulate as the child grows older. That is, a child from an impoverished background who is one year below grade level by age 6 may fall back to two full years below grade level by age 12. Just as the intellectually rich get richer, so too do the intellectually poor get poorer. Such studies lend dramatic support to the mounting evidence regarding the environment's power in affecting mental growth.

Ironically, the evidence from one of Jensen's own studies goes a long way toward providing perhaps the most damaging evidence yet obtained against the purely genetic interpretation. Jensen studied large groups of children, both black and white, from an area in the rural South. According to Jensen, the blacks in this locality were "as severely disadvantaged, educationally and economically, as can be found anywhere in the United States today" (Jensen, 1977, p. 185). Yet what Jensen found was that for black children there was a progressive *decline* in IQ scores. And what caused the decline? The cumulative effects of an impoverished environment:

> It was found that blacks (but not whites) showed significant and substantial decrements in both verbal and nonverbal IQs as a linear function of age . . . from about 5 to 16 years of age (p. 184).

Studies of this type, though not refuting the importance of heredity on intelligence, make it clear that time and environment are extremely important in determining later levels of intellectual functioning. "To overstress the genetic factor is inevitably to assert that the blame belongs on the shoulders of the victim. This whole method of diagnosis and treatment takes us into the theatre of the absurd" (Daniels and Houghton, 1972, p. 75).

Sir Cyril Burt and the Taint of Scandal

Sir Cyril Burt had allegedly conducted a large number of studies in which the IQs of monozygotic twins reared apart were compared with the IQs of mono-

zygotic twins reared together. However, in 1977, three years after Burt's death, Leon Kamin tried to prove that many of Burt's data were not only flawed but fraudulent (Kamin, 1977). At least some of the raw IQ data that Burt had used to support his hereditarian view could not be found among his papers. The suspicion grew that Burt had simply created correlations out of nonexistent data (Eysenck & Kamin, 1981).

Even Jensen began suspecting the authenticity of Burt's data, but then said that if the Burt studies were thrown out, the total heritability of IQ would have to be lowered from .80 to .70 (Jensen, 1981). Even if newer studies indicated the true heritability value to be only .50, Jensen asserted, that would still show the effect of heredity to be as great as that of any environmental variables. Today some scholars are now arguing that Burt actually did have the data, and that the charges leveled at him were grossly exaggerated and not borne out by the facts (Fletcher, 1991a). In fact, Bert Green says that the charge of falsifying data cannot be proved and that even the allegation itself, with Burt no longer able to defend himself, may have permanently scarred one of England's most prestigious psychologists (Green, 1992). No credible case of data falsification has yet been unequivocally presented (Fletcher, 1991b). We do know now that all of Burt's data have stood the test of time. Burt had stated that the IQ correlation between MZ twins reared apart was .77. The Minnesota study, which has been hailed as meticulous in its scientific rigor, reported that correlation to be .78 (Bouchard et al., 1990). So, if Burt was a fraud, he was one of the most prescient frauds in the history of science.

Brain Size and Intelligence: Myth or Fact?

J. Philippe Rushton, a Canadian psychobiologist, has examined cranial measurements on a random sample of more than 6,000 U.S. Army personnel and found IQ differences to be a function of brain size, even after adjusting for weight, stature, and race (Rushton, 1992). These data are consistent with those found by Andreasen and colleagues (1993), who conducted a study using magnetic resonance imaging (MRI) on 67 live, healthy subjects (37 men and 30 women). Andreasen found significant correlations, of approximately .40, between the volume of certain brain structures and WAIS-R IQ scores. Among the various brain-tissue components measured, only gray matter seemed to produce the significant IQ correlations. The greater the volume of gray matter, (1) the greater the number of nerve cell bodies, (2) the more dendritic expansion, and (3) the more neu-

SPOTLIGHT ON NATURE AND NURTURE

The Debate Continues

As we have seen in earlier chapters, the nature-nurture debate has been with us at least since Socrates, Plato, and Aristotle. The inspired argumentation of the medieval scholastics pales beside the debates that modern academicians have waged on this issue over the years. And the shouting matches are not over. During the 1970s and 1980s the IQ controversy typically focused on intellectual differences between black and white children; today researchers are becoming increasingly interested in the high educational achievements shown by Asian Americans. It has been found that Asians have higher IQs than do whites both in the United States and in Europe.[a] On the math portion of the SAT and in high school grade-point averages, Asian Americans also score significantly higher than other American students. One study found that of those precocious children who scored 700 or higher on the SAT in math before age 13, 43 percent were Asian, whereas less than 3 percent of the population at large were Asian.[b] Even among the Southeast Asian boat people, those poverty-stricken refugees who finally arrived in the United States with nothing more than the clothes they were wearing, the children still tend to excel in school. One study found that the children of these refugees had higher grade-point averages, especially in math

and science, than were the norms for their schools and that they also scored above the median on the California Achievement Test.[c] These children had limited exposure to Western culture and knew virtually no English when they arrived. Because of their low economic status, virtually all these children were attending slum-area U.S. schools. Although they did less well in liberal arts courses, where more extensive language skills are required, their combined GPA was 2.64.

To explain these data, the two long-standing rivals, hereditarians versus environmentalists, have rejoined battle. On the side of heredity, Richard Lynn suggests that the most parsimonious explanation of these Asian advantages must be based on the genetic component, especially since even cross-adoption studies (abandoned Korean babies reared in the homes of white Americans) show significantly higher IQs for these children than those of even the adopting family. Lynn suggests that Asians may have a genetic predisposition toward hard work—an inherited motivational variable. On the other side, environmentalists such as Stanley Sue and Sumie Okazaki maintain that the difference is due to the Asians' reaction to U.S. discrimination. Because they encounter prejudice, both in school and in the workplace, Asian Amer-

icans tend to compensate by working and studying much harder in order to obtain educational credentials for entry into the job market, especially the professions. Because of the language barrier encountered by newly arriving Asians, these children tend to concentrate especially in the areas of math and science, where quantitative rather than verbal and cultural skills are emphasized.[d] Finally, it has also been noted that most of these transported Asian family units are extremely close and have an especially strong commitment to accomplishment and education. It seems safe to say that this nature-nurture argument, heard even in the days of Socrates and Plato, will continue well into the twenty-first century, perhaps with other racial groups and probably even in other parts of the world.

---

[a] Lynn, R. (1991). Educational achievements of Asian Americans. *American Psychologist, 46,* 875–876.

[b] Sue, S., & Okazaki, S. (1990). Asian-American educational achievements: A phenomenon in search of an explanation. *American Psychologist, 45,* 913–920.

[c] Caplan, N., Choy, M. H., and Whitmore, J. K. (1992). Indochinese refugee families and academic achievement. *Scientific American 266,* 36–42.

[d] Sue, S., & Okazaki, S. (1991). Explanations for Asian-American achievements: A reply. *American Psychologist, 46,* 878–880.

ronal connections—all of which the researchers suggest are thought to be closely related to higher cognitive functions. Andreasen concludes that the correlation between gray-matter volume and IQ suggests

that some factors influencing intelligence and brain size operate relatively early in human development. Since head size in humans is influenced by brain growth, brain size is to some extent determined by the second year of life, when the sutures in the skull close, and is nearly complete by the sixth year. As has been shown throughout our discussions of growth and development, factors that might influence all forms of development, and especially cranial development, include genetics as well as such important environmental variables as nutrition, general health, and the amount and quality of environmental stimulation.

From his analysis of the cranial capacity of the Army personnel, Rushton also found that officers scored higher than enlisted personnel and that Asian Americans averaged higher than white Americans and African-Americans. Since others have found significant correlations of between .35 and .40 between brain size and intelligence (Willerman et al., 1991), these systematic relationships are seen by Rushton to be of great scientific interest, even though they may fly in the face of political correctness. All these data have come long after Gould (1981) seemingly put to rest the brain-size difference theories that were so prevalent in the 1920s and 1930s.

Testing the Teachers?

Robert Carkhuff, an expert in the fields of counseling and human relations, observed that although the mean IQ of black children is about 86 when they enter first grade, it drops even lower by the time they reach fifth grade. Carkhuff has attributed this drop to environmental forces working on the black child in the school setting. Since teachers and counselors often treat black children as if they were devoid of intellectual resources, the children begin to fulfill this expectation as the school years go by. Says Carkhuff, "The teachers and counselors respond to black children as if Jensen were correct" (Carkhuff, 1971, p. 125).

To compound the felony, Carkhuff argues, the least competent teachers are assigned to ghetto and predominantly black schools. It is not surprising, then, that black children often do not achieve beyond the eighth- or ninth-grade level, since it may be that the level of their teacher's own competence does not extend beyond this point. One study found that two-thirds of the teachers tested scored lower than junior high school level on tests of proficiency in the teacher's own specialty area (Brenton, 1970). Says Carkhuff of these teachers, "They could not pass their own exams" (Carkhuff, 1971, p. 264). In fact, the recent movement in this country to force teachers to take standardized competency tests in order to enter or remain in the teaching profession has met with considerable resistance from teachers. Teachers have suddenly been placed in the ironic position of seeming to say that testing is not a good way to judge people.

The Confluence Model: The Family Environment

Robert B. Zajonc (rhymes with "science") has proposed a provocative theory of intellectual development that views the family unit as the key ingredient in the formation of IQ growth. Although Zajonc interprets his data on the basis of the family's influence as an environmental variable, there may again be a hint, as some critics suggest, of an interaction effect between the family's gene pool and its ability to produce a stimulating intellectual environment. Zajonc has interpreted the relationship between family size and intelligence as a product of general environmental stimulation. The data are as follows:

1. Firstborn children tend to have higher IQs than their younger siblings.

2. The more children there are in a family, the lower the IQs of all the children.

3. Twins have lower IQs than nontwins.

4. Children in one-parent homes have lower IQs than children from homes in which both parents are present. (The younger the child at the time of parental loss, the more severe the resulting IQ deficit.)

5. The only child has a lower IQ than does the firstborn in a two- or three-child family (Zajonc, 1976).

In his interpretation of these facts, Zajonc uses what he calls the **confluence model,** a model that predicts that the intellectual growth of each child is a function of the intellectual levels of all the other family members. A given child's intellectual environment is based on the average of the intellectual levels of all the family members, and since children contribute less than their parents to the absolute level of the family's intellectual environment, the more children there are, the lower the absolute level. However, the more spacing between children, the less the damage to the family's intellectual environment. The data on only children do reveal a discontinuity in this prediction, and Zajonc suggests that a child in some way benefits from having younger siblings. The only child has less opportunity to be a "teacher," to show a younger brother or sister how to hold a pencil, grip a baseball bat, or tie shoes.

Zajonc has provided an interesting and provocative explanation, also based on his confluence model, of the steady decline in SAT scores that occurred during the 1970s. The decline was simply a reflection of the fact that, following World War II, American parents decided to have large families and to have these children close together. Further, since the size of American families began decreasing in the early 1960s, Zajonc predicted an upswing in SAT scores for the 1980s. To some extent this prediction proved accurate. For example, from 1980 to 1986 the average verbal SAT score went from 428 to 437, and the average math score from 491 to 501. The uptrend has recently reversed, however, with the 1991 verbal average at 426 and the math average at 497. It must also be pointed out that during 1991 more students, well over a million, took the SAT than ever before, and it has been shown, by Zajonc and others, that the larger the population of test takers, the lower the average scores. For example, in South Carolina, where almost 60 percent of seniors took the test, the average SATs were the lowest in the nation, with a verbal score of only 395 and a math score of 437. In Iowa, on the other hand, where only 5 percent of seniors took the test, the average scores were the highest in the nation, with a verbal of 515 and a math of 578.

There has also been an alternate explanation for the rise in SAT scores that occurred in the 1980s. Since the population of students taking the test is self-selected, average SAT scores may be a function of the overall strength of the nation's economy. When economic times are good, more students are in a financial position to elect to go to college and therefore take the test. According to this explanation, during the 1981–1983 recession, the rise in SAT scores may have been due to the fact that fewer students were taking the test, and the very ones who opted not to take it were most likely to be at the economic margin. Financially disadvantaged students as a group have traditionally not done well on the SAT. According to this theory, then, as the economy improves, SAT scores go down, and as the economy weakens, SAT scores go up (Wainer, 1986).

Regardless of whether Zajonc's model is correct or incorrect with respect to SAT scores, Zajonc believes it can be used to explain another phenomenon: racial IQ differences. Since black families generally have more children (and have them closer together) than do average white families, that fact alone could explain the difference in average IQ scores between the two groups. Add to this the further fact that more black than white families are one-parent families. Zajonc's conclusions are based on studies conducted on well over 1 million subjects from the United States, France, the Netherlands, and Scotland. His predictions have held up regardless of nationality, race, social status, or income level.

Critics suggest that since the confluence model has been analyzed using correlational techniques, perhaps Zajonc has overinterpreted the direction of the relationship. Although it may be that Zajonc is correct and that large numbers of children in a family do tend to lower overall average IQ levels (an environmental argument), the reverse might also be true: that parents with lower IQs tend to have more children in the first place (a genetic argument).

Trying to Define Intelligence

At the beginning of this chapter we asked "What is intelligence?" Even professional psychologists have trouble providing an adequate definition. When Yale psychologist Robert Sternberg polled a sample of 24 professional psychologists and asked them for a definition of intelligence, he got 24 somewhat different answers (Sternberg & Detterman, 1986). However, the situation is not as bleak as the Sternberg poll might indicate. There are certain aspects of intelligence that apparently the majority of theorists currently agree on. As one researcher has indicated, there is virtual unanimity that intelligence is based on one's ability to understand complex ideas, adapt effectively to the environment, learn from experience, engage in various forms of reasoning, and overcome obstacles via the thought process (Niesser et al., 1996). And Betsy Waterman (1994), in recapping the major findings concerning the research on intelligence and intelligence testing, states that:

1. IQ scores are typically more stable for school-aged children than for preschoolers, as well as being more stable for individuals without disabilities than for those with disabilities.

2. IQ scores may at times change somewhat from childhood to adulthood.

3. IQ scores may be a function of environmental factors, socioeconomic status, family structure and values, and of course genetic components.

4. Such physiological factors as low birthrate, malnutrition, fetal alcohol syndrome, and anoxia have all been shown to impact IQ.

5. Academic achievement and IQ appear to be highly related.

Above all else, however, we must be reminded that intelligence does not act in a vacuum; it must always be seen in contextual terms. As Charles Locurto puts it, intelligence is the "ability to master the skills and information necessary to succeed within a given cul-

ture, that is, to succeed at a given point in time within a defined context" (Locurto, 1991, p. 165).

SUMMARY

Psychologists have generally assigned three meanings to the concept of intelligence: intelligence as a genetic capacity, intelligence as observed behavior, and intelligence as a test score.

The history of intelligence testing begins with Sir Francis Galton. Galton believed that intelligence was largely an inherited characteristic and attempted to measure intelligence through the use of simple sensorimotor tests. Galton's test results led him to emphasize what later became the theme of all measurement practitioners—individual differences. Galton's student and colleague Karl Pearson analyzed the testing data and, in order to make some meaningful comparisons, introduced a new statistical technique, the correlation coefficient.

Charles Spearman, a friend of both Galton and Pearson, used the correlational approach to factor out what he thought were the true components of intelligence. His data told him that intelligence was made up of several factors: an underlying general factor, *g;* and a series of very specific factors, *s*'s. Later, in the 1930s, L. L. Thurstone theorized that intelligence was made up only of specific factors, and he identified a total of seven of these, which he called primary abilities of intelligence.

Following Galton's lead in attempting to test for intelligence, Alfred Binet established an important tradition just after the turn of the century. Binet discarded Galton's idea of measuring intelligence through the use of sensorimotor tasks and adopted instead the approach of using intellectual tasks. Binet used the concept of mental age in order to assign a numerical value to performance on his test.

In 1916 an American psychologist, Lewis M. Terman, published an American revision of the Binet test. The scoring of this test, the Stanford-Binet test, was based on the concept of the intelligence quotient, or IQ.

In 1939 David Wechsler introduced the first of a series of new individual IQ tests. Wechsler felt that the Stanford-Binet test was too heavily laden with verbal items, and so he created a series of performance tasks to be presented along with the more traditional verbal tests.

During World War I, group tests of intelligence were introduced, allowing for the testing of large numbers of people in one sitting. Because of their ease of administration and lack of expense, group tests of intelligence quickly became popular throughout most school systems.

Since the mid-1980s, two new approaches to intelligence have been introduced. Harvard's Howard Gardner argues, as Thurstone had, that there is not just one intelligence, but instead there are a number of intelligences. Although, again like Thurstone, he began with seven components, he has since introduced two new ones. Yale's Robert Sternberg has theorized that intelligence should be viewed as triarchic, consisting of componential intelligence, experiential intelligence, and contextual intelligence. Both Gardner and Sternberg share a more humanistic view of intelligence than did either Galton or Spearman.

What do tests of intelligence tell us that we couldn't determine before? Studies have shown that IQ tests do predict how well a child will perform in school. Studies also indicate that high IQ scores correlate with success in later life as measured by such factors as physical health, emotional adjustment, financial income, and literary and scientific contributions.

Intelligence, like all human behavior, is a product of heredity interacting with environment interacting with time.

1. *Heredity:* Studies show that the closer the genetic similarity between people, the higher the resulting IQ correlation.

2. *Environment:* Similar environments also produce similar IQs. The specific environmental parameters studied include home factors (such as number of books in the home and parental attitudes toward schooling), nutrition, stimulus variety, past experience, and parental encouragement.

3. *Time:* The Bloom curve indicates that environmental influences on intelligence are most pronounced during the first few years of life.

The transactional model of development states that the interplay between parent and child affects not only the intellect and personality of the growing child but also the ongoing behavior of the parent, which in turn further shapes the child.

Bornstein has provided evidence indicating that fairly reliable measures of infant intelligence can be achieved and that these measures correlate both with later IQ measures and with the quality of the interaction between mother and child.

Arthur Jensen's hypothesis that there are racial differences in intelligence finds no substantiation. Although the average IQs of black and white children do differ, there is no reason to assume that this difference is due more to genetic than to environmental factors.

Zajonc's theory, called the confluence model, predicts that the more children there are in a family, especially if the children are close together in age, the lower the IQs of all the children will be. Birth order is also important, since firstborns have the highest IQs, unless there is wide spacing between the children. Zajonc's findings have held up regardless of nationality, race, income level, or social status.

KEY TERMS AND NAMES

Alfred Binet
Bornstein's infant intelligence test
confluence model
deviation IQ
factor approach
group tests of intelligence
J. P. Guilford
heritability
intelligence
intelligence quotient (IQ)
Arthur R. Jensen

mental age
performance IQ
Charles Spearman
Stanford-Binet test
Lewis M. Terman
L. L. Thurstone
transactional model
WAIS (WAIS-R)
David Wechsler
Wechsler Intelligence Scale for Children
(WISC-III)

THEORY INTO PRACTICE: TESTING FOR INTELLIGENCE-LEARNING

As we have seen, the concept of intelligence can be one of the most confusing in all of educational psychology. People commonly confuse issues of IQ, scholastic aptitude, and academic achievement, and creativity. Even the experts have not yet arrived at a consensus as to what behaviors should be labeled as intelligent (Snyderman & Rothman, 1987). All too often, discussions of intelligence become discussions of qualitatively different things (Sternberg, 1990). However, the central focus has been on the concept of intelligence, the goals as well as the measurement procedures.

To help you keep these goals and procedures clearly in mind, we have created a simulation of an intelligence test for children. In one column we list examples of questions similar to those found on the most widely used of the individually administered child IQ tests, the WISC-III (the Wechsler Intelligence Scale for Children.) In the second column you are to name the subtest being used. Finally, you are to list the reasons for your selection along with a brief comment on the subtest. Coming up with a valid reason for your choice will force you to think over the concepts involved and prevent you from simply trying to rely on rote memory. Before beginning, you should reread the section on the Wechsler tests found on pages 483–485.

Here's an example of our test quiz:

Question: How is a car like a bus?

Answer: Similarities subtest.

Reasons and explanation: This must be a test of Similarities, because to answer this item, the child must be thinking in abstract terms. Different levels of abstraction can also be demonstrated here. For example, the child who says, "They both have wheels" is operating at a lower conceptual level than the child who says, "They are both modes of transportation."

Here is another example:

Question: Repeat after me the following numbers: 1, 7, 3, 2, 8.

Answer: Digit Span subtest.

Reasons and explanation: This must be a test of Digit Span, since the ability to immediately echo a series of random digits taps the child's short-term memory bank. To get a more precise measure here, we could start with, say, three random digits—2, 5, 3—and then increase the length of the series until it results in failure.

Remember that an IQ test has the goal of assessing each person's capacity to think rationally, act purposefully, and deal effectively with the environment. Intelligence is thus seen as a general or global capacity. To measure the traits that make up intelligent thinking, Wechsler designed his test to assess cognitive functioning in a variety of areas. This was, in fact, Wechsler's rationale for including a whole series of subtests, since no single subtest by itself could be sufficient as an overall measure of intellectual capacity.

For this exercise, we will focus only on subtests that are common to both the WISC and the WAIS: Information, Arithmetic, Comprehension, Vocabulary, Picture Completion, Object Assembly, and Similarities.

ITEM	YOUR ANSWER	REASONS AND EXPLANATION
1. What does the word *stalagmite* mean?	_____ subtest	
2. If a minivan holds 8 people, how many vans do you need to carry 48 people?	_____ subtest	
3. How is a mouse like an elephant?	_____ subtest	
4. What should you do if you noticed large amounts of smoke in the back of the school auditorium during an assembly?	_____ subtest	
5. Look at the picture and tell what important part is missing.	_____ subtest	

6. What does the word *nail* mean?	_____ subtest	
7. What does this saying mean? "A rolling stone gathers no moss."	_____ subtest	
8. What should you do if you found another student's homework assignment lying on the floor of the school's hallway?	_____ subtest	
9. How many states are there in the United States?	_____ subtest	

ITEM	*YOUR ANSWER*	*REASONS AND EXPLANATION*

10. Here are some pieces, as in a jigsaw puzzle. As quickly as possible, put them together to make something.

_____ subtest

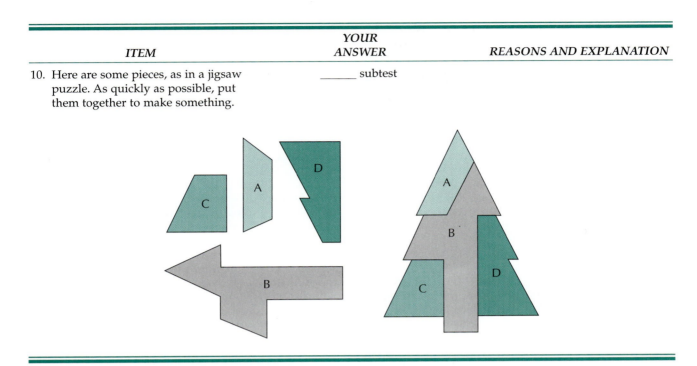

Discussion of the Reasons

1. Vocabulary   Discovering whether a child knows the correct definition of a sample of words aids in predicting the size of the child's total vocabulary. A definition of *stalagmite,* such as "a cylindrical deposit projecting upward from the floor of a cave" is perfect. But even here, in this relatively objective area, there can still be shades of gray. For example, the child who says that "the stalagmite projects downward from the roof of a cave" has a better idea of the meaning than someone who says it is "a German prison camp." A list can easily be drawn up that begins by requiring relatively easy definitions, such as, What is a banana? and goes on to words so difficult as to tax the limits of any child's vocabulary.

2. Arithmetic   Math items can be easily ordered as to difficulty. Also, an item such as the one shown requires an understanding of mathematical principles, not just the ability to recite the multiplication table or divide in one's head. Having a general concept of how to apply number facts is crucial to arriving at the correct answer of six vans.

3. Similarities   Here the ability to abstract is critical and indicative of the child's ability to organize facts into a meaningful and coherent structure. For example, saying that both the mouse and the elephant have tails is a lower-order answer than that they are both living creatures, or both animals or mammals. However, any of the above answers would be better than saying that they both squeak, except for the elephant.

4. Comprehension   A question such as this, although aimed at a child's overall level of comprehension, may also produce an indication of the child's level of social understanding. Notice that the children are not asked what they *would* do, but what they *should* do. Do they at least know what the right thing to do *should* be? The child who says he'd sneak out the side door, although certainly indicating a strong sense of self-preservation, is not showing the same degree of overall comprehension as the child who says she would quietly tell the teacher. The interaction between intellectual and personality factors can be seen in many of the answers to this question. For example, the child who says she would go up on the stage and order the band to play the "Star-Spangled Banner" and would then direct rows A through J to leave by exit 1 and rows K through Z by exit 2, could be illustrating a self-aggrandizing approach that typifies her general personality structure. Also, the child who answers by repeatedly insisting that he would not yell fire may be wrestling with an underlying problem of impulse control.

5. Picture completion   In this test, attention to detail and listening carefully to the instructions play key roles in the child's ability to succeed. For example, the question asks, "What is missing in the picture?" *not* "What is wrong with the picture?" The child who does not pay attention to the question is likely to jump in quickly and say that the steering wheel is on the wrong side rather than that one of the headlights is missing or even that the license plate is missing.

6. Vocabulary   The child who shows an understanding that a nail is a metal object used for holding pieces of wood together is giving us some indication of the extent of his or her vocabulary. This subtest is unusually rich in its ability to pull out overtones of personality. The trained examiner learns to use this subtest to ferret out personality as well as intellectual factors. The child who defines a nail as "something on the finger that can be polished, manicured, and made to look pretty" may be demonstrating needs that transcend any straight, cognitive interpretation.

7. Comprehension   The child who realizes that this saying is allegorical, not literal, shows a high degree of comprehension and developmental maturity. For example, an answer such as "People who are always on the move, who are overly restless, never stay in one place long enough to accumulate wealth or put down any lasting roots," is one that certainly shows an abstract understanding of the phrase. Even an answer such as "Busy people get their jobs done quickly, and are not bogged down by side issues and excuses," is qualitatively better than an overly literal answer such as "A stone that keeps rolling down a hill has all of its moss worn away and doesn't have any of its own moss left."

8. Comprehension   The child who says she would find the student who lost it and quietly hand it over is showing a marked degree of comprehension and social awareness. This is certainly a better

answer than "I'd look at the homework, and if it's better done than mine, then I'd write my name on the top and pass it in." Even the child who answers by saying he'd make an appointment with the principal and then go down to the office and, perhaps even waiting for a fanfare, personally present the homework to the principal, is probably showing a higher need for recognition than the situation demands. Is this the same child who went up on stage after detecting smoke at the back of the school auditorium?

9. Information   Knowing the correct answer— fifty states—indicates an alertness to one's surroundings and the existence of an informational base that may have been effortlessly and almost automatically created by an inquiring and absorbent young mind. Again, even factual and informational questions can indicate degrees of knowledge and understanding. An answer such as five or 450 shows a lack of any conceptual base, whereas answers such as forty-eight or fifty-two, while not hitting the bull's-eye directly, are at least somewhere close to the target.

10. Object assembly   A test such as this one, which measures not just eye-hand coordination or motoric speed, is especially valuable in determining the strength of the child's powers of recognition. Responses to this test may also be used to infer something of the child's mode of perception, the degree to which the trial-and-error approach is used, and even frustration tolerance in reaction to mistakes. The child who is easily upset, even to the point of not being willing to complete the problem, shows a different level of frustration tolerance than the child who, despite making some mistakes, stoically continues trying. Also, cognitive approaches to this problem can vary dramatically. For example, one child may blindly rush in and randomly flip the pieces around without the vaguest notion of what the parts represent. This approach may work, but it would certainly be a case of success by accident. Another child may spend a brief time looking over the parts, using this time to internally reorganize his or her perceptions, and only then begin to accurately and quickly put the pieces together. In many cases, you may even hear the child verbally announce the moment of insight with a phrase such as "Oh, I get it."

REFERENCES

Alexander, K. L., & Entwistle, D. R. (1988). Achievement in the first 2 years of school: Patterns and processes. *Monographs of the Society for Research in Child Development 53*(2, Serial No. 218).

Andreasen, N. C., Flaum, M., Swayze, V., O'Leary, D. S., Alliger, R., Cohen, G., Ehrhardt, J., & Yuh, W. T. C. (1993). Intelligence and brain structure in normal individuals. *American Journal of Psychiatry 150,* 130–134.

Ankney, C. D. (1992). Sex differences in relative brain size: The mismeasure of woman too? *Intelligence 16,* 329–336.

Armstrong, T. (1994). Multiple intelligences: Seven ways to approach curriculum. *Educational Leadership 52*(3), 29–31.

Baghurst, P. A., McMichael, A. J., Wigg, N. R., Vimpani, G. V., Robertson, E. F., Roberts, R. J., & Tong, S. L. (1992). Environmental exposure to lead and children's intelligence at the age of seven years: The Port Pirie cohort study. *New England Journal of Medicine 327,* 1279–1284.

Barrett, G. V., & Depinet, R. L. (1991). A reconsideration of testing for competence rather than for intelligence. *American Psychologist 46,* 1012–1024.

Binet, A., and Simon, H. (1905). Application des méthodes nouvelles au diagnostic du niveau intellectuel chez des enfants normaux et anormaux d'hospice et d'école primaire. *L'Anne Psychologique 11,* 245–266.

Bloom, B. S. (1964). *Stability and change in human characteristics.* New York: Wiley.

Bornstein, M. (1985). How infant and mother jointly contribute to developing cognitive competence in the child. *Proceedings of the National Academy of Science 82,* 7470–7473.

Bornstein, M. H. (1989). Stability in early mental development: From attention and information processing in infancy to language and cognition in childhood. In M. H. Bornstein & N. A. Krasnegor (Eds.), *Stability and continuity in mental development* (pp. 147–170). Hillsdale, NJ: Erlbaum.

Bouchard, T. J., Lykken, D. R., McGue, M., Segal, N. L., & Tellegen, A. (1990). Sources of human psychological differences: The Minnesota study of twins reared apart. *Science 250,* 223–228.

Bradley, R. H. (1989). HOME measurement of maternal responsiveness. In M. H. Bornstein (Ed.), *Maternal responsiveness: Characteristics and consequences* (pp. 63–74). San Francisco: Jossey-Bass.

Brenton, M. (1970). *What's happened to teachers?* New York: Coward.

Brody, N. (1992). Intelligence (2nd ed.). San Diego: Academic Press.

Caldwell, B. M., & Bradley, R. H. (1984). *Home observation for measurement of the environment.* Little Rock: University of Arkansas Press.

Calvert, S., & Cocking, R. (1992). Health promotion through mass media. *Journal of Applied Developmental Psychology 13,* 143–149.

Carkhuff, R. R. (1971). *The development of human resources.* New York: Holt, Rinehart & Winston.

Carroll, J. B. (1989). Factor analysis since Spearman: Where do we stand? What do we know? In R. Kanfer, P. L. Ackerman, & R. Cudeck (Eds.), *Abilities, motivation and methodology* (pp. 43–67). Hillsdale, NJ: Erlbaum.

Clifford, M. M. (1991). Risk taking: Theoretical, empirical, and educational considerations. *Educational Psychologist, 26*(3, 4), 263–297.

Couchon, A. R. (1983). Approaches to the normal level. *Personality Assessment System Journal 2,* 2–13.

Cravens, H. (1992). A scientific project locked in time: The Terman genetic studies of genius. *American Psychologist 47,* 183–189.

Daniels, D., & Houghton, V. (1972). Jensen, Eysenck and the eclipse of the Galton paradigm. In K. Richardson and D. Spears (Eds.), *Race and intelligence.* Baltimore: Penguin.

Daniels, D., & Plomin, R. (1985). Origins of individual differences in infant shyness. *Developmental Psychology 21,* 118–121.

Deary, I. J. (1995). Auditory inspection time and intelligence: What is the causal direction? *Developmental Psychology 31,* 237–250.

Dennis, W. (1960). The mental growth of certain institutional children: Iran. *Journal of Genetic Psychology 96,* 47–59.

Dennis, W. (1969). *The mental growth of certain foundlings before and after adoption.* Paper delivered at American University, Beirut, Lebanon.

Duncan, O. D., Featherman, D. L., & Duncan, B. (1972). *Socioeconomic background and achievement.* New York: Seminar Press.

Eickenwald, H. F., & Fry, P. C. (1969). Nutrition and learning. Science, 163, 644–648.

Erlenmeyr-Kimling, L., & Jarvik, L. F. (1963). Genetics and intelligence: A review. *Science, 142,* 1479–1488.

Eysenck, H. J., & Kamin, L. (1981). *The intelligence controversy.* New York: Wiley.

Farber, S. L. (1981). *Identical twins reared apart.* New York: Basic Books.

Feingold, A. (1988). Cognitive gender differences are disappearing. *American Psychologist, 43,* 95–103.

Fine, M. (1991). Framing dropouts: *Notes on the politics of an urban public high school.* Albany: State University of New York Press.

Fletcher, R. (1991a). Intelligence, equality, character, and education. *Intelligence, 15,* 139–149.

Fletcher, R. (1991b). *Science, ideology, and the media: The Cyril Burt scandal.* New Brunswick, NJ: Transaction.

Flynn, J. R. (1980). The mean IQ of Americans: Massive gains 1932 to 1978. *Psychological Bulletin, 95,* 29–51.

Forrester, B. J., & Klaus, R. A. (1964). The effect of race of the examiner on intelligence test scores of Negro kindergarten children. *Peabody Papers in Human Development, 2(7),* 1–7.

Galton, F., & Schuster, E. (1906). *Noteworthy families: Modern science.* London: John Murray.

Gardner, H. (1985a). *Frames of mind: The theory of multiple intelligences.* New York: Basic Books.

Gardner, H. (1985b). *The mind's new science: A history of the cognitive revolution.* New York: Basic Books.

Goleman, D. (1995). *Emotional intelligence: Why it can matter more than IQ.* New York: Bantam Books.

Gottfried, A. W. (1984). Home environment and early cognitive development: Integration, meta-analyses, and conclusion. In A. W. Gottfried (Ed.), *Home environment and early cognitive development* (pp. 329–342). Orlando, FL: Academic Press.

Gould, S. (1981). *The mis-measure of man.* New York: Norton.

Graham, S. (1989). Motivation in Afro-Americans. In L. G. Berry & J. K. Asaman (Eds.), *Black students: Psychosocial issues and academic achievement* (pp. 40–68). Newbury Park, CA: Sage.

Green, B. (1992). Exposé or smear? The Burt affair. *Psychological Science 3,* 328–346.

Guilford, J. P. (1967). *The nature of human intelligence.* New York: McGraw-Hill.

Haan, N. (1963). Proposed model of ego functioning: Coping and defense mechanisms in relation to IQ change. *Psychological Monographs 11.*

Hardy-Brown, K., Plomin, R., & Defries, J. (1981). Genetic and environmental influences on the rate of communicative development in the first year of life. *Developmental Psychology 17,* 704–717.

Harlow, H. F., McGaugh, J. L., & Thompson, R. F. (1971). *Psychology.* San Francisco: Albion.

Hebb, D. O. (1978). Open letter to a friend who thinks the IQ is a social evil. *American Psychologist 33,* 1143.

Herrnstein, R. J., & Murray, C. (1994). *The bell curve: Intelligence and class structure in American life.* New York: Free Press.

Hirsch, J. (1971). Race, intelligence, and IQ: A debate. In N. Chalmer, R. Crawley, and S. P. R. Rose (Eds.), *The biological bases of behavior* (pp. 244–245). London: Open University Press, Harper & Row.

Hoerr, T. R. (1994). How the new city school applies the multiple intelligences. *Educational Leadership 52(3),* 29–31.

Hummel, R., & Sprinthall, N. A. (1965). Underachievement related to interests, attitudes, and values. *Personnel and Guidance Journal 44,* 388–395.

Jensen, A. R. (1969). How much can we boost IQ and scholastic achievement? *Harvard Educational Review 39,* 1–123.

Jensen, A. R. (1977). Cumulative deficit in IQ of blacks in the rural south. *Developmental Psychology 13,* 184–191.

Jensen, A. R. (1981). *Straight talk about mental tests.* New York: Free Press.

Jones, L. V. (1984). White-black achievement differences. *American Psychologist 39,* 1207–1213.

Kamin, L. (1977). *The science and politics of IQ.* Harmondsworth, England: Penguin.

Locurto, C. (1991). *Sense and nonsense about IQ: The case for uniqueness.* New York: Praeger.

Lynn, R. (1991). The role of nutrition in secular increases in intelligence. *Personality and Individual Differences 11,* 273–285.

Maccoby, E. E., & Martin, J. (1983). Socialization in the context of the family: Parent-child interactions. In P. Mussen (Ed.), *Handbook of child psychology* (4th ed.). New York: Basic Books.

Mackenzie, B. (1984). Explaining race differences in IQ. *American Psychologist 39,* 1214–1233.

McKean, K. (January 1986). Intelligence: New ways to measure the wisdom of man. *Current,* 15–23.

Messick, S. (1980). Test validity and the ethics of assessment. *American Psychologist 35,* 1012–1027.

Mikelson, R. A. (1989). Why does Jane read and write so well? The anomaly of women's achievement. *Sociology of Education 62,* 47–63.

Neisser, U., Boodoo, G., Bouchard, T. J., Boykin, A. W., Brody, N., Ceci, S. J., Halpern, D. F., Loehlin, J. C., Perloff, R., Sternberg, R. J., & Urbina, S. (1996). Intelligence: Knowns and unknowns. *American Psychologist 51,* 77–101.

Nelson-LeGall, S. (1991). The condition of sex equity in education: Sex, race, and ethnicity. In J. Pfleiderer (Ed.), *Proceedings of the 1991 ETS Invitational Conference: Sex equity in education, opportunity, achievement, and testing* (pp. 91–102). Princeton, NJ: Educational Testing Service.

Newman, H. H., Freeman, F. N., & Holzinger, K. J. (1937). *Twins: A study of heredity and environment.* Chicago: University of Chicago Press.

Ogbu, J. U. (1990). Literacy and schooling in subordinate cultures: The case of Black Americans. In K. Lomotey (Ed.), *Going to school: The African-American Experience* (pp. 113–131). Albany: State University of New York Press.

Piel, G. (1975). The new hereditarians. *The Nation 19,* 457.

Plomin, R., Corley, R., DeFries, J. C., & Fulker, D. W. (1990). Individual differences in television watching in early childhood: Nature as well as nurture. *Current Directions in Psychological Science 6,* 371–377.

Pollard, D. S. (1993). Gender, achievement, and African-American students' perceptions of their school experience. *Educational Psychologist 28,* 341–356.

Powell, G. J. (1989). Defining self-concept as a dimension of academic achievement for inner-city youths. In L. G. Berry & J. K. Asaman (Eds.), *Black students: Psychosocial issues and academic achievement* (pp. 69–82). Newbury Park, CA: Sage.

QEM—Quality Education for Minorities Project. (1990). *Education that works: An action plan for the education of minorities.* Cambridge, MA: Massachusetts Institute of Technology.

Ree, M. J., & Earles, J. A. (1992). Intelligence is the best predictor of job performance. *Current Directions in Psychological Science 1,* 86–89.

Ricciuti, H. N. (1993). Nutrition and mental development. *Current Directions in Psychological Science 2,* 43–46.

Rose, S. A. & Feldman, J. (1995). The prediction of IQ and specific cognitive abilities at 11 years from infancy measures. *Developmental Psychology 31,* 685–696.

Rose, S., & Weinberg, R. (1976). IQ test performance of black children adopted by white families. *American Psychologist 31,* 731.

Rushton, J. P. (1992). Cranial capacity related to sex, rank, and race in a stratified random sample of 6,325 U.S. military personnel. *Intelligence 16,* 401–413.

Sameroff, A. (1975). Early influences on development: Fact or fancy? *Merrill-Palmer Quarterly, 21,* 267–294.

Scarr, S. (1971). Race, social class, and IQ. *Science 174,* 1285–1295.

Scarr, S. (1981). *Race, social class, and individual differences in IQ.* Hillsdale, NJ: Erlbaum.

Scarr, S., & McCartney, K. (1983). How people make their own environments: A theory of genotype-environment effects. *Child Development 54,* 424–435.

Scarr, S., & Weinberg, R. (1976). IQ test performance of black children adopted by white families. *American Psychologist 31,* 726–739.

Scarr, S., & Weinberg, R. (1978a). The rights and responsibilities of the social scientist. *American Psychologist 33,* 955–957.

Scarr, S., & Weinberg, R. (1978b). Attitudes, interests, and IQ. *Human Nature 1,* 33.

Schoenthaler, S. J., Amos, S. P., Eysenck, H. J., Peritz, E., & Yudkin, J. (1991). Controlled trial of vitamin-mineral supplementation: Effects on intelligence and performance. *Personality and Individual Differences 12,* 351–362.

Sherman, M., & Key, C. B. (1932). The intelligence of isolated mountain children. *Child Development 3,* 279–290.

Shurkin, J. N. (1992). *Terman's kids: The ground-breaking study of how the gifted grow up.* Boston: Little, Brown.

Smolak, L. (1986). *Infancy.* Englewood Cliffs, NJ: Prentice Hall.

Snyderman, M., & Rothman, S. (1987). Survey of expert opinions on intelligence and aptitude testing. *American Psychologist 42,* 137–144.

Spearman, C. (1904). General intelligence objectively determined and measured. *American Journal of Psychology 15,* 201–293.

Sternberg, R. J. (1990). *Metaphors of mind: Conceptions of the nature of intelligence.* Cambridge, England: Cambridge University Press.

Sternberg, R. J., & Detterman, D. K. (Eds.) (1986). *What is intelligence: Contemporary viewpoints on its nature and definition.* Norwood, NJ: Ablex.

Sternberg, R. J., & Lubart, T. I. (1992). Buy low and sell high: An investment approach to creativity. *Current Directions in Psychological Science 1,* 1–5.

Sternberg, R. J., & Wagner, R. K. (1993). The g-centric view of intelligence and job performance is wrong. *Current Directions in Psychological Science 2,* 1–5.

Streissguth, A. P., Barr, H. M., Sampson, P. D., Darby, B. L., & Martin, D. C. (1989). IQ at age 4 in relation to maternal alcohol use and smoking during pregnancy. *Developmental Psychology 25,* 3–11.

Terman, L. M. (1925; revised 1926, 1930, 1947, 1959). *Genetic studies of genius.* Stanford: Stanford University Press.

Thorndike, R. L., Hagan, E. P., & Sattler, J. M. (1985). *Stanford-Binet* (4th ed.). Chicago: Riverside.

Thurstone, L. L. (1935). *The vectors of the mind.* Chicago: University of Chicago Press.

Turner, G. (1996). Intelligence and the X chromosome. *Lancet 347* (9018), 1814–1816.

Vernon, P. E. (1969). *Intelligence and cultural environment.* London: Methuen.

Vincent, K. R. (1991). Black/white IQ differences: Does age make the difference? *Journal of Clinical Psychology 47,* 266–270.

von Mayrhauser, R. T. (1992). The mental testing community and validity. *American Psychologist 47,* 244–253.

Vygotsky, L. (1978). *Mind in society.* Cambridge, MA: Harvard University Press.

Wainer, H. (1986). Minority advances in test performance: A response to Jones. *American Psychologist 41,* 103.

Waterman, B. B. (1994). Assessing children for the presence of a disability. *News Digest 4,* 1–25. (Published in Washington DC by the National Information Center for Children and Youth with Disabilities.)

Wechsler, D. (1944). *The measurement of adult intelligence.* Baltimore: Williams & Wilkins.

Wechsler, D. (1991). *Wechsler Intelligence Scale for Children manual* (3d ed.). New York: The Psychological Corporation, Harcourt Brace Jovanovich.

Weinberg, R. A. (1991). Intelligence and IQ: Landmark issues and great debates. *American Psychologist 44,* 98–104.

Willerman, L., Schultz, R., Rutledge, J. N., & Bigler, E. D. (1991). In vivo brain size and intelligence. *Intelligence 15,* 223–228.

Zajonc, R. B. (1976). Family configuration and intelligence. *Science 192,* 227–236.

Zelazo, P. R. (1989). Infant toddler information processing and the development of expressive ability. In P. R. Zelazo & R. Barr (Eds.), *Challenges to developmental paradigms: Implications for theory, assessment, and treatment.* Hillsdale, NJ: Erlbaum.

Zelazo, P. R., Weiss, M. J., & Tarquinio, N. (1991). Habituation and recovery of neonatal orienting to auditory stimuli. In M. J. Weiss & P. R. Zelazo (Eds.), *Newborn attention: Biological constraints and the influence of experience.* Norwood, NJ: Ablex.

Zuckerman, M. (1990). Some dubious premises in research and theory on racial differences. *American Psychologist 45,* 1297–1303.

MANAGING STUDENTS IN GROUPS

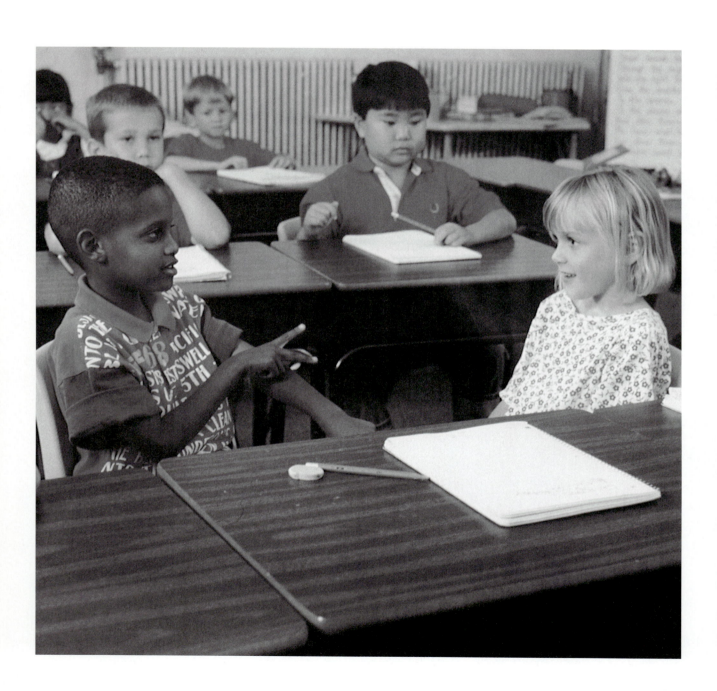

THE CLASS
AS A SOCIAL UNIT

Every classroom is a distinct social unit with its own set of norms, its own psychological atmosphere, its own set of role relationships, its own special blend of behavioral expectancies. Every classroom has a social climate unlike that of any other classroom. An observer walking from room to room in a typical elementary school finds one room charged with excitement and enthusiasm; another, tense, with submissive pupils going through the motions; and still another, bordering on anarchy.

The psychology of the classroom does not operate in a vacuum, for every classroom is part of the larger social unit, the school itself. Again, the observer traveling from school to school can sense differences in social climate among the various schools. The differences among schools may not be as flagrant as the differences among classrooms, but the differences are there, and do have an effect.

What causes these differences among rooms, among schools, among any different number of groups? The quick and easy answer is the personality of the teachers or principal. This, however, is only part of the answer. Just as the principal's behavior helps shape the teachers', so the teachers' behavior shapes the principal's actions. And just as the teacher's behavior influences the pupils' behavior, so the pupils' behavior has a profound effect on the teacher. Teachers may firmly believe that their classrooms have the same social climate year in and year out, despite the shifting student population, but these same teachers will stare in shocked disbelief at a videotape showing one of their classes two or three years ago, or even last year. The shifting student population creates a shifting social climate. Sometimes the shift is subtle, but often it is dramatic. Many teachers freely confess that with one particular class they barely weathered the year, or the opposite: "For the first time in my life my class this year was an absolute dream." This chapter takes a look at some of the findings of social psychology, which, we hope, will increase your understanding of the classroom as a social unit.

SOCIAL PSYCHOLOGY DEFINED

Social psychology attempts to understand human behavior in the context of the social situation. Social psychologists study the ways people affect and are affected by other people. As a subfield of psychology, social psychology still uses the behavior of the individual as its unit of analysis—the individual's behavior in the social context. The social psychologist would probably not be interested in the lonely figure of Hermann Ebbinghaus going about the business of memorizing long lists of nonsense syllables,

Different schools have different social climates.

but would be very much interested in how Ebbinghaus's performance might have been affected by the presence of other people. The very first studies in the field of social psychology were concerned with the effect of a group situation on a person's behavior.

SOCIAL FACILITATION

Even before the turn of the century, studies indicated that on certain tasks a person's performance would improve when others were around (Triplett, 1897). This phenomenon later became known as **social facilitation.** It was also found that this was not a universal phenomenon. Social facilitation was most pronounced in the case of fairly simple mechanical tasks. The more difficult and the more intellectual the task, the less the effect of social facilitation. Later studies have revealed the operation of **social inhibition;** that is, on some tasks, a person's performance suffers when there are others around. On easy tasks, students did better when in the presence of others (social facilitation), but on difficult tasks they did much worse when in the presence of others (social inhibition) (Guerin, 1993).

The Risky Shift

When people get together in group situations, one effect that has been demonstrated in several experiments is the **risky shift** (Pruitt, 1971). The group situation apparently produces an environment in which individuals become far less cautious than they would be if they were alone; consequently, an attitudinal shift in the direction of "throwing caution to the winds" occurs. Individuals are suddenly willing to take greater risks regarding their **attitudes** and behavior. They become less conservative and more willing to gamble. One explanation of this phenomenon is that individuals who are basically risk takers to begin with also happen to be more persuasive and better able to have their opinions prevail in the group setting. These high-risk people become opinion leaders when interacting in the group. Another explanation is that in our culture the daredevil is more revered than the individual who prudently and cautiously weighs all the outcomes before acting. We are more apt to honor an Evel Knievel than a stodgy, trust-department banker. Thus, many individuals would prefer to have the group see them as risk takers. They prefer the public image of being a "gutsy gambler" and therefore shift in the culturally approved risky direction when in a group situation.

Whatever the explanation, the risky shift is an empirical fact. The teacher who is aware of this is less apt to be overconcerned when some budding daredevil disrupts the class with an image-building display of bravado. Perhaps a short session alone with the student will be sufficient to restore the equilibrium and integrity of the classroom.

Brainstorming

The concept of social facilitation has also been used to promote a technique called **brainstorming,** in which individuals get together in an attempt to solve problems in new and creative ways. The idea is that because of the mutual stimulation of a brainstorming session, each participant will individually produce more creative solutions than when in isolation. Individuals in a brainstorming session are urged to interact freely, to call out any ideas no matter how bizarre, and to hold nothing back. The technique is used in many businesses, especially in areas in which creativity is crucial, as in an advertising agency mapping out a new campaign.

The techniques involved in brainstorming can be taught, even to persons not considered to be overly creative. In one study, the presentation of a short course in innovative problem solving (IPS) demonstrated that individuals could be trained to improve their brainstorming skills. However, whether the improvement in brainstorming techniques actually translates into an increase in problemsolving ability is still somewhat at issue (Rice, 1984).

Studies performed over the years have found that brainstorming is not as effective a procedure when used in the group setting as when people are asked to brainstorm alone. In fact, alone, individuals were twice as effective as when in the group setting (Paulus et al., 1995).

Differential Effects on Behavior

Research in the area of social facilitation thus suggests that people do behave differently when in a group. The seemingly contradictory results of the studies (groups sometimes enhance performance and sometimes inhibit it) show that the group has differential effects on behavior.

Working in a group has two main effects: It in-

Cooperative learning may lead to group cohesion.

creases feelings of competition and motivation, on the one hand, and it increases feelings of anxiety and provides distractions, on the other. The presence of other people explicitly or implicitly creates a competitive situation. However, the research studies in this area may be slightly artificial, for it has been found that in these studies the subjects tend to become somewhat self-conscious. The subjects assume that the researcher may be making comparisons among them and/or they hope to impress other members of the group. As might be expected, training for group activities as such is far more effective when done in group settings than when taught on an individual basis (Wang et al., 1995).

Cohesiveness

When individuals interact in a group situation, one possible by-product is the spread of a group phenomenon that social psychologists call **cohesiveness.** When cohesiveness develops, group members tend to stick together more and have more of a sense of "we-ness" than "I-ness." Some teachers have been known to feel threatened by this turn of events.

Cohesiveness is one of the few truly group concepts in social psychology. It is the cement that binds the group together, or the attraction of the group for its members. Groups can range from collections of unrelated individuals (strangers waiting together at a bus station) to highly cohesive groups, in which norms are shared and status and role relationships are highly structured. When students and teachers meet in the classroom for the first time in September, they resemble a collection of individuals more than they do a cohesive group. As the weeks go by, however, the social situation may change dramatically as the loosely knit collection of individuals becomes more cohesive. Cohesiveness may be enhanced by the following:

1. *Friendly interaction:* Interaction per se is not the crucial ingredient; a husband and wife fighting it out in divorce court are interacting. The interaction must be on friendly terms.

2. *Cooperation:* The more the group works together to achieve superordinate goals, the more cohesiveness is allowed to develop.

3. *Group status:* High-status groups tend to be more cohesive than low-status groups. If a classroom is broken down into various reading groups, for example, and if it is obvious to every child that the groups have been rank-ordered on the basis of ability, the top group will feel more cohesive than the bottom group. A teacher may also increase the status of the entire classroom by pointing out that it is in some way a special group and will have special privileges.

4. *An outside threat:* A group's cohesiveness may be dramatically increased by the presence of an outside threat. This is true of large and small groups. In wartime, when a country's very existence is threatened by an outside force, the country's morale and cohesiveness are often at their highest level. In a classroom this same kind of situation may inadvertently occur when a coercive teacher is perceived by the class as overly threatening. The class may band together and form a highly cohesive group—a group, incidentally, that does not include the teacher.

5. *Style of leadership:* We will look at this phenomenon in more detail in a later section. Suffice it to say here that groups in which the leadership is based on democratic factors are usually more likely to be cohesive than are groups in which more authoritarian leadership techniques are employed.

Cohesiveness and productivity   Research indicates that there is no simple one-to-one relationship between cohesiveness and productivity. A cohesive group is one in which the members stick together, but this doesn't necessarily mean that the group is more productive. For example, a highly cohesive labor union is more likely to be able to call a strike (during which production on the job goes down to zero) than is a union whose members are not so attracted to one another. Highly cohesive groups may be more productive than less cohesive groups when the motivation of the members is positive, yet when the motivation is negative, the more cohesive group will be even less productive than the less cohesive group (Schachter, 1951).

Cohesiveness and conformity   Any group brings a certain amount of pressure to bear on its members to conform to the group's standards and norms. In a highly cohesive group the pressure to conform is greater than in a less cohesive group. This helps explain the previously mentioned relationship between cohesiveness and productivity. When the group norm is for high productivity, the highly cohesive group conforms to that norm; likewise, when the group norm is for low productivity, the highly cohesive group conforms to that norm, especially in matters of consequence to the group (working conditions and salary, for example).

Within a group, great pressure exists for conformity, and group pressure to conform is highest when the group is highly cohesive.

Conformity

One of the most striking facts about life on this planet is that human beings form groups and live out their lives in group situations. Equally striking is the fact that while in the group situation, people tend to behave in a uniform way. **Conformity** is a fact of life. Wherever we look we find groups of people, and within each group almost everyone is behaving alike. The behavior of an individual may change from group to group, and the norms of any particular group may shift from time to time, yet the phenomenon of conformity remains. We may like to feel as if we can act with some degree of independence, and yet in truth our freedom of action is severely limited by group pressure.

In a structured situation such as a church service, conformity may be most obvious. People stand, sit, and kneel with the precision of a marching band. The pressure to conform, however, can be just as compelling in less structured situations. If, during the give and take of a dormitory "rap" session, someone suddenly stood up and started singing "Onward Christian Soldiers," that person might be referred to the counseling center.

The message from the group is always the same: Be like us! The pressure to conform is virtually irresistible and may come in a variety of forms. It may be physical force, as in the case of a bouncer's throwing a rowdy customer out of the local tavern—a customer who has exercised too much individuality. Or it may be more subtle, as when the hostess at a formal dinner party raises her eyebrow when one of the guests chooses the wrong fork for the salad. Regardless of the form it takes, the pressure on the individual to conform makes itself known. Conformity has been demonstrated experimentally in many studies. The two most famous, however, are the classic studies by Muzafer Sherif and Solomon Asch.

Sherif and the autokinetic effect   A stationary, pinpoint source of light in an otherwise darkened room will appear to move. You may have noticed this phenomenon yourself. You may have been looking up at a certain star, and out of the corner of your eye it appears that another star has suddenly moved. Or you may have been driving on a turnpike when the rear light of the car in front of you suddenly starts to dance crazily before your eyes. Some plane crashes have even been caused by this **autokinetic effect.** The stationary runway lights suddenly appear to move just before the pilot lands the plane. The effect is even more dramatic if the subject doesn't know how far away the light really is.

FIGURE 17.1   Asch used a card such as this to study group pressures to conform.

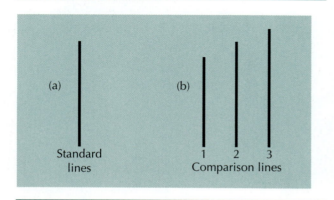

Standard lines   Comparison lines
(a)   (b)   1   2   3

Sherif utilized this autokinetic effect to demonstrate conformity (Sherif, 1936). He put his subjects in a darkened room in groups of three, presented them with the pinpoint source of light, and asked them to call aloud their estimates of how far the light moved. The first subject might estimate that the light moved 16 inches; the second subject, 3 inches; and the third subject, 24 inches. After a few trials, however, all three subjects reported essentially the same distance—a group norm emerged. Repeating this procedure with other groups, Sherif found that conformity occurred in every case. The groups formed different norms, to be sure, but they all created some standard to which every member conformed.

Another interesting result of Sherif's study was

that when he later tested many of the subjects individually, they still perceived the light on the basis of the norms created in the group situation. A member of a "7-inch" group, for example, when later tested alone, would continue to conform to the 7-inch standard. A member of a "22-inch" group would continue to see the light moving that distance, even when tested individually.

Sherif's study shows us that in a relatively unstructured situation, group norms will be created and individuals will follow these norms not only when they are in the group, but even when they are alone.

Asch and group pressure   Sherif had shown that conformity occurs in a fairly unstructured situation, and Asch wondered whether the same result would be obtained in a more structured setting (Asch, 1952). Asch presented his subjects with cards showing four lines: three comparison lines and a standard (see Figure 17.1). The subject was asked to indicate which of the three comparison lines was closest in length to the standard line on the left of the card. As you look at the illustration, you may feel that the task is too easy, that the solution to the problem is too obvious. Yet when Asch conducted this study, his subjects were in error one out of three times. The difference is that as you look at the lines, you are not being exposed to group pressure, whereas Asch's subjects were. Asch's subjects sat in a room with what appeared to be eight other subjects. In fact, these other "subjects" were really stooges, told beforehand just what to say and how to respond. Each group contained one naive subject and eight previously re-

"Well, heck! If all you smart cookies agree, who am I to dissent?"

Drawing by J. B. Handelsman; © 1972 The New Yorker Magazine, Inc.

hearsed bogus subjects. The subject was thus in a situation in which his eyes told him one thing, while all the other people in the room made a unanimous judgment that contradicted his own. The stooges were set up in advance so that every once in a while they would all agree on a certain line, even though that line could not possibly be the correct one. In this setting, the subjects were incorrect one-third of the time; that is, 33 percent of their judgments were errors in the direction of the majority. As we have already said, group pressure is tremendous in its insistence on conformity.

As a matter of fact, the majority does not have to be so large. Asch's later studies revealed that a majority of three to one has just as much effect as a larger majority; that is, the naive subject made as many errors with three stooges as with eight. A two-to-one majority caused errors to drop only to about 12 percent, while the influence of only one stooge was negligible.

When the situation was reversed, when there was a naive majority of 16 against one lone stooge, the errors of the stooge were met with uncontrolled laughter from the rest of the group. Scholars consider the Asch study to be one of the watershed events in the understanding of conformity behavior (Rock, 1990).

In studies that have replicated various features of the original Asch study, it has been found that females tend to be more influenced by the majority pressures than are males (Eagly, 1987). It appears, therefore, that females are more prone to social forces than are males but they are also more likely to offer social *support* (advice, encouragement, and nurturance) to persons in distress (Shumaker & Hill, 1991). This may be one of the reasons why women have become so successful in the field of psychology and in fact now outnumber men in the number of new Ph.D.s entering the field (NCES, 1991).

Sherif and Asch thus demonstrated experimentally the compelling power the group exerts on the individual to conform. Sherif was able to produce norms in the laboratory and show how they govern individual behavior, and Asch, though artificially creating the norms, showed us the force of the group's influence in a relatively structured situation.

Can group pressure be liberating? So far, conformity and group pressure have been shown to be repressive and limiting, generally robbing people of their individuality. Sherif showed us how a group of people can come to believe that a stationary light is moving a certain distance; Asch showed that our need to conform to group standards will cause us to distort our perceptions and judgment. In fact, virtually all the studies done in the area of conformity follow this theme: The noble individual is robbed of human integrity by the insidious pressure of the group.

The experiment by Stanley Milgram that was discussed in Chapter 7 shows the reverse side of the coin (Milgram, 1965). Milgram, in a somewhat frightening experiment, shows us that group pressure can also have a liberating effect. We say "frightening" experiment because Milgram's study also points up the destructive potential of human beings and shows what a thin veneer of socialization we have.

To establish a baseline for our potential for hostility, Milgram asked subjects to deliver increasing amounts of electric shock to another person. Despite the "victim's" anguished cries and pleas for mercy, the experimenter urged the subject to keep increasing the voltage all the way up to 450 volts. The dial in front of the subject contained 30 voltage levels, from 15 to 450 volts, and was printed with such warnings as "Danger" and "Severe Shock." The subject had witnessed the "victim" being strapped into the electric chair and could clearly hear the "victim's" cries.

Milgram established his baseline. Fully 65 percent of his subjects were willing to administer the maximum 450 volts; that is, almost two-thirds of the subjects were willing to risk killing a fellow subject.

Who were these subjects? Where and when was this experiment conducted? Were these Gestapo agents being trained in some sadistic Nazi laboratory during the 1930s? In fact, these subjects were ordinary American citizens, from 20 to 50 years of age, from all walks of life, and living in New Haven, Connecticut. The study was done at Yale University during the 1960s. The subjects were unaware that the "victim" did not really get shocked: The wires connecting the control panel to the electric chair did not really carry any electricity, and the victim was really an ally of the experimenter. Presumably, the subjects thought the shocks were effective and were nevertheless willing to deliver the shocks as the experimenter instructed.

The second phase of Milgram's study was to see what would happen in a group situation. How would subjects react if they were placed in the same situation with two other subjects who refused to follow the experimenter's commands? The results were dramatic. Under the condition of group pressure, only 10 percent of the subjects still pushed the lever all the way to 450 volts. The majority of the subjects refused to go beyond the halfway point. In this case, then, group pressure liberated the individual from the experimenter's authoritarian control and had a positive effect.

(a)

(b)

(c)

(d)

(e)

Asch found, in studying conformity, that some subjects are able to maintain independent judgment throughout. Most, however, are unable to do so and yield to group pressure on at least one trial. (a) The experimenter gives instructions. (b) The critical subject, seated in the middle, listens to the instructions. (c) He makes his first judgment that disagrees with the consensus. (d) He leans forward as the next set of lines appears. (e) He feels conflict as he listens to new, incorrect peer judgments.

Conformity and group pressure may often be beneficial to the individual. Milgram's study suggests that they may help a person act in a more humane and less destructive manner.

Milgram stressed the fact that the aggressive nature of humans can be fairly easily displayed when the external pressures are perceived as demanding, or allowing for, a hostile expression. This explanation has been challenged, however, on the grounds that a person who is confronted by a seemingly professional scientist wearing the obligatory white coat and situated on the hallowed grounds of Yale Uni-

versity has to assume that the situation is either really safe or that the medical results gained from the study are going to be worth the apparent suffering of a few individuals. The subject, therefore, is in conflict over the contradictory nature of the situation, a trusted hall of science versus an open challenge to an authoritative power figure (Nissani, 1990).

Locus of control   Despite the insistent demands of group pressure, people differ in how readily they yield to the seductive lure of conformity. Studies have shown that a person who has a low self-concept, who is unsure of his or her private beliefs, and who is fearful of being perceived as different is the very person who is most likely to conform (Santee & Maslach, 1982).

Psychologists have categorized people on the basis of whether their **locus of control** is internal or external. Persons who have been identified as having an *internal* locus of control typically view themselves as being personally in control of their actions and in charge of their own destinies. Persons measured as having an *external* locus of control, however, feel that they are largely at the mercy of environmental circumstances (Kobasa, 1982). It follows, then, that the individual who is externally controlled is more easily swayed by group pressures, whereas the internally controlled person is more apt to stand up to the group's demands and be more *flexible under conditions of stress* (Parkes, 1984).

Persons are more apt to develop an internal locus of control in areas in which they excel. Thus, locus of control and achievement typically go hand in hand, and the locus of control may change as a function of the general area of activity in which the child is involved (Weiner, 1980). The outstanding athlete may have a strong internal locus of control on the football field and exhibit poise and confidence while there but, because of past academic problems, develop an external locus of control in the classroom and appear to be timid and insecure. Sometimes a person reacts in a particular manner in one type of situation, but in another context seems like a different person with a different personality. Typically, the child who develops a strong sense of internal control has greater ego strength, greater feelings of personal competence, and is less likely to go along with the crowd.

As we have seen, pressures for conformity are pervasive in our society, and even the internally controlled person is not totally immune. In fact, the power of the group is enhanced even further when that group is composed of persons we tend to like (Marks & Miller, 1985).

SOCIALIZATION

Conformity is a key issue in social psychology because it is a driving power of socialization. **Socialization** is the process of learning society's rules and customs and is accomplished through pressures to conform. The newborn infant—at best an innocent little hedonist and at worst a savage bundle of Freudian instincts—is slowly transformed into a conforming member of society. The individual slowly but surely gives up personal independence as socialization continues, learning how and when to eat, where and when to urinate and defecate, how to interact with other people, and so on. Finally, the

Socialization is the process of learning society's rules and customs. True nonconformists are rare.

mature adult emerges who has learned these lessons so well that he or she conforms with the instinctive precision of a homing pigeon.

Are there any nonconformists? There are only a few, and most of them are either in prison or in a psychiatric hospital. For example, you might think that members of a nudist colony are nonconformists, and yet they are all conforming to their own group norm. The only nonconformist in a nudist camp would be the person who is fully dressed. Or you might assume that members of a commune are nonconformists, and yet they are conforming as rigidly to their norms as middle-aged Rotarians are to theirs.

The so-called generation gap may be essentially a difference in group norms. Both groups may be marching in unison but to different drummers. Sociologists have been insisting that the norms of today's young people are in such conflict with those of the "Baby-Boomer" generation that American society is moving toward genuine cultural conflict. Yet some studies are now showing that the generations have more in common than conventional wisdom has been proclaiming (Ladd, 1995). Even though today's youths are buying different CDs, clothes, and magazines, they do not appear to be buying into value systems fundamentally different from those of their parents.

Who is the drummer in the classroom? Who sets the beat for the in-unison march of classroom members? To a large extent, it is the norms of society at large. After all, most students and teachers have been socialized in a common culture. The way they dress, the ideas they consider important, the way they interact, the way they express feelings are all determined by the core culture. The fact that most students feel a sense of competition is in large part culturally determined and already part of their characters before they ever set foot in the classroom. The fact that they are in the classroom at all, pursuing an educational goal, is a cultural dictate. But this doesn't explain it all, for each classroom has its own distinct set of norms that exists within the larger context of society's norms. The teacher contributes much of the tone, but so does every single member of the class. The crucial ingredient in the formation of a norm, and thus conformity, is interaction among group members. Interactions produce group norms, which then set the limits within which further interactions can take place. Status and role relationships begin to emerge, and further demands and expectancies are set for each individual's behavior. Who sets the beat? The classroom, within the context of the larger social situation, sets its own beat, and every single member of the class participates in the process.

Cognitive Dissonance

Another aspect of socialization has been described by Leon Festinger. According to Festinger, people strive to achieve a state of equilibrium among their various attitudes (or learned predispositions to persons, situations, or things) and behaviors (Festinger, 1957). This is because we prefer consistency, or consonance, to inconsistency, or dissonance. Therefore, whenever we have a thought that is not consistent with our behavior, we experience **cognitive dissonance** and are motivated to restore the equilibrium. To avoid self-contradiction, we can either change our thinking so that it conforms to our behavior or change our behavior so that it conforms to our thinking. For example, someone who enjoys smoking and who hears that smoking is a health hazard can either conclude that the evidence linking smoking with disease is flimsy or stop smoking. One smoker, it has been said, became so nervous after reading the evidence linking smoking with cancer that he gave up reading.

The point is that whenever our thoughts and deeds conflict, we are driven to reduce the anxiety-provoking dissonance. Teachers should be alerted to the possible consequences of cognitive dissonance when it occurs in the classroom. The desire for consonance operates within the individual and within the group. The chances against finding a classroom in which all 30 pupils and the teacher have totally compatible interests, attitudes, and values are so great that it is safe to say that dissonance is inevitable. The important thing is the way that dissonance is resolved. If the teacher decides to always "fight and never switch," if the pupils have to do all the changing, then the reduction of dissonance in the classroom will be more apparent than real. We will see in Chapter 19 that the way in which a teacher handles pupil discipline will help define the educational atmosphere of the class. The imposition of too strict a set of sanctions may reduce dissonance, but the resulting compliance is likely to be begrudging at best. Pupil discipline is just one instance of the general problem of the incongruity between the individual and the group.

Attribution Theory

Many years ago, the social psychologist Fritz Heider introduced the term *attribution* to refer to the explanations people give for their own or another person's actions or beliefs (Heider, 1958). When the attribution is based on an internal factor it is called a *dispositional* attribution, and when it is based on ex-

SPOTLIGHT ON LEARNING DISABILITIES

*Beyond the School Day and the Social Dilemma of Nonconformity**

Learning-disabled (LD) children, as we saw in Chapter 11, may experience deficits in a broad range of measurable skills, such as attention span, memory, motor control, perception, emotional control, and especially social skills. A teacher may report that a child who has perceptual deficits has difficulty copying from the board, organizing written work, and/or writing neatly, especially on or between the lines. However, these perceptual deficits also reveal themselves in areas far beyond the academic setting. The child who has deficits in depth perception, for example, is the child who in all innocence hugs everyone just a bit too tightly, or is just a little too rough when playing with the baby, or seems to tip over the milk at virtually every meal. If a child cannot judge the distance between himself and the person he is talking to, he will tend to get too close to another child's face and then, to make matters worse, talk too loudly. It is not long before the other children begin to avoid this child because they lose patience with his or her clumsiness or intrusive style. Because of these inappropriate social skills, learning-disabled children are frequently labeled "nerds" or "jerks" by their peers and siblings and thus become rejected by their peer groups. As LD children become ever more isolated from meaningful interactions with age-mates, they have fewer chances to practice social skills, and the cycle of isolation becomes increasingly difficult to break.

If a learning-disabled child has a short attention span, which is certainly common, teachers will report that the child is not attending to instructions and parents complain that their child never listens to directions. Other children will say that the child with the short attention span is no fun to play with because he or she always leaves the game before it's finished. These LD children can in fact be very poor listeners; they tend to become restless and walk away when people are talking to them, often in midsentence. Playmates are simply not tolerant of the child who leaves games or conversations before they are finished. The LD child becomes an *unwitting nonconformist* and eventually is excluded from the peer group and is no longer asked to play games at all.

If the child also has a language-based learning disability, there will almost certainly be an academic difficulty in reading and writing. But the problem doesn't stop there. A language-based learning disability also affects the learning-disabled child *socially* because such a child does not always understand the language and jargon of the peer group. These are the children who just never "get" the jokes or puns and as a result are perceived as being humorless or even stupid. The youngster who appears to be "not much fun to play with" is pressured by peers to leave the group. As a result, the rejected child is no longer exposed to age-appropriate humor, and the development of both language and social skills is further delayed.

Parents of an LD child are particularly and painfully aware of the child's social difficulties. Parenting the LD child presents challenges not even dreamed of by other parents. To further compound the problem, the difficulties experienced by the learning-disabled child come to weigh heavily upon all the family members. Parents consistently report feeling frustrated, anxious, and sometimes even helpless in dealing with their LD child. And brothers and sisters also report suffering from and becoming embarrassed by the social blunders of their LD sibling. Thus, learning disabilities extend far beyond the school day and involve the LD child's whole life. Tragically, the untreated learning disability may then become a life disability.

---

* This Spotlight was especially prepared for this volume by Dr. Nancy Hayes, Educational Psychologist and School Consultant, Longmeadow, Massachusetts.

---

ternal factors it is called a *situational* attribution. For example, if a teacher attributes a child's poor performance on a test to basic laziness or general stupidity, that would be a dispositional attribution. If, however, the teacher views the poor performance as resulting from the child's temporarily feeling ill or having had a fistfight on the way to school, that would be a situational attribution. According to **at-**

tribution theory, when people attempt to explain another person's actions, they tend to overestimate dispositional factors and to underestimate situational factors (Reeder, 1982). This is called the *fundamental attribution error.* Notice that this occurs mainly when someone is explaining another person's behavior. For example, a teacher who has an unruly child in class may explain the behavior in terms of the child's basic aggressiveness. When explaining our own behavior, however, we are far more likely to use a situational attribution. Thus, we are more likely to interpret another person's actions on the basis of the latter's inherent personal traits, whereas we see our own actions as logically fitting the reality demands of the situation. During a pupil-teacher conference, for example, the teacher might patiently listen to the pupil's list of situational reasons for failing the math quiz, but may privately view them as alibis for the pupil's inherent laziness. It has even been found that some members of minority groups make an effort to protect self-esteem by always attributing negative feedback to prejudice or discrimination, when in fact the negative consequences may at times be deserved (Vivian and Berkowitz, 1992).

Stereotypes are reinforced by erroneous assumptions of outgroup homogeneity and the use of illusory correlations as explanations of outgroup behavior (Oakes et al., 1994). Research also suggests that students who really begin to believe that their academic failures are due to dispositional factors are apt to lose motivation and stop trying altogether. If, however, the students become convinced that their failures are due more to transitory situational factors, academic motivation may increase (Wilson & Linville, 1982).

The fundamental attribution error is more likely to occur when the behavior in question is perceived as negative, such as rudeness, disruptiveness, or academic failure. When a student performs brilliantly, say on a standardized test, then the teacher is more willing to attribute this victory to a situational factor—in this case the teacher's own elegant instructional style.

Children who rarely experience success in the classroom, for example the learning-disabled, often attribute their failures to dispositional factors and eventually can be heard making statements like "I am too dumb to learn" (Bryan & Bryan, 1986). Such children need to be taught coping strategies for dealing with their failures.

Finally, in assigning reasons for another's behavior, two other variables must be included—how well liked the other individual is and how personally attractive. Thus, for example, when you dislike some-

one, your list of dispositional attributes will be extremely negative, and may include terms such as *manipulative, greedy, stupid, hostile.* When you're in love with the individual, your list will overflow with terms expressing noble and saintly qualities (Harvey & Weary, 1984).

AGGRESSION

Social psychologists have long been interested in the phenomenon of aggression. Human society is obviously fraught with violence. The United States has the dubious distinction of leading the world in rates of homicide, rape, assault, and robbery.

Guns and Society

In terms of injury-related deaths, homicide is now the second leading cause of death among adolescents, regardless of ethnic or racial grouping (Rodriguez, 1990). And among blacks, male adolescents are now more likely to die from gunshot wounds than from *any other cause* (Fingerhut et al., 1992). In fact, the number of homicides among young black males is far higher than among young white males or among any other ethnic group. The rate for young black males is 10 times higher than for white males of the same age, and twice as high as the rate for young black females (NCHS, 1992). We cannot hope to comprehend these statistics without considering the social interactions and social systems in which they are embedded. At least part of the problem might be solved given some changes in society's social, economic, and political systems (Henggeler, 1989). As another example, family violence is certainly a social issue, especially violence against women, who often become so trapped in dysfunctional marriages that they resort to killing or maiming the men they cannot leave—a bizarre outcome for those segments of our society that still view women as possessions (Walker, 1989).

The gruesome statistics on firearm deaths in the United States are compelling. In just one year during the mid-1990s, 38,317 Americans were killed by firearms in assorted homicides, suicides, and accidents (Herbert, 1994). To dramatize this, visualize a macabre scene in which a dead body was placed in every seat (bleachers, grandstand, box seats, luxury boxes, dugouts) in Fenway Park, Boston, and there would still be over 3,000 bodies outside waiting to be accommodated. During that same year handguns were used in the murders of 13 in Australia, 33 in Britain, 36 in Sweden, 97 in Switzerland, 128 in

Canada, and 60 in Japan (ibid.). Gunshot wounds are now the leading cause of death for both black and white teenage boys in the United States.

Researchers Richard Lore and Lori Schultz (1993) firmly believe that more stringent gun controls would reduce the high homicide rate. In 1990, 60 percent of all murders were committed with firearms, and all but 10 percent of those were with handguns (U.S. Department of Justice, 1991). The homicide results were as follows: firearms, 60 percent; knives and blunt instruments, 30 percent; hands, fists, and feet, 5 percent. A number of studies over the years have shown that the more physically removed the perpetrator can remain, the easier it is to kill someone. For example, it is less personally horrifying to drop bombs on civilian targets from 30,000 feet than to see the victims personally. And it's easier to shoot someone from a distance than to kill that person with a knife. Ethologists speculate that humans have inborn mechanisms for controlling violence and that we must learn more about the neural mechanisms that trigger or inhibit aggressive behavior, and how these mechanisms might be altered under changing environmental situations (Karli, 1991). Are the neural responses the same or different under differing conditions, and at different ages? And at what point does normal aggressive behavior cross the social line and become pathological?

Over 3,000 children are murdered by their parents or caretakers every year in the United States, and even more common are the tiny broken bodies resulting from the *battered child syndrome*. As every football, hockey, and boxing fan knows, violence also has crowd appeal. And "hit 'em again harder" apparently is not reserved for the sports arena. On September 23, 1967, at a large southwestern university, when a depressed student crawled to the edge of a dormitory roof and threatened suicide, thousands of students stood below and chanted in unison, "Jump! Jump! Jump!" As for major conflicts, the world has rarely seen a day since the beginning of recorded history when there wasn't a full-scale war going on somewhere on the globe. These facts seem to argue that aggression is an inevitable by-product of people getting together in groups.

Theories of Aggression

Psychology has generated four basic positions regarding the issue of aggression:

The Freudian According to Sigmund Freud, aggression is built into the organism and is as basic to human behavior as sexuality. The urge to violence is a result of pressure from our innate and irrational id instinct. The trouble with the Freudian hypothesis is that, by explaining so much, it may in fact not explain anything. To say that people are aggressive because they have a built-in aggressive instinct smacks of circular reasoning. This was referred to in Chapter 2 as the nominal fallacy.

The ethological Konrad Lorenz and other ethologists view aggression as a constant potential in virtually all organisms. If the proper releaser occurs, the potential for aggression will quickly be translated into action. For example, the male stickleback fish attacks whenever stimulated by the color red. Other ethologists have even found that among fish the attacking behavior itself has a profound effect on the physiology of the fish, especially its brain. In aggressive males, brain cells in the hypothalamus that control mating behavior have been found to be six to eight times larger than among more passive male fish. Further, these brain cells will change in size as a result of environmental clashes. For example, when an aggressive male is defeated in battle, these neurons in the hypothalamus begin to shrink, followed by a similar shrinking of the testes, and eventually the loss of any desire to either mate or fight (Bond et al., 1991).

As for humans, Lorenz feels that aggression actually has survival value for the species. Since population density often outruns available food supplies, aggression acts both to reduce the size of the population and to spread the remaining population over a larger area (Lorenz, 1966). Another ethologist, Robert Ardrey, suggests that aggression results from a fundamental territorial need. Ardrey says that all organisms have an innate drive to own, defend, and gain territorial areas (Ardrey, 1966). The ethological explanation runs the risk of possibly having ventured beyond the actual observed data. Since Lorenz has based his theory on observations of lower organisms, more research is needed before extrapolation to the human level can become convincing.

Frustration-aggression Led by Neil Miller and John Dollard, a group of Yale psychologists in the late 1930s introduced the now famous **frustration-aggression hypothesis** (Dollard et al., 1939). Aggression was explained as the result of being frustrated, or of having one's goals blocked. Said Miller, "The occurrence of aggression always presupposes frustration" (Miller, 1941). In many instances the Miller-Dollard hypothesis is obviously valid. We have all seen people become angry, sometimes to the point of irrationality, over having a goal blocked: An individual already late for an important appointment becomes furious when the car won't start; a teenage boy gets into a fistfight on the way home from school after having been dropped from the varsity basketball team.

One psychologist has identified five important sources of frustration in modern life, frustrations that in some cases can become persistent sources of irritation (Morris, 1990):

1. *Delay:* As in the case mentioned above of the person made late for a meeting because the car wouldn't start

2. *Failure:* As in the case of the young man cut from the basketball team or a high school student being rejected for admission to a preferred college

3. *Lack of resources:* As when a lack of finances prevents the purchase of some dearly sought item

4. *Losses:* As when a close friend moves to a far-off city or an affair of the heart is abruptly ended

5. *Discrimination:* As when a society prevents some of its citizens from full participation in its resources on account of race or gender

The frustration-aggression hypothesis, however, has some major drawbacks as an explanatory model. Some people react to frustration not with overt aggression but merely by sitting quietly and seething inwardly. Another person may respond to goal blockage by regressing, that is, acting in a less mature fashion. Also, there are countless examples of aggressive behaviors that are not triggered by frustration. Being annoyed or attacked by another person often results in aggression aimed at the source of the annoyance. A student was playing poker in the dorm when, without provocation, another student moved quietly behind his chair and playfully poured beer on his head. Five seconds and two punches later the "playful pourer" was on his back and nursing a bruised eye and jaw.

For these and other reasons, the original frustration-aggression hypothesis has been revised, most recently by Leonard Berkowitz (1983). Berkowitz says that frustration may produce a range of emotions from disappointment and depression to anger. Although anger may lead to aggression, other emotions generated by frustration usually do not. Also, how someone responds to frustration is in large measure a direct function of how the person handled frustration in the past. In summary, Berkowitz says, "anger is only one of the possible emotional responses to frustration, and aggression is one of the possible behavioral responses."

"This will teach you not to hit people."

Social learning or modeling   As we noted in Chapter 10, Albert Bandura's social learning theory has been used to explain aggressive behavior. Children who watched an adult model punch and kick a large Bobo doll themselves punched and kicked the doll when they later got the chance. In this instance, the children were imitating the adult's aggressive behavior. The children had not been provoked, annoyed, or frustrated, and yet because of modeling they exhibited aggressive responses. It has also been shown that if children watch a film of an aggressive adult model, they, too, will imitate the aggressive behavior (Bandura et al., 1963).

That social learning is at least one of the factors involved in the development of aggressive behavior seems now to be in little doubt. Many studies have reported that children who exhibit high levels of overt aggressive behavior typically have parents who use physical punishment. In fact, the parents of aggressive children are more apt to use punishment than reward when attempting to shape their children's general behavior. That this tends to be a potent influence is shown by the fact that the level of a boy's aggressiveness is usually formed by about the age of eight (even before the onset of puberty) (Eron, 1982).

It seems clear that children can and do learn aggressive responses by watching the aggressive behavior of parents and other adults. It is also true that children may learn to modify their aggressive responses by observing the consequences others have earned for their aggression (Slife & Ryschlak, 1982). For example, children are not so quick to imitate adult aggression when they also witness the adult being punished for that behavior.

Aggression in the Classroom

Teachers must expect that there will be an occasional scuffle in the schoolyard and even in the classroom itself. A few overt manifestations of aggression should not cause undue alarm. However, teachers should not just rationalize away every display of fisticuffs with a "boys-will-be-boys" attitude. There are some children who repeatedly express themselves with their fists, and other children who are repeatedly selected as the targets of these fists. In both cases, oddly enough, the reasons may be similar. Problems at home, such as an impending divorce or severe financial strain, have often been found to be precursors of childhood aggression. These children often blame themselves for the family difficulties, and then either beat up other children or in some cases offer themselves as victims. In the latter case, the child might feel so deserving of punishment that he sets himself up to be beaten as a cry for attention and help. We must not forget, however, that part of the aggressive syndrome, especially among young boys, may be due to societal pressures. Television and movies often project the view that the only honorable way to settle an argument is to resort to violence. Children also may get this message from their parents, who, through words or actions, communicate the clear signal that to be respected you have to punch a few faces. Children who are consistently violent, however, must be taken seriously. The children who are always in fights are often found to be serious lawbreakers in adolescence and early adulthood. In fact, the vast majority of adolescents who are in repeated trouble with the law have a long history of violent behavior, *many as far back as kindergarten.*

Controlling Violence in the Schools

As stated previously, Lore and Schultz (1993) contend that the ability to control violence has been grossly underestimated. In fact, they believe that humans are "exquisitely sensitive" to control by the social environment. "Humans are easily capable of inhibiting their use of violence in predictable ways in response to seemingly minor changes in their physical and social environment" (p. 24). In one large-scale study, Dan Olweus (1991) found that 10 percent of all students in grades one through nine report having been *frequent* victims of aggression while in school, and that this regular bullying is produced by only 8 percent of the students. To counter this problem, Olweus implemented a special program among teachers, school administrators, and parents, specifying the extent of the problem and also teaching a variety of educational techniques for handling the problem. The program consisted of (1) providing printed information to both students and their parents describing what is known of bully-victim relationships, (2) presenting a 25-minute video depicting episodes in the lives of bullies and victims, and (3) administering a questionnaire to be completed anonymously by all students. The questionnaire was both a measuring instrument and a form of sensitizing the students to the problem. The program also involved the development of *clear rules by the school,* and, importantly, *rapid enforcement of those rules* through the consistent use of teacher sanctions—not including physical punishment. Finally, the school provided support and even protection for the victims. Over the next two years, incidents of school violence decreased by 50 percent; a side benefit was a sharp reduction in theft, vandalism, and truancy, as well as a concomitant increase in positive attitudes toward school. Perhaps the most important aspect of this study was the sharp reduction in aggressive behavior that resulted from a rather limited intrusion on the life of the school. It did not demand a complete restructuring of the school system or a thorough revamping of the home environment. It centered on (1) making persons aware of the problem; (2) achieving cooperation among parents, teachers, and administrators; and (3) enforcing the school's rules. The enforcement aspect provided a social control that worked to prevent initial aggressiveness and concomitant behavioral contagion.

The School Bully: What Makes Him Tick?

Dan Olweus has challenged several of the most popular beliefs about the so-called school bully. For example, Olweus has found that in general the bullies are not necessarily poor academic achievers who are using their aggressiveness as a reaction to frustrations brought about by school failure. Nor are they especially insecure. As a group, they are not anxiety-ridden waifs hiding under a tough exterior. In fact, the bullies scored at least in the average range on a number of anxiety measures as well as on measures of self-esteem. A portrait of the *victims,* however, revealed the pattern so often thought to be the hallmark of the bully, that is, high levels of anxiety and low levels of self-esteem. Olweus characterized the typical victim as having an anxious personality pattern combined with physical weakness. He found a large statistical difference between the bullies and the victims in terms of physical strength: the bullies were found to be physically stronger than average and also much stronger than their victims.

Aggression and the Mass Media

Social psychologists, like most other Americans, have expressed concern about whether the portrayal of violence in movies and on TV encourages aggressive acts in viewers. This question is especially important with regard to TV, since most children are avid television viewers. One survey report indicates that the average 16-year-old has spent more hours of his or her young life in front of the TV than in class. Some of the studies done in this area have shown a relationship, especially among boys, between watching violence on television and the acting out of aggression. In the typical study a group of boys are asked to indicate which TV shows they watch, and these results are then correlated with the peer group's evaluation of each boy's overt aggressiveness. Significant relationships have been discovered; that is, boys who report watching the most TV violence are also the ones rated most aggressive by their peers (Eron, 1982). As we pointed out in Chapter 15, such studies are difficult to evaluate in terms of cause and effect. Does the violence on TV cause the boys to be aggressive, or does aggressiveness in the boys cause them to select violent TV shows? Or are some boys aggressive by nature, and because of this do they act out their aggression more and do they also choose to watch more aggressive TV shows?

Milgram attempted an experimental evaluation of this problem by using a large portion of the United States as his laboratory. Milgram talked CBS into creating two versions of a popular TV program, one version having far more aggressive cues than the other. Milgram was unable to detect any difference in the rates of violence among the cities on the basis of whether they received the aggressive or the nonaggressive programs, even though the cities were equated for prior levels of violent crimes (Milgram & Shotland, 1973).

One study attempted to subject this problem to controlled, experimental analysis by actually manipulating the TV fare (as an independent variable)

(Feshback & Singer, 1970). The subjects, again all boys, were enrolled in private boarding schools or state residential schools. By random assignment, the boys were required to watch either violent or nonviolent shows. Both before and after six weeks of this controlled-viewing regimen, the boys were measured for both overt and covert aggressiveness. Overt aggressiveness was determined by a supervisor's daily tally of each boy's aggressive incidents. Covert aggressiveness was measured by projective personality testing.

The results showed that the boys who watched the violent TV shows expressed more covert or fantasy aggression as measured by the Thematic Apperception Test. The boys who watched the nonviolent shows, however, were involved in twice as many fistfights and exhibited far more overt verbal aggression. The results suggest that TV violence may have a cathartic effect on boys, rechanneling their hostility so as to inhibit overt aggression. The authors of the study caution, however, that watching real-life violence on newscasts may increase rather than decrease the expression of aggressive responses in viewers. They say that "violence presented in the form of fiction is much less likely to reinforce, stimulate, or elicit aggressive responses than violence in the form of a news event" (Feshback, 1969). Thus, whereas TV's coverage of a violent news story may increase viewer aggression, fictitious violence may possibly even inhibit overt viewer aggression. This is obviously a very difficult area to research. As we have seen, the interpretations of the results in this area vary widely.

It is not clear from any of these studies whether TV violence causes behavioral aggressive or whether children who are more overtly aggressive choose to watch the more violent TV programs. The NIMH report did point out that young boys watch more violent TV programs than do young girls. It is also known that young boys are more overtly aggressive than young girls.

Some researchers are now suggesting that exposure to media violence of any sort does cause a small to moderate increase in aggressiveness among young boys, even among those not necessarily prone to aggressiveness (Wood et al., 1991).

For those who are "fantasy prone," TV may act in a more forceful and direct manner. Some children may spend up to half their waking time in active daydreaming, living out their wishes in a make-believe world of their own creation. These "fantasy-prone" persons make up about 5 percent of the population. For this group, TV may be even more realistic and influential than it is among the rest of the population. Studies have shown that TV stimulates spontaneous daydreaming but may also act to diminish a child's creative and more purposeful fantasies (Valkenburg & van der Voort, 1994).

One cannot casually dismiss the possibly profound effects that television has on viewer behavior. Advertisers obviously believe that television affects behavior, and they back up their belief by spending millions of dollars for commercials.

Nature or Nurture?

Like the great intelligence debate, the question of whether aggression is primarily innate or learned has also stirred controversy among psychologists. The nature theorists see humans as instinctively violent, destined by their genes to be aggressive. The nurture position is that humans, being products of environmental stimulation, can be shaped into peaceful and loving beings. Indeed, the four positions on aggression just outlined can be categorized according to this issue; both the Freudian and ethological positions rest on the assumption that aggression is largely inherited; both the frustration-aggression and social learning explanations view aggression as basically a product of the environment.

The genetic argument   As pointed out in Chapter 3, white mice have been selectively bred for aggressiveness. In one study, a large group of mice was separated on the basis of the amount of aggressiveness displayed. The most aggressive and least aggressive mice were then selectively bred, and after seven generations two nonoverlapping groups were identified. That is, the least aggressive of the aggressive strain were more aggressive than the most aggressive of the nonaggressive strain (Lagerspetz, 1964).

At the human level, a number of studies have compared monozygotic (MZ), or identical, twins with dizygotic (DZ), or fraternal, twins on the criterion of aggression. Since MZ twins result from a single fertilized egg, they have identical genetic endowments. DZ twins derive from separate eggs fertilized at the same time and are thus no more alike genetically than other siblings. Regarding crimes of violence, the concordance rate (the percentage of cotwins having the trait) was significantly higher for MZ than for DZ twins (Rosenthal, 1970).

The environmental argument   Psychologists holding the environmental view see aggression as resulting from the way society reinforces and punishes its members' attitudes and behavior. The environmentalists state that the attitudes of the majority of people in each society determine whether or not

violence will be tolerated. Cultures are cited in which aggression is apparently almost nonexistent, and other cultures have been found in which hostility is a major characteristic. In short, the environmentalists argue that aggression is determined by group norms and the frustrations of day-to-day living.

Is there an answer?   As is the case with so many areas in psychology, not all the answers are in on the issue of human aggression. It is known, however, that behavior is caused by many factors, and perhaps the safest prediction is that aggression will be found to result from heredity interacting with environment interacting with time. The genetic component in aggression seems to be fairly well established. Also, the built-in aggressive tendencies emerge at different times through maturation, depending on individual differences, gender, and species. Just as certainly, since aggression can be expressed in so many ways and in so many different situations, there is obviously a very large learning component to it. Harry Harlow comments:

> There is little disagreement among comparative psychologists that aggression is part of the biological heritage of primates. However, some social psychologists who limit their studies to the human animal still believe that aggression is basically a learned behavior, and that the differences which occur between the sexes or among individuals within their sex group are accountable solely on the basis of experience. No doubt the late appearance of aggression in the developmental sequence has led some observers to underestimate its biological basis (Harlow et al., 1971).

Finally, we cannot ignore the role of drug use in understanding some of the root causes of aggression, especially among those prone to hostility. A study of a large number of delinquent youths found that drug use is a reliable predictor of later violent behavior (Martin & Hoffman, 1990).

STATUS AND ROLE

If you met someone for the first time and she suddenly put her hand into your mouth, you might be pretty startled. Or, suppose a perfect stranger told you to take off all your clothes. Your reaction might be hard to predict. Yet all of us have been in situations like these and have hardly blinked. When the individual putting her hand into your mouth is a dentist, or the stranger telling you to undress is a

SPOTLIGHT ON EXPECTATIONS AND "LOOKS"

Never Judge a Book by Its Cover

It has long been assumed that some individuals tend to get by on their looks. That is, the individual's appearance, his or her own physical stimulus value, seems to influence the kinds of expectations and treatments provided by other people. Much research evidence suggests that this is indeed the case. In one study, now a classic, attractive individuals were judged to possess more positive personality traits, to hold more prestigious occupations, and to have more potential for future success than were unattractive people.[a] This stereotype about physical attractiveness apparently begins early in life, at least by the time the child reaches kindergarten.[b] By the time children are five years old they can differentiate between handsome and homely classmates. Attractive first-graders are thought by their peers to be more independent and better-liked.

Asked whom they would pick as someone who "scares you" or as someone who's "afraid of lots of things," children generally select unattractive peers. Studies have also shown that during the elementary and adolescent years, perceptions of physical appearance and social acceptance correlate strongly with a child's feeling of self-worth.[c]

But this type of bias is not just a childish, schoolroom phenomenon. Studies have consistently shown that employers pay unattractive people less money, bar or restaurant patrons offer smaller tips to unattractive waiters, jurors tend to find unattractive witnesses less believable, and voters tend to think that unattractive candidates for public office are less worthy of being elected.[d] A study of sexual harassment cases found that guilty verdicts are significantly more

likely if the defendant (in this study the male) is unattractive and the female plaintiff is highly attractive.[e] "Even in the anti-glamor, egalitarian feminist movement, leader Betty Freidan says that her rival, Gloria Steinem, jumped ahead of her because of her looks."[f] Gloria Steinem, however, had underestimated her physical attractiveness and remained seemingly unaware of her good looks; for years she felt that she was really an ugly duckling. It wasn't until she increased her own inner feelings of self-esteem that she finally realized that she was also a beautiful woman on the outside.[g]

This relationship between self-esteem and attractiveness can be reciprocal, since the research shows that when people overestimate their physical attractiveness (as opposed to underestimating it, as Steinem had), they also tend to

---

physician, the situation has a context in which the behavior is expected.

Social psychologists use the terms **status** and **role** to describe expected behavior of this type. Status is the position we occupy in society's prestige hierarchy. Role is the behavior that is expected of us because of the particular status we have. Conformity is essential to status and role because status gives us an obligation to behave (act out the role) in the way society expects us to behave (conform to society's expectations). For example, our society expects far different behavior from a used-car salesman than from a college president. People might smile if the used-car salesman created a drunken scene in public, but they would be severely disapproving if the college president did the very same thing. Our behavior is expected to conform to society's norms for our position in life. If it does not conform to these expectations, society has ways of exerting great pressure to bring us back into line.

Because of the complicated nature of our society today, most people find themselves occupying different status positions at the same time. A man may have a job as a clerk in a shop and spend each day quietly taking orders, while at night he issues directives with an authoritative flourish in his capacity as Boy Scout executive. In each case his role conforms to his status. A given status often has multiple roles. A woman may have a number of status positions and roles, as mother, clubwoman, wife, and corporate executive. The variety of roles may create conflict and a feeling of frustration and despair if she feels that she cannot carry out all her roles—that, for example, she can't continue to work and also fulfill the role of a good mother. Yet if she doesn't work, she may feel frustrated and perhaps even guilty over the fact that she isn't living up to her full potential as a woman.

It is crucial to understand role behavior in order to understand human behavior. People tend to behave

have higher levels of self-esteem.[h] This phenomenon can be especially damaging to the teenager who is making the transition from school to the workplace. Research shows that overweight girls and short boys tend to earn significantly less money after joining the labor force than do their more attractive age-mates.[i] Some researchers have suggested that this relationship between obesity in girls and their later lack of earning power is as much a result of socioeconomic status as it is of attractiveness per se (since girls of low socioeconomic status have been found to be more obese than their wealthier peers). Sargent and Blanchflower suggest, however, an alternate view—that the obesity itself may be one of the determining factors of social class among women. For example, women who marry men of higher education

and more earning power have been found to be significantly thinner than women who marry men of less education and earning power. Apparently it's all over for the fat lady—even before she sings.

Although we've all been warned not to judge a book by its cover, it is all too easy to ignore that sage advice. What this means to the teacher should be obvious: the attractive and docile child should not be overrewarded with high grades and praise—"looks" should not be confused with achievement.

---

a   Dion, K., Berscheid, E., & Walster, E. (1972).What is beautiful is good? *Journal of Personality and Social Psychology, 24,* 285–290.
b   Berscheid, E., & Walster, E. (1972). Beauty and the best. *Psychology Today, 5,* 42–46.
c   Wigfield, A., & Karpathian, M. (1991). Who am I and what can I do? Children's self-concepts and motivation in achievement situations. *Educational Psychologist, 26,* 223–261.
d   Umberson, D., & Hughes, M. (1987). The impact of physical attractiveness on achievement and psychological well-being. *Social Psychology Quarterly, 50,* 227–236.
e   Castellow, W. A., Wuensch, K. L., & Moore, C. H. (1990). Effects of physical attractiveness of the plaintiff and defendant in sexual harassment judgments. *Journal of Social Behavior and Personality, 5,* 547–562.
f   Grieve, F. (1987, February 19). For ugly people a hard cold world. *Boston Globe,* 67–68.
g   Steinem, G. (1992). *Revolution from within: A look of self-esteem.* New York: Little, Brown.
h   Gurman, E. B., & Balban, M. (1990). Self-evaluation of physical attractiveness as a function of self-esteem and defensiveness. *Journal of Social Behavior and Personality 5,* 575–580.
i   Sargent, J. D., & Blanchflower, D. G. (1994). Obesity and stature in adolescence and earnings in young adulthood. *Archives of Pediatrics and Adolescent Medicine, 148,* 681–687.

---

in the way society (as embodied by the people around them) treats them.

The Influence of Expectations

Expectations and personality

Even the developing child's basic personality structure is largely shaped by social expectations, especially those of the parents. Much of what a child begins to expect of himself or herself develops from the child's attempts to gain parental approval and to live up to parental expectations. According to personality theorists Joseph Perez and Alvin Cohen, "For the developing self, 'Mom and Dad are me'" (Perez & Cohen, 1969).

One of the contributing factors in adolescent rebellion is the lack of consistency with which society treats these nonchildren-nonadults. When adolescents are treated like children, they tend to respond like children, no matter how many speeches they hear about their failure to assume responsibility or act maturely. The parents' words are often drowned out by the volume of their own contradictory behavior. Physically attractive children are apt to regard themselves as good, smart, and lovable because that's the way they are typically treated by others. Unattractive children tend to have lower self-esteem because they have more often been treated as unlovable and perhaps even bad (Aronson, 1992).

Expectations and older siblings

Just as a teacher's expectations and consequent treatment of a pupil may be in part a function of the child's looks—that is, overrewarding the good-looking child and underrewarding the unattractive child (see the Spotlight on Expectations and "Looks")—so, too, teacher expectations may be influenced by the past performance of a pupil's older sibling. Although teacher remarks such as "I never had this kind of trouble with your sister" tend to frustrate and burden a child, they can also work to the child's advantage. One study found that a child received higher grades from teachers who knew and admired an older sibling than from teachers who had no such previous knowledge (Seaver, 1973). This is simply one more example of the Rosenthal effect in the classroom—teacher's judgments are clearly affected by expectations.

A summary of the research on the relationship between teacher expectations and student achievement again demonstrates the power of this important phenomenon (Good, 1981). Because of its power, efforts have been made to train teachers to guard against this source of bias. The Teacher Expectations and Student Achievement (TESA) program was designed to sensitize teachers to their own, often subtle, negative treatment of those perceived as low-achieving children. The TESA technique appears to have had a positive impact when used as part of the Connecticut School Improvement Program (Proctor, 1984).

Expectations and teacher behavior   Just as the teacher's evaluation of a student is often clouded by certain preconceived expectations, so students' ratings of their teachers are influenced in the same manner. If a student has been told that her new teacher "really knows her stuff" or "has her act together," or that "she's a hard marker but you're really going to learn something," then the student will almost certainly perceive that teacher in a positive manner. As the weeks go by, however, the teacher must really earn the positive image that the student brought into the class. Some teachers have the ability to generate positive feelings in students from the very first day, even if the students have not received any information about the teacher's reputation. Research has shown that the teacher's physical appearance is the most important single source of initial student expectations (Hurt et al., 1978). The teacher who "looks good" is immediately perceived as a person who is good—at teaching, counseling, whatever. But again, as the term wears on, the students begin using more substantive measures of effectiveness. A teacher can get by on looks and style for only a limited time. Even first-graders are soon able to spot the phony, the teacher who is really not doing the job. Style without substance is like a book with a pretty cover but filled with blank pages.

Sex Roles in Society and in the School

Right from the day the child is born, parents tend to perceive and then treat differently their male and female children. Even in the absence of objective differences, parents are apt to rate newborn girls as softer and smaller than newborn boys, whereas newborn boys are rated as bigger, stronger, and hardier than newborn girls. These differential perceptions tend to persist and strengthen as the child develops. Parents play different types of games with their male and female children, the boys virtually always being involved in more rough-and-tumble games (especially when playing with the father) (Huston, 1983). When all this is added to the fact that the bedrooms of boys and girls are decorated differently, that the toys they are given are different, that the activities planned for them are different, and that the *expectational demands* on them differ dramatically, it is little wonder that intellectual and temperamental gender differences emerge (Snow et al., 1983). Eleanor Maccoby, however, reminds us again that personality is not just a function of environment, that children are not just passive recipients of cultural pressures. We should remember psychology's important axiom concerning the interaction of environment, heredity, and time in the formation of personal traits and behaviors. Although society treats boys and girls differently, some elements of those differences are contributed by the children themselves. The influence between adult and child is a two-way street, and some of the treatment differences between the sexes reflect differences in the ways boys and girls react to these treatments (Maccoby, 1991).

Yet even in this seemingly enlightened age, the message of sexism can be stark. One of the authors of this text witnessed the following scene at a Vermont ski area: The mother of a small boy reprimanded him for being, as she thought, overly cautious in his skiing. To dramatize her point, she suddenly pointed to a girl who was gliding effortlessly down the slope (a girl who was, incidentally, at least two years older than her son) and further admonished the boy by loudly proclaiming, "Look how brave she is, *and she's only a girl.*"

Just as the school often acts to transmit the traditional values of the larger culture in general, it also transmits society's version of the sex role. Boys are encouraged to be more "masculine" and girls to be "ladylike." One analysis indicated that this transmittal is done, often inadvertently, in three ways:

1. Schools encourage gender typing by separating male and female activities and interest areas. Young boys are more apt to be sent to the "block corner," whereas girls are placed in the "housekeeping" and art areas.

2. Teachers project gender-typed expectations—exactly the kind of situation that role theory would predict. If teachers expect little boys to be less manageable than little girls, the boys pick up these cues and don't let the teachers down.

3. Schools have typically created an ideal "pupil role." The ideal pupil is conforming, docile, dependent, and manageable—that is, the pupil exhibits the very traits that have traditionally defined the female role. By more easily adopting this role, girls learn to be more receptive than active. Boys, in contrast, have more difficulty in conforming to this ideal-pupil image and thus often find school to be a stressful and alienating experience (Lee & Gropper, 1975).

Gender stereotypes are not just products of U.S. culture. In one study, children from 30 different countries were read stories and then asked to identify the central character's gender. There was great consistency across cultures in terms of what the children used to make their choices. For example, males were chosen when the characters were strong, dominant, and aggressive, whereas females were chosen on the basis of traits such as being affectionate, emotional, and soft-hearted (Williams & Best, 1990). One psychologist has urged that we stop doing studies on gender differences, or at least not divulge the results of such studies to the general public. His concern is that the information itself tends to accentuate the differences and strengthen the stereotypes, especially when they are reported and distorted by the media (Baumeister, 1990).

Role and Personality

Although the pressure of group expectations is a powerful influence on our behavior, our basic personality will determine the way in which our role in the group is interpreted and carried out. The fact that individual behavior is consistent across different roles in different groups shows that we each bring an integrated and coherent behavioral unity to our groups. The way in which role and personality interrelate is reciprocal. The role we play in a group also has a definite impact on our personality. For example, an actor who for years plays the "tough guy" in the movies may slowly incorporate this image into his personality and may begin to believe and act as if he *is* that tough guy.

The therapy technique called *psychodrama* is based on this notion. Neurotic patients are put on the stage and given roles that they typically find uncomfortable to act out. With encouragement, and in the context of a nonthreatening situation, they learn the behavior required for certain roles and experience a concomitant personality change. The relationship between role and personality also works the other way. We will consciously or unconsciously select roles that are consistent with our underlying personality. Extroverted personalities usually assume roles that allow them to stay in the limelight, while introverts adopt roles that keep them away from the stage front.

Studies have shown that the majority of college seniors majoring in education prefer to work with people rather than things and describe themselves as "conventional in opinions and values" (Davis, 1964). Teachers also tend to score above average in such personality areas as friendliness, sociability, and personal relations. A summary of the research on teacher personality profiles as determined by the Minnesota Multiphasic Personality Inventory (MMPI) describes teachers as (1) responsible, conscientious, conforming, and friendly; and (2) likely to emphasize control of self and adaptation to the needs and demands of others (Johnson, 1970, p. 57).

Evidence indicates that the personalities of teachers are fairly consistent with the role demands of their job. However, the research in this area is correlational, meaning that the interpretations can go either way. In other words, teachers may have a personality style that causes them to select the role of teacher, or the role demands of the teaching position may shape the personalities of those involved in the teaching profession. The best guess is that both selection and shaping are involved.

LEADERSHIP

The highest position in the status hierarchy of any group is that of leader. The leader has the most influence in shaping the group's norms and expectations. Before relating styles of leadership to group functioning, we must first get some understanding of the concept of leadership itself.

Is leadership something we either have or don't have? Are there people who, regardless of the group, the social setting, the cultural norm, will always rise to the top? Or is leadership strictly a function of the group norms, the task being performed, or the social context? In other words, is leadership a quality of the individual or a quality of the group?

Theories of Leadership

The great-leader theory
The **great-leader theory** sees leadership as a quality of the individual. In its boldest form the theory states that certain individuals possess just the right blend of looks, personality traits, and intelligence to be almost automatically thrust into leadership positions. These individuals—who are said to have **charisma**—will always become leaders in any situation or in any group. Charisma is a kind of personal magnetism and hypnotic appeal. When a charismatic person walks into a room, the room is suddenly charged with excitement, and the others in it become submissive and willing to follow the individual anywhere. As one theorist explains it, "charisma is a compulsive, inexplicable emotional tie linking a group of followers together in adulation of their leader" (Lindholm, 1990, p. 6). Some of history's charismatic leaders include Mahatma Gandhi, Joan of Arc, Winston Churchill, Cleopatra, John F. Kennedy, Martin Luther King, Jesse Jackson, and Pope John Paul II. Charisma also has its dark side in the form of Adolph Hitler and his Third Reich, Charles Manson and his "family," and Jim Jones and the "People's Temple." Each charismatic leader had a personal appeal that was spellbinding, almost mystical. People such as these, says this theory, have to become leaders regardless of the times in which they live.

In one study, the relative charisma ratings of past U.S. presidents, from Washington to Reagan, were deduced on the basis of historical records. It was found that charisma ratings were a function of both the president's personality and the situations and events occurring around him. Charisma was positively correlated with the president's need for power and the magnitude of the crises he had to face. The ratings of some of our more recent presidents were as follows: Franklin Roosevelt, 2.5; Lyndon Johnson, 1.5; John Kennedy, 1.3; Ronald Reagan, 1.2; Dwight Eisenhower, .6; Richard Nixon, .3; Harry Truman, 0; Gerald Ford, −.10; and Jimmy Carter, −.40 (House et al., 1991).

The group theory
According to the group theory, almost anyone who fulfills some basic need of the group can be a leader. And, since the needs of the group shift, so too does leadership. For example, a group on a camping trip would see leadership constantly changing according to the dictates of the situation. If the group became lost, the individual with the compass would become the leader. If someone became injured, the person with first-aid knowledge and supplies would become the leader.

Even history's great leaders are explained on this basis. Winston Churchill became a leader late in his career, when the times called for someone with his special talents. Hitler would have found no followers and would have probably had to spend his entire life painting portraits in Austria had Germany not been rocked by runaway inflation and crushing depression. The group theory suggests that the unfolding of history is like the opening of a combination lock—only when a certain sequence of events occurs will a certain individual be called upon to lead.

In fact, one theorist has suggested that the situational approach to understanding leadership should not be called a leadership theory at all. By overly stressing the situation, it tends to downplay the notion that leaders can do much of anything to change the dynamics of the forces acting on both them and their followers (Dipboye et al., 1994).

A blending of the theories
The actual evidence regarding leadership now suggests that the best explanation lies somewhere between these two theories. Both theories are needed to account for the data. Certain individual qualities do seem to be more common in leaders than in other group members. For example, leaders tend to be taller but not too much taller, and more intelligent but not too much more intelligent, than other members of the group. Leaders also seem to possess more social skills than followers. For example, leaders are apt to give more information, ask for more information, and make more interpretations about a situation (Cartwright & Zander, 1953). Among other personal traits that appear to enhance a leader's effectiveness are:

Self-confidence

Ability to manipulate others

Ability to satisfy the needs of others

Great personal persistence

Strong motivation to attain a group goal (Barker et al., 1983)

But it has also become increasingly evident that the demands of the situation are crucial in determining the group's choice of a leader. One study of schoolchildren found that the boy who could spit the farthest was the leader in the first grade. By fourth grade it was the child who "sassed" the teacher the most. In high school the girl who had always stayed in the background in grade school suddenly blossomed into leadership because of her "dating power" (Cunningham, 1984). Former major league pitching star and philosopher extraordinaire Bill Lee

SPOTLIGHT ON SOCIAL SKILLS

*Training in the Classroom**

There is a great deal of clinical and descriptive literature regarding the social behavior of many learning-disabled youngsters. This research has generated a growing recognition that most LD children experience significant social difficulties. Accumulated evidence supports the hypothesis that adequate peer social skills do play an important role in child development and academic success, as well as in the long-term adjustment of individuals. In fact, in terms of total-life functioning, social ineptitude tends to be more disabling than academic difficulties.[a]

Can social skills be taught in the classroom? And are teachers equipped to teach these skills? The answer to both questions is quite simply, yes! In fact, the same methods used to teach academic skills can be used to teach social skills. The emphasis on increasing prosocial behaviors should be of benefit to all students in the classroom, not just the learning-disabled. Social skills interventions can be readily incorporated into the general management of the classroom so that no time is needlessly taken from academic lessons.[b] In addition, evidence suggests that social skills training is directly translated into improved academic performance by increasing the child's self-esteem, attend-

ing behavior, on-task behavior, and ability to follow directions and complete tasks. Intervention strategies should target behaviors that are valued in the child's environment, for example, improving conversation skills or learning how to express feelings more appropriately. However, determining what is considered appropriate for a given child demands an understanding of the child and the child's background.

Appropriate behavior may vary according to age, gender, socioeconomic level, race and, of course, the situation itself. At the risk of stating the obvious, contextual variables must always be considered. Effective interventions include the following:

1. *Positive reinforcement*—should be given whenever behavior is appropriate
2. *Cooperative learning strategies*—help create an environment that increases the probability of positive social interactions
3. *Modeling appropriate behavior*—both in a natural setting or by observing a videotaped model
4. *Direct coaching*—involves verbal instruction concerning the appropriate behavior
5. *Rehearsal*—provides the opportunity for the child to practice the modeled behavior

6. *Constant feedback*—helps the child monitor improved behaviors
7. *Self-talk*—helps the child develop strategies for retrieving the newly learned social skill and maintain a focus on the use of that skill

Research evidence shows clearly that the most important aspect in the teaching of social skills is to teach the specific skills directly rather than spend time sermonizing about general rules of conduct.[c]

---

* This Spotlight was especially prepared for this volume by Dr. Antoinette Spinelli-Nannen, Director, School Psychology Program, American International College, Springfield, MA.
[a] Spinelli-Nannen, A. (1987). *An investigation of the personality assessment system as a discriminator of socially misperceptive tendencies in elementary students.* Unpublished doctoral dissertation, American International College.
[b] Gresham, F. M. (1990). Best practices in social skills management. In A. Thomas and J. Grines (Eds.), *Best practices in school psychology.* Washington, DC: National School Psychology Association.
[c] Elliot, S. N. (1988). *Acceptability of behavioral treatments in educational settings.* In J. C. Witt, S. N. Elliot, & F. M. Gresham (Eds.), Handbook of behavior therapy in education (pp. 121–150). New York: Plenum Press.

---

said that he never did think much of leadership as a unitary trait. "As far as I was concerned the best leadership is provided by a grand slam home run that overcomes a three-run lead, or by a shutout that stops a losing streak" (Lee, 1985, p. 98). Even the mystique of charisma has by some been partially de-

fined in situational terms. In this view, the leader is imbued with charisma by his or her followers when the number and intensity of the leader's behaviors are perceived as compellingly relevant to the current situation (Conger, 1989). Thus, the demands and values of the group are just as important in determining

SPOTLIGHT ON SINGLE-SEX EDUCATION

Because of the gender bias found in many schools, there has recently been more discussion of the possible advantages of a return to single-sex education. Since many studies have shown that girls in coeducational settings receive less attention, more criticism, and less reinforcement than boys, some educators are now arguing that girls are better served in single-sex classes, which allow the girls, who typically lose confidence and self-esteem in high school classes (especially classes in math and the sciences), the opportunity to be assertive and to excel in a nonthreatening atmosphere. In fact, one study has shown that when teenage females were trained as math tutors for fifth-grade girls, not only did the math achievement scores of the fifth-graders go up, but also there was a significant increase in the level of psychological growth shown by the female tutors.[a] Advocates claim that girls have to learn to be assertive before they can compete successfully with men. On the other side of this issue, however, is the notion that since men and women eventually have to live and work together, delaying a child's opportunity to practice these skills may be damaging to both genders.[b] Other evidence is somewhat contradictory. One researcher has found that high school girls are not low in self-esteem and that by the tenth grade more girls than boys said that their teachers called on them and listened to what they had to say.[c]

Debate has now spilled over to the male side of the ledger, and some are suggesting that even boys may learn better in single-sex classrooms. Since boys seem to mature more slowly than girls, giving them their own classes may produce a better learning environment by leveling the maturational playing field. This argument has been especially forceful with regard to African-American boys, who may need more opportunity for male bonding, both with their peers and with male role-model teachers. It is thought that all-male and all-black classrooms allow for more discipline and more male camaraderie that will better prepare young black males for life outside the classroom.[d] On the other side of this debate are those, including the NAACP, who maintain that this movement is in effect caving in to racial segregationists.

Throughout history and certainly within the field of psychology, most theoreticians have used the behavior of men as normative, and when women's behavior differed from that norm it was seen as a negative deviation from that universal standard.[e] Only a few researchers have recognized that this deviation might instead be positive. For example, Carol Gilligan has long argued, though not always with supporting data, that women are morally superior to as well as morally different from men. Also, there is a strong suspicion that psychological theories in general are biased toward men and that developmental theories in particular have consistently used male development as the norm. Traditional developmental theories, for example, typically establish independence and a need for separation as the norm for both sexes, thus portraying women, who have significantly more concern with relationships and feelings of dependence, as somehow weak or even pathological.[g] The point is that maybe the world would be better off if all people, both men and women, developed more concerns with relationships and less need to separate.

In reviewing the research on gender differences during this age of the new hereditarians, we must all be careful to retain a scientific outlook of dispassionate objectivity. It is all too easy for those with built-in biases, such as an avowed political agenda, to seek out in nature only those data that might confirm their prejudices and to reject any observations that might disturb their preconceptions. The recent seemingly relentless search for innate genetic mechanisms to explain complex human behavior may produce easy answers to difficult questions—and, worse, easy excuses for the status quo.[h]

---

[a]   Sprinthall & Scott, (1989).
[b]   de Groot (1994).
[c]   Sommers, C. H. (1994, April 3). The myth of school girls' low self-esteem. *The Wall Street Journal*, 4.
[d]   Ascher (1992).
[e]   Tavris (1992).
[f]   Gilligan, C. (1982). *In a different voice*. Cambridge, MA: Harvard University Press; Gillipan, C. (1991).
[g]   Guisinger & Blatt (1994).
[h]   Mednick (1989).

leadership as many of the personal qualities listed above. Leadership results when the individual's qualities match the group's demands.

As has been shown, leadership effectiveness is predictable on the basis of certain personality factors, but only *as they relate to the group in question.* The same personality factors that lead to success as, say, an academic leader may differ substantially from those leading to success in more entrepreneurial ventures (Hogan et al., 1994).

Leadership and Gender

Of all the personal traits usually assumed to correlate with effective leadership, perhaps the most pervasive is simply that of being a male. This is undoubtedly the result of conscious or unconscious bias and, of course, gender stereotyping. The facts, however, tend to dispel this leadership myth. When men and women *of equal leadership experience* are compared on the basis of their actual influence on a group in getting the job done, there are usually no significant differences between them (Hollander & Yoder, 1980). Of course, differences in leadership skills do exist between experienced men and inexperienced women. However, despite the equal effectiveness of men and women, groups still tend to evaluate autocratic female leaders more negatively than they do autocratic male leaders (Jago & Vroom, 1982). This bias against women leaders may be due in part to the fact that people in general have had less experience dealing with autocratic women in leadership positions.

Recent studies indicate that women have already caught up to men in their ability to handle leadership positions. The evidence now seems to show that women are just as effective as men in carrying out leadership demands (Eagly et al., 1995).

Styles of Leadership

Most of you have been members of several different groups—scout troops, athletic teams, school clubs, whatever. You have thus been exposed to various styles of leadership, and you may have noticed that the efficiency of the group's performance and the satisfaction of the group's members were due in large measure to the style of the group's leadership. You may recall a coach who was so lenient that the team failed to perform according to expectations. Or perhaps you remember a scout leader who was so rigid and domineering that most of the members quit and the troop had to fold.

Many years ago Kurt Lewin, who had once been a student of Max Wertheimer, conducted an experiment to assess the ways in which groups respond to different kinds of leadership (Lewin et al., 1939). One aspect of the study was to compare the effects of **authoritarian** and **democratic styles of leadership** on group activity. The subjects were young boys who were placed in "club" groups under the direction of adult leaders. The authoritarian leader was domineering, never asking for suggestions about group activities and controlling every aspect of the group situation. The democratic leader, in contrast, guided the group gently, constantly asking for suggestions and allowing the group to make decisions. The results of the study indicated that completely different atmospheres were generated in the two groups. The democratic group's members were more satisfied, more cooperative, less hostile, and better able to carry on group activities when the leader was not present. Though the authoritarian group did have a higher rate of production (building model planes), the work of the democratic group was of a higher quality.

Leadership style has been shown in study after study to affect the behavior, perceptions, and feelings of group members. Clearly, group members perceive democratic leaders more favorably than they do authoritarian leaders. Leaders who use the participatory leadership style are liked better by the group members than are those using the autocratic style. In one study, college students were placed in groups led by either a participatory (democratic) leader or an autocratic leader. The leaders who utilized the participatory style received more positive evaluations than did those using the autocratic style (Jago & Vroom, 1982).

Classroom Leadership

Although the teacher is handed the main leadership role in the classroom, other leaders are also present. In large measure, the broad base of influence from which the teacher operates shapes the social climate in the classroom. The degree to which the teacher is authoritarian or submissive or coercive or democratic sets the tone for norm formation in the classroom. But once school has been in session for a few weeks, student leaders begin to emerge. Again, it is the teacher who, to a large extent, may determine which students attain leadership positions. The teacher may encourage and reinforce the leadership behavior of one child and withhold reinforcement when the same behavior is exhibited by another child. Yet the teacher can also succumb to reinforcement. One prominent sociologist has said that "influence over others is purchased at the price of allowing one's self to be influenced by others" (Homans, 1961, p. 116). This sociologist feels that an influential leader must have the esteem of everyone in the group. This means that students can exert considerable pressure on a teacher by giving or withholding their esteem

KENNETH B. CLARK

Kenneth B. Clark, noted educator and psychologist, was born in the Panama Canal Zone in 1914. Clark's father, Arthur B. Clark, was a passenger agent for the United Fruit Company in Panama. When Clark was five years old, his mother left Panama for the United States, bringing her children with her. To support the children, Mrs. Clark worked as a seamstress in a New York garment factory, where she also helped organize a union. Clark says his first contact with social issues was listening to his mother tell of her problems in trying to organize the union in her shop.

Clark graduated from Howard University in 1935 and received his M.A. in 1936. For the next two years Clark taught psychology at Howard, but the following year he enrolled as a Ph.D. candidate in experimental psychology at Columbia University. He was awarded his degree in 1940, and during the academic year 1940–1941 he became an assistant professor of psychology at the Hampton Institute in Virginia. The following year, Clark worked as a social science analyst for the Office of War Information, traveling throughout the country studying morale problems in black population centers. In 1942 he joined the psychology department of the College of the City of New York; he became a full professor in 1960.

In 1946 Clark and his wife, Dr. Mamie Clark, established the non-profit Northside Center for Child Development in New York City. The center is devoted to treating children with emotional problems. In 1950 Clark worked on a report that showed that segregation in the schools is detrimental to the growth and development of white as well as black children. The U.S. Supreme Court relied on Clark's study when, in 1954, it made its important decision that segregation in public schools is unconstitutional.

Clark has devoted his life to improving school conditions for all children. He has found racial prejudice to be a two-edged sword that harms both the prejudiced and the objects of the prejudice. In 1970 Clark received his colleagues' highest honor when he was named president of the American Psychological Association. During his presidency, he established the Board of Social and Ethical Responsibility for Psychology. His many articles and books include *Desegregation: An Appraisal of the Evidence* (1953), *Prejudice and Your Child* (1955), *Dark Ghetto* (1965), *A Relevant War against Poverty* (1968), and *Pathos of Power* (1974).

In 1978 Clark was selected by the American Psychological Association to receive its Distinguished Contribution to Psychology in the Public Interest Award.

As an educator and psychologist, Clark ranks at the top of his profession. Though a brilliant theorist, he has not sought refuge in an ivory tower but prefers to remain on the front lines, working, doing, and making things happen. He is without question psychology's most prominent spokesperson for social justice.

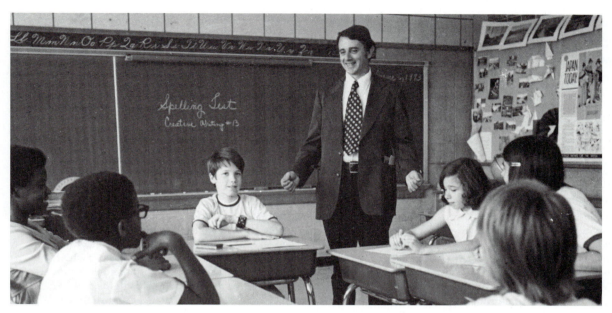

Changing the role of one individual in the group may change the whole group, since the classroom is a collection of interdependent individuals and the dynamics of their interrelationships depend on roles established through interaction.

and that they can, by this means, shape their teacher's behavior. It also explains why a given teacher might be a successful leader with one group of students and not so successful with a different group.

Social psychology assumes that leadership ability is a set of behavioral skills that most people can learn. One psychologist says that effective leadership depends on the following:

1. Flexible behavior

2. The ability to know what behaviors are needed at a particular time in order for the group to function most efficiently

3. The ability to behave as required or to get other members of the group to do so

An effective leader must learn to spot what the group needs in a given situation and then be flexible enough "to provide diverse types of behaviors that are required under different conditions" (Johnson, 1970, p. 128). The effective leader must also get the cooperation of various members of the group so that they will help perform the necessary group functions.

GROUP DYNAMICS IN THE CLASSROOM

The classroom is a collection of interdependent individuals. The dynamics of their interrelationships depend on the roles that have been established through interaction. Whenever there is a change in the expected behavior of any group member, the dynamic interrelationships of the entire group—that is, the **group dynamics**—must necessarily change. The pressure on role behavior is so great that if a group has certain expectations about an individual's behavior, that individual usually responds in a way consistent with those expectations. The group's expectations become a self-fulfilling prophecy.

In a two-person group, or dyad, the expectations of the superordinate member clearly determine the behavior of the subordinate member. Suppose a mother is convinced that red hair causes a child to have a quick temper. She will then tolerate the temper tantrums of her red-haired child while extinguishing these same responses in her blond or brunette children. Or, suppose a high school student complains that his mother treats him as if he were a child; an objective analysis of the student's behavior may reveal that he indeed doesn't let his mother

SPOTLIGHT ON BILINGUAL EDUCATION

*A Social, Psychological, and Educational Concern**

Approximately 10 percent of the school-age population in the United States speaks a native language other than English. These second-language learners, or bilinguals, present special problems to educators. Until the early 1960s, such children were typically placed in the traditional English-language curriculum alongside their native English-speaking counterparts, in the belief that all ethnic groups should forced to blend into a single "all-American" cultural group. During the 60s, however, public schools suddenly experienced an influx of several thousand Cuban children. These non-English-speaking children were dropping out of school at what soon became alarmingly high rates. The educational establishment was confronted with several major issues. Because schools had experienced great difficulty in obtaining valid evaluations of the academic ability of these bilingual children, many were being incorrectly placed in classes for the mentally retarded. This rather widespread, and certainly unfortunate, practice led in part to the 1974 Supreme Court decision (*Lau* v. *Nichols*) that set care-

ful guidelines and regulations designed to reverse this trend. School districts were required by the Department of Health, Education and Welfare, as it was then called, to develop bilingual educational programs whenever they had 20 or more students from a single language background. In 1984, federal legislation reauthorized school systems to amend these programs to include placing bilingual children in regular school programs with the proviso that instructional aides be available to assist the classroom teacher.

There has been a lively debate among educators over which method is better for educating these children. Two very different approaches are currently in use. One method, the native-language approach, sometimes called the indirect method, provides reading instruction in the child's native language. Proponents argue that disadvantaged children learn to read and understand concepts best by having their own native language structures reinforced. This allows the bilingual child to perceive the native language as worthwhile and also promotes the

child's personal sense of self-esteem.

The second approach, the direct method, totally immerses the bilingual children in the language of their new culture. Its proponents believe this will more fully prepare the children for the language demands inherent in their eventual careers and life responsibilities. Advocates of this approach are not concerned with the development of reading skills in the children's first language. Because the numbers of bilingual students are increasing, the prevailing federal and local philosophy appears to be in line with this "direct" approach.

Some educational psychologists argue for a more integrative approach to close the gap between these two methods. This compromise approach is based on the belief that bilingual education methods should focus on assisting children to move as quickly as possible into English-based classes. Two key beliefs are fundamental to this approach: (1) that the integration of first-language goals into the curriculum helps develop in children an understanding of the basic components of reading and writ-

down—he acts like a child. Or, imagine a husband who complains that his wife is domineering. During the conversation he mentions that he recently dropped one of his wife's plant pots and was thereupon banished to the cellar, where his son later brought him his supper. In each case, the dynamic relationship between the people involved could exist only if both members played their expected roles. If the student who was being treated like a child stopped acting like a child, his mother would have to change her expectations and thus her behavior to-

ward him. The man with the domineering wife must have played the role of a dominated husband to the hilt. Why else would he meekly allow himself to be served dinner in the cellar? In the words of a once-popular song, "It takes two to tango," there can be no tango, or any other consistent form of interaction, unless both partners play their expected roles.

In a classic case reported by learning theorist Edwin R. Guthrie, a group of male college students decided to make an all-out effort to cater extravagantly ing,[a] and (2) that the fostering of classroom conditions that allow students to utilize life experiences in their native language helps them build self-confidence and the self-esteem-necessary tools for optimal learning (see Chapter 18 on motivation in the classroom). Sarah Hudelson cites an extensive 1987 U.S. General Accounting Office report in which 10 experts were asked to review bilingual education research. The conclusion drawn was that quality bilingual education is beneficial for English-language acquisition.

Experts in the field would agree that not enough evidence is yet available to show us which is the better method. There are problems inherent in both models currently in use, and integrative methods, though seemingly viable, are still unsubstantiated alternatives. The direct method, for example, is not always implemented effectively, especially among Spanish-speaking children. In addition, there appears to be a growing interest in the maintenance of ethnic languages, identities, and cultures to sustain a pluralistic society. Our schools have begun to recognize what Catherine

R. Stimpson of Rutgers University has called cultural democracy, or an understanding that we must listen to a "diversity of voices" in order to be knowledgeable about our culture, past and present.[b]

For these and other reasons, some educators seem to lean toward the native-language approach. However, because of certain methodological problems, including the lack of adequate control groups and the possibility of confounding variables, studies have failed to fully support the superiority of that approach. More research is needed in the areas of learning and information processing to shed light on double-language learning in early childhood. As we have seen, the problems produced by proactive and retroactive inhibition are significant under the best of circumstances and may be especially acute for the young child faced with having to learn two languages at the same time. However, we have learned that bilingualism does not necessarily have to impede cognitive development and that cognitive skills acquisition is transferable across cultures and languages.[c]

Currently no definitive answer exists to the question of how best to teach bilingual children. We are a long way from having enough evidence to show us the most effective method. And so the controversy continues, particularly in regions where the concentration of immigrant families is especially high. It would be important to keep in mind that "the fact that we live in a culturally and ethnically diverse society can present problems; but . . . this diversity can be turned into a positive experience for all of us."[d]

* This Spotlight was especially prepared for this volume by Carol S. Spafford, Chair, Department of Education, American International College, Springfield, MA.
[a] Hudelson, S. (1987). The role of native language literacy in the education of language for minority children. *Language Arts 64*, 827–841.
[b] Ravitch, D. (1990). Multiculturalism. In J. Epstein (Ed.), *The American Scholar*. Washington, DC: Phi Beta Kappa.
[c] Ovando, C. J. (1983). Bilingual/bicultural education: Its legacy and its future. *Phi Beta Kappan 64*, 564–568.
[d] Hessong, R. F., & Weeks, T. H. (1991). *Introduction to the foundations of education*. New York: Macmillan.

to a shy, socially inept coed. They made sure she was invited to all the social functions, constantly flattered her with gifts and attention, and in general saw that she was the "belle of the ball." By the end of the college year she had developed an easy, confident manner and had become a popular campus favorite even among those not aware of the original plot. Says Guthrie, "What her college career would have been if the experiment had not been made is impossible to say, but it is fairly certain that she would have resigned all social ambitions and would have found interests compatible with her social ineptitude" (Guthrie, 1938).

The influence of group expectations on individual behavior can also be seen in the area of racial prejudice. Although prejudice is learned primarily in the home, teachers may also implant prejudice, especially during the first few grades. They may not directly teach hatred, but the message still comes through loud and clear. The teacher's differential treatment of minority races and religions sets the stage for differential student responses. African-

American children, for example, can hardly be expected to act maturely in the classroom when they are not treated with dignity and respect. The mass media have also helped to communicate this social distortion. Until the last few years movies typically cast African-Americans in subservient roles, as servants. The movies also played up stereotypes, often characterizing an African-American as a wide-eyed, frightened fool. This sort of thing could hardly lend dignity to the black race.

Group expectations can be so powerful that the minority group members may learn to hold the prejudices and stereotyped attitudes toward their own group that the majority group holds. This can be very destructive to the minority group member's self-image (Sprinthall et al., 1971).

The classroom teacher is obviously a potent reinforcer, and through the judicious use of social approval he or she can shape the behavior of the entire class. The teacher must realize, however, that the classroom is a social unit with a dynamically balanced set of role relationships. Any shift in the role of one student necessarily results in a change in the social balance of the entire group. If the teacher clamps down on the class joker, for example, the social climate could shift in a negative direction. The joker may be fulfilling the important role of relieving group tensions in moments of social stress. Removing that function could lead to a far more anxious social climate in which the conditions for learning could deteriorate. By the same token, shutting off the antics of a loudmouth who is motivated more by compulsive attention-seeking than by reducing class tensions could produce better learning conditions for the rest of the class. Some tinkering and adjusting can be attempted, but remember that changing the role of any individual in the group produces changes in the whole group.

All the variables that have been mentioned in this chapter will be operative at one time or another in almost any classroom. The question is: What kind of a group will the classroom become? The teacher as leader can clearly exert a major influence on the definition of the group. We have noted that classes can run the entire gamut from a collection of egocentric individuals "doing their own thing" to a smoothly functioning machine in which each individual may be defined only as a group member. If the teacher does not know about the social variables or chooses not to exert definitional leadership, the students will impose their own definition. This is likely to create a very awkward situation: The teacher's role will be totally defined by the group. The opposite extreme, in which the teacher sets the classroom atmosphere and educational objectives solely in terms of his or her own needs and values, is equally undesirable. Thus, the way in which a teacher uses concepts such as social facilitation, conformity, competitiveness, cohesiveness, and group pressure is part of the teaching problem. A question of equal significance involves the whole area of social goals and objectives. A knowledge of social psychology can truly help the teacher promote human development through education.

SUMMARY

Social psychology is the study of human behavior in the context of the group situation. Each classroom is a social unit with its own unique set of norms, role relationships, and behavioral expectations. Though the social atmosphere of the classroom is in large part shaped by the teacher, it is also a function of each student's behavior.

Sometimes the influence of the group acts to increase an individual's performance (social facilitation), and sometimes the group's influence decreases an individual's performance (social inhibition). Working in a group situation can increase feelings of competition and anxiety. A student's performance will be facilitated by the group's influence when (1) the student's motivational level is on the low side and (2) the task is neither overly difficult nor overly intellectual.

The risky-shift phenomenon occurs in group situations and seems to promote more risk-taking behavior among group members than they would display were they alone. The group situation has also been used to foster the growth of creative ideas through a process called brainstorming, in which individuals are encouraged to call out any ideas they might have on a given subject, no matter how seemingly bizarre.

Cohesiveness is defined as the amount of attraction the group has for its members. Cohesiveness can be increased in a group as a result of (1) an increase in the amount of friendly interaction, (2) an increase in the amount of cooperation, (3) an increase in the group's feeling of status, (4) an outside threat, or (5) a change in the style of leadership.

One result of group life is the overwhelming desire of individuals to conform to the norms of their group. Two major studies indicate the compelling nature of conformity: Sherif's research on the autokinetic effect and Asch's study of group pressure. In each case, the behavior of individuals conformed to the group norm. Though most conformity studies tend to show the power of the group as being repressive to the individual, a study by Milgram showed that the influence of the group may actually allow an individual to act in a more humane and less aggressive fashion.

Despite the pressure to conform exerted by the group, some individuals are less likely to yield than others. Individuals whose locus of control is internal (that is, who see themselves as being personally in control of their actions and in charge of their destinies) are less likely to conform than individuals whose locus of control is external.

The process of socialization is essentially produced by pressures to conform, whereby the child is literally forced into adopting society's standards. Socialization is necessary to society but produces some loss of personal independence.

Another aspect of socialization is dissonance. When a person feels a lack of consistency between attitudes and deeds, he or she undergoes cognitive dissonance, an uncomfortable feeling of disequilibrium. To reduce the anxiety, the individual attempts to restore consistency by changing actions to conform with attitudes or attitudes to conform with deeds.

Attribution refers to the explanations people give for their own or another person's actions or beliefs. When the attribution is based on internal factors it is called a dispositional attribution, and when based on external factors it is called a situational attribution. The fundamental attribution error occurs when we assign dispositional factors to the actions of others and situational factors to our own actions.

Social psychologists are also concerned with aggression. The Freudian and the ethological positions assume that a major portion of aggressiveness is innately determined; the frustration-aggression hypothesis and social learning theory view aggression as a product of the environment. Studies of the effect of violence in the mass media on aggression have had equivocal results: some indicate that violence on TV has increased aggressive behavior in viewers, while other studies suggest that it may have a cathartic effect.

The behavior of the individual also conforms to the expectations society forms on the basis of one's status and role. Status is one's position or niche in society's prestige hierarchy, and role is the behavior expected of a person having a particular status.

Society assigns roles by gender, and schools typically encourage these gender-based roles. Although society influences behavior by the role playing it encourages, the personality of each individual determines how a role is interpreted and carried out.

Leaders seem to be chosen on the basis of both personal characteristics and the demands of the group. In a study comparing democratic versus authoritarian styles of leadership, it was shown that democratic leaders (those who gently guided the group, asked for suggestions, allowed for group decisions, etc.) were apt to have groups in which the members were more satisfied, more cooperative, less hostile, and better able to follow through on group projects even when the leader was absent.

Because of the present status and role requirements of the classroom, the teacher automatically holds the leadership position. He or she is not the only leader, however, for student leaders inevitably arise and can influence the behavior of both the teacher and the other students.

The group dynamics of the classroom, or of any group situation, are based on interdependent status and role relationships. When a group has a certain expectation regarding an individual's behavior, the individual usually responds in a way consistent with that expectation. This can be especially damaging to the minority group child when the group's expectation is based on prejudice and stereotyping.

KEY TERMS AND NAMES

attitudes
attribution theory
authoritarian leadership
autokinetic effect
brainstorming
charisma
Kenneth B. Clark
cognitive dissonance
cohesiveness
conformity
democratic leadership

frustration-aggression hypothesis
great-leader theory
group dynamics
locus of control
risky shift
role
social facilitation
social inhibition
social psychology
socialization
status

THEORY INTO PRACTICE: IMPACT OF STATUS AND ROLE ON BEHAVIOR

In this chapter, we have seen, among other things, the impact of status and role on behavior. The influence of a group's expectations on the behaviors of group members can be truly enormous. As has been pointed out, a child who is treated as a baby will soon begin responding in less mature ways, and a child who is treated as an outcast will play the role of the object of the group's scorn. Perhaps even worse, the child who is perceived and treated as though he were stupid, after a while begins to believe it and act in ways that confirm the expectations of those who are applying this label. For a fairly dramatic illustration of this phenomenon, try the following:

From your class select two students at random and ask them to leave the room for a few moments and wait outside in the corridor. During their absence, assign roles to each of them. Give one student a high-status position, such as that of a world-famous cultural anthropologist who is visiting your college as part of your institution's faculty development program. Assign a low-status role to the other student, say, a college "flunk out" who is still in the process of trying to find a job. When they are brought back into the classroom do not tell the returning students that these roles have been assigned. The class, or perhaps five or six students selected from the class, should engage in a round-table discussion on a certain topic, for example, how the alumni of your college might be persuaded to make donations to a special fund designed to increase faculty salaries. During this discussion, the students must keep firmly in mind the roles that have been assigned to the two naive subjects. Treat the high-status student with dignity and respect, and the low-status student with derision and inattention.

This technique has been tried many times in the classroom of one of the authors, and it typically results in rapid and sometimes severe behavioral changes on the part of the role players. Within 15 or 20 minutes the group's expectations usually begin affecting the subjects' behaviors. The high-status student will probably try to dominate the discussion, perhaps even pontificating grandly for minutes at a time. The low-status subject will at first probably make repeated attempts to become involved, but as time passes these attempts will probably become increasingly less frequent. You may even observe the low-status person showing signs of regression. If a male, even the pitch of his voice may rise until it borders on an adolescent squeak. Or you may witness the low-status person slowly withdrawing from the scene to the point of even sitting stiffly in tight-lipped silence.

After completing the role play, question the subjects about their feelings. Usually the high-status subject will admit to having had a great time, and will probably volunteer to take part in other class demonstrations. The low-status subject may admit to feelings of frustration and perhaps even anger. Personality differences will naturally have some effect on how each of the subjects reacts. However, the group's pressure, if strong enough, should still affect the subjects enough to produce predictable behavioral results, despite any original personality differences.

The lesson to be drawn from this demonstration is an important one that you as a prospective teacher should never forget. If just a few minutes of artificial group pressure can change the behavior of fairly mature college students, imagine the impact that real and long-term pressure might have on the lives of youngsters in the lower grades.

REFERENCES

Ardrey, R. (1966). *The territorial imperative.* New York: Atheneum.

Aronson, E. (1992). *The social animal* (6th ed.). New York: Freeman.

Asch, S. E. (1952). *Social psychology.* Englewood Cliffs, NJ: Prentice Hall.

Bandura, A., Ross, D., & Ross, S. (1963). Imitation of film-mediated aggressive models. *Journal of Abnormal and Social Psychology 66,* 3–11.

Barker, L. L., Wahlers, K. J., Cegala, D. J., & Kibler, R. J. (1983). *Groups in process* (2d ed.). Englewood Cliffs, NJ: Prentice Hall.

Baumeister, R. F. (1990). Should we stop studying sex differences altogether? *American Psychologist 43,* 1092–1095.

Berkowitz, L. (1983). Aversively stimulated aggression. *American Psychologist 35,* 1140.

Bond, C. T., Francis, R. C., Fernald, R. D., & Adelman, J. P. (1991). Characterization of complementary DNA encoding as the precursor for gonadotropin-releasing hormone and its associated peptide from a teleost fish. *Journal of Molecular Endocrinology 5,* 931–937.

Bryan, T. H., & Bryan, J. H. (1986). *Understanding learning disabilities.* Palo Alto, CA: Mayfield.

Cartwright, D., & Zander, A. (1953). *Group dynamics* (p. 536). Evanston, IL: Row, Peterson.

Conger, J. A. (1989). *The charismatic leader: Behind the mystique of exceptional leadership.* San Francisco: Jossey-Bass.

Cunningham, R. (1984). Leadership and the group. *Group dynamics and education.* Washington, DC: National Education Association Division of Adult Education.

Davis, J. A. (1964). *Great aspirations.* London: Aldine.

Dipboye, R. L., Smith, C. S., & Howell, W. C. (1994). *Understanding industrial and organizational psychology.* New York: Harcourt Brace.

Dollard, J. M., Doob, L. W., Miller, N. E., Mourer, O. H., & Sears, R. R. (1939). *Frustration and aggression.* New Haven: Yale University Press.

Eagly, A. H. (1987). *Sex differences in social behavior: A social-role interpretation.* Hillsdale, NJ: Erlbaum.

Eagly, A. H., Karau, S. J., & Makhijani, M. G. (1995). Gender and the effectiveness of leaders: A meta-analysis. *Psychological Bulletin 117,* 125–145.

Elliot, S. N. (1988). Acceptability of behavioral treatments in educational settings. In J. C. Witt, S. N. Elliot, & F. M. Gresham (Eds.), *Handbook of behavior therapy in education* (pp. 121–150). New York: Plenum Press.

Eron, L. D. (1982). Parent-child interactions, television, violence and aggression of children. *American Psychologist, 37,* 197–211.

Feshback, S. (1969). *Film violence and its effect on children: Some comments on the implications of research for public policy* (p. 5). Address to the American Psychological Association, Washington,DC.

Feshback, S., & Singer, R. D. (1970). *Television and aggression.* San Francisco: Jossey-Bass.

Festinger, L. (1957). *A theory of cognitive dissonance.* Stanford: Stanford University Press.

Fingerhut, L., Ingram, D., & Feldman, J. (1992). Firearm and nonfirearm homicide among persons 15 through 19 years of age. *Journal of the American Medical Association 267,* 3048–3053.

Good, T. (1981). Teacher expectations and student perceptions: A decade of research. *Educational Leadership 38,* 415–421.

Gresham, F. M. (1990). Best practices in social skills assessment. In A. Thomas & J. Grines (Eds.), *Best practices in school psychology.* Washington: National School Psychology Association.

Guerin, B. (1993). *Social facilitation.* Cambridge, England: Cambridge University Press.

Guthrie, E. R. (1938). *The psychology of human conflict* (p. 158). New York: Harper & Row.

Harlow, H. F., McGaugh, J. L., & Thompson, R. F. (1971). *Psychology* (p. 114). San Francisco: Albion.

Harvey, J. H., & Weary, G. (1984). Current issues in attribution theory and research. *Annual Review of Psychology 35,* 427–459.

Heider, F. (1958). *The psychology of interpersonal relations.* New York: Wiley.

Henggeler, S. W. (1989). *Delinquency in adolescence.* Newbury Park, CA: Sage.

Herbert, Robert (March 2, 1994). Deadly data on handguns. *The New York Times,* A15.

Hogan, R., Curphy, G. J., & Hogan, J. (1994). What we know about leadership: Effectiveness and personality. *American Psychologist 49,* 493–504.

Hollander, E. P., & Yoder, J. (1980). Some issues in comparing women and men as leaders. *Basic and Applied Social Psychology 1,* 267–280.

Homans, G. C. (1961). *Social behavior: Its elementary forms.* New York: Harcourt, Brace & World.

House, R. J., Spangler, W. D., & Woycke, J. (1991). Personality and charisma in the U.S. presidency: A psychological theory of leader effectiveness. *Administrative Science Quarterly 36,* 364–396.

Hurt, H. T., Scott, M., & McCroskey, J. C. (1978). *Communication in the classroom.* Reading, MA: Addison-Wesley.

Huston, A. (1983). Sex-typing. In P. Mussen (Ed.), *Handbook of child psychology* (4th ed.). New York: Basic Books.

Jago, A. G., & Vroom, V. H. (1982). Sex differences in the incidence and evaluation of participative leader behavior. *Journal of Applied Social Psychology 67,* 776–783.

Johnson, D. W. (1970). *The social psychology of education.* New York: Holt, Rinehart & Winston.

Karli, P. (1991). *Animal and human aggression.* London: Oxford University Press.

Kobasa, S. C. (1982). Commitment and coping in stress resistance among lawyers. *Journal of Personality and Social Psychology 42,* 707–717.

Ladd, E. C. (January 1995). Exposing the myth of the generation gap. *Reader's Digest 1,* 49–54.

Lagerspetz, K. (1964). *Studies on the aggressive behavior of mice.* Helsinki: Soumalainen Tiedeakatemia.

Langer, P. A. (1986). *Preventing domestic violence against women.* Washington, DC: U.S. Government Printing Office.

Lee, B. (1985). *The wrong stuff.* New York: Penguin Books.

Lee, P. C., & Gropper, N. B. (1975). A cultural analysis of sex roles in the school. *Journal of Teacher Education 26*(4), 335–339.

Lewin, K., Lippitt, R., & White, R. K. (1939). Patterns of aggressive behavior in experimentally created social climates. *Journal of Social Psychology 10*, 271–299.

Lindholm, C. (1990). *Charisma*. Oxford: Blackwell.

Lore, R. K., & Schultz, L. A. (1993). Control of human aggression: A comparative perspective. *American Psychologist 48*, 16–25.

Lorenz, K. (1966). *On aggression*. New York: Harcourt, Brace & World.

Maccoby, E. E. (1991). Gender and relationships: A reprise. *American Psychologist 46*, 538–539.

Marks, G., & Miller, N. (1985). The effects of certainty on consensus judgments. *Personality and Social Psychology Bulletin 11*, 165–177.

Martin, B., & Hoffman, J. A. (1990). Conduct disorders. In M. Lewis & S. M. Miller (Eds.), *Handbook of developmental psychopathology*. New York: Plenum Press.

Milgram, S. (1965). Liberating effect of group pressures. *Journal of Personality and Social Psychology 1*, 127–134.

Milgram, S., & Shotland, R. L. (1973). *Television and antisocial behavior*. New York: Academic Press.

Miller, N. E. (1941). The frustration-aggression hypothesis. *Psychology Review 48*, 338.

Morris, C. (1990). *Contemporary psychology and effective behavior* (7th ed.). Glenview, IL: Scott-Foresman.

NCES—National Center for Educational Statistics. (1991). *Digest of education statistics, 1991*. Washington, DC: Office of Educational Research and Improvement, U.S. Department of Education.

NCHS—National Center for Health Statistics. (1992). *Data tables from the NCHS mortality tapes* (FBI-SHR). Atlanta: Centers for Disease Control.

Nissani, M. (1990). A cognitive reinterpretation of Stanley Milgram's observations on obedience to authority. *American Psychologist 45*, 1384–1385.

Oakes, P. J., Haslam, S. A., & Turner, J. C. (1994). *Stereotyping and social reality*. Oxford: Blackwell.

Olweus, D. (1991). Bully/victim problems among school children: Basic facts and effects of a school-based intervention program. In D. Pepler & K. Rubin (Eds.), *The development and treatment of childhood aggression* (pp. 411–448). Hillsdale, NJ: Erlbaum.

Parkes, K. R. (1984). Locus of control, cognitive appraisal, and coping in stressful episodes. *Journal of Personality and Social Psychology 46*, 19–84.

Paulus, P. B., Larey, T. S., & Ortega, A. H. (1995). Performance and perceptions of brainstormers in an organizational setting. *Basic and Applied Social Psychology 17*, 249–265.

Pearl, D. (1984). Violence and aggression. *Society 21*, 17–22.

Pearl, D., Bouthilet, L., & Lazar, J. (Eds.) (1982). *Television and behavior: Ten years of scientific progress and implications for the eighties* (Vols. 1 and 2). Washington, DC: U.S. Government Printing Office.

Perez, J. F., & Cohen, A. I. (1969). *Mom and dad are me* (p. 7). Monterey, CA: Brooks-Cole.

Proctor, C. P. (March 1984), Teacher expectations: A model for school improvement. *Elementary School Journal*, 469–481.

Pruitt, D. G. (1971). Choice shift in group discussion: An introductory review. *Journal of Personality and Social Psychology 20*, 339–360.

Reeder, G. D. (1982). Let's give the fundamental attribution error another chance. *Journal of Personality and Social Psychology, 43*, 341–344.

Rice, B. (May 1984), Imagination to go. *Psychology Today*.

Rock, I. (Ed.) (1990). *The legacy of Solomon Asch: Essays in cognition and social psychology*. Hillsdale, NJ: Erlbaum.

Rodriguez, J. (1990). Childhood injuries in the United States. *American Journal of Diseases of Childhood 144*, 527–646.

Rosenthal, D. (1970). *Genetic theory and abnormal behavior*. New York: McGraw-Hill.

Santee, R. T., & Maslach, C. (1982). To agree or not to agree: Personal dissent amid social pressure to conform. *Journal of Personality and Social Psychology 42*, 690–700.

Schachter, S., Ellertson, N., McBride, D., & Gregory, D. (1951). An experimental study of cohesiveness and productivity. *Human Relations 4*, 229–238.

Seaver, W. B. (1973). Effects of naturally induced teacher expectancies. *Journal of Personality and Social Psychology 28*, 333–342.

Sherif, M. (1936). *The psychology of group norms*. New York: Harper & Row.

Shumaker, S. A., & Hill, D. R. (1991). Gender differences in social support and physical health. *Health Psychology 10*, 102–111.

Slife, B. D., & Ryschlak, J. E. (1982). Role of affective assessment in modeling aggressive behavior. *Journal of Personality and Social Psychology 43*, 861–868.

Snow, M., Jacklin, C., & Maccoby, E. E. (1983). Sex-of-child differences in father-child interactions at one year of age. *Child Development 54*, 227–232.

Sprinthall, R. C., Lambert, M., & Sturm, M. (1971). Anti-Semitism: Some perceptual correlates among Jews and non-Jews. *Journal of Social Psychology 84*, 57–63.

Triplett, N. (1897). The dynamogenic factors in pacemaking and competition. *American Journal of Psychology 9*, 507–533.

U.S. Department of Justice (1991). *Uniform Crime Re-*

ports. Washington, DC: U.S. Government Printing Office.

Valkenburg, P. M., & van der Voort, T. H. A. (1994). The influence of TV on daydreaming and creative imagination: A review of research. *Psychological Bulletin 116*, 316–339.

Vivian, J. E., and Berkowitz, N. H. (1992). Anticipated bias from an outgroup: An attributional analysis. *European Journal of Social Psychology, 22*, 220–230.

Walker, L. E. (1989). *Terrifying love: Why battered women kill and how society responds.* New York: Harper & Row.

Wang, D. W., Moreland, R., & Argote, L. (1995). Group versus individual training and group performance: The mediating role of transactive mem-ory. *Personality and Social Psychology Bulletin 21*, 384–393.

Weiner, B. (1980). *Human motivation.* New York: Holt, Rinehart & Winston.

Williams, J. E., & Best, D. L. (1990). *Sex and psyche: Gender and self viewed cross-culturally.* Newbury Park, CA: Sage.

Wilson, T. D., & Linville, P. W. (1982). Improving academic performance of college freshmen: Attribution theory revisited. *Journal of Personality and Social Psychology 42*, 367–376.

Wood, W., Wong, F. Y., & Chachere, J. G. (1991). Effects of media violence on viewers' aggression in unconstrained social interactions. *Psychological Bulletin 109*, 371–383.

MOTIVATION
IN THE CLASSROOM

But practice without zeal—with equal comfort at success and failure—does not make perfect, and the nervous system grows away from the modes in which it is exercised with resulting discomfort. When the law of effect is omitted—when habit formation is reduced to the supposed effect of mere repetition—two results are almost certain. By the resulting theory, little in human behavior can be explained by the law of habit; and by the resulting practice, unproductive or extremely wasteful forms of drill are encouraged.

E. L. Thorndike (1913)

MOTIVATION AND
THE LAW OF EFFECT

If you were told that people learn more when they try harder, you would probably stifle a yawn and ask wryly, "So what else is new?" The fact that motivation is a crucial component in learning is so taken for granted that such a thought now seems like a statement of the obvious. Yet it wasn't always so. When Hermann Ebbinghaus spent those dismally boring months learning long lists of nonsense syllables, his motivation level must have been unbelievably high, and yet he didn't mention it. Perhaps he didn't even notice it. Perhaps his motivation, like the air around him, was so all-pervasive that it was virtually impossible for him to sense it.

It wasn't until early in the twentieth century that anyone experimentally validated the link between learning and motivation. E. L. Thorndike accomplished this task in his famous law of effect. Learning, Thorndike stated, is strengthened when it is followed by a *satisfying state of affairs*—satisfying, of course, to the learner. There it is—the obvious—but what a Pandora's box Thorndike opened with that innocent-sounding truism! Several people had articulated such a notion before Thorndike. But it was Thorndike who provided both the experimental evidence and (because of his own personal prestige) the sounding board for getting the message heard.

Educators throughout the country listened when Thorndike spoke. Other psychologists also listened, but they didn't like what they heard. Thorndike was immediately challenged, first, on the grounds that the law of effect was circular in its logic, and second, on the basis that it was totally illogical to assume that an event (satisfactory state of affairs) can work backward in time to influence a previous event (pairing of stimulus and response).

In answer to the first criticism, Thorndike correctly maintained that the law of effect was *not* circular (see *nominal fallacy* in the glossary), since he had given an independent, operational definition of the satisfying state of affairs. Said Thorndike, "By a satisfying state of affairs is meant one which the animal does nothing to avoid, often doing things which maintain or renew it" (Thorndike, 1913). In answer to the second objection, Thorndike argued that the intricacies of deductive logic cannot be used to refute an observable, experimentally validated fact. It would be like using a deductive proof to indicate that the moon is in a gaseous state despite the fact that Neil Armstrong brought back rock-hard evidence to the contrary. Though there remained a few diehards like Edwin Guthrie who said that motivation need not be directly involved in learning, Thorndike's answers were powerful enough to silence most of the critics, and by 1920 motivation was a firmly established concept in education and psychology.

A Current Appraisal

Today virtually all psychologists acknowledge the impact of motivational variables on human behavior. It is little wonder that past students of educational psychology could never fully appreciate the concepts of growth, development, learning, and achievement without taking into account motivation. Teachers have long recognized that these motivational, or nonintellectual, factors are critical in determining the achievement of their students. Even if we were to develop an absolutely reliable, valid, and culture-fair measure of intelligence, no totally accurate prediction of academic achievement could be made without consideration of the motivational variables.

Implicit in the entire literature on underachievement and overachievement is the assumption that motivational and emotional variables play a crucial, if not *the* crucial, role in academic success. We have probably all known individuals loaded with IQ points and able to learn with seemingly little or no effort who nevertheless flunk more courses than they pass. It is more than just a glib cliché that some students seem to be desperately (though probably unwittingly) trying *not* to achieve academically. The student's veiled smile when the parents are presented with a report card filled with low grades is obvious evidence of a tragically self-defeating yet concerted effort at "striking back." "Show *this* around the country club" is the hidden message to many a coercive parent.

Although we have stressed throughout this book the extreme importance of early experience on the developing child, the environmental impact does not, of course, cease abruptly at age five or six. From the very first day the child—especially the middle-class child—enters school, society exerts enormous pressure to succeed academically. The young child often comes to see the entire adult world as joined in an enormous conspiracy to urge, cajole, or threaten him or her into believing that scholastic success is the single most important thing in the world. First-grade teachers, and certainly parents of first-graders, have been known to admonish a child who might be having some difficulty in following the plot of a "See Puff jump" epic with the awesome threat, "You'll never get into college!"

The pressures often increase geometrically as the child progresses into high school. Some high school guidance counselors seem to believe that their very existence depends not on guiding the student toward opportunities for taking advantage of his or her greatest potential and aptitudes, but on what percentage of the senior class is accepted for college. One counselor proudly boasted that all but three of her graduating seniors had been placed in college, and two of those three would have gone on to college but because of emotional problems they had to be institutionalized. "But as soon as they get out, I'll get them into college," she proclaimed.

Motivation Never Acts in a Vacuum

Motivation never operates in isolation from either learning or perception. Psychology's "big three"—learning, perception, and motivation—are in a constant state of interaction, each affecting and being affected by the other two. Not only does motivation affect learning, but learning also affects motivation. As we shall see, most human motives are learned or acquired. Nobody is born with a built-in motive for acquiring three-and-a-half-by-six-inch slips of green paper with a picture of George Washington printed on one side and the words "In God We Trust" on the other. Yet dollar bills have certainly been known to motivate people. The entire advertising industry is devoted to training and shaping our motives and, indeed, to supplying us with new ones.

Motives also affect perception. We often "see" what we want to see and even fail to see what displeases us. We have probably all had the experience of waiting to meet someone at an airport, train, or bus terminal and then prematurely "seeing" that person—only to find on closer inspection that we were in error. We "saw" the person we were hoping and wanting to see. The extent of our momentary embarrassment is a direct function of the volume of our greeting and of how dramatically we waved our hand.

Many years ago, a psychologist performed an experiment in which he showed people an extremely ambiguous picture, simply a blob of different colors daubed across a piece of cardboard. When persons who were hungry looked at this picture they reported seeing steak dinners, french fries, loaves of bread, and so on. The study clearly demonstrated that people tend to see the world from the point of view of their own motivational states (Sanford, 1936). As Shakespeare said in *A Midsummer Night's Dream:*

> Or in the night, imagining some fear
>
> How easy is a bush supposed a bear!

And we even use our own motives as unwitting guides in our perceptions of another person's motivational state. When feeling angry, we might erroneously attribute anger to another person, a phenomenon that can lead to an attribution error (Bierhoff, 1989).

Another important psychological concept is that of perceptual defense. A number of studies have noted that people tend not to see those things in their environment or in themselves that for some reason they find distasteful (Postman et al., 1948). A student with a strong distaste for math may literally not see the next day's assignment, even though the teacher clearly inscribed it at the top of the chalkboard. That same student, however, might have eyes like a Mount Palomar telescope if the announcement on the chalkboard had read, "Half day of school tomorrow."

Thus, perception depends on motivation, motivation depends on perception, and both depend and are dependent on learning.

THE MOTIVE AND ITS COMPONENTS

Psychologists who have analyzed motivation have found that a **motive** has two identifiable components—a need and a drive. **Needs,** on the one hand, are based on some deficit *within* the person. The deficit may be physiological or psychological, but in either case the deficit must lie within the person. Physiological needs are often obvious, such as needs for water, food, sex, sleep, warmth—and all are based on a physical deficit within the body. Psychological needs, though potentially just as powerful, are often more subtle and less easily identified, such as needs for approval, affection, power, and prestige. **Drives,** on the other hand, though certainly based on needs, have the added feature of an observable change in behavior. Drives imply motion of some sort. The person is not considered to be in a drive state until the need has goaded that person into action. The term **motive** refers to a drive (an activated need) that is directed toward or away from some sort of goal. Technically, then, the inner deficit (need)

pushes the person into action (drive) toward or away from some particular goal (motive). Finally, the individual's ultimate behavior may rest on a series of goals, separately or in combination, and is therefore more often than not multimotivated. Human beings are complex creatures, seldom acting on the basis of a single motive. Real life is not like a Skinner box, in which the whole thrust of the rat's existence depends on whether or not the lever is pressed. Thus, the motive cycle can be expressed as:

1. Need
2. Drive = Need + Action
3. Motive = Drive + Goal

PHYSIOLOGICAL MOTIVES

As we said, motives may be physiological or psychological. The satisfaction of physiological motives is typically beyond the role of the teacher (although an obviously hungry or improperly clothed child should be reported and helped). However, we should take a brief look at the physiological motives in order to make the whole topic more understandable.

Biological deficits are, of course, regulated within the organism. For example, it is known that the hypothalamus (a part of the brain) plays an important role in regulating the body's need for fat (Bennett & Gurin, 1982). **Physiological motives** are therefore based on physiological needs, or tissue deficits, within the body. At that level the motive, governed to some extent by the brain, will be aimed at reducing this deficit and returning the body to its natural state.

Physiologists use the term *homeostasis* to describe that process. Homeostasis is the tendency of the body to maintain a "steady state," or balance, among its various physiological components, such as the internal organs, the blood, and the hormones. The body does this more or less automatically, but often some overt, motivated behavior is also needed. For example, if one's body becomes too hot, sweating occurs and the automatic evaporation of the skin's moisture helps cool the skin area. However, the person also may *act* in ways designed to cool off the immediate environment, such as removing some clothing, opening windows, or turning on the air conditioner. Similarly, under conditions of extreme cold, the body shivers, and this reaction increases the metabolic rate. Burning the body's fuels faster generates extra heat. However, the individual also adds clothing, goes indoors, and generally seeks conditions that will reduce the discomfort. (Interestingly, the brain mechanisms involved in homeostasis may at times be misled by contrary cognitive information. For example, in one study, when subjects were told that the room temperature was higher than it really was, they all reported being just as comfortable as when the temperature was actually set at that higher level [Rohles, 1980].

Thus, physiological needs can be adjusted to some extent by the internal mechanisms of homeostasis, but goal-directed action may also be involved. Deficits of water and food cannot be compensated for internally, and the individual *must* seek out replacements from the external environment. Complicating matters is the fact that the individual will probably be faced with a host of alternative goals in the environment. If a person is hungry, for example, the choice of which food to select is overlaid with all sorts of learned, or *acquired*, habits and tastes. In an extremely interesting study, Clara Davis took a group of 6- to 12-month-olds and allowed them to select their own diets from a menu of natural, unprocessed, and unpurified foods (Davis, 1967). She found that these infants, not yet brainwashed by adults and various commercials, could be trusted to select a balanced diet if given a series of free choices among wholesome foods. Contrast this with adolescent and adult eating habits, such as taking in too many sweets, eating too little at breakfast, or snacking too much at bedtime. Not only human infants but also young and adult mammals generally have this ability, called *specific hunger*. Only human adults seem to lose it, through learning.

ACQUIRED MOTIVES

Earlier, we stated that motivation and learning are in constant interaction in the determination of behavior. Even physiological motives can have a heavy learning component, for example, in choosing *how* to satisfy such basic needs as those for food, warmth, and sex. It seems, however, that some motives are acquired—that is, they are entirely learned; they seem not to be continuously dependent on biological needs.

Functional Autonomy

The famous Harvard personality theorist, Gordon Allport, has proposed a theory of motivation called **functional autonomy** (Allport, 1967). In this theory Allport attempts to account for the myriad human motives for which no biological needs seem present. Allport tells us that many human motives arise when *a means to an end becomes an end in itself*. That is, the route chosen to search out a goal for satisfying a

more primitive need may itself become a goal. We have all read newspaper accounts of some miserly recluse living in squalor, existing on 50-cent cans of dog food, yet owning stocks and bonds and innumerable bankbooks worth hundreds of thousands of dollars. The original reason for saving the money— perhaps to satisfy the biological needs of food and warm shelter—was eventually taken over by the need for money itself, and this began to override the original intent. The means (saving money) to the end (food and shelter) became an end (saving money) in itself. Thus, the motive of saving money began to function autonomously, or independently. The motive came to have a life of its own and was no longer historically connected to its origin.

Suppose a young boy will practice on his violin only if his mother gives him an ice cream cone. Playing the violin is thus dependent on the primary reinforcer of ice cream. Then, one fine day the boy begins to play not for the ice cream but for the sheer joy of creating beautiful music. The motive for playing the violin comes to function autonomously and is no longer dependent on any earlier goal, or on any *external* goal. Someday perhaps that boy will play his violin on stage at Lincoln Center, and it is certainly fondly hoped that he won't have to go off into the wings between concertos and munch on a Dairy Queen special.

Emotions and Motivation

The types and levels of various emotions also have a strong impact on motivation. A child who is fearful reacts very differently to a situation than a child who feels confident and is self-assured; a teacher who for one reason or another is feeling temporarily depressed will respond to the class in ways the pupils may find baffling. A child who is happily walking home from school carrying a report card filled with grades of A may not respond as aggressively to a classmate's taunts as a child whose report card is laden with grades of F.

Psychologists have even found that the physiological arousal associated with certain emotions can transfer from one motivational area to another. For example, people who were emotionally aroused by watching a violent hockey or football game later found themselves more easily aroused sexually than those who had not seen the game. Also, young males who have just finished working out (doing calisthenics and lifting weights) tend to respond far more aggressively to a problem situation than if they had previously been involved in some more sedentary activity (Riesenzein, 1983).

Finally, conquering the feelings associated with

what one perceives to be a negative emotion may itself be extremely motivating. Some young daredevils even appear to be "addicted to their own adrenaline." Jumping from high places or climbing the tallest trees may at first fill the youngster with feelings of terror. But after a few attempts, although the initial fear is reduced, the emotional arousal may still be present, and the child looks for even taller trees in order to recreate the excitement. Not climbing the tree has now itself become an aversion. Psychologists explain this phenomenon in terms of the **opponent process theory** of acquired motivation. It can sometimes put children in the ironic position of needing to show off their bravado by recklessly talking back to the teacher in front of the entire class. Not doing so has now become aversive (Solomon, 1980).

Intrinsic versus Extrinsic Motivation

Intrinsic motives are those which are satisfied by internal reinforcers. Behavior that is intrinsically motivated is engaged in for its own sake, for the sheer joy and satisfaction derived from the performance itself. **Extrinsic motives,** on the other hand, depend on needs that must be satisfied by external reinforcers. Extrinsically motivated behaviors are performed not out of interest in the behavior itself but because they are seen as instrumental to some separate goal (Deci et al., 1991).

As we discovered in Chapter 9, Jerome Bruner, the great cognitive psychologist, is convinced that learning will be far longer-lasting when it is sustained by intrinsic motivation than when it is driven by the more transitory push of external reinforcers. Bruner does admit, however, that extrinsic motivation may be necessary to get the learner to initiate certain actions or to get the learning process started and off dead center. But once on its way, the sometimes fragile process of learning is better nourished and sustained by intrinsic motives. Bruner's position is similar in many ways to Allport's. Intrinsic motivation may require an external reinforcement to get it under way, but once it comes to function autonomously—that is, independently of the external reward—real learning can become a solid, lifetime pursuit.

Some psychologists are creating techniques for increasing the intrinsic motivation of children by helping them meet their needs for autonomy, competence, and self-mastery (Raffini, 1996). Intrinsic motivation, when it is present, usually builds on itself, thus producing an increased sense of motivation to continue the activity. Some people who are intrinsically motivated in a certain area often make extra efforts to seek out even more challenging situations (Deci & Ryan, 1980). Those who are willing to seek

Intrinsic motivation: learning for its own sake.

the challenge, to literally rise to the occasion, are also said to be high in self-efficacy (Schunk, 1991). One educator has provided parents and teachers with a list of five principles for fostering intrinsic motivation in young children:

1. Provide a novel and varied home environment.

2. Provide experiences in which children may have an effect on their environments.

3. Provide environments that are responsive to a child's actions.

4. Respond positively to children's questions while still encouraging children to seek their own solutions.

5. Reward children often with praise, which gives them a feeling of competence (Gottfried, 1983).

Self-Regulated Learning

Psychologists have long been aware that there are certain "self-starting" learners who are extremely self-disciplined, able to postpone gratification, and virtually able to teach themselves with little supervision. These individuals don't even seem to need any external reinforcers because their own internal feelings of success and accomplishment provide motivation enough. These are the self-regulated learners, those high achievers whose own inner resources, intrinsic motivation, and self-reliance produce an almost irresistible formula for success. In fact, one study found that students' scholastic achievements could be predicted with 93 percent accuracy on the basis of their measured self-regulation (Zimmerman, 1991). **Self-regulated learning** and motivation are interdependent processes. A learner's perception of personal academic self-worth is both a cause (motive) of learning and an effect (outcome) of learning. Self-regulated learners don't just react to their learning environments; they deliberately seek out further opportunities to learn (Zimmerman, 1989). They initiate activities designed to promote self-awareness of their learning styles (Zimmerman & Martinez-Pons, 1990), and their increased motivation prods them into setting increasingly higher learning goals, a trait that Bandura calls "self-regulation" (Bandura, 1989).

Research on self-regulation and development is fairly clear on this point: the ability to self-regulate and the age of the child go hand in hand. Young children (below age seven) may be motivated, but too often they lack awareness of their metacognitive strategies and seem overly naive about their ability to learn, in some cases regardless of outcome. As children approach adolescence, however, both their capacity for self-regulation and cognitive self-awareness increase (Zimmerman, 1991).

Maslow's Need Hierarchy

Abraham Maslow, an important psychologist in the area of motivation theory, has suggested that there is a definite order in which individuals attempt to satisfy their needs. When a person is in a situation in which several needs are operating simultaneously, the person strives to accommodate the need that is of the highest order of importance at that particular time. Maslow sees this order of importance as universal among human beings. Furthermore, he maintains that a person will remain at a given need level until those needs are satisfied, and then move on to the next level.

At the most basic level are physiological needs. Maslow contends that until these needs are at least partially satisfied, the individual will not be concerned with the needs of the next level, those of safety and security.

The Maslow **need hierarchy** is as follows:

1. *Physiological needs:* food, drink, sex, and shelter

2. *Safety needs:* security, order, protection, and family stability

3. *Love needs:* affection, group affiliation, and personal acceptance

4. *Esteem needs:* self-respect, prestige, reputation, and social status

5. *Self-actualization needs:* self-fulfillment and achievement of personal goals, ambitions, and talent

Maslow does not mean to imply that every human being achieves full success in satisfying all those needs. For example, not everyone gets to enjoy prestige and social status, let alone the ultimate goal of self-actualization. What Maslow does mean is that we must be alert to the fact that persons cannot even consider some of their more social needs when their basic needs are left unfulfilled. The hungry child or the child filled with anxiety because of a traumatic family situation may not wholeheartedly pursue goals of prestige and self-actualization (Maslow, 1954).

Maslow's model has not gone unchallenged. In fact some theorists now insist that there are cases in which the failure to satisfy lower and more basic needs may actually motivate people to seek the fulfillment of higher-level needs, as when a family that has to struggle through difficult economic times becomes closer as a result of the shared experience. In this case, the needs for self-esteem and a sense of belonging become stronger because of the lack of more basic satisfactions. Thus, adversity, it has been argued, may even promote self-actualization (Neher, 1991).

Acquired Motives and Social Forces

Acquired motives, such as competition, power, status, approval, and even achievement, are dictated by social rules and pressures—either in origin or in the form in which they are expressed. The cultural anthropologists, who have swarmed over every remote nook and cranny on earth, have been unanimous in telling us of the great variation in human motivation and in *how these motives are expressed.* Before the days of the great field treks by such anthropologists as Margaret Mead and Ruth Benedict, many early Western psychologists took the parochial view that what they observed in their own culture was true the world over. Because it was assumed that all these motives were present among all people everywhere, the term *instinct* was used.

William McDougall, who in 1908 wrote the first book to carry the title *Social Psychology*, felt that group life was an inherent part of our basic nature (McDougall, 1908). Therefore, to McDougall, all so-

SPOTLIGHT ON SELF-REGULATION AND TEACHING

A Cognitive Approach

Self-regulated learners obviously do not need a lot of help from either teachers or researchers. The point of doing research on them is that if we can understand more about these children—the strategies they use, the reasons for their motivation, and the developmental nature of these abilities—maybe we can teach other, less motivated children how to increase their levels of academic achievement. Several teaching strategies have been identified as promoting self-regulated learning.[a]

1. Children can be taught to use inner speech to enhance personal motivation. For example, the child can learn to repeat phrases such as "I'll do better next time" or "I know I can succeed."

2. Children can be taught to change their implicit cognitive theories. This has been called the "top-down" approach. Since many children have faulty beliefs about the best methods to employ in the learning situation, they can benefit from the direct teaching of certain tactics. Teaching children to use more efficient learning strategies, however, should not be done in an arbitrary or domineering fashion, but in such a way that the children come to appreciate the value of these strategies. The child who simply follows a set of seemingly arbitrary cognitive rules will not retain the

strategy nearly as well as the child who understands the reasons for, and makes a personal commitment to, the new approach. When the child comes to realize that these tactics lead to better learning and to more positive beliefs about learning, especially learning that can be transferred to other situations, this approach often spontaneously leads to the self-controlled use of increasingly sophisticated strategies.

3. Children can be taught to make their thinking public. Open class discussions allow thinking to be observed by the teacher as well as shared among classmates. In fact, some theorists believe that freewheeling and open-ended discussions are at the heart of metacognitive training.[b] There is a double benefit to this approach, since it allows the teacher to hear and "see" the way the students are thinking, and thus diagnose processing difficulties, while evaluating how well the children are understanding the curriculum content.

4. Children can be taught strategies involving active participation and collaboration. Getting children to become active participants in the learning process promotes both increased motivation and more effective learning techniques. For example, peer tutoring owes much of its success to the

fact that a child can't simply be a passive bystander, but must actively collaborate in the learning process. Reciprocal teaching demands that the students swap roles, from tutor to student, and it forces them to pay attention and monitor the other's thinking. As Paris and Newman have stated, "When students act as teachers, they are also given another opportunity to relearn what they may only have thought they knew. As students teach others, they develop a personal commitment to the strategies they are teaching."[c] And as these strategies are found to be successful, motivation also increases.

5. Children can be taught to ask themselves questions as they read and then to summarize paragraphs. Studies have shown that this metacognitive strategy can have dramatically positive effects on comprehension.[d]

---

[a] Paris, S. G., & Newman, R. S. (1990). Developmental aspects of self-regulated learning. *Educational Psychologist, 25,* 87–102.
[b] Paris, S. G., Cross, D.R., & Lipson, M. Y. (1984). Informed strategies for learning: A program to improve children's reading awareness and comprehension. *Journal of Educational Psychology, 76,* 1239–1252.
[c] Paris & Newman (1990).
[d] Nolan, T. (1991). Self-questioning and prediction: Combining metacognitive strategies. *Journal of Reading, 35,* 132–138.

cial life was a result of our inherited instincts. For example, McDougall stated that people get together in groups because of their gregarious instincts. Furthermore, he said that these instincts carried an emotional quality that made their fulfillment irresistible. McDougall's bleak psychology meant that people were destined to play out the preprogrammed instincts that were built into their biological natures.

Because of the *nominal fallacy* involved in the instinct approach, McDougall's version of social motivation finally became discredited and an object of real scorn. To declare that students achieved academically because of an achievement instinct meant that those students who were not so blessed were doomed to a school life of academic frustration and that *nothing could be done to change it.* By the mid-1920s psychology in general had dismissed instinct theory as unscientific and ludicrous. And ludicrous it was. By 1924 it was found that McDougall and other instinct theorists had compiled lists of more than 6,000 instincts to explain behavior. Virtually any conceivable bit of behavior had been "explained" by the simple expedient of calling it instinctive. Everything from twiddling one's thumbs to "inserting the fingers in crannies to dislodge small animals hidden there" was seriously cited as a legitimate instinctive behavior. It is now clear that social motives differ widely among peoples throughout the world because social motives are in fact learned, or acquired.

Need for Approval

In retrospect, it is easy to see how instinct theory got started. Though social motives are learned, people tend to learn these lessons so well that they begin to behave with almost the kind of automatic precision of a homing pigeon. One of the best-learned social motives is the **motive for social approval.** An infant soon learns to associate the sound of the mother's voice with his or her own satisfactions. Since the mother is usually the one to provide food and warmth for the infant, her voice and its various intonations come to matter a great deal. The infant eventually learns that the sounds of approval follow some responses and the sounds of disapproval (and then perhaps punishment) follow other responses. As words are learned, the mother's voice becomes even more potent, and the child usually attempts to modify behavior in accordance with her verbal reactions.

Usually during the second year, the child also begins to learn that many of the things he or she really wants to do, like eating candy before meals or drawing on the wall, are constantly followed by disapproval. That is, the child begins to associate personal satisfaction with the sounds of disapproval. This reaction on the part of the child helps to explain the negativism of the "terrible twos," a dilemma for both parent and child. To make matters worse, the child is also faced with many situations in which the sounds of approval follow behaviors the child does *not* want

to do, like helping to rake leaves, washing dishes, or going to bed. It is little wonder that most children are caught in an approval-disapproval conflict situation, the overtones of which can last for a lifetime.

Teachers must be alert to this conflict. Since approval, in the form of good grades, gold stars, a friendly "well done," is the teacher's most powerful ally, it is to the definite advantage of both teacher and student that this motive not be stifled. A teacher may unwittingly reduce the intensity of the child's approval motive by using approval too liberally in situations that the child finds distasteful. Conversely, too much self-sacrifice on the part of the child in order to receive approval may create a boomerang effect—even to the point at which approval is no longer sought. This may be one facet of the underachievement syndrome. The student has learned that approval can be gained only at a terrible price. Therefore, seeking it no longer seems worthwhile.

Although the approval motive obviously originates in the infant's need for physiological satisfaction, it is one of those many acquired motives that eventually seem to have lives of their own. The approval motive comes to function autonomously—even to the extent of overriding more primitive motives. People have been known to go hungry rather than give up the opportunity to hear the sounds of applause. Acquired needs, however, such as the need for approval, should be understood within their social context. The overt expression of such needs takes very different forms, depending on the social situation, such as when dealing with parents or teachers versus peers (Geen, 1995).

Peer approval   Though the teacher, like the parents, is in an especially powerful position to shape a child's behavior through the vehicle of approval, adults are not the only source of this potent reinforcement. Students often play to the applause of their peers—a situation that can be extremely disruptive when the students and teacher have widely different goals. When peer approval becomes more important than the approval of the teacher, the classroom situation may get out of hand. In order to avert too many open confrontations, it is sometimes wise for a teacher to ignore a certain amount of student horseplay. This approach must be handled carefully and judiciously because the teacher should not be perceived as a doddering fool in whose classroom anything goes. The students will certainly test the limits of the teacher's permissiveness.

It is known that aggressive children tend to be less accepted by their peers, but the direction of this relationship is still not clear. Do the children become aggressive because they are not popular, or is their lack of popularity a result of their aggressive behavior? The importance of this issue is underscored by the fact that these unpopular children, who do not make friends easily and who are not accepted by their peers, are more at risk when it comes to personal adjustment in later life. As adults, they are more apt to engage in antisocial activities and show more signs of psychopathology than those who enjoyed higher levels of peer acceptance (Parker & Asher, 1987).

Peer approval is closely linked to the need for affiliation. People differ in the degree of their desire to be with other people. Some children feel compelled to constantly seek out the company of others, while other children need more time to be alone. Students who can't stand being alone often find homework, a solitary activity, especially burdensome. Typically, people feel stronger needs to affiliate under conditions of stress. This seems to be especially true when the others with whom we might affiliate appear to be competent and strong (Rofe, 1984).

The ripple effect   Sooner or later, usually sooner, every teacher confronts the situation in which a student seeking peer approval acts out in some inappropriate way. Perhaps it begins with a student's surreptitiously making animal sounds, groaning, or throwing a paper airplane. Soon another student joins in, then another, and quickly bedlam ensues. This phenomenon, in which one disruptive student triggers disruption by the entire class, is known as the ripple effect (Kounin, 1970). Studies have shown that the ripple effect is far more prevalent in classes in which the motivation to learn is low. However, these same studies indicate that in highly motivated classes, the teacher's immediate attempt to restore order is greeted by student approval. In the studies, students in the highly motivated classes seemed to want an environment conducive to learning, and they stated that the teacher's efforts to scold the instigator made them even more willing to do their work. In the classes with low levels of motivation, students took every student-teacher confrontation as a fresh opportunity for more catcalls and general disruption.

Teachers differ in their ability to contain the ripple effect, and the difference seems to depend on the teacher's personality and level of control. The teacher whose style seems best suited to prevent the ripple effect has been called "with it" or "hip." This is the teacher who creates the impression that "firm hands are on the wheel," that the situation is well under control. On the one hand, the "hip" teacher doesn't always jump in as soon as a child acts out. However, when the hip teacher does move into the fray, she confronts the instigator one on one. In con-

trast, the teacher who is not "with it" usually lets the situation run on for too long, thereby allowing the ripples to become tidal waves. Then, when she does finally step in, she compounds the felony either by reprimanding *the class as a whole* or by punishing the last child she spots acting up.

Achievement

Perhaps no other acquired motive has been the object of as much discussion and research among educational psychologists as **achievement motivation.** Although it probably originates in the service of physiological needs, or at least in association with the need for approval, the achievement motive may itself become autonomous. When it does, the student is in the happy position of possessing an intrinsic motive to achieve, that is, to achieve for the sake of the achievement itself. One study that appears to support the back-to-basics movement found that children show higher levels of overall achievement when teachers spend larger amounts of time in the *direct* teaching of reading, math, science, and social studies than in music, art, or social awareness (Rosenshine, 1980).

The now-famous Coleman report found that a student's personal feeling of self-directed competence was the most important factor in determining academic achievement. This factor was discovered to be more important than a whole host of seemingly crucial variables, including social-class differences, race, pupil-teacher ratios, the number of books in the library, and even the educational background of the teachers. Academic achievement depended most heavily on the student's personal conviction of being in charge of his or her own fate. The high achievers did not ascribe their fate to luck or to the vagaries of chance but rather to their own personal decisions and efforts. Society's "losers" are far more apt to see their lot determined by impersonal, fatalistic forces than are the "winners" (Coleman et al., 1966).

Underachievers   Society's "losers," however, need constant study, evaluation, and help, for unless their condition can be reversed, society itself will be the real loser. When the student has the ability to learn and profit from the educational experience, it is indeed frustrating to witness, as every teacher has, the wasted talent of the underachiever. It is like an Indianapolis racing car with a high horsepower engine going no more than 20 miles per hour because of a mechanical failure that prevents the driver from depressing the accelerator.

The problem of the underachiever illustrates par

SPOTLIGHT ON LEARNED HELPLESSNESS

Where Has All the Motivation Gone?

Just as higher levels of motivation can be learned, so too can lowered levels. Some children (as well as adults) seem to lose their sense of motivation and become apathetic, extremely passive, and even emotionally depressed. This defeatist attitude appears to be learned through a series of frustrating situations in which the child has been treated in inconsistent and unpredictable ways. The result is that children feel they have no control over the consequences of their actions, that whatever they do results in failure, so why try?[a] This condition should in most cases be brought to the attention of the school psychologist, especially if it occurs during adolescence. Among teenagers, learned helplessness, and the possibility of concomitant depression, can become incapacitating and should be taken seriously. Depression during adolescence has been found to be a powerful predictor of depression

in adulthood.[b] Although this condition often requires the assistance of a professional psychologist, the teacher can also be an important source of help. Such pupils should be provided with opportunities for frequent, little successes, given in small steps, and then followed by immediate feedback. Computer-assisted instruction (CAI) could also be tried, since with CAI the small steps and immediate feedback can be built right into the program. Above all, however, the teacher's expectations and rewards should remain as consistent and predictable as humanly possible.

Children who rarely experience success in the classroom and perceive themselves as academic failures (as in the case of the learning-disabled) often develop a syndrome that includes a variety of self-defeating motives. For example: (1) such children are far more apt to develop an external

locus of control, (2) they are more easily influenced by extrinsic reinforcements, (3) they are low in self-regulated learning strategies, (4) they have low levels of self-efficacy, and (4) they are more apt to develop feelings of learned helplessness, showing little in the way of competence motivation.[c] Obviously, such children can be extremely difficult for the classroom teacher to handle, and they need the special help of the school psychologist in learning coping strategies for dealing with failure.

---

[a] Rosehan, D. L., & Seligman, M. E. P. *Abnormal psychology* (2d ed.). New York: Norton.
[b] Garber, J., Kriss, M. R., Koch, M., & Lindholm, L. (1988). Recurrent depression in adolescents: A follow-up study. *Journal of the American Academy of Child and Adolescent Psychiatry 27,* 49–54.
[c] Hallahan, D. P., & Kauffman, J. M. (1988). *Exceptional children.* Englewood Cliffs, NJ: Prentice Hall.

---

excellence the importance of the motivational variables in academic success. In one study the researchers, holding intelligence constant, found that academic achievement was a function of the student's ego strength or reality orientation (Hummel & Sprinthall, 1965). The study demonstrated that the underachiever possessed a weak ego and was unwilling to postpone pleasure. Underachievers were more easily distracted and less able to set about tasks in an organized manner. In short, these students were less able to control their own basic impulses and, therefore, their destinies.

Another study, in which achievement motivation was related to whether or not women went on to college, found that achieving women were more in tune with the norms of their peer group or reference

group than were nonachieving women. The achieving women were better able to predict how members of their peer group would react in various situations (Sprinthall & Bennett, 1978).

It's clear that achievement motivation and success are highly correlated, but, as is so often the case, it is sometimes difficult to determine the direction of this relationship. Was Sally's high achievement motivation in basketball a result of her superior athletic skills, or was it the other way around? Was Billy's low achievement motivation in reading a result or a cause of his poor comprehension skills? The evidence suggests that the two are reciprocal, each being sustained by and sustaining the other (Gottfried, 1985). One way of taking advantage of this reciprocity is through the use of peer tutoring. Giving help to another student, especially when it involves explanation and elaboration, produces higher learning and increased motivation in the *helper* (Webb, 1983; Goodenow, 1992). In other words, tutoring increases both the skill level *and* the motivation of the tutor.

Achievement and gender differences

Academically, females definitely outperform males, especially in the lower school grades. By the time they get to high school and college, however, the males catch up, and in the posteducational world the males move ahead of the females in virtually every area—arts, professions, sciences, corporate life, and so on (Maccoby & Jacklinn, 1974). Without doubt, this phenomenon is cultural and not genetic. Men are expected to achieve more; they are given more opportunities to achieve and are rewarded more for their achievements. Young men are constantly reminded that they are going to be the breadwinners in the family and that even the social status of their wives and children will depend on their efforts. By the time he reaches high school and college, the average male in our society definitely hears this cultural message and begins to work harder, knowing that not only his own fate but that of his future family rests with his ability to achieve.

Sexism in society

The message of sexism is often subtle, but it seems ever present. One theorist has suggested that men and women converse in ways that are in some ways so different as to be likened to cross-cultural communication. According to this view, women are more apt to communicate in a language of connection and intimacy, whereas men converse in a language of status, independence, and power. As children, little girls use talk as a way of maintaining intimacy, and when playing in groups they tend to make more suggestions and give fewer orders than do little boys. For boys, talk is used more as a method of negotiating status. High-status boys give orders and push around (or even bully) the low-status boys (Tannen, 1990). Males have also been found to use conversational ploys to gain the upper hand in interactions with females (Parlee, 1979). These verbal power ploys were dubbed *conversational politics,* in which the men tended to ignore topics that the women raised and the women usually picked up on the subjects raised by men. The men were also more apt to interrupt women, even in mid-sentence—in the same way that parents interrupt children. In general, cultural pressures are so strong that both males *and females* accept conversational power ploys like these as normal.

Several years ago an interesting attempt was

"Oh, Helen—I saw the counselor today, and he told me to start paying more attention to you."

From *The Wall Street Journal,* by permission, Cartoon Features Syndicate.

made to discover whether the women's movement had made any impact on sexism. A number of couples were selected to visit various restaurants in order to discover whether the man or woman would get the check. Almost always, the check went to the man. Even when a female executive was taking a male friend to dinner and was clearly in charge—asking for the table, ordering for both, answering all questions—she still received the check only 5 out of 36 times. And waitresses, it turned out, were even less apt to give the woman the check than waiters (Laner, 1979).

Sexism in schools

Although it appears that women are not typically given the check in restaurants, they certainly often get the "shaft" in most American school systems. Public schools still seem to be strongly organized around the gender variable. By the last decade of the twentieth century, 72 percent of all K–12 classroom teaching was being done by women, whereas only 28 percent of school principals and less than 5 percent of school superintendents were women (American Association of School

Administrators, 1990). In high school, science teachers are more apt to be male, whereas less than 10 percent of all home-economics courses are taught by men. Similarly, among industrial arts teachers, only 4 percent are women (U.S. Department of Education, 1992). It's apparently considered all right for women to teach our children but often not all right if they concern themselves with administering the educational enterprise.

Fear of success   **Matina S. Horner** has noted that an important factor in creating lower levels of achievement (and sustaining sexism) is the **fear of success** (Horner, 1968). She has also noted that females, because of their cultural brainwashing, are more prone to this condition than males. Many females assume that achievement brings with it many extremely unpleasant side effects, not the least of which is a "loss of femininity." Women also tend to perceive that competing for success is somehow too aggressive an activity to be consistent with their stereotyped self-image of "being a lady."

Horner asked college women and men to complete a series of stories that began like this one: "After first-term grades are out, Joan [John for the males] finds herself [himself] at the top of her class." The vast majority of women wrote stories clearly showing the fear-of-success theme, whereas the men typically wrote stories that implied a positive outlook toward success. The women's fear-of-success stories were of three general types: First, and most common, were stories indicating fears of being socially rejected, unmarriageable, unpopular, lonely, and isolated; second were stories that showed doubts about femininity and normality; and third were stories that flatly denied that such success was possible ("It was later discovered that there had been a mistake in the registrar's office, and Joan was really not first") (Horner, 1969).

More recently, a group of junior high school girls was tested, and although the majority did show evidence of a fear of success, there was an interesting and important sidelight. The girls whose stories predicted a more positive outlook (admittedly a minority) actually performed better by a margin of six to one on an intellectual task than did the girls whose stories reflected a fear-of-success theme (Harvey, 1975).

Finally, the 17-year-old daughter of one of the authors wrote the following. It perhaps indicates that the situation may be improving.

Joan realizes that she has had to work very hard to get where she is, but having done so well, she de-

cides she must keep it up. Joan faces a lot of pressure from her friends, who tell her she should put away the books and go to more parties—that she has already proven herself, so why keep pushing? Though Joan is tempted by her friends, she realizes that she wouldn't really be happy unless she was working up to her potential. One night, while in bed, Joan said to herself, "I want to do my best these next two years because this is the only life I have, and I want to make it a successful one."

Although there is obviously an element of conflict in the story, achievement does win out in the end.

Fear of failure   Fear of failure has also haunted some schoolchildren to the point where they won't take any problemsolving risks. To be judged as having failed is seen as so terrifyingly traumatic that an almost trancelike state sets in, causing the child to cling so tenaciously to "safe" knowledge that curiosity, discovery, creativity, and even cognitive growth itself may become stunted. To prevent this, "schools without failure," such as Summerhill, have been introduced. The theory is that the threat of failure does not motivate students but instead acts as a detriment to a secure and efficient learning environment. For these and other reasons, social promotions, whereby children are kept with their age-mates regardless of academic performance, have become increasingly common.

This view has not gone unchallenged. Robert Ebel believes that the removal of the threat of failures has, in fact, removed an important academic incentive (Ebel, 1980).

Competence

Robert White, a personality theorist, has suggested that one of the most fundamental human motives is based on a strong personal desire to master one's environment. White calls this *competence motivation* (White, 1959). Competence motivation is without question an intrinsic motive and one that may even have survival value for the species. To become competent—to achieve a degree of mastery over one's environment—allows the individual to take charge of his or her own life, in fact, to be the author of his or her own fate. There is a real question as to whether the human race could have survived so long on this harsh planet without that strong desire for mastery. If we were, instead, simply passive blobs of protoplasm being buffeted about by an impersonal and seemingly cruel environment, perhaps our species would have died out thousands of years ago.

Competence motivation need not depend on culturally acquired achievement motivations but may itself have deep biological roots. Even at 19 months, infants may display smiles of satisfaction on completing a job (a simple job, but nevertheless a job well done). Jerome Kagan calls these *mastery smiles* and presumes that they are indicative of an inner feeling of pride at having completed the task (Kagan, 1984).

A teacher can certainly take advantage of competence motivation in the classroom. Students are always going to be more interested in what they are good at, whereas it is nearly impossible to motivate them in areas in which they have no competence. In a sense, it's like J. McV. Hunt's problem of the match (see Chapter 4) or Piaget's *only* motivational concept, that of equilibration (see Chapter 5). The teacher must attempt to match the new stimulus inputs to the student's level of competence. The most effective technique is to keep the new material a shade or two above the level at which the student is currently operating, always a little out of reach. Some degree of challenge helps initiate and maintain competence motivation.

Curiosity

Closely linked to competence motivation is **curiosity motivation.** Indeed, the two may be inseparable. There is much recent speculation that the curiosity motive is not an acquired motive at all but is, in fact, based on the physiological functioning of the nervous system. There seems to be mounting evidence that the curiosity motive functions autonomously right from birth, that it never depends on food or drink or on any other biological predecessor. **Harry F. Harlow** tells us, for example, that monkeys have been observed taking apart and reassembling a metal lock arrangement. Just like the child who takes a clock apart to see what makes it tick, monkeys will manipulate mechanical puzzles for no reinforcement other than the sheer joy of manipulation. One monkey continued taking a complicated metal lock apart for 10 straight hours. "At this point the experiment was terminated because of experimenter fatigue; the monkey was still going strong" (Harlow et al., 1971).

In another study, a monkey was trained to push a certain panel inside the cage, with food as the posi-

Curiosity may be inborn.

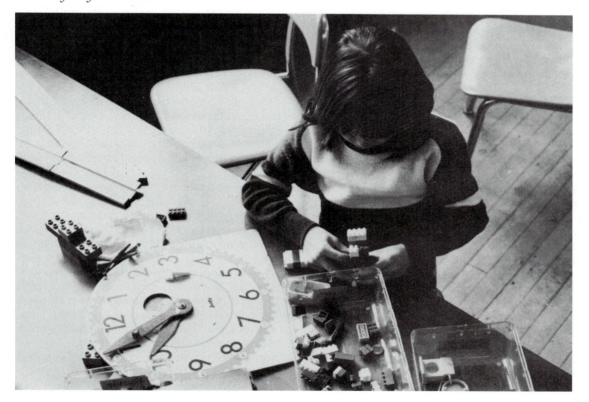

tive reinforcer. In order to observe the monkey during the learning trials, the experimenter made a small peephole in the screen that separated him from the monkey. The peephole, however, immediately became an object of great fascination for the monkey, and when the experimenter tried to peer through the hole, all he could see was the eye of the monkey peering back.

Monkeys are also seemingly fascinated by watching the playback of color videotapes of the activities of other monkeys, especially when male monkeys are allowed to observe tapes of female monkeys (Swartz & Rosenblum, 1980). Monkeys have actually been conditioned to discriminate between stimuli (a blue card and a yellow card), with the only reinforcer being the opportunity to open a small door in the training box and look out. Thus, the drive to manipulate objects and to explore the world visually "is fundamental and primary in monkeys and man" (Harlow et al., 1971, p. 272).

D. E. Berlyne has suggested that when a person (or animal) is in a situation in which conflicting responses are possible, a curiosity drive is generated, and the person (or animal) is motivated to seek further information just to satisfy the drive. That could mean that discovery learning, as Bruner has suggested, is indeed self-reinforcing. Berlyne believes that there is an optimum level of arousal that is physiologically based. He sees arousal level as a function of brain excitation: If the arousal level is too low, the child may attempt to increase it by taking in new stimuli; if the arousal level is too high, however, the child will attempt to lower it by reducing the stimulus inputs (Berlyne, 1960).

Self-Esteem

Effects on academic performance   Since the more academically successful students tend to display higher levels of various affective components, including **self-esteem** (at least when tested in a school setting), it might seem to follow that increasing any student's feeling of self-esteem would then be translated into an increase in academic performance. It is also assumed that children who feel good about themselves will be less likely to bully other children. If you value yourself, goes the argument, you will so value others around you. On the basis of these premises, many elementary schools throughout the nation, especially schools in economically distressed areas, have been implementing a variety of programs aimed at increasing student feelings of self-esteem. Most of the programs rely on teaching the children songs and even rap phrases, such as "I'm beautiful, I'm wonderful, I know I'm a star" or "I'm

good enough, I'm smart enough, and doggone it people like me" or "No matter what you say or do to me, I'm still a worthwhile person." The results of these efforts, however, have been questionable (Strein, 1988). Although the measured student feelings of self-esteem have often been shown to rise as a result of these training programs, there seems to be no concomitant rise in academic achievement or any reduction in aggressive behavior. In fact, critics of the self-esteem movement maintain that these programs lead to the practice of lavishing praise on the most modest of accomplishments. Constantly hearing how wonderful one is may eventually tend to cast some doubt on the legitimacy of the message and even perhaps of the messenger. In one school, children were asked to finish a sentence that began with "I am special because . . ." The children used such completions as "I can ride a bike," "I can color," or "I can play with my friends." How long will it take these children to discover that these are actually rather trivial accomplishments? As Lilian Katz suggests, if everybody is that special, then perhaps nobody is special at all (Katz, 1993). Katz further explains that self-esteem can be better conveyed to students when others, especially adults, treat them with respect, ask for their views and preferences, and provide opportunities for choices about the things that matter to them. Also, sometimes children fail, and when this happens they shouldn't be praised for it (or punished either). Learning to deal realistically with reversals and learning to persist are integral parts of a child's long road to mastery, and mastery, as both Erik Erikson and Robert White have observed, is the real foundation for a lasting self-esteem. Says Katz, "children who are helped to develop these qualities will surely respect themselves—though they probably will have better things to think about." Psychologist William Damon says that the self-esteem programs have no empirical base whatever to support their claims of positive educational accomplishments or higher grades (Damon, 1995). And Robyn Dawes suggests that the self-esteem mystique is simply a myth, and that in fact these programs may do more harm than good, since they may mislead children into thinking that learning a few easy rap lyrics will take the place of the effortful work needed to achieve their goals (Dawes, 1994). However, there are documented studies that show a positive and significant relationship between the teacher's levels of interpersonal functioning and student gains *both* on achievement test scores and in enhanced self-concepts (Aspy et al., 1984).

It is becoming increasingly clear that the surest route to student self-esteem is through the child's own personal competence and mastery (which should result from effective teaching), not through learning songs and rhymes about how good children feel about themselves. Both Erik Erikson and Robert White have theorized that all children have an in-born drive to master and explore the environment, and that this mastery is self-rewarding and crucial to feelings of self-esteem. Children should be offered opportunities for these explorations as a means of allowing for the natural unfolding of mastery and self-esteem. Critics also worry that the time spent on these self-esteem programs may be time taken away from more traditional academic pursuits, like arithmetic and spelling. There is also concern that a gain in self-esteem may be short-lived when the youngsters discover that they don't have the skills to count their change after ordering a Big Mac.

Effects on later success   Closely related to the issue of self-esteem is the notion that students will be more motivated and work harder in school if they believe that their efforts will later pay off in the job market. John Ogbu has argued that African-American children know that they will someday face a job ceiling that completely prevents them from receiving economic rewards that are anywhere near commensurate with their educational efforts (Fordham & Ogbu, 1986). In fact, says Ogbu, this is the main reason that black children don't put their full efforts into their homework assignments. In a partial test of this hypothesis, one study asked students to respond to two questions: "Suppose you do get a good education in high school, how likely is it that you will end up with the kind of job you hope to get?" and "Suppose you don't get a good education in high school, how likely is it that you will still end up with the kind of job you hope to get?" (Steinberg et al., 1992). The results tended to support Ogbu, in that the more that students believed that doing well in school paid off, the better they performed in school. This result held up for white, African-American, and Asian American students. It was also found that the second question, concerning the negative consequences of school failure, was an even better predictor of school success. Academically successful Asian American and white students were far more apt to believe that a good job will *not* follow a poor education.

The results of such studies must be interpreted carefully, for, as we have seen over and over, it is sometimes extremely difficult to extract the reason for *post hoc* relationships. It may well be that students do better in school because they believe that educational effort pays off in the job market, or it may be that because they are doing well in school they believe that it will pay off later, that is, that all this effort can't be a total waste. This latter explanation

would be consistent with the concept of cognitive consonance (see Chapter 17).

Cooperation and Competition

Two other acquired motives of importance for teachers are cooperation and competition. First, there is no clear evidence that competition is built into the human species as some kind of biologically determined instinct. In fact, cultural anthropologists claim to have found groups of people, such as the Zunis, in the American Southwest, in which competition is said to be virtually nonexistent. We are told that for the Zunis, the act of winning at anything is so frowned on that it brings disgrace and social ostracism. One young teacher who got a job working with Zuni children attempted to invoke a competitive spirit in order to increase their motivation. She had them all at their desks doing arithmetic problems, and she then asked that the first one to finish proudly stand. Instead, the Zuni children patiently waited for the last one to finish, and then *stood* in unison.

Our culture, in contrast, reinforces competitive behavior, often at the expense of cooperation. Bruner, however, has suggested that a case can be made for cooperativeness as the more fundamental of the two motives. Even biologists have long fretted over this seeming irony. After all, it would seem that the urge to survive is fundamentally selfish, and yet cooperative behavior can be observed in species after species, from bacteria to humans. Certain bacteria cells hunt their prey in cooperative groups, cornering their targets just like a pride of lions homing in on a wounded gazelle or a group of vampire bats sharing food with unrelated but needy bats. Even fish will take on high-risk forays on behalf of their schools by scouting the surrounding waters for potential enemies. Therefore, Bruner says that reciprocity, which is a motive for working with others cooperatively, may in fact be built into human species and that society itself developed as a result of this most basic motive (Bruner, 1966).

Cooperation in the classroom   American schools have traditionally utilized a competitive grading system in evaluating students. This is certainly a major reason why the competitive motive is so strongly ingrained among Americans. That schools reflect the cultural norms of the society as a whole should come as no surprise. Actually, one study has shown that the longer a person remains in school, the more competitive he or she becomes (Nelson & Kagan, 1972). Social psychologists have been concerned, however,

Harlow's evidence supports the theory of an innate curiosity drive. One monkey continued to take apart a complicated metal lock for ten straight hours.

that competitive grading may in fact have several harmful side effects. For example, negative attitudes, both toward the teacher and toward school in general, may result from too high a competitive level. Competition also engenders a general hostility, which causes many students to be highly critical of one another (perhaps in hope of building their own images). One social psychologist, **Morton Deutch,** in comparing students in competitive versus cooperative classrooms, found that the competitive group atmosphere tended to create the following:

1. Students with higher levels of anxiety

2. Students who think less of themselves and their work

3. Students with less favorable attitudes toward their classmates

4. Students with a lowered feeling of responsibility toward others (Deutch, 1979)

Deutch has been studying these factors for almost 50 years (Deutch, 1949), and his message to teachers is clear: The more cooperative the group tasks students can be involved in, the more positive will be the general classroom atmosphere. He urges that, when possible, grades be assigned to group efforts—efforts in which the individual's goal can be achieved only if all the individuals in the group reach their goals. The focus should be on interdependence among members of the class and not simply on dog-eat-dog competition.

In another example of cooperative learning, Robert Slavin had students work in mixed-ability groups of four members each. The individual members of each group were forced to cooperate in order to reach their academic goals, since the group was rewarded on the basis of how much *all the group members learned*. The students were thus motivated to help one another, and as a result the cooperative group effort produced an increase in student achievement. Slavin's cooperative learning methods have also been used effectively to reduce student prejudices in racially mixed classes and classes in which special-education students have been recently mainstreamed (Slavin, 1983). Studies also seem to indicate that cooperative learning approaches lead to higher levels of *intrinsic* motivation, especially among less able children (Knight, 1982).

Deutch has been successfully using cooperative learning techniques to combat dropout problem among inner-city adolescents (Deutch, 1988). Says Deutch, "The probability of reward is positively linked so that as one's personal situation improves or worsens so do those of the others . . . To the extent I win, you win, and to the extent I lose, you lose" (Deutch, 1979, p. 398).

However, there are problems inherent in group-grading practices—a fact that Deutch freely admits. These include

development of vested interests in one's specialized role in the cooperative system, the growth of in-group favoritism that may lead to discrimination against out-group members, and the evolution of excessive conformity and reluctance to question the majority opinion (1979, p. 400).

Cooperative learning modes don't always lead to success. Some students simply don't have the needed motivation to cooperate with a genuine sense of responsibility. When this lack of motivation is combined with a cooperative group effort that fails, the consequences are decidedly less than positive. When a cooperating team fails to reach its goal, the low performers in the group are often blamed for

SPOTLIGHT ON COOPERATION IN THE CLASSROOM

The Jigsaw Approach

One interesting attempt to utilize both competitive and cooperative motivation is called the jigsaw approach, which was first introduced in the late 1970s.[a] Since then this technique has been applied successfully in a broad range of educational and even business settings. Recognizing the importance of both cooperative and competitive motives, adherents of this approach set up classrooms or skill groups that combine an individual reinforcement structure, in which grades are assigned on the basis of individual performance, and a cooperative structure, in which groups of students must share their work in order to carry out assignments. In the latter case interdependence and the cooperation needed to attain a superordinate goal are vital for success. The group effort literally becomes a jigsaw puzzle in which each member receives a part, but only through interaction can the parts be formed into a whole. For example, a textbook chapter may be cut up into paragraphs, and each group member will receive only one paragraph. Using the jigsaw technique for at least part of every day helps reduce some of the destructive elements inherent in the competitive structure and can increase a students' feeling of interdependence and cooperation.[b]

---

[a] Aronson, E., Blaney, N., Stephan, C., Sikes, J., & Snapp, M. (1978). *The jigsaw classroom*. Beverly Hills: Sage.
[b] Aronson, E. (1986, August). *Teaching students things they think they know all about*. Paper presented at the meeting of the American Psychological Association, Washington, DC.

---

the loss, and these individuals tend to feel both shame and frustration (Harris & Covington, 1993). In fact some researchers have suggested that the low performers in groups that fail are subjected to double jeopardy—they experience both individual shame and team blame.

Another experiment in cooperative learning, in which a group of children write their themes together, has been greeted with underwhelming enthusiasm by some students, although in this case cooperative student efforts considerably lessened the teacher's work load: by grouping her students, she had to correct only 8 term papers instead of 25 (Brockman, 1994).

Group effects Groups by their very nature change behavior. Working in a group situation has two main effects: on the one hand, it may increase feelings of competition and motivation, and on the other it may increase feelings of anxiety and provide distractions. The presence of other people explicitly or implicitly create a competitive situation. In research studies the subjects seem to assume that the researcher will be making comparisons and/or they hope to impress other members of the group. If the subject's motivation is high to begin with, increasing it may have a damaging effect. However, if the subject's motivation is low, the competitive atmosphere of the group situation may enhance performance.

The nature of the task is also of great importance. When an individual in a group situation begins feeling simultaneously more competitive and more anxious, his or her performance on simple, nonintellectual tasks is enhanced. As the task becomes more difficult and more intellectual, the effect of working in a group becomes increasingly detrimental to performance. Before using any of the group techniques in a learning situation, the teacher should carefully take into account both the level of the students' motivation and the nature of the task.

The classroom is always going to promote some competitive feelings. Students, like the subjects in the previously mentioned research studies, assume that performance comparisons will be made. They will also try to gain the attention of their teacher and peers by various methods of "trying to impress." Despite these facts, the teacher can choose to emphasize competition in certain areas and to deemphasize it in others. Highly motivated students who are working on difficult math problems would probably be better off if left alone at their desks. Less motivated students who are working on simpler rote tasks might do better if the work were done openly, for example,

Does competitive activity produce harmful side effects?

by using flashcards to drill the whole class in multiplication tables.

Competition can probably never be completely ruled out of an American classroom situation. Social psychologists have shown over and over again that even in situations in which cooperation is the most efficient route to success, competition continues to dominate. Even when subjects fully realize that the rewards will be greater for cooperative group interaction, they still prefer to compete with one another (Minas et al., 1960).

Despite the powerful competitive tendency of American students, the teacher can set up conditions that reduce it. Preparing group projects for which a single grade is assigned helps promote cooperation. Any situation in which the students are working toward a superordinate goal—a goal none of them can attain independently—will help to reduce competitive responses.

Cooperation and cognitive development   Cognitive psychologists like Jerome Bruner and Jean Piaget, though suggesting that motives toward cooperation and reciprocity may have strong biological underpinnings, warn that the strength of these motives may vary with the age of the child. For example, Piaget tells us that young children are limited in their ability to cooperate by *egocentricity*—the inability to take another person's point of view (Piaget, 1932). As the child grows older, however, and acquires more sophisticated levels of thought, cooperative behavior becomes more possible. Moral principles like "mutual respect" can be acted on only when the child's level of cognitive growth allows for their full incorporation (Krebs, 1979). A great deal of research in this area is obviously needed—research that compares in general the effects of competitive versus cooperative structuring and that also makes particular comparisons at various age levels (Nelson & Dweck, 1977). The young child who firmly believes that obedience to adults is more important than loyalty to peers will have great difficulty appreciating the group spirit inherent in cooperative structuring.

UNCONSCIOUS MOTIVATION

Sigmund Freud stated that roughly two-thirds of all human motivation lies below the threshold of conscious awareness; in other words, most human behavior is motivated by reasons of which we are totally unaware and which are therefore largely irrational. Thus, to Freud and to many modern psychologists, any effort to understand why people behave as they do must take into account **unconscious motivation**—the irrational needs that lurk beneath the level of conscious awareness.

Although these motives may be unconscious to the person having them, a trained observer can often make sense out of this apparent irrationality. For example, a second-grade student is totally unaware of the reasons for his or her sudden change in behavior—using baby talk, wetting the bed at night, and not concentrating in class. The school psychologist might ascribe these responses to a general motive to regress—perhaps the young student has recently been presented with a baby brother. Similarly, a 10-year-old suddenly develops symptoms of a full-blown school phobia; the child becomes a truant, getting to school only when brought in kicking and screaming. Again, the school psychologist might find that the youngster's home situation presents great conflict—perhaps the parents are getting a divorce. The teacher certainly should be alert to any dramatic behavior change and be ready, if it continues, to make the proper referral.

Repression

One form of unconscious motivation that may be particularly perplexing to the teacher is repression, as when a child does something—perhaps in full view of the teacher and class—and then later denies any personal memory of the event.

Fourth-grade student Kenny D. comes from a home where parental standards are exacting and nonpermissive. Kenny is typically quiet and conforming. He is what has been called an "overly steered" child. One day in class, Kenny uncharacteristically has a verbal confrontation with John H., a youngster suffering from cerebral palsy. Suddenly, Kenny knocks away John's crutches, pushes him to the ground, and begins to pummel the handicapped child. Both the teacher and the other students quickly pull Kenny away and accuse him of being evil. Later, in the principal's office, Kenny flatly denies that the event has ever taken place. He cries and says he is being falsely accused and even asks to take a lie-detector test.

In this instance, Freud might say that Kenny has repressed any memory of the guilt-provoking situation. Repression is the exclusion from consciousness of anxiety-producing memories, thoughts, or impulses. Repression differs from ordinary forgetting in two ways: first, with repression the memory loss is total, and second, repression is always triggered by anxiety.

Less dramatic cases of repression abound in the classroom—a student with a distaste for math constantly "forgetting" to do his assignment; a student with a fear of being in front of the class "forgetting" to prepare her oral report (and being genuinely surprised when called on); a student, traumatized by the thought of the physical contact involved in athletics, "forgetting" to bring his sneakers to gym class.

Some of these situations, of course, require the professional intervention of the school psychologist, but in many cases an understanding and compassionate teacher can provide the student with enough insight to minimize the trauma that caused the repression. A caring, nonjudgmental, and accepting teacher can often defuse the underlying anxieties.

The Zeigarnik Effect

The other side of the repression coin is a phenomenon called the **Zeigarnik effect.** In some learning situations, the thought of an unfinished assignment motivates the student in such a way that the memory is actually *enhanced*. Students are better able to recall unfinished assignments than those that have been completed (Zeigarnik, 1927).

Think of the time that you had a term paper to write and tried mightily to put it off and out of your mind. Perhaps you went to a movie but couldn't enjoy it because the nagging thought of the unfinished paper haunted your every waking moment. That's the Zeigarnik effect. To alleviate the tension of the memory, you finally had to "bite the bullet" and start the paper.

To a large extent, therefore, the Zeigarnik effect plays into the hands of the teacher, since memory *enhancement* is obviously more positive than memory destruction or repression. It may at first seem as if the Zeigarnik effect and repression are self-contradictory. It may seem that the thought of an unfinished term paper must itself be so anxiety-provoking that the whole idea of it would be repressed. To some extent this is true. More recent studies have shown that if the unfinished task is so threatening that the individual's entire feeling of self-esteem is at stake, it is possible for the Zeigarnik effect to boomerang. In this situation, the finished tasks will be remembered more than the unfinished ones.

Thus, the teacher who attaches too many dire consequences to an assignment may find the Zeigarnik effect being reversed. When this happens, the assignment is no longer self-motivating through memory enhancement, and it may become repressed into the never-never land of "out of sight, out of mind."

MOTIVATIONAL CONFLICTS

Human behavior does not result from the simple action of a single motive. People constantly seek a number of goals, often simultaneously. One of these goals may act antagonistically to another, thus creating **motivational conflicts.**

Sources

Dependence and independence   Every child is faced with the conflict of dependence versus independence—a conflict that seems to reach a roaring crescendo during adolescence. The conflict arises on the one hand from the need to remain dependent, to have somebody else make one's decisions, to have a shoulder to cry on, and on the other hand from the equally strong drive to be free, to make one's own decisions, and to become self-reliant. This can become a major issue during adolescence. There is usu-

ally at least a temporary increase in family conflict during the early and middle adolescent years, the added stress involving these issues of dependence-independence, or autonomy and control. These issues are usually renegotiated during this developmental period, and these negotiations are often stormy, as it is not easy for parents to decide the optimal levels of autonomy and control, or for the adolescent to understand and conform to these changing rules (Eccles et al., 1993). Leaving the cocoon of womb and family can be a highly stressful stage of life. From birth on, the child is engaged in the long and sometimes painful process of slowly giving up dependence in order to attain independence; and even as an adult, there is compromise and balance between these two competing needs.

Sex   Another source of motivational conflict occurs in the area of sex. As children advance through puberty, they are confronted with the dilemma of becoming aware of their own sexual needs together with society's demand that these needs not be satisfied. Our society does not yet fully condone any form of premarital sexual release. The conflict is further heightened in today's society, for with advancing technology and the need for more and more education and training to compete successfully, marriage and its privilege of socially sanctioned sexual expression are further delayed.

Aggression   Aggression is still another source of motivational conflict. When persons occasionally have hostile tendencies (and who doesn't?), society allows very few opportunities for this hostility to be overtly expressed (see Chapter 17). Although overt aggression is acceptable in certain prescribed situations such as contact sports and warfare, it typically results in very serious legal consequences when practiced in day-to-day interactions.

Achievement and altruism   The child also faces the cultural paradox of competitive achievement versus the Judeo-Christian ethic of "Love thy neighbor." Our children are urged to compete, to win, to succeed at all costs, and yet they are told that this should not be a dog-eat-dog world and that they should be good Samaritans.

Reactions

In the course of these and many more assorted conflicts, individuals react differently. Some children,

SPOTLIGHT ON PERSONALITY

The Big Five Personality Traits

Despite the many versions of what personality is or is not, and despite the innumerable personality characteristics that have been formulated over the years, teachers should know that psychology now believes that there are only five basic personality categories, known in the trade as the Big Five. The great majority of personality theorists endorse this model and see it as a great advantage over psychology's past use of hundreds of different personality structures and concepts, many of which are now seen as simply redundant duplicates. Virtually all the past personality studies can be reinterpreted using this new terminology.[a] The Big Five model asserts that all the known personality characteristics can be categorized on the basis of the following broad dimensions: surgency, agreeableness, conscientiousness, emotional stability, and intellectance:

1. *Surgency:* The individual who is high in this personality dimension is sociable, gregarious, assertive, and leaderlike—as opposed to withdrawn, reserved, quiet, and mannerly. Older concepts, such as Adler's "need for power" or Jung's "introversion-extraversion," are now seen as part of this factor.
2. *Agreeableness:* This factor identifies the person who is warm, sympathetic, cooperative, and good-natured—as opposed to grumpy, cold, unpleasant, and disagreeable. Other traits now considered to be part of this factor are "need for affiliation" and "likeability."
3. *Conscientiousness:* This factor measures the degree to which an individual is hard-working, responsible, dependable, persevering, and organized—as opposed to impulsive, irresponsible, undependable, and lazy. Under this heading the "need for achievement" has now been subsumed, as has the Freudian concept of "ego strength."
4. *Emotional stability:* This factor measures the degree to which a person is calm, steady, cool, and self-confident—as opposed to anxious, insecure, worried, and emotional. Older concepts, such as "neuroticism" and "nervousness," are now placed in this category.
5. *Intellectance:* This factor evaluates the person's ability to be imaginative, creative, broadminded, and curious—as opposed to closed-minded, concrete, dogmatic, and rigid. The distinction between divergent and convergent thinking applies here, with *divergent* thinking being placed in this category.

With this new, streamlined model, psychologists and educators are better able to look at the personality factors that may now be used to predict academic and personal success.

---

[a] Goldberg, L. R. (1993). The structure of phenotypic personality traits. *American Psychologist 48*, 26–34.

and adults too, seem to thrive in times of motivational crisis, while others simply fold up and perhaps develop a whole series of psychological symptoms. As Allport once said, "The same fire that melts the butter hardens the egg" (1967, p. 7).

Teachers must be made aware that the manifestations of emotional symptoms may not always be obvious. The teacher usually devotes much time and attention to the rebellious child. Thus, by "acting out" conflicts, the overtly aggressive child receives the attention and recognition of the teacher. However, a more serious psychological symptom, that of withdrawal, may easily escape the attention of the teacher (and parent, too). The child who withdraws, perhaps into a make-believe world of fantasy, does not upset the school routine and therefore does not seem to present a problem. Some teachers—at times, perhaps all—actually wish they had more withdrawn children, more "little angels," in their classes. This syndrome, however, can be serious since the withdrawn child who does not get needed attention and recognition may slip into further withdrawal and even a complete loss of contact with reality.

The Teens and Academic Motivation

Tied in with family conflicts in early adolescence are changes in academic motivation and achievement. Several studies have noted a marked decline in academic performance as youngsters move from sixth grade into junior high. Is this just a case of raging hormones and the need for more student autonomy? Eccles believes that the shift from sixth grade to junior high creates a dramatic environmental change that in fact contributes to adolescent motivational problems (Eccles et al., 1993). For example, research in something as obvious as the size of the school (small school versus big school) has demonstrated the motivational advantages of small schools, especially for marginal students. But Eccles suspects other culprits, and homes in on five important differences between the sixth-grade environment and that of the typical junior high. Compared with elementary classrooms, junior high classrooms are characterized as:

1. Based far more on teacher control and rigid discipline, allowing fewer opportunities for student decision making at the very time these youngsters are yearning for more autonomy at home and at school (Buchanan et al., 1992)

2. Less personal and less conducive to positive teacher-student relationships

3. Using whole-class learning with little concern for small-group instruction and virtually no individualized instruction (in contrast to sixth-grade classrooms, which often mix whole-class and small-group instruction)

4. Staffed by teachers who feel they are less effective, especially with low-ability students, than elementary teachers

5. Using a higher grading standard: junior high teachers typically demand more than sixth-grade teachers in the way of academic performance for a given grade, and as grades decline so too do student expectations and motivation levels

Eccles suggests that the fit between adolescence as a *developmental stage* and the educational structure the youngsters are assigned to can be a woeful mismatch. By creating a climate that undermines both teacher and student motivation (the larger size of the schools, departmentalized teaching, larger student loads), the structure of the typical junior high actually creates many of the problems that are so often blamed exclusively on the teenagers. Such a structure may even prevent teachers and students from forming close, mutually respected, relationships.

There is a dire need for developmentally responsible educational environments for all ages, and this is especially true for the adolescent.

MOTIVATION AND DEVELOPMENT

Broad types of motivational systems will vary according to both age and stage. With children in the preschool and elementary grades, the predominant motivators will be extrinsically determined. Young pupils may become "interested" in learning because the teacher is much bigger and physically more powerful, or because they can win a candy bar, a gold star, a smiling face on a paper, or personal recognition and approval from the teacher or the other children. Such motivators are largely extrinsic or separate from the learning material itself.

This does not mean that intrinsic motivation is impossible at this age. However, to expect that elementary-age children will focus on basic skill learning (the three R's) solely for intrinsic reasons may be unrealistic. The romantic notion that teachers can constantly reveal the mysteries of academic disciplines so ingeniously that pupils will be filled with a devouring compulsion to learn results in frustration for the teacher and puzzlement for the pupil. Thus, the teacher's role at that level is to employ a variety of extrinsic motivators in addition to finding material that is intrinsically interesting. In this way, the likelihood of shaping the attention and time on task of the pupils will be increased.

During adolescence, intrinsic motivation is more likely to become a major factor in learning because of the adolescent's ability to perform formal operations. Thus, with the increased ability for self-direction and abstract reasoning, secondary school pupils can, for greater time periods, enjoy learning for its own sake. On their own, pupils can now seek out new ideas, new sources, and new concepts. Intrinsic motivation then becomes self-reinforcing.

However, this does not mean that the problems of motivation and learning are fully solved as a result of the onset of formal operations. In the first place, as we noted in Chapter 5, most secondary school pupils do not employ formal operations even though that potential exists. In the second place, pupils may become intrinsically motivated to study material totally unrelated to the required school topics. Thus, there is no guarantee at all that adolescents will be bursting with enthusiasm to find out what the reasons are behind the Triangle of Trade, why the Tigris and Euphrates were so important, how English poetry changed with Wordsworth's "Tintern Abbey," what the Pythagorean theorem means. It is also apparent that the "time bomb" effect will not work as a motivational device unless the students are at extremely high levels of intrinsic motivation. If a teacher simply resorts to the plea, "Twenty years from now, class, you'll be glad that you learned about gerunds, the ablative case, and parsing," the class may react with glazed eyes, slouched postures, and puzzled expressions. The nonverbal message back to the teacher will be loud and clear—"Oh yeah? Why?"

Thus, from a developmental point of view, the continuum of motivational factors from extrinsic to intrinsic presents the teacher with an array of strategies to be matched with the pupil's age, stage, and interest level. It is most important to remember both White's and Allport's concepts. A teacher can employ a variety of extrinsic rewards as motivators, such as learning to please, to earn "tokens," to work for extra recess time, and so on. Such methods do not necessarily mean that the pupils will always be dependent on these specific external and extrinsic motivators. There can be, as we have seen, an intrinsic drive toward self-directed competence as well as toward functional autonomy. Students may start out learning to please the teacher and to earn material rewards and then find that the means (learning) becomes an end in itself. In the long run, of course, this is what is truly wanted—students capable of the enjoyment and stimulation that intrinsic learning experiences provide.

THE TEACHER'S ROLE

The teacher is in an especially advantageous position regarding a child's motivational conflicts, because aside from the parents, perhaps nobody else is able to observe the child for so many hours and in such a variety of situations. The teacher can observe how the child relates to adults, to the peer group, or to frustration, and can detect when these reactions seem at all deviant. This is not to suggest that teachers must all become professional psychologists, but like it or not, we do "psychologize" whenever we make inferences about how or why people behave as they do.

The study of motivation in the classroom, especially as it relates to academic achievement, is indeed fascinating. As people come to better understand themselves, master themselves, and free themselves, all of humankind will be the beneficiaries. To paraphrase the late Lawrence K. Frank, the fundamental motives of the individual are precisely the same as the fundamental motives of society (Frank, 1969). Ideally, the school and the learning tasks in school should be organized in such a way as to promote the growth of personal competence and self-mastery. Therefore, important goals of the school should include fostering, nurturing, and facilitating personal growth in a learning context, thus counteracting debilitating effects and enhancing the full realization of human potential.

SUMMARY

Thorndike was the first psychologist to document experimentally the link between learning and motivation. He explained this link on the basis of his law of effect. Motivation has since become a firmly established concept in psychology and education. Motivation never acts in a vacuum but is always acting on and being acted on by both learning and perception. Motives are composed of needs (deficits within the person) and drives (needs that cause the person to act). The whole sequence, or cycle, is called motivational when the drive is goal-directed. Although all people have physiological motives based on physical needs for food, sex, warmth, and so on, of more importance to the educational psychologist are the acquired motives. Allport's concept of functional autonomy suggests that motives may be acquired when a means to an end becomes an end in itself.

Various emotional states may act to influence motivated activity. People will respond differently, despite similar motivations, when under different emotional sets. The physiological arousal associated with

an emotion may even transfer from one motive to another. When the arousal activates motives, especially acquired motives, that are in opposition to each other, psychologists explain this phenomenon in terms of the opponent process theory of acquired motivation. A distinction is made between intrinsic and extrinsic motives, or between motives that can be satisfied from within and those that demand external satisfaction. In addition, Maslow has suggested a universal order in which people try to satisfy their needs, from physiological and safety needs, to love, esteem, and self-actualizing needs. Some critics of Maslow insist that the order in which needs must be satisfied can vary, especially as a function of the situation.

Self-regulated learning occurs when the student achieves an intrinsic motivational set and is able to postpone gratification and rely on inner resources. Self-regulated learning and motivation are seen as interactive processes, with the learner's perception of personal academic self-worth as both the cause of a strengthened motivation for further learning and the effect of past outcomes. Techniques have been proposed, especially by cognitive psychologists, for teaching self-regulation to those who don't seem able to achieve it on their own.

One of the most potent acquired motives is for the social approval of one's parents, teachers, and peer groups. The skilled teacher takes advantage of this need and uses it to help nourish a genuine love of learning in his or her students. Another important motive is the need for achievement. This need may become autonomous and function as an intrinsic drive to succeed. Research in the area of achievement has found, for example, that gender differences in achievement are culturally determined; some women fail to achieve because they have learned to fear success. Robert White suggests the importance of competence motivation, an intrinsic drive to master one's environment. This motive is even thought to have had an evolutionary survival value for the human race. Research in the area of self-esteem consistently shows that academic achievement and self-esteem go hand in hand, but it is difficult to determine which is the cause and which the effect. Critics of the self-esteem movement complain that using class time for the teaching of self-esteem is too often done at the expense of the time needed for the teaching of more traditional subject areas. The critics feel that when areas such as math and reading are conquered, self-esteem will naturally follow.

Harlow has shown the significance of the curiosity motive, an intrinsic and self-reinforcing motive to discover how things work. Bruner's discovery learning takes advantage of the motive. Cooperative and competitive motives are acquired by the developing child, and these, too, can be brought into action in the classroom. A classroom spirit of cooperativeness, especially in the older child, can be manipulated to create a less anxious atmosphere. The competitive motive may not be instinctive and is probably just as culturally determined as an acquired taste for certain foods.

Freud pointed out the importance of unconscious motivation and insisted that most human behavior is so determined. One example of unconscious motivation is repression, a form of motivated forgetting. The Zeigarnik effect, in contrast, is a kind of motivated remembering of tasks that have not yet been completed.

Humans are beset by many motivational conflicts, such as needs for both dependence and independence. Some of these seem to reach their climax as the child enters adolescence. How these conflicts are resolved depends on a host of cultural and personality factors. For example, some people may react to motivational conflicts by procrastinating, putting off for tomorrow (or forever) whatever produces the conflicts and its resulting anxiety.

The school is best organized when it promotes the growth of personal competence and self-mastery. The teacher's role is crucial in this process.

KEY TERMS AND NAMES

achievement motivation
acquired motives
approval (need for)
Morton Deutch
drives
extrinsic motives
functional autonomy
Harry F. Harlow
   curiosity motivation
Matina S. Horner
   fear of success
intrinsic motives

motivational conflicts
motives
need hierarchy
needs
opponent process theory
physiological motives
self-esteem
self-regulated learning
unconscious motivation
Robert White
Zeigarnik effect

THEORY INTO PRACTICE: MOTIVATION AND PROCRASTINATION

Of all the threats to achievement motivation, perhaps one of the most damaging is procrastination.

The child who constantly puts off assignments soon begins to lag so far behind that new material becomes virtually impossible to understand. The teacher may sequence the topics in elegantly logical steps, but the child who hasn't attempted to take step one will find step five to be all but incomprehensible.

Obviously, everyone at one time or another becomes involved in procrastination, but the underachieving student may be making an absolute fetish of this self-defeating trap. Research has shown that habitual procrastinators typically use one or all of three basic delaying tactics for allowing themselves the apparent luxury of putting things off.

Mañana   In this case the student is convinced that what is perceived to be an unpleasant task will be done . . . but later. Homework is not done during study-hall time but will be done later, at home. Studying cannot be done at home during the afternoon because a "break" is needed after a long, tiring school day. Studying cannot be done that evening because the parents have the TV on, and sister is listening to records—"But I'll catch up on the weekend, and if not this weekend, then the next one."

Contingency mañana   This method is used when the student sets up contingent conditions for completing a task, such as "I can't start writing my essay until my room is properly set up for studying." An entire term may pass before the room conditions become just right—pencil sharpener installed, new lights put in, cross-ventilation worked out, soundproof doors set up—the contingencies may be endless. And even then, "I can't write this essay until I've read all the books in the library on the topic, and I haven't gone to the library yet because I missed the session early in the term when they explained the card system."

Catch-22   The two previous methods allowed the student to retain the blissful hope that someday the job would be done—maybe not today, maybe not tomorrow, but sometime in the distant future. Catch-22, however, typically leads to the feeling that the job will never be done, "but it's not my fault." In this situation, circumstances are perceived as conspiring against the student so that whatever way the child turns, the goal of finishing the task is blocked. "Since the teacher doesn't like me I'll flunk anyway, even if I do my homework." "I can't ask Sally to the dance because my teeth aren't straight, and my family can't afford big dental bills." While this type of excuse often may bring on gloomy and depressed moods, the logic of the excuse seems to be so airtight that giving

up becomes easy and even rewarding. The situation may even progress to the extent that the student begins assuming the role of a self-declared martyr, while still feeling good because he or she is so noble in facing impossible conditions. The motive, of course, is to fail, but also to enjoy the failure.

Select someone you know who has obviously been using one of these tactics (this search will not be difficult) and work with that person, using the following guidelines:

1. Ask the person to make a list of at least six things currently being put off: term paper, diet, exercise, whatever. Having the reality of a definite list helps prevent allowing the student to just forget about the various goals.

2. Establish an objective, limited as it might at first be, for each of the delayed plans: write at least one paragraph of the term paper, take off one pound of weight.

3. Slowly increase the rate and strength of the goals.

4. Ask the student to verbalize aloud several key phrases: It's just as hard to start tomorrow as today. If I can take the first step, I can take the second. Even if I don't yet have the ability to complete the task, I will develop my skills as I go along.

5. Indicate to the student that using cop-outs such as "I'm basically lazy" is itself simply a diversionary tactic.

6. Finally, convince the student that all the smoke screens and diversions being used are indeed very creative and that these creative powers can be channeled toward solid academic gains.

We are indebted to William Knaus, an expert in the field of motivational conflict, for providing us with the ideas for the preceding material. For a more complete coverage of the procrastination syndrome, read Knaus's *Do It Now*, published by Prentice-Hall in 1979.

Even with a carefully sequenced approach to the problem of procrastination, success may not always be ensured. One of the authors recently tested the model above on an advanced graduate student who was a notorious procrastinator: late assignments, papers always delayed, urgent requests for recommendations always at the eleventh hour, thesis topics in constant flux, and so forth. Finally, an action plan was developed. The student made out the list, established manageable objectives, and slowly increased the rate of accomplishments. She was also told to verbalize key phrases and *very directly* told to stop using her favorite cop-out phrase, "I'm overwhelmed and overworked, and I want my work to be the best you've ever seen." Shortly after these sessions ended, a Christmas card arrived from the grateful student. Along with the traditional greetings of the season she had penned a note of thanks, saying how well the new system was working. The Christmas card's envelope was postmarked January 9.

REFERENCES

Allport, G. W. (1967). Functional autonomy. In J. F. Perez, R. C. Sprinthall, G. S. Grosser, & P. J. Anastasiou (Eds.). *General psychology: Selected readings* (pp. 157–159). New York: Van Nostrand.

American Association of School Administrators (1990). *Women and minorities in school administration: Facts and figures, 1989–1990.* Arlington VA: Author.

Aspy, D., Roebuck, F., & Aspy, C. B. (1984). Tomorrow's resources are in today's classroom. *Personnel and Guidance Journal 12,* 455–459.

Bandura, A. (1989). Human agency in social cognitive theory. *American Psychologist 44,* 1179–1184.

Bennett, W., & Gurin, J. (1982). *The dieter's dilemma.* New York: Basic Books.

Berlyne, D. E. (1960). *Conflict, arousal, and curiosity.* New York: McGraw-Hill.

Bierhoff, H. W. (1989). *Person perception and attribution.* New York: Springer-Verlag.

Bornstein, P. H. (1985). Self-instructional training: A commentary and state of the art. *Journal of Applied Behavior Analysis 18,* 69–72.

Brockman, E. B. (1994). English is not a team sport, Mrs. Brockman. *English Journal 1.*

Bruner, J. S. (1966). *Toward a theory of instruction.* Cambridge, MA: Harvard University Press.

Buchanan, C. M., Eccles, J. S., & Baker, J. B. (1992). Are adolescents the victims of raging hormones? Evidence for the activational effects of hormones on moods and behavior at adolescence. *Psychological Bulletin 111,* 62–107.

Coleman, J. S., et al. (1966). *Equality of educational opportunity.* Washington, DC: U.S. Department of Health, Education and Welfare.

Damon, W. (1995). *Greater expectations: Overcoming the culture of indulgence in America's homes and schools.* New York: Free Press.

Davis, C. (1967). Results of the self-selection of diets by young children. In J. F. Perez, R. C. Sprinthall, G. S. Grosser, & P. J. Anastasiou (Eds.), *General psychology: Selected readings* (pp. 166–171). New York: Van Nostrand.

Dawes, R. (1994). *House of cards: Psychology and psychotherapy built on myth.* New York: Free Press.

Deci, E. L., & Ryan, R. M. (1980). The empirical exploration of intrinsic motivational processes. In L.

Berkowitz (Ed.), *Advances in experimental social psychology* (vol. 13). Orlando, FL: Academic Press.

Deci, E. L., Vallerand, R. J., Pelletier, L. G., & Ryan, R. M. (1991). Motivation and education: The self-determination perspective. *Educational Psychologist 26,* 325–346.

Deutch, M. (1949). The effects of cooperation and competition upon group process. *Human Relations 2,* 199–231.

Deutch, M. (1979). Education and distributive justice. *American Psychologist 34,* 391–401.

Deutch, M. (1988). Use of innovative educational techniques with dropouts. In *William T. Grant Foundation Annual Report.* New York.

Ebel, R. L. (February 1980). The failure of schools without failure. *Phi Delta Kappan,* 386–388.

Eccles, J. S., Midgley, C., Wigfield, A., Buchanan, C. M., Reuman, D., Flanagan, C., & MacIver, D. (1993). Development during adolescence: The impact of stage-environmental fit on young adolescents' experiences in schools and in families. *American Psychologist 48,* 90–101.

Fordham, S., & Ogbu, J. U. (1986). Black students' school success: Coping with the burden of "acting" white. *Urban Review 18,* 176–206.

Frank, L. K. (1969). The fundamental needs of the child. In R. C. Sprinthall & N. A. Sprinthall (Eds.), *Educational psychology: Selected readings* (pp. 70–74). New York: Van Nostrand-Reinhold.

Geen, R. G. (1995). *Human motivation: A social psychological approach.* Pacific Grove, CA: Brooks/Cole.

Goodenow, C. (1992). Strengthening the links between educational psychology and the study of social contexts. *Educational Psychologist 27,* 177–196.

Gottfried, A. E. (1983). Intrinsic motivation in young children. *Young Children 39,* 64–73.

Gottfried, A. E. (1985). Academic intrinsic motivation in elementary and junior high school students. *Journal of Educational Psychology 77,* 631–645.

Harlow, H. F., McGaugh, J. L., & Thompson, R. F. (1971). *Psychology.* San Francisco: Albion.

Harris, A. H., & Covington, M. V. (1993). The role of cooperative reward interdependency in success and failure. *Journal of Experimental Education 61*, 151–168.

Harvey, A. L. (1975). Goal setting as compensator for fear of success. *Adolescence 10*, 137–142.

Hechinger, F. M. (May 29, 1979). The principal is the secret to better schools. *The New York Times*, D34.

Horner, M. S. (1968). Women's will to fail. *Psychology Today 3*, 36–38.

Horner, M. S. (1969). Fail: Bright women. *Psychology Today 3*, 46–48.

Hummel, R., & Sprinthall, N. (1965). Underachievement related to interests, attitudes and values. *Personnel and Guidance Journal 44*, 388–395.

Kagan, J. (1984). *The nature of the child*. New York: Basic Books.

Katz, L. (July 15, 1993). Reading, writing and narcissism. *New York Times*, A25.

Knight, C. J. (May 1982). Cooperative learning: A new approach to an old idea. *Teaching Exceptional Children*, 233–238.

Kounin, J. (1970). *Discipline and group management in classrooms*. New York: Holt, Rinehart & Winston.

Krebs, D. (1979). Reconsiderations. *Human Nature 2*, 93–95.

Laner, M. R. (1979). Sex and the single check. *Psychology Today 12*, 45.

Maccoby, E., & Jacklin, C. (1974). *The psychology of sex differences*. Stanford: Stanford University Press.

Maslow, A. H. (1954). *Motivation and personality*. New York: Harper & Row.

McDougall, W. (1908). *Social psychology*. London: Methuen.

Minas, J. S., Scodel, A., Marlowe, D., & Rawson, H. (1960). Some descriptive aspects of two-person non-zero-sum games. *Journal of Conflict Resolution 4*, 193–197.

Neher, A. (1991). Maslow's theory of motivation: A critique. *Journal of Humanistic Psychology 31*, 89–112.

Nelson, L., & Kagan, S. (1972). Competition: The star-spangled scramble. *Psychology Today 6*, 53–91.

Nelson, S., & Dweck, C. (1977). Motivation, competence, and reward allocation. *Developmental Psychology 13*, 192–197.

Parker, J. G., & Asher, S. R. (1987). Peer relations and later personal adjustment: Are low-accepted children at risk? *Psychological Bulletin 1*, 357–389.

Parlee, M. B. (1979). Conversational politics. *Psychology Today 12*, 48–56.

Petersen, C., Maier, S. F., & Seligman, M. E. P. (1993). *Learned helplessness: A theory for the age of personal control*. New York: Oxford University Press.

Piaget, J. (1932). *The mortal judgment of the child*. New York: Harcourt, Brace.

Postman, L., Bruner, J. S., and McGinnies, E. M. (1948). Personal values as selective factors in perception. *Journal of Abnormal and Social Psychology 43*, 142–154.

Raffini, J. P. (1996). *150 ways to increase intrinsic motivation in the classroom*. Boston: Allyn & Bacon.

Riesenzein, R. (1983). The Schachter theory of emotion: Two decades later. *Psychological Bulletin 94*, 239–264.

Rofe, Y. (1984). Stress and affiliation: A utility theory. *Psychological Review 91*, 235–250.

Rohles, F. H. (1980). Temperature or temperament: A psychologist looks at thermal comfort. *ASHRAE Transactions 86*, 541–551.

Rosehan, D. L., & Seligman, M. E. P. (1989). *Abnormal psychology* (2nd ed.). New York: Norton.

Rosenshine, B. V. (1980). How time is spent in elementary classrooms. In C. Denham & A. Liberman (Eds.), *Time to learn* (pp. 107–126). Washington, DC: National Institute of Education.

Sanford, R. N. (1936). The effects of abstinence from food upon imaginal processes. *Journal of Psychology 2*, 129–136.

Schunk, D. H. (1991). Self-efficacy and motivation. *Educational Psychologist 26*(3,4), 207–231.

Slavin, R. E. (1983). *Cooperative learning*. New York: Longmans.

Solomon, R. L. (1980). The opponent process theory of acquired motivation. *American Psychologist 35*, 691–712.

Sprinthall, R. C., & Bennett, B. (1978). Conformity and non-conformity among married women: The Reisman typologies. *Psychological Reports 42*, 1195–1201.

Steinberg, L., Dornbusch, S. M., & Brown, B. B. (1992). Ethnic differences in adolescent achievement: An ecological perspective. *American Psychologist 47*, 723–729.

Strein, W. (1988). Classroom-based elementary school affective education programs: A critical review. *Psychology in the Schools 25*, 288–296.

Swartz, K. B., & Rosenblum, L. A. (1980). Operant responding by bonnet macaques for color videotape recordings of social stimuli. *Animal Learning Behavior 8*, 322–331.

Tannen, D. (1990). *You just don't understand: Women and men in conversation*. New York: Morrow.

Thorndike, E. L. (1913). *Educational psychology: The psychology of learning* (p. 2). New York: Teachers College Press.

U.S. Department of Education (1992). *A comparison of vocational and nonvocational public school teachers of grades 9–12*. Washington, DC: U.S. Government Printing Office.

Webb, N. (1983). Predicting learning from student

interactions: Defining the interaction variables. *Educational Psychologist 18*, 33–41.

White, R. (1959). Motivation reconsidered: The concept of competence. *Psychological Review 66*, 197–233.

Zeigarnik, B. (1927). Uber das behalten von erledigten und unerledigten handlugen. *Psychologische Forschung 9*, 1–85.

Zimmerman, B. J. (1989). A social cognitive view of self-regulated learning. *Journal of Educational Psychology 81*, 329–339.

Zimmerman, B. J. (1991). Self-regulated learning and academic achievement: An overview. *Educational Psychologist 25*, 3–17.

Zimmerman, B. J., & Martinez-Pons, M. (1990). Student differences in self-regulated learning: Relating grade, sex, and giftedness of self-efficacy and strategy use. *Journal of Educational Psychology 82*, 51–59.

19

STUDENT DISCIPLINE: A DEVELOPMENTAL MODEL

Ask almost any teacher or adult to identify the most difficult problem of education and childrearing, and he or she will usually mention discipline. In this chapter, we provide some historical background, showing the timeless nature of the problem and looking at some of the old theories and beliefs about character formation. We then outline the developmental approach to discipline, based largely on Lawrence Kohlberg's theory and illustrated with positive and negative modes of discipline at each stage. A chart outlines the answers to four related discipline questions: who makes the rules, who keeps them, how are the rules enforced, and why do the students obey? The chapter concludes with some case studies illustrating different methods of humane control according to developmental level.

HISTORICAL BACKGROUND

An archaeologist reportedly found evidence of the antiquity of the problem of discipline in the ruins of ancient Sumeria. He is supposed to have dug up some clay tablets recording a conversation between an adult and a teenager. According to the archaeologist's translation, the adult harangued the teenager as follows, "Grow up. Stop hanging around the public square and wandering up and down the street. Go to school. Night and day you torture me. Night

and day you waste your time having fun" (National Geographic Society, 1968).

These words were spoken some 4,000 years ago; the problem—lack of discipline, unruliness, wasting time. The more recently discovered memoirs of President Edward Everett of Harvard suggest that he spent the most miserable three years of his life (1846–1849) dealing with problems of student discipline. As a scholar, Everett was regarded as equal to Pericles in Athens, yet he complained bitterly about his students:

> Hateful duties in the morning to question three students about beckoning to loose women in the College Yard on Sunday afternoon; to two others about whistling in the passage; to another about smoking in the College Yard. Is this all I am fit for? . . . The life I am now leading must end, or it will end me.
>
> My time taken up all day with the most disgusting details of discipline, such as make the heart perfectly sick—fraud, deception, falsehood, unhandsome conduct, parents and friends harassing me all the time and foolishly believing the lies their children tell them (1965, p. 583).

If we turn to fiction we find similar sentiments. The tragic figure of the father in John Updike's novel, The Centaur, is likewise upset and in despair concerning student behavior and discipline. Mr.

Caldwell, perhaps overstating the problem for effect, turns to a particularly "slow-witted" pupil, Deifendorf:

> "The Founding Fathers," he explained, "in their wisdom decided that children were all an unnatural strain on parents. So they provided jails called schools, equipped with tortures called an education. . . . I am a paid keeper of society's unusables—the lame, the halt, the insane and the ignorant. The only incentive I can give you, kid, to behave yourself is this: if you don't buckle down and learn something, you'll be as dumb as I am and you'll have to teach school to earn a living" (Updike, 1963, pp. 80–81).

It seems safe to conclude that problems of student behavior and discipline have been with us for a long time and will probably be with us for a long time to come. Studies of teachers' attitudes toward children's behavior have revealed concerns exactly like those revealed by the ruins of ancient Sumeria and by President Everett of Harvard. In 1928, for example, a study found that the greatest concern of most teachers was acting-out, loud, disruptive children (Wickman, 1928). Some 30 years later, in a replication, another researcher came to very much the same conclusion (Beilin, 1959). And recently Michael Tulley and Lian-Hwang Chiu (1995) analyzed student teachers' reports of their classroom disciplinary problems and found that 91 percent of the discipline problems related to disruptions, defiance, and inattention. A particularly tragic effect of this preoccupation is that teachers may fail to recognize one of the most common mental-health problems—excessive inhibition—because their attention is diverted by the noisy, aggressive pupils. Even though educational psychologists have been trying to convince teachers to look beyond the obvious and recognize that withdrawn children may be a more serious problem than loud, active ones, there is still a very strong tendency to equate activity and noise with a discipline problem and to ignore passivity.

STUDENT DISCIPLINE AND THE FALLACY OF CHARACTER EDUCATION

A general assumption we all tend to make about discipline is that pupils learn best when they are quiet. When we say, "Learn with your eyes and ears but not with your mouth," we are assuming that we can't learn anything if we are talking, making noise, or moving around. When all the students are sitting quietly, listening in rapt attention to the teacher, it

does look as if they are learning. However, as we have already noted, appearances are deceiving.

If we accept the idea that a quiet atmosphere promotes learning, it follows that any breach of that atmosphere is not to be tolerated. In fact, to carry this logic a step further, it becomes the teacher's moral duty to keep peace in the classroom, because it is by this means that pupils develop the proper moral character. Thus, the teacher's role is seen in terms of simple-minded **character training,** or moral education.

Because of the seriousness with which moral education is viewed, no latitude or flexibility can be allowed. Student behavior is an indication of character, and so teachers may react strongly to noncompliant behavior: There is no room for give-and-take when we are dealing with issues of character.

Finally, to make matters even worse, this view assumes that by forcing obedience and conformity on children in school, self-directing and self-controlled adults will result. To many, however, it seems strangely paradoxical to teach self-control, personal independence, and responsibility by forcing students to be dependent and controlled. The discontinuity between demanding one set of behaviors when people are young and expecting a completely opposite set when they are older strikes some as counterproductive. Education will simply not promote personal independence if dependence and conformity are insisted on during the formative years. We noted earlier in this volume the almost indelible effect of early experience on later behavior. Teaching dependence and conformity will tend to enhance those behaviors rather than promote independence, inquiry, and self-direction. Or, as the eminent 19th-century educator Horace Mann put it, "We cannot educate for freedom with the methods of slavery."

DISCIPLINE: A DEVELOPMENTAL METHOD

Although the problems of classroom discipline have been with us from the beginning of formal instruction, solutions have been elusive. Most approaches to classroom discipline have been too singular, recommending a single procedure almost regardless of the age of the pupil or the situation. It's like writing a single prescription to be used in any emergency situation. For example, it is common to find a particular dictum or discipline law promoted as *the* answer. There is a view that strongly suggests that a teacher can never permit any departure from a policy of strict obedience. Even the most minor breach of classroom peace is to be met with instant punish-

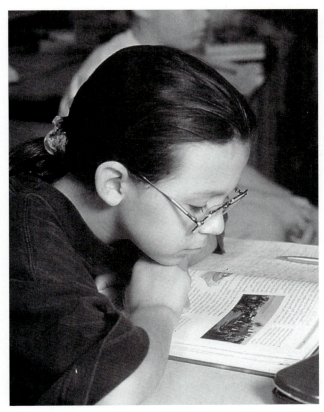

Teachers often assume that silent attention is a sign of learning and that orderly obedience is a sign of character building. The teacher must face the conflict between the need for classroom control and the encouragement of self-reliance and responsibility.

nizing activities and were literally unaware of the noise, confusion, spitballs, and paper airplanes all about. This permissive, **laissez-faire approach** somehow assumes that a classroom group on its own will always be so interested in the learning activities that teacher sanctions and reminders are unnecessary. In either case, however, whether the recommendation is for strict obedience or the permissive approach, the solutions are really bound to fail. The assumption is that one method is best since consistency is important.

A developmental approach to discipline in the classroom rests on a different set of assumptions. Alternatives to the single methods of power or permissiveness include methods that encourage student self-management, emphasize prevention, motivate student behavior, reinforce cooperation, encourage student self-esteem, help students solve problems, and intervene in negative behavior. The alternatives presented in this chapter are based on a developmental approach to discipline and classroom management. As we have stressed throughout this volume, pupils process and make meaning from their own experiences in qualitatively different methods. We have stressed the importance of tailoring or matching curriculum materials and teaching strategies to the developmental levels of the pupils. Thus, it will certainly come as no surprise to find that we recommend a similar approach to pupil discipline.

ment. With this **authoritarian approach to discipline,** there is no room for variation or negotiation, regardless of circumstances. The dictum states, "Lay down the rules." In other words, permit no deviation, or chaos and anarchy will reign. Such a single-variable solution to interactions as complex as teaching inevitably fails. Either the teacher gets so caught up with enforcement that there is little time for teaching, or the pupils get so caught up with the game that their energy is spent in constantly testing the limits.

As if in reaction to the absolute-obedience approach, an opposite extreme is often employed. Again, a single solution is proposed, only in this case the recommendation is to ignore misbehavior. We have all had teachers who seemed studiously indifferent to our antics. They seemed to be busy orga-

Stages of Development and Discipline

In order to avoid the trap of single prescriptions, the **developmental method of discipline** requires that we view the problem from a complex perspective. We have made the point that the way in which a

pupil understands intellectual or academic material (Piaget), value questions (Kohlberg), and personal issues (Erikson) depends on the child's stage. The same is true for discipline. Therefore, if we apply Kohlberg's framework of general value judgment to the question of how pupils understand rules and or-

TABLE 19.1   STAGES OF DEVELOPMENT: PUPIL DISCIPLINE

DESCRIPTION	POSITIVE	NEGATIVE
Stage I		
Use of physical means to require compliance. Obedience because of unequal power. Generally effective only in short term.	Helen Keller's teacher in *The Miracle Worker.* Placing an out-of-control child in a time-out room. Holding the arms of a child in the middle of a temper tantrum. Walking up to a child, standing over him or her. Making eye contact. Nonverbally indicating that the behavior is unacceptable.	Punching, kicking, breaking bones to teach a child a lesson. Locking a child in a dark closet. Punching the child with fists. Paddling.
Stage II		
Use of materialistic consequences such as rewards or withdrawal of privileges for acceptable or unacceptable behavior. Generally effective in the short run while the reinforcers (either positive or negative) are in effect.	The Premack principle (see Chapter 10). Use of Skinnerian positive reinforcers such as a token economy. A balance between positive reinforcers and negative reinforcers (withdrawing privileges). Selective positive reinforcers. Positive teacher comments exceeding negative by 2:1. Positive reminders and cues on classroom rules.	Exclusive use of aversive conditioning. Exclusive use of negative reinforcers (withholding food or restricting rations, e.g., bread and water only; use of criticism, sarcasm). Predominant use of negative verbal statements.
Stage III		
Use of social group (peer and adult pressure) to promote individual conformity to group norms and classroom rules. Concern for feelings of the group. Can be highly effective for significant periods as long as the individual remains in the group.	Setting classroom rules with group participation. Running classroom meetings to discuss general effects of misbehavior. Use of positive peer pressure. Rewarding the group as a whole to promote cooperative learning. Promoting group cohesiveness: "Our class—our team—our group." Cooperative learning materials. Using I-messages.	Turning the class members into a collective to scapegoat an individual child. Using the group to shame or shun a pupil publicly. Using a group to make individual pupils feel like outcasts (making a pupil sit in a "dunce chair"; standing the child in the wastebasket and having others throw trash in, etc.)

TABLE 19.1 *(continued)*

DESCRIPTION	POSITIVE	NEGATIVE
Stage IV		
Governance and sanctions according to legal standards. Individual responsibility and choice are stressed. Inner direction and individual decisionmaking toward rules and laws. Can be highly effective over long periods.	Careful observance by both adults and other pupils of each person's individual rights. Clear understanding of reasons for school laws. A point and contract system for grading. Understandable and reasonable consequences known to all for misbehavior. Teaching children self-management skills, such as self-directed behavior modification. Teaching children peer mediation and conflict resolution skills. Assertiveness training.	Excessive reliance on individual competition for grades. Exclusive stress on individual achievement. Narrow interpretation of laws and rules without regard to principles behind them.
Stage V		
Governance and sanctions based on general democratic principles; fairness, equity, toleration, freedom of thought, and the like.	Rules and laws developed democratically by open participation of adults and pupils. Sanctions imposed by student and teacher councils. Due process followed. Town meeting procedures; each person has one vote. Individual autonomy and responsibility to the group stressed. Interdependence a focus. Appropriate only for secondary-age or older students.	

Note: *In applying sanctions, the same developmental rules apply. Usually it is most appropriate to use methods that are one stage up from the learner.*

der, we'll have a more appropriate scheme for discipline. Essentially, the questions become: Which sanctions should I use as a teacher? What procedures may be more effective with which children? What is the repertoire of methods I should use as opposed to an exclusive reliance on any single type?

Table 19.1 outlines stages of moral development in relation to disciplinary methods. Most important, the table includes examples of what can be considered to be **positive disciplinary techniques** versus negative disciplinary techniques within each stage.

For example, at Stage I, the basic approach involves superior physical force. This can be manifested as brutality in such forms as whipping, breaking bones, bludgeoning, or maiming. A gym teacher instructing a class in sit-ups places his foot on the back of an overweight pupil and pushes his neck hard enough to force the boys' chin to his knee, all the while making the sarcastic comment, "Gee kid, you bend easy!"

Compare that approach to the technique used by the teacher in the movie *The Miracle Worker*. Anne

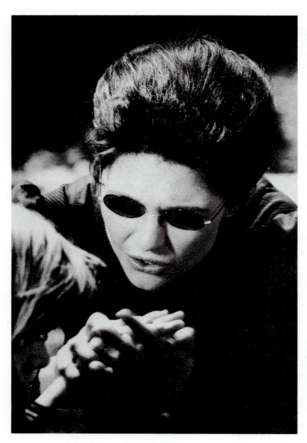

Annie Sullivan (as portrayed by Anne Bancroft) used humane physical constraints to start Helen Keller's learning process.

Bancroft portrayed Annie Sullivan, a young Irish teacher-companion to Helen Keller. Helen, who was born both blind and deaf, had been raised with almost no limits set on her behavior. During the initial phase of the relationship, Sullivan literally had to use physical force to restrain Helen. She would not allow Helen to hit her and ended up in exhausting wrestling matches, holding Helen's arms until finally her reluctant pupil was willing to start the process of growth and self-development.

In the life of any teacher, there may be times when physical force is the only appropriate solution. A young child in a temper tantrum, beating up a peer, may need to be physically removed, gently yet firmly, and placed in a time-out room. A teenager, out of control on drugs, may have to be physically restrained from doing harm to himself or herself as well as to others.

Thus, the old adage "Spare the rod and spoil the child" does not ring true. Not only isn't it true, but, as the Spotlight makes clear, the rod was used as a guide, not as a beating stick. The use of aversive physical force does not achieve positive results, even with highly motivated persons. A series of studies reviewed by Roger Brown and Richard Herrnstein (1974) indicated that even with a variety of novel techniques (a cigarette case that electrically shocks the would-be smoker, a remotely controlled "bug in the ear" device by which an out-of-sight therapist could shock a patient up to 300 feet away), the outcomes were not positive. As soon as the aversive stimulus was removed, the individuals reverted to their normal behavioral patterns. Physical punishment produced no long-lasting changes. The more up-to-date recommendations suggesting that teachers use physical punishment have no supportive research base.

Paddling (a form of corporal punishment) is a form of negative discipline at Stage I. Paddling has been abolished in 27 states, but 23 states still allow school districts this use of physical discipline. Students with disabilities (behavioral, emotional, learning, mental) are often more at risk for this negative form of discipline. So, too, are certain minority groups. African-American and Hispanic males, for example, from low socioeconomic homes are more likely to be physically punished than their Anglo-American peers (Evans & Richardson, 1995). Alternatives to paddling and corporal punishment can be found if we consider forms of discipline more appropriate to students' developmental stages. The Council for Exceptional Children has taken a strong stand in supporting no conditions for which corporal punishment is to be used in special education. American Association for Mental Retardation (AAMR) recommends positive, more complex humanistic discipline strategies such as training in conflict resolution, involving students in making discipline rules, using positive self-regulation skills, teaching prosocial skills, involving parents in behavior management programs, and preparing students with cooperative learning and peer mediation skills. We will discuss some of these strategies in the next few sections—and the importance of the teacher's having the flexibility to consider the developmental stage of the student when using discipline strategies.

In particular situations there may be little choice except the application of physical force. The key is the choice between brutality and humane control. There are basically two questions to answer. First, is Stage I the appropriate level on which to base the sanction? Second, is the pupil in such a state that more complex methods will not work? For a variety

SPOTLIGHT ON DISCIPLINE

Spare the Rod . . . What Does It Really Mean?

In almost every election for local school boards across the country, there will be at least one candidate who campaigns on the slogan "Spare the rod and spoil the child." Such a candidate will make it very clear that the cause of nearly all school problems derives from a lack of firm corporal punishment: School violence, drug abuse, lack of respect, indeed, the decline of Western civilization as we know it result from schools' having put the rod away. The image is stark. Give teachers the rod or the cane, and unruly students will be remolded into motivated, attentive learners. Civilization will be preserved. If anyone doubts the validity of such claims, then the school board can-

didate will surely cite the Bible as the source. And who can dispute such a formidable citation as justification?

As is often the case, however, such biblical references may not be entirely accurate. What zealots for corporal punishment fail to realize is that the metaphor "spare the rod" actually means the opposite of a justification for physical beating. The Bible was written in an age when each town grew crops and raised its own herds of animals for food. Shepherds used a long rod with a crooked neck while tending their flock. When moving the herd to the next pasture, the shepherd would use the rod to guide occasional strays back

to the fold. There was no beating or flailing of the animals. The shepherds were careful husbandmen, gently but firmly redirecting the flock to greener pastures—quite a different picture from the one painted by our school board candidate. Thus, if you don't provide guidance and gently redirect those few strays in your class back into the life of the classroom, you will be spoiling the child. Firm and fair discipline does not, however, involve physical abuse. The rod is not a stick for beating. By comprehending the original use of the shepherd's crook, you can respond to the common misunderstanding of the concept and tend your flock like a good shepherd.

of psychological reasons there are times when a child may be, literally, out of control. If that seems to be the case, then the second choice is most important, that is, between negative and positive applications of physical force. The amount of physical force employed should be just enough to restore control to the child or teenager. There is no point in massive retaliation. Also, it is important to remember that such physical control is effective only in the short run and in the immediate situation. Naturally, the educator's goal is to employ more complex methods that will aid the pupil in the development of self-control. Reaching such a goal, however, is a gradual process; it is not achievable overnight (Hart, 1991).

At the second stage, positive discipline involves the use of extrinsic or materialistic rewards to aid in the shaping of pupil behavior. Pupils at Stage II are still egocentric; their dominant point of view is "What's in it for me?" The great variety of so-called Skinnerian techniques (described in detail in Chapter 10) fit here. The key is to use generally positive reinforcers such as extra recess time, special trips, or treats as rewards. Point systems and token economies are extensions of the same approach.

Skinner is convinced that his operant conditioning works most effectively when the teacher uses rewards rather than relying exclusively on aversive conditioning. For example, studies of teacher-pupil verbal interaction show ratios as high as eight negative teacher comments for every positive one. A balance of teacher comments, in which the positive exceeds or at least equals the negative-critical, would improve classroom control. This recommendation does not mean that the teacher should never make negative evaluative comments. To praise uncritically every activity of every child does not improve learning outcomes. However, a balance is clearly appropriate.

Thus, in selecting goals for reinforcement, choose the positive. If you set up a token economy (so many points for handing in homework on time, for doing seatwork, for listening to directions, etc.), the goal could be special reading time or avoiding detention. The more that teachers and principals use the latter category, the more schools become like prisons. Aversive measures and goals teach the child to seek a psychological escape, to learn not to learn.

It is clear that the Stage II positive approach is

more effective as well as easier on both teacher and pupils than Stage I. Using behavioral principles to reinforce positive behavior is a powerful educational strategy. However, it does require extreme consistency. The teacher must remain absolutely consistent in providing immediate reinforcement for positive behavior and must never (even inadvertently) reinforce negative behavior. For example, if a teacher mistakenly yells at loud, noisy children, the yelling reinforces the children's noise rather than achieving the opposite effect. Thus, for the system to work, the teacher has to monitor reinforcers with vigilance.

As in Stage I, the major responsibility for control is still with the adult. The system will work as long as the adult applies the contingencies with humane goals. Naturally, the system can be employed in the service of out-and-out demeaning manipulation and at-risk children are particularly vulnerable to excessive control (Edwards, 1994). A most graphic example is found in the movie (and novel) *One Flew Over the Cuckoo's Nest*. Nurse Rachett expertly manipulates the patients. She controls all the activities of the ward, allowing no individuality or choice. Like an absolute despot, she employs behavioral principles to prevent human growth. The importance for teaching is obvious. The choice of goals is critical. The means, that is, the disciplinary strategies, should be consistent with educative and growth goals.

At the Stage III level, the overall objective is to begin sharing the responsibility for control and discipline with the children as a group. The social group as a community can be an extremely strong influence on class effort and behavior. The ability to experience how the group feels about individuals and vice versa means that control and direction no longer need to be exclusively determined by the adult. The group can participate in setting classroom norms and rules for appropriate behavior. Classroom meetings, in William Glasser's sense, are now possible for discussions on content as well as on feelings about appropriate and inappropriate behavior. The procedures recommended by Glasser (1975, 1992) are useful at this level. Also, the use of so-called I-messages by the teacher can now be effective. When children have the ability to understand their own emotions as well as the feelings of adults, the system of I-messages developed by Thomas Gordon (1974), becomes an important technique. There are three components of I-messages:

1. A nonjudgmental, precise, objective statement of the pupil's behavior: "When you interrupt Nancy . . ." not "When you rudely/inconsiderately/thoughtlessly blurt out/shout out/ scream out at the answers Nancy is giving . . ."

2. A statement explaining why the behavior is troublesome: "The class can't hear what Nancy is trying to say . . ." not "I cannot let you steamroller your classmates/cut people off/have your own way/be so self-centered . . ."

3. A statement of how you feel: "I feel frustrated trying to listen to two people at once . . ." not "I feel ashamed to have such an unproductive student in my class who casts such a terrible reflection on the rest of us. How do you ever expect not to end up on welfare when you grow up?"

Thus, an I-message has three parts: an objective description of troublesome behavior, an explanation of consequences to the teacher and the rest of the class, and a personal statement of the teacher's feelings. It may sound very awkward as a procedure, especially since it may appear that you are leading with your chin, so to speak. To be sure, an I-message will not always work, but teachers trained in Gordon's method report that it has a very substantial probability of success, especially if the teacher pauses and waits through the silence that usually follows.

In addition to classroom meetings and I-messages, the use of cooperative groups is a third important procedure at this level. Students can be taught to think and act in accordance with the welfare of the group as a whole. The decline in egocentric materialism of Stage II means that pupils can be enlisted as peer teachers and can benefit from small group-learning activities. Rewards such as grades or treats can be granted to groups rather than to individuals. Loyalty and cooperation to one's own class or small group act as powerful motivators.

Procedures outlined by Robert Slavin (1990) are most appropriate for setting up small groups to enhance such cooperative learning. Under such conditions, children can monitor the members of their group who may not be positive contributors. "Come on, Henry and Althea, help the rest of us finish the project so we can all go on the museum trip!" or "You know you're leaving us holding the bag because you haven't learned your part yet for the play." Both the approval and the disapproval of the group are powerful conditioners of individual behavior. Also, it is obvious that the direction is more shared than at Stage I or II. The cohesiveness and group togetherness act as a bond. Children are no longer completely at one end of the classroom with the teacher at the other. There is more interaction, more collegueship, and more mutual decisionmaking. Classroom norms, written on the blackboard, are derived with student input and participation.

There is, however, a negative aspect of the general Stage III approach. It is relatively easy for a teacher, if he or she desires, to use the system to effect a kind of totalitarian approach. With manipulation, a teacher can use the class group to squelch any kind of individuality. In the educational system of the former Soviet Union the purpose was exactly that—to promote loyalty to the state at the expense of individuality. It is possible in any classroom to use group process toward such ends. Any pupil deviation or individual initiative (even relatively mild acting up) can be subject to public shaming. Group punishment for individual misdeeds is another way to turn members of a group against one of their colleagues. The novel and movie *Lord of the Flies* provide a dramatic example of how far a group of children can go to enforce absolute conformity. Adults can mastermind such activities through scapegoating and forcing individual confessions in kangaroo-court atmospheres.

A teacher can unconsciously use the class group to reinforce an existing classroom social order in which diversity of race, gender, social class, and culture is not valued. Thus, the teacher using a Stage III approach will want to notice discipline problems in the classroom that may result from the social system in the classroom, and not be located just in an individual student. Thus, as is the case at the two earlier stages, the procedures for discipline at Stage III are not fail-safe. The overall goals and learning activities as well as the methods help to determine if the techniques are educationally sound. However, at Stage III the effects can be longer-lasting than at either Stage I or II. The system is no longer directed exclusively by a single adult. The group is more pervasive and more powerful.

At Stage IV, the overall goal is to move the major responsibility for discipline from the group to the individual. This goal is clearly a democratic ethic. Self-governance and direction provide scope for individuality and autonomy. The shift is from social conformity and other-directedness to individual conscience and inner direction. The laws that govern behavior are applied equally to teachers and pupils. There is clear public knowledge, and acceptance of consequences.

At this level, the teacher may instruct pupils in so-called self-management techniques. There is a difference between this instruction and the control exercised by the teacher at Stage II. At the lower level the teacher regulates the reinforcers. At this higher level the teacher essentially gives the psychology of behavior modification away to the pupils. They are helped in setting up their own schedules of reinforcement in certain problem areas, in monitoring the outcomes, and in setting their own rewards. Thus, rather than punish a pupil for not handing in a term paper, the teacher and pupil (together) could work out a schedule, keep track of study time, and provide short-term and longer-term positive reinforcers. Ultimately, only the pupil can learn how to apply behavioral principles to his or her own problem areas.

A second approach involves what is called *assertiveness training*. Individuals are taught to speak up for themselves, to exercise their right of choice, and most important, to negotiate solutions to conflict situations. There is an important distinction here between assertiveness and aggression. These procedures are not designed to encourage a kind of Stage II egocentric aggressiveness. Rather, pupils are helped to develop the ability to speak up for themselves, quietly yet firmly. An outgrowth of the cooperative learning focus in classrooms is the use of peer mediation for resolving conflicts between students. David Johnson and Roger Johnson from the University of Minnesota have developed peer-mediation training programs ("Teaching Students to Be Peacemakers") that focus on training students in negotiation and mediation procedures and skills. Results of five years of research in suburban, middle-class, and inner-city elementary schools show the effectiveness of training students to be conflict managers to mediate schoolmates' conflicts (Johnson & Johnson, 1995; Johnson et al., 1996). Most of the conflicts brought for mediation strategies involve physical and verbal attacks involving physical aggression, playground activities, access to or possession of objects, turn taking, put-downs/teasing, and academic work. Observations of hallways, lunchroom, playground, and gymnasium months after training show that discipline problems were eliminated as the students became more autonomous in managing their conflicts constructively. There is some evidence that school-based peer-mediation training transfers acquired conflict management skills from school to the home setting for use during sibling conflicts.

With these abilities in the hands of the students, the overall teaching role naturally shifts more to that of a manager and consultant. Instruction and projects can be highly individualized. Learning contracts between teacher and pupils can be negotiated *and* renegotiated. In fact, at this level even the choice of consequences can be mutually determined. Goal setting can vary in accordance with pupils' differential abilities. Thus, for a particular pupil in a physical education class, improving from 5 to 15 pushups may be just as valued as a Dominique Dawes type of performance by the star female gymnast in the class. Joint decisionmaking and monitoring increase the likelihood of individual commitment and motivation.

Naturally, there is another side to Stage IV. Essentially, the possible difficulty of this system is that it can lead to excessive individualism. Any particular pupil can become so achievement-oriented that there is almost no concern for anyone else. Unmoderated competition can become so intense, the rugged individualism so rugged, that pupils may drive themselves to the brink of psychological breakdown. The achiever may become the overachiever. A pupil's life can become organized in the exclusive pursuit of grades or test scores. Highly "competitive" high schools with public class rankings, published college admission results, and posted SAT score profiles can create personal nightmares for those pupils who are already highly achievement-oriented. The same is true at the college and graduate levels. The signs are all too familiar, such as cheating, bribing, hiding assigned library books, or tearing out critical passages from them.

When the individual loses sight of the overall purposes of education and confuses grades as ends in themselves rather than as means, then negative consequences follow. Part of the challenge for the teacher is that much of this problem may remain hidden. The student who is overly achievement-oriented is hardly a discipline problem in the usual sense. Thus, it is important to monitor the level of individual competition in the classroom and to keep in mind that the goal of Stage IV is to promote self-management and self-direction and not rampant self-aggrandizement.

The risk at Stage IV is that responsibility for oneself cannot be emphasized at the expense of responsibility and care for others. Responsibility and care for self and others become paramount as a sense of teachers' solidarity with and among students develops at Stage V. At Stage V, negotiation in a democratic community is the basis for teachers sharing power with students, not holding power over students. James McLaughlin (1994) extends the notion that student obedience is one kind of discipline system at the lower stages, whereas student responsibility is an advanced form of discipline which we describe at Stage IV; and student and teacher solidarity in a democratic community is the most advanced form of classroom management, which we describe as corresponding to Stage V.

One further point at this level: since law becomes a reference point for decisions, it is possible to stick too closely to literal interpretations. Schools and state departments of education publish the legal aspects of students' rights, which call for highly detailed procedures. Access to file information (under the so-called Buckley amendment); the steps that must be followed before searching student lockers; liberalized court rulings on matters of suspension, hair length, dress codes, and legitimate student protests—all these areas are now regulated at the Stage IV due-process level. Such legal codes provide for more stability and equality in how schools and teachers may apply sanctions. Before these changes, children and teenagers could literally be pushed out more on the basis of their social class or ethnic background than on anything else.

There is, however, a possible danger in reliance on legalism. It can lead to a narrow interpretation of law. In this view, the rules must always be obeyed; under no circumstances can a teacher, principal, or pupil change or adjust the rule. The reasons for the laws can be forgotten almost too easily. Stage IV has its limits, particularly because in exceptional cases the principles and reasons for the law may be ignored. Thus, there may be unique and admittedly rare occasions when exact recourse to the letter of the law is not appropriate. For example, a school nurse noticing an incoherent pupil in the midst of an extremely "bad" drug trip may need to know what drug has been taken in order to make a decision on an antidote. Obviously, examining the contents of the locker may be crucial for speedy action. In this case, as in some others, strict adherence to the letter of the law may have to be set aside.

At the Stage V level, the teachers, administrators, and pupils essentially form a democratic community. Each person participates in the creation of sanctions, laws, and rules that include all aspects of schooling. The organization that is set up is much like the town meeting; there is literally no difference between adults and pupils. Through parliamentary-style debate, rules are established and enforced across the board—honor codes, homework assignments, grading practices, attendance requirements, social-service obligations, and so on. Governance by students and teachers is according to majority rule. Arbitrary decisions by either teachers or students are not permitted. All issues are debatable and all consequences carefully examined. The overall concept is that of a community of teachers and pupils based on **democratic** principles of justice and equality—a kind of Jeffersonian, grass-roots, direct democracy.

The Stage V level of discipline does sound somewhat idealized as a goal and is perhaps unattainable. A basic assumption is that all members of any such community are far enough along developmentally to process at a Stage V level. In other words, such a plan simply will not work unless the participants are capable of understanding issues at a level of principled thought.

There are a few examples of such procedures actually working at the eleventh- and twelfth-grade level in public schools as well as at the college level. Such experiments suggest that this level of discipline may be possible but that it is also extremely difficult to achieve. The system demands a very high level of commitment by both teachers and pupils, huge amounts of goodwill, and high levels of cognitive ability. Genuine democracy is an extraordinarily fragile commodity. Such procedures should be applied only after the most careful examination of the assumptions and required procedures. Ralph Mosher, this country's leading innovator in democratic high school organization, wryly sums up four years of experience with a quote from democratic theorist D. W. Brogan: "Non-democratic government is like a splendid ship, with all its sails set; it moves majestically on, then it hits a rock and sinks forever. Democracy is like a raft. It never sinks, but damn it, your feet are always in the water" (Mosher, 1979, p. 497).

Matching Discipline Levels and Pupils

With this five-stage scheme in mind, we can now turn to specific applications. We haven't outlined a Stage VI approach for two reasons—one theoretical and one practical. At the theoretical level, Stage VI individuals would always follow universal principles; therefore, any system would be unnecessary and clearly redundant. At the practical level, so few persons operate at Stage VI that the school itself might be the size of a phone booth.

As we noted at the outset, the role of the teacher in discipline is to discern in a general way the approximate range of levels within the class. Table 19.2 presents the overall trends by school grades (obviously a very general framework).

TABLE 19.2   STAGE OF REASONING ABOUT DISCIPLINE AND GENERAL AGE LEVELS

AGE	PREDOMINANT REASONING LEVEL	NEXT MODEL STAGE UP
Preschool (3–4 years)	I	I (II)
Kindergarten to grade 3	I (II)	II
Elementary grades 4 to 8	II (III)	III
Grades 9 through 12	III (IV)	IV–V*

* Under special circumstances.

The table provides a guideline for choice and expectation. Remember, there is individual variation within any class, yet in general the class as a group will function at these levels. Also remember that even though the children cluster at a particular level, there is the plus-one concept. They are capable of understanding and being attracted to a slightly more complex level of discipline. Thus, even if you find yourself confronted with a prekindergarten class with everyone at the collective-monologue stage, you can still use some Stage II rewards and treats. In other words, the matching of discipline to stage can be a slight mismatch in which you try to use some techniques and strategies from the next level up. If there are occasions when that does not work, you can still employ the humane or positive strategies precisely at the level of the pupils. The overall choice is to select the least restrictive alternative, given the age and stage of the pupils.

In addition to the plus-one idea, a second aspect of the discipline system is important to remember. Each stage is slightly more complex and more effective than the prior level. At the higher levels, more of the responsibility is shared with the pupils. They require less monitoring by you. Thus, the overall goal of discipline is not simply to keep the peace so that children will all sit still and listen, with teachers applying power to control recalcitrant pupils. The developmental approach employs sanctions in the service of general growth. Pupils can gradually take on some of the responsibility and learn self-management. It's like a creative abdication. The teacher gradually shifts some power, control, and responsibility to the pupils in accordance with their stage of development and readiness. Teaching children to care, says Ruth Charney (1992), made her love being a disciplinarian because she has grown to appreciate helping children to take better care of themselves, each other, and their classrooms. Her anecdotes about and guidelines for student discipline strategies such as rule setting, logical consequences, problemsolving class meetings, time-out, power struggles, social conferences, empowering language, clear positives, and critical contracts provide practical, authentic examples of teaching appropriate to the developmental stages we list in Table 19.1.

Certainly, the major procedure to avoid is gross mismatching either way. Using procedures way over the heads of the pupils will simply confuse them and frustrate you. To expect second- or third-graders, for example, to understand the principles of participatory democracy (Stage V) is obviously unrealistic. Similarly, to expect pupils at straight Stage II levels to understand and to behave in accordance with a Stage IV "honor code" is to invite noncompliance. Finally, the teacher should not use methods substantially below the stage levels of the pupils. Such a procedure would clearly be regressive.

With the stage characteristics in mind, it is possible to organize classroom **discipline strategies** based on the following **four questions:**

1. Who makes the rules?

2. Who keeps the rules?

3. How are the rules enforced?

4. Why do students obey the rules?

Strategies at Stage I

At Stage I, the teacher sets the rules: "During seatwork time, students are expected to remain at their desks," or "Please raise your hands if you know the correct answer," or "In this class we will all line up by twos before we go out to recess." The teacher has carefully selected a minimum yet essential number of rules to preserve the classroom as an orderly, humane workplace for children. Understanding the developmental stage of the pupils means that the teacher does not expect the pupils to figure out what kind of learning environment is most appropriate to their needs. Thus, the answer to the first question is that the teacher makes the rules.

For similar reasons the teacher also monitors compliance. This means keeping careful track of pupil behavior. If a rule is broken a number of times without a response by the teacher, such silence actually encourages further testing of the limits. At the same time it is important to remember that positive monitoring is more effective than negative and/or aversive control. So praise for those who remain seated not only increases their obedience but also is a message quickly heard by the others. In addition, positive, nonverbal body language such as smiles, pats on the back, and nods of the head are other means of humane physical control. At this level, then, the answer to the question "Who keeps the rules?" is that it is mostly the teacher and through a positive mode.

For the third question of how the rules are enforced, it is important to remember the system of judgment that the child uses. For those still reasoning at Stage I, what makes the rules effective is the physical presence of the teacher. Children in preschool and early elementary grades vary quite substantially in their ability to monitor their own behavior without an adult actually visible or at least within earshot. Research indicates that a few preschool children can monitor their own behavior and delay gratification even without an adult present and with a tempting choice at hand (Mischel &

Peake, 1982). While it is certainly a positive sign that children even at this early age possess some internal self-control, the researchers also found that young children make life most difficult for themselves in such tempting situations. They focus on what they cannot have, making the "forbidden fruit" even more attractive.

By the third grade, however, most children are fully capable of resisting temptation without an adult monitor. The idea of a positive reward is strong enough that the pupil can postpone the immediate temptation. Yet even in this instance, remember that the findings come from studies of children one at a time and thus indicate a potential. Placing children in group situations, such as a classroom, can lower their ability to resist temptations. As we pointed out in Chapters 5–7 and 18, children, like adults, can be swayed quite substantially by pressure to conform to the peer group. Thus, the teacher in preschool and the early elementary grades needs to proceed slowly toward a more complex and humane system at Stage II. This means that outside physical force is still a strong "reason" why children this age will keep the rules. Desire for physical approval or fear of punishment is the answer to the fourth question in our scheme.

One final point: Remember that children can process reasons at different levels. Some children, especially those reared by parents who follow the model of effective parenting outlined in Chapter 6, will show an ability to verbalize and exhibit a higher level of self-control. Not so with other children: If parents of kindergarteners regularly use negative physical force (severe corporal punishment), the children will most likely show very little capacity for self-control without an adult close at hand. In this case much patience and support are needed to prepare the child for discipline based on material rewards rather than physical presence (Lickona, 1991).

Strategies at Stage II

At Stage II, during the first part of elementary school, the teacher still makes and keeps the rules. The big change occurs with the pupil's ability to delay gratification and to work for concrete rewards instead. Thus, the answers are the same for the first two questions but different for the last two.

Rules can be enforced through material rewards simply because that method fits the reasoning level of the children. This does not mean that the children are not capable of working and learning for intrinsic reasons. As we pointed out in Chapter 5, there is an innate drive to learn, a motivation for competence. However, new learning is not universally pleasant.

SPOTLIGHT ON CLASSROOM RULES

Within the developmental framework, there are some overall criteria for setting up classroom rules that are posted.

1. Rules should encourage *positive behavior*. This means using phrases and concepts in a positive mode. Instead of "No putting down your classmates," the rule could read "Each student will show respect to other students." Or instead of "No talking out of turn" (or "No call outs") the rule could be "Raise your hand and take turns in answering without interruption."
2. Rules should be *specific*, especially in elementary and middle school. Stating general principles to young students seldom affects their behavior. Thus, it is better to say in middle school, "Each student is expected to be seated, with school materials at hand, and ready to learn at the beginning of class" instead of "Learning requires effort and attention."
3. Rules should be *enforceable* yet fair with logical consequences. For example, in the case of cheating, the grade for both pupils might be a single grade divided by two; thus, an 80 percent paper provides a 40 percent grade to each. If the sanctions are too severe, students will withdraw and learning will cease. For minor transgressions, a sincere apology may be most effective.
4. Use as *few rules* as possible. It would be disheartening to anyone to enter a room and be confronted with a list of 25 to 50 rules of conduct. General guidelines from experienced teachers suggest from 2 to 4 rules in the primary grades, 4 to 6 in middle school, and up to 8 in high school.
5. The rules can be modified through increased participation by the students as they progress developmentally. Most important, include a discussion with the students as to the *reasons* for the rules. Resist the tendency to give a long lecture. Instead promote dialogue and extensive participation.

Finally, do not despair over the prospect of carrying all of this off effectively. In the long run you'll find that your reputation as a "firm but fair" teacher will gradually reduce the need for careful monitoring. The student grapevine is swift and usually accurate. In fact, one experienced teacher simply announced to her high school class without sarcasm, "I've been teaching for 10 years. I know all the 'creative' reasons for being late, for incomplete homework (a computer glitch has replaced the dog who eats term papers), and for missing class. If all those sick and dying grandmothers were really hospitalized, there wouldn't be room for anyone else. So dispense with those plans. Instead, we'll work together to make it a good learning experience for all of us." You will also see a grudging admiration for your with-it-ness and your savvy.

Instead, a part of each person's learning and processing stage likes the present "just fine, thank you." We all have a way of thinking and behaving that is comfortable and habitual. As noted in Chapter 5, the pupils are in part "old fogeys," conservatives who like to keep in touch with the past. Certainly, if students have difficulty learning new material (and we all do at some point), then discouragement can set in, and out-of-seat behavior increases. Thus, especially with elementary-age children, the teacher who does not use a systematic approach in dispensing concrete rewards is giving up a powerful ally. Discipline problems and pupil anxieties can be addressed simultaneously through a careful sequence of positive reinforcers. It is not manipulative if, in a humane way, you help children give up a reliance on outside physical control and replace it with reliance on point systems, a token economy, gold stars, "smiling faces," special time to work on puzzles and games, and the like. You are then aiding the children in the process of growth toward self-control. The Stage II methods help students gain a level of self-control and as a result facilitate the process of learning new and difficult material.

Strategies at Stage III

Not until pupils begin to reason at a Stage III level can further shifts be made toward greater student participation. There is some potential for discipline in this mode by the late elementary and the middle-school years. Interaction in both rulemaking and rulekeeping can increase. The teacher can use much

Discussing classroom rules through a play activity reduces discipline problems.

more discussion in formulating rules and deciding on appropriately positive group sanctions. (See the Spotlight on Classroom Rules.) The reason that both making and monitoring rules need to be "managed" by the teacher is that Stage III reasoning can be over-scrupulous. We noted a concern about scapegoating. Other research has shown that junior high students can be little short of draconian in their ideas of fair punishment (Sprinthall, 1985). (The Greek lawgiver Draco set up a system of excessively harsh and downright cruel sanctions). Students at this age apparently quite easily suggest similarly fearful punishments even for minor misdeeds. As they emerge from childhood, it's almost as if they immediately identify with adults as authoritarians rather than as authorities. Thus, teacher monitoring is needed to ensure that mercy is mixed with their conception of justice.

As we have pointed out elsewhere in detail, junior high students often exhibit open streaks of racism and sexism. This is part of the Stage III social-conformist mode. Students show little tolerance, often outright intolerance, toward anyone obviously different in ethnic background or social class.

Strategies at Stage IV

At the high school level students are developmentally ready to participate more fully in making, keeping, and participating in the sanctions when the rules are broken. They have reached the point of initial individuality and identity as autonomous people. To be sure, there are still strong aspects of social conformity, but the students now have a real potential for reasoning for and by themselves.

Perhaps the most important aspect of this stage is the rational or abstract understanding of what are sometimes called "natural consequences." It is true that younger children can learn about concrete consequences. Yet by high school, students have a deeper understanding. Thus, in setting up a learning contract for, say, a term paper, the student can learn the importance of doing each step in sequence and, most of all, that he or she can't wait until the night before the project's due to start on it. The wise teacher sets up the contract with a series of checkpoints: "After two weeks, list the references used and the key points of each reference . . . After four weeks prepare the first draft in outline form." Dividing a large task into manageable pieces developed with the student assures a much greater chance for compliance. Similarly, in contracting for homework assignments, students can discuss how many points toward their final grade each assignment is worth, whether makeup homework counts, and if so, how much.

In preparing for and taking "chapter" tests, students and teacher can work out a comparable system of points. Then comes the most important part of the contract approach: failure. You must be firm but not harsh in dealing with failure. Students (and parents) need to know quite clearly that failure to study, to submit homework, and to prepare long-term assignments does have consequences such as not passing the course. At this point each classroom teacher needs the support of the school administration, so that failing one or a number of required courses will have a real consequence—to repeat the class, to attend summer school, to be ineligible for extracurricular activities, or even to receive inschool suspensions. Such negative sanctions are sometimes necessary even though, as with the other stages, the positive aspects of the contract system yield better and more cooperative results. For the slow or handicapped learner, the contract specifies a reachable level of improvement through an individualized education plan (discussed in more detail in Chapter 20).

Strategies at Stage V

Finally, with some high school students, some teachers, and some administrators, it may be possible to go to the last step. The community as a whole handles all three aspects of the rules (who makes them, who keeps them, and how they are kept), and the group can reason through discipline dilemmas on the basis of principles of justice. There are some ongoing **school-within-a-school** programs in which this process is actually followed. A town meeting format is employed, and all major disciplinary decisions are made after full debate. Careful examination is made of alternatives, and consensus is achieved through voting. Such a program cannot work overnight, however. Democratic governance needs to be cultivated slowly. Otherwise, as soon as the first real crisis comes along, students will move quickly to their prior levels and either become excessive sticklers for the letter of the law or conform to their friendship groups. Nevertheless, it is possible for students at this age to act responsibly. Decision-making can be based on Stage V principles.

From a preventive approach, the **democratic high school model** is the comprehensive solution. Recent studies have shown that the atmosphere is significantly more positive than in the usual secondary school format. The quality of both the peer relationships and the student-to-teacher relationships make a major difference. Discipline problems are reduced to such a minimal level that they almost disappear. Studies of these programs found that in a variety of public settings, such as a school for gifted and talented, a suburban district, a "blue-collar" school, and a school for high-risk students in the "Fort Apache" district of New York City, cheating and stealing ceased altogether, fighting was reduced to one incident in five years, drug and alcohol abuse virtually disappeared, and racial integration increased (Kuhmerker, 1991). The students not only learned their academic lessons but also learned to care for one another. Such students were very likely

Using a contract approach sets clear guidelines for student projects.

to offer help to a member of their school even though the student was not from their clique. In contrast, students from regular schools generally ignored peers who were in some way different. Also, students participating in the democratic format were more likely to behave proactively in activities in the surrounding community. It is an old-fashioned word, but they were better "citizens" both in and out of school—they were better informed and more likely to read about public affairs, and they had a greater respect for society's laws. Finally, their assessed level of value development on the Kohlberg system (see Chapter 7) also improved (Sprinthall & Collins, 1995).

Similar approaches to this democratic community milieu have been successfully implemented at the college level. The management of college dormitory rules and regulations can be turned over to the students and staff as a community (Sprinthall & Collins, 1995). Such a process promotes maturity and responsibility. Just think what life would have been like for President Everett if such a method had been tried earlier.

Table 19.3 summarizes the answers to the four questions as an approach to discipline at the various stages.

One point needs further mention. In order to match discipline strategies to students' behavior at higher stages, a teacher will need to be able to reason at these levels. Judith MacCallum's (1993) study in Australia with 24 high school teachers really cross-validates a number of studies in the United States on the relation between discipline and stage. The 24 teachers in MacCallum's study completed tests of moral reasoning and were interviewed before and after an inservice course on a new discipline program adopted by their school district.

The interviews were about four hypothetical school discipline incidents: 1) fighting in the playground, 2) defaming a fellow student, 3) wearing a school uniform, and 4) calling a teacher by a nickname. The first two incidents are concerned with moral issues and the last two are concerned with social-conventional issues. MacCallum separated and analyzed the interview data for the nine teachers who scored highest on moral reasoning and the nine teachers who scored lowest on moral reasoning. She found that the moral reasoning of teachers was related to their overall approach to discipline. The low group viewed their approach to discipline as one of controlling, in which they policed the school rules and felt confident that they were doing the right thing. The high group viewed their approach as one of facilitating discipline, trying to balance the rights of all concerned, and they appeared less confident because they were aware of the difficulty of trying to find this balance.

The high group tended to focus on providing students with explanations of rules or assisting students in viewing rules from different perspectives, whereas the low group tended to focus on rules and authority. The low group were less able to separate themselves from the situation to look at other perspectives when the discipline problem occurs in

TABLE 19.3   PREDOMINANT STAGE OF PUPIL'S REASONING AND APPROACHES TO DISCIPLINE

	STAGE I	*STAGE II*	*STAGE III*	*STAGE IV*	*STAGE V*
1. Who makes the rules?	Teacher	Teacher	Teacher and pupils	Teacher and pupils	Pupils and teacher
2. Who keeps the rules?	Teacher	Teacher	Teacher and pupils	Pupils and teacher	Pupils and teacher
3. How are the rules enforced?	Physical methods	Concrete rewards	Group discussion and class meetings	Pupils monitor own "contracts" and mediate peer conflicts	Town meetings and student-controlled discipline committees
4. Why do students obey the rules?	Out of fear of punishment or to seek physical approval	To gain some materialistic rewards or to avoid losing rewards	To belong to the class as a group (social conformity) or to avoid being isolated	To develop individual responsibility or to avoid an identity only as a member of a group	Out of an understanding of principles of justice and the meaning of democratic community of rights and responsibilities and care

At Stage V, a democratic approach to school discipline is a workable option.

their own classroom or when it involves themselves; they see rules as made by the authorities and given to the students. The high group see rules as necessary for the rights of individual students as well as the group. They can work with students to set up the rules so that students understand the rules and their responsibilities. They encourage students to talk about the value of the rules, the reasons for them, and the consequences of breaking the rules; the high group of teachers talk with students about the reasons behind rules.

MacCallum also makes an interesting comment about gender. Although she found no difference between males and females in their levels of moral reasoning, she did find that in the high group females were more consistent over time than males in using their moral reasoning ability to deal with school discipline incidents. In Chapter 14, we talked more about teachers and the implications of their own stages of development on their classroom interactions and strategies of teaching.

Effects of Discussion

The more you discuss reasons for rules of discipline and engage students in these discussions, the greater the likelihood of improvement in their level of un-

derstanding. In fact, one study has shown that the discussion approach helped even first-graders become somewhat more reflective and less impulsive in classroom behavior. There was a reduction in Stage I behavior, in kids hitting other kids and in other acts of physical violence (Enright, 1981). The teacher, of course, still set the rules and monitored compliance. Discussions about the reasons for rules, conducted at the child's level of understanding, can aid in promoting growth. In addition, you should not accept the current level of stage-linked reasoning about discipline problems as a permanent classification. Instead, always be on the watch for evidence of higher and more complex reasoning as you provide the opportunity for classroom discussion about rules and reasons.

The final and most positive point to remember is that students do have potential for developmental growth even in the worst-case discipline situations. They may at times behave in a manner approaching the level of the children in *Lord of the Flies*. There still is some part of each student, as the assimilation-accommodation balance makes clear, that is attracted to a more complex and more humane system of controls. The advantage to you as a teacher is obvious. The greater the growth, the less time you must spend setting, keeping, and monitoring the rules. Then there is more time for learning.

Discipline Stage and Individual Differences

Developmental stages should be considered only as general frameworks for students at different age groupings. Obviously, not every student fits neatly into his or her appropriate modal stage. There are **individual differences.** Anyone who has worked with children or teenagers in any capacity such as a teacher, camp counselor, coach, or den leader can quickly relate examples of students who don't quite fit. Such students are the ones who clearly do not respond well to the average prescriptions matched to stage. It works both ways. Some students, developmentally advanced, may show signs of boredom or acting-up behavior, whereas others, for a variety of reasons, may be mismatched the other way, displaying an inability to attend to the material and methods you are employing.

The first step, then, is to review the student interaction with your teaching. How many different models are you using? Do you vary the assignments and promote a positive classroom atmosphere? For example, an eighth-grade honor student began acting up when a teacher assigned the same rotelike homework exercise for three days in a row: "Look up and identify the following 50 names of people and places from today's newspaper." Each day a new list. In another case an otherwise attentive student started an underground newspaper as a reaction to a classroom taught exclusively through a didactic high-structure method. Preventing discipline problems by modifying the classroom environment should always be the first line of defense (Burden, 1995, Wolfgang, 1995).

After such a review of methods and materials, the next step is to deal with the misbehavior by individualizing your discipline strategies. There is always a debate between psychologists and educational psychologists as to how much time and effort should be directed at finding the psychological causes of misbehavior through family history. Naturally, it is helpful to understand any unusual circumstances that may be affecting a student (divorce, family abuse, loss of a grandparent), yet such "causes" cannot be used to overlook behavior that is truly disruptive and prevents not only the student in question but also peers from learning.

Initiating and Preventive Teacher Behaviors

Robert MacDonald (1991) has provided a useful list of what he calls *initiating* and *preventive* teacher behaviors to deal with students who are disrupting the classroom atmospheres. Under **initiating** he suggests the following:

1. *Nonverbal cues:* Body posture position in the room, hand signals, and eye contact

2. *Tuning:* Verbal cues to start the discussion and reminders about taking turns

3. *Pausing:* Waiting quietly for extra comments to gradually subside

4. *Restarting:* Pausing halfway through giving directions and then restating the instructions

For **preventive** strategies he suggests a parallel set of teacher behaviors also designed to structure and remind in a low-keyed manner what the appropriate classroom behaviors are for those out of phase with the general procedures. This includes teacher activities such as

1. *Scanning:* To be able to spot possible trouble in advance

2. *Synchronizing:* To manage common tasks such as passing out or collecting homework, editing a particular page in an assignment, or shifting from lecture to small groups by guiding such transitions quickly

3. *Prepping:* To provide very clear and understandable directions for new classroom activities, including having students restate their understanding of the required tasks (especially important when using small cooperative learning activities)

4. *Renewing:* To review at both the beginning and end of each class the progress that the class is making toward the learning goals

5. *Positive framing:* To use positive reinforcement statements (remember the Walberg meta-analysis finding discussed in Chapter 12—avoid sarcastic comments)

In dealing with minor classroom management problems, then, from callouts to inattention, an array of initiating and preventive procedures will usually smooth out the learning process.

Transition to Corrective Methods: I-Messages

Generally, as MacDonald points out, when students feel treated fairly though firmly, antagonism and hostility will subside, and cooperation will increase. This is a reminder of the Flanders research on classroom atmosphere (see Chapter 12), which demonstrated an increase both in achievement and in pupil self-concept as a learner in a democratic atmosphere.

There still may be a student or two who don't respond to the initiating and preventive methods. At this point we recommend, at least for upper elementary and older pupils, the use of I-messages in an individual conference. The approach can be an effective confrontation yet must not be used in front of the entire class. If you do so, you run the risk of a "secondary gain," undue notoriety as well as the cornering of the student in front of his or her peers. The advantage of the individual conference is that you can calmly describe the annoying behavior, express your feelings and disappointment, and describe the adverse effects upon the teaching process and your role. In many cases such a meeting and I-message will be enough to curb the disrupting behavior. If it doesn't, you'll need to consider corrective measures.

Corrective Techniques

Here MacDonald recommends a series of more deliberate low-profile methods followed by higher-profile disciplinary strategies. **Corrective low-profile methods** include

1. Stern eye contact

2. Gestures, including moving toward the student

3. Relocating the student

4. The "broken record" (e.g., repeating the instructions: "I said raise your hand first . . . I said to raise your hand . . .")

5. Defusing potentially explosive situations by coolly redirecting the challenge: "Your question on my personal plans is not relevant to the causes of WW I; now back to August 1914 . . ."

Corrective high-profile methods include:

1. Individual conferences with the student and the parent

2. Referral to other school procedures such as time-out rooms or, for more serious misbehaviors, inschool suspension

Unfortunately, the more you move to high-profile measures, the less effective the outcome will be, especially with adolescents. Such last-resort measures because of their punitive nature are relatively ineffective. Physically removing a student from the class may be necessary in some extreme cases. Yet the older the student, the less likely it is to produce positive behavior. With young children a short time-out is generally sufficient for them to regain enough self-control to return to the classroom. With the onset of adolescence such an exclusion policy takes on a different meaning. Thus it is a difficult tradeoff.

To provide you with some specific examples of how to deal with more serious behavior problems, we now outline two common difficulties, cheating and acting-out behavior, and describe the various procedures you may wish to follow.

Dealing with Cheating

You may recall from Chapter 7 that the two subgroups of adolescents most likely to cheat are either high-IQ/low-moral-judgment students or the low-IQ/low-moral-judgment group. This sends an important message. Do not assume that either high IQs or, for that matter, high GPAs are also functioning at an average or above-average level in value development. In reality, both of the subgroups cheated over 80 percent of the time when given the opportunity. In this case, then, a preventive strategy is clearly the best choice. However, it will also take skill to create an atmosphere that reduces cheating but does not result in a punitive or prisonlike environment. This means that you must take positive action such as reinforcing the importance of students' doing their own work. With adolescents you can even lighten up the situation a bit by reminding them that you were a teenager once and observed many of the common techniques, for example, formulas behind a watch crystal, hand signals for true-false tests, "gifted" peripheral vision by students reading other's answers two seats away. Such "friendly" reminders indicate in the Kounin sense that you are "with it." You might even comment that you know the "Woody Allen story." Allen has said he got thrown out of college for cheating: on a metaphysics exam he peered into the soul of a classmate.

A second procedure is to be sure that the exam or the paper assignment is structured to minimize temptation. For example, if the students' chairs are close together and the room crowded, use alternate forms of the exam by row and be sure to scan the room to prevent test swapping. A second method is to use broader questions or an open-book exam. For such a method to work you'll need to raise the level of the questions by asking the higher-order questions on Bloom's taxonomy. You could present the students with some material from the text and then ask them to either defend or criticize the position together with their reasons for such a view. Or you could present a case study based on the lessons and require a critical analysis.

A third method is to have the students read and sign an "honesty" pledge. By itself this doesn't work, but it does serve as a reminder of the importance of doing one's own work. In elementary and secondary schools, however, it is not recommended that students act as "radar" detectors for their peers. Some colleges with honor codes require peer monitoring. The written and signed pledge, then, is a verbal reminder to all the students but does not require peer enforcement—that is still your responsibility. From a developmental stage perspective, requiring peers to report cheating places students who blow the whistle in a nearly-impossible situation.

> I   *(name)*   pledge to use my own effort exclusively on the examination. I will not use notes or any other outside source for my answers.

When prevention fails, you'll need to be prepared for corrective action. For example, as you are reading answers you may note that two papers are almost exactly alike. In fact years ago there was a famous example (perhaps apocryphal) of two such papers: One student on the final question wrote, "This one has me stumped. No matter which formula I try I can't compute the answer." The next paper commented on the same question, "I couldn't do it, either." While this scenario is very unlikely, you will see less fanciful examples of extremely suspicious similarities. Thus, following our format, you start by holding a conference with the two students and send a straightforward I-message.

1. "When I read your papers and saw that they were almost exactly alike . . ." (*describe the situation*)

2. "I felt upset and discouraged" (*the impact on you at a feeling level*)

3. "I realized that you hadn't learned what I've been trying to teach you" (*effect on you*)

At this point you stop and wait for their responses, which can vary widely from denial to admission. It is important to remain somewhat dispassionate, allowing some of your feelings to show but not to the point of really "unloading." Then you can restate your disappointment, that they failed to live up to their agreement. Of course, you can't really tell who helped whom, and helping in this case is as bad as receiving. As a result, whatever grade the exam is worth should be divided in half. For example, if the grade on one was 80, they both receive a 40. At the conclusion of the meeting, which should be relatively brief and brisk, indicate that the event is over.

There will be no further penalties, so they can start now with a clean slate on future classroom interactions, papers, and exams. Obviously, it is important not to over- or underreact to the situation. Even persons reasoning at principled levels (Stage V) do not always resist temptations. On the other hand, with appropriate use of sanctions, students at all levels of development can learn from such a cheating experience that there are serious consequences. Probably the most difficult lesson of all is that helping a peer is also cheating. Not helping a friend seems to run counter to much of the Stage III social conformity ethic and a definition of friendship. It takes a more mature perspective to understand just what the cheater has learned by being helped, that is, to avoid the normal consequences of one's own behavior. Such issues can be discussed individually with the students involved or in general with the class as a whole. A specific incident, however, should not be used as an object lesson in front of the classroom as a whole. Such public shaming is inappropriate.

When All Else Fails: Behavioral Contract Form

The final set of examples concerns more serious behavior problems in the classroom such as fighting, disrespectful racist and sexist comments, and displays of genuinely antisocial and antiacademic behavior such as truancy, repeated lateness, and homework either never done or done carelessly. In fact, the test of severity is the repetitive nature of the behaviors. It means that the usual stage-appropriate methods, plus initiating, preventive, and corrective activities, have failed. In such instances, the next procedure is the use of a contract, monitored by you, regardless of the age of the student. If behavior improves, the emphasis can be shifted to the student, but not at the outset. An example is found in the Spotlight on Behavioral Contracting. The first step is to assess the level of mismatch between the student and the modal strategy for that age and then calibrate down until you find a match between current behavior and strategy. Also, it may be necessary to create both positive rewards and aversive consequences in order for some students to really understand the importance of giving up their disruptive behaviors. However, the ratio of positive to aversive rewards must greatly favor the positive. Thus, if the contract specifies points gained for attending behavior, the list should be long. You'll need to provide many examples of positive behavior which can earn points; for example, be on time for class and ready to start (5 points), bring books and writing material (5

SPOTLIGHT ON BEHAVIORAL CONTRACTING

Extremely Inattentive in Class

The hypothetical example here focuses on either middle school or high school. You are the teacher. (Since behavioral contracting is commonly employed and is stage-appropriate in elementary schools, we haven't included an example for the elementary level here.)

The context of the situation is as follows. One student's extreme inattention, the problem behavior, has continued in this classroom in spite of your use of stage-appropriate methods (Stages III and IV), effective teaching methods (use of a variety of models), and appropriate subject matter (of general interest to most students). You conference with the student. Send an I-message, listen to his or her comments, and then set up the contract. You outline the behaviors

necessary for positive points. Then add one or two of the "worst" inattentive behaviors commonly used. In this case it is either sleeping or poking classmates.

The reward was selected by the student from your list, and in this case you had already approached the local arcade owner for help in improving the academic achievement of certain students who were falling behind in their work.

After a week you notice a steady improvement, and after two weeks the student begins to show a genuine interest in the material. You conference, congratulate, and discontinue, explaining that the improvement in grades is now the indicator of real progress. You also call the parents to indicate how well things are going as the stu-

dent brings home the first B ever. You suggest, if they haven't already mentioned it, their continued verbal approval and perhaps the giving of a special treat.

Remember, however, that the system of behavior shaping through extrinsic rewards has genuine limits. To avoid decay, do not employ such a system for long periods. Instead, view it as a short-term procedure to get the student back on the learning track. The signs of decay will be obvious: a return of the original nonlearning behavior. On the other hand, the signs of success will be the emergence of genuine interest in the learning material as you switch to generic methods appropriate to the entire class.

POSITIVE ACTIVITIES	POINTS	DAYS				
		1	2	3	4	5
1. Takes notes without reminding	5					
2. Notes are organized	10					
3. Positive contributions to classroom discussions	5					
4. Attends to instructions	5					
5. Brings necessary materials to class	5					
				(Maximum in 1 week = +175)		
DISRUPTIVE ACTIVITIES						
1. Sleeps in class	–10					
2. Pokes classmates	–5					
				(Maximum in 1 week = –75)		
Goal for the first week	150 or 125					
Reward: Coupons for the video arcade	10 or 5					

points), listen to directions quietly (5 points), use an "inside" voice (5 points), keep hands and feet to self (5 points), turn in homework on time (5 points), and so on. Then give a few examples of disruptive behavior that will cost points or "fines"; for example, antagonize other students (minus 5 points) or leave the seat constantly (minus 5 points). In the latter instance, carefully select only one or two of the most annoying behaviors. You cannot extinguish multiple behaviors simultaneously.

You'll also need to assess the general developmental level as to the type of activities that will gain points. If the student is still very concrete in orientation even though an adolescent, then an array of extrinsic/materialistic rewards may be the only effective rewards. Remember the examples of Stage II reinforcers. Sprick (1985) suggests that points can be earned for rewards such as: free time, food treats, a no-homework day, computer game time, free time in the shop, art, or weight room, tickets to the roller rink, video arcade, or movies, or free time to read magazines or, for teenagers, a driver's manual.

As you can see, the rewards have no direct connection to the learning experiences. If you have difficulty developing such a list, you can ask the student for ideas as long as you reserve the right to veto the dangerous or the illegal. For example, in a camp for early adolescents, points were gained for a wide variety of positive behaviors, such as early preparation, at reveille, hands washed *before* eating, quiet at table, neat bunks. Small monetary fines were instituted for foul language. By the third day the language had improved and the positive behaviors increased substantially. The camper with the worst record at the end of the first day turned completely around and won the Camper of the Week award and the largest share of the "fine" pot.

You probably cannot fine students in dollars and cents in public schools, but you can devise some system of small penalties. The problem, of course, is that the system will fail if the penalties get too large and the student loses hope from the realization that he or she "owes" more points than could ever be earned. Also realize that you can shape only relatively small amounts of behavior, but this may be enough to get the student back on track for classroom learning.

For students who function at a higher and less concrete level, you can use more intrinsic or learning-related activities. Again set up the system so that there are multiple behaviors for earning points and a few ways to lose or "owe" points. Then develop, perhaps with student input, a list of rewards: special lessons, an educational field trip, extra time in some school activity, extra help in some activity, special

recognition, informal reading, or extra time with the computer.

Otherwise the procedure is the same. The only difference is that with more advanced students, providing intrinsically interesting learning experiences is more likely to shape behavior. The reward is closer to their level of development.

Every so often educational practice seeks a quick-and-easy solution to the problems of classroom management, especially with the growing concern over delinquency, fighting, and the appearance of guns in the classroom. Teachers, counselors, and principals despair and yet hope there is a simple solution. Such was the case a few years ago with the famous Scared Straight program in Rahway, New Jersey. The idea was to send the worst offenders for a day at the state prison to receive lectures from hardened "lifers." Surely that would make the point. Stay in school, behave, or face a future in crime and ultimately land in the "slammer." In spite of all the favorable publicity, a follow-up study showed that the plan backfired. First, it had no effect on reducing delinquent behavior; and, second, visiting the prison became a badge of distinction, desired by both delinquent and non-delinquent students. Needless to add, the program was suspended (Finkenauer & Kuhmerker, 1979). A more systematic study on the effects of different approaches to discipline will be described from the work of Damon, to which we now turn.

DISCIPLINE AND PARENTING

Damon's Implications for Teaching

William Damon, of Brown University, summarized much of the research on parenting styles and discipline (1990). His analysis raises some important general issues for teachers. In the past it has been common to classify parenting in three separate categories: democratic-authoritative, authoritarian, and permissive. Damon finds, however, that the authoritarian and permissive styles are not really different from the point of view of the child. Both approaches have the same negative outcomes, since both approaches meet the parents' needs, not the child's. Thus, authoritarian parents confront the child in a harsh and arbitrary manner when they *feel* like it, not when the child needs it. Similarly, the permissive (laissez-faire) parent uses sentimental overindulgence to protect the child from consequences in order to make the parent feel good. However, when such an overindulged child's behavior directly affects the parent, then severe punishment may be suddenly invoked.

Thus, according to Damon, both the authoritarian and the permissive parents make the same error, effecting arbitrary intrusions into the child's life. The paths are different but lead to the same outcome. On the one hand, authoritarian parents fail to confront the child on a regular basis so as to provide direction, but instead confront the child in response to their own moods and temper. This clearly limits the child's opportunities for exploration, since the child doesn't really know when the hammer will come down but only that it will come down at some seemingly arbitrary point. On the other hand, permissive parents, by not setting reasonable, evenly enforced limits, shelter the child from the natural consequences of inappropriate behavior. In both the authoritarian and the permissive cases, the adverse effects on self-control and initiative are the same, since it is the parental power that is at issue.

The real difficulty with power as the exclusive means of control is that the effectiveness is very short-lived. In developmental terms, this means that discipline at Stage I is extremely limited. An observational study demonstrated that major use of power may actually reduce compliance with adult directives. One group of children threatened with severe punishment for playing with one specific toy actually played with the forbidden toy much more frequently than a second group who were only mildly admonished.

These studies, then, show that the humane application of a stage approach actually implies an **authoritative** method. According to Diana Baumrind's findings (1989), the authoritative parent, or in our case the authoritative teacher, combines kindness and control with clear communication. Authoritative parents support the natural empathy in children by helping them understand when their actions hurt others. The parental commands are direct and honest rather than deceitful or manipulative. The demands imposed are realistically moderate and tuned to the child's developmental abilities. The parents also expect growth toward maturity and increasing amounts of independence with self-control. Thus, the pattern is clear as well as the effects. Baumrind finds that such children move toward social responsibility and are friendly, facilitative, and cooperative with adults.

Children of authoritarian and/or permissive parents behave similarly, but their behavior is quite different from that of the children of authoritative parents. The former have difficulties in developing self-reliance, appropriate assertiveness, and a sense of social responsibility. One somewhat surprising finding is that both the authoritarian and permissive pattern produced children low in impulse control.

Neither group could tolerate normal ups and downs. From a developmental viewpoint, then, we can now say that at any stage, discipline models that are administered in either an authoritarian or permissive manner will fail. Authoritative implementation, in contrast, helps induce growth toward higher stages and more self-control. In fact, almost all studies of family discipline come to the same conclusion, namely, that adult modeling is important. What you do as well as how you do it will make lasting impressions on children. In a Kenyan tribe, parents chose to actively discourage aggression in children by severe beatings. You can guess what the observer noticed when the children played alone (Edwards, 1987).

Thus, we can return to the overall framework as a reminder of the importance of the different stages as well as the process of managing. Stage sets some broad limits as to how far "up" the scale you can proceed. For example, direct attempts to train elementary students in empathy (being able to understand how another child feels) did not generalize (Damon, 1990). However, empathy training at the high school level by means of programs such as peer counseling has been shown to generalize in follow-up. The developmental map, then, outlines the general reasoning levels that are most typical of the different age groups. The authoritative process is clearly the most effective means of getting the messages across at each level and of inducing maturity.

Parents' Night

It is clear that discipline strategies by stage complemented with individualized methods will help you become an authoritative teacher with your students. But what about parents? Student teachers and beginning teachers often dread the prospect of parents' night. Their journal entries often contain commentary like "What am I to do? The parents are much older. They will probably think I'm still wet behind the ears" or "Maybe I can come down with a fever so I won't have to appear tonight. I'm really nervous. What can I say without appearing defensive?" One beginning teacher summed it up: "I've just become comfortable in setting rules and following through with the kids. Now I have to face _the parents_. Will the dissonance ever end?"

From a developmental point of view, the first steps you take in advance of parents' night are critical. Generally, this means that early in the school year you can send a letter home introducing yourself and describing some of your general goals, such as improving basic skills and promoting self-directed

SPOTLIGHT ON PARENTS

A Sample Letter at the High School Level*

Dear Parent of _____ Fall 199__

I am writing to introduce myself to you, to explain my expectations for the year, and to give you some information about our rules. To help each student have a successful experience, I do expect that each will do the following:

1. Keep a notebook organized by our topics, assignments, and notes.
2. Usually there are daily assignments with some homework each night.
3. For each absence, the student is given two days to make up the missed work. Longer absences require an individualized plan. I am usually available after school for assistance and for makeups.
4. I expect each student to be seated and with materials ready at the appointed time for class.
5. I usually test the students on a weekly basis, with a major unit test each month.
6. To build a positive learning atmosphere, I expect students to be respectful to me and to each other. There are sanctions such as detention and inschool suspension for inappropriate behavior. I will, however, try to conference with you in advance of major difficulties.

Also please let me know if there are unusual difficulties at home that may affect student learning.

You are a most important person to your (son/daughter) and to me. By working cooperatively we can ensure a good year. If you have any questions, please let me know.

Sincerely,

---

* Adapted from a letter written by Cynthia Carter Crabtree of the Wake County, North Carolina, school system. The letter exemplifies the points made in the text on the importance of parent-teacher communication.

learning. This can be followed by a few statements on your posted classroom rules. Then end the letter with positive comments and an open invitation to discuss any special questions, circumstances, or concerns. The goal is to build a working relationship with the parent(s) early in the term. A sample letter would look like the one in the Spotlight on Parents.

It is also most important to realize that at least some parents may dread parents' night as much as you do. If you realize just how many adults did not experience success in schools, with estimates as high as 40 to 50 percent, and for whom schooling would still be associated with negative feelings, then parent reluctance is understandable. This means you'll need to watch for signs of parental discomfort and try to set them at ease. It is not an inquisition, either way. Also remember that the basic framework for families has changed. For example, 25 percent of schoolchildren now live with a single parent, 33 percent of remarriages have created blended families, and another 25 percent of children are cared for by a step-parent (Burden, 1995). This obviously means that even scheduling conferences is now compli-

cated, as well as the increase in the complexity of family dynamics; for example, who is really in charge of discipline in a blended family, or is the step-parent unsure or overly authoritarian in dealing with the student?

At the same time, it is most important for you to avoid stereotyping these changed family structures. Unfortunately, research on this issue is not positive. Even experienced teachers fall into such stereotypes. As we noted in Chapter 14, if a child was described as from a one-parent home then the common tendency was for a teacher to label the child as a behavior problem, even though the video excerpts described similar behaviors for the pupils of single parents and intact families. The same is true for students from minority versus majority backgrounds. And as we point out in Chapter 20, similar stereotyping takes place for students with disability labels. Thus, you will need to work very hard to avoid the stereotyping trap even though you'll hear such statements from experienced colleagues. This is particularly important because such stereotypes are most often conveyed at nonverbal levels, such as eye contact, voice tone, and body attitude. This is simply another way of saying that genuine understanding and caring cannot be "faked" in dealing with parents from different backgrounds or nontraditional structures.

With all this as background or context, the actual conferences are not really all that complicated. In conferring, remember to accentuate the positive. Enumerate the good points about what the pupil has accomplished. Then pick out one area for improvement. A single focus will allow for manageable discussions without either you or the parent(s) becoming defensive. Also collaborate in setting a realistic goal for improvement and help in discussing procedures that the parent could use in working with the student. Another possibility would be to discuss the use of a peer tutor if your school has older students available for peer tutoring. Parents who are working long hours often welcome such assistance, and peer-tutoring programs benefit both the tutor and the student. As the conference closes, reiterate the positive aspects and indicate that you will follow up by discussing the plan with the student, and in a week or two will make a phone contact for a progress report. In the long run genuine collaboration between you and the parent(s) will pay important dividends in student achievement.

SUMMARY

One of the potentially most stressful aspects of teaching involves student discipline. Policing, monitoring, and keeping the peace often seem like the most unpleasant aspects of the role of the teacher. Individuals who choose teaching generally are not authoritarian personalities who enjoy and seek power and control over others.

Too often the most common approach has been to enforce a kind of "might-makes-right" dictum. Teachers are expected to enforce obedience and mold character almost at any cost. Failing that, teachers can be expected to rely on a series of tricks and games to bring about order. These may range from studied indifference (the head in the sand) to constant classroom entertainment (the teacher as Mary Poppins). There is no particular theory to guide the choice of disciplinary techniques. An alternative, however, is the developmental model. In using this framework, teachers must ask: (1) Who makes the rules? (2) Who keeps the rules? (3) How are the rules enforced? (4) Why do students obey? Answering these questions requires an application of stage theory: The choice of technique depends on the stage of reasoning of the students. Very young pupils at Stage I may require the humane use of physical constraint. In the early elementary grades, pupils at Stage II may respond best to extrinsic behavior modification. In the later elementary grades, pupils at Stage III can be disciplined by peer pressure. In junior high and beyond, students at Stages IV and V are ready for more self-governance. Contract systems can be effective in those years.

There are humane and inhumane applications of methods within each stage, which involve carrying the approach too far or using it too literally. For example, harsh physical punishment versus firm physical constraint for an out-of-control child represent the wrong and right ways to approach discipline at Stage I. Excessively zealous application of stage-appropriate methods is a problem at all stages.

At the most complex level, teachers and pupils can form a democratic community along the lines of the New England town meeting. This form of democratic citizenship training, while rare, can nonetheless serve as an ideal goal for student discipline.

When the developmental approaches do not work, the teacher may follow a series of steps to individualize the process. In our outline of these steps, we included a continuum of preventive, initiating, and corrective methods from Robert MacDonald as well as a system for behavioral contracting.

The chapter closed with a discussion relating effective parental discipline to models for teacher strategies. The democratic-authoritative system was shown to have clear advantages over either the permissive or authoritarian models. Avoiding stereotyping of your students and their family structures is important as you begin to develop more collaborative connections with the parents of your students. Conferring with parents can be extremely helpful to your teaching and disciplinary responsibilities. Building a working relationship with parents can begin early in the year when you inform parents of your classroom expectations; it continues through the year as you share positive information about the students and use parental help to address recurring discipline problems.

KEY TERMS AND NAMES

authoritative versus laissez-faire or authoritarian methods
character training
William Damon
democratic high school model
developmental method of discipline
discipline strategies: four questions

individual differences
Robert MacDonald
matching of discipline to stage
positive vs. negative disciplinary techniques
preventive, initiating, and corrective methods
school-within-a-school

THEORY INTO PRACTICE: MATCHING DISCIPLINARY STRATEGIES

In this section we present a series of case studies. Your task is to read through each case carefully. List some of the main characteristics of the children in question and then review each of the four suggested disciplinary strategies. Next, make your selection and list the reasons for your choice. Also, for practice, identify the stage strategies in the other choices as well as your reasons for rejecting those choices. Finally, check out your answers in the last section to clear up any possible misunderstandings.

Case Study One: Elementary School

You are a third-grade teacher. Your pupils are just beginning their year with you. You notice, in the lunchroom and playground, that the boys and girls are beginning to square off at each other. The amount of shoving, pushing, and name calling is on the increase. Also, during class itself, you begin to spot "little" incidents—a girl accidentally shoves her spelling book into the ribs of a boy nearby; a boy just happens to slip his foot into the aisle and trips a girl on her way to your desk. What are possible solutions within a stage framework?

As you read the four suggestions that follow, try to assess the approximate developmental level of the strategy, whether it seems humane, and whether it would be appropriate to the level of development of third-graders, who are probably mostly Stage II with some mix of Stage III. Which would seem most effective and which least effective as discipline strategies?

1. I'd set an example so that they would know how such abuse physically feels. Every time I'd catch a culprit, I'd make the kid take punishment in kind. For example, I'd take the book

and shove it into the ribs, not hard enough to leave a mark, but enough so she'd remember what it feels like! I'd teach her a lesson—it's called "an eye for an eye."

2. I'd approach it through the use of positive reinforcement. I'd explain that there is too much fighting at recess, in the lunchroom, and in class. As a class we would discuss some rewards for not fighting—a class field trip, a special movie, extra time for special projects, or things like that. Then we'd set up a chart to keep track of the amount of fighting, shoving, hair pulling, etc. I would show them the chart I kept on them last week. Then we would keep track of misbehaviors next week and compare.

3. I'd try using some classroom discussions and some of the semistructured materials like Robert Selman's filmstrips on interpersonal problem-solving and Henry DuPont's units on affective development. These materials are like case studies showing difficulties that children have in getting along with each other. We'd also have a chance to talk about alternative methods besides hitting back. Then I'd stress the importance of understanding each other's feelings and that as a class we will have to learn to work together. If this began to help, then I'd put in a few small-group cooperative learning games.

4. I'd talk to the class as a whole. I'd explain that they were acting like different countries in the world—fighting all the time. I would show them the need for a United Nations as a means of governance. Each person, like each country in the world, would have to learn that we are interdependent. I would demonstrate that our classroom is like our planet and that we are all

on the same spaceship as a unit. In order to survive we all must pull together. I would show them a brief film on Eric Toffler's *Future Shock* and have them read about the Mayflower Compact and then the UN Charter.

Case Study Two: The Middle School

You are an eighth-grade English and social studies teacher who also heads a guidance "bloc." You notice that most of your students seem to be social outcasts. There is a small group of 10 or so (out of 35) who form a clique. They dominate the discussion sessions in class, deliberately exclude most of their classmates from extracurricular activities, and even determine the mode of dress. Recently, the clique (about half boys and half girls) decided to wear good clothes to school—boys in suits and ties, girls in dresses and stockings. Pretty soon the others did the same. Then the "leading crowd" reverted to jeans and laughed among themselves at the "sheep." The clique tends to do well on exams, but there is a strong trend toward "white superiority" in their comments. They also put down the kids who have to work after class as know-nothing "hard hats." Tension in the class is increasing. You overhear some of the working-class kids and a few of the black kids talking about getting even.

1. I would get the class together and talk about the need for brotherhood and sisterhood. I'd explain that the world is full of hatred and prejudice. I would point out that it is up to each of us to live according to the "Golden Rule." Then I'd show excerpts from the film *Brian's Song* and have each student write an essay on Donne's meditation "No Man Is an Island."

2. I would excuse the clique early one day and talk to the rest of the class. I would indicate that I heard rumors of a possible fight. I would point out that fighting is against the school rules and that anyone caught would be put on detention or suspended, with the assistant principal's approval. I would make sure that they all knew that fighting, for whatever reason, was wrong and that we would not tolerate that kind of behavior.

3. I would develop a unit on cross-age teaching and counseling. This would involve classroom practice units in listening to feelings (communication exercises), sending I-messages, and learning to lead open-ended value-dilemma discus-

sions. The values-clarification material, some Kohlberg-type dilemmas, and similar units would lead to an overall focus on values and relationships. We would include some material on the nature of prejudice, including some role-taking exercises. When the students, as teams, started teaching in the fifth- and sixth-grade classes, I'd be sure to assign team membership to prevent the clique from remaining together.

4. I would simply ignore the whole thing. My job as teacher is to teach the standard curriculum. We cover the material that the school board requires. If fighting occurs during class, I'd punish the class as a whole. All students would stay after school. If that didn't work, then I'd cancel the field trips and so forth.

Case Study Three: Secondary School

You are a twelfth-grade social studies teacher. It is the first week of the second semester. One of the immediate problems is the students' lack of initiative and independence. It isn't really a disciplinary problem in the usual sense. The students don't throw erasers or drop books, and most of them are on time for class. The problem is more hidden but just as troubling. There is a kind of passivity tinged with hostility. They do the assignments and with some urging will answer questions reasonably well. The atmosphere is closer to boredom than anything else. There is very little volunteering. The feeling is one of going through the motions. They have let you know somewhat subtly that this is how they behave in their other senior classes. They will put their time in, do enough to pass, and don't want to be hassled by a lot of work. Their college applications are in and their SATs completed.

1. I would develop a unit on the value of hard work and stress the importance of high achievement. I would try to persuade them that though the college decisions would be made before the term ends, the colleges would still be interested in their senior semester. For those not going to college, the work in the senior semester would still be important for job recommendations. I would also talk about the importance of self-respect and how good they will feel to do well in the last semester even though it wouldn't really count for much.

2. I'm really not sure of the best way to handle this situation. My inclination would be to set up a re-

ward schedule for playing their favorite rock videos at the end of each week if they were willing to put out more effort. I would rate their performance as a class each day. If they achieved three "outstandings" each week, they would earn a 15-minute video during the last period. If they earned no outstandings in a week, then I would assign extra homework or make them stay after school.

3. In order to promote more independence in learning, I would set up a series of assignments on key topics to be covered. I would indicate that my own role would be to serve as a resource person and that I could direct them to material in the library. I would provide a handout detailing how to use the new computerized catalog system. We would have group discussions on how to find and select resources. Each student would be given a topic and an outline of activities. The grades would be earned according to the number of points assigned for completing each section. Initially each student would write an outline on the topic and be prepared to present the information to the class as a whole on a first trial. Then after class discussion and more comment, the student would refine the topic and turn it into a complete project to be presented to the class at the end of the semester. The information from all the topics would be collected and published in "desktop" form and filed in the library.

4. I would show a film of the "just community" approach as a demonstration of how high school students their age can set up their own classroom rules and norms. I would assign some readings on the topics to four small groups. The task of each group would be to develop sections of the overall plan. Included would be (1) participation rules, (2) means of protecting the rights of those holding minority opinions, (3) disciplinary strategies, and (4) responsibilities to others. By midsemester, the goal would be to start functioning as a just community in discussing the key concepts of democratic governance. The community meetings would be chaired by different students. At the end, each student would write a paper detailing his or her own experience in the town meeting. Their weekly journals would form the raw material for their end-of-semester synthesis paper. The overall program, complete with video excerpts of the classroom just community meetings, would also be presented to a local conference on innovations in education.

Suggested Answers

The elementary school strategies are quite straightforward. Suggestion 1 represents Stage I negative, the use of force to teach a lesson. Suggestion 2 illustrates the use of reinforcement principles (Stage II positive) to create a significant positive reward for "attending behavior." Suggestion 3 demonstrates a Stage III positive method of helping the children begin to experience and to reflect on issues of relationships and feelings. Suggestion 4 is essentially a Stage V approach and would be far too abstract and ideal for elementary school students to understand. One teacher, in fact, tried the "UN Day" method, and the fighting on the playground increased. "Don't countries go to war all the time?" was the children's comment. The most appropriate method, given the stage of the children, would probably be either suggestion 2 or suggestion 3, or maybe both in combination.

The middle school strategies cover a broad range. Suggestion 1, outlining a Stage V strategy, would probably go almost totally over the heads of junior high adolescents. Suggestion 2 represents a Stage IV negative method, since the solution, though legally correct, in essence misses the point of the problem. Suggestion 3 details the most complicated response, since, in order to be effective, the unit would require considerable time. In the long run, however, this would be the most effective approach. The actual role-taking experiences of "helping" others in small groups would aid in breaking down some of the barriers. This solution is essentially a combination of Stage III positive and Stage IV positive. The pupils learn to identify feelings in themselves and others (III), to send I-messages (III), and to speak up for themselves (IV). Suggestion 4 is a combination of Stage IV negative (a narrow legal definition of teaching) and Stage II negative (the use of aversive techniques to control behavior).

At the secondary level, suggestion 1 outlines a Stage III strategy of trying to gain compliance with the norm of hard work through exhortation. The students have all heard these exhortations before and would probably listen, agree with the substance of your comments, and not change their behavior at all. There might be some small change in the next day or two, but soon they would lapse back into semipassivity.

Suggestion 2 represents a humane Stage II positive reinforcement strategy. You are not changing the teaching-learning interaction or content but rather are attempting to shape their behavior by an extrinsic reward system. The strategy may work in the short run, but, given the age of the students, it is really an example of undermatching. The use of punishment at the end changes the strategy from Stage II authoritative (or humane) to Stage II authoritarian. Compliance is likely to be low.

Suggestion 3 is basically a positive Stage IV method based on individualized learning contracts. You are providing some structure intended to wean them from dependence and tasks that require greater independence on the students' part. The requirements that they make a presentation before the class and eventually create a product will also help to promote responsibility. In teaching them the skills of finding, compiling, and presenting the information, your role is more that of a coach or supervisor. De-

velopmentally, they are ready for such independence as learners, and it is what they'll need either in college or in their career.

Suggestion 4 is quite clearly a Stage V positive. You are providing the background and steps to move the class into a just community. Small-group and leadership experience through participatory decisionmaking will help to promote both individuality and a caring community, a microcosm of a democratic ideal. As indicated in connection with the discussion of suggestion 3, the students are developmentally ready for a guided and gradual transition to such a community.

REFERENCES

Baumrind, D. (1989). Rearing competent children. In W. Damon (Ed.), *Child development today and tomorrow.* San Francisco: Jossey-Bass.

Beilin, H. (1959). Teachers' and clinicians' attitudes toward the behavior problems of children: A reappraisal. *Child Development, 30,* 9–25.

Brown, R., & Herrnstein, R. (1974). *Psychology.* Boston: Little, Brown.

Burden, P. R. (1995). *Classroom management and discipline: Methods to facilitate cooperation and instruction.* White Plains, NY: Longman.

Charles, C. M. (1992) *Building classroom discipline.* New York: Longman.

Charney, R. S. (1992). *Teaching children to care: Management in the responsive classroom.* Greenfield, MA: Northeast Foundation for Children.

Damon, W. (1990). *The moral child.* New York: Macmillan.

Edwards, C. H. (1994). Learning and control in the classroom. *Journal of Instructional Psychology, 21(4),* 340–346.

Edwards, C. P. (1987). Socialization in Kenya. In J. Kagan and S. Lamb (Eds.), *The emergence of morality in young children.* Chicago: University of Chicago Press.

Enright, R. D. (1981). A classroom discipline model for promoting social cognitive development in early childhood. *Journal of Moral Education, 11(1),* 47–60.

Evans, E. D., & Richardson, R. C. (1995, Winter). Corporal punishment: What teachers should know. *Teaching Exceptional Children, 27(2),* 33–36.

Finkenauer, J. O., & Kuhmerker, L. (1979). "Scared straight." *Moral Educational Forum, 4,* 1–7.

Glasser, W. (1975). *Schools without failure.* New York: Perennial Library.

Glasser, W. (1992). *The quality school: Managing stu-*

dents without coercion (2d ed.). New York: Harper-Collins.

Gordon, T. (1974). *Teacher effectiveness training.* New York: Longman.

Hart, S. (1991). From property to person status: Respect for the dignity of children. *American Psychologist, 46,* 66–71.

Harvard Alumni Bulletin (1965, May), Cambridge, MA: Harvard University.

Johnson, D. W., & Johnson, R. T. (1995). Teaching students to be peacemakers: Results of five years of research. *Peace and Conflict: Journal of Peace Psychology, 1(4),* 417–438.

Johnson, D. W., Johnson, R., Mitchell, J., Cotten, B., Harris, D., & Louison, S. (1996). Effectiveness of conflict managers in an inner-city elementary school. *Journal of Educational Research, 89(5),* 280–285.

Kuhmerker, L. (1991). *The Kohlberg legacy.* Birmingham, AL: REP.

Lickona, T. (1991). *Educating for character.* New York: Bantam.

MacCallum, J. A. (1993). Teacher reasoning and moral judgement in the context of student discipline situations. *Journal of Moral Education, 22(1),* 3–17.

MacDonald, R. E. (1991). *A handbook of basic skills and strategies for beginning teachers.* New York: Longman.

McLaughlin, H. J. (1994, Spring). From negation to negotiation: Moving away from the management metaphor. *Action in Teacher Education, 16(1),* 75–84.

Mischel, W., & Peake, P. (1982). Beyond *déjà vu* in the search for cross-situational consistency. *Psychological Review, 89,* 730–755.

Mosher, R. L. (1979). *Adolescents' development and education.* Berkeley, CA: McCutchan.

National Geographic Society. (1968). *Everyday life in Bible times.* Washington, DC: Author.

Slavin, R. (1990). *Cooperative learning: Theory research and practice.* Needham Heights, MA: Allyn & Bacon.

Sprick, R. S. (1985). *Discipline in the secondary classroom.* West Nyack, NY: Center for Applied Research in Education.

Sprinthall, N. A. (1985). Early adolescence and opportunities for growth in the 1980s: Ships passing in the night, again. *Journal of Early Adolescence, 5*(4), 533–547.

Sprinthall, N. A., & Collins, W. A. (1995). *Adolescent Psychology: A developmental view.* New York: McGraw-Hill.

Tulley, M., & Chiu, L. (1995). Student teachers and classroom discipline. *Journal of Educational Research, 88*(3), 164–171.

Updike, J. (1963). *The centaur.* New York: Knopf.

Wickman, E. K. (1928). *Children's behavior and teachers' attitudes.* New York: Commonwealth Fund.

Wolfgang, C. H. (1995). *Solving discipline problems: Methods and models for today's teachers.* Boston: Allyn & Bacon.

20

INCLUSION OF STUDENTS WITH SPECIAL NEEDS

As a result of both a gradual revision of educational theory and a series of milestone legal decisions, special education for so-called atypical and exceptional children is undergoing a period of major reformulation. Traditionally, societies have followed one of three practices with regard to children and teenagers labeled handicapped or difficult: (1) **remolding,** (2) **exclusion,** or (3) deviate-status placement **(segregation).** Different civilizations, and the same societies at different times, have naturally used a variety of methods to achieve each policy goal. In this chapter we describe these methods and discuss their shortcomings in view of both our current psychological understanding of such children and the emergence of a series of new "right-to-education" laws. We follow this with a discussion of current policy in special education, called **inclusion,** and its implications for classroom teachers.

TRADITIONAL PRACTICES REGARDING PLACEMENT

Remolding

As noted in Chapter 6, practically all societies have practiced remolding and reshaping their children during the early formative years, using methods that vary from the somewhat benign to the most gro-

tesque. For example, one old wives' tale suggests that it is important to play soft music to very young children to soothe the beast within their breasts; at the other extreme might be the medieval practice of exorcism, popularized in a movie.

The objective of all remolding methods is essentially to fit the child to the society. This means that, at least to some degree, the process of socialization was and is designed to eliminate individual variation or difference. Remolding can take the form of physically reshaping a child (for example, binding the feet or elongating the neck), alteration of physiological characteristics (such as conditioning feeding patterns—recall the old debate of demand versus scheduled eating), or psychological reshaping (for example, brainwashing). Thus, societies have attempted through physical, physiological, and psychological means to remake children.

Of course, not every society seeks to rebuild each child completely in its own adult image. It is clear, however, that a major goal of the practice is to eliminate some real or imagined negative attributes in children. Thus, in general, we should take a careful look at some of the procedures in early education to ensure that the programs are in the child's best interests and reflect effective methods toward promoting individual development. We have certainly stressed this view throughout this volume: Children are not miniature adults. For our purpose here, however, the critical questions are: What happens when children do not fit, when the procedures for remolding and reshaping do not work? What policies have societies followed when some children remain different? One policy is obvious—simply exclude such children from the rest of society.

Exclusion

The implementation of exclusionary policies can vary from an extreme—for example, murder—to psychological avoidance and exile. Ancient Sparta placed children with physical disabilities on a mountainside; in seventeenth-century Salem, Massachusetts, teenaged girls and boys were put to death because they were thought to be witches. David Bakan has provided a detailed account of such bloodcurdling procedures in his appropriately titled work, *The Slaughter of the Innocents* (1971).

Of course, not all exclusionary policies necessarily result in death. In some instances a society simply pretends that the atypical or different child doesn't really exist. Thus, it is not unusual to find children who are labeled as retarded living a marginal existence, hidden from view most of the time or, even if they do appear in public, generally not acknowledged. Such "different" children are spoken of only in hushed voices, in the hope that they will soon return to attic rooms, cellars, or garages. Every so often newspaper stories announce the "discovery" of such a child in a headline story; the famous case of the "wild boy" of Aveyron may be an instance of this exclusion.* It goes without saying that such children have literally no chance to grow and develop; they suffer either actual physical or, perhaps even worse, psychological death at an early age.

Segregation

Deviate-status placement   A more common policy, at least recently, has been the system of categorizing some children as deviate and placing children so designated in segregated environments. Various societies employ scores of different methods of classification—physical handicaps, racial characteristics, ancestry, intelligence testing, degrees of skin color, and so on. Naturally, a critical question here is the validity of the assessment procedures so employed,

and we will discuss this issue more fully in a later section. At this point, we wish to emphasize that the effect of the overall policy is to exclude, separate, and segregate such children from the mainstream of society.

Sometimes the segregation policy is referred to as *warehousing:* States and nations build human warehouses, usually in remote areas, and place designated children within those walls for safekeeping. This policy is, of course, almost the same as deportation. So-called undesirables are literally shipped out and thus are effectively removed from citizenship roles in a manner similar to sending the French emperor Napoleon to the island of St. Helena. The obvious natural tendency is for a society then to feel it has solved the problem; the education and growth of such children are now taken care of, and we can all turn our attention to other concerns. The exclusionary policy eliminates designated children from society while the deviate-status-placement procedure segregates. "Out of sight, out of mind" is the hoped-for result.

To show that such a segregated approach has not totally disappeared, we need only recall a study of adolescents with multiple disabilities. The teenagers were placed in a rural residential facility. Besides the professional staff, they had contact with persons from the "outside" world on an average of less than one visitor per month. The isolation was so substantial that the teenagers' psychological development appeared halted (Dormer, 1975). In such a barren interpersonal environment, those adolescents would hardly have had a chance to develop any kind of identity in the Eriksonian sense. Without interaction, growth does not occur. Today fewer children with disabilities are kept in such isolated residential units. Such children may require medical assistance, yet they also have genuine interpersonal needs.

Segregation policies: A mockingbird   One scene in Haper Lee's Pulitzer Prize–winning novel *To Kill a Mockingbird* (1962) depicts the first day of school for a new second-grade teacher, Miss Caroline Fisher, in a small rural southern community. In the middle of a lesson a small "cootie" jumps out of Burris Ewell's hair, scaring Miss Caroline half to death. In the process of examining the youngster more closely, Miss Caroline concludes that he should be sent home to wash his hair with lye soap and the rest of himself with soap and water. As the novel's little-girl heroine "Scout" remarks, Burris "was the filthiest human I had ever seen. His neck was dark grey, the back of his hands were rusty and his fingernails were black deep into the quick. He peered at Miss Caroline from a fist-sized clean space on his face." Miss Caroline

---

*   An 11-year-old boy was found living like an animal in the woods in southern France in 1799. He had been left there some years earlier. He was subsequently cared for and educated by a famous French special educator, Jean Marc Gaspard Itard.

emphatically comments then that Burris is to go home immediately and return "tomorrow" for the second day of school, clean as a whistle and ready to learn. But the boy balks:

> The boy laughed rudely. "You ain't sendin' me home, Missus. I was on the verge of leaving. I done my time for this year."
>
> Miss Caroline looked puzzled. "What do you mean by that?"
>
> The boy did not answer. He gave a short contemptuous snort.
>
> One of the elderly members of the class answered her. "He's one of the Ewells, Ma'am—Whole school's full of 'em. They come the first day every year and then leave. The truant lady gets 'em here cause she threatens 'em with the sheriff, but she gives up trying to hold 'em. She reckons she's carried out the law just gettin' their names on the roll and running 'em here the first day. You're supposed to mark 'em absent the rest of the year" (Lee, 1962, 31–32).

The Ewell children, then, were deviates and segregated from the other pupils. The letter of the law in this case was honored, but the educational future of the children was ignored. The school itself could then avoid having to cope with the special problems of the Ewell children, cooties and all. Unfortunately, many of the segregated special-class placements for children have had the same effect. For the past 40 years or so, the common educational policy has been to place children with mild to moderate educational disabilities (IQ scores roughly in the 50–70 range) in special classes, separated from the other schoolchildren. This practice has continued until recently, even though a long series of studies, beginning in the 1930s, has consistently indicated that such special-class placements are not superior to regular-class placements. In fact, no research evidence supports such special-class placements for "mild to moderately" retarded children; there are no academic gains for children placed in these classes and only equivocal social gains. A comprehensive review suggests that the pupils placed in segregated classes suffer a lowered self-concept—as a result of separation (Baroff, 1974).

A NEW POLICY: INCLUSION

An alternative policy for children and teenagers with disabilities is called inclusion. Essentially, the goal here is to expand the boundaries and reduce the barriers that have segregated such children from the mainstream of society. For many centuries this country legally sanctioned a segregated public school system that prevented black children from attending our society's mainstream white schools. The famous *Brown* v. *Board of Education* decision by the Supreme Court in 1954 ruled that separate facilities were inherently not equal. Thus, even if black children attended schools in new buildings filled with books, new carpets, and well-trained teachers, their schooling experience would still not be equal to that of mainstream white children. "Segregation equals second-class citizenship" was the dictum of the Court. At a philosophical and psychological level, equal educational opportunity means that each child should have access to the same educational experience. To rule otherwise is a logical absurdity. A public school is for the public's children.* Segregation is inherently separate and *not* equal.

In a manner similar to the 1954 *Brown* decision, a number of legal rulings have struck down the segregation of children with disabilities. Following the reasoning of the Supreme Court decision of 1954, legislation such as the Pennsylvania Right to Education Law (1971) clearly commits educational policy to a goal of integrated education. The schools in Pennsylvania as well as other states are to provide public education for all children, regardless of the "label," "condition," "potential," or any other characteristic of the child.

Public Law 94-142 and Its Successor, IDEA

In the early 1970s as many as 15 states had no legislation at all for children with disabilities (Ysseldyke and Algozzine, 1990). In 1975 a landmark federal law was enacted—Public Law 94-142, the Education for All Handicapped Children Act—which lays down the following requirements for all public school systems in all states:

1. Identification of all children with disabilities, aged 4 to 21

2. Assessment of their educational needs

3. Individualized program planning

4. Procedural (due-process) safeguards for students and their parents

5. Education in the least restrictive alternative that meets the child's needs

6. Nondiscrimination

---

*   We are emphasizing the legal grounds on which the segregation laws were changed. This still doesn't touch the issue of so-called de facto segregation—a system of housing patterns, school-district lines, and the like—that produces a separate, segregated educational system in spite of the legal sanctions.

The successor to 94-142, the **Individuals with Disabilities Education Act (IDEA)** of 1992, includes all children with disabilities from infancy to age 21. Public Law 94-142 and IDEA have been referred to as an educational Magna Carta for all children who have been excluded from regular classes by reason of any disabling condition. Included are children and adolescents who may be classified in one or more of the following **disability categories:**

Specific learning disabilities

Speech or language impairments

Mental retardation

Serious emotional disturbance

Multiple disabilities

Hearing impairments

Orthopedic impairments

Deaf-blindness

Visual impairments

Other health impairments

Autism

Traumatic brain injury

These 12 disabling categories are deliberately broad so as to include practically all children and teenagers with disabilities. It is no longer optional for schools to educate or not. The law is clear. Provision must be made from birth until graduation from high school (or its equivalent) or to the age of 21.

Americans with Disabilities Act

The **Americans with Disabilities Act (ADA)** of 1990 affirms the right of all citizens with disabilities. ADA comprehensively prohibits discrimination in employment practices, public services, privately operated settings, and telecommunications. Together, IDEA and ADA assure equality and protect the rights from birth to death of all persons with disabilities.

The "Least Restrictive" Dictum

The most far-reaching and controversial aspect of this legislation is the term *least restrictive alternative.* This means that each pupil must be educated in an environment that is as normal as possible. The intention of the law is clear. Schools must include rather

than exclude. Regular classroom environments must be expanded both physically and psychologically so that children with special needs can function in the mainstream. This aspect of the law may translate into such changes as barrier-free classrooms for wheelchairs and special apparatus for the hearing- and sight-impaired, as well as a greater variety of curriculum materials.

The controversy arises from the so-called due-process provision. Before the school system can move a child out of the mainstream, it must prove its case. If parents disagree with the school's plan to place a child elsewhere than in the regular class, they have the right to a hearing, representation by a lawyer, and access to all the assessment information. Finally, they have the right to appeal the decision. In everyday language, this means that the burden of proof is on the school for every decision to exclude children with disabilities from regular classes. It does not mean, however, that all children, including those with major and multiple-disabilities, must be in regular classrooms all the time. When special services, and even special residential schools, may be required, the school needs to be able to demonstrate that such a facility is indeed the least restrictive alternative for that particular child. As a result of the legislation, literally thousands of segregated special classes have been closed, special-school enrollments have declined sharply, and special residential schools have dramatically reduced their populations.

The legal requirement has created a bias toward placement in regular classrooms, as **Maynard Reynolds (**1990) has pointed out. The ambiguity of the key word *appropriate,* however can create a barrier to mainstream inclusion. Any observer of public schools will be struck by the increase in children with special needs attending regular classes. The movement is not without controversy, since to a large degree the assessment of the learning potential of such children has not been achieved. How can we as educators decide what is an appropriate learning environment if the basis for diagnosis and placement is less than valid? We consider this question first and follow with a discussion of effective educational programming.

THE DIAGNOSTIC PROBLEM

IQ Testing: Is It Valid?

The traditional system of classifying children or teenagers as "retarded" or "deviate" has been criticized on at least two grounds: (1) the system of assessment is too narrowly based, and (2) the labels become permanent. The traditional method was based on an attempt to group children by degree of retardation, using an IQ test as the major assessment procedure. This resulted in three major categories:

1. *Educable mentally retarded (EMR):* IQ score is generally between 50 and 80 on standard tests. The child is usually classed as a slow learner and a "concrete" thinker but can be successfully employed later in life.

2. *Trainable mentally retarded (TMR):* IQ score is generally between 25 and 50 on standard tests. The child is considered not capable of "ordinary" academic learning but can learn self-care and safety rules. "Sheltered" workshops can provide an employment environment. The child can learn social adjustment.

3. *Profoundly retarded:* IQ score is between 0 and 25. The child requires constant supervision. Many children are bedridden.

As you can immediately see, the IQ score becomes extraordinarily important in deciding on the assignment of children to the EMR, TMR, or profoundly retarded groupings. Also, you may notice that these three labels can easily become euphemisms, or "softer" words replacing the older categories of moron, idiot, and imbecile. The primary difficulty, of course, is the effect of such a global classification based on a somewhat singular method of assessment. The major criticism is that we are overgeneralizing from a limited evaluation system. Maynard Reynolds has provided an incisive critique of this issue. He notes the following:

1. There is no sharp discontinuity in mental ability between people with IQs of 79 and 81, or 49 and 51, yet the tests can lend themselves to such absurd assumptions.

2. The test scores are also subject to the limitations of examiner influence and culture bias. Examiners either consciously or unconsciously do influence the scores achieved by their pupils. Also, few if any tests can claim to be completely culturally fair.

3. The tests themselves are not assessing the complete range of the child's functioning. For example, a "blind" child is usually not completely blind, nor is he or she necessarily incapable of functioning well in other areas. In the same way, a low-scoring-IQ child is not necessarily without school achievement potential, nor is he or

she necessarily incapable of functioning well in other areas.

4. The tests themselves are virtually useless for making educational decisions with regard to placement. Educational classifications for special education make sense only when the classification is related to programs.

5. We should spend far less time predicting how children with special needs may perform in "traditional" classrooms as a result of an IQ score. Instead, we should develop more effective instructional procedures that will reach more children—that is, increase the educational potential of each classroom to teach almost all children.

6. Special education should talk less about dysfunction, low IQs, deficits, impairments, and disabilities. Instead, school offerings should be differentiated sufficiently so that all children receive the help they need to develop maximally.

Reynolds sums up the generic assessment problem as one of "remote dispositional analysis" (1990, p. 427). By this he means that there is a great distance between a static concept like an IQ and the way children actually learn in the classroom. An IQ score has no relationship to effective teaching strategies or to what Reynolds calls "the level of the lesson" (ibid.).

The most trenchant examination of the failures of diagnostic testing for special-education pupils has been provided by John Salvia of Pennsylvania State University and James Ysseldyke of the University of Minnesota. Their work details clearly how most common normative tests discriminate against such children (1991). Essentially, they literally indict almost all tests as having entirely inadequate norm groups. They point out that most of the test items have been selected after excluding all pupils with mental retardation. In a sense, this is the same argument that was used against the early forms of intelligence tests, which systematically excluded black children from the norm groups and then used the unrepresentative norm-group scores to classify black children.

Salvia and Ysseldyke also note that most national tests of academic ability such as those for reading, arithmetic, and other primary mental abilities do not provide local schools or particular classroom teachers with any useful information on which to base an educational program. As a result, the authors appeal for great caution in the continued use of most of the common national assessment tests of ability. Those

Dr. James Ysseldyke

in new learning in each of those previous four levels. A current debate (Macmillan et al., 1996) focuses on the fact that mild mental retardation (MMR) may deserve its own category. MMR has received little attention. Cases of MMR are often based in biological and psychosocial contexts. MMR is by far the largest segment of the population with retardation. MMR can be understood in terms of the transaction (match or mismatch) between the child's cognitive inefficiencies and the environmental demands for problemsolving (p. 357), but social competence has to be included in diagnosing mental retardation.

A study by Penelope Peterson provides telling commentary on the negative effects of the special-education categories (1988). With two groups of students of equivalent ability, one labeled and the other not, the results favored the nonlabeled group. The difference in academic achievement was half a standard deviation, an effect size approximately equal to the difference between a C– and a C+. Apparently, the combination of the label and the lowered teacher expectation interacts to reduce achievement. Can there be a special-education label without a stigma? The labels so developed become in the careful and somewhat arcane language of scientific researchers, "powerfully biasing stimuli" (Ysseldyke & Algozzine, 1990, p. 89).

Assessment: The Problematic Nature of the Specific Learning Disabilities Category

The assessment of children with special needs, however, does not end with an IQ test. There are 11 other categories. If there are genuine validity problems with the mental retardation (EMR) grouping, what of the others? To understand this problem more clearly, it is necessary to outline the difference between the so-called high-incidence and low-incidence groups. The high-incidence group lists the categories in which most children with special needs are placed. The latter group contains a relatively small number of the total population. Table 20.1 presents the percentage differences. As you can readily see, over 90 percent of all children with disabilities are grouped in just four categories: (1) specific learning disabilities, (2) speech or language impairments, (3) mental retardation, and (4) serious emotional disturbance. While there seems to be no major difficulty in identifying a speech impairment, there are grave problems with all the remaining high-incidence groups. We have already pointed out the problems with the MR area. The greatest problem, however, concerns the largest single category. Surveys have shown that the criteria are so slippery that almost all

procedures too often misclassify and misdiagnose, to the detriment of pupils from special-education backgrounds. Special-education interventions designed to match students' aptitudes show disappointing outcomes and small effect sizes, causing continuing calls for system reform both in conceptions about disabilities and in special-education methods (Reschly & Ysseldyke, 1995).

Controversy continues about the categories of disability. New categories have been added. For example, autism and traumatic brain injury were added in 1993. Older categories are debated. For example, in 1992 the description of the mental retardation category was changed by the American Association on Mental Retardation. The AAMR abolished the levels of mental retardation that were based on cognitive impairment (mild, moderate, severe, and profound). Instead the AAMR differentiates cases of mental retardation according to the needed levels of supports

TABLE 20.1 FREQUENCY OF DISABILITY CONDITIONS IN STUDENTS, AGES 6–21

HIGH INCIDENCE	PERCENTAGE
Specific learning disabilities	51
Speech or language impairments	21
Mental retardation	12
Serious emotional disturbeance	9
Total high incidence = 93%	

LOW INCIDENCE	PERCENTAGE
Multiple disabilities	2.3
Hearing impairments	1
Orthopedic impairments	1
Deaf-blindness	0.03
Visual impairments	0.5
Autism	0.4
Traumatic brain injury	0.1
Other health impairments	1.7
Total low incidence = 6+%	

Source: *U.S. Department of Education (1995).*

schoolchildren (80 percent) could be classified as learning disabled (LD) according to the definitions in use. Also, there is substantial variation in different states. For example, Maryland classified 5.2 percent of pupils as LD while New York had "only" an 0.8 percent incidence (Gelb & Mizokawa, 1986). Follow-up research has shown that even with such broad and variable definitions, many students who were clustered in the learning disability category did not, in fact, meet the criteria. In one state, over 45 percent of the students enrolled were erroneously classified (Reynolds et al., 1987).

An even more telling problem with the specific learning disabilities (SLD) category is that the incidence changes over relatively short periods. As Figure 20.1(a) shows, during the period 1976–1994 the number of students so labeled increased 208 percent, while the number grouped as MR declined 38 percent. In fact, it has been suggested that the amount of criticism leveled against IQ tests, especially with regard to their use with minority students, has encouraged schools to avoid the MR category for fear of due-process litigation (Reschly, 1988). In actual numbers, this could suggest that 300,000 pupils who were originally MR are no longer denoted as "retarded" while 1 million students who were "normal" are now "learning-disabled." The actual reason for

the shift probably has little to do with the learning potential of the children. Instead it is, in all probability, a reflection of a major court case, as we note on page 621.

To summarize, then, we note that the validity of the SLD label is extremely doubtful if most normal students fit the definition. Also, the incidence varies substantially from state to state; even more to the point, there is major variation in percentages in each category over short periods as a result of litigation. Maynard Reynolds has referred to this phenomenon as the **hydraulic model of assessment,** which reduces the number in one container and increases the number in the closest container regardless of the initial accuracy of the distribution. This could mean that children are simply moved from category to category regardless of their learning potential.

FIGURE 20.1 (a) Changes in special-education classifications, 1976–1994; (b) Growth in number of students classified in disability categories.

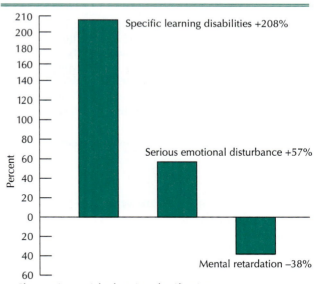

(a) Changes in special-education classifications

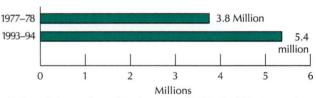

(b) Growth in numbers of students classified in disability categories

Source: *U.S. Department of Education (1995).*

SPOTLIGHT ON ASSESSMENT

Teachers Don't Want to Be Labeled

Harry W. Forgan

When teaching a course on tests and measurements at Kent State University recently, I decided to administer an adult group intelligence test to the class. I wanted the students to "feel" what it was like to take such a test and realize what items we use to measure intelligence. I also thought they might be more aware of the short time it takes to obtain a number which is regarded as very important by many educators.

The students were told not to write their names on the test papers, but rather to use a code such as their house number, physical measurements, or any less obvious symbol. I explained that I really didn't have faith in IQ scores; therefore, I didn't want to know their IQs.

The administration of the test required only 50 minutes. The students seemed to enjoy taking it and chuckled at some of the tasks they were expected to perform. I had to laugh myself when I saw some of them looking at their hands and feet when responding to items concerning right and left.

Upon scoring the test I found that the lowest IQ was 87 and the highest 143. The mean IQ for the 48 students was 117. I was not astonished by the 87, even though all the students had successfully completed the general education courses and student teaching at Kent State and were ready to graduate by the end of the term. After all, IQ tests have many limitations.

Then I got an idea. I decided to prepare a report for each student, writing his code on the outside and "IQ 87" on the inside of each. I folded and stapled each paper—after all, an IQ is confidential information!

At the next class period I arranged all the folded papers on a table at the front of the room. I wrote the range and the average IQ on the chalkboard. Many students snickered at the thought of somebody getting an 87. The students were eager and afraid as I began by explaining the procedures for picking up their papers. I made a point of telling them not to tell others their IQ score, because this would make the other person feel as if he too had to divulge this "total endowment." The students were then directed to come up to the table, row by row, to find their coded paper. I stood sheepishly—ready to laugh out loud as I watched the students carefully open their papers and see "IQ 87." Many opened their mouths with astonishment and then smiled at their friends to indicate they were extremely happy with their scores. There was dead silence when I began to discuss the implications of the IQ scores. I explained that in some states a person who scores below 90 on an IQ test is classified as a slow learner. The fact that group intelligence tests should not be used to make such a classification was stressed. I also emphasized the fact that *someone* in this class could have been classified

Assessment: The Problem with the Serious Emotional Disturbance Category

As is shown in Table 20.1, the fourth special-education category in the high-incidence area is that of serious emotional disturbance (SED). Approximately 9 percent of the students are so grouped, yet there are serious shortcomings with these assessment procedures. Some estimates run from 50 to 80 percent of students misclassified. The problem of accuracy remains a major issue.

Also, as was the case with SLD, the period of classification makes a difference. Over the recent period, the number of children in the group has changed. While not as dramatic as for SLD, nonetheless there was a 57 percent increase in the numbers of students categorized as SED. Because of validity problems,

we cannot say that there has been a 57 percent increase in emotionally disturbed students, but only that use of the category is becoming more frequent. In fact, one very alarming trend is that the total number of children grouped in the high-incidence categories is increasing—from 3.7 million for the period 1977–78 to 5.4 million for the period 1993–94. See Figure 20.1(b). This means that not only is there a hydraulic system at work shifting identified pupils from one category to another, but there is also an increase in the population itself. It is difficult to accept the legitimacy of labeling ever more children with designations that are of doubtful validity. Ysseldyke and colleagues refer to this as a problem of *categorical drift*, which looks more like a psychometric version of Dow Jones averages than accurate assessments (1992, p. 105).

as a slow learner and placed in a special class on the basis of this test.

I told how many guidance counselors would discourage a child with an 87 IQ from attending college. Again I emphasized the fact that one person in this room was ready to graduate from college having passed several courses in history, biology, English, and many other areas.

I then went on to explain that the majority of elementary and secondary school teachers believe in ability grouping. This is usually done on the basis of intelligence tests, so I explained that I would like to try ability grouping with this class—again to see "how it feels." Some students objected right away, saying that "I did not want to know their IQ scores." I calmed them by saying it would be a worthwhile learning experience and assured them that I really didn't believe in IQ scores.

I told the students not to move at this time, but I would like all of those with an IQ below 90 to come to the front so they could sit nearer to me for individual help. I told the students who had an average IQ (between 90 and 109) to go to the back of the room and then take the seats in the middle of the class. The students with an above average IQ were asked to go to the side of the room and take the seats in the back

because they really didn't need much more extra help.

"O.K., all those who got an IQ below 90 come to the front of the room." The students looked around to find those who scored below 90. I said that I knew there was an 87 and maybe a couple of 89's. Again, there was dead silence.

"O.K., all those students whose IQ is between 90 and 109 go to the back of the room." Immediately, to my amazement, 8 or 10 students picked up their books and headed for the back of the room. Before they could get there I said, "Wait a minute! Sit down! I don't want to embarrass you, but you would lie and cheat—the same way we make our students lie and cheat—because you don't want to be classified as "slow." I wrote 'IQ 87' on every paper!"

The class erupted. It was in an uproar for about five minutes. Some of the women cried. Some indicated that they needed to use the restroom. All agreed it was a horrifying and yet valuable experience.

I asked them to do one thing for me: Please don't label kids. Because we are all "gifted," "average," and "slow," depending on the task at hand. They promised.

From *Phi Delta Kappan,* September 1973. Reprinted by permission.

Assessment: The Confounding Effects of Social Class, Ethnicity, and Gender

As if there weren't enough problems with the high-incidence categories, the effects of social class and ethnicity further complicate the issue. A major study of all 50 states compared the use of the high-incidence and low-incidence groupings. The findings indicated that the low-incidence categories were not related to factors such as social class or ethnicity. Just the opposite was the case in the high-incidence categories, especially MR and LD. Using a combined index of socioeconomic status (SES), the study reported a series of very strong correlations between SES and MR, accounting for about 50 percent of a predicted relationship between SES and the MR label. The actual correlations were + .70 and + .63, re-

spectively, to indices of poverty, and infant mortality and − .60 to family income (the higher the income, the less likely the MR classification) (Gelb & Mizokawa, 1986).

There was a very strong correlation of +.65 between race and MR for black students. There is every reason to believe that the overrepresentation of such minorities in special education is the result of faulty diagnosis. For example, in a very large urban system the rosters indicated that the system had three times more black students assigned to MR classes than did any other school system in the country. For this to occur, either a huge concentration of retarded people all had to be living in a single city, or the method of assignment was at fault. Investigation has shown that the method was the cause. A major flaw in the use of high-incidence categories is that a dispropor-

SPOTLIGHT ON BIAS IN SPECIAL EDUCATION

Systemic Discrimination

Jim Ysseldyke, who leads a major assessment program at the University of Minnesota, and his colleague Bob Algozzine conducted a series of studies on the relation between parental social status and special-education placement.[a] For a sample of over 200 educational decisionmakers (teachers, counselors, and school administrators), they provided identical educational data for students referred for evaluation. They varied the parental background; for example, in half the cases the student had a father who was a bank vice-president and a mother who was a real estate agent, and for the other half, the father was a janitor and the mother a supermarket clerk. The referrals for special education were substantially higher for the students from lower socioeconomic backgrounds even though there was no objective difference in academic performance, test scores, or classroom behavior for the students involved. Though unintentionally, the educators were consistently biased in referring for special classes or resource room simply on the basis of family occupation. This is sometimes called *systemic discrimination*, a subjective prejudice that is built into the educational system. Although each decisionmaker would certainly claim that there was no bias on an individual basis, the Ysseldyke-Algozzine studies illustrated the opposite. Their findings should remind all educators to become conscious of the effects of such prejudice on referral and placement, particularly in the high-incidence areas of special-education categories.

Robert Gaylord-Ross[b] points out the paradox: Public Law 94-142 calls for unbiased assessment; yet the single largest category (SLD) is most strongly influenced by political, economic, and social factors rather than accuracy in classification.

---

[a]   Ysseldyke, J., Algozzine, B., & Thurlow, M. (1992). *Critical issues in special education,* Boston: Houghton Mifflin.
[b]   Gaylord-Ross, R. (1990). *Issues and research on special education* (Vol. 1). New York: Teachers College Press.

---

tionate number of minority pupils are often classed as deviates. The label stigmatizes even when accurate; when inaccurate, it not only stigmatizes but leads to negative self-fulfilling prophecies. Research has shown consistently that minorities are the groups most often misclassified. In one study the MR label was applied to 16 percent of the school's minority population. A careful reassessment of the children indicated that 2 percent were accurately classified. In the words of Maynard Reynolds, "Racial and ethnic minorities often deeply resent the high rates of classification of their children as 'retarded,' 'disturbed' or 'maladjusted'" (1984, p. 77). In the cases cited, the resentment appears more than justified.

Unfortunately even the most recent evidence indicates further errors rather than effective solutions. It has been reported that the IQ testers favored middle-class children through positive feedback, a supportive environment, and a "lenient" (27 percent increase) scoring system. The reverse was true for children from working-class and impoverished backgrounds (Rothman and Semmel, 1990, p. 357).

An extensive study by Sally Shaywitz and associates (1990) has also shown a bias against females in the classification of reading disability. It has long been a part of folklore that boys have more difficulty learning to read than girls. Shaywitz found that this view was apparently effecting a different referral rate for developmental or remedial reading assistance. Regular school referral procedures were compared to a careful reassessment method. The teachers in the early grades systematically overreferred boys and underreferred girls even though there were no objective differences between the groups in the extent of reading disability.

Currently about 5.4 million children are classified in some special-needs category, but the current view is that such a figure is grossly underestimated. Reynolds (1990) suggests that by the late 1990s the figure may well approach 8 million, almost double the current level. He sees four factors as "producing" children with special needs: (1) more school-age children, (2) more children living in poverty, (3) more low-birth-weight babies, and (4) more children victimized by drugs, alcoholism, neglect, and abuse.

The sheer numerical increase is a cause for concern and adds to the urgency of solving the assessment problem.

ASSESSMENT: SOME NEW PROPOSALS

One recent attempt to improve testing has been termed *dynamic assessment*. The idea is based on the work of Vygotsky (see Chapter 5) to evaluate learning potential by a sequence of test-teach-test. The examiner through observation seeks to identify the child's "zone of proximal growth" as a first step. This is followed by direct instruction of learning material, for example, teaching the child how to solve a school problem. Then the child is tested again to see if he or she understood the problem. The early results of this approach are mixed, since there is little evidence of increases in actual learning. Also the approach is both expensive and time-consuming, since it is done on an individualized basis over extended periods. The other difficulty is the relation between assessment and effective teaching strategies (Rothman & Semmel, 1990). The theory for dynamic assessment may hold an important key to developing accuracy in classification, but current practice will need further revision.

A second method calls for a completely different sequence in the assessment procedures. The first step, when a child isn't keeping up, would be to assess the learning environment in the classroom, carefully reviewing the teaching methods, materials, and classroom atmosphere. Also, pupil achievement would not be measured by traditional nationally normed achievement tests or the standard IQ method.

Nationally normed achievement tests measure only about one-third of the content of a given grade, which stacks the deck against a child if the test is used to measure current classroom learning. The problems with IQ tests have already been noted. In the words of Samuel Messick (then vice-president of research for the Educational Testing Service), "An individual assessment of the pupil would be permitted only after deficiencies in the learning environment had been ruled out" (1984, p. 5). Thus, a careful look at the quality of instruction would become the first step. As a second step, a new method of assessment that emphasized actual problemsolving or "work samples" would be used. Testing would be used only as a last resort; otherwise, the pupil would be unnecessarily "exposed to the risks of stigma and misclassification in referral and individual assessment" (Messick, 1984, p. 8). The final step, after ruling out the classroom environment and using a careful and comprehensive valid assessment of learning ability, would be to consider the special-class placement *temporary*, no more than one year at a time. The reason for such a time limit on assignment to segregated special classes is simply that the longer a pupil remains outside regular classes, the less likely it is that the pupil will ever return. In the classes themselves, there is often "a sharply reduced curriculum and little cognitive demand" (Finn and Resnick, 1984, p. 11).

In the San Francisco District Court in 1979, Judge Robert Peckham presided over a now-famous court case, *Riles* v. *Larry P.* After an exhaustive examination of placement practice and the learning environments in a large urban district, he declared that the special classrooms were "dead-end classrooms." The doors, once closed, seemed permanently sealed.

To give you a greater personal sense of the effects of misdiagnosis, we present a brief case study drawn from the case files of a famous child psychotherapist.

Dibs: A case of misdiagnosis   Virginia Axline, a gifted child psychotherapist and author, has provided a dramatic case study of a little boy, Dibs. From parental description and nursery school behavior, it appeared that Dibs was grossly mentally defective. His parents reported that from birth on he was always remote, untouchable, slow to talk and walk, unable to play, and striking out at people.

The nursery school teachers were baffled by him. The school psychologist had been unable to test him. The pediatrician had concluded he was "strange," perhaps mentally retarded, psychotic, or brain-damaged. Apparently no one was able to get close enough to Dibs to find out the causes of his difficulties.

The parents themselves were both brilliant and successful yet terribly ashamed, fearful, and anxiety-ridden over their "problem" child. Deep down they believed that the awful truth was that Dibs was an "idiot."

The mother told Axline about a terrible fight between Dibs and her husband at home. The four-year-old had apparently hurled a chair at his father, kicking and screaming all the while, "I hate you." This was in response to the husband's direct comment to Dibs that he was babbling like an idiot. The mother reported to the therapist the following scene with her husband.

> "Dibs wasn't babbling like an idiot now. 'He said he hated you.' Then, my husband sat down in a chair and actually wept! It was terrible; I had never seen a man cry before. I had never thought anything could

cause my husband to shed a tear. I was afraid, suddenly terrified, because he seemed to be just as scared as I was. I think we were closer to each other than we have ever been. Suddenly, we were just two frightened, lonely, unhappy people with our defenses crumpled and deserted. It was terrible—and yet a relief to know that we could be human, and could fail and admit that we had failed! Finally, we pulled ourselves together and he said that maybe we had been wrong about Dibs. I said I would come and ask what you thought about Dibs."

The mother then looked at Axline with an expression of fear and panic in her eyes. " 'Tell me,' she said. 'Do you think that Dibs is mentally defective?' " (Axline, 1967, p. 90).

Dibs was "defective" only in the sense that he had suffered enormous emotional deprivation. For whatever reason, neither parent had been capable of forming a warm, supportive, nurturing early environment for him. In the language of a psychiatrist who interviewed the family, Dibs was "the most rejected and emotionally deprived child" he had ever seen.

In the case study itself, Axline describes the emotional reeducation she provided for Dibs, as well as the assistance to the parents so that they could maintain the gains. Dibs gradually yet dramatically emerged from his shell into the world of human relationships. The work stands both as a moment of high drama and as a reminder of our basic human needs for supportive relationships to encourage healthy psychological development—an essential first step to becoming a person. The word "Dibs" is a common expression in England for "self."

To give you a greater sense of the effects of reluctance to acknowledge a specific learning disability, we next provide a short history of dyslexia.

Dyslexia: A Type of Specific Learning Disability

A lengthy debate has been waged over the question of word *blindness* in children and teenagers. Though given various labels such as *dyslexia* (word disability), *streptosymbolia* (twisting symbols), and *minimal brain dysfunction,* the symptoms are all the same. Essentially, children and teenagers afflicted with this disability reverse words and numbers and have enormous difficulty in spelling, remembering telephone numbers, looking up words in a dictionary, keeping number columns straight, and learning a foreign language—to name just a few of the most common symbol-processing areas.

Dyslexia has a long history and has afflicted many famous people. Public figures such as Albert Einstein, George Patton, Woodrow Wilson, and Nelson Rockefeller have all described in the most poignant way what it was really like during their difficult school days, when they were asked to perform activities that they literally could not understand. In math, for example, a child might be asked to add 783 and 227, but might actually read these numbers as 873 and 272 without realizing the reversal. Thus, when the answer was marked wrong, the reason for the failure would remain a mystery. Similarly, in writing, *no* might become *on, god* might become *dog,* and so on.

In spite of the long history of personal accounts, systematic research studies, and a wide variety of documentation, there continues to be substantial opposition within educational circles to acknowledging the existence of the disability. Estimates run as high as one of seven pupils affected, with a large preponderance of males over females. Too many teachers, however, continue to resist admitting that some pupils actually suffer from the disability. At an intuitive level, the common view is that it is just a question of willingness and motivation; somehow the child with dyslexia doesn't really work hard enough.

A second common misperception is that if dyslexia isn't a fancy psychological label for laziness, it's just a coverup for mental retardation. The reason Johnny can't read, or add, or spell is simple—he's stupid. Even though studies have shown that individually administered IQ scores do not correspond with dyslexia, this second myth persists.

If teachers have experienced difficulty in accepting the reality of dyslexia, psychologists and researchers have had difficulty in documenting the causes. In fact, for too long researchers have attempted to discover the single crucial factor. Some feel the problem is basically a physical-coordination deficiency. Others suggest a chemical basis, from bad reactions to artificial food coloring to hyperactivity due to a drug imbalance. Still others think of it as a psychoanalytic problem resulting from anal fixation, a lack of training during formative preschool years, or a problem of birth order, parental neglect, or fatherlessness.

But human behavior cannot be reduced to a single cause. Emphasis needs to be placed on what dyslexia means for how an individual child learns. The child's strengths in learning are just as important. If some pupils cannot employ the usual channels for processing symbols, than an educational program needs to include a broader array of techniques and experiences. Multisensory programs allow the child quite obviously to use all the senses—see the letter, trace it in sand, cut it out of cardboard, say it out loud, pick it out of magazine ads and street signs, and touch it in block form.

The techniques really come down to "good" instruction—namely, an array of alternatives to help children learn the code. The same solutions apply to helping pupils learn to produce symbols. Since regular writing is a difficult task even to regular learners, other channels can be employed. In addition to paper and pencil, fat crayons, and chalk and chalkboard, pupils can also be allowed to tape-record reports, give oral reports in class, or use a typewriter.

Employing multiple techniques is, of course, not enough. In learning new and difficult tasks, any pupil will need extra human support and encouragement—and this support is crucial for the child with dyslexia. Signs of impatience, despair, and discouragement by a teacher are quickly transmitted to a child afflicted with word blindness, and such a child will be hyperalert to teacher feelings. Positive human support is necessary to create a low-anxiety atmosphere that will help the pupil take risks and not feel it necessary to cover up his or her difficulty. Some children with dyslexia learn magnificent social skills to prevent a teacher from finding out that they can't read or write. Probably the best tutoring in this instance would be from older children and adults who themselves have struggled with the problem. Given support, encouragement, and a multisensory approach, word-blind children do learn to read.

Other Health Impairments: ADHD

Attention deficit hyperactivity disorder (ADHD) is a disability that is included in the category "other health impairments." This category appears to be increasing; greater numbers of students are being identified as having ADHD and are being serviced by special education (U.S. Department of Education, 1995). For every five boys diagnosed with ADHD, only one girl is diagnosed. Broad characteristics of children with this disability include short attention spans, distractibility, inability to organize, and high level of movement. Students with ADHD will also be impulsive and disorganized. When the student's academic skills are average or above average, and the features of this disability are mild, the student may often be able to compensate and to function reasonably well in the classroom. If impulsive and distracting behaviors are prevalent and academic abilities are weak, the student may experience many adjustment problems in the classroom. As with any disabling condition, it is important to remember that

the behaviors of students with ADHD are not deliberate. It takes a long time for them to learn to compensate and/or control their disabling behaviors, and students with ADHD may experience much failure and much discouragement in their classes. A growing sense of inadequacy may increase as the students with this disability move from elementary to middle and high school. Teachers can be more successful with students with ADHD if they match teaching strategies (using David Hunt's model) to the conceptual level of the student and the severity of the disability. For example, high structure will help ADHD students with low conceptual level to function more successfully as they learn what works best for themselves. Even ADHD students with high conceptual level will appreciate a teacher's efforts to get their attention and then to give clear and brief directions. Paul Burden (1995, p. 357) recommends three videotapes for teachers and parents to learn more about attention deficit hyperactivity disorder: (1) *ADHD in the Classroom: Strategies for Teachers;* (2) *ADHD—What Can We Do?* and (3) *ADHD—What Do We Know?* All three videos are produced by Menninger Video Productions.

To learn more about the ADHD disability we need to investigate the ways in which youngsters negotiate their ADHD experiences; in what ways are these different? We also need to investigate the relationship of age, maturation, and the classroom structure (including duration and scheduling of classroom lessons) as children with ADHD move through the primary, elementary, and secondary grades. Finally, because most of the research has been cross-sectional or single-grade-level in design, we also need longitudinal research to follow individual children with ADHD as they move from less formal preschool and kindergarten experiences to more formal experiences in elementary and secondary grades (Pellegrini & Horvat, 1995). Teachers could inquire further about these issues within their classrooms and schools by using collaborative action research, as we discussed in Chapter 14. In the Spotlight we present excerpts from second-grade teacher Katharina Fachin's (1996) action research study "Teaching Tommy."

An Alternative Classification Procedure

Test interpretation is a critical process, for it indicates how we make meaning and judgments. We certainly need a more comprehensive system of educational diagnosis for all children and particularly for those with special needs. Evelyn Deno (1970), an eminent theorist-practitioner in this field, developed a **cas-**

SPOTLIGHT

Teaching Tommy: A Second-Grader with Attention Deficit Hyperactivity Disorder (ADHD)

Katharina Fachin was a second-grade teacher. Her report of her year-long collaborative efforts with the school psychologist and the neurologist, the instructional support teacher and the school principal, the resource room teacher and in-class aide, Tommy's parents and classroom peers is a moving account of her successive attempts to learn more about Tommy's form of ADHD and to develop behavioral and academic programs to fit Tommy's needs. She begins her narrative:

When Tommy walked into my second-grade classroom on the first day of school, I was happy to see a familiar face. I looked at him with sympathy and hope, wanting to make the year one of learning and of building self-esteem.

Tommy was coming to my class with a difficult year behind him. He had spent first grade in a highly structured classroom, and he had not conformed to its behavioral standards. The behavior modification used with him in that class had included the removal of rewards, and Tommy had experienced little success in keeping the rewards he earned. He was often in trouble, and everyone in the school knew his name. He was three-fourths of a year behind his peers in reading and writing. These experiences led Tommy to believe that he was stupid and bad. I was determined to replace his negative self-image with a positive one based on academic and social success.

Tommy and I already had a history before that first day of school, for I had tutored him once a week from May through July. Originally, Tommy had qualified for home tutoring because of a myringotomy and an adenoidectomy. In preparation for teaching Tommy at home, I talked to his first-grade teacher to find out about his capabilities and to see if she could recommend any materials. I was disappointed when I talked to her because she seemed so negative about him, yet she lacked any precise descriptions of his learning. I met Tommy with the impression that he had had a tough break—a little child facing a teacher who had no hope in him and who lacked the flexibility to meet his needs. Tommy's mother reaffirmed this impression when she described how the teacher wanted him tested and how she was afraid that they just wanted to drug her child so he would be easier to handle.

Tommy snacked on cupcakes and soda as we worked at the kitchen counter. The phone would ring, and siblings would be preparing to go off to after-school activities. Tommy wiggled and slid about on the chair, and he would often take bathroom breaks. By remaining firm, I was able to get Tommy to read and write with me. We talked about his interests, and I got to know him. He had a very limited sight vocabulary and could not predict vowel sounds. He could identify most consonant sounds, but could not identify the correct vowels, nor was he familiar with how to spell common endings. Although Tommy did not like to read and write because it was such a struggle, he loved math. Using his fingers, he could calculate all first-grade-level addition and subtraction problems quickly and accurately. Tommy felt very confident of his mathematical abilities.

I became attached to this rough-and-tumble boy

cade system (see Figure 20.2) that respects both the complexity of the problem and the need to employ careful assessment in the service of the children. She suggests that instead of viewing the problem from society's perspective first, we start with the fundamental needs and rights of children. In this way we can keep our educational priorities in mind. The system is also based on a positive assessment concept designed to uncover the areas of positive educational potential. Instead of generalizing from one negative aspect of a child's functioning, the system seeks to differentiate general functioning into a se-

ries of elements. This helps prevent classifying children into negative categories. Instead, the children can be grouped into one of seven levels of educational environments, from regular classes to "total" care. The dynamic commitment in the plan is always to move children upward in the system as far and as fast as possible. Thus, assignments are at first based on the level of activity the child brings to the environment. The educational goal of any particular level, then, is to prepare the child for the next level up, so to speak; none of the levels, two through seven, is regarded as a permanent placement.

with blue eyes and the big smile. He told me about his daredevil biking stunts and about jumping out of tree houses. Grass stains on his jeans, scrapes on his knees and elbows, and dirty hands were his hard-won war wounds. Tommy struck me as very inquisitive. He spoke of such experiments as creating a pocket of air under water with a bucket. I wondered how I could tap into his creativity in the classroom. Tommy was a very active boy who had trouble maintaining eye contact and concentration, but I attributed these characteristics to his personality, immaturity, diet, and environment. I couldn't understand why a teacher would be so negative about handling him in the classroom.

Over the course of the next school year, I found out why. But I also discovered the joys of teaching Tommy.

In her story, Katharina Fachin describes in rich detail Tommy's behavior in the second-grade classroom, the token economy of rewards for Tommy, her analyzing and reanalyzing of her own teaching, and the interventions she tried with the advice and help of others. In the end, medication was added to the intervention. She writes:

I do not mean to argue for the use of medication to address the needs of all ADHD students. I see medication as a last resort and one that should be used in combination with a comprehensive behavioral academic program. I offered Tommy an activities-based curriculum to tap into his energy and creativity. I taught abstract ideas concretely and contextu-

ally. I consistently used and adapted behavior modification techniques and tried other techniques like relaxation techniques. I let Tommy know that I thought he was a great kid and a talented person, too. I had the class support Tommy as peer tutors and as members of project teams, literature study groups, and cooperative learning groups. The district provided instructional and noninstructional support. But Tommy needed something more to enable him to benefit from these interventions. Tommy's ADHD was severe, and the medication helped him achieve success in the classroom.

From my experience with Tommy and his family, I have come to believe even more strongly that it is vital to gain the trust of parents. Their faith in our efforts and concern for their child must be the basis for communication and teamwork between home and school. I also realize how painful it can be for parents to accept that their child might need extra help and even medication. By fielding my colleagues' complaints about Tommy's behavior, I got a small taste of what parents must feel when they are told by friends, family members, and doctors that they don't know how to discipline their children. More painful than the frustration of trying to deal with the condition of ADHD itself is enduring the criticism and condemnation that come from others. I think that this holds true for the student, the parents, and the teacher.

Excerpts from Fachin, K. (1996). Teaching Tommy: A second-grader with attention deficit hyperactivity disorder. *Phi Delta Kappan, 77*(6), 437–441. Copyright © 1996. Reprinted by permission of the publisher and author.

Alternative Educational Environments: Promoting Development

Deno's system clearly implies the need for differential service. The diagnostic problem, as we indicated, involves broad assessment procedures in all areas of functioning. The critical assumption, however, is not the initial prescription, but the developmental program. From this point of view, the various categories of disabling conditions are, at best, only immediate and temporary stations for the child. Growth is determined by interaction. The labels are dangerous,

since it's so easy to assume that the problems are safely locked up inside the child. The frameworks of Jean Piaget, Jerome Bruner, Robbie Case, J. McV. Hunt, and Robert White suggest the following educational assumptions:

1. Students with special needs develop through the same sequence of stages as other pupils but at slower rates in the areas of their impairments.

2. The growth of these children depends on the same set of principles applicable to all children,

FIGURE 20.2   Deno's Cascade: The "cascade" classification system.

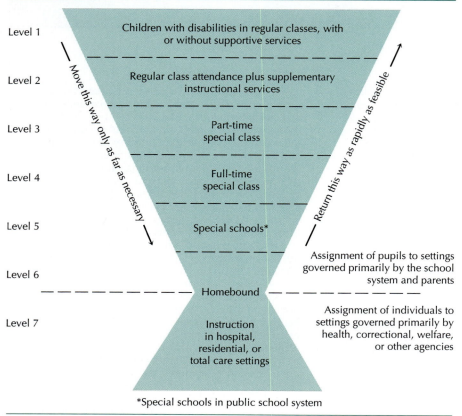

Level 1   Children with disabilities in regular classes, with or without supportive services

Level 2   Regular class attendance plus supplementary instructional services

Level 3   Part-time special class

Level 4   Full-time special class

Level 5   Special schools*

Level 6   Homebound

Level 7   Instruction in hospital, residential, or total care settings

Move this way only as far as necessary

Return this way as rapidly as feasible

Assignment of pupils to settings governed primarily by the school system and parents

Assignment of individuals to settings governed primarily by health, correctional, welfare, or other agencies

*Special schools in public school system

Adapted from Deno (1970), 229–237. Copyright © 1970 by The Council for Exceptional Children. Reprinted with permission.

namely, a rich, stimulating, and abundant early environment (Hunt) and an active rather than a passive learning environment, including a heavy emphasis on practice and participation from the early years onward (Piaget and Bruner).

3. Careful educational preparation is needed for stage growth and transition to the next stage up. This includes the process of *equilibration,* Piaget's term for a constructive match between the child's functioning stage and the learning environment—for example, a rich, stimulating sensory environment during the very early years. Developmental growth depends on interaction between the child and the environment. The opposite of this developmental assumption is the isomorphic view—that the learning problem is a deficit locked up inside the body of the designated child.

A number of studies, including a classic one by Maria Skodak and Harold Skeels (1949), the Perry Preschool Program (see Chapter 3), and one by Sandra Scarr-Salapatek and Richard Weinberg (1975), indicate rather clearly that intellectual functioning and general development can be positively influenced by a rich, stimulating early environment. Skodak and Skeels demonstrated that cognitive functioning could be dramatically increased for young children by modifying an extremely barren orphanage environment. The Perry Preschool Program showed the positive effects of a stimulating preschool environment, while Scarr and Weinberg showed the positive effects of modifying early-home-care environments. Whether the actual environment was an orphanage, a nursery school, or a home, significant increases were found in cognitive functioning as a result of "active" learning, positive interaction, and developmental-stage equilibration. In all these studies, many preschool children were initially classified, on

Several studies conducted during the last thirty-five years all clearly indicate that intellectual functioning and general development can be positively influenced by a rich, stimulating early environment.

the basis of an IQ test, as "retarded" or as "slow learners."

The Case for Inclusion

A major longitudinal study by Susan Osborne and associates (1991) provides substantial cross-validation for inclusion of students with disabilities in regular classrooms. Over a three-year period in elementary school, the team studied 42 LD children from the standpoint of academic outcomes. The students were culturally diverse (62 percent African-American and 38 percent white), and the families were largely working class in background. Initially all the students were in a part-time, resource-room (pull-out) program based on the same discrepancy between their intelligence score and their academic achievement. Overall, the IQ scores averaged just below the fiftieth percentile, for example, 95.5, and academic achievement was in the vicinity of the twentieth percentile. During the school years, 14 students were fully included in the mainstream of regular classrooms, 25 remained in the resource room program, and 3 were moved to a self-contained room.

The outcomes are presented in Figure 20.3 for math, reading recognition, and reading achievement. The results indicate clearly that the mainstreamed LD students outperformed their resource-room counterparts in all three areas. Moreover, the resource-room students with learning disabilities ex-

FIGURE 20.3 Inclusion versus resource room achievement over three years.

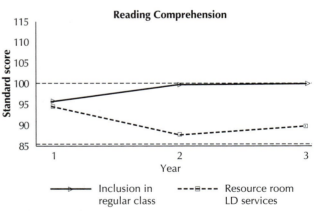

Source: *Osborne et al. (1991), pp. 81–95.*

perienced a *12-point drop* in verbal IQ score over the period of the study. Theories of intelligence are based on the concept of stability over just such a period (three to five years). It is also relevant that such a drop is almost equal to a standard deviation of such a test. Both results, the decline in learning po-

TABLE 20.2   SUMMARY OF POSITIVE LEARNING AND SOCIAL RESULTS FROM INCLUSION OF STUDENTS WITH DISABILITIES IN REGULAR CLASSROOMS, 1991–1994

SKILL AREA	RESULTS
Academic/learning	• Higher quality Individual Education Plans compared to those in special classes
	• Higher level of engaged time in general education compared to students in special education
	• Higher level of engaged time for elementary students with and without disabilities in classrooms in which there are students with more significant disabilities
	• Disruptions to classroom learning time not associated with students with significant disabilities
	• Students with disabilities learn targeted skills in general education classrooms
	• No decline in academic or behavioral performance of nondisabled classmates on standardized test and report-card measures
Social	• High school students report that interactions with students with disabilities produced positive attitudes, increased responsiveness to needs of people, and increased appreciation for diversity
	• Students with disabilities in general education settings are alone less often and display more social contact than students in special classes
	• Demonstrated gains in social competence for students in inclusive settings compared to that of students in segregated placements
	• Social acceptance and opportunity for interactions not uniquely associated with the child's level of functioning
	• Regular class participation is an important factor in determining the composition and stability of social networks for high school students with disabilities

Source: *U. S. Department of Education (1995), p. 496.*

tential (IQ) and in actual achievement, create concern about the resource-room model and reinforce the reasons for inclusion.

In searching for possible causal factors, Osborne noted that prior studies had found that such students were pulled out of regular classes during academic instruction, particularly language arts. The same was true for Osborne's study. Also, prior research had indicated that there was very little interaction between special-education teachers and regular class instructors. This also proved true. Almost two-thirds of the mainstreamed SLD students in Osborne's study were never observed by the special-education teachers. On average, these teachers interacted only five minutes per month with these students (Osborne et al., 1991). Thus the results seriously question the efficacy of the resource-room approach. Another recent study (Hibbert, 1992) with three- and four-year-olds came to similar conclusions. In a study of preschoolers with serious emotional disturbance, those fully included in regular classrooms were assessed at higher levels of adjustment after one year versus a comparison group of re-

source-room children, even though the control group received slightly higher initial ratings. These two studies provide a strong case for inclusion versus resource-room approaches. "Stay put" appears more defensible than "pull out." In a national report to Congress in 1995 a number of additional studies showed gains in academic learning and social skills for students with disabilities who are included in regular classrooms. See Table 20.2. And as Figure 20.4 indicates, from 1990 to 1995 there was a positive shift (from 30 to 40 percent) in the share of students with disabilities who are served in regular classrooms, while the share of students in resource-room pull-outs has decreased from 39 to 32 percent. Inclusion of students with disabilities is on the increase.

Unfortunately, a recent national review of pupil placement policies indicates a strong migration from inclusion as students with disabilities get older. Table 20.3 presents the most recent survey of classroom assignments across four age groupings: three to five years, 6 to 11 years, 12 to 17 years and 18 to 21. There is a major reduction in the number of special-education pupils in regular classes, from 50 to 30

FIGURE 20.4   Special-education services.

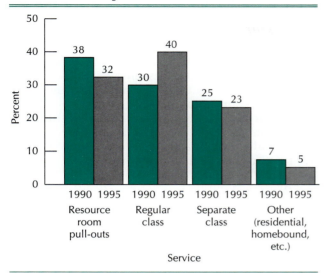

Source: *U.S. Department of Education (1990, 1995).*

percent, and an increase in resource-room placement (27 to 32 percent), and separate classes (20 to 27 percent). Figure 20.5 compares regular classes to resource rooms separately.

Some fear that teacher training is not adequate and that teachers may need more variety in teaching techniques when working with disability conditions in regular classrooms. But a substantial body of literature supports the view that regardless of regular education or special-education teacher role, there is a common knowledge base for good teaching. Regardless of role, special-education teachers and regular education teachers were almost identical ($r = .95$) in their ratings of the important teaching variables: (1) time on task (student time engaged actively in learning), (2) time spent in direct instruction on basic skills in reading and mathematics, (3) providing frequent feedback to students about their performance, (4) comprehension monitoring by the teacher, and (5) explicitly promoting self-responsibility and effective metacognitive learning strategies. These similarities combine with the current emphases in both special education and regular education on classroom contexts for learning such as (1) embedding instruction in meaningful activities, (2) promoting classroom dialogue for self-regulated learning, (3) responding to individual learner needs and realities, and (4) establishing learning communities in classrooms (York & Reynolds, 1996, p. 825.)

The trend toward greater inclusion appears in-

evitable (Ysseldyke et al., 1992), and a major step is the framework to eliminate the distinctions among three of the high-incidence categories. We now turn to the issue of cross-categorical, or noncategorical, proposals.

Cross-Categorical, or Noncategorical, Systems

While there is strong interest in inclusion in regular education, it is clear that not all pull-out programs should be eliminated. The plan, however, is to reduce substantially the current reliance on separate teaching-learning experiences.

The first step will be to continue to move toward the elimination of the high-incidence categories, such as MR, SLD, and SED. The goal is to propose a single functional category of low achievement. The creation of such a broad category is often referred to as a **cross-categorical,** or **noncategorical, approach.** Under this approach, the new category is defined in terms of school achievement rather than some deficit within the child. Thus, the idea is to include the previously labeled students as part of a general educational continuum of learners. The "old" categories too easily became the cause of low achievement in spite of their questionable validity.

The other major problem, never resolved in the old system, was the lack of relationship between the teaching strategy and the categories of disability. As we note further, citing Haberman's work, effective teaching strategies for SLD, MR, and SED students are not that different from those for regular pupils. The specific prescriptions offered in the past as to special teaching methods for SLD, MR, or SED hardly varied from the general methods, again raising the question as to the utility of the labels in the first place. And, finally, research has shown that special teacher certification in these high-incidence categories has no noticeable effect upon pupil achieve-

TABLE 20.3   *PERCENTAGE OF SPECIAL-EDUCATION STUDENT PLACEMENT, SCHOOL YEAR 1992–93*

TYPE OF CLASS	AGE			
	3–5	6–11	12–17	18–21
Regular	48	50	30	24
Resource room	9	27	32	33
Separate class	31	20	27	29
Other	11	3	5	14

Source: *U.S. Department of Education (1995).*

FIGURE 20.5   Differences in special-education placement: Regular classes versus resource rooms, by age group.

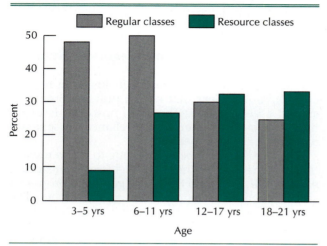

Source: *U.S. Department of Education (1995).*

ment in those special areas (Ysseldyke et al., 1992, p. 359).

INTERVENTION PROGRAMS

Increasing the Accommodative Capacity of Classrooms

As inclusion programs increase, educational environments will need careful preparation, including attention to teacher attitudes and use of imaginative materials and methods. Studies have shown patterns of teacher behavior—namely, discomfort, anxiety, and stress—that teachers experience when dealing with children who are different. We noted earlier that in some urban classrooms white teachers were not responsive to the needs of black children: Teachers engaged in less eye contact, made more negative statements, displayed more punitive behavior toward black children than toward white children. Whether inclusive schooling succeeds, then, will depend the ability of teachers to become more responsive to the fundamental needs of all children. In the special-education literature this is referred to as the need to increase the accommodative capacity of regular classrooms—to broaden the learning environment so that all pupils are genuinely included in positive learning activities. For example, it does little good to legalize racial integration in a school, only to

have the school operate as a segregated institution, with students eating separately, occupying different spaces in the same building, participating in separate activities, being treated separately by school rules and teachers. In the same way, if previously separated special-education pupils are included in regular classes only to be resegregated there, changing the form but not the substance will merely perpetuate the status quo.

Jack Birch (1974) summarized a series of studies in mainstreamed school districts. The cluster of positive attitudes of regular teachers was the most effective force for excellent special education.

1. Belief in the right to education for all children

2. Readiness of special-education and regular-class teachers to cooperate with each other

3. Willingness to share competencies as a team on behalf of pupils

4. Openness to including parents as well as other professional colleagues in planning for and working with children

5. Flexibility with respect to class size and teaching assignments

6. Recognition that social and personal development can be taught and that they are as important as academic achievement

Birch also noted that in the school districts that successfully included students into the mainstream of regular classes at elementary and secondary levels and across disciplines, three factors stood out:

1. There was genuine appreciation of the teamwork with the special-education teachers, particularly the help the regular classroom teachers received with the children already in their rooms.

2. Regular classroom teachers found that special-education pupils were usually no more difficult to include in their classes than some children already there.

3. The spirit that all the children are in the same school system was expressed time after time.

Research by Stanley Deno and associates (1990) has shown that regular-education teachers can work effectively with special-needs children and that in fact they often view the behavior of such students more positively than do the special-education teachers. It is also clear that the key to successful inclusion

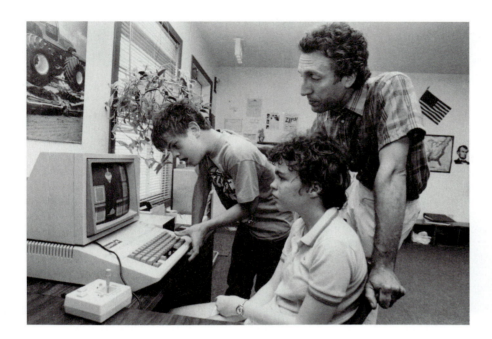

Special-education studies have demonstrated the critical importance of positive teacher-child interaction in promoting intellectual growth.

continues to be the skill of the classroom teacher and the collaboration with special education. At first in response to Public Law 94-142 special educators used the model of expert consultation to help improve what went on in regular-education classrooms that included students with disabilities. Over time the consultation model shifted toward collaborative problemsolving with regular-education teachers. But to achieve the goals of inclusive schools we need to move beyond both past and present-day views, say Marleen Pugach and Lawrence Johnson (Stainback & Stainback, 1996, chap. 15). Beyond problemsolving, they challenge us to move to a view of collaboration in which all members of a school and community are working together, inquiring together, and supporting each other to provide higher-quality teaching that is increasingly responsive to diversity and to the individual needs of all students.

Developing the Requisite Teaching Skills

In addition to the obvious importance of teacher attitudes, we also need to consider new teaching skills for the classroom itself. It will do teachers little good to have highly positive attitudes toward exceptional children, but not have the requisite teaching skills to help them. We noted earlier the critical developmental assumptions:

1. Exceptional children can develop through the same Piagetian stages (especially sensorimotor, preoperational, and concrete), in a manner similar to regular children, yet at slower rates.

2. Interaction with a rich, stimulating environment and active learning will promote growth.

Educational researcher David Hunt (1974) has shown repeatedly in a key series of studies that it is important to match the educational environment with the stage of development of the child. Pupils who are functioning at relatively low levels of conceptual thinking tend to learn best in a highly structured teaching environment. Thus, in elementary schools, as pupils are attempting to master the initial stages of concrete thinking, Hunt's work would support carefully structured teaching. The educational tasks assigned should be (1) carefully explained, (2) relatively brief, (3) monitored quickly, (4) systematically varied, and (5) set up to achieve learning through multiple senses.

At first, this approach may strike you as one that overmanages the child, shutting out the possibility of creativity and being too preplanned or programmed. If you view it from the child's position, however, Hunt's plan may not seem as negative. Children starting school at low conceptual levels can be easily confused by ambiguity. They may also be

MARIA MONTESSORI

Maria Montessori (1870–1952) was in the forefront of change and innovation throughout her life. She was raised in the small, conservative Italian town of Chiaravelle. Her aspirations, however, led her to seek admission to the prestigious University of Rome to study medicine. At the time it was unheard of for a woman to pursue a medical career; there were no female physicians in Italy. Such barriers, however, did not deter Montessori. Her intellect, personal drive, and dedication soon won her respect at the

all-male university, and at age 24, she became the first female physician in Italy.

Her interest in practicing general medicine, which at that time consisted largely of treating symptoms, soon waned. She began to ask larger questions about life and compassion, and her focus shifted toward the problems and needs of what at that time were called "idiot" or "insane" children. The streets of one section of Rome (the San Lorenzo district) were inhabited by gangs of unruly young delinquents, most of whom had been rejected by the traditional school system and all of whom were economically and culturally deprived. These roaming bands of street urchins engaged in vandalism and aimless violence and were destroying the neighborhood as an economically viable entity. To remedy this situation, a school was set up, called the Casa dei Bambini ("Home for Children"), and Maria Montessori, then 29, became its first director. At first the school was considered to be more of a reform school than a real educational institution, and the authorities would have been happy if it did nothing more than keep the children off the streets, making the area safe again.

Montessori's success, however, far surpassed the hopes of the sponsors. Using techniques inspired by her study of the works of Edouard Seguin (who had worked with children with mental retardation) and Jean Marc Itard (who had worked with the "wild boy" of Aveyron), she soon taught these slum children how to read, write, and count, often before the age of five. As a by-product, delinquency in the area was greatly reduced, even on nonschool days. Montessori continued to create new learning materials, and always applied her theories to the classroom. Using her highly structured materials and multisensory procedures, she soon revolutionized the entire educational approach for these street urchins, who became perhaps the first generation of children with special needs to be included in the mainstream of regular education.

Montessori's work expanded in scope as she became increasingly interested in the general learning problems of all children, not just those of the disadvantaged or "disturbed." She began to suspect that learning was dependent on the interaction between the child and the environment, between nature and nurture, an unpopular view at that

afraid to ask for clarification, especially if they see that other children apparently understand the directions. Under such conditions children may revert to lower-stage thinking. If you were just on the threshold of learning to think concretely and became confused, anxious, and unsure of an educational task, you might understandably fall back into an earlier mode, namely, preoperational thinking.

From an educational standpoint, the careful use of a structured approach to teaching is legitimate as a means of helping children with lower conceptual

levels to master some initial tasks. However, we are not suggesting that all problems of retardation or other types of exceptionality can be "cured" through high-structured learning. Although there may be individual cases of dramatic improvement within a group of children previously segregated in special classes, those will remain the exception. In the nineteenth century in this country an early pioneer in special education, Edouard Seguin, suggested that slow learning and retardation could be stamped out. With training and responsive environments all chiltime. David Elkind, an American expert in cognitive-developmental theory, has noted that many of Montessori's concepts were highly similar to some of Piaget's later age-stage theories. She viewed development as occurring in a sequence of stages, or *sensitive periods,* as she called them, and she felt that such development proceeded by leaps and bounds and was followed by slower periods of integration. She used the term *growth explosions* to denote these qualitative shifts to new cognitive stages.

Montessori's other obvious similarity to Piaget was her absolute genius for developing empathy with children. Without doubt, this sensitivity, which enabled her to understand both the thoughts and feelings of young children, was the central ingredient in her educational system.

Above all else, Maria Montessori was committed to educational practice. Whereas Piaget focused mostly on the theoretical aspects of how children learn, Montessori always viewed every problem with an eye to practical application. She was a bridge between theory and practice; she both described how children learn at a theoretical level and pre-scribed teaching methods to accom-plish developmental goals. Thus, like Bruner many years later, she at-tempted to synthesize a theory of learning with a theory of instruc-tion. From her naturalistic observa-tions of how young children learn, she developed her now-famous "prepared environment." She wished not to accelerate growth or to force children to grow up overnight but rather to help chil-dren develop their own competen-cies maximally at each stage of growth. The environment, if care-fully matched to the child, provides the nourishment for such growth. The child should not be over-matched, but provided with inputs that cause the child to "stretch." This notion was later picked up by both J. McV. Hunt (problem of the match) and L. S. Vygotsky (zone of proximal development).

Despite the credibility that Montessori's theories have for us today, she was long treated with disdain by psychology's inner cir-cle, especially here in the United States. Part of the scorn stemmed from the fact that she was a woman and didn't fit the American stereo-type of the woman's role. Second, her notions about child develop-ment were too divergent from the dominant theories of psychoanaly-sis, behaviorism, and the IQ testers. After all, Montessori was insisting to everyone who would listen that intelligence was *not* fixed and *not* determined only by heredity, and further, that early experience *did* play a key role in the cognitive growth process.

As seems to be the case with all major innovators, a few of Montes-sori's "disciples" have misunder-stood her intentions and have cre-ated some lockstep environments that do not always serve children well. For Montessori, development involved the matched environment of repetitive learning and multisen-sory materials, as well as spontane-ity and empathy. Children do not learn best in prescriptive educa-tional straitjackets.

Montessori's long life was de-voted to increasing our theoretical and practical knowledge of devel-opment for both the normal and atypical child. In her lifetime she addressed many audiences: the teacher, the educational researcher, the curriculum-materials devel-oper, and the parent. By the time of her death at 82, Montessori had fi-nally become accepted and contin-ues to be a powerful voice for chil-dren.

dren could be normalized. Such overly optimistic hopes created a backlash of disappointment when reality indicated that improvement was slow and limited. The goal of the educator is to stimulate de-velopment. Small gains, in the long run, may in fact be the most significant and longest-lasting.

The differences in learning aptitudes between normal and mildly handicapped children—those in the high-incidence categories of SLD, MR, and SED—can be associated with stages of cognitive growth. This means that at any particular point, the latter may not process the teaching information as ef-ficiently as their peers. Their cognitive strategies, or (as we outlined in Chapter 11) their system of infor-mation processing, may not be as well developed. Thus, one important variable is engaged learning time, its purpose being to provide extra experience as a means of catching on to the lesson at hand. While there are differences in the speed of acquisi-tion between children with mild learning disabilities and their nondisabled peers, problemsolving, infor-mation processing, and strategies of memorizing appear to be important additional factors in determining how much learning actually takes place. Certainly we have emphasized, throughout this book, that the goal of instruction is not so much rote repetition of answers as it is comprehension of both the content and the process. Thus, the aim for children with special needs is the same as for all others: to improve their cognition and problemsolving capacity (sometimes called *metacognitions*) as learners.

FROM DIAGNOSIS TO TEACHING

Assuming we develop a more valid base for classifying individuals with disabilities, particularly in reducing the overassignment of minority children, what are the teaching implications for you? Just how different is it to teach a handicapped child? What knowledge of special education and teaching strategies do you need? What are the special learning characteristics of the child so designated? These questions are central to inclusive teaching. If there are 12 disability conditions, are there 12 different teaching strategies?

Martin Haberman (1980), former dean of the University of Wisconsin at Milwaukee, has carefully examined inclusion from the teacher's point of view. He reviewed the variety of special-education techniques, the curriculum materials needed for special-education pupils in regular classrooms, and the procedures and strategies that are common to all effective teachers. He then estimated how much special content and strategy are needed, as well as general procedures for all children. When you look at Table 20.4, you may be quite surprised and encouraged by his conclusions.

For example, the table estimates that from 5 to 10 percent of the time you will need to employ new materials and from 5 to 10 percent of the time, special methods of communication. For students with visual impairments this would mean giving them access to books in braille, having them use a tape recorder for answering an essay exam, setting up the room to minimize changes in furniture placement, and having them sit close to the front of the room. Many students with visual impairments have some residual vision. Students with hearing impairments would need a different set of materials, the use of a signer (a person adept at signing your words to the pupil), and similar accommodations to their special needs. For those with orthopedic impairments, the room would be set up to reduce barriers to mobility for a wheelchair, and the playground would have a lowered hoop for basketball. In one sense these are small changes, but they make a substantial difference to an individual student. Try maneuvering in the average school room or getting to the bathroom in a wheelchair, and you'll understand at an experiential level how different the world of a wheelchair user can be in activities we take for granted.

Consistent with these ideas, there has been a major shift in the training of special-education teachers themselves. Reynolds (1990) has shown that the fastest-growing speciality in teacher training is the noncategorical area. In one year in the 1980s, the number almost doubled, from 16,000 to 26,000, further supporting the idea of generic teaching approaches, especially in the high-incidence areas.

In the area of special teaching methods, as Haberman notes, there is a very small body of unique approaches, involving perhaps 5 percent of the teaching time. Many educators would argue that even these special methods are not that unique. In any case the special-education resource teacher or school psychologist can provide you with the current recommendations. The consistent use of a time-out room for a hyperactive child, the close monitoring of individualized seatwork with frequent positive reinforcement for a child with MR, or the use of different standards in judging penmanship for palsied children represent some examples of somewhat specialized teaching methods. Probably the most significant special technique is more psychological than pedagogical—what psychologists call learned helplessness.

Learned Helplessness

Some years ago a theorist, Martin Seligman, discovered a particular type of personality response that was common to many types of people who had been excluded from full participation in the mainstream of society (1975). Although Seligman originally focused on migrant workers and on impoverished or ethnically different people, his theory can also be applied to children with disabilities, many of whom suffer from a similar kind of exclusion and resultant stigma. His central point is that such people learn to appear helpless. They acquire a set of behaviors intended to give an impression that they are not competent. Seligman stresses that these responses (giving up quickly, crying, refusing to try) have been *learned*—hence the term **learned helplessness.** Daniel Reschly (1988) has reviewed much of the literature on attitudes and motivation and finds that such pupils do not attribute success to themselves and show a dependence on other persons and on external reinforcement.

Research has also shown that parental attitudes and practices often impede growth for children with

TABLE 20.4   EFFECTIVE TEACHING STRATEGIES FOR INCLUDING PUPILS WITH DISABILITIES *(Summarized by Martin Haberman)*

APPROXIMATE PERCENTAGE OF TIME SPENT IN ACTIVITY	TEACHING ACTIVITIES FOR WHICH HELP MAY BE SOUGHT BY CLASSROOM TEACHERS LEARNING TO INCLUDE ALL STUDENTS
5–10	Using special materials that are new to the teacher. This involves becoming familiar with materials and equipment and being shown how they operate.[a]
5–10	Communicating with students who have special handicaps (e.g., hearing, visual). This involves receiving straightforward direction.[b]
5	Special methods of teaching. There is a very small body of special teaching behaviors for working with handicapped students that teachers can learn through observation and develop through practice (i.e., usually supervisory procedures).[c]
75–85	Engaging in normal classroom teaching practices that are, in large part, effective with all children.[d]

[a]*Reynolds, Maynard C. & Birch, Jack W. (1977). Teaching exceptional children in all America's schools (pp. 569–571 and 632). Reston, VA: Council for Exceptional Children. Copyright © 1977 by The Council for Exceptional Children. Reprinted with permission.*

[b]*Ibid., pp. 562–563 and 630–631.*

[c]*Ibid., pp. 565–569 and 633–636.*

[d]*Ibid., pp. 303–304.*

disabilities. Although it is a complex story, reduced to its simplest terms, parents tend either to reject or to overprotect such children. Parental anxiety and guilt result in the parents' quite unintentionally fostering dependency. However, do not make the mistake of simply blaming the parents, any more than you should blame teachers (remember Rosenthal's studies) for negative expectations. The syndrome is learned, and it can be unlearned. In fact Martin Seligman now makes that point most emphatically with the title of his book, *Learned Optimism* (1991). The challenge is to turn feelings of helplessness into feelings of competence.

Unlearning Helplessness

In dealing with learned helplessness it is most important, especially at the outset, to employ a careful set of behavioral strategies. Find some positive behavior of the child that you can positively reinforce, and do not under any circumstances positively reinforce helplessness when an activity is well within the child's ability. These two rules go together; unless you follow both, you will quickly undo your gains. You will probably find this process extremely difficult at a personal level. The child has spent years learning the process. It is as if individual competence has been frustrated, so the child now becomes competent in getting others to wait on him or her. In

some cases the act is very convincing, having been polished through many performances. Such children can make you feel guilty and perhaps even heartless. At such times it's important to review your own role. They need your support to nurture their growth, but that does not mean you should do for them those things they can learn to do for themselves. Dealing with your feelings of compassion and concern for a child struggling with a disabling condition may well be your most difficult experience as a teacher. As your own experience grows, you will gain more confidence in your ability to identify areas of positive accomplishment to reinforce and become even more consistent in avoiding reinforcing the appearance of helplessness.

In the long run you will see the gradual emergence of the child's positive competence drive. The first sign may be most dramatic. The child lets you know, "Look here, I can do this myself." That's when you'll realize you have made progress—as an educator for all children.

TEACHING STRATEGIES FOR INCLUSION

As clearly suggested, the greatest need in inclusive classrooms is the development of competent general teaching strategies. In this realm certain approaches need emphasis. These procedures are not unique to special-education pupils; they are useful with all children. Yet they are not used often enough in general and so must be underlined here as a system of instruction.

One of the major difficulties in developing teaching strategies for inclusive classrooms has been the lack of diversity in teaching methods employed in separate special-education classes before passage of Public Law 94-142. In fact, criticism of the profession of special education itself has increased substantially in the past decade. As more research is done, the weaknesses in the old methods of classification become more apparent, thus emphasizing the need for better and more valid classifications, especially in the high-incidence areas. So too with teaching. There has been almost a complete reliance on behavior modification as the only method for such high-incidence areas. A highly structured and simple-task approach is helpful (indeed the next section will provide an extensive outline of a behavior modification system that is most appropriate), but effective teaching for special-education children cannot begin and end there. Richard Snow, one of the originators of attribute-treatment interaction (ATI), commented on the weakness of a singular approach: "A truly adaptive instructional system is needed, not a new blanket panacea chosen because it produces some average improvements" (Snow, 1984, p. 14).

As you read these recommendations, keep in mind that the various elements can become a system. We do not advocate any one as a "blanket panacea," a single and final solution. The system includes (1) precise teaching, (2) cooperative learning, (3) tutoring, (4) social skills training, (5) matching and gradual mismatching, and (6) portfolio assessment.

Precise Teaching

Substantial work has been done in a method of **precise teaching** as a means of providing high structure for children newly included in regular classes. Essentially, the method is derived almost directly from learning theory and Skinnerian principles. The specific advantages of the method are that it allows the learner to focus on a structured task, proceed at his or her own pace, receive positive reinforcement for accomplishments, and build up feelings of being a successful learner. The overall process, then, represents a method of tailoring educational tasks to fit each child, or, as it's sometimes called, individualizing instruction. A discussion of the key elements involved in setting up this process follows.

Select a manageable task   The task to be learned by the child needs to be very specifically defined. Thus, the educational objective should not be too cosmic. To become more human, to appreciate American civilization, to be spontaneous, and so on are all too ambiguous as manageable tasks for precise teaching (see Chapter 10). Instead—and this may sound hopelessly pedestrian to you—it is important to identify a highly specific task: learning to count from one to 10, to recognize vowels, to read 10 single words without an error, or similar highly structured learning activities. This approach is useful not just in special-education classes but in almost any new learning situation, especially where the ambiguity of a task may generate anxiety. Thus, the first problem is to pinpoint the specific area. Some examples of specific areas are:

1. *Subject areas:* Multiple mistakes in oral reading, faulty knowledge of the multiplication table, erratic completion of homework assignments, not enough divergent products in artwork, and so on. (These must be described in behavioral terms—that is, in terms of something you can see and count with a very low level of inferences.)

2. *Deportment areas:* Hitting others, out-of-seat behavior, shouting out, not talking, never volunteering, excessive profanity, poor attendance, too much staring out of the window, and so on. (Be careful in picking out areas here. We don't want to turn all pupils into "Goody Two Shoes.")

3. *Personal areas:* Negative feelings toward self, putting self down, overly apologetic, hostile feelings, not speaking up for self, never trying a new activity, and so on.

Set up a contract with the pupil   The contract should specify who will keep track of the counting, how the chart is to be set up, and how the count is to be kept. Contracts can be developed in almost any area and can even employ pictures to describe the activities for nonreaders. For example, in the contracts depicted in Figures 20.6 and 20.7 the positive behavior and desired reinforcements are described pictorially.

Other, more sophisticated contracts naturally are possible and may specify more complex behaviors. Also, other methods of keeping track of the counting are available. The important point is that the record be visible to the pupil so that he or she can see on a cumulative basis how the score is mounting. This

FIGURE 20.6 Behavioral contracts for pupils who are not yet readers.

Source: *B. Dollar, Leadership Training Institute, University of Minnesota, Minneapolis. Used with permission.*

feedback is essential to the system. You could have pupils keep paper charts and graphs, use a plastic grocery-store counter, or have them make a leather bracelet containing small movable beads on strings of pipe cleaners. The one thing to avoid is asking them to keep track of the behaviors in their heads.*

---

* The classic research of George Miller has shown that humans in general can keep about five to seven discrete pieces of "knowledge" in their consciousness at one time. After that point, unless we employ chunking, we become easily confused (see Chapter 11).

Negotiate a significant "award" There is a debate among behavioral theorists as to whether just seeing a line on a chart "improve" is sufficient. In general, with younger pupils the more concrete the reinforcer, the better. There are thousands of funny stories about erroneous choices of reinforcers. For example, one teacher had pupils collect red chips for not speaking out of turn, then exchange five red for one blue, collect two blues and exchange for one gray, and exchange one gray for extra recess time. The children wouldn't exchange blue for gray. They didn't like the color.

It is certainly permissible to discuss the choice of

FIGURE 20.7   A behavioral contract for pupils who can read.

Contract

Date: _____

I will earn checks ✓ each day for

✓ raising hand to speak . . .

✓✓✓ helping others . . .

✓✓ working at each center . . .

I will lose checks ✓ each day for

✓ talking out . . .

✓✓✓ fighting . . .

✓✓ not working . . .

At the end of each week . . . I may . . .

✓✓✓✓✓✓✓
✓✓✓✓✓✓   =   1. extra recess time
2. "good" note home
3. extra art time
4. Hershey bar

Teacher: _____

Student: _____

M   T   W   TH   F   M   T   W   TH   F

Source: B. Dollar, *Leadership Training Institute, University of Minnesota, Minneapolis. Used with permission.*

reinforcers with the children. Also realize that you don't have to select conventional reinforcers, like a candy bar, gold stars, or extra recess time. Other possibilities might include open discussion time with you—setting aside a few moments of "special time" between an adult and a child can be an unusually powerful reinforcement. Remember that the quality of time, not the quantity, is the crucial aspect. A few moments of focused individual attention can be most meaningful to a child and to an adult, too.

In setting up the contract, specify rewards for positive behavior. For example, if a student is in constant motion, the contract should reward time spent at his or her desk. As we noted in Chapter 19, positive reinforcement is both more effective and more humane than punishment. If you set up the contract so that the pupil loses privileges for disruptive behavior, you will find that the pupil will become less cooperative in general and more negative toward you in particular. It is also important that the reward be offered for a genuine achievement. Special-needs children are similar to children in general in their ability to spot the real meaning of unsolicited help, sympathy, and overly generous praise (Graham & Barker, 1990).

A final point on the reinforcement schedule is to make sure that the reinforcement itself follows close on the heels of the desired contracted behavior. Long delays between accomplishment and reinforcement are ineffective, in spite of what we may think about building character through self-denial and discipline. B. F. Skinner has commented that a person would never learn to play the piano if he or she had to wait a week to hear the sound of the note. In baseball parks, electric scoreboards explode the very moment a home-run ball lands in the seats. The opera audience does not wait a month to reward the diva for an outstanding aria. A doctor is congratulated on the spot after a successful operation.

Don't employ the method too broadly   Try the method in single areas for relatively brief periods. It would be a mistake to bombard a child with an endless series of contracts. If we have children "charting" in all their subject areas, in a series of personal-management domains, and in extracurricular activities, the entire method of contracting may soon become aversive. The pupils will feel trapped, hemmed in, and rebellious.

The point of contracts is to help pupils become successful in mastering a variety of tasks. The contracts can provide positive motivation to help children focus their energies, receive positive feedback, and develop a sense of personal mastery in learning. The chart obviously should be used to help a child see how he or she is improving. Each child compares present performance only with his or her past performance. It would be destructive to have children compare themselves with each other, since the whole point of precise teaching to individualize instruction would be lost amid a flurry of competition. If I initially don't know how to read and then learn to recognize *cat, hat, bat,* and *sat,* that achievement should be regarded as significant in its own right. I should not be asked to compare my progress with that of another pupil who's learning to distinguish cases in Latin.

Cooperative Learning

We have provided a discussion on the use of the cooperative approach in Chapter 18, which will not be repeated here. It is important to remember that the cooperative method means mixing regular and special-education children together. For example, two researchers, Ray McDermott and Jeffrey Aron, set up a video recorder to examine teacher-pupil interaction in recently mainstreamed classes. Unfortunately, the teachers tended to isolate the four or five "new" special-education pupils in each class as a separate group in their classrooms. Thus, instead of four reading groups, there would be five, with similar groupings for math and other small-group activities. As you can see, almost from the start the new pupils were resegregated and clearly identified as different. To make matters worse, when the amount of teacher time was calculated from the video, it became apparent that the pupils in the segregated group had received almost no instruction. The special-education pupils were interrupted 40 times in a 30-minute reading group, whereas the top group of readers was interrupted only 2 times in the same interval. Thus, time on task virtually disappeared for the special-education pupils. The source of the interruptions was either the pupils in the top group or the teacher! The researchers observed, "Almost two-thirds of the time in the reading lesson is spent in either getting a turn or waiting for the teacher to attend to the group" (McDermott & Aron, 1978, p. 57).

Robert Slavin, of Johns Hopkins University, has done a series of studies on actual classroom achievement when special-education children are included in the mainstream. The learning tasks are set up as small-group activities with group problemsolving. He calls one method the **student teams-achievement divisions (STAD).** The students are divided into groups of four or five, with high- and low-achieving students in each. After introducing the lesson content for the week through either direct or indirect teaching methods, the teacher hands out worksheets to each group. The students then quiz each other on the material, have a small-group discussion, and engage in a variety of activities. The final quiz scores within each small group are averaged and extra points are assigned during the semester for "improving" students in each small group. Slavin finds that this protects the student with learning disabilities from becoming a dead weight, or, in baseball terminology, "an automatic strikeout."

The advantage of this approach, according to Slavin, is that it reduces destructive competition. Conventional approaches to grading basically lead to an unequal distribution of positive reinforcers. A few excellent students receive all the positives; the rest do not. This does not happen with the cooperative approach, even though the so-called top students are recognized individually as well as through the team efforts. Most important, of course, are the learning outcomes for the students with disabilities.

Rather than being allowed simply to "be," the students show both academic and social acceptance gains. Also, and in some ways this may be the most important point of all, the achievement of the other students does not decline; it improves.

More recently, Slavin has shifted his focus from the use of cooperative learning programs as a supplement to their use in regular instruction. He has tested a method of integrating the cooperative approach with some aspects of individualized instruction. The results are most promising. Academic achievement in mathematics and language arts at the elementary school level improved substantially (Slavin, 1990).

Overall, recent meta-analysis of deliberately formed mixed groups of students engaged in cooperative learning activities supports the approach. Academic achievement improves on the average of about three-quarters of a standard deviation—almost one grade level higher (Reynolds, 1990, p. 430).

Currently there are multiple approaches to cooperative learning methods in addition to Slavin's student teams–achievement divisions. A partial list (Furtwengler, 1991) includes:

Teams, games, tournament

Team-assisted individuation

Cooperative integrated reading

Jigsaw I and II

Learning together

Group investigation

These systems improve the achievement of everyone in a class.

Tutoring

Individual tutoring has a long tradition as a teaching method. Studies have consistently found that effective tutoring is the single most valuable instructional tool in all of teaching. Benjamin Bloom has called it the "two sigma problem" (1984, p. 4). Tutoring yields achievement that is two standard deviations above the level of conventional group instruction. In Bloom's study, the average tutored student ranked above 98 percent of the students in the controlled classes.

Since most studies of tutoring were not done with children with disabilities, we can't be sure whether the benefit for them would be as great. (Perhaps it would be greater.) We can say, however, that some overall benefit would accrue to children included in regular classrooms. We also need to note that the study was done with trained tutors. Placing a child with special needs with an untrained tutor does not guarantee success. Under appropriate conditions, however, working with students on an individual basis will promote their learning more effectively than any other technique or even combination of techniques.

How can teachers employ tutoring for students with disabilities when they have to teach all the other students as well? The answer is that other students or community volunteers can be used as tutors. Research shows clearly that children, teenagers, or volunteers can learn fundamental tutoring skills and that such tutoring improves the academic performance and attitudes toward school of the students helped (Sharpley et al., 1983). This means that regular classroom students can participate as tutors for children with special needs to help such children learn and prevent them from falling behind. Such tutoring programs are becoming widely available.

Would we be shortchanging regular-classroom students by having them spend time tutoring other students? Naturally, if students were expected to spend 15 to 20 hours per week tutoring, it would reduce the time they have for their own tasks. But if the time involved is reasonable (one to 4 hours per week), tutoring does not adversely affect the student tutor; in fact, it has the opposite effect. Some studies have shown that student tutors actually improve their own level of achievement at a greater rate than those they tutor. Some students have shown psychological gains as well. Student tutors exhibit higher rates of maturity, leadership, and empathy than peers who did not tutor. A carefully run tutoring program, then, benefits both groups. For example, a program of high school females doing math tutoring with underachieving fifth-grade females resulted in two sets of benefits. The secondary students improved on measures of leadership and conceptual complexity. The fifth-graders made an 11-point gain on the California Achievement Test in math, and changed their attribution of success from others to self. Control groups showed no gain at either level on any measure (Sprinthall & Scott, 1989).

For those tutoring children with disabilities, it is especially important to provide systematic training. Otherwise, volunteer student helpers may end up with more negative attitudes to children with special needs than they had before the experience (Sprinthall & Blum, 1980).

The objectives of tutoring are similar to those of cooperative learning, but the academic gains for tutoring are more clear-cut. Both methods reduce invidious competition. Neither method impairs the

Tutoring may prove to be mutually beneficial to this high schooler and her preschool student. The student will progress with his class, and the tutor may advance academically beyond her peers because of her participation in the tutoring program.

achievement of the normal-progress students. "Used expertly and in selected ways, peer teaching can have good effects on all participants and on both academic and social outcomes" (Reynolds, 1990, p. 430).

Social Skills Training

Children with disabilities are different from their peers not only in learning achievement but even more so in social skills. Because of both past isolation and current lack of interaction with normal peers, children with disabilities often lag behind in rudimentary social abilities. Numerous studies have found that children included in regular classrooms unfortunately are not necessarily accepted socially by their peers. The base rates of interaction are low. The children are often ignored, or allowed to just "be."

Social role-taking refers to a process central to Erik Erikson's concept of personality development in stages—namely, the ability to understand where another person is "coming from," or to practice a kind of interpersonal perspective taking. It is an ability that develops from interaction with other people. We aren't born understanding relationships; our role-taking ability grows slowly. Studies have shown that children with disabilities lag behind peers in social role-taking (Perry & Krebs, 1980). During adolescence the difference increases. For example, before adolescence deaf children are approximately 5 to 10 percent behind on estimates of social and emotional

maturity; with the onset of adolescence that figure climbs to 20 percent (Dupont, 1978). Similar shifts are reported with other types of disability. An important aspect of the child's interpersonal development, then, is being ignored.

The results also suggest something else. Without some planned programs, mixing students with disabilities and students without disabilities produces negative effects on social interaction. Virginia Bruininks has shown that students with learning disabilities received the lowest peer-status ratings of all groups in school. Perhaps the most upsetting finding was that students with SLD were unaware of their low social status (Bruininks, 1978). They did not apparently "understand" that they were actually being ignored and thus weren't aware of the need to improve their social skills to gain some acceptance. For their part, the regular children were content to avoid the "others" as much as possible. We mentioned earlier that Public Law 94-142 was based on the concept of the least restrictive environment for such children. The irony is that, especially during adolescence, inclusion can result in a more restrictive social environment.

Although you obviously cannot alter the social environment of an entire school, by employing some techniques such as social skills training, cooperative learning groups, and individual tutoring you can reduce some of the isolation. You can also search out counselors and support their efforts to improve the social skills of the children and teenagers. An extensive review points out that some methods are effective in helping children with disabilities fit into the school environment. Also, programs such as peer counseling have been shown to be effective as a means of socialization (Sprinthall et al., 1992). In general, this aspect of development has been sadly neglected during the inclusion process (Gresham, 1981).

Henry Dupont, who reviewed the studies demonstrating the increasing gap in emotional development of special-education students, suggests quite accurately that nearly all such children desperately need more adequate and responsive teaching-learning environments. The vocational adjustment and job success of these pupils are most directly related to their social-emotional adjustment. Social skills and interpersonal competence apparently are central ingredients of success after school. Dupont concludes that children with special needs require more acceptance as persons of individual worth and that they also need an instructional climate to help them develop higher levels of emotional-social maturity (1978–1989). This is as true for the gifted as for the learning disabled (Reynolds, 1990; Sapon-Shevin, 1996).

Matching and Gradual Mismatching

This strategy is mostly a reminder of Snow's point, presented at the outset of this section. Effective teaching for children with special needs requires a variety of methods, not one "blanket." In Chapter 13 we suggested that matching and gradual mismatching were in fact central to the process—or the art—of teaching. In David Hunt's sense, then, the same rules apply. Especially if you suspect that a particular student is functioning at a very concrete, or even preoperational, level in Piaget's scheme (low CL in Hunt's scheme), then it is clearly most appropriate to use high structure and all the elements of that approach. You also need to watch academic performance for signs of growth toward more independence as a learner. Watch for possible differences in levels of functioning in different subject areas or in different parts of the same subject. The major mistake to avoid is assuming that a child who may be classified with a special learning disability is disabled in all areas. Because none of the common assessment methods really taps all the different components of what we commonly call "intelligence," be alert to any variation in school performance. By adjusting the teaching strategy, then gradually mismatching, you will increase the probability of developmental growth. Stages of development are not permanent classifications.

It is important to remember that effective teaching

does not remain singular in its approach. While the direct, concrete, and focused approach may be the appropriate match or starting point for most children with mild learning disabilities, it is not the only method. The debut does not have to become the finale. In fact, Penelope Peterson reminds us that attribute-treatment interaction is still the rule for all learners. If we retain the singular approach of high-structured teaching, which has been the hallmark of most pull-out programs, then the possibility of ever developing higher-order thinking skills is reduced. She correctly notes that research in mathematics and reading points to the importance of teaching for meaning and understanding while also teaching the lower-order skills through drill and practice. She suggests that in math, for example, word problems should be introduced early, while the students are engaged in mastering computation skills ("If there are two horses in one yard and three horses next door, how many horses all together?" rather than "Two plus three equal?").

Also in reading, asking beginners to discuss the meaning of what they have just read is another example of going beyond the drill-and-practice system. If students are taught only to memorize, then transfer becomes most difficult. Peterson provided the following example of a student who had memorized the multiplication table without understanding the meaning.

The problem: Twenty-nine students are to go on a field trip. Each van holds eight students. How many vans are needed?

The response:

Student: You have to multiply 8 by 9, um, then you have to multiply 9 by 7. Then you have to multiply 8 by 2.

Interviewer: Tell me everything that you're thinking.

Student: Um, then you multiply 7 by 2. Then you add 2, um, and you add 6 and 3. Then you add 6 and 1.

Interviewer: OK. Are you done? Yes? What do you think the final answer is?

Student: 14,992.

Interviewer: OK. What were you thinking about besides the problem?

Student: Um, the answer (Peterson, 1988, p. 344).

The question of how 29 students could fit on 14,992 buses had apparently not occurred to the student. The student's own experience of riding to school on a bus had not been brought to bear on the question. Such are the difficulties with an exclusive focus on drill and practice.

Portfolio Assessment

This strategy incorporates new thinking on teaching methods of constructivism and their success with children with special education needs. The State of Vermont uses portfolio assessment with all students, including students with disabilities. This strategy often includes the concepts of writing process. Teachers have documented the progress of special-education learners who are included in their regular-education classes and who are involved in the writing process (Five, 1991). In portfolio assessment and the writing process, learners create meanings, present their learning from their own point of view, develop their own voice. Classroom teachers set up dialogues with and among students, helping students to voice their opinions and hear others' voices. Students express themselves verbally and in writing. Students research issues that concern them, share with other students, revise their thinking, share again, listen again, research and revise again. They learn to act and reflect in a continuous cycle. Each student's portfolio provides documentation of his or her process. Teachers come to understand better the linguistic, cultural, and special-need differences that exist in the inclusive classroom. Similarly, teachers find themselves more aware of the special strengths of each of their students.

THE INDIVIDUALIZED EDUCATION PLAN

With these six strategies in mind, we now turn to the issue of inclusive classrooms and lesson planning. In general, Madeline Hunter's system is a most effective method for instructional planning. However, as more and more special-education students enter the regular classroom, the range of individual differences increases. To ensure that the newly included are not lost in the shuffle, the law includes a provision for an **individualized education plan (IEP),** which is basically a lesson plan for one child at a time.

The plan is created by a team made up of the teacher, the psychological assessment specialist, the special-education resource consultant, a school administrator, and the parent. Its purpose is to set out specific learning objectives in a timetable and to identify how the outcomes are to be evaluated. Perhaps the most unique feature of this approach is that the plan must be accepted and approved by the parent. When first proposed, this feature of the IEP met with some resistance from school professionals, since in effect they would have to share the author-

ity for the plan with parents. Also, further underlining the importance of this new approach, the parents had the right to bring in their own specialists, such as an independent psychological consultant and even a lawyer. After an initial period, however, the IEP approach has been largely accepted. School personnel and parents have found common ground in working out realistic goals and strategies for specific children. The plan starts where the learner is currently functioning and outlines the details. Each plan must be reviewed annually. The IEP includes:

1. Current academic performance level

2. Goals and objectives

3. Specific services to be provided

4. The designation of school personnel and their roles

5. Where and on what schedule the service will be provided

6. An evaluation plan

After many years of experience, the IEP is no longer seen as a radical change in educational philosophy but rather as a useful method to prescribe manageable learning objectives for children who otherwise might be overlooked in the fast pace and complex environment of a regular class. The document does protect the child's interests and serves as a reminder of his or her individual needs. You may find it initially awkward to set up IEPs. With so many points of view represented, the first few conferences will be somewhat confusing and perhaps even frustrating. After a while, though, you will see that an IEP is just a lesson plan that is very concrete and specific. You will have a clearer sense of what you can accomplish plus access to a resource team to help with the implementation. You will also find that, as your confidence increases, you will provide more and more suggestions for goals and methods to improve classroom performance. As a plan, The IEP is no guarantee of the outcome, but it does represent the best abilities of people at the time. Because the IEP is not carved in stone, it can be revised as often as people wish.

It will also be helpful for you to remember our discussion of the Concerns-Based Adoption Model (CBAM, Chapter 14). Susan Loucks-Horsley and Deborah Roody (1990) applied that framework to the issue of including students with disabilities in regular classrooms. They found that the phases of concern—from phase 0, awareness, to phase 6, refocusing—can apply directly to the inclusion issue. As a result, each of you confronted with the need to improve the accommodative capacity of the classroom will probably experience these phases of concern in sequence. They point out that the personal agenda of how you feel about these changes is critical. "Teachers may feel challenged, hopeful and desirous of what can be accomplished, but they also may feel frustration, burden, fear, lack of support and inadequacies about their ability to teach children with different kinds of problems. These feelings need to be resolved before teachers can energetically tackle the task of teaching difficult youngsters" (1990, p. 54).

To provide teachers with help, a new program was developed (Tindal et al., 1990). The idea is that the responsibility for the IEP and its implementation should be shared between the regular and special-education teachers. In an attempt to promote colleagueship and collaboration, a consultation agreement was drawn up to define ongoing cooperation between such teachers. Although the initial research results were problematic, the idea still appears promising, given the need to increase fruitful and co-equal collaboration between both sets of teachers. Perhaps if such a program were combined with the CBAM approach, greater collaboration would result.

It is a good idea to teach the children in regular classes more about children with special needs. There are a number of children's books accompanied by teacher guides that will help sensitize children to certain disability conditions. The Council for Exceptional Children is an excellent resource. Such readings help spread the word that exceptional children may have difficulties in one area but have many talents in other areas. Often adults forget this too. Simply observe an adult trying to communicate with a sightless person by shouting or simplifying the language by dropping all prepositions and qualifiers.

THE INDIVIDUAL TRANSITION PLAN: SCHOOL TO WORK

With the IDEA of 1992 came greater emphasis on the transition from school to work for individuals with disabilities. By law at age 16 **an individual transition plan** needs to be developed with each person with a disability. A transition plan needs to cover education, recreation, housing, employment, and community issues. Findings from the National Longitudinal Transition Study show that during their five years after high school students with disabilities in secondary schools who were included in regular classes are more likely to be employed, have higher yearly wages, and live independently. The relationship between more time in regular education and positive results as a young adult needs to be studied

further. The promising results of the 1993 study (Blackorby & Wagner, 1996) suggest that increased time in regular education enhanced students' overall intellectual and social competence by providing better preparation for postsecondary experiences. Two-thirds (66 percent) of those living independently after high school had participated in regular education 75 percent or more of their time in high school (see Table 20.5). Also, students with disabilities who spent more time in regular education in high school were more likely to be employed and to make higher salaries in the three years after high school than students who had taken fewer regular education courses in high school. Students who had spent more time in regular education were also more likely to be fully participating in their communities. Over 50 percent of students with disabilities who had spent 75 percent or more of their time in regular classes were employed or in post–high school education; they were not socially isolated, and they were either married or engaged.

The modifications of the disability classification system by AAMR in the 1990s is also leading to significant changes in the individual transition plans. Mental retardation, for instance, is no longer conceived as an absolute trait expressed solely by the individual, but rather an expression of the interaction of the individual and his or her environment. The individual's strengths and weaknesses are described in relation to all of these four dimensions: (1) cognitive functioning and adaptive skills, (2) psychological and emotional well-being, (3) health and physical well-being, and (4) life activity within home and community. Thus, individual transition plans don't focus on strengths and weaknesses of the individual in isolation; instead they focus on types of supports needed within the school, home, and community to optimize an individual's functioning. Supports can take the form of personal maintenance services,

TABLE 20–5   *STUDENTS WITH DISABILITIES IN REGULAR EDUCATION AND INDEPENDENT LIVING*

Time in high school spent in regular classes (%)	LIVED INDEPENDENTLY AFTER HIGH SCHOOL (%)	
	Yes (N = 552)	*No* (N = 1316)
0–25	8	20
26–74	26	37
75–100	66	43

Source: *U.S. Department of Education (1995), p. 85.*

homemaker services, home health aides, inhome living assistance, medical-alert devices, architectural modifications, technology services, financial planning, employee assistance, community and school access, as well as teaching and befriending. The individual transition plan matches an individual with a particular community living situation and considers the supports needed for the person to live there, not whether the person is capable of living there. Transition planning is collaborative. Supported living is to be designed not "for" but "with" individuals with disabilities. Paid staff act as friends, advocates, brokers of services, and counselors, working with the individual. Paid staff no longer control people with disabilities; they serve them. This changing role of staff is critical to the individual transition plan. The Americans with Disabilities Act has been called the civil rights bill for people with disabilities. Its guarantee of nondiscrimination toward all people with disabilities has helped focus greater attention on community integration of individuals with disabilities and on community-based systems of services in the individual transition plan (Stainback & Stainback, 1996).

THE CASE FOR INCLUSION

In 1975, just before his death, Nicholas Hobbs, an eminent educational psychologist and clinician, headed a national commission charged with examining the problems of special-education classification systems. In a work significantly titled *The Futures of Children* (1975), Hobbs advanced the thesis that a comprehensive educational plan is required to classify children according to the services they need rather than the capabilities they lack. Special education and regular education essentially need the same point of view—namely, to create and emphasize educational programs that start where the learner is and then stimulate and nurture positive development. Both new skills and positive attitudes are needed for educational success. For too long we have been satisfied to follow policies that have too often been designed to exclude or segregate significant numbers of children not only from the mainstream of schooling but from life as well. When so-called retarded children are placed in regular classrooms containing effective accommodative capacities, the pupils make as much educational progress as they would if they remained in separate classes, and sometimes more. In addition to academic learning, all such pupils gain socially: their self-concepts become more positive, less stigmatized, and less characterized by self-hatred and self-contempt (Gartner and Lipsky, 1987).

A key factor in the concept of inclusion is the phrase *"increasing the accommodative capacity* of all classrooms to respond to a broad range of *individual differences."*

We end this chapter with a particularly promising study. Is there a difference between inclusive classrooms that have equal numbers of children with and without disabilities and those that have just a few children with disabilities? This question was investigated as part of a recent study (Hibbert & Sprinthall, 1995). The study compared two kinds of inclusive classrooms for preschool children with identified disabilities. Both preschool programs in the study contained state-of-the-art developmentally appropriate curriculum and resource staff. In the model program there were approximately equal numbers of typically developing children and children with identified disabilities in the same preschool classrooms for the entire morning. In the comparative program, there were fewer children with disabilities mainstreamed into the regular education classroom for a portion of the preschool day. In addition, in the comparative program there was another, regular-education classroom of typically developing preschool students, and no children with identified disabilities; this third class formed the control group for the study. The total sample included 54 children, with an equal number of boys and girls, and they were divided into the three classrooms as described above. The researchers assessed the children individually using pre- and post-tests over the nine-month period of the intervention. The children were assessed on the Social Skills Rating Schedule and the Dupont Test of Affective Development. The outcomes for the typical inclusive approach (that is, one or two children with disabilities being included in a regular preschool classroom) produced positive gains for all members of the class. In the fully inclusive classroom (that is, an equal number of children with and without disabilities) the outcomes were even more positive. The children with disabilities and the children considered typically developing both made positive social, emotional, and cognitive gains. The outcomes support the claim that both groups of children can gain when inclusion principles are applied effectively. A second finding of the study was that there were no negative effects for any subgroups of either of the inclusive classrooms. None of the children moved toward negative or unhealthy emotional development as a result of being placed in an inclusive classroom. Neither the children with disabilities nor the typically developing children were sacrificed to benefit the gains made by the others. It seems that if there are enough resources, all can benefit in inclusive classrooms.

SUMMARY

Traditional educational practices for dealing with children with disabilities involved remolding their characters so that they fitted into society, excluding them from a society into which they did not fit, or segregating them from other so-called normal children. Under a new policy, inclusion in the mainstream, legislation requires that previously excluded groups of children now enter regular classrooms and be educated in the least restrictive environments possible.

Twelve designations of disability have been set up; however, problems of accurate diagnosis and effective placement are substantial. The rate of error in diagnosis is highest in the categories that include the most children—mental retardation, learning disability, and emotional disturbance. As a result, traditional methods of dealing with children with disabilities cannot be relied on. New approaches, such as Deno's system of graded educational environments that stress movement up as far and as fast as possible, and other educators' emphasis on active learning and short-term, temporary placements for the exceptional, offer more promising alternatives.

The question of teaching strategies for special-education students is also important. Haberman has demonstrated that teaching strategies that are effective with "regular" students are just as effective with children with disabilities; only a few procedures are needed in addition. Teachers must especially guard against fostering and maintaining the sense of learned helplessness that is so common among students with special needs.

The most useful teaching methods that can also be employed with special-education students are (1) precise teaching, (2) cooperative learning, (3) tutoring, (4) social skills training, (5) matching and gradual mismatching, and (6) portfolio assessment. These strategies, taken as a whole, would help increase the accommodative capacity of regular classrooms and hence increase the learning potential of all pupils.

In using these methods, teachers can benefit their pupils most by also employing an individualized education plan (IEP). The plan is formulated by a school services team and is revised as the student progresses. Careful attention to teaching strategies can help students with disabilities progress both academically and socially, as they gain more positive self-concepts.

KEY TERMS AND NAMES

Americans with Disabilities Act
Individuals with Disabilities Education Act (IDEA)
attention deficit hyperactivity disorder (ADHD)
cascade system
cross-categorical, or noncategorical approach
Evelyn Deno
disability category
exclusion
Martin Haberman
hydraulic model of assessment

individualized education plan (IEP)
individual transition plan (ITP)
learned helplessness
Maria Montessori
precise teaching
Public Law 94-142
remolding
Maynard Reynolds
segregation
student teams—achievement divisions (STAD)

THEORY INTO PRACTICE: PEER TUTORING

A very effective method of increasing the educational resources of schools is to create a student tutoring program. Generally, this involves selecting older and more psychologically mature pupils as helpers. There is no optimal age difference between tutor and tutee; however, some amount of difference is usually more effective such as fourth- or fifth-graders with first-graders and tenth- or eleventh-graders with middle schoolers.

The second issue is to provide the helpers with careful and systematic training. In a tutoring program, this means that you as a teacher become a tutor trainer. You teach the helpers some fundamental elements of effective teaching, have them practice with each other, and then set up the actual tutoring. Basically, this involves a role shift for you from teaching to supervising. What follows is a sample series of tutor-training lessons that were used to teach fourth-grade students to serve as *buddies* to trainable mentally retarded children. These activities provide enough of a framework to enable you to add specifics to our suggestions in working with student tutors.

Unit 1

Objective: To learn similarities and differences between themselves and the children with disabilities.

Materials: Blindfolds, wooden blocks of varying shapes (ten for each pair of tutors).

Plan: Each pair of students is to take turns as a tutee and a tutor. To help the students experience the feelings of a disability condition, the "tutee" is blindfolded and then asked to build a block tower. The tutor is to give verbal directions only and no other form of help. Then the students switch roles.

After each pair has experienced the role of teacher and of pupil with special needs, conduct a discussion with the group as a whole to promote reflection.

What was it like to tutor a person with a visual impairment using only verbal directions?

What was it like to try to build a tower without being able to see?

How did it feel to be given only verbal help? Was it frustrating?

What do you have to do to give good directions to someone who has a hard time with blocks and puzzles? (Encourage many ideas for altering the style of communication: speaking more slowly, giving more verbal clues, using shorter phrases.)

Should you give more help than you did? What kind of help? (Encourage the students to talk about hands-on help.)

Then, help the students draw conclusions about effective helping. Remember to use wait-time in questioning and to call on students by name for answers.

Note: Other simulations of a disability condition include a blindfolded "trust" walk. Arrange a pathway through a maze of chairs and have the helpers direct the blindfolded peer with verbal directions only. Or have all the students write their own name, address, and phone number either with the non-dominant hand (left if right-handed) or while looking into a mirror. These experiences help the stu-

dents learn more about how it feels to struggle over otherwise ordinary tasks.

Unit 2

Objective: To learn to give clear directions.

Materials: Games or puzzles that are typically used with low-functioning students.

Plan: Remind the students of the outcome of Unit 1. Ask for a summary. Outline effective direction-giving and model the behavior with one of the students. (Deliberate talk: one- or two-syllable words; be prepared to help.)

Then, have the children pair up and use one of the games. After five minutes or so have everyone switch roles. (During this experience, be sure to circulate and provide lots of positive reinforcement to anyone using one of the four techniques.)

After the practice, conduct the discussion session with questions such as:

Did you hear your tutor give clear directions?

How did you feel when the directions weren't clear?

How does this experience relate to working with children with disabilities?

Again, remember to call on specific children by name rather than addressing a general question to all. Also remember to use both wait-time for a response and cues to help students answer more completely.

Unit 3

Objective: Learn to give positive feedback.

Materials: Games from the special-education resource room.

Plan: Form pairs for role-play and ask the tutor to give instructions to the tutee and then say nothing at all if the student does well. Repeat the same exercise but provide praise whenever the tutee succeeds.

Reconvene the group as a whole and ask questions such as:

How did you feel with silence?

How did you feel with praise?

How might you feel if instead of silence you were criticized?

Can you see yourself giving praise to the "buddy" from the special class?

Remember to review the guidelines for effective praise (Chapter 12) so that the students don't over-praise or "gush over" the tutees.

Unit 4

Objective: Never say no—or hardly ever: how to handle discipline. Sometimes special-class children have not learned to play games by the rules. This doesn't mean that they are naughty but rather that they sometimes need extra help and encouragement. The objective is to help the tutor learn constructive ways to redirect attention and teach the buddy to follow directions.

Materials: Blocks of different colors.

Plan: Start by modeling the techniques. The first technique is verbal redirection. Demonstrate with a student; for example, hold out two colored blocks, one red and one blue. Then say, "Mary, give me the red one." Mary chooses blue. "Mary, this is blue. Here is the red one. Now give me the red one." Then when Mary hands over the red one be sure to use positive reinforcement. This will often be sufficient to keep the tutee on task.

The second technique is behavior redirection. Demonstrate the previous scene with Mary, but in this case, Mary has no interest in that particular game and starts to poke a nearby student. Say, "Mary, let's go over to this corner (away from others) and do some drawing with crayons. Let's see if you can draw a red line for me." Take Mary by the hand and walk with her to the corner. Then use positive reinforcement for Mary's appropriate behavior.

The third technique is a combination of physical restraint and redirection. Demonstrate the first scene again, but in this case Mary is about to hit a nearby tutee with the wooden box holding the game. You say, "Oh, Mary, I can't let you do that." Then move quickly to grab the box and hold Mary's arm. Follow this with the steps in the second technique.

After completing the demonstrations, have the tutors pair off and practice the three techniques, again verbally reinforcing good examples.

Reconvene the group and ask questions such as:

How did you feel about using the different techniques?

Why do you suppose you should not hit the child when she (or he) was about to bop another tutee?

Do you find it difficult to distract and redirect?

Does it bother you to find out that sometimes the child might not follow the rules of the game?

It will be most important to conduct the above discussion at length. Many children either from their own experience or from observation of adults may feel that behaviors such as physical retaliation, spanking, or the knuckle on the head, are appropriate. These ideas need to be aired, but you must also firmly indicate that physical retaliation is not permitted, while restraint is. Recall the discussion in the previous chapter on the differences between humane and inhumane control. Children with disabilities may sometimes need firm external control, that is, positive methods suited to levels of Kohlberg stages I, II, and III. They do not need the negative methods.

A final point: The use of student tutors can be a positive educational resource for children with disabilities. The student tutors, however, need systematic training and continuous monitoring. Without training, the tutors may end up with more negative attitudes toward the peers with disabilities. With training, the students learn some important lessons themselves while helping others.

For further information see Sprinthall and Blum's (1980) article, Peer and cross-age training.

REFERENCES

Axline, V. (1967). *Dibs.* Boston: Houghton Mifflin.

Bakan, D. (1971). *The slaughter of the innocents.* San Francisco: Jossey-Bass.

Baroff, G. S. (1974). *Mental retardation: Nature, cause, and management.* New York: Wiley.

Birch, W. J. (1974). *Mainstreaming.* Reston, VA: Council for Exceptional Children.

Blackorby, J. & Wagner, M. (1996). Longitudinal post school outcomes of youth with disabilities: Findings from the National Longitudinal Transition Study. *Exceptional Children 62*(5), 399–413.

Bloom, B. S. (1984). The 2 sigma problem: The search for methods as effective as one-to-one tutoring. *Educational Researcher 13*(6), 4–16.

Bruininks, V. (1978). Actual and perceived peer status of learning-disabled students in mainstream programs. *Journal of Special Education 12*(1), 51–58.

Burden, P. R. (1995). *Classroom management and discipline*. White Plains, NY: Longman.

Deno, E. (1970). Special education as developmental capital. *Exceptional Children 37*, 229–237.

Deno, S., Maruyama, G., Espin, C., & Cohen, C. (1990). Educating students with mild disabilities in general education classrooms: Minnesota alternatives. *Exceptional Children 57*(2), 150–161.

Dormer, S. (1975). The relationship of physical handicap to stress in families with an adolescent with spina bifida. *Developmental Medical Child Neurology 17*, 765–776.

Dupont, H. (1989). The emotional development of exceptional students. *Focus on exceptionality 21*(9), 1–10.

Dupont, H. (1978). Meeting the emotional-social needs of students in a mainstream environment. *Counseling and Human Development 10*(9), 1–11.

Fachin, K. (1996). Teaching Tommy: A second-grader with attention deficit hyperactivity disorder. *Phi Delta Kappan 77*(6), 437–441.

Finn ,J. D., & Resnick, L. (1984). Issues in the instruction of mildly mentally retarded children. *Educational Researcher 13*(3), 9–11.

Five, C. L. (1991). *Special voices*. Portsmouth, NH: Heinemann.

Furtwengler, C. B. (1991). How to observe cooperative learning classrooms. *Educational Leadership 49*(7), 59–62.

Gartner, A., & Lipsky, D. K. (1987). Beyond special education: Toward a quality system for all students. *Harvard Educational Review 57*, 367–395.

Gaylord-Ross, R. (1990). *Issues and research in special education* (Vol. 1). New York: Teachers College Press.

Gelb, S. A., & Mizokawa, D. T. (1986). Special education and social structure: The commonality of "exceptionality." *American Educational Research Journal 23*(4), 543–557.

Graham, S., & Barker, G. (1990). The down-side of help: An attributional-developmental analysis of helping behavior as a low-ability cue. *Journal of Educational Psychology 82*, 7–14.

Gresham, F. M. (1981). Social skills training with handicapped children: A review. *Review of Educational Research 51*(1), 139–176.

Haberman, M. (1980). Principles of inservice training for implementation of mainstreaming in the public schools. In D. C. Corrigan & K. Howey (Eds.), *Concepts to guide the education of experienced teachers* (pp. 53–64). Reston, VA: Council for Exceptional Children.

Hibbert, M. T., & Sprinthall, N. A. (1995). Promoting social and emotional development of preschoolers: Inclusion and mainstreaming for children with special needs. *Elementary School Guidance & Counseling 30*, 131–142.

Hibbert, M. (1992). *Assessing the social and educational development of preschool children in two mainstreamed programs*. Unpublished doctoral dissertation, North Carolina State University.

Hobbs, N. (1975). *The futures of children*. San Francisco: Jossey-Bass.

Hunt, D. (1974). *Matching models in education*. Toronto, Canada: Ontario Institute for Studies in Education.

Lee, H. (1962). *To kill a mockingbird*. New York: Popular Library.

Loucks-Horsley, S., & Roody, D. S. (1990). Using what is known about change to inform the Regular Education Initiative. *Remedial and Special Education 11*, 51–56.

Macmillan, D. L., Siperstein, G. N., & Gresham, F. M. (1996). A challenge to the viability of mild mental retardation as a diagnostic category. *Exceptional Children 62*(4), 356–371.

McDermott, R. P., & Aron, J. (1978). Pirandello in the classroom: On the possibility of equal educational opportunity in American culture. In M. C. Reynolds (Ed.), *Futures of education for exceptional students*. Reston, VA: Council for Exceptional Children.

Messick, S. (1984). Assessment in context: Appraising performance in relation to instructional quality. *Educational Researcher, 13*(3), 3–8.

Osborne, S., Schulte, A., & McKinney, J. (1991). A longitudinal study of students with learning disabilities in mainstream and resource programs. *Exceptionality 2*, 81–95.

Pellegrini, A. D., & Horvat, M. (1995). A developmental contextualist critique of attention deficit hyperactivity disorder. *Educational Researcher 24*(1), 13–19.

Perry, J., & Krebs, D. (1980). Role-taking, moral development and mental retardation. *Journal of Genetic Psychology 136*, 95–108.

Peterson, P. L. (1988). Selecting students and services for compensatory education: Lessons for aptitude-treatment-interaction research. *Educational Psychologist 23*(4), 313–352.

Reschly, D. (1988). Learning characteristics of mildly handicapped students: Implications for classification, placement and programming. In M. C. Wang, M. C. Reynolds, & H. J. Walberg (Eds.), *The handbook of special education* (Vol. 2). Oxford, England: Pergamon.

Reschly, D. J., & Ysseldyke, J. E. (1995). School psychology paradigm shift. In A. Thomas & J. Grimes

(Eds.), *Best practices in school Psychology III* (pp. 17–31). Washington, DC: National Association of School Psychologists.

Reynolds, M. C. (1984). Classification of students with handicaps. In E. W. Gordon (Ed.), *Review of research in education* (pp. 63–92). Washington, DC: American Educational Research Association.

Reynolds, M. C. (1990). Educating teachers for special education students. In R. Houston (Ed.), *Handbook of research in teacher education* (pp. 423–436). New York: Macmillan.

Reynolds, M. C., Wang, M. C., & Walberg, H. J. (1987). The necessary restructuring of special and regular education. *Exceptional Children 53*(5), 391–398.

Rothman, H., & Semmel, M. (1990). Dynamic assessment: A comprehensive review of the literature. In R. Gaylord-Ross (Ed.), *Issues and research in special education* (Vol. 1) (pp. 355–386). New York: Teachers College Press.

Salvia, J., & Ysseldyke, J. (1991). *Assessment in special and remedial education.* Boston: Houghton Mifflin.

Sapon-Shevin, M. (1996). Including all students and their gifts within regular classrooms. In W. Stainback & S. Stainback (Eds.), *Controversial issues confronting special education: Divergent perspectives* (2nd ed.) (pp. 69–80). Boston: Allyn & Bacon.

Scarr-Salapatek, S., & Weinberg, R. (1975). The war over race and IQ. *Psychology Today 9*(7), 80–82.

Seligman, M. E. P. (1975). *Helplessness.* San Francisco: Freeman.

Seligman, M. E. P. (1991). *Learned optimism.* New York: Knopf.

Sharpley, A., Irvin, J., & Sharpley, C. (1983). An examination of the effectiveness of a cross-age tutoring program in mathematics for elementary school children. *American Educational Research Journal 20*(1), 103–111.

Shaywitz, S., Shaywitz, B., Fletcher, J., & Escobar, M. (1990). Prevalence of reading disability in boys and girls. *Journal of the American Medical Association 264*(3), 998–1002.

Skodak, M., & Skeels, H. M. (1949). A final follow-up study on one hundred adopted children. *Journal of Genetic Psychology 75*, 85–125.

Slavin, R. E. (1990). *Cooperative learning: Theory, research, and practice.* Englewood Cliffs, NJ: Prentice Hall.

Snow, R. (1984). Placing children in special education. *Educational Researcher 13*(3), 12–14.

Sprinthall, N. A., & Blum, M. (1980). Peer and cross-age teaching: Promoting social and psychological development in mainstream classes. In M. C. Reynolds (Ed.), *Social environment of the schools.* Reston, VA: Council for Exceptional Children.

Sprinthall, N. A., Gerler, E. R., & Hall, J. S. (1992). Peer helping. *The Peer Facilitator 9*(4), 11–15.

Sprinthall, N. A., & Scott, J. (1989). Promoting psychological development, math achievement and success attribution of female students through deliberate psychological education. *Journal of Counseling Psychology 36*, 440–446.

Tindal, G., Parker, R., & Germann, G. (1990). An analysis of mainstream consultation outcomes for secondary students identified as learning disabled. *Learning Disability Quarterly 13*, 220–228.

U.S. Department of Education (1990). *Twelfth annual report to Congress on the implementation of the Education of the Handicapped Act.* Washington, D.C.: Author.

U. S. Department of Education (1995). *Seventeenth annual report to congress on the implementation of the Individuals with Disabilities Education Act.* Washington, DC: Author.

York, J. L., & Reynolds, M. C. (1996). Special education and inclusion. In J. Sikula (Ed.), *Handbook of research on teacher education* (2d ed.) (pp. 820–836). New York: Simon & Schuster Macmillan.

Ysseldyke, J., & Algozzine, B. (1990). *Introduction to special education.* Boston: Houghton Mifflin.

Ysseldyke, J., Algozzine, B., & Thurlow, M. (1992). *Critical issues in special education.* Boston: Houghton Mifflin.

GLOSSARY/
STUDY GUIDE

This glossary/study guide has been prepared to help you develop familiarity with the key concepts and contributions of the major theories and theorists described in the book. A good way to use this guide is to review the key concepts and names just as you finish each chapter. Then, on notepaper, jot down a brief paragraph or two for each concept or person on the list. Try to figure out one or two main reasons why the person or idea is important to educational psychology. After you've given that activity your best effort, turn to this glossary/study guide and review your answers by comparing them with the ones provided. Then, since the concepts and names are keyed to the chapter numbers (in parentheses) for easy cross-referencing, clarify any ambiguities by going back to the chapter and rereading the appropriate section.

Of course, all this also means that it is important to understand the reasons behind the concepts. Jerome Bruner once said that a student needs to have a background of facts, what he called "the stuff of learning," before understanding and discovery learning can take place. The glossary/study guide will help provide you with the "stuff" for creative thinking in educational psychology. Just listening to lectures or reading text material, the student new to the field often becomes dismayed over the number of technical terms and the seemingly endless jargon. But what at first may seem like forbidding language is really an attempt to be precise. In order to understand the more global concepts in educational psychology, the student should master the tools of the trade, that is, the methods and terms used by educational psychologists in presenting their views.

The items in the guide define specific terms, outline broad theoretical positions, or provide brief biographies of some of the significant individuals in educational psychol-

ogy. Although each entry is essentially a self-contained unit, in some cases you will be directed to one or two additional entries in order to develop a more complete thought. The number in parentheses at the end of each entry indicates the chapter in which the concept has been discussed.

Rote memorization will not serve you well, since if you don't have an underlying understanding, you may easily fall into the trap of repeating "nearly accurate" phrases that may, unfortunately, signify nothing. On an exam given by one instructor in educational psychology, it is alleged that a student wrote a brief essay that included a discussion of means and modians as well as a section on the standard devotions. So to avoid being caught without a prayer (sorry), study for understanding, not just for mere memorization.

Accessibility Channels

David Hunt uses this term to denote the meaning of conceptual development stages. Teachers achieve their significant educational objectives by tuning up the materials and methods in accordance with the different *channels* the pupils prefer to use. Similar to Vygotsky's notion of the zone of proximal development. (13)

Accommodation

Concept used by Piaget in his discussion of cognitive development. Accommodation is the adjustment the individual makes when incorporating external reality. Piaget uses this concept in conjunction with *assimilation*, which is the individual's ability to internalize and conceptualize his or her environmental experiences. Accommodation is the individual's response to the immediate and compelling environmental demands that have been and are being assimilated. *See also* Assimilation. (5)

Achievement Motivation

A possibly intrinsic motive to achieve just for the sake of achieving, rather than in the service of some other motive. Research shows that the most important single ingredient in achievement motivation is a feeling of self-directed competence. (18)

Acquired Motives

Motives that are based on the activation of psychological needs, such as approval, affection, power, and prestige. Such motives are said to have been learned. (18)

Active School

Based on Jean Piaget's ideas, the concept suggests that learning will be enhanced through active, or hands-on, experiences in combination with thoughtful reflection. Piaget's dictum states, "To know by heart is not to know." Passive memorization does not necessarily mean that the pupil has really learned or understood the concepts. (5)

American Question

According to Jean Piaget, any question about how to accelerate cognitive-stage growth. Piaget suggested that Americans may be preoccupied with a concern for developmental teaching programs that are designed to speed up the naturally unfolding stages of cognitive growth. Some recent programs of infant stimulation are examples of Piaget's concern. (5)

Americans with Disabilities Act (ADA)

Affirms the rights of all citizens with disabilities. The ADA of 1990 prohibits discrimination in employment practices, public services, privately operated settings, and telecommunications. ADA has been called the civil rights bill for people with disabilities. Together ADA and IDEA assure equality and protect the rights from birth to death of all persons with disabilities. (20)

Anal Stage

Second of Freud's psychosexual stages of development. During this stage, the child takes great pleasure, first in the act of defecating, and later in the act of withholding the fe-

ces. This stage usually takes place between the ages of 18 months and three years. The first part of this stage is called the *anal expulsive stage*, which later develops into the *anal retentive stage*. Freud says that the way in which the child is treated during this stage (toilet training, etc.) makes a permanent imprint on the later adult personality. (6)

Anastasi, Anne

A past president (1971) of the American Psychological Association, Anne Anastasi has written on a wide variety of subjects in the field, ranging from the psychology of art to the nature-nurture controversy. She is best known, however, for her work in statistics and test construction. A firm believer in IQ tests, she feels that discontinuing the IQ test would be like asking a physician to throw away the thermometer just because children who are ill register an undesirable deviation from the norm. In her 1958 paper "Heredity, Environment, and the Question 'How?'" Anastasi put the nature-nurture controversy in perspective. Instead of asking which component, heredity or environment, contributes more to the child's development, the better question is *how* heredity and environment interact in the development of behavioral differences. She also cites the importance of early experience on intellectual growth and development. (15)

Approval (Need for)

A social or acquired need for being accepted and positively evaluated by other persons. The need for approval is thought to be based on the individual's desire, learned in infancy, to be loved by his or her mother or primary caregiver. (18)

Archer, Sally

Developmental psychologist who has shown the importance of identity formation for teenage females, especially with regard to career development. Archer found that these females do not receive sufficient help and guidance to balance the problems of family responsibilities and careers. Too often females suffer from the costs of invisibility and the resultant delay in reaching an achieved identity. (6)

Arlin, Patricia

Developmental psychologist who has investigated the relationship between Piaget's stages and adult development. She suggests that there may be a fifth stage called *postformal operations*, which is characterized by abstract thought and problem finding. (5)

Artificial Intelligence

The simulation of human thinking by the use of a computer program. Programs attempt to parallel the human thought process. Artificial intelligence is based not only on our current understanding of how humans think but also on the hope that through the use of the program as a model our current understanding of thought processes will be increased. (11)

A/S Ratio

The A/S ratio is a concept developed by D. O. Hebb, the Canadian physiological psychologist. Hebb developed the ratio by comparing the amount of brain space devoted to association areas with the amount devoted to sensory areas. As he went up the phylogenetic ladder from rat to monkey to humans, Hebb found an ever-increasing A/S ratio. Rats, with their lower A/S ratio, are more sensory-bound, whereas humans, with a higher A/S ratio, are capable of far more varied and greater amounts of learning. (4)

Assimilation

Concept used by Jean Piaget in his theory of cognitive development. Assimilation is the process of taking within, or internalizing, one's environmental experience. Assimilation is used by Piaget in conjunction with the concept of accommodation. Piaget believes that assimilation is a spontaneous process on the part of the child. *See also* Accommodation. (5)

Attention Deficit Hyperactivity Disorder (ADHD)

A form of attention deficit characterized by distractibility, inability to sustain focused attention, and high levels of restlessness, fidgeting, and squirming and a low level of impulse control. (11)

Attention Deficits

A syndrome that results in an inability to focus attention or concentrate for an extended period. This condition is often, but not always, accompanied by hyperactivity. (11, 20)

Attitudes

Learned predispositions to respond either positively or negatively to persons, situations, or things. Attitudes carry a strong emotional component and therefore can never be neutral. When a negative attitude is generalized to include an entire group of people, it is called a *stereotype*. This can be destructive to the holder of the stereotype as well as to the group about which it is held. It can be especially destructive to the minority group member's self-image. (17)

Attribute-Treatment Interaction (ATI)

Framework, devised by David Hunt, that suggests that effective teaching should be a match between the developmental-stage characteristics of the learner and both the process and content of the teaching program. At different conceptual levels (CLs), students have different needs regarding the amount of structure a teacher should employ and how concrete or abstract concepts being presented should be. Effectiveness requires starting where the learner is, then gradually removing the structure and increasing the abstractness of the concepts being taught. The term *stage* in Hunt's system refers to the currently preferred learning style rather than to any sort of permanent classification. (13)

Attribution Theory

The term *attribution* refers to the explanation a person gives for his or her own or another person's actions or beliefs. An attribution based on internal factors is called a dispositional attribution, and one based on external factors is called a situational attribution. The fundamental attribution error occurs when we assign dispositional factors to the actions of others and situational factors to our own actions. (17)

Ausubel, David

Educational theorist who has contributed, among other things, the concept of advance organizers to a model of teaching. His system involves providing learners with a clear set of objectives in advance of the presentation so that the learners become oriented to the planned goals of the lesson. This model forms the basis for much of what is called the *direct instruction* approach. (12)

Authoritarian Leadership

Style of leadership in which the individual holding the leadership position retains all the decisionmaking power. (17)

Authoritative versus Laissez-Faire or Authoritarian Methods

William Damon, a developmental psychologist at Brown University, has translated much of the research on parental styles into an overall framework for understanding and implementing classroom discipline. Laissez-faire and authoritarian methods, though seemingly different on the surface, both typically lead to the same outcome, namely, a lack of self-control by the pupil. (18, 19)

Autokinetic Effect

A visual effect produced when a small but stationary pinpoint of light in an otherwise darkened room *appears* to move. Since the light remains physically stationary and since the perceived movement is only apparent, the autokinetic effect has been used to further our understanding of how group norms emerge. Experiments using the autokinetic effect have been performed by social psychologist Muzafer Sherif. (17)

Bandura, Albert

Originator of social learning theory, which suggests that learning may take place not just on the basis of straight reinforcement principles, but also as a result of a process called *modeling.* Bandura insists that people may learn new responses simply by observing the behavior of others. (10)

Bayley, Nancy

Developmental psychologist and author of the famous Berkeley Growth Study. Bayley was the first woman to win the American Psychological Association's Distinguished Scientific Contribution award. Bayley's major findings have been that (1) IQs are not constant; (2) IQ variability is greatest during the first few years of life; (3) intellectual growth may continue throughout life; and (4) the components of intellect change with age level. (4)

Becker, Howard

Investigator of the relationship between the social class of the teacher and pupil attitudes. He found that many teachers from the lower middle class had difficulty accepting students from either lower or higher socioeconomic levels.

Behavior Genetics

A subfield of psychology concerned with the effects of genotype on behavior. The behavior geneticist is interested in the effect of genetic differences or behavioral differences within a defined population. With animals the main method of study is that of selective breeding and/or the use of inbred strains. At the human level comparison studies of MZ twins with less genetically related individuals are typically the current methods of choice.

Behaviorism

A school of thought in psychology usually considered to have originated in the work and writings of John B. Watson. In 1913 Watson outlined the behaviorist position in his paper "Psychology as the Behaviorist Views It." Watson argued there against the use of introspection in gathering psychological data. He considered observable behavior the only valid data in psychology. According to Watson, any concepts, like mind or consciousness, that have mentalistic overtones must be purged from the field of psychology. The most famous recent representative of this tradition was Harvard University's B. F. Skinner. (8)

Behavior Modification

A system for changing behavior based on the principles of conditioning. The term *behavior modification* is usually applied either to the classroom or to a patient undergoing therapy. When desirable behavior is exhibited, it is followed by a reinforcing stimulus; when undesirable behavior is emitted, it is followed either by no reinforcement (extinction) or, less commonly, by punishment. It is important when using this system that (1) goals be defined precisely *and in behavioral terms* and that (2) the conditioning schedule be followed with absolute consistency. (10)

Berkowitz, Marvin

One of Kohlberg's students, who examined different methods of leading value-dilemma discussions. He found that effective discussion leaders combined support and challenge as well as indirect teaching methods. (7)

Big Five Personality Traits

The Big Five model of personality structure holds that the phenotypic (observable) personality can be categorized on the basis of only five broad dimensions: surgency, agreeableness, conscientiousness, emotional stability, and intellectance. (18)

Binet, Alfred (1857–1911)

Originator of psychology's first modern intelligence test (1905). In assembling his test, this French psychologist set up a series of intellectual tasks, as opposed to the sensorimotor tasks previously used by Sir Francis Galton. Binet also introduced the concept of mental age as the basis for scoring his later tests (1908). The original Binet test items were later used as the basis for the famous Stanford-Binet intelligence test (1916), published in the United States by Lewis M. Terman. The test was scored on the basis of the ratio between the test taker's mental age and chronological age. This ratio, multiplied by 100, is known as the *intelligence quotient*, or IQ. *See also* Intelligence Quotient; Stanford-Binet Test. (16)

Bloom, Benjamin S.

American educational psychologist and professor at the University of Chicago and Northwestern. He is most widely known for his work in two important areas in educational psychology:

1. Bloom sought to describe systematically the classroom teacher's educational goals, and methods for achieving those goals. This work is called his *taxonomy for educational objectives.*

2. Bloom also published the now-classic *Stability and Change in Human Characteristics* (1964), which outlined an early-experience position regarding intellectual growth. Bloom maintained that the positive effect of a beneficial environment on intellectual growth decreases as the children get older. Three-year-old children profit far more from enriching experiences than do seven- or eight-year-old children. (4)

Bonding

A process occurring between mother and child, seen by some to be similar to imprinting. Bonding requires direct physical contact between the mother and child and must occur within the baby's first three days of life. It produces a strong emotional attachment between the two. Failure to form this bond has been hypothesized as the cause for later episodes of child neglect and even abuse. (3)

Bornstein's Infant Intelligence Test

Intelligence test used on six-month-olds and based on how long it takes a baby to process information about moving stimuli. Marc Bornstein discovered significant correlations between infant test scores and the IQ scores on Wechsler scales taken four years later. (16)

Brainstorming

A technique for generating new ideas in which individuals get together in a group and are urged to interact freely and call out any idea, no matter how seemingly bizarre. Brainstorming is used in many businesses, especially in areas in which creativity is important, as in an advertising agency's mapping out a new campaign. The actual research on brainstorming, however, casts some doubt on its effectiveness with regard to both the number of new ideas and the quality of the ideas produced by the group. (17)

Bruner, Jerome S.

Researcher of such varied subjects as propaganda techniques, the effect of need on perception, and most important, how people obtain knowledge and how they develop intellectually. In 1960 Bruner founded Harvard's Center for Cognitive Studies, and although he didn't invent cognitive psychology, he went a long way toward making it systematic and consistent with the rules of science. Perhaps Bruner's most famous statement is that any subject can be taught effectively in some intellectually honest form to any child at any stage of development. He stresses discovery learning and communication at three levels: enactive, iconic, and symbolic. (9)

Cascade System

A dynamic system used to group special-education services on a continuum with the aim of providing handicapped children with an environment that incorporates the fewest possible restrictions. The ultimate goal of this system is to move special-education children toward regular services. The cascade system has seven different levels and was created by teaching expert Evelyn Deno. (20)

Case, Robbie

Developmental psychologist who has become the major contemporary researcher in cross-validating and extending the work of Piaget (through his research teams at Stanford and Toronto). His research includes cross-cultural studies, comparisons by gender, giftedness, and special education—all of which cut across intellectual, interpersonal, and social domains. (5)

Cattell, James McKeen (1860–1944)

A pioneer in the field of intelligence testing. Cattell, an American, studied both in Germany under Wilhelm Wundt and in England under Sir Francis Galton. He brought the message of European psychology back to the United States, and in 1888 he was appointed to the first professorship in psychology anywhere in the world. Cattell is credited with fathering the mental-testing movement in the United States, and in fact it was Cattell, in 1890, who first used the term *mental test.* (2)

Cell Assembly

Concept used by D. O. Hebb in describing cognitive growth. The cell assembly defines the action of a group of brain cells organized into a coherent unit and enabling the young child to learn at an ever-increasing rate. The child learns slowly and ploddingly when operating at the single-cell level, but after cell assemblies are formed in the brain, learning speed increases dramatically. (4)

Character Training

Education to develop character through inculcation and brainwashing. Research has shown that such education is ineffective; rather, character appears to develop in stages as more democratic and humane values are incorporated. Careful reviews show that many of the current methods of character education such as D.A.R.E., "Scared Straight," and moral lessons from literature seem to have no lasting positive effects on moral maturity. (7)

Charisma

Term used in describing a leader or a leadership trait or quality. An individual who has charisma is thought to possess a kind of animal magnetism or hypnotic appeal. The power of a charismatic leader is seen by some as being almost mystical in its spellbinding appeal. When a charismatic person enters a room, the room is supposed to be suddenly charged with excitement. (17)

Chomsky, Noam

American psychologist interested in cognitive growth through language development. Chomsky has severely criticized the typical American learning-theory explanation of language as the result of straight conditioning. Chomsky insists that children learn the use of language far more quickly than the conditioning theory can explain. Chomsky explains this rapid rate of language development on the basis of a built-in capacity for language acquisition. That is, a baby enters the world genetically prewired, or born with a biological readiness that directs the course of language development. (9)

Chromosome

Long, threadlike bits of protein. Each cell of the human body contains 23 pairs. Egg and sperm cells, however, carry only 23 individual chromosomes, or just half the number contained in other body cells. An infant receives half of its chromosomes from each parent at conception, 23 from the sperm cell and 23 from the egg cell, thus achieving the full complement of 23 pairs. (3)

Chunking

The grouping together of several separate items in order to aid in their recall. Remembering digits that have been grouped in threes is an example of chunking. It is easier to retrieve the number 103 than the separate numbers 1, 0, and 3. (11)

Clark, Kenneth B.

Noted black educator, psychologist, and professor at City College of New York. Clark's 1950 report on the effects of segregation in the schools was used extensively by the Supreme Court in the historic 1954 decision declaring segregation in public schools unconstitutional. Clark has worked and written in a wide variety of areas in the fields of educational and social psychology. (17)

Classical Conditioning

Term used to describe conditioning techniques introduced by Ivan Pavlov. It is the pairing of a conditioned stimulus with an unconditioned stimulus over long numbers of trials until the conditioned stimulus alone has the power to elicit the conditioned response. During the conditioning trials, the conditioned stimulus acts as a signal that the unconditioned stimulus will follow, and the organism thus eventually learns to respond to the conditioned stimulus alone. In Pavlov's basic experiment, a dog was conditioned to salivate at the sound of a tone. The tone was presented (conditioned stimulus), followed by meat powder (unconditioned stimulus), until the dog began salivating just at the tone. (8)

Cognitive Dissonance

Concept introduced by social psychologist Leon Festinger. Individuals prefer to maintain a state of equilibrium among their various attitudes, beliefs, and behavior. Inconsistency between thoughts and actions sets up within the individual a state of cognitive dissonance, an uncomfortable state that the individual attempts to resolve by changing either his or her actions or beliefs. It is far more comfortable, and thus desirable, from the individual's point of view to attain cognitive consonance over cognitive dissonance. (17)

Cognitive Learning

The view that learning is based on a restructuring of perceptions and thoughts occurring within the organism. This restructuring allows the learner to perceive new relationships, solve new problems, and gain understanding of a subject area. Cognitive-learning theorists stress the reorganization of one's perceptions in order to achieve understanding, as opposed to the conditioning theorists, who stress the importance of associations formed between stimuli and responses. Gestalt psychology has been oriented toward the cognitive view of learning. (8)

Cohesiveness

Concept introduced by social psychologist Leon Festinger. Cohesiveness describes those positive forces that hold a group together and prevent its deterioration. Cohesiveness is one of the few truly group concepts in social psychology. It can be thought of as the cement that binds the group together, or the attraction of the group for its members. Group cohesiveness can be increased by (1) friendly interaction, (2) cooperation, (3) increased group status, (4) an outside threat, or (5) democratic rather than authoritarian leadership. (17)

Collaborative Action Research

An approach to research that takes place in actual classrooms, where the teacher becomes both a participant and an observer. When problems arise such as in management or course content, the teacher engages in a sequence of planning, acting, observing, and replanning steps to solve the specific problem at hand. Teachers often work with colleagues and share decisionmaking. This is similar to the original John Dewey "project method" and scientific problemsolving methods in the natural setting of the classroom or school building. It has been shown to have beneficial effects on both teachers and their students by helping teachers become more reflective inquirers (e.g., theoretical practitioners). (14)

Competence Motivation

Theory developed by personality theorist Robert White. White feels that all humans, and even some animals, have a basic drive to achieve competence as a way of developing control over their environments. People have a need to be competent in some area. Of course, as competence increases, so too does enjoyment. Competence is a key concept for many educators and is viewed as being synonymous with personal mastery and self-direction. (6, 18)

Computer-Assisted Instruction (CAI)

Use of the computer, especially the microcomputer, as a "private tutor" constantly monitoring a student's progress and allowing a student to proceed at his or her own rate. The program, or software tutorial, may take a student through a discrete lesson unit and during its running allow many choices. A student's error, if it occurs, automatically triggers a program review of the material not fully comprehended. (10)

Concept Formation

In the information-processing model, the processing of data by identifying certain characteristics of incoming information and then organizing the information in such a way as to provide encoded meaning. (11)

Conceptual Level

Applied to teachers, David Hunt's concept that teachers process experience at different levels according to their stage of conceptual development and behave in the classroom accordingly. At the least complex level, stage A, teachers tend to view knowledge as fixed truth and pupils as passive memorizers of rote facts. At a more advanced level, stage B, teachers perceive their role as more interactive, and they emphasize a combination of goals, including promoting pupil development. Teachers functioning at the highest level, stage C, exhibit the broadest variety of teaching methods keyed specifically to pupil needs and their levels of understanding. *See also* Hunt, David. (13)

Concordance Rate

Term used in behavior genetics to denote the percentage of cotwins exhibiting a specific phenotypic trait. (3)

Concrete-Operations Stage

A stage of thinking, according to Jean Piaget, that is characteristic of the period from ages 7 to 11. At this stage thinking is based on specifics and literal-mindedness. The child using this mode of thought is objective and logical, but almost too literal-minded. The child wants facts and wants the facts to be specific, but cannot separate facts from hypotheses at this stage. (5)

Conditioned Reinforcement

Sometimes called *secondary reinforcement*, it describes the situation in which a previously neutral stimulus acquires reinforcing power by being repeatedly associated with a primary reinforcer. The sequence of events for establishing conditioned reinforcement is as follows: (1) response; (2)

neutral stimulus, such as a light or buzzer; (3) primary reinforcer, such as a pellet of food. In the classroom, conditioned reinforcers might be good grades, prizes, promotions, and generalized social approval. The use of tokens by behavior-modification proponents is another example of conditioned reinforcement at work in the classroom. (9)

Conditioned Response

Term used both in classical conditioning and in operant conditioning. In classical conditioning, the conditioned response is the response being elicited by the conditioned stimulus. The stronger the conditioning, the greater the magnitude of the conditioned response and the shorter its latency. In Pavlov's experiment the conditioned response was the dog's salivation to the tone.

In operant conditioning, since the response must precede the reinforcer, the conditioned response is defined not in terms of magnitude or latency, but in terms of either the rate of the response or its resistance to extinction. For example, a strongly conditioned operant will occur far more rapidly than one that has been only weakly conditioned. Also, a strongly conditioned operant will be far more difficult to extinguish. (8)

Conditioned Stimulus

In classical conditioning, the previously neutral stimulus takes on the power to elicit the response through association with an unconditioned stimulus. For this to occur, the conditioned stimulus must precede the unconditioned stimulus on enough occasions to cause the conditioned stimulus to serve as a signal that the unconditioned stimulus will follow. In Pavlov's experiment on conditioning the dog, the tone was used as the conditioned stimulus. The tone was consistently followed by the meat powder, until the dog began salivating to the tone alone. (8)

Conditioning

Process of learning whereby stimuli and responses become associated through training. There are two general types of conditioning, classical and operant. In classical conditioning a conditioned stimulus is presented, followed by an unconditioned stimulus. Conditioning is exhibited when the organism learns to respond to the conditioned stimulus alone. In operant conditioning the operant is allowed to occur and then is followed by a reinforcing stimulus. Operant conditioning is exhibited when the rate of responding increases over the original, preconditioned rate. (8)

Conduct Disorders

A psychiatric diagnosis that identifies the child whose behavior is overly aggressive (bullying, threatening, and physically abusive). These children impact the basic rights of other children in particular and/or society in general. Unless treated, this condition has been shown to remain stable for at least 30 years. (10)

Confluence Model

A theory of intelligence proposed by R. B. Zajonc that proposes a strong relationship between the number of children in a family and the family's overall intellectual level. The model predicts that the more children there are in a family and the closer together they are in age, the lower the IQs of all the children will be. (16)

Conformity

Term used in social psychology to describe the fact that individuals in group situations tend to behave in a uniform way. Group pressure acts on the individual to force him or her into acting in accord with the rules and norms of the group. Important studies in this area include: (1) Muzafer Sherif's study, in which individuals formed a common estimate of how far a light appeared to move (autokinetic effect); (2) Solomon Asch's study, in which a naive subject's estimate of the length of a line conformed to the group's estimate, even though the group was obviously wrong; and (3) Stanley Milgram's study, in which subjects who believed they were administering an electric shock to their lab partner were less apt to deliver high voltages when acting in a group situation than when acting alone. (17)

Congruence

One of the three necessary and sufficient conditions (the others being empathy and unconditional positive regard) for the promotion of learning, according to Carl Rogers. By congruence, Rogers means total and complete honesty. To promote learning, the teacher must be "real" and honest in dealing with students. Teachers can't go through the motions of liking students. A teacher without congruence should probably try a different line of work. (12)

Connected Teaching

Based largely on the work of Belenky, Clinchy, Goldberger, and Tarule, connected teaching emphasizes the importance of personal experience, cooperation, consensus, and a supportive classroom atmosphere as ways of enhancing growth. In many ways it is similar to the Carl Rogers model of teaching. (13)

Conservation

Term used by Jean Piaget in his theory of cognitive growth and illustrated by the idea that water from a tall, thin glass can be poured into a short, wide glass *without a change in the amount of water involved*. According to Piaget, the concept of conservation is typically acquired by a child reaching the stage of concrete operations or operational thinking (at about the age of seven). (5)

Constructivism

Theory that learners construct knowledge from experience. The child's mind is seen as being like an erector set, and meaning is built in increasingly complex ways. Meaning is not given to the learner but is instead created by the learner. (1)

Correlation

A numerical statement of the relationship among two or more variables. A correlation is said to be positive when high scores on one variable are associated with high scores on another variable, and when low scores on the first variable are associated with low scores on the second. A correlation is said to be negative when high scores on the first variable are associated with low scores on the second, and vice versa. Correlations range in value from +1.00 to –1.00. Correlations that fall around zero indicate no consistent relationship among the measured variables. In psychological research a correlation is usually based on taking several response measures of *one group of subjects*. (15)

Criterion-Referenced Test

A test scored on the basis of how an individual's performance compares to an arbitrarily fixed standard of performance. Most teacher-made tests are criterion-referenced. (15)

Critical Periods

Concept used by Konrad Lorenz and other ethologists to define certain age periods in the organism's life in which learning can occur more easily than in any other age period. For example, Lorenz found that goslings imprint on moving stimuli only between hatching and an age of about 30 hours.

The concept of critical periods was also used in de-scribing human growth and development by Myrtle McGraw in her study of the twins Johnny and Jimmy. The critical-period hypothesis is usually used by psychologists who favor an early-experience position on growth and development. *See also* Imprinting. (4)

Cross-Categorical, or Noncategorical, Special Education

Because most of the categories in the high-incidence areas of special education, particularly SLD, SED, and MR, are so problematic and also because there are few unique teaching strategies for students in these high-incidence categories, a new system of classification has emerged. Instead of separate designations, a single broad category is now being used that includes all students experiencing low levels of achievement. It is now one of the fastest-growing specialties in the training of special educators. (20)

Curiosity Motivation

An inborn motive that is satisfied not by food, drink, or praise but simply by getting the answer. Harry Harlow feels the curiosity drive is fundamental and primary in monkeys and humans. (Why else would a child take apart a watch just to find out what makes it tick?) Daniel Berlyne, another theorist who posits the existence of curiosity motivation, believes that there is an optimum level of curiosity arousal that is a function of brain excitation. (18)

Damon, William

Educational psychologist who has studied the process of peer interactions, particularly at the elementary school level. He suggests that these relationships are important foundations to the development of empathy and moral judgment. This work forms an important basis for understanding the teacher's role in promoting such growth through *authoritative discipline*. (7, 19)

Darling-Hammond, Linda

Professor of education and codirector of the National Center for Restructuring Education, Schools, and Teaching (NCREST) at Teachers College, Columbia University. She is outspoken on policy issues related to teaching quality and educational equity. She is a member of the National Academy of Education and the National Board for Professional Teaching Standards and is past president of the American Educational Research Association. Her research spans the areas of teacher evaluation, professional development schools, authentic assessment, and restructuring for the twenty-first century. As executive director of the National Commission on Teaching and America's Future she published *What Matters Most: Teaching for America's Future* (1996). (14)

Deciles

Points that divide a distribution into tenths. Each decile represents ten percentiles, such that the 1st decile represents the tenth percentile and the 9th decile the ninetieth percentile. (15)

Declarative Memory

Storage of long-term memory (LTM) information about names, dates, and past events—anything that can be put into words and "declared." Declarative memory has both semantic and episodic components. (11)

Democratic High School Model

A model in which pupils and teachers together are responsible for making and keeping the rules. Rules are enforced through town meetings and student-controlled discipline committees. Students obey the rules out of an understanding of principles of justice and the meaning of democratic community rights and responsibilities. Research illustrates that the students in the democratic high school model not only learn their academic lessons, but also learn to care for one another. The quality of peer relationships and student-to-teacher relationships make such a difference that discipline problems are reduced to a minimal level. (19)

Democratic Leadership

Style of leadership in which the decisionmaking power is shared by members of a group. (17)

Deno, Evelyn

Eminent theorist and practitioner in the field of special education. She was among the first to call for alternative classification procedures for children with disabilities. She focused upon the fundamental rights and needs for children with disabilities and their positive educational potential. She developed the cascade system of assessment of students with disabilities. (20)

Deoxyribonucleic Acid (DNA)

Rather large organic molecules located in the chromosomes (which lie in the nucleus of every one of the body's cells). These molecules act to direct the body's growth and development. DNA has been called the building block of genetic organization and, along with RNA, makes up the chemical composition of the gene. Geneticists say that DNA acts as a blueprint for the formation of certain enzymes that guide the development of the organism. The coded information stored in the DNA molecule is transmitted to other parts of the cell by the RNA molecules. (3)

Deutch, Morton

Social psychologist who has studied, among other things, the issue of cooperation versus competition. Deutch believes that schools should be less competitively organized and that students will reap significant benefits from more cooperatively managed classrooms. (18)

Developmental Method of Discipline

A method of classroom control that matches discipline to the developmental stage of the pupils. Depending upon the stage, the teacher may use physical restraint, behavior modification, peer pressure, contracts, or democratic decisionmaking. There are both humane and inhumane ways of implementing each of these techniques. (19)

Developmental Model

In teaching, the model that suggests that the teacher's role is to stimulate the natural growth process of all pupils. The developmental framework assumes that each child has a basic learning potential and that the teacher's role is to arrange the most appropriate learning environment in order to nurture that growth. Since by definition teaching cannot be value-free, a goal for the professional development of each teacher is to become increasingly reflective about teaching while "doing." Teachers can then reduce the amount of pupil stereotyping and improve their attitudes. (14)

Developmental Stage

A growth and/or behavior organization category that satisfies the following four criteria: (1) it is qualitatively different from the preceding stage; (2) it represents a new and more comprehensive system of organization; (3) it occurs in a maturationally fixed sequence; and (4) it is age-related within general confines. (5)

Deviation IQ

A technique for measuring intelligence based on calculating the percentage of individuals in each age category achieving a given score and then assessing how far a certain individual's score deviates from the mean score for the age group in which he or she belongs. The IQ score is thus determined on the basis of age standards and is considered to be norm-referenced. (16)

Dewey, John (1859–1952)

The philosopher and psychologist best known for his educational philosophy of "learning by doing." At the time of this pronouncement by Dewey, American education was still in the grip of the formal-discipline theorists, educators who were convinced that children should sit quietly in a classroom and "strengthen their minds" through the study of a classical curriculum. Dewey attempted to change this traditional method of education by creating learning environments in which children engaged actively in learning. To some extent, Dewey anticipated the ideas of Jean Piaget and the open classroom. Dewey's curriculum came to be known as *progressive education* and was incorrectly translated by many into meaning totally unguided education.

Before moving to Columbia University, where he spent most of his professional career, Dewey was involved with the functionalist school of psychology at the University of Chicago. (1)

Disability Category

A physical, mental, emotional, or other condition recognized by Public Law 94-142. The law specifies 12 categories and says that education must be provided for all those in these categories until graduation from high school or until the age of 21. Recent study has shown that about 93 percent of the disability conditions are grouped into four high-incidence types: (1) specific learning disabilities, (2) speech or language impairments, (3) mental retardation, and (4) serious emotional disturbance. All other disability conditions total just over 6 percent and include multiple disabilities, hearing impairments, orthopedic impairments, deaf-blindness, visual impairments, autism, traumatic brain injury, and other health impairments. The main difficulty with this classification is that the validity and accuracy of the diagnosis is lowest in the areas of high incidence, and vice versa. (20)

Discipline Strategies: The Four Questions

In assessing the different levels of discipline used in the classroom, it has been suggested that four basic questions should be asked: who makes the rules, who keeps the rules, how are the rules enforced, and what are the reasons for student compliance? (19)

Discovery Learning

Term used by Jerome Bruner to describe a form of learning that results not from rote memorization or conditioning but from the active exploration of alternatives on the part of the learner. Bruner maintains that the learning attained through discovery is more meaningful and long-lasting than that from memorization. (9)

Discrimination

A term used by learning theorists to describe the ability of an organism to respond to one stimulus and not to respond to another similar stimulus. Ivan Pavlov first demonstrated this phenomenon by conditioning dogs to salivate to a given conditioned stimulus—say, a 2,000-cycle tone—while not salivating to a similar stimulus—say, a 1,900-cycle tone. This was accomplished by continuing to reinforce (with the unconditioned stimulus) the presentation of the 2,000-cycle tone, while withholding reinforcement of responses following presentation of the 1,900-cycle tone.

B. F. Skinner has identified essentially the same phenomenon in the area of operant conditioning. Skinner reinforces a response that occurs in the presence of a given stimulus (S^D), while extinguishing the response when it occurs in the presence of the other similar stimulus (S^Δ). (9)

Dispositions of Thoughtfulness

A major recent effort in educational goals has been to improve the thinking skills of students. From a developmental perspective, such skills can be conceptualized as representing higher-order dispositions of thoughtfulness. They can be seen as a synthesis of formal operations (Piaget), understanding democratic principles (Kohlberg), constructed knowledge (Belenky), and critical thinking (Glaser). The dispositions are generic and involve problemsolving and problem posing. (13)

Distribution

A statistical term defined as the arrangement of measured scores in order of magnitude. Listing scores in distribution form allows the researcher to notice general trends more readily than the unordered set of raw scores would allow. A frequency distribution is a listing of each score achieved, together with the number of individuals receiving each score. In graphs of frequency distributions, the scores appear on the horizontal axis (abscissa) and the frequency of occurrence appears on the vertical axis (ordinate). (15)

Divided Attention

The ability to attend to more than one source of incoming information, such as when a child studies with the radio on. (11)

Dizygotic (DZ) Twins

Fraternal twins resulting from eggs that are fertilized at the same time but that are not identical. Thus, DZ twins are no more alike genetically than any other set of brothers and sisters. (3)

Dominant Gene

Gregor Mendel's term for the unit of heredity whose characteristics are expressed when paired with a like gene or with a recessive gene. Recessive gene characteristics are not expressed unless paired with a like gene. (3)

Drives

Parts of the motivational cycle that are really just activated needs. Drives always result in some observable change in behavior. (18)

Dyslexia

A form of learning disability characterized by what is literally *word blindness,* which prevents the child from developing a reading level that would by typical for his or her IQ level and age. Dyslexia may be acquired, for example, either from a brain injury or from poor educational experiences, or it may possibly be inherited. (11, 20)

Early-Experience Position

A position taken by researchers and theorists who stress the crucial importance of an individual's early environmental experiences in determining later adult characteristics. The early-experience proponents typically argue that the child goes through various periods when certain cognitive and other skills can best be learned. Attempting to develop these skills either too early or too late can result in wasted effort on the part of the teacher and possible permanent damage to the student. (4)

Ebbinghaus, Hermann (1850–1909)

The father of the experimental study of learning. Ebbinghaus spent many hours memorizing long lists of nonsense syllables. Later he would relearn the lists, and he mea-

sured his retention capacity on the basis of how much more quickly he could learn the lists the second time. This technique is known as the method of savings. He drew two major conclusions from this work: (1) forgetting occurs at an uneven rate, most of what is forgotten being lost very quickly; and (2) in learning new material it is more efficient to space the practice sessions rather than mass them together. (8)

Elaborative Rehearsal

Technique used for consolidating long-term memory (LTM) information based on expanding, embellishing, and/or relating new information to other items or concepts already stored. (11)

Elkind, David

Researcher who has demonstrated the difference between concrete and formal operations in thinking. In discussing Stonehenge, for example, concrete thinkers are more impressed by a long list of facts than a theory in deciding whether Stonehenge was a fort or a temple. Elkind has also described the extreme forms of egocentric thinking, such as the imaginary audience and the personal fable that young adolescents often use. (5)

Embryo

The second stage of prenatal development, which for the human begins at two weeks after conception and lasts until about eight weeks after conception. During this stage the heart begins beating, and sex organs, hands and feet, and all the internal organs are formed. At the end of the embryonic stage, the organism may be clearly identified as human. (3)

Empathy

The ability to realize, understand, and appreciate another person's feelings, or the ability to experience and "feel" the world through another person's eyes. Also, one of the three necessary and sufficient conditions for the promotion of learning, according to Carl Rogers. The other two are unconditional positive regard and congruence. (12)

Enactive Representation

Stage of cognitive development and method of communication introduced by Jerome Bruner. During this first stage of development, the child thinks and communicates with "wordless messages." Young children understand things best at the action level: A chair is to sit on, a spoon is to eat with, and so on. Even adults may, and perhaps should, revert to this level of thinking when learning a new skill, especially a motor skill. An adept ski or tennis instructor often will ask the student (child or adult) to imitate his or her actions physically, rather than just teach at the verbal level. (9)

Encoding

In the information processing model, the creation of memory traces, or abstractions, based on the salient features of the incoming information. The encoded information, which represents the external object or event, can thus be used for storage. (11)

Engram

Term used, usually by the physiological psychologists, to denote the hypothesized physical location of memory. (11)

Epigenetic Principle

Erik Erikson's notion that human beings have an inherent or inborn tendency to grow. It represents the ground plan for personality development through the psychosexual stages he describes. Each stage involves the resolution of opposite tendencies; successful resolution involves acquisition of a sequence of virtues—hope, will, purpose, competence, and fidelity—from birth through adolescence. (6)

Episodic Memory

Information contained in long-term memory (LTM) that holds past episodes in one's life and is stored in the form of images. (11)

Equilibration

Term used by Jean Piaget to describe the motivational force for arriving at an adjustment between the twin concepts of assimilation and accommodation. Equilibration makes it possible for the child to go on to new, higher-level assimilation and accommodation. (5)

Erikson, Erik H. (1902–1996)

German-born personality theorist who studied under Sigmund Freud at the Psychoanalytic Institute in Vienna. Erikson was in the United States since 1936, and he taught human development at Harvard University. Although his theory of personality development has its roots in psycho-

analytic theory, it is definitely not just "warmed-over" Freud. His theory describes stages of personality development extending throughout life, though there is special emphasis on childhood. The focus is always on the normal and healthy personality. Erikson sees development progressing through eight stages, each typifying a particular crisis. Through the attempt to resolve these crises, the healthy personality emerges. (The stages are sequential, and when a healthy adjustment to a particular crisis does not occur, it is even more difficult to resolve a similar crisis at a later stage.) The mature personality should have a sense of identity, and although the climax of this search occurs during adolescence (identity crisis), residues of the conflict can emerge throughout life. (6)

Ethology

The study of the behavior of organisms in the organism's natural habitat. Unlike experimental psychologists, who often study animal behavior in artificial, laboratory situations, ethologists (like Konrad Lorenz) study behavior in the animal's natural environment. Ethologists have introduced such terms as *innate releasing mechanism* and *imprinting* into the working vocabulary of psychologists. *See also* Lorenz, Konrad. (2)

Extinction

Term used by conditioning theorists to describe a forgetting process in which the stimulus-response associations are eroded. In classical conditioning, extinction occurs when the conditioned stimulus is presented without being followed by the unconditioned stimulus. Extinction is then defined as occurring when the magnitude of the conditioned response returns to zero. In operant conditioning extinction occurs when the conditioned operant is allowed to occur without being followed by a reinforcing stimulus. Extinction is defined as occurring when the rate of responding returns to its preconditioned level (operant level). (8)

Extrinsic Motives

Motives that are driven by external reinforcers. Such motives are often considered necessary in order to initiate the learning process. *See also* Intrinsic motives. (18)

Factor Approach

A mathematically based model of intelligence in which correlational statistical methods are used for determining the components of intelligence. Among the most widely known factor approaches are those of Charles Spearman (two factors), Louis Thurstone (seven factors), and J. P. Guilford (120 factors). (16)

Fear of Success

A basic fear that may be due to the perceived unpleasant side effects brought about by being overly successful. Women appear to be especially prone to this condition as a result of a conscious or unconscious belief that success may make them appear to lose their femininity. (18)

Fetus

The third stage of prenatal development, lasting from the eighth week after conception until birth. The fetus is definitely a behaving organism, and its behavior can be studied. (3)

Flanders, Ned

American educational psychologist known primarily for his work on defining teacher effectiveness. Using the concepts of direct and indirect teaching, Flanders found that despite various subject matters, different grade levels, and different school settings, teachers using indirect teaching styles were producing higher levels of student learning than were direct teachers. (12)

Flashbulb Memory

A person's extremely vivid recollection of an event or situation that was etched into long-term memory because the individual was in a highly charged emotional state. (11)

Formal Discipline (Theory)

Early educational theory that stressed a curriculum designed to discipline the mind. The theory rested on the assumption that the mind was like a muscle and must be systematically exercised until it became so strong it could learn and understand almost any new material. Subjects such as logic, Latin, and Greek were included in the curriculum not because they were thought to have any immediate practical use, but because they were thought to strengthen the mind. The theory of formal discipline originated in ancient Greece and remained in vogue until the early twentieth century. It was finally challenged by three psychologists, William James, E. L. Thorndike, and Charles Judd, whose independent studies in the area of positive transfer refuted the formal discipline position. *See also* Transfer. (1)

Formal-Operations Stage

A stage of cognitive development, according to Jean Piaget, occurring during early adolescence. The period of formal operations (11 to 16 years) is the last of Piaget's stages and is characterized by the youth's ability to develop full, formal patterns of thinking based on abstract symbolism. The youth is able to reason things out logically at the abstract level, develop symbolic meanings, and generalize to other situations. This is the highest level of thinking and, according to Piaget, must await the maturation of certain structures in the brain for its full development. (5)

Four-Way Agenda of Teaching

The four elements that are always interacting during the process of education. They include (1) student characteristics, (2) the subject matter, (3) teaching strategies, and (4) teacher characteristics. (1)

Frank, Lawrence K. (1890–1968)

The researcher who reviewed a wide variety of cross-cultural methods of childrearing and found that too often adults attempt to remold children as if they were midget-sized adults. (6)

Freud, Sigmund (1856–1939)

Perhaps psychology's single most famous figure, he originated the school of thought called *psychoanalysis*. A physician in Vienna, Freud treated patients with "nervous disorders" during the day and wrote down his thoughts and observations at night. From these observations and his own genius for speculating came the theory of psychoanalysis. It stated that all behavior is motivated and that the motives are usually hidden from the individual, thus causing much behavior to appear to be irrational. The basic source of energy for these motives is the libido, or pleasure-seeking drive. Freud described the personality as being composed of three structural components: id, ego, and superego. Most human anxiety results from inner conflict among these three components. Adult personality disorders can always be traced to and found to be directly caused by childhood trauma and anxiety. *See also* Psychoanalytic theory. (6)

Frustration-Aggression Hypothesis

Neil Miller and John Dollard's theory to explain aggressive behavior. The hypothesis states that aggression results from environmental causes. When a person is frustrated, or experiences goal blockage, aggressive behavior results. (17)

Fuller, Frances (1918–1975)

Educational researcher who created a framework for tracing the type and level of personal concern exhibited by teachers during their early experiences in the classroom. Among other things, she outlined three general levels of concern: self, management, and impact. (14)

Functional Autonomy

Concept introduced by Gordon Allport and used to explain the great number of human motives for which no biological needs seem present. A means to an end becomes an end in itself, and an acquired motive comes to function independently (autonomously). The resulting motive comes to have a life of its own and is no longer dependent on its biological base. (18)

Furth, Hans

A leading contemporary Piagetian theorist interested in the interaction between "new" learning and "old" learning. He used the example of the young German boy and the church that looked like a house to point to what he called a *knowledge disturbance*. He traced the process of such knowledge disturbances to show how a child gradually develops more complex cognitive structures to take in new and strange information. (5)

Gage, Nate

One of the first educational researchers to accumulate a series of studies on teacher effectiveness. He created the first scientific basis for the art of teaching and showed that different modes work better at the secondary than at the elementary level. (12)

Galloway, Charles

One of the first researchers to study teaching from the nonverbal perspective of body language. He demonstrated that clusters of teacher nonverbal behaviors either facilitate or impair student learning so that teacher actions in the classroom may speak louder than words. (12)

Galton, Francis (1822–1911)

Considered the "father of intelligence testing," Galton put together the first series of tests designed to measure intellectual ability. Although his tests seem somewhat naive by modern standards, his emphasis on the relationship between sensory ability and intellect foreshadows much of today's research on the importance of sensory stimulation in determining cognitive growth. Galton assumed that intelligence was dependent on the quality of the human sensory apparatus, and so his tests measured such abilities as reaction time, visual and auditory range, and sensory acuity. Galton firmly believed that one's sensory apparatus was largely inherited. Thus, the testing movement, from its very inception, sided with nature in the nature-nurture debate. Galton emphasized individual differences and, more than any other person, set psychology on the road to quantifying its data. (2)

Gardner, Howard

Psychologist and intelligence expert who has proposed that intelligence, rather than being made up of a single, unitary, underlying factor, is really composed of a variety of different traits and talents. He suggests that there are at least eight different intelligences: linguistic, logicomathematical, spatial, musical, bodily-kinesthetic, interpersonal, intrapersonal, and naturalistic. He has recently announced that a ninth trait may be added, to be called "existential." (16)

Gender Equity Testing

Since some researchers feel that there still seem to be gender-based differences in a number of standardized ability and aptitude tests (for example, on the SAT, females score lower on the math section that do males), test makers should compensate for this difference by setting up separate scoring systems based on gender. (15)

Gene

The fundamental unit of analysis in genetics. The gene is a tiny particle that contains hereditary information. Genes are located in the chromosomes of each of the body's cells and are composed of rather large organic molecules called *nucleic acids*. (3)

Genetics

The study of the rules and lawful relationships of heredity. Geneticists are interested in how inherited characteristics are transmitted from generation to generation. They study both the continuity and the variation of traits across generations. The first studies in genetics were those of Gregor Mendel (1860s), who determined that the color of flowers could be predicted from one generation to the next. Thomas Hunt Morgan (1910s) studied the fruit fly and suggested that genes are arranged in the chromosomes in an ordered sequence. James Watson and Francis Crick won the Nobel Prize in 1962 for their pioneering work on genetic composition. A subfield in genetics, called *behavior genetics,* is of special interest to psychologists, since it studies the effects of genotype on behavior. *See also* Behavior genetics. (3)

Genotype

The genetic properties of the organism, often latent (as opposed to the phenotype, which is always expressed). A brown-eyed individual may carry a gene for blue eyes (genotype), but since the gene for brown eyes is dominant over the gene for blue eyes, that particular genotype would not be expressed. (3)

Gestalt Psychology

A school of thought maintaining that the organized whole, configuration, or totality of psychological experience should be the proper object of study. Founded in Germany by Max Wertheimer in the early 1900s, gestalt psychology's first interest was in the field of perception. Later, under Wolfgang Kohler's direction, studies were done in the area of learning and, under Kurt Lewin's direction, in the area of motivation. Gestalt psychologists tend to emphasize cognitive processes in the study of learning. They stress that true understanding occurs only through the reorganization of ideas and perceptions, not through memorization or conditioning. *See also* Wertheimer, Max. (8)

Gilligan, Carol

Researcher who has charged that Lawrence Kohlberg's stage theory of moral development and his scoring system are biased against women. Extensive reviews of the research literature, however, have cast substantial doubt on her position. (7)

Goddard, Henry H. (1866–1957)

Early psychologist and strong hereditarian who researched the Kallikak family and concluded that intelligence was as directly controlled by heredity as eye color. Goddard studied at Clark University under G. Stanley Hall and was the first psychologist to translate the Binet intelligence test into English. (2)

Great-Leader Theory

Theory that leadership is a function of personal traits rather than of the social situation. Great leaders possess just the right blend of looks, personality traits, and intellect to be almost automatically thrust into power roles, regardless of the times in which they live. (17)

Greene, Maxine

A philosopher of education who conceptualizes the teacher's role as a "stranger"—that is, he or she is to be with pupils in the classroom but also apart from them in order to nurture their growth toward freedom. Greene is the leading exponent of the positive existential theory of educational practice. Self-direction and democratic values are her dual goals for teaching and learning. (1)

Group Dynamics

A subfield of social psychology that studies the processes that create and maintain group life. Group dynamics has as its goals the systematic understanding of group functioning, the discovery of general laws concerning group properties, and the application of those laws to enhance group life. Generally, there are two broad positions within the field of group dynamics—the basic research wing and the applied wing. (17)

Group Tests of Intelligence

Tests sometimes called "paper-and-pencil tests" and designed to measure large groups of individuals at a single sitting. Originally devised during World War I and called the Army Alpha test, the group test became immediately popular because of its ease of administration and low cost. Many psychologists believe the group tests to have less validity than the individually administered tests. (16)

Guilford, J. P.

A specialist in the area of statistics and measurement theory, Guilford has constructed, through the use of factor analysis, a model of the "structure of intellect." Guilford concluded that intelligence is not just a single trait but is made up of a series of distinctly different modes of thought. He has grouped similar modes together into appropriate categories, and his famous phrase "the three faces of intellect" suggests that intelligence can be separated into three categories: operation, content, and product. Each of these three categories contains a further series of dimensions. So far, he has identified 70 separate traits of intelligence (out of a possible 120 traits provided for by his model). Among the traits identified so far are those responsible for what is usually called creativity. (16)

Guthrie, Edwin R. (1886–1959)

Behaviorist and learning theorist in the tradition of John B. Watson. Guthrie believed that all learning could be explained on the basis of a single law—the law of contiguity:

Learning resulted from the contiguous association of stimuli and responses. He also believed that forgetting was entirely the result of retroactive inhibition. (8)

Haberman, Martin

Investigator who examined the variety of teaching strategies that research has found to be effective with mainstreamed children. He concluded that between 75 and 85 percent of the time, teachers should use regular teaching strategies that are effective with all children. There is only a very small body of highly specialized teaching methods specifically appropriate for special-education children. (20)

Harlow, Harry F.

An American psychologist who has spent most of his professional career at the primate lab of the University of Wisconsin. Harlow's research, usually on rhesus monkeys, has shed light on many important topics in psychology. Perhaps his three most famous studies were on (1) surrogate mothers—in which frightened young monkeys preferred cloth-covered, cuddly surrogates to wire-framed surrogates that delivered food; (2) learning sets—in which monkeys solved oddity problems by developing solution rules or strategies rather than on the basis of either insight or the slow accumulation of stimulus-response associations; and (3) curiosity drive—in which monkeys exhibited a motive to manipulate novel items in their environment despite the fact that no primary reinforcement was presented. (18)

Hartshorne, Hugh (1885–1967)

Researcher who, together with Mark May, studied the process of value inculcation with a large sample of children in the 1920s. The results exploded the myth that values could be ingrained in children. Hartshorne and May found almost no relationship between character-training programs and how children behaved in tempting situations. (7)

Head Start: Perry Preschool Program

A longitudinal study of the effects of Head Start, a government-funded preschool program designed to enhance the intellectual potential of disadvantaged children. Measures were taken on 19-year-olds who as children had been in the Head Start program, and these were compared with measures taken on a control group who had not attended Head Start. The results for this particular Head Start program showed a variety of positive effects, ranging from an increase in academic achievement to a decrease in criminal activity. (4)

Hebb, Donald O. (1904–1985)

Canadian physiological psychologist who, in *Organization of Behavior* (1949), revolutionized psychological thought, especially in the United States. In this work Hebb dared to infer the existence of some possible physiological correlates of behavior. He stated that there was a relationship between intelligence and the way brain cells are organized. This organization occurs first at the level of cell assemblies, then as phase sequences, and finally in the total organization of the brain cells. Hebb also proposed a distinction between Intelligence A and Intelligence B, the former being one's innate potential, and the latter, one's present ability level on the intellectual growth continuum. *See also* A/S ratio; Cell assembly. (4)

Helms, Janet

Contemporary African-American theorist who has created a system outlining the phases of racial identity formation: pre-encounter, encounter, immersion/emersion, and internalization. (6)

Heritability

The proportion of the total variability of a given trait in a population that is due to genetic as opposed to environmental factors. Heritability is expressed as a value running between 1.00 and zero. Thus, regarding measured intelligence, if all the variation in IQ scores in a given population were due to genetic factors, the heritability of IQ would be 1.00. If all the variability were due to environmental factors, the heritability would be zero. The concept of heritability applies only to a particular population of a single generation under one set of environmental conditions. (16)

Hidden Agenda

Basic teacher attitudes toward the instructional process, perceptions of students, and self-knowledge that have been found to have a major influence on student learning. The influence can be either positive or negative. (14)

Higher-Order Thinking

Related to formal operational thought, postconventional moral thinking, and categories of analysis, synthesis, and evaluation. Teaching strategies like scaffolding, issue-based unit planning, and connected teaching can help teachers focus on the goal of students' higher-order thinking. (13)

Holophrase

Between about 12 and 18 months of age, the child will begin using the "holophrase," a single word to express a whole phrase. For example, "down" can mean "Don't keep holding me, put me down," or "I want to go downstairs," or "I want to get down out of the car," and so on. (3)

Homozygosity

An organism (diploid) that carries identical alleles at one or several genetic sites. (3)

Horner, Matina S.

Professor at Harvard University and then president of Radcliffe College. Horner achieved almost instant recognition in the area of the psychology of women's attitudes and motives. She contends that society often conditions women both to expect and to want to fail. Since motivational differences between the sexes are a result of social pressures, educators must revise their ideas, practices, and policies concerning young women in schools and colleges. (18)

Human Genome Project

Research effort whose goal is to discover the exact genetic locations of a wide variety of human traits and conditions. (3)

Hunt, David

Researcher who, in applying developmental concepts to teachers and pupils, classified both groups according to conceptual level of development (CL). Hunt found that pupils' learning styles varied by CL stage according to preferences for the amount of structure provided. He also found certain teaching patterns (labeled A, B, and C) that were reflective of the CL stages of teachers. Teaching effectiveness was partly defined as the ability to "read and flex" with pupils and was correlated particularly with the higher conceptual levels. (13)

Hunter, Madeline

Theorist who outlined a systematic approach to lesson planning. Hunter suggested a sequence of (1) anticipatory set, (2) stated objectives, (3) input, (4) modeling, (5) checking, (6) guided practice, and (7) independent practice. It is not necessary to use all these steps, but independent practice should be used as a guide to assessing the quality of the final product and modifying a plan. (13)

Hydraulic Model of Assessment

Term used by Maynard Reynolds to refer to shifts in special-education classifications for political or economic reasons rather than on the basis of any valid assessment. The students labeled as emotionally disturbed increased by 57 percent over 18 years, while those labeled mentally retarded declined by 38 percent. (20)

Icon

The visual image of a stimulus held in the sensory register for only a brief duration. (11)

Iconic Representation

Jerome Bruner's second stage of cognitive growth and mode of communication, the first stage being the enactive level. At the iconic level, objects become conceivable without resorting to muscular action. The child can now visualize an object or concept. He or she possesses an image that no longer depends on action. The use of pictures and diagrams illustrates the iconic mode of communication. (9)

Imprinting

A special form of learning that is acquired early in life, usually during a very specific time interval; that is triggered by a releasing stimulus; and that is not reversible. Konrad Lorenz demonstrated this phenomenon by presenting himself as a moving stimulus to a group of newly hatched goslings. The goslings then imprinted on Lorenz himself and followed him around as though he were the mother goose. *See also* Critical periods; Lorenz, Konrad. (2)

Inclusion

Placement of persons with disabilities within the mainstream of society. Children with disability conditions are not placed in special classes but are "included" in regular classrooms. Inclusion of students with disabilities in regular classrooms has been shown to result in positive academic and social learning. The success of inclusion depends upon the ability of teachers to learn to become more responsive to the fundamental needs of all children. Inclusion depends upon collaborative problemsolving in which all members of a school and community are working together, problemsolving together, and supporting each other to provide higher-quality teaching that is increasingly responsive to diversity and to the individual needs of all students. (20)

Individual Differences

The fact, first noted scientifically by Sir Francis Galton, that people tend to differ on a whole host of measured traits. Investigators disagree about the causes of these variations in abilities, traits, and performance measures, but there is no doubt about their existence. (15)

Individualized Education Plan (IEP)

A plan of instruction mandated by Public Law 94-142 for all children classified in any category of special education. A team establishes a series of educational goals and timetables for each child. The plan is reviewed on a regular basis. At each point in the child's schooling, he or she must be placed in the least restrictive environment that is consistent with achievable educational attainments. This may vary from a regular classroom to other environments that offer much greater structure, such as a self-contained special class or even a special residence. (20)

Individualized Transition Plan (ITP)

By law, at age 16 an Individual Transition Plan needs to be developed with each person with a disability. The ITP needs to cover education, recreation, housing, employment, and community issues. The emphasis is on the transition period from school to work for individuals with disabilities. (20)

Individuals with Disabilities Education Act (IDEA)

The successor to Public Law 94-142. Enacted in 1992, IDEA ensures that all people from infancy to age 21 are guaranteed appropriate identification, assessment of educational needs, individualized program planning, procedural (due-process) safeguards, education in the least restrictive alternative that meets the child's needs, and nondiscrimination. (20)

Inductive Fallacy

An error in logic resulting from overgeneralizing on the basis of too few observations. The inductive fallacy results when one assumes that all members of a class have a certain characteristic because one member of that class has it.

It would be fallacious to assume that all Mongolians are liars on the basis of having met one Mongolian who was a liar. (15)

Information Processing

Theory of learning and remembering that is based on the computer as a model. Information is seen as flowing into and within the organism. The sense organs respond to incoming information, and it is passed along and encoded in the memory and nervous system. The encoded information may then be stored and processed and finally retrieved and acted on. As with the computer, there is information input, storage and/or processing, and output. (11)

Innate Releasing Mechanism (IRM)

Reflexive stimulus-response mechanism involving responses to certain specific environmental stimuli. Used currently instead of the discredited term *instinct*. Environmental inputs are said to automatically trigger a certain response or series of related responses. (2)

Insight

A suddenly realized solution to a problem, sometimes called the "A-ha! phenomenon." Introduced by Wolfgang Kohler, the concept of insight is used to explain the apparently spontaneous appearance of a solution to a problem. Insight results from the reorganization of ideas and perceptions rather than from simple trial-and-error behavior. The concept of insight is typically used by gestalt psychologists. (8)

Instinct Theory

A now-discredited theory that attempted to explain behavior by simply describing it and then calling it "instinctive." For example, humans were seen as going to war because of an "aggressive instinct," forming groups because of a "gregarious instinct," or even twiddling thumbs because of a "thumb-twiddling instinct." Instinct theorists committed a logical error called the *nominal fallacy. See* Nominal fallacy. (2)

Intelligence

Widely varying definitions—from Wechsler's "global capacity of the individual to act purposefully, to think rationally, and to deal effectively with his environment" to E. G. Boring's positivistic definition of intelligence as simply that which an intelligence test measures. The problem with intelligence as a concept is that it cannot be directly observed. It must be inferred from behavior. Rather than *being* intelligent, one can be viewed as acting intelligently.

As a hypothetical construct, intelligence has come to mean higher-level thought processes, or intellectual abilities, as opposed to Francis Galton's original notion of acute sensory powers. Statistical studies of intelligence utilize the concept of measured intelligence, which is the score received on a standardized intelligence test. *See also* Intelligence quotient. (16)

Intelligence Quotient (IQ)

Originally, a measure of intelligence calculated by dividing a subject's mental age by the chronological age and multiplying by 100. That is, IQ = MA/CA × 100. This is called the *ratio method* of obtaining an IQ.

More recently, IQ has been computed by the deviation method. One's deviation IQ is defined by one's relative standing among peers. The deviation IQ is computed on the basis of how far one's score deviates from the mean score obtained for the entire group of individuals of the same chronological age. This technique is based on the standard, or *z*-score, concept and assumes a normal distribution for each age group. (16)

Intrinsic Motives

Motives that are sustained by internal factors—for example, the need for self-satisfaction. Learning that is based on intrinsic motivation has been found to be longer-lasting than that based on the more transitory external reinforcers. *See* Extrinsic motives. (18)

Introspection

A technique used for ferreting out psychology's data by having a subject look within himself or herself and then report all feelings, sensations, and images. This technique was the basic method for obtaining data in the days of Wilhelm Wundt and the structuralist school of psychology. J. B. Watson, the founder of behaviorism, attacked the use of introspection as being too subjective for an objective, scientific discipline like psychology. The technique is rarely used in psychology today. (8)

Invariant Sequence

The notion in developmental theories that development occurs in stages arranged in a sequence that moves in only one direction. Further, these stages cannot be skipped. The growth process is thus seen as a sequence of steps that must be taken one at a time. (5, 7)

James, William (1842–1910)

America's first, and probably most revered, psychologist. James spent his entire academic lifetime at Harvard University, first as a student and later as a professor. Though he received an M.D. degree, James carved out a career as a professor of both psychology and philosophy. In 1876 he created and taught the first psychology course ever offered in the United States. In 1890 he published *Principles of Psychology*, a book that still provides a relatively modern version of psychology. Later, in his famous "Talks with Teachers," James pointed out that the entire enterprise of education is determined by the performance of the teacher in the classroom. James is credited with originating the school of functionalism in psychology, a school of thought interested not so much in what the elements of consciousness are but in what they are for. (1)

Jensen, Arthur R.

Researcher and professor of educational psychology whose special interest is IQ. Jensen's 1969 article "How Much Can We Boost IQ and Scholastic Achievement?" created a big stir in educational psychology because of its pronounced emphasis on genetic factors in the development of intellect. Jensen has been criticized for one of the implications of his article, namely, that the difference between the IQs of black and white children are partly due to genetics. (16)

Joyce, Bruce

Theorist who conceptualizes effective teaching methods as a repertoire of different teaching models. Joyce suggests that teachers should deliberately employ a variety of modes. Exclusive reliance on any one mode will lead to boredom for both pupils and teachers. (12)

Just Community

System developed by Lawrence Kohlberg and Ralph Mosher, in which a subgroup of high school students is organized on the basis of Stage V principles. The students and staff jointly determine and carry out all school rules. Research indicates that such communities have had some success in dealing with the usual problems of discipline and that levels of academic achievement increase while drug use and absenteeism decrease. (19)

Kallikak Family

Case name (taken from the Greek words for good and bad) for a family that was studied in great detail by Henry Goddard during the early years of this century. Goddard traced back two branches of the Kallikak family, both deriving from the Revolutionary War soldier Martin Kallikak. One branch, the "good Kallikaks," resulted from Martin Kallikak's marriage, while the "bad Kallikaks" were a result of Martin's affair with a barmaid. Goddard found that the two branches were significantly different in virtually every way, especially in regard to intelligence: Most good Kallikaks were superior, and most bad Kallikaks were retarded. This "good seed–bad seed" account is regarded as totally fanciful by today's students of genetics. (2)

Kohlberg, Lawrence (1927–1987)

Psychologist whose Ph.D. thesis, written at the University of Chicago, outlined a theory of how moral reasoning develops in children. His theory of moral development states that children proceed through a series of developmental stages—preconventional, conventional, and postconventional. Like Jean Piaget's theory of cognitive development, Kohlberg's theory sees moral development occurring in an invariant sequence, with each stage qualitatively different from the preceding stage. *See also* Moral development. (7)

Kohler, Wolfgang, (1887–1967)

One of the founders of gestalt psychology. Having been a student of Max Wertheimer's at the University of Frankfurt, just before World War I, Kohler spent the war years in the Canary Islands, where he performed gestalt psychology's most famous animal-learning study. He discovered, while studying apes, that some learning occurs on the basis of insight rather than solely on the basis of the slow accumulation of specific associations. Insight, or the "aha! phenomenon," is learning that occurs suddenly as a new relationship among perceptions is discovered. *See also* Insight. (8)

Language Competence

The underlying knowledge of the structure and rules of language (as opposed to language performance, which is the overt language response). (3)

Law of Effect

One of E. L. Thorndike's main laws of learning. It states that when an association between a stimulus and response is followed by a satisfying state of affairs, the association (or connection) is strengthened. When the association is followed by an annoying state of affairs, it is weakened. In brief, reward strengthens and punishment weakens any

connection between stimuli and responses. In a later version of the law, Thorndike soft-pedaled the importance of punishment as a weakening agent. Thorndike's law of effect is considered by many psychologists to be the cornerstone on which B. F. Skinner built his system of operant conditioning. (8)

Law of Exercise

One of E. L. Thorndike's three main laws of learning. It states that the more frequently a stimulus-response connection occurs, the stronger the resulting association and, hence, the stronger the learning. The law was later amended to incorporate the importance of the consequences of the action; thus, practice without knowledge of results is not nearly as effective as when the consequences become known to the learner. (8)

Law of Readiness

One of E. L. Thorndike's three main laws of learning. It states that learning occurs when neurological conduction units are primed or ready to conduct. The reference here is to momentary readiness rather than to maturational readiness. (8)

Learned Helplessness

The appearance of helplessness that is characteristic of some handicapped children. The term, from Martin Seligman, suggests the need for teachers to pay careful attention to such children in order to prevent them from being caught in the syndrome, especially since some of the children can be expert performers. Setting reasonable objectives in a firm yet supportive atmosphere will avoid reinforcing learned helplessness. (20)

Learning

A very general term referring to a process that leads to a relatively permanent change in behavior resulting from past experience. Thus, such activities as acquiring physical skills, memorizing poems, acquiring attitudes and prejudices, or even tics and mannerisms are all examples of learning. Learning may be conscious or unconscious, adaptive or maladaptive, overt or covert. Although the learning process is typically measured on the basis of a change in performance, most psychologists agree that an accompanying change occurs within the nervous system. Though there are a great many theories and explanations concerning learning, there is general agreement regarding its definition. (8)

Learning Curve

A graphic presentation of learning performance, with the measure of learning being plotted on the vertical axis and the amount of practice on the horizontal axis. Though learning curves take many shapes, depending on what is being learned and under what conditions, the classical, or ideal, curve is negatively accelerating. That is, acceleration (improved performance) becomes less and less as the amount of practice increases. When there is no further increase in performance, the curve levels off into a plateau. (10)

Learning Sets

Concept developed by Harry Harlow and used as a modern explanation for the gestalt term *insight*. Harlow insists that what the gestaltists had viewed as insight does not come about as a sudden reorganization of perceptions but rather occurs on the basis of learning how to learn, or the learning of general rules. The learning set does not occur "in a flash" but takes many trials and much experience in which to develop. The concept of learning sets is also in opposition to the straight stimulus-response learning model in that the learning set involves the development of a learning strategy rather than the slow accumulation of stimulus-response associations. A learning set is a form of nonspecific transfer. (10)

Locus of Control

Concept that identifies the type of personal control used by an individual. When the locus of control is internal, individuals view themselves as personally in charge of their own destinies. When the locus of control is external, the person feels he or she is at the mercy of external circumstances. (17)

Logicomathematical (LM) Learning

Concept developed by Jean Piaget to describe a form of learning that results not from the physical environment's acting on the learner but from the actions of the learner on the environment. LM learning is the result of an individual's continuous experience of organizing and reorganizing actions—a process that leads to the goal of understanding. Piaget says that LM learning is internally motivated. The discovery of a new relationship is self-rewarding. *See also* Physical (P) learning. (9)

Lomawaima, K. Tsianina

Professor and researcher in history and contemporary policy issues in the areas of Indian education, economy, and the law. She cautions that although research in some Native American communities strongly suggests the importance of cooperating learning strategies, teachers need to recognize the diversity among native cultures and not assume that one teaching method will be appropriate to all Native Americans. Teachers need to be flexible in using a variety of learning strategies to best meet the needs of each individual learner. (12)

Long-Term Memory (LTM)

In the information processing model, the second of the two main storage systems. Information that is in short-term memory may, under certain conditions, be passed along for processing and consolidation into a more permanent storage site, long-term memory. Long-term memory has the potential for holding encoded information for a lifetime. (11)

Lorenz, Konrad (1903–1989)

Austrian ethologist and winner of the Nobel Prize in medicine in 1973. Lorenz insisted that to understand animal behavior one must study the animal in its natural habitat, not in the artificial confines of the laboratory. In 1937 Lorenz first described the phenomenon of imprinting, a form of learning that dramatically illustrates the interaction of heredity, environment, and time in the determination of behavioral characteristics. Lorenz was able to revive the long-discredited instinct theory and, by carefully analyzing the biological mechanisms involved, to make the theory scientifically respectable. *See also* Imprinting. (2)

Low and High Structure

Different teaching methods, particularly variation in levels of structure, are appropriate for pupils operating at different conceptual levels (CLs). Lower-CL pupils learn material in significantly greater amounts when teachers use high-structure activities like advance organizers and the rule-example-rule sequence. Higher-CL pupils learn best under methods using low-structure like examples only or discovery. (13)

MacDonald, Robert

Educational specialist and teacher trainer who has outlined several new techniques for dealing with individual differences in classroom discipline. He particularly emphasizes initiating and preventive methods, with corrective techniques as a last resort. (19)

Maintenance Rehearsal

Technique used for consolidating long-term memory (LTM) information based on rote memorization and repetition. (11)

Marcia, James

Educational psychologist who analyzed the process of identity formation during late adolescence by identifying four separate and distinct identity "statuses": foreclosure, diffusion, moratorium, and achievement. (6)

Massed Learning

Learning that occurs in massive doses, without a break, as opposed to spaced learning. Studies show that for many activities, especially motor activities, massed learning is less efficient than spaced learning. (10)

Matching and Mismatching

Method of teaching that involves discovering a student's cognitive stage of development, matching content and structure to that stage, and gradually introducing mismatches to stimulate development one stage up. Teachers should be alert to the fact that some pupils may experience anxiety when new material is introduced or when going through developmental transitions. Also, some pupils may be "advanced thinkers" in certain subjects but not in others. Watching for such variability in pupil responses can guide teachers in changing the level of structure when necessary. (13)

May, Mark (1891–1973)

See Hartshorne, Hugh.

Mean

A statistical measure of central tendency, found by adding all the scores in a distribution and dividing by the number of scores. It is also called the *arithmetic average*. (15)

Measurement

The assigning of numbers to observations according to certain rules. The rule used to assign the numbers determines which scale of measurement is being employed—nominal, ordinal, interval, or ratio. (15)

Measurement-Driven Instruction (MDI)

The general term now used for the use of standardized testing to evaluate both the children and the classroom teacher. This has led to charges that teachers have gone too far and, instead of just teaching to the test, have taught the test itself. (15)

Measures of Central Tendency

A statistical term used for describing the typical, middle, or central score in a distribution of scores. Measures of central tendency are used when the researcher wants to describe a group as a whole with a view toward characterizing that group on the basis of its most common measurement. The researcher wishes to know what score best represents a group of differing scores. The three measures of central tendency are the mean (or arithmetic average), the median (or the midpoint of the distribution), and the mode (the most frequently occurring score in the distribution). (15)

Median

A statistical measure of central tendency found by identifying the middlemost point in a distribution of ordered values. (15)

Menarche

The time of the first menstruation, which signals the onset of puberty and/or adolescence among females. The girl who is secure in her sexual identity and has had adult support and guidance is less likely to feel anxiety when reaching this developmental milestone. (3)

Mendel, Gregor (1822–1884)

Austrian monk whose work with the flower color of garden peas led to the theory of genetics that states that some genes are dominant and some recessive. When paired with a recessive gene, the dominant gene is the one whose characteristics will be expressed. (3)

Mental Age

Term first used by Alfred Binet as the unit for measuring intelligence. Binet defined mental age in terms of the age at which a given number of test items are passed by an average child. If, for example, the average six-year-old could correctly answer a certain number of items, then any other child correctly answering the same number of items would be assigned at least a mental age of six. (16)

Metacognition

Internal awareness of cognitive abilities, including self-awareness of both learning and retrieval strategies. If cognition is learning's pilot, then metacognition is the copilot. (11)

Milgram, Stanley (1933–1986)

Researcher who studied, among other subjects, human aggression and conformity. In one series of studies, Milgram, a professor of social psychology at the City University of New York, asked subjects to deliver increasing amounts of electric shock to another person. He found that almost two-thirds of those tested were willing to risk killing someone they perceived to be a fellow subject. When tested in groups, however, only about 10 percent of the subjects pushed the shock lever all the way. Milgram interpreted this behavior in terms of the liberating effects of conformity and group pressure on individual behavior. Milgram's experiments also demonstrated the relationships between Kohlberg's stages and moral development. Most subjects at the conventional and preconventional levels were willing to follow orders and administer seemingly painful electric shocks. (7)

Miller, Alan

Researcher who has reviewed a large number of studies that support the idea that pupils at more complex conceptual levels benefit from indirect instruction while those at lower levels need more direct methods. Thus, teacher methods and content should vary in accord with pupils' attributes. (13)

Mnemonic Devices

Memory aids used to increase retention powers. Mnemonic devices typically utilize one of the following learning strategies: (1) visual imagery, (2) rhyming, and (3) associations with past learning. Using the word *homes* for recalling the names of the Great Lakes (Huron, Ontario, Michigan, Erie, and Superior) is an example of a mnemonic device based on association with past learning. (11)

Mode

A statistical measure of central tendency found by identifying the most frequently occurring score in a distribution of scores. (15)

Modeling

Concept used in Bandura's social learning theory. Learning can occur not only through response conditioning but also through modeling, which is the imitation of the behavior of others. Learning by modeling can occur even when the imitative responses are not themselves being directly reinforced. *See also* Social learning theory. (10)

Monozygotic (MZ) Twins

Identical twins who have identical genetic backgrounds. They result from the fertilization of a single egg, which then divides. The two individuals thus have precisely the same genetic makeup (3).

Montessori, Maria (1870–1952)

Italian educator, psychologist, and physician. Montessori was one of the first theorists to stress the developmental nature of humans in an evolutionary setting. Her approach to education was based on her work first with mentally retarded children and later with culturally deprived children living in the slums of Rome. Her educational technique, now called the Montessori method, stressed sensory training in a prepared environment. She stressed the importance of early experience in cognitive development, and although her approach was rejected by most American behaviorists, it is now receiving renewed attention by serious educational psychologists. (20)

Moral Development

The process whereby children come to adopt guiding principles of right and wrong and achieve the ability to resist the temptations of unacceptable conduct. The view that morality develops in a series of growth stages originated in the work of Jean Piaget, who believed the development of moral stages was similar to cognitive development. One of the leading representatives of this view was Lawrence Kohlberg, who saw moral development occurring in a series of stages: preconventional, conventional, and postconventional. Like Piaget, Kohlberg described moral development as occurring in an invariant sequence, with each stage qualitatively different from the preceding stage. *See also* Kohlberg, Lawrence. (7)

Moratorium

Erik Erikson's term for a stage of identity formation during late adolescence. It is thought to be a time for possible experimentation, which precedes a commitment to an adult career. (6)

Morine-Dershimer, Greta

Educational psychologist who studied interpersonal communication in the classroom between teachers and students and peers in a multiethnic community. One interesting finding was that the use of nonstandard English in interpersonal communication was not a causal factor in school achievement, whereas negative teacher expectations based upon students' usage of the language may influence how much a student learns. (12)

Motivation

A general psychological term used to explain behavior initiated by needs and directed toward a goal. Motives may be biogenic (that is, stemming from tissue needs within the organism) or acquired (that is, learned through interaction with the environment, especially the social environment). Almost all personality theorists have developed their own lists of important human motives, and great debates have occurred over which motives are of greatest importance or which can rightly be called universal. Among learning theorists, Jerome Bruner makes much of the principle of motivation, assuming that almost all children have a built-in "will to learn." (18)

Motivational Conflicts

Conflicts that result when individuals seek a number of goals, one (or some) of which may be antagonistic to others. The conflicts that most affect the lives of school-age children are (1) the need for independence versus the need for dependence, (2) internal sexual needs versus society's demand to leave those needs unsatisfied, and (3) internal feelings of aggression versus society's rule that such feelings not be directly expressed. (18)

Motives

Activated needs (drives) that are directed toward or away from some specified goal. (18)

Nature-Nurture Controversy

Debate over which component, nature (heredity) or nurture (environment), is more influential in determining behavior. In psychology the behaviorists consistently argued on behalf of nurture, and the intelligence testers favored nature. Educational psychology has long been the battleground on which this issue has been fought, since the psychologists primarily concerned with the issue were the learning theorists (largely behaviorists) and measurement practitioners. (2)

Need Hierarchy

Theory proposed by Abraham Maslow that suggests that humans place their needs on the following universal, order-of-importance scale: (1) physiological needs, (2) safety needs, (3) love needs, (4) esteem needs, and (5) self-actualizing needs. (18)

Needs

The part of the motivational cycle seen as deficits that lie within the individual. These may be physiological (e.g., the need for food) or psychological (e.g., the need for approval). (18)

Negative Discipline Techniques

Inhumane methods of classroom discipline, such as brute physical force, aversive conditioning, and scapegoating, that do not generally produce long-lasting results of a positive nature. (19)

Negatively Accelerated (Intellectual) Growth Curve

A graph of the relationship between intellectual growth and age. Benjamin S. Bloom suggests that this relationship is negative—that is, as a child increases in age his or her potential for continued intellectual growth decreases. (4)

Negative Reinforcement

Any stimulus whose *removal* increases the rate of responding. If a rat is in a cage with an electrified floor grid and the electricity is turned off only after the rat presses a lever, the rate of lever-pressing responses will tend to increase dramatically. Unlike punishment, which reduces response rates, negative reinforcement often increases response rates even more quickly than positive reinforcement. (9)

Negative Transfer

Phenomenon whereby the learning of A inhibits the learning and retention of B. For example, learning to type by the hunt-and-peck method may create bad habits that make the later learning of touch typing more difficult. (10)

Nieto, Sonia

Educational psychologist who investigated the relationship between teacher expectations and racial or sexual bias. She advocates that schools and teachers set goals of increasing racial diversity in the staff and that the curriculum be restructured to include a specific focus on valuing diversity and pointing out the negative effects of racism and discrimination. (14)

Nominal Fallacy

A logical error resulting from the attempt to explain an event on the basis of a redescription of that same event. Saying that sleeping pills work because they have dormative power or maintaining that people fight because they have aggressive instincts is an example of the nominal fallacy. The instinct theorists of the early 1900s built an entire system on the soft sands of the nominal fallacy. (2)

Nonverbal Behavior

Body language. Based largely on the theory of Charles Galloway and some research by Robert Rosenthal, the teacher's nonverbal behavior represents an important avenue for the transmission of teacher expectations. Galloway has shown how nonverbal behavior can promote or reduce pupil learning. Rosenthal has shown how his test (Profile of Nonverbal Sensitivity) can identify the channels for communicating how teachers really feel about their pupils. (12)

Normal Curve

A frequency distribution curve in which scores are plotted on the horizontal axis (X), and frequency of occurrence is plotted on the vertical axis (Y). The normal curve is a theoretical curve shaped like a bell, on which (1) most of the scores cluster around the center, and as we move away from the center in either direction there are fewer and fewer scores; (2) the scores fall into a symmetrical shape, each half of the curve being a mirror image of the other; (3) the mean, median, and mode all fall at precisely the same point, the center; and (4) there are constant area characteristics regarding the standard deviation. (15)

Normal Curve Equivalent (NCE)

A standardized set of scores (based on the normal curve) in which the mean is set at 50 and the standard deviation at approximately 21. (15)

Norm-Referenced Test

A test scored on the basis of how an individual's performance compares to the average performance of the group to which the individual is being compared. Most of the nationally standardized tests are norm-referenced. (15)

Occam, William of (1300–1349)

British-born philosopher and Franciscan monk who warned that explanations are dangerous when they carry excess meaning. He believed that unnecessary assumptions should be avoided in order that explanations be kept as simple and straightforward as possible. This principle is now called the *law of parsimony,* and the concept of "shaving away" excess meaning is now referred to as using *Occam's razor.* Though primarily an empiricist, Occam tried to guide theorizing toward an objective approach that avoided both "wooly-headed" rationalism and "narrow-minded" empiricism. (1)

Ogbu, John

Educational anthropologist who documented the negative effects of the job ceiling upon the motivation for achievement by devalued groups such as African-Americans, Native Americans, and Hispanic Americans. The program was set up by a successful entrepreneur, Eugene Land, in a New York City ghetto school. The results validated Ogbu's contention that removing the ceiling can dramatically increase academic motivation and achievement. (14)

$O = H \leftrightarrow E \leftrightarrow T$

One of psychology's basic principles, which states that the organism is a product of heredity interacting with the environment interacting with time. (3)

Operant Conditioning

Form of conditioning, described by B. F. Skinner, in which the free operant is allowed to occur and is followed by a reinforcing stimulus that is, in turn, followed by an increased likelihood of the operant's occurring again. For optimum conditioning the reinforcing stimulus should follow the operant immediately. The rate of responding for a conditioned operant may jump dramatically over the preconditioned rate (operant level). (9)

Operant Level

The original, or preconditioned, rate of operant responding before any reinforcing stimuli have been introduced. If a rat happens to press the lever in a Skinner box four times an hour (without being reinforced), the operant level for that response is established at four per hour. Thus, the operant level is the rate at which the free operant is typically emitted prior to conditioning. (9)

Operants

Responses, according to B. F. Skinner, for which the original stimuli are either unidentified or nonexistent. The consequences of operant behavior can be observed even though the stimulus is not known. For example, if a rat presses the lever in a Skinner box and this results in reinforcement, an increase in operant rate will be observed despite the fact that no stimulus could be identified as initiating the original lever-pressing. In operant conditioning, reinforcement is contingent on the operant's first being emitted. The organism must in some way "operate" on the environment in order that the reinforcement will follow. Operant responding at one time was called *instrumental responding* by some psychologists. (9)

Oral Stage

First of Freud's psychosexual stages of development. During this stage, the baby lives through and loves through its mouth. This stage occurs between birth and about age 18 months and permanently affects the child's later feelings of independence and trust. (6)

Paired-Associate Learning

A method used in the study of verbal learning and memory. A subject is presented with a list of word pairs (blue-moon, red-dog, play-toy, etc.) and is then tested by being asked to repeat the second word of the pair (response) each time the first word (stimulus) is introduced. This is one of the most common techniques employed in the study of verbal learning, since many psychologists believe the learning of item pairs is a fundamental process in thinking and memory. (9)

Pavlov, Ivan (1849–1936)

Russian physiologist who won the Nobel Prize in medicine in 1904 for his work on digestive activity in dogs. His lasting fame, however, resulted from his observation that dogs salivated not only when meat powder was placed in their mouths but also when stimuli occurred well ahead of time (for example, when they heard Pavlov's footsteps coming down the stairs to the laboratory). Pavlov coined the term *conditioned reflex* to describe this phenomenon. Pavlov attempted to relate these behavioral observations to neural activity in the brain; for example, he introduced the concept of *cortical inhibition*, which he believed important in producing sleep. Though most modern psychologists consider

his theory of neurological activity as something of a historical curio, his laboratory findings on conditioning are still of great importance. Pavlov's system of conditioning is now generally called *classical conditioning*. (8)

Pearson Product-Moment Correlation (Pearson *r*)

Statistical test introduced by Karl Pearson for showing the degree of relationship between two variables. It is used to test the hypothesis of association, that is, whether or not there is a linear relationship between two sets of measurements. Computed correlations range from +1.00 (perfect positive correlation) through zero to –1.00 (perfect negative correlation). The further the Pearson *r* is from zero, whether in a positive or negative direction, the stronger the relationship. The Pearson *r* may be used for making better-than-chance predictions but may not be used for directly isolating causal factors. (15)

Percentile

The percentage of cases falling at or below a given score. Thus, if an individual were to score at the ninety-fifth percentile, that individual's score would exceed 95 percent of the scores of all persons taking that particular test. If test scores are normally distributed, and if the standard deviation of the distribution is known, percentile scores can easily be converted from the resulting *z* scores. (15)

Performance IQ

Term used by David Wechsler to describe the nonverbal component of intelligence. Wechsler believed that the Stanford-Binet test was too heavily loaded with verbal items; thus, when constructing his own test, he included a section designed to tap visual-motor abilities. The Wechsler IQ tests are scored on the basis of verbal IQ, performance IQ, and full-scale IQ. Scores are computed in each of the three categories. (16)

Periodization

Stages through which the brain passes in developing. This growth appears to parallel the Piagetian stages of cognitive development. As yet, there is no evidence to support the idea that learning cannot take place during the transitional phases of periodization. (5)

Permastore

That part of long-term memory (LTM), both semantic and episodic, which is said to be permanently stored. (11)

Peterson, Penelope

Researcher who has investigated attribute-treatment interaction (ATI). Peterson has shown the positive effects of systematically varying the amount of structure in teaching according to levels of pupil ability, anxiety, and attitudes toward learning. (13)

Phallic Stage

Third stage of personality development in Freud's theory of psychosexual development. During the phallic stage (ages three to seven years) the child focuses on the genital area. Conflict results as the child projects its sexual desires on the opposite-sex parent and feels the fear of retaliation from the same-sex parent. The conflict is resolved, at about age seven, when the child identifies with the same-sex parent. The major crisis for the child during this stage centers on the struggle for sexual identification. (6)

Phenotype

The observable properties or the inherited traits that are expressed in the organism. (3)

Physical (P) Learning

Form of learning described by Jean Piaget that results from the actions of the physical environment on the child rather than the actions of the child on the environment. Piaget's P learning (physical event acting on the learner) is very similar to B. F. Skinner's concept of operant conditioning. *See also* Logicomathematical (LM) learning. (9)

Physiological Motives

Motives that are based on the activation of physical needs, such as the need for food, water, sleep, sex, and warmth. (18)

Piaget, Jean (1896–1980)

Swiss psychologist who spent most of his adult life studying cognitive development. Through carefully detailed, hour-by-hour observations of the developing child, Piaget formulated a theory of how children learn to know or form concepts. Piaget stated that children learn concepts only as they go through a series of developmental stages that are sequential and biologically based. Thinking processes are a biological extension of newborn motor processes. Piaget's developmental stages are (1) sensorimotor (birth to

2 years), (2) preoperational or intuitive (2 to 7 years), (3) concrete operations (7 to 11 years), and (4) formal operations (11 to 16 years). (5)

Polygenic Inheritance

Inherited traits that result from the combination of large numbers of genes, as opposed to traits, such as eye and hair color, determined by a single pair of genes. (3)

Portfolio Approach

A system for evaluating student progress that is based on selected examples of a student's best work over a term or even an entire year of study. It is said that the portfolio approach places more emphasis on a student's overall accomplishments than on the ability merely to score well on a battery of tests. Typical portfolios include original poetry, plays, short stories, essays, and art projects. At the end of the term, the student hands over the portfolio to the teacher for evaluation. (15)

Positive Discipline Techniques

Humane methods for classroom discipline that are geared to the developmental stage of pupils. (19)

Positive Reinforcement

Any stimulus that, when added to the situation, increases the likelihood of the response's recurring. A pellet of food may be a positive reinforcer to a hungry rat only if it can be observed that the rat emits the same response (pressing the lever in the Skinner box) in order to get another pellet. In the classroom positive reinforcement may be provided by primary reinforcers, such as milk, cereal, or candy, or by conditioned reinforcers, such as gold stars, high grades, or social approval. (9)

Positive Transfer

Phenomenon whereby the learning of A aids in the learning and retention of B. For example, learning the rules of algebra makes the later learning of the principles of physics more efficient. (10)

Power, Clark

Researcher who found no significant relationship between stages of moral development and self-esteem. (7)

Precise Teaching

Teaching technique used with newly included children. Precise teaching provides maximum structure in the learning environment and utilizes behavior modification to aid students in mastering a variety of educational tasks. (20)

Preferred Style of Learning

The current system of problemsolving preferred by a student at his or her stage of conceptual development. David Hunt believes that this learning mode is not fixed, nor is it a permanent classification. With appropriate matching and mismatching of material and methods, pupils can be encouraged to grow conceptually and increase the complexity of their thinking. (13)

Premack Principle

A principle of behavior modification introduced by David Premack. Premack states that behavior that occurs at a naturally high rate of frequency may be used to reinforce behavior that occurs at a naturally low rate. The establishment of high- and low-frequency responses must be done through careful observation. (10)

Preoperational Stage

The second of Jean Piaget's stages of cognitive growth (from ages two to seven). It is really the beginning of symbolic thinking and frees the child from the thinking of the sensorimotor period that is so directly tied to immediate experience. Oral vocabulary increases by a huge amount, and the child exhibits little concern over the accuracy or even the reality of perception. Imaginary friends, animals that talk, and very "tall" stories mark the period as one of freewheeling creativity. (5)

Proactive Inhibition (PI)

The disruption of information retrieval due to interference from other encoded and stored information. When learning task A and then later learning task B, the encoded information of A works forward to disturb efforts to retrieve the encoded information of B. In effect, old learning is preventing the recall of new learning. (11)

Procedural Memory

Storage of long-term memory (LTM) information concerning motoric patterns and conditionings. Procedural memory allows us to remember how to tie our shoes, ride a bike, or play scales on the piano. (11)

Profile of Nonverbal Sensitivity (PONS)

Robert Rosenthal's measuring instrument to assess the ability to identify aspects of nonverbal communications. The PONS measurement results have indicated that most adults in this culture are not aware of their own nonverbal behavior. The correlation between self-awareness and accuracy was zero. (14)

Programmed Instruction

An arrangement of instructional material in a step-by-step sequence designed to lead the student to a specified goal. The material being presented is broken down into small units called *frames*. There are two general approaches to programming: (1) *linear* programs, in which all students go through the entire program and the frames gradually increase in difficulty; and (2) *branched* programs, in which the student skips forward or backward in the program (the order of the frame presentation varies) as a result of the success or failure experienced in responding.

Programmed instruction can be in book form, or it can be presented through the use of a teaching machine and/or computer. The concept of programmed instruction is credited to B. F. Skinner. (10)

Protein Synthesis (in Memory)

Part of a physiological memory theory that sees permanent memory as the result of RNA's role in synthesizing new brain protein. The new protein is assumed to contain the memory and is thus seen as the ultimate engram. *See also* Engram. (11)

Psychoanalytic Theory

Theory of human behavior and method of treating mental illness presented by Sigmund Freud at the turn of the century. The theory attempts to give a rational explanation for irrational thoughts and responses. Psychoanalytic theory states (1) that all behavior is determined by specific motives; (2) that most human motives lie at the unconscious level, and therefore people are unaware of the reasons for most of their own behavior; (3) that neurotic symptoms result from an individual's inner conflicts; and (4) that inner conflicts are a product of childhood trauma and anxiety. The technique is based on the therapist's revealing to the patient the source of his or her anxiety and helping the patient to thus achieve insight and emotional release. *See also* Freud, Sigmund. (6)

Psycholinguistics

Branch of psychology whose main focus is the study of the acquisition and function of language. There are three basic theoretical positions: (1) conditioning theories, which assume that language acquisition is based on the external reinforcement of randomly emitted vocalizations; (2) cognitive theories, which view language development as based on the learning of basic rules and strategies of words and syntax; and (3) genetic theories, which assume that the child comes into the world genetically prewired or born with biological givens that direct the course of language development. (3)

Public Law 94–142

Major legislation in the 1970s, the law required access to public schools for children with disabilities in the least restrictive educational environment. Other provisions included due process, individualized planning, identification, assessment, and nondiscrimination. This law and its successor, IDEA, are regarded as the Magna Carta for all such children. (20)

Punishment

A method for controlling behavior through the use of aversive stimulation. Punishment, though not itself causing the extinction of a conditioned response, does severely reduce that rate of responding *while the punishment is in force*. Punishment should not be confused with negative reinforcement. *See also* Negative reinforcement. (10)

Qualitative Development

The notion in stage theory that cognitive growth and maturation occur in a sequence of qualitative transformations in a manner similar to the change from an egg to caterpillar to butterfly. Each change leads to a major shift to a more complex system of thinking. (5)

Quantitative Development

Theory of intellectual development that sees growth occurring in a linear fashion. Cognitive growth is assumed to be based on steady additions to the intellect, not on any changes in the structure of thought. (5)

Quartiles

Points that divide a distribution into quarters. Each quartile represents 25 percentiles: the 1st quartile is equal to the twenty-fifth percentile, the 2d quartile to the fiftieth percentile, and the 3d quartile to the seventy-fifth percentile. (15)

Race Norming

An attempt to make testing fairer by using separate racial and ethnic norms for the groups under study. For example, since some test items may tend to favor white culture over the cultures of blacks and other minorities, test score adjustments can be used to compensate for the cultural imbalance that may have been built into these tests. (15)

Racial Identity Stages

Based on the work of Janet Helms, racial identity among whites can be considered as progressing through a series of six stages, from *contact* to *autonomy*. In a parallel sense, the work of Cross has focused on the same process among devalued groups, such as African-Americans. The process for majority whites and for devalued groups suggests a gradual movement toward genuine understanding and respect among all such groups as the highest stage of racial identity development. (6, 14)

Random Sample

A method of selection in which everyone in a population that is being researched has an equal chance of being chosen. This approach helps to ensure that the sample will be representative of the population being studied. (15)

Range

A statistical measure of variability found by subtracting the lowest score from the highest score. It measures the entire width of a distribution. (15)

Recessive Gene

Gregor Mendel's term for the unit of heredity whose characteristics are expressed only when paired with a like gene; those characteristics are not expressed when paired with dissimilar (dominant) genes. (3)

Rehearsal

In the information processing model, the critical component of intentional learning. It consists of practice or repetition and is perhaps the key method whereby incoming information may become permanently encoded and stored. (11)

Reinforcement

Any stimulus that increases the likelihood of a response's recurring. Reinforcement, as a Skinnerian concept, should not be confused with reward, feelings of pleasure, or any other concept with subjective or mentalistic overtones. Reinforcement may be used in either classical (respondent) or operant conditioning. In respondent conditioning the unconditioned stimulus serves as the reinforcement. In operant conditioning the presentation of any stimulus following the emitted response can be considered a reinforcement *if it results in a higher response rate. See also* Positive reinforcement; Negative reinforcement. (9)

Reliability

The consistency of a measuring instrument over time. A reliable test tends to produce roughly the same results when used repeatedly under the same conditions. (15)

Remolding

An early method of physically transforming children who did not fit adult perceptions of normalcy. (20)

Respondent Conditioning

B. F. Skinner's term for classical conditioning, in which a conditioned stimulus that has been paired several times with an unconditioned stimulus comes to evoke the conditioned response. (9)

Respondents

Name given by B. F. Skinner to those responses that are sometimes called *reflexes*. Respondents are those responses that may be automatically elicited by a specific unconditioned or unlearned stimulus. Respondents are also called *unconditioned responses. See also* Unconditioned response. (9)

Rest, James

Creator of an objective measure of Kohlberg's stages. It is the most widely used measure of moral development and so far has shown a number of strong cross-cultural similarities, but no significant gender differences. (7)

Retrieval

In the information processing model, the output end of the memory process. Retrieval is the utilization of stored in-

formation and must be not only available but also accessible to the individual. (11)

Retroactive Inhibition (RI)

The disruption of information retrieval due to interference from other encoded and stored information. RI occurs when the learning of new material (task B) works backward to prevent the recall of older material (task A). Encoding new information thus hampers efforts to retrieve information already in storage. (11)

Retrograde Amnesia

The loss of memory for recent events as a result of a head injury accompanied by a loss of consciousness. (11)

Reynolds, Maynard

A leader in the inclusion movement who has been critical of the use of a single IQ test for diagnosis and placement of retarded pupils. Reynolds has also shown how the common approaches to special-education classification often penalize students from minority backgrounds and lead to negative self-fulfilling prophecies. (20)

Ribonucleic Acid (RNA)

Molecules, located in the chromosomes, that carry the hereditary instructions contained in the DNA to other parts of the cell. RNA can be thought of as the "builder" that translates the DNA "blueprint" into a finished product. (3)

Risky Shift

Concept from social psychology suggesting that persons in a group situation are less cautious and more prone to risk taking than are persons who are alone. The group situation apparently allows individuals to become less conservative and more willing to take chances in terms of both attitudes and behavior. (17)

RNA Theory (of Memory)

Theory of memory based on chemical changes occurring within the organism. The life-controlling nucleic acid RNA (ribonucleic acid) is seen as being, if not the physical site of memory itself, at least part of the chain of events leading to the physiological formation of memory. (11)

Rogers, Carl (1902–1987)

Founder of the client-centered, or nondirective, approach to personality. Rogers challenged the orthodox psychiatric and psychological treatment techniques in vogue when he started practice. He felt that psychiatrists often harmed more than helped their patients. Rogers insisted that all persons have a natural tendency to grow in healthy directions and that the role of the therapist is to provide conditions in which the patient (or client) can fulfill his or her destiny of self-actualization. The famous Rogerian triad of unconditional positive regard, empathy, and congruence became the crucial ingredients in the helping process. Good teaching, like good counseling, is based on this same triad. Classroom interaction should be based on the development of equal and genuine relationships. (12)

Role

Term used by social psychologists to denote the dynamic aspect of status. Role is the behavioral repertoire associated with an individual's status—the bundle of responses available to a person as a result of his or her niche in society's prestige hierarchy. Society *expects* individuals of a given status to act in certain ways, and the individual feels obliged to act according to society's expectations. *See also* Status. (17)

Rosenthal Effect

Concept introduced by Robert Rosenthal, who found that teachers often form expectations about the performance of students, and the students then respond on the basis of a self-fulfilling prophecy. If a teacher assumes a child to be intellectually inferior, the teacher treats the child in such a way as to reinforce inferiority. The child thus begins to act in accordance with the teacher's expectations. (14)

Saber-Tooth Curriculum

An educational spoof that clearly points out the current debate over educational goals: Should we teach specific skills (how to scare away fierce tigers with firebrands) or general abilities (how to be courageous)? Educational leaders often take extreme positions on teaching goals that fit the examples taken by the tribal elders in this mock history. (13)

Schedules of Reinforcement

According to B. F. Skinner, the arrangement of reinforcers on the basis of either time elapsed or number of responses emitted. Responses that are reinforced periodically, rather than each time they are emitted, tend to be conditioned more strongly and are thus more resistant to extinction. The major schedules of reinforcement are (1) continuous, (2) fixed ratio, (3) fixed interval, (4) variable ratio, and (5) variable interval. (9)

Segregation

A method of dealing with children who do not conform to societal perceptions of normalcy by providing separate facilities, such as residential schools in remote areas. (20)

Selective Attention

The ability to focus on one source of incoming information while ignoring possible distractions. This ability is developmental and increases with age. (11)

Self-Esteem

Sense of personal self-worth. Research among school-age children has not yet settled the issue of whether self-esteem may act to increase academic achievement, or whether self-esteem is the result of academic achievement.

Self-Regulated Learning

Occurs when the learner achieves an intrinsic motivational set and is able to postpone gratification and rely on inner resources. The self-regulated learner is said to have an internal locus of control. (18)

Semantic Memory

Information in long-term memory (LTM) that is based on language (words and the meaning of words), including names, dates, and facts. (11)

Sensitive Period

A period when an organism is susceptible to a change in behavior as a result of certain kinds of environmental stimulation. The sensitive periods typically occur early in the organism's life and tend to produce behavior changes that are relatively long-lasting. The process of mother-infant bonding is said to occur only during the baby's first three days of life. (2)

Sensorimotor Stage

First stage of cognitive development, according to Jean Piaget, in which the child learns to distinguish himself or herself from the external environment, begins to notice and follow objects in the environment, and develops the rudiments of trial-and-error learning. This stage lasts from birth to age two years, and the child operates at the level of raw, immediate stimulation as experienced through the senses. A milestone during this stage is the development of the concept of object permanence, the thought that objects still exist even though they are not, at the moment, being seen. Piaget insists that mental processes are developed directly from inborn motor processes. The child's ability at birth to make certain motor responses forms the basis for the cognitive processes that come later. (5)

Sensory Register

In the information processing model, the first stop for incoming information. When information first impinges on sensory receptors, there is a brief moment when it is held as raw, unprocessed information in the sensory register. It is the "buffer" or "way station" situated between the external environment and internal memory. (11)

Shaping (Successive Approximations)

Technique used by B. F. Skinner to encourage the acquisition of new conditioned operants. The learner is differentially reinforced for making ever-closer approximations of the behavior being conditioned. (10)

Short-Term Memory (STM)

In the information processing model, the first of two main storage systems. Sometimes called "working" or "active" memory, it may encode only about seven separate items. Estimates of how long information may be retained in short-term memory vary from about 20 seconds to over a minute. (11)

Sissy-Boy Syndrome

Psychiatrist Richard Green's suggestion that there may be growth trends in the development of adult male homosexuality. Green asserts that he has identified a pattern of early male development, called the *sissy-boy syndrome*, which he claims can be used to predict the later onset of homosexuality. (3)

Skinner, B. F. (1904–1990)

Psychology's most important and honored behaviorist, Skinner is the originator of the system of operant conditioning. Using E. L. Thorndike's law of effect as a starting point, Skinner has shown that conditioning can take place

when responses are allowed to occur and are then followed by reinforcing stimuli. Reinforcement is thus contingent on the fact that the response (operant) has been emitted. Skinner's emphasis is on response analysis. He is concerned not with what goes on inside the organism but with specifying the environmental conditions associated with and affecting the organism's response repertoire. Skinner's most notable contributions to education are the techniques of programmed instruction and behavior modification. (9)

Snarey, John

Investigator who used cross-cultural studies to determine whether Lawrence Kohlberg's system of classifying moral development was as universal as originally claimed. He found that Western and non-Western urban cultures were similar in the sequence of stages Kohlberg described, but tribal and/or feudal cultures exhibited a different pattern. (7)

Snow, C. P. (1905–1980)

Popularizer of the idea that science and the humanities are separate cultures, or distinct worldviews. The differences are often found in how the objective psychological scientist and the subjective educational practitioner view the world of schools and classrooms. (1)

Social Facilitation

A concept from the field of social psychology used to explain the fact that in some circumstances individuals perform more quickly when in a group situation than when alone. Social facilitation is most pronounced in the case of fairly simple mechanical tasks. The more difficult and the more intellectual the task, the less the effect of social facilitation. (17)

Social Inhibition

The fact that individuals, in some circumstances, perform less well when in the presence of other people. This is especially true when the tasks being performed are perceived as being difficult by the individual being measured. The opposite of social inhibition is called *social facilitation*. (17)

Socialization

Process by which an individual learns and internalizes society's rules and norms, thought by social psychologists to be brought about through societal pressures to conform. (17)

Social Learning Theory

Theory, proposed by Albert Bandura, suggesting that a large part of what a person learns occurs through imitation or modeling. Bandura's major concern is with learning that takes place in the context of a social situation in which individuals come to modify behavior as a result of how others in the group respond. Social learning does not require primary reinforcement. (10)

Social Psychology

The study of individual behavior in the context of the social situation. Social psychology analyzes the ways in which people affect and are affected by other people. Major topics in the field include conformity, cohesiveness, status and role, attitudes and attitudinal change, social perception, and group structure and leadership. (17)

Social Role Taking

Significant social role taking, such as peer helping and tutoring, along with self-reflection, has been shown to produce a positive effect on moral development (as opposed to ordinary role playing, which seems to have no effect). (7)

Spacing Effect

The efficiency of spaced learning over massed learning. Documentation of the spacing effect, as a valid phenomenon goes back at least to the seminal work of Hermann Ebbinghaus in about 1905–1909. Ebbinghaus had stated that spreading learning sessions over a period of time is more efficient than completing them all at a single time. *See also* Massed learning. (10)

Spearman, Charles E. (1863–1945)

English psychometrician and psychologist who proposed that intelligence was not a simple unitary process but could be separated into an underlying general factor (*g*) and a series of very specific factors (*s*), such as verbal ability, math ability, and even musical ability. Spearman used a statistical approach, mainly correlational, to segregate these components of intelligence. (16)

Spontaneous Recovery

The fact that a conditioned response that has been extinguished will, after a brief time, tend to recur on its own, with no additional conditioning trials. (9)

Standard Deviation (SD)

A statistical measure of variability that is based on how *all the scores* in a distribution vary from the mean. A large SD indicates a group of heterogeneous measures; a small SD indicates homogeneity. (15)

Standard Score

See z score.

Stanford-Binet Test

Intelligence test developed by Lewis M. Terman in 1916 at Stanford University. The Stanford-Binet test was an American revision of the original Binet test, first published in France in 1905. It has since gone through numerous updates and revisions but is still considered to be more "verbally loaded" than its Wechsler counterparts. The Stanford-Binet, like the Wechsler, is an individual test of intelligence. (16)

Stanines

A set of standardized scores (based on the normal curve) arranged across nine intervals. The mean is set at 5, and the standard deviation at approximately 2. (15)

Status

Term used in social psychology to define an individual's niche in society's prestige hierarchy, or the individual's standing in a social system. The behavior expected of an individual of a given status is called his or her "role." *See also* Role. (17)

Stem and Leaf

A technique for graphing data in which the first digit is displayed in the first column, the stem, and the trailing digits in the second column, the leaf. (15)

Sternberg, Robert J.

Yale psychologist who has created a new view of intelligence that is based on an information processing model and is called the triarchic theory of intelligence. The three major constituents are (1) componential intelligence (the acquisition of new information, as well as the storage and retrieval of that information), (2) experimental intelligence (the solving of new problems, acting creatively, and using insight), and (3) contextual intelligence (the use of practical knowledge and common sense). (16)

Stimulus Generalization

Term used in conditioning to describe a situation in which a previously neutral stimulus similar to the actual stimulus used in the training procedure takes on the power to elicit the response. In classical conditioning the neutral stimulus is similar to the conditioned stimulus, whereas in operant conditioning the neutral stimulus is similar to the discriminated stimulus S^D. (9)

Stimulus-Response Theory

A theory that stresses the importance of the buildup of stimulus-response *associations* in defining learning. Most behaviorists adhere to stimulus-response learning theories, the major exception being E. C. Tolman. The leading stimulus-response theorists are E. L. Thorndike, Ivan Pavlov, J. B. Watson, Edwin Guthrie, C. L. Hull, and B. F. Skinner. Stimulus-response theorists stress the importance of nurture in the nature-nurture debate. Most theories of learning during the first half of the twentieth century, especially in the United States, were stimulus-response theories. The cognitive-gestalt position, in contrast, was not based on a stimulus-response theory. (8)

Stimulus Variety

Variation, at all sensory modes, of stimulus inputs. Stimulus variety was seen by many early-experience theorists as the crucial ingredient in intellectual development. J. McV. Hunt states that the more the child hears, sees, and touches, the more he or she will want to hear, see, and touch, and the more intellectual growth will occur. (4)

Storage

In the information processing model the organism's internal memory. When information is stored, it may persist over time. Currently, theorists refer to at least two storage components, short-term and long-term. (11)

Structure

Part of Jerome Bruner's theory of instruction, which states that any given subject area can be organized in an optimal fashion (structured) so that it can be transmitted to and understood by almost any student. Bruner feels that if a subject area is properly structured, then "any idea or problem or body of knowledge can be presented in a form simple enough so that any particular learner can understand it in a recognizable form." (9)

Student Teams–Achievement Divisions (STAD)

A system created by Robert Slavin to promote mainstreaming. He integrates special-education and regular-class children and sets up achievement groups (teams) composed of a mix of students. By offering a variety of rewards, the system increases both group and individual achievement. It does not drain resources from the "regular" pupils to meet the needs of special-education children. (20)

Summerhill School

English boarding school whose curriculum and way of life are based on the permissive orientation of its founder, A. S. Neill. The school stresses the free expression of ideas without the rigors of required exams or the demands of required class attendance. (4)

Symbolic Representation

The third stage of cognitive development and method of communication introduced by Jerome Bruner, the first two being the enactive and iconic levels. At the symbolic level, the child is able to translate experience into language. Words can then be used for communication and for representing ideas. Symbolic representation allows us to make logical connections between ideas and to think more compactly. (9)

Teacher Enthusiasm

According to research by Jacob Kounin and Barak Rosenshine, the characteristic of being "with it" and alert that has been shown to have a consistent, positive relationship with student behavior. (12)

Teacher Expectations

A teacher's attitude toward student learning and achievement. Numerous factors have been found to influence teacher acceptance of pupils, including social class, ethnicity, gender, rearing in a single-parent home, personality, and academic achievement. Some estimates suggest that as many as 50 percent of current teachers harbor one or more stereotypes and as a result provide children with less than optimal learning opportunities in the classroom. (14)

Teaching Machine

A device used to present an instructional program one step (or frame) at a time. The student either writes in answers or presses a button corresponding to the correct alternative. The advantages of the teaching machine are that (1) the student can proceed at his or her own pace, (2) the student receives immediate feedback, and (3) for many students the machines are intrinsically motivating. *See also* Programmed instruction. (10)

Terminal Behavior

Concept used by experts in the field of behavior modification. Terminal behavior defines the educational goals for the class as a whole or for individual students. It defines these goals in objective, behavioral terms. Instead of using what they consider to be vaguely stated goals like "understanding," the behaviorists insist that the goals describe specific behaviors that will result when the objective is attained. For example, students can be said to have learned how to multiply when they can recite the multiplication table with no errors. (10)

Theory and Practice

The twin pillars of educational psychology. The discipline represents a bridge, or connector, between psychology as the science of human behavior and the profession of education. (1)

Thinking Skills

An effort to teach children strategies of thinking that will increase their abilities to comprehend. The thinking-skills approach has been adopted as a result of outcome studies indicating that even though students may be mastering basic skills, they still show reduced levels of comprehension. The goals of this approach are similar to those proposed at the higher levels of Bloom's taxonomy. (13)

Thorndike, Edward L. (1874–1949)

One of America's most renowned educational psychologists. Thorndike studied at Harvard under William James and later taught at Columbia University's Teachers College. Early in his career, Thorndike did important laboratory studies of learning, using animals as subjects. From the results of these studies he constructed the first internally consistent learning theory. He created three major laws of learning (the law of readiness, the law of exercise, and the law of effect) and many subordinate laws. Thorndike believed learning occurs in a trial-and-error

fashion and thought of learning itself as the result of a buildup of connections between stimuli and responses. He insisted that educational psychology must utilize the scientific method in establishing its own "book of knowledge." (8)

Thurstone, Louis L. (1887–1955)

One of the developers of the factor approach to the understanding of intelligence. Thurstone originally gave 60 different tests of special abilities to large groups of children and then grouped those test scores that correlated highly with each other. He discovered that out of the original list of seemingly separate tests, there were only seven underlying correlated groupings (or *primary abilities*): verbal comprehension, word fluency, numerical ability, spatial visualizations, associative memory, perceptual speed, and reasoning. (16)

Time-Out Room

A separate room for handling extremely difficult children by segregating them from other students for a relatively short period. Excessive use of such a room can become aversive, making the technique ineffective. (19)

Tip-of-the-Tongue (TOT) Phenomenon

Momentary retrieval problem that occurs when one is trying to access semantic information from long-term memory (LTM). An example is the momentary inability to remember the name of a friend or family member. (11)

Token System

A system of reinforcement used by proponents of behavior modification, in which tokens of varying point values are awarded to students for fulfilling specific behavioral objectives. The tokens (conditioned reinforcers) may be cardboard or poker chips of various colors that the student may earn to achieve some desired prize or privilege. The system is said to have two main advantages: (1) it maintains a high daily rate of desirable responses, and (2) it teaches delayed gratification. (10)

Tolman, E. C. (1886–1959)

Creator of *purposive behaviorism*, a bridge between rigid behaviorism and doctrinaire gestaltism. Tolman was a behaviorist to the extent that he accepted observable responses as psychology's basic data, but he insisted that, far from being random or based on trial and error, learning was purposive, or goal-directed. He agreed with the gestaltists that people learn by forming cognitive maps of their environment. People can form hypotheses, see relationships, and then respond on the basis of these cognitive maps, rather than responding solely on the basis of a conditioned stimulus-response connection. Tolman's system is called an S-S (sign-significate) theory rather than an S-R (stimulus-response) psychology. (8)

Transactional Model

The interplay between individuals, especially the parent and child, in which each, in effect, shapes the other's environment. This phenomenon has given rise to a view of general development called the *transactional model*. These reciprocal influences affect not only the child's cognitive growth, but also the formation of the child's temperament, attitudes, and general personality. And, of course, the actions of the child also affect the future actions of the parent. Bruner has used a variant of the transactional model to describe language acquisition, which he feels depends strongly on the myriad of small but continuing interactions between parent and child. (9, 16)

Transfer

The influence of the learning of one activity upon the learning of a second ability. If the learning of A facilitates the learning of B, it is called *positive* transfer. If the learning of A inhibits the learning of B, it is called *negative* transfer. (10)

Trivia in the Classroom

A teacher's rapid-fire series of questions to students, calling for rote-memory answers. A series of classroom observation studies dating from the beginning of this century to the 1980s has indicated that too often this is the common mode of teacher-pupil interaction. (1)

T Score

A standardized score (based on the normal curve) in which the mean is set at 50 and the standard deviation at 10. *T* scores range from a low of 20 to a high of 80. (15)

Two-Stage Memory Theory

In the information processing model, the theory that memories are encoded and stored in at least two stages—in short-term memory, which lasts from about a few seconds to up to a minute; and in long-term memory, which may last a lifetime. (11)

Unconditional Positive Regard

Concept used by Carl Rogers in dealing both with clients in therapy and with students in the classroom. Unconditional positive regard means accepting people for what they are, without passing judgment, and without exacting any condition for full acceptance. According to Rogers, this is one of the three necessary and sufficient conditions for the promotion of learning, the other two being empathy and congruence. (12)

Unconditioned Response

A reflex response or, in Skinnerian terms, a respondent. An unconditioned response is any response that can be elicited automatically by the presentation of a certain stimulus, without any training or learning. The term is used in classical conditioning, and in Ivan Pavlov's original experiment the unconditioned response was salivation to the stimulus of meat powder being placed in the dog's mouth. (8)

Unconditioned Stimulus

Any stimulus that will elicit a given response automatically, without any training or learning. The term is used in classical conditioning, and in the case of Ivan Pavlov's own experiment, the unconditioned stimulus was meat powder placed in the dog's mouth. (8)

Unconscious Motivation

Freudian view that most of a person's behavior is motivated by forces of which the person is unaware—irrational needs that lurk beneath the level of conscious awareness. (18)

Validity

The extent to which test instruments are true indicators of what they purport to measure. A valid history test, for example, should measure a person's knowledge of history, not his or her neatness, penmanship, or spelling ability. (15)

Variability Measures

Measures that give information regarding individual differences, or how individuals vary in their measured scores. The two most important measures of variability are the range and the standard deviation. (15)

Visual Cliff

The perceived dropoff at the edge of any steep place. Research has shown that the newborn of many species, including human babies, will avoid the "deep" side of a specially built platform. This seems to show that depth perception is innate rather than learned. (3)

Vygotsky, Lev S. (1896–1934)

A major Russian cognitive psychologist, educator, and researcher who added two important concepts to stage theory: (1) the zone of proximal development and (2) the importance of peer and teacher interaction to "tow" cognitive development through stages. Vygotsky maintained that the child should be stretched into new areas of learning that are just beyond that child's comfort level. His work was considered too controversial by the Communist regime of Stalin and was banned for many years. (4, 5, 18)

Walberg, Herbert

A leading educational researcher who has applied the technique of meta-analysis to the study of teaching effectiveness. Walberg has outlined the relative importance of a variety of teaching strategies. Most important is providing positive reinforcement, followed by other methods such as giving cues and feedback, promoting cooperative learning, and establishing a positive classroom atmosphere. Other relevant factors are time on task, the incidence of higher-order questions, and use of advance organizers. (12)

Waterman, Alan

Working within the identity-formation framework of James Marcia, Waterman traced the pathways of identity development and demonstrated the number of multiple directions that were possible. Waterman asserts that the moratorium stage cannot be maintained indefinitely. *See also* Moratorium. (16)

Watson, John B. (1878–1958)

Founder of behaviorism and, at one time, psychology's most vocal critic of subjectivism, mentalism, and especially the technique of introspection. Watson was a strong believer in the importance of environment (as opposed to heredity) in shaping virtually all human behavior. He also believed that learning resulted from a buildup of stimulus-response connections, or what he called "habits." He was a strong advocate of Ivan Pavlov's concept of classical conditioning and utilized this method in his study of the ac-

quisition of fear in the baby Albert. Watson taught psychology at Johns Hopkins and later spent many years working for an advertising agency in New York. *See also* Behaviorism. (2)

Wechsler, David (1896–1981)

America's premier psychologist in the area of intelligence testing and test construction. Beginning in 1939 with the publication of the Wechsler-Bellevue test, David Wechsler spent his life creating, standardizing, and refining a long list of individual IQ tests (see below). He defined *intelligence* as "the global capacity of an individual to think rationally, act purposefully, and deal effectively with the environment." All the Wechsler tests report three separate IQ scores: a verbal IQ, a performance IQ, and a full-scale IQ. (16)

Wechsler Tests

Individual IQ tests, developed by David Wechsler, currently including the Wechsler Intelligence Scale for Children (WISC-III), the Wechsler Adult Intelligence Scale (WAIS-R), and the Wechsler Preschool and Primary Scale of Intelligence (WPPSI). All the Wechsler tests are administered by a trained examiner to one person at a time. All the tests yield three scores: a verbal IQ, a performance IQ, and a full-scale IQ. Wechsler believed that many of the intelligence tests of the day were too heavily laden with verbal items. To correct for that tendency, all the Wechsler tests include a performance section that tests an individual's visual-motor abilities. Wechsler tests use the deviation IQ method of scoring. In the hands of a skilled examiner, the Wechsler test can be used as a projective test for ferreting out a subject's personality traits. *See also* Intelligence quotient. (16)

Wertheimer, Max (1880–1943)

Founder of the gestalt school of psychology in the early 1900s. Wertheimer had criticized the structuralists and their insistence that all psychological phenomena should be analyzed into the smallest possible parts. He felt that the whole was more than just the sum of its parts. In order to understand psychological phenomena, one had to study all the parts together in their particular *Gestalt*, a German word meaning "whole," or "totality of configuration." Wertheimer's first studies were in the area of perception, especially the perception of apparent movement. Later he became interested in education and the principles of learning. He urged educators to teach for "understanding" instead of relying on repetition and rote memorization. *See also* Gestalt psychology. (8)

White, Robert

Harvard psychologist who has suggested that one of humankind's most fundamental motives is based on a strong personal desire to master the environment. White calls this the "competence" motive and believes it to be an intrinsic one that may even have survival value for the species. (18)

Wundt, Wilhelm (1832–1920)

German psychologist and founder of the structuralist school of thought. Wundt created the world's first laboratory of psychology at the University of Leipzig in 1879. He believed that psychology should devote itself to the study of the basic elements that make up conscious experience. To ferret out these individual elements, Wundt used trained subjects who looked within themselves and reported all their most fleeting and minute thoughts, feelings, and sensations. This technique of looking within the self is called *introspection*. Wundt's goal was to take psychology out of the field of philosophy and give it scientific respectability. (8)

Zeigarnik Effect

The propensity, in some situations, to remember unfinished tasks rather than those that have been completed. Memory is enhanced by the thought of the job still left undone. (18)

Zygote

First of the prenatal stages of development. The zygote is formed at conception and results from the fertilization of an egg by a sperm cell. The zygote floats freely within the uterus for about two weeks and finally attaches itself to the uterine wall. (3)

z Score (Standard Score)

A number that results from the transformation of a raw score into units of standard deviation. The z score specifies how far above or below the mean a given score is in these standard deviation units. The normal deviate, z, has a mean equal to 0 and a standard deviation equal to 1.00. (15)

PHOTO CREDITS

Chapter 1

xx: David Young-Wolff/PhotoEdit. **3:** *Left,* Instructional Material Production Center, North Carolina State University; *right,* Spencer Grant/Photo Researchers. **10:** Brown Brothers. **14:** Courtesy Office of Public Information, Low Library, Columbia University. **16:** Courtesy Office of Public Information, Low Library, Columbia University. **21:** Elizabeth Crews/Image Works. **22:** Courtesy Maxine Greene. **23:** David S. Strickler/Picture Cube.

Chapter 2

30: Myrleen Ferguson/PhotoEdit. **32:** Alan Carey/Image Works. **35:** Renate Hiller/Monkmeyer. **36:** Courtesy Ferdinand Hamburger, Jr., Archives of the John Hopkins Archive. **40:** Clark University Archive. **40:** Stanford University News Service. **42:** Tim Calson/Stock Boston. **44:** Dennis Stock/Magnum. **45:** From *The Kallikak Family* by H. H. Goddard.

Chapter 3

50: Tony Freeman/PhotoEdit. **55:** Sybil Shelton/Monkmeyer. **60:** Bruce Anderson. **64:** Marie Geggis. **70:** J. M. Tanner in Gardner, ed., *Endocrine and Genetic Diseases in Childhood* (Philadelphia: W. B. Saunders Co., 1969). **71:** Ellis Herwig/Picture Cube.

Chapter 4

86: Philip & Karen Smith/Tony Stone Images. **89:** Elizabeth Crews/Stock Boston. **90:** Courtesy The Bancroft Library, University of California at Berkeley. **93:** Rosemary Good. **97:** AP/Wide World Photos.

Chapter 5

106: Michael Newman/PhotoEdit. **109:** Gessell Institute of Child Development. **110:** Bill Anderson/Monkmeyer. **118:** Thad R. Wisehart. **122:** Cary Wolinsky/Stock Boston. **124:** Joel Gordon. **134:** Jean-Claude Lejeune. **139:** Robert A. Isaacs/Photo Researchers.

Chapter 6

150: J. Nourok/PhotoEdit. **154:** Historical Pictures Service. **158:** *Top,* Vinnie Fish/Photo Researchers; *bottom,* Harry F. Harlow, University of Wisconsin Primate Laboratory. **160:** Elizabeth Crews/Image Works. **162:** Courtesy Erik Erikson. **164:** Diane Schaefer/Design Works. **166:** *Left,* Dan Bosler/Tony Stone Images; *right,* Elizabeth Crews. **168:** David S. Strickler/Picture Cube. **173:** Gale Zucker/Stock Boston.

Chapter 7

188: David Young-Wolff/Tony Stone Images. **195:** Michael Siluk/Image Works. **196:** Courtesy Harvard Office of News & Public Affairs. **204:** Copyright 1965 by Stanley Milgram, from the film *Obedience,* distributed by New York University Film Library. **210:** MacDonald Photography/Picture Cube.

Chapter 8

228: David Young-Wolff/PhotoEdit. **231:** Bettmann. **282:** Courtesy The Graduate Faculty, The New School for Social Research.

Chapter 9

246: Penny Tweedie/Tony Stone Images. **248:** Courtesy B. F. Skinner, photo by Christopher Johnson. **254:** Wally Huntington. **256:** Monkmeyer. **258:** Thad R. Wisehart. **260:** Courtesy the Publicity Department, Harvard University Press, photo by Sue Klemens. **262:** Joel Gordon. **264:** Joel Gordon.

Chapter 10

272: Michael Newman/PhotoEdit. **287:** Thad R. Wisehart. **293:** Robert E. Daemmrich/Tony Stone Images.

Chapter 11

302: Vic Bider/Tony Stone Images. **305:** Ian Shaw/Tony Stone Images. **307:** Mimi Forsyth/Monkmeyer. **317:** Steve Payne. **328:** Nita Winter/Image Works. **331:** *Left,* Tom McCarthy/PhotoEdit; *right,* Tony Stone Images.

Chapter 12

340: R. Hutchings/PhotoEdit. **342:** Courtesy Herbert J. Wahlberg. **350:** Al Parker/Far West Lab. **353:** Kevin Horan/Tony Stone Images. **356:** Carl Rogers. **359:** David Young-Wolff/PhotoEdit. **364:** Instructional Materials Production Center, North Carolina State University.

Chapter 13

370: Dennis MacDonald/PhotoEdit. **376:** Marshall Henrichs. **381:** Mimi Forsythe/Monkmeyer. **383:** Jean Clough, Evanston, Illinois. **386:** Elizabeth Crews/Image Works. **393:** AP/Wide World Photos.

Chapter 14

400: Terry Vine/Tony Stone Images. **403:** Susie Fitzhugh/Stock Boston. **405:** Wally Huntington. **425:** Bob Daemmrich/Stock Boston.

Chapter 15

440: Lawrence Migdale/Tony Stone Images. **442:** Marie Geggis. **457:** Tony Freeman/PhotoEdit. **463:** Brown Brothers. **465:** Courtesy Duane Library Archives, Fordham University, photo by Tom Weber.

Chapter 16

472: Jeff Greenberg/PhotoEdit. **478:** Historical Picture Service. **479:** Courtesy National Library of Medicine. **481:** Courtesy National Library of Medicine. **482:** Wally Huntington. **483:** Psychological Corporation, New York. **484:** Courtesy David Wechsler. **497:** Courtesy Sandra Scarr.

Chapter 17

512: Robin Sachs/PhotoEdit. **514:** Marshall Henrichs. **515:** Bob Kramer/Picture Cube. **517:** Shirley Zeiberg. **520:** Marshall Heinrichs. **521:** Jean-Claude Lejeune. **538:** Wally Huntington. **539:** Courtesy Clark, Phipps, Clark & Harris, Inc., photo by Raimondo Borea.

Chapter 18

548: Robin Sachs/PhotoEdit. **553:** Thad R. Wisehart. **561:** Thad R. Wisehart. **564:** Harry F. Harlow, University of Wisconsin Primate Laboratory. **566:** David Young-Wolff/Tony Stone Images.

Chapter 19

578: Wayne Eastep/Tony Stone Images. **581:** Mary Kate Denny/PhotoEdit. **584:** Bob Henriques/Magnum. **592:** Instructional Materials Production Center, North Carolina State University. **593:** Jean-Claude Lejeune/Stock Boston. **595:** David Strickler.

Chapter 20

610: Frank Siteman/Tony Stone Images. **616:** Courtesy James Ysseldyke. **627:** The Boston Globe. 631: Paul Conklin/Monkmeyer. **632:** Reverend William J. Codd, S. J. **641:** Paul Conklin/Monkmeyer.

INDEX